Also by Joe Kane

THE PHANTOM'S ULTIMATE VIDEO GUIDE

The Phantom of the Movies'

VIDEOSCOPE

The Phantom of the Movies'

VIDEOSCOPE

The Ultimate Guide to the Latest, Greatest, and Weirdest Genre Videos

Joe Kane

*The Phantom of
the Movies®*

THREE RIVERS PRESS • NEW YORK

Published by Three Rivers Press, New York, New York. Member of
the Crown Publishing Group.

Random House, Inc. New York, Toronto, London, Sydney, Auckland
www.randomhouse.com

THREE RIVERS PRESS is a registered trademark and the Three Rivers
Press colophon is a trademark of Random House, Inc.

THE PHANTOM OF THE MOVIES and VIDEOSCOPE are registered in
the U.S. Patent and Trademark Office. All rights reserved.

Portions of this work have been previously published in the
New York *Daily News* and on its website, in *VideoScope* magazine
(and on its website), and in *The Phantom's Ultimate Video Guide*
(Dell Pub., 1989).

Printed in the United States of America

Design by BTD NYC

Library of Congress Cataloging-in-Publication Data
Phantom of the Movies.
The Phantom of the Movies' videoscope : the ultimate guide to the
latest, greatest, and weirdest genre videos / Joe Kane, The Phantom of
the Movies.
p. cm.
Includes index.
ISBN 0-8129-3149-1 (alk. paper)
1. B films—United States—Catalogs.   2. Video recordings—
Catalogs.   I. Title.
PN1998.P46 2000
016.79143'75'0973—dc21   99-086034

10 9 8 7 6 5 4 3 2 1

First Edition

For Nancy Naglin (a.k.a. The Phantomess),
without whose tireless love, assistance,
and support—
Fuhgedaboudit!

Phantom Foreword

So many movies, so little time.

That's the prospect faced by critics and movie lovers alike in an era when more films are being produced for more outlets than ever before. Major and smaller studios, independent filmmakers, "outlaw video" auteurs, cable-TV and direct-to-video suppliers, among others, have all upped their volume with "product" that, sooner or later, finds its way to homevideo. Add to their number the steady stream of foreign fare as well as older films of all stripes continually making their homevid debuts, often in remastered "director's cut" or "collector's" editions (especially for the burgeoning DVD market), and you have an annual output that reaches into the thousands.

It's been your Phantom's virtually lifelong mission (see *The Great 1960 Summer Bijou Binge*) to search out quality (usually low-budget) genre flicks that often get lost in the celluloid shuffle. Since covering the genre beat for the New York *Daily News* and launching *The Phantom of the Movies' VideoScope* magazine in 1993, we've waded through countless movies and videos, discovering obscure pearls aplenty embedded in the expected cinematic seaweed. Enough, in fact, to literally fill a book—hence, *The Phantom of the Movies' VideoScope*. With the wealth of choice videos available today, there's no reason for viewers to have to settle for bad or boring flicks (unless, of course, they're *good* bad or boring flicks—we're nothing if not open-minded here) or look for other, lesser ways to spend their time, like watching network television or going to the gym.

THE GEMS FROM THE JUNK

And speaking of futile exercises, we've all experienced the heartbreak of traipsing to our nabe vid store with maybe two or three desired titles in mind, only to find that all available copies have been rented. What's left is a vast array of "obscure" titles. Rather than leave empty-handed, many customers will choose an unknown video on the basis of cover art, recognizable cast names, or genre identification. All too often, underinformed consumers quickly learn they've wasted their time and bucks on a turkey—a tragedy that could have been avoided had the public been warned. One of *VideoScope*'s primary aims is to steer viewers toward those films deserving of their time and away from those that aren't— especially when it comes to those lower-profiled titles that proliferate on homevideo but receive little or no review coverage in the mainstream media. There are, we feel, enough overlooked quality films covered in this book to translate into thousands of hours of honest entertainment.

We'd like to take this op to proffer the following guarantee: All titles reviewed herein (with the exception of Nancy Naglin's erudite *Robot Monster* critique) were actually watched, albeit with occasionally bleary eyes, by yours truly. The Phantom believes that, in a book of this nature, a single voice can be more valuable than a consortium of disparate critics. Once readers get a sense of how a single reviewer's mind works (or malfunctions, as the case may be), the better they'll be able to gauge their own probable reaction to an individual video. In this service, The Phantom has sacrificed more than a few of his own brain cells so that you might preserve your own.

WHAT, WHERE, HOW

Watch what *you want,* when *you want.*

That's long been the homevideo credo, and one The Phantom fully supports. Too often, however, the *when* is easier to arrange than the *what.* Discounting specialty outlets, most video stores—from dominant chains like Blockbuster to the increasingly endangered "mom-and-pop" independents—tend to be chronically understocked on what we genre fans want to see. Worse, they increasingly rely on multiple copies of the same mainstream releases (*depth of copy,* in vid-biz parlance; *breadth of copy* refers to the number of *different* titles a site carries). Vintage genre films, worthy obscurities, and imports are frequently frustratingly difficult to locate via normal channels.

In addition to separating the gems from the junk, then, we've devoted considerable time and energy seeking out sources for hard-to-find titles of *all* kinds. Our Video Source Guide and Hot CyberCinema Sites sections offer detailed info re a wide spectrum of video suppliers. With a slight bit of detective work, readers can use those sections to ferret out every title, no matter how rare, mentioned in this book, along with thousands more—indeed, just about every title that's ever been issued on homevideo.

MORE IS MORE

From the outset, we envisioned *VideoScope* to be something more than a standard movie-review guide. To that end, we've also included numerous exclusive interviews with and sound bites from filmmakers, actors, and behind-the-scenes personnel responsible for the movies we want to see—from famous cult figures like John Waters, Pam Grier, and Jackie Chan to undeservedly obscure auteurs like José (Coffin Joe) Mojica Marins—to provide the back story on many of the films' geneses and to supply a greater feel for the filmmaking process, told the untamed way. We've likewise incorporated sidebars embracing everything from timeless movie quotations to the making of genre classics like Alfred Hitchcock's *Psycho* and Ishiro Honda's original *Godzilla.* Our goal is to furnish a book that can be read straight through, rather than used solely as a reference work to look up individual titles or personalities.

REVIEW *THIS*

For inclusion in this volume, a film first and foremost must answer "yes" to the question: "Are you now, or have you ever been, available on homevideo?" Regrettably, because of legal constraints or marketing doubts, many genre films otherwise worthy of inclusion (e.g., *Burn, Witch, Burn!, Wink of an Eye*) are still forced to answer in the negative. And since this *is* a *video* book, they'll have to wait until the video equivalent of the velvet ropes open and allow them deserved, if belated, entry.

Second, we've focused our attention on those titles that fit the (admittedly often loose and subjective) distinction of being *genre* films. What *is* a genre film? (So sorry I asked.) Broadly, that appellation applies to any film geared to appeal to a specific cinematic appetite. Say you're in the mood to be frightened ("I'm in the mood to be frightened") but you don't want to watch the evening news; for videos designed to fill that bill, you'll want to 'scope out our Inside the Frightgeist: Homevideo Horrors chapter. We've conveniently organized *VideoScope* according to *all* major genres—from Action to Wild Youth—to allow fans of a particular type of flick instant access to their prime area of interest and also (hopefully) to present a better picture of the intra-genre ebb and flow of filmmakers, personalities, and trends over the years.

For each title reviewed, we've listed the release date, Phantom rating (on a scale of 0–4), director, leading cast members, running time, availability in separate editions (e.g., "R" or "Unrated"), and video label. For titles released on now-defunct labels, we indicate the companies' belly-up condition with the notation "n.i.d." (not in distribution). Many labels have changed corporate names (as when Vidmark became Trimark or Live became Artisan); in such cases, we cite the current handle, even though you may find the video itself carrying the original name.

Titles listed with more than one label: In addition to offering licensed original material, invaluable archival companies such as Anchor Bay Entertainment, Englewood Entertainment, Home Vision Cinema, Kino International, Sinister Cinema, Something Weird Video and VCI Home Video, among others, frequently re-license copyright-lapsed titles that earlier surfaced on now-defunct labels. In most cases, we mention the (usually improved) edition that's currently available. Certified public domain titles routinely appear on several different labels simultaneously, with varying audiovisual quality; wherever possible, we've listed the label featuring the best-available quality.

We also indicate which VHS titles are currently available on DVD as well. This number continues to expand exponentially; many titles not yet available on DVD as of this writing (early 2000) *will* be when this volume appears in print. While VHS will continue to dominate in the near future (despite the relentless corporate push DVD has been getting), the new format is inarguably here to stay (at least until a shinier one comes along, like recordable DVD [not too far off], or Internet retrieval) and is projected to reach close to 10 percent penetration in American homes by the end of 2000 (VHS remains well over 90 percent). Virtually all major-label new releases are now routinely issued in both formats.

REMOTE POSSIBILITIES

Whatever the format of preference, today's homeviewer can be his or her own creative programmer. Video places viewers firmly in control, allowing access to a wealth of movie material that was once the private province of privileged film collectors. It's *VideoScope's* goal to help you, the homeviewer, not only to relive fond movie memories but to explore previously unsampled, often hard-to-find fare.

Homevideo has also granted a second life to countless films. The indie boom that kick-started with Steven Soderbergh's 1989 *sex, lies & videotape* owes its ongoing survival less to loud but fleeting film-fest buzz than to its video afterlife. And without homevideo, genre films, formerly largely the domain of B-movie producers, would likely exist only in their bloated, mutant, megabudget "event-movie" form (e.g., the *Batman, Jurassic Park,* and *Star Wars* franchises). Homevideo enables modest, thoughtful genre fare, like Vincenzo Natali's *Cube,* Andrew Niccols's *Gattaca* and Darren Aronofsky's *Pi*—to cite but three recent examples of films that, despite mostly favorable notices, couldn't compete in a fast-turnover, short-attention-span multiplex environment—to find their audiences, turn a back-end profit and encourage more films of their offbeat ilk to be financed and produced. Still more titles, like the solid Jean-Claude Van Damme actioner *Legionnaire,* receive their *first* life on homevideo, bypassing even token theatrical exposure, and manage to live long and prosper. On video, a title doesn't have to rack up instant powerhouse numbers; its potentially eternal shelf life grants viewers the chance to discover it at their leisure. It's our intent with *VideoScope* to help speed that discovery process.

DEPARTMENT OF CORRECTIONS

Since this is essentially a one-Phantom enterprise, we're ready to accept the blame for the occasional errors that are bound to surface in a volume this massive and detailed. We hope you'll find it in the goodness of your human hearts to forgive The Phantom any factual *faux pas* that may creep their way into this book. You're entirely free, of course, to disagree with his *opinions,* so long as you realize that to do so would mean running the risk of being terribly, terribly WRONG!

That said, we more than welcome your pheedback and encourage you to send your comments and queries to *The Phantom of the Movies' VideoScope* magazine, P.O. Box 216, Ocean Grove, NJ 07756 or e-mail us via our website at www.videoscopemag.com

In the meantime, and at *all* times, don't forget to . . .

Keep watching the screens!

Contents

RATINGS KEY

Titles are followed by year, Phantom rating, director, lead actors, running time (with tapes released in separate editions, the running time refers to the unrated version), video label, and DVD availability.

★★★★	Couldn't be better
★★★ ½	Excellent
★★★	Good
★★ ½	Not bad; worth watching
★★	Mediocre, worthwhile for a particular thesp, director, or genre
★ ½	Poor but may have points of interest
★	Just plain bad
½ ★	Even worse than that
0★	The pits
n/a	Not available on video
n.i.d.	Not in distribution
DVD	Also available on DVD

ACKNOWLEDGMENTS

It took a lot of help from a lot of sources over a lot of years to compile this volume. An appreciative tip of the Phantom hood goes to: The American Museum of the Moving Image, Anchor Bay Entertainment, AnimEigo, Inc., A-Pix Entertainment, Steve Apple, Arrow Video, Inc., Artisan Entertainment, Avalanche Entertainment, Andre Barcinski, Clive Barker, Richard Blackburn, Bob Blair, BMG Independents, Ron Bonk, Brian Boucher, Laura Boucher, Matthew Bright, Conrad Brooks, Buena Vista Home Video, Eric Caidin, Bruce Campbell, John Carpenter, Peter Castro, Central Park Media, Jackie Chan, Chris Chiarella, Peter Chow, Clein+White, Kevin Clement, Larry Cohn, Columbia/TriStar Home Video, Roger Corman, Wes Craven, Critics' Choice Video, Dan Cziraky, Joe Dante, Guillermo Del Toro, Dimension Home Video, Simon Drax, Terry DuFoe, Christian Duguay, EI Independent Cinema, Englewood Entertainment, Robert Englund, Ellen Enke, Jason Evers, Falco Ink., Tim Ferrante, Abel Ferrara, First Run Features, Evan Fong, Fox Lorber Home Video, David Franklin, Robert Freese, Tom Friedman, Roy Frumkes, Full Moon Studios, John Gallagher, Ken Goddard, Bruce Goldstein, Stuart Gordon, Rudolph Grey, Greycat Films, Pam Grier, Guidance Ro-Man, John Gullidge, Hallmark Home Entertainment, Herk Harvey, Rutger Hauer, Wings Hauser, HBO Home Video, Kevin Hein, Cliff Henderson, Frank Henenlotter, Candace Hilligoss, Hollywood Pictures Home Video, Home Vision Cinema, Image Entertainment, Incredibly Strange Filmworks, Ivy Film & Video, Peter Jackson, Steve James, Walt James, Jeff Kaplan, Dwight Kemper, Kino International, Craig Ledbetter, Corky Lee, Johnny Legend, Ivan Lerner, Greg Luce, Zoe Lund, William Lustig, Guy Maddin, Mike Maimone, Manga Entertainment, Jose Mojica Marins, MGM Home Entertainment, Milestone Film & Video, Miramax Pictures Home Video, Charles P. Mitchell, Monarch Home Video, Michael D. Moore, John Morthland, MPI Home Video, MTI Home Video, Mr. and Mrs. H. Lawrence Naglin, Nashville Cinema, Kevin Neal, New Horizons Home Video, New Line Home Video, New Video, New Yorker Video, Joan Kane Nichols, Peter M. Nichols, Chuck Norris, Gary Oldman, Open City Communications, Terry O'Quinn, Palm Pictures, Paramount Home Video, Fred Patten, PM Entertainment, Tom Poster, Michael Powell, Sue Procko, Thomas C. Rainone, Darrin Ramage, Rhino Home Video, Debbie Rochon, Michael Rooker, Lynn Samuels, Julian Sands, John Sayles, Screen Pix Home Video, Katt Shea, Andy and Arlene Sidaris, Sinister Cinema, Something Weird Video, the Spirit of Ed Wood, Ray Dennis Steckler, Sterling Home Entertainment, George Stover, Jeff Strate,

Streamline Pictures, John Swenson, Tai Seng Video, John Thonen, Jennifer Tilly, Tony Timpone, Tony Todd, Susan Toepfer, Alan Trembly, Trimark Home Video, Troma, Inc., Turner Home Entertainment, 20th Century Fox, Universal Studios Home Video, Jean-Claude Van Damme, Mario Van Peebles, VCI Home Video, Mark Voger, Mike Vraney, Warner Home Video, Water Bearer Films, John Waters, Tom Weaver, Michael Weldon, Wade Williams, WinStar Entertainment, World Artists Home Video, Xenon Entertainment, Yossarian, Zontar (Official Phantom Feline), and anyone we may have momentarily misplaced (you know who you are and we saw what you did).

Special thanks to my loyal agent and friend Anthony Gardner,
ever-alert editors Philip Turner and Pete Fornatale, and Benjamin Dreyer
and the entire hardworking Random House gang.

The Phantom of the Movies'

VIDEOSCOPE

Inside the Frightgeist:
HOMEVIDEO HORRORS

THE ABOMINABLE DR. PHIBES: THE SERIES

THE ABOMINABLE DR. PHIBES (1971) ***

D: Robert Fuest. Vincent Price, Joseph Cotten, Terry-Thomas. 94 mins. (MGM)

AIP's deadpan send-up of Hammer's horror flicks features a witty script, gaudy Art Deco sets, a flamboyantly florid perf by masked fright pro Price, plus the memorable tag line "Love means never having to say you're ugly." Price/Phibes strikes anew in the solid sequel *Dr. Phibes Rises Again* (Orion).

THE ADDICTION (1995) B&W **½

D: Abel Ferrara. Lili Taylor, Christopher Walken, Edie Falco, Annabella Sciorra, Paul Calderon, Fredro Starr, Kathryn Erbe. 82 mins. (Hallmark)

Set in and around Greenwich Village's New York University, *The Addiction* stars a game but baffling Taylor as an embittered grad student prone to waxing obvious via frequent apoplectic, apocalyptic rants re the world's sundry injustices. One night Taylor is brutally assaulted and bitten by equally attitudinal street vampire Sciorra. Soon after, our sour antiheroine is talking her stuffy professor (Calderon) into shooting heroin, then nips his neck, along with those of fellow students Falco and Erbe and strangers of all stripes. In the vampire vision of Ferrara and scripter Nicholas St. John, the bites don't prove fatal but transform their recipients into surly bloodsuckers. Walken has a showy role as a veteran vampire who volunteers a few inside tips to Taylor while, like nearly everyone else in this mouthy movie, spouting Philosophy 101–type snippets. Characters and motivations seem murky and arbitrary throughout this rage-choked exercise, but you have to credit the ever offbeat Ferrara and St. John for at least having the courage of their conniptions. Taylor, meanwhile, enjoys another antisocial downtown-'tude rampage as hostile lesbian writer/ would-be assassin Valerie Solanis in Mary (*American Psycho*) Harron's fact-based *I Shot Andy Warhol* (Evergreen).

ALICE, SWEET ALICE (1977) ***½

D: Alfred Sole. Louisa Horton, Tom Signorelli, Brooke Shields, Paula Sheppard, Linda Miller, Lillian Roth. 108 mins. (Anchor Bay) DVD

Originally (and more aptly) titled *Holy Terror,* this is the best Catholic-themed verité-styled chiller ever lensed in New Jersey, a wonderfully perverse, low-budget *Bad Seed–*type tale. Ten-year-old Shields barely makes it past the first reel before being strangled on her First Communion day. Is her hostile older sister (Sheppard) the culprit? Is the latter also responsible for the brutal slayings that follow in Brooke's wake? It will cost you less than $15 to find out via Anchor Bay's uncut, remastered edition of a film previously available in oft butchered public-domain versions, legally permissible due to a technical copyright screwup. Director Sole has since helmed the 1981 Vanity production *Tanya's Island* (see index) and the frightcom *Pandemonium* (MGM).

ALLIGATOR (1980) ***

D: Lewis Teague. Robert Forster, Robin Riker, Henry Silva, Dean Jagger. 92 mins. (Lightning, n.i.d.)

John Sayles supplies the in-joke-laden script, Forster the low-key heroics, and Silva (as a Great White Hunter stalking urban sewers!) the sardonic comic relief in a generally fun—if occasionally self-conscious—fright film about a giant alligator on the loose. Unfortunately, the cassette itself has become a rarity since Lightning flashed out. Perhaps equally unfortunately, the toothless retread, *Alligator II: The Mutation* (with popular character thesp Richard Lynch in the Silva role), *is* readily available (Columbia/TriStar).

ALONE IN THE DARK   (1982) ***1/2

D: Jack Sholder. Donald Pleasence, Jack Palance, Martin Landau, Dwight Schultz, Deborah Hedwall, Erland van Lidth. 92 mins. (Columbia/TriStar)

Wacko war vet Palance ("I'm here because I enjoy the social life") and paranoid preacher Landau head a quartet of crazies who run amok in Jersey during a blackout caused by a faulty nuclear power plant. Imperiled psychiatric aide Schultz tries to protect his endangered family from the psychos' wrath, while nutty head doc Pleasence insists that his errant charges, whom he dubs "voyagers," are merely "confused." Sholder's sharp satiric splatter pic—which sometimes approximates the feel of a live-action *Simpsons* Halloween special gone *way* over the edge—pokes fun at 'burb life, Laingian shrinks, punk rock, American media addiction, and voyeurism in general and features one of the best nightmare sequences ever lensed. *Alone in the Dark* is an almost seamless genre movie that's funny, scary, and equipped with a bright central metaphor. Who could ask for anything more?

AMERICAN GOTHIC   (1988) **1/2

D: John Hough. Rod Steiger, Yvonne De Carlo, Sarah Torgov, Michael J. Pollard, Fiona Hutchison, Mark Lindsay Chapman. 90 mins. (Trimark)

After a slow start that finds three yuppie couples landing their fuel-

THE FAMILY THAT SLAYS TOGETHER: Yvonne De Carlo and Rod Steiger strike classic poses as the heads of a brain-dead killer clan in the island-set slaughter-fest *American Gothic.*
Courtesy of Trimark Home Video

depleted plane on a scary uncharted isle *miles* from Seattle, *American Gothic* revs up into high gear once our castaways encounter loony locals Ma (De Carlo) and Pa (Steiger), their two psycho sons, and their equally demented daughter. You know what direction the flick is headed in as soon as one of Ma and Pa's infantile middle-aged offspring asks a bewildered yuppie, "Wanna ride our swing?" Its pedestrian, Ed Gein–inspired plot notwithstanding, *Ameri-*

can Gothic comes through with an impressive array of truly sicko surprises, involving wholesale slaughter, necrophilia, and other activities seemingly at odds with traditional family values. Steiger and De Carlo (erstwhile Mrs. Munster) are consistently entertaining in what may be the most humiliating roles of their long and checkered careers, while Pollard giggles and drools convincingly as one of their dim-witted sons.

AN AMERICAN WEREWOLF IN LONDON (1981)***

D: John Landis. David Naughton, Jenny Agutter, Griffin Dunne. 97 mins. (Artisan) DVD

Landis's lycanthrope lampoon rates as one of those rare comedy/horror hybrids that succeeds in supplying honest laughs without sacrificing the chills. Rick Baker's bubbling-bladder makeup FX netted him a well-deserved Oscar. Anthony (*Mute Witness*) Waller's seriously belated 1998 follow-up, *An American Werewolf in Paris* (Hollywood Pictures, DVD), on the other bubbling bladder, may be the ultimate low-impact *whatever* movie (a lycanthropic sex act performed on Jim Morrison's Parisian grave while Bush's "Mouth" whines on the soundtrack represents a case in point).

AMITYVILLE HORROR:
THE SERIES

THE AMITYVILLE HORROR (1979)**

D: Stuart Rosenberg. James Brolin, Margot Kidder, Rod Steiger. 117 mins. (Warner)

Rosenberg (of *Cool Hand Luke* fame) assembles a familiar, overblown but marginally watchable schlock shocker, based on Jay Anson's bestseller, wherein poltergeists frighten the new inhabitants of the haunted Long Island title site. Since gaining fright franchisehood, the pic has inspired (thus far) no fewer than seven sequels: *Amityville II: The Possession* (Nelson); *Amityville 3D: The Demon* (Vestron); the made-for-TV (and relocated to California) *Amityville 4; The Amityville Curse* (both Trimark); Tony (*Hellbound*) Randel's *Amityville 1992: It's About Time*, about an accursed Amityville clock; *Amityville: A New Generation*, about a haunted Amityville mirror; and the highest concept to date, *Amityville Dollhouse* (all from Republic).

ANACONDA (1997)**½

D: Luis Llosa. Jennifer Lopez, Ice Cube, Jon Voight, Eric Stoltz, Jonathan Hyde, Owen Wilson, Kari Wuhrer. 90 mins. (Universal) DVD

A documentary crew looking to locate the elusive Amazon tribe known as the "People of the Mist" instead encounters the 40-foot, people-eating title critter in this generally fun if thoroughly formulaic throwback to the monster movies of yore. The cast members are polished off one by one, in a fairly predictable pecking order, by the peckish snake. South American scenery specialist Llosa (*Sniper*) yields the max from his authentic locales, to say nothing of Lopez's supremely photogenic bod. In the thespian department, the snake finishes a close second to Voight, who turns in at once menacing and witty work as a dangerous Paraguayan "river rat."

ANGUISH (1988)**

D: Bigas Luna. Zelda Rubinstein, Michael Lerner, Talia Paul. 92 mins. (Anchor Bay) DVD

Luna's metaphorical, metaphysical, perhaps even meta-brain-damaged *Anguish* is less a straight-ahead horror film than a meditation on the movie medium itself. Four-foot *Poltergeist* psychic Rubinstein plays the supportive mom of eye-gouging oedipal wreck John (Lerner), an optometric aide whose hobby is slicing out—and collecting—human eyeballs. After following John on his ocular rounds, director Luna cuts to the audience *watching* the above pro-

ceedings on-screen. John himself then ducks into a *different* theater, where the silent version of *The Lost World* is unspooling; also present is the same audience we saw in theater 1, a few of whom John surreptitiously relieves of their eyes. Meanwhile, a second, "real" maniac turns up in theater 1, responds to the on-screen Zelda (in a fictitious film called *The Mommy*), and runs around shooting patrons. (Is this *heavy* or what?) While thematically akin both to Lamberto Bava's *Demons* (whose febrile feel it shares), Fulvio Wetzl's *Rorret*, and Peter Bogdanovich's *Targets* (see index), *Anguish* dares to venture onto some relatively virgin turf for its time, but in our view the pic's not worth keeping an eye out for. You may feel differently, especially if you enjoyed such later Luna-tic fare as *Jamón, Jamón* (New Yorker).

THE APE MAN (1943) B&W***

D: William Beaudine. Bela Lugosi, Louise Currie, Wallace Ford. 64 mins. (Sinister Cinema)

Prolific Poverty Row auteur William ("One-Take") Beaudine assembles a moving account of ailing mad scientist Lugosi's complex love-hate relationship with his pet guy-in-an-ape-suit. Bela delivers some creative line readings. Better than Boris Karloff's simian stint *The Ape* (Sinister Cinema).

ARACHNOPHOBIA (1990)**½

D: Frank Marshall. Jeff Daniels, Harley Jane Kozak, John Goodman, Julian Sands, Stuart Pankin, Henry Jones. 109 mins. (Hollywood Pictures) DVD

Marshall's megabuck scare epic gets off to a fairly bright start, as a single mutant spider stows away in a coffin shipped from Venezuela to scenic small town Canaima, California. When the alien arachnid mates with its California counterparts, Canaima's unsuspecting citizens fall prey to an outbreak of fatal spider bites. It's up to spider maven Sands and arachnophobic hero Daniels to end the insects' reign of terror. Unfortunately, this Steven Spielberg–produced "thrillomedy" begins its steady decline as soon as we're introduced to the wimpy Daniels and the rest of his Typical American Family—levelheaded spouse Kozak and a pair of standard-issue sitcom offspring. A mechanical script crammed with clichéd creature setups, hoary horror-film gags, and Spielberg's patented brand of anvil whimsy likewise conspire to keep *Arachnophobia* from having any real bite. On the plus side, director Marshall, abetted by the expected intricate FX, delivers several genuine shocks, including an excellently staged basement battle between Daniels and the lead spider. But *Arachnophobia* would have worked better with fewer Spielbergian 'burb antics and more authentic arachnid anarchy.

THE ASPHYX   (1972) ***

D: Peter Newbrook. Robert Stephens, Robert Powell, Jane Lapotaire. 98 mins. (Something Weird) DVD

The title refers to a spirit that exits the body at the moment of death; photographer Stephens captures one in the hope it will make him immortal. This fairly novel period horror pic was previously available as *Spirit of the Dead* (Media), no relation to *Spirits of the Dead* (see index).

ASYLUM   (1972) ***

D: Roy Ward Baker. Barbara Parkins, Richard Todd, Peter Cushing. 100 mins. (Prism, n.i.d.)

The title facility serves as the frame for four Robert (*Psycho*) Bloch–penned scare tales in Baker's tight fright anthology. No relation to the lame 1996 psycho chiller of the same name (Monarch).

THE ATTIC   (1979) **½

D: George Edwards. Ray Milland, Carrie Snodgress, Rosemary Murphy. 92 mins. (Hallmark)

This familial fright flick—occasionally funny, in its own grim way—pits resentful spinster Snodgress against her dictatorial dad (interpreted with elaborate unpleasantness by Milland). Caught in the middle is Carrie's surrogate kid, Dickie the Chimp. Played with utter sincerity, *The Attic* proffers a strange idea of entertainment, to put it mildly.

THE AWFUL DR. ORLOFF   (1962) B&W ***

D: Jesús Franco. Howard Vernon, Perla Cristal, Ricardo Valle, Conrado Sanmartín, María Silva, Diana Lorys. 86 mins. (Something Weird)

Sadly overappreciated (in some quarters) but undeniably prolific auteur Franco fashions a solid fright flick in this early effort, presented, in a crisp transfer, by Frank (*Basket Case*) Henenlotter and the dedicated genre archivists at SWV. A Jack the Ripper-ized variation on Georges Franju's superior *Eyes Without a Face* (see index), the film finds obsessed surgeon Dr. O. (Vernon), with the aid of servile blind psycho Morpho (Valle), shearing hapless harlots of their skin in a bid to restore his comatose daughter's disfigured face. Genuinely atmospheric and well-paced without sacrificing any sleaziness, *The Awful Dr. Orloff* should appeal even to non-Francophiles in search of vintage celluloid scares. Other available Franco flicks include *Angel of Death* (Video Treasures); *Attack of the Robots, The Diabolical Dr. Z* (Sinister Cinema); *Bloodsucking Nazi Zombies* (a.k.a. *Oasis of the Zombies,* Lightning); *Deadly Sanctuary* (Monterey); *The Invisible Dead* (Lightning); *Bloody Moon, Manhunter, Revenge in the House of Usher* (TWE); *The Castle of Fu Man-chu, Kiss and Kill* (Moore); *Count Dracula, 99 Women, Venus in Furs* (Republic); *The Demons* (Unicorn); *Dr. Orloff's Monster* (Something Weird); *Ilsa, the Wicked Warden* (CIC); *Jack the Ripper* (Vestron); *Kiss Me, Monster, Succubus,* and *Two Undercover Angels* (Anchor Bay); *The Loves of Irina* (Private Screenings), a.k.a. *Erotikill* (Lightning); *Lust for Frankenstein, Marie Cookie and the Killer Tarantula,* and *Tender Flesh* (EI); *The Perverse Contessa, Sex Is Crazy* (VSOM); *Revenge of the Dead, The Screaming Dead* (Wizard); and *A Virgin Among the Living Dead* (Lightning).

THE BAD SEED   (1956) B&W ***

D: Mervyn LeRoy. Patty McCormack, Nancy Kelly, Henry Jones. 129 mins. (Warner)

Little blond brat Patty is literally a born psychopath in this extravagantly febrile adaptation of Maxwell Anderson's controversial Broadway play. She might have been happier if Norman Bates had adopted her. The mature Pat has since gone the madmater route in Max Allan Collins's *Mommy* and *Mommy 2: Mommy's Day* (see index).

THE BEAST WITH FIVE FINGERS (1946) B&W ***

D: Robert Florey. Robert Alda, Peter Lorre, Andrea King, J. Carrol Naish, Victor Francen. 88 mins. (MGM)

One of the few fright titles released during Hollywood's post–World War II horror drought, *Beast* benefits mightily from Lorre's typically intense, pop-eyed perf as an astrology-obsessed aide to ailing, semiparalyzed pianist Francen. A remote Italian village in the early 1900s provides an exotic setting, though most of the major characters, save for Lorre and local police chief Naish, are Americans gathered to hear Francen's will. Florey's creepy atmospherics and disembodied-hand effects (several trick scenes feature the director's own digits!) plus an earnest cast fully compensate for the minor detail that not much actually happens. Naish's extraneous, mood-killing coda constitutes *Beast*'s only serious flaw.

BEDLAM   (1946) B&W ***

D: Mark Robson. Boris Karloff, Anna Lee, Ian Wolfe. 79 mins. (Turner, n.i.d.)

Producer Val Lewton's look at the notorious Brit insane asylum, inspired by a series of Hogarth sketches that serve here as brief on-screen entr'actes, doesn't pretend to be a horror movie and even plays a bit tame as a belated exposé. But Boris has a great role as Bedlam's alternately toadying and bullying warden, while actor Robert Clarke, in his pre–*Hideous Sun Demon* daze, turns in a bizarre bit as an inmate with a canine complex. Karloff's confrontations with feisty heroine Lee—a sworn enemy who's wrongfully entrusted to Boris's creepy "care"—are also vividly rendered.

BEGOTTEN   (1991) B&W ***

D: E. Elias Merhige. Brian Salzberg, Donna Dempsey, Stephen Charles Barry, TheaterOfMaterial members. 78 mins. (World Artists)

Painstakingly lensed in supergrainy B&W and scored with a genuinely eerie minimalist soundtrack (birdcalls, heartbeats, buried, dirgelike melodies), Merhige's biblical avant-gore indie opens with a spazzed-out "God" (Salzberg) committing hara-kiri with what looks like a straight razor (!). That painful tableau sets the mood for a parade of primordial images as a tribe of hooded figures proceed to perform stark, arcane sex-and-death rituals on "Mother Earth" (Dempsey) and "Son of Earth" (Barry). A feature-length fever dream, *Begotten* unspools sans dialogue or formal narra-

tive. At 78 minutes, Merhige's hallucination eventually becomes an audience endurance test; the film would have been twice as effective at half the length. Still, Merhige deserves full credit for achieving his avowed goal, carefully crafting a surreal exercise that really does play like an "anthropological documentary," as though one of Eric Von Daniken's ancient aliens had brought a camcorder (or, more precisely, an Arri-S 16-millimeter) along to record primitive earthlings at grisly religious play.

THE BELIEVERS   (1987) **¹/₂

D: John Schlesinger. Martin Sheen, Helen Shaver, Robert Loggia, Harley Cross, Elizabeth Wilson, Harris Yulin, Richard Masur. 114 mins. (HBO)

Schlesinger's high-budget horror film opens with a hot Mr. Coffee Massacre sequence, then settles into a less inspired groove as widowed police shrink Sheen, aided by squeeze Shaver and cop Loggia, seeks to save his young son (Cross) from the creepy clutches of a kid-sacrificing *brujeria* (witchcraft) cult led by Yulin. *The Believers* is a polished, professionally crafted pic, but its then-heralded gore FX had been done before and in far ghastlier fashion by Dario Argento, while the voodoo hook was employed to more visceral effect in Alan Parker's superior suspenser *Angel Heart* (see index). With its lack of sustained tension and emphasis on child mutilation, *The Believers* is ultimately more depressing than chilling.

THE BEYOND   (1981) ***

D: Lucio Fulci. Catriona MacColl, David Warbeck, Sarah Keller. 87 mins. (Anchor Bay) DVD

Erecting a hotel on the site of one of the seven gateways to hell proves a predictably bad idea, as new owner MacColl and friend Warbeck discover in Fulci's *The Beyond*, earlier out on the defunct Vestron label as *Seven Doors of*

Death. Widely considered to be the late, great Italo frightmaster's masterpiece, this Louisiana-set gorefest, resurrected for a highly successful summer 1998 national midnight theatrical run by Quentin Tarantino's Rolling Thunder Pictures, fully lives up to its advance chiller billing. The simple plot serves as a sturdy frame for Fulci and makeup-FX genius Giannetto De Rossi to fashion a truly stunning series of over-the-top terror tableaux, ranging from bloody crucifixions and acid baths to a faceful-of-spiders sequence and the requisite climactic zombie assault. The pic also sports one of frightdom's more memorable endings. Other available Fulci fear films include *Cat in the Brain* (Blackest Heart), *Gates of Hell* (Paragon), *The House by the Cemetery* (Artisan), *Manhattan Baby* (Vestron), *The Psychic* (Lightning), *New York Ripper,* and *Zombie* (both Anchor Bay, DVD).

THE BIRDS   (1963) ***¹/₂

D: Alfred Hitchcock. Rod Taylor, Tippi Hedren, Jessica Tandy. 120 mins. (Universal)

Hitch launches a high-flying horror classic that finds man's fine-feathered friends turning into formidable fiends. The film has lost none of its original impact, though the big screen remains the best place to see it. Avoid the notorious "Alan Smithee"–directed low-flying 1994 made-for-cable update *The Birds II: Land's End* (Universal), its oblique last-reel homage to the immortal *The Killer Shrews* (see index) notwithstanding.

THE BLACK CASTLE   (1952) B&W ***

D: Nathan Juran. Richard Greene, Boris Karloff, Stephen McNally, Paula Corday, Lon Chaney, Jr., John Hoyt, Michael Pate, Tudor Owen. 81 mins. (Universal)

More of a terror-tinged period suspenser than an all-out fright film,

The Black Castle manages to entertain more often than not. Future TV "Robin Hood" Greene plays a Brit gentleman who, accompanied by faithful manservant Owen, hies to the Black Forest's darkest heart to investigate the fates of two former cronies he suspects have been murdered by evil Austrian nobleman McNally (in a sneer-driven perf), henchmen Hoyt and Pate, personal physician/resident poisoner Karloff, and castle brute Chaney. Greene not only finds his worst suspicions confirmed but, much to his own dismay, tumbles for McNally's beautiful but neglected wife (Corday). A near live-burial sequence, an alligator pit, creepy castle accoutrements, and Boris and Lon's lurking presence comprise *The Black Castle*'s prime horror elements.

THE BLACK CAT   (1934) B&W ***1/2

D: Edgar G. Ulmer. Bela Lugosi, Boris Karloff, David Manners. 65 mins. (Universal)

Boris and Bela's maiden screen teaming is a suitably bizarre bout pitting good guy Bela against devil-worshipper Boris. Surreal sets, Ulmer's atmospheric direction, and Karloff's New Wave hairstyle also help make this a memorable scare gem. The fleeting appearance of a lone black feline supplies the only link with Edgar Allan Poe's famous tale of the same name. No relation to the forgettable 1941 comedy/mystery *The Black Cat* (Universal). Other available *Black Cat* titles include the 1965 Texas-lensed indie (Sinister Cinema), Lucio Fulci's 1981 incarnation (Rhino), and Luigi Cozzi's 1990 edition (Columbia/TriStar), with Caroline Munro and Brett Halsey.

BLACK CHRISTMAS   (1975) ***

D: Bob Clark. Olivia Hussey, Margot Kidder, Keir Dullea, Andrea Martin, John Saxon. 98 mins. (Warner)

Also released as *Silent Night, Evil Night* and *Stranger in the House*,

Bob *(Porky's)* Clark's Canadian campus-set fearfest supplied several scream-screen firsts. Its holiday-horror theme predated John Carpenter's *Halloween* by three years, while its key phone hook, with the killer calling from inside the murder site, was later lifted by *When a Stranger Calls* (Columbia/TriStar). Clarke even throws in a brief hockey-mask scare shot that anticipated the long-running *Friday the 13th* series' similarly costumed killer, Jason Voorhees. Though not in the same league as *Halloween* or Clark's own *Deathdream* (see index), *Black Christmas* holds up as an effective fright pic laced with dark wit. It opens with several sorority sisters, portrayed by such A-level thesps as Hussey, Kidder, and *SCTV*'s Martin, being plagued by an obscene caller/killer. Suspicion ultimately falls on Olivia's neurotic pianist boyfriend (Dullea). But even after perennial B-movie detective Saxon seemingly solves the case, Clark and company spring a clever surprise in the film's final moments.

Other yuletide terror outings that have their redeeming moments include 1980's *Terror in Toyland,* a.k.a. *Christmas Evil; You Better Watch Out* (Academy); and Brian Yuzna's *Silent Night, Deadly Night 4: Initiation* (see index). Edmund Purdom's *Don't Open Till Christmas* (Vestron) still holds Best Killer Christmas Tag Line honors. To wit: "'Twas the night before Christmas/and all through the house/not a creature was stirring…They were all DEAD!" Your Phantom's all-time fave Christmas freak-out scene, however, unfolds in John Waters's *Female Trouble* (see index) when Divine erupts in a fit of abrupt and senseless violence upon failing to find her desired cha-cha heels under the family tree. Now, *that's* scary!

THE BLACK ROOM   (1935) B&W ***

D: Roy William Neill. Boris Karloff, Marian Marsh, Robert Allen. 67 mins. (Goodtimes)

The *Black Room* offers two Karloffs for the price of one: Boris plays twins—one good, one evil—who labor under an ancient curse in this generally effective gothic tale. No relation to 1981's *Black Room* (Vestron), a bloody psychosexual yarn.

BLACK SUNDAY   (1960) B&W ***

D: Mario Bava. Barbara Steele, John Richardson, Ivo Garrani. Dubbed. 83 mins. (Sinister Cinema) DVD

The pic that put graveyard beauty Barbara Steele—cast here as a reanimated witch—on the horror-movie map also represents one of gothic great Bava's most atmospheric excursions. Sinister Cinema carries the British version of the film, with different thesps dubbing the voices and with the original Italo score intact. We likewise recommend Bava's superior 1964 fright anthology, *Black Sabbath* (Sinister Cinema, DVD), hosted by Boris Karloff and highlighted by the classic tale "A Drop of Water"; Karloff also stars in the whistling vampire episode "The Wurdulak." Bava scores again with 1964's *Blood and Black Lace* (VCI, DVD), an inventively perverse bloodbath about a masked maniac who murders models in Cameron Mitchell's employ.

BLACULA   (1972) ***

D: William Crain. William Marshall, Denise Nicholas, Vonetta McGee, Thalmus Rasulala, Ketty Lester, Elisha Cook, Jr., Gordon Pinsent. 92 mins. (Orion)

Longtime Shakespearean thesp Marshall is excellent as a culture-shocked 18th-century African vampire, cursed by the original (and apparently racist) Dracula, loose in 1970s L.A. Though the pic takes an eventual turn toward the predictable, it's a better-than-average bloodsucker romp. Singer Lester, as a nipped cabbie, and vet Cook contribute memorable support.

Followed by *Scream, Blacula, Scream* (Orion), with Marshall and Pam Grier.

BLADE (1998) ***

D: Stephen Norrington. Wesley Snipes, Stephen Dorff, Kris Kristofferson, N'Bushe Wright, Donal Logue, Udo Kier, Traci Lords. 123 mins. (New Line) DVD

While subtlety's not a strong point, Stephen (*Death Machine*) Norrington's *Blade* succeeds in its primary aim, bringing Marv Wolfman and Gene Colan's cult 1970s Marvel Comics characters to lavish, contemporary, and consummately bloody big-screen life. Snipes, in a role that requires more action than acting, stars as Blade, a half vampire whose mother was bitten by a bloodsucker just prior to his birth, an event dramatized in a harrowing opening sequence. Blade has dedicated his life to eradicating as many members of the bloodsucking breed as he semi-humanly can, with the assistance of terminally ill but still murderously active mentor Whistler (an ultragrizzled Kristofferson), and employing everything from high-tech automatics loaded with silver bullets to ultraviolet-light machines to kung fu to his trusty namesake titanium sword. Crowd-pleasingly violent and visually inventive in the MTV-inspired quick-cut style (with further fast-motion photography borrowed from Godfrey Reggio's influential impressionistic 1983 *Koyaanisqatsi* [Pacific Arts]), *Blade* boasts an impressive amount of mayhem.

THE BLAIR WITCH PROJECT (1999) B&W/COLOR **1/2

D: Daniel Myrick and Eduardo Sánchez. Heather Donahue, Joshua Leonard, Michael Williams. With "newly discovered footage." 87 mins. (Artisan) DVD

This megahyped homemade horror—a true progeny of the Internet age—floats somewhere between a fitfully effective *Out Alone* for Generation Y and risible fodder for Count Floyd's *Monster Horror Chiller Theater* ("You hear that twig snapping! Look—a pile of stones! Oooh, that's scary, boys and girls!") (And didn't *Cannibal Holocaust* already use *Blair*'s central riff some two decades earlier?) But *Blair Witch* undeniably boasted one of the most brilliant, relentless promo campaigns in movie history. William Castle must be *kvelling* in his grave. (We hear he's buried in Burkittsville!)

CURSE OF THE BLAIR WITCH (1999) ***

D: Daniel Myrick and Eduardo Sánchez. Frank Pastor, Heather Donahue. 45 mins. (Artisan)

While the actual film drew mixed, often heated reactions from genre fans, few deny the entertainment value of *Curse of the Blair Witch*, *Blair Witch* directors Myrick and Sánchez's ingenious chronicle of the "legendary" Blair Witch's back story. The "documentary" interweaves interviews with law-enforcement officials, private investigators, local citizens, and friends and neighbors of the three young filmmakers who disappeared in *The Blair Witch Project* with historical accounts of the witch's wicked alleged exploits and even ersatz vintage "newsreel" footage of murderer Rustin Parr (Pastor), driven by "voices" to slay seven Burkittsville children back in 1940. This utterly straight-faced account is an example not only of brilliant marketing but an utterly compelling hoax that can take its place beside Orson Welles's infamous 1938 *War of the Worlds* radio broadcast.

BLOOD AND ROSES (1960) ***

D: Roger Vadim. Mel Ferrer, Elsa Martinelli, Annette Vadim. 74 mins. (Paramount)

Vadim's update of Sheridan Le Fanu's venerable vampire story "Carmilla" is an atmospheric affair that neatly contrasts gothic and modern elements. This handsome, crisply told terror tale features a terrific nightmare sequence, color and B&W photography within the same frame (à la Lars von Trier's 1991 hallucination *Zentropa* [see index] and the more widely hyped *Pleasantville*), relatively daring lesbian imagery, and an eerie *danse macabre* that prefigures *Carnival of Souls*, all in a compact 74 minutes. The cassette's considerable downside has to do not with the film but with Paramount's briefly heralded "MasterSharp" process, which purported to lend greater audio and visual quality to tapes recorded in the inferior E.P. (slow-speed) mode. While the audio is adequate, the transfer drains the richness from Vadim's original Technicolor, leaving the film with a faded, fuzzy look. (The same label's *Frankenstein and the Monster from Hell* comes doubly cursed, since it's transferred from an edited TV version of the original Hammer release.) Gregory (*Slime City*) Lamberson's low-budget but effective *New York Vampire* (EI) offers a modern, downtown Manhattan variation on the "Carmilla" fable.

BLOOD BEAST TERROR (1967) **

D: Vernon Sewell. Peter Cushing, Robert Flemyng, Wanda Ventham. 81 mins. (Monterey, n.i.d.)

Entomologist Flemyng turns daughter Ventham into an outsized death's-head moth with vampiric tendencies. Must have seemed like a good idea at the time.

BLOOD CLAN (1991) ***

D: Charles Wilkinson. Gordon Pinsent, Michele Little, Robert Wisden. 91 mins. (Monarch)

This offbeat, 1910-set drama/horror hybrid stars Little as the sole survivor of Scotland's mass-murdering, flesh-eating Bane clan, saved from the gallows by the same judge (Pinsent) who'd ordered the execution of the family's adult members. Pinsent relocates to a remote western Canadian village, where, with his resentful wife, he raises the girl with his own biological daughter. When a rash of ritualistic killings plague the area, suspicion naturally points to the now-adult Little. Winner of several Canadian film awards, *Blood Clan* may rely too heavily on domestic drama to please hard-core horror fans, while its extreme exploitation elements—psycho slayings and cannibalism—may turn off more genteel viewers. Still, *Blood Clan*, like the unsung 1988 Aussie outing *Celia: Child of Terror* (see index), makes for an engrossing, thoughtful blend of realism, mystery, and gore.

BLOOD FEAST (1963) **

D: Herschell Gordon Lewis. Thomas Wood (William Kerwin), Connie Mason, Mal Arnold. 70 mins. (Something Weird) DVD

The movie that invented the hardcore gore genre, from the fertile mind of H. G. Lewis. Lewis's cynical mutilation tableaux are relieved by this legendary lunch-loser's consummate bad acting, particularly by ex-Playmate Mason. When in North Miami Beach, be sure to visit the luxurious Suez Motel, where much of this pioneering work was shot. *Blood Feast* has been endlessly ripped off, referenced, and virtually recreated in flicks ranging from *Blood Diner* (Vestron) to Fred Olen Ray's *Hollywood Chainsaw Hookers* (see index). Something Weird Video, meanwhile, has all but cornered the market in Lewis titles of every genre.

BLOOD FOR DRACULA (A.K.A. *ANDY WARHOL'S DRACULA*) (1974) ***1/2

D: Paul Morrissey. Udo Kier, Joe Dallesandro, Arno Juerging, Vittorio De Sica, Maxime

McKendry, Roman Polanski. 93 mins. (Image Entertainment) DVD

After the uneven but consistently over-the-top *Flesh for Frankenstein* (a.k.a. *Andy Warhol's Frankenstein* [Image, DVD]), Morrissey fashions one of the screen's best horror/comedy combos here, with an anemic Drac (Kier) and loyal minion (Juerging) scouring the 1920s Italo countryside in search of "wirgin" blood. Dallesandro, likewise fresh from *Flesh*, resurfaces as a Brooklyn-accented Marxist gardener (!), while noted directors Polanski and De Sica cameo as a hostile villager and the windbag dad of a quartet of sisters, respectively. Kier makes for a semisympathetic Drac, summed up by his now famous lament "The blood of these whores is killing me. I just want my coffin back…to sleep in." Image's Eurohorror Redemption line, meanwhile, has the early Clive Barker experimental terror shorts *Salome* and *The Forbidden* and the 1975 gothic lesbian-vampire romp *The Bloodsucker Leads the Dance*, among many others.

BLOOD LINK (1982) **1/2

D: Alberto De Martino. Michael Moriarty, Penelope Milford, Cameron Mitchell. 98 mins. (Video Treasures)

A nightmare-plagued doc (Moriarty) discovers he has an evil twin brother in this interesting, overlooked though uneven sleeper highlighted by Mike's ever unpredictable work and by Mitchell in one of his better later roles.

THE BLOOD ON SATAN'S CLAW (1971) ***

D: Piers Haggard. Patrick Wymark, Linda Hayden, Barry Andrews. 93 mins. (Cannon)

Devil-worshipping kids in 17th-century England cause havoc for locals in a stylish, genuinely unsettling Brit fear flick with a strong period flavor.

BLOOD TIES (1991) ***

D: Jim McBride. Harley Venton, Patrick Bauchau, Bo Hopkins, Kim Johnston Ulrich, Michelle Johnson. 84 mins. (New Horizons)

Onetime underground auteur Jim (*David Holzman's Diary*) McBride —who's also directed such mainstream Hollywood fare as the Richard Gere *Breathless* remake (Vestron) and *The Big Easy* (HBO)—fashions a neat vampire variation that originally aired on cable TV. In *Blood Ties*, produced by Gene (brother of Roger) Corman, nonlethal Carpathian vampires, living for generations in L.A., are periodically victimized by mouth-foaming fundamentalists (led by Hopkins) obsessed with the vamps' "blasphemous" presence and envious of their comparative material success. McBride tackles several themes simultaneously—assimilationism versus cultural isolationism, cross-ethnic romance (between vampire hero Venton and normal Johnston Ulrich, a tryst that incurs the wrath of Venton's Carpathian ex, Johnson), and the eternal conflict between group loyalty and individual ambition. Not that *Blood Ties* is a dry, serious treatise. Anything but—the flick also features several bloody FX scenes, vampire bikers amok, a last-reel rumble between bloodsucker and fundamentalist forces, and dark wit aplenty. *Blood Ties* delivers the genre goods with smarts and style to spare.

BLOODY PIT OF HORROR (1965) **1/2

D: Max Hunter (Massimo Pupillo). Mickey Hargitay, Walter Brandi, Louise Barrett, and the Cover Girls. 87 mins. (Sinister Cinema)

Former Mr. Jayne Mansfield Mickey Hargitay stars as the Crimson Executioner, a muscle-bound torturer Iron-Maidened back in 1848 (in an opening scene that blatantly rips off Mario Bava's *Black Sunday*). He reawakens to impale and slaughter anew when a bunch of badly dubbed models and photographers invade his castle to snap cover photos for a lurid line of horror paperbacks. As an actor, Mickey doesn't really get to stretch here, though at least one of his victims does when he winds up on the rack. The best exchange takes place between a catty brunette model and her bleached-blond counterpart, to wit:

BLONDE:
I'm not just a dumb blonde, y'know.

BRUNETTE:
Who says you're a blonde?

For a work based on "the writings of Marquis de Sade," *Bloody Pit* is woefully lacking in discipline.

BLOODY WEDNESDAY   (1985) ***

D: Mark G. Gilhuis. Raymond Elmendorf, Pamela Baker, Navarre Perry, Jeff O'Haco. 89 mins. (Prism, n.i.d.)

Bloody Wednesday is one truly strange movie. The twisted script—by former more-or-less mainstream scenarist Philip (*Johnny Guitar, Studs Lonigan*) Yordan, who later specialized in bizarre B titles—tells of chronic screw-up Harry (Elmendorf), who, after losing his job, holes up in an empty L.A. hotel owned by a client of his concerned older brother (Perry). Here Harry unravels at an accelerated pace, enjoying the warped, pulpy fantasy life of a man who's seen too many B movies. (Hey, we can definitely relate to *that*!) He converses with his pet teddy bear (voiced by the late midget actor Billy Curtis, of *Terror of Tiny Town* fame), befriends a bonkers imaginary bellhop (sort of a precursor of *Barton Fink's* Chet [Steve Buscemi]), and crosses paths with a violent street hood (ace stuntman O'Haco), who turns out to be all too real. *Bloody Wednesday* may not be up there with such agoraphobic epics as Polanski's *The Tenant* or Kubrick's *The Shining* (from which this flick lifts), but it displays as much sheer weirdness.

Only the cheap, if inevitable, slaughter climax detracts from its mood of sustained dementia.

BLUEBEARD   (1944) B&W ***

D: Edgar G. Ulmer. John Carradine, Jean Parker, Nils Asther, Iris Adrian. 73 mins. (Goodtimes) DVD

Carradine carries the day as a Parisian puppeteer who spends his spare time strangling unsuspecting women in a tight thriller aided by cult auteur Ulmer's atmospheric direction. Other Ulmer outings recently added to the video ranks include the surreal 1945 mystery *Strange Illusion* and 1959's *Journey Beneath the Desert* (a.k.a. *L'Atlantide*), both from Sinister Cinema.

BODY BAGS   (1993) **½

D: John Carpenter, Tobe Hooper. Stacy Keach, Alex Datcher, Mark Hamill, Robert Carradine, David Warner, Deborah Harry, Twiggy, David Naughton, Sheena Easton. 95 mins. (Republic)

Wearing Rick Baker makeup, John Carpenter hosts (as a morgue attendant with a penchant for bad puns) and helms two segments of this Showtime cable scare anthology. Episode #1, "The Gas Station," is a virtual minicompendium of the *Halloween* horrormeister's patented fright moves as foxy attendant Datcher dodges a psycho at the all-night title site. Effective jolts and in-jokes abound—the station is situated outside *Halloween's* Haddonfield; customers include David (*An American Werewolf in London*) Naughton, Wes Craven, and Carpenter regular Buck Flower, while Sam Raimi cameos as a corpse. Unfortunately, the payoff doesn't match the buildup. Carpenter and crew employ a more original idea in "Hair," with a balding Keach unwisely signing on as a client of miracle-cure TV pitchman Warner and henchnurse Harry; again, a weak ending undermines

an otherwise funny fear fable. Hooper takes the reins for the third and grisliest installment, "Eye," which, despite appearances by John Agar, Roger Corman, John Landis, and Hooper himself, plays like an ocular variation on the same director's overwrought 1990 pyromania exercise, *Spontaneous Combustion* (Video Treasures). Still, *Body Bags* harbors enough horrific highlights to justify the price of an overnight rental.

THE BODY SNATCHER   (1945) B&W ***½

D: Robert Wise. Boris Karloff, Bela Lugosi, Henry Daniell. 77 mins. (RKO/Turner, n.i.d.)

Boris is at his menacing best as a 19th-century grave robber who graduates to murder to meet his quota in a typically atmospheric Val Lewton chiller based on a Robert Louis Stevenson story. Bela lends sinister support in a secondary role. The film sports a terrifically chilling ending.

BOWERY AT MIDNIGHT   (1942) B&W **½

D: Wallace Fox. Bela Lugosi, Dave O'Brien, Tom Neal. 60 mins. (Sinister Cinema)

Bela is a madman who keeps zombies in the basement of his Bowery mission. *Bowery at Midnight* represents pretty shoddy filmmaking, but the evocative title, downbeat atmosphere, and fine cult cast—including (beyond the immortal Bela) Dave (*Reefer Madness*) O'Brien and Tom (*Detour*) Neal—makes this *Bowery* worth a visit.

BRAM STOKER'S DRACULA (1974) **½

D: Dan Curtis. Jack Palance, Fiona Lewis, Nigel Davenport, Simon Ward. 105 mins. (MPI)

Following the theatrical success of Coppola's vampire epic of the same name, MPI exhumed Dan (*Dark Shadows*) Curtis's earlier TV adaptation, starring Palance as the thirsty count. While modestly mounted and often static, Curtis's version represents a fairly earnest attempt to remain relatively faithful to its source. The production design may be threadbare compared with Coppola's extravaganza—Drac's Carpathian castle looks downright cheery here—but Palance, as might be expected, makes for a singularly intense Transylvanian, ably conveying Dracula's rage and bringing out the famed bloodsucker's inherent pimp qualities as he convincingly abuses his stable of distaff vamps. (The bug-munching Renfield is lost in this particular translation.) Longtime TV vet Curtis occasionally manages to overcome the medium's limitations, as when he compresses Drac's shipboard slaughterfest into a single striking image of a petrified seaman clutching an obviously ineffective crucifix, a *tableau vivant* that's artfully expanded in John Badham's 1979 *Dracula* (Universal), starring Frank Langella as the caped count, Laurence Olivier as Van Helsing, Kate Nelligan as Lucy, and the ever dependable Donald Pleasence as Dr. Seward.

BRAM STOKER'S DRACULA
(1992) ***1/2

D: Francis Ford Coppola. Gary Oldman, Winona Ryder, Anthony Hopkins, Sadie Frost, Keanu Reeves, Bill Campbell, Richard E. Grant, Cary Elwes, Tom Waits. 123 mins. (Columbia/TriStar) DVD

Eschewing the slimmed-down, stagebound approach established by Tod Browning's Bela edition—the basis of most straightforward Drac adaptations to come—Coppola returns the tale to its pulp Victorian roots by adhering to Stoker's then-contemporary 1897 concerns, biases, references, and themes. These range from the nature of romantic love to venereal-disease fears (with their current AIDS corollary), new tech-

---

GARY OLDMAN: *A DRAC FOR ALL SEASONS*
As Told to The Phantom

British actor Gary Oldman has played many an offbeat biographical role. He was self-destructive punk rocker Sid Vicious in Sid & Nancy *(Nelson), impulsive gay playwright Joe Orton in* Prick Up Your Ears *(Virgin Vision), accused Kennedy assassin Lee Harvey Oswald in Oliver Stone's* JFK *(Warner), and Beethoven in* Immortal Beloved *(Columbia/TriStar). One historical figure the versatile Oldman never expected to add to his list was Dracula. Oldman shared his thoughts with yours truly shortly after* Dracula's *theatrical opening.*

PHANTOM: Dracula's a character many flamboyant actors have sunk their teeth into—Bela Lugosi, Christopher Lee, and Jack Palance, to name a few. Was it a role you consciously wanted to play?

OLDMAN: No, I never thought about Dracula, really. It never occurred to me to play anything like that. In fact, when I heard they were doing *Dracula*, my initial response was "Why?"

PHANTOM: What changed your mind?

OLDMAN: When I learned it was Francis doing it, I thought, "Then he must see something in it. It's not going to be like the others. There's going to be a vision."

PHANTOM: How did you feel about Coppola directly linking Stoker's vampire with the real-life fifteenth-century warrior Vlad the Impaler?

OLDMAN: When you show Vlad, at least you get an idea of the origin of the vampire. I saw there was goodness in him, that he was a soul who'd fallen from grace.

PHANTOM: Do you feel the film is really faithful to Stoker's book?

OLDMAN: Of course, we cheated a bit. We all sat around at Napa and read the book. It took us two or three days. I hardly said a word the whole of the reading, because Dracula doesn't say that much. It's all seen through the eyes of Mina and Dr. Seward and Van Helsing. You couldn't really make Stoker's book, which is a collection of letters; you'd have a boring six-hour movie. But Coppola's taken the spirit of the book.

PHANTOM: In the course of your career, you've already portrayed a Southern prison inmate [*Chattahoochie*], a Boston attorney [*Criminal Law*], and a Hell's Kitchen Irishman [*State of Grace*]. How did you arrive at your Dracula voice?

OLDMAN: The story is that the real Prince Vlad was held captive by the Turks from the age of six to fifteen, a very formative period in one's life. So I thought, "Well, I suppose he would speak Turkish." And I know someone who's Hungarian, so I sort of borrowed from him as well. I worked on my voice for two months, to lower it, with a singing teacher; instead of having them do anything electronic to my voice, I wanted to do all these sounds. And as an homage to Bela, I said to Francis, "Can I do one take where I say, 'I never drink...*wine*'?"

nological advances (including the nascent motion picture medium), and even America's Wild West. In Coppola's version, Bowie knives, cinematographs, and then-shocking books like Sir Richard Burton's *Arabian Nights* (the *Joy of Sex* of its day) share a crossroads world with decaying Carpathian castles and mysterious, threatening foreigners embodied by the dread Dracula himself. The result is a grand-scale blend of dangerous erotica, febrile romance, rousing adventure, and charnel-house horror.

Bram Stoker's Dracula unfolds as a series of lush, detailed paintings brought to life by Coppola's bulging bag of cinematic tricks, from affectionate re-creations of the medium's earliest in-camera FX magic to clever shock cuts (e.g., a severed head to a slab of roast beef). One of FFC's neatest conceits is Drac's outsized shadow, which wanders with a will of its own. Unlike earlier, visually stunning but contentually empty Coppola exercises such as *One from the Heart* (Columbia/TriStar), here the spectacular visuals support their mythic source material.

The ever versatile Oldman gives Drac a fresh spin. He first appears as a fierce 15th-century warrior (the real-life Vlad the Impaler, whose connection to Stoker's bloodsucker is tenuous but whose inclusion adds plenty of production-design opportunities) enraged by his wife's suicide, his bouts with doubt, and the church's inability to ease his subsequent pain. When he welcomes Jonathan Harker (Reeves) into his cob-webbed castle, he's an ancient but energetic shadow of his former sturdy self. After draining a ship's crew of their invigorating blood, Drac surfaces in London as an elegant gent with shoulder-length hair. Oldman handles each of Dracula's incarnations with equal aplomb.

Hopkins makes for a cruder but wittier Van Helsing than such screen fore-bears as Edward Van Sloan and Peter Cushing. Asked if he intends to perform an autopsy on the late Lucy Westenra,

Hopkins casually replies, "No, I just want to cut off her head and take out her heart." Frost is excellent as Drac's spirited victim Lucy, while Ryder convinces as her shyer friend, Mina. Bill (*The Rocketeer*) Campbell is properly laconic as visiting Texan Quincy, and Elwes is appropriately bland (sort of a David Manners for the '90s) as Lucy's aristocratic beau. Less serendipitous are a miscast Reeves and a Renfield interpreted by Tom Waits (!), who, while better than expected, demonstrates he's no Dwight Frye. In what well may be the film's greatest casting coup, Sofia Coppola *doesn't* appear at all. On the downside, *Bram Stoker's Dracula* is a tad slow to get rolling and, while creepy, isn't particularly scary (admittedly not Coppola's priority here). Annie Lennox's haunting "Vampire Love Song" extends the pic's bittersweet mood into the closing credits.

BRAM STOKER'S THE MUMMY (1997) **¹/₂

D: Jeffrey Obrow. Louis Gossett, Jr., Amy Locane, Eric Lutes, Richard Karn, Mark Lindsay Chapman, Lloyd Bochner, Victoria Tennant. 99 mins. (A-Pix) DVD

Drawn from Stoker's novel *The Jewel of the Seven Stars*—previously the basis for the 1980 Charlton Heston mummy movie *The Awakening* (Warner)—*Bram Stoker's The Mummy*, from scare specialist Jeffrey (*Servants of Twilight, The Kindred*) Obrow, arrives as a mostly entertaining, if occasionally awkward, mix of Victorian gothic-styled dramatics and contempo Southern California characters. Light in the gore department, save for a discreetly lit dismemberment sequence and some faux nightmare tableaux, the pic compensates with effective suspense, an earnest tone, and sturdy perfs by a cast of veteran thesps and network-TV refugees, notably hero Lutes (*Caroline in the City*) and *Home Improvement*'s Karn as his portly, femme-crazed colleague. Vic-

toria Tennant can be glimpsed in an eye-blink cameo as a blind landlady. *Bram Stoker's The Mummy* also contains a candidate for The Phantom's Famous Last Words file, when a maid calls out, "I'm just down in the basement getting a space heater for Mr. Wyatt!" Stoker, meanwhile, is less adroitly plundered in 1997's *Bram Stoker's Shadowbuilder* (Sterling), despite the presence of Michael (*Henry*) Rooker and Tony (*Candyman*) Todd.

THE BRIDE (1985) ***

D: Franc Roddam. Sting, Jennifer Beals, Anthony Higgins, Clancy Brown, David Rappaport, Geraldine Page, Quentin Crisp. 118 mins. (Columbia/TriStar)

The Bride answers the venerable fright-film question: What might have happened if, in the original *Bride of Frankenstein*, the rejected Monster *hadn't* given in to his rage and blown up the lab but instead had gone off to "find himself" and granted his intended mate time to do likewise? In Roddam's revisionist version of the Frankenstein story, the Monster (inventively interpreted by Brown) hits the road, hooks up with an enterprising dwarf named Rinaldo (Rappaport), and achieves a measure of showbiz success as part of a comedy high-wire act in a Budapest circus. A parallel thread follows the Pygmalion-esque progress of the Bride (*Flashdance*'s Beals, shown briefly sans leotards here) under the tutelage of her creator, Baron Frankenstein (played by a largely zingless Sting), who wants to mold her into the perfect woman (i.e., "the equal of any man"). The stage is thus set for any number of other, equally relevant queries. Can the Monster redeem himself in the eyes of his beloved? Can the Bride—an independent, sophisticated creature (at least when she's not tearing her food apart or snarling at the castle cat)—escape the baron's increasingly possessive clutches? Though it runs on about a reel too long, *The Bride* addresses these issues in a genuinely entertaining and imaginative way. Watch it with someone you love.

BRIDE OF FRANKENSTEIN (1935) B&W ★★★★

D: James Whale. Boris Karloff, Elsa Lanchester, Ernest Thesiger, Colin Clive. 75 mins. (Universal) DVD

From Whale's atmospheric direction to Thesiger's supremely perverse Dr. Pretorius to Elsa's electric hairdo and Boris's alternately poignant and pushy Monster, *Bride* ranks as one of horrordom's towering achievements. For the inside story on Whale and his *Bride*, scope out Bill Condon's excellent biopic, *Gods and Monsters* (see index).

THE BRIDE WITH WHITE HAIR: THE SERIES

THE BRIDE WITH WHITE HAIR 2 (1993) ★★★½

D: David Wu and Ronny Yu. Brigitte Lin, Leslie Cheung, Sunny Chan, Christy Chung, Joey Memg, Lily Chung. 80 mins. (Tai Seng) DVD

"Having been misunderstood by her lover, Cho Yi Hang, Lien Ni Chang went on a killing rampage and slaughtered everyone in Wu Tang." So goes the written prologue to Wu's sequel to Ronny Yu's equally excellent *The Bride with White Hair* (Tai Seng, DVD), a mesmerizing period fantasy-horror-martial-arts romance about angry (to put it mildly!) bride-to-be Lin, who transforms into a witch, complete with a nest of wild white hair that doubles as a lethal weapon. While a chastened Cho hies to a remote mountain in hopes of retrieving a "majestic flower" that might reverse Lin's symptoms, 'tude, and tresses, the vengeful bride snatches Lyre, the wife of Cho's nephew Kit, on her wedding night. Kit leads a disparate crew of kung fu fighters, including a wisecracking sidekick, a tomboy (who's secretly in love with Kit), and a tough old lady, who vow to terminate the bride and her cadre of demonic femme minions' reign of terror. Battles rage and blood flows, both in the present and via flashbacks, with most of our heroes meeting horrible deaths at the hands and hair of the bride. This breathlessly paced exercise in mythic escapism boasts shocks aplenty, a mega body count, and a moral to boot.

THE BRIDES OF DRACULA (1960) ★★★

D: Terence Fisher. Peter Cushing, Martita Hunt, David Peel. 86 mins. (Universal)

Cushing repeats his *Horror of Dracula* Van Helsing role, this time in pursuit of Dracula disciple Peel, in a bloody good vampire outing from director Fisher and the horror mavens at Britain's Hammer Films.

THE BROOD (1979) ★★★

D: David Cronenberg. Oliver Reed, Samantha Eggar, Art Hindle. 92 mins. (Embassy, n.i.d.)

Cronenberg's oft brilliant meta-shocker sees Eggar's hostilities come to vengeful life as a killer crew of mallet-wielding munchkins! (Woody Allen employed a similar conceit for a very funny throwaway gag, involving a gorilla, in *Stardust Memories*.) Cronenberg's bleak vision may be light on science, but it shapes up as a genuinely creepy, downright disturbing viewing experience and represents D.C. at his megaphobic best.

BROTHERHOOD OF SATAN (1971) ★★★

D: Bernard McEveety. Strother Martin, L. Q. Jones, Anna Capri. 92 mins. (Columbia/TriStar)

An earnest, eerie, imaginative indie—produced by character thesps Alvy *(Green Acres)* Moore and L. Q. Jones—*Brotherhood* follows a satanic coven that covets the children of a small Southern town. Moore also turns up in the less effective *The Witchmaker* (Media).

THE CABINET OF DR. CALIGARI (1919) B&W ★★★½

D: Robert Wiene. Conrad Veidt, Werner Krauss, Lil Dagover. 92 mins. (Kino) DVD

The surreal journey of the mad Dr. Caligari and his somnambulistic slave, Cesare, through a distorted dreamscape of expressionist sets retains its dark, disorienting power, thanks to Wiene's masterful direction. Though the film is available on several public-domain labels, Kino has the definitive edition. The grim but pale 1962 remake, *The Cabinet of Caligari*, scripted by Robert *(Psycho)* Bloch, remains unavailable on tape. Stephen *(Cafe Flesh)* Sayadian's 1989 downtown "avant-garde" black comedy, *Dr. Caligari* (SGE), is well worth avoiding.

CANDYMAN: THE SERIES

CANDYMAN (1992) ★★★

D: Bernard Rose. Virginia Madsen, Tony Todd, Vanessa Williams, Xander Berkeley, Kasi Lemmons. 98 mins. (Columbia/TriStar) DVD

As John Sayles did in his 1980 chiller *Alligator*, director/coscripter Rose, working from Clive Barker's short story "The Forbidden," literalizes an urban fright folktale. Instead of sewer-dwelling gators, Rose's film deals with the myth of Candyman, a century-old African-American avenger who magically materializes to massacre anyone foolhardy enough to say his name five times while looking in a mirror. But Candyman

(Todd) is more than mere myth, as grad student Madsen and associate Lemons learn the hard way when they unwittingly invoke the hook-handed spirit while investigating his gory legend at Chicago's already ominous Cabrini-Green Housing Project. When Madsen refuses to volunteer to become Candyman's willing victim, the vengeful specter commits a fresh round of bloody atrocities for which Madsen gets the blame. Another story thread concerns Madsen's disintegrating relationship with her smug, generally useless academic hubby (Berkeley), an unraveling accelerated by her sudden status as an accused serial killer.

Auteur Rose, who skillfully explored childhood horrors in 1989's *Paperhouse* (see index), manages to wring parallel lines of tension from Madsen's unstable personal life and the story's grisly supernatural overlay. Rose's blend of the bleakly realistic, epitomized by the projects' detailed squalor (lensed mostly in harsh winter daylight), and the supernatural weaves a genuinely disturbing spell. Our heroine's plunge into near-madness is also harrowingly delineated. *Candyman*'s only major flaw lies with the titular bogeyman, a character who's far too specific to be treated as vaguely as he is here. (A flashback sequence might have helped.) While Todd conveys a convincing sense of both majesty and menace, *Candyman* resorts to too many Freddy Krueger moves as the reels roll on. A comic epilogue also serves to cheapen the film's better, darker instincts. Still, *Candyman* offers strong performances, especially by Madsen, Todd, and Williams, and contains its fair share of legit jolts.

CANDYMAN: FAREWELL TO THE FLESH (1995) ***

D: Bill Condon. Tony Todd, Kelly Rowan, Timothy Carhart, Veronica Cartwright, William O'Leary, Bill Nunn, Matt Clark. 99 mins. (PolyGram)

A CANDID CONVERSATION WITH *CANDYMAN* TONY TODD

As Told to The Phantom

Veteran film and stage actor Tony Todd first attracted genre fans' attention via his visceral turn as vicious gang leader "the Count" in 1987's Enemy Territory. *He's since gained greater recognition as the screen embodiment of Clive Barker's undead avenger Candyman.*

PHANTOM: **Do you think Candyman's streak of gratuitous cruelty undercuts our sympathy?**
TODD: **Yeah, it does, but I think it also makes him more complicated. This is not an easy guy to pin down. Obviously, he's in need of therapy, but, you know, he is dead. What's a therapist gonna say? "Get a life"?**
PHANTOM: **And he can't really take up painting again.**
TODD: **Unless he did it left-handed. Or did that kind of Jackson Pollock stuff. Just spray-paint his chest, open it up, and let the bees fly where they want. He'd make a fortune!**
PHANTOM: **Did you have an easier time with the bees [in the sequel]?**
TODD: **No, I had a *worse* time. I *thought* I would have an easier time. The same entomologist was there, and again he assures me, "No problem." But he also tells me, "Tony, it really is better to work with bees early in the morning." He says this at about two-twenty P.M. This is the big bee day. He says, "The bees get a little temperamental after a long time under the hot lights." That's the last thing I hear him say. Then they come over and pin a rose on me to make me look like a queen bee to confuse these poor guys. They're unhappy because they get on me and say, "Wait a minute, where's the honey?"**
PHANTOM: **Any injuries?**
TODD: **I had twenty-seven stings. That scene where I'm on the log, that was a horrible day. But the worst day was when we kill Thibideaux [Matt Clark]; I was in a restraining board, so I can't open my coat. I was trussed in there; I couldn't move. We shot this late at night—like ten-thirty—after I'd already been warned they work better in the morning. He brings the bees into the studio with the hot lights and strange people walking around giving instructions. Then they dump them on *me*—in the cavity in the chest piece. I feel them buzzing; something happened, they released the floodgate, and a whole bunch of them landed on my ear and went to work. And the director says, "Don't hold them yet; let's just try to get the shot."**
PHANTOM: **And there are hundreds of them that you work with?**
TODD: **Hundreds? *Thousands!***
PHANTOM: **Is there any special kick to doing power-fiend roles like Candyman?**
TODD: **You know there is. Look at the perks. I can go to a lot of newsstands and pick out any candy bar I want. "No problem, man. Take the candy, man." I love the genre!**

Candyman (Todd) returns, to a new city (New Orleans, during Mardi Gras), in search of fresh victims in Condon's continuation of the Clive Barker–spawned series (the latter scores exec-producer and story credits here). In the opening scene an author (Michael Culkin), who's penned a book about the

Candyman "myth," joshingly repeats the dread Candyman chant. To his terminal regret, it works. Following Culkin's gory slaughter in a saloon men's room, young O'Leary—whose father, like Virginia Madsen in the original *Candyman,* had been branded a Candyman-copycat killer—is charged with the crime. His sister, teacher Annie Tarrant (Rowan)—aided by ailing mom (Cartwright) and loyal hubby (Carhart)—attempts to prove her bro's innocence. Bugged by her young students' belief in Candyman's reality, she likewise repeats Culkin's earlier error and calls Candyman forth. From that point on, the sequel pretty much follows in *Candyman's* footsteps, with the revived hook-handed fiend stalking our heroine while systematically dispatching her loved ones and anyone else—like amateur Candyman maven Thibideaux (Clark)—foolish enough to interfere with his agenda. The sequel further clarifies Candyman's roots, supplying the expos-itory flashbacks missing from the initial outing and establishing a stronger con-nection between Candyman and his cur-rent victims. *Candyman: Farewell to the Flesh* doesn't stint on the horrific FX (by the Ultimate Effects team, with a major assist from bee wrangler Norman E. Gary) as our title fiend bleeds bees, guts his prey, and confronts Rowan and allies in an at-once violent and atmospheric finale. Todd returns in the 1999 direct-to-video sequel, *Candyman 3: Day of the Dead* (Artisan, DVD). Director Condon went on to helm the James Whale biopic *Gods and Monsters.*

CANNIBAL HOLOCAUST (1979)0 *

D: Ruggero Deodato. R. Bolla (a.k.a. Robert Kerman), Francesca Ciardi, Perry Pirkanen, Pio Di Savoia, Salvatore Basile. Subtitled. 95 mins. (Blackest Heart)

Unless close-ups of slaughtered ani-mals, rotting corpses, amputa-tions, castrations, and sundry other, more arcane forms of self- and other

mutilation are your movie meat, you'd be advised to steer clear of this unde-niably popular Italo turkey. The film *does* boast a great score, itself a consis-tently hot-selling CD, available from Blackest Heart, and a "found footage" hook that presaged the even more pop-ular *Blair Witch Project.* Cannibalis-tic companion pieces include *Emerald Jungle* (Cinema Group), *Make Them Die Slowly* (IVE), *Jungle Holocaust* (Video City), and *Slaves of the Cannibal God* (Wizard).

CANNIBAL MAN (1971) ***1/2

D: Eloy de la Iglesia. Vicente Parra, Emma Cohen, Eusebio Poncela, Vicky Lagos, Ismael Merlo, Charlie Bravo. Subtitled.. 92 mins. (Anchor Bay) DVD

Despite a half-dozen gory slayings, Iglesia's excellent, if radically mis-nomered, *Cannibal Man* (the Spanish title translates as *Apartment on the Thir-teenth Floor*) exudes more sadness than horror. A lethal argument with an obnoxious cabdriver leads slaughter-house worker Marcos (Parra) to elimi-nate a chain of unlucky witnesses and interlopers, including his own fiancée and brother, who unwisely insist on vis-iting him. The central story, though, details Marcos's budding friendship with a lonely homosexual neighbor (Poncela) who lives in one of several high-rises that overlook Marcos's mod-est but extremely conspicuous house, itself tagged for eventual demolition. Even while claiming nearly a victim a day, Marcos adheres to his mundane routines, reporting to work (where he even receives an unexpected promo-tion!), hanging at a local café, and deal-ing with his increasingly malodorous abode by dousing it with air fresheners and perfume. *Cannibal Man* is quite unlike any American film dealing with the subject matter; rather than experi-encing psychotic glee, extreme remorse, or alienated indifference, Marcos settles instead into a dull depression allevi-

ated only by his melancholy neighbor's platonic (or at least sublimated) over-tures. *Cannibal Man* is well worth seek-ing out.

CAPTAIN KRONOS: VAMPIRE HUNTER (1973) ***

D: Brian Clemens. Horst Janson, Caroline Munro, John Carson, John Cater, Shane Briant, Lois Dane. 91 mins. (Paramount)

Captain Kronos, which shared a Hammer horror double bill with *Frankenstein and the Monster from Hell* during its original 1973 release, stars Janson as the titular bloodsucker-basher who also comes equipped with samurai-styled sword skills. Janson travels the 19th-century countryside accompanied by trusty hunchbacked vampire scholar Professor Grost (Cater). (As Horst at one point puts it, "What he doesn't know about vampirism wouldn't fill a flea's codpiece.") Rounding out the anti-vampire crew is Kronos groupie Carla, played by fan fave Munro. The plot pits our trio against an initially unidenti-fied fiend who's been busily depleting local virgins of their lifeblood, adding a mystery element to the already hybrid blend of swashbuckler and horror. The flick is also filled with deft visual touches, such as the flowers that wither and die at the hooded monster's mere approach.

CAPTIVE WILD WOMAN (1943) B&W **1/2

D: Edward Dmytryk. John Carradine, Evelyn Ankers, Milburn Stone, Acquanetta, Martha Vickers, Lloyd Corrigan. 61 mins. (Universal)

Universal honchos' efforts to add a recurring female fiend to their '40s monster roster came up short with their Ape Woman trilogy—*Captive Wild Woman, Jungle Captive,* and *Jungle Woman* (all Universal). *CWW* is the first and best of the threesome, but that's a less-than-gala testimonial. Indeed, with Stone as a Clyde Beatty wannabe (matched with lots of actual Beatty footage), *Captive Wild Woman* plays more like a circus picture than a horror flick, with wild-animal acts eating up much of the screentime. Mad doc Carradine easily steals his scenes. While second-rate compared with *Man Made Monster* and *The Mad Ghoul* (see index), *Captive Wild Woman* supplies modest fun for nostalgia-minded fear fans.

CARNIVAL OF SOULS (1962)
B&W**

D: Herk Harvey. Candace Hilligoss, Sidney Berger, Frances Feist, Stan Levitt, Art Ellison, Herk Harvey. 81 mins. (Sinister Cinema, VidAmerica) DVD

This legendary indie classic may represent the ultimate triumph of talent and care over budgetary constraints. The film works both as a straight-ahead horror outing in an understated but genuinely eerie Val Lewton vein and as a dramatization of a mental breakdown, as alienated Mary Henry (an indelible Hilligoss), after surviving a car crash, finds herself drifting ever further from reality. Director Harvey (who doubles as one of the cadaverous phantoms pursuing our ever endangered heroine) contrasts the determinedly mundane world of Mary's daily life (spent in such unotherworldly locales as Lawrence, Kansas, and Salt Lake City) with the haunting nocturnal images of a pier-front pavilion where the title specters perform a nightly *danse macabre*. While *Carnival of Souls*'s cult rep had grown steadily via its regional TV screenings over the decades, few viewers saw it in its entirety and sans disruptive commercials. Several public-domain labels have carried *Carnival,* but only Sinister Cinema had the complete original print until VidAmerica's edition, complete with an intro by Harvey, appeared following the film's selective 1989 the-

SOULS *SURVIVOR:* Candace Hilligoss (top) seeks to elude relentless phantoms in imaginative box art for Englewood's reissue of Herk Harvey's cult chiller *Carnival of Souls.* Courtesy of Englewood Entertainment/Wade Williams Distribution

atrical reissue. *Carnival of Souls* is must viewing not only for horror buffs but for cinema fans of all stripes. Avoid the awful 1999 Wes Craven–presented remake-in-name-only, *Carnival of Souls* (Trimark).

THE CARPENTER (1989) **

D: David Wellington. Wings Hauser, Lynne Adams, Pierre Lenoir. In R and unrated editions. 87 mins. (Republic)

Hauser returns with another of his patented wacky hack-'em-up perfs in a Canadian-lensed chiller that can't decide whether it's a hallucinatory thriller or a cheap slasher flick. Our story centers on unhappy housewife Adams, whose sour relationship with her unfaithful academic prig of a hubby (Lenoir) leads to a nervous breakdown (in the course of which Lynne shares a hospital room with a patient given to reciting, in a relentless monotone, the lyrics of Sam and Dave's "Knock on Wood" [!]). Lynne and Pierre eventually repair to a country home being renovated by not only a hired crew but the mysterious, chivalrous Wings, who soon acts as Lynne's instrument of revenge, treating her sundry enemies to a faceful of chainsaws and power drills. Is "the Carpenter" an actual psycho? The vengeful ghost of a mass murderer? A violent figment of Lynne's unstable imagination? Unfortunately, *The Carpenter* opts for the cheapest possible answers to those potentially intriguing queries.

CARRIE:
THE SERIES

CARRIE (1976) ***

D: Brian De Palma. Sissy Spacek, Piper Laurie, William Katt, Amy Irving, John Travolta. 98 mins. (MGM) DVD

Telekinetic teen (Spacek) strikes back at nutzoid mom (Laurie) and sadistic classmates (including a young Travolta) in De Palma's mostly successful Stephen King adaptation, highlighted by Spacek's shyly spooky perf, the frenzied finale, and the since oft imitated graveyard kicker. Katt (*Dance of the Damned*) Shea assumed the

---

Filmmakers in Focus!

HERK HARVEY: THE LAST INTERVIEW

As Told to The Phantom

Horrordom lost a visionary auteur and a class act when Carnival of Souls *creator Herk Harvey passed on in 1996. The Phantom spoke with Harvey prior to* Carnival's *theatrical rerelease.*

PHANTOM: When did you first become aware that *Carnival* was a cult movie?

HARVEY: I think it was when I started getting letters, usually from young people in New York and California. They would call the chamber of commerce in Lawrence, Kansas, and they'd say, "Do you know Herk Harvey?" And my name is *Harold* Harvey. So they'd say, "No, hell, we don't know him." So finally they got used to it and they would send me the letters. And I answered some of these kids.

PHANTOM: Do you identify with her [Mary Henry]?

HARVEY: I only do intellectually, I never do emotionally, because she's so cold, she won't let anybody in. We did that on purpose. We all build up defense mechanisms to keep from getting hurt, but if you get to the place where you do it like she does, you get to a place where you isolate yourself, where you're not living. And that's basically what the whole point of the film is—she gets to a place where she no longer communicates with life. Then the only thing left is for the ghoul to come up and say, "You're mine." We always hoped that people would get that, but in the drive-in situation, the people who saw it there never did....I got a Swedish review of *Carnival*. They really got excited about the concept of death. Was this all mental? Or was it physical? Was this spiritual? What actually happened?

PHANTOM: The music is a strong element.

HARVEY: It's interesting. I hate organ scores usually. A man in Kansas City used to play the organ in the Orpheum Theater. At that time, he wasn't scoring movies, he would just play before the movie. But there was a huge pipe organ he used to play. He said, "I'll write you an original score for this if you're interested." And I was, so he did it. I sent him the sixteen-millimeter version, and he scored it to that, did it on a Thomas organ, an electronic organ. And when I first heard it, I thought, "Eh, okay." But it really didn't have some of the elements that I wanted. And yet, I think that's one of the strongest features of the film today. The synthesizer wasn't big in those days, and he created on that organ sound effects, really, that helped things go along. Like when she's in the car and beginning to have motor problems. You know, to score that with an organ—a car having trouble—I couldn't imagine that. And yet it works. One of the things about organ music, calliope music, and carnival music, if it's a little off, if it goes a little minor, it really gets strange. For some reason, it goes back to the thing of having fun and tragedy being that close; to laughing, then serious, then getting *way* out.

PHANTOM: I don't think anyone was prepared for the dancing scenes in 1962. The closest thing might be scenes from *Beauty and the Beast*.

HARVEY: Well, that's really where I got a lot of the feel, from Cocteau. The

---

one that made a terrific impression on me was when she goes down the hallway—I couldn't figure if they had her on a roller or what—but it's like she's floating down the hall, and that wind is blowing on her. The face in the fireplace, the hands with the chandeliers, those were all great.

PHANTOM: Were you ever tempted to go back and "correct" *Carnival*'s glitches, like the footsteps?

HARVEY: The way I feel about the film is it's almost like colorizing. I can remember so well the night that I did the footsteps, sitting there with a piece of three-quarter-inch plywood in my lap and two high-heeled shoes, beating them on the plywood. Then when I looked at it, I thought, "God, that's terrible." But, I gotta show this, I gotta go to print stage, I can no longer fool around 'cause we're running out of money—so it went. And I wouldn't change that today. People can say, "God, that's really out of sync, and some of that dubbing in the very front—*God*, that's out-of-sync!" As a filmmaker, when I watch that film—and I've watched it an awful lot of times now with the festivals, more than I'd want to admit—it's like Chinese water torture. But I wouldn't change it, because that was the way it was. We had seventeen thousand dollars cash to make it. We were just in an absolute frenzy that last week to get it done, so we could actually come in on budget, because we had to save six hundred dollars so I could take a trip to New York to talk to Embassy Films about distribution. And we came in exactly on budget. It wasn't a case of us saying *this is good*. It was just a case of *had to have it*....We never made a cent from *Carnival*. Oh, I take that back! Once a year I would get a call from either the Waverly or the Thalia saying, "Could we rent *Carnival of Souls* for the New York University students for Halloween?" And I would send it to them, and I'd get a check for a hundred dollars. Which just barely covered the postage.

reins for the belated, ill-received 1999 sequel, *The Rage: Carrie 2* (MGM).

THE CARRIER (1988) ***

D: Nathan J. White. Gregory Fortescu, Stevie Lee, Steve Dixon, N. Paul Silverman. 95 mins. (Magnum)

The Carrier, sort of a *Blue Velvet* Meets *Masque of the Red Death*, centers on an unidentified flesh-melting disease sweeping through the isolated hamlet of Sleepy Rock, circa 1962. The plague is being unwittingly spread by the title character (Fortescu), a local pariah who appears to have contracted it from "the black thing"—a mysterious Bigfoot-like creature who may or may not be a hallucination. The predominantly Christian population promptly panics, eventually splitting into rival factions and waging an all-out gore war (!). *The Carrier*'s originality lies less in its bizarre plot, though, than in its pervasive aura of paranoia, its abundant religious imagery, and its almost Dark Ages sense of dread. White's Michigan-lensed indie is sometimes crude—though the sight of crazed fundamentalists, wrapped in protective plastic trash bags (!), cheerfully chopping one another to bits is a novel and compelling one—but it is rarely less than genuinely disturbing.

CASTLE FREAK (1995) ***

D: Stuart Gordon. Jeffrey Combs, Barbara Crampton, Jonathan Fuller, Massimo Sarchielli, Elisabeth Kaza, Raffaella Offidani, Jessica Dollarhide. 95 mins. (Full Moon) DVD

Re-Animator alums Gordon, scripter Dennis Paoli, and lead thesps Combs and Crampton combine their considerable talents to come up with a strong, textured terror film. Combs stars as an American who unexpectedly inherits an Italo castle. He visits the site with his wife (Crampton) and sightless daughter (Dollarhide), unaware that a twisted, naked freak (who turns out to be Combs's own sibling) is alive and sick in the castle dungeon and eager to vent his pent-up hostility. Combs, meanwhile, is hounded by guilt for having inadvertently killed his young son and blinded his daughter in a drunk-driving accident, an act that embittered spouse Crampton is unable to forgive. While never stinting on gore (including a cat-eating scene) or suspense, Gordon and Paoli craft a solid horror movie that doubles as a layered, often wrenching meditation on the themes of parental guilt and responsibility. Combs contributes strenuous work as the self-tortured family man, while Fuller lends a genuine sense of brute rage and pathos to his grunt-heavy role as the ugly embodiment of the assembled characters' collective guilt. Lensed on location in Giove, Italy, and buoyed by a first-rate Richard Band score, this disturbing, grimly moving chiller shapes up as a true thinking-phan's horror film.

CASTLE OF BLOOD (1964)
B&W ***

D: Antonio Margheriti. Barbara Steele, George Riviere, Montgomery Glenn. 85 mins. (Sinister Cinema)

A night-in-a-haunted-house flick shot with earnestly creepy flair and featuring the sepulchrally seductive Steele in the lead, *Castle of Blood*, based on Poe's "Berenice," rates as a good bet for Italo gothic horror fans, as does the same year's *Castle of the Living Dead* (Sinister Cinema), with Christopher Lee and

Donald Sutherland, in an early screen appearance.

CAT GIRL   (1957) B&W **½

D: Alfred Shaughnessy. Barbara Shelley, Robert Ayres, Kay Callard, Paddy Webster. 69 mins. (Columbia/TriStar)

Starlet Shelley's subtly sexy presence supplies welcome visual distraction in a professional but second-rate Brit rehash of Val Lewton's *Cat People*. Shelley's alleged feline condition, a family curse passed on by her late uncle, remains somewhat open to doubt throughout, while a pursuit scene is lifted practically intact from the original. The flick originally double-dated theatrically with the superior Bert I. ("Mr. B.I.G.") Gordon "stretcher" *The Amazing Colossal Man* (likewise Columbia/TriStar).

CAT PEOPLE:
THE SERIES

CAT PEOPLE   (1942) B&W ****

D: Jacques Tourneur. Simone Simon, Kent Smith, Jane Randolph, Tom Conway. 73 mins. (Turner, n.i.d.)

The first of RKO producer Val Lewton's "quiet" horror films, directed by protégé Tourneur, chronicles architect Smith's troubled marriage to a withdrawn Simon, who's convinced she's part feline. The film's subtly disturbing atmosphere and painstakingly choreographed shock scenes retain their original power. The infamous "Alan Smithee" scripted director Paul Schrader's 1982 *Cat People* (Universal, DVD), a more explicit but less effective remake.

THE CURSE OF THE CAT PEOPLE (1944) B&W ***

D: Robert Wise, Gunther von Fritsch. Simone Simon, Kent Smith, Jane Randolph, Elizabeth

Russell, Ann Carter, Sir Lancelot. 70 mins. (Turner, n.i.d.)

It's seven years after *Cat People*'s conclusion. Oliver and Ann Reed (Smith and Randolph reprising their original roles) have married and moved to Tarrytown, but all is not well in the Reed household. Daughter Amy (Carter) frequently retreats into a fantasy world, where she encounters her spiritual mother, Irena (Simon). The title is a downright cheat—*Curse* isn't really a horror film at all—but this is still an extremely haunting, often moving, and poetic pic contrasting Amy's melancholy hallucinations with the overinsistent clarity and relentless reality of her suburban surroundings. Another neat job by producer Val Lewton, scripter DeWitt Bodeen, and the entire RKO crew.

CAT'S EYE   (1985) **½

D: Lewis Teague. Drew Barrymore, James Woods, Alan King, Kenneth McMillan, Robert Hays, Candy Clark. 93 mins. (Key)

While he lifts freely from everything from EC Comics to *Gremlins*, writer Stephen King strings together a generally entertaining trilogy framed by the peripatetic journey of a versatile feline thesp. The pacing is swift, the stories generate sufficient suspense, and the tone remains refreshingly throwaway throughout. Even the multiple in-jokes (e.g., cameos by King's killer car, Christine, and murderous mutt, Cujo) are more self-mocking than self-aggrandizing. *Cat's Eye* is no *Creepshow* (see index), but it stacks up as an adequate time-filler chiller.

CEMETERY MAN   (1993/1996) ***

D: Michele Soavi. Rupert Everett, François Hadji-Lazaro, Anna Falchi, Mickey Knox, Fabiana Formica, Clive Riche, Katja Anton. 100 mins. (20th Century Fox)

Lensed by Dario Argento disciple Soavi in 1993 as *Dellamorte Del-*

lamore (a longtime bootleg video fave) and based on an Italo *Dylan Dog* graphic novel, *Cemetery Man* belatedly hit these shores for a select 1996 theatrical run. Brit thesp Everett (*My Best Friend's Wedding*) goes the hard-core horror-comedy route as graveyard watchman Francesco Dellamorte, whose buried charges, dubbed "returners," won't stay dead, compelling Rupe to dispatch them with bullets in the head (the old Romero technique). Abetted by mute, television-addicted assistant Gnaghi (chrome-domed Hadji-Lazaro, sort of a cross between Curly Howard and Tor Johnson), Francesco is kept busy as a succession of fatal accidents replenishes the cemetery's zombie supply. Our alienated hero ("We all do what we can not to think about life," he sighs) tumbles for femme mourner Falchi ("the most beautiful living woman I've ever seen"), who's in turn turned on by Francesco's underground ossuary. Loosely plotted but determinedly bizarre, *Cemetery Man* is rich in gallows humor, disgusto (though not groundbreaking) makeup FX, and a deadpan tone all its own. Manuel De Sica's deft score helps keep the demented story line bouncing along.

CHILD'S PLAY:
THE SERIES

CHILD'S PLAY   (1988) **½

D: Tom Holland. Katherine Hicks, Chris Sarandon, Alex Vincent, Brad Dourif, Dinah Manoff, Tommy Swerdlow. 87 mins. (MGM) DVD

Sort of a *Garbage Pail Kids* Go Psycho, Tom (*Fright Night*) Holland's influential killer-doll chiller has a slender premise: Dying madman Dourif transfers his evil soul into a singularly homely but seemingly benign "Good Guy" doll, which winds up in the possession of Chicago tyke Andy (Vincent), who unwittingly aids the demonic toy in a vengeful plot to waste Windy City cop Sarandon. The result is a watchable, occasionally fun but thoroughly contrived outing. While director Holland knows how to deliver a decent scare scene—as when Chucky assaults hero Sarandon during a high-speed car chase—and even names a character in honor of legendary Ed Wood regular and telepsychic Criswell, *Child's Play* is neither as funny nor as terrifying as *SCTV*'s memorable send-up "Slinky: Toy from Hell!"

CHILD'S PLAY 2   (1990) **½

D: John Lafia. Alex Vincent, Jenny Agutter, Gerrit Graham, Christine Elise, Brad Dourif, Grace Zabriskie. 84 mins. (Universal) DVD

The return of Chucky, the killer "Good Guy" doll (with voice again supplied by Dourif), and his intended victim, Andy (Vincent), is a routinely plotted affair lensed with dash, panache, and style—particularly young Andy's POV shots and a showdown set in a toy factory—and further bolstered by Kevin Yagher's dependable FX work. Here Good Guy manufacturers unwisely decide to reassemble the demented doll in a bid to exonerate themselves of any blame in Chucky's prior rampage. Naturally, this bad move revives the minuscule maniac, who sets out after Andy in order to complete the voodoo soul-transference ritual thwarted in the original. If you enjoyed the first one, *CP 2* shouldn't disappoint, its clichéd *Terminator*-type climax notwithstanding.

CHILD'S PLAY 3   (1991) **½

D: Jack Bender. Justin Whalin, Perrey Reeves, Jeremy Sylvers, Travis Fine, Andrew Robinson, Peter Haskell, Brad Dourif. 89 mins. (Universal)

With *Child's Play 3*, Chucky strengthens his position as a Froggy Gremlin for the '90s. The pic picks up eight years after *CP 2*, with toy manufacturers again rather inexplicably deciding to revive the Good Guy line.

Naturally, Chucky, who continues to harbor the twisted soul of serial killer Charles Lee Ray (Dourif), is one of the first dolls off the assembly line. Chucky pauses to orchestrate an attack-of-the-terror-toys sequence that polishes off top exec Sullivan (Haskell, in a role tailor-made for Leslie Nielsen) before making his way to Kent Military School, where his perennial victim, Andy (with Whalin replacing an aging Vincent), has been exiled. When the demonic doll—who plays such impish practical jokes as substituting live ammo for paint pellets during the cadets' mock war games (!)—targets black tyke Tyler (Sylvers) as his next host body, Andy and distaff cadet De Silva (Reeves) swing into action. The military school offers a reasonably novel setting, a carnival spookhouse ride provides an excellent locale for the climactic fright scenes, and the film is laced with dark humor throughout.

BRIDE OF CHUCKY   (1998) ***

D: Ronny Yu. Jennifer Tilly, Brad Dourif, Katherine Heigl, Nick Stabile, Alexis Arquette, John Ritter. 89 mins. (Universal) DVD

Chucky's back and Tilly's got him! That's Chucky, America's fave foulmouthed sociopathic Good Guy doll (still housing the evil soul of executed serial killer Charles Lee Ray, again wittily voiced by Dourif), and Jennifer Tilly, as the Chuckster's patient white-trash sleaze squeeze, Tiffany. Under veteran Hong Kong fantasy/horror helmer Ronny (*The Bride with White Hair*) Yu's direction, Chucky returns with a vengeance in what easily rates as the series' best entry. The pic opens with Tiffany repairing the severely scarred and damaged doll, who resembles a sort of a FrankenChucky. With the dubious aid of a manual titled "Voodoo for Dummies" (!), Tiffany tries to transfer

---

JENNIFER TILLY TELLS ALL

As Told to The Phantom

Since following her sister Meg into the movie biz in 1984, actress Jennifer Tilly has added her seductive, over-the-top talents to dozens of A and B comedies, noirs, and offbeat indies. Best known as the squeaky-voiced would-be actress Olive in Woody Allen's Bullets Over Broadway, *the suburban temptress in the Jim Carrey showcase* Liar Liar, *and lesbian Gina Gershon's partner in crime in the cutting-edge noir* Bound, *Tilly made her full-fledged horror-film debut in* Bride of Chucky.

PHANTOM: What attracted you to the role?

TILLY: Well, actually, when my agent first called up and said, "Do you want to do a *Child's Play* movie?" of course I said, "Absolutely not." Because people associate horror roles with something you do at the beginning of your career or the end of your career. But my agent sort of was saying it's not like that. They want to make a really cool movie. And with horror films being really big right now, it's a good way to reach another audience, like a young, hip audience, which is really good for your demographics. So he sent the script over, and I read it. I've never seen any of the other *Child's Play* movies, and I just thought it was really clever and funny and fresh and kind of unexpected.

The other thing I thought was really interesting was when he said Ronny

(continued)

Yu was gonna be the director. And he's just this brilliant Hong Kong director, a protégé of John Woo's, who directed this movie called *The Bride with White Hair*. There were several elements that made me think that they wanted to do something interesting....Ronny seemed the perfect type of director to reinvigorate the Chucky genre. I don't know if it's a cultural thing, but I think a lot of times that films in America, especially formulaic films, are very predictable. Not only have you seen the script, you know what's gonna happen, but you've seen the camera shots. The Hong Kong films—I was struck by their ability to make stuff phantasmagorical and grotesquely violent almost within the same frame....It just seemed that everything sort of coexisted. You know, the romance, the silliness, the humor, the violence. These films seem almost epic in their format. So I thought it's very interesting they hired Ronny Yu to do it and that they want me to play a part. I just thought it would be kind of a fun romp and that I'd have a good time.

PHANTOM: You've been in a ton of movies, especially the last few years. And you've mostly been attracted, it seems, to offbeat kinds of roles.

TILLY: Right. That was the thing too. I really liked the way Tiffany was written. I thought she was just a lot of fun. She's this odd mixture—she's really into mayhem, and she's kind of turned on by violence and murder. But at the same time she's a Martha Stewart aficionado, she's really romantic and sort of naïve in a way. You could really go over the top to a large extent and it would be appropriate. And going over the top is what I do best.

PHANTOM: You've done a lot of comedy before, but I think this is your first horror film.

TILLY: Yes, absolutely. I don't think I'd take on a horror film where I'm being chased, like where the murderer is chasing me, killing all my friends, because I think when you act it takes a lot out of you. And if you're going through that amount of extreme trauma, you would hope that you could save that kind of acting for something that's maybe a little more worthy of all the stress. I think that's too much emotional output in terms of the creative satisfaction returned.

Chuck's soul into a fresh human body (Arquette). A typical mix-up instead transports Tiff's essence into a tacky bridal doll. The diminutive duo dupe a pair of eloping teens (Stabile, Heigl) into driving them to Charles Ray's Hackensack, New Jersey, gravesite, where they hope to retrieve a magic amulet that will set the situation right. Along the way the deadly dolls rack up a sizable human body count, indulge in suitably bizarre domestic squabbles (Tiff's a Martha Stewart fan), and even enjoy an over-the-top sexual tryst. (When Tiffany queries, "Do you have a rubber?" Chucky replies, "I'm *all* rubber!"). Ritter contributes an amusing cameo as a power-crazed local police chief, while a clip from *Bride of Frankenstein* also sneaks its way in.

CHILDREN OF THE CORN:
THE SERIES

CHILDREN OF THE CORN   (1984)**

D: Fritz Kiersch. Peter Horton, Linda Hamilton, R. G. Armstrong. 93 mins. (Anchor Bay)

Vacationing couple Horton and a pre-*Terminator* Hamilton encounter brainwashed Midwestern yokel kids fond of sacrificing adults to their harvest god, "He Who Walks Behind the Rows." This weak adaptation of the Stephen King source material nonetheless scored well enough at the box office and on home vid to spawn (so far) five sequels.

CHILDREN OF THE CORN II: THE FINAL SACRIFICE   (1993)*½

D: David Price. Terence Knox, Paul Scherrer, Rosalind Allen, Ned Romero, Ryan Bollman, Christie Clark. 94 mins. (Paramount)

This belated, unnecessary sequel blends *Corn*-again fundamentalism with the standard quota of cheap chills. The surviving kid cultists who'd eliminated the adult population of Gatlin, Nebraska, conspire anew under the leadership of young Bollman (who shouts his lines like maybe boom mikes haven't been invented yet). While *Children of the Corn II* is a thoroughly by-the-numbers affair, it does offer one novel scene, wherein the corn kids turn an elderly sawbones into a human pincushion with a dozen or so hypos, then leave the dead doc with complimentary lollipops (!). *COTC II* also contributes a new addition to The Phantom's ever expanding Famous Last Words file, when one imminent victim wrongly surmises, "This might be a shortcut to the highway." Otherwise, *Children of the Corn II* is pretty close to a total shuck.

CHILDREN OF THE CORN III: URBAN HARVEST   (1995)***

D: James D. R. Hickox. Daniel Cerny, Ron Melendez, Jim Metzler, Nancy Lee Grahn, Michael Ensign. 91 mins. (Buena Vista)

Following an impressive cornfield crucifixion engineered by young killer-corn kid Cerny, the latter and his older adoptive brother (Melendez) journey to Chicago, where they're taken in by an unsuspecting corn commodities broker (Metzler) and wife (Grahn). While Melendez gradually adapts to urban high school life, Cerny lives only for the greater glory of He Who Walks Behind the Rows, planting his demonic seeds in the backyard and working to convert local kids to his cause. Under FX ace Screaming Mad George's supervision, *COTC III* easily emerges as the goriest and most crowd-pleasing of the King *Corn* lot.

CHILDREN OF THE CORN V: FIELDS OF TERROR   (1998) **

D: Ethan Wiley. Stacy Galina, Alexis Arquette, Adam Wylie, Eva Mendez, Ahmet Zappa, Angela Jones, Fred Williamson, David Carradine. 85 mins. (Dimension)

Writer/director Wiley constructs a serviceable but utterly routine return to King's *Corn* country, further elaborating on a horror hook that lent new meaning to the term *stalk*er flick and only marginally improving on the utterly dull 1996 entry, *Children of the Corn 4: The Gathering* (Touchstone). Here a half-dozen *Scream*-age airheads encounter supernatural killer kid Wylie and his corny crew for a series of slice-and-burn (the latter via a fiery sacrificial silo) set pieces that deliver the gory goods without scaring up much excitement or suspense. Carradine appears briefly as their strangely serene spiritual mentor, Luke. (As one corn kid says to a concerned "outsider," "Don't feel bad for Luke. He's been dead for years.") Carradine shares a mutual head-cleaving scene with local sheriff Fred ("the Hammer") Williamson in the pic's undisputed highlight. Two Zappas also show up—Ahmet plays one of the leads, while Diva Zappa *is* "Drill Girl." Followed by 1999's *Children of the Corn 666: Isaac's Return* (Dimension DVD).

A CHINESE GHOST STORY:
THE SERIES

A CHINESE GHOST STORY (1987) ***½

D: Siu-Tung Ching. Joey Wang (Wang Tsu-hsien), Leslie Cheung, Wu Ma. 91 mins. (Tai Seng) DVD

This film from Hong Kong producer Tsui Hark—since transplanted to Tinseltown—tells the story of young pilgrim Cheung, who wanders into a rural village in search of free lodging. Like strangers in many a Western fear film, he's soon sadistically directed to the worst site around, in this case the haunted Lan Ro Temple. There Cheung not only discovers alluring ghostess Wang but a superwitch equipped with an Amazing Colossal Tongue, several living-dead studs drained of their precious bodily fluids, and an aggressively eccentric Taoist swordsman (Wu Ma) who prefers ghosts to people but who agrees to guide Cheung through his perilous new surroundings. While a love story at heart, this kinetic tale also incorporates subversive humor, copious swordplay, horrific FX, and even scattered musical interludes, as when swordsman Wu performs what amounts to a Taoist version of "My Way." Followed by *Chinese Ghost Story II*, *Chinese Ghost Story III*, and the animated remake, *Chinese Ghost Story: The Tsui Hark Animation* (all Tai Seng, DVD). For a racier take on the theme, see *Erotic Ghost Story* (Tai Seng, DVD).

THE CHURCH   (1988) **½

D: Michele Soavi. Asia Argento, Hugh Quarshie, Tomas Arana, Feodor Chailiapin. Dubbed. 110 mins. (Southgate, n.i.d.)

Produced and coscripted by Soavi's mentor, Dario Argento, *The Church* emerges as a well-mounted but mostly routine gothic frightfest. The film opens with the bloody medieval massacre of scores of suspected satanists. A church is erected over the victims' mass grave, setting the scene for a violent payback that unfolds in the present. The simple premise serves as a broad canvas, which Soavi and Argento fill with bizarre Catholic/satanic imagery, visual flourishes, and gore galore. Deliberately paced, slight on characterizations, and light on (dubbed) dialogue, *The Church* partially compensates with impalings, face rippings, horse hooves trampling severed heads, and other, similarly bracing sights, set to a pumping Keith Emerson organ score.

CIRCUS OF HORRORS   (1960) ***½

D: Sidney Hayers. Anton Diffring, Erika Remberg, Yvonne Monlaur, Donald Pleasence. 89 mins. (HBO)

A superior, surprisingly sadistic for its time, and often haunting horror film, *Circus* casts Diffring as a homicidal fugitive plastic surgeon disguised as a circus owner. Pleasence impresses as the circus's soon-to-be-late (courtesy of an ill-advised drunken waltz with a dancing bear who would have preferred to sit that one out) original proprietor, as does the contrapuntal theme song "Look for a Star." John Moxey's *Circus of Fear* (Saturn), starring Christopher Lee, is likewise worth a look.

THE CLIMAX   (1944) **½

D: George Waggner. Boris Karloff, Susanna Foster, Turhan Bey, Gale Sondergaard, Thomas Gomez, June Vincent, George Dolenz. 86 mins. (Universal)

Phantom of the Opera director Waggner recycles lavish sets, actress Foster, and several plot elements from that 1943 hit in *The Climax*. Boris plays it somber indeed as a quietly deranged opera-house physician whose obsession with since-vanished diva Vincent resurfaces when her sound-alike

(Foster) reprises her part in an operetta titled *The Magic Voice*. Boris turns a routine throat exam into a mad hypnotism session, during which he convinces an unconscious Susanna that she can no longer sing. It's up to Su's composer beau (Bey) to save her from Karloff's psychic clutches, while B.K.'s mysterious servant (Sondergaard) nurtures a plot of her own. Karloff gives a largely one-note performance as the demented medico. While the operetta snippets sent yours truly reaching for his volume control, the rich Technicolor tones are pure music to the eye.

THE CLOWN AT MIDNIGHT (1998) **

D: Jean Pellerin. Christopher Plummer, Margot Kidder, Sarah Lassez, James Duval, Tatyana Ali. 91 mins. (Artisan)

Assorted teen weens eat psycho-opera-clown death in a flimsy but serviceable slayfest from up high-glam Winnipeg way. Plummer appears almost openly contemptuous of his surroundings in his brief wraparound role as the opera-house owner who entrusts the space—site of a 17-year-old murder in which a jealous stage Pagliacci butchered coed Lassez's diva mom—to college prof Kidder (looking a *long* way from her Lois Lane days) and a cross section of brain-dead theater students. You can guess the rest. (If you can't, the tag line—*Clown's* cleverest stroke—gives it away: "So many victims. So little time.") Other killer-clown flicks include the recommended *Clown House* (Forum), John Candy in the dreary *Clown Murders* (TWE), Tobe Hooper's fairly frightening *The Funhouse*, the unfunny *Funland* (Artisan), the atrocious *Judge & Jury* (A-Pix), the intermittently imaginative *Killer Klowns from Outer Space* (Media), the fitfully effective *Out of the Dark*, *Poltergeist*, Bobcat Goldthwait's inspired *Shakes the Clown* (see index), the comic-book-drawn *Spawn* (New Line), and the TV miniseries *Stephen King's It* (Warner).

THE COMEBACK   (1978) **½

D: Pete Walker. Jack Jones, Pamela Stephenson, David Doyle, Bill Owens, Sheila Keith. 100 mins. (Warner)

In *The Comeback*—also out as *Encore* on the Saturn label—idiosyncratic Brit fright auteur Walker has singer Jones playing a former pop star looking to get his recording career back on track after the collapse of an ill-advised marriage. He rents an isolated estate inhabited by an eccentric caretaking couple (including the always welcome Keith) and an uninvited guest—i.e., his ex-wife's decomposing cadaver (!). While occasionally slow, *The Comeback*, with scripter Murray Smith replacing former Walker collaborator David McGillivray, stacks up as a perverse, highly watchable chiller.

THE COMPANY OF WOLVES (1984) **

D: Neil Jordan. Angela Lansbury, David Warner, Graham Crowden, Brian Glover, Sarah Patterson, Stephen Rea. 95 mins. (Vestron)

A series of visually striking but otherwise vapid variations on the venerable Little Red Riding Hood Meets the Wolf Man myth, *The Company of Wolves* plays like a classy Hammer period piece gone pretentious. While Lansbury is effective as the archetypal eccentric Granny and Patterson is appropriately fetching as Little Red (herein redubbed Rosaleen), Jordan's Freudian fright mosaic left yours truly longing for Maria Ouspenskaya and Lon Chaney, Jr.

THE CONFESSIONAL   (1975) **½

D: Pete Walker. Anthony Sharp, Susan Penhaligon, Stephanie Beacham, Norman Eshley, Sheila Keith. 104 mins. (Prism, n.i.d.)

Hot on the heels of their *Frightmare II* (see index), the director/writer team Walker and David McGillivray come up with *The Confessional* (a.k.a.

House of Mortal Sin), switching their concerns from family life to organized religion. Sharp is convincingly demented as a psycho priest who tapes confessions, harasses young women, and offs suspicious parishioners with poisoned Communion wafers (!). *The Confessional* contains several effective shock scenes and another wonderfully disturbed perf—this time as the killer confessor's caretaker—by the excellent Keith.

THE CONQUEROR WORM (1968) ***½

D: Michael Reeves. Vincent Price, Ian Ogilvy, Hilary Dwyer, Rupert Davies, Robert Russell, Patrick Wymark. 96 mins. (Orion)

Most genre fans know the story by now: how, after directing just three films—*She-Beast* (Sinister Cinema), *The Sorcerers* (n/a), and this one (more appropriately titled *The Witchfinder General* in England)—auteur Reeves checked out in 1969 at a radically premature 25. There seems little doubt that Reeves was on his way to carving a significant career as a major genre craftsman (at the very least). Both Reeves and his cast are in good form here, with Price leading the charge as mercenary witch-hunter Matthew Hopkins, who, assisted by torturer John Stearne (Russell), roams the English countryside ridding local villages of their suspected "witch" population—always for a handsome fee. A solid, flawlessly performed blend of period action, horror, and suspense—with a moral message tossed in—*The Conqueror Worm* makes one wonder about the films that might have been made had Reeves managed to survive his reportedly crushing bouts of acute depression.

THE CORPSE VANISHES   (1942) B&W ***

D: Wallace Fox. Bela Lugosi, Luana Walters, Tristram Coffin. 64 mins. (Sinister Cinema)

Bela murders and body-snatches hapless brides for use in his home beauty experiments and receives able support from henchdwarf Angelo Rossitto in a swiftly paced, precociously sicko Monogram chiller, a model of Poverty Row efficiency.

CORRIDORS OF BLOOD (1958) B&W***

D: Robert Day. Boris Karloff, Betta St. John, Finlay Currie, Christopher Lee. 86 mins. (Sinister Cinema) DVD

Boris is a compassionate surgeon seeking to perfect an effective anesthetic whose troubles begin when he gets embroiled with grave-robber Resurrection Joe (sleazily enacted by Lee). Day's downbeat but generally entertaining chiller went unreleased in England until 1963.

THE CRAFT (1996)***

D: Andrew Fleming. Fairuza Balk, Robin Tunney, Neve Campbell, Rachel True, Assumpta Serna, Skeet Ulrich, Cliff De Young. 100 mins. (Columbia/TriStar) DVD

A mostly serious-minded horror fable revolving around the theme of empathy, *The Craft* shares similarities with *Carrie, Heathers* (though it's heavier than that), and the latter's 1976 model, *Massacre at Central High*. Tunney is a transfer student who falls in with a trio of emotionally scarred students— "white trash" Balk, "Negroid" True, and bad-skinned Campbell—who've formed a self-protective secret sorcery society to lend their isolated lives more meaning. All they need, they believe, to attain true empowerment is a fourth witch to complete their coven. Tunney, an unwitting "natural witch," at first embraces an invitation to join their group, which initially results in fairly harmless fun as the girls get back at their former tormentors. Mentally unstable leader Fairuza begins to wield her powers in more overtly

wicked ways, leading Tunney to balk. Peter Filardi's organic script, Fleming's urgent direction, a top rock soundtrack, a compelling cast, and the expected FX expertise combine to put *The Craft* over the top.

THE CREEPING FLESH (1973)***

D: Freddie Francis. Peter Cushing, Christopher Lee, Lorna Hellbron. 89 mins. (Columbia/TriStar)

Cushing is an Edwardian scientist out to rid the world of evil. Major obstacles include sinister rival Lee, an escaped maniac, Peter's own demented slut of a daughter, plus a prehistoric demon waiting to come to vengeful life. In the hands of vet Hammer helmer Francis, it all adds up to frightful, multitiered fun.

CREEPSHOW:
THE SERIES

CREEPSHOW (1982)***

D: George Romero. Hal Holbrook, Adrienne Barbeau, Ed Harris, E. G. Marshall, Fritz Weaver. 120 mins. (Warner) DVD

Romero and Stephen King neatly capture the spirit (and flesh) of the beloved, verboten EC Horror Comics of yore in this lively anthology of ghoulishly funny fear tales. The late Marshall gives the performance of his career as a rich, Howard Hughes–like recluse at war with a labful of roaches.

CREEPSHOW 2 (1987)**1/2

D: Michael Gornick. Lois Chiles, George Kennedy, Dorothy Lamour, Tom Savini. 92 mins. (New World)

Creepshow 2 employs essentially the same framework as the original. A comics-crazed kid receives the latest issue of "Creepshow Comics," personally delivered by The Creep

(makeup-FX maven Savini), and delves straightaway into three sinister stories involving a killer statue, a killer oil slick, and your ever reliable killer corpse. The tales proper are imaginatively bridged by brief animation sequences, and King contributes his customary cameo as a thick-witted trucker in the final (and funniest) episode, "The Hitchhiker." While it lacks *Creepshow*'s freshness, 2 is a suitably sick crowd-pleaser in its own right.

CRONOS (1993)***

D: Guillermo Del Toro. Federico Luppi, Ron Perlman, Claudio Brook, Margarita Isabel, Tamara Shanath. Subtitled. 92 mins. (Trimark)

Mexican auteur Del Toro makes an impressive feature-film debut with his Guadalupe-set horror fable, putting a boldly original spin on traditional celluloid vampire lore that separates his film from its bloodsucking brethren. While Del Toro's pivotal invention, the mysterious, immortalizing "Cronos Device," is reminiscent of the "Lament Configuration Box" from Clive Barker's *Hellraiser* series, the device itself is a wonderfully creepy item, a small 24-carat-gold box encasing an ancient, life-giving insect that creates an immediate addiction and a lust for blood among all who make use of it. Its current possessor, aging antique-store owner Jesus Gris (Luppi, in what would have been an ideal role for the older Boris Karloff), stumbles upon it by accident with the help of his ever present young granddaughter Aurora (Shanath). Actively seeking the same device is dying millionaire Dieter de la Guardia (Brook), who dispatches his brutal thug of a nephew, Angel (Perlman), to wrest it from Gris. Alternately menacing, poignant, and darkly funny, Del Toro's meditation on mortality eschews the vampire genre's usual interplay between Eros and Thanatos, instead dwelling almost exclusively on the latter.

Cronos should please horror buffs and adventurous crossover viewers alike.

CRY OF THE BANSHEE (1970) ***

D: Gordon Hessler. Vincent Price, Elisabeth Bergner, Essy Persson, Hugh Griffith, Hilary Dwyer, Sally Geeson, Robert Hutton. 87 mins. (Orion)

When 16th-century witch-hunter Whitman (Price) slaughters heathen followers of sorceress Oona (Bergner), the latter swears vengeance against him and his family. Hessler's period horror outing, which opens with a quote from the oft plundered Poe, contains several effective scare sequences and an authoritative performance by Price as the sadistic magistrate.

CULT OF THE COBRA (1955) B&W ***1/2

D: Francis D. Lyon. Faith Domergue, Marshall Thompson, Richard Long, Kathleen Hughes, David Janssen, Jack Kelly, William Reynolds. 82 mins. (Universal)

Lyon's underrecognized chiller takes an almost Lewton-esque approach to its tale of supernatural reptilian revenge. A half-dozen happy-go-lucky flyboys attend a secret Indian cobra-cult ritual at World War II's end. When one of the GI jerks (James Dobson) disrupts the ceremony by snapping a forbidden photo, the cult leader swears vengeance on the six interlopers. Beautiful snake lady (and former Howard Hughes protégé) Domergue is the instrument of said revenge, claiming Dobson that very night. The five survivors, New Yorkers all, more or less forget the incident until Faith arrives to put the bite on the infidels one by one. After taking a Greenwich Village apartment conveniently located next door to targets Long and Thompson, she begins succumbing to the latter's all-American charms, causing her to question the wisdom of her lethal mission.

What separates *Cult* from many '50s B-horror yarns is the strength of its core story and the specificity of its central characters. While the fright elements are imaginatively handled on a low budget via Faith's serpentine POV shots—unlike the thematically similar Val Lewton–produced classic *Cat People* (see index), there's no ambiguity about Faith's abilities; she really *does* turn into a killer cobra—there's a legit tragic quality to the impossible attraction of the melancholy Thompson and the self-doubting Domergue. *Cult* also exhibits a strong eye for subtle period details and, though shot on a Universal back lot, presents a credible portrait of 1945 Manhattan that ranges from Greenwich Village to Broadway.

THE CURSE:
THE SERIES

CURSE IV: THE ULTIMATE SACRIFICE (1988) **1/2

D: David Schmoeller. Timothy Van Patten, Laura Schaefer, Jeremy West, Ian Abercrombie. 84 mins. (Columbia/TriStar)

Adhering to homevid horror tradition, the fourth installment in this fright-franchise series has nothing to do with any of its previous namesakes, which in turn bore no resemblance to one another. The original *Curse* (Media)—a rural American-gothic rip-off of H. P. Lovecraft's "The Colour Out of Space" (earlier bastardized in the Nick Adams/Boris Karloff outing *Die, Monster, Die!* [HBO]), featuring a frothing Claude Akins—logically led to *Curse 2: The Bite* (TWE), offering Jamie Farr and radioactive snakes (!), which naturally evolved into *Curse III: Blood Sacrifice* (Columbia/TriStar), a voodoo tale set in 1950s Africa and costarring Christopher Lee. *Curse IV*—originally an entirely unrelated project called *Catacombs*—opens in 1506 in an Italian abbey, where an albino demon is being sealed alive by the assembled abbots,

then flashes to the present, when said demon is about to be unwittingly unleashed. While fairly feeble in the fear department—a strong live-burial scene and a Christ-as-psycho-killer sequence (!) represent the exceptions—*Curse IV* is oddly successful at conveying the modern monks' (nicely shaded characters portrayed by mostly low-key Euro thesps) cloistered lifestyles and petty frictions. (A dying monk's "confession" re his sexual regrets is a particularly poignant piece of writing.) The prolific Pino (*Don't Look Now, Dressed to Kill*) Donaggio contributes an appropriately hymnal score.

THE CURSE OF FRANKENSTEIN (1957) ***

D: Terence Fisher. Peter Cushing, Christopher Lee, Hazel Court. 83 mins. (Warner)

Cushing is the infamous baron and Lee his misbegotten creation in the film that launched Hammer's long-lived horror-movie line. Not as good as *Horror of Dracula* but briskly entertaining in its own right.

CURSE OF THE DEMON (1958) B&W ****

D: Jacques Tourneur, Dana Andrews, Peggy Cummins, Niall MacGinnis. 96 mins. (Goodtimes)

Val Lewton protégé Tourneur helms an absolutely brilliant horror tale (originally titled *Night of the Demon*) pitting rational psychologist Andrews against sinister mystic MacGinnis. Despite the demon's sporadic appearances—a decision director Tourneur had actively protested (though, truth to tell, the creature cameos work quite well)—*Curse of the Demon* ranks right up there with any of producer Lewton's '40s fright classics. The Goodtimes video is recorded in LP (middle speed), but the transfer quality is quite good—plus you get the complete 96-minute print.

CURSE OF THE UNDEAD (1959)
B&W **¹/₂

D: Edward Dein. Eric Fleming, Michael Pate, Kathleen Crowley, John Hoyt, Bruce Gordon, Edward Binns, Jimmy Murphy. 79 mins. (Universal)

Curse of the Undead is an uneven attempt to blend the western and vampire genres. Released at the height of the television-western craze, the flick sports the claustrophobic, unatmospheric look of a TV episode and suffers from some glaring miscasting, most notably urban-thug specialist Gordon (The Untouchables's Frank Nitti) as the local heavy. Rawhide boss Fleming is a tad too understated as Preacher Dan, who goes up against hired gun/vampire Drake Robey (Pate, who turns in the best work here). The vampire elements fare a bit better than the dull sagebrush clichés but don't come into play until midflick.

THE CURSE OF THE WEREWOLF (1961) ***

D: Terence Fisher. Oliver Reed, Clifford Evans, Yvonne Romain. 91 mins. (Universal)

Reed turns in energetic work as a Spanish lycanthrope on the loose in another superior, atmospheric shocker from the Hammer horror crew. A cleavage-driven Romain also impresses as Oliver's hapless mom.

THE CURSE OF THE WRAYDONS (1946) B&W **¹/₂

D: Victor M. Gover. Tod Slaughter, Bruce Seton, Gabriel Toyne. 94 mins. (Sinister Cinema)

Set in 1805 England, this typical mix of melodrama, romance, and madness offers a strong showcase for Britain's fave movie maniac, Slaughter. Here the portly, gleefully sadistic villain plays an outcast who's determined to wreak revenge at the expense of the

family that spurned him. There are some dull stretches, but the flick picks up considerably whenever Tod strides across the screen with spine-snapping mayhem in mind. Other available Slaughter showcases include Crimes at the Dark House, The Crimes of Stephen Hawke, Demon Barber of Fleet Street, The Face at the Window, The Greed of William Hart, Murder in the Old Red Barn, Never Too Late to Mend, Sexton Blake and the Hooded Terror, and The Ticket of Leave Man (Sinister Cinema).

DANCE OF THE DAMNED (1988) ***¹/₂

D: Katt Shea Ruben. Starr Andreeff, Cyril O'Reilly. 83 mins. (Virgin Vision, n.i.d.)

Katt (Stripped to Kill) Shea Ruben's Dance of the Damned is a strange and quite eloquent romantic encounter between a self-destructive vampire and a suicidal stripper. This extremely odd couple—Jodi (Andreeff) and the Vampire (O'Reilly)—spend a single intense evening together exploring nothing less than the nature of the human (and vampiric) condition. Essentially a two-character screenplay featuring strong work by both leads, Dance of the Damned conveys a sense of fear and dread despite its minimal bloodshed. Dance is a stylish and consistently involving flick, a legit low-budget sleeper for those in the market for thoughtful fright fare. Remade (and poorly at that) as To Sleep with a Vampire and ripped off (and pretentiously at that) by Club Vampire (both New Horizons). Also worth skipping is producer Roger Corman's 1993 attempted Bram Stoker's Dracula rip-off, Dracula Rising (New Horizons), which is to Coppola's vampire epic what Drac's reflection is to the count himself. Coppola's nephew Christopher actually beat unc to the punch with the 1987 fang-in-cheek cheapie Dracula's Widow (HBO), with Emmanuelle starlet Sylvia Kristel, though all positive comparisons end there.

DARIO ARGENTO'S WORLD OF HORROR (1985) ***

D: Michele Soavi. With Dario Argento. 76 mins. (Trimark) DVD

A behind-the-scenes look at the Italo terror maestro at work, deftly assembled by acolyte and fellow fright filmmaker Soavi (Cemetery Man), World of Horror alternates interesting segments detailing Dario's screen techniques with occasionally repetitious interviews with the man himself. A must for Argento advocates.

THE DARK (1994) **¹/₂

D: Craig Pryce. Stephen McHattie, Jaimz Woolvett, Brion James, Cynthia Belliveau, Dennis O'Connor. 90 mins. (Imperial, n.i.d.)

Scientist McHattie and ruthless ex-cop James pursue separate competitive paths to the lair of an elusive prehistoric creature that dwells beneath a graveyard, where it feasts on human remains (and the occasional live treat, when such appears). The laconic McHattie, abetted by Belliveau—a waitress he rescued from unruly bikers—wants to take the beast alive, the better to study its mysterious self-healing abilities, while a vindictive James wants it dead. The Dark maintains an admirably low-key approach most of the way, offers some imaginative shots of the critter's busy underground lifestyle, and generates legit suspense.

DARK ANGEL: THE ASCENT (1993) ***

D: L. Hassani. Angela Featherstone, Daniel Markel, Charlotte Stewart, Michael Genovese, Nicholas Worth, Michael C. Mahon, Milton James. 83 mins. (Paramount)

Dark Angel: The Ascent offers an offbeat, oft original twist on the angel/human love-story genre, inventively penned by Matthew (Freeway) Bright. With its successful blending of seemingly radically disparate elements—terror, comedy, pathos—the film comes close to capturing the loopy surrealism of a Hong Kong horror fantasy. Set stateside but lensed in a Romania that couldn't pass for *Toronto*, let alone an American city—an on-screen squad car reads POLITIA (!)—and lends the film a Kafkaesque look, *Dark Angel* opens in hell (imaginatively rendered on a low budget, with spinning-head tricks copied from *Jacob's Ladder*). As distant descendants of the original fallen angels, restless little devil Veronica (a very effective Featherstone), her family, and their fellow fiends view themselves not as satanic minions but as angels assigned to do God's dirty work—i.e., torturing malefactors for eternity. When Veronica expresses her desire to flee "the pit" long enough to visit Earth, her stern dad (Worth), who resembles a demonic Tor Johnson, threatens severe consequences. Complains Featherstone to her somewhat mellower mom (Stewart), "He means to dismember me like all those other religious schismatics!" Once Veronica, accompanied by her faithful hellhound, Hellraiser (played by pro canine Heros), makes good her escape to Earth, she can't restrain herself from morally judging and violently intervening when she witnesses acts of human cruelty, resulting in gory demises for a pair of muggers and two bigoted cops, as well as triggering an all-out manhunt for the "serial killer" assumed responsible. In another *Taxi Driver* touch, Veronica asks the kindly young doctor with whom she's fallen in love (Markel) to take her to a porn movie, a spectacle that moves her to sentimental tears (!). Clever details abound, and *Dark Angel*'s images linger in memory long after the end credits roll.

THE DARK HALF   (1993) **1/2

D: George A. Romero. Timothy Hutton, Amy Madigan, Michael Rooker, Julie Harris, Robert Joy. 122 mins. (Orion) DVD

The Dark Half benefits from frightmeister Romero's finely honed scare skills while suffering somewhat from Stephen King's ultimately one-note story line. Tearing a page from the more fully realized King adaptation *Misery* (see index), S.K. again utilizes an imperiled-writer plot. Rather than being imprisoned and abused by a rabid fan, author Thad Beaumont (Hutton) literally becomes his own worst enemy when his pseudonymous alter ego, George Stark (also Hutton)—the alias Thad attaches to his lucrative line of sadistic slasher novels—transforms into a flesh-and-blood doppelgänger with demands of his own. When Thad refuses to cooperate with his titular dark half, Stark executes a series of vicious slayings that implicate his creator as the perp. Hutton's Thad is bland enough to make us root for dark half Stark, a black-clad redneck greaser with a ready razor and lust for blood.

The trouble is that the convergent threads leading to Thad and Stark's inevitable showdown grow increasingly predictable. The film's strong opening—juvenile writing hopeful Thad (Patrick Brannan), afflicted by mysterious seizures, is laid open by brain surgeons who find bits of an unborn twin buried therein (says a medical aide to an understandably screaming nurse, "Hilary, please remember where you are!")—promises more than it delivers. That this stillborn parasite should eventually assert itself as its host's depraved (and more commercial!) writing "partner" is the type of notion with which David Cronenberg might have had a visceral and cerebral field day. Strained through King, the concept receives more standard scream-screen treatment, with simply creepy cruelty often subbing for true perversity. Still, on the creepy, cruel level, *The Dark Half* works fairly well, as director Romero manages to milk maximum shock and gore value from Stark's escalating rampage.

DARK NIGHT OF THE SCARECROW (1981) ***

D: Frank De Felitta. Charles Durning, Robert F. Lyons, Lane Smith. 100 mins. (Key)

Durning heads a group of small-town bigots who unwisely kill a retarded man. De Felitta's offbeat, serious-minded made-for-TV fear film has garnered its share of fans.

DARK OF THE NIGHT   (A.K.A. *MR. WRONG*) (1985) **1/2

D: Gaylene Preston. Heather Bolton, David Letch, Margaret Umbers. 89 mins. (Lightning, n.i.d.)

New Zealand director Preston helms an interesting haunted-car horror yarn that places almost as much emphasis on single gal Bolton's big-city tribulations as it does on the *Christine*-styled fear elements. Our fave scene sees our plucky heroine defend herself with a Venus de Milo statuette (!), lending fresh meaning to the term "well-armed."

DARKEST SOUL   (1994) ***

D: Doug Ulrich. Al Darago, Jeff Witte, Heather Brown, Doug Ulrich. 62 mins. (Salt City)

Less a horror flick than a verité-styled study of two overaged Baltimore Beavis and Butt-head types—leather-jacketed lowlife Tommy (Darago, who also cowrote and coproduced) and his hefty stooge, Mark (Witte)—*Darkest Soul* unspools like an early John Waters movie played utterly straight. We follow the duo as they drink, dabble in drugs, party with their twentysomething peers, and blow a succession of dead-end jobs. The scare elements kick in when they land grave-digger gigs, which prompts them to go into the corpse-robbing racket, copping jewelry from both newly interred and long-buried cemetery residents. *Darkest Soul* ends arbitrarily and abruptly but supplies its share of grim grunge fun along the way.

DAUGHTER OF DARKNESS (1989) **¹/₂

D: Stuart Gordon. Mia Sara, Anthony Perkins, Jack Coleman, Robert Reynolds, Deszo Garas. 93 mins. (Trimark)

Stuart (*Re-Animator*) Gordon's made-for-cable fang flick showcases the fetching Sara as an American tourist who journeys to Romania in search of the father she's never met. Sporadically assisted by diplomat Coleman and native cabbie Garas, Sara eventually finds her "man" in vampire Perkins. While *Daughter* isn't up to Gordon's highest standards, the offbeat auteur does his best to bring this obviously for-hire assignment to atmospheric life. The result is an occasionally contrived but consistently involving effort highlighted by Perkins's typically quiet but intense perf as the reluctant vampire (with a fanged tongue!).

DAUGHTER OF HORROR (1955) B&W ***

D: John Parker. Adrienne Barrett, Bruno VeSota, Angelo Rossitto. 60 mins. (Sinister Cinema)

Easily the best silent (or nondia-logue, anyway) movie of 1955, Exploitation Productions' florid Freud-voidian descent into the mad mind of a femme maniac (*woman*iac?) must be seen to be believed. Lensed in murky black and white by Ed Wood cine-matographer William C. Thompson, *Daughter of Horror* (originally titled *Dementia*) tracks our unhinged heroine through flashbacks in which she kills her drunken dad (who's already slain her bimbo mom), paranoid fantasies of relentless pursuit, and a rough night at the Club Pronto (informal successor to *Cocaine Fiends*'s Dead Rat Cafe and forerunner of *Blue Velvet*'s Slow Club).

Daughter of Horror also features the sci-fi vocal stylings of Marni Nixon, "New Concepts in Modern Sound" courtesy of Shorty Rogers and his Giants, and Angelo Rossitto as a dwarf. While the pic is perhaps best remembered as part of the midnight horror show the titular alien invades in 1958's *The Blob*, *Daughter* deserves to be seen in its idiosyncratic entirety.

DAUGHTERS OF DARKNESS: DIRECTOR'S CUT (1971) ***

D: Harry Kumel. John Karlen, Delphine Seyrig, Danielle Ouimet, Andrea Rau. 100 mins. (Anchor Bay) DVD

Daughters of Darkness is a lyrical, erotic vampire thriller highlighted by Seyrig's sweetly sinister interpreta-tion of ancient but well-preserved bloodsucker Elizabeth Bathory, who intrudes her evil self on a susceptible honeymooning couple at an isolated hotel in modern-day Belgium. The violence is fairly restrained—save for a brilliantly executed razor-induced death scene—while the sexual mes-sages are more explicit. Originally out, in truncated form, on the defunct Cin-ema Group label (as well as the dead AIR label, under the title *Children of the Night*), *Daughters of Darkness* makes its stateside "director's cut" debut via Anchor Bay, with 12 minutes of additional footage missing from the earlier editions. Film archivist/auteur William Lustig performed the restora-tion chores and penned the liner notes. Anchor Bay's handsomely packaged, letter-boxed edition returns the film to its original 1.66:1 theatrical aspect ratio.

DEAD AND BURIED (1981) **¹/₂

D: Gary A. Sherman. James Farentino, Jack Albertson, Melody Anderson. 92 mins. (Vestron)

Dark Star writer Dan O'Bannon's agreeably perverse script pits small-town sheriff Farentino against local undertaker Albertson and a num-ber of homicidal cadavers who refuse to stay dead in this uneven but entertain-ing sickie.

DEAD MEN WALK (1943) B&W **¹/₂

D: Sam Newfield. George Zucco, Mary Carlisle, Dwight Frye. 67 mins. (Sinister Cinema)

It's Mondo Zucco time as George gets to portray twin brothers—one's good, the other's a vampire. Frye, of *Drac-ula*'s Renfield and *Frankenstein*'s Fritz fame, plays a crazed assistant in this typical but fun Poverty Row outing.

DEAD OF NIGHT (1945) B&W ***¹/₂

D: Alberto Cavalcanti, Robert Hamer, Charles Crichton, Basil Dearden. Mervyn Johns, Michael Redgrave, Googie Withers. 102 mins. (HBO, Congress)

This Brit anthology of chilling tales (the "comic relief" golf sequence excepted), framed by an authenti-cally disturbing wraparound, rates as one of horrordom's best. Redgrave's psycho ventriloquist and his demented dummy—a hook later used to decent effect in the 1964 Brit chiller *The Devil Doll* (MPI) before being mangled by *Magic* (Embassy)—are enough to give the hardiest fright fan sleepless nights.

THE DEAD ZONE (1983) **¹/₂

D: David Cronenberg. Christopher Walken, Brooke Adams, Martin Sheen. 104 mins. (Paramount)

Cronenberg meets Stephen King in a horror tale about an accident vic-tim (Walken) who develops sudden psy-chic powers that alert him to a devious political conspiracy involving presiden-tial candidate Sheen. The pic could have been bolder, but it's still worth a look.

DEATHDREAM (1972) ***1/2

D: Bob Clark. John Marley, Richard Backus, Lynn Carlin. 90 mins. (MPI, n.i.d.)

With *DeathDream*, Clark crafts a brilliantly sick allegory about a Vietnam fatality (Backus) who returns home unexpectedly and alive—sort of. The final scene is a fright-film classic in this Ernest Hemingway's "Soldier's Home" Meets *Night of the Living Dead*.

DEATHMASK (1984) ***

D: Richard Friedman. Farley Granger, Lee Bryant, John McCurry, Arch Johnson, Ruth Warrick, Danny Aiello. 102 mins. (Prism, Parade)

Friedman's underrated 1984 thriller stars Granger as an NYC cop whose young daughter's accidental drowning leads to his subsequent obsession with the senseless murder of an unidentified four-year-old boy. Granger is grimly convincing as the detective so consumed by the unsolved case that, over the course of a decade, he unwittingly alienates the affections of his own family, especially his neglected surviving daughter. *Deathmask* is ultimately less a chiller than a muted but unsettling psychodrama, but Friedman works in enough grisly details to honor the genre's basic conventions while taking his story in unexpected directions.

DEE SNIDER'S STRANGELAND (1998) *1/2

D: John Pieplow. Dee Snider, Kevin Gage, Elizabeth Peña, Brett Harrelson, Robert Englund. 90 mins. (Artisan) DVD

Infamous Mr. Twisted Sister Snider makes a less-than-Dee-lightful big-screen debut with this eponymous heavy-metal horror. Sort of an imagination-challenged *Hellraiser* variation minus the latter's supernatural angle, the determinedly sicko flick stars the shock rocker (who also coscripted) as "Captain Howdy," a cyberpsycho who lures unsuspecting teenettes to his house of horror via on-line frat-party invites. Snider crams the screen with some legitimately squirm-inducing torture tableaux, but not even these crowd-pleasing, over-the-top terror elements can compensate for the film's sorry structure, countless lapses in basic genre-movie logic, and a plot stretched thinner than Snider himself. As additional fear-buff bait, Robert ("Freddy") Englund scores a supporting role as a local white-trash lynch-mob leader. Rocker Bret Michaels, of Poison, makes *his* stab at celluloid glory with 1998's *A Letter from Death Row* (ETD).

DEEP RED (A.K.A. *THE HATCHET MURDERS*) (1975) ***

D: Dario Argento. David Hemmings, Daria Nicolodi, Gabriele Lavia. 100 mins. (HBO)

Hemmings finds himself drawn into a hunt for a hatchet psycho; Argento's expertly rendered bloody set pieces are the film's raison d'être. Unfortunately for Dario disciples, the video represents an edited, less gruesome version of the original.

DEEP RISING (1998) ***

D: Stephen Sommers. Treat Williams, Famke Janssen, Kevin J. O'Connor, Anthony Heald, Wes Studi, Derek O'Connor, Jason Flemyng, Djimon Hounsou, Uma Damon, Trevor Goddard. 106 mins. (Hollywood Pictures) DVD

A fun entry in the subaqueous-monster subgenre, writer/director Sommers's *Deep Rising* casts Williams and Kevin J. O'Connor as a maverick sea captain and his comic sidekick, characters seemingly sprung from the serials and B flicks of yore. With femme partner Damon, our heroes hire out to a band of hard cases headed by Studi (in a rare non–Native American role) to transport mysterious sealed cargo through South Seas plagued by marauding monsters up from the murky depths. While *Deep Rising* (like dozens of other modern monster movies) obviously owes a major debt to *Alien*, Sommers and crew imbue the bloody proceedings with sufficient spirit to make the scares and laughs play relatively fresh. Jerry Goldsmith's full-throated score adds a pulse-pounding aural dimension. Avoid the similarly themed 1999 yawner *Virus* (Universal, DVD).

DEF BY TEMPTATION (1990) **1/2

D: James Bond III. Cynthia Bond, Kadeem Hardison, James Bond III, Bill Nunn, John Canada Terrell, Rony Clanton. 95 mins. (Troma) DVD

This urban fear film stars sultry Cynthia Bond in the title role (as Temptation, not Def), an ancient demon in youthful guise given to staging kinky sex-and-death affairs with guys she picks up at a local bar. Cynthia ultimately sets her sights on young actor Hardison and his innocent North Carolina divinity-student friend (appealingly played by auteur Bond III). Despite its terror trappings, *Def* actually plays best during its early social-comedy phase as Bond III offers a perceptive look at the cross section of characters who hang at the tavern where Cynthia selects her victims. The contrived segue into full-blown horror leads to an overreliance on fear-film clichés that conveys an ultimately retro message. Still, Bond III, his skilled cast, and some decent low-budget FX—highlighted by Hardison's *Videodrome*-styled battle with a possessed TV set—instill enough life to keep *Def* entertaining, while longtime Spike Lee lensman Ernest Dickerson lends the proceedings a slick look.

DEMENTIA 13 (1963) **1/2

D: Francis Ford Coppola. William Campbell, Luana Anders,

Patrick Magee. 81 mins. (Sinister Cinema) DVD

Notable more for being Coppola's first "legit" feature film (after the awful soft-core sex comedies *Playgirls and the Bellboy* and *Tonight for Sure*) than for being a memorable frightfest in its own right, *Dementia 13* has its atmospheric moments, especially the justly famous opening rowboat-murder scene.

DEMONS:
THE SERIES

DEMONS (1985) **1/2

D: Lamberto Bava. Natasha Hovey, Urbano Barberini, Paolo Cozzo, Fiore Argento, Bobby Rhodes. 88 mins. (Anchor Bay) DVD

Produced and coscripted by Dario Argento, Bava's *Demons* attempts to exploit every fear-film fan's fondest paranoid fantasy: Random passersby are given free theater passes to attend a horror-pic premiere. The fright-flick-within-a-fright-flick is a *Living Dead*–type gruefest about a group of kids who violate the tomb of Nostradamus and mutate into sharp-clawed, pus-oozing, cannibalistic zombies. Before long, the unwitting movie patrons also start turning into—you guessed it—sharp-clawed, pus-oozing, cannibalistic zombies. Imbued with the wit of a George Romero or Larry Cohen, *Demons* might have emerged as a splendid blend of blood and black humor, sort of a splatter version of *The Purple Rose of Cairo*. In Bava's heavier hands, *Demons* ultimately degenerates into a mondo disgusto FX exercise, albeit a well-wrought one. Lamberto and Dario return with 1988's still weaker *Demons 2* (Anchor Bay, DVD), wherein the antisocial title characters emerge not from a theater but from a TV screen, where the same movie-

within-a-movie we saw in *Demons* happens to be playing.

THE DENTIST:
THE SERIES

THE DENTIST (1996) ***

D: Brian Yuzna. Corbin Bernsen, Linda Hoffman, Ken Foree, Earl Boen, Molly Hagen, Jan Hoag. 93 mins. (Trimark) DVD

The Dentist charts a decay-obsessed Encino, California, dentist's rapid descent into orthodontal dementia. As portrayed by Bernsen with repressed intensity, Dr. Alan Feinstone makes *Marathon Man*'s Nazi dentist (Laurence Olivier) seem like a regular Dr. Feelgood. Dr. Feinstone's final day of disintegration kicks off on a negative note when he hallucinates blond 'burb trophy wife Hoffman doing the deed with a leering pool cleaner. The situation worsens when the doc arrives at his ultra-modern office (complete with soothing music, sky walls, and even a "Rain Forest Room" [!]), eyes his waiting patients, and, via voice-over, concludes, "The filth was everywhere. The infection was spreading." A visit from a corrupt IRS agent (*The Terminator*'s shrink Boen) finally pushes Feinstone over the edge, and he launches his lethal dental rampage in earnest. The handiwork of *Re-Animator* alumni Stuart Gordon and Dennis Paoli (who coscript) and Brian Yuzna (who directs), *The Dentist* is a must for devotees of *way* over-the-top, tongue-in-bloody-cheek terror. The sound FX alone when Feinstone puts his various drills, needles, and forceps into play may be enough to send fainter-hearted viewers screaming from the couch. *The Dentist* is best watched with plenty of novocaine and nitrous oxide nearby. Yuzna fails to recapture the orthodontal magic with the routine, redundant 1999 sequel, *The Dentist 2* (Trimark, DVD), wherein an escaped Bernsen drills again.

DERANGED (1974) ***1/2

D: Jeff Gillen, Alan Ormsby. Roberts Blossom, Leslie Carlson, Cosette Lee, Marion Waldman, Robert Warner. 82 mins. (Moore Video) DVD

Inspired, like the same year's *Texas Chainsaw Massacre* and the 1960 Hitchcock classic *Psycho,* by killer/cannibal Ed Gein's real-life exploits, *Deranged* manages to be, by turns, gross, scary, and blackly funny. Under the supervision of auteurs Ormsby and Gillen, who'd earlier collaborated on *Children Shouldn't Play with Dead Things* (VCI), *Deranged* opens with backward, unsocialized Ezra (Blossom) tending to his dying mom, whose last words are a warning against the wiles of wicked women—*all* women, in fact, save for one Maureen Selby: "Maureen's the only woman I ever did trust. She's fat, that's why." Mater's death leaves Ez so lonely that, after a year, he decides to exhume and "repair" her (!), using flesh sheared from fresh cadavers. When Ezra finally meets the aforementioned Maureen (Waldman), a sex-starved widow, the only way he can save himself from imminent seduction is by shooting her, thus launching his entry into the world of big-time crime and psychosis.

As Ezra, Blossom is nothing short of brilliant, lending considerable idiosyncratic shading to what could easily have been a one-dimensional role, and he receives ample support from a cast of unknowns. The film's simple but effective framing device features an omniscient reporter (Carlson) who pops in and out of the action with updates on Ezra's career. Moore's digitally remastered video exclusive also contains a short, postfeature documentary, *Ed Gein: American Maniac,* which offers a look at Ezra's real-life model. No relation to Chuck Vincent's 1987 dementia-fueled hallucinatory horror *Deranged* (Republic). Moore also has the fascinating making-of documentary *The Deranged Chronicles.*

THE DEVIL BAT:
THE SERIES

THE DEVIL BAT   (1941) B&W **½

D: Jean Yarbrough. Bela Lugosi, Suzanne Kaaren, Dave O'Brien. 69 mins. (Sinister Cinema) DVD

One of Lugosi's livelier PRC outings finds him training the title creatures to carry out his vengeful schemes. Nearly every public-domain video label carries this, many under the alternate title *Killer Bats*.

DEVIL BAT'S DAUGHTER   (1946) B&W **½

D: Frank Wisbar. Rosemary La Planche, John James, Molly Lamont. 66 mins. (Image) DVD

This belated nominal sequel to Bela's *Devil Bat* is far from a classic but does offer more atmospheric touches than many PRC quickies. Bela, alas, didn't hang around for this one. Veteran German-émigré auteur Wisbar went on to direct the effective *Strangler of the Swamp* (see index) that same year.

DEVIL'S ADVOCATE   (1997) ***

D: Taylor Hackford. Al Pacino, Keanu Reeves, Charlize Theron, Jeffrey Jones, Judith Ivey, Craig T. Nelson, Delroy Lindo. 144 mins. (Warner) DVD

Sort of a *Rosemary's Lawyer*, *Devil's Advocate* provides Pacino with a fiendish field day as a literal attorney from hell (then again, whence else does the breed hail?). While overlong, overproduced, and frequently formulaic, director Hackford and scripters Jonathan Lemkin and Tony Gilroy's adaptation of Andrew Neiderman's novel is executed with enough wit and flair to rate as the best entry in the late-'90s spate of fallen-angel-themed fright films (e.g., *Fallen*, *The Prophecy*). Reeves, as the young hotshot Florida lawyer lured to "wicked" NYC by a rep from Pacino's

global firm, wisely abstains from competing with Pacino's alternately wry and fiery performance, while Theron contributes Ashley Judd–styled work (and we mean that in the most positive sense) as Keanu's increasingly unhappy spouse. Despite its millennial references, *Devil's Advocate* sometimes feels like a refugee from the late-'80s cycle of cautionary yuppie-temptation fables (e.g., *Wall Street*). The penultimate scene, set in Pacino's penthouse office, represents mainstream horror filmmaking at its lavish best. (Ironically enough, it also earned the film a lawsuit for copyright infringement, filed by sculptor Frederick E. Hart, whose famous bas relief "Ex Nihilo" was allegedly imitated in the scene; following a settlement, Warner agreed to alter the on-screen artwork for future video, laser, and DVD editions and TV airings.)

THE DEVIL'S DAUGHTER   (1991) ***

D: Michele Soavi. Kelly Curtis, Herbert Lom, Angela Giordano, Tomas Arana. 112 mins. (Republic)

Cowritten and produced by Dario Argento, *The Devil's Daughter* (a.k.a. *The Sect*) opens (to the strains of "Horse with No Name") in "South California 1970," where a hippie band is ritualistically slaughtered by a pack of satanist bikers. We next flip to Frankfurt 1991, where schoolteacher Curtis runs afoul of Lom, who turns out to be anything but the harmless old-timer he initially appears. Lom literally puts a bug up Kelly's nose (!) while she sleeps, leading to a lurid nightmare rich in cheap religious imagery. It soon becomes clear that, à la *Rosemary's Baby*, Kelly's been selected to serve as Satan's mater. What differentiates *The Devil's Daughter* from its paler Anglo counterparts is its typically Italo over-the-top treatment. In addition to the insect-snorting segment, we witness a pickpocket inadvertently snatch a human heart from a cultist's pocket (!), a psycho attack rab-

bit, a face-shearing scene, and a diabolic variation on Leda and the Swan—sort of a Kelly and the Stork from Hell—when our heroine is raped by a crazed devil bird. No relation to Hammer's middling Peter Sykes horror *To the Devil, a Daughter* (Republic), with Richard Widmark, Nastassja Kinski, and Christopher Lee.

THE DEVIL'S PARTNER   (1958) B&W **½

D: Charles R. Rondeau. Ed Nelson, Edgar Buchanan, Jean Allison, Richard Crane, Spencer Carlisle, Byron Foulger. 75 mins. (Sinister Cinema)

The Devil's Partner (coscripted by former Bowery Boy Stanley Clements) stars AIP regular and future *Peyton Place* mainstay Nelson in dual roles as ancient conjurer Pete Jensen and young Nick Richards, Jensen's mysterious "nephew," whose arrival in desolate Furnace Flats, New Mexico, sparks an outbreak of local tragedies. Buchanan gives his patented folksy perf as the town doctor; Carlisle is the puzzled sheriff ("Doesn't make sense—a hunk of beef killing Dr. Marx!"); and Allison and Crane (of *Rocky Jones* fame) play a couple whose lives are disrupted by the seemingly helpful Richards.

THE DEVIL'S RAIN   (1975) ***

D: Robert Fuest. Ernest Borgnine, Ida Lupino, William Shatner. 85 mins. (VCI) DVD

Borgnine and fellow high-profile satanists melt down real good in a luridly enjoyable, star-studded chiller that not only features a post–*Star Trek* Shatner but marked John Travolta's big-screen debut.

THE DEVIL-DOLL   (1936) B&W **½

D: Tod Browning. Lionel Barrymore, Maureen O'Sullivan, Frank Lawton. 79 mins. (MGM/UA)

Another strange tale from Tod (*Freaks*) Browning: Barrymore, who plays much of the movie in old-lady drag, is an escaped con who invents living killer dolls to do his deadly bidding. The film doesn't always work, but it does succeed in being honestly different.

THE DEVILS   (1971) ***

D: Ken Russell. Oliver Reed, Vanessa Redgrave, Dudley Sutton. 109 mins. (Warner)

More fun antireligious hysteria from auteur Russell, centering on 17th-century French witch trials and loosely based on Aldous Huxley's *The Devils of Loudon. The Devils* is one of Ken's most compelling efforts and a must for orgiastic-nuns buffs.

DIARY OF A MADMAN   (1963) **½

D: Reginald LeBorg. Vincent Price, Nancy Kovack, Chris Warfield, Ian Wolfe, Nelson Olmstead. 96 mins. (Wood Knapp, n.i.d.)

Price is a French magistrate infiltrated by the evil "Horla." A band of blue light frames his eyes whenever the sinister spirit exerts its homicidal will. Based on stories by Guy de Maupassant, the movie is deliberately paced but fair enough fun in an old-fashioned way. Actor Warfield went on to direct and costar in the worthy obscurity *Teenage Seductress,* among other exploitation indies. The best line belongs to a prison guard, who confides to Price, "Murderers—they're all the same. Humanity would be better off without them!"

DIE! DIE! MY DARLING!   (1965) **½

D: Silvio Narrizano. Tallulah Bankhead, Stefanie Powers, Donald Sutherland. 97 mins. (RCA/Columbia)

Tallulah joins the then-popular parade of moviedom's mad matrons,

launched by Robert Aldrich's *Whatever Happened to Baby Jane?* (see index), in a performance whose strength is not restraint. Sutherland is her geeky Igor-like henchhunchback; Powers plays their victim.

THE DIVIDING HOUR   (1998) ***

D: Mike Prosser. Brad Goodman, Greg James, Mike Prosser, Brian Prosser, Jillian Hodges, Max Yoakum, Jay Horenstein. 89 mins. (Playground Films)

Writer/director Mike Prosser crafts a compelling *Reservoir Dogs* Meets *Carnival of Souls* variation that, despite the obvious comparisons, manages to sport a mood and tone all its own. After pulling off a successful drive-through bank heist, four amateur crooks—Goodman, James, and real-life bros Mike and Brian Prosser—head for the Canadian border, bickering all the way. When their getaway car breaks down, the criminal quartet take shelter in a remote house occupied by gentle femme Hodges and her deaf/blind dad, Yoakum. All efforts to leave the house fail, and it soon becomes clear that Canada isn't the border the boys are about to cross. Earnest perfs, a disturbing ambience, and occasionally inspired dialogue—e.g., dope-smoking robber James's stoned but cogent analysis of the existential profundity of Bugs Bunny and Daffy Duck's contentious relationship (!)—keep the action engrossing throughout.

THE DOCTOR AND THE DEVILS (1985) **

D: Freddie Francis. Timothy Dalton, Jonathan Pryce, Twiggy, Stephen Rea, Julian Sands, Phyllis Logan. 93 mins. (Key)

Based on an original screenplay by Dylan Thomas and directed with relative restraint by Hammer horror vet Francis, *The Doctor and the Devils* draws its inspiration from the real-

life exploits of infamous 19th-century grave robbers Burke and Hare (herein renamed Fallon and Broom), who weren't above resorting to murder to meet their cadaver quota. Pryce and Rea turn in credible work as the unsavory stiff-lifters; Dalton is properly self-righteous as Dr. Rock, who buys the bodies for "progressive medical purposes," and ex-anorectic Twiggy emotes effectively as blond pub tart Jenny Bailey. Unfortunately, the script needs work (sorry, D.T., wherever you are), and the film grows less compelling with each passing reel.

DR. GIGGLES   (1992) **

D: Manny Coto. Larry Drake, Holly Marie Combs, Cliff De Young, Michelle Johnson, Richard Bradford. 96 mins. (Artisan) DVD

Manny (*The Playroom*) Coto and coscripter Graeme (*Sonny Boy*) Whifler's hackneyed hack-'em-up stars Larry (*Darkman, L.A. Law*) Drake as an escaped loony out to terrorize the town that terminated his killer-quack dad some three decades earlier. After a promising asylum-set surgical sequence, this unimaginatively sicko pic quickly degenerates into a typical slashed-teens throwback as our demented amateur medico employs his trusty tools to carve out an admittedly impressive body count (final tally: Dr. Giggles 16, Townsfolk 1). Drake's dialogue is limited to largely lame, sub–Freddy Krueger one-liners (some truly antique). There's also a flashback wherein the young Dr. G. slices his way out of his late mater's body, where he's been sewn up by his mad dad, a sequence that comes this close to very nearly bordering on bad taste.

DR. JEKYLL AND MR. HYDE   (1932) B&W ****

D: Rouben Mamoulian. Fredric March, Miriam Hopkins, Rose Hobart, Holmes

Herbert, Halliwell Hobbes. 97 mins. (MGM/UA)

Back in 1990, MGM/UA Home Video belatedly debuted Mamoulian's thematically complex, cinematically adventurous, and generally intense adaptation of Robert Louis Stevenson's classic identity-crisis caper in its original, uncensored 97-minute form. A fresh air of honest sensuality and candor pervades this 1932 pre-Code production. March, who copped an Oscar for his schizoid work, is excellent as the progressive, life-embracing Dr. Jekyll, whose efforts to break the stifling bonds of Victorian constraint eventually transform him into the simian sadist Hyde; outsized dentures force him to talk like Humphrey Bogart while his unharnessed id prompts antisocial behavior worthy of Al Pacino's Tony (*Scarface*) Montana. Hopkins projects raunchy vulnerability as Ivy, the hooker with a heart of champagne, who's aided by Dr. Jekyll and bestially abused by his badder half, Hyde. Mamoulian's active B&W camera brings the dramatic action into sharp, compelling focus.

DR. JEKYLL AND MR. HYDE   (1941) B&W ***

D: Victor Fleming. Spencer Tracy, Ingrid Bergman, Lana Turner. 114 mins. (MGM/UA)

Gone With the Wind director Fleming's lavish "classics" treatment of Stevenson's study of good versus evil is a solid show, but the accent is on Dr. J.'s emotional turmoil rather than on the horror aspects and the production pales a bit beside Mamoulian's more urgent approach. In other takes on the Stevenson tale, Kirk Douglas does double duty in the 1973 *Dr. Jekyll and Mr. Hyde* remake (Sony), as does Jack Palance in *The Strange Case of Dr. Jekyll* (Artisan). Variations include Hammer's clever *Dr. Jekyll and Sister Hyde* (Anchor Bay), 1995's not-so-clever *Dr. Jekyll and Ms. Hyde* (HBO),

Charles B. Griffith's wacky *Dr. Heckyl and Mr. Hype* (Paragon), and the "blaxploitation" edition *Dr. Black, Mr. Hyde* (Xenon). John Barrymore's 1920 silent version, *Dr. Jekyll and Mr. Hyde*, is also available (Kino, DVD). More tangential titles include *Dr. Jekyll's Dungeon of Death* (Wizard) and the Paul Naschy Spanish horrors *Dr. Jekyll and the Wolfman* and *Dr. Jekyll vs. the Werewolf* (both Sinister Cinema).

DR. TERROR'S HOUSE OF HORRORS (1965) ***

D: Freddie Francis. Peter Cushing, Christopher Lee, Donald Sutherland. 98 mins. (Republic)

Brit horror titans Cushing and Lee are in top form in Francis's fun fright anthology, offering five terror tales framed by fortune-teller Cushing. Sutherland puts in one of his earliest screen appearances as a doctor who mistakenly stakes his suspected vampire wife.

DOLLS   (1987) **1/2

D: Stuart Gordon. Carrie Lorraine, Ian Patrick Williams, Carolyn Purdy-Gordon, Guy Rolfe, Hilary Mason, Stephen Lee. 77 mins. (Vestron, n.i.d.)

This outing by *Re-Animator* auteur Gordon involves a sensitive little girl named Judy (Lorraine), part of a group of otherwise largely obnoxious travelers stranded at your standard old dark manse, this one inhabited by a pair of elderly doll-makers (Rolfe, Mason). The dolls come to aggressive life and begin eliminating those guests who deserve that fate, while befriending the empathetic Judy. Gordon does what he can with the mediocre material, and in its defense, *Dolls* includes the best killer-teddy-bear sequence we've seen since *Bloodbath at the House of Death* (see index). It's a lot better than the 1992 *Child's Play* rip-off, *Dolly Dearest*

(Paramount), costarring a temporarily hard-up Rip Torn.

DON'T BE AFRAID OF THE DARK (1973) **1/2

D: John Newland. Kim Darby, Jim Hutton, Barbara Anderson. 74 mins. (IVE, n.i.d.)

Darby is bedeviled by sneaky humanoid gremlins—a riff later recycled in Stephen King's *Cat's Eye*—in a pretty good made-for-TV terror effort that's easily stolen by the lilliputian predators and has won its fair share of fans.

DON'T LOOK NOW   (1973) ***1/2

D: Nicolas Roeg. Donald Sutherland, Julie Christie, Hilary Mason. 110 mins. (Paramount)

Drawing from a Daphne du Maurier story, Roeg crafts a supremely creepy, disorienting, and generally downbeat horror outing involving grief-stricken parents Sutherland and Christie (who indulge in a then-controversial erotic scene) and their ill-advised Venice vacation. In short, *Don't Look Now* is not just another axe-wielding-dwarf-in-a-red-raincoat thriller.

DOPPELGÄNGER: THE EVIL WITHIN (1992) **1/2

D: Avi Nesher. Drew Barrymore, George Newbern, Dennis Christopher, Leslie Hope, Sally Kellerman, George Maharis. 105 mins. (Fox)

Petite pre-*Scream* Barrymore dominates in dual brunette roles, as the Good Drew and the sunglassed Bad Drew. After Bad Drew butchers their (more or less) mutual mom, Good Drew splits for L.A., where she's soon sharing a pad with sympathetic aspiring screenwriter Newbern. Though she's set to collect a sizable inheritance, all is not well in Good Drew's world: She suffers from disturbing flashbacks involving sicko sexual malpractices performed by her doctor guardian (Christopher, of *Fade to Black* fame), takes blood showers, can't shake her seemingly supernatural twin, and eventually transmogrifies into two—count 'em—two full-fledged, identical (and much taller) slime monsters. While *Doppelgänger* sports its effective moments, the flick ultimately smacks of desperate last-minute interference by producers fearful of not covering all the B-movie horror bases. *M°A°S°H* alum Kellerman briefly materializes as an ex-nun/phone-sex slut/amateur doppel-gänger authority (you know the type).

DRACULA (1931) B&W ***

D: Tod Browning. Bela Lugosi, David Manners, Helen Chandler, Dwight Frye, Edward Van Sloan. 75 mins. (Universal) DVD

What can we add? While some-times static and stage-bound, Browning's *Dracula* is still perverse and powerful after all these years, with a groundbreaking performance by Bela (reprising his long-running Broadway role) as Bram Stoker's thirsty count and manic work by Frye as his insect-starved slave, Renfield. A remastered 1999 edition features a new Philip Glass score performed by the Kronos Quartet.

DRACULA: THE SPANISH VERSION (1931) B&W ***½

D: George Melford. Carlos Villarias, Lupita Tovar, Barry Norton, Pablo Alvarez Rubio. Subtitled. 103 mins. (Universal)

Although lensed simultaneously with Tod Browning's better-known 1931 Bela edition, using the same sets and basic script, *The Spanish Version* emerges as a much different—in many ways superior—fear film. According to a video intro by actress Tovar, who plays Eva (a renamed Mina), director Melford didn't even speak Spanish. Fortunately, he had a top cast to work with. Villarias makes for a suitably menacing

Dracula, while Rubio, as the insect-eating Renfield, goes even further over the top than his Anglo counterpart, Dwight Frye. Far more than a curio, *Dracula: The Spanish Version* is a highly effective fright film in its own right.

DRACULA—PRINCE OF DARKNESS (1966) ***

D: Terence Fisher. Christopher Lee, Barbara Shelley, Andrew Keir. 90 mins. (Anchor Bay) DVD

While not up to Hammer Films' 1958 *Horror of Dracula*, Fisher's bloodsucking sequel is still fun to watch for Lee's typically charismatic interpre-tation of the toothy title fiend, along with some creatively gruesome tableaux and a novel Dracula-destruction scene.

DRACULA'S DAUGHTER (1936) B&W ***

D: Lambert Hillyer. Otto Kruger, Gloria Holden, Marguerite Churchill, Irving Pichel, Edward Van Sloan, Nan Grey. 70 mins. (Universal)

Universal's Lugosi-less sequel is an oddly calm but engrossing affair that opens with vampire-hunter Van Helsing (reprised by *Dracula*'s Van Sloan) applying the stake to the count in Carfax Abbey. The good doctor is promptly arrested for murder by a pair of vigilant bobbies. Asks one constable re the deceased Drac, "How long has he been dead?" Replies the ever earnest Van H., "About five hundred years." Van Helsing looks to psychiatrist and former student Kruger for moral support and legal assistance. The case grows more complex when the titular offspring (somberly interpreted by Holden) and overbearing minion Pichel surface just as a fresh rash of bitings breaks out. The unhappy Holden invites Kruger to her digs, where she echoes the thirsty count's famous line, "I never drink… wine." The astute shrink observes, "This is the first woman's flat I've been in that

didn't have at least twenty mirrors in it." While a later scene involving Hol-den (pretending to be a painter) and model Grey boasts lesbian overtones, the vampire's victims are recruited from both sexes and rather joylessly dis-patched.

DREAM DEMON (1988/1993) **

D: Harley Cokliss. Jemma Redgrave, Kathleen Wilhoite, Timothy Spall, Jimmy Nail, Mark Greenstreet. 89 mins. (Warner)

When New Wavy American emi-grant Wilhoite returns to the Brit abode of her traumatic youth, her arrival sparks a series of vivid night-mares in current resident Redgrave, a virginal lass engaged to wealthy cad Greenstreet. (Jemma's opening night-mare is a knockout—scoring a perfect 10 on the Official Phantom Squirm-ometer—that the pic never comes close to duplicating.) While this 1988-lensed *Elm Street* wannabe has its effective nightmare moments, "cult movie-maker" (per the Warner box) Harley (*Black Moon Rising*) Cokliss tosses all manner of cheap tangential "scares" into the mix, irrevocably diluting the pic's potential impact.

THE DUNWICH HORROR (1970) **

D: Daniel Haller. Dean Stockwell, Sandra Dee, Ed Begley. 90 mins. (Embassy, n.i.d.)

Longtime Roger Corman set designer Haller offers up a medi-ocre movie version of a classic H. P. Lovecraft tale that pales beside Stuart Gordon's later exercises in Lovecraft-ian lunacy, *Re-Animator* and *From Beyond* (see index); nonetheless it should be of interest to Lovecraft followers.

DUST DEVIL (1993) ***

D: Richard Stanley. Robert Burke, Chelsea Field, Zakes Mokae, Rufus Swart, William

Hootkins, Marianne Sagebrecht. 87 mins. (Paramount)

We haven't seen *Hardware* (HBO) helmer Stanley's original 108-minute director's cut of *Dust Devil*. But the 87-minute video version plays so well that we wonder if *Dust* doesn't represent a rare case of a film being salvaged, or at least improved, by radical reediting. In the available edition, Robert (*RoboCop 3*) Burke stars as a carrier of demonic evil who roams the African desert, drawn to victims already burdened with strong death wishes. Burke splatters several cases in point before hitching a ride with heroine Field, who doesn't share his opinion that she's looking to die. Brimming with imaginative nightmare imagery and rife with genuine jolts, *Dust Devil* doesn't readily fade from memory.

EATEN ALIVE   (1976) **¹/₂

D: Tobe Hooper. Neville Brand, Mel Ferrer, Carolyn Jones, Stuart Whitman. 96 mins. (Prism)

Brand enjoys a thespic field day as a crazed cracker who leads unsuspecting strangers to his croc-stocked swamp. Hooper's low-budget horror is no *Texas Chainsaw Massacre* (see index), but it's better than a lot of his later, more lavish Hollywood work.

EDGE OF SANITY   (1989) *¹/₂

D: Gérard Kikoïne. Anthony Perkins, Sarah Maur Thorp, Glynis Barber, David Lodge, Ben Cole. 85 mins. (MCEG/Virgin, n.i.d.)

Perkins finds himself trapped in an unusually twerpy interpretation of Stevenson's oft lensed *Dr. Jekyll and Mr. Hyde.* Here Perkins plays Hyde (who, in this version, is also Jack the Ripper) as a sort of demented "Crackula" who acts out his misogynistic fantasies after freebasing the cocaine used by his more enlightened half, Dr. Jekyll, as an anesthetic. Most of the movie unfolds at a brothel, where Hyde wiles away his

evening hours torturing tarts while still finding time to slice and dice his way through London's streetwalker populace. Auteur Kikoïne attempts to kinkify *Edge*'s primer-level script—this is the type of pic wherein a doctor straight-facedly asks an obviously lash-marked hooker, "Did someone beat you up?"—with nudity and odd erotic obsessions that do little to relieve the boredom. Perkins's strange line readings and twitchy style supply some diversion but can't compensate for *Edge*'s otherwise colorless cast (save for Dr. Jekyll's pet baboon, a simian talent who goes sadly uncredited here), inept shock scenes, and general air of lethargy. The late, great thesp continued to wind down his career with the early-'90s terror duds *I'm Dangerous Tonight* (Universal), *In the Deep Woods* (Atlantic), and *A Demon in My View* (Trimark).

THE EIGHTEENTH ANGEL (1997) **¹/₂

D: William Bindley. Christopher McDonald, Maximilian Schell, Rachael Leigh Cook, Stanley Tucci, Wendy Crewson. 90 mins. (Columbia/TriStar)

The *Omen* author David Seltzer pens a fairly sturdy satanic chiller. Schell plays a crazed priest who devises a scheme to lure teenage beauty Cook from Boston to Italy with the promise of a modeling career. Natch, Max and his minions harbor far more sinister plans for the naïve nymphette, plans that include nothing less than returning Lucifer to earth, and it's up to Cook's suspicious dad, McDonald, to thwart the evil plot. While it doesn't scale the scary heights of *The Omen*, *The Eighteenth Angel* is an eerily efficient fear film that fills the homevid chiller bill.

THE ELEPHANT MAN   (1980) B&W ***¹/₂

D: David Lynch. John Hurt, Anthony Hopkins, Anne Bancroft. 125 mins. (Paramount)

Lynch crafts a haunting, heartrending, elegaic biography of the hideously deformed but bright and kindly title character, saved from a sideshow hell by physician Hopkins. Hurt gives an amazing performance under a ton of makeup. *Elephant Boy* (HBO), starring Sabu, is *not* a prequel.

EMBRACE OF THE VAMPIRE (1995) **¹/₂

D: Anne Goursaud. Alyssa Milano, Martin Kemp, Harrison Pruett, Charlotte Lewis, Jennifer Tilly. In R and unrated editions. 93 mins. (New Line) DVD

Sort of a teenage *Interview with the Vampire* wannabe, *Embrace* may not rate as a great vampire movie, but as an Alyssa Milano travelog, it's pretty hot. The former Amy Fisher/*Who's the Boss?*/*Charmed* girl plays a studious, virginal college frosh three days away from her 18th birthday. Awaiting that event with open lips is vampire Kemp, who believes Alyssa is the reincarnation of the virgin that got away centuries ago. (A flashback set in a *Legend*-like forest dramatizes Kemp's vampiric origins when he's nipped by three nearly naked vampirettes in a sequence blatantly "inspired" by *Bram Stoker's Dracula*.) Kemp intermittently materializes on campus to tempt Alyssa and plant doubt in the mind of her supremely patient beau (Pruett), who's been dating her chastely for over a year, even as the rest of the student population seems to seethe with abundantly requited lust. Alyssa really lets it all hang out here—at least in the unrated version—performing several nude scenes, two lesbian sequences (with older student photog Lewis), and a mixed human/vampire orgy. Unlike most so-called "erotic thrillers" that rely on token noirish plots to frame dull, gauzy sex scenes, *Embrace of the Vampire* gets honestly steamy via a series of truly febrile (as opposed to merely feeble) erotic encounters.

Femme director Goursaud works in a fair amount of reasonably bloody nape-nippings too. Oscar-nominated Tilly (*Bullets Over Broadway*) turns up in a last-reel leather cameo as Kemp's distaff minion and makes the most of her brief part. If you go for vampire tales that stress jugs over jugulars and gonads over gore, *Embrace of the Vampire* (actually *Nosferatu: Embrace of the Vampire* in the on-screen credits) shapes up as a fair rental bet.

ENTER THE DEVIL   (1972) ***

D: Frank Q. Dobbs. Josh Bryant, Irene Kelly, Dave Cass, John Martin, Carle Bensen, Norris Domingue. 83 mins. (Something Weird)

A deftly constructed, well-acted regional horror about an outlaw religious cult partial to human sacrifices, *Enter the Devil* traces the efforts of a deputy sheriff (a charismatic Cass, who also coscripted with director Dobbs) and a cult researcher (Kelly) to solve a rash of deaths and disappearances in and around a remote hunting lodge near Terlingua, Texas. One Happy Shahan sings the original tune "Green Green Green" and doubles as the cult's first on-screen victim. (Hey, it wasn't *that* bad bad bad.) A "Rex Reddneck" plays another deputy, while the pic concludes with the credit "Beer Sequences, Courtesy of Pearl Brewing Company."

THE ENTITY   (1983) ***

D: Sidney J. Furie. Barbara Hershey, Ron Silver, Jacqueline Brooks. 115 mins. (Fox)

H ershey is raped repeatedly by the invisible titular demon and is also forced to contend with nonbelievers who think she's out of her mind in this perverse, effective offbeat chiller. Barbara has since found less grueling work under Woody Allen.

EQUINOX   (1967/1971) B&W ***

D: Jack Woods. Edward Connell, Barbara Hewitt, Fritz Leiber, Jack Woods. 80 mins. (Lightning, n.i.d.)

A mateur acting and a nonexistent budget can't kill the hallucinatory thrills provided by David Allen's stop-motion animation and the solid story line (adapted from a story by Fritz Leiber, who cameos on-screen) that informs this enduring cult fright fave. The devil appears as a forest ranger (!) played by director Woods. The rare pic is also out as *The Beast* (Wizard).

ERASERHEAD   (1978) B&W ***1/2

D: David Lynch. Jack Nance, Charlotte Stewart, Allen Joseph. 90 mins. (Columbia/TriStar)

T he legendary midnight movie that put director David Lynch on the cult-film map is a one-of-a-kind hallucination that plays like a nightmare experienced by a nuclear-holocaust survivor: consistently creepy and often brilliant, with one of the best hemor-rhaging-chicken scenes ever captured on celluloid. The cassette itself rated as a rarity until Columbia/TriStar reissued it, then placed it on moratorium again.

ETERNAL EVIL   (1987) **1/2

D: George Mihalka. Winston Rekert, Karen Black, John Novak, Andre Bednarski. 85 mins. (Lightning, n.i.d.) DVD

I n this Canadian scare tale, Rekert is a depressed commercial director who dabbles in astral projection (beats watching hockey, eh?), a pastime apparently linked to the sudden, violent deaths of several associates. Complicating the case are a pair of ancient souls trapped in dying bodies and currently searching for suitable replacements. *Eternal Evil* fails to exploit its plot to the max, but it does feature some deft, free-floating aerial photography in the astral-projection

sequences. Black proffers another of her patented wacko performances, as the free-spirited lesbian dancer/astral-projection expert who starts our misguided protagonist down the flight path better not taken.

THE EVIL DEAD:
THE SERIES

THE EVIL DEAD   (1982) ***

D: Sam Raimi. Bruce Campbell, Ellen Sandweiss, Betsy Baker. 85 mins. (Anchor Bay) DVD

G ore auteur Sam Raimi topped his feature debut with the even wilder *Evil Dead 2*, but this surreal regional fearfest is still well worth catching for its own raw, kinetic splatter moves and frenetic camera work. Anchor Bay presents the formerly long-absent fave in a special remastered "collector's edition" with several "extras."

EVIL DEAD II: DEAD BY DAWN   (1987) ***1/2

D: Sam Raimi. Bruce Campbell, Sarah Berry, Dan Hicks, Kassie Wesley, Theodore Raimi, Denise Bixler. 85 mins. (Anchor Bay) DVD

R aimi's energetically brain-damaged sequel (remake, really) may be the most maniacal and wildly hallucinatory of horrordom's popular '80s spate of anything-for-a-gasp comic-nightmare movies. Raimi's hyperactive POV camera remains in constant frenzied motion throughout, even though most of the flick unfolds in a single claustrophobic cabin. As in the original, there's no real story here, just a simple situation. Five characters battle a succession of grotesque evil spirits (and one another) in a series of gross encounters of the absurd kind. One especially memorable tableau sees Campbell—reprising his role as Ash, the lone survivor of *The Evil Dead*—at war with his own left hand, now possessed by the title demons. When

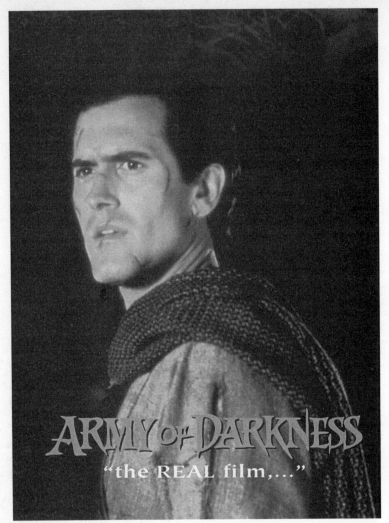

ARMY of DARKNESS

"the REAL film,..."

KICKING ASH: Bruce Campbell returns as much abused one-fisted hero Ash in Part 3 of Sam Raimi's splatstick *Evil Dead* trilogy, *Army of Darkness,* restored by Anchor Bay. *Courtesy of Anchor Bay Entertainment*

said hand begins *giggling* at its owner (!), Ash responds by plunging a knife into it and shouting triumphantly, "Who's laughing *now*!?" Raimi's live-action cartoon style, exploding-id imagery, and outrageous FX make *Evil Dead II: Dead by Dawn* essential viewing.

ARMY OF DARKNESS   (1993) ***

D: Sam Raimi. Bruce Campbell, Embeth Davidtz, Ian Abercrombie, Marcus Gilbert. 81 mins. (Anchor Bay) DVD

After languishing in legal limbo for nearly two years, Part the Third of Raimi's *Evil Dead* series finally swooped into national bijous in 1993—albeit in slightly truncated form, following a few cuts from its earlier overseas edition. (Anchor Bay's 1999 *Army of Darkness: The Special Edition* includes the original ending.) Despite its relatively scant running time, *Army* amply delivers in the black slapstick and Ash-kicking departments. An oft battered Campbell returns sans the hand he'd

self-amputated in *Evil Dead II* but with his trusty trademark chainsaw and Remington shotgun in tow.

Picking up where *Evil Dead II* left off, our story cuts to medieval Europe, where Ash and his Oldsmobile had been rudely deposited by the dread "Book of the Dead." Our unlikely hero receives a less-than-warm welcome from the locals, who promptly toss him into a "Deadite" pit wherein feisty cadavers await fresh victims. Once Ash displays his zombie-combat prowess, however, he's sent on a quest to recover the offending book, a botched job that leads to the widespread resurrection of the titular army. Most of the flick chronicles the ensuing battle between the skeletal warriors and their undermanned flesh-and-blood foes in an intricately choreographed comic conflict. Highlights include a scene that finds our hero besieged by malicious *homonculi* versions of himself spontaneously generated from the shards of a broken mirror; a hostile encounter with zombified former love object Davidtz; and nods to everything from *Commando* to *The Day the Earth Stood Still* to the Japanese obscurity *The Manster.*

Campbell again excels as the intrepid Ash, who compensates with confidence what he lacks in competence, greeting each new peril with direct (if often ill-advised) action and a macho quip. Look also for eye-blink cameos by Bridget Fonda and Raimi's thespian brother Theodore. While *Evil Dead II* remains The Phantom's fave series entry, *Army of Darkness* succeeds in steering the concept in a less grisly but still crazed direction.

THE EVIL MIND   (1934) B&W ***

D: Maurice Elvey. Claude Rains, Fay Wray, Jane Baxter. 80 mins. (Evergreen)

Claude's a phony seer whose predictions start coming true in an excellent, complex thriller (originally titled *The Clairvoyant*) marred only by a somewhat bland epilogue. Evergreen has the definitive edition of the film, which has popped up on countless public-domain labels.

THE EXORCIST:
THE SERIES

THE EXORCIST: 25TH ANNIVERSARY SPECIAL EDITION (1973) ***½

D: William Friedkin. Ellen Burstyn, Linda Blair, Jason Miller, Max von Sydow, Lee J. Cobb. 121 mins. (Warner) DVD

The framing story grows tedious at times, but Linda's demonic freak-out scenes, with vocal help from Mercedes McCambridge and some high-tech audio wizardry, remain as fresh and shocking today as they were in '73, despite dozens of pale imitations. The DVD includes Blair's infamous "spider crawl," deleted from the theatrical release, along with a slew of additional audiovisual "extras." Followed by John Boorman's ill-received *Exorcist II: The Heretic* (Warner), wherein an older but not much wiser Linda learns she's still got a bit of the devil in her.

THE EXORCIST III (1990) *½

D: William Peter Blatty. George C. Scott, Ed Flanders, Jason Miller, Viveca Lindfors, Brad Dourif, Zohra Lampert, Barbara Baxley. 110 mins. (Fox)

Original *Exorcist* author Blatty takes the devil by the horns, writing and directing this sequel, based on his own novel *Legion*. The pic opens with Georgetown detective Scott—his patented screen screaming jags intact—investigating a fresh rash of gruesome priest slayings. The murders match the M.O. of a supposedly dead serial psycho called the Gemini Killer (Dourif), who's back with a little help from his fiend, Satan, and now occupying the still-breathing body of Father Karas (Miller). With its emphasis

---

Kicking Ash!
BRUCE CAMPBELL COMES CLEAN
As Told to The Phantom

Actor Bruce Campbell came up through the ranks with Sam Raimi and has since gone on to establish himself as an extremely versatile thesp whose credits include the title role in the Fox-TV tongue-in-cheek cult western series The Adventures of Brisco County Jr.

PHANTOM: How did you and Sam Raimi first hook up?

CAMPBELL: In high school drama class in Bloomington, Michigan. That was back in '75, so I've known Sam for many, many moons. On weekends, myself and some of the other guys he grew up with would go up and help Sam make some of the movies he made at college.

PHANTOM: What were you doing at that point?

CAMPBELL: Making Super-eights—these real cheeseball, kind of Three Stooges rip-offs.

PHANTOM: So you were both into comedy?

CAMPBELL: Very much. That's why we've always been kind of surprised at this whole horror thing. I think it was a result of us feeling pressured that we raised money from investors in Michigan and we really wanted to get them their money back. This was the late '70s, just after *Halloween*, Jason—all that stuff. So we decided to make a horror film. But because we were new to it, we decided not to crap around. We wanted to make something that would really be kind of a balls-to-the-wall film. Whether it's good or bad. We just didn't want to get lost in the shuffle.

PHANTOM: Was it a long shoot?

CAMPBELL: It took four years, ultimately. We started in '79 down in Tennessee. Then we ran out of money. Then we raised a little more, ran out—you know, that whole routine—until it finally got its U.S. theatrical release in '83. It had opened overseas in '82.

PHANTOM: Was that a different version?

CAMPBELL: No. It was just that no U.S. distributors would touch it because it was so violent—*until* it opened overseas and made money. And then they called back claiming that they'd always loved it.

PHANTOM: Sam Raimi's intricate camera work must have added some time to the filming.

CAMPBELL: That's Sam's trademark. We had stuff on the first *Evil Dead* where we did one shot in a day. Part of it was because we didn't know what the heck we were doing, but also because the stuff could be pretty tricky. Sam comes from a magic background. Once he discovered films, he saw them as ninety-minute magic tricks.

PHANTOM: *Army*'s not as gory as the earlier *Evil Dead* films.

CAMPBELL: *Evil Dead* and *Evil Dead II* were technically unrated; we were contractually obligated for an R on *Army*. We actually weren't going for the gore most of the time anyway; we were actually leaning more to the adventure/humor side. It's in a horrific setting—we have our kind of creepy cool sequences—but there's nothing in this movie that comes anywhere close,

(continued)

to give you an example, to *Goodfellas*. To me, the scene in *Goodfellas* where they're stabbing the guy in the trunk is more violent—*true* violence, real, live, you-are-there sort of violence—than all our movies *combined*. We've never pretended to have *real* violence. There's always these monsters with silly white eyes—how seriously can you take it? The ratings board, they hate us. Universal wanted to change the title because they wanted it to stand on its own, and I can relate to that. We were all for it. But the ratings board says, "Oh, this is *Evil Dead* 3, huh? You didn't go to us the first two times, so let's take a look at this one." And they just came down real hard. It's completely arbitrary. It depends on how big the studio is, how big the filmmakers are. I don't think it's fair.

PHANTOM: They didn't put *Silence of the Lambs* through those kinds of hoops.

CAMPBELL: That's got Jodie Foster and Anthony Hopkins, these are classy actors, not Bruce Campbell—a guy who's been in a bunch of horror movies. And Jonathan Demme. Once you put those big shots behind it, it becomes judged in a different light. I'm all for ratings, but let them not be judged on the economics involved.

PHANTOM: Like *Evil Dead*, didn't *Army* play overseas first?

CAMPBELL: That's a different version. That's got what we call the "sad" ending; it's appropriate for the character, we thought. We then tested here in the United States. The response was they weren't so thrilled with the ending. Those countries that could wait (contractually) got the new ending too.

PHANTOM: Ash, the "Rambo of Gore," becomes more of an action hero in *Army*.

CAMPBELL: I think so. He's willing to take on creatures most action heroes don't take on. Rambo doesn't come across people who are possessed. He also takes way more of a beating than Rambo.

PHANTOM: Would you do another *Evil Dead* installment?

CAMPBELL: I'd be happy to do it if Sam wrote it. Even though they're the most difficult things I've done, they're also the most rewarding.

---

on pretentious theological patter, mannered perfs, and self-indulgent dark humor, *Exorcist III* is closer in spirit to Blatty's 1979 cult fave *The Ninth Configuration* (see index) than it is to the original *Exorcist*. While Blatty's jejune Jesuit vaudeville approach—exemplified by a nutsy nightmare sequence featuring hoop star Patrick Ewing as the Angel of Death (!)—fails more often than not, he does exhibit a flair for creative casting. Linda Blair may be nowhere in sight, but vet thesps Barbara Baxley, Harry Carey, Jr., Don Gordon, Viveca Lindfors, Zohra Lampert, Nicol Williamson, and Scott Wilson contribute brief turns, while Larry King and Everett Koop cameo as themselves. *Exorcist III* offers little in the scare or gore departments, and its token exorcism sequence is but a pale shadow of

the original's. The flick is not, however, without its ardent defenders.

EYES OF FIRE (1983) **½

D: Avery Crounse. Dennis Lipscomb, Guy Boyd, Rebecca Stanley, Fran Ryan, Rob Paulsen. 86 mins. (Vestron, n.i.d.)

Set on the "American frontier" circa 1750, Crounse's *Eyes of Fire* follows the exodus of some rather eccentric pioneers, led by Lipscomb and Boyd, into a "promised land" that quickly turns into a valley of death. Crounse adopts a Val Lewton–like approach, and his hallucinatory horror tale definitely has its black-magic moments—naked ghosts come and go, living faces form on haunted trees, and blood flows from the

earth. *Eyes* also succeeds in conveying the tenuous nature of frontier survival as our frightened pioneers try desperately to fight the elusive forest phantoms—the restless souls of innocent murder victims—that are destroying them one by one. Though flawed by a sluggish pace and slack acting, *Eyes of Fire* is worth a look.

EYES WITHOUT A FACE (1959)
B&W ***½

D: Georges Franju. Pierre Brasseur, Alida Valli, Edith Scob. 88 mins. Subtitled. (Interama)

French filmmaker and cinephile Franju's haunting horror outing, originally released stateside in an Anglicized version dubbed *The Horror Chamber of Dr. Faustus* (Sinister Cinema), receives royal treatment from Interama in this pristine, letter-boxed edition. Brasseur stars as an obsessed surgeon seeking to perfect "heterograft" techniques to restore daughter Scob's horribly disfigured face. Aided by reluctant assistant Valli, Brasseur relieves abducted young women of their visages (via extremely strong operation footage), but triumph continues to elude his grasp and violent tragedy ensues. Franju's blend of poetry and terror is ably abetted by Maurice Jarre's bittersweet score, and the film sports one of the most memorable fade-outs in genre history. Franju's infamous slaughterhouse shockumentary, *Blood of the Beasts,* is also out (Video Yesteryear).

FADE TO BLACK (1980) **½

D: Vernon Zimmerman. Dennis Christopher, Linda Kerridge, Tim Thomerson, Mickey Rourke. 100 mins. (Anchor Bay) DVD

This slasher tale is enlivened by countless in-references to genre-film lore—plus clips from *Public Enemy, Creature from the Black Lagoon, Kiss of Death,* and *Night of the Living Dead*—

as a maladjusted movie maniac known as "the Celluloid Killer" (Christopher) adopts the personas of famous thriller-film characters when carrying out his killings. Unfortunately, auteur Zimmerman ultimately runs out of inspiration before his movie runs out of reels. Anchor Bay has the "Special Edition."

FALL OF THE HOUSE OF USHER (1960) ***

D: Roger Corman. Vincent Price, Mark Damon, Myrna Fahey. 85 mins. (Warner)

Floyd Crosby's lush color cinematography and Daniel Haller's set designs lend this well-dressed low-budget Corman/Poe collaboration (the first of many) a classy, Hammer-like look. The 1928 silent and 1949 B&W British versions of Poe's claustrophobic tale are likewise available (Sinister Cinema), while Martin Landau stars in a 1980 version of the story (label unknown). The 1988 remake *House of Usher* (Columbia/TriStar), with Oliver Reed in the lead, is well worth avoiding.

FALLEN (1998) **

D: Gregory Hoblit. Denzel Washington, John Goodman, Donald Sutherland, Embeth Davidtz, James Gandolfini, Elias Koteas. 124 mins. (Warner) DVD

The hooks of *Shocker* and *The Hidden* meet the look of *Se7en* in a mainstream chiller directed by Hoblit (*Primal Fear*) from Nicholas Kazan's derivative script: The evil spirit of an executed killer (Koteas) lives on in a series of otherwise innocent citizens who unwittingly transmit it by simple touch. Cop Washington, whose efforts had placed Koteas on death row, is the ultimate target of this elaborate game of lethal tag, which, over *Fallen*'s two-hour running time, ultimately goes from supernatural to *stupor*natural. The Stones' "Time Is on My Side" serves as an ironic mantra (the same song was sim-

ilarly, and more adroitly, referenced in Jim McBride's 1971 postapocalyptic parable, *Glen and Randa* [see index]), sung first by Koteas prior to his execution and later picked up by his clueless carriers. *Fallen* sports a neat twist ending worthy of a superior *Twilight Zone* episode but fails to supply enough entertainment along the way to make it worth the wait.

5 DEAD ON THE CRIMSON CANVAS (1996) **1/2

D: Joseph F. Parda. Liz Haverty, Joseph Zaso, Xavier Domingo, Veronica James, Lynn Marri, Mony Damevsky. 96 mins. (El Independent Cinema)

It's Dario Argento, Long Island–style, and Glen Cove auteur Parda and crew do a fair job approximating a vintage D.A. chiller in this gory tale of murder and madness in the local art world. Abetted by Jerry Djerrasi's evocative score (with a further assist from Beethoven, whose "Sonata in C-minor, op. 13, Pathetique" Djerassi performs), Parda manages to keep his *hommage* involving despite some rough edges and uneven acting. Brit indie director Mario Baiano fashions an even better Italo-horror salute with his *Dark Waters*, available stateside as *Dead Waters* (York).

FLOWERS IN THE ATTIC (1987)0 *

D: Jeffrey Bloom. Victoria Tennant, Louise Fletcher, Kristy Swanson, Jeb Stuart Adams, Ben Granger, Lindsay Parker. 95 mins. (New World)

Unless watching four bland blond kids languish in the title site, as circles spread under their pale eyes and cobwebs gather over yours, is your idea of grand entertainment, we'd advise you to avoid this lame TV-movie-type loser like your proverbial plague. Tin-eared dialogue, a total lack of action and suspense, plus cardboard performances, like Fletcher's (who goes from Ratched

to wretched here) as a Granny from Hell, combine to make *Flowers* one of moviedom's all-time worst; not even a director named Jeffrey Bloom could keep this horticultural horror from wilting on the celluloid vine. Still, we admired *Flowers*'s big climactic shock line. To wit: "Eat the cookie!"

THE FOG (1980) **1/2

D: John Carpenter. Adrienne Barbeau, Jamie Lee Curtis, Hal Holbrook. 91 mins. (Columbia/TriStar)

While *The Fog* doesn't find frightmeister Carpenter at his creative peak, the pic still shapes up as a more-than-serviceable scarefest, as spectral seagoing lepers (!) slip through coastal mists to massacre unsuspecting citizens.

THE FORCE (1994) **

D: Mark Rosman. Jason Gedrick, Kim Delaney, Gary Hudson, Cyndi Pass, Dennis Lipscomb, Lyman Ward, Aki Aleong. 94 mins. (Republic)

A Canadian-produced, L.A.-set *policier* with a *Ghost* (Paramount) hook, *The Force* sees the troubled soul of murdered cop Hudson take temporary shelter in the mind of confused rookie Gedrick, who must solve Hudson's killing to reclaim sole occupancy of his own person. While competently acted and assembled, *The Force* is a mostly dull whodunit unabetted by its supernatural overlay.

THE FORGOTTEN ONE (1990) ***

D: Phillip Badger. Terry O'Quinn, Elisabeth Brooks, Kristy McNichol. 98 mins. (Academy, n.i.d.)

Badger's quietly effective fright tale stars *The Stepfather*'s O'Quinn as a writer and recent widower drawn to Denver, where he unwittingly moves into a haunted house. Even more unsettling is the fact that the resident poltergeist, the fetching Brooks, is convinced that Terry is actually her former paramour, survivor of a tragic tryst that culminated in her murder at the hands of her jealous spouse nearly 100 years before. Terry's own emotions gradually shift from fear to infatuation with the beguiling ghostess (who apparently can become flesh and blood at will). While *The Forgotten One* makes up its own spirit rules as it goes along, the film unfolds with sufficient depth, feeling, and eeriness to qualify as a rewarding genre entry.

FORTRESS OF THE DEAD (1965) B&W ***

D: Ferd Grofé, Jr. John Hackett, Conrad Parham, Eddie Infante, Jennings Sturgeon, Ana Corita. 75 mins. (Sinister Cinema)

A Filipino *Carnival of Souls* in reverse, *Fortress of the Dead* is a grimly effective, almost solemn chiller produced, written, and directed by Ferd Grofé, Jr., who also helmed *Samar, Warkill*, and other Filipino flicks (and whose composer dad wrote the score for *Rocketship X-M*, among others). In *Fortress*, American Hackett, sole survivor of a Corregidor battery unit, returns 20 years later in hopes of putting to rest his all-consuming guilt about his failure to save his doomed comrades. *Fortress of the Dead* looms as an unusually thoughtful fear film that, in the Val Lewton tradition, relies more on mood and atmosphere than cheap shocks.

FRANKENSTEIN (1931) B&W ****

D: James Whale. Boris Karloff, Colin Clive, Mae Clarke, John Boles, Edward Van Sloan, Dwight Frye. 71 mins. (Universal) DVD

K enneth Branagh's megabudgeted remake, *Mary Shelley's Frankenstein* (see index), sent us scurrying back to Whale's original, and truth be told,

we'd forgotten just what an over-the-top rock-'n'-roll rendition of the Shelley story Whale's version really is. Unlike Branagh's extravagant edition— and such other semifaithful modern adaptations as the 1975 Swedish-Irish production *Terror of Frankenstein* (Super) and the telefilms *Frankenstein* (1973, MPI), *Frankenstein* (1982, Lightning), *Frankenstein* (1993, Turner), and *Frankenstein: The True Story* (1973, DVT)—Whale's pic, by making the originally motormouthed Monster mute, stripped Shelley's tale of most of its philosophical discourse, gleefully emphasizing the story's exploitation elements instead. The result is a wonderfully unhealthy celluloid nightmare. From the refreshing bad taste of the opening funeral scene to Clive's classic "It's alive!" reverie, hyperactive hunchback Frye's enthusiastic sadism and Karloff's intense interpretation of the Monster, Whale's 71-minute movie emerges as a masterpiece of streamlined Grand Guignol and pure illicit fun.

FRANKENSTEIN MEETS THE WOLF MAN (1943) B&W ***

D: Roy William Neill. Lon Chaney, Jr., Ilona Massey, Patric Knowles, Bela Lugosi, Lionel Atwill, Maria Ouspenskaya. 72 mins. (Universal)

F rankenstein Meets the Wolf Man marked the first time two celebrity monsters shared the same marquee and screen. The sequel picks up where both the original *The Wolf Man* (see index) and *Ghost of Frankenstein* (Universal) left off. Lycanthrope Larry Talbot (Chaney) is reawakened by a pair of grave robbers, finds his way to the dread Frankenstein castle, and stumbles across the Monster encased in ice. Actually, it's Bela—in his only appearance as Frankenstein's creation (he rejected the original role back in 1931)—who does most of the stumbling. As initially scripted, the Monster is blind. That detail was omitted in the final cut, how

ever, which leaves Bela looking like he's perpetually drunk and searching desperately for the nearest men's room! That and other flaws prevent the film from rising to classic status, but there's enough Universal back-lot charm, skilled thesping, and cheap thrills to keep it consistently entertaining.

FRANKENSTEIN UNBOUND (1990) **½

D: Roger Corman. John Hurt, Raul Julia, Bridget Fonda, Jason Patric, Nick Brimble, Michael Hutchence. 86 mins. (Fox)

C orman's first directorial effort since 1970's *Von Richtofen and Brown* (Fox) covers much of the same ground as Ivan Passer's *Haunted Summer* and Ken Russell's *Gothic* (see index), fueled by a *Back to the Future*–type time-travel twist. Twenty-first-century American scientist Hurt conducts laser-weaponry experiments that inadvertently open a "time slip" through which he, accompanied by his talking, computerized supercar, is propelled back to 1817 Geneva. There he encounters not only Mary Shelley (Fonda), Lord Byron (Patric), and Percy Shelley (INXS's Hutchence) but Dr. Frankenstein (Julia) and his infamous Monster (Brimble). Based on Brit writer Brian Aldiss's novel, *Frankenstein Unbound* emerges as an uneven but often thoughtful attempt to merge futuristic sci-fi with its 19th-century roots—i.e., Mary Shelley's seminal novel *Frankenstein, or A Modern Prometheus* (though by recasting her fictitious Frankenstein as a living neighbor, the film belittles Mary's literary imagination a mite).

As in Franc Roddam's *The Bride* (see index), the Monster here is not only articulate but occasionally downright motormouthed; when he's not demanding a mate, he's pestering both his creator and the visiting Hurt with all manner of ontological queries (e.g., "Who made *you*?"). The outsized, starfish-faced Monster also has his violent side, supplying the movie with its scattered splatter moments by gore-killing several irritating humans. *Frankenstein Unbound* often unfolds at the kind of leisurely pace usually accorded far longer films (reports hold that the flick was subjected to extensive trims prior to its theatrical release), and the characterizations probably would have worked better had Brit Hurt and Yank Julia switched roles. The convincing period sets provide a plus, recalling the best of Corman's 1960s Poe adaptations. *Frankenstein Unbound* is a flawed but ambitious thinking-phan's fright film that delivers an essentially serious message re amoral science through the ages.

FREAKS   (1932) B&W ***1/2

D: Tod Browning. Wallace Ford, Leila Hyams, Olga Baclanova, Henry Victor, Harry Earles, Daisy Earles, Violet and Daisy Hilton, Angelo Rossitto, Johnny Eck, Prince Randian. 66 mins. (MGM)

The video version, transferred from an excellent print, loses none of *Freaks*'s original shock value. The simple plot—beautiful trapeze artist femme fatale Baclanova, in league with callous strongman Victor, woos, weds, and slowly poisons lovesick midget Harry Earles, the better to lay claim to his lucrative estate—is a perfectly serviceable excuse to draw the viewer into "freak" society, with its attendant bonds, codes, and rituals. Director Browning took a costly risk in recruiting actual circus freaks to play essentially themselves: "Human Torso" Prince Randian, legless Johnny Eck, dwarf (and steadily employed thesp) Angelo Rossitto, Siamese twins Violet and Daisy Hilton (later of *Chained for Life* fame), and other anatomical anomalies. Highlights include the freaks' sylvan frolic, the wedding-banquet sequence, and, of course, the fierce finale. The video also includes a choppy "happy" ending. When mainstream exhibitors refused to book *Freaks*, MGM sold the rights

to road-show sleazemeister Dwain (*Maniac*) Esper, who showed it in urban grindhouses and rural bijous under the title *Nature's Mistakes*. (It was still playing into the '50s as *Forbidden Love*.) Unfortunately, nothing ever came of the much anticipated rumored gala '80s remake, set to star Madonna, Arnold Schwarzenegger, Danny DeVito, and Dr. Ruth Westheimer, with Francis Ford Coppola at the helm. Tsk.

FRIDAY THE 13TH:
THE SERIES

FRIDAY THE 13TH   (1980) *1/2

D: Sean S. Cunningham. Betsy Palmer, Adrienne King, Harry Crosby, Laurie Bartram, Kevin Bacon. 95 mins. (Paramount) DVD

Director Cunningham and Paramount unleashed *Friday the 13th* back in 1980, essentially as a cheap rural rip-off of John Carpenter's wildly successful *Halloween*. When *Friday* and *its* mindless slasher icon, Jason Voorhees, proved equally boffo at the old B.O., Paramount spewed out *Friday the 13th Parts 2* (DVD) and *3*, the unfortunately misnomered *Friday the 13th: The Final Chapter; Part V: A New Beginning; Part VI: Jason Lives; Part VII—The New Blood; Part VIII: Jason Takes Manhattan* (lensed mostly in Vancouver); and *Jason Goes to Hell: The Final Friday* (New Line), with a rumored *Jason vs. Freddy* still in the works. Unlike the up-and-down *Halloween* and *Nightmare on Elm Street* series, *Friday the 13th* has maintained an umblemished record, with nary an entry that rises above the utterly forgettable.

FRIGHT NIGHT:
THE SERIES

FRIGHT NIGHT   (1985) **1/2

D: Tom Holland. Chris Sarandon, William Ragsdale, Roddy McDowall, Amanda Bearse,

Stephen Geoffreys, Jonathan Stark. 105 mins. (Columbia/TriStar) DVD

Fright Night starts out looking like another dumb assembly-line teen-horror comedy, as young Charlie Brewster (Ragsdale) tries to convince girlfriend Amy (Bearse) and creepy pal Evil Ed (Geoffreys, doing an irritating junior Jack Nicholson imitation) that his suave new next-door neighbor (Sarandon) is really a vampire. The pace picks up considerably, however, once these screen-teen nonentities are usurped by polished pros Sarandon and McDowall (aptly tacky as hack-actor-cum-horror-show-host Peter Vincent). The kids recruit a reluctant Roddy to subject Sarandon to the "vampire test"—an exam Chris flunks with flying colors (ranging from plasma scarlet to blood red). From that point on, *Fright Night* wisely leaves the low comedy behind and shifts into high fear gear. Sarandon's vampiric transformations rank among the best, while a femme blood-sucker who appears near film's end sports the champ vamp choppers of all time, stalactitic fangs gleaming from a crimson kisser that takes up half her face. The jolts are a long time coming but definitely worth the wait.

FRIGHT NIGHT PART II (1988) **1/2

D: Tommy Lee Wallace. Roddy McDowall, William Ragsdale, Traci Lin, Julie Carmen, Brian Thompson, Merritt Butrick. 104 mins. (Artisan)

Roddy returns as TV horror host and self-described "fearless vampire killer" Peter Vincent to help fellow returnee Charlie Brewster (Ragsdale) rid his life of a new slew of fanged fiends led by slinky "performance artist" Regine (Carmen). While *Fright Night II* is content to tread water (or, more accurately, blood), the pic plays as a highly watchable, light-veined horror vehicle in its own right.

FRIGHTMARE II (1974)***

D: Pete Walker. Rupert Davies, Sheila Keith, Deborah Fairfax, Peter Greenwood, Andrew Sachs, Kim Butcher. 86 mins. (Prism)

Like Larry Cohen and David Cronenberg, Brit auteur Pete Walker explores weighty themes within genre contexts and usually succeeds on both planes. Walker kicked off his screen career by producing, writing, and directing several late-'60s soft-core sexploitation quickies bearing such provocative titles as *The Big Switch* (a.k.a. *Strip Poker*), *Cool It, Carol!* and *Hot Girls for Men Only* (a.k.a. *I Like Birds*). He took his first plunge into the fright-movie maelstrom with 1973's *The Flesh and Blood Show* (Monterey), wherein a troop of Grand Guignol–type actors fall fatal prey to a crazed, frustrated thesp. In 1974 Walker began a fruitful collaboration with critic-turned-scripter David McGillivray. After crafting the S&M-flavored fearfest *House of Whipcord* (see index), the terror twosome hit their sinister stride with the same year's *Frightmare II*.

Despite its generic title (the "II" was added for the flick's vid release to avoid confusion with the unrelated fear anthology *Frightmare* [Vestron]), *Frightmare II* shapes up as strong, original stuff. Walker regular Keith gives a chilling perf as Mrs. Yates, a matronly maniac whose addiction to human flesh causes no end of stress for weak-willed accomplice/hubby Davies and decent stepdaughter Fairfax. Her 15-year-old biological offspring (the aptly named Butcher), on the other hand, enthusiastically embraces mater's decidedly perverse appetites, even helping to supply and prepare her human comestibles. Walker and McGillivray unravel their sicko but disturbingly credible psychodrama with a sly irony bolstered by ample grue; the pic works both as a deft horror exercise and a grotesque meditation on dysfunctional family life.

FROGS (1972)**

D: George McCowan. Ray Milland, Sam Elliott, Joan Van Ark. 91 mins. (Warner)

Wildlife destroyer Milland, in one of his patented petulant-patriarch parts, pays the price for his polluting proclivities when the title creatures exact their revenge. While nearly the whole cast croaks, *Frogs* doesn't quite fulfill the promise of its inspired tag line: "Today the pond, tomorrow the world!"

FROM DUSK TILL DAWN (1996)**½

D: Robert Rodriguez. George Clooney, Harvey Keitel, Quentin Tarantino, Juliette Lewis, Cheech Marin, Michael Parks, Tom Savini, Fred Williamson, John Saxon, Marc Lawrence. 108 mins. (Miramax) DVD

The first half of this disappointing collaboration of Rodriguez (director) and Tarantino (scripter/costar), (which we'll dub *Dusk*) shapes up as an exciting put-on pulp actioner in a *Reservoir Dogs* vein. The *second* half (which we'll call *Dawn*) is a well-executed (with gore FX by the busy KNB EFX team) but derivative and, save for the obligatory wooden stakes, ultimately pointless *Evil Dead* meets *Night of the Living Dead* rehash with morphing vampires subbing for zombies. On balance, *From Dusk Till Dawn* delivers enough high-voltage entertainment to cover the cost of an overnight rental, but it should have been two much better movies. A documentary, *Full Tilt Boogie* (n/a), provides an inside look at the making of *Dusk*. The mayhem continues, mostly minus the intermittent imagination, in Scott Spiegel's gore-driven 1999 direct-to-video sequel, *From Dusk Till Dawn 2: Texas Blood Money* (Dimension, DVD).

FROZEN TERROR (1980)***

D: Lamberto Bava. Bernice Stegers, Stanko Molinar. 93 mins. (Vestron, n.i.d.)

Cowritten by Pupi (*Revenge of the Dead*) Avati, directed by Bava, and inspired, according to the opening credits, by "true incidents that took place in New Orleans a few years ago," *Frozen Terror* (originally *Macabro*), which casts dubbed Euro thesps as Americans, begins with a bad day experienced by bored housewife Stegers. Seems that while Stegers is busy doing the deed with her lover in an apartment leased from blind repairman Molinar, her psychotic young daughter is expressing her disapproval by drowning her little brother in the bathtub. The situation worsens when, on their way to the tragedy site, Stegers and her paramour crash their car, resulting in his decapitation. The action picks up a year later when Stegers, released from a mental hospital, moves into her old trysting place, where she builds a shrine to her late lover, whose severed head she now stores in the fridge (!). While not as riveting as Avati's *Revenge of the Dead* (see index), *Frozen Terror* certainly ranks among the best frozen-head-in-a-fridge necro chillers we've seen.

FULL ECLIPSE (1993)**½

D: Anthony Hickox. Mario Van Peebles, Patsy Kensit, Bruce Payne, Anthony John Denison, Jason Beghe, Paula Marshall. In R and unrated editions. 97 mins. (HBO)

Van Peebles is an honest cop with a briefly dead partner who returns to life with a new gung-ho attitude and nearly supernatural vigor. While TV's *Nick Knight* (Starmaker) earlier mined a vampire-cop vein, *Full Eclipse* is the first werewolf-fuzz hybrid your Phantom can recall. Frightmeister Hickox (*Hellraiser III*) gets the over-the-top action/horror aspects right but can't steer the flick clear of last-reel clichés. *Full Eclipse* delivers on enough of its promise to make it worth a look, though we felt compelled to dock the pic for using the line "I'm getting too old for

That was a role not written for a brother—just a situation where a British director came out and said they needed a name and how about Mario? They didn't make a big deal about the racial issue; they just did it, and no one in reviewing it said anything, and that was refreshing. They sent me the script and told me it was about cops who turn into werewolves. I figured, in light of the Rodney King beating, it's not *that* much of a stretch.

It was my first time in that kind of makeup. There was something very cathartic about playing the monster. As a kid, I liked to play the monster; it sets you free in a way. If you look at the old Greek statues or Egyptian hieroglyphics, man's always had a fascination with his animal side, or dark side. So it was a chance to tap into some of that.

this." And Mario shouts "Nooooo!" in audio-distorted slo mo not once but *twice*, which is at least once too often.

THE FURY   (1978) ***

D: Brian De Palma. Kirk Douglas, John Cassavetes, Amy Irving, Carrie Snodgress, Charles Durning. 117 mins. (Fox)

De Palma plays with the fear genre and an extravagant budget in this overlong but generally fun story of psychokinetic destruction crammed with lavish cheap thrills galore. Bad guy Cassavetes blows up *real* good.

GARGOYLES   (1972) ***

D: B.W.L. Norton. Cornel Wilde, Jennifer Salt, Grayson Hall, Bernie Casey, Scott Glenn. 74 mins. (VCI/Liberty) DVD

Gargoyles is one of a handful of network-TV fright films (e.g., *Don't Be Afraid of the Dark, The Night Stalker, Trilogy of Terror*) to earn a legit cult rep. Author Wilde and daughter Salt happen upon the hatching title creatures in a Southwest desert and soon realize that the gargoyles will inherit the earth if they, along with a few locals (including a young Glenn), don't destroy the rapidly multiplying monsters. Among the cast, Casey literally stands tall as the gargoyles' winged, English-speaking chieftain.

THE GATE:
THE SERIES

THE GATE   (1987) **1/2

D: Tibor Takács. Stephen Dorff, Louis Tripp, Christa Denton, Kelly Rowan, Jennifer Irwin, Scott Denton. 92 mins. (Vestron, n.i.d.)

Takács's fantasy focuses on two kids (Tripp and a since-ascendant Dorff) who dig a hole in their backyard that leads directly to a satanic lair. ("We accidentally summoned demons who used to rule the universe," one youth blandly explains.) With the aid of an older sister (Denton) and an arcane heavy-metal LP, our half-pint heroes confront sundry forces of darkness over the course of a single harrowing night. *The Gate* was something of a surprise hit in its day and is not without its pluses. The on-screen tykes are likable for a change; the dialogue rings true (one kid's cry of "Suck my nose till my head caves in!" ranks as one of moviedom's more imaginative taunts); and the story unfolds with genuine suspense. The demons—more of your clichéd *Gremlin*-esque minimonsters—are disappointing, though, and the murky night photography pointlessly oppressive.

GATE II   (1992) **

D: Tibor Takács. Louis Tripp, Pamela Segall, James Villemaire, Simon Reynolds. 95 mins. (Columbia/TriStar)

Takács's belated follow-up finds a now-teenaged Tripp determined to return to the scene of the slime to "do it right" this time. ("It's hard to believe the world almost ended right here on our block," he wistfully reminisces.) Our young hero's plans go awry, however, when three local youths interrupt his demon-summoning ceremony, unleashing a diminutive infernal "minion" and eventually transforming two of the bad kids into full-sized stop-motion monsters. Despite these eerie events, Takács seems bent on presenting a "feel-good" fright fable here, even supplying a series of gratuitous "happy" endings that do little to juice a film saddled with slow pacing, flat dialogue, uncharismatic actors, and sub-Freddy surrealism. The pic's wittiest bit doesn't arrive until after a seemingly endless end-credit crawl, when few viewers will likely be around to appreciate it.

THE GHOUL   (1933) B&W **1/2

D: T. Hayes Hunter. Boris Karloff, Cedric Hardwicke, Ernest Thesiger. 73 mins. (Evergreen)

Boris plays an avenging corpse out to eliminate the thieves who broke into his tomb in this atmospheric but often painfully slow Brit chiller. The rediscovered complete print, sans the Czech subtitles that appearsd on previous video versions, is also available from Sinister Cinema. No relation to 1975's *The Ghoul* (Media), with Peter Cushing and John Hurt.

THE GIRL IN A SWING
(1989) ***

D: Gordon Hessler. Meg Tilly, Rupert Frazer, Nicholas Le Prevost, Elspet Gray, Lorna Heilbron, Helen Cherry. 112 mins. (HBO)

Hessler's adaptation of Richard Adams's novel is a lot more compelling than it has any right to be. As a German girl with a secret who weds wealthy, reserved Brit antiques dealer Frazer (sort of a poor man's Jeremy Irons), Tilly casts an irresistible spell that lends *Girl* a distinctly hypnotic aura. The normally unsurprising Hessler invests *Girl* with a sense of inevitable doom amid bursts of passion, resulting in a film that, though bleak, implausible, and overlong, is impossible to forget.

THE GIRL WITH THE HUNGRY EYES
(1994) **

D: Jon Jacobs. Christina Fulton, Isaac Turner, Leon Herbert, Bret Carr. 84 mins. (Columbia/TriStar)

"Inspired" by the Fritz Leiber short story of the same name, *The Girl with the Hungry Eyes* opens with model Fulton (late of *Bram Stoker's Dracula*) ending it all in a Miami Beach hotel room in 1937. She returns to life in the remodeled South Beach Deco District of the '90s as a vampire driven by the electronically enhanced voice of her late lover, who sounds something like Freddy Krueger with a bad flu. The large-lipped Fulton gives a curiously spazzed-out perf as the reborn bloodsucker who specializes in telepathically retrieving the past crimes of her deserving victims before draining their bodily fluids and, in some cases, decapitating them. (As fashion photographer Turner understates the case, "Is there no end to your attitude?") Unless you, like The Phantom, happen to be a big South Florida fan, watching *Girl* can make for a long 84 minutes.

GOD TOLD ME TO:
THE COLLECTOR'S EDITION
(1976) ***½

D: Larry Cohen. Tony LoBianco, Sandy Dennis, Deborah Raffin, Sylvia Sidney, Sam Levene, Richard Lynch, Mike Kellin. 95 mins. (Anchor Bay)

One of the strangest genre films ever made, Cohen's sci-fi/horror hybrid stars LoBianco as an NYPD detective whose obsessive investigation into a series of seemingly religious-themed mass murders brings him face-to-face with a far more bizarre plot. The film features terrific Gotham location lensing, from Little Italy to Harlem. One standout sequence sees a uniformed cop—a young, pre-*Taxi* Andy Kaufman in a one-line ("God told me to!") cameo—go berserk during the St. Patrick's Day Parade (which Cohen lensed sans permits). *God Told Me To* (a.k.a. *Demon*) remains an essential addition to every genre fan's vid library, and Anchor Bay does a typically excellent job in granting the film the care it deserves.

GODS AND MONSTERS
(1998) ***½

D: Bill Condon. Ian McKellen, Brendan Fraser, Lynn Redgrave, Lolita Davidovich, David Dukes. 105 mins. (Universal) DVD

McKellen fully earns his Best Actor Academy Award nomination for his complex interpretation of haunted, caustic, openly gay *Frankenstein* director James Whale. Based on Christopher Bram's novel *Father of Frankenstein*, Condon's powerful drama chronicles Whale's last days as a self-styled Hollywood exile who wrestles with his past while carrying on a platonic but increasingly intense relationship with his hunky hetero young gardener (an effective Fraser). Director/writer Condon, who won a well-deserved Best Screenplay Adaptation Oscar for his work here, seamlessly weaves Whale's real and reel lives, past and present, into a moving tapestry laced with wry wit. Best Supporting Actress nominee Redgrave is sheer brilliance as Whale's loyal Eastern European housekeeper/surrogate mother. *Gods and Monsters* may have been too modest to score big-time box office bucks, but the film makes for ideal home viewing.

THE GORGON (1964) **½

D: Terence Fisher. Peter Cushing, Christopher Lee, Barbara Shelley. 83 mins. (Goodtimes)

Shelley is an innocent possessed by the serpent-tressed spirit of the title creature; the peerless Pete and Chris shine as a battling brain surgeon and an investigator, respectively, in a stylish Hammer outing that ultimately falls a bit short of the monstrous mark.

GOTHIC (1987) **

D: Ken Russell. Gabriel Byrne, Julian Sands, Natasha Richardson, Miriam Cyr, Timothy Spall. 90 mins. (Vestron)

Russell's filmic fever dream traces a dark and stormy night in the laudanum-laced lives of a quintet of literary crazies—Lord Byron (Byrne), Percy and Mary Shelley (Sands, Richardson), Mary's half-sister Claire (Cyr), and Byron's unstable physician, Dr. Polidori (Spall). In 1816, at Byron's Swiss summer retreat, Villa Diodati, this rather self-indulgent lot set their febrile imaginations to conjuring demons who represent their deepest fears. The eventual result of this histrionic encounter was the birth (cesarean all the way, if you accept Russell's account) of Mary Shelley's immortal novel *Frankenstein*. There are some striking raging-id images and suitably sick sight gags on view but not enough to challenge Russell's own *Lair of the White Worm* (see index). Ivan Passer's *Haunted Summer* (see index) covers much the same ground.

GRANDMOTHER'S HOUSE (1989) ***

D: Peter Rader. Eric Foster, Kim Valentine, Brinke Stevens, Ida Lee, Len Lesser, David Donham. 89 mins. (Academy, n.i.d.) DVD

Grandmother's House (later rechristened Grandma's House) represents yet another troubled report from the Embattled American Family front: Newly orphaned teen Valentine and younger brother Foster move into the seemingly normal title abode, only to discover that their outwardly kindly grandfolk (Lesser, Lee) appear willing to kill to keep a deep, dark family secret. And that's only the beginning of the plot complications in this clever, stylishly lensed low-budget chiller. For further geriatric terrors, scope out Luca Bercovici's *The Granny* (WarnerVision) (with Stella Stevens in the title role), 1999's *Granny* (Spectrum), and the splatstick Euro import *Rabid Grannies* (Media).

GRAVEYARD SHIFT (1987) **½

D: Gerard Ciccoritti. Silvio Olivierio, Helen Papas, Cliff Stoker. 89 mins. (Video Treasures)

Ciccoritti's grimly effective low-budget horror yarn stars Oliviero as a vampire cabbie attracted by dying video director Papas in a pic that compensates with style and offbeat eroticism what it lacks in flashy FX. Ciccoritti followed with *Understudy: Graveyard Shift II* (Virgin) and also helmed the largely execrable *Psycho Girls* (MGM/UA) and the steamy NC-17 erotic outing *Paris, France* (A-Pix), no relation to Wim Wenders's *Paris, Texas* (Fox).

GRAVEYARD SHIFT (1990) *½

D: Ralph S. Singleton. David Andrews, Stephen Macht, Kelly Wolf, Brad Dourif. 89 mins. (Paramount)

After doing demented dogs (*Cujo*), rampaging werewolves (*Silver Bul-*

let), and killer cats not once but five times (*Cat's Eye, Pet Sematary, Pet Sematary II, Stephen King's Sleepwalkers,* and *Tales from the Darkside: The Movie*'s "Cat from Hell" segment), Stephen again puts the "King" in "animal kingdom." This time around, rats supply the initial scares, though the little rodents serve largely as red herrings—or rat herrings, if you will—with the major menace provided by a mutant mega-rat monster sequestered in the basement of a run-down Maine textile mill. Sort of a lower-budgeted *Ratnophobia, Graveyard Shift* shapes up as a numbingly routine horror outing, certainly nothing to rat home about. Rat lovers, meanwhile, are also referred to the Peter Weller rodent thriller *Of Unknown Origin* (Warner), costarring Shannon Tweed, along with *Deadly Eyes* (Warner), *A Rat's Tale* (Warner), *Rats* (Lightning), Andy Milligan's *The Rats Are Coming! The Werewolves Are Here!* (Sinister Cinema), *Willard* (Paramount), and sequel *Ben* (Prism).

THE GUARDIAN (1990) *½

D: William Friedkin. Jenny Seagrove, Dwier Brown, Carey Lowell, Brad Hall, Miguel Ferrer. 93 mins. (Universal)

Exorcist director Friedkin's shrug-a-minute story line, coadapted by Dan Greenburg from his novel *The Nanny*, finds a dull West Coast yup couple (Brown, Lowell) and their newly minted offspring (played by no fewer than four infant thesps, not counting stunt babies) endangered by young Brit nanny Seagrove. Seems Jenny's actually a secret druid who spends her nights frolicking nude with frothing hellhounds and delivering innocent babes unto voracious monster trees (!). While Friedkin manages to craft a few effective shock tableaux, he's fatally (to say nothing of fetally) burdened by a hack script, colorless characters, and an uninvolving mainstream milieu. The best segment details bland hero Brown's cli-

mactic chainsaw showdown with the killer tree, whose bark proves every bit as bad as its bite.

HABIT (1997) ***½

D: Larry Fessenden. Larry Fessenden, Meredith Snaider, Aaron Beall, Patricia Coleman, Heather Woodbury, Jesse Hartman. 112 mins. (Orion) DVD

Multitalented Fessenden scripts, directs, edits, and stars in this haunting indie gem, a totally naturalistic NYC-set fable about identity anxieties, life choices, romance, loss, and (we nearly forgot) vampires. Sort of a Gen-X "Carmilla" update, the pic opens, appropriately enough, at a Halloween party, where Sam (an engaging Fessenden, somewhat reminiscent of a young Jack Nicholson), depressed over his explorer dad's recent death and his own breakup with longtime squeeze Liza (Woodbury), is drinking heavily and behaving sloppily ("committing suicide on the installment plan," as he later puts it). At the bash, Sam meets Anna (Snaider), a serious, mysterious, kinky brunette whom he later dates. While shaken by Anna's penchant for sex in unsafe places and "playful" taste for blood (she nips his lip during one early session), Sam remains innocent of the darker threat she poses. Anna, meanwhile, insinuates herself ever deeper into Sam's life, short-circuiting his halfhearted attempts to reconnect with Liza. *Habit* saves its overt horror elements for the last reel, where the indecisive Sam proves a poor match for the aggressive, narrow-focused Anna.

Working on an obviously meager budget, Fessenden performs wonders with this complexly but seamlessly woven, thoroughly hypnotic exercise in stately grunge. His supporting actors hit nary a false note, while his camera captures the seediness, excitement, and glories of Sam's Lower Manhattan streets and surrounding environs. Like most classics of "quiet horror," from Jacques

Tourneur's *Cat People* to Herk Harvey's *Carnival of Souls, Habit* has an air of mundanity and specificity that serves to heighten the horror. Fessenden's feature debut, the sci-fi-tinged *No Telling: USA*, is also available (World Artists).

HALLOWEEN:
THE SERIES

HALLOWEEN (1978) ***

D: John Carpenter. Donald Pleasence, Jamie Lee Curtis, P. J. Soles. 93 mins. (Anchor Bay) DVD

John Carpenter's scare-crammed horror hit—the unfortunate inspiration for several inferior sequels and countless imitations—deserves its vaunted status as a true terror trailblazer. The first installment sees an imperiled Curtis and shrink Pleasence encounter indefatigable madman Michael Myers. Anchor Bay issued a separate "special edition" in 1999.

HALLOWEEN II (1981) *½

D: Rick Rosenthal. Jamie Lee Curtis, Donald Pleasence, Charles Cyphers. 92 mins. (Universal) DVD

Carpenter coscripts a thoroughly pedestrian sequel, which boasts higher blood and body counts but offers less suspense and atmosphere than its pioneering predecessor.

HALLOWEEN III: SEASON OF THE WITCH (1982) ***

D: Tommy Lee Wallace. Dan O'Herlihy, Tom Atkins, Stacey Nelkin. 98 mins. (Universal) DVD

A rad departure (to say the least) from earlier series entries, this entertainingly demented fable finds evil toy manufacturer O'Herlihy out to destroy America's tyke population. The endlessly repeated "Silver Shamrock"

toy jingle burned its way into the brains not only of its intended child victims but of viewers as well.

HALLOWEEN IV: THE RETURN OF MICHAEL MYERS (1988) *½

D: Dwight H. Little. Ellie Cornell, Danielle Harris, Donald Pleasence, George Wilbur. 88 mins. (Fox) DVD

After rotting on his laurels for nearly a decade, Halloween-masked misanthrope Michael Myers (a.k.a. "the Shape") returns for another pointless slaughter spree in a slack hack job that proceeds with none of the original's *joie de morte.*

HALLOWEEN 5: THE REVENGE OF MICHAEL MYERS (1989) *½

D: Dominique Othenin-Girard. Donald Pleasence, Danielle Harris, Wendy Kaplan, Ellie Cornell. 96 mins. (Fox)

In this relentlessly predictable retread, Mad Mike once again stalks hapless Haddonfield, Illinois, in a bid to reduce the local teen population. Pleasence's presence as the loony Dr. Loomis, young Danielle's thesping, and the KNB EFX Group's contributions represent the pic's only pluses.

HALLOWEEN: THE CURSE OF MICHAEL MYERS (1995) *

D: Joe Chappelle. Donald Pleasence, Paul Stephen Rudd, Marianne Hagen, Mitchell Ryan. 88 mins. (Dimension)

The series' sixth installment rates as the lamest of the lot. Most of the flick is devoted to the usual slice-and-dice set pieces, executed with few directorial flourishes and only middling gore FX. Relying largely on deafening soundtrack stings to up the terror ante, this barely coherent mess measured a perfect zero on the Official Phantom Squirmometer.

HALLOWEEN H2O (1998) ***

D: Steve Miner. Jamie Lee Curtis, Adam Arkin, Michelle Williams, LL Cool J, Janet Leigh, Josh Hartnett. 86 mins. (Dimension) DVD

Miner's update of the original *Halloween* is the first film to recapture some of Carpenter's black magic. Curtis is in fine form as dysfunctional adult Laurie Strode, who comes on strong in a final confrontation with her unstoppable homicidal brother.

HAUNTED (1995) ***

D: Lewis Gilbert. Aidan Quinn, Kate Beckinsale, Anthony Andrews, Sir John Gielgud. 108 mins. (Evergreen)

Vet Brit helmer Gilbert (*Alfie, Moonraker*) delivers a suitably chilling adaptation, co-exec-produced by Francis Ford Coppola, of James Herbert's novel. Quinn plays an American-educated psychology prof in 1928 England, whose guilt over the drowning death of his twin sister some 23 years earlier has steered his career in a supernatural-exposé direction. Summoned to the estate of a trio of aristocratic siblings who want him to dispel their aged nanny's fear of lingering ghosts, Quinn undergoes a series of surreal, emotionally draining encounters that include a temporary reunion with his late twin. Gilbert handles the trippy material with a *Dead of Night*–styled flair, and while the effects are excellent, they refreshingly serve rather than overwhelm the twisty storyline.

THE HAUNTED STRANGLER (1958) B&W ***

D: Robert Day. Boris Karloff, Elizabeth Allan, Anthony Dawson. 78 mins. (Sinister Cinema) DVD

Boris is in top form in this atmospheric story of a Victorian novelist who unconsciously reenacts the violent crimes of the dead killer whose exploits he's been researching. The plot eventually takes a twist that prefigures *Angel Heart*.

HAUNTED SUMMER (1988) **

D: Ivan Passer. Philip Anglim, Laura Dern, Alice Krige, Eric Stoltz, Alex Winter. 115 mins. (Media, n.i.d.)

Passer's *Haunted Summer* covers much of the same ground as Ken Russell's 1987 fever dream *Gothic* (see index), although Passer forgoes Russell's determinedly grotesque burlesque treatment in favor of a more traditional approach. Mary (Krige), Shelley (Stoltz, boasting an ersatz English accent), and Byron's soon-to-be-spurned squeeze, Claire (Dern, whose lone tearful outburst here fails to match her memorable crying jag in *Blue Velvet*) accept an invitation from the infamous Byron (Anglim) to join him at his Swiss retreat. Unfortunately, while Russell went over the top, Passer plays it too low-key. Much screen time is devoted to our self-enamored poets' posturing before Mary and her immortal Monster (glimpsed briefly during a shared opium vision) are allowed to take center stage.

HAUNTED SYMPHONY (1994) **1/2

D: David Tausik. Ben Cross, Beverly Garland, Jennifer Burns, Doug Wert, Lev Prygunov. 98 mins. (New Horizons)

Roger Corman resumes his celluloid relationship with Russia—an alliance that dates back to the early '60s, when he purchased a Soviet space epic and proceeded to construct several films (e.g., *Planet of Blood*) around its more spectacular footage—in this decently mounted attempt to recapture the gothic grandeur of his Poe pics of yore. While Ben Cross may be no Vincent Price, Beverly Garland *is* still Beverly Garland, and it's good to see the former feisty '50s femme fiend-fighter

in a meaty (and villainous) fright-film role. A prologue finds early 19th-century French composer Prygunov having a bad wig day when his latest composition, the *Devil's Symphony*, fails to score with an audience of local clerics. After Prygunov is drawn and quartered by those same self-appointed critics, his fetching niece Burns commissions alcoholic composer Cross to complete the unfinished piece. With sinister housekeeper Garland's help, Prygunov exerts his influence from beyond the grave, compelling Cross to keep at his sacrilegious labors, with the occasional time out to slay local tarts with a length of piano wire. Featuring full-frontal femme nudity and rough-sex tableaux, *Haunted Symphony* is more openly daring but decidedly less atmospheric than Corman's earlier gothic works. New Horizons reissued the video in 1997 under the title *Blood Song*—no relation to the 1982 psycho romp of the same name (Coast-To-Coast Video), featuring a flute-playing Frankie Avalon.

THE HAUNTING (1963) B&W ***

D: Robert Wise. Julie Harris, Claire Bloom, Russ Tamblyn, Richard Johnson. 112 mins. (MGM)

This gothic horror, adapted by Val Lewton protégé Wise from Shirley Jackson's *The Haunting of Hill House*, may be somewhat overrated but still supplies ample atmosphere, subtle chills galore, and an excellent turn by Harris as a raging neurotic. Remade by Jan (*Speed*) De Bont in an ill-received 1999 FX-driven version (Warner, DVD), starring Liam Neeson and Lili Taylor.

HELL HIGH (1986) **

D: Douglas Grossman. Christopher Stryker, Christopher Cousins, Jason Brill, Maureen Mooney. 84 mins. (Prism, n.i.d.)

A precursor of Kevin (*Scream*) Williamson's unpopular 1999 black-

comedy thriller *Teaching Mrs. Tingle* (Dimension), *Hell High* focuses on a foursome of adolescent pranksters—one of whom, Dickens (Stryker), emerges as more dangerously disturbed than his mates—who play a disastrous practical joke on their secretly bonkers bio teacher, Ms. Storm (a tense but appealing Mooney). *Hell High* eventually lurches from high school hijinks turf into *I Spit on Your Grave* territory, as the volatile Ms. Storm violently turns the terror tables on her young tormentors. Auteur Grossman succeeds in creating a stark, autumnal atmosphere, and the movie's post-slaughter fade-out scenes are likewise well rendered. But the pic gets on track way too late to compensate for its meandering setup reels and occasionally risible dialogue. (Says Stryker of an allegedly haunted swamp, "That legend is a myth!")

HELLRAISER:
THE SERIES

HELLRAISER (1987) ***

D: Clive Barker. Andrew Robinson, Clare Higgins, Ashley Laurence, Sean Chapman, Oliver Smith, Robert Hines. 94 mins. (Anchor Bay) DVD

A surreal, claustrophobic gruefest, Clive Barker's *Hellraiser* depicts a Brit degenerate named Frank (Chapman) whose addiction to an arcane Beelzebubian puzzle box (the infamous "Lament Configuration Box") capable of supplying unimaginable pleasure and pain ultimately results in his gory demise. When Frank's brother Larry (Robinson) buys the house wherein Frank's splattered remains lie undetected, a few drops of Larry's blood bring his sinister sibling to gradual slime-creature life. After that, it's up to Larry's unhappy wife and Frank's former lover (Higgins) to lure fresh victims to the house to complete Frank's physical restoration. Hot on Frank's trail, meanwhile, are the box's original owners, four demonic Cenobites who resemble refugees from a late-'80s CBGB hard-core punk matinee. Though better known for his fright fiction, Barker demonstrates in his directorial debut that he knows how to deliver perverse visual chills as well.

HELLBOUND: HELLRAISER II (1988) ***

D: Tony Randel. Clare Higgins, Ashley Laurence, Kenneth Cranham, Imogen Boorman, William Hope, Doug Bradley In R and unrated editions. 98 mins. (Anchor Bay) DVD

Hellbound represents one of those rare cases wherein a scare sequel equals, and in some instances surpasses, the original. Directed by Randel from a story by Barker (who also coproduced), Hellbound offers an ever escalating procession of nightmare set pieces that succeed in being both darkly comic and genuinely chilling. (As Pinhead at one point proclaims, "Your suffering will be legendary—even in hell!") Highlights include imaginatively grotesque sets, horrific FX that outnightmare Elm Street, and one of the sickest heavy-petting scenes The Phantom's ever seen on-screen. The video is available in both the R-rated and a gorier, unrated version.

HELLRAISER III: HELL ON EARTH (1992) ***

D: Anthony Hickox. Doug Bradley, Terry Farrell, Kevin Bernhardt, Paula Marshall. 97 mins. In R and unrated editions. (Paramount)

Scripted by Peter Atkins, Hellraiser III forgoes much of II's sinister surrealism but provides Pinhead with far more of a showcase. What the pic lacks in plot invention is more than compensated for by lots of colorful carnage, complete with some effectively revolting FX work (courtesy of Bob Keen). Especially impressive are a club-set

slaughterfest with a mega body count and a scene that sees a Pinhead victim instantly filleted before our very eyes. Helmer Hickox, meanwhile, goes Hitchcock one better by giving himself two cameos—as a soldier in a 'Nam-set flashback and as himself in a split-second TV clip. The unrated version promises an "extra 5½ minutes of extreme gore."

HELLRAISER: BLOODLINE (1996) *½

D: "Alan Smithee." Bruce Ramsey, Valentina Vargas, Doug Bradley. 81 mins. (Dimension)

It's usually a pretty sure sign a flick's in big trubs when an auteur signs his work "Alan Smithee," the standard pseudonym adopted by disgruntled directors. Unhappily for horror hounds, Hellraiser: Bloodline is no exception to this celluloid rule. The film's actual helmer, veteran FX ace Kevin Yagher, does accept design credit for Pinhead's pet hellhound, "Chattering Beast," which ranks as one of this otherwise weak sequel's few horrific highlights. The earlier Hellraisers' trademark surrealism is nowhere in sight, while their ruminations on the subjects of evil and suffering are reduced to a few Pinhead wisecracks here.

HENRY:
THE SERIES

HENRY: PORTRAIT OF A SERIAL KILLER (1986/1990) ***½

D: John McNaughton. Michael Rooker, Tracy Arnold, Tom Towles. 90 mins. (MPI) DVD

After building a cult rep via various regional playdates and festival screenings, McNaughton's disturbing, offbeat chiller, lensed in 1986, finally arrived on homevid in 1990. Filmed in a stark, semiverité style, Henry chronicles the Chicago-based slay career of the title psycho, a part-time freelance exterminator (!) given a deliberately flat, gen-

uinely creepy interpretation by Rooker. Henry, sociopathic product of a traumatic oedipal-wrecked childhood, hooks up with the equally trashy Otis (Towles) and his naïve younger sister Becky (Arnold), a former topless dancer. Henry soon introduces petty criminal Otis to the joys of abrupt and senseless violence as the pair perpetrate a series of intentionally random, aggressively pointless slaughters. They eventually begin videotaping their murderous misdeeds for leisurely reviewing in the privacy of their squalid digs.

While Henry lacks the layered perversity of David Lynch's Blue Velvet (see index), for sheer relentless, painstakingly rendered ugliness, McNaughton's snuff-fest is fairly unparalleled in the annals of quality genre cinema. The pic's penultimate sequence alone piles on the atrocities as if they were going out of style, in crazed but uncomfortably credible profusion. Henry: Portrait of a Serial Killer plays it both ways, simultaneously exposing and exploiting our mundane modern monster's vile crimes. The movie—like the later Secret Life: Jeffrey Dahmer (see index)—succeeds in leaving the viewer with the sense that society supplies little in the way of effective treatment for, or protection from, Henry's bland brand of alienated, impulsive fiend. Similarly, there's almost no barrier separating the audience from the on-screen abominations. Henry is not your standard fantasy fear-figure but a true contempo grotesque you're not likely to forget.

HENRY: PORTRAIT OF A SERIAL KILLER PART 2 (1997) **½

D: Chuck Parello. Neal Giuntoli, Rich Komenich, Kate Walsh, Carri Levinson, Daniel Allar, Penelope Milford. 84 mins. (MPI) DVD

Writer/director Parello's belated sequel is a virtual revamp of the original's basic plot: Laconic drifter Henry (Giuntoli, creepily competent but no match for the blood-freezing Rooker)

again insinuates himself into a low-life family—here headed by part-time arsonist Kai (Komenich), whom Henry gradually converts to his one-maniac cult of abrupt and senseless violence. A subplot charts Kai and wife Cricket's (Walsh) neurotic young niece Louisa's (Levinson) increasingly obsessive crush on the antisocial killer. On its own, *Henry 2* is a reasonably well executed (so to speak) descent into slaughter and sleaze, sort of what *Stepfather II* (see index) was to the original. But as a successor to a true pioneer, this unnecessary reprise is little more than a faint echo of the original's shout of celluloid rage.

HIDEAWAY   (1995) **½

D: Brett Leonard. Jeff Goldblum, Christine Lahti, Alicia Silverstone, Alfred Molina, Jeremy Sisto, Rae Dawn Chong, Kenneth Welsh. 103 mins. (Columbia/TriStar)

Director Leonard (*Lawnmower Man, Virtuosity*) continues to corner the screen virtual-reality market. While not keyed directly to a VR motif, his adaptation of Dean R. Koontz's novel—about a pair of resuscitated souls who share the same crowded psychic space (a concept less adroitly explored in the ludicrous 1989 campfest *Retribution* [Virgin, n.i.d.])—is dependent on similarly styled FX. Here, under doc Molina's care, antiques dealer Goldblum is revived after undergoing a 20-minute life-after-death experience where he crosses paths with another retrieved goner, young misogynistic psycho Sisto, who dispatched his own mom and sis in the pic's prologue. Jeff's better half (Lahti) and his endangered teen daughter (Silverstone) think he's nuts—as Alicia puts it, "I mean, he's really on edge. Dying and all, y'know?"—when he starts channeling the killer and his heinous crimes. The flick culminates in an impressive FX duel between Goldblum and Sisto, set in an abandoned amusement park, that briefly drifts into Miltonian *Paradise Lost* territory (!).

HIGH DESERT KILL   (1990) **

D: Harry Falk. Chuck Connors, Anthony Geary, Marc Singer, Micah Grant. 93 mins. (Universal)

Originally lensed for cable, *High Desert Kill* boasts a potentially fun premise that's largely done in by poor, often boring execution. Three friends (Geary, Singer, Grant) on a hunting trip are being covertly manipulated by an unseen behavioral scientist from outer space, who later appears in the image of a dead crony. (As Geary sighs, "I just don't understand how a being obviously so advanced can be so cruel.") The trio encounter hunter Connors (in one of his livelier old-coot turns) and a pair of feminist campers who, also via the intrusive alien's intervention, briefly transform into sex-crazed bimbos who lust after Chuck's bod (!). Unfortunately, this latently perverse *Predator* variation suffers from torpid, made-for-TV pacing, a paucity of action and FX, and an awkward story structure that's ultimately more muddled than mysterious.

THE HILLS HAVE EYES:
THE SERIES

THE HILLS HAVE EYES   (1977) ***

D: Wes Craven. Dee Wallace, James Whitmore, Michael Berryman. 89 mins. (Magnum, Starmaker, n.i.d.)

Desert mutants seek to ruin innocent campers' road trip in the best of Craven's early low-budget epics and the movie that launched screen monster man Berryman. Director Craven's sharp sense of suspense and his willingness to go "too far" help overcome a slender story line and uneven cast. *The Hills Have Eyes Part II* (HBO) doesn't hack it (though giving the surviving dog his own flashback is a neat touch). A planned second *Hills* sequel instead mutated into the unrelated *Wes Craven's Mind Ripper* (WarnerVision).

THE HITCHER   (1986) ***

D: Robert Harmon. Rutger Hauer, C. Thomas Howell, Jennifer Jason Leigh, Jeffrey DeMunn, John Jackson. 98 mins. (HBO) DVD

We'll say this much for *The Hitcher:* It may burn up a lot of octane, but it doesn't waste any time. No sooner does naïf Howell pick up highway menace Hauer than *The Hitcher* revs into high homicidal gear. Hauer flashes his trademark sneer as icy superpsycho John Ryder, an archetypal everyfiend who, sans identity or motive, embroils Howell in a harrowing desert intrigue that finds our young hero hounded not only by the nutjob but by a veritable army of enraged redneck cops who think *he's* the killer. Howell is so rattled by this revolting development that, before the movie's halfway through, he barfs twice *and* tries to kill himself. Sympathetic waitress Leigh does her best to help our persecuted protag, but the paranoiac plot twists—and the body count—continue to mount. When *The Hitcher* first appeared in '86, its *Terminator*-rip-off climax played more plagiaristically than it does today. There's a sly edge that threatens to push *The Hitcher* to the brink of self-parody, but this is a flick that's stood the test of time. Scripter Eric Red has gone on to contribute several other worthy genre items, from *Near Dark* to *Cohen and Tate* (see index).

HOLLYWOOD GHOST STORIES (1986) B&W/COLOR***

D: James Forsher. Elke Sommer, William Peter Blatty, Susan Strasberg, Frank De Felitta. 75 mins. (Warner)

John Carradine hosts an entertainingly tacky, brain-damaged investigation into the title subject, wherein heavyweights like Elke Sommer describe spooky Tinseltown incidents, interspersed with some choice frightflick clips. The pic also offers a classic example of high-concept Hollywoodthink when *Amityville Horror* producer Elliott Geisinger explains why that allegedly haunted house's original owners couldn't have been perpetrating a hoax: "What kind of gain could they possibly get from leaving the house and walking away from it? They didn't have a book contract when they left the

house. Even if they *did* have a book contract, there was no guarantee the book would possibly be a best-seller. They did not have a movie contract. And if they *did* have a movie contract, there was no guarantee the movie would come out and be successful." Now, *that's* scary!

HORROR EXPRESS   (1972) ***½

D: Gene Martin. Peter Cushing, Christopher Lee, Telly Savalas. 88 mins. (Anchor Bay) DVD

Just about every public-domain video outfit stocks this immensely entertaining chiller about a brain-sucking alien loose aboard the Trans-Siberian Express, circa 1906, but Anchor Bay has the definitive version. Pete and Chris excel as rival scientists, while Savalas cameos as an overbearing Cossack in a pic rich in characterization and period flavor (if not in budget), offering everything from trepanning close-ups to mad monks to brain-drained zombies. Not to be missed.

HORROR HOTEL   (1960) B&W ***½

D: John Moxey. Christopher Lee, Dennis Lotis, Betta St. John. 76 mins. (Anchor Bay) DVD

Set in New England but lensed in Britain, Moxey's moody scarefest, scripted by mystery novelist George Baxt, about a reincarnated Salem witch who lures sacrificial victims to the title establishment has garnered a sizable (and well-deserved) cult following over the years. Anchor Bay presents a pristine print of *Horror Hotel,* previously available mostly in muddy public-domain transfers.

HORROR OF DRACULA   (1958) ***½

D: Terence Fisher. Peter Cushing, Christopher Lee, Michael Gough. 82 mins. (Warner)

Frequent Hammer helmer Fisher crafts one of the studio's classiest

scare productions, with Lee perfectly cast as the caped count and Cushing shaping up as an equally ideal Van Helsing. *Horror* was widely condemned in its day for its high violence quotient, including the count's still-impressive climactic meltdown. Great fun all around. Hammer was less successful with its snarky 1970 *Horror of Frankenstein* (HBO).

HORRORS OF THE BLACK MUSEUM (1959) ***½

D: Arthur Crabtree. Michael Gough, June Cunningham, Graham Curnow, Shirley Ann Field, Geoffrey Keen, Gerald Anderson, John Warwick. 94 mins. (VCI)

A wonderfully sardonic Gough stars as a successful crime author who—with the help of chemically "hypnotized" assistant Curnow and using instruments inspired by Scotland Yard's "Black Museum" weapons collection, as well as lethal artifacts purchased at a macabre antiques shop—commits the hideous murders he then goes on to chronicle. Gough has also assembled his own secret murder museum in his basement, a terrific set with wax figures of his victims, an active acid vat, and even an electronic death ray of his own design. *Horrors of the Black Museum* is chockful of justly infamous money shots: the steel-pronged binocs that claim the film's first fatality, a grisly guillotine sequence, and an ice-tongs slaying, among others. (We also liked the purple-tinted transition scenes and the generally lurid color schemes.) While it falls a tad short of matching Michael Powell's then-contempo scare classic *Peeping Tom* (see index), *Horrors,* deftly scripted by director Crabtree and writer Abel Kandel, shares many of the same modern, media-themed touches. The flick's only questionable element is its tagged-on "HypnoVista" prologue, a 13-minute hypno-demonstration short, hosted by mesmerist Emil Franchel, that's tackily entertaining enough in its own right but proves totally extraneous to the pic proper.

HOUSE:
THE SERIES

HOUSE (1986) *½

D: Steve Miner. William Katt, George Wendt, Richard Moll, Kay Lenz. 93 mins. (Starmaker)

Stephen King–type fright writer Katt moves into his late nutty aunt's haunted house to work on his Vietnam memoirs. *House* opens as a straightforward, if mostly ineffectual, chiller, cluttered with grim 'Nam flashbacks, before careening into broad comedy and finally collapsing into a failed EC Comics–styled gruefest. For some inexplicable reason, *House* did well enough to merit a somewhat improved sequel, Ethan Wiley's 1987 *House II: The Second Story* (Starmaker), which maintains a refreshingly throwaway attitude toward its largely senseless but livelier material, emerging as a sort of EC Comics Meets *Pee-wee's Playhouse*. What had been intended as a *House III* (it screened under that title in Europe) mutated stateside into 1989's irredeemably awful *The Horror Show* (MGM), a *Nightmare on Elm Street* wannabe that featured the same executed-killer's revenge plot as Wes Craven's *Shocker* (see index), unleashed the same year. This rickety series concluded (hopefully) with 1992's lame *House IV: Home Deadly Home* (New Line), starring original *House* inhabitant Katt.

HOUSE OF DREAMS (1964) B&W **½

D: Robert Berry. Robert Berry, Pauline Elliott, Charlene Bradley, Lance Bird, David Goodnow. 80 mins. (LSVideo)

Add to the lengthy list of one-shot auteurs Robert Berry, who fash-

ioned this moody horror-tinged dream drama (it reportedly played a few Midwest drive-ins). Berry takes the lead role of a blocked, headache-plagued writer. The budget-constrained nightmare sequences unfold within the abandoned title abode and foretell several tragedies that befall our beleaguered hero. Berry seems to have been an early *Carnival of Souls* student; the alienation theme and discordant organ score recall Herk Harvey's 1962 cult chiller. Unfortunately, *House of Dreams,* while effective in stretches, succeeds mostly in being simply bleak rather than bleakly disturbing.

HOUSE OF HORRORS (1946) B&W ***

D: Jean Yarbrough. Rondo Hatton, Robert Lowery, Virginia Grey, Martin Kosleck, Bill Goodwin, Alan Napier, Howard Freeman. 65 mins. (Universal)

Stricken with a bone-distorting, ultimately fatal case of acromegaly, thesp Rondo Hatton—once tastefully billed as "the monster man who needs no makeup"—appeared in several low-budget 1940s fear flicks, with *House of Horrors* rating as the sturdiest of the lot. Set in a Hollywood B-movie version of the NYC art world, *House of Horrors* is richer in grim irony than horror. The film focuses on lowly regarded "mad" sculptor Kosleck, who shares his humble, candlelit Greenwich Village studio with his faithful cat, Pietro, and a clutter of surreal anatomical sculptures. When arrogant art critic/newspaper columnist Napier ruins a potential sale, Kosleck grows so depressed he decides to end it all in the Hudson River. Already floating in same is Hatton, a presumed-dead serial killer called "The Creeper," who unwittingly rekindles the artist's nearly extinguished life spark by providing him with the ideal model ("the perfect Neanderthal man!") for a new work. An equally grateful Rondo joins Kosleck's already odd household, posing for his

benefactor by day while pursuing his own hobby—strangling stray femmes (!)—by night.

When callous critic Napier boasts of his cruelty to Kosleck in print, the artist strongly hints that the world would be a more harmonious place with Napier out of the picture. Since Kosleck's wish and Hatton's command are nothing if not synonymous entities, Rondo promptly pays Napier a covert nocturnal visit and snaps the critic's spine. Initial suspicion for the crime falls on a second artist, commercially successful Vargas-like painter/illustrator Lowery, who'd engaged in a public shouting match with Napier the night before. In direct contrast with Kosleck's stripped-down lifestyle, Lowery lives in posh uptown digs where he sketches a sexy succession of scantily clad models while romancing art critic Grey (though he openly disapproves of her "independence").

Tidily constructed and laced with witty dialogue, *House of Horrors* tells its tale in a streamlined yet atmospheric 65 minutes. Unfortunately for Rondo, he checked out before either *House of Horrors* or his other 1946 showcase, *The Brute Man* (Image, DVD), saw the light of day. Rondo Hatton completists can also catch their idol in these video-available titles: *Hell Harbor* (Glenn Video), *The Hunchback of Notre Dame* (RKO), *In Old Chicago* (Fox), *The Pearl of Death* (Fox), and *The Princess and the Pirate* (HBO). Rondo also received an extended tribute in 1991's *The Rocketeer* (see index).

HOUSE OF WAX (1953) ***

D: Andre de Toth. Vincent Price, Carolyn Jones, Phyllis Kirk. 88 mins. (Warner) DVD

Price hams it up with his usual élan as the scarred sculptor who turns his enemies into wax dummies. Charles Bronson (then "Buchinski") is his brain-damaged assistant. Originally lensed (and very effectively) in 3-D, the pic plays even funnier without it as all sorts of objects—for no apparent reason—hurl themselves at the camera with *Poltergeist*ian frenzy.

HOUSE OF WHIPCORD   (1974) **¹/₂

D: Pete Walker. Barbara Markham, Patrick Barry, Penny Irving, Ray Brooks, Anne Michelle, Sheila Keith. 102 mins. (Monterey) DVD

Another genre-framed assault on warped religious/family values by frequent Brit collaborators Walker (director) and David McGillivray (writer), *House of Whipcord* leans more toward pure exploitation than horror. The film, recycling a familiar Walker/McGillivray story structure, finds "Mark E. DeSade" (Robert Tayman) luring swinging London birds to an allegedly abandoned jail, where his mad mom (Markham) continues to operate the correctional facility, flogging and frequently hanging her "promiscuous" charges. While often predictable, enough of the W/M team's patented dark wit—here justice, represented by doddering Judge Barry, is not only literally blind but senile into the bargain—seeps through to make *House of Whipcord* worth a visit. In her turn as a volunteer prison matron named "Walker," ever dependable Walker regular Keith provides the film with another plus. Walker and McGillivray also contribute cameos.

HOUSE ON HAUNTED HILL   (1958) B&W ***

D: William Castle. Vincent Price, Carol Ohmart, Richard Long. 75 mins. (Key) DVD

The late, great Vincent Price warns viewers not to be late for their own funerals as he presides over a group of endangered invitees to the title manse in a typically fun William Castle gimmick pic, given the gala remake treatment in 1999 (Warner, DVD), with Geoffrey *(Shine)* Rush in the Price role.

HOW TO MAKE A MONSTER (1958) B&W **¹/₂

D: Herbert L. Strock. Robert H. Harris, Gary Conway, Gary Clarke, Paul Brinegar, Malcolm Atterbury, Morris Ankrum. 74 mins. (Columbia/TriStar)

With *How to Make a Monster*, AIP officially entered its self-referential, postmodern phase. The shoestring studio was already notorious for inserting plugs for its other movies—via on-screen posters, marquees, and even dialogue (see *Earth vs. The Spider*) but *HTMAM* is actually set on the glorious AIP lot, a property swarmed by eager sightseers on studio tours (only in Sam Arkoff's wildest dreams!). In the movie, the studio's been bought by soulless corporate creeps who decide to phase out fright films in favor of more upbeat fare. Fired makeup ace Harris exacts revenge by applying his special zombie powder (!) to actors portraying the Teen Frankenstein and Werewolf (Conway, reprising his original role, and Clarke, replacing a then-upwardly mobile Michael Landon) and ordering them to kill the interlopers. The result is 74 minutes of good dumb fun, highlighted by "guest star" John Ashley singing the unforgettable "You've Got to Have Ee-Ooo." Like *I Was a Teenage Frankenstein*, *How to* originally featured a climactic color sequence missing from the Columbia cassette.

THE HOWLING:
THE SERIES

THE HOWLING   (1980) ***

D: Joe Dante. Dee Wallace, Patrick Macnee, John Carradine. 91 mins. (Columbia/TriStar)

Dante's mostly on-target, John Sayles–scripted lycanthrope update, crammed with vet-thesp cameos, deals with werewolf troubles at a New Age California therapy center. Steer clear of Philippe Mora's 1982 *Howling*

II: Your Sister Is a Werewolf (HBO), a total misfire. Mora makes amends with his *Howling III: The Marsupials* (1987, Vista), a deadpan spoof of self-serious celluloid lycanthrope lore, a consistently twisty affair with some neat original set pieces, including a grisly ballet rehearsal and a movie wrap party invaded by a trio of werewolf nuns (!). Followed by John Hough's weak *Howling 4: The Original Nightmare* (1988), Neal Sundstrom's even feebler *Howling 5: The Rebirth* (1989), Hope Perello's inventive (if typically tangential) *Howling 6: The Freaks* (1991, all Artisan), and the latest and least, *The Howling: New Moon Rising* (see index).

THE HUMAN GORILLA   (1948) B&W **¹/₂

D: Budd Boetticher. Richard Carlson, Lucille Bremer, Douglas Fowley, Tor Johnson. 62 mins. (Sinister Cinema)

The *Human Gorilla*, billed as a Tor Johnson movie, is actually a retitling of a terror-tinged noir originally known as *Behind Locked Doors*, in which Tor appears briefly (albeit memorably) as an insane ex-boxer and which rates as an effective B flick in its own right. Future *Macumba Love* auteur Fowley is especially vivid as a sadistic asylum attendant. Director Boetticher would gain greater fame helming several classic 1950s Randolph Scott westerns.

THE HUMAN MONSTER   (1939) B&W **¹/₂

D: Walter Summers. Bela Lugosi, Hugh Williams, Greta Gynt. 73 mins. (Sinister Cinema)

Based on an Edgar Wallace novel, this Brit-lensed flick is ultimately more bleak than scary as Bela (in dual roles) operates a home for the blind and victimizes its sightless inhabitants. Still, a must for Bela buffs.

THE HUNCHBACK OF NOTRE DAME (1939) B&W ***1/2

D: William Dieterle. Charles Laughton, Maureen O'Hara, Edmond O'Brien. 117 mins. (RKO) DVD

Still the definitive version of Hugo's novel, with Laughton not only poignant and menacing but *believable* as the ill-fated Quasimodo. Painstakingly detailed sets and crisp black-and-white cinematography likewise aid in making *Hunchback* a precious nugget from RKO's Golden Age. Kino Video, meanwhile, offers a pristine, remastered edition of Lon Chaney's 1923 silent classic (also DVD). Touchstone has the less successful 1957 *Hunchback of Notre Dame,* with Anthony Quinn in the title role and Gina Lollabrigida as Esmeralda. Other video-available versions include 1997's made-for-cable *The Hunchback* (Turner), starring Mandy Patinkin, the 1982 made-for-TV *Hunchback of Notre Dame* (Trimark), with Anthony Hopkins, and, of course, the widely hyped 1996 Disney animated musical (Touchstone).

THE HUNGER (1983) ***

D: Tony Scott. David Bowie, Catherine Deneuve, Susan Sarandon. 97 mins. (MGM/UA)

Bowie and Deneuve play decadent Gothamites who seek eternal life by draining the blood of others. Gerontologist Sarandon becomes Bowie's unwitting replacement in Scott's generally effective MTV-styled vampire variation.

I BURY THE LIVING (1958) B&W ***

D: Albert Band. Richard Boone, Theodore Bikel, Peggy Maurer, Herbert Anderson. 76 mins. (VCI)

Albert (Father of Charles) Band helms an offbeat chiller with sur-

real touches supplied by veteran Czech montage master Slavko Vorkapich. Reluctant cemetery overseer Boone finds that by sticking black pins (for deceased) into a burial-grounds map, he can cause the demise of the plot's owner /future resident, an entirely unwanted power. Folksinger/thesp Bikel (in Captain Kangaroo–type makeup) plays an elderly caretaker with a wandering Scottish accent. Marred by a disappointing ending, *I Bury the Living* is still well worth watching for its fresh story line, Boone's uncharacteristically subdued performance, and Vorkapich's eerie contributions.

I DRINK YOUR BLOOD (1971) **1/2

D: David Durston. Bhaskar, Jadine Wong, Rhonda Fultz, George Patterson. 83 mins. (Something Weird)

Originally paired (by aptly named producer Jerry Gross) with *I Eat Your Skin*—a rather fanciful retitling of Del (*Horror of Party Beach*) Tenney's tame 1964 terror turkey *Voodoo Bloodbath* (a.k.a. *Zombie*), available from Sinister Cinema—our story centers on a roving band of Manson-oid "hippies" led by one Horace ("Satan was an acidhead!") Bones (overacted by the monomonikered Bhaskar). When our itinerant lowlifes slip LSD to an unsuspecting elderly local, the latter's enterprising 12-year-old grandson strikes back by selling them a batch of meat pies that he's injected with rabid-dog's blood (a cogent argument for the vegetarian lifestyle). In no time, the frothing free spirits are not only literally at one another's throats but infecting the citizenry, including a band of already volatile hardhats. Rated X for violence before last-minute cuts altered it to R status, *I Drink Your Blood* is at once professional and raw enough to make for fairly compelling, if doggedly unpleasant, viewing. Auteur Durston went on to direct a pre–*Miami Vice* Philip Michael

Thomas in the instructive social-disease exploitationer *Stigma* (Vista).

I KNOW WHAT YOU DID LAST SUMMER (1997) **1/2

D: Jim Gillespie. Jennifer Love Hewitt, Sarah Michelle Gellar, Freddie Prinze, Jr., Ryan Phillippe, Anne Heche, Johnny Galecki. 100 mins. (Columbia/TriStar) DVD

The high-glam allure of femme telestarlets Hewitt (*Party of Five*) and Gellar (*Buffy the Vampire Slayer*) plus the imprimatur of *Scream/Scream 2* scripter Kevin Williamson (adapting Lois Duncan's novel) must have been the main magnets that drew millions of young 'plex-goers to this slicked-up rehash of the hoary '80s slasher genre. Williamson certainly brings more skill to the terror table than most of his hack '80s predecessors; like Clive Barker with *Candyman*, he employs a venerable American fright folktale involving a severed hook/hand as a clever wraparound for what's otherwise fairly standard chase-and-slash fare. Followed in 1998 by the feebler *I Still Know What You Did Last Summer* (Columbia/TriStar, DVD). No relation to the 1999 USA Network TV movie *I've Been Waiting for You* (PM), beyond being based on another novel, *Gallows Hill*, from *Summer*'s source novelist, Duncan.

I SAW WHAT YOU DID (1965) B&W **1/2

D: William Castle. Joan Crawford, John Ireland, Sarah Lane, Andi Garrett, Leif Erickson, Sharyl Locke, Patricia Breslin, John Archer. 82 mins. (Anchor Bay) DVD

Legendary gimmick guru Castle semi-blows a terrific premise here. Two bubbleheaded 'burbettes (Lane, Garrett) pull a prank call ("I saw what you did and I know who you are") on the wrong "victim," a no-nonsense lowlife (Ireland) who's just murdered his wife (in a genuinely shocking reverse varia-

THE EYES HAVE IT: Gimmick guru William Castle delves into the mysterious realms of voyeurism and uxoricide in *I Saw What You Did*. *Courtesy of Anchor Bay Entertainment.*

tion on Hitchcock's *Psycho* shower sequence). Castle undercuts the potential tension via annoying actors (the teens and accompanying tyke Locke), an irritating sitcom-styled score, and an overly hurried wrap-up. The pic ends with overhead shots of telephone lines and the corny sign-off "The End of the Line." Anchor Bay's deluxe widescreen cassette/DVD, which also contains two original trailers, is still well worth catching for the watery slay scene and Ireland's authentically scary perf (though Crawford is wasted, figuratively and literally, in a largely humiliating role). But *I Saw What You Did* repre-

sents a relatively rare case when the normally excessive Castle should have gone further over the top.

I WALKED WITH A ZOMBIE   (1943) B&W ***1/2

D: Jacques Tourneur. Frances Dee, Tom Conway, James Ellison, Edith Barrett, Christine Gordon, Sir Lancelot, Darby Jones. 69 mins. (Turner, n.i.d.)

The extremely fetching Dee plays a Canadian nurse assigned to care for Gordon, the comatose wife of plantation owner Conway, on the gloomy Caribbean isle of San Sebastian, where locals "cry when a child is born and make merry at a burial." Is Gordon really a zombie, victim of a voodoo curse? You'll enjoy finding out in this typically low-key but immensely disturbing Val Lewton chiller. You have to look closely to catch RKO's in-joke addition to the standard credit-sequence disclaimer: "Any similarity to actual persons, living, dead or possessed, is purely coincidental." Novelist/film critic James Agee recognized producer Lewton's genius early on and helped establish the latter's cult status long before the word was routinely applied to filmmakers working the B-movie beat.

I WAS A TEENAGE FRANKENSTEIN (1957) B&W **1/2

D: Herbert L. Strock. Whit Bissell, Phyllis Coates, Gary Conway, Robert Burton. 72 mins. (Columbia/TriStar)

While not on a par with *I Was a Teenage Werewolf*, *Teen Frank* is not without its virtues, most of them supplied by Bissell's dry, wry perf as an arrogant descendant of the original Dr. Frankenstein. Whit invests his role with considerable deadpan wit, as when he commands reconstructed adolescent Conway, "Speak! You have a civil tongue in your head. I know; I sewed it there myself." Unlike the original theatrical print, the cassette doesn't switch to color for the film's finale and is also missing the vital head-in-a-birdcage image.

I WAS A TEENAGE WEREWOLF (1957) B&W ***

D: Gene Fowler, Jr. Michael Landon, Whit Bissell, Yvonne Lime, Tony Marshall. 75 mins. (Columbia/TriStar, n.i.d.)

Landon makes a memorable screen debut as an adolescent lycanthrope with an attitude in Fowler's at-once clever and effectively chilling blend of the horror and troubled-youth genres, while Bissell again proves aces as the authority-figure villain. No relation to the postmodern genre parodies *I Was a Teenage Mummy* (Ghost Link) or the atrocious *I Was a Teenage Zombie* (Image, DVD).

I, MADMAN (1989) **¹/₂

D: Tibor Takács. Jenny Wright, Clayton Rohner, Randall William Cook, Steven Memel, Bruce Wagner. 89 mins. (Anchor Bay)

Blond bookstore clerk Wright (*Near Dark*) is addicted to backdate horror novels, particularly those penned by the mysterious Malcolm Brand. Brand, it soon develops, is himself a serious psycho who goes Van Gogh several better by slicing off not only his ears but his nose, lips, and other facial accoutrements. When the grisly murders described in Brand's book (likewise titled *I, Madman*) begin occurring in real life, only Wright realizes what's happening. Trouble is, she can't get local authorities—not even her cop boyfriend (Rohner)—to believe her far-fetched tale. After a strong 1950s-set start featuring a stop-motion animation creature called "Jackal Boy," director Takács (*The Gate, Gate 2*) accords his promising material increasingly static treatment. Some thrills survive, though, most of them provided by our faceless fiend (played by makeup FX ace Cook).

ICE CREAM MAN (1995) **

D: Norman Apstein. Clint Howard, Sandahl Bergman, Olivia Hussey, Lee Majors II, JoJo Adams, Justin Isfeld, Jan-Michael Vincent, David Naughton, David Warner, Steve Garvey. 96 mins. (A-Pix)

Veteran screen geek Howard lands a showcase role as a sort of Bad Humor man, a confectionary fiend whose ice cream truck is a frozen hell on wheels (serving such unlisted Monty Python–esque flavors as Crunchy Dog). Alas, a tasty concept—a fright fable based on kids' natural paranoia re their local ice cream vendor—quickly turns sour in what degenerates into an aimless parade of B-star cameos. Howard, replete with outsized orthodontic prosthetics, tackles his role with obvious

relish, but the pic, like Fred Dekker's *Monster Squad* and Bob Balaban's somewhat better realized 1989 cannibal comedy, *Parents* (both Artisan), lacks the wit and focus to put it over as a dark modern 'burb fairy tale. No relation to the even lower-budgeted indie *Mr. Ice Cream Man* (EI).

IN THE MOUTH OF MADNESS (1995) ***

D: John Carpenter. Sam Neill, Julie Carmen, Jürgen Prochnow, Charlton Heston, David Warner, John Glover, Bernie Casey. 95 mins. (New Line)

Halloween helmer Carpenter's *In the Mouth of Madness*—written by then–New Line production head

---

Filmmakers in Focus!

JOHN CARPENTER: *IN THE MOUTH OF MADNESS*

As Told to The Phantom

PHANTOM: What was it about the script that appealed to you?

CARPENTER: It was the first movie I'd ever seen that deals with dual reality. It's couched in horror terms, but it's very, very fascinating. And I loved the humor of it. Everyone's a character in a generic horror book. Our rather cynical private investigator, who represents the point of view of the audience—which is, come on, this couldn't really be happening—discovers that he in fact is being written and that this writer is God. When you discover that, it's enough to drive you crazy.

PHANTOM: The main theme is about shared belief systems; if enough people believe it, it isn't nuts. You can see that on some Christian channels.

CARPENTER: That's one of my favorite pastimes, watching Christian channels! Oh, man, is it great! It is so fascinating. They have more fears than anyone who's ever watched any one of my movies. They really do. They're frightened people.

PHANTOM: Didn't Lovecraft deal with essentially religious themes?

CARPENTER: Lovecraft wrote about the old ones, the creatures from the other side who are waiting to take back the world. He invented this inverted Christian myth. Very, very talented, very brilliant writer—very frightening stories. He's very hard to adapt. Once you start reading it, you realize it's in his language. He describes things that are indescribable, the indescribable horror. Some of his best stories are just impossible to visualize. There have been some pretty good attempts at it, but they never really caught it. The original movie *Alien* owed a whole lot to H. P. Lovecraft; just replace a planet with New England, and you've got it.

Mike De Luca—posits that best-selling books penned by Stephen King–like horror novelist Sutter Cane (Prochnow) are turning readers into homicidal cultists on the brink of bringing about nothing less than the end of Civilization As We Know It. Carpenter and De Luca explore the idea that "sanity" and "reality" are shaped by consensus: Ultra-skeptical private investigator Neill *may* be Western Civ's last bastion of sanity, judged insane because of his adherence to a "niche" belief system; more likely, he's truly nuts.

Mouth opens with a straitjacketed Sam stuck in a padded cell into which is piped the Carpenters' saccharine "We've Only Just Begun" (admittedly enough to drive anyone crazy) in a *Caligari*-esque asylum overseen by a clearly bonkers administrator, grinningly interpreted by Glover. Neill next relates his tale in flashback for the benefit of somewhat better-balanced visiting shrink Warner. Sam's troubles begin when publisher Heston hires him to locate vanished "cash cow" Cane, who disappeared before delivering his latest manuscript. Cane's crazed followers are already engaging in scattered riots outside bookstores where his promised chiller (the eponymous *In the Mouth of Madness*) has failed to turn up. Heston sends Cane's editor (Carmen) to accompany Sam, who's sure he can find the "fictional" town of Hobbs End, New Hampshire, where Cane's novel takes place. Cane himself surfaces to assure Sam that he—and everyone else in the world—are merely figments of his imagination, and the evidence soon mounts, in crazed, surreal, and often gory profusion (with elaborate FX handled by the KNB EFX Group), that Cane is right, despite Sam's claim that "God isn't supposed to be a hack horror writer." De Luca's scenario brims with Lovecraftian allusions, starting with the title, a takeoff on H.P.'s *In the Mountains of Madness. In the Mouth of Madness* is rich in dark satire and delivers a goodly number of genuine jolts. Besides, it's

hard not to admire any flick savvy enough to include a choice clip from *Robot Monster*.

INNER SANCTUM
COLLECTION

THE FROZEN GHOST (1945)
B&W **½

D: Harold Young. Lon Chaney, Jr., Evelyn Ankers, Milburn Stone, Douglas Dumbrille, Martin Kosleck, Elena Verdugo. 61 mins.

WEIRD WOMAN (1944)
B&W ***

D: Reginald LeBorg. Lon Chaney, Jr., Anne Gwynne, Evelyn Ankers, Ralph Morgan, Elisabeth Risdon, Lois Collier, Elizabeth Russell. 63 mins. (Universal)

Despite his suave pencil-line moustache and relatively flab-free form, Chaney makes for an unlikely object of unbridled female lust, but that's the role he's assigned in both ends of this entertaining *Inner Sanctum* doubleheader. In *The Frozen Ghost* Lon plays Gregor the Great, a stage mentalist who believes he's responsible for the death of a drunken audience volunteer. Gregor chucks both his lucrative career and beautiful (and subsequently heartbroken) fiancée, Maura (perennial Universal heroine Ankers), for a gig at the wax museum of Madam Monet (Tala Birell). Our tortured hero is too busy guilt-tripping to respond to the inexplicable amatory advances of either Tala or her niece Nina (Verdugo). Kosleck supplies some fun as a discredited plastic surgeon turned sinister wax-museum sculptor, while Dumbrille delivers a droll perf as a Shakespeare-spouting detective. Our fave scene, though, finds Gregor's press agent (future *Gunsmoke* "Doc" Stone) and Ankers sharing drinks and expository dialogue at a bistro whose large windows open onto expansive rear-projected stock street footage

that looks a good two decades old (a horse-drawn truck is seen rambling by!). Some of said footage is even *re*used within the same brief sequence—a guy sitting beside a newsstand kiosk can be glimpsed repeating the same motion twice—while the grain contrast between the studio foreground and the stock background is extreme, to say the least, lending the tableau a truly surreal quality. True, Universal B honchos weren't anticipating the more demystifying media of video or even television—and didn't hold their targeted bijou audience's collective attention span in high regard in any event—but this particular mismatching wouldn't elude the notice of the most comatose viewer. Why they didn't shoot the pair seated in a corner remains a mystery far more intriguing than any found in the story. Like most *Inner Sanctum* entries, the pic emerges as a hastily assembled, clumsily plotted pastiche bald on supernatural elements but worth watching for its curio value.

Director LeBorg and crew have more fun with *Weird Woman*. Loosely adapted from Fritz Leiber's *Conjure Wife* (more definitively remade as the George Baxt–scripted 1962 Brit chiller *Burn, Witch, Burn!* [n/a] and less felicitously retooled as the 1979 satire *Witches' Brew* [Embassy]). *Weird Woman* finds Lon again badly miscast, this time as author/academic Professor Norman Reed. Norm and his safely white Hawaiian bride, Paula (a fetching Gwynne), encounter all manner of grief, engineered by Lon's jealous ex, Ilona (Ankers), at otherwise idyllic Monroe College. Ilona eventually comes to believe that Gwynne has used her voodoo expertise on her, condemning her to die and leading to an unintentionally hilarious rapid-fire impending-doom montage. *Weird Woman* is richer in yoks (a back-lot island voodoo flashback represents another prime example) than shocks but furnishes enough of the former to make for lively viewing. Universal completes the series with the duo *Calling Dr. Death* and *Strange Confession* (the latter a loose remake of the 1934 Claude Rains decapitation-themed thriller *The Man Who Reclaimed His Head*), and *Dead Man's Eyes* and *Pillow of Death* (a literally suffocating bore).

INTERVIEW WITH THE VAMPIRE (1994) ***¹/₂

D: Neil Jordan. Tom Cruise, Brad Pitt, Antonio Banderas, Stephen Rea, Christian Slater, Kirsten Dunst, Domiziana Giordano. 123 mins. (Warner) DVD

Though short in stature, Cruise proves credibly long in the tooth as battered but immortal vampire Lestat in scripter Anne Rice's deft adaptation of her own bloodsucking best-seller. Pitt is equally strong as the tale's main character and existential center—Louis, 'the depressed Louisiana landowner Lestat saves for a fate worse than death (i.e., *un*death) in the last decade of the 18th century. It's Pitt who poses the pic's primary query: Is it "evil" to take others' lives if their sacrifice is essential to your own survival? Terrific set pieces and details abound in Jordan's screen translation. The subterranean decor for Banderas's Parisian *Theatre des Vampires,* Rea and Pitt's macabre variation on the Marx Brothers' "mirror" routine, the torching of the Parisian vamps, and Dunst and adoptive mom Giordano's dread ordeal in a sunlit pit comprise but a few of the lyrically horrific highlights. Pitt's eventual addiction to movies—the only venue where it's safe to see sunrises (his viewing choices range from F. W. Murnau's *Sunrise* to Robert Towne's *Tequila Sunrise* some 60 years later)— provides another innovative, strangely poignant touch. Like most modern vampire films, *Interview* makes several alterations in traditional celluloid bloodsucker lore. Rice's vamps are unburdened by religious phobias, immune to crucifixes, holy water, mirrors, and stakes; but they *are* required to sleep in coffins and remain vulnerable to the lethal influence of sunlight and fire. As

most fright fans doubtless recall, Rice went public with her criticism of Cruise's casting, then later recanted via a full-page *New York Sunday Times* ad. (Oprah Winfrey also grabbed a piece of the *Interview* action by making an early, conspicuous exit from an advance *Interview* screening, ostensibly because of the pic's gore content [kudos to FX ace Stan Winston!].) For all the prerelease static surrounding it, *Vampire* emerged as a vastly entertaining horror entry that proved a hit with most critics and audiences alike.

VAMPIRES SAY THE DARNDEST THINGS!

"I never drink…wine."
—Bela Lugosi, *Dracula*

"I don't think Betty Ford takes vampires."
—Rick Springfield, *Forever Knight*

"Being a vampire in the twentieth century is a nightmare."
—Lauren Hutton, *Once Bitten*

"Whining again! I've been listening to that for centuries!"
—Tom Cruise to Brad Pitt, *Interview with the Vampire*

"Eternity is a long time—get used to it."
—Christopher Walken to Lili Taylor, *Addiction*

"I don't mind being a vampire, but a man oughtta be able to see himself."
—William Marshall, *Blacula*

"He's so ugly, he makes my gums ache."
—Joshua Miller re victim, *Near Dark*

AND SO DO THEIR VICTIMS . . .

"I just don't like things that suck your blood and have conversations afterward."
—Michael Moriarity, *Return to Salem's Lot*

"She was in great pain. Then we cut off her head and drove a stake through her heart and burned her and then she was at peace."
—Anthony Hopkins, *Bram Stoker's Dracula*

"I may be dead, but I'm still pretty—which is more than I can say for you."
—Buffy to the Master, *Buffy the Vampire Slayer*

"My! What a big bat!"
—David Manners, *Dracula*

INVISIBLE GHOST (1941)
B&W **1/2

D: Joseph H. Lewis. Bela Lugosi, Polly Ann Young, Clarence Muse. 64 mins. (Sinister Cinema)

Bela spends much of his screen time staring out windows in a fairly creaky Monogram quickie. Not as good as *The Corpse Vanishes* but a must for Lugosi lovers. Director Lewis went on to helm the cult fave *Gun Crazy*, among many others.

ISLE OF THE DEAD (1945) B&W ***

D: Mark Robson. Boris Karloff, Jason Robards, Ellen Drew, Marc Cramer. 72 mins. (Turner, n.i.d.)

Boris is superb in another atmospheric Val Lewton chiller, this time cast as a Greek-army officer stranded, with an assortment of unlikely strangers, on a plague-endangered island. As usual with producer Lewton, the horror is hinted at rather than openly revealed, but the fog-enshrouded ambience here provides genuine visual chills.

JACK BE NIMBLE (1993) ***

D: Garth Maxwell. Alexis Arquette, Sarah Smuts-Kennedy, Bruno Lawrence, Tony Barry, Elizabeth Hawthorne. 93 mins. (Triboro) DVD

Debuting New Zealand auteur Maxwell establishes his celluloid mood with a brilliant exercise in dark visual poetry that fully captures the haunting quality of a primal childhood nightmare. As the film opens, a desperate housewife (Hawthorne) weeps while tending to her outdoor clothesline, breaking down with abrupt finality when a wind-whipped sheet literally slaps her in the face. The scene ends with her two children, Dora (Smuts-Kennedy) and younger brother Jack (Arquette), being taken by separate sets of adoptive parents. From that point on, the siblings' paths radically diverge. Dora lands a stable domestic situation in a loving home, while Jack winds up trapped in a gothic outback hell, where he's tormented by an abusive foster dad, brittle mom, and their four spooky, witchlike daughters. Jack proceeds to eliminate the parents with ingenious efficiency, only to be relentlessly pursued by the deranged daughters. While Maxwell can't quite sustain the poetic precision of his knockout opening sequence, there's no shortage of imaginative scares, surreal nightmare imagery, and grim irony on view, as the adult siblings reunite and Jack conducts a violent search for identity and completion. Arquette convincingly projects an intense sense of resentful dementia, and *Jack Be Nimble* works on a straight-ahead horror as well as an allegorical level.

JACK THE RIPPER (1959)
B&W/COLOR***

D: Robert S. Baker, Monty Berman. Lee Patterson, Eddie Byrne, Betty McDowall, Ewen Solon, John Le Mesurier, George Rose, the Montparnasse Ballet. 88 mins. (Sinister Cinema)

An atmospheric and, for its time, fairly graphic account of one of Western Civ's most infamous celebrity serial killers, *Jack the Ripper* features future *Surfside Six* telestar Patterson (who appeared in a number of '50s Brit genre films) as an American detective who journeys to 1888 London to lend an investigative hand to Scotland Yard inspector Byrne. Red herrings abound as a black-clad Jack lurks about London's back alleys, surgically slaying not only trollops but barmaids and dancing girls while posing the guttural query, "Are you Mary Clark?" Filmmakers Baker and Berman maintain suspense throughout but *do* unveil the real "Jack" at film's end. Stage thesp George Rose contributes a brief but colorful cameo as a Cockney crook, while members of the Montparnasse Ballet display their terpsichorean talents as music-hall cancan girls. In an obviously William Castle–influenced move, an opening voice-over urges viewers to pay close attention to the upcoming on-screen clues to the Ripper's real I.D. Sinister Cinema's tape includes the climactic switch to color, where bright crimson blood drips from the victim of an elevator crushing.

JACK'S BACK (1988) **1/2

D: Rowdy Herrington. James Spader, Cynthia Gibb, Rod Loomis, Rex Ryan, Chris Mulkey. 97 mins. (Paramount)

Though it sounds like the most craven of clones, Herrington's *Jack's Back*—about a modern Ripper amok in L.A.—bears scant resemblance to Nicholas Meyer's clever *Time After Time* (Warner), wherein the *real* Ripper time-trips to modern Frisco, with H. G. Wells in pursuit. In fact, *Jack's Back* begins just as the current spate of Ripper-like hooker murders is about to end. The plot twists in an entirely different direction, into contempo thriller rather than gory gothic horror turf. And for a time, the pic generates considerable tension and surprise, as Spader scours the Angel City streets and his own subconscious for clues to the killer's whereabouts and identity. While *Jack's Back* gradually grows too convoluted for its own good and fails to approach Meyer's 1979 variation, the film is very much worth a look.

Other video-available Ripper-related films include *Deadly Advice* (see index); *The Diary of Jack the Ripper* (Image, DVD); *Fatal Exposure* (HHE), featuring Jack's psychotic great-grandson; Hammer's solid 1971 *Hands of the Ripper* (VidAmerica), dealing with Jack's daughter; *He Kills Night After Night After Night* (Monterey), about a Ripper copycat; Alfred Hitchcock's 1926 silent *The Lodger* (Video Yesteryear); 1976's *Jack the Ripper* (Vestron), with Klaus Kinski; the made-for-TV miniseries *Jack the Ripper* (Artisan), with Michael

Caine; *A Man with a Maid* (Video Dimensions); *The Monster of London City* (Sinister Cinema); Bob Clark's 1979 Sherlock-Holmes-Meets-the-Ripper cult fave, *Murder by Decree* (New Line); *Phantom Fiend* (Facets); the recommended *The Ripper* (Universal), with Patrick Bergin; *Room to Let* (Sinister Cinema); Peter Medak's 1972 *The Ruling Class* (Water Bearer), with Peter O'Toole; the other Holmes-versus-Ripper caper, *A Study in Terror* (Columbia/TriStar); *Terror at London Bridge* (Fries); *Terror in the Wax Museum* (Artisan); and *Waxworks* (Artisan).

JACOB'S LADDER (1990) **¹/₂

D: Adrian Lyne. Tim Robbins, Danny Aiello, Elizabeth Pena, Matt Craven, Pruitt Taylor Vaughn, Jason Alexander. 113 mins. (Artisan) DVD

Smoke-machine-crazed auteur Adrian *(Fatal Attraction)* Lyne's hallucinatory thriller is sort of a bad-acid, 'Nam-based *Carnival of Souls* update. Like *Carnival* and the Roger Corman–produced *Brain Dead* (see index), *Jacob's Ladder* gives us what may be the terminal paranoid fantasies of a dying protagonist, in this case critically wounded GI Jacob Singer (Robbins). The script, by Bruce Joel *(Ghost)* Ruben, contains vividly realized moments but ultimately crosses the line separating complexity from contrivance. *Jacob's Ladder* is relentlessly grim, frequently irritating but rarely dull; some of Lyne's nightmare imagery is as creepy as anything you'll find in a David Lynch, Clive Barker, or Alejandro Jodorowsky movie, and the disco-party scene is almost too intense to take. But *Jacob's Ladder*'s overly manipulative treatment betrays its own integrity by including scenes that couldn't have been manufactured by the mind of a single character—a nebulous, contradictory character at that. The basic concept was resurrected yet again and fused with *Ghost* for the wildly overrated 1999 Bruce Willis supernatural

smash *The Sixth Sense* (Buena Vista, DVD).

JAWS:
THE SERIES

JAWS (1975) ***¹/₂

D: Steven Spielberg. Roy Scheider, Robert Shaw, Richard Dreyfuss. 124 mins. (Universal) DVD

Spielberg put sharks on the big-time movie map and scared the swimsuits off viewers in the process in his terrifying adaptation of the Peter Benchley novel. Shark-fighter Scheider returns in the mediocre *Jaws 2*. Dennis Quaid takes over in the marginally related *Jaws 3* (originally *Jaws 3-D*), while Lance Guest and Michael Caine surface in the utterly awful 1987 *Jaws: The Revenge* (all Universal, DVD).

JOHN CARPENTER'S VAMPIRES (1998) ***

D: John Carpenter. James Woods, Daniel Baldwin, Sheryl Lee, Thomas Ian Griffith, Maximilian Schell, Tim Guinee, Gregory Sierra. 108 mins. (Columbia/TriStar) DVD

Hard-core horror hounds aren't likely to be disappointed with this straight-ahead gore orgy hampered only by a relatively weak ending. An intense Woods leads the way as Jack Crow, head of a hard-partying, supermacho vampire-hunting team hired by the Vatican (!) to eradicate hidden nests of vile bloodsuckers. Jack's group stakes out rural New Mexico, and the movie opens with an over-the-top scene of unrelenting carnage as the heavily armed mercenaries slaughter a vampire brood holed up in an abandoned ranch house. The situation quickly reverses, however, when a surviving "master vampire" (menacingly embodied by erstwhile action-star manqué Griffith) interrupts our heroes' premature celebration, bloodily slaying most of the crew along with a

slew of local hookers. Only Jack, partner Baldwin, and call girl Lee escape with their lives—but Sheryl's already been bitten and has since sunk her teeth into Baldwin. With novice priest Guinee, the reduced group goes after Griffith, who's in search of a magic crucifix that will enable the vamps to walk the earth in daylight, setting the stage for their potential conquest of the planet.

While *Vampires* bears a passing resemblance to *Blade* (see index), Carpenter, drawing from John Steakley's novel, takes less of a comic-book and more of a vintage-western tack (à la his urban *Rio Bravo* update, *Assault on Precinct 13*). Subtlety and subtext are not strong points here, but Carpenter amply delivers the horror goods in a film abetted by evocative location lensing and an aggressive guitar-and-synthesizer score composed by the multitalented auteur.

THE JOHNSONS (1992) ***

D: Rudolf van den Berg. Monique van de Ven, Esmée de la Bretonière, Kenneth Herdigein. 98 mins. (Anchor Bay) DVD

Van den Berg's bizarre Holland horror, based on a script by Yank writers Roy Frumkes and Rocco Simonelli *(The Substitute),* traces the efforts of seven psychotic siblings, dubbed the Johnsons, to capture adolescent gal Emalee (de la Bretonière) to complete their unholy plan to summon pure evil into the world. Quirky, swiftly paced, and boasting its share of shocks, *The Johnsons* should appeal to fright buffs hungry for offbeat fare.

KILL, BABY, KILL (1966) ***¹/₂

D: Mario Bava. Giacomo Rossi-Stuart, Erika Blanc, Fabienne Dali, Giana Vivaldi, Piero Lulli, Max Lawrence. Dubbed. 83 mins. (Sinister Cinema) DVD

In some ways similar to the Fellini segment "Toby Dammit" in the 1969

Poe-derived fright anthology *Spirits of the Dead* (see index), *Kill, Baby, Kill* (originally titled *Operation Fear* and released stateside, in a dubbed version, as *Curse of the Living Dead* on an *Orgy of the Living Dead* triple bill) dramatizes the lethal spell the ghost of a little girl (with an ominous bouncing ball) casts over the citizenry of a small Transylvanian hamlet, circa 1907. Investigating physician Rossi-Stuart finds little cooperation among the frightened villagers, except for benign sorceress Dali, who knows the culprit is the long-dead daughter of vengeful local baroness Vivaldi. Bava cowrote as well as directed, while son and future fright filmmaker Lamberto served as assistant director. Bava senior's earlier cinematography experience, on films like *Caltiki, the Immortal Monster* (n/a), shows in nearly every frame of this intensely atmospheric Eastmancolor affair, from a *Seventh Seal*–like hilltop tableau to Rossi-Stuart's murky descent into a local crypt.

KILLER NUN   (1978) ***

D: Giulio Berruti. Anita Ekberg, Lou Castel, Joe Dallesandro, Alida Valli, Laura Nucci, Massimo Serato. Dubbed. 82 mins. (Image/Redemption) DVD

Anita is a hospital nun with a whole wardrobe of bad habits. After suffering a cancer scare, she becomes addicted to morphine, slips into something more comfortable for zipless trysts with handsome strangers, seduces fellow nun Nucci into a lesbian affair, steals and stomps on an elderly patient's dentures (!), and finally undertakes a full-blown murder spree. "Based," according to the opening credits, "on actual events in a Central European country not many years ago," *Killer Nun* strives for realism without neglecting the promised dosages of sleaze and gore. Anita is convincingly overwrought and receives solid support from an established Euro cast, along with former Warhol superstar Dallesandro as a young doc.

KING KONG:
THE SERIES

KING KONG   (1933) B&W ****

D: Merian C. Cooper, Ernest B. Schoedsack. Fay Wray, Robert Armstrong, Bruce Cabot. 103 mins. (Warner)

The titular supersimian's affections for fragile Fay lead to his imprisonment, abortive showbiz career, and literal downfall in one of Hollywood's truly towering achievements, crammed with powerful iconic imagery, breakthrough special effects (courtesy of FX pioneer Willis O'Brien), seat-squirming scares, and more subtexts than you can shake a banana at. Beware the computer-colorized version, still out there on the Turner label, and the awful, soulless 1976 Dino De Laurentiis remake, *King Kong* (Paramount, DVD), with Jeff Bridges, Charles Grodin, and Jessica Lange.

SON OF KONG   (1933) B&W **1/2

D: Ernest B. Schoedsack. Robert Armstrong, Helen Mack, Victor Wong. 70 mins. (Warner)

Disgraced showman Carl Denham (a returning Armstrong) flees his creditors and hies to Skull Island, where he encounters Kong junior (though mater remains a mystery; he bears no resemblance to Fay Wray). A shockingly cheesy follow-up for its time, generously padded with footage lifted intact from the first film, *Son* set a bad sequel precedent for decades to come. Still fun going, though, with Schoedsack and crew emphasizing humor and pathos over thrills.

KING KONG LIVES   (1986) **1/2

D: John Guillermin. Linda Hamilton, Brian Kerwin, John Ashton. 105 mins. (Lorimar)

The belated sequel to the 1976 remake posits that a comatose Kong survived his World Trade Center plummet but needs giant-gorilla blood transfusions before his body can accept the outsized artificial heart designed by Atlanta University doc Hamilton. Meanwhile, back on "Kong Island," a cut-rate Indiana Jones (Kerwin) captures Lady Kong and peddles her to Linda, who uses her blood for the operation. To make a slow story fast, the King awakes and springs his mate, and together they flee Atlanta for an idyllic romp in rural Honeymoon Ridge (!). Any comparisons with the original *King Kong* would leave *King Kong Lives* barely breathing, but our celebrity apes, alternately formidable and poignant, supply some fun, far outshining Kerwin/Hamilton's parallel romance, and the King kicks enough homo-sap butt to keep fans glued to their seats.

KING OF THE ZOMBIES   (1941) B&W **1/2

D: Jean Yarbrough. John Archer, Mantan Moreland, Dick Purcell, Joan Woodbury. 67 mins. (Sinister Cinema) DVD

Black comedian Moreland carries the day in this otherwise wooden back-lot chiller. The pic's offhanded but relentless racism (which extends to Irishman Purcell as well) is truly appalling, though Mantan manages to transcend. Like many B movies of its era, this one is more interesting as sociology than as horror. Sinister Cinema stocks the uncut edition.

THE KINGDOM   (1994) ****

D: Lars von Trier. Ernst Hugo Järegård, Søren Pilmark, Kirsten Rolffes, Birgitte Raaberg, Ghita Nørby, Jens Okking, Udo Kier. Subtitled. 265 mins. (Evergreen)

Produced for Danish TV, *The Kingdom* rates as a video great, a four-episode hospital-set ghost-story-cum-dark-medical-satire directed and coscripted by Dogma 95 mastermind von Trier, of *Zentropa* (see index) and *Breaking the Waves* (Evergreen) fame.

The Kingdom ranks with the best of David Lynch's work, combining horror—Episode 4 is titled "The Living Dead" and features cannibalistic zombie nightmare sequences right out of Romero—gallows humor (a reappearing severed head supplies one typical running riff; another involves a squeamish medical student who ducks out on operations but can watch *The Texas Chainsaw Massacre* repeatedly), brain-surgery close-ups, the grottiest birth scene ever seen on-screen, voodoo, and a truly scary take on the medical mentality. (One doc, obsessed with retrieving the world's largest liver tumor from a still-breathing patient, thoughtfully assures the latter's reluctant relatives, "Dissection would take place only *after* death.") The linking story thread involves elderly spiritualist Rolffes—whose son (Okking) works in Copenhagen's "the Kingdom" hospital—who keeps checking in with bogus ailments in order to locate the ghost of a little girl she's sure is haunting the hosp. The late Järegård is brilliant as an arrogant Swedish neurosurgeon who considers his banishment to Denmark a fate worse than death, while Pilmark is appealing as the compassionate Dr. Hook, a medico so hooked on healing that he secretly makes his home in the hospital basement (!). À la Alfred Hitchcock, von Trier appears on screen at the end of each episode to offer a brief wry commentary, while veteran Euro genre thesp Kier puts in a sinister last-episode cameo. The film received a selective stateside theatrical run, as did the sequel, *The Kingdom II* (n/a).

THE KISS   (1988) **

D: Pen Densham. Joanna Pacula, Meredith Salenger, Nicholas Kilbertus, Mimi Kuzyk, Jan Rubes. 101 mins. (Columbia/TriStar)

Tough times for troubled teen Amy Halloran (appealingly portrayed by Salenger): her mom's been mashed by a runaway RV, her best friend's been mauled by a mall escalator, and her dad's been scratched by a ferocious feline from hell. And that's only the beginning of the hapless Halloran clan's calamities when Amy's voodoo vampire-queen aunt Felice (Pacula) decides to pay a deadly visit. Densham's Albany-set, Canada-lensed horror delivers its share of decent scares in the early going before careering headlong into dangerously brain-dead terrain that finds Aunt Felice—aided by FX ace/future director Chris Walas—performing increasingly elaborate stupid voodoo tricks in her venomous quest to steal young Amy's innocent soul. In its errant plunge into over-the-top hysteria, *The Kiss* supplies, if little else, enough flamboyantly bad entertainment to make it worth a look.

KISS OF THE VAMPIRE   (1963) ***½

D: Don Sharp. Clifford Evans, Noel Willman, Edward DeSouza, Jennifer Daniel, Barry Warren, Jacqueline Wells. 88 mins. (Orion) DVD

Rarely has the union between vampirism and venereal disease, or the theme of the decadent rich preying on their innocent social inferiors, been more cogently presented than in Hammer's *Kiss of the Vampire* (*Kiss of Evil* in Britain), set circa 1905. Following a nicely paced opening funeral scene that concludes with a terrific shock moment, our story focuses on honeymooning Brits DeSouza and Daniel, whose antique auto runs out of petrol near the posh digs of the cordial but mysterious Ravna family, headed by an impeccably sinister Willman. After registering at an inn deserted but for the aloof, brandy-swilling, vampire-hating Professor Zimmer (Evans), the pair unwisely accept an invitation to the Ravna estate, where their literally draining relationship with the fanged family begins. Director Sharp mixes suspense and horror in equal measure, while the perfs (particularly by sworn foes Willman and Evans) and textured character-izations are uniformly excellent, and the elaborate period re-creation—most notably during a masked-ball sequence that prefigures Roger Corman's *Masque of the Red Death* (released the following year)—greatly abets the film's atmosphere. *Kiss* concludes with an extended exorcism sequence that adds a fresh twist to screen vampire lore.

LADY IN WHITE   (1988) ***

D: Frank LaLoggia. Lukas Haas, Len Cariou, Alex Rocco, Katherine Helmond, Jason Presson, Renato Vanni. 112 mins. (Virgin Vision) DVD

A strange mélange of the good, the bad, and the self-indulgent, LaLoggia's *Lady in White* ranges from trite to pretentious to downright brilliant. This ambitious one-man project (LaLoggia wrote, produced, directed, and composed the music), a ghost story with a psycho subplot, relates nine-year-old Haas's encounter with the wandering spirit of a little girl murdered a decade earlier by a still-rampaging serial killer. *Lady in White* is at its best when LaLoggia applies a Val Lewton–like approach to his intricate fright material, powerfully conveying, via evocative writing and inspired imagery, a feeling of pervasive menace roiling just beneath the surface of Haas's small-town life—a life outwardly normal but for death's frequent, irrational intrusions. LaLoggia's earlier fright entry *Fear No Evil* (Embassy) is also worth scoping out, as is his 1994 *Mother* (Trimark).

THE LAIR OF THE WHITE WORM (1988) ***

D: Ken Russell. Amanda Donohoe, Hugh Grant, Catherine Oxenberg, Sammi Davis, Peter Capaldi, Stafford Johns. 93 mins. (Vestron) DVD

Russell assembles a wild parody that sends up the complete catalog of monster-movie clichés old and new in an outing further enhanced by his typically loopy overlay of demented erotic-religious imagery. Our story, loosely based on Bram (*Dracula*) Stoker's final novel, concerns a quartet of young British locals who stumble upon the title site *and* a venomous, vampiric snake-woman, the aristocratic Lady Sylvia. Of our fearless foursome, Davis especially impresses as the pic's petite but feisty blond heroine, while Donohoe contributes a fine, sexy turn as the serpentine seductress Lady Sylvia. Director Russell keeps a firm grip on the improbable ins and absurdist outs of his mock-serious story line. Deadpan visual and verbal puns abound, and the film is abetted by generous doses of gratuitous nudity and cheap but gaudy gore FX.

THE LANGOLIERS   (1995) ***

D: Tom Holland. Patricia Wettig, Dean Stockwell, Bronson Pinchot, David Morse, Mark Lindsay Chapman, Frankie Faison, Baxter Harris, Kimber Riddle, Christopher Collet, Kate Maberly. 180 mins. (Republic)

Based on the novella from the Stephen King collection *Four Past Midnight*, *The Langoliers* emerges as a deft translation that scores on several levels—as an atmospheric fear flick, a trippy time-travel adventure, and an engrossing disaster drama populated with complex characters brought to life by an excellent cast. Ten passengers aboard an airliner mysteriously depleted of fellow riders ultimately find themselves trapped in an immediate past barren of other human life. Further complicating their situation is rapidly unraveling tycoon Toomey (a showy perf by Pinchot), who begins raving about the approach of the "Langoliers," insatiable little monsters who eat slackers and layabouts "alive and screaming." Under Holland's direction, *The Langoliers* represents a rare case of an elongated running time being used to add nuance, ambience, and suspense, with no unnecessary filler to kill the story flow. *The Langoliers* plays far better on

video, where it can be watched straight through, sans commercial interruptions. Other video-available King miniseries include *Stephen King's It* (Warner), *Stephen King's Golden Years* (Worldvision), *The Stand* (Republic), *Storm of the Century* (Trimark), and *The Tommy-knockers* (see index).

THE LAST WAVE   (1977) ***

D: Peter Weir. Richard Chamberlain, David Gulpilil, Olivia Hamnet. 109 mins. (Rhino)

Future *Truman Show* helmer Weir follows his acclaimed period mood piece *Picnic at Hanging Rock* (Home Vision) with an interesting, if not entirely satisfying, chiller about an Aussie attorney (Chamberlain) who becomes involved with Aboriginal magic, courtesy of his accused-killer client (Gulpilil).

THE LEECH WOMAN   (1960) B&W ***

D: Edward Dein. Coleen Gray, Grant Williams, Philip Terry, Gloria Talbott, John Van Dreelen, Estelle Helmsley. 77 mins. (Universal)

"Old women always give me the creeps," says doc Terry. But

when 152-year-old (!) patient Helmsley produces a youth serum and points out that more can be obtained in her native Africa, the phobic physician can't wait to get there and try it out on his own "old lady"—alcoholic Gray. An even more profound treatise on 1950s sexism and female self-image than its Roger Corman–produced counterpart of the previous year, *Wasp Woman* (see index), *The Leech Woman* abounds with intentional ironies while simultaneously working on a cheap-scare level. Gray's ultimately doomed "rejuvenation" allows her plenty of opportunities for feminist vengeance, since fluids extracted from male pineal glands are required additives to her artificial-youth formula. While the windup's a bit abrupt, *The Leech Woman* shapes up as a good bet for couch tomatoes.

THE LEGEND OF HELL HOUSE (1973) **1/2

D: John Hough. Roddy McDowall, Pamela Franklin, Clive Revill. 94 mins. (Fox)

Richard Matheson's solid script hoists this decent if unspectacular pre-*Poltergeist* tale of flying furniture and

ROCK OF CAGES: Innocent Christian wench Cheryl Smith is kept under lock and key in Richard Blackburn's moody lesbian-vampire fable *Lemora.*
© 1994, 1999 Michael D. Moore/T/A MDM Productions

similar telekinetic terrors witnessed by a team of parapsychologists. The electronic score represents another plus; Randy Newman's "Short People" would have made for an ideal closer. Remade by producer Roger Corman, also as *The Legend of Hell House* (New Horizons), in 1999.

LEMORA: A CHILD'S TALE OF THE SUPERNATURAL   (1973) ***

D: Richard Blackburn. Cheryl Smith, Leslie Gilb, William Whitton, Richard Blackburn, Steve Johnson, Hy Pyke, Maxine Ballantyne. 115 mins. total (Moore Video) DVD

Fright fans who've seen Blackburn's long-elusive *Lemora* only on late-night TV broadcasts are in for a pleasant surprise: Moore Video replaces those mangled prints with a crisp director's cut that restores this underseen cult chiller's dark beauty. (*Lemora* was also exhibited as *Lemora, Lady Dracula* and *The Legendary Curse of Lemora*.) Condemned by the Legion of Decency for its perceived sacrilegious elements (though its MPAA rating is a wholesome PG!), *Lemora* unfolds as a sort of "Alice in Horrorland." The film opens with rural 1930s gangster Alvin Lee (Whitton) shotgunning his unfaithful wife and her beau before wrecking his car. His estranged daughter, angelic 13-year-old church ward Lila (Smith, who'd soon graduate to greater celluloid infamy as exploitation-pic mainstay "Rainbeaux" Smith in flicks like Jack Hill's *Swinging Cheerleaders* [Anchor Bay]), receives a mysterious note apprising her of her damaged dad's whereabouts and unquestioningly sets off on a peril-fraught journey into the deepest backwoods. Like a Southern Little Red Riding Hood, the innocent Lila travels a gamut of male lechery just to reach the bus terminal, where a maniacal driver (Pyke) waits to transport her through nocturnal forests inhabited by rabid fiends. Our heroine soon lands in the clutches of lesbian vampire Lemora

Filmmakers in Focus!

RICHARD BLACKBURN ON *LEMORA*
(Excerpted from *The Making of Lemora*)

It was banned by the Legion of Decency. And since one of my favorite movies, *Baby Doll*, was banned by the Legion of Decency, I figured I was in pretty good company....I was trying to do a vampire film crossed with *Night of the Hunter*. *Lemora* is set in the thirties, same as *Night of the Hunter*. When you make a low-budget film, there are three things you're not supposed to do: (1) you're not supposed to do period; (2) you're not supposed to have heavy makeup; and (3) you're not supposed to have a lot of night shooting. We did all three. We made more mistakes, and then probably *invented* some mistakes and made them too.

I had tried to storyboard it. I had to throw 'em out in half a day. It was just so frantic and crazy the way we were shooting. In fact, at the lab that was developing the dailies, they said they had never seen, *ever*, so many setups for a low-budget [$250,000] movie like this. I felt like that guy William ("One-Take") Beaudine, the guy who would be shooting a scene and the flat would fall down and he'd go, "Cut! Print it!"

I came up with something that's not really an art film, but it's not really an exploitation film, so it was very hard to market. We were fortunate enough, after having done everything wrong, to get distribution by a company whose big movie was *Executive Action*, on the lower half of double bills. When it came out, *The Exorcist* had come out, so the poster was all about exorcism, which had nothing to do with the movie. [The television prints] were hacked up so much that it's sometimes hard to tell *what* the story is.

Cheryl [Rainbeaux] Smith was at that time basically a Sunset Strip waif. She was my first choice, and I think she is quite amazing. That she could register this innocence—Cheryl was *not* an innocent child at all. When I was trying to explain to her how to play the part, I said, "You're an innocent girl, you're a ward of the church, you don't know anything about the outside world, all these people come on to you, and you don't know what they're doing." And she goes, "You mean like when a rounder flashes a twenty at me from a Cadillac?"

(Gilb), who launches a leisurely campaign to seduce the child into voluntarily joining the undead ranks.

Director Blackburn is less concerned with plot than with capturing the alternately horrifying and bittersweet illogic of Lila's rite-of-passage nightmare—a task at which he succeeds quite admirably, despite a low budget, troubled production, and California locations subbing for the rural South. Evocative sets, disorienting camera movements (especially during a *Carnival of Souls*–like dance sequence), spare but faithful period details, and effec-

tively grisly makeup FX contribute to *Lemora*'s vivid nightmare quality. On the downside, the pacing becomes a shade *too* deliberate during Lila's lengthy escape scene, and some of the secondary thesps lack the leads' dramatic expertise. The Moore cassette includes *The Making of Lemora*, a fascinating interview with auteur Blackburn conducted by West Coast TV host Art Fein, assisted by Hollywood Book & Poster Company owner/genre maven Eric Caidin. *Lemora*'s assistant director, Art Names, meanwhile, went on to helm the recommended black comedy *Snakes* (see index), while a since-underutilized Blackburn's sole other major genre credit was as coscripter of Paul Bartel's *Eating Raoul* (see index).

THE LEOPARD MAN (1943)
B&W ***

D: Jacques Tourneur. Dennis O'Keefe, Margo, Jean Brooks. 66 mins. (Fox Hills, n.i.d.)

Producer Val (*Cat People*) Lewton returns to his trusty feline fright theme: A series of brutal Southwest slayings may or may not be the claw work of an escaped circus leopard. The blood-under-the-door sequence, considered shocking in its day and much imitated since, still packs a punch in this nearly seamless, streamlined mystery chiller.

LET'S SCARE JESSICA TO DEATH (1971) ***

D: John Hancock. Zohra Lampert, Kevin O'Connor, Barton Heyman. 89 mins. (Paramount)

The title is admirably up-front re what this nongory but thoroughly sadistic and generally suspenseful thriller's about, as conspirators conjure all manner of terrors in a bid to loosen an unstable Lampert's cerebral screws.

LORD OF ILLUSIONS (1995) ***

D: Clive Barker. Scott Bakula, Famke Janssen, Kevin J. O'Connor, Daniel Von Bargen, Sheila Tousey, Vincent Schiavelli, Joel Swetow. 121 mins. In R and unrated editions. (MGM) DVD

Fear and fantasy novelist Barker's third directorial effort shapes up as a mostly successful fusion of the horror and noir genres that plays better in its longer, unrated video form. The first screen appearance of Barker's print P.I. hero Harry D'Amour offers fewer outright fright moves than his earlier *Hell-*

Filmmakers in Focus!

THE BRAINS BEHIND THE PAIN
CLIVE BARKER ON *LORD OF ILLUSIONS*

As Told to The Phantom

PHANTOM: What was your intent with *Lord of Illusions*?

BARKER: The movie *isn't* an homage to noir. I deliberately sat down with the DP [Ronn Schmidt] and said, "Look, we're not going to do what *Angel Heart* did brilliantly." Which was to reference noir visually. You know, sunlight through venetian blinds falling on a desk with a P.I. with a slouch hat on. It wasn't going to look like a Raymond Chandler novel....The references are much more to things like *Night Stalker*, which was a favorite series of mine, with a bit of Hammett or Chandler thrown in. I didn't want to make a movie that was self-consciously self-referential, because that's not what I do.

I go back to the Cronenberg pictures, to Lynch, to *Texas Chainsaw Massacre*, which I still think is a really smashing picture. *The Omen* was a particular model for us, because it's a very classy movie with some very visceral things in it, particularly for its time. I wanted to make a picture that aspired to that kind of level—good storytelling, solid performances, and, well, David Warner's head bouncing on a pane of glass.

PHANTOM: There seems to be an emphasis on pain, in *Lord of Illusions*, the original *Hellraiser*, and both *Candyman* movies.

BARKER: It's a lot about the flesh. I mean, I got that from Cronenberg. It's a lot about the fact that we're born vulnerable. What David does in his movies over and over again, he creates a situation where the flesh transforms, where the vulnerable flesh becomes more vulnerable, or becomes transmutated—a vagina opens up in Jimmy Woods's belly and he loses his gun inside [!]. I'm in some senses less fantastical—the flesh rots, the flesh is pierced, and occasionally the flesh supplies pleasure.

However metaphysical your drama gets, however much it's about good and evil, the manifestation of how these things happen, if you're really trying to get to the audience, they've got to happen in concrete terms, where the audience says, "Okay, however fantastical this has got, it's something that I can make sense of." I always give as the perfect example of this John Carpenter's *The Thing*, in which [Rob] Bottin produces all these magnificent transformations of things, but the scene that gets everybody going is when they take a blood sample and they take a scalpel to the ball of their thumb—and this is after an hour of watching heads explode, bodies erupt, and all that kind of thing. Clearly, the difference is—and this is nothing to say about Bottin's effects, which are *spectacular* throughout the whole picture—it's just about what you can relate to. We've all of us cut our fingers chopping vegetables. Because of that, you know what that feels like.

I think what you want to be able to do in a horror movie is draw the audience in to the point where they say, "Okay, I believe this character. I trust this character. I *like* this character." That's part of the problem I have with the set-'em-up, knock-'em-down pictures—I *don't* really care. I've read reviews where *you've* made this point—if you can't remember the names of the victims, if they're sort of interchangeable camp counselors who don't realize they're in number seven of a series, there's no investment in the character. And so the chances of any harm, large or small, genuinely affecting the audience is pretty minuscule.

PHANTOM: As a writer, how do you view directing?

BARKER: This is *not* my primary profession. When you're concentrating on one thing, it obsesses your life. Then you move on to something else. For the time when I was making the movie, it was consuming my life completely. Now I look back, I think, "Well, I'm a writer who makes movies, and not a movie director who writes." I come from the position of firstly being a novelist and a short-story writer. Occasionally I make movies. But when I was actually making the movie, it seemed like that's all I did.

PHANTOM: So you didn't write at all while you were making the movie?

BARKER: I don't think anybody does anything while they're making a movie. I remain agog at people who can both *be* in the movies and direct them. That is phenomenal to me. Ken Branagh. I mean, I'll write the movie, then I'll direct it, but they are essentially different processes. They're not concurrent functions, which is not the case if you're acting and directing. You're pretty much having to do the two things at the same time.

PHANTOM: Which current directors do you enjoy?

BARKER: Lynch is wonderful with a kind of casual horror. The ant-covered ear. That's a very different kind of horror than the big gothic stuff, which is what Universal did so brilliantly in the thirties. Or even the kind of stuff that's very special-effects-driven we've seen in the last ten years where you do feel sometimes, in the late Freddy pictures, the narrative's just gonna grind to a halt while you watch these really amazing FX. As a consequence, I think most audiences will step back from the movie. They can admire it and have a good time: "Gee, is that girl *really* turning into a giant cockroach?" What makes a good horror movie is where you both want to see the horror and *don't*. What good horror movies do is put you in the position where you want something which is terrible. The desire to see the resolution of the story even though you know that resolution is inevitably going to have to take you into an even darker place than you are right now. Any horror story, whether it's on the screen or page, is a journey into a darker and darker and darker place—and it's going to be resolved in the darkest arena of the lot. Sometimes that arena is going to be a place that the audience does genuinely not want to go.

raiser but is a more coherent and compelling affair than *Nightbreed* (see index.)

Our story opens in the Mojave Desert, where four armed ex-members of a cult headed by the evil, preternaturally puissant Nix (Von Bargen) invade the cultists' dilapidated HQ to retrieve young captive Theodora (Ashley Lyn Cafagna). While isolated with Nix, the rebel cultists' leader, Swann (O'Con-

nor), strikes an unholy bargain with his former guru that grants him magical powers. We cut to 12 years later, when down-and-out NYC shamus D'Amour (an effective Bakula, of TV's *Quantum Leap* fame) accepts an offer to follow up on a routine insurance-fraud case in L.A. While there, he's approached by an adult Theodora (Janssen), who's married to Swann, now a wealthy, world-famous "illusionist" in a Doug Henning/David

Copperfield mode. Seems that Swann's former cultist cronies are turning up dead—but the mystery doesn't end there. *Lord* boasts its share of legit shocks. Particularly gripping are an elaborate homage to *Circus of Horrors* that finds Swann's new sword trick taking an unexpectedly bloody direction; Harry's encounter with two memorable Nix minions, Butterfield (Barry Del Sherman) and Miller (Jordan Marder), which ends with the latter lovingly removing shards of glass from his happily battered body; and Harry's visit to an asylum where ex-cultist Jennifer (Tousey) unravels before his eyes. Our hero manages to land a valuable ally in young illusionist Billy Who (Lorin Stewart) who helps him solve the mystery of Swann and leads to the film's FX-laden climactic confrontation.

THE LOVE WANGA   (1936) B&W ***

D: George Terwilliger. Fredi Washington, Philip Brandon, Sheldon Leonard. 63 mins. (Something Weird)

In this obscure vintage chiller, originally titled *Ouanga* ("a love or death charm," a narrator informs us, "created through the magic of deadly voodoo gods"), Washington turns in strong work as a light-skinned black woman spurned by local plantation owner Brandon, while Jewish thesp and future TV mogul Leonard is oddly cast as a Haitian suitor (!). A reportedly problem-plagued production that suffered several on-set casualties while lensing in Haiti and Jamaica, *The Love Wanga* makes for compelling viewing today.

MAD AT THE MOON   (1992) **½

D: Martin Donovan. Mary Stuart Masterson, Hart Bochner, Stephen Blake. 98 mins. (Republic)

Apartment Zero (see index) auteur Donovan and costar Bochner reteam for this offbeat, Old West–set mood piece. Hart is a mysterious loner lusted after by Masterson, who gives in to social pressure and weds shy farmer Blake instead. Turns out Blake's more than a mite strange in his own right, suffering as he does from what he terms "full-moon sickness," an apparently harmless form of lycanthropy. *Mad at the Moon* is by no means your standard werewolf story; unfortunately, it's hard to say exactly what it is, besides an evocative but vague fable about sexual repression. It's definitely different, though, and if mood were money, *Mad* would be rich indeed. For another offbeat werewolf entry, scope out the South American import *Plenilunio* (Sub Rosa).

THE MAD GHOUL (1943) B&W ***1/2

D: James Hogan. George Zucco, David Bruce, Evelyn Ankers, Turhan Bey, Charles McGraw, Robert Armstrong, Rose Hobart, Milburn Stone. 65 mins. (Universal)

This ingenious, wryly scripted (by Paul Gangelin, Hans Kraly, and Brenda Weisberg) scarefest details the adventures of one Dr. Morris (Zucco), who, assisted by med student and clean-cut All-American Boy Ted (Bruce), is working on a series of seemingly harmless experiments. Little does the ever innocent Ted realize, however, that the doc is actually perfecting a gas designed to induce a zombielike trance in anyone who inhales it, making that unlucky person a slave to the good doctor's ruthless bidding. Dr. Morris harbors another obsession in his dark, droll soul: Ted's professional concert-singer lady friend, Isabel (perennial Universal monster-bait Ankers). But not only is Isabel indifferent to the doc's oblique amatory overtures—"You need someone who knows the book of life," he assures her, "and can teach you how to read it"— she's rapidly losing interest in Ted in favor of her exotic pianist Eric (a typically suave Bey). The rejected Ted, meanwhile, finds himself doubly

cursed: He's being turned into the mad ghoul of the title and led by Dr. Morris on nocturnal graveyard junkets, where he practices his surgical techniques by removing the hearts from recently buried cadavers in order to sustain his own increasingly worthless life. Ted and Doc Morris trail Isabel and Eric's concert tour, where an odd series of "coincidences" occur—at each small city they visit, another grave is desecrated, another heart carried off. Notes wise-acre reporter Armstrong to his paper's music critic, "You mean to say that your gal and my ghoul are workin' the same circuit?" (A bit later, Zucco gets to echo the famous Mark Twain line when he discovers a live Armstrong playing dead in a local morgue: "Reports of your death have been greatly exaggerated.") *The Mad Ghoul*'s mix of over-the-top horror elements and subtle black humor qualifies it as one of the era's best and brightest fright flicks. Zucco lends a terrific deadpan acerbic edge to Dr. Morris, while Bruce's hapless Ted ranks as one of the most abused innocents in fear-film history.

MAD LOVE (1935) B&W ****

D: Karl Freund. Peter Lorre, Frances Drake, Colin Clive, Isabel Jewell, Ted Healy, Keye Luke, Edward Brophy. 68 mins. (MGM)

Mad Love, with Lorre as smooth-skulled surgical genius Dr. Gogol, not only marked the German thesp's American debut but prompted no less a luminary than Charlie Chaplin to dub him "the greatest living actor." In this early adaptation of Maurice Renard's oft filmed novel *The Hands of Orlac*, Lorre's unrequited love for fetching Grand Guignol–type actress Drake prompts the scientist to save her pianist hubby Clive's crushed hands by grafting on the mitts of a professional knife-thrower/murderer (Brophy). A crest-fallen Clive soon finds that, while he can no longer tickle the ivories, he's suddenly quite adept in the dagger-tossing

department. Lorre kills Clive's stepfather, connives to have the ex-pianist framed and plots to possess Drake as his own. Running an intense 68 minutes, *Mad Love* not only boasts a bravura turn by Lorre as the alternately abject and arrogant scientist ("I, a poor peasant, have conquered science!" he rages. "Why can't I conquer love!?") but fine supporting work by Drake, Clive, and Luke as Gogol's aboveboard medical assistant (a rare nonstereotypical role for an Asian-American actor in those days). Lorre's breathy delivery, maniacal laughter, and metal makeup in an eerie scene where he poses as one of his own patients are truly unforgettable. *Mad Love* ranks among the best shockers ever made.

THE MADDENING (1995) **1/2

D: Danny Huston. Burt Reynolds, Angie Dickinson, Mia Sara, Brian Wimmer, Josh Mostel, William Hickey. 97 mins. (Trimark)

Burt and Angie go nutzoid in Danny (*Becoming Colette*) Huston's Southern white-trash gothic, partially lensed on Reynolds's Jupiter Bay, Florida, ranch. The ever endangered Mia (*Born to Be Violated*) Sara plays a neglected house mouse who petulantly packs her bags and young daughter and hits the road to spite workaholic hubby Wimmer. Unfortunately, Mia's first stop is Burt's remote gas station, a detour that leads to imprisonment at his rural home. There Mia and offspring are mistaken for Burt's wife Angie's long-missing (read murdered) sis and kid; they're subsequently tortured by Angie and her own demented ten-year-old daughter. Burt, sporting a generous salt-and-pepper skyrug, smokes cigars, broods, and contemplates raping Mia while suffering the raspy taunts of his dead evil dad (a wheel-chair-bound Hickey). Some surprisingly sicko moments, including a backyard exhumation, elevate *The Maddening* to watchable status.

MAN OF A THOUSAND FACES (1957) B&W ***

D: Joseph Pevney. James Cagney, Dorothy Malone, Jane Greer. 122 mins. (Universal) DVD

Cags gives his all, in a variety of elaborate disguises, as Lon Chaney in Pevney's sturdy study of the pioneering silent star's rigorous screen career and sometimes troubled personal life. In a flattering bit of casting, handsome 77 *Sunset Strip* costar Roger Smith plays Lon junior.

THE MANGLER (1994) **½

D: Tobe Hooper. Robert Englund, Ted Levine, Daniel Matmor, Vanessa Pike. 106 mins. (New Line)

Texas Chainsaw Massacre auteur Hooper and career Freddy Krueger Englund, who'd earlier worked together on the 1976 horror *Eaten Alive* (see index), reunite for this sometimes mangled, more often effective frightfest, drawn from a Stephen King story, about a possessed Hadley-Watson industrial speed-iron and folding machine. While shorn here of his Freddy gear, Englund is nearly as elaborately disguised as William Gartley, the ancient, one-eyed, leg-brace–encased owner of the Blue Ribbon Laundry and its titular death device. Gartley successfully thwarts all efforts to shut down his demonic machine, even when it starts folding, spindling, and mutilating workers with renewed vigor. Pragmatic cop Levine and his more mystical-minded bud (Matmor) conduct an investigation that uncovers the Mangler's evil roots and a long-standing local conspiracy. Their troubles multiply when the Mangler begins transferring its evil powers to other objects it touches, including a refrigerator and a bottle of antacid tabs (!). While loose in the logic department, old horror hand Hooper and his roving camera succeed in keeping things creepy most of the way. *The Mangler* was

partially lensed in South Africa, which accounts for the strange outbreak of Brit-flavored accents among the on-screen Maine natives. Final score: Mangler 6, Townsfolk 1.

MANIAC COP:
THE SERIES

MANIAC COP (1988) ***

D: William Lustig. Tom Atkins, Bruce Campbell, Laurene Landon, Richard Roundtree, William Smith, Sheree North, Robert Z'dar. 85 mins. (TWE, n.i.d.) DVD

Writer/producer Larry Cohen, abetted here by director Lustig, again displays his patented flair for taking a simple but solid premise and cleverly exploiting every story hook with wit and style. The plot peg finds the mysterious title character—a psycho killer cop played by the hulking Z'dar—rapidly reducing Gotham's population via his nocturnal slaughter sprees, while frightened citizens respond by shooting innocent cops on sight (an angle that could have been explored more fully). Cohen also pens credible-sounding dialogue and has a great cast of B-movie veterans to deliver it: Atkins as the detective assigned to the case, *Evil Dead* alum Campbell as the honest flatfoot wrongly accused of the crimes, former *Shaft* Roundtree and Big Bill Smith as police officials, and Landon and North as femme officers.

MANIAC COP 2 (1990) ***

D: William Lustig. Robert Davi, Claudia Christian, Michael Lerner, Bruce Campbell, Laurene Landon, Robert Z'dar, Leo Rossi, Clarence Williams III, Charles Napier. 90 mins. (Artisan)

Maniac cop Matt Cordell (Z'dar) is alive, if not quite well, and hell-bent on protecting NYC's criminal element in Lustig's lively reprise, also written and produced by Larry Cohen.

Filmmakers in Focus!
The Men Behind the Maniac
WILLIAM LUSTIG ON *MANIAC COP*
As Told to The Phantom

Larry Cohen had just been fired from the movie *Deadly Illusion,* with Billy Dee Williams. In the Larry Cohen tradition, he decided he was gonna go into production right away and make his own movie while he was still in New York. He happened to call my uncle, Jake La Motta, from *Raging Bull.* My name came up, so we go out to lunch. Larry asked me why I never made a sequel to *Maniac.* I told him I'd sold the sequel rights 'cause I really didn't know what to do. So we started tossing around some ideas and came up with *Maniac Cop.* Then we came up with the copy line, "You have the right to remain silent...forever." On the basis of that I said, "Larry, no matter how the movie turns out, that's gonna sell. I want to go make it."

This was in February. We had this idea that somehow we were going to incorporate the St. Patrick's Day Parade into the movie. [Cohen had previously worked the same parade into his 1977 cult classic *God Told Me To.*] So on St. Patrick's Day in March, I got my pal Sam Raimi to go out and be the announcer. We didn't have a script at this time; we were just winging it. We took the footage back and we cut it, and Larry sort of worked out a story that led to the St. Patrick's Day Parade and then expanded after the parade. And that was it!

The sequel rewinds the first film's finale, then picks up with cops Campbell and Landon finding evidence of the allegedly dead title fiend's return. Authorities represented by commissioner Lerner, detective Davi, and police psychologist Christian naturally doubt their fellow officers' contention—until the blue body count around town reaches epic proportions. This successfully sicko sequel, which works in a clever *Bride of Frankenstein* hook, benefits from crisp lensing, an excellent genre cast (plus a cameo by director Sam Raimi as a TV announcer), and a full complement of killings, car crashes, and action set pieces. Particularly impressive is the elaborate pyrotechnic work, as those unsung men in the gray asbestos suits perform some truly scary daredevil fire stunts. The movie is dedicated to the late, great character thesp Joe (*Maniac*) Spinell.

MANIAC COP 3   (1992) **¹/₂

D: William Lustig. Robert Davi, Robert Z'dar, Caitlin Dulany, Gretchen Becker, Julius Harris, Robert Forster. 85 mins. (Artisan)

Scripter Larry Cohen and director Lustig (with unspecified "additional scenes" credited to Joel Soisson, one of the pic's producers) pretty much lose touch with *Maniac Cop*'s original high concept in this unlikely sequel, which premiered on HBO cable, as *Maniac Cop 3: Badge of Silence*. Voodoo priest Harris chants hulking dead-fuzz-from-hell Matt Cordell (reprised by Z'dar) into a reanimated state. The lenient-judicial-system theme reaches ridiculous proportions here, but the action sequences and Z'dar's menacing presence help salvage the day. *MC3* also features the best death-by-defibrillator scene seen on-screen since the 1985 David McCallum hospital romp *Terminal Choice* (a.k.a. *Death Bed*) (Vestron). Forster shows up briefly as a blithe supervising physician who incurs Z'dar's wrath, while Ted (brother of Sam) Raimi cameos as a newsman.

THE MANSTER   (1960)
B&W ***

D: George D. Breakston, Kenneth Crane. Peter Dyneley, Jane Hylton, Tetsu Nakamura. 72 mins. (Sinister Cinema)

In *The Manster,* an Occidental journalist in Japan discovers a second head growing from his shoulder. It turns out it's no brighter than the one that's already there. The sharp Brit comedy *How to Get Ahead in Advertising* (Video Treasures) mined a similar premise for more satirical purposes.

MARK OF THE DEVIL
(1970) **¹/₂

D: Michael Armstrong. Herbert Lom, Udo Kier, Olivera Vuco, Reggie Nalder, Herbert Fux. 96 mins. (Anchor Bay) DVD

Your Phantom is proud to report he has not one but two authentic *Mark of the Devil* barf bags in his archival collection—both sent (empty, fortunately) by generous phans, who may or may not have been making oblique editorial comments. As for the movie, though its barf is ultimately worse than its bite, *Mark* remains a fairly kinky, sadistic flick, featuring strong turns by fright vets Lom, as an 18th-century witch-finder, Nalder (*Dracula's Dog*), and Kier (*Blood for Dracula*). Some of the Inquisitional dialogue is worthy of Monty Python, as when a suspected witch is accused of having "killed an embryo, boiled the cadaver together with snakes and toads into a witch's brew, made a sign over the devil's broth, and then hid it in the earth under the porch of a convent so that Lucifer's wooden leg could step over the threshold and the nuns who serve God may receive large, pus-infected welts on the arms" (!). A "hell" of a mouthful, to be sure. Anchor Bay also carries the sequel, *Mark of the Devil II*, while Moore Video has the related-in-name-only indie *Mark of the Devil: 666.*

MARK OF THE VAMPIRE   (1935)
B&W **¹/₂

D: Tod Browning. Bela Lugosi, Lionel Barrymore, Lionel Atwill. 61 mins. (MGM)

Tod (*Freaks*) Browning does a nice atmospheric job with this *London After Midnight* (the lost Lon Chaney silent) remake that further benefits from fine perfs delivered by Bela and a couple of Lionels (Atwill and Barrymore). Unfortunately, it's all an elaborate hoax, as *Mark* contorts itself to the point of breaking to avoid being an actual horror film. Red-herring Bela's few lines at film's end are eerily prophetic.

MARTIN   (1978) ***

D: George Romero. John Amplas, Lincoln Maazel, Christine Forrest, Tom Savini. 96 mins. (Anchor Bay)

Romero devises a new twist on traditional vampire lore: Amplas is an otherwise sympathetic adolescent who happens to be addicted to human blood and is willing to kill to get it. This impressive, offbeat approach to modern horror is revived in a remastered edition by the invaluable archivists at Anchor Bay. Bedford Entertainment offers something of a Brit zombie variation on the theme, 1999's *I, Zombie*, distributed by *Fangoria* magazine.

MARY REILLY   (1996) **¹/₂

D: Stephen Frears. Julia Roberts, John Malkovich, George Cole, Michael Gambon, Glenn Close. 108 mins. (Columbia/TriStar)

The mainstream big screen proved the wrong venue for *Mary Reilly*, which came a monstrous box-office and critical cropper. *Mary Reilly* might have enjoyed a kinder reception had it arrived as a PBS or A&E TV movie, where its sometimes funereal pacing, visual understatement, and unrelievedly dreary mise-en-scène would have been less glaring. Drawing from Valerie Martin's novel, director Frears, of *The Crying Game* (Artisan) fame, retells the Jekyll and Hyde saga from the eponymous servant's POV, resulting in a sort of "Jekyll and Hyde" Meets *Upstairs, Downstairs*. While not wholly successful, *Mary Reilly* explores some interesting notions re the nature of (specifically male) evil by switching between Mary's present harassment at the hands of Malkovich's Hyde (who, in one scene, is at least chivalrous enough to kiss her rat bites) and her past mistreatment by her drunken dad (Gambon). Roberts is quite credible in her change-of-pace part, while Close registers brightly as a sleazy madam, and Malkovich demonstrates he can brood with the best of them, in both his melancholy Jekyll and drooling Hyde personas. The flawed *Mary Reilly* deserves credit for taking the time-honored tale in fresh directions.

MARY SHELLEY'S FRANKENSTEIN (1994) **

D: Kenneth Branagh. Kenneth Branagh, Helena Bonham Carter, Robert De Niro, Tom Hulce, John Cleese. 123 mins. (Columbia/TriStar) DVD

Multithreat Branagh's aggressive mounting of *Mary Shelley's Frankenstein* succeeds admirably in its gala rendering of traditional Frankenstein "money shots"—e.g., the lightning-lit creation sequence, wherein actor Branagh, as ambitious scientist Victor Frankenstein, brings the Monster to life single-handedly, sans the assistance of an Igor or Fritz. But Branagh choreographs his film like an elaborate *Sound of Music* audition: His characters are forever running, jumping, dancing, and flouncing like Trapp Family members trapped in an early Richard Lester flick. As the Monster, De Niro sounds vaguely like Marlon Brando's Don Corleone while look-

ing uncomfortably close to Ed Wood makeup man Harry Thomas's squashed-nose creature design for Richard Cunha's notorious 1958 quickie *Frankenstein's Daughter* (Englewood). While De Niro does what he can with the role, the acclaimed actor fails to match the poignancy or menace of such previous Monsters as Boris Karloff or even Randy Quaid. Branagh's exercise in gothic overkill might have been better served had the thundering score calmed down a mite and the hyperactive camera kept its cool. Still, with its emphasis on the issues of child support and paternal responsibility, there's no questioning the movie's timeliness, and Old Vic would certainly seem prime Promise Keeper material.

THE MASK (1961) B&W ***½

D: Julian Hoffman. Paul Stevens, Claudette Nevins, Bill Walker, Anne Collings, Jim Moran. 83 mins. (Rhino)

Issued, complete with 3-D specs that really work, by the offbeat vid specialists at Rhino, *The Mask* offers a pretty tame wraparound—shrink Stevens inherits an ancient mask from a suicidal patient—but the 3-D sequences are surprisingly hot. Shot in black and white, the chiller (Canada's first feature-film export) boasts genuinely disturbing 3-D shock FX—not designed, as widely misreported, by famed Czech montage master Slavko Vorkapich; he was approached, but his design ideas were deemed too costly and thus rejected—as we follow the on-screen Stevens through a hallucinatory hellscape alive with clawed demons, floating skulls, hissing snakes, sacrificial maidens, and other infernal perils. *The Mask* (a.k.a. *Eyes of Hell*) makes for unique late-night viewing and an ideal Halloween-party tape. Rhino also has 3-D editions of Arch Oboler's *The Bubble* (a.k.a. *The Fantastic Invasion of Planet Earth*), the camp classic *Cat-Women of the Moon*, the Tony Anthony

spaghetti western *Comin' at Ya!*, and the immortal *Robot Monster* (see index).

MASQUE OF THE RED DEATH (1965) ***

D: Roger Corman. Vincent Price, Hazel Court, Jane Asher, David Weston, Patrick Magee, Skip Martin. 88 mins. (Orion)

The best of Corman's Edgar Allan Poe adaptations, *Masque* is arguably Rog's greatest directorial effort ever, even reaching into Ingmar Bergman territory—especially in those eerily poignant tableaux showing a crimson-cloaked Death marching wearily but inexorably through ravaged, fog-enshrouded forests. Price plays decadent, sadistic, devil-worshipping Prince Prospero, who gathers his fellow nobles at his castle for what proves to be a final round of degenerate revels as the plague steals ever nearer. While there are touches of humor here—as when Prospero, busily tormenting the local peasantry, sighs, "I have to do everything myself!"—*Masque* is a generally somber affair reeking of depravity and doom. Aiding immeasurably are the contributions of set designer Daniel Haller, who works miracles on a modest budget, and cinematographer/future auteur Nicolas Roeg. Avoid the awful Corman-produced 1989 remake (MGM) and the barely related 1990 *Masque of the Red Death* (Columbia/TriStar), with Frank Stallone. Other poor Poe adaptations include *Buried Alive*, despite the fleeting presence of John Carradine in one of his final screen appearances, and 1988's *House of Usher* (both Columbia/TriStar).

THE MEPHISTO WALTZ (1971) ***

D: Paul Wendkos. Alan Alda, Jacqueline Bisset, Curt Jurgens. 108 mins. (Fox)

Journalist Alda and spouse Bisset serve Satan in one of Hollywood's hotter A horror films, based on Fred Mustard Stewart's novel, laced with several genuine jolts and helped along by Jerry Goldsmith's moody score.

MR. FROST (1990) **

D: Philip Setbon. Jeff Goldblum, Kathy Baker, Alan Bates. 92 mins. (SVS, n.i.d.)

Goldblum stars as the title weirdo, an Ed Gein–like psycho who later lays fairly convincing claim to being nothing less than the devil incarnate. We first meet the mad Mr. Frost as he greets Brit inspector Bates with several strange, Gracie Allen–styled non sequiturs, an impromptu cooking lesson (!), and finally a calm confession detailing the fates (which, like serial killer *Henry*, he's also taken the trouble to videotape) of the 24 cadavers buried under his lawn. Frost is consigned to an asylum, where he breaks a two-year silence by telling shrink Baker that it's his mission as the devil to restore "the age-old spirit of the wild side." To that end, Frost wills a formerly harmless fellow patient to kill several local religious figures and further demonstrates his "mysterious ways" by curing Baker's brother of his lifelong paralysis. Though the movie can't decide whether it's an illustrated good-versus-evil debate, à la William Peter Blatty's *Exorcist 3,* or an all-out frightfest, *Mr. Frost* is not without its interesting elements.

THE MONSTER CLUB (1980) **1/2

D: Roy Ward Baker. Vincent Price, John Carradine, Donald Pleasence. 97 mins. (Live)

Journalist Carradine journeys to a Transylvanian disco (!), where he pumps vampire/author Price for three macabre tales of varying quality. The three leads alone make this one a must for fright fans.

THE MONSTER MAKER (1944) B&W **1/2

D: Sam Newfield. J. Carrol Naish, Ralph Morgan, Wanda McKay. 62 mins. (Sinister Cinema)

The Monster Maker is an authentically creepy flick that sees mad scientist Naish afflict victim Morgan with disfiguring acromegaly—the disease that horror star Rondo Hatton suffered and died from. Pretty sick for its time.

THE MONSTER OF PIEDRAS BLANCAS (1957) B&W **1/2

D: Irvin Berwick. Les Tremayne, Forrest Lewis, Don Sullivan. 71 mins. (Rhino, VCI)

Relatively gruesome for its day, with a fairly explicit decapitation scene, Berwick's low-budget indie has the title monster—an uglier version of the *Creature from the Black Lagoon*—terrorizing inhabitants of a remote lighthouse. Perennial Z-movie teen hero Sullivan is on hand to save the day. This effectively atmospheric effort has developed a loyal video following.

MOTEL HELL (1980) ***

D: Kevin Connor. Rory Calhoun, Paul Linke, Nancy Parsons. 102 mins. (MGM)

Former sagebrush star Calhoun toplines as enterprising sausage mogul "Farmer Vincent" in Connor's sometimes broad but more often witty cannibal comedy. Rory's last-reel confession rates as a classic.

THE MUMMY (1932) B&W ***

D: Karl Freund. Boris Karloff, Zita Johann, David Manners. 72 mins. (Universal) DVD

Boris (billed as "Karloff, the Uncanny") steals the horror show via his solemn portrayal of ancient Egyptian high priest Im-ho-tep, who returns to agitated life following a 3,700-year snooze. Freund imbues the eerie proceedings with a darkly hallucinatory quality, while young archaeologist Bramwell Fletcher delivers the best nervous breakdown we've ever seen onscreen. Universal reissued the film in a "special edition" to tie in with the theatrical bow of its 1999 big-screen hit *The Mummy* (DVD), a blend of CGI-driven horror and smarmy *Indiana Jones*–styled adventure elements. The same label has also released the loose 1940s sequels *The Mummy's Hand, The Mummy's Tomb, The Mummy's Ghost,* and *The Mummy's Curse,* lesser entries (the last three with Lon Chaney, Jr.) that nonetheless command their share of fans.

THE MUMMY (1959) **1/2

D: Terence Fisher. Peter Cushing, Christopher Lee, Yvonne Furneaux. 88 mins. (Warner)

While essentially a back-lot hack job, Hammer's remake of Freund's original is such a thoroughly professional pulpfest that it's fun to watch anyway. Cushing is typically crisp as the tomb-desecrating archaeologist, though Lee has little to do in his limited mummy role. Anchor Bay has the Hammer sequel, *The Mummy's Shroud.* Other mummy movies not mentioned elsewhere in this volume include *Attack of the Mayan Mummy* (Loonic); *The Awakening* (Warner), with Charlton Heston; the 1950s Aztec-mummy epics *Curse of the Aztec Mummy, The Robot vs. the Aztec Mummy* (Rhino) and *Wrestling Women vs. the Aztec Mummy* (Sinister Cinema); the Euro gorefest *Dawn of the Mummy* (HBO); the animated *Mad Monster Party* (Deluxo); *The Monster Squad* (Artisan); the Paul Naschy romp *The Mummy's Revenge* (Unicorn); and *Timewalker* (Charter).

MURDERS IN THE ZOO (1933) B&W ***1/2

D: Edward Sutherland. Lionel Atwill, Kathleen Burke, Charlie Ruggles, Randolph Scott,

Gail Patrick, Harry Beresford, John Lodge. 62 mins. (Universal)

A deft mix of the droll and the horrific, *Murders* opens with an indelible shock scene that finds jealous millionaire zoologist Atwill surgically sewing shut an imagined rival's mouth (!). The action swiftly shifts from French Indochina to the States, where Lionel installs his newly captured menagerie, ranging from chimps to poisonous mamba snakes, in Beresford's zoo. When the deliciously loony Lionel (correctly) deduces that wealthy young Lodge is about to run off with his captive spouse (Burke), he slips him a mamba mickey in the midst of a highly publicized dinner arranged by zoo press agent Ruggles (amusing here as the decidedly eccentric comic relief). Atwill is wonderful as the gleefully sadistic animal lover, while future western star Scott turns in stalwart work as the zoo toxicologist who eventually catches on to Lionel's evil activities. Lodge, meanwhile, later abandoned his acting career to become governor of Connecticut. The pre-Code film infuriated several state censor boards, reportedly resulting in a multitude of reedited versions playing in different theaters. The best line, meanwhile, belongs to Atwill, when he protests, "You don't think I just sat there with an eight-foot mamba in my pocket!" A thought that surely would have tickled Mae West's fancy (to speak only of her fancy).

MUTE WITNESS (1995) ***

D: Anthony Waller. Marina Sudina, Fay Ripley, Evan Richards, Oleg Jankowskij, Igor Volkov, "Mystery Guest Star." 98 mins. (Columbia/TriStar)

E uro-based TV director Waller makes an impressive feature-film debut with his blackly comic, Moscow-lensed horror outing, a clever exercise somewhat reminiscent of early De Palma efforts like *Sisters*. A variation on the venerable handicapped-damsel-in-distress subgenre (e.g., *Hear No Evil*, *Wait Until Dark*), *Mute Witness* centers on speechless makeup-FX artist Billy (appealingly portrayed by Russian actress Sudina), currently working on a low-budget Russia-set slasher flick. After Billy witnesses a late-night snuff movie being shot on the sly by two Russki crewmembers, she's relentlessly pursued by the killers and their mobster boss, "the Reaper" (played by an immediately recognizable veteran thesp identified only as "Mystery Guest Star").

Waller amply demonstrates his expertise in executing surgically precise, irony-edged shock set pieces that manage to keep the viewer simultaneously alert and amused. He yields the max from his exceedingly bleak locations, from the dilapidated film studio to the frigid Moscow streets to Billy's own stark, icy apartment (where the cold doesn't prevent her from enjoying a lengthy, peril-fraught bath). *Mute Witness* also contains what may be filmdom's funniest death scene, courtesy of an overly intense Russian actress, during an opening film-within-a-film sequence.

THE MYSTERY OF EDWIN DROOD (1935) B&W ***

D: Stuart Walker. Claude Rains, Heather Angel, Douglass Montgomery, David Manners, Valerie Hobson, Francis L. Sullivan. 85 mins. (Universal)

S ince Charles Dickens never completed his novel *The Mystery of Edwin Drood*, it remains a mystery how the famed author intended to resolve the central murder plot. Universal arrived at its own resolution, based on one of the more likely scenarios that Dickens may have had in mind. Depressed choirmaster John Jasper (Rains) is hopelessly obsessed by his beloved nephew Edwin Drood's (Manners) teenage bride-to-be, the subtly monikered Rosa Bud (played by Heather Angel, no slouch in the subtle-name department herself), unaware that Edwin and Rosa are planning to cancel their arranged marriage. Rosa, meanwhile, finds herself taken with Ceylonese visitor Neville (Montgomery), who becomes the chief suspect when Drood disappears during a dark and stormy Christmas Eve. Punctuated by typically eccentric Dickensian comic relief—e.g., Forrester Harvey's drunken mausoleum keeper Durdles, E. E. Clive's officious Mayor Sapsea— *Drood* emerges as a satisfying suspenser, enacted by a more-than-capable cast (particularly Rains as the tortured Jasper), that also offers a deft sketch of 1860s England. While not a true horror film, *Drood* incorporates many effectively creepy atmospheric gothic elements, including the crypt set from the original 1931 *Dracula* and unsettling nightmare imagery engendered by Jasper's clandestine opium sessions.

MYSTERY OF THE WAX MUSEUM (1933) ***1/2

D: Michael Curtiz. Lionel Atwill, Fay Wray, Glenda Farrell. 77 mins. (MGM)

T he inspiration for the later 3-D *House of Wax*, future *Casablanca* helmer Curtiz's early two-strip Technicolor outing boasts great sets, swift pacing, pre-Code candor, and a vivid performance by the ever dependable Atwill as the mad sculptor, with Fay supplying the screams and Glenda the wisecracks. *Mystery* endures as a Golden Age fright film worthy of the name.

NADJA (1995) B&W ***

D: Michael Almereyda. Suzy Amis, Peter Fonda, Galaxy Craze, Martin Donovan, Elina Lowensohn, Karl Geary, Jared Harris, David Lynch. 92 mins. (Hallmark)

A lmereyda's NYC-set vampire fable details the downtown exploits of the toothy title character, a direct descendant of Dracula (we're told) exotically interpreted by Lowensohn. Nadja sets her sights and fangs on a local lass named Lucy (Craze), whom she soon seduces. When Lucy's spouse, Jim (Hal Hartley regular Donovan), notices his wife's gradual descent into somnambulism and vampirism, he seeks the aid of his uncle, vampire-hunter Van Helsing (Fonda). Van Helsing pursues Nadja in a labyrinthine chase that leads to Brooklyn's darkest heart, where Nadja's twin bloodsucker brother, Edgar (Harris), with the help of Renfield (Geary), is trying to kick the plasma habit. From there, our protagonists journey to Transylvania (with upstate New York filling in) for a climactic showdown.

Lensed, like Abel Ferrara's contemporary *The Addiction* (see index), in evocative black and white, *Nadja* suffers from some slow stretches but compensates with several inventive variations on traditional screen-vampire lore and an eccentric but able cast, including a strong contribution from Fonda as the manic Van Helsing. David Lynch cameos as a morgue security guard. Almereyda returns with 1999's less arresting *The Eternal* (Trimark), starring Christopher Walken.

NEAR DARK   (1987) ***

D: Kathryn Bigelow. Adrian Pasdar, Jenny Wright, Lance Henriksen, Bill Paxton, Jenette Goldstein, Tim Thomerson. 95 mins. (HBO)

A vampire revamp of *Bonnie and Clyde*, Bigelow's *Near Dark* is a high-concept combo of the rural-outlaw and vampire genres starring Henriksen and Goldstein as the leaders of a gang of fanged rednecks who leave their victims' throats a similar hue. Accompanied by new inductee Caleb (Pasdar), an innocent Oklahoma ranch boy recruited by cute blond bloodsucker Mae (Wright), they steal cars, run up an impressive nightly body count, and keep one step ahead of both the law and

the light. *Near Dark* features great trashy locations (from seedy motels to funky roadside dives), stylish direction, and enough blood to paint a small town red.

NECRONOMICON: BOOK OF THE DEAD   (1994) **½

D: Christophe Gans, Shusuke Kaneko, Brian Yuzna. Jeffrey Combs, Bruce Payne, David Warner, Millie Perkins, Bess Myer, Richard Lynch, Maria Ford, Dennis Christopher, Don Calfa. 97 mins. (Universal)

Producer/codirector Yuzna's *Necronomicon* arrives as an uneven but consistently over-the-top terror anthology, loosely drawn from H. P. Lovecraft's scare stories and featuring gross-out FX (courtesy of, among others, Steve Johnson and Screaming Mad George). Warner and Perkins topline in the best of the three episodes, Kaneko's "The Cold," with Warner in fine form as a literal "iceman" who employs the arcane science of "cryptobiosis" to retard the aging process—at the expense of several unwitting victims. Other members of Yuzna's culty cast include Lynch and busy B starlet Ford, who appear in Gans's gothic "The Drowned," detailing Payne's encounter with a demon who resurrects the former's late wife and son; Calfa as a subterranean alien in the third and goriest story, "Whispers"; and a made-over Combs as H. P. himself in the anthology's 1932-set wraparound, both directed by Yuzna.

NEEDFUL THINGS   (1992) **

D: Fraser C. Heston. Max von Sydow, Ed Harris, Bonnie Bedelia, John Heard, Amanda Plummer. 119 mins. (New Line) DVD

Despite a few funny lines—as when diabolical antiques-store owner von Sydow commends a pleading

Heard, "You're disgusting. I like that in a person"—Fraser C. (Son of Charlton) Heston's puerile Stephen King adaptation is a mostly tedious, one-joke job stretched to nearly two hours. Occasionally effective FX and performances that go beyond the story's feeble demands—von Sydow, sheriff Harris, café owner Bedelia, and waitress Plummer all put out with admirable enthusiasm—also help hoist the film to a watchable level. But only hard-core King completists are likely to rate *Needful Things* as necessary viewing.

NIGHT MONSTER   (1942) B&W ***

D: Ford Beebe. Bela Lugosi, Lionel Atwill, Irene Harvey, Ralph Morgan, Leif Erickson, Don Porter, Nils Asther, Fay Helm. 73 mins. (Universal)

Though top-billed, Bela is wasted as a butler with a squeamish streak in what emerges as one of Universal's weirder story lines, involving congenital madness, multiple murders, yogism, and mystically regenerated flesh. *Night Monster* offers an early depiction of Eastern mysticism triumphing over modern Western medical science, represented here by three less-than-shining exemplars—a supremely arrogant Atwill, gland-obsessed crony Francis Pierlot, and neurological convert Frank Reicher—whose inept surgical efforts have left mansion owner Morgan a double amputee. When said doctors, along with sundry potential witnesses and troublemakers, start turning up strangled, local police investigate the scene. Also onboard is breezy mystery writer Porter, who sees (and seizes) the situation as an excuse to get next to femme shrink Harvey—the only medical professional to receive the scripters' respect, though Erickson, as Morgan's leering lout of a chauffeur, at one point scoffs, "She's no doctor, she's just a dame." *Night Monster* is often outlandish and verbose but rarely dull.

NIGHT OF THE DEMONS: THE SERIES

NIGHT OF THE DEMONS (1987) **

D: Kevin S. Tenney. William Gallo, Hal Havins, Linnea Quigley, Mimi Kinkade. 89 mins. (Republic)

At the urging of "weird" cohort Angela (Kinkade), several over-aged high school party animals stage a Halloween bash at a local haunted manse. The party proceeds with mind-less, if rather mild, abandon until one of the teens takes lyrical note of "the noise, the stink, and the chill" (which, if little else, would have made for a more mem-orable title than *Night of the Demons*). One by one, our revelers transform into drooling demons and start knocking one another off. Aside from a neat animated opening-credits sequence, *Night*'s sole saving grace is the always welcome pres-ence of scream queen Quigley, who makes a memorable rearview entrance here and sticks around long enough to perform one of her patented topless scenes before transmogrifying into a screeching devil-creature further bur-dened by poor orthodontal work.

NIGHT OF THE DEMONS 2 (1994) **1/2

D: Brian Trenchard-Smith. Christi Harris, Bobby Jacoby, Amelia Kinkade, Merle Kennedy, Rod McCary, Jennifer Rhodes, Johnny Moran, Zoe Trilling. 96 mins. (Republic)

Tenney passes the directorial torch to genre vet Trenchard-Smith, who populates his follow-up with better-drawn characters and employs a less obnoxious tone while still delivering the gory goods. The hoary Halloween-set story line finds imperiled Catholic-school teens up against returning demoness Angela (Kinkade). While no single moment is as memorable as scream queen Linnea Quigley's disap-pearing-lipstick trick in the original, FX ace Steve Johnson compensates with a number of fairly imaginative disgusto tableaux. Perhaps more important, according to the end credits, "No bug was harmed in the making of this film." Followed by the 1997 yawner *Night of the Demons 3* (Republic).

NIGHT OF THE HOWLING BEAST (1975) **

D: M. I. Bonns. Paul Naschy, Grace Mills, Gil Vidal. Dubbed. 87 mins. (Super)

Naschy (Jacinto Molina) scripts and stars in this Spanish horror that opens with a striking moment of cross-cultural confusion—an establishing shot of London accompanied by a rousing bagpipe rendition of "Scotland the Brave" (!). Otherwise, it's a fairly desper-ate Naschy lycanthrope adventure that also works in a ludicrous yeti plot. Naschy is not without his fans, though, and the lat-ter can catch their Catalan fright fave in *Beyond the Living Dead, Fury of the Wolfman, The Mummy's Revenge* (Uni-corn), *The Craving* (Vestron), *Crimson* (TWE), *Curse of the Devil, The Devil's Possessed, Dr. Jekyll and the Werewolf, Inquisition* (Sinister Cinema), *Dracula vs. Frankenstein, Dracula's Great Love* (MPI), *Exorcism* (HHT), *The Hanging Woman, Horror Rises from the Tomb* (WesternWorld), *House of Psychotic Women* (Super), *People Who Own the Dark* (Moore), *Rue Morgue Massacre, Vengeance of the Zombies* (All Seasons), and *Werewolf vs. the Vampire Women* (Hollywood Select).

NIGHT OF THE LIVING DEAD: THE SERIES

NIGHT OF THE LIVING DEAD: COLLECTOR'S EDITION (1968) B&W ****

D: George Romero. Duane Jones, Judith O'Dea, Russell Streiner, Karl Hardman, Keith Wayne. 96 mins./108 mins. total. (Anchor Bay) DVD

When Romero unleashed *Night of the Living Dead* on an unsus-pecting public back in 1968, the pic rep-resented a radical, truly shocking departure from the usual run of formu-laic fear flicks. *Night* chucked all roman-tic and most pseudoscientific fright-film conventions and went straight for the jugular (to say nothing of the entrails), conveying a sense of visceral terror through its unrelieved atmosphere of frantic despair as much as through its relentless army of staggering ghouls.

Like a legit nightmare, *Night of the Living Dead* simply *starts,* sans rhyme or reason, and never lets up as the can-nibalistic title zombies launch their blind but tireless assault against the liv-ing. Embattled Sanity, embodied by beleaguered hero Jones, takes fragile shelter in a ramshackle house, while lethal (and seemingly limitless) Irra-tionality rages without. *Night*'s popular-ity led not only to two Romero sequels, *Dawn of the Dead* and *Day of the Dead,* and an ill-advised remake, but to count-less imitations, lensed here and abroad (most notably in Italy, where directors like Lucio [*Zombie*] Fulci and Umberto Lenzi forged careers colorfully robbing the *Dead*), and the separate, lighter-veined *Return of the Living Dead* series (see index). Anchor Bay's remastered "collector's edition" is by far the best available on VHS/DVD; the label also issued a "30th anniversary edition" that includes newly filmed (by original coscripter John Russo) scenes inserted into the original film, along with a new score. Best Film & Video carries a col-orized version.

NIGHT OF THE LIVING DEAD (1990) *1/2

D: Tom Savini. Tony Todd, Patricia Tallman, Tom Towles, McKee Anderson, William Butler, Bill Mosley. 92 mins. (Columbia/TriStar)

It's all here all over again, with a few minimal, uninspired twists, minus the truly nightmarish atmosphere and visceral shocks that made the first so memorable. Tony (*Candyman*) Todd turns in the best work, offering a thoroughly professional imitation of the late Duane Jones's perf as hero Ben. Tallman plays a shotgun-toting, Sigourney Weaver–ized Barbara; as an actress, she makes for a fine stuntwoman (though she does deliver the Ed Wood–like line "Whatever it is I lost, I lost a long time ago and I don't plan on losing it again!" with startling conviction). Towles, excellent as the title psycho's accomplice in *Henry,* can do nothing with his monotonous role as the perennially P.O.'d Cooper (a part tailormade for Joe Besser), whose on-screen lament "Damn it, we've heard all this before!" rings all too sadly true.

NIGHT OF THE LIVING DEAD: 25TH ANNIVERSARY EDITION (1993) **½

D: Thomas Brown. With George A. Romero, John A. Russo, Russell W. Streiner, Karl Hardman, Marilyn Eastman. 83 mins. (Drive-In Cinema)

Brown's feature-length look at the making of a cult classic intercuts scenes from the 1968 original with filmed comments from participants ranging from auteur Romero to makeup maven Eastman, who reminisce about the film's often arduous genesis. Adding to the fun are testimonials from "Famous Fans" of the pioneering fear flick. The latter include such legit industry heavyweights as Sam Raimi, Wes Craven, and Tope Hooper, along with more questionable "celebs," like director David (*Sorority Babes in the Slimeball Bowl-O-Rama*) DeCoteau (who, in his defense, *does* know Linnea Quigley personally). Indefatigable low-budget auteur Fred Olen (*Hollywood Chainsaw Hookers*) Ray also manages to squeeze sufficient time from his busy

sked to contribute his two cents' worth. On that subject, budgetary restrictions are obvious throughout this *Dead* doc, but such involuntary penury is nothing if not in the spirit of the original. Occasionally slack editing and an underdeveloped profile of late *Living Dead* star Duane Jones represent more serious drawbacks. Still, Brown comes through with a group portrait compelling enough to keep dedicated *Dead*heads entranced.

Drive-In Cinema also stocks such other shock docs as David Del Valle's *Cult People,* a collection of interviews with, among others, Russ Meyer and Patrick Macnee, the James Karen–narrated alfresco bijou salute, *Drive-In Madness,* and *Linnea Quigley's Horror Workout* (shower included).

DAWN OF THE DEAD: THE DIRECTOR'S CUT (1979) ****

D: George Romero. David Emge, Ken Foree, Scott Reiniger, Gaylen Ross, Tom Savini. 138 mins. (Anchor Bay) DVD

Romero's *Night of the Living Dead* sequel rates as a horror-movie masterpiece, the *Gone With the Wind* of gore. In the midst of the mall-set *Dawn*'s abundant carnage, Romero also manages to get off some sardonic zingers re McAmerica's rampant brainwashed cult of consumerism. Couple Emge and Ross and ex-soldiers Foree (who's since become a genre mainstay) and Reiniger all turn in naturalistic perfs, while makeup-FX ace Savini lends conviction to his sadistic-biker role (loosely reprised in the Quentin Tarantino/Robert Rodriguez collaboration *From Dusk Till Dawn* [see index]). *Dawn* is an ideal blend of black comedy and chunk-blowing horror that, like its predecessor, never wears out its welcome. Anchor Bay's letter-boxed version restores 12 minutes of footage slashed from the original theatrical release. For the complete inside scoop, scope out Roy (*Street Trash*) Frumkes's

excellent documentary *Document of the Dead* (Synapse, DVD).

DAY OF THE DEAD (1985) **

D: George Romero. Lori Cardille, Terry Alexander, Joseph Pilato, Jarlath Conroy, Richard Liberty, John Amplas. 102 mins. (Anchor Bay) DVD

In *Day,* Romero's zombies find themselves all messed up with no place to go, doomed to stagger on empty sans the shock value of *Night* or *Dawn*'s brilliantly retch-ed excesses. *Day* centers on a dozen or so soldiers and scientists who hole up in an underground bunker in a bid to find out what makes the cannibalistic corpses "tick." Much infighting and stale, obscenity-driven dialogue ensue between the disharmonious factions, while the mindless zombies marshal their forces on the terra firma above, preparing for the inevitable assault on the grossly outnumbered human survivors. *Day of the Dead* is not entirely bereft of redeeming moments, such as the scene that sees wacky scientist Dr. Logan (Liberty) attempt to "civilize" a captive zombie (whom he dubs "Bub") via standard behavioral techniques. When the student ghoul grows unruly, petulantly upsetting a lab bench, the doc douses the lights and testily admonishes, "You can just sit there in the dark and think about what you've done" (!). *Day* also generates some genuine last-reel suspense (full of Tom Savini's usual expertly revolting makeup FX), but here it's a case of too much, too late.

THE NIGHT STALKER (1971) ***½

D: John Llewellyn Moxey. Darren McGavin, Carol Lynley, Simon Oakland, Ralph Meeker, Barry Atwater. 73 mins. (Anchor Bay) DVD

Richard Matheson's ingenious script puts a new spin on traditional horror motifs as hardboiled reporter McGavin tracks a Las Vegas vampire in a made-for-TV movie that begat the cult teleseries *Kolchak.* Anchor Bay archivists perform their typically exemplary job in remastering and repackaging the cult fave. The label also has the made-for-TV follow-up *The Night Strangler,* wherein McGavin reprises his role as reporter Kolchak, this time sleuthing a series of grisly murders in Seattle; the top-notch cast includes John Carradine and Margaret *(The Wizard of Oz)* Hamilton.

NIGHT TIDE   (1961) B&W ***½

D: Curtis Harrington. Dennis Hopper, Linda Lawson, Gavin Muir, Luana Anders, Ben Roseman. 84 mins. (Milestone)

Obviously inspired by the Val Lewton–produced, Jacques Tourneur–directed classic *Cat People,* Harrington's moody seaside chiller emerges as a sort of "Cat*fish* People." Like its model, *Night Tide* is less an all-out horror film than a supremely eerie mood piece, heightened by B&W cinematography that captures the otherworldly aura of Santa Monica and Venice, California's seedy piers and amusement parlors. Hopper gives a layered perf as lonely young sailor Johnny Drake, entranced by the mysterious, alluring Mora (Lawson), who works as a midway mermaid—but there may be a stronger link than mere sideshow whimsy binding Mora to the denizens of the deep. A West Coast cousin to *Carnival of Souls, Night Tide* rates as an essential addition to any genre-film library. And we'd swear that's Ed Wood's rubber octopus from *Bride of the Monster* (by way of *Wake of the Red Witch*) seen wrestling with Hopper during a nautical nightmare sequence.

THE NIGHT WALKER   (1964) B&W **

D: William Castle. Barbara Stanwyck, Robert Taylor, Lloyd Bochner, Hayden Rorke, Rochelle Hudson. 86 mins. (Columbia/TriStar)

One of gimmick guru Castle's hokier efforts, *The Night Walker* stumbles at a slow pace as victim Stanwyck first suffers unpleasant blind hubby Rorke's infidelity accusations (barks a bitchy Barb, "My lover is only a dream, but he's still more of a man than you!"), then a plot to drive her insane. A few creepy touches—a cheaply surreal nightmare prologue and a scene that finds Barb scared by a shish kebab—help relieve the tedium, but the self-styled "Master of Movie Horror" is in far-from-top form here. The pic signs off with "Pleasant Dreams!" in place of the standard "The End."

NIGHTBREED   (1990) ***

D: Clive Barker. Craig Sheffer, David Cronenberg, Anne Bobby, Charles Haid, Douglas Bradley, John Agar. 99 mins. (Media)

The victim of several reshoots, scheduling delays, and skirmishes with the MPAA, Barker's (literally) multilevel story line traces suspected mass murderer Sheffer's troubled journey through two infernal locales: rural Canada and the mythical Midian. The latter is a secret city of freaks—survivors of various vanquished mutant races—situated under a remote cemetery. A living-dead Sheffer finds sanctuary in the mostly benign monsters' midst, while psycho shrink Cronenberg (supplying well-modulated menace) and Sheffer's understandably worried lover (Bobby) follow in his wake. While *Nightbreed* doesn't quite sustain the intensity level of Barker's best work, there are more than enough demented diversions—including a cameo by '50s B fave Agar—to satisfy quality-seeking scare buffs.

A NIGHTMARE ON ELM STREET:
THE SERIES

A NIGHTMARE ON ELM STREET (1984) ***

D: Wes Craven. John Saxon, Ronee Blakeley, Heather Langenkamp, Amanda Wyss, Nick Conti, Johnny Depp, Robert Englund. 92 mins. (Media, Anchor Bay) DVD

Craven delivers the chills via several scary set pieces while introducing shockingly popular dream demon Freddy Krueger. Unfortunately, Craven is far less adept here at crafting credible dialogue or coaxing convincing perfs from some of his cast members, who include a young Johnny Depp. Still, *Nightmare* indisputably remains one of the genre's most influential and genuinely jolt-driven affairs.

A NIGHTMARE ON ELM STREET 2: FREDDY'S REVENGE   (1985) **

D: Jack Sholder. Mark Patton, Kim Myers, Robert Rusler, Clu Gulager, Hope Lange, Robert Englund. 84 mins. (Media, Anchor Bay) DVD

Fred returns to infiltrate the somnolent psyche of young Jesse (Patton), an unsuspecting teen whose family has unwisely moved into a house last occupied by one of Freddy's victims. While *Nightmare 2,* under Jack *(The Hidden)* Sholder's direction, contains its fair share of shock yoks, particularly in the early going, the chill factor—the original *Nightmare*'s strength—is virtually nil.

A NIGHTMARE ON ELM STREET 3: DREAM WARRIORS   (1987) ***

D: Chuck Russell. Heather Langenkamp, Craig Wasson, Robert Englund, Patricia Arquette, John Saxon, Zsa Zsa Gabor. 96 mins. (Media, Anchor Bay) DVD

Nightmare 3 finds "the last of the Elm Street children" undergoing group therapy for their Freddy Krueger–caused sleep disorders. Few of 3's nondream sequences possess much in the way of logic, serving simply as convenient frames for the flicks's real raison d'être; happily, the numerous nightmare set pieces save the day, as

F.K. adopts such unlikely guises as a sexy blond nurse, a TV set, and smarmy talk-show host Dick Cavett (!). *Nightmare 3* remains the sickest, funniest, and most outlandishly surreal of the series.

A NIGHTMARE ON ELM STREET 4: THE DREAM MASTER   (1988)**

D: Renny Harlin. Robert Englund, Andras Jones, Tuesday Knight, Brooke Theiss, Danny Hassel, Toy Newkirk. \93 mins. (Media, Anchor Bay) DVD

Here since-ascendant auteur Harlin lets Fred coast his way through sundry slaughter scenes as he slays three survivors from *3*, along with several new recruits, in a variety of increasingly predictable ways. Only an imaginative bijou-set sequence—wherein Fred invades a *Reefer Madness* screening (!)—approaches the wacky inspiration that informed much of the film's immediate predecessor. Scream queen Linnea Quigley is tragically wasted as a "Soul from Freddy's Chest" (though ex-Playmate/former Andy Sidaris starlet Hope Marie Carlton fares better in her mute but eloquent "Waterbed Bunny" bit). Despite its expanded budget and isolated FX highlights, *Nightmare 4* is pretty old hat—and we're not talking about Freddy's famous fedora.

A NIGHTMARE ON ELM STREET 5: THE DREAM CHILD   (1989)***

D: Stephen Hopkins. Robert Englund, Lisa Wilcox, Kelly Jo Minter, Beatrice Boepple, Danny Hassel. 90 mins. (Media, Anchor Bay) DVD

Freddy's fifth fearfest finds our fedo-rad fiend in fine form; unlike its immediate forebear, this edition takes its tormented teens' fright plight seriously. *Dream Child* opens with a vivid Marat/Sadean dramatization of Freddy's conception, as a "hundred maniacs" (an on-screen caretaker confirms the exact count) attack hapless nun Amanda Krueger (Boepple) when she finds herself trapped in an institution for the criminally insane. That vision is witnessed by *Dream Master* survivor Alice (Wilcox), a pregnant high school grad whose own dreaming fetus unwittingly provides the dread, not-quite-dead Fred with convenient reentry into the waking world. The movie taps into and effectively exaggerates the normal insecurities experienced by adolescents too old to cling to childhood illusions and too young to enjoy adult autonomy. *Nightmare 5* also boasts its share of surreal FX work: Particularly impressive are Freddy's natal flashback (even if it does borrow from Larry Cohen's mutant-baby opus *It's Alive*), a gross-out dinner scene that could well put less intestinally fortitudinous couch

potatoes off their popcorn for months, and a suspenseful journey through Alice's womb.

FREDDY'S DEAD: THE FINAL NIGHTMARE   (1991)**

D: Rachel Talalay. Robert Englund, Lisa Zane, Shon Greenblatt, Lezlie Deane, Ricky Dean Logan, Breckin Meyer, Yaphet Kotto. 96 mins. (New Line) DVD

Freddy's Dead unfolds "ten years after" in the familiar environs of Springwood, Ohio. The town's last teen survivor, an amnesic "John Doe" (Greenblatt), literally falls from the sky following an in-flight nightmare. His vague memories of Freddy's lethal reign prompt therapist Zane to visit the now-childless Springwood, populated solely by bonkers adults (Roseanne and Tom Arnold among them), like the teacher who gives a crash course in "Freddy 101" to an empty classroom. Said Fred (Englund) soon resumes his old tricks, invading the nightmares of Greenblatt and cronies. At the urging of "dream doctor" Kotto, Lisa vows to turn the terror tables on Freddy by entering his twisted brain. Before you can say "Put the mask on now!" we're treated to a 3-D tour of the inside of Fred's ugly little head. (Unfortunately, the 3-D sequence is lost on VHS, while Alice Cooper's silent cameo is not; the DVD edition restores the 3-D elements.) The results, alas, are fairly brainless. Fred again dispatches his victims with his patented blend of splatter and patter while transmogrifying into a psychedelic Freddy (to the strains of Iron Butterfly's "In-a-Gadda-Da-Vida," no less!), a video-game Freddy, et al.

WES CRAVEN'S NEW NIGHTMARE (1994)***

D: Wes Craven. Heather Langenkamp, Robert Englund, John Saxon, Miko

Hughes, David Newsom. 111 mins. (New Line) DVD

When we first heard that Freddy Krueger's resurrection would be a self-referential outing that would find the razor-fingered fiend frightening such actual New Line Cinema personnel as actress Langenkamp, Freddy's real-life interpreter Englund, and director Craven, we feared the worst—a campy attempt to wring a few final bucks from the *Nightmare on Elm Street* concept's corpse. Instead, Craven and crew play their unlikely story line totally straight—indeed, with an earnestness absent from most of the earlier Freddy sequels. Freddy even keeps his patented one-liners to a minimum here; spiritually and physically, the character is less the supernatural child-killer from Craven's original *Nightmare on Elm Street* than an all-purpose, universal demon in Freddy drag.

Playing herself, original *Nightmare* heroine Langenkamp is married to FX ace Chase Porter (Newsom), who's about to embark on a new Freddy flick when Fred gets his infamous claws on him. An earthquake rocks Chase's subsequent funeral, where Heather and young son Dylan (Hughes) encounter Freddy and, from there, a series of events recorded in director Craven's script-in-progress for the film we're watching. Seems that Craven is nothing less than mankind's potential savior; by keeping Freddy "imprisoned" in celluloid, he's effectively prevented the *real* demon Freddy represents from intruding on our reality. That this rather immodest conceit actually works is a credit to Craven's creative prowess. Craven lenses his *New Nightmare* in a nearly verité style that lends the film a radically different look from that of its predecessors. While *New Nightmare* lacks the pure shock value of the original and the dark wit and wild surrealism of *Nightmare 3*, it handily bests the rest of the series.

Filmmakers in Focus!

CRAVEN IMAGES
WES CRAVEN ON HIS *NEW NIGHTMARE*

As Told to The Phantom

Following a less-than-amicable split with New Line honcho Robert Shaye, Wes Craven set out to "bury Freddy" with his competing 1989 scare pic Shocker *(see index). Craven and Shaye later buried the celluloid hatchet to collaborate on Freddy's "final" fling.*

PHANTOM: *New Nightmare* is probably the most serious Freddy film since your original *Nightmare on Elm Street*.

CRAVEN: That's what I wanted to do. I didn't quite know *how* to do it at first, but I knew I wanted to bring it up to a different level. I went back and looked at all the films—I must say, after a while, it was sort of a dulling experience—and I thought I had to just jump the context, jump the paradigm somehow. I had lunch with Heather [Langenkamp], whom I hadn't seen in a while—I felt I wanted her to star in the film if I did it—and we found ourselves talking about what it meant to have done this film. So that was the first half, just realizing that whole thing was kind of fascinating to talk about.

The other half was a dream I had. It was this wacky dream where we were all at a cocktail party to celebrate the tenth anniversary of the original *Nightmare* and the demise of Freddy. Robert Englund comes in dressed up like Freddy and was dancing around, slapping high-fives, and I was thinking it was kind of a long way from the spirit of the first film. Then I noticed that the shadow he was throwing against the wall was much larger than he was and not moving quite with him. When I tried to figure out what the dream was, I concluded that whatever was that thing out there that we gave the name Freddy Krueger is eternal, just part of human nature, part of our history in many different forms. It doesn't have a fixed shape or name, but I, as a writer, gave it this persona; because this persona stops doesn't mean this thing stops. That in some way this thing contains or controls certain frightening aspects of our lives.

PHANTOM: In *New Nightmare*, he's less Freddy the child-killer than an all-purpose demon or symbol of evil.

CRAVEN: If we'd had the money, he'd have gone through a lot of different permutations. We tried to keep him more unknown, unknowable.

PHANTOM: The body count is the lowest of any *Nightmare* film.

CRAVEN: It's very low. As a matter of fact, at one point, that was a specific note from New Line: "Not enough people die." Bob [Shaye] kept giving me suggestions: "What if the postman gets killed?" He had all these different characters we could concoct and kill off! But that wasn't what this one's about.

PHANTOM: The hospital scenes in *New Nightmare* are especially unnerving.

CRAVEN: When I was nineteen, I came down with a devastating paralysis—Joseph Heller the writer had it also—so I was in a hospital for about six months. I have very accurate memories of hospitals and what's scary about

(continued)

NOSFERATU   (1922) B&W ***½

D: F. W. Murnau. Max Schreck, Alexander Granach, Greta Schroeder. 84 mins. (Kino) DVD

Most prior versions of Murnau's vampioneer run 63 minutes, but Kino's restored edition clocks in at 84. In addition to rediscovered scenes, Kino's *Nosferatu* also features new intertitles translated from the original German prints. Heavy on shadow and gloom but fairly swiftly paced, *Nosferatu* sticks pretty close to Bram Stoker's *Dracula*—too close, it seemed, to suit the then-recently deceased author's estate: English courts ordered all negatives burned. Fortunately, German authorities ignored the decree; though Murnau's piratical tactics may have been sleazy, few fright-film fans today would begrudge *Nosferatu* its celluloid survival. Murnau devotes most of his attention to the novel's earlier passages: real estate agent Harker's (rechristened "Kuller") journey to Dracula's (now Count Orlok) creepy castle (actual Carpathian locations were used for these scenes); his victimization at the fangs of the skeletal vampire (Schreck's count easily cops Ugliest Vampire of All Time honors); and the fiend's stormy cruise to Wisborg (subbing for London). Indeed, the section chronicling the vampire's voyage is arguably *Nosferatu*'s strongest, with Murnau granting considerable screen time to the count's pitiless annihilation of the hapless crew. Arrow Video, meanwhile, offers *Nosferatu: The First Vampire*, an "updated" edition, hosted by David Carradine and featuring a new score composed and performed by the Goth rock group Type O Negative.

NOSFERATU: THE VAMPYRE (1979) ***½

D: Werner Herzog. Klaus Kinski, Isabelle Adjani, Bruno Ganz, Roland Topor. 107 mins. (Anchor Bay) DVD

Herzog crafts an eerily lyrical reinterpretation of Murnau's silent classic. Idiosyncratic screen heavy Kinski delivers a chilling portrayal of the bloodthirsty count, with makeup modeled on Murnau's Max Schreck, while Adjani projects pale beauty and quiet courage as Lucy, the wife of bitten Jonathan Harker (Ganz) and the most formidable foe Drac faces in his scheme to infest London with plague-bearing rats. Haunting imagery abounds (*vide:* the death-surrounded street banquets held by a maddened citizenry), imagery pristinely preserved in a digitally mastered wide-screen edition, spoken in English by the heavily accented cast.

THE OFFSPRING   (1986) **½

D: Jeff Burr. Vincent Price, Clu Gulager, Cameron Mitchell, Rosalind Cash, Terry Kiser, Susan Tyrrell. 99 mins. (Artisan)

The Offspring (formerly *From a Whisper to a Scream*) is a slow-moving fear anthology that muffs more opportunities than it exploits. The feeble though well-acted wraparound features a restrained Tyrrell as a reporter who quizzes Oldfield, Tennessee, librarian Price re the town's sinister rep. Price obligingly reels off four fright vignettes centering on such wholesome small-town activities as necrophilia, glass eating, and torture of every insidious stripe. Of course, any film dealing with such eternal topics would have a hard time being *completely* lame, and *The Offspring* occasionally succeeds in creating an honestly creepy atmosphere. Best here are the first story, with Gulager as a milquetoast who—in one of the pic's sicker twists—sires a living-dead mutant, and the Lovecraft's Traveling Circus episode, wherein pigging out on razor blades leads to a gory case of indigestion. Also of interest is the stellar supporting cast: Cameron Mitchell, ex-Hammer starlet Martine Beswick, and the late Angelo Rossitto (typecast, once again, as a dwarf).

THE OLD DARK HOUSE   (1932) B&W ***

D: James Whale. Boris Karloff, Melvyn Douglas, Charles Laughton, Gloria Stuart, Lillian Bond, Ernest Thesiger, Raymond Massey. 71 mins. (Kino) DVD

Loosely based on the J. B. Priestley novel *Benighted* and laced with deadpan wit, Whale's film spins on the even then hoary premise of a group of travelers being stranded at the mysterious title site during the course of a dark and stormy night. First to arrive are newlyweds Massey and Stuart (of *Titanic* fame) and their caustic pal Douglas, a card-carrying member of the post–World War I Lost Generation. They're soon joined by self-made businessman Laughton (in wonderfully eccentric form) and his companion Bond, who promptly tumbles for Douglas. As for the house's inhabitants, the Femm Clan is spooky enough to make the Addams Family look like the Brady Bunch (or is it the other way around?). The constantly quarreling brother-and-sister act of atheist Thesiger and religious zealot Eva Moore are in turn dominated by their brutish, bearded butler Karloff. Eerier surprises await our guests when they meet the family's 102-year-old progenitor (John Dudgeon) and his craziest offspring (Brember Wills), a pyromaniac who spends most of the film locked away in an upstairs room.

The Old Dark House exudes more black humor and musty melancholy than full-blown scares, but the pic, previously available only in poorly transferred bootleg tapes, easily succeeds in living up to its advance rep as a prime showcase for Whale's directorial talents and his ensemble cast's considerable skills. At the time, though, Universal honchos were more obsessed with pushing Karloff, who, fresh from his triumph in Whale's *Frankenstein,* not only receives top billing but is the subject of a fanciful precredits "Producer's Note." To wit: "Karloff, the mad butler in this production, is the same Karloff who created the part of the mechanical monster in *Frankenstein.* We explain this to settle all disputes in advance, even though such disputes are a tribute to his great versatility."

THE OMEN:
THE SERIES

THE OMEN (1976) ***

D: Richard Donner. Gregory Peck, Lee Remick, David Warner. 111 mins. (Fox)

Beleaguered parents Peck and Remick try to cope with a brat from hell in Donner's genuinely scary mainstream horror flick, which spawned three uninspired sequels: *Damien: Omen 2; The Final Conflict;* and *Omen 4: The Awakening* (all Fox).

ONIBABA (1964) B&W ****

D: Kaneto Shindo. Nobuko Otowa, Jitsuko Yoshimura, Kei Sato. 104 mins. (Home Vision)

For sheer unrelieved eeriness, Shindo's *Onibaba* is tough to beat. Set in a war-torn medieval Japan, the film follows life-hardened Otowa and her young war-widow daughter-in-law, Yoshimura, on their at-once grim and greedy rounds as they routinely finish off wounded warriors, selling their swords and armor to a sleazy forest fence. Deserter and neighbor Sato returns home and begins a torrid affair with Yoshimura, much to Otowa's chagrin, since *she* covets his sexual attention. After leading a grotesquely masked samurai to his death, Otowa dons the hideous demon visage herself in a bid to throw a scare into Yoshimura.

Shindo's erotic terror tale is greatly abetted by an atmospheric setting—endless undulating reed fields—stunning B&W cinematography, a subtle kodo drum score, and an overwhelming aura of human depravity. Home Vision presents this hypnotic classic in a pristine, digitally remastered wide-screen edition.

THE OTHER (1972) ***

D: Robert Mulligan. Chris and Martin Udvarnoky, Uta Hagen, Diana Muldaur, Norma Connolly, Victor French, John Ritter. 100 mins. (Fox)

Mulligan's adaptation of thesp-turned-writer Tom (*I Married a Monster from Outer Space*) Tryon's best-seller deals with towheaded twins who wreak lethal havoc on an otherwise idyllic Kansas farm in the 1930s. *The Other* isn't formulaic mainstream pseudo-scare fare in an *Audrey Rose* (MGM) vein but a genuinely creepy thriller that sneaks up on the viewer.

PALE BLOOD (1991) **½

D: V. V. Hsu. George Chakiris, Wings Hauser, Pamela Ludwig, Darcy DeMoss. 93 mins. (SVS, n.i.d.)

Pale Blood stars an almost eerily youthful-looking Chakiris, of *West Side Story* immortality, as a courtly, nonlethal Euro vampire who carries his own collapsible canvas travel coffin (!). George journeys to L.A., where he hires femme shamus Ludwig to investigate the gruesome handiwork of the " Vampire Killer," the type of amateur psycho bloodsucker who gives legit vampires a bad name. Also in the mix are the always welcome Hauser, who contributes his typically over-the-top all as a demented video artist, and the rock band Agent Orange. *Pale Blood* stacks up as a neat variation on standard vampire lore executed with flair on a low budget.

PAPERHOUSE (1989) ***

D: Bernard Rose. Glenne Headley, Charlotte Burke, Elliott Spiers, Ben Cross. 94 mins. (Vestron)

When 11-year-old Brit schoolgirl Anna (Burke) sketches a crude house on her notepad, she seems at first to be engaging in harmless play. That outwardly innocent artistic activity soon takes a scarier turn, however, when Anna begins visiting that selfsame haunt in a series of vivid nightmares that find her communing with the isolated abode's lone, unlikely inhabitant—a sickly adolescent named Marc (Spiers). Events grow downright spooky when Anna learns that Marc is not a figment of her imagination but an actual patient of Anna's own physician, a boy she's never met in her waking life. While Rose's *Paperhouse* hinges on potentially life-threatening nightmares, the pic is situated a safe distance from Elm Street. Rock-video vet Rose forgoes gore and standard haunted-house hallucinations in favor of a Val Lewton–like approach to his semi-supernatural story line, adapted from Catherine Storr's novel *Marianne Dreams.* The result is a largely successful mix of mystery, poignancy, and dread.

PARANOIAC (1963) B&W ***

D: Freddie Francis. Janette Scott, Oliver Reed, Liliane Brousse, Alexander Davion. 80 mins. (Universal)

Greedy playboy Reed is three weeks away from inheriting a bundle from his late parents' estate but wants his unstable sister's (Scott) cut as well. He sets up Davion to impersonate his dead younger brother in hopes of pushing her over the edge. As our story unfolds, it becomes increasingly clear that Reed is the crazy one, escalating from mere destructive irresponsibility—"There are certain standards," aunt Sheila Burrell reproaches him, "even for the rich!"—to attacks of acute paranoia. Though much of Francis's directorial debut is fairly routine, a few scenes stand out, most memorably the movie's consummately macabre finale, and Reed offers a textured, blackly funny turn as the paranoid plotter.

PEEPING TOM (1960) ****

D: Michael Powell. Carl Boehm, Moira Shearer, Anna Massey, Brenda Bruce, Maxine Audley, Martin Miller. 101 mins. (Home Vision, Criterion) DVD

The pre-*Psycho* world wasn't ready for a snuff-movie thriller, particularly one directed by a distinguished auteur like Michael Powell, whose previous work (with writer/partner Emeric Pressburger, a team known as "the Archers") included such beloved classics as *The Red Shoes, The Tales of Hoffmann* (both Home Vision), and *Stairway to Heaven* (a.k.a. *A Matter of Life and Death* [see index]). That *Peeping Tom* was not just a chiller but a meditation on those voyeuristic impulses that make a film industry possible (even mandatory) in the first place was lost on most critics of the day. Ocular imagery dominates, from the opening shot of an arrow hitting a round target's center (the Archers' standard logo) to a hooker's eye seen in extreme close-up through photog

Filmmakers in Focus!
MICHAEL POWELL ON *PEEPING TOM*

* *

The following is excerpted from an address delivered by Michael Powell, on August 13, 1989, at the American Museum of the Moving Image in Astoria, New York. Martin Scorsese, who'd long cited Peeping Tom *as one of his fave films, was instrumental in locating and restoring a mint 16-millimeter print for screening at the AMMI's Powell fest. Powell—whose often ironic inflections, cadence, and anecdotal powers are unfortunately diminished in the translation to print—died in 1990, at age 85.*

First of all, of course, comes the writer. Leo Marks was a remarkable little demon. His father had a very famous bookshop in Charing Cross Road—they made a film about it....Leo Marks had been watching me for some time, at various meetings and with other people. This morning he says to me, "Mr. Powell, how would you like to make a film about a young man who photographs the women he kills." I said, "Ooh, yes, that's me. That's a great idea. Let's go." He said, "Well, how do we go about it?" I said, "Well, you've probably got the idea in your head now. Why don't you come in twice a week, bring me what you've written, and we'll go over it and talk about it and evolve the script that way together. You'll write without me bothering you in the room. That should work."

And that's what we did. Evenings at nine o'clock he would turn up at my apartment, twice a week, smoking this new cigar and always very formal. And always with very good ideas. I said, "There's too much dialogue." He said, "Mr. Powell, you can't tell a story without dialogue." I said, "Oh, yes, I can. If you write these long dialogue scenes, you'll find they're on the cutting room floor." He said, "No doubt we can compromise."

So we completed the script and were rather pleased with it. I took it to Anglo-Amalgamated, a little firm run by two delightful fellows called Nat Cohn and Stuart Levy. Nat Cohn was very keen on it. And I said to him, "What do you think of Laurence Harvey for the young man in the story?" "Oh, that'd be great. Can you get him?" I said, "Well, yes, he's working next door at Shepperton and he's just finishing up a film, he's making *Room at the Top,* and I've told him about this and he wants to do it."

Then suddenly Laurence Harvey came into my stage from his stage: "They're crazy about my film. They've seen all the rushes in Hollywood. I've got an offer to play opposite Elizabeth Taylor in *Butterfield 8.* And what's more, they want to sign me up and I'll play with all the Hollywood leading ladies. Because they haven't had a new leading man to play with [or go to bed with] for a long time." I said, "Well, can't you do it first, Larry—do the film first and then the rest of the program?" But he wouldn't. And I don't blame him. You've gotta grab a chance like that when it comes.

So then I had to find somebody. At a party I ran into Carl Boehm, who was a young Austrian, the son of Karl Böhm, the great conductor. And he wanted to be a conductor too, but of course his father didn't like that idea very much. And so he was thinking of turning actor. I had seen him in a film in Austria. So Nat Cohn said, "Is everything going all right?" "Everything's going splendidly. Oh, by the way, Laurence Harvey can't be in the film. I've got Carl Boehm instead." He says, "Who?" I said, "Carl Boehm." He wasn't pleased about that at all. I said, "Well, he's very good, very sensitive, I'm sure he can play the part." So we got over that hurdle for a bit.

This film was good because we all loved doing it. And we all understood what the other one wanted. And we all cared what the other one wanted. And I can assure you that is very rare in the film business....That was a film that was made with love, by everybody. And yet, when it was shown to the critics, they hated it. They didn't just think it was unnecessary to make it; they just *loathed* it. And they couldn't say why. But they killed it. They killed it for twenty years.

Carl and I, just two dreamers, we came to the premiere in London in dinner jackets, black tie, and saw it together, with everybody, the special-critics invitation people, and they all came out afterwards and passed by us and nobody spoke to us—just like in the movies! And the press came out saying, "What a terrible, disgusting, loathsome piece of shit. For God's sake, wash it down the toilet. Take it off." They used language like that. I was just—dazed. I had no idea the critics were so innocent. So I said to the distributor, Nat Cohn, "Look, let's do what somebody did years and years ago when they made a film of a Broadway play, *Mother Goddamn*." It all took place in a whorehouse, and that was a bit new then. I said, "Let's take space in all the papers and say this is what the critics said—this unbelievable abuse—come and judge for yourselves. Keep the film running. It'll do." But they wouldn't do it. They took it off that night; they yanked it. And it was booked already for all 'round the country. They probably made about fifty prints....They took it out of release, and Anglo-Amalgamated sold it to somebody for television and showed it in black and white here. It took me a long time later on, when I had the chance, with the help of Martin Scorsese; we discovered where the negative was and what sort of state it was in and saved it.

Boehm's lens, to his own three-eyed camera and cyclopean projector. Boehm is alternately timid and creepy as the camera-obsessed film technician, part-time pornographer, and full-time psycho determined to capture verité death on film, while Audley is strong as the sightless, hard-drinking downstairs neighbor who's on to his madness. (Says she, "The blind always live in the rooms they live under.") Massey, as Audley's sensitive, appealing daughter, is herself at work on a children's book about a magic camera; she and Boehm form a mutual attraction.

Though there's no gore in evidence, Boehm's bladed tripod makes for a terrifying weapon and the murder sequences are intensely intimate. Powell shot the home-movie scenes—both Boehm's and his sinister biologist father's (a silent cameo by Powell him-self)—in black and white. Black humor also abounds as Powell aims satirical barbs at the hack, economy-minded side of the British film industry and entrusts the killer's investigation to three semicomic detectives. ("I don't want to spoil anyone's fun," says one, "but we do have a maniac on our hands.") Powell, unjustly, had a celluloid scandal on *his*. Fortunately, through the efforts of cinephiles like Martin Scorsese, the critically devastated *Peeping Tom* has at last reached the audience it has always deserved. Home Vision's new "restored" video is identical to the earlier version issued on Canada's Admit One label, except for the inclusion of the original Anglo-Amalgamated logo. The transfer quality is superior, though. Both clock in at 101 mins., not the 109 that most sources list.

PET SEMATARY: THE SERIES

PET SEMATARY (1989) **

D: Mary Lambert. Dale Midkiff, Denise Crosby, Fred Gwynne, Brad Greenquist, Michael Lombard, Blaze Berdahl. 102 mins. (Paramount)

Trouble begins when the Creed family (dad Midkiff, mom Crosby, their two kids and pet cat) move into an otherwise idyllic New England home that has one serious drawback: It's situated on a road thick with high-speed monster-truck traffic—not a primo spot for raising pets and tots. Elderly neighbor Gwynne (affecting a heavy Yankee twang) confirms that assessment when he leads the Creeds to the titular graveyard, final resting place for decades' worth of hapless roadkill. When Church the cat becomes a hit-and-run victim, Gwynne directs Midkiff to another, secret cemetery, a former Indian burial ground possessed of magical restorative powers, where they inter the felled feline. Church returns to life all right, but as a four-legged fiend. The same fate awaits the Creeds' two-year-old son after he likewise joins the ranks of road fatalities, with even darker results. *Pet Sematary* emerges as a sick, tasteless, but not very successful attempt to exploit common familial fears. A few genuine shocks survive, and fans of author King (who contributes his usual on-screen cameo, as a local minister) should find *Pet Sematary* of at least passing interest.

PET SEMATARY II (1992) **½

D: Mary Lambert. Edward Furlong, Anthony Edwards, Clancy Brown, Darlanne Fluegel. 100 mins. (Paramount)

Minor improvements here include less emphasis on explaining the stupid premise, more over-the-top gore FX (courtesy of Steve Johnson), and Brown's scenery-and-flesh-chewing turn as one of scare screendom's most animated—nay, downright hyperactive—zombies. (*Pet Sematary II* features what may be the first necrophilia scene where the corpse is the sexual aggressor!) In the hands of returning auteur Lambert, *Pet Sematary II* doesn't break any new ground (burial or otherwise), but it does deliver on a straight-ahead horror level.

PHANTASM:
THE SERIES

PHANTASM   (1979) ***1/2

D: Don Coscarelli. A. Michael Baldwin, Bill Thornbury, Reggie Bannister, Kathy Lester, Angus Scrimm. 87 mins. (MGM) DVD

On the surface, Coscarelli's *Phantasm* would seem to be just another simpleminded scare pic. But when viewed as the understandably lurid nightmare of an otherwise ordinary adolescent boy, Mike (Baldwin), trying to adjust to the unfathomable loss of his parents and his own vanishing childhood, *Phantasm* weaves a powerful primal spell and introduces a memorable celluloid bogeyman in "Tall Man" Scrimm, an evil, otherworldly mortician. It's easy to see why *Phantasm* became an enduring one-of-a-kind cult fave and why Coscarelli and crew couldn't quite recapture the black magic in the widely separated sequels.

PHANTASM II   (1988) **1/2

D: Don Coscarelli. James LeGros, Reggie Bannister, Angus Scrimm, Paula Irvine, Samantha Phillips. 90 mins. (Universal)

In Coscarelli's first, belated sequel, Mike (LeGros), now 19, is being released from a mental institution where he's passed the last seven years being treated for his horrific "hallucinations." No sooner does Mike set foot in

"reality" than the Tall Man (reprised by a spectral Scrimm) is at it again, robbing graveyards of their cadaverous contents and unleashing his new, improved flying silver spheres—replete with brain-draining drills—whenever the urge arises (which, as you might imagine, is fairly often). Mike enlists the aid of fellow *Phantasm* survivor Bannister to fight this formidable embodiment of their deepest fears with a Rambo-esque arsenal of chainsaws, flamethrowers, and four-barreled shotguns. Like its model, *Phantasm II*, while operating on a lower plane, works less on a logical than on a filmic fever-dream level, but most of the original chill is gone.

PHANTASM III: LORD OF THE DEAD (1994) **1/2

D: Don Coscarelli. Reggie Bannister, Angus Scrimm, A. Michael Baldwin, Bill Thornbury, John Davis Chandler. 91 mins. (Universal)

For *Phantasm III*, auteur Coscarelli recycles the most crowd-pleasing elements from his earlier films—original cast members Baldwin, Bannister, and Thornbury, those ever popular flying silver spheres with the retractable spikes, the malevolent Tall Man (Scrimm) and his hooded mutant-dwarf minions (or "lurkers"), elaborate morgue sets, furtive glimpses into a demonic dimension, and even Bannister's trusty four-barreled shotgun. Still, *Phantasm III* adds up to considerably less than the sum of its parts, a plotless repetitive journey through a nearly deserted rural Idaho ("Half the county's been wiped out, and nobody's figured it out yet," notices Reg), spiced only by sporadic bursts of effective nightmare imagery and an admittedly vivid sense of ominous desolation. Like the other sequels, Coscarelli's overly busy 1998 *Phantasm: Oblivion* (Orion) boasts its share of effective scenes but ultimately seems more willed than organic.

THE PHANTOM OF THE OPERA (1925) B&W/COLOR***1/2

D: Rupert Julian. Lon Chaney, Mary Philbin, Norman Kerry. 101 mins. (Kino) DVD

An ever amazing Chaney dominates as the deranged, disfigured but oft sympathetic title character in Rupert Julian's opulent, poignant, and creepy silent-film giant. Kino's definitive edition comes complete with the lavish two-strip Technicolor "Bal Masque" sequence.

PHANTOM OF THE OPERA (1943) ***

D: Arthur Lubin. Claude Rains, Susanna Foster, Nelson Eddy. 92 mins. (Universal)

While it could have used more Phantom and less Opera, Lubin's gala Technicolor rendering of Gaston Leroux's timeless terror tale boasts its share of highlights, including the chandelier scene and Claude's disastrous encounter with a crass music publisher.

THE PHANTOM OF THE OPERA (1962) ***

D: Terence Fisher. Herbert Lom, Heather Sears, Edward DeSouza, Michael Gough, Thorley Walters. 84 mins. (Universal)

Veteran Hammer horror hand Fisher helms a highly enjoyable version of the Leroux tale. Lom, in a role originally planned for Christopher Lee, has little to do till the last couple of reels, when he proves his thespian mettle via his complex interpretation of the masked madman. The opening scene retains its shock value, the single tear dripping from the Phantom's mask provides a nice touch, and there's a gratuitous gore moment when Lom's personal jerk, identified only as "The Dwarf" (Ian Wilson), stabs an errant rat-catcher in the eye for no particularly urgent reason. Miles Malleson, indelibly imprinted in fright fans' minds as the cheerfully ominous omnibus conductor in the 1945 anthology *Dead of Night* ("Room for one more, sir"), enjoys an in-joke turn as a comic-relief carriage driver. The falling-chandelier money shot caps a somewhat rushed climax. An extra six minutes of footage added to pad the pic's 1960s television release have been excised—to the good, since even at 84 minutes this *Phantom* suffers from occasionally slack pacing.

THE PHANTOM OF THE OPERA (1989) **½

D: Dwight Little. Robert Englund, Jill Schoelen, Alex Hyde-White, Stephanie Lawrence. 93 mins. (Columbia/TriStar)

In its fourth official celluloid mounting, Leroux's venerable opus serves primarily as a vehicle for Englund, who doffs his Freddy Krueger duds to don the Phantom's classier cloak. This *Phantom* sticks fairly close to the original in retelling the familiar tale of crazed, disfigured composer Erik's obsessive efforts to see his masterwork produced at the Paris Opera House with aspiring diva/unrequited-love object Christine (*The Stepfather*'s Schoelen) in the lead. The filmmakers try to inject a novel note or two by shifting the action to Jack the Ripper's London (an underutilized thread) and sandwiching the main story within a contempo wraparound that finds a modern-day Christine being propelled back to Erik's time after discovering his charred *Don Juan Triumphant* score in an NYC music library. Despite these alterations, Little's *Phantom* is essentially a straightforward, old-fashioned fright film reminiscent of a standard 1960s Hammer horror and encompassing the latter's typical virtues and flaws. There's also a good deal more gore than we saw in the *Phantoms* of yore (Englund's Erik alternately skins and decapitates his victims), with makeup FX courtesy of Kevin Yagher. Dario Argento's over-the-top interpretation *The Phantom of the Opera* arrived in late '99 (A-Pix, DVD), with Julian Sands as the Phantom and Asia Argento as his reluctant protégée.

PHANTOM OF THE PARADISE (1974) ***

D: Brian De Palma. William Finley, Paul Williams, Jessica Harper, Gerrit Graham, George Memmoli. 92 mins. (Key)

De Palma's clever takeoff/update is a *Phantom of the Opera* Meets *Faust*, set against a decadent backstage rock world. Finley plays naïve composer Winslow Leach, who suffers unceasingly at the hands of diabolical impresario Williams (whose smarmy presence represents the film's only serious drawback) while trying to help ingenue Harper gain singing stardom. *Phantom* is a bright, savvy satire on the music industry that also delivers its fair share of chills, twists, and texture. Special kudos go to Graham as fey glitter-rock animal Beef, the key figure in the wittiest *Psycho* shower-scene send-up we've seen. And Sissy Spacek designed the sets! Richard Friedman's 1989 *Phantom of the Mall: Erik's Revenge* (Fries) and Allen Plone's 1988 *Phantom of the Ritz* (Prism) are two additional updates that are well worth avoiding.

THE PICTURE OF DORIAN GRAY (1945) B&W/COLOR***

D: Albert Lewin. Hurd Hatfield, George Sanders, Donna Reed, Angela Lansbury. 110 mins. (MGM)

Lewin's stately original remains the best of several adaptations of Wilde's darkly witty fable. Those truly wild about Oscar's work can also obtain the 1971 remake, with Helmut Berger as Wilde's young/old antihero (Republic); the 1974 made-for-Brit-TV version (Thriller Video), starring Shane Briant; and 1982's *Sins of Dorian Gray* (Playhouse), with Anthony Perkins and Joseph Bottoms. For an excellent portrait of the writer himself, scope out 1997's *Wilde* (Columbia/TriStar), starring Stephen Fry in an uncanny performance.

PIN (1988) ***

D: Sandor Stern. David Hewlett, Cyndy Preston, Terry O'Quinn, John Ferguson, Bronwen Nantel, Jacob Tierney. 103 mins. (New World, Starmaker)

Subtitled *A Plastic Nightmare* for its video incarnation, *Pin* was barely released theatrically until NYC's Film Forum rescued it for a critically acclaimed two-week run in 1992. Stern's strange thriller features O'Quinn in another superlative bad-dad perf (though a subtler one than his two *Stepfather* stints). Terry plays Dr. Linden, a normally grim grammar-school physician who indulges in one odd bit of whimsy—working a ventriloquism act with his life-sized anatomical dummy, Pin (short for Pinocchio, because the dummy never lies). Young daughter Ursula understands the trick, but disturbed son Leon begins to believe in Pin's autonomy, a belief that only grows after dad O'Quinn and mom Nantel expire in a car crash. A college-age Leon (Hewlett) later employs Pin to control teen sis Ursula (Preston), and the lines between Leon and Pin continue to blur as the reels advance. While *Pin* owes an obvious debt to Hitch's *Psycho* (as do hundreds of other films) in its plot and antirepression sentiments, the pic still scores high marks in the suspense and originality departments.

THE PIT AND THE PENDULUM (1961) **½

D: Roger Corman. Vincent Price, Barbara Steele, John Kerr. 80 mins. (Warner)

As usual, this Corman production has precious little connection with Poe, beyond the admittedly vital presence of the titular torture devices. It's fun enough in its own sometimes slow-moving right, though, and represents Price and Steele's only screen pairing.

THE PIT AND THE PENDULUM (1991) ***

D: Stuart Gordon. Lance Henriksen, Rona De Ricci, Oliver Reed, Jonathan Fuller, Jeffrey Combs, Tom Towles. 97 mins. (Paramount)

The dark, subversive wit of Gordon and scripter/fellow Organic Theater alum Dennis Paoli surfaces early in this Poe redo, in a scene, set in 1492 Spain, that sees deranged Inquisitor Torquemada (an ideally cast Henriksen) posthumously punish an alleged heretic by applying 20 lashes to his exhumed cadaver (!). Gordon and Paoli proceed to satirize the Inquisition's S&M insanity by detailing Lance's lustful persecution of an innocent wench (the fetching De Ricci), while recycling elements from Poe's "Premature Burial" and "The Cask of Amontillado," among others. While it doesn't reach *Re-Animator*'s heights, this *Pit*—bolstered by supporting thesps Reed, Combs, and Towles—is the most creative Poe-inspired fear flick to turn up since Roger Corman's *Masque of the Red Death*.

POLTERGEIST:
THE SERIES

POLTERGEIST (1982) ***1/2

D: Tobe Hooper. JoBeth Williams, Craig T. Nelson, Heather O'Rourke, Zelda Rubinstein. 114 mins. (MGM) DVD

After a sometimes cloyingly cute opening reel, this Spielberg production gets down to serious business with one of the most visually spectacular spook-outs in celluloid history. While the film is undeniably more effective on the big screen, video at least adds a certain verité note to the evil spirits' initial entry via our Typical American Family's TV. And pint-sized psychic Rubinstein gets a bit less lost in the smaller surroundings.

POLTERGEIST II: THE OTHER SIDE (1986) **1/2

D: Brian Gibson. JoBeth Williams, Craig T. Nelson, Will Sampson, Geraldine Fitzgerald, Julian Beck, Heather O'Rourke, Zelda Rubinstein. 91 mins. (MGM)

This much maligned first sequel to the Spielberg/Hooper horror hit follows the fleeing Freeling family as they kiss their haunted hacienda good-bye and light out for hopefully greener pastures. Unfortunately for them, they're tailed by the evil spirit of the deranged Reverend Kane ("Living Theater" cofounder Beck in a suitably sinister, serpentine turn), former leader of a 19th-century Jonestown-type cult, and the restless ghosts of his followers. "Magic munchkin" Rubinstein returns, accompanied by Native American shaman Sampson, to help the embattled Freelings win their latest spooky duke-out. While *Poltergeist II* can't hold a bell, book, or candle to its predecessor, there are enough grisly surprises here to keep the ghostly goings-on from growing dull. A scene wherein young Robbie Freeling (Oliver Roberts) is nearly strangled to death by his own braces (!) adds a fresh dimension to the realm of orthodontal terror, and the floating chainsaw's good for a cheap chill. *Poltergeist II* even coughs up 1986's best credit line—"Vomit Creature played by Noble Craig" (even if his barf *is* worse than his bite).

POLTERGEIST III (1988) *

D: Gary Sherman. Tom Skerritt, Nancy Allen, Heather O'Rourke, Zelda Rubinstein, Richard Fire, Nathan Davis. 97 mins. (MGM)

The slack, lifeless *Poltergeist III* makes the merely passable *Polter-geist II* look like, well, *Poltergeist*. This ghostly go-round finds the persistent Preacher Kane (Davis replacing the late Beck) shadowing Carol Ann (O'Rourke, who died, at age 12, shortly after the film's completion) to a Chicago condo. Nearly an hour passes before Kane even deigns to claim his first and only victim. Not even the weak FX work offers much relief from the hack script and Sherman's stilted direction. Richard Fire, as the pic's obnoxious shrink, sums it up best when he shouts, "Enough! Stop this stupid sideshow!" MGM pulled the plug on this fright franchise shortly thereafter, before resurrecting it nearly a decade later as a cable-TV series, launched by the feature-length pilot *Poltergeist: The Legacy* (MGM).

THE PREMATURE BURIAL (1962) **1/2

D: Roger Corman. Ray Milland, Hazel Court, Richard Ney. 81 mins. (Vestron)

Milland has a phobia about being buried alive, which leads to the film's highlight—a nightmare sequence that finds our protagonist in precisely that predicament. The rest of the film is pretty forgettable—until, of course, Ray *does* get buried alive, in the movie's other memorable scene.

PRINCE OF DARKNESS (1987) **1/2

D: John Carpenter. Donald Pleasence, Lisa Blount, Jameson Parker, Victor Wong, Dennis Dun, Peter Jason. 102 mins. (Universal) DVD

Carpenter's *Prince of Darkness* pits a team of physicists against an agitated vat of vile living liquid holed up in the basement of an abandoned L.A. church. Priest Pleasence determines that the churning green gunk, protected over the centuries by the secret Brotherhood of Sleep sect, is actually none other than the son of Satan struggling to be reborn. And that's Carpenter's cue to crowd the screen with a dizzying procession of gore slaughters, demonic possessions, rampaging maggots, dark transmissions from the future, and other fun fright stuff. JC also composed the minimalist score, while Alice Cooper contributes a thankfully silent cameo as a "street schizo." The movie's ultimate message, though, relayed midway through via a possessed computer, hails from the devil himself: "You will not be saved by the Holy Ghost. You will not be saved by the god Plutonium. In fact, *you will not be saved!*"

PRISON (1988) ***

D: Renny Harlin. Lane Smith, Viggo Mortensen, Chelsea Field, Lincoln Fitzpatrick, André De Shields, Ivan Kane. 102 mins. (New World, Starmaker)

The vengeful spirit of a convict that Creedmore Prison warden Smith railroaded into the chair a couple of decades ago is back for blood, and he's not particularly choosy about whose he spills. Even liberal prison-board rep Field can do little to improve the supernatural situation; as might be imagined, however, future major mainstream-movie helmer Harlin's *Prison* ("Horror Has a New Home!") is less an impassioned plea for penal reform than a straight-ahead slayfest. Surprisingly, the pic actually works better as a traditional men's-prison movie than it does as a horror outing. The characters are deftly sketched—especially Kilpatrick as a lifer who knows the warden's deep, dark secret, and Kane as Lasagna, a would-be Sly Stallone clone—the script is tight, and the inmate intrigues are kept fairly credible. While the FX are pretty routine, the decaying Creedmore set aids immeasurably in augmenting the movie's genuinely claustrophobic feel.

THE PROPHECY:
THE SERIES

THE PROPHECY (1995) ***

D: Gregory Widen. Christopher Walken, Virginia Madsen, Elias Koteas, Eric Stoltz, Amanda Plummer, Viggo Mortensen. 97 mins. (Dimension) DVD

Scripter *(Highlander)*/debuting auteur Widen fashions an original, surreal fright fantasy about a "Second War in Heaven" that spills onto earth. After a dead angel—with no eyes but dual sex organs, no less—turns up in an alley, "good" angel Simon (Stoltz) contacts failed-priest-turned-cop Koteas to warn him of an insidious plot. Trumpet-toting "bad" angel Gabriel (a showy Walken, playing the role in glib living-gargoyle style) shows up to steal the soul of a newly dead military strategist, a maniac who performed unspeakable atrocities during the Korean War, to help his troops plan their attack. Stoltz, meanwhile, has stashed the late officer's evil soul in the body of a little Indian girl (portrayed by the imaginatively monikered Moriah Shining Dove Snyder) who begins speaking in Freddy Krueger tones (!). While Widen apparently lacked the budget to give *The Prophecy* (originally titled *God's Army*) the sweeping treatment it deserved, he still offers many a memorable tableau, such as an infernal field of impaled angels, and concocts interesting twists on angel lore (e.g., they possess heightened olfactory abilities to compensate for their weak vision). Plummer is terrific as a dying woman "recruited" by Walken to serve as his combo zombie slave and chauffeur (!), while Mortensen is creepily intense in a last-reel cameo as the devil himself. Not every riff works and loose threads are left hanging, but *The Prophecy* stacks up as a thoughtful, chilling addition to the religious-horror subgenre. No relationship to John Frankenheimer's ill-conceived 1979 ecohorror, *Prophecy* (Paramount).

THE PROPHECY II (1997) **½

D: Greg Spence. Christopher Walken, Jennifer Beals, Russell Wong, Eric Roberts, Brittany Murphy, Glenn Danzig, Bruce Abbott, Tom Towles. 83 mins. (Dimension) DVD

Original auteur/now-producer Gregory Widen entrusts the directorial reins to Greg Spence. The result is a diluted but generally entertaining continuation of the conflict between evil angels led by Gabriel (Walken) and good angels headed by Michael (Roberts, in a last-reel cameo). Visiting angel Wong seduces good-hearted nurse Beals, instantly impregnating her with an angel/human hybrid (or "Nephalim"). Walken stalks Beals in a bid to destroy her and her threatening spawn; along the way he waxes philosophical, accumulates a sizable human-body count, and saves a suicidal punkette (Murphy) to serve as his slave and computer expert, leading to the pic's best line: "So you're keeping me alive because you don't know DOS?" Followed by *Prophecy 3: The Ascent* (2000, Dimension, DVD).

PSYCHO (1960) B&W ****

D: Alfred Hitchcock. Anthony Perkins, Janet Leigh, John Gavin, Vera Miles, Martin Balsam. 109 mins. (Universal) DVD

What more can we add about a film that's had entire books devoted to it and that virtually founded one of horrordom's most durable genres? Only that if you haven't seen it already, avail yourself of the video at once. (One final thought: If Anthony Perkins had played the Vincent Price role, the Fly might still be alive today.) Beware Gus Van Sant's mega-pointless, nearly note-for-note 1998 *Psycho* "recreation" (Universal, DVD), notable only for Vince Vaughn's giggle-driven Norman Bates interpretation and Robert Forster's last-reel turn as the windy shrink originally played by Simon Oakland.

PSYCHO II (1983) **½

D: Richard Franklin. Anthony Perkins, Vera Miles, Meg Tilly, Robert Loggia. 113 mins. (Universal) DVD

Franklin's belated sequel doesn't approach the original—though it proved a big-time summer-'83 box-officer winner—but turned out better than might have been expected, thanks largely to Perkins's on-target reprise of his role as Norman Bates, now "cured" of his psychoses following a long asylum stretch.

PSYCHO III (1986) ***

D: Anthony Perkins. Anthony Perkins, Diana Scarwid, Jeff Fahey, Roberta Maxwell, Hugh Gillin, Lee Garlington. 93 mins. (Universal) DVD

Norman Bates is alive and sick and again running the Bates Motel. Into our loony's lonely life comes convent runaway Maureen (Scarwid), who (unfortunately for her) puts Norm in mind of former thwarted flame Marion Crane (Janet Leigh in Hitch's original). While snoopy journalist Maxwell dogs his twisted trail, Norman digs Mom's knife and wig out of mothballs and reverts to his old nasty habits. All things considered, scripter Charles Pogue and director Perkins do a decent job with *Psycho III* (except when Tony the director lets Tony the thesp over-act, stuttering and twitching as if there were no tomorrow—or at least no *Psycho IV*). There's a neat ironic twist on the original shower scene, a number of choice lines (as when Norman under-states, "I feel a little sick!"), and even a tender moment or two between needy nutcases Norman and Maureen.

PSYCHO IV: THE BEGINNING (1991) **

D: Mick Garris. Anthony Perkins, Olivia Hussey, Henry Thomas, CCH Pounder, Warren Frost. 96 mins. (Universal)

PSYCHO: THE SERIES
MONDO PSYCHO:
BEHIND THE SCENES OF HITCHCOCK'S CLASSIC

THE *GEINESIS* OF *PSYCHO*

In 1959 Alfred Hitchcock acquired the rights to Robert Bloch's short novel *Psycho,* a pulp shocker loosely based on Ed Gein's real-life atrocities. Author Bloch received a princely $9,000 for the rights (before taxes and agent fees), while Hitch sent his people out to buy up as many copies of the book as possible to keep the title and concept secret from the public. After rejecting initial screenwriter James Cavanaugh's attempt to adapt the book, Hitchcock worked closely with relatively unknown scenarist (and future *Outer Limits* producer) Joseph Stefano to hone the final script for what, forty years later, many viewers still hail as the scariest movie ever made (though *Exorcist* disciples and *Night of the Living Dead* heads might put up a fight).

THE REEL DEAL

Honchos at Hitchcock's then-current studio, Paramount, initially wanted no part of what they perceived as a perverse project, grudgingly granting their star director a paltry $780,000 budget, 30-day shooting sked, and TV back lots to work in. When Hitch proposed to pony up his own dough in exchange for 60 percent of the profits, with Paramount serving solely in a distribution capacity, many industryites and even close friends wondered whether the legendary Master of Movie Suspense wasn't undergoing a psychotic breakdown of his own. (Bottom line: *Psycho* would earn over $14 million in its first quarter of release alone and would eventually make its creator one of Hollywood's wealthiest auteurs.) Hitchcock stretched his tight budget by hiring the crew from his popular teleseries, *Alfred Hitchcock Presents,* and shooting in black and white (which had always been his intent) with ultra-streamlined efficiency.

THE BATES ESTATE: HELL'S MOTEL

After researching the look of its seedy real-life counterparts, Hitchcock built the Bates Motel on the back lot. The propinquitous Victorian manse where homicidal hotelier Norman and mater Bates resided cost a mere $15,000 and was creatively cobbled together largely from leftover sets. (The infamous foreboding tower was borrowed from rabbit-happy James Stewart's home in 1950's *Harvey.*) With Hitchcock dead set on keeping the project shrouded in secrecy from the get-go, *Psycho* started rolling in 1959 under the working title *Wimpy* (!) but was more often referred to simply as "Production 9401."

THE CASTING OUCH

Several actresses were considered for the pivotal Marion Crane role—including glam queen Lana Turner and future *Carrie* mom Piper Laurie—but budgetary restrictions narrowed Hitch's list. The director was reportedly happy to land versatile (and ever game) starlet Janet Leigh, whose taboo-breaking role would abruptly and violently terminate 45 minutes into the film, and young anxiety specialist Anthony Perkins as Norman. He felt less sanguine about casting future ambassador to Mexico John Gavin as Marion's adulterous lover (preferred thesps included Jack Lord, Rod Taylor, and future "Billy Jack," Tom Laughlin). Hitch came up with his cleverest casting ploy by spreading rumors re who might play

"Mrs. Bates," bandying about the names of such celluloid grand dames as Judith Anderson and Helen Hayes. The director soon found himself deluged with offers from scores of established actresses "of a certain age" eager to tackle the nonexistent role. Hitch screen-tested the actual "Mrs. Bates" at Leigh's expense, placing the ossified mannequin, sans warning, in the actress's dressing room. Leigh later claimed her resultant real-life shrieking easily topped her on-screen screams.

THE SHOWER MUST GO ON

Few scenes before or since pack the visceral punch of the infamous shower scene where fugitive Marion Crane meets her high-decibel demise at the business end of granny-dressed Norman's flashing knife. Hitchcock ate up a full week of his skimpy shooting schedule to craft one of filmdom's most masterful and influential sequences: The 45-second scene required more than 70 camera setups and 90 editing cuts, with chocolate sauce subbing for the black-and-white blood. For the flesh-shearing sound effects, Hitch employed a knife stabbing a casaba melon while composer Bernard Herrmann's screeching violins further upped the auditory anxiety level. Censors originally rejected the scene due to perceived nudity; when Hitchcock resubmitted it, without making a single change, it was passed uncontested. Though it was widely accepted that a stand-in performed the scene, Leigh later stated in her autobiography, *There Really Was a Hollywood,* that she did much of the work herself, wearing a flesh-colored moleskin that quickly melted under the water's heat. An outsized, specially constructed, partially plugged nozzle kept the shower stream from splashing the camera but not from thoroughly soaking the crew. After Hitchcock had expended so much time and attention to detail, it was his wife, Alma, who pointed out a major glitch in the original cut—the "late" Ms. Leigh could be seen swallowing after Norman had delivered the coup de grâce. Hitchcock quickly corrected the error. In other bathroom-fixture breakthroughs, *Psycho* is commonly credited with being the first mainstream American film ever to show a flushing toilet (!).

HYPE MAKES RIGHT

Since he sank his own simoleons into the risky picture, Hitchcock, ever the showman in any case, revved into high promotional gear. The secrecy that had cloaked the filming was extended to the classic trailer, where, in lieu of revealing any actual *Psycho* snippets, the droll director leads the viewer on a teaser tour of the Bates Estate. Hitchcock's true stroke of ballyhoo genius was instructing bijou owners not to let patrons into the theater after the film began. Hitchcock read his era and audience with uncanny insight. That potentially offputting ploy ordained *Psycho* as *the* picture everyone *had* to see; failure to do so would be to risk becoming a cocktail-party, water-cooler, or schoolyard pariah.

LAUGHING LAST IN THE AFTERMATH

While *Psycho* succeeded in changing forever the face of movie horror and making its already comfy creator wealthy beyond his wildest dreams, the film also drew some negative feedback. The shocker scored a mixed response from stateside reviewers, but London critics almost universally reviled it, much as they had Michael Powell's ultra-edgy, thematically related *Peeping Tom* (see index) a few months earlier. Hitchcock himself received a letter from one disgruntled male viewer who reported that his wife, who'd refused to take baths after watching 1955's *Diabolique,* now shunned showers after seeing *Psycho.* Replied the ever wry Mr. H.: "Send her to the dry cleaners."

Psycho IV betrays its made-for-cable roots via static lensing and a pat framework: A supposedly rehabilitated Norman (Perkins in his final go-round) finds his homicidal impulses aroused when he hears his former shrink (Frost) expounding about oedipal killers on a local radio talk show. Norman calls in to air his feelings to host Pounder, paving the way for multiple flashbacks (with ex-*E.T.* tyke Thomas playing the adolescent Norman) chronicling his sicko relationship with his late mom (Hussey) and his early murders of several sexually provocative gals. While original *Psycho* scripter Joseph Stefano peppers his teleplay with grotesque tableaux and dark humor (young Norman even repeats his "Mother hasn't been herself lately" line), he ultimately serves to demystify Hitchcock's powerful original by reducing Norman's story to an unpleasant issue-of-the-week case history. Returning *Psycho* composer Bernard Herrmann's score rates as a plus.

PSYCHOMANIA   (1973) **½

D: Don Sharp. George Sanders, Beryl Reid, Nicky Henson. 95 mins. (Goodtimes, others)

A living-dead Brit biker gang (!) rides amok in this intermittently entertaining genre hybrid. Sanders, as a butler/occultist, projects boredom with stunning conviction. No relation to 1964's *Psychomania* (Sinister Cinema), an off-the-wall psycho chiller that's not without its own tacky virtues.

PUMPKINHEAD:
THE SERIES

PUMPKINHEAD II: BLOOD WINGS (1994) *

D: Jeff Burr. Andrew Robinson, Ami Dolenz, Kane Hodder, R. A. Mihailoff, Linnea Quigley, Roger Clinton. 88 mins. (Artisan)

E rstwhile scream queen Quigley goes topless and lets loose a loud one for old times' sake, while Roger (half-brother of Bill) Clinton, as small-town "Mayor Bubba," shows promise as a screen geek in this otherwise stale sequel to Stan Winston's mediocre but, compared with this, far superior 1988 *Pumpkinhead* (MGM).

PUPPET MASTER:
THE SERIES

PUPPET MASTER   (1989) **

D: David Schmoeller. Paul Le Mat, Irene Miracle, Matt Roe, Kathryn O'Reilly, Jimmie F. Skaggs, William Hickey, Barbara Crampton. 90 mins. (Paramount)

Puppet Master concerns a mad puppet maker (Hickey) who uses ancient Egyptian rites to animate his killer creations: Blade, Jester, Ms. Leech, Pin Head (no relation to *Hellraiser*'s Cenobite of the same name), and Tunneler. Fifty years after Hickey's suicide, several far-flung psychics gather at California's Bodega Bay Inn to attend the funeral of evil magician and former colleague Skaggs. They spend the rest of the pic attempting (mostly unsuccessfully) to elude the puppets' relentless wrath. The puppets, created by FX animation ace David Allen, are easily the best component here. Particularly effective is a bizarre erotic encounter pairing leech-extruding femme puppet Ms. Leech and a blindfolded human. Unfortunately, *Puppet Master* fails to sustain this lofty level of invention, degenerating into a series of unimaginative gore set pieces. Which didn't prevent it from spawning (thus far) six sequels: *Puppet Master 2* (1990), *Puppet Master 3: Toulon's Revenge* (1991), *Puppet Master 4* (1993), 1994's *Puppet Master 5: The Final Chapter* (all Paramount), *Curse of the Puppet Master* (1998), and *Retro Puppet Master* (1999) (both Full Moon).

THE PYX   (1973) **½

D: Harvey Hart. Karen Black, Christopher Plummer, Donald Pilon. 111 mins. (Prism)

This earnest, well-produced Canadian chiller (a.k.a. *The Hooker Murders*) stars Black as a spiritual-minded hooker and Plummer as a perplexed cop. The pic is relentlessly depressing, however—a mood in no way relieved by Karen crooning her own musical compositions on the soundtrack.

Q: THE WINGED SERPENT (1982) ***

D: Larry Cohen. Michael Moriarty, David Carradine, Candy Clark, Richard Roundtree, Malachy McCourt. 92 mins. (Anchor Bay) DVD

Moriarty is an antsy junkie who happens to know where the titular Aztec horror is nesting in NYC. And he wants a million tax-free bucks for the info. Q, meanwhile, munches on vulnerable Gothamites, while detective Carradine tries to track down the outsized bird, in another witty monster romp, presented in a remastered "collector's edition," from Cohen at the top of his subversive fright-film form.

RACE WITH THE DEVIL   (1975) ***

D: Jack Starrett. Peter Fonda, Warren Oates, Lara Parker, Loretta Swit, R. G. Armstrong. 88 mins. (Key)

Devil worshippers give high-speed pursuit to the hapless RV-driving vacationers (Fonda, Oates, Parker, Swit) who've witnessed a ritualistic killing in an underrated, exciting merger of the chase and chiller genres, with an unforgettable ending. An upscale entry from actor/auteur Starrett, who also cameos as a suspicious pump jockey.

RASPUTIN—THE MAD MONK (1966) ***½

D: Don Sharp. Christopher Lee, Barbara Shelley, Richard Pasco, Francis Matthews, Dinsdale Landen, Suzan Farmer, Renee Anderson. 92 mins. (Anchor Bay) DVD

Rasputin emerges as a happily Hammerized portrait of the sinister Svengali who mesmerized the czarina's court in pre–World War I Russia. Lee consumes mass quantities of scenery as the lusty, power-mad country monk, who comes complete with healing abilities and terpsichorean skills. After a run-in with some locals, one of whom our hero gorily unhands with a farm implement, Lee decides to make his fortune in St. Petersburg. He wins a drinking contest with a dissolute doctor (Pasco), seduces lady-in-waiting Shelley (whom he later successfully commands to "go away and destroy yourself"), and cozies up to czarina Anderson. Lee also makes the mistake of alienating doc Pasco, who plots to put an end to the avaricious monk's destructive schemes. While there are no true supernatural elements in play, Lee's intense interpretation of the title fiend manages to throw a scare or two into the viewer. Director Sharp, cinematographer Michael Reed, and production designer Bernard Robinson lend the film an impressively large look. All that's missing is the free Rasputin beard promised to patrons who caught the pic during its initial bijou run.

THE RAVEN   (1935) B&W ***½

D: Lew Landers. Bela Lugosi, Boris Karloff, Irene Ware. 62 mins. (Universal)

This compact Universal classic bears no connection to Poe, beyond mad plastic surgeon Bela's avowed interest in that much-purloined author. He's even more interested in his home torture equipment and in bedeviling escaped con Boris.

THE RAVEN   (1963) **½

D: Roger Corman. Vincent Price, Boris Karloff, Peter Lorre, Jack Nicholson. 86 mins. (Warner)

This Corman production has *absolutely* nothing to do with the

Poe poem. Instead, Price, Karloff, and Lorre play a feature-length game of "dueling sorcerers," which is at least as much fun as the Poe poem anyway, though the flick doesn't find young Jack at his best.

RAWHEAD REX   (1986)**

D: George Pavlou. David Dukes, Kelly Piper, Niall Tobin, Heinrich Von Schellendorf. 89 mins. (Vestron, n.i.d.)

Clive Barker has more or less disowned this celluloid version of his novella of the same name, and we more or less can't blame him. The flick plays like just another B monster movie, sans the visceral verve and sinister surrealism of Barker's original tale. Our story, shifted to rural Ireland from pastoral England, involves a gardener who inadvertently unearths the title fiend, a nine-foot-tall, face-eating demon who proceeds to devour much of the local populace while simultaneously enlisting an evil church deacon to serve as his earthly minion. Yank tourist Dukes strives to end Rawhead's reign of gustatory terror and is not above wildly overacting to achieve that goal.

RAZOR BLADE SMILE   (1999)***

D: Jake West. Eileen Daly, Christopher Adamson, David Warbeck, Jonathan Coote, Kevin Howarth, Heidi James. 101 mins. (A-Pix) DVD

Brit writer/director West crafts a cool, relentlessly but not pretentiously stylish postmodern variation on vintage Hammer vampire films (themselves then-postmodern variations on vintage Universal vampire films) with additional La Femme Nikita flourishes. A black-and-white 18th-century-set prologue dramatizes the forced conversion of Lilith Silver (the stunning, statuesque Daly) to the bloodsucker ranks by Blake (Adamson), a nobleman who's just killed her lover in a pistol duel. Following a

flashy opening-credits sequence deftly employing a kinetic razor-blade motif, we pick up Lilith in the present, where she works as an assassin whose targets, it transpires, are enemies of the legendary Illuminati who secretly control world governments and economies. Lilith combines work with pleasure (and nutritional necessity) by draining her marks of their plasma after she's mortally wounded them. (A self-styled jugular wine critic, she then rates her victims on a taste basis!) In West's take on ever mutating movie-vampire lore, the blood addicts can operate in bright daylight but suffer from acute ocular sensitivity, while massive blood loss can result in fatal anemia. West achieves a lavish look on a low budget and brings his darkly witty story to a satisfyingly ironic conclusion.

RAZORBACK   (1984)**

D: Russell Mulcahy. Gregory Harrison, Bill Kerr, Janet Morris, Chris Haywood, David Argue. 95 mins. (Warner)

Tusks would have been a more fitting title for future Highlander auteur Mulcahy's imitative exercise in porcine paranoia, a Jaws clone transplanted to the landlocked Australian outback. Razorback is at its best when exploring the outback's authentically eerie alienoid landscape (credit ace cinematographer Dean Semler). But while a polished, professional affair, Razorback is, in the end, more bore than boar.

THE RED HOUSE   (1947) B&W**½

D: Delmer Daves. Edward G. Robinson, Lon McCallister, Judith Anderson. 100 mins. (Sinister Cinema) DVD

Robinson stars as a haunted, guilt-obsessed farmer who knows but can't confront the title site's dread secret in a fitfully effective borderline horror pic released during America's postwar fright-film drought.

THE REFLECTING SKIN   (1991)**

D: Philip Ridley. Viggo Mortensen, Lindsay Duncan, Jeremy Cooper, Sheila Moore, Duncan Fraser. 106 mins. (Artisan)

Ridley's The Reflecting Skin, a high-strung meditation on the "nightmare of childhood," is a red-herring horror film that's way too gratuitously grim and self-consciously grotesque. The early-'50s rural childhood of eight-year-old Seth Dove (Cooper) is definitely not out of Norman Rockwell: His mom (Moore) is a literally slap-happy nutjob, his passive, pulp-addicted dad (Fraser) hides a secret "pervert" past, and his brother (Mortensen) has just returned from radioactive duty A-bombing islands in the postwar Pacific. On top of that, Seth's widowed Brit neighbor, Dolphin Blue (Duncan), is a suspected vampire, while four leather boys cruising the area in a black Cadillac of death have apparently murdered Seth's only friends. The latter tragedy leads to an immortal exchange. When Mortensen asks his kid bro', "Why don't you go play with your friends?" Seth replies, "They're all dead!"

On the upside, The Reflecting Skin explores several worthy themes—primarily the "beauty" of violence, illustrated by an exploding frog, a self-immolation scene, Seth's "adoption" of a dead fetus, and a photo of an infant Hiroshima victim whose irradiated flesh supplies the film with its title. The vivid cinematography and expansive yet sinister Alberta, Canada, locales (subbing for Idaho), green fields dotted by gnarled trees, represent additional pluses, but they aren't enough to overcome Ridley's fatal flair for grating pretentiousness. An end credit thanks "Bialystock and Bloom Limited" (Zero Mostel and Gene Wilder's characters' company in Mel Brooks's The Producers). Ridley returned a half decade later with the equally offbeat allegory The Passion of Darkly Noon (Turner).

THE REFRIGERATOR (1991) **½

D: Nicholas Jacobs. David Simonds, Julia McNeal, Angel Caban, Phyllis Sanz. 86 mins. (Monarch)

The Refrigerator is an oft intriguing but ultimately frustrating near miss that supplies some chills before defrosting in its final reels. The flick opens as a sort of "Rosemary's Refrigerator": Ohio newlyweds the Batemans (Simonds, McNeal) unwisely relocate to NYC's Avenue D to pursue Manhattan careers—she as an actress, he as a kind of conscientious yuppie. The pair's plans are soon sidetracked by the eerie title appliance, a fridge from hell that torments McNeal with grim images of mysterious traumas from her buried past and exerts a negative influence over Simonds as well, who grows increasingly conservative and power-crazed. Unfortunately, director/scripter Jacobs never centers the killer fridge as a consistent menace or metaphor, an imbalance that strips the film of its potential impact.

REPULSION (1965) B&W ***½

D: Roman Polanski. Catherine Deneuve, Yvonne Furneaux, Ian Hendry. 105 mins. (Trimark)

*P*aranoia, claustrophobia, sexual hysteria, abrupt and senseless violence, and other of auteur Polanski's fave themes are expertly woven in this harrowing account of the life and crimes of dissatisfied razor murderess Deneuve.

THE RESURRECTED (1991) ***

D: Dan O'Bannon. Chris Sarandon, John Terry, Jane Sibbett, Roberts Blossom, Laura Briscoe. 108 mins. (Artisan)

*L*ike Stuart Gordon's enduring cult fave *Re-Animator*, *The Resurrected* is based on an H. P. Lovecraft story dealing with the reanimation of the dead. O'Bannon eschews Gordon's black-humor approach in favor of a straight-

forward mystery treatment. Terry plays a P.I. hired by Sibbett, whose hubby (Sarandon) has been dabbling in bizarre occult experiments at their rural Rhode Island manse. O'Bannon gives the story a slow, steady build, and the film scores high in the shock department via a classic sequence that unfolds in a lightless catacomb. *Re-Animator* composer Richard Band's score supplies another plus.

THE RETURN OF THE LIVING DEAD:
THE SERIES

THE RETURN OF THE LIVING DEAD (1985) ***

D: Dan O'Bannon. Clu Gulager, James Karen, Don Calfa, Thom Mathews, Beverly Randolph, Linnea Quigley. 90 mins. (HBO)

*I*f farcical flesh-eaters are your movie meat, you won't be disappointed with O'Bannon's satirical splatcom. The plot posits that George Romero's *Night of the Living Dead* was based on a true incident involving army-owned corpses inadvertently revived by a toxic chemical. Said dead were subsequently sealed in airtight drums and erroneously delivered to the Uneeda Medical Supply Company in Louisville, Kentucky. Needless to say, it's not long before they're on their unsteady feet again, joined by the similarly reanimated residents of a nearby graveyard. *Return* works as a fairly faithful form parody of *Night* and sequels as Uneeda owners Burt (Gulager) and Frank (Karen), along with a pack of seemingly already brain-dead punks, are put through their paces by the cerebrum-starved ghouls. Unlike Romero's, these corpses can talk, and spend much of their time chanting for "Brains!" and "More brains!" Scream queen Quigley made her B-movie bones by baring lots of living flesh in this one. In the heavy hands of director/scripter Ken (*Meatballs Part II*) Wiederhorn, 1988's *Return of the Living Dead Part II*

(Lorimar) merely mimics the surface machinations of the first, minus that flick's satiric thrusts. Brian Yuzna's 1993 *Return of the Living Dead 3* (Trimark), at heart a nihilistic love story about a boy (J. Trevor Edmond) and his punkette zombie (Mindy Clarke), injects a bit more life into the series, but not enough to prevent producers from pulling the franchise plug.

THE RETURN OF THE VAMPIRE (1943) B&W **½

D: Lew Landers. Bela Lugosi, Frieda Inescort, Nina Foch. 69 mins. (Goodtimes)

*T*his often aimless Bela vehicle—slightly better produced than his Monogram and PRC efforts of the period—has our hero wandering wartime London with his werewolf minion (Matt Willis). There's a memorable face-melting fade-out, though, and Bela, as ever, wears his cape well. No relation to Paul Landres's 1958 *Return of Dracula* (MGM/UA), a low-budget but well-done vampire tale set in a small American town and starring Francis Lederer in the title role.

A RETURN TO SALEM'S LOT (1987) ***

D: Larry Cohen. Michael Moriarty, Sam Fuller, Andrew Duggan, Ricky Addison Reed, June Havoc, Evelyn Keyes. 101 mins. (Warner)

A very loose semisequel to Stephen King's TV movie *Salem's Lot* (see index), Cohen's *Return* is a lively fang-in-cheek tale detailing anthropologist Moriarty's visit to the title locale, where he's inherited a ramshackle farmhouse from a late, distant relation. At first he feels the scenery change might benefit his troubled young son (Reed). But that's *before* he gets acquainted with the native populace—vampires and their undead slaves all. Director/writer Cohen has fun playing with traditional vampire lore—we learn, for example, that most of the local bloodsuckers enjoy considerable financial security since, as town patriarch Duggan explains, real estate accrues in value and vampires live long enough (i.e., in the ideal scenario, forever) to capitalize on that trend—and peppers his cast with such veteran thesps as Havoc and Keyes. It's the late cult auteur Sam Fuller who steals the show, though, as a manic vampire-hunter who arrives in Salem's Lot with wholesale slaughter in mind.

REVENGE OF FRANKENSTEIN (1958) ***

D: Terence Fisher. Peter Cushing, Francis Matthews, Michael Gwynn. 89 mins. (Columbia/TriStar)

The late, great Cushing continues his unorthodox medical experiments in Hammer's literate, atmospheric follow-up to the previous year's *Curse of Frankenstein* (see index) and prequel to *Evil of Frankenstein* (Columbia/TriStar).

REVENGE OF THE DEAD (1984) ***1/2

D: Pupi Avati. Gabriele Lavia, Anne Canovas, Paola Tanziani, Cesare Barbetti, Bob Tonelli, Ferdinando Orlandi. 100 mins. (Lightning, n.i.d.)

Not to be mistaken for a typical Italo zombie gore romp (the late Lightning label's misleading box art notwithstanding), *Revenge of the Dead* is a generic retitling of a masterful exercise in supernatural suspense originally called *Zeder*. Though he's since moved on to nongenre fare (e.g., *The Story of Boys and Girls* [Fox Lorber] and the jazz bio *Bix* [Rhapsody Films]), auteur Avati has won a deserved cult rep for his work on this film and his script for the earlier *Macabro* (a.k.a. *Frozen Terror* [see index]). Avati eschews explicit gore but delivers several original shocks in a

sinister story that begins when a young writer (Lavia) reads the impressions found on an old discarded typewriter ribbon. That chance discovery, like the severed ear in David Lynch's *Blue Velvet* or the errant beer can in *The Clonus Horror,* leads to a labyrinthine descent dealing with nothing less than the secrets of human resurrection. To say more would be to risk ruining the multiple pleasures of Avati's intricately woven tale.

REVENGE OF THE ZOMBIES (1976) ***

D: Meng-Hwa Ho. Lung Ti, Lily Tu. (Loonic)

Not to be confused with the 1943 John Carradine–starrer of the same name (n/a) or the singular *Revenge of the Zombie* (Genesis), a.k.a. *Kiss Daddy Goodnight,* starring former teen heartthrob Fabian, this Run Run Shaw production rates as a decidedly surreal scare item that crams the screen with a truly bizarre array of lunch-losing imagery, including brain-draining, eye-eating, and worm-infestation scenes. Toss in ghosts, zombies, new twists in necrophilia, and your requisite kung fu action—all lensed with a heavy reliance on frantic pans and zooms—and you have, well, something for everyone. Asian-horror fans should also check out the similarly themed *Black Magic* (SB Video).

RORRET (1987) ***

D: Fulvio Wetzl. Lou Castel, Anna Galiena, Rossanna Coggiola, Patrizia Punzo. 105 mins. (Fox Lorber)

Joseph Rorret (*terror* spelled backward—but you already figured that out) is the ultimate voyeur. Not only does he own and inhabit Rome's Peeping Tom Cinema, but he spies on his patrons from his perch behind the screen. Rorret, who programs only extreme thrillers and horror pics, is

especially interested in the reactions of his comelier femme customers, whom he later (a) befriends and (b) strangles. While too mannered to generate much suspense on a thriller level, *Rorret* is a relatively unpretentious, generally entertaining meditation on the nature of fear, film, and voyeurism. Former Fassbinder thesp Castel conveys the right note of vulnerable menace as the cinemaniac who adopts movie-related aliases and even patterns his wardrobe after Peter Lorre's psycho in Fritz Lang's *M*—while Galiena, Coggiola, and Punzo are uniformly fine as the kind of bright, classy babes most guys would be happy just to meet, let alone strangle. Auteur Wetzl also incorporates brief, B&W re-creations of famous scenes from Hitch's *Psycho* (herein redubbed *Blood in the Shower*), *Strangers on a Train,* and *Dial M for Murder,* as well as Michael Powell's *Peeping Tom.*

ROSEMARY'S BABY (1968) ****

D: Roman Polanski. Mia Farrow, Ruth Gordon, John Cassavetes, Sidney Blackmer. 134 mins. (Paramount) DVD

Director Polanski and producer William Castle—a match happily made in Hollywood hell—transform Ira Levin's novel into a modern scare-screen classic as ambitious actor Cassavetes makes a pact with demonic neighbors Gordon and Blackmer that spells big trubs for pregnant wife Mia. This utterly mesmerizing horror giant is now available in a remastered "30th anniversary edition."

RUMPELSTILTSKIN (1996) **

D: Mark Jones. Kim Johnston Ulrich, Tommy Blaze, Max Grodénchik, Allyce Beasley, Vera Lockwood, Jay Pickett. 91 mins. (Republic)

Producers of the largely lame *Leprechaun* series—*Leprechaun, Leprechaun 2, Leprechaun 3, Leprechaun 4:*

In Space, Leprechaun in the Hood (Trimark), all starring Warwick Davis—repeat their Little Fairy Tale Fiend formula with *Rumpelstiltskin*. Like *Leprechaun*, the pic opens with a medieval-set prologue (the film's best sequence), wherein the diminutive baby-snatcher (Grodénchik) is vanquished by a local witch. Back in late-20th-century L.A., the grieving widow (Ulrich) of a slain cop (Pickett) unwittingly purchases Rump's remains at a curio shop run by a contempo witch (Beasley). It's not long before the minimonster's back on his feet, determined to relieve Ulrich of her infant son. Following a decent start, *Rumpelstiltskin* degenerates into a *Leprechaun* clone, with Rump bumping off extras to run up a high body count, capping his kills with lame anachronistic wisecracks. The best thing here is Kevin Yagher's makeup design for the title fiend. Marginally more compelling than Kevin S. Tenney's *Pinocchio's Revenge* (Trimark), which peaks with its title.

SALEM'S LOT: THE MOVIE (1979) ***

D: Tobe Hooper. James Mason, David Soul, Bonnie Bedelia. 112 mins. (Warner) DVD

This made-for-TV vampire outing represents one of the tube's better Stephen King translations, due in no small measure to Mason's expert thesping as the brains behind the bloodsuckers. The video version represents the European theatrical release, reedited from the original two-part teleseries, and contains more violence than the TV print.

SANTA SANGRE (1989) ****

D: Alejandro Jodorowsky. Axel Jodorowsky, Blanca Guerra, Guy Stockwell, Thelma Tixou, Sabrina Dennison, Adam Jodorowsky. 123 mins. In R and NC-17 editions. (Republic)

Imagine a mix of *Circus of Horrors*, Fellini's *The Clowns*, Bigas Luna's

Anguish, and just about any Dario Argento fright film, and you'll have at least a faint idea of Alejandro (*El Topo*) Jodorowsky's *Santa Sangre (Holy Blood)*. The film was produced and coscripted by none other than Dario's bro' Claudio Argento and exec-produced by Mexican genre vet Rene Cardona, Jr., of *Night of the Bloody Apes* (MPI) infamy. (To balance the cinematic scales a mite, Jodorowsky also grants a credit to Marcel Marceau.) An ambitious, at-once deadpan and elaborately surreal fear-film send-up, Jodorowsky's English-language opus chronicles the psychotic sufferings of young Phoenix (son Axel Jodorowsky), offspring of lecherous circus owner Orgo (a bloated Guy [brother of Dean] Stockwell) and nutzoid religious fanatic Concha (Guerra). Years after Dad cuts off Mom's arms (!) before killing himself, our nearly catatonic hero reunites with his disturbed mater and serves literally as her absent upper limbs, both in private and in their bizarro act at a Mexican burlesque house. We won't attempt to catalog *Santa Sangre*'s full gallery of geeks, freaks, and grotesqueries here. Suffice it to say that the pic includes clips from the original *Invisible Man* (our tortured protagonist's personal idol), a cemetery-set "Night of the Living Dead Naked Ladies" scene, transsexual wrestlers, tattooed stripteasers, and other imaginative hallucinations of the sort that oughtn't be missed. The NC-17 version offers three additional minutes of cinematic excess.

SATAN'S PRINCESS (1990) **1/2

D: Bert I. Gordon. Robert Forster, Lydie Denier, Caren Kaye, Phillip Glasser, Ellen Geer, Jack Carter. 90 mins. (Paramount)

Gordon abandons his usual celluloid stretchers (*Amazing Colossal Man*) and shrinkers (*Attack of the Puppet People*) in favor of more infernal concerns. Originally titled *Malediction*, *Satan's Princess* stars Forster as an alco-

holic ex-cop who's searching for a teen runaway. The corpse-littered trail ultimately leads to demonic 500-year-old (give or take a century or two) fashion mogul Denier. While not big in the credibility department, *Satan's Princess* is consistently entertaining and mightily elevated by Forster's multifaceted perf. In a more bizarre casting coup, Borscht Belt comic Jack Carter contributes a one-line cameo as a 17th-century Spanish monk (!).

SAVAGE INTRUDER (1968) ***

D: Donald Wolfe. John David Garfield, Miriam Hopkins, Gale Sondergaard, Florence Lake, Lester Matthews, Joe Besser, Minta Durfee. 90 mins. (Unicorn, n.i.d.)

Sort of a *Sunset Boulevard* on angel dust, John David (Son of John) Garfield's first and last star vehicle casts the famous thesp's offspring as a sarcastic, perverted literal lady-killer who signs on as the male nurse of elderly ex-starlet Hopkins (in her filmic farewell). This entertainingly depraved affair features decapitations, torture tableaux, old-timers Gale (*The Spider Woman*) Sondergaard, Edgar Kennedy's one-time screen spouse Lake, silent-film ingenue Durfee, and a too-brief cameo by former Stooge Besser as a Beverly Hills tour-bus driver.

SAWBONES (1995) ***

D: Catherine Cyran. Adam Baldwin, Nina Siemaszko, Barbara Carrera, Nicholas Sadler, Don Harvey, Don Stroud. 78 mins. (New Horizons)

A solid, occasionally sicko B flick, *Sawbones* stars Baldwin as a cop investigating a rash of surgically mutilated corpses, the spazzed-out handiwork of med-school reject Harvey. Crisply acted and swiftly paced, with some effectively disgusto surgical-gore flourishes—including a bloody liposuction procedure (!) and an ever popular death-by-defibrillator scene—*Sawbones* rates as a better-than-average entry in the mad-medico sweepstakes. Clint Howard appears in a silent cameo so brief it seems likely that most of his role was gutted from the final cut.

SCARED TO DEATH (1947) *½

D: Christy Cabanne. Bela Lugosi, George Zucco, Nat Pendleton. 65 mins. (Englewood) DVD

Bela's only appearance in a color movie supplies viewers with the only reason to sit through this clunky chiller produced to showcase a cheap color-film process that looks a lot like the computer-colorized flicks of the late '80s/early '90s. Zucco and Angelo Rossitto fans may also want to tune in.

SCHIZO (1977) **½

D: Pete Walker. Lynne Frederick, John Leyton, Stephanie Beacham, John Fraser. 109 mins. (VCI)

Schizo sees the Peter Walker/David McGillivray director/scripter team return to domestic concerns (see *Frightmare II*), as long-institutionalized Leyton torments stepdaughter Frederick—or so it seems. While it lacks *Frightmare II*'s morbid magic, *Schizo* sports a solid central plot twist, several brutal slayings, and crisp performances. *Schizo* is also one of several Walker picks to prefigure *Henry* by having its psycho slayer escape unpunished at film's end.

SCREAM:
THE SERIES

SCREAM (1996) ***

D: Wes Craven. Neve Campbell, David Arquette, Courteney Cox, Skeet Ulrich, Drew Barrymore, Matthew Lillard, Henry

Winkler, Jamie Kennedy. 111 mins. (Dimension) DVD

Scream represented Craven's second metahorror movie in three years. While his 1994 *Wes Craven's New Nightmare* rates as the more compelling exercise, *Scream* obviously proved the more popular, ringing up surprise mega-smash numbers (a whopping $100 mil). Kevin Williamson's script constantly comments on the genre, with vid-store clerk and movie expert Randy (Kennedy) reciting his horror-movie "rules" (a riff earlier used in Rolf Kanefsky's *There's Nothing Out There* [Prism], which also sent up the type of cheap cat scare Craven winkingly employs here). Craven uses his entire bag of terror tricks to satiric yet intense effect in a fright flick somewhat marred by an elongated running time and a rather weak resolution. Movie references run rampant right from the ghoulish get-go. In the effectively creepy opening scene, Barrymore is grilled by her potential killer via cell phone re the scariest movie she's ever seen. Craven and Williamson generously let her answer, "*Halloween.*" The killer opts for *Nightmare on Elm Street;* "The first one was," he's quick to clarify; "the rest sucked." There's also a mention of "Wes Carpenter" and clips from *Frankenstein* and *Halloween*. Craven's lingering bitterness about the MPAA also surfaces when Ulrich describes his affair with fellow high-schooler Campbell as going from "NC-17 to edited for television." Campbell replies, "Would you settle for a PG-13 relationship?"

Among the assembled thesps, Campbell is very good as the teenette terrorized by a killer (wearing a mask cleverly modeled on Edvard Munch's *The Scream*) whose horrific handiwork has been claiming the lives of several of her friends, while Arquette supplies amusement as an aw-shucks young deputy, as does Cox as a craven newscaster (pardon our redundancy). Former Fonz Winkler turns in sharp comedic work as

Principal Himbry but, unlike the other major cast members, isn't included in the closing-credit close-ups. The KNB EFX Group crafted the state-of-the-art gore FX.

SCREAM 2 (1997) ***

D: Wes Craven. Neve Campbell, Courteney Cox, David Arquette, Liev Schreiber, Jerry O'Connell, David Warner, Jamie Kennedy, Jada Pinkett. 120 mins. (Dimension) DVD

The megahit *Scream 2* rates as one of those rare scare sequels that succeeds in at least equaling the original. In the capable hands of returning *Scream* weavers, director Craven and writer Williamson, *Scream 2* cleverly honors vintage horror conventions *and* the *Scream* "tradition." Set two years after *Scream*'s conclusion, *Scream 2* opens with a sequence that mirrors the original Drew Barrymore murder scene and takes it a self-referential step further. At a promotional theatrical premiere of *Stab*—the fictional flick based on the best-seller *The Woodsboro Murders* by TV reporter Gale Weathers (Cox) and shot in "Stab-O-Vision" (!)—the Barrymore slaying is re-created on-screen before an enthusiastic crowd wearing free "Stab" masks while a patron (guest victim Pinkett) gets slashed to death in her seat. The fresh killing lures both Cox and deputy Dewey (an amusing Arquette) to the college that fellow *Scream* returnees Campbell and Kennedy are attending. It's not long before more bodies pile up, with initial suspicion pointing to falsely accused Cotton Weary (Schreiber, likewise reprising his original role). Craven and Williamson don't disappoint their fans here, fashioning at least three classic scare set pieces—Campbell and a crony trapped in a car, a scene set in a soundproof studio, and the climactic unmasking on a college theater stage. The performers are likewise uniformly strong, including drama teacher Warner, replacing the original's Winkler as the pic's token adult (a clip from 1922's *Nosferatu* also puts in a cameo). Followed by Craven's *Scream 3* (2000, Dimension, DVD). *Scream and Scream Again*, meanwhile, is *not* yet another sequel but a creepy 1970 Brit frightfest featuring the terror troika of Vincent Price, Peter Cushing, and Christopher Lee. No relation to the low-budget 1981 regional turkey *Scream* (Vestron).

SCREAM BLOODY MURDER (1973) **

D: Marc B. Ray. Fred Holbert, Leigh Mitchell, Robert Knox. 90 mins. (Troma) DVD

As the box so eloquently explains, "Michael was a strange little boy. His steel claw which replaced the hand he mangled while murdering his father is a weapon to punish his mother." (Sounds like Jerry Springer, or at least Ricki Lake, material to us.) Young Mike also suffers from hallucinations that provoke him to off strangers as well as loved ones in this troubling low-budget report from the Embattled American Family front.

THE SECRET LIFE: JEFFREY DAHMER (1993) ***

D: David R. Bowen. Carl Crew, Lisa Marks, Aaron Braxton, Jeanne Bascom, LP Brown. 93 mins. (Magnum)

While we expected a low-rent crass exploitation exercise in a fictionalized *Faces of Death* vein, *Secret Life*— lensed in deliberately flat, verité style, with Buenaventura, California, subbing for Ohio and Wisconsin—is instead a deadly serious, convincingly acted, and thoroughly disturbing account of the late mass murderer's foul misdeeds. In fact, *Secret Life*'s chill factor is easily the equal of such vaunted serial-killer counterparts as John McNaughton's *Henry* and Alan Ormsby and Jeff Gillen's *Deranged* (see index). On-screen doppelgänger Crew (who also coproduced

and wrote the stark, utterly believable script) plays Dahmer as a lonely loser— at once miswired and disconnected, and incapable of forming relationships with other living beings. (The film shows a juvenile Dahmer prepping for his coming career by mutilating roadkill.) Disapproving of his own homosexual leanings ("I should have stayed with God" goes his oft repeated refrain), Dahmer deals with his confusion by murdering and dismembering his victims, starting, in 1978, with a hetero hitchhiker at the Ohio house Dahmer shares with his grandmother (Bascom). ("I knew he'd leave," narrator Crew explains re his victim, "and I'd be left alone again.") Dahmer begins his "collection" in earnest after renting a Milwaukee apartment, where he lures his prey by offering them money to pose for Polaroids, ultimately mounting a well-documented body count of 13 in roughly as many months.

While *Henry* had earlier exposed a system sufficiently lax to enable an obvious (and largely careless) psycho to kill at will simply by keeping mobile and selecting mostly "unimportant" victims, *Secret Life* dramatizes an even scarier situation: Not only doesn't Dahmer cover his tracks, but his crimes unfold in the same small apartment. Neighbors repeatedly complain of the stench and even report an injured teenager fleeing Dahmer's death domicile—and still no action is taken; it's simply no one's job to follow up. Traumatized escapee Braxton ultimately convinces two cops to enter Dahmer's two-room charnel house, where they finally bust the depraved perp. Despite an opening disclaimer promising to spare viewers the most gruesome of Dahmer's atrocities, *The Secret Life: Jeffrey Dahmer* depicts some truly sicko scenes, particularly the surgical experiments the killer performs on several still-living victims. (Having Dahmer wear a *She-Devils on Wheels* T-shirt seems a cheap shot, though.) *The Secret Life: Jeffrey Dahmer* is an extremely powerful document that suc-

ceeds in humanizing the killer's undeserving victims, indicting indifferent authorities, and bringing new meaning and menace to the phrase "the banality of evil."

SEDUCED BY EVIL (1994) *1/2

D: Tony Wharmby. Suzanne Somers, James B. Sikking, John Vargas, Mindy Spence, Julie Carmen, Nancy Moonves. 88 mins. (Paramount)

Cast as a Southwestern journalist, Somers takes two—count 'em— two on-screen showers, has sex with a *brujo,* and, in her dramatic pièce de résistance, briefly shape-shifts into a wolf (!). *SBE* also features lots of prophetic nightmares, slo-mo pursuit sequences, and domestic conflicts among Somers, hubby Sikking, and teen daughter Spence. The end result, alas, is a slow night in the desert for all but the most dedicated of Suzanne fans, of which there are no doubt many.

THE SENDER (1982) ***

D: Roger Christian. Kathryn Harrold, Zeljko Ivanek, Shirley Knight. 92 mins. (Paramount)

Ivanek is an unwitting psychic whose telepathic transmissions are received by concerned shrink Harold in a solid paranormal thriller hoisted by some inventive story hooks and vivid nightmare imagery.

THE SERPENT AND THE RAINBOW (1988) **1/2

D: Wes Craven. Bill Pullman, Cathy Tyson, Zakes Mokae, Paul Winfield, Brent Jennings, Michael Gough. 98 mins. (Universal) DVD

"Inspired" by Wade Davis's nonfiction book of the same name, Craven's voodoo adventure charts the experiences of an anthropologist (Pullman) dispatched to Haiti by the Biocorp pharmaceutical company to retrieve some potent authentic "zombie powder" to market as an anesthetic. While tracking down a local zombie, our hero runs afoul of one of Port-au-Prince's meanest—secret-police chief Peytreaud (Mokae), who doubles as an evil voodoo sorcerer. Bill recruits physician Tyson and benign voodoo priest Winfield to help him defeat his powerful new enemy. While calling to mind *The Believers, Macumba Love,* and Craven's own *A Nightmare on Elm Street, Serpent* beats around the graveyard bush for nearly an hour before deciding it's a horror film. Once it does, Craven delivers a number of effectively frightening tableaux, especially when Peytreaud launches a full-scale voodoo "mind invasion." We get a creepy live-burial scene, several elastic limbs à la Freddy, rotting corpses, and a dinner party ruined by a live zombie hand in the soup (hey, we've all been *there*). Though there are some insights along the way—plus a detailed look at the art of zombie-powder preparation—viewers searching for a lucid exegesis of the role voodoo may have played in the Duvalier-dominated Haitian political system will probably be disappointed. For a more verité take on Haiti's troubled recent past, scope out the recommended documentary/mondo-movie combo *Krik? Krak! Tales of a Nightmare* (Facets Video).

SERPENT'S LAIR   (1995) **½

D: Jeffrey Reiner. Jeff Fahey, Lisa B., Heather Medway, Patrick Bachau, Taylor Nichols. 90 mins. (Republic)

After suffering a severe bout of "virtual-reality sickness" in the same year's *Virtual Seduction* (New Horizons), Fahey gets systematically drained of his precious bodily fluids by insatiable succubus Lisa B. in Reiner's watchable terror tale in erotic-thriller mufti. Frequent heavy Bachau plays Ms. B.'s secret partner-in-satanism with his usual cheerful menace, while Whit Stillman regular Nichols receives rough

treatment at Lisa's hands in a last-reel cameo. Romania stunt-doubles for L.A.

SERVANTS OF TWILIGHT (1991) ***

D: Jeffrey Obrow. Bruce Greenwood, Belinda Bauer, Grace Zabriskie, Richard Bradford, Jarrett Lennon, Carel Struycken, Kelli Maroney. 95 mins. (Trimark)

Director Obrow, who struck out with the 1987 Rod Steiger slime-monster movie *The Kindred* (Artisan), fares far better in bringing Dean Koontz's satanic novel to the screen. A slick, kinetic combo of action and horror, *Servants* stars Bauer as a panic-stricken single mom whose seemingly benign young son (Lennon) has been targeted for destruction by a band of brain-dead Christian cultists, headed by an intense Zabriskie, who's convinced that young Lennon is Satan's son. P.I. Greenwood and cronies do their best to shield mother and child from the armed cultists' wrath. Exciting chase sequences and sporadic bloodbaths lead to a chilling twist ending.

THE SEVENTH SIGN   (1988) *½

D: Carl Schultz. Demi Moore, Michael Biehn, Jürgen Prochnow, Manny Jacobs, Akosua Busia, Arnold Johnson. 97 mins. (Columbia/TriStar) DVD

A torpid exercise in 1980s yuppie egocentricity masquerading as a supernatural thriller, *The Seventh Sign* casts Moore as a pregnant West Coast yup who fears she's about to give birth to a baby with no soul. (Who *said* they could have it all?) What's worse, this event will signal the end of the world as we know it, since 11 other signs of impending apocalypse—hailstorms, solar eclipses, blood moons, et al.—have already manifested themselves. *The Seventh Sign* relays its muddled mélange of New Testament prophecies, moral messages, and modern horror clichés with

such unrelenting languor that, by that time, you'll be *ready* to sign off. If *The Seventh Sign* is any indication, the world will end with neither a bang nor a whimper but a protracted yawn.

THE SEVENTH VICTIM   (1943) B&W ***

D: Mark Robson. Kim Hunter, Tom Conway, Jean Brooks. 71 mins. (RKO, n.i.d.)

Producer Val Lewton and director Robson work with a suitably sinister theme—satanism in Greenwich Village—and get their film off to an ominous, atmospheric start as schoolgirl Hunter's search for her errant weird sister leads her into a web of genteel evil. Trouble is, the filmmakers play it a bit *too* subtle here as the movie meanders a mite through its middle reels and doesn't deliver enough of a payoff. Conway virtually reprises his fatuous *Cat People* shrink role in a film that, despite its flaws, still rates as a must for Lewton buffs.

SHATTER DEAD   (1993) ***

D: Scooter McCrae. Stark Raven, Flora Fauna, Daniel "Smalls" Johnson, Marina Del Rey, Robert Wells, Candy Coster. 84 mins. (Tempe)

A grim variation on George Romero's celluloid *Living Dead* lore, McCrae's shot-on-video, "filmlook"-processed *Shatter Dead* works well on a surreal, depresso nightmare level. In McCrae's movie ("inspired," the auteur claimed in an interview, by Dante's *Inferno* [!]), people no longer die naturally, but many are eager to commit suicide to achieve a sort of functioning-zombie immortality. (Even a shotgun blast will leave a zombie victim eternally handicapped but still alive.) McCrae's zombies are less dead than nonliving, leading homeless existences and becoming easy converts to the religious rantings of the deceased but active "Preacher Man" (Wells). The minimalist plot finds exhausted, heavily armed heroine Susan (Raven) trying to make her way back to her beau's (Johnson) place. *Shatter Dead,* which effectively strips death (to say nothing of life) of its glamor, is almost too grindingly downbeat to recommend. But McCrae's is an exceedingly well-crafted and original vision. If Romero, Ingmar Bergman, and H. G. Lewis ever decided to share a camcorder over a weekend, the results might look something like *Shatter Dead.*

SHE FREAK   (1967) ***

D: Byron Mabe. Claire Brennan, Lee Raymond, Lynn Courtney, Bill McKinney. 87 mins. (Something Weird)

As an uncredited *Freaks* remake, *She Freak* is admittedly pretty weak. But as a slice of Southwestern lowlife, Mabe's carnal carny parable, produced and well-written by frequent H. G. Lewis cohort David F. Friedman, is fairly riveting fare, a John Waters–type parody played almost straight. Brennen is especially memorable as desperate blond bimbo Jade, whose idea of upward mobility is to quit her greasy-spoon waitressing job to work a concession stand at a seedy traveling carnival. There she's torn between her animal lust for stud ride-operator Raymond and the class yearnings that tilt her in the direction of relative high-roller McKinney, who owns the carny sideshow. The unbelievably inept *Freaks*-inspired climax shifts the flick from authentic sleaze to utter camp and plays as if Friedman and company had simply run out of money (entirely possible).

THE SHINING   (1980) **½

D: Stanley Kubrick. Jack Nicholson, Shelley Duvall, Scatman Crothers. 143 mins. (Warner) DVD

The Phantom has to fess up that he was among that faction bored rather than held spellbound by much of the usually mesmerizing Kubrick's slowly paced adaptation of the Stephen King novel. King himself was reportedly far happier with the TV-miniseries remake.

SHOCKER   (1989) **½

D: Wes Craven. Michael Murphy, Peter Berg, Mitch Pileggi, Cami Cooper, Theodore Raimi, Timothy Leary. 110 mins. (Universal) DVD

Take *Horror Show*'s electrocuted psycho, *The Hidden*'s body-invasion riff, *Videodrome*'s telehallucinations, *Dracula*'s dread crucifix, Freddy's nightmare motifs and one-liners, and Relax Video's *Fireplace TV*, put 'em all together, and you've got *Shocker.* Craven's grab-bag scare affair features future *X-Files* regular Pileggi as Horace Pinker, a.k.a. "the Family Slasher," a skinheaded TV repairman, closet occultist, and all-purpose mass murderer who specializes in carving up entire nuclear-family units. Horace encounters an unexpectedly formidable foe in young Jonathan Parker (Berg), who, it soon develops, is actually H.P.'s biological son. When Jon witnesses his own adoptive family's slaying via telepathic dream transmissions, he and stepdad cop Murphy move in for the kill. But Horace has only begun to fight. He's sent to the electric chair, and afterward his evil spirit infiltrates a series of unsuspecting citizens who carry out his lethal handiwork.

Craven's relentlessly eclectic chiller is not without its effectively malevolent moments. One such unfolds when the late Horace's spirit transforms a cheerful little girl into a foulmouthed, tractor-driving (!) killer. The casting of the late Timothy Leary as a sleazy televangelist (pardon our redundancy) adds another novel touch (*Elm Street* alum Heather Langenkamp and Craven himself also surface in eye-blink cameos). Unfortunately, *Shocker*'s derivative imagination and ill-advised last-reel lurch into broad black comedy keep Craven's flashy, FX-laden flick from really taking off, and its attempts to refute its own recurrent phrase "If you don't like the news, change the channel" rate as fairly hollow. Timothy Leary lovers, meanwhile, can also sight the late guru as a toxic-waste mogul in 1990's *Fatal Skies* (AIP) and *Roadside Prophets* (New Line).

THE SHOUT   (1978) ***

D: Jerzy Skolimowski. Alan Bates, Susannah York, John Hurt. 87 mins. (Columbia/TriStar)

Skolimowski's *The Shout,* based on a novel by Robert Graves, is an effectively offbeat, metaphorical fright film about a mysterious nomad (Bates) who can kill by unleashing the title sound.

THE SILENCE OF THE LAMBS (1991) ***½

D: Jonathan Demme. Jodie Foster, Anthony Hopkins, Scott Glenn, Ted Levine, Anthony Heald, Diane Baker. 118 mins. (Orion) DVD

Hopkins gives his all as the serenely inhuman, flesh-famished psychiatrist (says he re a slain ex-patient, "Best thing for him, really; his therapy was going nowhere"), while Foster is at once vulnerable and resilient as his mentally violated "partner." Russ Meyer alum Charles Napier gets eaten alive, while auteur Roger Corman contributes a brief bit as a Bureau honcho. (Award yourself an extra ten points if you can spot *Night of the Living Dead* director George Romero in a wordless cameo.) Director Demme yields original shocks from such seemingly innocuous props as night-vision glasses and a self-storage unit. On the downside, the flick is overly stylized, a tad too ponderous for its lurid material, and occasionally gaping in the plot-hole department. The retro emphasis on FBI training techniques harks back to the weakest elements of '40s noir classics like *T-Men* and *White Heat*, where on-screen seminars on the latest advances in police science served mostly to drag the pics' pacing. Still, *The Silence of the Lambs* is undeniably strong stuff. What's even more impressive is how this creepy, authentically depraved descent into the Demme-monde managed to incorporate many traditional exploitation elements not yet normally seen in A movies—such as the detailed forensic examination of a week-old corpse—without alienating mainstream critics or Academy members. An even bigger surprise is that licensed "Hannibal the Cannibal Face Restraint Masks" never turned up at a mall near you.

SILENT NIGHT, DEADLY NIGHT:
THE SERIES

SILENT NIGHT, DEADLY NIGHT 4: INITIATION (1990) **1/2

D: Brian Yuzna. Maude Adams, Neith Hunter, Tommy Hinckley, Allyce Beasley, Clint Howard, Reggie Bannister. 90 mins. (Artisan)

W hile far from a classic, *Initiation* is easily the best entry in a stupid seasonal-slasher series started back in '84, doubtless due to the fact that, beyond the tagged-on franchise title and a marginal Christmas motif, the movie bears no connection to the earlier flicks (*Silent Night, Deadly Night; Silent Night, Deadly Night 2; Silent Night, Deadly Night 3: You Better Watch Out!* [all Live/Artisan]). Instead, *Initiation* is an extremely gross, semifeminist fright film about your typical lesbian Lilith cult, led by Adams (*Octopussy*), out to recruit femme reporter Hunter. Director Yuzna succeeds in extracting genuine creepiness from outwardly mundane situations and ups the film's fear quotient with sicko apparitions and makeup FX fashioned by Screaming Mad George.

SISTERS (1973) ***

D: Brian De Palma. Margot Kidder, Jennifer Salt, Charles Durning. 93 mins. (Home Vision) DVD

D e Palma achieves a deft balance between the sinister and the satiric in his story of distaff Siamese twins (a versatile Kidder) brain-twisted by an evil surgeon (William Finley).

THE SKULL (1965) **

D: Freddie Francis. Peter Cushing, Christopher Lee, Patrick Wymark, Nigel Green, Jill Bennett, Michael Gough. 83 mins. (Paramount)

B rit thesps tend to be uncommonly adept at lending an air of dignity or at least drollery to the dullest, most risible of projects. Few actors have done dumb material more undeserved credit than Cushing and Lee, and their presence is about all this Amicus snoozefest, penned by Robert (*Psycho*) Bloch, has to offer. A rehash of *The Mask* minus the latter's surrealism and 3-D effects about collector Cushing's ill-advised obsession with the remains of the Marquis de Sade's demented dome, *The Skull* provides little in the way of brainpower, originality, or chills. The final two reels unspool with virtually no dialogue (Sade's skull remains closemouthed throughout), but this gimmick fails to redeem the proceedings.

SLUMBER PARTY MASSACRE:
THE SERIES

SLUMBER PARTY MASSACRE (1982) **1/2

D: Amy Jones. Michele Michaels, Robin Stills, Michael Villela, Andre Honore, Debra Deliso, Gina Mari. 78 mins. (Nelson, n.i.d.)

SLUMBER PARTY MASSACRE II (1987) *1/2

D: Deborah Brock. Crystal Bernard, Atania Ilitch, Kimberley McArthur, Juliette Cummins, Patrick Lowe. 75 mins. (New Horizons)

SLUMBER PARTY MASSACRE III (1990)1/2*

D: Sally Mattison. Keely Christian, Brittain Frye, M. K. Harris, David Greenlee, Maria Ford, Hope Marie Carlton. 76 mins. (MGM)

T his mysteriously long-lived series began in 1982 when the unlikely distaff tandem of director Amy (*Love Letters*) Jones and novelist Rita Mae (*Rubyfruit Jungle*) Brown spawned the original *Slumber Party Massacre*, a mostly standard slasherfest fraught with unsubtle sexual symbolism and scattered stabs at dark wit (e.g., a local radio station sports the call letters KDED). A simple plot—peppered with jiggle basketball games and one of the genre's more prolonged shower scenes—places a gaggle of giggly Venice, California, beach bimbos in an unchaperoned house for the titular bash. A few jerky male friends crash the affair (the better to add to the body count), which is later visited by an escaped mass murderer equipped with a decidedly phallic power drill. The total tally adds up to six femme victims (five drilled, one stabbed), five male fatalities (two drilled, one stabbed, one eye-gouged, one decapitated), and one doll (hatcheted). While it straddles the line between satire and pure exploitation, *Slumber Party Massacre* offers several high points, notably a starkers appearance by up-and-coming B-screen scream queen Brinke Stevens and a couple of successful gags (as when one of the gals touches a dead pizza-delivery guy and shudders, "Boy, is he cold!" To which a famished fellow femme replies, "Is the pizza?").

Still, *SPM I* should have marked the end of the *Slumber Party* saga. Instead, enter the ever enterprising Roger Corman, who, five years later, hatched

Slumber Party Massacre II, also written and directed by a femme auteur (Brock). With the slasher subgenre already on the wane, Brock blends blatant *Nightmare on Elm Street* elements—she openly tips her hand by naming a cop character "Officer Krueger"—with the original story: *SPM I* survivor Bernard suffers from nightmares that not only rehash the initial massacre (a convenient excuse to incorporate gory clips from the first flick) but introduce new, improved maniac Ilitch, a rock-'n'-roll animal with a drill-equipped electric guitar (!). Actor Ilitch, who resembles a cross between John Travolta and Andrew "Dice" Clay (now, *that's* scary!), even takes time out to perform a couple of rock tunes between slaughters (!). Those moments and some decent disgusto FX raise *SPM II* slightly above the level of the utterly useless, though the actual body count is fairly paltry: three males (drilled) and three females (two drilled, one tossed from a roof).

Nothing, unfortunately, redeems the most recent (hopefully last) *SPM* entry, another Corman quickie. Observing the odd, by this time totally meaningless, tradition of employing a femme writer and director—Catherine Cyran and Sally Mattison, respectively—*SPM III* shapes up as a total retro fiasco. The flick finds the usual slew of overaged high school bimbos at the mercilessness of a singularly dull driller killer, deranged college boy Frye. Frye is revealed after a pair of red herrings— voyeuristic neighbor Harris and a "weirdo" who follows the girls home from the beach—are perfunctorily presented, then quickly eliminated as suspects. Minimalist in the extreme (the pic uses all of four locations), *SPM III* is likewise unabetted by such sparkling lines as "I wish the pizza would get here" and "I can't believe somebody killed the weirdo!" Worse, the gals here are unusually helpless for post–Sigourney Weaver Era heroines; these shrieking wimpettes botch at least three easy chances to waste the rather clumsy

killer. *SPM III* also falls short in the gratuitous-nudity and simulated-sex departments and squanders the talents of foxy Ford and Andy Sidaris jiggle vet Carlton. While the body count matches the original's total of twelve—seven females (five drilled, one stabbed, one electrocuted), five males (three drilled, one chainsawed, one run through with a HOUSE FOR SALE sign!)—*III* exhibits none of *I*'s sporadic wit or suspense. *SPM III* also came along at a time when formula slasher pics had all but vanished from the genre-movie zeitgeist, though they've since been revived by such postmodern entries as *Scream, I Know What You Did Last Summer,* and *Urban Legend* (see index). No relation to Carol Frank's 1986 *Sorority House Massacre* (Warner).

SON OF FRANKENSTEIN (1939) B&W ***1/2

D: Rowland V. Lee. Basil Rathbone, Boris Karloff, Bela Lugosi, Lionel Atwill, Josephine Hutchinson. 99 mins. (Universal)

The third installment in Universal's classic *Frankenstein* series casts Rathbone in the title role, Lugosi as the broken-necked Ygor, Karloff in his final fling as the Monster, and Atwill as the one-armed police inspector covertly investigating a rash of murders that coincide with Herr Frankenstein, Jr.'s ill-advised return to his father's infamous castle. All four principals turn in unforgettable work here, especially Basil as the increasingly agitated scientist whose plans to correct his dad's costly procedural errors are continuously compromised by the rest of the cast. Add Lee's atmospheric direction, Jack Otterson's majestically macabre sets, and a deft script laced with unobtrusive dark humor, and you have one of the legit giants of the fright-film industry. While not quite of the same rank, Robert Siodmak's 1943 bayou-set *Son of Dracula* (Universal), starring Lon Chaney, Jr., as Dracula's *dad* (cleverly

called Count Alucard), also supplies its share of retro fright fun.

SPIRIT OF THE BEEHIVE (1973) **1/2

D: Víctor Erice. Fernán Gomez, Teresa Gimpera, Ana Torrent. Subtitled. 95 mins. (Interama)

Not a horror film but a film inspired by a horror film: When young Gimpera witnesses a screening of *Frankenstein* in her rural Spanish village in 1943, she becomes obsessed with the image of the lonely Monster and leads her older sister on a search for same. Erice's lyrical exploration of childhood fears and longings gets off to a fine start but proceeds at too leisurely a pace.

SPIRITS OF THE DEAD (A.K.A. *HISTOIRES EXTRAORDINAIRES D'APRES EDGAR ALLAN POE*) (1968) ***

"Metzengerstein," D: Roger Vadim. Jane Fonda, Peter Fonda, Carla Marlier. "William Wilson," D: Louis Malle. Brigitte Bardot, Alain Delon, Katia Christine. "Toby Dammit," D: Federico Fellini. Terence Stamp, Salvo Bandone, Fabrizio Angeli, Marina Yaru. 117 mins. (Water Bearer) DVD

Water Bearer presents a letterboxed, French-language, English-subtitled edition of this hitherto elusive terror trilogy loosely drawn from a trio of Edgar Allan Poe tales. The film opens with its weakest segment, "Metzengerstein," originally published in the *Saturday Courier* in 1832. A French-speaking Jane Fonda, then wed to director Vadim, portrays debauched noblewoman Countess Frederica, who runs an alternately cruel and orgiastic court. While out for a sylvan romp on her favorite steed (Fonda's an accomplished equestrian off-screen as well), Jane is rescued from a bear trap by her estranged cousin, Baron Wilhelm (a

French-dubbed Peter Fonda, in an incestuous touch). When the latter fails to respond to her overtures, she orders his stables burned, a blaze that takes his life as well (not part of her plan). A mysterious horse soon shows up at Jane's castle, seemingly animated by Peter's spirit, and beckons her to her fate. While lushly photographed by Claude Renoir, "Metzengerstein" is slackly paced, with a predictable payoff, and Jane, fresh from *Barbarella,* seems more Hollywood petulant than imperiously decadent.

The pace picks up with Malle's "William Wilson," adapted from Poe's 1839 seasonal story "The Gift: A Christmas and New Year's Present for 1840." Delon stars as a depraved medical officer who's haunted early on by his apparent doppelgänger, also named William Wilson and likewise played by Delon, who interrupts him at strategic points (like when he's about to surgically eviscerate naked blonde Christine) in his infamous career. The story's centerpiece is a card game between Delon and Bardot, an upscale courtesan who has naught but contempt for the sadistic bully. Much of the tale is told in flashback, in the form of Delon's desperate confession to a local priest. While there are few true surprises, "William Wilson" is well handled by Malle and his cast.

By far the best segment is Fellini's satiric yet creepy contribution, "Toby Dammit," based on Poe's "Never Bet Your Head" (published in *Graham's Magazine,* 1841). Stamp plays the title part of a tipsy wastrel of a Brit actor who accepts the starring role in a "Catholic western" produced by priest Bandone. At a gaudy, fatuous awards ceremony where Fellini pokes wicked fun at the Italo media's expense, a drunken Stamp mocks his audience and himself, then roars off in his Ferrari. Throughout, Stamp is haunted by the vision of a coyly smiling little girl in a white dress who bounces a white ball. While fairly far from Poe—who quite likely never attended a single film-awards cere-

THE STRANGE WORLD OF COFFIN JOE
THE FILMS OF JOSÉ MOJICA MARINS

Imagine a mix of Mario (*Black Sunday*) Bava and John (*Pink Flamingos*) Waters, and you still won't come close to a complete picture of outrageous Brazilian underground actor/auteur José Mojica Marins. Though bootlegs of his raw, surreal but professional "Coffin Joe" movies (he's made more than 30, along with numerous TV shows) had been making the rounds for a while, Something Weird Video became the only label to form a legal arrangement with Marins himself, issuing a slew of Coffin Joe cassettes featuring sharp visual clarity and large, easy-to-read subtitles.

In *At Midnight I Will Take Your Soul* (1963, B&W), Marins introduces his self-portrayed Coffin Joe ("Ze de Caixao") character, a sadistic, black-clad, top-hatted, philosophical undertaker who greets the camera with "I wish you an awful evening." Director Marins follows actor Marins on his evil rounds as he terrorizes local barflies, kills his mistress in a protracted spider-torture scene, gouges a local doctor's eyes out with his (real) Freddy Krueger–like nails, slays a friend and rapes his fiancée, and even insists on eating meat on Friday. While *At Midnight* follows a fairly linear story line, the flick introduces many of Marins's soon-to-be-trademark psychosexual, sacrilegious, and bourgeoisie-baiting antics.

The action turns far wilder in *Awakenings of the Beast* (1968, B&W/Color). Coffin Joe—who, by this time, even boasts his own theme song—serves less as an active participant than a hands-on guide through a drug demimonde highlighted by all manner of depraved, color-lensed LSD-freak-out sequences. In one scene, the monomaniacal Marins, as himself, is judged by a panel of critics on a fictional TV show. (According to SWV, the Brazilian military dictatorship banned *Awakenings* from theaters and video for 18 years.)

In *The Strange World of Coffin Joe* (1968, B&W/Color), Marins uses a twisted *Twilight Zone* format to frame a trio of tales that emphasize black humor along with the usual perverse horror and erotic elements. Story 1, "The Dollmaker," demonstrates the filmmaker's fondness for climactic excess as he drives his punchline home with unswerving relentlessness. The less predictable "Obsession" charts a geeky balloon-seller's infatuation with a woman who, for him, loses none of her appeal after death. Installment 3, "Theory," returns Coffin Joe to the fore. Here, after again being attacked by TV critics, C.J. stages an elaborate burlesque featuring such fun stuff as sadomasochism, cannibalism, necrophilia, and murder—sort of a more violent version of "Lady Divine's Cavalcade of Perversions" in the aforementioned John Waters's *Multiple Maniacs.*

For those who want to fast-forward straight to the hot parts, SWV has *Hallucinations of a Deranged Mind* (1978, B&W/Color), wherein Marins conveniently assembles censored scenes from more than ten of his films.

This Night I'll Possess Your Corpse (1968) sees the filmmaker indulge his Antichrist complex in a direct sequel to his Coffin Joe debut, 1963's *At Midnight I Will Take Your Soul.* Abetted by disfigured henchhunchback Bruno, C.J. resumes his search for the ideal woman to bear his son—the quicker to spur the evolution of the "perfect man," one governed by pure instinct rather than

(continued)

mony—"Toby Dammit" is a terrific piece of work that can stand on its own (and in fact enjoyed Italian bookings as a separate short film).

STEPHEN KING'S SLEEPWALKERS (1992) **¹/₂

D: Mick Garris. Brian Krause, Mädchen Amick, Alice Krige, Ron Perlman. 91 mins. (Columbia/TriStar)

The title refers to a race of feline shape-shifters, represented by Krause and an excellent Krige as an incestuous mother-and-son team who must suck the life force from virginal human females for continued survival. Making life tough for said sleepwalkers, beyond the expected scarcity of virgins, is the fact that they're vulnerable to attack by ordinary cats. The movie sports its fair share of honest shocks, crowd-pleasing splatter moments, and vivid makeup FX but is frequently undermined by King's campier impulses. Cameos by King and cohorts Clive Barker, Joe Dante, and John Landis serve only to dilute the mood and slacken the tension. Other available King titles not covered elsewhere include the fair airborne vampire chiller *The Night Flier* (HBO), 1997's *Thinner* (Republic), the supernatural revenge tale *Sometimes They Come Back*, sequels *Sometimes They Come Back...Again* and *Sometimes They Come Back for More* (all Trimark, DVD).

STRAIT-JACKET (1964) B&W **¹/₂

D: William Castle. Joan Crawford, Leif Erickson, Diane Baker. 89 mins. (Columbia/TriStar)

Castle strikes again with this suitably lurid axe-murder tale hinged on former psycho Crawford's current guilt or innocence. George Kennedy is one of the cast members who gets it in the neck.

"superstitious" morality. (It's not enough for Coffin Joe to be full of himself; he wants a woman to be full of him too: According to a *Fangoria* article, the sixtysomething Marins, then wed to his seventh wife, has sired some 23 offscreen offspring!) After slaying a number of losing contestants via creepy snake and spider rampages and eliminating a male enemy in a lovingly executed head-crushing scene, Joe meets himself in hell, a color-lensed sequence that showcases Marins's talent for crafting truly original, surreally sadistic tableaux.

Described in the Marins trailer collection, *Visions of Terror,* as "a luxurious production for people of good taste" and "a majestic story for intelligent people," 1971's *The End of Man* shapes up as Coffin Joe's *King of Hearts.* This time out, Marins indulges his *Christ* complex: We first sight our hero walking naked from the sea and into the streets of São Paulo, where he performs *numero uno* of several unwitting "miracles": frightening a wheelchair-bound woman (played by Marins's real-life mom) into jumping up and running to warn her fellow citizens of his arrival (!). Eventually acquiring a wizard-esque wardrobe and adopting the name Finis Hominem (End of Man), Marins becomes a guru to the local hippie population, a savior to a modern Mary Magdalene, and a miracle worker for an ersatz Lazarus. By film's end, an entire nation, its frenzy fueled by an eager Brazilian media, turns its lonely eyes to Coffin Joe for guidance and salvation (!). *The End of Man* is Marins's most accessible (and funniest) flick, an oft clever, drop-deadpan satire that understates its most outrageous moments. It's also reminiscent of John Waters's *Mondo Trasho* in its use of found music, including instrumental Muzak arrangements ranging from "Goldfinger" and "Raindrops Keep Falling on My Head" to the Josephine Baker tune "La Petite Tonkinoise" (later recycled to deft comic effect in Richard Elfman's cult musical *Forbidden Zone* [Media]).

The Bloody Exorcism of Coffin Joe (1972) is Marins's meditation on the creative process. Jose plays himself, a moviemaker between projects and ideas who accepts a friend's invitation to spend the Christmas season at his country home. Marins portrays himself as distinctly separate from his fictional alter ego, the determinedly diabolical Coffin Joe, who, Marins fears, is more popular than his creator. During his stay, events turn sufficiently surreal that Marins winds up meeting his badder half at a wedding ceremony in hell (!), an exercise in vintage Coffin Joe excess: Naked zombie babes cavort while demons perform satanic rites incorporating mutilations, cannibalism, and other flagrant acts of religious irreverence. Happily, Marins heads home with a headful of fresh celluloid ideas.

Hellish Flesh (1971) boasts a more conventional, though clever, story line. Marins abandons his C.J. persona to portray cuckolded scientist George Medeiros. George's wife and her covert lowlife lover set fire to George's lab. The scientist survives the resultant inferno, but his disfiguring burns lead to painful reconstructive surgery. George takes to wearing a mask and hires a local detective to shadow his unfaithful spouse and her beau as they squander his money. Several twists add up to a victorious denouement for George.

An excellent outre party tape, *Visions of Terror* compiles trailers from 14 Marins movies, from pet projects like *Perversion* ("The cast of this daring movie includes Cacador Guerreiro and dozens of other actors!") to freelance directorial jobs like the "erotic comedy" *The Woman Who Makes Doves Fly,* the steamy *Women of the Violent Sex,* and the exploitation adventure *Sex and Blood in the Trail of the Treasure* (where "suspense unknown to the public is shown").

Visions of Terror concludes with Marins's "Macabre Nightmare," a live-burial-themed shock short that packs mucho jolts into a mere 20 minutes.

The sex-, surrealism-, and voodoo-drenched *Strange Hostel of Naked Pleasures* (1975, "presenting José Mojica Marins playing an enigmatic character, like only a genius like him could do"), directed by Marins protégé Marcello Motta, and the above-mentioned bizarre erotic thriller *Perversion*, starring Marins as a mad millionaire, complete Something Weird's J.M.M. set.

COFFIN FIT: Jose Mojica Marins's Coffin Joe sizes up potential victim in typically surreal tableau from Something Weird Video's C.J. series.
Courtesy of Something Weird Video

THE STRANGE DOOR (1951) B&W **½

D: Joseph Pevney. Charles Laughton, Boris Karloff, Sally Forrest, Richard Stapley, Michael Pate, Paul Cavanaugh. 81 mins. (Universal)

Universal Pictures had obviously lost, or at least misplaced, its classic-chiller chops when the studio made a rusty return to the fright field with the Nathaniel Hawthorne–drawn *The Black Castle* (see index) and the Robert Louis Stevenson adaptation *The Strange Door*. Fortunately, Laughton was aboard for this one, and the film belongs to him. Laughton obviously enjoys himself here as the extravagantly perverse Sire Alan de Maletroit, a rude nobleman whose lust for revenge inspires him to lock his own brother (Cavanaugh) in the castle dungeon for two decades while he searches for the worst possible mate to foist on the latter's daughter (Forrest). Boris is largely wasted as Cavanaugh's faithful servant (out of apparent desperation, he even throws in a vintage Frankenstein Monster gyrating-wrist gesture), but Laughton's thespian glee, imaginative set direction (by Russell A. Gausman and Julia Heron), and a taut protracted climax save *The Strange Door* from frequently encroaching torpor.

STRANGLER OF THE SWAMP (1945) B&W ***

D: Frank Wisbar. Rosemary La Planche, Charles Middleton, Blake Edwards. 60 mins. (Image) DVD

A moody mise-en-scène adds much to this swamp-set story of retribution directed by German émigré Wisbar and based on an earlier Teutonic film of his creation. Slow pacing and PRC's no-budget production values hinder the pic's progress, but *Strangler* remains well worth seeing. That's *the* Blake Edwards, by the way, cast as the unlikely love interest.

SUNDOWN: THE VAMPIRE IN RETREAT (1991) ***

D: Anthony Hickox. David Carradine, Jim Metzler, Morgan Brittany, John Ireland, Bruce Campbell, Deborah Foreman, Maxwell Caulfield. 104 mins. (Vestron, n.i.d.)

Sort of a Southwestern *Salem's Lot* with a more over-the-top approach, Hickox's *(Waxwork)* stylishly directed vampire pic combines black comedy with abundant violence capped by an all-out war between rival camps of armed vamps. Carradine heads a group of reform vampires who prefer the civilized practice of drinking artificial blood, while vet thesp Ireland leads a more traditional faction in favor of taking liquid refreshment the old-fashioned way. Metzler and Brittany play the human couple who unwisely wander into the vampire village of Purgatory, where Metzler resumes an old rivalry with former nemesis-turned-bloodsucker Caulfield. Campbell surfaces as the bumbling great-grandson of venerable vampire-hunter Van Helsing.

SUPERNATURAL (1933) B&W ***½

D: Victor Halperin. Carole Lombard, Randolph Scott, Vivienne Osborne, Alan Dinehart, H. B. Warner, Beryl Mercer. 64 mins. (Universal)

The same Halperin brothers (Victor and Edward) responsible for the atmospheric Bela Lugosi indie *White Zombie* (see index) hit heady horror heights with this chiller. *Supernatural* unfolds with pre-Code candor and often feels more like a modern movie in a period setting than an actual product of its time. Following on-screen quotations from Confucius, Matthew, and Muhammad (!), the film opens with scientist Warner petitioning a condemned murderess (a terrific Osborne, who conveys a sense of evil alternately destructive and seductive) to will him her body

---

Filmmakers in Focus!
OUR COFFEE WITH COFFIN JOE

It's not every day your Phantom gets to shoot the celluloid breeze with the likes of José Mojica (Coffin Joe) Marins over a cup of *café con leche*. For starters, the sixtysomething Brazilian cult actor/auteur had arrived for his first visit to these shores only the day before. Secondly, the Portuguese-speaking Marins knows barely four words of English (either "nice to meet you" or "thank you very much," we forget which), so we conducted our NYC-set confab with the vital assistance of writer/translator Andre Barcinski, quite probably the English-speaking world's foremost Coffin Joe authority.

The first thing we were struck by—or, more accurately, hoped *not* to be—were the trademark elongated nails curling from Marins's fingers. "Nine out of ten of them are real," Barcinski is quick to point out. The tenth, he explains, had been broken by an overenthusiastic fan on the flight up. Sure enough, a discreet glance revealed an obvious prosthetic—a pale imitation of the real thing—gracing Marins's left pinky.

Though José Mojica Marins has written and/or directed scores of feature films—including Brazil's very first Cinemascope movie, the 1959 western *The Adventurer's Fate*—he's best known, revered, and, in some quarters, reviled for his portrayal of fictional alter ego Ze de Caixao (Coffin Joe). Marins has actually devoted only two full features to Coffin Joe's exploits, but the character pops up in several others, as well as on TV shows, radio programs, and in comic books. In 1982 Marins even ran for the Brazilian Congress, losing, he claims, only because so many voters wrote in "Coffin Joe" instead of "José Mojica Marins"!

Marins first encountered his screen doppelgänger in a nightmare. "I was being dragged to my grave, a tombstone with my name and birthdate on it, by a faceless man," the self-taught auteur recalls. The man resembled an "Exu—a macumba saint people keep in their houses." (To illustrate his point, Marins asks Barcinski to bring forth his original costume—a black top hat, matching cape, and a medallion featuring a phoenix rising from the ashes.) As Marins views the character, Coffin Joe's mission is to shock people into taking responsibility for their own actions, rather than relying on the crutches of religion, be it Catholicism, the Africa-imported macumba, or Brazil's many strange convergences of the twain. "Whether you worship God or Satan," Marins opines, "it's the same thing."

Marins spent a nomadic youth traveling Brazil's more remote regions with his circus-performer parents and claims he was kidnapped by gypsies, held against his will until his father could raise the ransom money (a not-uncommon crime, even today, in Brazil). Marins developed his celluloid jones when his dad later managed a movie theater. "I saw *Tower of London*," Marins recalls, among other Universal fright films. When his father bought him an 8-millimeter camera, young Marins was on his way.

Marins cites Roman Polanski's *Rosemary's Baby* as his fave fear film. Among his own efforts, he admits a special affection for his 1971 social satire *The End of Man*, a film whose aim was to "expose false prophets."

Financing has been a constant problem for the prolific, iconoclastic auteur. Most Brazilian films are—or at least were—funded by a government film office.

Marins's maverick methods, perverse themes, and subversive messages failed to endear him to those appointed to dispense the *dinero,* forcing him to raise funds where he could, which often meant dealing with fly-by-night producers, distributors, or investors. His films didn't travel well because there are few Portuguese-speaking markets beyond Brazil and his work was considered too niche (to put it politely) to warrant the expense of adding subtitles. Marins credits more mainstream Brazilian director Glauber (*Antonio Das Mortes*) Rocha with helping him get at least a few of his films shown at various Euro festivals.

In addition to low budgets, Marins works with the specter of censorship hanging overhead. ("*Siempre!*" he sighs.) He attracted the authorities' negative attention early on when word of his unorthodox actor auditions reached their ears. To test his potential thesps' intestinal mettle, Marins would ask them to perform feats above and beyond the normal casting call, like ingesting live roaches (!). The acts were performed strictly on a voluntary basis, and Marins discovered no lack of actors willing to do virtually anything to score roles in his films.

Marins's movies themselves have routinely suffered unkind cuts at the hands and scissors of Brazilian censors. Before the release of one Marins film, his producer threatened to jump out a government-building window if censors refused to pass the film. Neither small minds nor undernourished budgets have deterred José Mojica Marins from his cinematic mission. He's already filmed (and, he claims, actively directed) his own eye operation. "I can't wait," the hitherto soft-spoken Marins suddenly exults with unconcealed glee, "till people talk about the FX!"

---

after death; it's the doc's belief that he can capture her wicked "soul" and prevent it from occupying another living person. Dinehart is a ruthless Greenwich Village spiritualist who shares a shady past with the now-late Osborne. When heiress Lombard's twin brother dies, Dinehart sneaks into the funeral parlor, makes a death mask, and contacts Lombard to scam her into staging a séance (a sequence that may have served as an early inspiration for Ed Wood's immortal séance in *Night of the Ghouls*). While those around her—including fiancé Scott—advise against the idea, Lombard agrees to Dinehart's proposal. The tables turn when Osborne's spirit returns to inhabit Lombard, who sets about settling an old score with the oily spiritualist. This swift, streamlined shocker is consistently strong on mood and ambience. Dinehart and Mercer (Cagney's saintly Hibernian mom in *Public Enemy*) as his avaricious landlady inhabit a Greenwich Village that's strictly and strikingly a figment of the set designer's imagination. Both future comedienne Lombard and soon-to-be saddle star Scott (then a supernatural specialist, with similar heroic roles in *Murders in the Zoo* and *She*) lend conviction to their characters, while Dinehart is equally credible as the coolly degenerate huckster.

THE SURGEON (A.K.A. *EXQUISITE TENDERNESS*) (1994) **¹/₂

D: Carl Schenkel. Isabel Glasser, James Remar, Sean Haberle, Peter Boyle, Malcolm McDowell, Charles Dance. 100 mins. (A-Pix) DVD

T*he Surgeon*'s producers were apparently thinking big-screen fright franchise when they sank a reported $11 mil into the operation, which subsequently sat for a couple of years before its belated homevid bow. An initially unknown surgical psycho plagues a Seattle hospital (with Vancouver filling in), collecting pituitary extract from unlucky patients, while also offing select medical personnel. It's up to docs Glasser and Remar (both appealing here) to stop the medical maniac. *The Surgeon* offers a fair measure of suspense and a plethora of gore, courtesy of makeup-FX ace Steve Johnson. Highlights include a zesty perf by McDowell as an arrogant surgeon, a crazed-baboon attack, and a mouth-sewing scene that mirrors the mother of all mouth-sewing scenes in 1933's *Murders in the Zoo.* Still, *The Surgeon* descends from a tense horror-mystery first half to a predictable series of standard slay tableaux.

SUSPIRIA (1977) ***¹/₂

D: Dario Argento. Jessica Harper, Stefania Casini, Joan Bennett, Alida Valli, Udo Kier. 92 mins. (Fox Lorber) DVD

A rgento's masterwork first surfaced on cassette in 1989 on the Magnum label, where it reportedly racked up impressive sales with Dariophiles willing to pay the full $90 freight for a copy. When the label went under, *Suspiria* again vanished from the shelves of all but the best-stocked specialty outlets. Finally, a major indie label, Fox Lorber, licensed Argento's gem, presenting a letter-boxed edition at a collectible price. For the uninitiated, Harper stars as a Yank ballet student who inadvertently dances into a witches' den. Vet actresses Bennett and Valli add to the gothic fun, while Argento's rock group, Goblin, contributes one of its best high-decibel, anxiety-provoking scores. *Suspiria* has lost none of its shock value over the ensuing years—the sight of a blind musician being gorily attacked by his own possessed Seeing Eye dog remains an indelible image—and rates as an essential addition to every serious horror buff's homevid library. Argento's recommended 1996 serial-killer chiller, *The Stendhal Syndrome,* received a 1999 VHS/DVD release via Troma.

SWINGERS MASSACRE (A.K.A. *INSIDE AMY*) (1975) ****½**

D: Ronald V. Garcia. Eastman Price, Jan Mitchell, Gary Kent, Marsha Jordan, Ushi Digart, Rene Bond. 90 mins. (Standard, n.i.d.)

A dorky middle-aged lawyer (Price), suffering from intense, self-inflicted Swingin' '70s peer pressure, persuades his lovely, loyal wife (Mitchell) to join him in an ill-advised swapping adventure. Ill-advised for our hero at least, since the experience proves to be nothing if not humiliating. While he fails to function among the seasoned swingers, *she* gets it on with abandon, sampling every intimidating stud in the house. Price can't get no satisfaction on *any* level—his better half neither repents nor loses her affection for him, all of which further enrages our frustrated protagonist. The logical solution? Why, kill the studs one by one with a variety of phallic instruments! Less a soft-core sex-and-gore orgy than an offbeat parable, *Swingers Massacre*—penned by femme scripter Elene Arthur—shapes up as a crude but compelling chronicle that contains more than its expected share of ironic twists and raw truths.

TALE OF A VAMPIRE (1992) *******

D: Shimako Sato. Julian Sands, Suzanna Hamilton, Kenneth Cranham. 93 mins. (Trimark)

Despite echoes of Coppola's *Bram Stoker's Dracula* and Katt Shea's *Dance of the Damned,* this British/Japanese coproduction arrives as a worthy addition to the video vampire genre in its own right. Sands stars as a sensitive, literate but lethal decades-old bloodsucker who, like Coppola's Drac, locates in contempo femme Hamilton a suitable replacement for a long-lost love (seen in flashbacks). Both Sands and research librarian Hamilton imbue their roles with charisma and complexity. Director Sato yields the maximum atmosphere from his modern-London

locales, and parts of this deliberately paced tale, while fairly generous in the blood-and-gore department, are downright poetic.

TALES FROM THE CRYPT:
THE SERIES

TALES FROM THE CRYPT: DEMON KNIGHT (1995) *******

D: Ernest Dickerson. William Sadler, Billy Zane, Jada Pinkett, CCH Pounder, Brenda Bakke, Dick Miller, John Schuck, Gary Farmer. 92 mins. (Universal) DVD

The initial *Tales* feature arrives as an *Evil Dead* with a more overt religious hook. While there's little that's essentially new on view, frequent Spike Lee cinematographer Dickerson keeps his grue stew at a sufficiently steady boil to satisfy fright fans, while a strong cast gives the material its all. The weakest element here is the crypt-keeper wraparound; the film proper, drawn from a script originally written independently of the series, stands on its own.

TALES FROM THE CRYPT PRESENTS "BORDELLO OF BLOOD" (1996) ******

D: Gilbert Adler. Dennis Miller, Erika Eleniak, Angie Everhart, Chris Sarandon. 89 mins. (Universal) DVD

You know you're in trouble when the best thing about a flick is smarmmeister Dennis Miller's presence. That's the sad case with the second theatrical *Tales from the Crypt* entry, *Bordello of Blood,* a decided descent from the middling heights reached by *Demon Knight.* Although some laughs, most engendered by Miller's deadpan asides (he serves as sort of an on-screen *Mystery Science Theater 3000* 'bot here), emerge from *Bordello,* the movie is gravely undermined by an inane story line and a misogynistic streak more pro-

nounced than the norm. Also worth a look are Freddie Francis's 1971 Brit *Tales from the Crypt* (Prism), likewise adapted from the EC Comics of the same name and starring Peter Cushing, Joan Collins, and Ralph Richardson; and Roy Ward Baker's EC-drawn 1973 *The Vault of Horror* (Media), with Curt Jurgens, Terry-Thomas, and Glynis Johns, More than a dozen volumes of the original *Tales From the Crypt* cable-TV series are also out (HBO).

TALES FROM THE DARKSIDE: THE MOVIE (1990) ****½**

D: John Harrison. Deborah Harry, Christian Slater, David Johansen, James Remar, Rae Dawn Chong, Robert Klein, Steve Buscemi, William Hickey. 93 mins. (Paramount)

The long-running TV terror series' big-screen debut adopts a three-tale format framed by a wraparound featuring Debbie (Blondie) Harry as a suburban cannibal. While not up to the same pair's *Creepshow,* the George Romero/Stephen King collaboration "Cat from Hell" emerges as the best of the trio, offering inventive sepia-toned lensing, imaginative gore FX, and quirky perfs by Hickey and Johansen. Solid acting and effects (courtesy of the KNB EFX Group) likewise highlight the otherwise routine companion tales "Lover's Vow," with Remar and Chong, and "Lot 49" ("inspired" by an Arthur Conan Doyle story), with Slater and Buscemi. Despite *Tales*'s generally mechanical story lines and overreliance on claustrophobic, interior-bound settings, the video should please *Darkside* devotees.

TEMPTRESS (1995) ******

D: Lawrence Lanoff. Kim Delaney, Chris Sarandon, Corbin Bernsen, Dee Wallace Stone, Jessica Walter, Ben Cross. 93 mins. (Playboy/Paramount)

Foxy photog Delaney returns stateside from a spiritually invigorating

India trip, only to transform into a Psycho Slut Slave of the Evil Sex Goddess Kali, leading her to whip a drunken Bernsen's groin with her long blond hair (!) in the midst of an art party. When Bernsen takes a sudden descent down an elevator shaft, Kim's corporate lawyer beau (Sarandon) starts to worry. To the potential rescue comes Indian scholar Cross, who clues Chris in to the awful truth (accent on *awful*). While *Temptress*, the second entry in *Playboy*'s short-lived Paramount-distributed video-feature line (following *Cover Me* and preceding *Playback*), tries to spook with hallucinatory glimpses of secret Indian rites presided over by the real-deal Kali, the pic seems more concerned with working in the requisite number of would-be "sizzling" sex scenes.

TERROR AT RED WOLF INN (1972) ***

D: Bud Townsend. Linda Gillin, Arthur Space, John Neilson, Mary Jackson, Michael Macready. 90 mins. (Academy, n.i.d.)

Alternately titled *Terror House* and *Red Wolf Inn*, Townsend's film is an authentically sick yet relatively subtle sleeper that functions as both a fun fright flick and an effective visual dietary aid. Our story involves a family of folksy suspected cannibals—an older couple (Space, Jackson) and their unhinged grandson (Neilson)—who lure unsuspecting gals to the isolated title locale via a "free vacation" mail scam. Our heroine, a lonely but ebullient coed named Regina (winningly played by Gillin), gradually catches on to her attentive hosts' unorthodox eating habits when the other guests begin vanishing one by one. Despite a food-stamp budget, *Terror* is rich in sly wit and suspense.

TERROR AT THE OPERA (1987) ***

D: Dario Argento. Cristina Marsillach, Ian Charleson, Urbano Barberini, William McNamara, Daria Nicolodi. 107 mins. In R and unrated editions. (Southgate, n.i.d.)

"Italian Hitchcock" (alternately known as the "Visconti of Violence," to say nothing of the "De Sica of Sickness," "Capra of Carnage," and "Godard of Gore") Argento's opus (originally simply *Opera*) shapes up as a simultaneously stylish and brutal exercise that shouldn't disappoint the director's fans. Argento sets *Opera*'s tone early by focusing on a squawking raven who gives a megalunged diva much sonic competition during a rehearsal of Verdi's *Macbeth*. Said diva is soon hit by a car, paving the way for singer Marsillach to assume the opera's starring role as Lady Macbeth. Unfortunately for her and the rest of the crew, a demented diva devotee, secretly in love with Cristina, decides to goreslaughter several of their number. In addition to putting scissors and knives to creative lethal use, the masked maniac indulges in much intense ocular torture, forcing young Cristina to witness his hideous atrocities by taping straight pins under her eyelids (!). *Terror at the Opera* represented Argento's costliest cut-'em-up to that point, a reported $8 mil. Other available Argento terrors include uncut, uncensored VHS/DVD editions of *Phenomena* (a.k.a. *Creepers*) and *Tenebrae* (a.k.a. *Unsane*), both via Anchor Bay.

THE TEXAS CHAINSAW MASSACRE:
THE SERIES

THE TEXAS CHAINSAW MASSACRE (1974) ***1/2

D: Tobe Hooper. Marilyn Burns, Ed Neal, Gunnar Hansen. 84 mins. (MPI) DVD

Not as gory as originally advertised, Hooper's semi-satiric exercise in celluloid Gein-ocology still rates as a must for fright buffs and casual viewers alike. Ed ("My family's always been in meat") Neal, as the middle brother in the cannibalistic clan, cops top acting honors, while Hansen's "Leatherface" proves worthy of his vaunted status in the horror-character pantheon.

THE TEXAS CHAINSAW MASSACRE 2: COLLECTOR'S EDITION (1986) *1/2

D: Tobe Hooper. Dennis Hopper, Caroline Williams, Bill Johnson, Jim Siedow, Bill Moseley. 111 mins. total (Anchor Bay)

For all its well-intended pokes at American (or Texan, anyhow) violence, an amoral free-enterprise system run amok, and other worthy targets, Hooper's sequel isn't nearly as funny or scary as the original. Hopper, as "Lefty" Enright, a hard-nosed Texas Ranger equipped with holstered chainsaws (!), exhibits little of the manic energy normally associated with the dynamic thesp. The plot finds Hopper hot on the trail of the sicko Sawyer clan—played in splatstick Three Stooges style by original chainsaw maniac Siedow, with Johnson and Moseley replacing Hansen and Neal—who butchered his wheelchair-bound brother 12 years earlier. A femme deejay (Williams) leads Hop to the loonies' labyrinthine lair, where most of this virtually one-set wonder unfolds. In fact, the Sawyers' ghoulishly appointed subterranean slaughterhouse is one of the pic's few pluses, along with Tom Savini's reliably revolting makeup FX and a few stray laughs, including a brief opening *Texas Chainsaw Massacre* rap song.

LEATHERFACE: TEXAS CHAINSAW MASSACRE III (1990) *1/2

D: Jeff Burr. Kate Hodge, Viggo Mortensen, William Butler, Ken Foree, Joe Unger. In R and unrated editions. 85 mins. (Columbia/TriStar)

Leatherface recycles the *TCM* brand name in the service of a routine slice-and-dicer. Director Burr and "splatterpunk" scripter David Schow ignore *TCM 2* (admittedly not a difficult chore) and join the somehow resurrected cannibal clan—expanded here to seven members, including a lethal little blond brat (Jennifer Banko) in a Patty McCormack/*Bad Seed* vein—some 15 years and 70 or so victims later. Into the flesh-famished family's web come unsuspecting yuppies Hodge and Butler and survivalist Foree. The flick ultimately degenerates into a series of predictable stalk-and-saw scenes as a skin-masked Leatherface (R. A. Mihailoff) gives his new golden chainsaw a bloody workout while his crazed kin torment a captive Hodge, predictable antics capped by a well-worn "surprise" ending.

TEXAS CHAINSAW MASSACRE: THE NEXT GENERATION (1994) **½

D: Kim Henkel. Renee Zellweger, Matthew McConaughey, Robert Jacks, Tonie Perenski, Joe Stevens. 94 mins. (Columbia/TriStar) DVD

Carrying a 1994 copyright, *Texas Chainsaw Massacre: The Next Generation* was sprung from the vaults in 1997 to cash in on the growing celebrity of Texas-natives-turned-Hollywood-stars Zellweger and McConaughey. Original *TCM* scripter Kim Henkel's remake can't hold a chainsaw to the original but earns higher marks than the earlier sequels. Zellweger impresses in her strenuous, scream-driven turn as Jenny, a prom-night nerdette who, with three other victims, wanders into the lair of the infamous family that slays together. McConaughey offers an unsubtle interpretation of demented clan leader Vilmer, who comes complete with a remote-controlled mechanical leg and who dominates brothers W.E. (Stevens) and a cross-dressing Leatherface (Jacks). A late-arriving corporate conspiratorial twist adds a conceptually clever but ultimately deflating note to the proceedings (seems simple,

hardworking, chainsaw-fearing cannibal folk can't cut it on their own nowadays).

THEATRE OF BLOOD   (1973) ***

D: Douglas Hickox. Vincent Price, Diana Rigg, Jack Hawkins, Robert Morley. 105 mins. (MGM)

Price is typecast as an incurable Shakespearean ham who strikes back at his sundry critics. It takes considerable filler to pad the pic's lone idea to feature length, but there are enough payoffs to make for satisfying viewing. The Grand Guignol–set *Theatre of Death* (VCI), with Chris Lee, is likewise worth catching.

THEY WATCH   (1993) ***

D: John Korty. Patrick Bergin, Vanessa Redgrave, Valerie Mahaffey, Nancy Moore Atchison, Brandlyn Whitaker. 100 mins. (Columbia/TriStar)

After the accidental death of his 11-year-old daughter (Atchison), rapidly unraveling architect Bergin finds himself drawn, by a sketch and a matching photo, to the house of blind but second-sighted seer Redgrave, on whose grounds frolic the "lost souls" of children trapped between life and death. Korty's oft haunting ghost fable, adapted and updated by Edithe Swenson from Rudyard Kipling's short story, gets off to a somewhat pedestrian start but picks up once an excellent Bergin and Redgrave assume center stage. Several *Carnival of Souls*–styled images punctuate the poignant proceedings— an embittered ghost called the Owl Girl is an especially inspired creation— and help elevate this South Carolina–lensed, made-for-Showtime poltergeist parable to an emotionally potent level.

TORMENTED   (1960) B&W **½

D: Bert I. Gordon. Richard Carlson, Juli Reding, Susan Gordon, Joe Turkel. 75 mins. (Sinister Cinema)

Jazz pianist Carlson finds himself in the titular condition after killing his troublesome ex to pave the way for his pending marriage to a California socialite. Gordon's ghost story relies on cheap FX and a moody lighthouse setting to nudge it along but stacks up as agreeably tacky '50s fun.

THE TORTURE CHAMBER OF BARON BLOOD   (1972) **½

D: Mario Bava. Joseph Cotten, Elke Sommer, Massimo Girotti. 90 mins. (Anchor Bay)

Cotten is a revivified 16th-century warlock/nobleman determined to torture his castle's current inhabitants, the ever foxy Elke among them. Previously out in a truncated version via HBO under the title *Baron Blood*, Anchor Bay's 1996 reissue represents Bava's complete Italo version. No relation to the surreal 1967 *Pit and the Pendulum*–based horror *The Torture Chamber of Dr. Sadism* (Magnum), with Christopher Lee, also out as *Blood Demon* and in a shortened version called *Castle of the Walking Dead* (Interglobal).

TORTURE GARDEN   (1967) ***

D: Freddie Francis. Jack Palance, Burgess Meredith, Beverly Adams, Peter Cushing. 93 mins. (Columbia/TriStar)

Meredith is the mysterious Dr. Diabolo, a sideshow barker who treats spectators to terrifying forecasts of their uniformly awful futures in Francis's fertile fright anthology. Fun going, with Palance particularly sharp as a crazed Poe fanatic.

TOWER OF LONDON   (1939) B&W ***

D: Rowland V. Lee. Basil Rathbone, Boris Karloff, Barbara O'Neil, Vincent Price, Ian Hunter, Rose Hobart, Nan Grey. 92 mins. (Universal)

Sort of a witty, horror-tinged *Classics Illustrated* take on "What Makes Richard III Run" (or, more accurately, "Hobble"), Lee's look at murderous court politics in 15th-century England becomes more fun once its intricate, incestuous intrigues grow easier to sort out. Highlights include an ultimately fatal drinking duel between Rathbone (terrific, if a tad too fit-looking, as the serpentine "crookback" Richard) and his brother Clarence (an equally excellent Price); Boris's textured turn as chrome-domed, clubfooted court executioner Mord; and a stellar supporting cast. The multiple conspiracies are enough to make Oliver Stone salivate. As a young, soon-to-be-dead Prince Edward muses, "It's very queer. One day everyone is so pleasant, and then the next they tell me I'm no longer king." That's life in the big tower, kid.

TRAUMA (1993) ***

D: Dario Argento. Christopher Rydell, Asia Argento, Piper Laurie, Laura Johnson, James Russo, Brad Dourif, Frederic Forrest. In R and unrated editions. 106 mins. (Worldvision)

After a somewhat disjointed start, *Trauma* (no relation to the 1962 American terror turkey of the same title [Sinister Cinema]) twists its way to a surprising, extremely revolting climax. Anorexic teen Aura (Dario's daughter Asia, whose petite frame houses one high-decibel set of scream-happy lungs) is saved from an attempted suicide by Rydell, an art-department staffer at a local TV station that's been tracking the grisly progress of a mysterious decapitator. The latter, dubbed "the Headhunter," targets select medical personnel and strikes only on rainy nights. Rydell's concern for the tormented teen soon draws him into the bloody case. While there are fewer trademark Argento flourishes here than in the Fellini of Fright's *Suspiria* or *Deep Red*, *Trauma* flaunts its fair share of disturbing imagery and graphic gore FX (cour-

tesy of Tom Savini). Laurie, sporting a deep-black dye job, gives her scariest perf since *Carrie,* while Dourif has a brief but characteristically twitchy turn as an ex-doctor/drug addict.

TRICK OR TREAT (1986) **½

D: Charles Martin Smith. Marc Price, Tony Fields, Gene Simmons, Lisa Orgolini, Doug Savant, Ozzy Osbourne. 97 mins. (Lorimar, n.i.d.)

Trick or Treat borrows liberally from both *Carrie* and *Nightmare on Elm Street* yet manages to emerge as a well-crafted, fairly funny homage to '80s heavy-metal hostility. Price toplines as high school scapegoat Eddie, who unwittingly conjures the disfigured ghost of his late rock idol, Sammi ("Rock's chosen warriors will rule the apocalypse!") Curr, to help rid him of his sundry tormentors. But it seems that Sammi (hammily interpreted by Fields) has more serious mischief of his own in mind. Director Smith—who played the nerd Terry in *American Graffiti* and appears here (in a clever cameo) as equally nerdy teacher Mr. Wimley—gives us a far darker vision of adolescent life in this lively but nongory allegory. Real-life rockers Simmons and Osbourne also turn up in brief bits, as a local deejay and an antirock evangelist (!), respectively.

TRILOGY OF TERROR:
THE SERIES

TRILOGY OF TERROR II (1996) **½

D: Dan Curtis. Lysette Anthony, Geraint Wyn Davies, Matt Clark, Geoffrey Lewis, Blake Heron, Richard Fitzpatrick, Thomas Mitchell. 90 mins. (Paramount)

Former Britcom star and '90s B-video mainstay Anthony assumes the Karen Black mantle in Dan (*Dark Shadows*) Curtis's belated sequel to his 1975 made-for-TV cult item, *Trilogy of Terror* (Anchor Bay, DVD). The follow-up

also marks "the return of a horror fan favorite: the African Zuni fetish doll" (per the sleeve copy), and as in the first go-round, that toothy little terror toplines in the best of the three episodes: "He Who Kills," a pitched battle between trapped scientist Anthony and the aforementioned Zuni doll, who's lost none of his menace (or teeth) in the intervening years.

TWINS OF EVIL (1971) **½

D: John Hough. Peter Cushing, Madeleine Collinson, Mary Collinson, Dennis Price. 85 mins. (VidAmerica, n.i.d.)

Matching *Playboy* Playmates and real-life twins Mary and Madeleine Collinson play "Which One's the Vampire?" in a slick if predictable Hammer period piece. The video, transferred from the original Brit print, contains restored footage not seen in the American theatrical release. Femme vampire fans are also referred to Roy Ward Baker's superior 1971 *The Vampire Lovers* (Nelson), a sexy redo of Sheridan Le Fanu's "Carmilla" that sees lesbian bloodsucker Ingrid Pitt drain Peter Cushing's daughters, and the sequel, *Lust for a Vampire* (HBO).

TWO EVIL EYES (1990) ***

D: George Romero, Dario Argento. Adrienne Barbeau, Harvey Keitel, E. G. Marshall, Ramy Zada, Madeleine Potter, Martin Balsam, Kim Hunter, Sally Kirkland, John Amos. 121 mins. (Fox)

The famous fear auteurs' double visions of Edgar Allan Poe constitute two hours of solid shocks. Up first is Romero's contempo account of Poe's "Facts in the Case of M. Valdemar," a sardonic narrative in a *Creepshow* vein that reunites *Creepshow* alums Marshall, as a lawyer, and Barbeau, as Jessica, soon-to-be-merry widow of a dying millionaire. Jessica's doctor beau (Zada) uses hypnotism to control the ailing codger's mind while keeping him alive long enough for his will to go into effect. Trouble ensues when those self-same hypnotic techniques prevent the tycoon's brain from expiring even after his body bids adieu. Romero draws upon his sharply honed scare skills to milk the straightforward story for a fair amount of chills.

Argento exhibits more ambition in his ultra-eclectic update of Poe's "The Black Cat," weaving in threads from such other Poe stories as "The Pit and the Pendulum" and "The Cask of Amontillado." Keitel contributes a strong perf as feline-phobic crime photog Rod Usher. Argento probably had enough material and energy to go feature-length with his segment, which, with a running time of roughly 65 minutes, ultimately suffers from a truncated feel. *Two Evil Eyes* may not break new genre ground, but the film covers its oft trod terror turf with sure footing by a pair of pros.

TWO THOUSAND MANIACS! (1964) ***

D: Herschell Gordon Lewis. Connie Mason, Thomas Wood, Jeffrey Allen, Ben Moore. 75 mins. (Something Weird) DVD

Lensed in scenic St. Cloud, Florida, *Two Thousand Maniacs!* is probably the closest goremeister Lewis ever came to crafting a crossover movie (or, for that matter, to crafting a movie). This splatter update of *Brigadoon* (more of a "Brigadoom") succeeds in being genuinely sardonic, slickly paced, memorably scored (by H.G. himself, with major assists from the Pleasant Valley Boys), and even downright entertaining.

THE UGLY (1997) ***

D: Scott Reynolds. Paolo Rotondo, Rebecca Hobbs, Roy Ward, Vanessa Byrnes, Paul Glover, Chris Graham. 94 mins. (Trimark) DVD

Debuting writer/director Reynolds injects fresh life (and much death)

into his New Zealand–set entry in the overworked serial-killer genre. Reynolds's tale focuses on the notorious Simon Cartwright (Rotundo), an innocent-looking youth whose violent behavior dates back to early adolescence when he offed his deranged, domineering mother. Employing a *Silence of the Lambs*–styled setup, our story opens with controversial, much publicized shrink Dr. Karen Schumacher (Hobbs) getting Simon to agree to a series of grisly interviews. Reynolds then intercuts between the current sessions and Simon's assorted childhood traumas ("the Ugly," the name Simon lends those personal demons who compel him to kill, derives from a torn copy of the fairy tale *The Ugly Duckling*) and re-creations of some of his most horrific razor-blade murders. Like the title killer in *Henry*, Simon deliberately avoids setting a predictable pattern, including men, women, children, acquaintances, and strangers alike among his victims (he's kind to animals, though). It becomes increasingly clear that Karen's obsession with the articulate killer represents her own guilt-driven flirtation with self-destruction.

What separates Reynolds's film from the rest of the serial-killer pack is its complex structure, momentum-gathering pace, and rapidly shifting POV—from Simon's flashbacks, fantasies, and truly chilling visions of "the Visitors" (those past victims who urge him to slay anew, seen as grotesque, gored, but oddly beautiful angels), to Karen's own frequent hallucinations, to the camera's seemingly "objective" eye when both characters share the same frame. While the film echoes *Se7en* and *Psycho* as well as *Silence*, *The Ugly* is a work whose images linger in the mind (though not always pleasantly) long after the end credits roll.

THE UNCANNY (1977) **1/2

D: Denis Heroux. Peter Cushing, Samantha Eggar, Ray Milland, Donald Pleasence. 85 mins. (Media)

Felines of the world unite against their human oppressors in a trilogy of tales linked to killer cats and lifted by a top vet cast. Cat lovers should lap it up. We also refer the latter to *Because of the Cats* (Prism), *Night of a Thousand Cats* (Paragon, n.i.d.), *Strays* (Universal), and *Uninvited*, all roundly endorsed by Zontar, Official Phantom Feline.

UNCLE SAM (1996) ***

D: William Lustig. Bo Hopkins, Timothy Bottoms, Robert Forster, P. J. Soles, William Smith, David "Shark" Fralick, Isaac Hayes, Christopher Ogden, Leslie Neale. 90 mins. (A-Pix) DVD

Maniac Cop series collaborators—scripter Larry Cohen and director Lustig—reunite for *Uncle Sam*, sort of a Gulf War variation on Bob Clark's 'Nam-themed cult horror film, *Deathdream* (see index). After his chopper is shot down by "friendly fire" in Kuwait, Desert Storm "hero" Sam Harper's (Fralick) charred remains are shipped back to his Midwest hometown of Twin Rivers, much to the relief of his abused ex (Anne Tremko) and resentful sister (Neale), both of whom had feared he might still be alive. Indeed, as military escort Sergeant Twining (Hopkins) soon discovers, Sam's preteen nephew Jody (Ogden) is about the only one who mourns the expired SOB, a right-wing hardcase whose "heroics" masked his outright sadism. When Jody unlocks Sam's coffin, resting in the Harper home, he inadvertently paves the way for his uncle's violent return to life. Under the cover of an Uncle Sam disguise and a Fourth of July pageant, the vengeful zombie targets several locals for termination, dealing death via hanging, decapitation, and, in the movie's most spectacular scene, fireworks. Writer Cohen's attack on misguided gung-ho values lacks the subtler satiric thrust of such Cohen classics as *It Lives* and *The Stuff* (see index). But *Uncle*

SAY UNCLE: Patriotic zombie Sam Harper (David "Shark" Fralick) looks forward to a "gore-ious" Fourth in William Lustig's holiday horror Uncle Sam.
Courtesy of A-Pix Entertainment

Sam delivers the goods as a straight-ahead horror flick peppered with darkly comic moments and makes for ideal July Fourth homeviewing.

THE UNDEAD   (1957) B&W **1/2

D: Roger Corman. Richard Garland, Pamela Duncan, Allison Hayes, Mel Welles, Val Dufour, Billy Barty, Richard Devon, Bruno VeSota, Dick Miller. 75 mins. (Allied Artists)

A bid to cash in on the then-hot Bridey Murphy reincarnation craze (itself the direct inspiration for 1956's *The Search for Bridey Murphy* [Paramount]), *The Undead*, may not be Corman's best pic, but it certainly ranks among his weirdest. Scripted by Mark Hanna and Charles (*Little Shop of Horrors*) Griffith, the movie—originally titled *The Trance of Dianna Love*—opens with a prologue featuring AIP vet Devon as Satan, then segues into the present (1957). Callous psychic researcher Dufour hypnotizes hooker Duncan ("No telling how many fathoms deeper we'll have to sink into that murky mind of hers!") into reliving one of her past lives, as a medieval French lass unfairly sentenced to die for witchery. From that point on, the flick flashes back and forward between the hypno session and the drama unfolding centuries earlier. The stellar cast includes Hayes (*Attack of the 50-Foot Woman*) as a legit witch, Welles as the film's token would-be Shakespearean low-comedy relief (a doggerel-singing grave-digger), Miller as a local leper, and Barty as an imp (as Allison explains, "We witches each have one, you know"). *The Undead* also offers the hottest graveyard choreography this side of Ed Wood's *Orgy of the Dead* (Rhino) and served as the foil for one of *Mystery Science Theater 3000*'s wittiest episodes.

THE UNDYING MONSTER   (1942) B&W **1/2

D: John Brahm. James Ellison, John Howard, Heather Angel. 60 mins. (Sinister Cinema)

Coastal residents try to ascertain the identity of the werewolf who's been terrorizing the Brit countryside. Director Brahm adds enough atmospheric touches to qualify this fairly unsung B chiller as an hour well spent.

THE UNEARTHING   (1993) ***

D: Barry Poltermann, Wrye Martin. Norman Moses, Tina Ona Paukstelis, Mildred Nierras, Jamie Jacobs Anderson, Victor DeLorenzo, Flora Coker. 83 mins. (Prism)

Lensed largely in rural Wisconsin under the original title *Aswang* and populated by talented but credibly unglamorous thesps, *The Unearthing*—like its most obvious model, *The Texas Chainsaw Massacre*—is an intense exercise in extreme claustrophobia and disorientation. Wealthy Peter Null (Moses) arrives at his family's sprawling estate accompanied by teen Janine (Paukstelis), a contracted surrogate who's about to bear his child, ostensibly to enable him to collect his eventual inheritance. In reality, Null, his weird, impaired mom (Anderson), and "real" wife (Coker) are secret "aswangs," mega-tongued vampires who must feed on living fetuses to ensure their survival. Assisting the creepy Null clan is a Filipina maid named Cupid (!), played with sly menace by Nierras. Filmmakers Martin and Poltermann, who share producing, scripting, and directing credits, convey terror through nuance and detail as well as selective splatter moments. Fright fans would be well advised to ignore the vid's unpromising packaging and snatch this winner off the shelf.

THE UNHOLY   (1988) *1/2

D: Camilo Vila. Ben Cross, Hal Holbrook, Ned Beatty, William Russ, Trevor Howard, Jill Carroll. 100 mins. (Vestron)

Coscripted by Philip Yordan, *The Unholy* plays like a belated, claustrophobic *Exorcist* clone, with New Orleans priest Cross (at least the name fits) battling a determined demon named Desidarius (though it's the movie's relentless off-screen wind machine that seems to do most of the damage). There are a few deft touches, as when Cross starts receiving crank calls from hell (!), but not enough to raise the flick's temp much above a low boil.

THE UNINVITED   (1944) B&W ***

D: Lewis Allen. Ray Milland, Ruth Hussey, Donald Crisp. 99 mins. (Universal)

New homeowners Milland and Hussey discover their house is haunted in Allen's atmospheric, ultimately poignant screen version of the Dorothy Macardle novel, a successful A-movie stab at Val Lewton–styled quiet horror.

URBAN LEGEND   (1998) **1/2

D: Jamie Blanks. Jared Leto, Alicia Witt, Rebecca Gayheart, Joshua Jackson, Loretta Divine, Robert Englund, John Neville, Danielle Harris. 100 mins. (Columbia/TriStar) DVD

A reasonably clever, campus-set youth-horror outing that borrows equally from *Candyman* and *Scream*, *Urban Legend* also lifts freely from several long-standing—you guessed it—urban legends. Witt, late of the superior *Fun* (see index), plays the main femme stalkee who's trying to uncover the truth behind Pendleton College's own legend involving a 30-year-old student massacre. Robert (Freddy) Englund surfaces as a professor of urban legends, while Brad Dourif puts in an unbilled cameo as a seemingly crazed gas-station attendant, and former endangered tyke Harris (*Halloween 4* and *5*) turns up here as an oversexed goth queen (!). While hardly a groundbreaker, *Urban Legend* at least exceeds the watchability level of *I Know What You Did Last Summer* and sequel. One question though, re the end credits: How do you distinguish "Nerdy Guy" from "Dorky Guy"?

UROTSUKIDÔJI:
THE SERIES

UROTSUKIDÔJI: LEGEND OF THE OVERFIEND   (1989) ***

D: Hideki Takayama. Animated. Dubbed. 108 mins. (Central Park Media) DVD

The first Japanese "erotic grotesque" to land a stateside theatrical release (with an NC-17 rating, no less), Takayama's *animé* epic—reedited from the first three episodes of the same animation director's popular video series, *The Wandering Kid*—mixes monsters, mutations, heavy-metal mythology, and kinky sex. The pic's involved plot centers on a search for the new "Chojin," or Overfiend, a superbeing who appears, in human form, once every 3,000 years. It's said Chojin's sacred mission is to destroy

the existing world and unite its three mutually antagonistic dimensions—the human world, the man-beast world, and the world of the monster demons—into a new, peaceful order. The film switches from these heady pop-mythological heights to a contemporary Japanese high school where star basketball players and teachers can transform sans warning into sex-crazed mutant demons (!). The budding romance between two student victims, Akemi and Nagumo (the latter may, in fact, be the reincarnated Overfiend), infuses *Legend*'s overkill action with a core love story. Followed by Takayama's 1991 sequel, *Urotsukidôji II: Legend of the Demon Womb* (Central Park Media). *Animé* horror buffs should also enjoy *Vampire Hunter D* (Central Park Media).

VAMPIRE AT MIDNIGHT
(1988) **1/2

D: Gregory McClatchy. Jason Williams, Gustav Vintas, Lesley Milne, Robert Random. 93 mins. (Key)

Jason (*Danger Zone*) Williams toplines as an L.A. cop in hot pursuit of a bloodsucking serial killer. The psycho in question—a chic, wealthy New Age hypnotherapist (Vintas) who's also equipped with a traditional Transylvanian accent—may or may not be a literal vampire but has no trouble claiming an ever climbing number of mostly female victims. While occasionally slow of pace, *Vampire at Midnight* represents an admirable attempt to fashion an earnest fright film that's at once visually stylish and narratively straightforward.

VAMPIRE JOURNALS   (1996) ***

D: Ted Nicolaou. Jonathon Morris, Kirsten Cerre, David Gunn, Ilinka Goya, Dan Condurache, Starr Andreeff. 90 mins. (Full Moon) DVD

As *Interview with the Vampire*–inspired B videos go, *Vampire*

Journals rates as one of the better ones, an engrossing, atmospherically designed (by Valentin Calinescu), and moodily scored (by Richard Kosinski) Romania-lensed chiller. In Nicolaou's vampire universe, bloodsuckers come in all forms, from monsters to "creatures of grace." Zachary (Gunn) is one of the latter, a decent (though still fitfully plasma-addicted) vampire youth looking to save visiting American pianist Sophia (Cerre) from the fangs and clutches of his evil nemesis, Ash (Morris). Ash and minions operate out of a subterranean cabaret called "Club Muse"—similar to though less elaborate than *Interview*'s "Theatre des Vampires"—an establishment owned by a corrupt Andreeff. Zachary's pursuit of Ash, and Ash's bloody countermeasures, proceed at a stately but rarely static pace, and the tale ends on a bittersweet note. Mark Rappaport Creature FX claims responsibility for a pair of decapitations, along with much traditional vampire bloodletting.

SANDS OF TIME: Handsome devil Julian Sands stars as time-tripping title character in Anthony Hickox's satanic sequel *Warlock: The Armageddon. Courtesy of Trimark Home Video*

VAMPYR (1932) B&W ***

D: Carl Dreyer. Julian West, Sybille Schmitz, Harriet Gerard. Subtitled. 75 mins. (Kino) DVD

Dreyer's loose "Carmilla" variation is longer on style than story, but the imagery is often original, striking, and supremely unsettling. Kino has the definitive edition, in German with English subtitles.

VOODOO (1995) **½

D: Rene Eram. Corey Feldman, Joel J. Edwards, Jack Nance, Diana Nadeau, Ron Melendez, Sarah Douglas. 91 mins. (A-Pix) DVD

If you like to see Corey Feldman suffer (and, let's face it, who doesn't?), *Voodoo* is the video for you. In this

escapee from producer Pierre David's busy Canadian direct-to-home-vid fright factory, Corey stars as a transfer student who unwittingly signs on with the college's only voodoo-cult frat house. Despite its unlikely story line, *Voodoo* is played completely straightfaced, refreshingly free of jerky fratboy dialogue and smirky sex jokes. The flick furnishes a fair measure of shocks and vivid gore effects (the KNB EFX Group notches another credit for its crowded résumé) and earns The Phantom's Fright-Film Squeal of Approval, despite director Eram's failure to reshoot a climactic scene where a background "corpse" is seen clearly breathing (!).

WARLOCK: THE SERIES

WARLOCK (1991) ***

D: Steve Miner. Julian Sands, Lori Singer, Richard E. Grant, Kevin O'Brien, Richard Kuss, Mary Woronov. 103 mins. (Trimark) DVD

Miner's terror tale/time-travel adventure, a *Terminator* with witches, sees stouthearted witch-hunter Grant and eternal enemy Sands catapulted from 1691 Boston to contempo L.A. Caught in the middle of the warlock war is Linda Hamilton stand-in Singer, a 20-year-old airhead who witnesses Sands's untimely arrival. The ever earnest Grant enlists Lori's aid in his pursuit of the time-sprung demon, whose ultimate diabolical goal entails nothing less than the destruction of the universe. *Warlock* yields considerable suspense and excitement from its time-worn story line. There are moments of wry mirth as well, with both the evil Sands and the virtuous Grant suffering severe culture shock in their new environment even as they steer their single-minded, antagonistic courses through modern America. *Warlock* also offers its share of legit visceral shocks as Sands sucks out one victim's tongue, slices the eyes out of phony psychic Woronov's sockets, and even brews the sheared skin of an unbaptized youth into a restorative potion (!). Another effective scene sees Singer, stricken with a curse that accelerates her aging process, attempt to break the spell before she's too old to move. *Warlock*'s imaginative FX and flashes of black wit make it a modest winner.

WARLOCK: THE ARMAGEDDON (1993) **1/2

D: Anthony Hickox. Julian Sands, Paula Marshall, Chris Young, Steve Kahan, R. G. Armstrong, Joanna Pacula. 98 mins. (Trimark) DVD

Sands's "son of Satan" character returns earthward on a mission from hell: If he can collect six magical rune-stones, he can muster the forces of evil to bring about the title catastrophe. Replacing warlock-fighter Grant are a pair of small-town teens (Young, Marshall) whose secret druidic powers are revealed to them by elders Kahan and Armstrong, who supervise the junior Satan-busters' training sessions. The most spectacular set piece sees Sands hoist entranced fashion mogul/rune-stone owner Pacula high above a sky-scraper, whence she literally falls for the handsome devil. Bob Keen's vivid FX and Sands's by-now patented portrayal of dignified evil (see also *Tale of a Vam-*

pire) represent the sequel's strongest points. Bruce Payne replaces Sands in the utterly routine 1999 follow-up, *Warlock III: The End of Innocence* (Trimark).

WAXWORK:
THE SERIES

WAXWORK II: LOST IN TIME (1991) **1/2

D: Anthony Hickox. Zach Galligan, Monika Schnarre, Alexander Godunov, Maxwell Caulfield, John Ireland, Patrick Macnee, Bruce Campbell, David Carradine. 104 mins. (Artisan)

Like its predecessor, *Waxwork* (Artisan), Hickox's sequel takes a kitchen-sink-and-Cuisinart approach to its frenetic story line. Here, time travel replaces dimension-hopping as returning lead Galligan and newcomer Schnarre escape the original wax museum only moments after the first film's finale. Actually, the flick is less a trip through time than a ride through older movies. Zach and Monika battle their way through affectionate color and B&W send-ups of *Frankenstein, Alien, Excalibur, Dawn of the Dead,* and *Nosferatu,* among others, as well as encountering Dr. Jekyll and Mr. Hyde, Jack the Ripper, and even Godzilla. The couple's adventures range from mindless to clever, but, while uneven, *Waxwork II* works hard to please. The culty cast also includes Drew Barrymore in a silent bit as a "vampire victim."

WEREWOLF OF LONDON (1935) B&W ***

D: Stuart Walker. Henry Hull, Warner Oland, Valerie Hobson, Lester Matthews, Spring Byington. 75 mins. (Universal)

The screen's first werewolf outing is a sometimes slowly paced but

rewarding chiller in a Jekyll/Hyde mode that locks in much of Hollywood's subsequent lycanthrope lore. The opening scene, set in an eerie back-lot Tibet, remains the scariest. Oland is most memorable as the mysterious Dr. Yogami (or, as terminally tipsy socialite Byington refers to him, "Dr. Yokohama"). An excess of low comic relief represents *Werewolf*'s only major misstep.

WHAT EVER HAPPENED TO BABY JANE? (1962) B&W ***1/2

D: Robert Aldrich. Bette Davis, Joan Crawford, Victor Buono. 132 mins. (Warner) DVD

Deranged former child star Davis wars with crippled sister Crawford in a grand gothic bitchfest handled with care, flair, and perversity to spare by auteur Aldrich. *Baby Jane* is still foremost in the middle-aged-madwomen genre it created. Bette returns as an aging, bonkers Southern belle in Aldrich's *Hush...Hush, Sweet Charlotte* (Key), a decent but overlong thriller that's no match for the earlier film. Real-life sisters Lynn and Vanessa Redgrave star in the redundant 1991 made-for-TV *Baby Jane* remake (Facets).

WHEN A STRANGER CALLS (1979) ***

D: Fred Walton. Carol Kane, Charles Durning, Colleen Dewhurst. 97 mins. (Columbia/TriStar)

While the pic gets pretty predictable—a psycho caller threatens to kill an ex-babysitter's kids—it does offer a great hook, and Kane convincingly conveys high anxiety of the hysterical kind. Kane and Durning return in Walton's fitfully chilling 1993 sequel, *When a Stranger Calls Back* (Universal, DVD).

WHITE ZOMBIE (1932) B&W ***

D: Victor Halperin. Bela Lugosi, Madge Bellamy, John Harron. 73 mins. (Sinister Cinema) DVD

Bela cuts a memorably menacing figure as zombie master "Murder" Legendre in Victor Halperin's sometimes melodramatic but genuinely atmospheric and admirably unhealthy tale of lust, death, and voodoo on a vintage Haitian plantation.

THE WICKER MAN (1973) ***1/2

D: Robin Hardy. Edward Woodward, Christopher Lee, Britt Ekland, Diane Cilento, Ingrid Pitt. 103 mins. (Magnum, n.i.d.)

From the talented pen of playwright/scenarist Anthony (Sleuth) Shaffer (whose name appears above the title on-screen) comes a wry, ingenious, subtly yet devastatingly unsettling chiller. Future Equalizer telestar Woodward is Officer Howie, an earnest, devoutly Christian "copper" summoned to the remote Scottish island of Summerisle to investigate reports of a missing girl. Shaffer and director Hardy perfectly capture the predicament of a somewhat odd stranger in an extremely strange land as Woodward's dealings with the colorful but not very forthcoming locals inexorably lead him into a web of doom. Under the supervision of the suave Lord Summerisle (Lee in one of his juiciest roles), the natives practice an arcane but all-consuming "heathen" religion that leans heavily on sexual symbolism (and activity) and work hard to please the gods who, with some help from Lee's agronomist grandfather, have granted them a yearly bumper crop of world-famous apples that have kept the small isle in relative prosperity. Officer Howie—whose straitlaced ways make him a bit of a joke even to his mainland law-enforcement mates— is properly shocked by the pagan rites, promiscuity, and joyful blasphemy he witnesses in all strata of Summerisle

society as the natives gear up for their major annual holiday, Mayday, at which ceremony our innocent public servant is slated to play a pivotal role.

Over a dozen songs are seamlessly woven into Shaffer's narrative, several of an amusingly bawdy nature (e.g., "The Landlord's Daughter"), but both they and the mostly alfresco daylight lensing add to rather than detract from the film's increasingly ominous mood. Beyond the male leads (Lee even performs a drag scene), three blond heroines—Ekland, Cilento, and Pitt—contribute strong turns, while the religious rituals smack of considerable authenticity. The climactic scene rates as one of the most powerful ever committed to celluloid. Unfortunately, most video versions (Republic, VidAmerica) offer truncated prints, ranging anywhere from 84 to 97 minutes; Magnum's out-of-circulation full-length edition is available via mail order rental specialists.

WISHMASTER:
THE SERIES

WISHMASTER (1997) ***

D: Robert Kurtzman. Tammy Lauren, Andrew Divoff, Robert Englund, Chris Lemmon, Tony Todd. 90 mins. (Artisan) DVD

Following a splatterific prologue set in 12th-century Persia, a dockside accident in present-day U.S.A. unleashes the title character, an ancient evil genie (or "djinn"). Said demon (menacingly enacted by ethnic specialist Divoff) must grant three wishes to an unwitting human in order to conquer our world. The victim is young gemologist Alex (an appealing and appropriately feisty Lauren), who spends the flick in fierce combat with the power-crazed fiend. Along the way, the djinn tricks a parade of doomed secondary characters into bloodily self-destructing via their own vain, ill-conceived wishes. That deft horror hook ("Be careful what you

look for!"), courtesy of scripter and frequent Clive Barker collaborator Peter Atkins, and the resultant gore FX make Wishmaster a creepy crowd-pleaser. Followed by Jack Sholder's so-so 1999 sequel, Wishmaster 2: Evil Never Dies (Artisan, DVD).

WITCHBOARD:
THE SERIES

WITCHBOARD (1985) **1/2

D: Kevin S. Tenney. Tawny Kitaen, Todd Allen, Stephen Nichols, Kathleen Wilhoite, Rose Marie. 98 mins. (New Star, n.i.d.)

Tenney's Witchboard starts out fairly strong: Amateur occultist Nichols contacts the spirit of a seemingly benign ten-year-old boy who's promptly (and understandably) smitten by Nichols's ex, a foxy Kitaen (who contributes the pic's key gratuitous shower scene). A series of violent deaths, coupled with Tawny's increasingly erratic behavior, lead our heroes to suspect that the ethereal kid is more of a deadly Dennis the Menace than a Casper the Friendly Ghost. Witchboard's pluses include an earnest if not always original script, decent acting—especially by Wilhoite as a punk psychic and Rose Marie in a cameo—and some suspense until its last-reel detour to Cliché City.

WITCHBOARD 2: THE DEVIL'S DOORWAY (1993) **1/2

D: Kevin S. Tenney. Ami Dolenz, John Gatins, Timothy Gibbs, Laraine Newman, Christopher Michael Moore, Marvin Kaplan. 98 mins. (Republic)

Dolenz stars as a budding artist who finds a Ouija board in her new loft. When a murdered stripper communicates with our heroine, suspicion falls on building super Moore, and possibly on his landlady wife (a rather demeaning retro-hippie role for Newman, whose career's been sliding ever since she left

Saturday Night Live, reaching its nadir during her stint hosting the lame *Mystery Science Theater 3000* precursor *The Canned Film Festival*) and her photog brother (Gatins). The spook scenes are decently crafted, but Dolenz is way too whiny ("You're right, I've fallen into progressive entrapment!").

WITCHBOARD III: THE POSSESSION   (1995) **½

D: Peter Svatek. David Nerman, Locky Lambert, Cedric Smith, Donna Sarrasin. 93 mins. (Republic)

Series creator Kevin S. Tenney is limited to a coscreenplay credit in the third *Witchboard* installment. Here busted investor Nerman finds his fortunes improving after he inherits the titular Ouija board from its previous owner, suicide victim Smith. While few true scares emerge, the sequel does boast a few horrific highlights, most notably a death-by-butterfly-impalement scene. Avoid the terminally cheesy, inexplicably long-lived *Witchcraft* series (various labels), as of this writing, up to its tenth unfathomable installment. Tenney tanked with his similarly themed 1989 effort, *Witchtrap* (Magnum), costarring Linnea Quigley.

WITCHFIRE   (1986) *½

D: Vincent J. Privitera. Shelley Winters, Frances De Sapio, Corrine Chateau, Gary Swanson, David Mendenhall. 92 mins. (Lightning, Video Treasures)

Winters swallows acres of scenery (which may partially account for her figure) in an out-of-control perf as Lydia, a mental patient who leads two fellow femme inmates on a break from a Texas asylum. They eventually return to Shel's childhood home, where they trap arrogant hunter Swanson and subject him to a series of witchcraft rituals. *Witchfire* is best remembered, though, for incurring the ire of the National Alliance for the Mentally Ill via its sensitive tag line: "Not since *Cuckoo's Nest* has insanity been so much fun!" But the best line is uttered by Shel herself (who also served as the pic's producer): "I may be insane, but I'm not stupid!" She couldn't prove it by *Witchfire*, recommended for Shel-from-Hell fans only.

WOLF   (1994) ***

D: Mike Nichols. Jack Nicholson, Michelle Pfeiffer, James Spader, Kate Nelligan, Christopher Plummer. 125 mins. (Columbia/TriStar) DVD

Wolf shape-shifts up as the type of film that a Mike Nichols might have made 25 to 30 years earlier sans the supernatural angle. As it stands, the horror hook adds juice to his midlife-crisis fable about a fallen editor (Nicholson) at a newly corporate-engulfed publishing house who's suddenly empowered by a chance encounter with a wayward wolf. The story, and Nicholson, work best in the early stages when, like Jeff Goldblum in David Cronenberg's imaginative update of *The Fly* (see index), Jack finds his senses radically sharpened, rediscovers his dormant libido, and generally gets in touch with his inner werewolf, inspiring him to fight back against those forces seeking to control his fate. *Wolf* lacks *The Fly*'s weight and aims to entertain rather than truly frighten or enlighten. Still, the pic achieves its goal with sweep and style, while Rick Baker brings his usual high-level skills to the subtle makeup FX.

THE WOLF MAN   (1941) B&W ***½

D: George Waggner. Lon Chaney, Jr., Claude Rains, Evelyn Ankers, Bela Lugosi, Maria Ouspenskaya. 70 mins. (Universal) DVD

Tightly scripted by Curt Siodmak and directed by Waggner, *The Wolf Man* can take its rightful, frightful place beside such other Universal gems as *Dracula* and *Frankenstein*. Chaney stars as the ill-fated Larry Talbot, doomed to wail the full-moon blues after being bitten by a lycanthropic gypsy (a neat cameo by Bela). Not even the formidable Ouspenskaya can save Lon from wandering the nocturnal woods of his father's (Rains) estate in search of fresh victims. *The Wolf Man* accentuates human tragedy over lupine horror in its exploration of its traditional good-versus-evil theme.

ZOMBIES OF MORA TAU   (1957) B&W **

D: Edward L. Cahn. Gregg Palmer, Joel Ashley, Autumn Russell. 70 mins. (Columbia/TriStar)

Zombies is a tame, cheap, but occasionally atmospheric '50s fright flick about underwater zombies guarding a sunken treasure. Hero Palmer, fresh from his ambulatory-tree turn in the immortal *From Hell It Came* (n/a), tries to get to the bottom of things.

WE'VE GOT THE ACTION

(And Adventure)

"It might have doubled the budget if they had to blow up a real helicopter!"

Debbie Rochon on *ABDUCTED II: THE REUNION*

ABDUCTED II: THE REUNION
(1994) **½

D: Boon Collins. Jan-Michael Vincent, Dan Haggerty, Raquel Bianca, Debbie Rochon, Donna Jason, Lawrence King. 91 mins. (Arrow/Bullseye)

Director/coscripter Collins fashions a belated sequel to his 1986 rural psycho yarn, *Abducted* (Prism), lensed in the Canadian Rockies. Lawrence King and Haggerty ("Grizzly Adams") reprise their original roles as the femme-snatching maniac and his disapproving dad, respectively (this despite the seeming fact that Dad had dispatched son at the end of the first one). This time out, a trio of distaff mountain tourists— Italian rich girl Maria (Bianca), fish-out-of-water urbanite Sharon (Rochon), and resourceful outdoorsperson Ingrid (Jason)—run afoul of revived forest fiend King (wavering between relative sanity and savage idiocy throughout), who makes off with Bianca, with whom he intends to mate and raise "pups." Meanwhile, pop Haggerty is sharing a chopper with fellow hunter (former *Airwolf* star and since-recovered real-life car-crash victim) Vincent, a friendship that gradually sours due to the duo's radically divergent hunting philosophies.

Collins manages to wring a fair amount of tension from his sequel (he had some eight years to prep), gets at least adequate perfs from his cast, and, in addition to topless glimpses (as when Rochon removes her T-shirt in an abortive bid to flag down a roughly mile-high helicopter!), manages to work in an outrageously tangential gratuitous sex flashback. At the very least, *Abducted II* delivers what its title and box art promise. No relation to the fact-based *Abduction* (Trimark, a.k.a. *The Abduction of Kari Swenson*), about real-life Olympic hopeful Swenson's ordeal at the hands of mad Montana mountain men.

ACTRESS DEBBIE ROCHON ON *ABDUCTED II: THE REUNION*
As Told to The Phantom

• •

Debbie Rochon has appeared in Broadcast Bombshells, Tromeo and Juliet, *and numerous other films, as well as working as a journalist and radio talk-show host.*

We shot *Abducted II* in British Columbia in March 1994. They purposely did it during the winter months so they'd have access to everything—from equipment to crew members—that you can't get in the summertime when all these American companies come up and book them. The blown-up chopper that you see is actually a flat designed by an incredible art department that had done a lot of theater. It might have doubled the budget if they had to blow up a real helicopter!

I have no problems with topless scenes—watching them or doing them—but I think if you do too many, you're not taken seriously. When I did that scene, the problem I had with it was that it might take viewers out of the story. It wasn't a necessary scene at all. I felt it was very silly and gratuitous. If it was a love-making scene, it would have made more sense to me.

THE ABDUCTION (1975)**

D: Joseph Zito. Leif Erickson, Dorothy Malone, Judith-Marie Bergan, Gregory Rozakis, Lawrence Tierney, David Pendleton. 100 mins. (Media)

The definitive drive-in version of the Patty Hearst kidnapping—drawn from a novel, Harrison James's *Black Abductors*, actually published *prior to* Pat's Symbionese Liberation Army snatch—is a generally inept though determinedly lurid outing purportedly originally earmarked as the first "crossover" film with hard-core sex scenes (which apparently never made it past the foreplay stage). *The Abduction* is of interest mainly as a companion piece to Paul Schrader's better-known 1988 *Patty Hearst* (Media, n.i.d.), with Natasha Richardson in the title role (the account Patty officially endorses). Pat's since gone the thespian route herself, as former porn starlet Traci Lords's uptight mom and a juror-victim of a high-heel–wielding Kathleen Turner in John Waters's *Cry-Baby* and *Serial Mom*, respectively (if not respectably), and can also be sighted in the same outre auteur's *Pecker* (see index).

ABOVE THE LAW (1988)***

D: Andrew Davis. Steven Seagal, Pam Grier, Henry Silva, Sharon Stone, Ron Dean, Daniel Faraldo, Thalmus Rasulala. 99 mins. (Warner) DVD

Seagal (pronounced "See*gal*," as he was fond of pointing out at the time) makes a fairly impressive screen debut, as karate-trained Chicago cop Nico Toscani, in an at-times overly plotted actioner that finds the former CIA employee uncovering a Company conspiracy to import controlled substances from Central America with the help of prominent Windy City hoods. The always welcome Grier is at once solid and foxy as Seagal's soon-to-retire partner, while vet villain Silva gives his ven-

omous all in a trademark sadistic slime-ball role.

ACROSS 110TH STREET (1972)**½

D: Barry Shear. Anthony Quinn, Yaphet Kotto, Anthony Franciosa, Antonio Fargas. 102 mins. (MGM)

Educated cop Kotto and old-liner Quinn square off in a violent, actionful, but unceasingly bleak Harlem-set caper (filmed on location) about a gang of amateurs' disastrous plan to rip off the mob (represented by former '50s heartthrob Franciosa in a convincingly vicious turn). Erstwhile "Huggy Bear" Fargas, who's enjoyed a recent comeback, contributes top work as one of the hapless would-be hoods. Formerly out via Fox, the video was more recently reissued, after a long layoff, by MGM.

ACTION JACKSON (1988)*½

D: Craig R. Baxley. Carl Weathers, Craig T. Nelson, Vanity, Sharon Stone, Bill Duke, Robert Davi, Sonny Landham. 95 mins. (Warner) DVD

If little else, *Action Jackson* at least offers viewers a crash course in "How to Make a Bad Joel (*Commando*) Silver Movie." Take one muscle-bound maverick hero (Weathers as legendary Detroit dick "Action" Jackson), mix with a megalomaniacal villain (evil auto magnate Nelson), add a ditsy ethnic bimbo who becomes the hero's unwitting partner (Vanity as a singing junkie whore), dose liberally with loud shootouts, car crashes, and explosions, and before you can say "Arnold Schwarzenegger," you have another brain-dead *Commando* clone. A few bright spots emerge: The opening action sequence and auto-plant montage are well executed, and it's always a treat to watch Vanity croon "Undress Me" while staring directly at the camera. But *AJ* didn't do much for Weathers, who—save for

the 1992 Australia-set obscurity *Hurricane Smith* (Warner)—hasn't landed a bona-fide starring role since.

THE ADVENTURES OF ROBIN HOOD (1938)***½

D: Michael Curtiz. Errol Flynn, Olivia de Havilland, Basil Rathbone. 102 mins. (MGM/UA)

Flynn brings mucho zest to the title role, particularly in his classic duel with villainous sheriff of Nottingham Rathbone, in what ranks as Hollywood's definitive version of the legendary Brit vigilante's adventures, courtesy of future *Casablanca* helmer Curtiz. In addition to Kevin Costner's 1991 *Robin Hood: Prince of Thieves* (Warner), other Sherwood Forest flicks include the 1991 made-for-cable *Robin Hood* (Facets) with Patrick Bergin, the Douglas Fairbanks silent *Robin Hood* (Grapevine), the animated 1973 *Robin Hood* (Disney), Richard Lester's *Robin and Marian* (Columbia/TriStar) with Sean Connery and Audrey Hepburn, the Mel Brooks send-up *Robin Hood: Men in Tights* (Fox), Hammer's 1967 *A Challenge for Robin Hood* (Anchor Bay), and episodes from both the 1950s Richard Greene series (DVT) and the 1980s BBC series (Fox).

AGUIRRE: THE WRATH OF GOD (1972)***

D: Werner Herzog. Klaus Kinski, Ruy Guerra, Del Negro. Subtitled. 94 mins. (New Yorker)

Frequent fright-film (*Nosferatu: The Vampyre*) and spaghetti-western thesp, the late, great Klaus Kinski shines as a power-crazed 16th-century conquistador leading a contingent of Pizarro's men through the perilous Amazon jungles in a delusional quest for the legendary Seven Cities of Gold. Herzog's hallucinatory lensing and a haunting Peruvian flute score have helped make this offbeat adventure parable an enduring cult fave.

ALWAYS OUTNUMBERED, ALWAYS OUTGUNNED (1998)***

D: Michael Apted. Laurence Fishburne, Natalie Cole, Bill Cobbs, Cicely Tyson, Bill Nunn, Isaiah Washington, Bridgid Coulter, Laurie Metcalfe, Art Evans, Bill Duke. 115 mins. (HBO)

Fishburne is forceful as Socrates Fortlow, an ex-con with a past and an attitude who's desperately seeking dignity and redemption in this engaging urban drama scripted by African-American crime novelist Walter (*Devil in a Blue Dress*) Mosley from his book of the same name. Socko's personal reclamation project also involves helping several other South Central residents (often, it seems, whether they want it or not), including runaway preteen murder witness Washington, the underappreciated wife (Coulter) of a currently unemployed Nunn, and, in the story's best thread, ailing old-timer Cobbs (who easily steals his scenes). Despite its bleak settings and situations and an often offputting lead character, *Always Outnumbered, Always Outgunned* works more often than not, largely due to an excellent cast and author Mosley's finely tuned ear for colorful but credible dialogue. Fishburne and Mosley co-exec-produced the made-for-cable film, which originally preemed on HBO, where it's also aired as simply *Always Outnumbered.*

AMERICA'S DEADLIEST HOME VIDEO (1993)***

D: Jack Perez. Danny Bonaduce, Mick Wynhoff, Mollena Williams, Melora Walters. 90 mins. (Random)

Good news for Danny Bonaduce fans: The former *Partridge Family* towhead and later talk-show penitent stars in his very own roadkill sleaze video. According to the credits (where our hero is listed as *Dante* Daniel Bonaduce), the onetime sitcom kid played an active role in getting this savvy, Wisconsin-lensed exercise in abrupt and senseless violence not only off the ground but on the road and in the can, even to the point of serving as a camera operator. Danny toplines as Doug, a video-compulsive jerk who, after catching his wife (portrayed by real-life spouse, Gretchen Bonaduce) *en flagrante,* attempts to heal his hurtin' heart by taking to the highway, camcorder in hand. When his van is commandeered by a trio of trigger-happy convenience-store desperadoes, the latter decide to keep Doug onboard to record their brutal exploits.

Writer/director Perez's neatest stroke is making Doug's impassive camera the real star here: The gang's random holdups and shootings have the verité feel of crimes captured on surveillance camcorders. In one scene, when Clyde Barrow wannabe Clint (Wynhoff) tapes an S&M tryst with his designated Bonnie (Walters), the camera flashes "low battery" and shuts off just before the going gets hot (!). Not at all the sort of amateurish shot-on-video quickie its title and minibudget suggest, *America's Deadliest Home Video* is a sharply acted, cleverly directed, and credibly unglamorous trek through a seedy stretch of American heartland, one that scores its satirical points far more entertainingly than Oliver Stone's bloated *Natural Born Killers* (see index) or Deran Serafian's hopelessly lost direct-to-video loser *The Road Killers* (Artisan).

AMERICAN ANGELS: BAPTISM OF BLOOD (1989)**1/2

D: Ferd and Beverly Sebastian. Jan MacKenzie, Tray Loren, Mimi Lesseos, Trudy Adams, Patricia Cavoti, Sue Sexton. 99 mins. (Paramount)

The B-movie Sebastian clan (Ferd, Beverly, and, on occasion, son Ben)—who earlier brought us *Gator Bait, Gator Bait 2: Cajun Justice* (both Paramount), and the heavy-metal horror *Rocktober Blood* (Vestron), among many others—turn their creative attention to the wild world of women's wrestling. Our literally gripping tale follows the progress of three breathless aspirants to the titular femme wrestling team, focusing mostly on feisty red-headed heroine Lisa (MacKenzie). We see the drop-kicking chicks deal with intense personal problems ("What's the matter," one is asked, "don't your parents *want* you to wrestle?"), learn the ropes from a hard-boiled instructress ("I'm a firm believer in pain!"), and make their way through the big-time canvas jungle. In the course of this educational effort, we also witness coed Crisco matches, gratuitous postbout showers, and the secret tricks of distaff grappling. This pleasantly cretinous exercise shapes up as fairly entertaining fare for jiggle-mat fans in the right frame of mindlessness. (Robert Aldrich's somewhat subtler take on the subject, *...All the Marbles,* is also available [MGM].) Cast member Lesseos, meanwhile, has since carved out a minor action-star career in mostly forgettable direct-to-homevid pics like *Beyond Fear* (Prism), *Final Impact* (PM), *Pushed to the Limit* (Imperial), and *Streets of Rage* (Monarch).

AMERICAN JUSTICE (1986)**1/2

D: Gary Grillo. Jameson Parker, Gerald McRaney, Jack Lucarelli, Wilford Brimley, Jeannie Wilson, Dennis A. Pratt. 96 mins. (Artisan)

Those erstwhile *Simon & Simon* boys (Lucarelli, McRaney) of prime-time prominence produced, topline, and find themselves on opposite sides of the moral fence in this semisocially semisconscious B actioner. *American Justice* (a.k.a. *Jackals*) is rife with implausibilities but supplies considerable suspense, along with some surprisingly sadistic set pieces. There's also a horse called "Brain Damage" afoot and a fellow trooper named Hobie Landreth, in honor of the obscure former New York Mets catcher of the same name. Other worthy border-beat movies include Tony Richardson's *The Border* (Universal)—a solid, straightforward B flick with an A budget and cast, led by a convincing Jack Nicholson as a guilt-stricken border patrolman who bucks the corrupt system—along with *Borderline* (Fox), with Chuck Bronson as a brave ranger, and *On the Line* (Nelson), with David Carradine.

AMERICAN NINJA:
THE SERIES

AMERICAN NINJA   (1985) **¹/₂

D: Sam Firstenberg. Michael Dudikoff, Judie Aronson, Steve James, Guich Koock, Tadashi Yamashita, Don Stewart. 95 mins. (MGM)

Firstenberg's Philippines-filmed chop opera pits Dudikoff as mysterious ninja-trained GI Joe (no relation to Jack) Armstrong against evil Black Star Ninja Yamashita (of *Sword of Heaven* obscurity) and his sinister arms-dealing boss, the highly unpopular Señor Ortega (Stewart). In the course of this predictable but swiftly paced actioner, our laconic hero woos the base commander's daughter (JAPpily interpreted by Aronson), wins the grudging support of his fellow soldiers (including the late, great Steve James as muscular sidekick Curtis Jackson), and dispatches evildoers by the dozens.

AMERICAN NINJA 2: THE CONFRONTATION   (1987) **

D: Sam Firstenberg. Michael Dudikoff, Steve James, Gary Conway, Larry Poindexter. 90 mins. (Video Treasures)

Again abetted by army topkick Curtis Jackson (James), Dudikoff returns as Joe Armstrong, assigned to an unnamed Carib isle where marine embassy guards are disappearing at an alarming rate. Turns out there's a rational explanation: They're being kidnapped by villain Conway as part of his master plan to coerce a cancer-research genius into creating a race of black-suited bionic "superninjas" to protect his lucrative island drug trade. Director Firstenberg supplies a number of creative stunts here, but the pic proceeds sans the visceral verve of either the original *American Ninja* or the same team's *Avenging Force* (see index). Coscripter Conway's thesping has, sad to say, diminished greatly since his promising debut as the lead in *I Was a Teenage Frankenstein* (see index) back in 1957. And on the subject of thesping, in a Cannes '87 press conference promoting the film, Dudikoff went on record saying he was ready to tackle more challenging fare, like Tennessee Williams plays. Alas, "A S.W.A.T. Chopper Named Desire" has yet to materialize.

AMERICAN NINJA 3: BLOOD HUNT (1989) *¹/₂

D: Cedric Sundstrom. David Bradley, Steve James, Marjoe Gortner, Michele Chan, Calvin Jung. 90 mins. (Cannon)

Bradley replaces Dudikoff in the title role as a ninja-trained Yank out to avenge the slaying of his kickboxer dad. His travels likewise take him to a Caribbean isle, where he tangles with "the Cobra" (ex-evangelist Gortner), a power-crazed criminal type who oversees a secret germ-warfare lab while still finding time to dabble in such arcane sciences as "electro-narcosis" and "designer death." This brain-dead retread consists mostly of a series of one-sided kung-fu set-tos that see the inexpressive Bradley chopping and socking his way through dozens of black-robed "bionic" ninjas. Fortunately, James returns as sidekick Curtis Jackson (wearing a T-shirt reading SHALOM Y'ALL [!]), and his low-key expertise

partially compensates for Bradley and Marjoe's emotive inadequacies. The dull duo of Bradley and original *American Ninja* Michael Dudikoff teamed for the 1991 follow-up, *American Ninja 4: The Annihilation*, while Pat Morita joined Bradley for 1995's *American Ninja 5* (both Cannon).

AMERICAN SHAOLIN: KING OF THE KICKBOXERS II   (1992) **¹/₂

D: Lucas Lowe. Reese Madigan, Daniel Dac Nim, Billy Chang, Trent Bushey, Alice Zhang Hung, Kim Chan. 103 mins. (Academy, n.i.d.)

This nearly nonviolent, Asian-financed outing—no relation to the David (*American Ninja*) Bradley/Mark Dacascos team-up *American Samurai* (Warner)—plays less like a modern martial arts movie than a lightweight backdate American service-training film. It's also one of the few films we've seen of *any* sort that segues from Ocean Grove, New Jersey (site of The Phantom's secret HQ), to Mainland China (!), where titular hero Drew (Madigan) journeys to fulfill his dream of becoming an official, full-fledged Shaolin fighting monk. Drew's growing kinship with his fellow trainees (all Chinese), related from a basically Asian POV, is, at times, surprisingly affecting. The authentic locales and Shaolin-training techniques add further color. As an amiable second-rate cross between *The Karate Kid* (Columbia/TriStar) and *Iron & Silk* (Artisan), *American Shaolin* has its moments.

AND THEN YOU DIE   (1988) ***

D: Francis Mankiewicz. Kenneth Welsh, R. H. Thomson, Wayne Robson, Tom Harvey, George Bloomfield, Graeme Campbell. 115 mins. (Trimark)

No relation to Rene Clement's Canada-lensed crime allegory *And Hope to Die* (see index), this CBC production presents a sturdy study of the banality of organized crime. Purportedly "based on a series of real events," the film follows indie-gang leader Eddie (Welsh), who tries to balance his brutal vocation with a difficult home life with his resentful wife and worshipful young son. Director Mankiewicz manages to avoid sensationalizing his material, and it's his straightforward treatment that lends the movie its strength.

ANGEL: THE SERIES

ANGEL (1984) **

D: Robert Vincent O'Neil. Cliff Gorman, Donna Wilkes, Susan Tyrrell, Rory Calhoun. 94 mins. (Starmaker)

"High-school honor student by day, hooker by night!" promised the original ad posters, but only the occasional dose of sleaze separates this undeniably popular exploitation flick from a "socially conscious" made-for-TV soaper, as the multitalented title teen (Wilkes) alternately hits the books, streets, and bad guys.

AVENGING ANGEL (1985) *1/2

D: Robert Vincent O'Neill. Betsy Russell, Rory Calhoun, Robert F. Lyons, Ossie Davis, Susan Tyrrell. 93 mins. (Starmaker)

Four years later, Angel (Russell, replacing Wilkes) has given up prostitution to enter the legal profession (though some may not see that as much of a leap). But when cop mentor Andrews is blown away by ruthless Mafia killers, Angel puts her career on hold, removes her purple halter top and hot pants from mothballs, and takes to the streets with mayhem in mind. To aid her in her self-styled jihad, Angel recruits a wild crew of would-be lovable street zanies, including former sagebrush star Calhoun as eccentric stuntman Kit Carson, foulmouthed lesbian street matriarch Sally Mosler (a high-

decibel Tyrrell), and Pat and Mike, a pair of two-fisted tranvestites. It's the scum of the earth versus the salt of same, and the scum don't stand a chance. As Angel sagely remarks, "Some things never change, do they?"

ANGEL 4: UNDERCOVER (1994) *1/2

D: George Axmith. Darlene Vogel, Shane Fraser, Sam Phillips, Patrick Kilpatrick, Roddy McDowall, Stoney Jackson, Kerrie Clark. 94 mins. (Artisan)

This seriously belated sequel has virtually nothing to do with the previous entries, Angel having wrapped its first cycle with the execrable (and misnomered) 1988 entry, Angel III: The Final Chapter (Starmaker). Angel 4's tag line—"Executive by Day/Hooker by Night"—perpetuates this air of imprecision, since new "Angel" (a.k.a. "Molly Stewart") Vogel is neither an exec nor a hooker but an ex-tart police photographer working undercover on a homicide case involving troubled rock star Piston Jones (Fraser) and his vicious keeper, Jade (Phillips). Vogel, the first blond Angel, rates as the top component in a pic that plays like an elongated, slightly sleazed-up, third-rate TV policier. No relation to the Maria Ford vehicle Angel of Destruction or femme wrestler Cat ("the Cat on the Mat") Sassoon's Angel Fist (both New Horizons); the latter can also be sighted in Bloodfist IV: Die Trying, Dance with Death (both New Horizons), and Tuff Turf (Anchor Bay).

ANGEL TOWN (1990) **

D: Eric Karson. Olivier Gruner, Theresa Saldana, Frank Aragon, Tony Valentino, Peter Kwong, Mike Moroff. 106 mins. (Imperial) DVD

In Angel Town, Olivier ("the Feet from France") Gruner, contender for

the celluloid kickboxing throne then occupied by Jean-Claude ("the Muscles from Brussels") Van Damme, plays the unlikely role of a champ Euro kickboxer taking postgrad engineering courses at a California university situated but a few blocks from a seething barrio overrun by evil Valentino and his brutal minions. Our hero soon forsakes his studies to protect embattled local mom Saldana and son Aragon from the nabe's rampaging thugs. Asian ally Kwong and crippled but well-armed 'Nam vet Moroff likewise lend a helping hand and a semiautomatic, respectively. While rarely straying from strict genre formula, Angel Town delivers the basic action goods. Gruner has since gone on to star in a slew of direct-to-home-vid actioners, including Automatic (Republic), The Fighter (A-Pix), Mars (Avalanche), Nemesis (Imperial), and Savage (Republic).

THE ANNIHILATORS (1985) **

D: Charles E. Sellier, Jr. Christopher Stone, Andy Wood, Lawrence Hilton-Jacobs, Gerrit Graham, Paul Koslo, Dennis Redfield. 84 mins. (Starmaker)

The title tough guys are a quartet of macho 'Nam vets who regroup in Atlanta to rid a seedy nabe of the vicious street scum who offed their buddy (Redfield). The hoods here are an especially heartless lot; they torture paraplegics, rape and murder innocent women, beat up on bag ladies, and even kick a defenseless teddy bear down the street (!). Since the police, as always, are "handcuffed by the courts," our heroes waste little time in training fed-up area residents in the fine art of fighting back—at which point the red dye copiously flows. While The Annihilators leaves no urban-action cliché unturned, its gradual buildup and professional thesping at least place it a notch above countless others of its concrete-western ilk.

APOCALYPSE NOW (1979) ***1/2

D: Francis Ford Coppola. Martin Sheen, Marlon Brando, Robert Duvall. 153 mins. (Paramount) DVD

Coppola's large-scale, hallucinatory take on the Vietnam War has lost none of its power over the years. Fax Bahr and George Hickenlooper's excellent 1991 documentary on the making of the film, *Hearts of Darkness: A Filmmaker's Apocalypse* (Paramount), rates as a must for buffs. Ever idiosyncratic auteur Nicolas Roeg manages to adapt Joseph Conrad's original, hitherto screen-elusive novella *Heart of Darkness* (Turner) without resorting to gimmicks in his 1994 film of the same name. War films enjoyed a late-'90s revival with Spielberg's *Saving Private Ryan* (Universal, DVD) and Terrence Malick's *The Thin Red Line* (Fox, DVD); the 1964 version of the latter James Jones adaptation, *The Thin Red Line,* is also available (Simitar).

ARMED RESPONSE (1986) **

D: Fred Olen Ray. David Carradine, Lee Van Cleef, Lois Hamilton, Mako, Brent Huff, Michael Berryman, Dick Miller. 86 mins. (Columbia/TriStar)

Indefatigable B auteur Fred Olen Ray steps up to the relative big time with this genre-star-studded affair. The pic pits the macho Roth clan (ex-cop Van Cleef and his three two-fisted sons) against Yakuza heavies led by Mako ("a two-bit thug in a three-piece suit"). Fred gets the flick off to a flying start with an energetic desert shoot-out over a purloined million-dollar statue belonging to the malevolent Mako; Van Cleef's number-three son expires in the exchange, prompting the remaining Roths to embark on the requisite revenge rampage. Conveniently enough, number-one son (Carradine) is a 'Nam vet haunted by combat flashbacks, which provides a perfect excuse for still more gratuitous on-screen bloodletting. And

when number-two son (Huff) is captured and tortured by Mako ("Have you ever had your bones scraped, Mr. Roth?"), Ray hurtles the film into updated Fu Manchu territory. Unfortunately, *Armed Response* ultimately degenerates from the creatively brain-damaged to the merely dumb.

ARMY OF ONE (1993) *

D: Vic Armstrong. Dolph Lundgren, Kristen Alfonso, George Segal, Geoffrey Lewis, Michelle Phillips, Bert Remsen, Ken Foree. In R and unrated editions. 102 mins. (Artisan) DVD

Lundgren remains in desperate need of charisma therapy (Van Damme has more charisma in his little finger than Dolph has in his whole, well, fist) in a one-note chase flick that casts him as a wrongly accused escaped con. Formerly deft comic actor Segal, in a mid-'90s career slide (he's since picked up with better parts in flicks like *Flirting with Disaster* [Touchstone]), lands an embarrassing role as a corrupt cop. (The lumbering climactic fight scene between hero and villain, sort of a "Godzilla Versus George Segal's Stunt Double," is particularly painful to behold.) Someone apparently realized that no body count was mounting, so Dolph detours to L.A., where he shoots a couple dozen Chinese hoods (how John Woo!). *Army of One* has since aired on TV under the title *Joshua Tree.* Other Lundgren losers worth avoiding include *Bridge of Dragons* (HBO), *Cover-Up, Pentathlon, The Punisher* (all Artisan), *Silent Trigger* (Touchstone), and *Sweepers* (Trimark).

ASPEN EXTREME (1993) *1/2

D: Patrick Hasburgh. Paul Gross, Peter Berg, Finola Hughes, Teri Polo, William Russ. 117 mins. (Hollywood Pictures)

Beyond its brain-dead timing—it was released theatrically at the

height of winter '93's gay-supportive Boycott Colorado campaign (!)—this staunchly hetero fantasy suffers from a terminal case of raging clone-itis, culling clichés from flicks old and new until it becomes sort of a *Rocky* on skis. *Aspen Extreme*'s frosty formulaics are occasionally relieved by high-camp interludes, such as auteur Hasburgh's unintentionally risible efforts to imitate *Midnight Express*'s drug-panic sequence. The pic ends, appropriately enough, on a freeze-frame.

ASSASSINS (1995) *1/2

D: Richard Donner. Sylvester Stallone, Antonio Banderas, Julianne Moore, Reed Diamond, Kai Wulf. 113 mins. (Warner) DVD

Sly gives a restrained—at times bordering on catatonic—perf in what's essentially a three-character actioner involving rival hit men Stallone and Banderas and cyberthief Moore. Stallone and Banderas receive separate orders to ice Moore and retrieve a mysterious disk she plans to sell to equally mysterious "Dutch buyers." While Sly emerges as one of the genre screen's kindlier contract killers, Banderas carries on like a cowboy and a half, racking up a body count of 16 (roughly half of them innocent bystanders) all by his lonesome. Producer Joel Silver and director Donner manage to keep *Assassins* on its feet until the action shifts from Seattle to a Caribbean isle and comes to an almost complete standstill. (Or, more accurately, sitstill: The three main characters literally sit, in three separate but proximitous locations, while the clock ticks, eating up nearly an entire reel of screen time.) The film fades out to the strains of the Stones's cover of Dylan's "Like a Rolling Stone," though any thematic connection between the tune and the events depicted on-screen is purely coincidental.

ASSAULT ON PRECINCT 13
(1976) ***1/2

D: John Carpenter. Austin Stoker, Darwin Joston, Laurie Zimmer. 91 mins. (New Line) DVD

Carpenter's urban *Rio Bravo* update emerges as a model of expert low-budget genre filmmaking. L.A. youth gangs unite to mount a relentless attack on the nearly abandoned title site, defended by cop Stoker and motley crew. The undeservedly obscure Joston (who checked out at age 60 in 1999) is particularly good as a cool con named Napoleon. Carpenter also composed the taut minimalist synthesizer score. New Line reissued this essential outing in wide-screen format.

THE ASSIGNMENT   (1997) ***

D: Christian Duguay. Aidan Quinn, Donald Sutherland, Ben Kingsley, Liliana Komorowska. 119 mins. (Columbia/TriStar) DVD

French-Canadian director Duguay, late of the underrated *Screamers* (see index), brings considerable craft to *The Assignment*, a morally complex caper originally titled *The Jackal* (a handle usurped by the dull Bruce Willis–topped *The Jackal,* itself an update of Fred Zinneman's 1973 suspenser *Day of the Jackal* [both Universal]). Versatile actor Quinn turns in deft work in a particularly tricky dual role, as real-life international terrorist Carlos ("the Jackal") Sanchez and as Cuban-American naval officer Anibal Ramirez, who just happens to be the Jackal's physical doppelgänger. As the film opens in 1975, slimy CIA agent Jack Shaw (a heavily made-up Sutherland, looking like a haggard version of son Kiefer) witnesses a bit of Carlos's handiwork when the latter blows up a Paris bistro. In Israel nearly a dozen years later, Massad agent Amos (a solid Kingsley) mistakes a visiting Ramirez for Carlos, beats him up, and tosses him

in prison. Once the mix-up is straightened out, Shaw makes a determined bid to recruit family man Ramirez to impersonate Carlos as part of an elaborate plot to facilitate the terrorist's downfall. The initially reluctant Ramirez is put through months of cruel, grueling training by Shaw and Amos in a frozen Montreal compound, where he's force-fed gallons of porridge *and* tabs of LSD (!). Once Ramirez poses as Carlos, he finds he must trash his own moral code to complete his mission. *The Assignment* flagged at the box office and failed to rally much critical support; while it features sufficient action, it's more a meditation on the nature of personal identity than a formula Hollywood blow-'em-up.

THE AVENGERS   (1998) **

D: Jeremiah Chechik. Ralph Fiennes, Uma Thurman, Sean Connery, Jim Broadbent, Fiona Shaw, Eddie Izzard. 89 mins. (Warner) DVD

Not quite the aggressively awful shambles most critics labeled it when the flick arrived theatrically (sans press screenings, which may have contributed to the prevailing mood of critical malcontent) during summer '98, *The Avengers* is more an exercise in arch tedium occasionally relieved by reasonably witty repartee, imaginative set designs, and eye-tickling FX sequences involving computer-generated storms and giant flying insects. Uma makes for a rather pale Mrs. Peel, Fiennes fares a bit better with his Steed interpretation, and Connery, as the mad meteorologist villain of the piece, accepts a role far beneath his talents (though obviously not his pay scale). Original Steed Patrick Macnee contributes an amusing voice-over cameo as pipe-smoking, transparent agent Invisible Jones. *The Avengers* is far less excruciating than director Chechik's earlier desecration of the H. G. Clouzot classic *Diabolique* (Warner). A&E Home Video, mean-

while, has been releasing episodes from the original *Avengers* teleseries.

AVENGING FORCE   (1986) ***

D: Sam Firstenberg. Michael Dudikoff, Steve James, John P. Ryan, James Booth, Bill "Superfoot" Wallace, Karl Johnson. 103 mins. (Anchor Bay)

Avenging Force reversed '80s action-movie trends by pitting good-guy liberals against evil right-wingers. The *American Ninja* team of Dudikoff and James battle sinister Pentangle fanatics who, under the sicko supervision of crazed corporate head John P. ("Hitler was right!") Ryan, blow up federal agents, waste hordes of innocent tourists in a Mardi Gras massacre, and even gun down little kids in their ongoing efforts to wipe "yellow-bellied liberals" off the face of the nation. The script, penned by costar Booth—who performed the same dual functions for Sho Kosugi's energetic *Pray for Death* (see index)—makes more noise than sense, but action auteur Firstenberg keeps things moving at a sufficiently swift pace to more than compensate for the many plot holes.

BACK IN ACTION   (1994) **

D: Steve DiMarco. Billy Blanks, Roddy Piper, Bobbie Phillips, Matt Birman, Nigel Bennett. 93 mins. (Universal)

Wrestler Rowdy Roddy improves his acting chops, while kickboxer and since-ascendant Tae-Bo mogul Blanks comes through with another of his typical hyperactive-zombie perfs in *Back in Action,* a nearly nonstop series of shoot-outs, chases, and punch-ups that, while energetically staged, grow too numbingly repetitive even for diehard action hounds. A few imaginative torture touches surface, including one involving antismoking acupuncture treatments (!), but this exercise in kinetic brawn would have benefitted from a bit more brain. In a rare move, Toronto doesn't sub for New York or L.A. but actually plays itself, even to the point of flaunting its tawdry Yonge Street porn dives. Roddy and Billy reteam in *Tough and Deadly* (Universal). Blanks buffs can avail themselves of such solo Billy bashfests as *Balance of Power* (Artisan), *Expect No Mercy* (WarnerVision), *The King of the Kickboxers*, *Showdown* (both Imperial), *Talons of the Eagle*, and *TC 2000* (both Universal).

BAD LIEUTENANT (1992) ***1/2

D: Abel Ferrara. Harvey Keitel, Frankie Thorn, Zoë Lund. 95 mins. In R and NC-17 (original theatrical release) editions. (Artisan) DVD

A bel (*Ms. .45, King of New York*) Ferrara's NC-17–rated *Bad Lieutenant* is both a sardonic, ultra-intense exercise in urban depravity and a twisted religious journey fueled by Keitel's dominant perf as a degenerate cop. Scripted by former *Ms. .45* star Zoë Lund, this crazed Keitel showcase sets its tone early when Harv, billed only as "Lt" (apparently, and understandably, no one wants to get close enough to address him by name), snorts coke in a Catholic-school zone after dropping off his two young sons at same. A contempo Dantean roller coaster, *Bad Lieutenant* is adroitly framed by a fictional baseball play-off series between the Dodgers and the Mets (WFAN's Mad Dog Russo and Bob Murphy lend their vocal talents) into which Keitel has unwisely sunk a considerable chunk of change. Ferrara follows his craven antihero on his rounds (which rarely include actual police work) as he scores crack in a tenement (pausing to warn potential passersby with a cry of "Police activity!"), shoots smack with his lyrical junkie mistress (the aforementioned Ms. Lund, who at one point existentially muses, "We have to eat away at ourselves 'til there's nothing left but

appetite"), drinks himself into numerous stupors, and otherwise carries on like a walking (or, more often, staggering) toxic-waste dump. An increasingly important story thread emerges when a nun (Thorn) is raped by two ghetto youths (in a scene lensed in fevered porn-video style) whose identities the victim refuses to divulge. The mystical masochist's depth of forgiveness bugs the hell out of our perverted protagonist, himself a seriously lapsed Catholic, and serves to intensify his obsessive quest. Real-life Russian-roulette fatality Johnny Ace's haunting doo-wop ballad "Pledging My Love" provides evocative musical accompaniment.

Bad Lieutenant is nothing if not a bold piece of work. Of all its shock-value tableaux, though, Keitel's naked, coked-up crying jag easily copped top honors in The Phantom's Not a Pretty Sight Department, Film Division, 1992. (Indeed, if David Lynch's best stuff smacks of hallucinogens, Ferrara's disturbing juxtapositions project a hard-edged clarity ever threatening to erupt into cocaine hysteria.) In short, *Bad Lieutenant* rates as serious sleaze of the highest order, and contains some very funny bits to boot.

THE BAD PACK (1998) **

D: Brent Huff. Robert Davi, Roddy Piper, Ralf Moeller, Larry B. Scott, Shawn Huff, Patrick Dollaghan, Brent Huff, Marshall Teague. 93 mins. (Avalanche)

Y et another *Magnificent Seven* update—John Sayles had previously scripted two, just by his lonesome—*Battle Beyond the Stars* and *Men of War,* while James Glickenhaus tried it with *McBain* (see index)—this one involves a Tex-Mex border town harassed by the rude residents of a nearby right-wing paramilitary compound ruled by a Nietzsche-spouting Teague. Biker merc Davi and ace driver Piper (with personalized plates reading BADASS 1) are on hand to make you for-

get Yul Brynner and Steve McQueen, while Scott more or less handles the Horst Buchholtz (whom most have forgotten without any help from this flick) role as the eager young hero wannabe. Director/coscripter Brent Huff pens a part for himself and *La Femme Nikita* manqué Shawn Huff as two of the heroic crew. *The Bad Pack* provides some early brain-damaged fun when oppressed illegal-immigrant brothers Amtrak it to L.A. to assemble the group but lets its targeted aud down with a rather limp climactic battle scene that leaves too many of our protagonists regrettably alive.

BAIL OUT (1989) *1/2

D: Max Kleven. Linda Blair, David Hasselhoff, John Vernon, Tom Rosales, Tony Brubaker, Buck Flower. 88 mins. (Vestron)

O riginally titled *W.B., Blue and the Bean* (it's since aired on cable under that title), *Bail Out* plays like an R-rated busted TV pilot. The movie chronicles the clichéd adventures of a multiethnic bounty-hunting team composed, not surprisingly, of W.B., Blue, and the Bean. Future *Baywatch* surf stud Hasselhoff, who also coproduced, stars as W.B. (short for "White Bread"), while second-billed Linda portrays the heiress daughter of a corrupt Vernon (her warden in the superior 1983 broads-behind-bars classic, *Chained Heat*). In a cheat move, the pic pauses long enough for Linda to take her then-customary on-screen shower, at a hot-sheets motel, but L.B. is never seen sans oversized bath towel. In the action department, Linda gets to show off her shotgun skills at the expense of a few bad guys, but overall, *Bail Out* ranks as a disappointing effort for Blair buffs. Other lame later Linda vehicles worth avoiding include: *The Chilling* (Hemdale), *Dead Sleep* (Vestron), *Moving Target* (Southgate), *Night Patrol* (Video Treasures), *Nightforce* (Vestron), *Silent Assassins* (MCEG), *Sorceress* (Triboro), *Up Your Alley* (Vestron), and *Zapped Again* (Columbia/TriStar).

BALLISTIC   (1994) *¹/₂

D: Kim Bass. Marjean Holden, Cory Everson, Richard Roundtree, Sam Jones, Charles Napier, Joel Beeson. 86 mins. (Imperial)

A "1994 Theatrical Production" (as opposed to Theatrical Release), *Ballistic* toplines an impressively sculpted Holden as an honest LAPD plainclothesperson out to nail erstwhile direct-to-home-vid hero-turned-heavy Jones (who apparently took nasty-laugh lessons to aid in that transition) and his corrupt-officer helpmates for framing her ex-cop/current-jailbird pop (Roundtree). Produced by former rising B-action auteur Peter Maris, *Ballistic* opens with some flashes of style but soon sinks into formulaic plot moves and exceedingly lethargic "action" tableaux. There's a fun rocket-launcher POV shot (it looks like a grip's running with the rocket on his shoulder while an equally breathless steadicam op tries to keep him out of frame) that will make you appreciate the technical wizardry of the POV arrows in the Kevin Costner *Robin Hood: Prince of Thieves,* the bullets in *Sniper,* and the nuclear warhead in *Under Siege.* Marjean, meanwhile, can also be seen in *Philadelphia Experiment 2, Stripped to Kill II: Live Girls* (see index), *Mortal Kombat 2: Annihilation* (Warner), and, opposite Billy Dee Williams, in *Secret Agent 00-Soul* (Xenon).

BANDIT QUEEN   (1994) ***¹/₂

D: Shekhar Kapur. Seema Biswas, Nirmal Pandey, Manoj Bajpai, Raghubir Yadav. Subtitled. 119 mins. (Evergreen)

Combining serious social drama with crowd-pleasing action elements, *Bandit Queen* chronicles the fact-based exploits of gun-toting outlaw rebel Phoolan Devi (Biswas), who led raids in rural India from the 1970s until

her capture in 1981. The film candidly details the crushing poverty, paralyzing caste system, and rampant sexism that led Phoolan's father to sell her, at age 11, into marriage/servitude. Our abused heroine eventually escapes, only to suffer not one but two vicious gang rapes. Phoolan finally finds fulfillment by pursuing a bandit lifestyle and falling for fellow raider Pandey; the pair go on to form a sort of Phoolan and Clyde team. *Bandit Queen* eschews the usual kitchen-sink approach found in many Indian films—there are no musical production numbers on view—for a straightforward but visceral treatment.

THE BARON   (1975) ***

D: Phillip Fenty. Calvin Lockhart, Marlene Clark, Richard Lynch, Charles MacGregor, Joan Blondell, Gail Strickland, Raymond St. Jacques. 90 mins. (Paragon, n.i.d.)

Written and directed by *Superfly* scripter Fenty, *The Baron* features standout perfs by Lockhart, as a black first-time filmmaker, and vet villain Lynch as the bigoted mobster who, through "Cokeman" (MacGregor, *Superfly's* Freddy), muscles in on our pressured hero. As he did with Superfly, Fenty takes an ironic stance re Lockhart's hard life lessons. Blondell & *Ganja & Hess's* Clark contribute deft turns, as does the late St. Jacques as Lockhart's cynical Hollywood connection.

THE BEAST   (1988) ***

D: Kevin Reynolds. Jason Patric, George Dzundza, Steven Bauer, Stephen Baldwin, Don Harvey, Kabir Bedi. 109 mins. (Columbia/TriStar)

Patric plays a disgusted Russki soldier who switches allegiance to a band of Afghani rebels led by *Scarface's* Bauer in future Kevin Costner director (*Robin Hood, Waterworld*) Reynolds's actionful antiwar film, one that could as easily have been set in Vietnam, with

Yanks subbing for Soviets. An earnest but unpreachy parable that was largely dismissed during its initial theatrical release, *The Beast* is well worth a look. No relation to Jack Woods's *Beast,* on the defunct Wizard label, a retitling of the cult fright item *Equinox.*

A BETTER TOMORROW:
THE SERIES

A BETTER TOMORROW (1986) ***

D: John Woo. Chow Yun-Fat, Ti Lung, Leslie Cheung, Emily Chu. Subtitled/dubbed. 90 mins. (Tai Seng) DVD

Woo's breakout action film seems positively subdued—the body count barely cracks the three-digit barrier—compared with such later gun-fu orgies as *The Killer* and *Hard-Boiled* (see index). Here Woo's contempo "Chinese knight" Yun-Fat takes a backseat to Lung and Cheung as brothers on opposite sides of the law. The trio resolve their differences by banding together for a climactic battle against the bad guys that, while spectacular for its day, now rates as one of Woo's lesser blood orgies. While Woo's since moved onward and upward (and westward), *A Better Tomorrow* serves as an excellent intro to his manic action ouevre and a compelling outing in its own right. Tai Seng also has the sequels, Woo's 1988 *A Better Tomorrow 2* and Tsui Hark's 1989 *A Better Tomorrow, Part 3* (a.k.a. *Love and Death in Saigon),* along with Woo's highly recommended *Deer Hunter* variation *Bullet in the Head* (all DVD).

BEYOND FORGIVENESS (1995) **¹/₂

D: Bob Misiorowski. Thomas Ian Griffith, Joanna Trzepiecinska, Rutger Hauer, John Rhys-Davies. 95 mins. (Republic)

Kickboxing thesp Griffith improves on his self-directed vehicle *Exces-*

sive Force (New Line) and the Michael Mazo–helmed *Crackerjack* (see index) with this comparatively exotic actioner. When a scar-faced thug kills Chicago cop T.I.G.'s brother, our hero follows his trail all the way to swinging contemporary Warsaw, where he hooks up with all-purpose ethnic sidekick Rhys-Davies (a J. Carrol Naish for the '90s). Through beautiful blond disco-dancing surgeon Trzepiecinska, Tom uncovers an insidious Russian Mafia–backed black-market human-organs racket run by suave hospital head Hauer. Authentic location-lensing, a sizable body count (one unlucky Polish extra even gets shot in the accordion), some unexpected plot twists, and Hauer's gleefully inhuman histrionics (particularly during a sequence wherein he begins to relieve a strapped-down but unsedated Griffith of his internal organs) help overcome Griffith's ongoing charisma shortage (there's never a donor around when you need one).

THE BIG DOLL HOUSE   (1971) ***

D: Jack Hill. Judy Brown, Roberta Collins, Pam Grier. 95 mins. (New Line) DVD

This Philippines-filmed fine-fettered-femmes flick from *Switchblade Sisters* (see index) helmer Hill helped set forth many of the chicks-in-chains genre's most sacred conventions. One of the genre's best offerings—also out as *Women's Penitentiary* (MCM)—is further hoisted by the popular Grier's pulchritudinous presence. Pam returns for more in Hill's sequel, *The Big Bird Cage* (Warner), another mostly successful mix of broad humor and random violence. Vonetta McGee takes over as the foxy force behind another major prison breakout in the similarly themed *Big Bust Out* (Embassy).

BILLY JACK   (1971) **½

D: "T. C. Frank" (Tom Laughlin). Tom Laughlin, Delores Taylor,

Bert Freed, Kenneth Tobey. 115 mins. (Warner) DVD

Laughlin, directing under the *nom du cinema* T. C. Frank, franchised the punch-for-peace Native American maverick he'd introduced in *Born Losers* (see index) in this unexpectedly boffo American fable, wherein our hero protects endangered ethnic kids from local racists. *BJ*'s a lot preachier than *Born Losers,* with less out-and-out sleaze, but stacks up as an authentic curiosity piece. Laughlin has since issued the unsuccessful sequels *The Trial of Billy Jack* (1974) and 1977's *Billy Jack Goes to Washington* (Ventura).

BLACK CAESAR   (1973) ***

D: Larry Cohen. Fred Williamson, Art Lund, D'Urville Martin. 95 mins. (Orion)

Former gridiron star Fred ("the Hammer") Williamson is smooth in this mostly successful replay of the old crime-lord's-rise-and-fall story. The pic could have used a few more of director/writer Cohen's patented perverse flourishes—though the funky bass guitar under the tearful Italo mandolin strains supplies a neat soundtrack touch. Auteur Cohen and star Williamson reteamed for the far weaker sequel, *Hell Up in Harlem* (Orion).

BLACK LIZARD   (1968) ***

D: Kinji Fukasaku. Akihiro Murayima, Isao Kimura, Kikko Matsuoka, Yukio Mishima, Junya Asami. Subtitled. 86 mins. (Cinevista)

In *Black Lizard*—filmed from soon-to-be self-executed writer Yukio Mishima's stage adaptation of a Rampo (*The Mystery of Rampo*) Edogawa novel—the titular femme fatale is portrayed in drag (!) by Japanese TV star Murayama as a narcissistic criminal esthete who matches wits with "Japan's number-one detective," Akechi (Kim-

ura). The object of the Liz and gang's illicit lusts is the priceless "Star of Egypt." To lay hands on same, they kidnap jeweler Usami's fetching daughter (Matsuoka) while attempting to keep the persistent Akechi at bay. *Black Lizard* emerges as a stylized but not especially campy caper; Murayama comes across as a typical cliffhanger villainess, interpreting his/her role with studied but rarely exaggerated witchiness. The film accentuates the master criminal and dedicated detective's mutual attraction, an attraction born less of physical desire than of a keen appreciation of the cat-and-mouse maneuvers in which they find themselves embroiled. *Black Lizard*'s chief departure from standard caper pics lies in its characters' frequent philosophizing re morality, Eros, and aesthetics. Several bizarre ingredients spice the film, most notably Black Lizard's collection of human "statues," one of whom is played by Mishima himself. No doubt there's a good deal of Mishima in Black Lizard's cunning, theatrical, and relentlessly egocentric character, as well as in that of Edogawa's detached but dogged Akechi.

BLACK ROSE OF HARLEM (1995) **

D: Fred Gallo. Cynda Williams, Nick Cassavetes, Joe Viterelli, Lawrence Monoson, Garrett Morris, Richard Brooks, Maria Ford. 90 mins. (New Horizons)

Set in 1931 Harlem, *Black Rose* is woefully bald on period flavor, and Roger Corman starlet Ford (as gangster Viterelli's brunette daughter) even mangles the classic Mae West line by cooing to costar Nick (son of John) Cassavetes, "Is that a gun in your pants or are you just glad to see me?" (Besides, West didn't make her screen debut until 1932's *Night After Night;* we're pretty sure the phrase "the skinny" wasn't around in '31 either.) Williams plays "the Black Rose," a poorly synched chanteuse at a black-owned club mobster Viterelli (doing his usual mumbling-Mafioso act, à la *Analyze This* [Warner]) wants to add to his collection. New Horizons has since reissued the flick as *Machine Gun Blues.*

BLACK SISTER'S REVENGE (1987) **¹/₂

D: Jamaa Fanaka. Jerri Hayes, Ernest Williams II, Charles David Brooks III, Eddie Allen, Robert Slaughter, Malik Carter. 100 mins. (Unicorn, n.i.d.)

The defunct Unicorn label pushed this vid as a new black action pic—an accompanying "still" depicts an entirely unrelated, obviously contempo fox brandishing a pistol and machine gun. *Black Sister's Revenge* is actually a 1976 Jamaa (*Penitentiary*) Fanaka flick originally (and more appropriately) titled *Emma Mae*, a funky slice-of-lifer featuring a few mild and ephemeral exploitation elements. Fanaka documents the social adjustment of heroine Emma Mae (Hayes), a naïve but resourceful Deep South college girl who moves in with her more sophisticated and cynical cousins, a clan of California African-Americans. It's only when Em hooks up with local lowlife Jess (Williams) that the plot detours in some unlikely directions—as when Em, out of nowhere, decides to operate a car wash to raise bail for her errant beau; when that fails, in a move that prefigures F. Gary Gray's *Set It Off* (see index), she sticks up a nearby bank. Ridiculous retitling and promo campaign aside, *Black Sister's Revenge* is an uneven but compelling character study, rich in regional detail. Unicorn honchos should have trusted the film they had and not tried to con customers into thinking they were getting something less. Fanaka, meanwhile, more recently returned with the 1991 ghetto guerrilla-warfare opus *Street Wars* (Triboro).

BLACKJACK (1997) *¹/₂

D: John Woo. Dolph Lundgren, Kate Vernon, Phillip Mackenzie, Kam Heskin, Fred Williamson, Saul Rubinek. 112 mins. (Dimension) DVD

True, English is Hong Kong émigré action ace John Woo's second language. But surely someone onboard could have clued him in to the hopelessness of *Blackjack*'s cheap-symbol-laden script, with its tin-eared dialogue and overripe dramatics, brought to static small-screen life by a cast that's largely short in the talent and restraint departments (Fred Williamson emerges as one of the *better* thesps here). Director Woo's own reliance on his patented but herein misplaced cinetechniques—slo mo, B&W scenes, freeze-frames—further plunges *Blackjack* into the depths of self-parody. (Then again, maybe TV's not his medium; his teleremake of his feature film *Once a Thief* likewise came up lame.) In the film, Lundgren lands a gig protecting Percodan-addicted model Vernon from a psychotic sniper and his motorcycle-riding pals, leading to one excellent woods-set extended-action sequence that recalls vintage Woo.

BLIND FURY (1990) **¹/₂

D: Phillip Noyce. Rutger Hauer, Lisa Blount, Terry O'Quinn, Brandon Call, Noble Willingham, Tex Cobb, Meg Foster, Nick Cassavetes, Rick Overton, Sho Kosugi. 85 mins. (Columbia/TriStar)

Sort of a *Zatoichi* Meets *Raising Arizona*, *Blind Fury* stars Hauer as Nick Parker, a sightless swordsman who lost his vision but gained his superior fighting skills after being wounded in 'Nam. The flick picks Nick up 20 years later as he arrives in Miami in search of former combat-buddy-turned-chemist O'Quinn, currently held captive by villain Willingham in far-off Reno, Nevada, where he's being forced to manufacture designer drugs to pay off his gambling debts. With Terry's initially hostile young son (Call) in tow, Rut sets off on a cross-country quest, pursued all the way by bad guy Cobb and assorted hired thugs who supply our blind hero with plenty of bloody slice-and-dice opportunities. Hauer turns in typically solid work as the self-effacing swordsman, with able support provided by Cassavetes and Overton as lowlife siblings Lyle and Tector Pike (named in honor of Ben Johnson and Warren Oates's characters in Sam Peckinpah's *The Wild Bunch*). Fans of screen ninja Kosugi will want to see their idol's grunt-driven cameo as the anonymous assassin who puts Rut through his most grueling swordfighting paces.

BLIND TRUST (1986) ***

D: Yves Simoneau. Marie Tifo, Pierre Curzi, Jacques Godin. Subtitled. 88 mins. (Cinema Group, n.i.d.)

Alone, gay armored-car guard fends off a quartet of desperate would-be thieves in a bleak but compelling French-Canadian heist caper (a.k.a. *Pouvoir Intime*) that strives for the offbeat and generally succeeds. Not the easiest cassette to locate but well worth seeking out.

BLOOD GAMES (1990) **¹/₂

D: Tanya Rosenberg. Laura Albert, Ross Hagen, Gregory Cummings, Shelley Abblett, Buck Flower. 88 mins. (Columbia/TriStar)

Imagine a *Road Warrior* set in the contemporary South with armed rednecks replacing *RW*'s future punks and a team of baseball-playing bimbos (!) subbing for the beleaguered postnuke nomads—a sort of *Broad Warriors,* if you will. Well, the good news is you don't have to imagine it because distaff director Rosenberg has already put that improbable scenario on film in *Blood Games.* When sore-loser male crackers blow a softball contest to the barnstorming "Babe and Her Ballgirls," the resultant bad vibes soon explode into violence. The locals kill male coach Hagen, so Babe (Albert) and troops try to flee their team bus. The scantily clad gals ultimately exhibit admirable cheek (figuratively and literally) by taking on the backwoods chauvinists *womano-a-mano* in a lethal, filmlong conflict that eventually eliminates most of the cast. While falling short of a home run, this audacious, bodacious exercise in suspenseful stupidity at least smacks a ringing double.

BLOOD ON THE SUN   (1945)
B&W***

D: Frank Lloyd. James Cagney, Sylvia Sidney, Robert Armstrong. 98 mins. (Goodtimes) DVD

While stationed in prewar Japan, Yank journalist Cagney smells a rat in a solid suspenser that saw the normally two-fisted Cags become the first high-profile screen Westerner to use then-exotic karate techniques.

BLOODSPORT:
THE SERIES

BLOODSPORT (1988)**½

D: Newt Arnold. Jean-Claude Van Damme, Donald Gibb, Leah Ayres, Norman Burton, Forest Whitaker, Roy Chiso, Bolo Yeung. 92 mins. (Warner)

Then-newcomer Van Damme stars as real-life karate champ Frank Dux, allegedly the first Westerner to win the clandestine full-contact *kumite* competition staged (according to the film) every five years in a different exotic locale (in this case, Hong Kong). Between bouts, J-C finds time to befriend fellow competitor Gibb, romance reporter Ayres, antagonize sadistic defending champ Yeung, and consistently elude army investigators Burton and Whitaker (in an early role) dispatched to return him to the special-

service branch from which he's gone AWOL. While the predictable plot is further padded with several boring rock-video segments, *Bloodsport* comes alive where it counts—in the *kumite* ring. Nearly half the flick, lensed largely within Hong Kong's exotic Walled City, consists of full-contact fight footage, expertly choreographed by Van Damme and far more compelling than the wraparound dramatics. You can also catch the young Jean-Claude in *Black Eagle* (Imperial), where, cast as a Russki heavy, he takes a thespian backseat to

hard-hitting hero Sho Kosugi. Daniel Bernhardt replaces a priced-out J-C in the belated late-'90s sequels *Bloodsport 2: The Next Kumite*, with Pat Morita and James Hong, *Bloodsport 3*, and *Bloodsport 4: The Dark Kumite* (all FM Entertainment, DVD).

BLUE THUNDER   (1983)***

D: John Badham. Roy Scheider, Malcolm McDowell, Candy Clark, Daniel Stern, Warren Oates. 108 mins. (Columbia/TriStar) DVD

Phantom Phlashback!
OUR COFFEE WITH JEAN-CLAUDE, NYC 1988
• •

"Coffee's not good for you! You should drink tea, my friend!"

So then–barely known Belgian martial artist Jean-Claude Van Damme advised The Phantom during a 1988 *Bloodsport* promo blitz. The self-described "Muscles from Brussels," who stands a modest five feet ten ("five-eleven in my boots") and weighs in at roughly 175, also revealed that he'd been competing in the martial arts ring since age 11.

"When I was young, I was very thin, so I trained in karate and weights and also did some ballet. That's why I'm so graceful. And why I catch not only the male but the female audience. Coffee is bad for the nerves, and the heart."

At age 24, Jean-Claude chucked the Brussels gym he owned to take a shot at Hollywood. After working as a bouncer and trainer, he landed the role of a mean Russki karate champ in the no-budget indie *No Retreat, No Surrender* (see index). That led to a meatier part as the ever mutating monster-suited title alien in the Arnold Schwarzenegger sci-fi actioner *Predator*.

"Well," Jean-Claude clarifies, "actually I only had part of the role. Do you remember the chameleon monster? That was me."

The muscular thesp still harbors fond memories of training with Arnold and Carl (*Action Jackson*) Weathers. "I really wanted to spar with them," he recalls almost wistfully, "but that never happened." As for Arn, J-C observes, "He's a strong man mentally. He's the type of guy who if you're gonna have a fight with him, he's going to take a table and put it on your face."

Of course, injuries are a necessary evil of the action-movie game. "There were two broken jaws and one broken nose in *Bloodsport*," admits Jean-Claude, who received some serious bruises himself, though they failed to dent his enthusiasm. "I'm so much in love with film—it's my life—that when I listened to the cameras rolling, I felt no pain. Are you sure you wouldn't rather have tea?"

While Van Damme cites Jon Voight, Robert De Niro, Bruce Lee, and the ever influential Arn as his screen idols, he's nothing if not bent on making a name for himself.

"It's bigger than Arnold Schwarzenegger's," he points out between sips of tea. "It takes up more space on the screen."

ction specialist Badham's lively thriller with a superchopper hook sees LAPD pilot Scheider and partner Stern pit their combat skills against slick villain McDowell. Spectacular aerial action further hoists this fun affair.

BLUE TIGER   (1994) **1/2

D: Norberto Barba. Virginia Madsen, Toru Nakamura, Harry Dean Stanton, Dean Hallo, Ryo Ishibashi, Sal Lopez. 88 mins. (Columbia/TriStar)

The versatile Madsen, of *Candyman* fame, stars as a revenge-minded L.A. mom whose young son is killed in the crossfire between a masked Yakuza hit man and his Yank targets. Her only clue to the assassin's identity is the blue-tiger tattoo on his chest. Retired skin artist Stanton recounts the legend that a blue tiger will reveal himself to a red tiger, so Madsen has the image of just such a crimson cat tattooed on her back, then poses as a hostess in a tough "Little Tokyo" Yakuza club. Romantic complications ensue between our heroine and a sensitive gangster, while an all-out war rages between the Yaks and the Yank tour-bus company head (Hallo) they're trying to extort. Director Barba brings considerable visual style to his stark story, but the pic falls short in the suspense department. For more Little Tokyo intrigues, see *American Yakuza* (Columbia/TriStar), starring Michael Nouri, and *Showdown in Little Tokyo* (see index).

A TALE OF THREE BODY COUNTS

BODY COUNT   (1995) **1/2

D: Talun Hsu. Robert Davi, Steven Bauer, Brigitte Nielsen, Sonny Chiba, Jan-Michael Vincent, Cindy Ambuehl. 93 mins. (A-Pix)

Erstwhile *Street Fighter* Chiba, sounding phonetic but looking fairly fit in glasses and ponytail, returns to the celluloid fray in an American-Japanese coproduction set in New Orleans, helmed by a Chinese director, and coproduced by former dancer/Action International Pictures honcho David Winters. Sonny plays a laconic assassin who, after knocking off a pair of kiddie-porn mogul Mafioso brothers, is wounded and captured by Big Easy cops Davi and a corpulent Bauer (who opens the film sporting a Jim Carrey *Dumb and Dumber*–styled 'do). Eighteen months later, ex–Mrs. Sly Stallone Brigitte breaks Sonny out of stir and the duo wage a violent vendetta against the NOPD, claiming Vincent as one of their victims (via a lethal roof-tossing incident), while Davi and Bauer seek to terminate the odd-couple killers' reign of terror. The result is a fairly brisk actioner of special interest to Chibaphiles, though Sonny resorts to using guns, swords, and blowtorches rather than his patented hands-on windpipe-tearing techniques. As for the veracity of the pic's title, a couple dozen corpses pile up during the proceedings, with Sonny, by our tally, claiming an even ten and Brigitte contributing at least an additional half dozen.

BODY COUNT   (1997) **

D: Kurt Voss. Alyssa Milano, Ice-T, Justin Theroux, Tom "Tiny" Lister. 88 mins. (Artisan)

Coproduced by star Milano (then in that difficult teenette-to-bimbo transitional phase), this *Body Count* stacks up as a sort of "*Die Hard* at Home," with a twist. Alyssa and rich beau Theroux attend a dysfunctional-family reunion at the latter's home, where, after witnessing several nasty domestic squabbles, they retreat to the basement for a dalliance. No sooner do they do the deed than a trio of vicious thugs led by Ice-T break in, shoot the entire clan, and make off with the family art collection. It's up to Milano and Theroux to thwart the armed miscreants, but doubt remains re who's the true mastermind behind this possibly inside job. Voss and crew generate a fair amount of suspense at first, but the excitement doesn't sustain and the bland cast fails to compensate for the lack of story thrills. Milano increasingly relies on her tight, short dress to supply visual diversion as the reels roll on.

BODY COUNT   (1997) **1/2

D: Robert Patton-Spruill. David Caruso, Linda Fiorentino, John Leguizamo, Ving Rhames, Donnie Wahlberg, Forest Whitaker. 94 mins. (PolyGram)

Still another *Body Count* about yet another art heist (!), this literal road-show *Reservoir Dogs* at least scores higher marks than Voss's *Body Count*. After a museum theft erupts in violence, antagonistic survivors Caruso, Leguizamo, Rhames, and Donnie (Brother of Mark) Wahlberg seek to flee to Miami, where they plan to fence their ill-gotten gains, but predictably prove their own worst enemies. Caruso is the most credible of the criminal quartet, while Fiorentino—as a stranded but none-too-innocent motorist—a hyper Leguizamo, and a cool Rhames basically reprise characters we've seen them play before. Still, there's enough fractured action, sharp dialogue, and thespian intensity to hook, if not enthrall, modern road-noir fans.

BOILING POINT   (1993) ***

D: James B. Harris. Wesley Snipes, Dennis Hopper, Lolita Davidovich, Viggo Mortensen, Dan Hedaya, Valerie Perrine, Tony Lo Bianco, Seymour Cassel, Jonathan Banks. 95 mins. (Warner) DVD

Adapted from Gerald Petievich's novel *Money Men* by scripter/director Harris—earlier responsible for the quirky James Woods vehicles *Cop* and *Fast Walking* (see index)—the nocturnal L.A.-set *Boiling Point* isn't the clichéd shoot-'em-up its original print ads implied but a savvy, expertly scripted, character-driven crime drama that's riveting from reel 1 to final fade-out. Snipes is excellent as a dedicated T-man obsessed with nailing his partner's killers. The culprits are career con man Hopper and his psychotic, shotgun-wielding assistant (Mortensen). In classic *policier* fashion, Snipes and partner Hedaya narrow the net over our colorful miscreants during the course of 95 swiftly paced, richly textured minutes. What makes *Boiling Point* spin is Harris's detailed examination of Snipes's and Hopper's shared criminal milieu and parallel private lives. Both are on the outs with their former squeezes (though waitress Perrine ultimately cops to Hopper's pathetic promises of a better life). Both Hopper and Snipes likewise romance Davidovich, who, as a too formulaic golden-hearted hooker, represents the flick's weakest link. Several sentimental 1940s standards supply an ironic, contrapuntal soundtrack.

BORN INNOCENT   (1974) **1/2

D: Donald Wrye. Linda Blair, Joanna Miles, Kim Hunter. 92 mins. (WesternWorld, n.i.d.)

Blair serves her first stretch in celluloid stir in a sanitized made-for-TV girls'-reformatory exposé that nonetheless earned its share of notoriety, principally for a girl-gang-rape vignette that put broomsticks on the genre-movie prop map. Not as compelling as Linda's later *Chained Heat* (see index).

BORN LOSERS   (1967) ****

D: Tom Laughlin. Tom Laughlin, Elizabeth James, Jeremy Slate, Jane Russell, William Wellman, Jr., Robert Tessier. 112 mins. (Vestron)

Star/director Laughlin (under the alias T. C. Frank) not only introduces his popular chop-for-peace char-

acter Billy Jack—the dude who put the *fist* in pacifist—but crafts what may well be the best biker movie ever made, an edgy, ahead-of-its-time epic worthy of a Sergio Leone. Jeremy Slate is great as the Harley hounds' vicious leader, while Russell puts in a rare post-'50s appearance.

BORN TO KILL   (1947)
B&W ***

D: Robert Wise. Lawrence Tierney, Claire Trevor, Walter Slezak. 92 mins. (Turner)

Tough guy Tierney—who more recently displayed his rough-edged charms in postmodern noirs like Tarantino's *Reservoir Dogs* and John Herzfeld's *2 Days in the Valley* (see index)—steals the show as a homicidal hubby who has the hots for his sister-in-law (Trevor). Elisha Cook, Jr., likewise shines as Tierney's passive pal.

BORN TO RUN   (1993) *1/2

D: Albert Magnoli. Richard Grieco, Jay Acovone, Joe Cortese, Shelli Lether. 97 mins. (Fox)

The high concept behind *Born to Run* was apparently to assemble a loose feature-length music-video update of *On the Waterfront*—minus the music and with an illegal Brooklyn drag strip replacing the Jersey docks. Former Prince auteur Albert (*Purple Rain*) Magnoli lends the pic a mid-'80s gloss; Grieco, of the piercing-looks school of thespianism, subs for Brando, Cortese takes the Lee J. Cobb role, Acovone pinch-hits for Rod Steiger, and newcomer Lether is an Eva Marie Saint transformed from a near nun to a prissy slut. Grieco and Cortese's climactic confrontation is virtually a line-for-line rewrite of Brando and Cobb's final exchange. As one character puts it, "It ain't right. It's disproportionate or somethin'." To quote original

Waterfront thug Tony Galento: "Definitely."

BOUNTY TRACKER   (1993) ***

D: Kurt Anderson. Lorenzo Lamas, Matthias Hues, Cyndi Pass, Paul Regina, Whip Hubley. 90 mins. (Republic)

Direct-to-home-vid hero and later *Renegade* syndie-TV star Lorenzo (son of Fernando) Lamas scores one of his best vehicles in a far-fetched but fast-paced flick that finds vengeance-driven skip tracer L.L. on the trail of the hit team, led by perennial villain Hues and vicious looker Pass, who terminated his brother. When the police prove typically hopeless, Lamas accepts the aid of a trio of East L.A. homeboys. High-powered shoot-outs, lively martial arts mayhem, and a no-nonsense tone place *Bounty Tracker* above most of the B-video action competition.

BOXCAR BERTHA   (1972) **1/2

D: Martin Scorsese. Barbara Hershey, David Carradine, John Carradine. 90 mins. (Vestron, n.i.d.)

Scorsese made his Hollywood directorial debut with this road-show *Bonnie and Clyde* variation from Roger Corman's celluloid stable. Not one of Marty's more deathless efforts but worth a look for Scorsese buffs and Carradine-clan fans.

BRANDED TO KILL   (1967)
B&W ***

D: Seijun Suzuki. Jo Shishido, Mariko Osawa, Koji Nambara. Subtitled. 87 mins. (Home Vision) DVD

Suzuki's wildly perverse existential noir stars Jo Shishido as Goro, Japan's number-three-ranked hit man, a guy who thoroughly enjoys his work and a kinky home life with his willing sex-slave wife (though his single biggest turn-on is the aroma of boiling rice!). Goro's situation darkens when he botches an assignment and falls under the spell of the mysterious woman (Ogawa) who arranged the hit. Goro ultimately finds himself in the crosshairs of Japan's hitherto "phantom" number-one killer, who delights in teasing and torturing our antihero; the two even briefly live together, sharing the same handcuffs. *Branded to Kill* and the same director's *Tokyo Drifter* (also Home Vision) were, in their time, viewed as radical, unpopular departures from traditional Yakuza-film form, and Nikkatsu Studio fired Suzuki for his eccentric efforts. Today the films make for fascinating viewing as forerunners of Takeshi Kitano's idiosyncratic '90s Yakuza epics, especially the brilliant *Sonatine* and *Fireworks* (see index).

BREAKDOWN   (1997) ***½

D: Jonathan Mostow. Kurt Russell, Kathleen Quinlan, J. T. Walsh, Jack Noseworthy, M. C. Gainey. 95 mins. (Paramount) DVD

As an entry in the fitfully popular "Gone with the Wife" subgenre, *Breakdown* doesn't quite match the creepiness quotient of George Sluizer's original *The Vanishing* but equals the adrenaline level of Roman Polanski's *Frantic* (see index). Troubles begin for relocating upscale couple Russell and Quinlan when their car breaks down in a Southwest desert. Seemingly obliging trucker Walsh—in another wonderfully sinister turn (see also *Black Day Blue Night* and *Sling Blade*)—gives Quinlan a lift to a nearby diner. When Kurt arrives at the same destination, he finds no sign of his errant spouse and receives little help from the assembled locals. Instead, he gets grief galore from lowlifes led by Gainey as the trail ultimately circles back to Walsh. Director/coscripter Mostow—whose less-than-glittering previous credits include *Beverly Hills Bodysnatchers* (SGE) and

Flight of Black Angel (Vidmark)—keeps his narrative thrust moving at a breakneck pace as Russell is run through the proverbial wringer in his quest to rescue his missing missus. *Breakdown* delivers so abundantly in the action, suspense, and atmosphere departments that the flick can be excused for a logical lapse or two.

BRING ME THE HEAD OF ALFREDO GARCIA (1974) ***½

D: Sam Peckinpah. Warren Oates, Isela Vega, Gig Young. 112 mins. (MGM/UA)

Peckinpah's violent south-of-the-border chase film works brilliantly both as a kinetic adventure story and as a metaphor for the director's own experiences within the cutthroat Hollywood system.

BROKEN ARROW   (1996) ***

D: John Woo. John Travolta, Christian Slater, Samantha Mathis, Delroy Lindo, Frank Whaley, Bob Gunton. 108 mins. (Fox) DVD

As he did in his American debut, the 1994 Van Damme–starred *Most Dangerous Game* update *Hard Target* (see index), action auteur Woo injects his second stateside effort with enough adrenaline to simulate a slightly diluted version of his Hong Kong classics *Hard-Boiled* and *The Killer* (see index). In *Broken Arrow,* high-soaring buddies-gone-sour—good guy Slater and villain Travolta—clash big time when the latter aborts a shared test flight as part of his plan to hijack a pair of thermonuclear devices. Woo enlivens his potentially routine chase plot with breakneck action tableaux, while cheerful psycho Travolta easily steals the show from his fellow thesps (as when he warns a trigger-happy minion, "How many times do I have to tell you: Don't shoot at the thermonuclear devices!") *Broken*

Arrow may be lacking in profundity, but it succeeds in supplying a swift celluloid ride.

BROTHER FROM RUSSIA (1997) ***

D: Alexei Balabanov. Sergei Bodrov, Victor Suhorukov, Svetlana Pismichenko, Maria Zhukova, Yury Kuznetsov. Subtitled. 96 mins. (Kino)

A hard-boiled action noir from post–Soviet Russia originally titled simply *Brother,* Balabanov's unsentimental crime drama tracks the low-life odyssey of ex-army youth Danila (Bodrov), who journeys to St. Petersburg to hook up with older bro' Viktor (Suhorukov), already deeply entrenched in the local underworld. Balabanov treats us to a wonderfully seedy travelog of a new Russia riddled with corruption and stoned on rampant consumerism (as well as an impressive array of psychedelic drugs). Danila sets his sights on earning easy money—at least enough to buy the latest CD by his fave Russki band, Nautilius—and finds no lack of opportunities for ruthless young "entrepreneurs" like himself. With Viktor's aid, Danila lands some choice assassination assignments rubbing out rival gangsters while also finding time for erotic assignations with abused wife/trolley driver Sveta (Pismichenko) and nonsexual dope orgies with hip street chick Kat (Zhukova).

Despite his qualmless relationship with situational brutality, Danila emerges as an oft charming, likable thug; like many of his American noir counterparts, past and present, Danila operates within his own moral code (albeit a highly flexible one) and truly cares for the people he, well, truly cares for. (All others are advised to beware!) Writer/director Balabanov's penchant for loose plotting can confuse viewers trying to sort out some of the film's minor players, but *Brother from Russia* is a winner no noir fan will want to miss

BROTHER'S LITTLE HELPER: Shotgun-toting Sergei Bodrov means business in Alexei Balabanov's gritty crime drama *Brother from Russia* (a.k.a. *Brother*).
© *Kino International Corporation 1999*

plies its fair of gratuitous brutality and genuine suspense. And the violence here looks like it's truly painful, as opposed to merely bloody, which at least makes *Bullies* more honest than many of its more cartoonish counterparts.

BULLITT (1968) ***

D: Peter Yates. Steve McQueen, Jacqueline Bisset, Robert Vaughn. 113 mins. (Warner) DVD

Highlighted by an elaborate car chase through hilly Frisco—an endlessly mimicked sequence, recently recycled in *The Rock* (see index) and the Eddie Murphy vehicle *Metro* (Touchstone)—*Bullitt* established many of the conventions—including the cynical, single-minded maverick antihero who bucks the bureaucracy to bag his prey—of the modern American *policier*.

BUMS (1989) *1/2

D: Andy Galler. Christopher McDonald, Haskell Phillips, Dawn Evans, Matt Mitler. 94 mins. (Monarch)

The high concept here sees exsoldier McDonald organize and train a literally dirty half-dozen homeless men after his derelict brother is murdered in a hit financed by ruthless developers. Lensed on the mean streets of Paterson, New Jersey, *Bums* blows its potentially promising premise early on, turning its unarmed heroes into sacrificial victims in the face of the thugs' superior firepower. Clumsily staged action sequences (creatively monikered stunt coordinator J. C. Brotherhood shoulders some of the blame here) and McDonald's poorly motivated romance with cop Evans don't help either. Kung-fu hero Charles Bonet, meanwhile, combats vile NYC slumlords in the equally jaw-dropping 1977 social-minded caper *Death Promise* (Paragon, n.i.d.).

and an apt companion piece for the 1998 Odessa-set crime drama *Friend of the Deceased* (New Yorker).

BULLIES (1986) **1/2

D: Paul Lynch. Stephen Hunter, Jonathan Crombie, Janet Laine-Green, Dehl Berti, Olivia D'Abo. 96 mins. (Universal)

Despite its tame title, *Bullies* is a no-nonsense stroll into second-rate *Straw Dogs* territory. The urban Morris clan—teenage Matt, mom Jenny, and wimpy stepdad, Clay—move to rural British Columbia, where they suffer at the hands (or, more accurately, at the fists) of the cruel Cullen clan—a loutish patriarch and his three sadistic sons. When push comes to shove (to say nothing of beat, slash, torture, and rape), the Morrises fight back in a bloody climactic showdown. While thoroughly predictable, *Bullies* is a solid pro job with a competent cast (we especially enjoyed Dehl Berti in what used to be the Chief Dan George role of a wise old Native American neighbor) that sup-

CABEZA DE VACA (1989) ***1/2

D: Nicholás Echevarría. Juan Diego, Daniel Giménez Cacho, Roberto Sosa, Carlos Castañon, Gerardo Villarreal. Subtitled. 108 mins. (New Horizons)

Something of a *Dances with Wolves* Meets *El Topo* by way of *Aguirre: Wrath of God*, Echevarría's *Cabeza de Vaca*—barely released theatrically but salvaged by Roger Corman (no less) for the home-vid market—is an intense hallucinatory experience that relies very little on dialogue. Diego proves a master mime in the title role of a Spanish ship's treasurer who survives a storm that washes him and a few fellows onto a precondoized Florida coastline, circa 1528. After being enslaved by a local shaman, Diego develops mystical abilities himself. His subsequent odyssey among the area's various tribes plays like an extended fever dream that avoids pretentiousness and sentimentality while packing mucho emotional punch. The film's final image is a classic.

CAGE (1989) ***

D: Lang Elliott. Lou Ferrigno, Reb Brown, Michael Dante, Marilyn Tokuda, James Shigeta, Mike Moroff. 101 mins. (Orion)

Cage casts ex-Incredible Hulk Ferrigno as a literally brain-damaged 'Nam vet cared for by his merely dumb buddy Scott (fellow low-budget beefcake icon Brown). A searing exposé of L.A.'s thoroughly nonexistent "cage-fighting" racket, *Cage* unfolds as a sort of *Bloodsport* Meets *Requiem for a Heavyweight* with some "Of Mice and Rambos" tossed in. If you can get past the pic's numerous plot lapses and Lou's painful Lenny-like perf, *Cage* stacks up as a fairly fun tale that features multiple shoot-outs, sadistic cage fights, and frequent stretches of entertainingly improbable dialogue. *Cage* plays even better on cassette, where you can watch Lou and Reb's historic (to say nothing

of hysteric) on-screen crying jag in the slo mo it deserves. Ferrigno, Brown, and helmer Elliott reunite for *Cage 2: The Arena of Death* (Paramount).

CAGED HEAT (1974) ***

D: Jonathan Demme. Juanita Brown, Erica Gavin, Barbara Steele. 84 mins. (Embassy)

Demme continued to pay his B-movie dues with this lively, semisatirical chicks-in-chains outing. Barbara Steele buffs will enjoy their femme fright fave's uptight turn as a wicked warden in a wheelchair. Followed by *Caged Heat 2: Stripped of Freedom* (New Horizons), the largely uninspired (and seriously belated) 1994 sequel by Roger Corman's prolific longtime Filipino connection, Cirio H. Santiago, starring Jewel Shepard.

CAPTAIN KIDD (1945)
B&W ***

D: Rowland V. Lee. Charles Laughton, Randolph Scott, John Carradine, Gilbert Roland. 89 mins. (HHT)

Lee's low-budget pirate adventure is significantly hoisted by Laughton's wonderfully sly and slimy titular portrayal, with a long-haired Scott serving as an ideal foil and Carradine sharp as one of Laughton's scurvy crew. Homoerotic subtexts abound. Laughton's fade-out exchange with several gallows hecklers is especially priceless.

CARJACK (1993) ***

D: Maximo T. Bird. Deborah Riecks, Kelsey, Adrianne Moore, Randy Potes, Mark Williams. 90 mins. (Light Films)

"Grand Prize Winner of the Winnetka Film Festival," this raw indie from flavorfully nomered auteur Maximo T. Bird (actually *Hell Comes to Frogtown*'s Donald G. Jackson) is less a

road noir than a naturalistic character study that makes selective, effective, ironic use of a cyclical story line, flash forwards, and tight close-ups to put its tale across. Much of the film unfolds like a two-character play on wheels, fueled by Bird's believable dialogue and credible perfs by a regional cast. Following an initially unrelated carjack-and-murder sequence, our story picks up bruised and abused wife Bobby (Riecks) as she drives off from her grotesque, sadistic yuppie hubby (Williams) and impulsively picks up young hitchhiker Ernie (the monomonikered Kelsey), who promptly waves a gun and commandeers her car. Bobby perceives the action as a straight carjack/kidnap; Ernie is actually looking to flee a parole violation and intends to leave both car and driver intact once they're a fair distance from town. Over the course of a single day and night, an unlikely romance develops between the twain, both of whom see themselves as victims. Perception versus reality is Bird's primary theme, and he manipulates his material with generally fascinating results. Highlights include a prolonged desert-set magic-mushroom trip during which Bobby and Ernie further cement their burgeoning bond. Like Jack Perez's *America's Deadliest Home Video* (see index), *Carjack* is a no-budget journey that detours into cinematic surprises galore.

CASINO (1995) **1/2

D: Martin Scorsese. Robert De Niro, Sharon Stone, Joe Pesci, Don Rickles, Alan King, Kevin Pollak, James Woods, L. Q. Jones, John Bloom. 179 mins. (Universal) DVD

"Goodfellas Go Las Vegas" in Scorsese's surprisingly unsurprising rehash of themes and situations he's dramatized, with far more passion, in pics past. De Niro goes through the emotions with a sort of tired intensity as a serious-minded gambling czar, Pesci regurgitates his speed-yapping armed-and-dangerous Chihuahua shtick, while Stone snorts the scenery as a high-rolling hooker with a nose for cocaine and a jones for gold. Raucous domestic dramatics, brutal mob violence, and a flawlessly rendered dissection of the casino's inner workings fail to add resonance to *Casino*'s hollow, recycled ring. Master craftsman Scorsese manages to make it all highly watchable, though, in a comfortably comatose way, and *Casino*'s three supremely polished hours succeed in delivering their rental's worth.

TIANA'S TRIP:
FROM HOLLYWOOD TO HANOI

• •

Tiana returns in a radically different mode in the 1993 documentary *From Hollywood to Hanoi* (n/a). Under her original Vietnamese name, Thi Thanh Nga, Alexandra directs, writes, and narrates a roots journey back to the Vietnam her family fled in 1966. Tiana also covers her checkered showbiz career, including an '80s stint as would-be disco diva "Tiana Banana," while her interview with a less-than-alert-looking General Westmoreland, wearing a conical peasant's hat at a Miss Saigon promo bash, easily rates as the film's grottiest sequence. Withal, a compelling mix of vanity showcasing and legit cultural-identity crisis that's worthy of a home-vid release.

CAT CHASER   (1989) **

D: Abel Ferrara. Peter Weller, Kelly McGillis, Charles Durning, Frederic Forrest, Thomas Milian, Juan Fernandez. In R and unrated editions. 90/92 mins. (Vestron)

The combo of auteur Abel (*King of New York*) Ferrara and noir novelist Elmore Leonard would seem a match made in hard-boiled heaven. Unfortunately, the results of that marriage, in this edition, is a largely listless, poorly motivated affair. The film explores a dangerous romantic link that forms between former marine Weller, now a Florida motel owner, and McGillis, desperate wife of deposed Dominican secret-police chief Milian. Looking to separate Milian from his stashed millions are sleazy ex-cop Durning, his boozing cohort Forrest, and would-be blackmailer Fernandez. Although *Cat Chaser*—the code name of Weller's onetime marine platoon—incorporates several effectively offbeat scenes, they're not enough to overcome the pic's unappealing characters, clunky voice-over narration, and frequent lapses in logic. It should be pointed out, though, that both the R and unrated editions available on video are reedited versions of Ferrara's original cut, since screened at various retro fests but still unavailable on cassette.

CATCH THE HEAT   (1987) **

D: Joel Silberg. Tiana Alexandra, David Dukes, Rod Steiger, Brian Thompson, Jorge Martinez, John Hancock. 88 mins. (Media, n.i.d.)

Steiger's kung-fu-film (!) debut pits the portly thesp against tiny Tiana Alexandra, a supremely fetching Vietnamese martial arts expert. Undercover agent Alexandra, aided by male cohort Dukes, travels to Argentina, where she poses as a naïve Chinese showgirl to infiltrate theatrical-agent-cum-druglord Steiger's inner org. Beyond offering a novel cast and a new wrinkle in drug-smuggling methods (in a Russ Meyer–esque move, the smack is transported by unwitting femmes who think they've just had silicone implants!), *Catch the Heat* never really ignites. Unlike his relatively energetic patriarchal-psycho turn in *American Gothic* (see index), Rod just looks weary here, while Tiana, we're afraid, is better seen and not heard. A last-reel drug raid supplies a serviceable dose of action sorely missing from the flick's middle, which is as flabby as Rod's.

CELLBLOCK SISTERS   (1995) **½

D: Henri Charr. Annie Wood, Gail Harris, Jenna Bodner, Ace Ross, Jamie Donahue. 95 mins. (PM)

Persistence pays off for chicks-in-chains specialist Charr, who, after helming two prison-set duds (*Caged Hearts* [PM], *Under Lock and Key* [Imperial]), gets the formula at least half right with *Cellblock Sisters*. The preposterous plot finds wild-and-crazy biker chick Harris reuniting with her British-bred college-student sister (Wood), with a secret plan to pop the lowlife stepfather who snuffed their junkie-hooker biological mom and sold them to separate adoptive parents some 16 years earlier (a Jerry Springer appearance would seem a slightly less violent alternative). An innocent Wood gets pinched for the slaying, setting the stage for the usual sluts-in-stir intrigues. Catfights, showers, catfights in showers, bloody riots, and other traditional frails-in-jail elements receive swifter treatment here than in Henri's earlier efforts.

CERTAIN FURY   (1985) ***

D: Stephen Gyllenhaal. Irene Cara, Tatum O'Neal, Nicholas Campbell, George Murdock, Moses Gunn, and a "Special Appearance" by Peter Fonda. 87 mins. (Starmaker)

Certain Fury is a distaff urban update of *The Defiant Ones*, exploitation-style: Tracy (Cara), a well-to-do black doctor's daughter, meets Scarlet (O'Neal), an illiterate, lower-class white lass, during a typical court-room shoot-out between a pair of shotgun-wielding femme defendants and a small army of cops. Wrongly impli-cated in the bloody incident (the body count's up to nine before five minutes of film's unspooled!), our heroines are forced to rely on each other to survive a series of fast-paced encounters with sewer rats, rapists, pornographers, dop-ers, and the ever pursuing police. *Certain Fury* consistently delivers the sleazy goods, with high-energy bashings, slashings, and chases galore, all set to an adrenalizing rock score. Cara even briefly bares her modest, upper-middle-class breasts in the pic's token gratuitous shower scene (though Tatum keeps her larger, lumpen ones chastely concealed throughout). Add a memorable tag line—"One way or another they'll blow you away!"—plus a "special appear-ance" by Peter Fonda, and who could ask for anything more?

CHAINED HEAT:
THE SERIES

CHAINED HEAT   (1983) ***

D: Paul Nicolas. Linda Blair, Stella Stevens, Sybil Danning, Henry Silva, John Vernon, Tamara Dobson. 97 mins. (Video Treasures/Anchor Bay)

Chained Heat, sequel to *Concrete Jungle* (Columbia/TriStar), rates as one of the sleaziest and best of the entire chicks-in-chains genre. Blair once again learns the prison ropes the hard way. The pic's bolstered by a great B cast, including Danning and Silva, with Vernon a standout as the warden who videotapes inmates in his office Jacuzzi while feeding them cocaine (!). Typical of the flick's tone is Warden Vernon's advice to a coke-injecting prisoner who's begging for a fix: "Oh, why can't you *snort* it like the rest of us?"

CHAINED HEAT 2   (1993) *1/2

D: Lloyd Simandl. Brigitte Nielsen, Paul Koslo, Kimberly Kates, Kari Whitman. 98 mins. (New Line)

This belated, related-in-name-only sequel fills the small screen with even more nudity and gratuitous show-ers but does so sans the original's juice and passion. Nielsen plays Magda, broad-shouldered, crack-smoking les-bian warden of a Prague prison ("a decaying remnant of the Communist regime," a voice-over informs us). When Commie cops plant drugs on visiting American Kates, our heroine suffers all the usual indignities until the inevita-ble last-reel bust-out. Brigitte's floating accent and Nazi-styled histrionics sup-ply moments of campy relief, but *Chained Heat 2* succeeds only in driving another nail into the coffin of a fast-expiring genre. As Brigitte/Magda her-self puts it, not once but twice: "This is very bad!"

CHARLEY VARRICK   (1973) ***

D: Don Siegel. Walter Matthau, Felicia Farr, Joe Don Baker. 111 mins. (Universal)

Bank robber Matthau as Varrick (self-styled "Last of the Indepen-dents") tries to elude sadistic mob hit man Baker (in one of his scurviest screen roles) in a tough modern noir ably directed by Clint Eastwood mentor and veteran action specialist Siegel.

CHINA GIRL   (1987) **1/2

D: Abel Ferrara. James Russo, Sari Chang, Richard Panebianco, Russell Wong, Joey Chin, Judith Malina. 88 mins. (Vestron)

Ferrara's *China Girl* is a semiex-ploitation reworking of *West Side Story* (Fox) set to blaster tunes and transplanted from Hell's Kitchen to the Little Italy–Chinatown border. The romance—or crush, anyway—that develops between teens Tony (Pane-bianco) and Tye (an appealing Chang) lacks the operatic, acrobatic passion that possessed the original Tony and Maria, but at least this pair gets to have sex once. More successful is Ferrara's depiction of the separate-but-equal col-lusion between elder Chinese and Ital-ian crime lords, who seek to quell rebellious immigrant Su Shin (Chin) and his gang. The pic ultimately resorts to illogical plot twists and a forced tragic climax, but Ferrara accomplishes a lot on a low budget.

CIA II: TARGET ALEXA   (1994) **

D: Lorenzo Lamas. Lorenzo Lamas, Kathleen Kinmont, John Savage, Pamela Dixon, John Ryan, Larry Manetti. 90 mins. (PM)

Lamas handles directorial chores while then-spouse Kathleen ("the next female Schwarzenegger") Kinmont cops costory credit on this slick but largely charmless actioner. A portable nuke-guidance system supplies the req-uisite McGuffin. Violently snatched by merc leader Savage, the high-ticket device is subsequently pursued by CIA spook Lamas and ex-opponent Kin-mont, as well as rival villains headed by Ryan, who, in a move torn, as they say, from today's headlines, plans to peddle it to North Korean interests. Savage seeks to rekindle sparks with former flame Kinmont with such romantic pre-ambles as "I remember our last night in Beirut…" (!). Adequate cable-surfing fodder, *CIA II: Target Alexa* achieves its chief aim of filling the small screen with excessive explosive mayhem. PM offered video retailers an added induce-ment in the form of free copies of the original *C.I.A.: Codename: Alexa*, costarring accused killer O. J. Simpson.

CLEOPATRA JONES   (1973) ***

D: Jack Starrett. Tamara Dobson, Bernie Casey, Shelley Winters, Brenda Sykes,

Antonio Fargas, Bill McKinney. 89 mins. (Warner) DVD

While she failed to unseat then-reigning "blaxploitation" queen Pam Grier, the indomitable Dobson proved a hit in her own right (and left) in Starrett's fun action entry. Winters lends loud support as the villainous "Mommy." The film was followed by the equally adrenalizing *Cleopatra Jones and the Casino of Gold*—a title that preceded *Indiana Jones* (no relation) *and the Temple of Doom* by more than a decade—with Stella Stevens as the supremely evil "Dragon Lady."

CLIFFHANGER (1993) ***

D: Renny Harlin. Sylvester Stallone, John Lithgow, Janine Turner, Michael Rooker, Paul Winfield, Ralph Waite, Max Perlich. 113 mins. (Columbia/TriStar) DVD

Lithgow's hammy histrionics and Harlin's icy action scenes steal the show in this snowy Sly vehicle. Relatively subdued, reasonably decipherable former mountain ranger Stallone, squeeze Turner, and ex-partner Rooker contend with unfriendly elements and Lithgow's killer crew in a search for sky-jacked loot lost in rocky terrain. Perlich, who displayed excellent character-thesp chops in *Drugstore Cowboy* and *Rush* (see index), is literally wasted as the alpine equivalent of a dim surfer dude. Like Perlich, ranger Waite seems penciled in mostly to beef up the body count. Still, *Cliffhanger* delivers on its pulp-movie promise.

CLOCKERS (1995) ***

D: Spike Lee. Harvey Keitel, John Turturro, Mekhi Phifer, Delroy Lindo, Spike Lee. 129 mins. (Universal) DVD

Lee and coscripter Richard Price's adaptation of the latter's novel manages to infuse 'hood crime clichés with enough personality to make *Clock-*

ers (slang for neighborhood pushers) work most of the way. Phifer is effective as lead character Strike, a young dealer whose debt to local crack honcho Lindo drags him deeper into danger and violence. Keitel, as a streetwise cop, dominates his scenes, while Turturro is relegated to an unchallenging secondary role as his partner.

COBRA (1986) *

D: George P. Cosmatos. Sylvester Stallone, Brigitte Nielsen, Reni Santoni, Brian Thompson, Andrew Robinson, Art LaFleur. 87 mins. (Warner) DVD

Simian psychos, who perform mysterious displays that involve clanging axes over their heads, are knocking off random Angel City citizens, seemingly sans rhyme or reason. Local humans are helpless against them, so Cro-Magnon cop "Cobra" Cobretti (Stallone) and his equally primitive partner, Gonzalez (Santoni), are summoned to take matters firmly in paw. The pair protect endangered nature girl Nielsen and slaughter the villains in an outbreak of intense gorilla warfare. And that's about all Sly wrote: *Cobra* boasts what has to be one of the skinniest scripts to surface since the advent of talkies (or, in prime-'80s Sly's case, "grunties"). The rest of the flick is largely given over to multiple product plugs—including a Toys "R" You-Know-Who commercial that just happens to be playing when Cobra turns on his kitchen TV—while Cobra the character even goes so far as to flaunt his own IQ, via a personalized license plate reading AWSOM 50. In yet another Sly move, the chief opposing apeman (Thompson) not only bears a striking resemblance to then-B.O. rival Arnold Schwarzenegger (Arn earlier offed the same thesp, playing one of three punks, in *The Terminator*) but suffers from similar elocution problems. Sly and Bri's climactic confrontation—a heady debate re American society's inefficacious judicial practices—cries

out for subtitles, as do several earlier scenes involving Sly, a heavily accented Brigitte, and Santoni, who delivers much of his dialogue with a mouth full of junk food.

COCKFIGHTER (1974) ***

D: Monte Hellman. Warren Oates, Millie Perkins, Harry Dean Stanton, Troy Donahue. 83 mins. (Platinum)

Consummate character thesp Oates turns in strong work as the mostly silent titular killer-rooster trainer in an effectively offbeat parable (a.k.a. *Born to Kill* from cult auteur Hellman (*The Shooting, Two Lane Blacktop* [Anchor Bay, DVD]). Couchside extreme-animal-sports fans can also scope out the thematically related *Rooster: Spurs of Death!* (WesternWorld).

CODE OF SILENCE (1985) *1/2

D: Andy Davis. Chuck Norris, Henry Silva, Molly Hagan, Bert Remsen. 101 mins. (HBO)

Chuck is maverick Windy City cop Hank (presumably no relation to John or Joan) Cusack, who—with the help of his police-robot pal—wages a one-man war (or, more accurately, a one-man, one-police-robot war) against Silva and his drug-dealing thugs. The best line has Chuck inform a local hood, "When I want your opinion, I'll *beat* it out of you!" *Code's* not as good as *The French Connection,* which admittedly benefitted from not having Chuck in its cast. But you have to give Chuck credit—otherwise he just might beat it out of you—for being the first of our modern crop of screen action heroes to lay waste to Chicago, far ahead of cinematic competitors Arnold Schwarzenegger (*Raw Deal*), Steven Seagal (*Above the Law*), and Keanu Reeves (*Chain Reaction* [Fox]), among others, all forced to conduct what were little more than mop-up operations after Chuck's groundbreaking rampage.

FIGHTIN' WORDS!

"Don't just stand there—kill something!"
—oceangoing villain Deacon (Dennis Hopper), *Waterworld*

*"I always thought I liked animals.
Then I discovered I liked killing people more."*
—supervillain Scaramanga (Christopher Lee),
The Man with the Golden Gun

*"He's a fed. So neat you could shoot him and bury him
in the same suit."*
—thug re G-man, *Dead-Bang*

"I cannot bring back the dead, only kill the living."
—hit man, *The Valachi Papers*

"I don't care if he's dead or alive—so long as he can talk."
—mob boss to henchman, *Personal Property*

"What hit him?"
"A complete state of death."
—cop and fellow officer Charles Bronson, *The Stone Killer*

"I never thought I'd use macramé to kill."
—teen strangler Lulu Fishpaw (Mary Garlington), *Polyester*

COFFY (1973)***

D: Jack Hill. Pam Grier, Booker Bradshaw, Robert DoQui. 91 mins. (Orion)

Two-fisted, shotgun-toting nurse Pam slams local pushers after her sister becomes addicted in Jack (*Switchblade Sisters*) Hill's swiftly paced "blaxploitation" effort, one that went a long way in solidifying Grier's rep as a formidable action starlet.

COHEN AND TATE (1989)***

D: Eric Red. Roy Scheider, Adam Baldwin, Harley Cross. 86 mins. (Nelson, n.i.d.)

Cohen and Tate represents a case of a lame name masking a lean, mean movie. The title characters are a pair of mismatched assassins—seasoned pro Cohen (Scheider) and redneck psycho Tate (Baldwin)—dispatched to kidnap nine-year-old mob-murder witness Travis (Cross). Trouble is, Cohen and Tate genuinely hate each other, a natural emnity that young Travis tries to play to his advantage during a long, violent drive from Muscogee, Oklahoma, to Houston. Auteur Red, who earlier scripted the road-movie fright faves *The Hitcher* and *Near Dark* (see index), shapes his narrow but intense (if occasionally derivative) tale with admirable precision. While not quite the modern equivalent of B noir classics like Edgar G. Ulmer's *Detour* (see index), *Cohen and Tate* rates as a minor genre gem.

COMBAT SHOCK (1986)**½

D: Buddy Giovinazzo. Ricky Giovinazzo, Mitch Maglia, Asaph Livni, Nick

Viet vet Frank Dunlan is *not* having an easy time of it. Not only is he jobless, about to be evicted, haunted by recurrent 'Nam nightmares, nagged by his blowsy bitter half ("You sure there's no shrapnel in your *skull*?"), and bugged by a mutant infant son right out of *Eraserhead,* but he's just awakened to find the toilet's broken. All this before breakfast (stale Cocoa Puffs and sour milk!). Giovinazzo's *Combat Shock* (originally titled *American Nightmare*) is a relentlessly depressing, bleakly surreal, often dim and amateurish, but weirdly compelling day in the downtrodden life of Dunlan (well played by bro' Ricky Giovinazzo, who resembles something of a skid-row Henry Winkler in his Fonz days). For long stretches nothing much happens: Frankie wanders a Staten Island hellscape that does nothing to boost that oft benighted borough's image, encountering local hoods, junkies, and hookers while simultaneously enduring violent wartime flashbacks. The "action" doesn't heat up until the final reel, when *Combat Shock* takes a belated turn into *Taxi Driver* turf. A family affair all the way—the credits are crammed with Giovinazzos galore (star Ricky G. also composed the pic's loopy synthesizer score)—this reportedly $40,000 16-millimeter-shot indie is definitely *not* corporate-culture schlock. There are images in this fiercely idiosyncratic flick we doubt we'll ever forget. Buddy G. returned over a decade later with the far more polished *No Way Home* (see index).

COMMANDO (1985)*

D: Mark L. Lester. Arnold Schwarzenegger, Rae Dawn Chong, Dan Hedaya, Vernon Wells, James Olson, Alyssa Milano, David Patrick Kelly. 90 mins. (Fox) DVD

In producer Joel Silver's combination comic-book-cum-video-game, Arnie unleashes his terminating powers at the expense of a gang of sadistic goons employed by a South American would-be dictator who wants our hero to off his country's present prez. These leering lowlifes commit the fatal error of snatching the muscle-bound ex-commando's young daughter (future sitcom starlet and "erotic thriller" slut queen Milano). Arn enlists the reluctant aid of foxy stewardess Chong, and the chase is on, followed in swift order by entire reels of wholesale slaughter (see table, right). Unfortunately, all the essential ingredients that helped make Arn's immediate predecessor, *The Terminator,* one of the best genre movies ever, turn sour here. Arnie unwisely switches from a killer cyborg—a role he was built to play—to a run-of-the-mill superman who only *emotes* like a robot, which is akin to casting King Kong as James Bond. Through it all, no matter how many hapless mortals are thrown against him, Arn comes off as a witless bully and the movie as a terminal bore.

CONDITION RED   (1995) ***

D: Mika Kaurismäki. James Russo, Cynda Williams, Paul Calderon, Victor Argo, Andre Degass. 85 mins. (Arrow)

Finnish auteur Mika (brother of Aki, of *Leningrad Cowboys Go America* [Orion] fame) Kaurismäki, late of the effective *Zombie and the Ghost Train* and the Sam Fuller–focused documentary *Tigrero* (see index), switches gears and nations for this English-language fiction film. Russo stars as a bottled-up Philadelphia prison guard whose frequent fractious encounters with inmates earns him a transfer to the jail's female wing. There, he gradually becomes involved with imprisoned songstress Williams, who's thus far refused to sing re her at-large employers, sleazy club owner Calderon and his even sleazier money-laundering boss, Argo. "Inspired" by a real case, *Condition*

COMMANDO:
A DAY IN THE DEATH

• •

Surrendering to morbid curiosity (admittedly one of our fave activities), we freeze-framed our way through Commando *to record Arn's exact kill count. To qualify as a Confirmed Kill, Arn's victim had to be hit directly by a lethal weapon or shown to be absolutely, positively kaput. Those merely belted, kicked, or karate-chopped and left in an ambiguous physical condition do not count here. We also list the primary weapons employed and the injuries sustained by our hero. Let's go to the videotape:*

TIME LOG

1:36: Villains claim first victim.

4:00: First extreme close-up of Arnie's lats and 'ceps.

13:35: Arnie claims his first victim, machine-gunning an enemy messenger.

20:20: Arnie coughs up his first killer quip: "I like you, Solly, so I'm going to kill you last."

22:00: Arnie breaks bad guy's neck.

29:15: Arn rips out Rae Dawn Chong's seat.

35:00: Arn punches out several mall security guards and a phone booth.

37:25: Arn is hit by a car, lands on his head. No apparent damage.

41:00: Arn throws Solly off a cliff.

45:10: Arn is kicked in the head. No apparent damage.

46:30: Arn impales bad guy Bill Duke on a furniture leg.

51:20: Arn karate-chops an airport sentry—fails to qualify as a confirmed kill.

54:00: Arn drives a bus through a gun-store window to facilitate some last-minute shopping.

57:05: Rae Dawn does her bit by destroying an innocent building and a police van with a four-barreled rocket launcher borrowed from Arn.

59:05: Arn busts another sentry upside the head. Kill unconfirmed.

60:30: Arn takes out two bad guys with a machine gun. Kills confirmed.

Intermission: The Phantom, taking a break, threatens his VCR with a sound thrashing. Appliance in question repeatedly flashes 12:00 in open defiance. Phantom lays down his remote, puts his hands on his head, and steps away from the TV.

67:00: Back to the couch as Arn dresses to kill in now-famous commando-fetish fashion montage.

69:45–78:00: Arn gets serious, launches one-man assault, employing knives, machine guns, grenades, axes, and a pitchfork in claiming 78—count 'em yourself—78 additional victims.

79:00: Grenade blows up in Arn's face. No apparent damage.

80:00: Arn wounded below right shoulder, the same spot he gets shot in in several subsequent films.

84:00: Arn receives severe beating before pummeling, electrocuting, and impaling his final foe.

Running time: 90 minutes.
Confirmed kills: 92.

Red—the title is prison jargon for "state of alarm"—betrays few of Kaurismäki's earlier flourishes but rates as a solid entry, along the lines of a *Fast Walking* (see index), that's a mite more serious-minded than your usual prison caper and features fine work by Russo and Williams. Andre Degass, meanwhile, scores an unusual troika of credits here—screenwriter, actor (as Russo's fellow guard Bishop), *and* second-unit director (!). Mika also directed the mostly maligned environmentalist adventure *Amazon* (Artisan), starring Robert Davi and Rae Dawn Chong.

COPKILLERS (1973) ***

D: Walter Cichy. Jason Williams, Bill Osco, Diane Keller, Michael D. White, Donna Stubbert, Judy Ross. 93 mins. (TWE, n.i.d.)

This regional rarity rates as a reel surprise. *Flesh Gordon* star/future *Danger Zone* biker-series hero Williams and frequent adult filmmaker Osco play border lowlifes whose botched coke deal leads to a police ambush that leaves several officers dead. Circumstances prolong the pair's motorized killing spree; friction ensues when Williams decides he enjoys their new pastime, much to partner Osco's disgust. Director Cichy and coproducers Osco and Howard Ziehm (responsible for the aforementioned *Flesh Gordon*) bring an unsensationalized verité tone to the violent but consistently credible action. That, along with believable perfs, raises *Copkillers* to the top of the exploitation heap. We also recommend *Corrupt*, with Harvey (*Bad Lieutenant*) Keitel again cast as a corrupt cop who chains nutcase John (ex–Sex Pistol Johnny Rotten) Lydon to his bathtub, and the quintessentially '70s exposé, *Shoot It: Black, Shoot It: Blue* (both HBO), wherein African-American student Eric Laneuville films killer Cauc cop Michael Moriarty committing a cold-blooded murder.

CRACKERJACK (1994) **

D: Michael Mazo. Thomas Ian Griffith, Nastassja Kinski, Christopher Plummer, George Touliatos, Lisa Bunting, Richard Sali. 96 mins. (Republic)

Ex–*Karate Kid* villain Griffith returns for another crack at B-action stardom but proves as charmless as ever in this Vancouver-lensed *Die Hard* in a Mountain Resort Meets *Cliffhanger* following a *Lethal Weapon* prologue. Moody Chicago cop Griffith is on a forced Rockies vacation when terrorists led by Plummer (doing a bad Dr. Strangelove imitation) violently appropriate the resort where T.I.G.'s staying. Kinski is completely wasted in a white-bread role as a Euro-accented blond resort hostess who helps our hero's cause. *Crackerjack* rates as a minor improvement over Griffith's earlier *Excessive Force*, mostly due to its occasionally ambitious action set pieces. Our screener came complete with voice-overs for a video retailers' promotional contest that sporadically drowned out the on-screen dialogue—"Crackerjack's missed out on a hidden code for a Crack-the-Ice Screener Game. If your game card matches, you have just won a really cool ice bucket!"—though not nearly often enough.

CRIME STORY (1993) ***½

D: Kirk Wong. Jackie Chan, Kent Cheng, Christine Ng, Law Hang Kang. Dubbed. 100 mins. (Dimension)

Jackie eschews his usual kung fu comedy and scenery-chewing moves in a straightforward *policier* loosely based on an actual case. *Crime Story* gets off to a torrid start with a high-speed "practice run" for a planned kidnap caper. The victim is super-rich (and mega-stingy) construction mogul Wong (Kang), who's snatched during a sloppy job that costs the life of a Hong Kong motorcycle cop and makes fellow fuzz Chan obsessed with cracking the case.

What Jackie doesn't know is that one of the key investigating officers, the rotund Detective Hung (Cheng), is the crime's covert mastermind. Chan and director Wong pepper their no-nonsense narrative with the expected spectacular action sequences, including a Taipei-set shoot-out and a prop-driven martial arts set-to between Jackie and the kidnappers in a 7-Eleven. In place of the usual comic outtakes, *Crime Story* ends with a voice-over stating some grim Asian kidnap stats and dedicating the film to those police officers who've lost their lives in pursuit of the perpetrators. The only drawback to this otherwise competently dubbed video edition is that Jackie doesn't handle his own vocal chores, and it's jarring to hear a bland Anglo voice in place of Chan's distinctive delivery. Followed by Wong's blistering semisequel, *Organized Crime & Triad Bureau* (Tai Seng, subtitled, DVD), starring Danny Lee.

CRIMSON TIDE (1995) **½

D: Tony Scott. Gene Hackman, Denzel Washington, Matt Craven, George Dzundza, Viggo Mortensen, James Gandolfini. 115 mins. (Hollywood Pictures) DVD

Crimson Tide stacks up as a high-tech update of James B. Harris's 1965 *The Bedford Incident* (Columbia/TriStar), which, while equally histrionic, at least unfolded within a somewhat more credible geopolitical context, following in the wake of the Cuban missile crisis. In Scott's '90s variation, sub captain Hackman is less crazed than his Richard Widmark counterpart, and Washington less pure than his predecessor, Sidney Poitier. EXO Washington relieves Hackman of his command when the latter okays a nuclear launch even after the abortive arrival of a second order that may be canceling the strike. Quentin Tarantino was reportedly involved in one of the script rewrites, adding unenlightening *Silver Surfer* and *Star Trek* allusions, and Jason Robards contributes an uncredited cameo. *Crimson Tide* succeeds in generating some claustrophobic tension but basically shakes down as an unnecessary, overproduced exercise in intense predictability. For a better underwater adventure, scope out John McTiernan's tense adaptation of the Tom Clancy best-seller *Hunt for Red October* (Paramount, DVD), a deft balance between human drama and high-tech thrills, with Alec Baldwin as an American naval expert tracking Russian sub commander Sean Connery's errant course.

CROSSCUT (1995) ***

D: Paul Raimondi. Costas Mandylor, Megan Gallagher, Casey Sander, Allen Cutler, Jay Acovone, Zack Norman. 90 mins. (A-Pix)

Crosscut plays like the contempo equivalent of a solid '50s western. Laconic Mafioso Mandylor is forced to flee after killing a weasely fellow mobster in NYC, ending up in a small Northern California logging town, where he eventually romances local vet Gallagher. In traditional sagebrush fashion, gunmen led by Acovone make their way cross-country for an inevitable showdown. While not in the same class as Carl Franklin's edgier *One False Move* (see index), *Crosscut* is deftly scripted, acted, and photographed.

CUP FINAL (1991) ***1/2

D: Erin Riklis. Moshe Ivgi, Mohammed Bakri, Suheil Haddad. Subtitled. 107 mins. (First Run)

Israeli director Riklis makes a hopeful but far from starry-eyed case for replacing actual combat with the sublimated warfare of international sports. The title refers to the 1982 World Cup Soccer Games in Barcelona, which Israeli reservist Ivgi had planned to attend, a trip abruptly canceled by his country's invasion of Lebanon. The rueful reservist meets an even harsher fate when he's taken captive by a ragged band of PLO guerrillas. In the course of the group's violent journey to Beirut, Ivgi and Euro-educated PLO leader Bakri gradually form a bond based on their mutual love of soccer in general and Italy's team in particular. All is not soft-headed harmony between prisoner and captors, though; Riklis humanizes his characters, creating sympathy for both sides, but stops short of romanticizing either. While the movie's ultimate outcome may be downbeat, *Cup Final* is an immensely entertaining, actionful, often comic, and always ironic opus that can take its place beside Sam Fuller's Korean War fable, *The Steel Helmet* (see index).

CURSE OF THE DRAGON (1993) ***

D: Fred Weintraub, Tom Kuhn. 87 mins. (Warner)

This obviously rushed but consistently compelling Bruce Lee documentary was keyed to capitalize both on *Dragon*'s (see index) 1993 theatrical release and Brandon Lee's senseless death on the set of *The Crow* in April of that year. Narrated by *Star Trek*'s George (Sulu) Takei, *Curse* assembles rare footage, film clips, and interviews with such famed Lee students as James Coburn, Chuck Norris, and Kareem Abdul-Jabbar to form a portrait of the martial artist as an often angry young man whose abrasive style aroused almost as much ire as admiration. (Unlike *Dragon*, *Curse* doesn't sidestep the issue of Lee's premature, still-mysterious demise.) An irritating technique that overlaps the interviewees' voices represents *Curse*'s only serious flaw.

CUTTHROAT ISLAND (1995) *1/2

D: Renny Harlin. Geena Davis, Matthew Modine, Frank Langella, Stan Shaw, Harris Yulin, Jimmy F. Skaggs. 118 mins. (Artisan) DVD

Harlin's megabudgeted valentine to the nautical epics of yore sank like a stone (and we're not talking Sharon or Oliver) during its maiden theatrical voyage, prompting Live (now Artisan) to launch it on home vid well ahead of the usual six-month window and following up with a sell-through "special edition" with still *more* footage that nobody wanted to see. According to a *New York Times* article, *Cutthroat Island* officially surpassed *Heaven's Gate* for Biggest Box Office Bomb in Hollywood History honors, yielding a domestic B.O. tally of $9.8 million from a production and marketing total estimated at $115 mil. While *Cutthroat Island* incorporates some grand seagoing battle scenes, its problem is that it's cornball for the '50s, instead of being cornball for the '90s,

---

TOP 10 CORSAIR CLASSICS ON CASSETTE

The Black Pirate (1926, Kino)
The Black Swan (1942, Fox)
The Buccaneer (1958, Paramount)
Captain Kidd (1945, HHT)
The Crimson Pirate (1952, Warner)
Nate and Hayes (1983, Paramount)
The Sea Hawk (1940, Fox)
Sinbad the Sailor (1947, RKO)
Swiss Family Robinson (1960, Disney)
Treasure Island (1950, Disney)

MOTION IN THE OCEAN: Douglas Fairbanks leads his corsair crew into high-seas adventure in a scene from the two-strip Technicolor swashbuckler *The Black Pirate.* © Kino International Corporation 1999

to rest at the bottom of Davy Jones's Locker.

THE DALLAS CONNECTION (1994) **¹/₂

D: Drew Sidaris. Bruce Penhall, Mark Barriere, Julie Strain, Samantha Phillips, Rodrigo Obregón. 93 mins. (Monarch)

While veteran jiggle-action auteur Andy Sidaris (who's described the flick as "basically a knockoff of *Wuthering Heights*") and coproducer spouse, Arlene Sidaris, produced *The Dallas Connection,* it's directed by son Drew, who handled identical chores on the clan's *Enemy Gold* (see index). While it doesn't match the quality of the Sidarises' best efforts—e.g., *Guns, Savage Beach* (see index)—*TDC* provides considerable sweep, globe-hopping from Paris to South Africa to Hong Kong to D.C. before settling down in Dallas and environs. *The Dallas Connection* is at its best when it's at its drollest, an attitude best embodied (accent on *body*) by Amazonian villainess Strain, cast here as a skimpily clad, leather-mad assassin called "Black Widow." ("I do justice to my code name," she blandly remarks to a minion after offing a French scientist during a lusty S&M session.) On the downside, the obligatory sex scenes tend to drag on, and the climactic action sequences could use more juice. (It may be time for Andy's Gang to take in a John Woo movie or two.)

DANGER ZONE:
THE SERIES

DANGER ZONE (1986) **¹/₂

D: Henry Vernon. Jason Williams, Robert Canada, Suzanne Tara, Dana Dowell, Cynthia Gray, Daniel Friedman. 90 mins. (Charter, n.i.d.)

Biker-flick fans should get a bang out of *Danger Zone,* a hog-wild affair produced and coscripted by Jason

despite the progressive PC casting of Davis (who tried to jump ship prior to lensing; projected star Michael Douglas wisely bailed out early on, entrusting his role to Modine) in the Errol Flynn/Burt Lancaster acrobatic-pirate role. The energetic Geena (who, in close-up, appears in danger of becoming a serious collagen casualty) and her stunt double give their all, as do her colorful crew members—most of whom would look more at home in a biker movie than a pirate pic—but the would-be rousing treasure-hunt story line recycles without reanimating the hoariest of celluloid corsair clichés. Given the reception earlier accorded Roman Polanski's *Pirates* (Live), James Goldstone's *Swashbuckler,* and Peter Benchley's updated variation *The Island* (both Universal)—even Spielberg's highly hyped *Hook* (Columbia/TriStar) proved a comparative B.O. disappointment—perhaps this benighted genre might best be left

ANDY'S GANG: Julie Strain (top left) and posse (left to right, back row, Mark Barriere, Sam Phillips; front row, Bruce Penhall, Julie K. Smith) prepare for action in Andy Sidaris and clan's *The Dallas Connection.*
Courtesy of Andy Sidaris

Krueger. After the Manson-oid Reaper is released from custody on your typical legal technicality, he wastes no time in kidnapping Williams's squeeze (Higginson) and kick-starting our hog-riding hero into action. In a neat touch, Williams's search for the cycle psycho (who leaves rhymed clues in his wake) leads him first to several strangers who also harbor serious gripes re the heinous Reaper. Even better, the filmmakers take admirable care in crafting their contempo western-on-wheels, and the flick goes a long way (from the California desert to Vegas, in fact) on a low budget. Followed by 1990's weaker *Danger Zone III: Steel Horse War* (Premiere) and the still-shoddier *Death Riders* (Monarch). Footage from *Death Riders* turns up in flashback form in *Danger Zone IV: Bad Girls, Mad Girls* (n/a), which preemed on cable's USA Network.

DANTE'S PEAK   (1997) **1/2

D: Roger Donaldson. Pierce Brosnan, Linda Hamilton, Jamie Renee Smith, Jeremy Foley, Elizabeth Hoffman, Charles Hallahan. 109 mins. (Universal) DVD

This family-oriented disaster flick didn't warrant the price of a first-run bijou ticket but shapes up as a fair rental bet. Brosnan plays virtually perfect seismologist hero Dr. Dalton (doubtless named in honor of his James Bond precursor, Timothy), with much screen time devoted to his noble efforts to rescue romantic interest/small-town mayor Hamilton; her kids, Smith and Foley; her stubborn mom, Hoffman; and the latter's dog, Ruffie. (Bottom line: Granny buys the farm but Ruffie's just fine.) Dependable craftsman Donaldson delivers the shake-and-bake volcanic thrills, while a nearly eight-minute end-credit crawl pads the pic's running time. Fox released *Peak*'s equally lava-ish coast-toasting competitor *Volcano.*

(Flesh Gordon) Williams, who also costars as an undercover narc who infiltrates a gang of coke-dealing Harley hounds headed by "the Reaper" (a convincingly menacing Canada). Six starstruck bimbos on their way to a Vegas talent show suffer the misfortune of having their car break down near the bad guys' desert hideaway, and you can more or less fill in the blanks from there. While not startlingly original, *Danger Zone* is a taut, tense, and tough entry in the Sixpack Cinema Sweepstakes.

DANGER ZONE II: REAPER'S REVENGE   (1989) ***

D: Geoffrey G. Bowers. Jason Williams, Robert Random, Jane Higginson, Alisha Das, Walter Cox, Barnes Wms Subkoski. 95 mins. (Forum, n.i.d.)

This actionful sequel again pits leather-jacketed undercover cop Williams (who again coproduces) against biker supernemesis the Reaper (Random), who solidifies his niche as screen cycledom's answer to Freddy

• •

1) *Born Losers* (1967, Vestron)
2) *Stone Cold* (1991, Columbia/TriStar)
3) *Easy Rider* (1969, Columbia/TriStar)
4) *Hells Angels on Wheels* (1967, Trimark)
5) *The Peace Killers* (1971, Starmaker)
6) *Satan's Sadists* (1969, Super)
7) *She-Devils on Wheels* (1968, Something Weird)
8) *The Wild Angels* (1966, Orion)
9) *Hell's Angels Forever* (1983, Media)
10) *Bury Me an Angel* (1971, Starmaker)
11) *Northville Cemetery Massacre* (1976, Paragon)
12) *The Last Riders* (1991, PM)
13) *The Long Ride* (1998, Salt City)

Best Biker: William ("Big Bill") Smith: *Angels Die Hard* (Starmaker), *C.C. and Company* (MGM), *Chrome and Hot Leather* (Orion), *Eye of the Tiger* (Live), *Hollywood Man* (Video Gems), *The Last Riders* (see above), *The Losers* (Academy), *Run, Angel, Run!* (VidAmerica).

THE DARKSIDE   (1987) ***

D: Constantino Magnatta. Tony Galati, Cyndy Preston, Peter Read, John Tench, Charles Loriot, David Hewlett. 95 mins. (Trimark)

Naïve cabbie Galati helps runaway Preston escape the clutches of killer porn-peddlers in a realistically played outing that also boasts a fair amount of sadistic set pieces. While not in the same league as *Blue Velvet* (the video box's brazen comparisons notwithstanding), *The Darkside* represents a suspenseful descent into the urban Canadian demimonde.

DAY OF THE WARRIOR   (1996) **½

D: Andy Sidaris. Julie Strain, Kevin Light, Christian Letelier, Julie K. Smith, Marcus Bagwell, Shea Marks, Raye Hollitt, Rodrigo Obregón, Gerald Okamura, Richard Cansino, Cassidy Phillips, Tammy Parks, Ted Prior. 105 mins. (Monarch)

You know you're in Sidaris territory right from reel 1 when a government-agency head (bodaciously, if cosmetically, sculpted Strain) conducts a high-level meeting while working a Stairmaster and wearing a leopard-skin bikini (!). The agency in question is LETHAL (that's Legion to Ensure Total Harmony and Law to you). Here its far-flung ops (including one, Smith, working "deep cover as an exotic dancer") are out to stop superbuff black marketeer "Warrior" (pro wrestler Bagwell) and his violent minions (ever colorful Sidaris regular Obregón among them). The Sidarises (writer/director Andy and producer spouse, Arlene) adopt an even spoofier tone than usual in playing out their convoluted intrigues. Among the assembled LETHAL agents are bearded Asian Presley imitator "Elvis Fu" (Okamura), buxom demolitionist Marks ("Everything I touch has a way of exploding!"), and the usual gang of hunky guys and top-heavy heroines.

The Sidarises spare no frequent-flyer mileage in offering a wide geographical canvas, as their tale unfolds in such exotic locales as Beverly Hills, Vegas, the Santa Monica Pier, and rural Louisiana.

DAYLIGHT   (1996) **½

D: Rob Cohen. Sylvester Stallone, Amy Brenneman, Viggo Mortensen, Dan Hedaya, Jay O. Sanders, Karen Young, Claire Bloom, Danielle Harris, Barry Newman, Stan Shaw, Sage Stallone. 115 mins. (Universal) DVD

An uncharacteristically humble Sly scores one of his better recent vehicles with this old-fashioned disaster flick. When flammable toxic waste erupts in NYC's Holland Tunnel, former (and unfairly disgraced) EMS hero Sly—who just happens to be on the scene—takes it upon himself to save a handful of stranded survivors (including real-life son Sage as a cyberthief on his way to jail). Brenneman is especially winning as a harried young writer looking to exit the city on a permanent basis, while Mortensen has an amusing (if brief) turn as an ego-driven daredevil who views the tragedy as a primo promo op. Some of the FX and elaborate escape maneuvers would have done late celluloid disaster master Irwin (*The Poseidon Adventure*, *The Towering Inferno*) Allen proud. But, like many contempo overblown mainstream genre films, *Daylight* doesn't know when to quit, dragging out the action to the point where suspense evaporates into sheer ennui.

DEAD BOYZ CAN'T FLY
(1992/1994) ***

D: Howard Winters. David John, Brad Friedman, Ruth Collins, Delia Sheppard, Mark McCulley, Jennifer DeLora. R and unrated editions. 109 mins. (VCI)

The second entry in VCI's short-lived No Bull B's line almost equals the label's debut flick, *Small Kill* (see index), and, like the latter, also features a killer transvestite (or, as the VCI ad copy puts it, an "androgynous, pansexual, face-painted punk!"), "Goose" (Friedman), who, with two fellow degenerates, systematically abuses and slaughters the occupants of a partially vacated office building at the start of a Memorial Day weekend. Thoroughly sick, sadistic, ultra-cynical trash, *Dead Boyz* spares no one, from the merciless miscreants to their mostly hypocritical victims to the gung-ho but dense slob cops on the track of a connected rape-and-murder case. Even nominal hero John—a writer, janitor, and 'Nam vet—is basically a drunken, self-pitying loser. After toting up an impressive body count that nets nearly every on-screen character, the movie ends with an anti-murder plea (!). The NYC-lensed pic's occasional sloppiness actually adds to its verité feel, and sleaze-video fans will appreciate the pulchritudinous presence of home-vid B queens Collins, Sheppard, and DeLora.

THE DEAD POOL   (1988) ***

D: Buddy Van Horn. Clint Eastwood, Patricia Clarkson, Liam Neeson, Evan Kim. 91 mins. (Warner)

Eastwood makes a smooth transition from Carmel, California, mayor to celluloid slayer in this, his first Dirty Harry entry since 1983's *Sudden Impact*. The pic, light on elaborate car crashes and spectacular stunts, plays like a lively B movie (in the most positive sense), even down to its choice of milieu: the horror/sleaze-flick scene. When random celebs whose names appear on a morbid betting list start turning up dead, suspicion points to the list's owner, slice-and-dice director Peter Swann (Neeson), currently shooting a headbanger horror called *Hotel Satan*. (Clips from *Time After Time*, *Cujo*, and *It's Alive III* fill in as samples of Swann's fictional ouevre.) While Clint seems a tad weary at times, *The Dead Pool* itself is an energetic-enough action

---

IN LIKE CLINT
Clint Eastwood's Top Cop Capers

COOGAN'S BLUFF   (1968) ***¹/₂

D: Don Siegel. Clint Eastwood, Lee J. Cobb, Tisha Sterling. 100 mins. (Universal)

One of Clint's best Siegel-directed cop capers casts him as a pre–*Dirty Harry* Arizona lawman forced to cope with the wilds of NYC while pursuing fugitive Don Stroud.

DIRTY HARRY   (1971) ***

D: Don Siegel. Clint Eastwood, Andy Robinson, Harry Guardino. 103 mins. (Warner) DVD

Clint made America's day in his debut as a quick-triggered San Francisco cop who don't need no stinkin' Miranda law. Robinson is likewise effective as an inordinately creepy killer.

THE ENFORCER   (1976) ***

D: James Fargo. Clint Eastwood, Tyne Daly, Harry Guardino. 96 mins. (Warner)

Clint's Dirty Harry returns to tangle with mayor-snatching psychos and new femme partner Daly in a typically high-energy series entry from Eastwood's pre-PC days.

THE GAUNTLET   (1977) ***

D: Clint Eastwood. Clint Eastwood, Sondra Locke, Pat Hingle. 111 mins. (Warner) DVD

Actor Clint protects then-off-screen squeeze Sondra from a ring of killers while director Clint calls the camera shots in what's essentially an elaborate update of the 1959 Richard Widmark chase film *The Trap* (Kartes, n.i.d.).

MAGNUM FORCE   (1973) ***

D: Ted Post. Clint Eastwood, Hal Holbrook, Mitchell Ryan. 124 mins. (Warner)

Clint, in his second Dirty Harry turn, tracks a series of slayings to corrupt forces in his own department in this typically actionful account.

SUDDEN IMPACT   (1983) ***

D: Clint Eastwood. Clint Eastwood, Pat Hingle, Sondra Locke. 117 mins. (Warner)

A more mature, if not especially mellow, Dirty Harry tracks a vengeful femme killer in a thriller directed by Eastwood for maximum action impact.

TIGHTROPE   (1984) ***

D: Richard Tuggle. Clint Eastwood, Genevieve Bujold, Dan Hedaya. 115 mins. (Warner)

Clint goes the kinky route—topped only by his involuntary bondage scene with Sonia Braga in 1991's *The Rookie* (see index)—as a detective on the trail of a notorious sex killer.

outing. Highlights include the butchering of a contrary movie critic who panned Swann's sicko pics (quips Clint's partner, Kim, "On a scale of one to ten, I'd give it an eight") and a *Bullit*-type chase parody that finds Clint speeding from a footlong remote-controlled model Corvette rigged with deadly explosives (!). Though slower on the draw than in days of yore, Clint still manages—with the aid of his trusty Magnum and a barely related subplot—to run up a decent body count.

DEAD PRESIDENTS (1995) ***

D: Albert Hughes, Allen Hughes. Larenz Tate, Keith David, Chris Tucker, Freddy Rodríguez, Rose Jackson, Bokeem Woodbine, N'Bushe Wright. 120 mins. (Buena Vista) DVD

The Hughes brothers follow their impressive *Menace II Society* (see index) with *Dead Presidents*, sort of an African-American variation on John Woo's *Bullet in the Head* and Michael Cimino's *The Deer Hunter*. The film tracks high school grads Tate, Tucker, and Rodríguez to Vietnam (in an extremely grisly and gory sequence that, like the otherwise inferior *Walking Dead* [HBO], captures combat's slaughterhouse reality), then focuses on their damaged postwar lives. The only one of the three to escape the war physically intact, Tate can't find the job he needs to support his former teen sweetheart/current wife (Jackson) and their daughter. Though sold as a heist film, the caper and its disastrous aftermath occupy only the film's final quarter and, while well-staged, rate as *Dead Presidents*'s least organic elements. The cast is fine, particularly David as a Korean War vet and the boys' original mentor. (Seymour Cassel and Martin Sheen also contribute unbilled cameos.) While a bit long and lopsided, *Dead Presidents* is an ambitious work that fuses contempo attitudes with a real feel for the early '70s "blaxploitation" era in which it's set, complete with a deftly assem-

bled period soundtrack that ranges from James Brown to Barry White.

DEAD-BANG (1989) **1/2

D: John Frankenheimer. Don Johnson, Penelope Ann Miller, William Forsythe, Bob Balaban, Tim Reid, Frank Military. 102 mins. (Warner) DVD

Burnt-out cop Johnson contributes one of the modern screen's more memorable upchuck scenes in an okay *policier* that makes up in action what it lacks in credibility, though the white-supremacist thugs here pale beside their more colorful counterparts in the similarly themed but superior James Woods vehicle *True Believer* (Columbia/TriStar). Forsythe is good playing against type as Johnson's uptight FBI-agent foil. Not one of Frankenheimer's best, but better than most critics originally rated it.

DEADBEAT AT DAWN (1987) **1/2

D: Jim Van Bebber. Jim Van Bebber, Paul Harper, Megan Murphy, Ric Walker. 90 mins. (Ketchum) DVD

From off of the streets of exotic Dayton, Ohio, comes the oft primitive but lively gang-war gore orgy *Deadbeat at Dawn*, written, directed by, and starring busy Dayton native Van Bebber. JVB plays "Goose," a street-gang leader who quits his violent ways to keep squeeze Murphy happy. When Megan has her intestines torn out by rival gang members led by the dim-witted "Bonecrusher"—who pauses to report, with much moist nostalgia, that said intestines looked "just like snakes"—Jim rejoins his posse with vengeance in mind. The hitherto rival gangs team up for an armored-car heist, where Jim seizes his chance to eliminate his enemies. *Deadbeat* features some effective thesping from the mostly amateur crew, a memorable confrontation between Jim and his estranged, paranoid junkie

dad (Charley Goetz), and lots of literally visceral close-ups. *Deadbeat* suffers most during its rushed, awkwardly staged action scenes, but the video definitely represents a first in its bid to combine extreme gore with gang warfare, as though H. G. (*Blood Feast*) Lewis had replaced Walter Hill as *The Warriors'* director.

DEADLY ILLUSION (1987) **1/2

D: Larry Cohen, William Tannen. Billy Dee Williams, Vanity, Morgan Fairchild, Jo Beck, Joe Cortese, Joe Spinell. 87 mins. (Columbia/TriStar)

Any flick that opens with a shoot-out on a gun-permit line (!) can't be all bad, and *Deadly Illusions* surely isn't. While not one of maverick moviemaker Cohen's best efforts, *Deadly* is a cleverly plotted low-budget urban actioner, with Williams at once suave and earthy as the embattled Hamberger, an unlicensed private eye on the trail of fashion-model-turned-mogul Fairchild, who's actually fronting for an elite corporate drug syndicate. In addition to concocting a literate script, Cohen makes extensive, inventive, if inexpensive, use of such exotic Gotham locales as the Rockefeller Center ice-skating rink (great place for a chase) and even the Mets' dugout at Shea Stadium, site of the pic's climactic gun battle. The cut corners occasionally intrude, but *Deadly Illusion* delivers its share of action. The late, great Joe (*Maniac*) Spinell puts in a neat cameo as (what else?) a maniac, and Vanity looks great in leather as Billy Dee's partner/main squeeze.

DEADLY RIVALS (1992) **1/2

D: James Dodson. Andrew Stevens, Joseph Bologna, Margaux Hemingway, Richard Roundtree, Francesco Quinn, Randi Ingerman, Celia Wise. 93 mins. (Universal)

An unlikely mix of Mafia intrigues, international espionage, and a raging sibling rivalry between screen sisters Ingerman and Wise, *Deadly Rivals* generates more excitement than might have been expected. Stevens plays against type as a semi-nerdy physics whiz; Bologna and Quinn make for an amusing mobster team; ex-*Shaft* Roundtree provides balance as an amiably callous FBI agent; and the sisterly bitterness theme adds a fun subtext. A lively, percussive soundtrack, bright Miami Beach locales, and prolonged torture tableaux furnish further flavor.

DEATH RING   (1993) *½

D: Robert J. Kizer. Mike Norris, Billy Drago, Chad McQueen, Don Swayze. 91 mins. (New Line)

"Norris! McQueen! Swayze!" trumpets *Death Ring*'s trailer. Unfortunately, that's *Mike* Norris (wooden chip off old-block Chuck), *Chad* McQueen (chunky son of Steve), and *Don* Swayze (ungainly bro' of Patrick). Billy Drago is *the* Billy Drago, but that skeletal perennial home-vid villain hams it up fairly unbearably here. Despite the clone cast, *Death Ring*'s plot shapes up as its most derivative aspect—yet another *Most Dangerous Game* rip-off. The action's predictable and lethargically staged; only a last-reel decapitation delivers any surprise. A free six-pack should be awarded to any viewer who survives that long.

DEATH WARRANT   (1990) ***

D: Deran Sarafian. Jean-Claude Van Damme, Robert Guillaume, Cynthia Gibb, Art LeFleur, Joshua Miller, Patrick Kilpatrick. 88 mins. (MGM/UA)

Back in 1989 both Sly Stallone (*Lock-Up*) and Tom Selleck (*An Innocent Man*) served stretches in celluloid stir. Here Van Damme does his bit to bring back the largely inactive boys-behind-bars genre. J-C is cast as a Quebec cop (the better to explain his stubborn Belgian accent) who goes undercover in an American prison to investigate a string of mysterious inmate icepick murders. There he enlists the aid of an initially reluctant cellblock-wise black con (convincingly played by Guillaume, of *Benson* fame) in a violent, labyrinthine search for the culprits. While comfortably formulaic most of the way, *Death Warrant* offers a few fresh grisly twists involving a black-market body-organ racket and a formidable serial killer called "the Sandman" (who, as enthusiastically interpeted by frequent heavy Kilpatrick, is anything but a candy-colored clown). J-C again demonstrates he can take a lickin' and keep on kickin', surviving a stabbing, repeated beatings, and even a spill from a cellblock tier without ruffling his strong, mostly (perhaps fortunately) silent demeanor.

DEATH WISH:
THE SERIES

DEATH WISH   (1974) **½

D: Michael Winner. Charles Bronson, Vincent Gardenia, Hope Lange. 94 mins. (Paramount)

This precocious, shamelessly manipulative trend-setting trash epic inspired a wave of violent vigilante movies. Architect Paul Kersey (Bronson) goes kill-crazy after his wife is slain and his daughter raped by a trio of Gotham goons (including a young Jeff Goldblum, playing against future type). When the cops and courts prove predictably useless, C.B. takes matters into his own lethal hands, declaring a one-citizen war on NYC's street scum. Still foremost in the field it contrived, especially when compared with its own weak sequels.

DEATH WISH II   (1982) *

D: Michael Winner. Charles Bronson, Jill Ireland, Vincent Gardenia. 89 mins. (Warner)

Chuck takes his vigilante act to L.A. in the first of *Death Wish*'s belated follow-ups. It's also the most feeble of the lot, lacking both the marginal originality of the first and the over-the-top excesses of *3*, *4*, and *5*.

DEATH WISH 3   (1985) *½

D: Michael Winner. Charles Bronson, Martin Balsam, Deborah Raffin, Gavan O'Herlihy, Ed Lauter, Kirk Taylor. 92 mins. (MGM)

Seems "the element" is at it again. A pack of wild street animals—a multiethnic mix of savage punks, bearded bikers, ghetto warriors, and leather-bar refugees who could coexist only in a hack screenwriter's addled imagination—bumps off an elderly pal of freelance vigilante Paul ("Have Grenade Launcher, Will Travel") Kersey. And what do our impotent police do about it? Why, they promptly bust our hero (who wasn't doin' nothin'), then lovingly violate his civil rights! On top of that inhospitable display, they toss him in the hoosegow with gang leader Fraker (O'Herlihy), who promises Chuck he'll "kill a little old lady just for you!" So once again Bronson is forced to chuck his "No More Mr. Vigilante" vow and dispense the only kind of justice these street scum understand: i.e., wholesale slaughter. "Look, Eli," exclaims one superannuated neighbor to her equally elderly spouse, "Mr. Kersey just shot some of the creeps!"

DEATH WISH 4: THE CRACKDOWN (1987) *½

D: J. Lee Thompson. Charles Bronson, Kay Lenz, John P. Ryan, Perry Lopez, Soon Teck-Oh, George Dickerson, Irwin Keyes. 100 mins. (Media)

This time around, Chuck tackles not one but three L.A. crack syndicates, including the bunch responsible for the demise of his latest disposable surrogate daughter, the offspring of girlfriend Lenz. While there's abrupt and senseless violence galore, many of the action scenes are shoddily staged, particularly a climactic roller-rink slaughterfest. On the plus side, Chuck's more laconic than ever here, limiting his motivation to a lone line ("It's those damn drugs!") and behaving more indiscriminately than ever in his one-man crusade against hapless young criminals. C'mon, C.B., pick on someone your own age, why don'tcha?

DEATH WISH V: THE FACE OF DEATH   (1994)**

D: Allan Goldstein. Charles Bronson, Lesley-Anne Down, Michael Parks, Robert Joy. 95 mins. (Warner) DVD

Any flick that flaunts *Death* twice within the same title has a lot to live up to, and in the faint-praise department, we'd have to rate *V* as the series's best entry since the original. For starters, *V* goes for gore over numbers—the body count's a comparatively modest 13—with victims being torched, shrink-wrapped, treated to involuntary acid baths, and even slipped cyanide-sprinkled cannolis (!). Director Goldstein frequently resorts to floor-angle shots to intensify the film's intimate, in-your-face approach. Our token story line finds geriatric vigilante Paul Kersey (Bronson) forced to unretire when police prove typically helpless in preventing thugs led by mannered Method thesp Parks from muscling in on future Mrs. Kersey Down's fashion biz. Kersey keeps a cool head at first. But once Parks's high-strung henchtransvestite (flavorfully played by Joy) smashes Down's face into a mirror, then waits until *after* she completes costly reconstructive surgery before finishing her off—well, it's time for even a mellowed Chuck to run amok. As usual, Bronson's longtime stunt double, J. P. Romano, scores almost as much screen time as our then-72-year-old hero, while Toronto stunt-doubles for NYC's mean streets.

THE DECEIVERS   (1988)***

D: Nicholas Meyer. Pierce Brosnan, Saeed Jaffrey, Sashi Kapoor, Helena Mitchell, Keith Michell, David Robb. 103 mins. (Warner)

Nineteenth-century Brit officer Brosnan dons turban and berry stains to infiltrate India's infamous "Thugge" strangler cult in Nicholas (*The Seven Percent Solution*) Meyer's fun throwback to the Korda brothers' historical actioners of yore (e.g., *Drums, The Four Feathers*). Hammer's similarly Thugge-themed *The Stranglers of Bombay* (1960) remains unavailable on cassette, but you *can* wrap your hands around 1955's *The Black Devils of Kali* (Sinister Cinema), starring Lex Barker.

DEEP COVER   (1992)***½

D: Bill Duke. Laurence Fishburne, Jeff Goldblum, Victoria Dillard, Gregory Sierra, Charles Martin Smith, Clarence Williams III, Sydney Lassick. 107 mins. (New Line) DVD

Fishburne impresses as an undercover cop in a fast-paced actioner that plays like a cross between an inner-city *Rush* and an updated, better-integrated *Superfly*. Posing as an ambitious L.A. pusher, Fishburne infiltrates a nest of high-living lowlifes that includes lawyer/dealer Goldblum, foxy money-launderer Dillard, and sadistic Latino blow mogul Sierra. To protect his cover, our increasingly confused hero finds himself forced to peddle crack to kids, kill local rivals, and adopt a high-profile criminal lifestyle. While Michael (*The Player*) Tolkin's script grows increasingly improbable, *Deep Cover* delivers the action goods on a grand scale, highlighted by a nerve- (and fender-) shredding car chase and several brutal slay scenes, all set to a pulsing score. The film's angry skepticism re the government's (represented by DEA weasel Smith) bogus "war on

drugs" (there's even a Noriega parallel here) is jackhammered home with relentless intensity. Eccentric genre vet Lassick lands one of his better recent roles as Sierra's obsequious flunky.

DELIVERANCE   (1972)***½

D: John Boorman. Burt Reynolds, Jon Voight, Ned Beatty. 109 mins. (Warner) DVD

Atlanta businessmen on a macho canoe trip run afoul of hostile rednecks in Boorman's tense adaptation of the James Dickey novel. A flick that launched a thousand imitations, none of which match the original's power.

DELTA FORCE:
THE SERIES

THE DELTA FORCE   (1986)**½

D: Menahem Golan. Chuck Norris, Lee Marvin, Robert Forster, George Kennedy, Martin Balsam, Shelley Winters, Joey Bishop, Hannah Schygulla, Bo Svenson. 125 mins. (Anchor Bay)

A revisionist exploitation-fantasy version of an actual Mideast skyjacking incident, *The Delta Force* supplies swift, tense, cheap entertainment for its first 80 or so minutes. Terrorist Forster (excellent in a rare villainous role) and his Arab minions menace a planeload of Hollywood has-beens—Kennedy, Balsam, Bishop, Susan Strasberg, Lainie Kazan, and Winters (in a brief but patentedly hysterical cameo)—while the titular commando team, headed by Marvin and Norris, prepare for an eventual assault. The flick abruptly crashes, however, when Chuck wrests control of the final two reels. With the aid of his trusty rocket-armed motorcycle, he doles out his trademark brand of bland justice and destroys not only scores of ragheaded extras but what slender credibility *Delta Force* had, to that point, possessed.

DELTA FORCE 2   (1990) *½

D: Aaron Norris. Chuck Norris, Billy Drago, John P. Ryan, Bobby Chavez, Richard Jaeckel, Begonia Plaza. 105 mins. (Anchor Bay)

Aaron (Brother of Chuck) Norris's muscle-headed sequel finds Chuck in fine laconic form. (After leveling three punks in a Chinese restaurant, he quips, "I didn't fight; I gave a motivational seminar.") This time Chuck & Co. take on South American cocaine king and all-around baby-killing, widow-raping monster Drago. The standard action elements work well in *DF 2*'s early going, highlighted by a genuinely exciting aerial sequence wherein Chuck, with a little help from his stunt double, gets to show off his high-flying Superman moves. Unfortunately, once Chuck and crew infiltrate Drago's stronghold, with the help of Begonia Plaza (an actress, by the way, not a subway stop in Brooklyn), the pic slips into numbing predictability, with our Yank commandos' utter invincibility in the face of formidable enemy firepower drastically detracting from any potential suspense. Mike (Son of Chuck) Norris takes over in 1991's *Delta Force 3: The Killing Game* (Warner), costarring Nick (Son of John) Cassavetes, Eric (Son of Kirk, Brother of Michael) Douglas, and Matthew (Brother of Sean and Chris) Penn. Director Aaron N. takes *his* turn before the camera in the not-recommended *Overkill* (Touchstone). Fred ("the Hammer") Williamson, meanwhile, nearly single-handedly topples the Sandinista government in 1987's violent hostage-rescue mission *Delta Force Commando* (Vista), returning three years later, with old hand Van Johnson, in *Delta Force Commando 2* (Artisan).

DESERT HEAT   (A.K.A. *COYOTE MOON*) (1999) **

D: Danny Mulroon. Jean-Claude Van Damme, Pat Morita, Danny Trejo, Gabrielle Fitzpatrick, Larry Drake, Vincent Schiavelli, Ford Rainey. 95 mins. (Columbia/TriStar) DVD

Desert Heat flirts with but fails to attain the delirium of the 1990 camp classic *Sonny Boy* (see index). The Muscles from Brussels plays a depressed merc who journeys to a beat-out Southwest desert burg to deliver a 1949 motorcycle to Native American pal Trejo. Our hero soon tangles with a gang of local lowlifes led by Drake and his three redneck sons, as well as a biker aggregate who hang at a roadhouse called the Bombay, run by versatile character thesp Schiavelli (testing an Indian accent here). J-C at first tricks the criminal factions into fighting each other but ultimately faces them alone. While sporting a formula plot, *Desert Heat* teems with oddball, brain-damaged touches, including an alien subplot. The town boasts an unusually large coot population, most eccentrically exemplified by Morita as a Japanese local with a proper Brit accent. Van Damme works in his customary bare-butt shot, croons a C&W tune, and emotes with his usual low-energy intensity. The closing credits end with "A John G. Avildsen" film, but the *Rocky* director's name is missing from the video box.

DESPERADO   (1995) ***

D: Robert Rodriguez. Antonio Banderas, Steve Buscemi, Salma Hayek, Joaquim de Almeida, Cheech Marin, Quentin Tarantino, Carlos Gallardo, Mike Moroff. 103 mins. (Columbia/TriStar) DVD

Rodriguez's comparatively mega-budgeted *El Mariachi* sequel/remake lacks the soul and surprise of his $7,000 original (see index) but partially compensates with spectacular action. With Banderas subbing for original hero Gallardo (relegated to a small role here as one of Antonio's compadres), our story picks up where the first one ended. Assisted by a typically twitchy Buscemi, Banderas rides out for revenge against the men responsible for his girlfriend's murder and his own ruined life: drug lord de Almeida and his hordes of disposable goons. Banderas locates a new squeeze in the slinky Hayek, who soon sides with our laconic hero as he mows down scores of bad guys, absorbing one bullet and three knife wounds along the way. Rodriguez tosses in some Peckinpah, Leone, and John Woo moves, even interrupting the abundant violence to detail Antonio's tender relationship with a guitar-playing street urchin. While Marin handles his sinister-barkeep role well, the best we can say about Tarantino's appearance as an Anglo drug courier is that it's a brief one.

DETROIT 9000   (1973) **½

D: Arthur Marks. Alex Rocco, Hari Rhodes, Vonetta McGee, Ella Edwards, Scatman Crothers, Rudy Challenger. 106 mins. (Miramax)

When a fund-raising bash for Congressman Clayton (Challenger) is ripped off by masked thieves, the titular city is thrown into a racial tizzy. Was the robbery a black-on-black crime? An attempt by white bigots to crush Clayton's campaign? Or a simple, nonracially motivated heist? It's up to slick African-American detective Rhodes and his embittered Caucasian cohort Rocco to find the answer—and fast. This genre chestnut unearthed by Quentin Tarantino's Rolling Thunder Pictures rates as a decidedly mixed bag. Much of this 1973 pic—directed and scripted by white B-movie vets Marks and Orville H. Hampton, respectively—plays like a standard made-for-TV *policier* of the period pumped up by raw racial frictions, salty R-rated dialogue, and over-the-top violence. Still, while *Detroit 9000* isn't one of the "blaxploitation" genre's best (it's no *Shaft* or *Superfly*), the film provides enough curio value and legit twisty mayhem, including a truly wild, bullet-flying finale, to justify its belated return to its big-screen roots and subsequent home-vid revival.

DICK TRACY (1990) **

D: Warren Beatty. Warren Beatty, Madonna, Al Pacino, Glenne Headly, Charlie Korsmo, Dustin Hoffman. 104 mins. (Touchstone)

Enough was written about this megahyped yawner when it first blanketed the nation's 'plexes back in 1990. Suffice it to say that the vivid comic-strip set design, creatively grotesque makeup FX, and Pacino's peppy perf as superhood Big Boy Caprice are the only elements separating Beatty's epic from utter emptiness. Vet villain Henry Silva is especially wasted here.

DICK TRACY MEETS GRUESOME (1947) B&W ***

D: John Rawlins. Boris Karloff, Ralph Byrd, Anne Gwynne, Edward Ashley. 65 mins. (Sinister Cinema) DVD

RKO, a studio that traditionally had fun with its B line, imbues *Dick Tracy Meets Gruesome* with surprisingly hip deadpan black humor, from its clever false-start opening (involving a seemingly ominous noose) to the deservedly top-billed Karloff's darkly funny turn as the relentlessly unpleasant Gruesome, a humorless walking criminal instinct. While rife with wit (including the then-obligatory Karloff in-jokes), the film wisely plays its action elements straight. Highlights include a bank heist, wherein unwitting customers are awkwardly freeze-framed by a powerful nerve gas, and an atmospheric climactic chase sequence. Byrd, returning to the role he'd pioneered in the earlier Tracy serials, replaces temporary Tracy Morgan Conway as the quick-thinking, jut-jawed detective, while Gwynne adds charm and allure as Tess Truehart. The other series films are also available—*Dick Tracy, Detec-*

tive (1945), *Dick Tracy Vs. Cueball* (1946) with Conway, and *Dick Tracy's Dilemma* (1947) with Byrd—via Sinister Cinema (DVD). VCI/Liberty put out the Byrd-starred Tracy serials: *Dick Tracy* (1937), *Dick Tracy Returns* (1938), *Dick Tracy's G-Men* (1939), and *Dick Tracy Vs. Crime Inc.* (1941). Also out are four two-episode volumes of the 1950–51 teleseries *Dick Tracy: The Lost Episodes* (Budget Video), likewise with Byrd. Paramount has six volumes of the early-'60s animated teleseries *Dick Tracy*.

DIE HARD:
THE SERIES

DIE HARD (1988) ***

D: John McTiernan. Bruce Willis, Alan Rickman, Alexander Godunov, Bonnie Bedelia, Reginald VelJohnson, James Shigeta, Robert Davi. 132 mins. (Fox) DVD

While Willis's painful Mickey Rourke meets Clint Eastwood act represents a serious detriment, and producer Joel Silver's Beverly Hills brand of anarchy grows more irritating with each passing pic, *Die Hard* remains an action outing that amply delivers the pulse-pounding goods. The film further benefits from a band of memorable villains led by Rickman and some patented Irwin Allen–type disaster-movie moves as said bad guys, with a big assist from Bruce and some fatally meddlesome FBI fumblers, lay lavish waste to a 40-story L.A. office building.

DIE HARD 2 (1990) ***

D: Renny Harlin. Bruce Willis, Bonnie Bedelia, William Atherton, Reginald VelJohnson, Franco Nero, William Sadler, John Amos, Dennis Franz, Art Evans. 124 mins. (Fox) DVD

Butt-kicking soliloquist Willis is again called upon to save the world,

this time from homegrown terrorists out to spring Noriega-like dictator General Esperanza (erstwhile Euro B-movie hero Nero) during a stopover at D.C.'s Dulles Airport. Actually, the sequel finds Bruce spending only a few minutes of screen time lost in self-conversation; the script thoughtfully supplies him with a host of other characters—most notably the excellent Art *(White of the Eye, Trespass)* Evans as a control-tower technician—with whom to trade insights and insults. *Die Hard 2* succeeds as a megabuck B movie staged on a James Bond scale, replete with high-speed chases, extravagant violence, and even dollops of outright gore. The sequence that sees Bruce eject from a burning plane right into the camera is alone worth the price of a rental. The fun fizzles a bit in 1995's *Die Hard with a Vengeance* (Fox, DVD), though Samuel L. Jackson lends entertaining support as B.W.'s reluctant NYC ally in a battle against mad terrorist Jeremy Irons.

DILLINGER AND CAPONE (1995) ***

D: Jon Purdy. Martin Sheen, F. Murray Abraham, Catherine Hicks, Stephen Davies, Sasha Jenson, Don Stroud, Jeffrey Combs, Michael C. Gwynne, Clint Howard, Joe Estevez, Maria Ford. 95 mins. (New Horizons)

Producer Roger Corman goes upscale with a good-looking, fun pulp caper that plays with classic American gangster myths. Purdy's pic posits that John Dillinger (Sheen) didn't die outside Chicago's Biograph Theater in 1934, that his brother (Sheen's real-life bro' Estevez) took the FBI bullets meant for him. By 1940, the real Dillinger has retired to a Bakersfield, California, farm he shares with his wife (Hicks) and their young son. John D.'s troubles begin when a former confederate sells him out to a pair of ambitious renegade agents (Gwynne, Combs); he escapes that trap only to learn his wife and son have been kidnapped by Al Capone (!) and are captives at the former crime kingpin's South Florida estate. Blitzed by untreated syphilis, the now deranged Capone (Abraham) coerces Dillinger, accompanied by Big Al's Brit butler (Davies), into pulling a final job, breaking into a Chicago vault to retrieve nearly $15 mil in hidden loot. In addition to explaining why Geraldo found Al's vault empty, *Dillinger and Capone* succeeds in putting a hip, contempo (but not smarmily postmodern) spin on characters otherwise long thought to have worn out their celluloid welcome. Sheen's deadpan portrayal of Dillinger as reluctant but ever professional provides a neat balance with Abraham's alternately manic and depressive interpretation of the rapidly deteriorating Capone. *Dillinger and Capone* commits one major movie gaffe, however, when Jenson lets loose a cry of "Top of the world" nine years prior to *White Heat*'s release.

CELEBRITY GANGSTERS ON VIDEO

AL CAPONE   (1959) B&W **1/2

D: Richard Wilson. Rod Steiger, Fay Spain, James Gregory, Nehemiah Persoff. 104 mins. (Fox)

Steiger chews cigars and scenery with equal aplomb in a solid if unsurprising chronicle of erstwhile Chicago crime king Capone's oft documented rise and fall. Recently reissued after serving a long stretch on moratorium. Capone and crew return in Roger Corman's 1967 *Untouchables*–styled docudrama, *The St. Valentine's Day Massacre* (Fox), while Al's fictional law-abiding youngest brother is the focus of the 1990 TV movie *The Lost Capone* (Turner).

BLOODY MAMA   (1970) **1/2

D: Roger Corman. Shelley Winters, Bruce Dern, Robert De Niro. 90 mins. (Vestron)

Shelley makes for a high-decibel Ma Barker, while a young De Niro plays one of her criminal sons, in Corman's satisfyingly sleazy salute to Depression-era Middle-American family values. Lurene Tuttle earlier portrayed the homicidal matriarch in 1960's middling *Ma Barker's Killer Brood* (Sinister Cinema). The 1996 Ma Barker retread, *Public Enemies* (Trimark), with Theresa Russell as the machine-gun mama, is well worth avoiding.

BONNIE AND CLYDE   (1967) ***

D: Arthur Penn. Warren Beatty, Faye Dunaway, Estelle Parsons, Michael J. Pollard, Gene Hackman, Gene Wilder. 111 mins. (Warner) DVD

Penn's bloody paean to rural outlaws Bonnie (Dunaway) and Clyde (Beatty) plays a bit self-consciously but remains arresting entertainment and was instrumental in furthering the cause of slo-mo movie violence. Karen Black and Fabian teamed up for the low-budget B&C rip-off *Little Laura and Big John* (VidAmerica). Roger Corman's 1958 account of the no-account criminals, *The Bonnie Parker Story*, with Dorothy Provine, Jack Hogan, and the inimitable Dick Bakalyan, has yet to join the home-vid ranks.

BUGSY   (1991) ***

D: Barry Levinson. Warren Beatty, Annette Bening, Harvey Keitel, Ben Kingsley, Joe Mantegna. 135 mins. (Columbia/TriStar) DVD

Beatty and director Levinson craft a compelling, violent account of gangster Bugsy Siegel and his pivotal role in the birth of Las Vegas. Bening is forceful as Beatty's on-screen squeeze, while Elliott Gould turns in strong character work as a doomed goon.

DILLINGER   (1973) ***

D: John Milius. Warren Oates, Ben Johnson, Cloris Leachman, Richard Dreyfuss, Harry Dean Stanton. 106 mins. (Artisan)

Packed with vivid gunplay, this is the best and bloodiest of Hollywood's many Dillinger bios. Oates is especially convincing as the erstwhile Public Enemy Numero Uno, while Dreyfuss makes for an obnoxious, oddly petulant Baby Face Nelson and Johnson and Leachman turn in solid work as G-man Melvin Purvis and the infamous Lady in Red, respectively. Stanton, as gang member Homer Van Meter, gets the best death scene. Lawrence Tierney joined the ranks of great movie tough guys with his gruff interpretation of the title criminal in 1945's *Dillinger* (Fox), a swift B movie scripted by Philip Yordan. Mark Harmon plays the celebrity gangster in the 1991 made-for-TV bio *Dillinger* (Warner), a.k.a. *The Last Days of John Dillinger*, while Robert Conrad does Dillinger in 1979's *The Lady in Red* (Vestron). *Baby Face Nelson* (1957), with Mickey Rooney in the title role, unfortunately has yet to join the video ranks, while 1997's *Baby Face Nelson*, with a mugging C. Thomas Howell in the title role, unfortunately has (New Horizons). Dillinger confederate Verne Miller receives his day in celluloid court in *Verne Miller* (New Line), starring Scott Glenn.

THE KANSAS CITY MASSACRE (1975) **1/2

D: Dan Curtis. Dale Robertson, Bo Hopkins, Robert Walden. 99 mins. (Trimark)

While it's not up there with Milius's *Dillinger*, Curtis's fact-based gangster yarn shapes up as a surprisingly punchy made-for-TV sequel to *Melvin Purvis, G-Man* (HBO), with Robertson returning as Purvis in a fast-paced story packed with gunplay. For more of the FBI POV on Dillinger, Nelson, and other celeb outlaws, scope out

The FBI Story (Warner) and *Guns Don't Argue* (Sinister Cinema).

THE KING OF THE ROARING '20S: THE STORY OF ARNOLD ROTHSTEIN (1961) B&W **½

D: Joseph M. Newman. David Janssen, Dianne Foster, Mickey Rooney, Jack Carson. 106 mins. (Fox)

Janssen plays high-roller, mobster, and 1919 World Series fixer Arnold Rothstein in a standard, shallow but well-acted account drawn from Leo Katcher's book *The Big Bankroll.*

LITTLE CAESAR (1930) B&W ***

D: Mervyn LeRoy. Edward G. Robinson, Douglas Fairbanks, Jr., Glenda Farrell. 80 mins. (Fox)

Edward G. sneers his way into the hearts of millions as the Al Capone–inspired Rico, a mug who makes it to the top of the racketeer heap. Still effective, though no match for Cagney's *Public Enemy* (Warner).

MACHINE GUN KELLY (1958) B&W ***

D: Roger Corman. Charles Bronson, Susan Cabot, Morey Amsterdam, Jack Lambert, Richard Devon, Connie Gilchrist. 84 mins. (Columbia/TriStar)

Bronson, in his first lead role, plays the phobic '30s outlaw encouraged to tote his trademark Thompson by ambitious moll Cabot. While Corman's offbeat gangster flick plays pretty loose with the facts, *MGK* does capture Kelly and real-life squeeze Cleo Shannon's reported relationship. The pic is further peppered with tasty turns by henchmen Devon, Wally Campo, and especially Lambert—who, knife extended, tenders Bronson an offer to "carve a map of hell in your face" (!)—Barboura Morris

as a kidnapped nurse, and Gilchrist as Cabot's bordello-owner mom. But unlikely top acting honors go to longtime comic and future *Dick Van Dyke Show* regular Amsterdam as Bronson's effeminate confederate and eventual enemy Fandango (or "Fanny," as Bronson tauntingly calls him). *Machine Gun Kelly* offers tough talk, taut action, and psychosexual subtexts galore.

ONCE UPON A TIME IN AMERICA (1984) ***

D: Sergio Leone. Robert De Niro, James Woods, Elizabeth McGovern, Treat Williams, Tuesday Weld, Joe Pesci, Danny Aiello. 225 mins. (Warner) DVD

Leone applies his trademark epic treatment, complete with Ennio Morricone score, to the Roaring '20s in this intricate gangster tale. While it doesn't quite match his earlier *Once Upon a Time in the West,* it's well worth a look. Avoid the truncated 143-minute version that's still out there in Vidland. Other treatments of the same era and players—notably, Meyer Lansky, Lucky Luciano, Dutch Schultz, and company—include *Billy Bathgate* (Touchstone), drawn from the E. L. Doctorow novel, *Hoodlum* (see index), the lame, made-for-cable *Lansky* (HBO, DVD), and *Lucky Luciano* (New Line). Murder, Inc. honcho Lepke Buchalter serves as the subject of Menahem Golan's eponymous *Lepke* (Warner), with Tony Curtis in the title role, while 1960's *Murder, Inc.* has yet to score a video release; *Mad Dog Coll, Portrait of a Mobster, Pretty Boy Floyd,* and *Young Dillinger* are also among the missing.

THE RISE AND FALL OF LEGS DIAMOND (1960) B&W ***

D: Budd Boetticher. Ray Danton, Karen Steele, Jesse White. 101 mins. (Warner)

Danton makes for a swift Legs in a lively, if not always accurate,

account of the famed Irish-American mobster's brief gangland reign.

THE UNTOUCHABLES (1987) **½

D: Brian De Palma. Kevin Costner, Sean Connery, Robert De Niro, Andy Garcia, Charles Martin Smith. 119 mins. (Paramount)

De Palma's version of agent Eliot Ness's (Costner) war against Chicago crime kingpin Capone (De Niro, in what's little more than a cameo) doesn't stack up with his earlier *Scarface* remake (see index) but is a superbly crafted account featuring charismatic work by Connery as a veteran Windy City cop.

DIPLOMATIC IMMUNITY (1991) ***

D: Peter Maris. Bruce Boxleitner, Billy Drago, Tom Breznahan, Meg Foster, Robert Forster, Robert Do'Qui, Ken Foree. 95 mins. (Fries, n.i.d.)

Boxleitner toplines as an incensed marine out to nail Breznahan as the wealthy, psychotic Paraguayan S&M artist (!) who's gotten away with his daughter's murder due to the titular protection. The pursuit picks up in Paraguay, where our hero teams with smuggler Drago, who has his own score to settle. Director Maris crams his action canvas with car chases, intrigues, and gunfights without resorting to impossible one-man-army heroics. The director also fleshes out his cast with topflight supporting thesps, including Foster as villain Breznahan's equally mad mater, Forster as a treacherous CIA agent, and Maris regular Foree (of *Dawn of the Dead* fame) as a helpful barkeep. Though some of Maris's movies fizzle out en route to their finales, *Diplomatic Immunity* delivers the action goods with energy and flair to spare.

DIRECT HIT (1994) **1/2

D: Joseph Merhi. William Forsythe, Jo Champra, George Segal, Richard Norton, John Aprea. 91 mins. (Republic)

Forsythe turns in intense work as a world-weary, guilt-torn government hit man whose retirement plans are sabotaged by superior Segal and ruthless senatorial hopeful Aprea. The pair order Forsythe to ice exotic dancer/single mom Champra—whose compromising photo with Aprea is being used to blackmail the corrupt candidate—but our antihero defiantly decides to protect her instead. Straight-arrow ex-jock/former Mr. Cyndi Garvey Steve Garvey contributes a competent eye-blink cameo as a TV field reporter (he enjoys a fatter role in *Ground Zero: Bloodfist VI* [New Horizons]). *Direct Hit* shapes up as an on-target genre entry that relies more on mood than by-the-numbers plotting.

THE DIRTY DOZEN (1967) ***

D: Robert Aldrich. Lee Marvin, Ernest Borgnine, Charles Bronson. 149 mins. (MGM) DVD

Aldrich's lively World War II pulp adventure established a since oft-imitated formula, with Marvin recruiting an all-star crew of uniformed criminals and misfits for a suicide mission. Telly Savalas lends able support as the psycho of the group. A trio of made-for-TV sequels followed in the '80s—*The Dirty Dozen: The Deadly Mission, The Dirty Dozen: The Fatal Mission,* and *The Dirty Dozen: The Next Mission* (all MGM).

DIRTY MARY, CRAZY LARRY (1974) **1/2

D: John Hough. Peter Fonda, Susan George, Adam Roarke. 93 mins. (Magnetic, n.i.d.)

Aimless racers Fonda and Roarke, accompanied by wild babe George, drift into crime in an updated *Bonnie and Clyde* variation that's developed a loyal cult following, largely due to the flick's shocker ending.

DO OR DIE (1991) **1/2

D: Andy Sidaris. Dona Speir, Roberta Vasquez, Pat Morita, Erik Estrada, Cynthia Brimhall, Pandora Peaks, William Bumiller, Skip Ward. 97 mins. (Columbia/TriStar)

Speir and Vasquez reprise their roles as Molokai-based agents Donna and Nicole. This time around, our hard-breathing heroines become the targets of a half-dozen hit teams dispatched by the villainous Kane (Morita, of *Karate Kid* fame). The Sidarises use this updated *Most Dangerous Game* framework to give their feisty foxes (further fleshed out by Brimhall and mega-mammaried newcomer Peaks) ample opportunity to display their athletic, dramatic, and scenic skills. Also along for the ride are former *C.H.I.P.S.*ter Estrada, Bumiller as the squad's nominal "brains" (this in a flick where most of the characters claim to do their "best thinking" in bathtubs or bedrooms!), and vet thesp Ward, looking far above his playing weight in his backdate *Kitten with a Whip* days. The Sidarises again crowd their celluloid canvas with loud shoot-outs, high-speed chases, sweeping locations (including Vegas and Shreveport, Louisiana), soft-core sex, and exotic gadgetry. The duo likewise lace *Do or Die* with anything-goes gags, ranging from the lame to the inspired, such as a sincerely awful "Down on the Bayou" production number staged at the Cowboy Lounge and a great femme variation on *Commando*'s famous "dressing to kill" scene.

DOG DAY (1983) **1/2

D: Yves Boisset. Lee Marvin, Miou-Miou, Jean Carmet, Victor Lanoux, David Bennent, Tina Louise. 101 mins. (Vestron)

Boisset's bizarre black comedy/crime caper stars Marvin as a fugitive Yank gangster who holes up with a family of French rednecks who easily outslob their American screen counterparts. (They would have done Yves Montand's *Jean de Florette/Manon of the Spring* character proud.) Many of the movie's determinedly degenerate machinations don't really work, but the pic picks up as the plots, counterplots, and body count climb in the final reels. Definitely different, and worthwhile for fans of such earlier Gallic gangster homages as Godard's *Breathless* (Connoisseur) and Truffaut's *Shoot the Piano Player* (Fox Lorber, DVD).

DOG DAY AFTERNOON (1975) ****

D: Sidney Lumet. Al Pacino, John Cazale, Charles Durning. 124 mins. (Warner) DVD

Pacino and Cazale shine as crooks whose bungled heist turns into a tense, daylong hostage situation at a Brooklyn bank. Lumet copped a well-deserved Oscar nomination for his nail-biting direction.

DOMINION (1995) ***

D: Michael Kehoe. Brad Johnson, Brion James, Tim Thomerson, Woody Brown, Glenn Morshower, Richard Riehle, Geoffrey Blake. 98 mins. (Turner)

Cowritten and coproduced by supporting actor Brown—whose earlier credits include a costarring stint in the less-than-impressive *Animal Instincts 2* (Academy)—*Dominion* is a taut, fairly brutal *Deliverance* variation with a *Hitcher* hook. A half-dozen hunter buds find themselves stalked by mountain madman James. When group leader Johnson searches for the elusive killer, he becomes the target of a second hunting party who believe *he's* the culprit. Director Kehoe manages to build genuine suspense, while the victimized hunters behave more credibly than usual, and James supplies his trademark menace as the relentless, vengeance-bent killer.

THE DON IS DEAD (1973) ***

D: Richard Fleischer. Anthony Quinn, Robert Forster, Frederic Forrest, Angel Tompkins, Charles Cioffi, Al Lettieri. 115 mins. (Universal)

While it pales beside *The Godfather*, whose success the filmmakers were obviously trying to duplicate, *The Don Is Dead* (a.k.a. *Beautiful but Deadly*) holds up as an intriguing film in its own right. Forster, Quinn, Forrest, Lettieri, and Cioffi are uniformly fine as various players caught up in a mob war begun via a romantic misunderstanding. Like *Family Enforcer* (see index), *Don* plays better now, free of its original imitative context, than it did upon its initial theatrical release. The John Turturro–starred *Macbeth* gangster update, *Men of Respect* (Columbia/TriStar), on the other gun, is well worth avoiding. The earlier *Joe MacBeth*, with Paul Douglas, remains unavailable on cassette.

DON KING: ONLY IN AMERICA (1997) ***1/2

D: John Herzfeld. Ving Rhames, Vondie Curtis-Hall, Jeremy Piven, Loretta Devine, Keith David, Ron Liebman. 112 mins. (HBO)

Adapted by director John (*2 Days in the Valley*) Herzfeld from Jack Newfield's nonfiction book, *Don King* is a thoroughly compelling, slyly subversive vivisection of the big-time boxing biz. The film traces King's (an outstanding Rhames) career from his rough-and-tumble days as a 1950s/60s Cleveland street hustler, through his incarceration on manslaughter charges, to his emergence as one of the ring game's most powerful, if resolutely eccentric and supremely manipulative, players. Curtis-Hall supplies riveting support as singer Lloyd Price (even contributing a slick impersonation of Price's distinctive

vocal style), whose long-term, increasingly quarrelsome relationship with King reaches a head when they form an uneasy partnership to present the famed Muhammad Ali/George Foreman "Rumble in the Jungle" fight amid the chaos of a postrevolutionary Zaire (a vividly realized sequence). *Don King* also dramatizes the mouthy promoter's alliances and battles with mobsters, rival promoters, Ali's Muslim coterie, the law, and even his own warriors (who included nearly every heavyweight of note). To portray the famed fighters, the filmmakers cast look-alikes who can also act, and viewers get the feeling they're watching the real Ali, Foreman, Larry Holmes, and Mike Tyson (Rhames's makeup is likewise impeccable). You don't have to be a fight fan to deem *Don King* a winner; the flick can take its rightful place among the best boxing movies ever made.

DONNIE BRASCO (1997) ***1/2

D: Mike Newell. Al Pacino, Johnny Depp, Michael Madsen, Bruno Kirby, James Russo, Anne Heche. 127 mins. (Columbia/TriStar) DVD

A bulked-up Depp lends convincing edge to his portrayal of FBI agent Joseph Pistone, from whose nonfiction book director Newell and scripter Paul Attanasio draw their narrative. In the late '70s, Pistone (using the alias Donnie Brasco) successfully cozied up to a crew of NYC Mafiosi in a sting that ultimately resulted in more than 200 arrests and 100 convictions. *Donnie Brasco*'s central tension spins on Pistone's escalating addiction to the gangster lifestyle and his growing loyalty to mob mentor Lefty (Pacino), a bedraggled hit man/hustler who opens his guarded heart to our young hero. While *DB* covers oft trod (if not downright trampled) turf—its *GoodFellas* echoes are unmistakable—the filmmakers and thesps work to make the familiar material fresh and compelling. The film contrasts the primal behavior of the core gangsters—who include a beefy, ambitious Madsen, wisecracking Kirby, and laconic Russo—with the 4H Club creepiness of the eavesdropping FBI contingent. Pacino brings terrific texture to his weary, wary, but obedient soldier role—his fondness for predatory-animal TV nature shows provides a neat character detail—while Depp comes across as a more reined-in variation on Ray Liotta's Henry Hill in *GoodFellas*. *Donnie Brasco* stacks up as a nearly flawless gangster yarn.

TALES OF THE TAPE
THE 10 BEST BOXING MOVIES ON VIDEO

•••

Body and Soul (1947, Republic)
Champion (1949, Artisan)
Fat City (1972, Columbia/TriStar)
Golden Boy (1939, Goodtimes)
The Great White Hope (1970, Fox)
Hard Times (1975, Goodtimes, DVD)
The Harder They Fall (1956, Columbia/TriStar)
Raging Bull (1980, MGM, DVD)
Requiem for a Heavyweight (1962, Columbia/TriStar)
The Set-Up (1949, Critics' Choice)

DOUBLE IMPACT (1991)**

D: Sheldon Lettich. Jean-Claude Van Damme, Geoffrey Lewis, Alonna Shaw, Bolo Yeung, Cory Everson. 107 mins. (Columbia/TriStar)

J-C attempts to stretch beyond his usual suspenseful splits by portraying twin brothers separated at birth: Chad, a wholesome L.A. aerobics teacher with a moderate Belgian accent (he was raised in France), and Alex, a tough-guy smuggler with a heavy Belgian accent (he was raised in Hong Kong). At the urging of Chad's mentor, Frank (Lewis), who saved the infant pair from certain death a quarter century earlier, the twain converge in Hong Kong to exact belated revenge against the bad guys who wasted their parents. Despite its double-trouble hook, *Double Impact* emerges as one of J-C's more numbingly one-note affairs, lacking the mean edge of *Death Warrant* and the elaborate kickboxing choreography of *Lionheart* (see index). Van Damme even risks soiling his shining celluloid image by having Alex belt blond squeeze Shaw, a cowardly move unbecoming an icon of J-C's stature; it's a lot more fun watching J-C beat himself to a bloody pulp, as he does when the twins square off to settle a simmering sibling dispute.

DOUBLE TEAM (1997)**

D: Tsui Hark. Jean-Claude Van Damme, Dennis Rodman, Mickey Rourke, Paul Freeman. 93 mins. (Columbia/TriStar) DVD

After a fairly rousing opening, courtesy of veteran Hong Kong action ace Hark, *Double Team* takes a terminal dip from which it never recovers. The dive occurs after agent J-C fails to nail superterrorist Rourke; Van Damme is given the option to immediately self-destruct or accept permanent banishment to an island redoubt where other disappeared agents while away their days. Our hero escapes, natch, and joins forces with flamboyant arms dealer Rodman (who's not bad here, at least com-

pared with Van Damme) for a globe-hopping spate of routine chases, shoot-outs, and *mano-a-mano* punch-ups.

DRAGNET (1954)**1/2

D: Jack Webb. Jack Webb, Ben Alexander, Richard Boone, Stacy Harris. 71 mins. (Universal)

LAPD officers Friday (uptight icon Webb) and Smith (Alexander) jump from TV to the big screen, in living color (make that living colorlessness), in a typically laconic tribute to the virtues of law and order. *Dragnet* makes a good warm-up for the amusing Dan Aykroyd/Tom Hanks spoof of the same name (Universal, DVD). Episodes from the original *Dragnet* teleseries are also on tape (Universal, DVD).

DRAGON: THE BRUCE LEE STORY (1993)***

D: Rob Cohen. Jason Scott Lee, Lauren Holly, Nancy Kwan, Robert Wagner, Michael Learned, Kay Tong Lim. 120 mins. (Universal) DVD

In *Dragon: The Bruce Lee Story*—based on widow Linda Lee Caldwell's memoir, *Bruce Lee: The Man Only I Knew*—director Cohen wisely emphasizes the action elements, augmenting lively re-creations of Bruce's death-shortened screen adventures with violent apocrypha from Lee's "real" life. Highlights include a dance-hall bash-up that sees our young hero, energetically interpreted by unrelated actor Lee (also on view in Vincent Ward's *Map of the Human Heart* [HBO], a part, ironically enough, for which Bruce's late son, Brandon, also reportedly auditioned), demolish a half-dozen obnoxious Aussie sailors and a San Francisco–set duke-out wherein Bruce chops and socks four cleaver-wielding Chinese cooks to the soundtrack strains of Booker T's "Green Onions" (!). In the dramatic arena,

Dragon scores some trenchant racial points. One scene shows a packed bijou audience cracking up over Mickey Rooney's Asian impersonation in *Breakfast at Tiffany's*. The camera pans to a stone-faced Lee viewing the Mick's antics with an unamused eye. Bruce also encounters trouble from other California-based Chinese martial arts masters who condemn him for teaching their "secret" techniques to "foreigners." That dispute is settled in the ring in a brutal bout that leaves Lee temporarily paralyzed. At the urging of wife Linda (Holly), Lee not only gradually heals himself but uses that down time to set forth his kung-fu philosophy in a book called *The Tao of Jeet Kune Do*, a martial arts fusion of Bruce's invention.

Lee's screen years are compressed into the final reels. He first attracts attention as Kato on the *Green Hornet* teleseries (original Green Hornet Van Williams cameos as the show's director), develops the *Kung Fu* series with a Hollywood producer (the ever suave Wagner) only to lose the leading role to David Carradine, then returns to Hong Kong, where he establishes his international stardom in films like *The Big Boss, Fists of Fury*, and *Enter the Dragon*. (The flick discreetly cops out on the unresolved issue of Lee's mysterious death at age 32.) Only when *Dragon* wanders into Bruce's domestic life does it descend into soap-opera histrionics. The occasional stretch of clichéd dramaturgy aside, *Dragon* brings Bruce Lee home in a way that's true to the late action icon's spirit.

DRAGON INN (1992)***

D: Raymond Lee. Maggie Cheung, Tony Leung, Brigitte Lin, Donnie Yen. 107 mins. (Tai Seng)

Set during the Ming Dynasty, producer Tsui (*A Chinese Ghost Story*) Hark's historical martial arts epic pits underhanded agents in the employ of evil eunuch Yin (Yen) against the warrior couple of Chow (Leung) and Mo (Lin) and their cohorts. All are temporarily stranded at the storm-swept, desert-set title site, a boisterous establishment run by the beautiful, fierce, and multifaceted Jade (Cheung), who seduces Chow and works both warring factions to her advantage. *Dragon Inn*'s most impressive kung-fu set-to is a climactic battle between our heroes and an acrobatic Yin, who, in one memorable moment, sees his limbs skinned to the bone via a few swift sword swipes. Yin's expert archers lend another exotic note by employing an array of vicious designer arrows bearing names like "Dog's Teeth," "Plum Blossom," and "Phoenix Tail."

DRAGONS FOREVER (1987) ***

D: Sammo Hung. Jackie Chan, Sammo Hung, Yuen Biao, Pauline Yeung, Benny ("The Jet") Urquidez. (Tai Seng) DVD

The "Three Kung-Fu-Teers" (Chan, Hung, Biao) star in this entertaining blend of action and comedy. When lawyer Jackie realizes he's on the wrong side of a toxic-waste case, he recruits buds Hung and Biao to take on his corrupt ex-client and the latter's hordes of standard-issue goons. A rematch between Chan and kickbox champ Urquidez, who'd earlier gone one-on-one in *Wheels on Meals* (Tai Seng Video, DVD), supplies a last-reel highlight.

DRIVE (1996) **½

D: Steve Wang. Mark Dacascos, Kadeem Hardison, John Pyper-Ferguson, Brittany Murphy, Tracey Walter, James Shigeta, Masaya Kato. (A-Pix) DVD

High-kicking Dacascos, in a role tailor-made for Don ("the Dragon") Wilson, is a "bioenergetically" enhanced martial arts courier assigned to deliver a high-tech gizmo to contacts in L.A. Director Wang (*The Guyver* and sequel) knows his Asian-movie moves—Dacascos even identifies himself to an inquisitive cop as "Sammo Hung"—and manages to approximate a hyperactive Hong Kong B flick within his budgetary constraints.

THE DRIVER (1978) ***

D: Walter Hill. Ryan O'Neal, Bruce Dern, Isabelle Adjani. 131 mins. (Fox)

Action specialist Hill crafts an effective, laconic, atmospheric noir, punctuated by adrenalizing high-speed car chases, that pits professional getaway driver O'Neal against aggressively corrupt cop Dern, in a typically galvanizing, over-the-top turn.

DROP ZONE (1994) ***½

D: John Badham. Wesley Snipes, Yancy Butler, Gary Busey, Luca Bercovici, Michael Jeter, Malcolm Jamal-Warner. 101 mins. (Paramount) DVD

Director Badham, who's exhibited his flair for milking the max from gimmicky plots in such past pics as *WarGames* and *Blue Thunder* (see index), fashions what stacks up as the *Stone Cold* of skydiving movies. Star Snipes continues to hone his action skills while again taking to the air (à la the far inferior *Passenger 57* [Warner]), this time as a U.S. marshal assigned, along with screen brother/former *Cosby Show* kid Jamal-Warner, to protect prison-sprung computer genius/government witness Jeter. Badham kicks off on a literally high note as a team of skydiving terrorists led by a typically toothy Busey stage a spectacular kidnap that costs some 14 lives, Jamal-Warner's among them. A suspended Snipes, determined to work the case on his own, infiltrates the South Florida skydiver culture, whose high-flying, heavy-drinking denizens come across as mutant hybrids of hard-core bikers and *Top Gun*–type cadets. Badham knows when to rip the cord for a rousing action sequence before plot mechanics threaten to turn dull, and *Drop Zone* contains some of the best aerial stunts we've seen. *Drop Zone*'s a much better bet than screen-skydiving rival *Terminal Velocity* (Hollywood Pictures, DVD).

DRUNKEN MASTER:
THE SERIES

DRUNKEN MASTER II (1994) ***

D: Jackie Chan, Lau Kar Leung. Jackie Chan, Anita Mui, Ti Lung, Andy Lau. Subtitled. 108 mins. (Tai Seng)

Set during the early years of the 20th century and lensed on location (with much visual sweep and attention to period detail) in Hong Kong, Manchuria, and Shanghai, *Drunken Master II* finds Chan—reprising his

Wong Fei-Hung role from 1978's *Drunken Master*—determined to thwart conniving Brits' efforts to pinch a priceless jade treasure. That basic premise provides J.C. with plenty of opportunities to demonstrate his "drunken fist" chops. Here Chan takes the fighting style to a literal level; à la Popeye with his spinach, Jackie pumps up his kung-fu prowess by pausing, midbattle, to enjoy generous slugs from his wine bottle (!), which in turn supplies him with a convenient excuse to dust off his patented mugging and slapstick moves. Jackie also finds time to help oppressed foundry workers resist their brutal British overseers. A subplot sees him fall into disfavor with his loving but stern dad (played by John Woo regular Lung) and subsequently search for ways to redeem himself without compromising his own principles. Both on-screen dad Lung and crafty mom Mui look more like (slightly) older siblings than the nearly 40-year-old Jackie's parents. But while Chan's face occasionally betrays his age, his nimble (if oft battered) body shows no signs of slowing down, as he again performs his own strenuous stunts and elaborately choreographed fight scenes. In *Drunken Master II* the latter include a painstakingly staged stick fight that rages under a stalled train and a fiery foundry-set set-to that finds our hero drinking industrial alcohol (!) to augment his strength—a development that leads to a bizarre sick-joke fade-out. Chan also continues his tradition of screening outtakes under the end credits.

DUEL (1971) ***

D: Steven Spielberg. Dennis Weaver. 90 mins. (Universal)

Spielberg's directorial debut remains one of his best efforts—a tense TV movie dealing with desperate driver Weaver's close encounter with a truck bent on his destruction. Less adroit variations on the theme include 1977's

The Car (Anchor Bay, DVD), with James Brolin, and 1998's Stephen King–drawn *Trucks* (Trimark, DVD).

EASTERN CONDORS (1987) ***

D: Sammo Hung. Sammo Hung, Yuen Biao, Dr. Haing S. Ngor, Chi Jang Ha, Corey Yuen. Subtitled/dubbed. 95 mins. (Tai Seng) DVD

While not on a par with John Woo's 1990 Vietnam-set epic *Bullet in the Head*, Hung's *Dirty Dozen* Meets *The Deer Hunter* variation rates as an exciting, actionful affair. Hung also stars as the most capable of ten Asian criminals sprung from U.S. jails to assist in a 1976 American mission to destroy a hidden arsenal left over from the Vietnam War's last days. Hung crams his wide-screen canvas with firefights, explosions, martial arts displays, tough-guy dialogue, a requisite Vietcong prison-camp Russian-roulette scene, and fleeting anti-VC *and* anti-American sentiments. The late Cambodian actor Dr. Haing S. (*The Killing Fields*) Ngor—who survived the Khmer Rouge's mass genocide only to be shot dead in L.A.—has a small role as a Chinese colonel.

EASY RIDER (1969) ***½

D: Dennis Hopper. Peter Fonda, Dennis Hopper, Jack Nicholson, Karen Black. (Columbia/TriStar) DVD

Hopper's hog odyssey virtually invented the modern road movie as he and Pete hit the highways in search of America. A New Orleans–set LSD trip and Jack Nicholson's turn as a Southern liberal lawyer supply unforgettable highlights.

ELECTRA GLIDE IN BLUE (1973) ***½

D: James William Guercio. Robert Blake, Billy "Green" Bush, Mitchell Ryan, Jeannine Riley,

Elisha Cook, Jr., Royal Dano. 114 mins. (MGM)

Though less than a blockbuster during its initial release, Guercio's visually inventive karmic cop caper has since acquired a deserved cult rep. Blake is a stunted Arizona cycle trooper who hankers to be a plainclothes dick, the better to tap his ratiocinative powers. A suicide-masked murder gives him his chance, but he learns the hard lesson that, in this life, ability often plays second fiddle to (in this case sexual) politics. Guercio's circular chain-of-pain plot is as effective as his ace directorial eye, even if said plot's cyclical imperative leads to what some view as a contrived climax. *Electra Glide in Blue* is a film that doesn't easily fade from memory.

THE EMERALD FOREST (1985) ***½

D: John Boorman. Powers Boothe, Meg Foster, Charley Boorman. 113 mins. (New Line)

Myth-minded auteur Boorman's stirring adventure about a white youth (real-life son Charley) raised by South American Indians blends all the necessary ingredients—exoticism, cultural clashes, violence, and mysticism—that make for topflight cinematic escapism.

ENEMY GOLD (1993) **

D: Drew Sidaris. Bruce Penhall, Mark Barriere, Rodrigo Obregón, Suzi Simpson, Tai Collins, Julie Strain. 93 mins. (Prism)

In the international tradition of such multigenerational genre-movie dynasties as Italy's Mario (*Black Sunday*) Bava and son Lamberto (*Demons*) and Mexico's Rene (*Wrestling Women Vs. the Aztec Mummy*) Cardona, Sr., and Rene Jr. (*Night of the Bloody Apes*), among many others (see sidebar), cleavage-driven outdoor-action specialists Andy and Arlene Sidaris pass the directorial torch (or, perhaps more accurately, kleig light) to son Drew Sidaris. *Enemy Gold* opens with an ambitious Civil War flashback that sees two Confederate soldiers stash a cache of stolen Union gold. We quickly cut to the present, where agent Penhall, pal Barriere, and their foxy new partner, Simpson, raid one of Bolivian importer Obregón's remote drug outposts. Obregón hires bikini-clad assassin Strain to eliminate the troublesome trio. The ever reliable Julie turns in another typically arresting tough-babe performance. When asked, "Do you kill federal agents often?" our violent vixen shrugs, "It's a living." Fans of Andy and Arlene's hard-breathing brand of alfresco actioners should enjoy Drew's debut entry too.

ENEMY TERRITORY (1987) **¹/₂

D: Peter Manoogian. Gary Frank, Ray Parker, Jr., Stacey Dash, Jan-Michael Vincent, Frances Foster, Tony Todd. 92 mins. (Media, n.i.d.)

A sort of ghetto *Rio Bravo* by way of *The Warriors, Enemy Territory* features Frank as a struggling insurance agent sent by his sadistic boss to finalize a policy in an NYC housing project so perilous that "even the window-washers wear bulletproof vests." Frank inadvertently incurs the wrath of "the Count" (played by talented thesp Todd in a black Michael Berryman mode), leader of the violent Vampires street gang. Thereafter, Frank is forced to battle his way out of the building with the aid of phone-company rep (and *Ghostbusters* composer) Parker, shapely concerned tenant Dash (in an ersatz Rae Dawn Chong role), and paranoid, wheelchair-bound Vietnam vet Vincent (in a brief but bravura turn), who's converted his besieged apartment into an armed bunker. *Enemy Territory,* which inspired some token (possibly self-

manufactured) protests in its day for its alleged racism, is a thoroughly trashy, consistently tense urban thriller featuring able performances by Parker, Frank, Todd, and Foster as Mrs. Briggs, a tough elderly policyholder who demonstrates she can also wield a pretty mean machine gun.

AMERICA'S B-MOVIE DYNASTIES

• New Zealand–born Victor (*Rawhide Romance*) Adamson directed and, under the *nom du saddle* Denver Dixon, acted in indie B westerns in the '20s and '30s. Begat Al (*Blazing Stewardesses, Satan's Sadists*) Adamson, busy Independent-International auteur from the '60s until his murder in 1996.

• Italian-born Albert (*I Bury the Living*) Band wrote, produced, and/or directed dozens of features, here and abroad, from the '50s to the '90s. Begat Charles (*Parasite*) Band, former Empire Pictures honcho/current Full Moon Studios mogul, whose onetime announced aim was to produce 2,000 films by the year 2000.

• Irvin Berwick directed from the '50s (*Monster of Piedras Blancas*) through the late '70s (*Malibu High*). Begat Wayne Berwick, the brains behind the late Jackie Vernon's only gore movie, 1983's *Microwave Massacre*.

• British helmer Douglas (*Theater of Blood*) Hickox directed from the '60s through the '80s. Begat busy Hollywood-based scare-sequel specialist Anthony (*Warlock: The Armageddon, Waxwork 2*) Hickox.

• Howco International mogul and sometime scripter Joy (*Women and Bloody Terror*) Houck, Sr., begat director Joy Houck, Jr., creative force behind, among others, *The Brain Machine, Night of Bloody Horror,* and *Soggy Bottom U.S.A.*

• Regional indie auteur Jim (*Charge of the Model T's*) McCullough, Sr., begat Jim McCullough, Jr., who directed *Video Murders* and scripted and coproduced Jim Sr.'s infamous *Mountaintop Motel Massacre,* which sported the deathless tag line: "Please do not disturb Evelyn. She already is."

• Magician/moviemaker Ron (*Mesa of Lost Women*) Ormond, who directed from the '40s (several Lash La Rue westerns) through the '60s (*The Monster and the Stripper*), and performer/producer wife, June (*White Lightnin' Road*) Ormond, begat actor/auteur Tim (*The Girl from Tobacco Road*) Ormond. June and Tim later produced fundamentalist fear films for the church circuit.

• Regional auteurs Ferd and Beverly (*Gator Bait, The Hitchhikers*) Sebastian begat actor/producer Ben (*Rocktober Blood, Running Cool*) Sebastian.

• Exploitation pioneer Louis (*Drums o' Voodoo*) Weiss begat producer George (*Glen or Glenda, Test Tube Babies*) and producer/director Adrian (*The White Gorilla, The Bride and the Beast*) Weiss.

ENTER THE DRAGON   (1973) ***

D: Robert Clouse. Bruce Lee, John Saxon, Jim Kelly. 98 mins. (Warner) DVD

One of Bruce's best Western efforts sees our hero crash a secret island-set martial arts tournament in what turned out to be his final complete film. With American kung-fu ace Kelly and distaff Chinese chop champ Angela Mao. In 1998 Warner reissued the video in an extras-laden "25th Anniversary Edition." Sammo Hung, meanwhile, sends up the genre with his amusing 1978 slapstick romp, *Enter the Fat Dragon* (Crash Cinema), a.k.a. *They Call Me Phat Dragon* (Xenon).

ERASER   (1996) ***

D: Charles Russell. Arnold Schwarzenegger, James Caan, Vanessa Williams, James Coburn, Robert Pastorelli, Andy Romano. 115 mins. (Warner) DVD

Arn rebounded from his then-recent duds *Last Action Hero*, *True Lies*, and *Junior* with former horror helmer Russell's *(The Blob) Eraser*, a stunt-driven crash-and-burn bonanza whose pacing and pyrotechnics effectively mask a routine chase plot. As secret "Witness Program Security" commando John Krueger (presumably no relation to Freddy), it's Arn's job to protect the endangered life of weapons-corp worker Williams, key figure in an FBI sting gone sour. Turncoat Caan, Arn's boss and mentor, leads the nonstop assault against the duo. In addition to running up a mega body count, *Eraser* incorporates no fewer than three memorable money scenes involving (a) a deplaned Arn and his runaway parachute, (b) a severely taxed bulletproof shield, and (c) a troupe of hungry zoo crocs who add some unexpected hardcore gore to the action proceedings. Another clever running riff has Arn calling in favors from former witness placements, most notably mob refugee Pastorelli, who's only too happy to help.

> ### BRUCE LEE VIDEOGRAPHY
> All tapes are from FoxVideo, except where indicated.
> •
>
> *Bruce Lee: The Legend* (1984, Documentary)
> *The Chinese Connection* (1973, DVD)
> *Fists of Fury* (1973, DVD)
> *Game of Death* (1979)
> *Marlowe* (1969, MGM/UA)
> *The Real Bruce Lee* (1979, Video Gems, n.i.d.). Contains footage from Lee's early films as a child actor.
> *Return of the Dragon* (1973)

Arn kills dozens of dastards while enduring two bullet wounds, a wooden stake through the leg, flying shrapnel through the hand, and countless blows to the head (apparently in the fleshy part of the brain) with fists, furniture, and other blunt instruments.

EXECUTIVE DECISION (1996) ***½

D: Stuart Baird. Kurt Russell, Halle Berry, John Leguizamo, Oliver Platt, Joe Morton, David Suchet, Steven Seagal, B. D. Wong, Whip Hubley, Marla Maples Trump. 133 mins. (Warner) DVD

Proceeding from Jim and John Thomas's precision screenplay and further abetted by crisp acting, editing, and direction, *Executive Decision* arrives as a near-perfect exercise in big-budget Hollywood thrillmaking. Though prominently billed, Seagal is literally (and thankfully) blown out of the picture early on, contributing little more than a cameo; the midair rescue of a terrorist-snatched, biochemical-weapons-equipped passenger plane is instead entrusted to a group of much better thesps: tuxedo-clad think-tank head Russell, conscripted engineer Platt, and commandos Leguizamo, Morton, Wong, and Hubley. *Executive Decision*, unlike most recent A action epics, hinges more on high-tech knowhow than on firepower. Anyone who's ever struggled with computers, complicated phone systems, or even recalcitrant camcorders can relate to the unending technical difficulties our heroes encounter in their attempts to maintain surveillance on the terrorists' activities, even with the aid of flight attendant Berry, who becomes the boys' onboard contact. (Marla Maples Trump plays her frightened fellow stew.) While ideally suited to the big screen, *Executive Decision* holds up well enough on video to provide a plethora of high-flying thrills.

THE EXTERMINATOR   (1980) **½

D: James Glickenhaus. Christopher George, Robert Ginty, Samantha Eggar. 101 mins. (Anchor Bay) DVD

A 'Nam-vet variation on *Death Wish*, *The Exterminator* proved wildly successful at the box office and launched both Ginty's and Glickenhaus's action-movie careers. Ginty returns, accompanied by his trusty flamethrower, in Glickenhaus's *Exterminator II* (MGM).

EXTREME JUSTICE   (1993) **½

D: Mark L. Lester. Scott Glenn, Lou Diamond Phillips, Chelsea Field, Yaphet Kotto. 96 mins. (Trimark) DVD

Extreme Justice is an allegedly fact-based variation on the badged-vigilante theme explored in *The Star*

Chamber, *Magnum Force*, *Gang in Blue* (see index), *Dark Justice* (Warner), and *Scarred City* (Sterling), among others. Glenn and Phillips are partners in an elite LAPD violent-offender unit that causes more bloodbaths than it prevents. Conflicts arise when Phillips decides to expose the trigger-happy Glenn. While the plot's nothing new, director Lester (*Class of 1984*) demonstrates he's lost none of his action-movie savvy, crafting a swift, kinetic outing undermined only by an anticlimactic nonending.

EXTREME PREJUDICE   (1987) ***

D: Walter Hill. Nick Nolte, Powers Boothe, Maria Conchita Alonso, Rip Torn. 104 mins. (Avid)

Nolte stars as a border sheriff at odds with friend-turned-drug-mogul Boothe. Hill's contemporary western offers an ace cast, action aplenty, and some of the choicest dumb macho dialogue on record (to say nothing of videotape).

EYE OF THE STRANGER (1993) *½

D: David Heavener. David Heavener, Martin Landau, Sally Kirkland, Don Swayze, Joe Estevez, Stella Stevens. 96 mins. (Monarch)

Actor, auteur, C&W singer, homevid hero, and all-around legend-in-his-own-mind David Heavener again indulges his Clint Eastwood complex (a sort of *High Plains Drifter* Meets *Pale Rider* in this low-budget snoozefest). As "the Stranger," Heavener's laconic, harmonica-blowing loner trucks into the troubled town of Harmony, a hamlet long under the thumb of corrupt mayor Landau and henchgoon Swayze. Since sheriff Estevez is a hopeless drunk, Heavener works alone to uncover the truth behind a seven-year-old murder and inspires the oppressed townsfolk to

stand up for their rights. In addition to the above-listed luminaries, this boring self-homage squanders the talents of such B stalwarts as Sydney Lassick and Sy (*Street Asylum*) Richardson. Heavener has scripted, directed, and toplined in at least nine other turkeys: *Border of Tong* (Monarch), *Deadly Reactor* and *Ragin' Cajun* (both A.I.P., the latter as actor only), *Dragon Fury* (Monarch), *Fugitive X* (Silverlake), *Kill Crazy* (Media), *Outlaw Force* (TWE), *Prime Target* (Hemdale), and *Twisted Justice* (K-Beech). DH can also be sighted in *Kill or Be Killed* and *L.A. Goddess* (Prism).

EYE OF THE TIGER   (1986) **½

D: Richard Sarafian. Gary Busey, Yaphet Kotto, William Smith, Seymour Cassel, Bert Remsen, Kimberlin Ann Brown. 90 mins. (Avid)

In *Eye of the Tiger*, the flick that kick-started Gary Busey's still-active B-movie career, Gar stars as 'Nam vet and ex-con Buck Matthews, who returns to his corrupt Southwestern town to tangle with a horde of uniformed Harley hellions-cum-crack-dealers led by veteran heavy Smith. When Buck saves a potential rape victim from the bikers' clutches, the bad guys retaliate by wrecking his house and killing his wife. With the aid of resourceful ex-army buddy Kotto, Buck mounts a climactic assault on the bikers' desert redoubt, driving his customized cannon-equipped RV while Kotto drops grenades from his flame-red biplane as James Brown wails from his onboard blaster (!). Though laced with lame lines and countless lapses in logic, *Eye of the Tiger* careens along at a fairly brisk pace and offers a number of imaginatively sicko touches—as when Buck employs steel wire to decapitate several enemy bikers, and their cronies retaliate by digging up his late wife and depositing her coffin on his doorstep. What *will* they think of next?

FACE/OFF   (1997) ***

D: John Woo. Nicolas Cage, John Travolta, Joan Allen, Gina Gershon, Alessandro Nivola, Nick Cassavetes. 135 mins. (Paramount) DVD

To prevent an L.A. terrorist catastrophe, lawman Travolta reluctantly agrees to undergo surgery that will literally give him the face (and voice) of his archenemy (Cage), a vile psychopath responsible for the shooting death of Travolta's young son some six years earlier. Woo's most lavish Hollywood caper to that point, *Face/Off* represents a case of more is less. Though Woo crafts some excellent, adrenalizing set pieces (e.g., the climactic high-speed boat chase) and Travolta and Cage both turn in strenuous work in tricky dual roles, the émigré auteur's mix of operatic Hong Kong–styled action and quintessentially American elements doesn't always mesh here. And the basic hero/psycho identity switch closely mirrors the plot of the modest but more organic 1994 French thriller *The Machine* (see index). There's no denying that *Face/Off* supplies mucho bang for the video bucks, but it would have been even more effective with some judicious trimming. John (Joe Bob Briggs) Bloom has a cameo as a prison medical technician, while FX ace Kevin Yagher crafts the crucial facial FX.

FAIR GAME   (1995) **

D: Andrew Sipes. William Baldwin, Cindy Crawford, Steven Berkoff, Christopher McDonald, Salma Hayek, Jenette Goldstein, Dan Hedaya. 91 mins. (Warner) DVD

For her debut star vehicle, super-model Crawford firmly places her filmic destiny in the hands of celluloid demolition specialist Joel Silver. The result is a thoroughly typical B video bulked up by lavish production values. *Fair Game* casts Cindy as a civil-suit lawyer dogged by a high-tech ex-KGB team headed by a hammy Berkoff, and protected by valiant Miami cop William

(Brother of Alec, Stephen, and Daniel) Baldwin. The script sheds its scant logic faster than Cindy doffs her duds, but *Fair Game* is far from the worst actioner on vid-store shelves. No relation to the 1982 (Imperial), 1988 (Charter), and 1989 (Trimark) actioners of the same name.

FAMILY ENFORCER (1975) ***

D: Ralph De Vito. Joseph Cortese, Lou Criscuola, Joe Pesci, Anne Johns, Keith Davis, Frank Vincent. 89 mins. (VCI)

De Vito's solid low-budget slice of Mafia lowlife, East Orange, New Jersey–style, may have followed too closely on the heels of Scorsese's *Mean Streets* and Coppola's *The Godfather* to please critics of the day, but as part of the ongoing wiseguy genre, *Family Enforcer* (a.k.a. *Death Collector*) rates as one of the best. Cortese is excellent as the snake-bitten small-time hood whose association with local mob middleman Criscuola results in a series of disasters not entirely of our hero's making. A then-unknown Pesci likewise shines as Cortese's unwanted partner, and a nightclub scene wherein the pair harass a fey lounge singer offers a prescient Jersey version of *GoodFellas'* Copa segments. At once tight, violent, and verité, *Family Enforcer* maintains a high degree of authenticity without sacrificing any sleaze or entertainment value. Also released on the sell-through Star Classics label as *The Collector* but recorded in the inferior E.P. slow-speed mode.

FAST-WALKING (1982) ***½

D: James B. Harris. James Woods, Kay Lenz, Tim McIntyre, Robert Hooks, M. Emmet Walsh, Timothy Carey, Susan Tyrrell. 116 mins. (Key)

James B. (*Boiling Point*) Harris's perverse *Fast-Walking* emerges as something of a *Blue Velvet* behind bars.

Based on Ernest Brawley's novel *The Rap*, the pic stars Woods as "Fast-Walking" Miniver, a pot-smoking prison screw who's also a chronic screw-up and a cousin of inmate Wasco (McIntyre), an amateur Nietzschean philosopher, scam artist, and leader of the white inmate population. Wasco sics his cycle-slut squeeze, Moke (a frequently unclad Lenz), on Miniver in a bid to persuade the sharpshooting guard to assassinate newly incarcerated black radical Galliot (Hooks). *Fast-Walking* successfully combines suspense with dark humor, kinky erotica, complex character studies, and pure sleaze. Woods gives a standout perf as the lazy, self-serving, oft stoned, but ultimately principled Miniver and receives ample support from not only Lenz, Hooks, and McIntyre but B vets Carey, Sydney Lassick, and a mega-decibeled Tyrrell.

FEAR CITY (1984) **

D: Abel Ferrara. Billy Dee Williams, Tom Berenger, Melanie Griffith, Jack Scalia, Rae Dawn Chong, Rossano Brazzi, Jan Murray. 96 mins. (HBO)

Pals Berenger and Scalia manage the mob-owned Starlite Talent Agency, suppliers of fine, quality exotic dancers to nearby Times Square strip joints. When the "New York Knifer"—a moralistic maniac who records his punitive *pensées* in a diary entitled "Fear City"— starts slashing their foxy clients, ex-boxer Berenger assigns himself the task of bringing the blade-wielding wacko to swift street justice. Though blessed with a bigger budget, *Fear City* lacks the kinetic punch of Ferrara's earlier cult fave *Ms. .45* (see index), spinning its mostly routine tale of retribution at a pace too languid to compensate for its thin characterizations and slender story line. Top-billed Williams puts in only sporadic appearances here, though his personal hairstylist receives a well-deserved screen credit. Our rating applies only to this severely edited ver-

sion of Ferrara's director's cut—which itself has yet to join the video ranks.

THE FIFTH MONKEY (1990) ***

D: Eric Rochat. Ben Kingsley, Mika Lina, Vera Fischer, Silvia De Carvalho, Milton Gonzalez. 101 mins. (Columbia/TriStar)

While this picaresque South America–set tale (lensed in Brazil) probably suffers from an overly literal translation of Jacques Zibi's source novel—it's sketchy and superficial in spots and hampered by awkward transitions—*The Fifth Monkey* still stacks up as entertaining, offbeat adventure fare. Kingsley plays an impoverished rural snake-killer whose discovery of four errant chimps leads him on an odyssey to an unspecified city, where he hopes to sell the simians for enough simoleons to afford the affections of an avaricious but buxom local widow. The pic's outcome is never in doubt, but getting there makes for colorful viewing.

FIGHT FOR YOUR LIFE (1977) ***

D: Robert E. Edelson. William Sanderson, Robert Judd, Catherine Peppers, Lela Small, William Cargill, Peter Yoshida, Daniel Paraldo. 89 mins. (After Hours, n.i.d.)

Exec-produced by low-budget 42nd Street–based mogul William Mishkin, *Fight for Your Life* puts a black spin on Wes Craven's *Last House on the Left* (itself "inspired" by Bergman's *Virgin Spring*) with elements from 1955's *The Desperate Hours* (Paramount) tossed in. Sanderson—best known for his lonely replicant-designer role in *Blade Runner*—plays a sociopathic redneck who, with Asian and Hispanic cohorts Yoshida and Paraldo, invades the upstate New York home of African-American minister Judd and his family. Sanderson subjects his captives to all manner of racial taunts and humiliations while lawmen gradually narrow the net over the three killers. As in *Last House*, the hostages eventually get their chance to turn the tables on their tormentors. *Fight for Your Life* is a taut, compelling trashfest that features a standout perf by Sanderson as the murderously insecure basket case with a quick trigger finger.

FINAL CUT   (1988) ***

D: Larry G. Brown. Joe Rainer, Jordan Williams, Brett Rice, T. J. Kennedy, Carla DeLene, J. Don Ferguson. 92 mins. (Trimark)

A quartet of movie stuntmen run afoul of corrupt sheriff Ferguson while second-unit shooting on location in Caddo County, Texas, in this entertaining obscurity. A solid script (by Williams, who costars as carefree stunt ace "Smiley"), credible characterizations, and a gradually unfolding conspiracy plot make for engrossing viewing. *Final Cut* also offers an authentic inside look at movie-stunt mechanics. More imaginative than Mark L. Lester's better-known *Stunts* (HBO), *Final Cut* rates high on the list of stuntman-directed movies, a list normally longer on quantity (e.g., John Gazarian's *Real Bullets*, Byron Quisenberry's *Scream*) than quality.

FIRE DOWN BELOW   (1997) ***

D: Félix Enríquez Alcalá. Steven Seagal, Marg Helgenberger, Harry Dean Stanton, Kris Kristofferson, Stephen Lang, Levon Helm, Brad Hunt, Richard Masur. 98 mins. (Warner) DVD

Seagal lands his best vehicle to date with *Fire Down Below,* evocatively lensed by cinematographer Richard Houghton on authentic Appalachian locations. After three federal agents are killed, EPA op Seagal goes undercover as a humble volunteer handyman (with a closetful of Rodeo Drive designer leather jackets!) to get the goods on toxic-waste-dumping industrialist Kristofferson. Jeb (*Switchback*) Stuart

and Philip Morton's script sports more in the way of texture and characterization than the usual Seagal bashfest, with Stanton, as an extremely low-key eco activist, and Helm, as a decent but compromised preacher, landing especially nuanced roles. Seagal rings up his lowest direct body count to date but compensates by repeatedly creaming the same goons, who keep coming back for more. Steve even gets to show off a few guitar licks during an outdoor concert scene, while Stanton strums and croons "Tennessee Waltz" over the closing credits. *Fire Down Below* represents a major improvement over Seagal's earlier eco turkey *On Deadly Ground* (Warner) and his 1999 made-for-cable right-wing militia exposé, *The Patriot* (Buena Vista, DVD).

FIREPOWER   (1993) **½

D: Richard Pepin. Chad McQueen, Gary Daniels, Joseph Ruskin, Alisha Das, George Murdock, Jim Hellwig. 91 mins. (PM)

Ruggedly staged and decently acted, *Firepower*—no relation to Michael (*Death Wish*) Winner's 1979 Sophia Loren–starred dud of the same name (Fox)—plays a lot better than its clichéd plot synopsis reads. McQueen and Brit kickboxing champ Daniels are gung-ho cops who infiltrate 2007 L.A.'s police-free "Hellzone" to nail counterfeit AIDS-vaccine manufacturer, lethal-combat promoter, and all-around slimeball Ruskin. Presenting a formidable obstacle is death-ring killer "the Swordsman," gruntingly interpreted by ex–"Ultimate Warrior" pro wrestler Hellwig, sporting impressive musculature and a tonsorial style to match his surname. Highlights include several excitingly choreographed matches, an *Assault on Precinct 13*–style shoot-out, and Das's foxy presence. While not in the class of once and future king of wrestlers-turned-actors Tor Johnson, Hellwig is at least easier to take than Hulk Hogan or Jesse Ventura. Daniels

has gone on to topline in several subsequent low-budget actioners, including 1997's *Bloodmoon* (BMG).

FIRESTORM   (1998) **

D: Dean Semler. Howie Long, Scott Glenn, Suzy Amis, William Forsythe. 90 mins. (20th Century Fox) DVD

Former gridiron star Howie's a courageous Wyoming "smoke jumper," newly appointed chief (replacing a retiring Glenn) of an elite woodland firefighting team. While on a prison work detail, Forsythe and four fellow cons break out under the cover of a spreading conflagration, snatch innocent birdwatcher Amis, and battle our persistent hero. *Firestorm* plays like bulked-up direct-to-video fare with an occasional flicker of brain-damaged charm, most strikingly represented by Long's uniquely vacuous stare, an oddly subdued Forsythe's fleeting attempts at a Canadian accent, and the thinly sketched characters' mouthy bouts with clumsy expository dialogue. In his directorial debut, longtime Aussie cinematographer Semler (*The Road Warrior, Waterworld*) yields occasional visual fun from his flame-driven tale.

FIREWORKS (HANA-BI) (1997) ***½

D: Takeshi Kitano. "Beat" Takeshi, Kayoko Kishimoto, Ren Osugi, Susumu Terajima, Tetsu Watanabe. Subtitled. 103 mins. (New Yorker Video)

One-man media machine Takeshi ("Beat") Kitano is an irreverent Renaissance man who simply has no known counterpart (definitely *not* Howard Stern) in the West *or* East, a satirist who appears on several weekly TV shows; pens newspaper and magazine columns; writes, directs, and stars in brilliantly idiosyncratic feature films; *and* acts in other director's movies (e.g., Nagisa Oshima's *Merry Christmas, Mr.*

Lawrence [Universal], Robert Longo's *Johnny Mnemonic* [see index]). Kitano follows his excellent 1993 *Sonatine* with the equally arresting *Fireworks* (a.k.a. *Hana-Bi*). Though he portrays a Yakuza soldier in *Sonatine* and a Tokyo cop here, Kitano is essentially the same character, a virtually expressionless stoic (the right side of his stone face was left paralyzed following a 1994 motor-scooter accident, but you'd never notice it) who uses minimal body language, with enigmatic eyes usually hidden behind round sunglasses. Except for his signature outbursts of abrupt, explosive violence that leave instant gory carnage in their wake, the almost totally silent Kitano comes as close to a living still-life as any actor in international screen history. Director Kitano employs the same rhythm, pace, and movements in assembling his films—stretches of serenity jolted by *Wild Bunch*–styled mayhem.

In *Fireworks* Kitano portrays Nishi, a veteran Tokyo detective in serious hock to Yakuza loan sharks (much to their eventual bloody regret) and burdened by personal tragedy. It's implied that the death of their young daughter contributed to his wife's (Kishimoto) illness, a condition (presumably terminal cancer) that's never uttered aloud, not even by her doctor; much of *Fireworks* details Nishi's final weeks with her as they drive around in silence deeply and lovingly communing via such innocent, even childlike activities as card games and picnics. After his partner (Osugi) is crippled in a shoot-out, Nishi quits the force and forges a new career as a bank robber (wearing a police uniform, no less!), diverting part of the loot to buy art supplies for his injured, increasingly suicidal friend. The latter later takes up painting in earnest, creating canvases featuring an array of flower-faced people and animals (actually drawn by the indefatigable Kitano, apparently in his "spare" time). Kitano likewise takes a painterly approach to his celluloid canvas, with images of blood, snow, and flowers emerging as running motifs woven into his visual narrative.

FIRST KNIGHT   (1995) ***

D: Jerry Zucker. Sean Connery, Richard Gere, Julia Ormond, Ben Cross. 133 mins. (Columbia/TriStar) DVD

ZAZ Team refugee Jerry (*Naked Gun*) Zucker—who earlier went "straight" with the box-office biggie *Ghost* (Paramount)—runs the Arthurian legend through a Camelot theme-park wringer, resulting in a reasonably entertaining medieval actioner for the '90s. Gere (Daniel Day-Lewis must have been otherwise engaged) interprets Lancelot as a swaggering, tight-britched, sword-slinging stud closer in spirit to Clint Eastwood's "Man with No Name" than anything out of Mallory. (If you didn't know much about the Camelot crowd going in, rest assured you'll know a little less coming out.) When Lance rescues Guinevere (Ormond) from the clutches of renegade knight Cross's brigands, romance gradually ensues, despite Lady G.'s resistance and the presence of her betrothed—stately idealist King Arthur (Connery, commanding as ever). The best scene involves Gere's balletic run through an elaborate gauntlet of perpetual-motion mallets and blades, an impressive invention that would make an ideal holiday gift for the sadist who has everything.

FIT TO KILL   (1993) **½

D: Andy Sidaris. Dona Speir, Roberta Vasquez, Bruce Penhall, R. J. Moore, Julie Strain, Rodrigo Obregón, Tony Peck. 93 mins. (Columbia/TriStar)

Andy and Arlene Sidaris's promised "swan song" trots out *Playboy* Playmates Speir and Vasquez for a "final" ride into the Hawaiian sunset. *Fit to Kill* also returns *Hard Hunted* villain R. J. (Son of Roger) Moore to the fore in a typically complex, multifactional scramble for the precious "Alexa Stone." As in the pair's past entries, "breasts, thighs, and spies" provide the flick with its raison d'être, and while *Fit to Kill* fails to scale the modest heights of the Sidarises' best efforts, this fast-paced actioner should please the series' longtime fans.

FLESH + BLOOD   (1985) ***

D: Paul Verhoeven. Rutger Hauer, Jennifer Jason Leigh, Tom Burlinson, Susan Tyrrell, Jack Thompson, Brion James. 126 mins. (Vestron)

Sort of a medieval spaghetti western, Dutch director Verhoeven's maiden English-language movie is a lusty, irreverent actioner charting the misadventures of a motley band of mercenaries led by a rugged Rut. Tyrrell is at her loudmouthed best as one of Hauer's followers, while Leigh plays a captive virginal princess whom Hauer takes under his wing (to speak only of his wing). Lots of violence and gratuitous nudity dot the film, which nonetheless received a virtually nonexistent theatrical release.

FLIGHT TO FURY   (1966) B&W ***

D: Monte Hellman. Jack Nicholson, Dewey Martin, Fay Spain, Jacqueline Hellman, Vic Diaz. 76 mins. (CBS/Fox, n.i.d.)

The first collaboration between helmer Hellman and actor/scenarist Nicholson, *Flight to Fury* is an exotic B actioner about a handful of disparate plane-crash survivors who battle Filipino bandits and one another over a cache of stolen jewels. Scripter Nicholson writes a juicy role for himself as a smooth, sardonic scam artist who gloms on to drifter/hero Martin. Hellman and Nicholson reunited for the excellent cult westerns *Ride in the Whirlwind* and *The Shooting* (VCI).

FORCED TO KILL (1993) **½

D: Russell Solberg. Corey Michael Eubanks, Michael Ironside, Rance Howard, Don Swayze, Mickey Jones, Kari Whitman, Clint Howard. 90 mins. (PM)

Professional stunt ace Corey Michael (Son of Bob) Eubanks reunites many of the same personnel—including director Solberg and actors Ironside and Swayze—who worked on his 1990 feature, *Payback* (Republic), and adds Ron Howard's dad and bro', Rance and Clint, respectively, to this mix of *Deliverance, First Blood,* and all manner of modern gladiator movies. The modestly proportioned, generally unglamorous Eubanks cuts a fairly appealing figure as a repo man abducted in the wilds of Arizona by redneck Rance, his throwback sons Swayze and Jones, and corrupt sheriff Ironside, who force him to train for a covert fight tournament. While illogic runs rampant—Eubanks's prowess as a champ kickboxer *and* a deadly sharpshooter *and* an ace driver *and* a deft horseback rider *and* a speedboat racer becomes a bit much—the action is well-staged and the villains sufficiently individualized to make their eventual comeuppance satisfying to witness. In addition to starring and overseeing the multiple stunts, Eubanks also wrote and produced. Tammy S. Eubanks designed the costumes, which consist mostly of Stetsons, jeans, and torn T-shirts.

FORTUNES OF WAR (1993) ***

D: Thierry Notz. Matt Salinger, Sam Jenkins, Haing S. Ngor, Michael Ironside, Michael Nouri, Martin Sheen, Vic Diaz. 107 mins. (Columbia/TriStar)

Director Notz moves up a notch from his Roger Corman roots (*The Terror Within, Watchers 2*) with a well-mounted action drama set in contemporary Cambodia, with the Philippines standing in. Salinger's a disgruntled relief worker who undertakes a dangerous mission to swap medicine for gold with a vicious Cambodian warlord (vet Filipino villain Diaz). Nouri and Sheen contribute Cambodian-jungle cameos as a priest and doctor, respectively.

FOXY BROWN (1974) ***

D: Jack Hill. Pam Grier, Peter Brown, Terry Carter, Antonio Fargas, Sid Haig. 92 mins. (Orion)

Hill's quintessential Grier vehicle covers all the "blaxploitation" bases as Pam's efforts to bail out her lowlife, largely undeserving brother (a typically effective Fargas) lead to her lawman lover Carter's demise. Pam poses as a hooker to get the goods on a gaggle of honky goons headed by one-time TV heartthrob Brown, whose privates end up in a pickle jar. (Ouch.)

THE FRENCH CONNECTION (1971) ***½

D: William Friedkin. Gene Hackman, Roy Scheider, Fernando Rey. 104 mins. (Fox)

Friedkin's *The French Connection* is another groundbreaking genre movie that established the antihero cop as a modern screen icon. Hackman gives a great gritty perf as narc Popeye Doyle (loosely based on real-life cop Eddie Egan, who has a cameo here and went on to appear in several other films), out to crack a Marseilles-based smack ring. The car/El-train race even tops *Bullitt*'s breakneck vehicular chase. *The French Connection II* (Fox), while a slight step down, is also worth catching, as Doyle is forcibly addicted to heroin while stalking his prey in France.

THE FUGITIVE (1993) ***

D: Andrew Davis. Harrison Ford, Tommy Lee Jones, Julianne Moore. 127 mins. (Warner) DVD

Action specialist Davis, abetted by a fine Ford as the wrongly accused Dr. Kimble and Jones as his relentless pursuer, crafts a rare remake that greatly improves upon its early-'60s small-screen model. The teleseries's original 1963 opening episode, "The Fugitive: Premier Episode," is likewise available (Goodtimes), as are several subsequent shows. The 1998 big-screen sequel, *U.S. Marshals* (Warner), wherein a returning Jones chases Wesley Snipes, failed to recapture the magic.

THE FUNERAL (1996) **½

D: Abel Ferrara. Christopher Walken, Annabella Sciorra, Chris Penn, Isabella Rossellini, Vincent Gallo, Benicio Del Toro, Paul Hipp, Patrick McGaw, David Patrick Kelly, Victor Argo. 96 mins. (Evergreen)

This collaboration between director Ferrara and frequent scripter Nicholas St. John (*Body Snatchers, Dangerous Game*) chronicles two days in the lives of a dysfunctional Mafia family in 1930s NYC. While a wake for a gunned-down Gallo is being held at the home of his oldest bro' (Walken), the latter looks to locate the killer. Much of the story unfolds in flashback, where young Gallo's antagonistic behavior angers union mobster Del Toro; another thread traces middle brother Penn's accelerating mental disintegration. Sciorra and Rossellini play Walken and Penn's long-suffering wives, respectively, in what's less a traditional gangster film than a showcase for the idiosyncratic cast's emotive talents. Ferrara followers will want to tune in.

GANG IN BLUE (1996) ***

D: Melvin Van Peebles, Mario Van Peebles. Mario Van Peebles, Josh Brolin, Melvin Van Peebles, Cynda Williams, Stephen Lang, J. T. Walsh. 99 mins. (Evergreen)

The actor/directorial father-son tandem of Melvin and Mario Van Peebles comes up with a more crowd-pleasing variation on Charles Burnett's subtler renegade-racist-LAPD-cops exposé, *The Glass Shield* (see index). Originally aired on Showtime cable, *Gang in Blue* stars an earnest Mario as a black officer who's on to the brutal, institutionalized vigilante tactics of a ring of white fuzz (who call themselves "The Phantoms," also the name of their softball team) covertly led by department head Walsh and enforced in the field by the vile "Moose" (Lang, in a truly malignant turn). Though prominently billed, dad Melvin is relegated to a supporting role as a vet cop who serves as Mario's unofficial mentor. While *Gang in Blue* lacks some of *The Glass Shield*'s texture and shading, it's a solid, gritty, excellently acted urban-action drama with a message that's all too rooted in contemporary reality.

THE GETAWAY (1994) ***

D: Roger Donaldson. Alec Baldwin, Kim Basinger, Michael Madsen, James Woods, Jennifer Tilly, Richard Farnsworth. In R and unrated editions. 115 mins. (Universal) DVD

While not as over-the-top as Peckinpah's exciting original, *The Getaway* (Warner, DVD), Donaldson's often note-for-note replay (original scripter Walter Hill cowrote this version too) is enjoyable in its own right. Baldwin's capable in the Steve McQueen role as a bank robber on the lam, while Basinger's an improvement over Ali McGraw (not the world's most formidable challenge) as his marital partner in crime. Woods has little more than a cameo as the high-rolling heist mastermind who springs Baldwin from a Mexican jail. Even if you love the Peckinpah version, this one's fun as a comparison model.

GETTING EVEN (1986) ***

D: Dwight Little. Edward Albert, Joe Don Baker, Audrey Landers, Caroline Williams, Ron Pilloud. 90 mins. (Vestron, Artisan)

Originally titled *Hostage: Dallas*, *Getting Even* opens with a pitched battle between world superpowers Russia and Texas, as two-fisted biochemical whiz "Tag" Taggar—played with mucho macho panache by former peacenik Edward (*Butterflies Are Free*) Albert—leads his crack commando crew in a lightning raid on a secret Soviet chem-warfare plant. Amid whoops of "Don't mess with Texas!" and "Remember the Alamo!" (where, if memory serves, Lone Star state patriots fought those selfsame Reds a century and a half back), our heroes make off with several canisters of nerve gas capable of melting the flesh right off your face. Back in Dallas, the animosity shifts from the pesky Russkis to homegrown archvillain and rival chemical mogul King Kenderson (deftly overplayed by paunchy B-movie vet Baker). Seems King and his machine-gun-toting minions have copped the lethal canisters from Taggar's redoubt and are threatening to explode them over Dallas. Whether this represents high tragedy doubtless depends on your regional loyalties. What *really* matters is that *Getting Even* is an enjoyably dumb, fast-paced throwback to the pulp serials of yore, packed with kidnappings, torture tableaux, shoot-outs, and high-speed horse, car, and copter chases. No relation to the 1992 Richard Roundtree actioner of the same name (Columbia/TriStar).

THE GHOST AND THE DARKNESS (1996) ***

D: Stephen Hopkins. Val Kilmer, Michael Douglas, John Kani, Tom Wilkinson, Emily Mortimer. 114 mins. (Paramount) DVD

An effective combo of old-fashioned adventure and traditional monster movie based on a true incident, *Ghost* casts Kilmer as an Irish architect commissioned to build a bridge in 1898 Africa. Two voracious, seemingly supernatural lions, the eponymous "the

Ghost" and "the Darkness," begin running up an epic body count among Kilmer's workers, many of whom believe them to be demons sent to stop white men from "stealing the world." When Kilmer and foreman Kani fail to nail the beasts, American big-game hunter Douglas and his hired Masai warriors take the assignment. Ultimately, though, Kilmer, Kani, and Douglas are left to battle the killer cats alone. The flick's only flaw is a lack of texture in William Goldman's script; he would have enhanced the film by digging a bit deeper under the main (as opposed to maned) characters' skins, especially Douglas as the enigmatic hunter. Still, beautifully lensed by ace cinematographer Vilmos Zsigmond and scored by Jerry Goldsmith, *The Ghost and the Darkness* is an admirably earnest account that delivers the promised jungle thrills.

GINGER (1971) **

D: Don Schain. Cheri Caffaro, Cindy Barnett, Herb Kerr. 90 mins. (Monterey)

Hard-core Cheri Caffaro fans will want to see the sleaze special that introduced the blond B-girl to drive-in-goers the nation over. Cheri reprises her tough-gal role in *The Abductors*, *Girls Are for Loving* (both Monterey), *A Place Called Today* (Unicorn, n.i.d.), and *Too Hot to Handle* (Warner). She went on to coscript the 1979 sorority exploitationer *H.O.T.S.* (Artisan), a.k.a. *T&A Academy*.

THE GLIMMER MAN (1996) *1/2

D: John Gray. Steven Seagal, Keenen Ivory Wayans, Bob Gunton, Brian Cox, Michelle Johnson. 92 mins. (Warner) DVD

The Glimmer Man may be a decent second-rate serial-killer/Russian Mafia/government-conspiracy *policier*, but with Seagal blocking the view, it's tough to tell. As a "mystical" ex-agency assassin/LAPD dick clad in loud Nehru jackets and Tibetan prayer beads (!), the Amazing Colossal Jowls performs his usual sadistic-thug chores, reaching new lyrical heights here by surgically slicing a silicon implant from a female corpse's chest (it was to prove a point). Wayans, as Seagal's partner, lends the flick its only shred of likability and shows his emotive range by crying during a *Casablanca* showing.

GOD IS MY WITNESS (1993) ***

D: Mukul S. Anand. Amitabh Bachchan, Sridevi. Subtitled. 180 mins. (Scarecrow)

Part musical, part sweeping romance, part curry western (complete with Ennio Morricone instrumental echoes), *God Is My Witness* delivers big-time bang for the video bucks. Anand's three-hour Indian epic offers plot, characters, and spectacle enough for a dozen domestic flicks: The pic kicks off to a rousing start when a heated *buzkashi* match (a violent polo precursor played with a goat corpse) between rival Afghan clans leads hero Badshah (sonorous matinee idol Bachchan) to tumble hopelessly for sporting foe Benazir (sexy Sridevi). After a supercharged musical number, wherein even sword-waving Afghan warriors make like Rockettes, Badshah hies to India, vowing to return with the head of the lowlife who murdered Benazir's father. (All this unfolds circa 1970, though it could easily be a century earlier.) Story twists eventually land our hero in prison, while Benazir pines from afar. *God's* second half, set 20 years later (in a radically modernized present), drags at the outset as we're introduced to a new generation of characters with complicated interlocking destinies. But we're soon enough thrust into a fresh round of intrigues, battles, and elaborate production numbers (including one that erupts during a shoot-out!) that carry the viewer to an over-the-top finale. Bursts of hysteria, occasionally risible dialogue ("Even angels don't make the sacrifices you have," a suffering Badshah is told), and exploding tear squibs galore add to the fun of this ever intense, unabashedly emotional affair. The percussive music tracks, chastely foxy choreography, and larger-than-life characters make for the type of grand-scale escapist entertainment you rarely see stateside.

THE GODFATHER: THE SERIES

THE GODFATHER (1972) ****

D: Francis Ford Coppola. Marlon Brando, Al Pacino, Diane Keaton, Robert Duvall. 175 mins. (Paramount)

Marlon mumbles to perfection as Mafia mogul Don Corleone. Coppola's multigenerational crime saga rates high among the top American movies ever made.

THE GODFATHER, PART II (1974) ****

D: Francis Ford Coppola. Al Pacino, Robert De Niro, Diane Keaton, Robert Duvall. 201 mins. (Paramount)

Coppola's tricky prequel-and-sequel combo manages to be as brilliant as the original, with top work turned in by Pacino, De Niro (as the young Don Corleone) and an ace ensemble cast.

THE GODFATHER, PART III (1990) **1/2

D: Francis Ford Coppola. Al Pacino, Diane Keaton, Talia Shire, Eli Wallach, Joe Mantegna, Bridget Fonda, Andy Garcia, Sofia Coppola. 161 mins. (Paramount)

Much of the Mafia-movie magic is missing in Coppola's unnecessary sequel, but the pic remains a must for *Godfather* completists. Daughter Sofia is all profile and no charisma as the token ingenue, while dad Francis Ford borrows the film's best ideas from Hitchcock's original 1934 *The Man Who Knew Too Much*—to say nothing of T. S. Eliot's *Murder in the Cathedral* and the famous framing device from Orson Welles's *Citizen Kane* (albeit with a tomato substitute). Pacino cops the best lines: "This pope has powerful enemies. We may not have time to save him. Let's get back to the opera." All three films are now offered in remastered, letterboxed special editions, individually or as a complete set. *The Godfather: The Complete Saga* (Paramount), Coppola's chronologically reedited combination of Parts 1 and 2, shown on network television, is no longer in distribution and has become a video rarity.

GOODFELLAS (1990) ****

D: Martin Scorsese. Ray Liotta, Robert De Niro, Joe Pesci, Lorraine Bracco, Paul Sorvino. 146 mins. (Warner) DVD

Scorsese's masterful direction propels this brilliant realization of the criminal misadventures of small-time Mafia hood Henry Hill (given a lively interpretation by the always galvanizing Liotta). Pesci especially shines as a hit man who loves his work, while De Niro, Bracco, Sorvino, and a sharp ensemble cast lend able support. *GoodFellas* is the best gangster flick to surface since Brian De Palma's *Scarface* (see index).

THE GREAT ESCAPE (1963) ***1/2

D: John Sturges. Steve McQueen, James Garner, Richard Attenborough. 173 mins. (MGM/UA) DVD

Sturges's expertly executed prisoner-of-war epic proceeds without a single static stretch in its nearly three-hour running time and features topnotch work by a terrific ensemble cast headed by a cycle-riding McQueen. Followed 25 years later by the not-so-great TV miniseries *The Great Escape 2: The*

Untold Story, reduced to feature length for its video release (via Trimark).

GUN MOLL (1949) B&W ***

D: Fletcher Markle. Franchot Tone, Jean Lawrence, Myron McCormick. 79 mins. (Sinister Cinema)

While it may seem mild now, *Gun Moll* (a.k.a. *Jigsaw*) was considered bold, in its anti-Commie day, for its story line about exposing a right-wing organization. The pic includes uncredited cameos by such liberal-minded stars as John Garfield, Henry Fonda, Marlene Dietrich, and Burgess Meredith—a pretty impressive list for a B flick.

GUNCRAZY (1992) ***

D: Tamra Davis. Drew Barrymore, James LeGros, Billy Drago, Michael Ironside, Joe Dallesandro, Ione Skye. 97 mins. (Academy/Maverick) DVD

While not quite up to speed with its two-word 1949 namesake, *Gun Crazy* (20th Century Fox), or Terrence Malick's similarly plotted *Badlands* (see index), Davis's Matthew Bright–scripted doomed-couple exercise—which premiered on cable before landing a limited theatrical run prior to its video release—has enough atmosphere and crisp thesping to qualify as a quality item. The pic's main problem is that its trigger-happy protagonists—naïve teen slut Barrymore and impotent ex-con LeGros—are so painfully braindead that it's hard to get behind them. Drago is cast in a rare nonvillainous role as a local snake-handling preacher/mechanic, while Ironside plays LeGros's unsympathetic parole officer and onetime Warhol "superstar" Dallesandro convinces as Drew's absent mother's sleazy boyfriend and our heroine's first (and most deserving) victim. (J.D.'s dead body sports some pretty vivid makeup FX for a nonhorror

film.) Some trademark Drew nudity and several inspired lines also help, as when Drew tenderly coos to LeGros, "I remember you wrote in your letter nine-millimeters were your favorites."

GUNS (1990) ***

D: Andy Sidaris. Erik Estrada, Dona Speir, Roberta Vasquez, Bruce Penhall, Cynthia Brimhall, Rodrigo Obregón, William Bumiller, Phyllis Davis, Chuck McCann. 95 mins. (Columbia/TriStar)

Writer/director Andy and producer Arlene Sidaris bottle another brew of top-heavy bimbos, two-fisted hunks, low-camp hijinks, and, as the succinct title implies, wild shootouts aplenty. Estrada turns in strong work as a high-strung international gunrunner ("Looks like my focus will be clouded—and I hate that!") who hires a pair of transvestite (!) hit men (Richard Cansino, Chu Chu Malave) to eliminate troublesome Molokai-based femme federal agents Speir and Vasquez. The botched assassination attempt leads to a filmlong series of fast-paced chases and violent confrontations between the opposing forces. As in other Sidaris outings, the James Bond–ian gadgetry and colorful location lensing (in this case, Las Vegas and Hawaii) endow the film with a cinematic sweep that belies its modest budget. *Guns* is also the A&A Team's funniest flick. Especially amusing are the "team meetings" held by the good guys and gals, whose collective IQ would appear to approach room temp only in deep winter. Obregón sheds his usual macho-menace image to don a drag costume as undercover agent "Large Marge."

HAND GUN (1994) ***

D: Whitney Ransick. Treat Williams, Seymour Cassel, Paul Schulze, Anna Thomsen, Frank Vincent, Michael Imperioli. 90 mins. (Triboro) DVD

Despite its obvious Tarantino overtones, debuting writer/director Ransick's *Hand Gun* is a neat, adroitly scripted actioner with an almost biblical story line that successfully blends black comedy with sudden violence against a grim back-alley Brooklyn backdrop. When career crook Cassel makes off with a half mil in cash after a heist, his whereabouts become a source of concern for corrupt cops, Brooklyn hoods led by sturdy character thesp Vincent (best known as the ill-fated inhabitant of Joe Pesci's trunk in *GoodFellas*), and Cassel's own professional lowlife son, Williams. Williams, in turn, enlists the aid of his comparatively straight younger bro' Schulze, who ekes out a shady living peddling bogus cemetery plots to gullible senior cits. Ransick's inventive take on dysfunctional-family values reaches its zenith in a scene that briefly reunites the fractious siblings with their less-than-loving dad. *Hand Gun* is an especially bright showcase for Schulze, who earlier impressed as an unhinged petty crook in Nick Gomez's *Laws of Gravity* (see index) and gained later exposure as *The Sopranos*' Father Phil.

HANGFIRE (1991) **½

D: Peter Maris. Brad Davis, Kim Delaney, Lee de Broux, Jan-Michael Vincent, Ken Foree, George Kennedy, Yaphet Kotto, Lou Ferrigno, Lyle Alzado. 89 mins. (Columbia/TriStar)

Despite a desperate original ad campaign flaunting the name of Saddam Hussein (!), *Hangfire* is about as far from Iraq as New Mexico—where, in fact, the film actually unfolds. Boasting a cast that represents a veritable B-movie who's who, *Hangfire* (the title refers to a delayed weapons discharge) stars the late Davis as a New Mexico lawman newly married to comely Delaney. The ever popular George Kennedy cameos as a warden at a nearby prison who's forced to evacuate his dangerous charges under the threat of an approaching toxic-gas cloud. Davis soon sees his normally somnolent town invaded by a busload of cons who've used the emergency to bust out. Among the escapees are the late former footballer Alzado and ex–*Incredible Hulk* Ferrigno (both of whom turn in fine knuckle-walking performances), while the good guys include Davis's buddy Foree and state trooper Kotto. The pic slows considerably in its second half when Davis and Foree (who take starry-eyed male bonding beyond even the Danny Glover/Mel Gibson *Lethal Weapon* level) resort to retro *Rambo* tactics to save the day. Still, *Hangfire* offers enough explosive action to make it worth a look.

HARD-BOILED (1992)****

D: John Woo. Chow Yun-Fat, Tony Leung, Teresa Mo, Philip Chan, Philip Kwok. Subtitled/dubbed. 127 mins. (Fox Lorber) DVD

Hong Kong action mainstay Yun-Fat stars as "Tequila," a trigger-happy cop on the trail of two warring arms-smuggling gangs. As in Woo's *The Killer,* Yun-Fat spends much of his screen time bonding and blasting away with a newfound comrade-in-arms, elusive undercover agent Leung, while a subplot details Chow's efforts to reunite with disaffected squeeze Mo. *Hard-Boiled* saves its best shots for the balletic battle sequences, culminating in a hospital-set siege that takes the genre about as far as it can go. Gangsters, police, hospital workers, and patients all contribute to a mounting body count, while Yun-Fat and Mo try to rescue dozens of maternity-ward babies. Yun-Fat even receives an unexpected assist from an infant he dubs "Sammy Saliva," who conveniently wets just when his adult benefactor's pants catch fire (!). An exciting jazz fusion score helps fuel the action, while, in one offbeat scene, the decoded melody to "Mona Lisa"

supplies our heroes with an important clue. Woo uses his entire arsenal of cinematic tricks, from wipes to slo mo, to yield the max from each of his action segments.

HARD HUNTED (1992)**

D: Andy Sidaris. Dona Speir, Roberta Vasquez, Tony Peck, R. J. Moore, Michael Shane, Rodrigo Obregón. 97 mins. (Columbia/TriStar)

Writer/director Andy and producer Arlene Sidaris steer foxy feds Donna (Speir) and Nicole (Vasquez) through another high-energy, low-alpha-wave adventure, one of the few films to have its world premiere in happening Lake Havesu, Arizona. This time around, the pair run afoul of criminal mastermind R. J. (Son of Roger) Moore, who's nicked a nuclear trigger for potential sale to the highest bidder. As always, the Sidarises milk the max from their primo location lensing, from Hawaii's lush tropical scenery to Arizona's striking desert terrain. Vet villain Obregón trades in the drag wear he donned in *Guns* for a simple but effective eye patch here. Among our top-heavy heroines, Speir scores best, especially during a bout with amnesia that leaves her clueless re her own identity but fully capable of dismantling and reassembling complex automatic weaponry (!).

HARD RAIN (1998)**1/2

D: Mikael Salomon. Morgan Freeman, Christian Slater, Randy Quaid, Minnie Driver, Ed Asner, Richard Dysart, Betty White. 96 mins. (Paramount) DVD

A name cast lends its considerable talents to a gimmicky actioner that drowned at the box office but bobs to the cassette surface as reasonably entertaining home-vid fare. Director Salomon and scripter Graham (*Speed, Broken Arrow*) Yost's wet and wild

premise sees a criminal quartet commanded by an overqualified Freeman (lending beyond-the-call dignity to his improbable role) pull off a daring armored-car heist during a driving rainstorm that results in serious flood conditions. Reluctant guard Slater (who also coproduced) floats off with the loot, with Freeman and fellows in soggy pursuit. Our hero finds dubious shelter with the evacuated small town's sheriff (a cranky Quaid) but ultimately receives more reliable assistance from architect Driver, who's stayed behind to protect the vintage church she's spent nearly a year restoring. Multiple conflicts, betrayals, and action set pieces ensue, with the game thesps literally up to their necks (and frequently beyond) in rising water, leading to some original, often risible, and always supersoluble situations. Much of the most spectacular destruction comes at the expense of Minnie's church—a stained-glass Jesus panel flies directly at the camera in one imaginative, if eye-blink, highlight—prompting yours truly to wonder whether the filmmakers were making a point: like how aggressive trash movies like this gleefully trample all in their way—the more beautiful, venerable, and vulnerable, the better. On the other hand, probably not.

HARD TARGET (1993)***

D: John Woo. Jean-Claude Van Damme, Yancy Butler, Lance Henriksen, Arnold Vosloo, Kasi Lemmons, Wilford Brimley, Chuck Pfarrar. 97 mins. (Universal) DVD

While *Hard Target* may be toned-down Woo, it's a giant step up for Jean-Claude on the heels of his tepid *Shane* update, *Nowhere to Run* (see index). (The action-savvy crowd at the bijou matinee The Phantom originally attended cheered when Woo's name flashed on-screen, then booed when Van Damme's came up!) Not that *HT*'s plot is exactly fresh. The pic's hoary story line gives us yet another *Most Dangerous Game* reworking and at least the second one set in New Orleans (see also *Avenging Force*). Henriksen and Vosloo play itinerant entrepreneurs who charge rich sleazeballs upward of a half mil to hunt human prey shanghaied from the Big Easy's homeless ranks. After heroine Butler's screen dad (scripter Pfarrar) falls fatal victim to the violent scam, she enlists unemployed seaman Van Damme to help her nail the perps. No sequence in *Hard Target*—which underwent multiple MPAA cuts as well as voluntary reediting prior to release—matches the madcap gun-fu displays found in Woo's Hong Kong faves *The Killer* or *Hard-Boiled*. But *Hard Target* still blows away most of the homegrown competition, especially during a lengthy climactic shoot-out that unfolds amid outsized Mardi Gras props. Terrif cycle stunts and evocative bayou ambience supply further pluses.

HARD TICKET TO HAWAII (1987) **1/2

D: Andy Sidaris. Ronn Moss, Dona Speir, Hope Marie Carlton, Harold Diamond, Rodrigo Obregón, Cynthia Brimhall. (Lorimar, n.i.d.)

Jiggle-action auteurs Andy and Arlene Sidaris chronicle the glamorous, amorous adventures of hunky hero Rowdy Abilene, screen cousin to Travis Abilene of *Malibu Express* (Universal). Here Rowdy (Moss) and chopsocky sidekick Jade (Diamond) take a backseat to fighting femmes Speir and Carlton, who tangle with your typical vicious drug ring on the sunny isle of Molokai, Hawaii. The result is a reasonably lively mix of exotic scenery, erotic escapades, sinister plot twists, and mucho distaff skin that owes as much to Russ Meyer as it does to James Bond. The Sidarises also toss in sumo wrestlers, transvestite spies, and—in an inspired subplot—an escaped giant snake "infected with

deadly toxins from cancer-infested rats." The pic's best moment plays off Rowdy's woeful lack of gun prowess: After running down a would-be skateboard assassin with his jeep, Rowdy completes the job by blasting the bad guy with a bazooka at point-blank range. Explains our hero, "It's the only gun I can hit a moving target with."

HARD TO KILL   (1990) **

D: Bruce Malmuth. Steven Seagal, Kelly LeBrock, Bill Sadler, Frederick Coffin, Bonnie Burroughs, Branscombe Richmond. 95 mins. (Warner) DVD

It's spring 1983, and all L.A. surveillance supercop Mason Storm (Seagal) wants to do is get the audiovisual goods on a gang of hired assassins and return home in time to catch the end of the Academy Awards. Instead, he's shadowed by said assassins, who invade his house, waste his wife and son, and pump enough lead into our hero to put him in what appears to be a terminal coma. (All this only moments before Ben Kingsley cops his *Gandhi* Oscar!) Steve awakes after seven years of brain death (his California tan miraculously intact), hides out from his instantly alerted enemies with the help of sympathetic nurse (and then—real-life wife) LeBrock, and initiates an Asian self-healing regimen involving acupuncture, jogging, and kung fu. Soon Steve is ready to embark on an all-out revenge rampage against a cabal of bad guys who include a 1992 VP hopeful, several corrupt cops, and a horde of sadistic hired henchmen, none of whom (natch) prove a match for our reawakened warrior. Though a revived Steve, reunited with his former partner (Coffin), assures the latter, "We'll win because of our superior state of mind," the fact is *Hard to Kill* remains as brain-dead as our "Coma Cop" (as the on-screen media dubs him). We were also forced to question Steve's

worthiness as a role model for younger viewers after he left one of his intended targets a death threat reading, "Your [*sic*] next."

HEART OF DRAGON (1985) ***

D: Sammo Hung. Jackie Chan, Sammo Hung, Mang Hoi, Wu Ma. Subtitled. 90 mins. (Tai Seng) DVD

Jackie exhibits his sensitive side: While extended action tableaux frame the film, most of the story details Hong Kong cop Chan's relationship with his childlike, mentally retarded older brother (a versatile Hung, who also directs). Jackie demonstrates an impressive dramatic range in an oft touching tale that still works in its share of comic scenes.

HEAT   (1995) ***1/2

D: Michael Mann. Robert De Niro, Al Pacino, Val Kilmer, Tom Sizemore, Ashley Judd, Jon Voight, Amy Brenneman. 171 mins. (MGM) DVD

Miami Vice creator Michael (*Thief, Manhunter*) Mann enhances his well-earned rep as Hollywood's most stylish and character-driven crime-movie specialist with this gala account of two dueling obsessives, career criminal De Niro and LAPD detective Pacino. On-screen, the two share only a pair of scenes, but one, set in a diner, gives both thesps a chance to shine. Subplots dealing with Pacino's strained relationship with his neglected wife and suicidal daughter and middle-aged De Niro's unlikely romance with wholesome young bookstore clerk Brenneman prove less compelling than the crime elements, which include several tense capers and a lengthy alfresco shoot-out that verges on John Woo–styled overkill. Mann's large, capable cast, striking cinematography, and abiding respect for traditional story values make *Heat* a great A genre outing.

HELLHOLE   (1985) *½

D: Pierre de Moro. Judy Landers, Ray Sharkey, Mary Woronov, Marjoe Gortner, Edy Williams, Terry Moore. 95 mins. (Columbia/TriStar)

It's apparent from the outset that all is not well at Ashland's all-femme sanitarium: Dr. Dane (Marjoe) is in the basement mixing up his new chemical-lobotomy formula. Lesbian-necrophiliac hospital head Dr. Fletcher (Woronov) keeps the doc's hopelessly deranged "rejects" caged under the boiler room, the hellhole of the title. A greasy mad strangler named Silk (hammily portrayed by the late Sharkey) infiltrates the asylum by posing as a leering, gutter-mouthed aide. As Silk's intended prey, large-breasted amnesia victim Landers, perceptively remarks, "This is crazy!" Crazy, yes; fun, no. Despite the pic's perverse premise (further abetted by sandbox catfights, a lesbian shower-room brawl, and mudbaths designed to "cure nymphomania"), *Hellhole* won't give Sam Fuller's *Shock Corridor* (see index) any sleepless nights.

HEROES STAND ALONE   (1989) **½

D: Mark Griffiths. Chad Everett, Bradford Dillman, Wayne Grace, Rick Dean, Michael Chieffo, Elsa Olivero. 83 mins. (MGM/UA)

Heroes Stand Alone rates as a tense, actionful entry in the traditional-western-as-contempo-war-movie genre. Onetime TV heartthrob Everett stars as the leathery leader of a covert military squad sent into the Central American bush to retrieve a potentially incriminating black box containing data from an unauthorized (and since massacred) U.S. spy mission. Also in on the hunt is Chad's opposite number, a USSR military advisor (played by American Grace, who frequently misplaces his Russki accent) and his Cuban minions. The rival bands' jungle cat-and-mouse tactics consume most of the movie's lean running time.

THE HEROIC TRIO   (1993) ***

D: Ching Siu Tung, Johnny To. Michelle Yeoh, Maggie Cheung, Anita Mui. Subtitled/dubbed. 87 mins. (Tai Seng) DVD

Hong Kong superstars Yeoh, Cheung, and Mui play superheroines out to stop a series of supernatural kidnappings in a swift, surreal adventure that rates as super viewing for Hong Kong action/fantasy fans.

HIDDEN ASSASSIN   (A.K.A. *THE SHOOTER*) (1995) ***

D: Ted Kotcheff. Dolph Lundgren, Maruschka Detmers, Assumpta Serna, John Ashton, Gavan O'Herlihy. 87 mins. (Buena Vista)

Dolph Does Prague in this better-than-average Lundgren vehicle filmed on location by vet director Ted (*First Blood*) Kotcheff. Here the big guy's a U.S. marshal who, with CIA partner Ashton, is looking to bag suspected political assassin Maruschka D. Soon enough, Dolph finds himself trapped in a web of multiple betrayals, leading to twisty pursuits and shootouts galore. While our hero remains resolutely expressionless throughout—despite losing quarts of blood via a variety of stab wounds—Dolph and Maruschka's developing relationship supplies some unexpected texture.

HIGH VOLTAGE   (1997) **

D: Isaac Florentine. Antonio Sabato, Jr., Shannon Lee, William Zabka, Lochlyn Monro, Mike Manis, George Kee Cheung, Amy Smart, Veralyn Venezio, Antonio Sabato, James Lew. 92 mins. (A-Pix) DVD

"Hyperkinetic John Woo Action!" So boasts the box copy for *High Voltage*, which also features an imitation Ennio Morricone Meets *Pulp Fiction* soundtrack, along with garish neon lighting, copious gun fetishism, meaningless twists and betrayals, and other requisites of your basic bad "edgy" contempo road noir. Hunky desperado Sabato (late of Kirk Wong's largely lame *The Big Hit* [Columbia/TriStar]) leads a crew of "hard-boiled" criminals (played by hopelessly white-bread young thesps, including tin-eared scripter Manis) on a heist that sees them unwittingly rob a bank that secretly specializes in laundering drug money for inordinately mean Vietnamese Mafia honcho Cheung. In one lachrymose sequence, blond gangsterette Shannon (daughter of the late Bruce, sister of the late Brandon) Lee marries a corpse (!). *High Voltage* barrels along with an energetic ineptitude and eagerness to please that border on innocence and might tickle the fancy of half-dozing late-night viewers.

THE HIT LIST   (1993) ***

D: William Webb. Jeff Fahey, Yancy Butler, James Coburn, Michael Beach, Randy Oglesby, Jeff Kober. 97 mins. (Columbia/TriStar)

After directing a number of low-budget clunkers—e.g., *Sunset Strip* (Vestron), the Leif Garrett psychofest *Party Line* (Sony), and the somewhat better serial-killer caper *The Banker* (see index)—Webb comes up with a winner with *The Hit List*. Professional assassin Fahey finds himself a fairly ignorant player at the center of an involved plot that begins when he accepts an assignment, arranged by power lawyer Coburn, to protect rich widow Yancy (*Hard Target*) Butler. By wisely unraveling the tale from Fahey's POV, Webb and scripter Reed Steiner keep the viewer in the dark but fully engrossed. An unpredictable, ultimately downbeat caper—a wounded Fahey conveys physical agony in a way rarely seen on-screen—lensed in bright California colors, *The Hit List* stays on target, while the final image offers an apt metaphor for eros in the '90s. No relation to the 1989 William Lustig actioner *Hit List* (Columbia/TriStar), with Jan-Michael Vincent, Rip Torn, and Lance Henriksen as a kinky shoe salesman/hired killer.

HONG KONG '97   (1994) *½

D: Albert Pyun. Robert Patrick, Ming-Na Wen, Brion James, Tim Thomerson, Andrew Divoff. 91 mins. (Trimark)

The ever prolific Pyun attempts to go the two-gun John Woo route but comes up empty-handed, with results more woeful than Wooful. Pyun selects a promising time and place—Hong Kong on the eve of the colony's 1997 annexation by mainland China—and proceeds to waste them on a routine action plot. Perennial screen thug James supplies a hammy turn as Patrick's Brit-accented (!) mentor, while villain Divoff speaks with an inflection floating somewhere between Russian and German. On the upside, most of the dialogue is unintelligible, prompting one character to remark, with doubtless unintended irony, "That's easier said than done." Authentic locales, including a detour to HK's famed floating "Jumbo" cathouse/casino, and flashes of distaff nudity provide fleeting visual distraction but not nearly enough to make Hong Kong '97 worth the yen of an overnight rental.

HONOR AND GLORY   (1993) *½

D: Godfrey Hall. Cynthia Rothrock, Donna Jason, Chuck Jeffreys, Gerald Klein, Robin Shou, Richard Yuen. 90 mins. (Imperial)

Cynthia plays second ninchucks to screen sibling Jason, a TV reporter out to expose corporate creep Klein, a muscled, untalented Maxwell Caulfield clone who's so mean he rejects a prayer breakfast with ex-President Reagan ("To hell with the old bastard"). *Honor and Glory* kicks off on a promising high-camp note but, plagued by poor thesping and unexciting fight scenes, quickly sinks into mere incompetence. Even Rothrock addicts will be disappointed by the petite pugilist's comparatively scant screen time.

HOODLUM   (1997) ***

D: Bill Duke. Laurence Fishburne, Tim Roth, Vanessa L. Williams, Andy Garcia, Cicely Tyson, Chi McBride, Clarence Williams III, Richard Bradford, William Atherton, Queen Latifah, Beau Starr, Mike Starr. 130 mins. (MGM) DVD

Violent action, strong perfs, and a colorful period canvas combine to overcome the gangster clichés in Duke's highly fictionalized chronicle of 1930s crime boss Bumpy Johnson's efforts to prevent white mobsters from muscling in on Harlem's lucrative numbers racket. Fishburne stars as Johnson (a role he'd earlier played in Coppola's *The Cotton Club*), a newly sprung con who volunteers his services when Dutch Schultz (a sneering Roth) threatens to dethrone numbers czarina Madame Queen (Tyson). Most of the film depicts a running power struggle between the rival racketeers, with time out for Johnson's bumpy romance with typical "good girl" Williams, while a parallel thread examines the attempts of Lucky Luciano (Garcia) to mediate the dispute and the latter's behind-the-scenes dealings with ambitious D.A. Thomas Dewey (Atherton). Among the assembled players, Clarence Williams (*Deep Cover*) adds another charismatic turn to his résumé as Bob Hewlett, a black enforcer in the white hoods' employ, Chi (*The Frighteners*) McBride brings nuance to his role as Fishburne's best bud, and real-life brothers Beau and Mike Starr contribute idiosyncratic work as a pair of sibling assassins. Veteran composer Elmer Bernstein's lush, old-fashioned score adds a stately note.

HORSEMAN ON THE ROOF (1995) ***

D: Jean-Paul Rappenneu. Juliette Binoche, Olivier Martinez, Pierre Arditi, Francoise Cluzet, Jean Yeanne, Gerard Depardieu. 132 mins. (Buena Vista)

Drawn from Jean Giono's 1951 novel, this entertainingly old-fashioned period adventure chronicles young Italo cavalry officer Martinez's toxic travels through a cholera-infected 1832 Europe as he seeks to return home after a self-exile in France. Trailed by relentless Austrian assassins and met with obstacles at every turn, Martinez hooks up with a dedicated but doomed country doctor, an abandoned cat (the feline thesp gets snubbed in the closing-credit crawl), and, ultimately, with beautiful, mysterious noblewoman Binoche, who's likewise looking for a way back home. The growing but long-unacknowledged attraction between the courtly and extremely fortunate Martinez ("Cholera avoids me like the plague," he quips) and enterprising Binoche and their peripatetic odyssey comprise the bulk of Rappenneau's sweeping, handsomely photographed epic. Depardieu contributes a cameo as a rattled police chief in a cholera-crazed village.

HOSTAGE (1987) **

D: Hanro Mohr. Wings Hauser, Karen Black, Kevin McCarthy, Nancy Locke. 94 mins. (Columbia/TriStar)

It's *Delta Force* Revisited as an African airliner carrying an international cast is skyjacked by the usual band of scurvy Arab cutthroats. In a move befitting his name, Wings hang-glides to the rescue of the downed plane and its steadily diminishing passenger list. Karen Black impresses as a soft-core smut starlet and scores the best line ("I'm tired, tired, *tired* of being a stupid sex symbol!"). Joey Bishop and Shelley Winters, we're sorry to report, apparently missed this flight. Back on terra firma, the similar 1997 *Hostage Train* (Republic), with Judge Reinhold and Carol Alt, is also worth avoiding.

THE HOT BOX (1972) ***

D: Joe Viola. Margaret Markov, Andrea Cagan, Charles Dierkop. 89 mins. (Embassy, n.i.d.)

Coscripted by Jonathan (*Philadelphia*, *The Silence of the Lambs*) Demme during his Roger Corman apprenticeship, this action-filled entry sees a quartet of distaff Peace Corps nurses turn jungle revolutionaries after being abused by Marcos's goons. Never screened at Imelda's Manila Film Fest.

HUDSON HAWK (1991) *

D: Michael Lehman. Bruce Willis, Andie McDowell, Danny Aiello, James Coburn, Sandra Bernhard. 95 mins. (Columbia/TriStar) DVD

Bernhard, as loudmouthed, super-rich villainess Minerva Mayflower, delivers the key line when she insists, "This is supposed to be torture, not therapy." Actually, this much-maligned vanity movie doesn't get truly grotty until its second reel, following a few merely mediocre setup scenes establishing Bruce as a newly freed cat burglar coerced by a local Mafioso (Sly's talented bro' Frank Stallone) into committing a Da Vinci–related heist. The flick degenerates in earnest when McDowell, as a nun working undercover for the Vatican (!), and CIA agent Coburn (in what may be the worst perf of his long career) join the would-be farcical fray. By the time Bruce enjoys a simulated quasi-erotic encounter with a dog named Bunny (!), all hope has long been abandoned. As for Bruce, all we can say is next time you feel the urge to "express" yourself, use the men's room, not the audience.

THE HUNTED (1995) **½

D: J. F. Lawton. Christopher Lambert, Joan Chen, John Lone, Yoshio Harada, Yoko Shimada. 111 mins. (Universal) DVD

Better known as a comic scenarist—his previous scripts include *Blankman* (Columbia/TriStar), *Cannibal Women in the Avocado Jungle of Death* (see index), *Pizza Man* (Monarch), with future *Politically Incorrect* host Bill Maher, the unexpected B.O. biggie *Pretty Woman* (Touchstone), and the Steven Seagal vehicle *Under Siege* (see index)—Lawton takes the directorial reins for this self-scripted, critically lambasted Lambert outing. Lawton's tongue-in-cheek ninja romp kicks off in high gear. *Gaijin* businessman Lambert (who delivers his lines in a Vincent Price whisper throughout) meets and mates with a mysterious Chen—with time out for a gratuitous visit to a kodo drums show (the pic's percussive soundtrack is a plus)—then witnesses her decapitation at the sword of mythical ninja assassin Lone. Our hero survives the encounter but soon finds himself relentlessly pursued by Lone's impatient minions. Up to this point, Lawton has a wonderfully giddy pulp fantasy going. Unfortunately, his flick totally collapses once Lambert lands on Harada's ninja island; the plot stops cold for entire aimless reels until Lone and cronies invade the site for an indifferently choreographed climactic showdown. Among the first half's inspired moments is a scene in which, to avoid violating the ninja code of being recognized, a defeated villainess shears her own face off (!). Though *The Hunted* eventually collapses into sheer cinematic rubble, the early reels offer enough rewards to make it worth a look.

I SPIT ON YOUR GRAVE (1978) **

D: Meir Zarchi. Camille Keaton, Eron Tabor, Richard Pace. 102 mins. (VidAmerica, Anchor Bay) DVD

Rape victim Keaton kills a quartet of attackers in sundry unpleasant ways in this illogical, ugly, vile, and highly popular action/exploitation staple, originally titled *Day of the Woman*. Anchor Bay has the definitive "special edition." The similarly themed *I Want to Get Even* (Lorimar) and *Naked Vengeance* (Lightning) are also out there, while director Zarchi strikes again with 1985's *Don't Mess with My Sister!* (VidAmerica). No relation to the 1963 French civil-rights thriller *I*

Spit on Your Grave (Audubon) or Al Adamson's Georgina Spelvin showcase *I Spit on Your Corpse* (Super).

ILLTOWN (1996) **1/2

D: Nick Gomez. Michael Rapaport, Lili Taylor, Adam Trese, Kevin Corrigan, Angela Featherstone, Tony Danza, Isaac Hayes, Paul Schulze, Saul Stein. 101 mins. (Artisan)

NYC native Nick Gomez, who brought us the intense urban anomic-youth capers *Laws of Gravity* and *New Jersey Drive* (see index), adopts a dreamier approach with this Lake Worth, Florida–set drug drama. Rapaport and Taylor topline as a smack-dealing couple who harbor oddly mainstream desires (like starting a family and playing golf). Trouble intrudes in the form of ex-partner Trese, whom the couple had ratted out to the fuzz a few years back, who assembles a crew of amoral teenage enforcers to kill and maim the pair's street sales force. As in Gomez's earlier films, the ensemble acting is excellent throughout and is further bolstered here by sitcom grad Danza, as a local dope kingpin with a jones for gardening, and Hayes as an honest cop. Unlike the urgent *Laws* and *Drive*, *Illtown* floats along in the celluloid equivalent of a heroin haze, one populated by emotionally deadened characters, severely distancing the viewer from the on-screen action. Still, Gomez devotees should find *Illtown* worth a video visit.

IN THE LINE OF FIRE (1993) ***

D: Wolfgang Petersen. Clint Eastwood, John Malkovich, Rene Russo, Dylan McDermott, Gary Cole, John Mahoney. 127 mins. (Columbia/TriStar) DVD

Secret Service vet Clint, still smarting from his decades-old failure to prevent JFK's rubout, engages in a filmlong battle of wits with multiguised psycho

Malkovich, who broadcasts his intent to off the current prez. The film's at its best when illustrating Eastwood's personal war with the ravages of advancing age, particularly during a foreplay-interruptus seduction scene with femme agent Russo. Petersen assembles this lavish thriller with such care that he nearly obscures the fact that *Fire* breaks nary a centimeter of new ground.

INCIDENT AT BLOOD PASS (1970) ***1/2

D: Hiroshi Inagaki. Toshirô Mifune, Shintaro Katsu, Nakamura Kinnosuke. Subtitled. 118 mins. (AnimEigo)

Mifune's legendary Yojimbo character puts in his final film appearance as a samurai for hire assigned, by a doctor portrayed by fellow Samurai Cinema mainstay Katsu (*The Razor, Zatoichi*), to hijack a shogunate convoy at a remote, snowy outpost. Much of the film dramatizes the multiple relationships and intrigues that play out among a disparate group of characters holed up at an otherwise abandoned inn. Plots and counterplots (to say nothing of bodies) mount as Yojimbo awaits his final confrontation. Combining the best of the samurai genre with Sergio Leone–style spaghetti-western moves (two cultures and genres that enjoyed a mutually beneficial cinematic cross-pollination at the time), *Incident at Blood Pass* rates as a must for action aficionados of all stripes.

AN INNOCENT MAN (1989) ***

D: Peter Yates. Tom Selleck, F. Murray Abraham, Laila Robins, David Rasche, Richard Young, Todd Graff. 113 mins. (Touchstone)

Tom proves he's no glamour boy or shower toy in this entertaining throwback to the men-in-manacles movies of yore. Framed by slick corrupt

dicks, virtuous Tom gets through prison life on the strength of his own guts and guile, plus a lot of help from his pen pal (Abraham). A mainstream movie with a B-flick soul, *An Innocent Man* is much better than Sly's males-in-jail effort *Lock-Up*, though a notch below Van Damme's intense *Death Warrant* (see index).

INTENT TO KILL (1993) **1/2

D: Charles Kanganis. Traci Lords, Yaphet Kotto, Angelo Tiffe, Scott Patterson, Michael Foley, Sam Travolta. NC-17 and unrated editions. 93 mins. (PM)

Cop Traci works undercover as a street hooker in a bid to bag *Scarface*-inspired Colombian drug honcho Tiffe while simultaneously trying to iron out her interpersonal kinks with fellow fuzz and live-in lover Patterson. Foley, late of the immortal *Divine Enforcer* (see index), plays a sympathetic, kick-boxing detective; the ever reliable Kotto lends support as Traci's harried boss. *Intent* delivers plenty of slick action and a high body count further raised by a *Terminator*-like police massacre that's executed a tad *too* easily (bulletproof vests are not popular at this precinct). Traci manages to hold her own and kick butt with aplomb, though she's oddly modest in the skin department, doubtless in an ongoing effort to erase all traces of her erstwhile porn-starlet image. The NC-17 version features more violence.

INVASION U.S.A. (1985) *

D: Joseph Zito. Chuck Norris, Richard Lynch, Melissa Prophet, Alexander Zale, Alex Colon, Eddie Jones, Dehl Berti. 108 mins. (MGM)

Americans have grown "soft," so Red hordes invade Miami (where were Crockett and Tubbs?) and have their heartless way with us. And don't miss it, brother: These Commies are *mean*. How mean are they? They're so mean, they crush a color TV set smack in the middle of a Merv Griffin/Phyllis Diller tête-à-tête! Then they blow up the Miami 'burbs on Christmas Day! Then they try to explode a school bus full of kids singing "Row, Row, Row Your Boat" (the kids, not the Commies)! Finally, they make their biggest mistake of all—they wreck the Everglades shack of ex-CIA agent Matt Hunter (Norris) and shoot his beloved old Native American pal John Eagle (Berti). So Chuck packs a pair of machine pistols, leaves his pet armadillo (!) behind, and hops aboard his airboat, hell-bent on going toe-to-toe with the Russkis. While never losing his cool (Chuck's performance here is nothing if not laid back—laid *out* might be closer to it), our hero, throwing caution and logic to the winds, single-handedly saves both nation and day in a nonstop orgy of patriotic violence. At that, *Invasion USA* doesn't end so much as it runs out of ammo. No relation (except in its shared anti-Commie fervor) to 1953's *Invasion, U.S.A.* (see index).

IRON EAGLE:
THE SERIES

IRON EAGLE   (1986)*

D: Sidney J. Furie. Louis Gossett, Jr., Jason Gedrick, Tim Thomerson, David Suchet. 108 mins. (Fox) DVD

If nothing else, *Iron Eagle* boasts the hottest rock score of any war movie since *Apocalypse Now*. (The similarity definitely ends there.) Gedrick plays junior jet ace Doug, whose dad (Thomerson) has been snatched by arrogant Ay-rabs, and it's up to Doug and mad-as-hell pilot Colonel Chappy Sinclair (Gossett) to spring him. So in a militaristic update of the old let's-put-on-a-show routine, Doug's teenage pals help him on his way by stealing vital computer data and secretly arming a souped-up F-16 in a lively let's-put-on-

a-war montage set to Twisted Sister's "We Ain't Gonna Take It Anymore" (!). And our flyboys really know how to get down before they go up too: Colonel Sinclair works out the covert flight plan while dancing to a James Brown ditty (the Godfather of Soul's first patriotic cameo since the previous year's *Rocky IV*). And young Doug gives the 'Rabs what-for while "Gimme Some Lovin'" roars from his airborne cassette deck! (The same song was used to score a similarly destructive sequence in the pallid *policier Number One with a Bullet* [MGM], proving once again the old Hollywood axiom that small minds think alike.) The climactic aerial scenes see Doug forcing Qaddafi-like Arab leader Suchet (a fine actor paying his B-movie dues here) to eat rock-'n'-roll justice. Gossett returns in the glasnost-influenced but otherwise unimproved *Iron Eagle 2* (Artisan), *Aces: Iron Eagle III* (see below), and *Iron Eagle IV: On the Attack* (Trimark, DVD).

ACES: IRON EAGLE III   (1992)**

D: John Glen. Louis Gossett, Jr., Rachel McLish, Horst Buchholz, Paul Freeman, Sonny Chiba, Christopher Cazenove. 98 mins. (Columbia/TriStar)

The third installment in this live-action cartoon series—navigated by downwardly mobile onetime James Bond director Glen—veers from the usual military teens-versus-terrorists plot to an airborne Over-the-Hill Gang variation. Here Gossett enlists three elderly "Axis and Allies" air-show aces—German Buchholz, Brit Cazenove, and Japanese sock-and-chop champ Chiba (all of whom would have been preteens during World War II, but hey, who's counting?)—to help flex-queen McLish free her Peruvian people from sneering Nazi drug lord Paul (*Raiders of the Lost Ark*) Freeman. Representing the youth element is wisecracking homeboy Tee Vee (Phil Lewis), who tags along to play Rambo with our geriatric crew. While

Gossett turns in his usual stalwart work, McLish divides her screen time battling hapless drug henchmen and her own uncooperative Spanish accent. Chiba fans, meanwhile, will be disappointed by Sonny's punchless (to say nothing of unintelligible) perf. From initial takeoff to final landing, *Aces* piles on clichés from all nations and generations, but the admittedly impressive last-reel aerial sequences may be worth the price of a rental for hard-core aviation buffs.

IT'S ALL TRUE   (1993) B&W/ COLOR***

D: Richard Wilson, Myron Meisel, Bill Krohn, based on an unfinished film by Orson Welles. Narrated by Miguel Ferrer. 86 mins. (Paramount)

An engrossing verité examination of Welles's long-lost, unfinished adventure film of the same working title, *It's All True* details Orson's ultimately losing struggle to bring his tripartite dramatized documentary to fruition. Most of the found footage, which dates from 1942, tells the true story of four Fortaleza, Brazil, fishermen's perilous raft journey to Rio, where they petition for economic justice. Surrounding this beautifully lensed set piece are running commentaries from the Brazilian participants' descendants and Welles's filmmaking cronies, as well as direct testimony from Orson himself, describing the project's origins, detours, dilemmas, and eventual defeat. Withal, an entertaining and enlightening job.

JACKIE CHAN'S FIRST STRIKE (1996)**1/2

D: Stanley Tong. Jackie Chan, Chen Chun Wu, Jackson Lou. Dubbed. 85 mins. (New Line) DVD

Jackie goes the James Bond route in one of the international action icon's lesser recent outings. The convoluted, map-hopping plot puts Jackie on the trail of Russian Mafia nuke thieves. Chan does come through in the action department, though, with snowmobile stunts, a kung-fu-on-stilts sequence, and a prolonged battle in a shark-infested aquarium tank. Apparently inspired by Van Damme, Jackie even resorts to bare-butt antics, while also taking time out to showcase his dubious vocal talents. In the end, *First Strike* is more manic than inspired. The flick concludes with the usual stunt-breakdown outtakes running under the credits.

JACKIE CHAN'S POLICE FORCE (A.K.A. *POLICE STORY*) (1985) **½

D: Jackie Chan. Jackie Chan, Bridget Lin, Maggie Cheung, Cho Yuen, Bill Tung. 88 mins. (Cinema Group, n.i.d.)

One of the very few films to go directly from the prestigious (to say nothing of pretentious) New York Film Festival—where it was a controversial 1987 entry supported by a few daring critics like Dave Kehr—to the late, lamented 42nd Street's Roxy Twin kung-fu video theater (!), *Police Story* stars Jackie as a Hong Kong cop assigned to protect a major drug lord's fetching government-witness mistress (Lin)—a task that leads to romantic complications and considerable flak from J.C.'s girlfriend (Cheung). Jackie the director keeps the familiar plot careering along at a brisk clip, leavening the well-staged action with slapstick sight gags and satiric pokes at the local judicial system (mirroring Dirty Harry's similar stateside laments) and exhibiting a fondness for fast cutting and frequent zoom-lensing. A modestly entertaining kung-fu comedy, *Police Force* is superior to most of Jackie's earlier American efforts (e.g., *The Big Brawl*, *The Protector*) but not as good as more recent capers like *Crime Story* and *Supercop* (see index).

JACKSON COUNTY JAIL (1976) ***

D: Michael Miller. Yvette Mimieux, Tommy Lee Jones, Robert Carradine. 84 mins. (Warner)

Traveling exec Mimieux suffers extreme Southern inhospitality at the hands of cracker lawmen, leading her to bond with redneck con Jones in Miller's excellent exercise in crossover exploitation. Yvette also stars in the unofficial *JCJ* remake *Outside Chance* (Charter).

JOHNNY FIRECLOUD (1975) ***

D: William A. Castleman. Victor Mohica, Ralph Meeker, Frank De Kova, Sacheen Littlefeather, David Canary. 97 mins. (Prism)

Mohica plays the title character (named after a desert atomic test blast), a post–Billy Jack, pre-Rambo Native American 'Nam vet who encounters prejudice in the modern West at the hands of racist rancher Meeker and his redneck goons. Mohica also spends much screen time engaging in an ongoing debate with his tradition-bound grandfather, De Kova. When the latter insists that Mohica's reservation home is "full of rich heritage," our hero replies, "It's full of bugs!" Boldly declaring that "tradition is still like always," De Kova dons his tribal gear, attempts a meeting with the vicious Meeker, and winds up getting lynched for his troubles. Meeker's minions further raise the ante by raping schoolteacher (and one-time Marlon Brando protégé) Littlefeather, paving the way for Firecloud's requisite last-reel revenge spree. It's here that the movie hits its sadistic stride, as Mohica employs venerable Native American means to goreslaughter the bad guys, scalping one, eliminating another with a poison snake, staking yet a third to an anthill, and otherwise putting tradition to creative use. Mohica also starred in *Ghost Dance* (Interglobal) and had smaller roles in the slasher tale *Don't Answer*

the Phone (Media); the big-budget sci-fi time-travel adventure *The Final Countdown* (see index); and the western *Showdown* (n/a). If you see only one Mohica movie in your lifetime, though, we'd strongly urge you to make it *Johnny Firecloud*.

JOHNNY HANDSOME (1989) ***

D: Walter Hill. Mickey Rourke, Ellen Barkin, Lance Henriksen, Morgan Freeman, Forest Whitaker, Scott Wilson. 95 mins. (Artisan)

Sort of a *Bonnie and Clyde* Meets *The Elephant Man*, *Johnny Handsome* features excellent perfs by Henriksen and Barkin as the gun-happy duo who double-cross Rourke and add insult to injury by making mock of his unattractive facial prosthesis. Lance and Ellen may not be the type of couple you'd want to spend a long weekend with, but their fab threads represented the then-ultimate in trash-fashion statements. Freeman also contributes a deft turn as the New Orleans cop dogging Rourke's trail, as does Whitaker as the surgeon who fixes Mick's formerly ugly mug. An ace job all around as Hill helms yet another fun A-budgeted sleazefest.

JOHNNY 100 PESOS (1993) ***

D: Gustavo Graef-Marino. Armando Araiza, Patricia Rivera, Willy Semler, Luis Gnecco, Paulina Urrutia, Cristian Campos. 95 mins. (Fox Lorber/Orion)

Something of a Chilean *Dog Day Afternoon* and likewise drawn from an actual incident, *Johnny 100 Pesos* relates the details of a heist gone haywire. The title character is a confused 17-year-old thief (Araiza) ill-advisedly recruited by a quartet of veteran crooks to accompany them on a robbery at an eighth-floor video club (a Spanish-language *Exorcist III* poster is visible throughout much of the film) that's actually a front for an illegal currency-exchange operation. When police get wise to the crime-in-progress, the thieves hold four employees and an elderly customer hostage while they plot their next move. At once suspenseful and ironic, *Johnny 100 Pesos* examines how a media-mad culture exploits the newsworthy situation and how a government in transition from military dictatorship to democracy deals with it. Auteur Graef-Marino also offers a deft portrait of the high-schooler in over his head at a time when much official concern was being expressed over the state of Chilean youth. Rarely screened outside of film festivals, *Johnny 100 Pesos* makes for a welcome home-vid arrival for art-house devotees and caper fans alike.

JON JOST'S FRAMEUP   (1993) **¹/₂

D: Jon Jost. Nancy Carlin, Howard Swain. 91 mins. (World Artists)

More experimental, less successful than his previous effort *Sure Fire* (see index), *Jon Jost's Frameup* sees the prolific indie auteur apply his patented collage approach to a two-character study in a road movie that rarely ventures outdoors for its key moments. Much of Jost's tale—shot over 3,000 miles in 10 days (!)—consists of monologues delivered by peripatetic criminal Swain and his blank-slate waitress squeeze Carlin as they motor from Idaho to California, with frequent stops for motel trysts and meandering exchanges. Jost's striking visual techniques—from painterly landscapes to minimalist long takes—and the improvisationally trained thesps (a real-life married couple) manage to exert a hypnotic effect during *Frameup*'s best stretches, and there are images haunting enough to remain forever etched in the viewer's mind.

JOURNEY OF HONOR   (1991) **

D: Gordon Hessler. Sho Kosugi, Christopher Lee, Polly Walker, Toshiro Mifune, Kane

Kosugi, David Essex, John Rhys-Davies. 107 mins. (Universal)

Sort of Sho's version of Kurosawa's *Ran* (Fox Lorber) crossed with James Clavell's *Shogun* (Paramount), the lavish *Journey of Honor,* set in 1602 Japan, opens with a sweeping battle scene pitting Sho's sword-wielding "West Army" against the musket-armed East forces. When local lord Mifune sees the necessity for improved firepower, he dispatches his teenage son (played by Sho's real-life offspring Kane Kosugi) and protector Sho to Spain to buy 5,000 rifles. There Sho and Kane encounter Christopher Lee as King Philip, treacherous priest Norman Lloyd, Rhys-Davies as a Moroccan potentate, golden-tressed damsel Walker, and, worst of all, Polly's fiancé, Don Pedro (Essex), an evil nobleman who's out to shaft Sho. Originally titled *Shogun Mayeda, Journey of Honor* boasts impressive scope; unfortunately, Sho's saga comes up short on most other counts. While the action scenes—from a full-scale pirate attack to Sho's expert samurai swordplay—work fairly well, the dialogue and plotting range from the risible to the downright dull. Sho has yet to master English—though son Kane has ("It's the one thing I do better than you," he tells his elder)—making the flick that much harder to follow. At times *Journey of Honor* plays so much like a '50s B swashbuckler that we expected a turbaned Jeff Chandler to swoop down from the nearest yardarm and save the day. While *Journey* may represent a failed stab at celluloid glory, it rates as a pic Kosugi completists won't want to miss.

JUDGMENT NIGHT   (1993) ***

D: Stephen Hopkins. Emilio Estevez, Cuba Gooding, Jr., Denis Leary, Stephen Dorff, Peter Greene. 110 mins. (Universal) DVD

As a slick, ghetto-set *Deliverance* variation, *Judgment Night* delivers

the genre goods. Four twentysomething guys on their way to a Windy City boxing match take an ill-advised detour, winding up in an urban wasteland where they witness Leary and goons' execution of a light-fingered drug dealer and spend the rest of a long night-of-passage fleeing the killers. Comedian Leary makes for a convincing villain and receives solid support from Greene; in fact, they're far more charismatic than our heroes, led by a laconic Estevez. While rarely surprising, *Judgment Night* achieves its limited goals with visceral and visual energy to spare.

JUNGLE WARRIORS   (1984) ***

D: Ernst R. von Theumer. Alex Cord, Sybil Danning, Nina Van Pallandt, Paul L. Smith, John Vernon, Marjoe Gortner, Woody Strode. 96 mins. (Media, n.i.d.)

Seven foxy fashion models crash-land in a South American jungle, where they run afoul of fat cocaine kingpin Cesar (Smith), his blond lesbian sis, Angel (Danning), and sundry gun-toting minions. One of the gals is really a secret drug agent, out to get the goods on Cesar and a team of visiting Mafiosi, headed by Vernon and Cord. After a slow buildup, *Jungle Warriors* (*Jiggle Warriors* would have been an apter title) delivers its promised quota of slashings, bashings, and decapitations, and culminates in a lengthy shoot-out in which our beleaguered gals get to give as good as they've gotten.

JUNGLEGROUND   (1995) **¹/₂

D: Don Allan. Roddy Piper, Torri Higginson, Peter Williams, Nicholas Campbell. 90 mins. (Triboro) DVD

It's *Escape from New York* Meets *Most Dangerous Game* time in this Rowdy Roddy romp. Fortunately, director Allan and crew keep the pace so blistering that this new sprint through old turf kept us pretty much glued. In the titular crime zone, a bloody shoot-out between cops and members of petty demagogue Williams's gang leaves Roddy the lone good-guy survivor. Williams sics a pack of his followers on Roddy's trail, while twin goons hold Roddy's artist squeeze (Higginson) captive "uptown" (where most Junglegrounders fear to tread), and gives our hero till dawn to (a) get out alive and (b) save his gal. The action is solid throughout—Roddy even gets to demonstrate a few of his old WWF moves—and an inventive suffocation sequence supplies a new wrinkle in traditional screen torture techniques.

KICKBOXER:
THE SERIES

KICKBOXER   (1989) **¹/₂

D: Mark DiSalle. Jean-Claude Van Damme, Dennis Chan, Haskell Anderson, Rochelle Ashana, Denis Alexio, Tong Po. 105 mins. (HBO) DVD

J-C stars as Kurt Sloane, an aspiring chopsocky champ who swears vengeance when his kickboxing bro' Eric (Alexio) is paralyzed by psycho fighter Tong Po (played by "himself") during an ill-advised Bangkok bout. While *Kickboxer*'s simple revenge story wouldn't strain the brain of a head of lettuce, it serves as an adequate frame for the film's real *raison d'être*: Jean-Claude's strenuous *Rocky*-like efforts to whip himself into shape under the tutelage of "Muay Thai" martial arts master Xian Chow (wryly interpreted by Chan, a sarcastic cross between *The Karate Kid*'s Pat Morita and *Remo Williams*'s Joel Grey). J-C also finds time to romance Chow's comely niece Mylee (Ashana), befriend black 'Nam vet Taylor (Anderson), and tangle with local lowlifes in league with the hateful Tong, sort of a Kung-Fu Manchu. *Kickboxer*'s inarguable highlight arrives with the expected climactic duke-out between J-C and Tong, who, in a creatively bloody touch, go at it wearing gloves coated with broken glass. In a lighter moment, J-C also gets to display his less impressive disco techniques while drunkenly dancing to a jukebox ditty. Like Van Damme's earlier *Bloodsport*, filmed within Hong Kong's exotic Walled City, *Kickboxer* makes evocative use of its authentic Asian locales.

KICKBOXER 2   (1991) **

D: Albert Pyun. Sasha Mitchell, Peter Boyle, Dennis Chan, Cary-Hiroyuki Tagawa, Matthias Hues, Michel Qissi, Vince Murducco. 90 mins. (Warner)

Kickboxer 2 continues the saga of the kickboxing Sloane brothers, sans the chopsocky services of priced-out original star Van Damme. Mitchell plays David, the lone surviving Sloane, a retired kickboxer who returns to the ring to (a) save his endangered gym and (b) avenge the death of his friend Murducco at the hands, feet, elbows, knees, and seemingly cement head of dread Thai terror Tong Po (Qissi). Mitchell, who displayed considerable comic flair in Paul Morrissey's underrated *Spike of Bensonhurst* (see index; he also appeared as J.R.'s illegit son in *Dallas*'s final season), is largely wasted as Van Damme's replacement, a part that utilizes little of the thesp's genuine acting skills. *K2* comes alive only during the kickboxing bouts, lensed in ersatz *Raging Bull* slo-mo style.

KICKBOXER 3: THE ART OF WAR (1992) **

D: Rick King. Sasha Mitchell, Dennis Chan, Richard Comar, Noah Verduzco. 92 mins. (Artisan)

While nearly as dim-witted as the L.A. ghetto-set 2, *KB3* at least relocates to the more picturesque environs of Rio, when Mitchell and diminutive mentor Chan journey for a match with a mad martial artist in the employ of scuzzy Yank pimp/promoter Comar. Mitchell's Brooklyn accent may not be as exotic as Van Damme's Belgian drawl, but he makes for a likable enough hero until he and Chan step out of character and violate a cardinal action-movie rule by shooting up a bunch of bad guys who haven't been seen committing any on-screen crimes. (This gratuitous siege scene may actually be an elaborate setup for an arcane cinematic in-joke. Chan asks Sloane, "How many did you kill in the kitchen?"—a variation on the famous query posed repeatedly in Sam Fuller's *Shock Corridor* [see index], "Who killed Sloane in the kitchen?" Then again, on the other hand, probably not.)

KICKBOXER 4: THE AGGRESSOR (1994) **¹/₂

D: Albert Pyun. Sasha Mitchell, Kamel Krifa, Brad Thornton, Jill Pierce, Michelle "Mouse" Krasnoo, Thom Matthews, Nicholas Guest. 90 mins. (Artisan)

In the Giving the Director His Due Department, much-maligned genre auteur Pyun deserves credit for delivering what ranks as the series' punchiest entry. The pic utilizes an *Enter the Dragon*–type premise that maximizes the oft lethal full-contact bouts while thankfully minimizing any attempts at manqué dramatics. Mitchell returns for his third go-round as Sloane, who's released from prison, where he's been serving time on a trumped-up murder conviction, to go undercover to nail the supremely evil and still-kickin' Tong Po (Krifa), currently hosting his annual full-contact sweepstakes at his south-of-the-border redoubt. What follows is virtually nonstop fight action in a variety of styles. Diminutive Michelle "Mouse" Krasnoo is particularly impressive as a feisty femme fighter and one of the few cast members to survive the carnage.

KILL LINE (1991)¹/₂*

D: Richard H. Kim. Bobby Kim, Michael Parker, Marlene Zimmerman. 91 mins. (Hemdale)

A family affair produced by Robert W. Kim and written/directed by Richard H. Kim, *Kill Line* stars diminutive Asian Bronson clone Bobby (*Manchurian Avenger*) Kim (print ads punched the resemblance home by listing Kim's on-screen name as Bone Crusher Bronson; actually, it's Joe Lee, but, hey, we're not here to split hairs, let alone crush bones) as an ex-con out to avenge the massacre of several relatives in obscure Salinas Park, Colorado. A squabble over stashed stolen cash soon pits our pint-sized hero against a corrupt local sheriff and assorted goons. That's about as much as we could follow, since this utterly senseless amateur-night mess seems to be missing entire scenes. Worse, the Kim clan can't execute the simplest fight stunts, a fairly fatal flaw in an alleged action pic. Bobby K. gives a sluglike perf—he's shot, burned, and tossed off a cliff before he throws so much as a single punch or kick in his defense—and his fellow cast members fare little better delivering their brain-dead English-as-second-language dialogue. *Kill Line* is so rife with confusion that the Kims actually tack on a flash card at film's end in a bid to explain what we've just witnessed (!). Even kung-fu-camp fans won't want to cross *this* line.

THE KILLER (1989) ***¹/₂

D: John Woo. Chow Yun-Fat, Danny Lee, Sally Yeh, Shing Fui-On. 110 mins. Subtitled/dubbed. In R and unrated editions. (Fox Lorber) DVD

Sort of a *Fistful of Yen*, Woo's ultraviolent pop-gangster melodrama plays like a Sergio Leone spaghetti western jacked to the max and transplanted from a stylized Old West to contempo Hong Kong. Woo's story chronicles the bloody exploits of titular hit man Jeff Chow, portrayed by Yun-Fat in a style that outcools even vintage Clint Eastwood. When Jeff accidentally blinds nightclub singer Yeh during a chaotic opening shoot-out, our sentimental antihero vows to score the bucks needed to pay for her cornea operation. Also central to the case is maverick cop Lee, who eventually teams up with intended target Jeff to take on mobster Fui-On and his ever multiplying hordes of highly expendable henchmen. While Woo leaves no action cliché unturned, his flick is so bold, manic, and over-the-top that the plot machinations take a distant second place to the director's wild style. Woo crams his action canvas with exploding bullets and squirting blood squibs galore (*The Killer* was originally rated X for violence), running up a mega body count. Hectic car and boat chases likewise contribute to the fast-paced fun. Woo is equally excessive in the tongue-in-cheek macho-heroics department. Killer Yun-Fat and cop Lee take male-bonding rituals to a whole new, sometimes risible plateau, affectionately addressing each other as "Mickey Mouse" and "Dumbo." Viewers in search of profundity won't find it here, the characters' running exchanges on the themes of honor, trust, and responsibility notwithstanding. But if it's spectacular, adrenalizing action you're after, only Woo's own *Hard-Boiled* (see index) supplies more bang for the video bucks. For a period costume variation on *The Killer*, scope out Woo's 1978 actioner *Last Hurrah for Chivalry* (Tai Seng), likewise starring Yun-Fat.

THE KILLING MAN (1994) ***

D: David Mitchell. Jeff Wincott, Michael Ironside, Terri Hawkes, David Bolt, Jeff Pustil. 93 mins. (A-Pix) DVD

This lean, mean, existential actioner qualifies as a reel surprise. Martial arts ace Wincott plays a partially amnesic, legally dead assassin repaired by government medics and coerced by sinister official Ironside (in another of his understatedly sadistic perfs) to terminate a trio of political troublemakers—a gay activist, muckraking journalist, and femme scientist—about to prove that the AIDS virus was initially manufactured and disseminated by our own government. Our tormented antihero carries out part of his assignment before falling for scientist Hawkes, a predictable twist but one that doesn't quite lead to the expected happy ending. Indeed, director/coscripter Mitchell imbues *The Killing Man* with a mood of futility that runs deeper than the usual posturing and attitude-copping common to contempo genre films. At the same time, he never lets his flick grow ponderous or pretentious, keeping the action in the forefront while adding shading even to his secondary characters.

KILLING ZOE (1994) ***

D: Roger Avary. Eric Stoltz, Julie Delpy, Jean-Hugues Anglade, Gary Kemp, Bruce Ramsay. 96 mins. (Artisan)

Onetime Quentin Tarantino bud (from their fabled Manhattan Beach, California, vid-store days) Avary makes his feature-film debut with a superviolent caper that lacks the fractured narrative and manic energy of Q.T.'s *Pulp Fiction* or *Reservoir Dogs* but works well on a pulp-fable level. Stoltz stars as Zed (the same name sported by Peter Greene's character in *Pulp Fiction*), a passive American explosives expert who arrives in Paris to help childhood friend Eric (Anglade) and his degenerate gang blow a bank on Bastille Day. Before the job, Zed enjoys a tryst with art student, bank worker, and part-time hooker Zoe (Delpy). Eric—an HIV-positive junkie, anarchist, and criminal sans the slightest shred of empathy—shows up and tosses a naked Zoe from the room; Zed observes but does nothing to prevent the abusive act. As Avary's story unfolds, it becomes apparent that Zoe represents humanity, sensuality, and creativity—handicaps rather than virtues in Eric's debased worldview. Eric and his smack-dazed, trigger-happy cohorts seduce Zed with the self-destructive, instant-grat lures of hard drugs, cheap booze, and senseless violence. When the gang breaks into the bank, Zoe is among the workers held hostage, forcing Zed to make a literal life-or-death choice between her and Eric. While not especially suspenseful, the heist scenes boast more than their fair share of perverse brutality, and Avary finds a satisfying variety of visual metaphors to illustrate his Eros-versus-Thanatos theme.

KING OF NEW YORK   (1990) ***1/2

D: Abel Ferrara. Christopher Walken, Larry Fishburne, David Caruso, Victor Argo, Wesley Snipes, Janet Julian, Steve Buscemi, Joey Chin. 103 mins. (Artisan)

Ferrara's *King of New York* supplies plenty of raw, brutal entertainment as several warring factions battle for control of the Gotham drug market. An unemotive Walken plays coke kingpin Frank White as a sort of charismatic zombie. Just out of stir, White seeks to reestablish his top-dog status while funneling part of his ill-gotten proceeds into worthy urban causes (a not especially plausible plot embellishment). Most of the movie involves Walken and troops' violent encounters with the opposition, who include local Mafiosi, a Chinatown gang, a squad of vigilante cops, and traitors within Walken's own ranks. While director Ferrara covered much the same turf in 1987's *China Girl* (see index), he does it far more lavishly and expertly here. Beyond the neatly staged action sequences, highlights include an erotic subway interlude that lends new meaning to the concept of unsafe sex. Ferrara also incorporates clips from F. W. Mur-

nau's 1922 vampire classic, *Nosferatu,* screened by Chinatown gang leader Chin, who tells Walken, "Why don't you stick around? I got *Frankenstein* coming on next." Greatly aiding and abetting the film are a number of talented thesps, ranging from Fishburne as Walken's wired, trigger-happy lieutenant, Jimmy Jump, to Buscemi as a cocaine chemist and James *(Frankenhooker)* Lorinz as a newly married young cop.

KINJITE: FORBIDDEN SUBJECTS (1989) **1/2

D: J. Lee Thompson. Charles Bronson, Juan Fernandez, Perry Lopez, Peggy Lipton, James Pax, Bill McKinney. 97 mins. (Cannon)

Kinjite: Forbidden Subjects* ranks as geriatric action star Bronson's least soporific suspenser in years. That's not to say that *Kinjite* is *good* exactly—the flick is, in fact, an unholy mess. But it's a consistently *compelling* mess. Its converging plot lines follow prudish LAPD vice dick Chuck (in an unusually testy turn) as he overprotects his own teen daughter while trying to nail notorious jailbait pimp Fernandez. Equally repressed Japanese businessman Pax, meanwhile, finds his fate inextricably bound with Bronson's. Until the formulaic final reel, *Kinjite* offers a fairly kinky, unpredictable mix of sleaze, suspense, and cross-cultural confusion, leavened with unintentional laughs (as when Chuck, in his big emotive moment, unleashes a garbled racist harangue at the expense of a crowd of understandably bewildered Japanese visitors).

LADY SNOWBLOOD   (1973) ***

D: Toshiya Fujita. Meiko Kaji, Toshio Kurosawa, Daimon Masaaki, Eiji Okada. 97 mins. (AnimEigo)

Another superior entry in Anim-Eigo's exemplary Samurai Cinema

line, *Lady Snowblood* (a.k.a. *Shurayuk-ihime*) presents an exquisitely lensed tale of bizarre vengeance. In 1873, shortly after the end of the shogunate period, a schoolteacher, mistaken for an official connected with Japan's new Universal Conscription Law, is brutally slaughtered by a quartet of murderous scam artists, three men and a woman, while his wife is beaten and raped. The widow survives long enough to become pregnant in a bid to spawn a living instrument of revenge. The resultant daughter, Yuki (Kaji), is trained in combat by a local priest. Upon reaching adulthood, she sets out on her kamikaze mission to slay her father's killers (hence the intriguing tag line: "Her Life Was Over Before She Was Born!"). In the title role, Kaji is alternately delicate and deadly, tracking the far-flung miscreants and slicing and dicing their unlucky minions along the way. Rich in period detail and color, *Lady Snowblood* represents another lively hybrid of history lesson and slaughterfest.

LAST ACTION HERO   (1993) *1/2

D: John McTiernan. Arnold Schwarzenegger, Austin O'Brien, Charles Dance, Robert Prosky. 122 mins. (Columbia/TriStar) DVD

What starts as a sub-ZAZ Team action-flick parody descends into utter stupidity—*Hudson Hawk*–like antics followed by a *Terminator 2*–type farewell scene between lonely tyke O'Brien and his muscle-bound stick-figure hero (you know who). *Last Action Hero* is peppered with star cameos, including turns by Tina Turner, Sharon Stone, and Jean-Claude Van Damme—just in time to remind us of their *own* then-upcoming summer '93 movies (*What's Love Got to Do with It?, Sliver,* and *Hard Target,* respectively). If nothing else, *LAH,* with its recreated 42nd Street backdrop, demonstrates the since-Disneyfied Deuce's undiminished hold on the national imagination. If 42nd Street didn't exist, Hollywood designers

THE LAST BOY SCOUT   (1991) **½

D: Tony Scott. Bruce Willis, Damon Wayans, Danielle Harris, Noble Willingham, Badja Djola. 105 mins. (Warner) DVD

Producer Joel Silver's megabuck kill orgy rates as one of the more gleefully sadistic actioners to come down the mainstream pike. Shane Black's screenplay is pretty senseless—cars, buildings, and plot threads all explode with equal regularity—but the pic definitely coughs up its share of memorable moments, among them the best sports sequence (featuring B-video martial arts hero and current Tae-Bo infomercial mogul Billy Blanks as an armed [!] drug-crazed running back) we've seen since *Naked Gun*'s extended baseball send-up. Wayans, as a drug-dependent ex-football star, easily outscores a sleazy, smirking Willis in the thespian department. The film is further buoyed by some of the most colorful henchmen (*Penitentiary*'s "Half Dead" Djola among them) seen on-screen since John Frankenheimer's *52 Pickup* (see index). We also liked the bit wherein our heroes are done in by their own short attention spans, destroying a vital audiotape by impatiently hitting the fast-forward control. It's just that kind of move that makes our culture, if not great, then certainly what it is.

LAST MAN STANDING   (1995) **½

D: Joseph Merhi. Jeff Wincott, Jillian McWhirter, Jonathan Fuller, Steve Estin, Jonathan Banks, Michael Greene. 96 mins. (PM)

The action specialists at PM— the people who put the *car* in *carnage*—again deliver big-screen spectacle on a home-vid budget. Here, LAPD dick Wincott (one of the few chain-smoking martial arts champs we've seen) finds himself caught between corrupt fellow officers and a vicious criminal ring, led by a grinning Fuller, who are in turn conducting a war of their own. (And it's a pretty sorry state of affairs when criminals and cops can no longer trust each other.) Perennial heavy Banks scores a rare good-guy role as Jeff's doomed partner.

**THE PHANTOM'S
Famous Last Words File**

"We've had big stars stay here. I'm talking Evel Knievel, Erik Estrada, Dionne Warwick. We had the entire cast of *American Gladiators* here once!"
—*hotel manager Jacobsen Hart
before being blown away*
Last Man Standing

LAST MAN STANDING   (1996) ***

D: Walter Hill. Bruce Willis, Christopher Walken, Alexandra Powers, Bruce Dern, Karina Lombard, David Patrick Kelly. 101 mins. (New Line) DVD

Action ace Hill fashions an expectedly violent, highly stylized re-creation of Akira Kurosawa's *Yojimbo*, transplanted from medieval Japan to 1920s rural West Texas. The film establishes a solemn tone early on with a Peckinpah-like death-of-the-West image of a horse carcass rotting in the middle of a street packed with dust-churning cars. In the original Toshiro Mifune samurai role, laconic lone-wolf gunman Willis, who seems to thrive on physical abuse (see also *Die Hard with a Vengeance, Pulp Fiction,* and *12 Monkeys*), absorbs bullets and bruises while playing both sides of a bootlegger war raging in a near-ghost town. In Hill's chilly retelling of Kurosawa's story, Bruce lends his two-gun expertise first to an Italo mob headed by Ned Eisenberg and Michael Imperioli, then to a more colorful Irish gang led by diminutive Kelly and a hoarse Walken. Our hero also finds time for old-fashioned chivalry, rescuing Mexican Indian lass Lombard (late of the steamy *Wide Sargasso Sea* [New Line]) from Kelly's clutches. The talented cast also includes Dern, in a relatively restrained but effective turn, as the beat-out burg's hands-off sheriff, William (*Blade Runner*) Sanderson as an idle local barkeep, and frequent villain Patrick Kilpatrick, who makes one of his earliest exits to date here, courtesy of Bruce's blazing .45s. Ry Cooder supplies an appropriately brooding guitar score.

THE LAST RIDERS   (1990) **½

D: Joseph Merhi. Erik Estrada, William Smith, Armando Sylvestre, Kathrin Lautner, Angelo Tiffe, Mimi Lesseos. 90 mins. (PM)

Former *C.H.I.P.S.*ter Estrada returns to the steel saddle, this time as a biker on the run from the law. After Erik kills a crooked cop while trying to recover a stolen coke stash, he splits from his gang, "the Slavers," and hooks up with mechanic Smith in small-town Sloane, Nevada, where he eventually finds love and stability with stranded motorist Lautner and her young daughter. Erik's modest mobile-home Eden is soon shattered when several Slavers, believing Erik has turned stoolie, show up to slaughter his new-found family, setting the scene for your requisite climactic revenge spree. While the action scenes are adequately handled, *The Last Riders* plays best during its domestic middle reels, dramatizing a naturalistic love story with admirable lowlife authenticity.

LAWS OF GRAVITY   (1992) ***

D: Nick Gomez. Peter Greene, Edie Falco, Adam Trese, Arabella Field, Paul Schulze. 107 mins. (Triboro)

Something of a downscale, Brooklyn-set *Mean Streets* (Warner), Gomez's vivid slice-of-lowlife crime drama is a mostly effective, often powerful, and always budget-defying (a reported $38,000) indie. The film profiles likable petty hustler Jimmy (a charismatic Greene), his softhearted barmaid spouse, Denise (Falco, who later gained fame as TV's Carmela Soprano), poorly chosen, hotheaded buddy Jon (Trese), and the latter's battered squeeze, Celia (Field). The minimalist plot centers on a stash of stolen guns Jimmy's unstable friend Frankie (Schulze) enlists him to help sell. When not reluctantly scouting for potential buyers, Jimmy acts as an unofficial neighborhood big brother—watching out for Jon, comforting the abused Celia, and generally trying to keep the peace. The sullen, self-destructive Jon may be the character with *doom* figuratively stamped on his forehead, but Jimmy is the flick's true tragic figure, a guy too decent and code-bound to flourish within his dead-end environs. Auteur Gomez goes for a verité look, achieved via handheld-camera work, that suits his material without calling attention to itself. The ensemble scenes, with rapid-fire overlapping dialogue delivered at high, profanity-laced decibels, play amazingly well for a film with a 12-day shooting sked. The largely rap-driven soundtrack supplies an apt sonic counterpoint while never dominating or serving as filler.

LEGACY OF RAGE (1986) ***

D: Ronny Yu. Brandon Lee, Michael Wong, Regina Kent, Bolo Yeung. Subtitled/dubbed. 86 mins. (Tai Seng) DVD

Long before the late Brandon (Son of Bruce) Lee's American vehicles *Rapid Fire* and *The Crow*, he starred in what may stand as his best genre film—Ronny (*The Bride with White Hair*, *Warriors of Virtue*) Yu's hard-edged Hong Kong actioner *Legacy of Rage*. The then-21-year-old Lee plays Brandon Ma, a martial artist/waiter framed

for murder by his ambitious criminal "friend" Wong. Lee registers strongly both in the action and acting departments, as the film follows him through a long prison term and a *Scarface*-influenced last-reel revenge mission.

LEGIONNAIRE (1998) ***

D: Peter MacDonald. Jean-Claude Van Damme, Steven Berkoff, Nicholas Farrell, Adewale Akinnuoye-Agbaje, Daniel Caltagirone, Jim Carter. 98 mins. (Sterling) DVD

With *Legionnaire*, Van Damme, director MacDonald, and crew pull off the not-inconsiderable feat of fashioning a credible, exciting 1950s-styled adventure. Reportedly the most expensive ($35 mil) feature film ever to go directly to video (following a Euro bijou run), *Legionnaire* stars Jean-Claude as a 1920s boxer who finds arduous shelter with the French Foreign Legion after refusing to take a dive for a Parisian gangster. Echoing such fun Legionnaire fare as 1977's superior *March or Die* (n/a), as well as classics like *Beau Geste* (Universal), the film takes a refreshingly no-nonsense stance as we follow J-C and several fellow new recruits—disgraced former Brit major Farrell and African-American enlistee Akinnuoye-Agbaje, among others—through their rigorous training paces and, ultimately, their bloody desert battle with rebellious Arab warriors. With the aid of top-notch cinematographer Douglas (*Full Metal Jacket*) Milsome, the filmmakers lend *Legionnaire* impressive sweep, employing a literal cast of thousands (well, hundreds anyway), while the rousing combat sequences are easily the equal of the Legion epics of yore. A thankfully laconic Van Damme acquits himself well as the flawed but honorable hero, a role that arrived as especially redemptive following his lame turn in Tsui Hark's surprisingly unwatchable *Knock Off* (Columbia/TriStar).

LETHAL WEAPON:
THE SERIES

LETHAL WEAPON (1987) **

D: Richard Donner. Mel Gibson, Danny Glover, Gary Busey, Mitchell Ryan, Tom Atkins, Darlene Love. 110 mins. (Warner) DVD

After "meeting cute," psychotic-white-cop/stable-black-cop tandem Gibson and Glover set out to nail a network of evil drug mercenaries headed by icy killer Busey (in albino makeup). While *Lethal Weapon* unspools with suitable manic energy, it's ultimately an exercise in overdrive jive. A calculated blend of *Commando*, *Mad Max*, *Miami Vice*, *Rambo* and *The Cosby Show*, the pic plays like a standard Schwarzenegger vehicle, with Mel subbing for the mighty Arnie. And despite its endless array of gun battles, exploding cars, and Fu Manchu–style torture sequences, *Lethal Weapon* is a painfully predictable affair. (Producer Joel Silver even lifts the climactic kung-fu fight from his earlier *Commando*.) As weary cop Glover at one point remarks, "Pretty thin stuff, huh?"

LETHAL WEAPON 2 (1989) ***

D: Richard Donner. Mel Gibson, Danny Glover, Joe Pesci, Joss Ackland, Patsy Kensit, Derrick O'Connor. 113 mins. (Warner) DVD

LAPD dicks Roger (Glover) and Riggs (Gibson) return for an improved if thoroughly implausible romp that pits the pair against vile South African emissaries who deal drugs, launder Krugerrands, and kill cops with impunity, all under the protective cover of diplomatic immunity. Dan and Mel spend much of their screen time apart; in fact, for a while there, Mel actually pays more attention to his new distaff amour (petite blonde Kensit) than he does to Danny (whose own screen wife puts in only token appearances). But fear not: Patsy is conveniently offed in time for our boys to enjoy their most overtly romantic moment to date when Mel, lying gravely wounded, whispers over Bob Dylan's soundtrack rendition of "Knockin' on Heaven's Door" (!) and beseeches Dan to "give us a kiss." For those uninterested in the vagaries of our heroes' complex relationship, Pesci supplies welcome relief as a garrulous government witness placed in the haphazard custody of a distracted Dan and Mel.

LETHAL WEAPON 3   (1992) **

D: Richard Donner. Mel Gibson, Danny Glover, Joe Pesci, Rene Russo, Stuart Wilson. 118 mins. (Warner) DVD

America's fave cop couple spend almost as much time bonding with their respective squeezes as they do with each other here. Otherwise, it's business as usual, with Mad Mel and Down-to-Earth Danny taking on a slew of unusually dull villains led by a renegade cop (Wilson). Not even Pesci's manic presence elevates this downwardly mobile retread. The series sinks to even lower depths with the desperate, deafening, barely coherent *Lethal Weapon 4* (1998, Warner, DVD), which nonetheless scored big-time with 'plex auds.

LIONHEART   (1991) **½

D: Sheldon Lettich. Jean-Claude Van Damme, Deborah Rennard, Harrison Page, Lisa Pelikan, Ashley Johnson, Brian Thompson. 105 mins. (Universal) DVD

Formerly titled both *A.W.O.L.* and *Wrong Bet*, *Lionheart* opens with our hero deserting the French Foreign Legion to avenge the death of his drug-dealing brother in the States. J-C arrives penniless in cold, cruel NYC but is soon rescued by black street-fight promoter Page (best remembered as the militant in Russ Meyer's *Vixen*) who steers him to ruthless blond martial arts mogul Rennard and her hulking bodyguard,

Thompson. J-C next journeys to warm, cruel L.A., where he engages in gladiatorial free-for-alls for the amusement of degenerate high-rollers, secretly turning his earnings over to his brother's widow (Pelikan) and five-year-old daughter (Johnson), who supplies the pic with a marginal "Kindergarten Kickboxer" angle. J-C shows he's learned how to cry on cue and apparently taught the same tearful trick to the rest of the cast, resulting in more on-screen bawling than we've seen in any actioner since *Cage*, when Reb Brown and Lou Ferrigno let the ocular moisture flow. The kickboxing choreography is first-rate, especially during J-C's climactic bout with an impressive kung-fu killer named Attila, who's fond of literally breaking his opponents in half.

LITTLE ODESSA   (1994) ***

D: James Gray. Tim Roth, Edward Furlong, Moira Kelly, Vanessa Redgrave, Maximilian Schell. 98 mins. (Artisan) DVD

Little Odessa is a downbeat but compelling crime-thriller/domestic-trauma combo that stars frequent Tarantino player Roth as a Russian-Jewish hit man who reluctantly returns to his old Brighton Beach nabe on an unwanted assignment. While waiting for the hit to go down, Roth is found by his emotionally needy younger bro' (Furlong), visits his brain-cancer-victim mother (Redgrave), resumes a long-standing feud with his father (Schell), and rekindles an abortive affair with ex-squeeze Kelly. Roth impressively fleshes out his unsympathetic role, while debuting director Gray manages to hold viewer attention despite a story line that's as grim as it gets. He also milks the max from his wintry Brooklyn and Queens locales and deserves credit for avoiding the flip crime-caper route that so many aspiring auteurs mine for their Hollywood demo reels. While the flick's inevitable violent denouement comes up short in the credibility depart-

ment, *Little Odessa* succeeds in providing a vivid picture of the dark side of an immigrant enclave.

LOCKDOWN   (1990) **

D: Fred Haines. Richard Lynch, Chris DeRose, Chuck Jeffreys, Joe Estevez, Elizabeth Kaitan. 94 mins. (Trimark)

Part *policier*, part prison pic, and part San Jose travelog, *Lockdown* shapes up as a sloppily assembled cliché compendium elevated only by B-screen supervillain Lynch's energetically malevolent turn as an opera-loving psycho. Director Haines grants the inventive thesp free reign, a wise move that makes this otherwise awkward actioner a must for R.L.'s fans.

LONE WOLF AND CUB:
THE SERIES

LONE WOLF AND CUB: SWORD OF VENGEANCE (KOZURE ÔKAMI: KOWOKASHI UNDEKASHI TSUKAMATSURU)   (1972) ****

D: Kenji Misumi. Tomisaburo Wakayama, Fumio Watanabe, Tomoko Mayama, Shigeru Tsuyuguchi, Yunosuke Inoo. Subtitled. 83 mins. (AnimEigo)

In presenting their debut Samurai Cinema entry, the Asian specialists at AnimEigo offer a pristine, uncut ("Not one drop of blood omitted!") letter-boxed edition of the first *Baby Cart* film, previously available only via bootleg tapes and a desecrated 1980 vid version titled *Shogun Assassin* (Media), dubbed by the likes of Marshall Efron and Sandra Bernhard. AnimEigo not only subtitles its edition but includes a running glossary, translating frequently used Japanese words like *ronin* (mercenary) and *seppuku* (ritual suicide). Produced by *Zatoichi* series star Shintaro Katsu, *Lone Wolf and Cub: Sword of Vengeance* (literal translation: "Child and Expertise for Rent") plays like

Yojimbo Meets Sergio Leone, complete with a pounding Morriconesque electric-guitar–dominated opening theme. Our story chronicles the violent quest of a 16th-century shogunate executioner, Itto Ogami (a portly Wakayama), who swears vengeance against his former employers and the Yagyu-clan assassins who murdered his wife and left him with the roughly year-old titular "cub" (Inoo). In a classic scene, Itto presents his uncomprehending young son with a choice between a samurai sword or a brightly colored ball; if the tot opts for the ball, Itto will send him to "join his mother." (Obviously, the toddler takes the sword, or the series would have ended there.) The first lap of the pair's journey leads them to a lawless "bathhouse" town, where, in a traditional Hollywood- (and spaghetti-) western setup, they encounter a gang of thugs terrorizing the local populace. It takes a good deal of provocation to get Itto to unsheath his trusty sword, but once he does, heads, limbs, and blood fly across the wide screen with gory abandon. AnimEigo follows with several worthy sequels, including *Lone Wolf and Cub: Baby Cart at the River Styx, Baby Cart to Hades, Baby Cart in Peril, Baby Cart in the Land of the Demons,* and *White Heaven in Hell.* AnimEigo also issues the recommended *Razor* and *Sleepy Eyes of Death* series.

THE LONG KISS GOODNIGHT (1996) *¹/₂

D: Renny Harlin. Geena Davis, Samuel L. Jackson, Patrick Malahide, Craig Bierko, Brian Cox, David Morse, G. D. Spradlin. 120 mins. (New Line) DVD

The deadly alliance of director Harlin and then-real-life wife, Davis—who'd earlier collaborated on the swashbuckling dud *Cutthroat Island* (see index), Hollywood's all-time biggest money loser—and scripter Shane (*Last Action Hero*) Black results in a loud, obnoxious, soulless, and suspense-free action "comedy," the epitome of low-wattage "high concept" and the worst of its ilk since the equally awful Michael J. Fox fiasco *The Hard Way* (Universal). Geena's an amnesic Jersey-'burb PTA type who learns she's really a former CIA killing machine. Aided by low-rent shamus Jackson, she sets out to foil an elaborate Company plot to blow up Niagara Falls and pin the blame on Arab terrorists. Geena's truly grotesque here, while the supporting thesps are likewise encouraged to mug, sneer, and leer their way through the empty, inorganic proceedings.

THE LONG RIDE (1998) B&W ***

D: Hal Singleton. Hal Singleton, Gina Galligan, Brian LeBoeuf, Vince DeSepio, Stephen Halcum, Dave Silva. 120 mins. (Salt City)

One-biker-show Hal Singleton proves himself a sort of camcorder Cassavetes on wheels, while his *Long Ride* emerges as a no-budget *Easy Rider* for the '90s. A believably battered, fortysomething Singleton takes the center role as J. T. Monroe, a basically decent sort but a lifelong loser whose understandable frustrations short-circuit a series of menial jobs and encourage minor but persistent scrapes with the law. Evicted from his squalid L.A. pad, J.T. hits the road, seeking salvation (or at least a better menial job) in the decidedly low-glam environs of Tuba City, Arizona. At first, J.T.'s luck remains consistent (i.e., bad) when a scuffle at a biker-owned topless bar leaves him severely beaten and stripped of his one important possession—his motorcycle. Our hero finds help in a rare sympathetic lawperson, local sheriff Dave (Silva), and fetching waitress Galligan (a former Miss Harley Davidson, according to the box). Singleton's utterly authentic odyssey supplies rewards aplenty for viewers patient enough to weather its rough start, where the raw tech quality, dense night photography, ambient sound, and ragged editing (the infamous "Alan Smithee" assumes credit/blame for the last-mentioned!) is offputting at best. But *The Long Ride* gains in both clarity and momentum once J.T. zooms off on his nearly verité journey through lowlife Americana and, astoundingly, sustains over the course of its two-hour (!) running time.

LOVE & A .45 (1994) ***

D: C. M. Talkington. Gil Bellows, Renee Zellweger, Rory Cochrane, Jeffrey Combs, Ann Wedgeworth, Peter Fonda, Jack Nance, Michael Bowen. 102 mins. (Trimark) DVD

An indie that struck out with most mainstream critics—who either compared it negatively with Oliver Stone's *Natural Born Killers* or confessed to being sick of the entire celluloid roadkill genre—during its scattered, eye-blink theatrical release, *Love & a .45,* while far from subtle, entertains and scores its points sans Stone's sledgehammer approach. Bellows plays a nonviolent, code-bound crook who totes an unloaded .45 while robbing convenience stores. He becomes a murder accomplice when his unstable, crank-crazed bud Cochrane blows away his own junkie-clerk girlfriend during a botched holdup. Gil's troubles escalate when squeeze Zellweger shoots a pair of Texas Rangers to save her beau's life. When the pair take it on the lam, they inadvertently become local TV celebs, a status Zellweger embraces with undisguised glee. Debuting writer/director Talkington keeps his mock potboiler moving at a swift pace. The pic is peppered with quirky perfs by *Re-Animator* mad doc Combs as an aggressive lowlife named Dinosaur Bob, a grotty-looking Fonda as Zellweger's drug-damaged "handicapped suburban hippie" dad (who speaks with the aid of an electronic larynx booster), and the late Jack (*Eraserhead*) Nance as the hapless justice of the peace who weds the fugitive lovers. Cochrane endures an especially painful role; in the course of the film, he's knifed through the hand, forked in the neck, skull-massaged with a tattooist's drill, beaten, and shot. Ex-Television guitarist Tom Verlaine composed the score, while the Flaming Lips ("She Don't Use Jelly") contribute a soundtrack tune.

LOWER LEVEL   (1991) **½

D: Kristine Peterson. David Bradley, Elizabeth Gracen, Jeff Yagher. 88 mins. (Republic)

Peterson's *Lower Level* is a downscale *Die Hard* that finds foxy architect Gracen and yuppie beau Yagher trapped in a deserted skyscraper controlled by crazed security guard David (*American Ninja 3*) Bradley. While ultimately predictable, *Lower Level* generates some legit suspense and benefits from several deft touches, including an especially striking fade-out.

THE MACK   (1973) **½

D: Michael Campus. Max Julien, Richard Pryor, Don Gordon, Carol Speed. 110 mins. (Nelson)

A former 42nd Street perennial and one of the "blaxploitation" genre's most durable hits, *The Mack* stars Julien as an ex-con-turned-pimp who, with a little help from his friend Pryor, rids the 'hood of pushers.

MACON COUNTY LINE (1974) ***

D: Richard Compton. Max Baer, Jr., Alan Vint, Cheryl Waters, Jesse Vint. 89 mins. (Anchor Bay) DVD

A tragic misunderstanding triggers sheriff Baer's vendetta against a trio of innocent Yankee youths in a tense B flick that helped establish the "Wish I Wasn't in Dixie" genre. Followed by *Return to Macon County* (Vestron), with Don Johnson and Nick Nolte. New Horizons added the seriously belated *Macon County Jail,* with Ally (*High Art*) Sheedy, in 1999.

MADE IN USA   (1988) **

D: Ken Friedman. Christopher Penn, Lori Singer, Adrian Pasdar. 92 mins. (Nelson, n.i.d.)

Young drifters Pasdar and Penn pick up an embittered Singer in dioxin-poisoned Town Beach (an actual site) and wander in and out of petty crime on a peripatetic journey to sunny California. Friedman's tour of America's real-life toxic-waste centers could have provided a powerful frame for a more pointed story. Unfortunately, *Made in USA* is done in by a meandering narrative, uninteresting characters, and a diffused focus. The Sonic Youth soundtrack helps some, but Friedman's potentially strong idea never really clicks.

MAGNIFICENT BUTCHER (1979) ***

D: Yuen Woo Ping. Sammo Hung, Yuen Biao, Wei Pai, Kwan Tak-Hing. 90 mins. Subtitled/dubbed. (Tai Seng)

Longtime Jackie Chan cohort, popular kung-fu comedian, and network-TV (*Martial Law*) star Hung dominates this fun, early showcase for the rotund actor/auteur. Here Hung takes the title role as a bumbling butcher and student of legendary martial arts master Wong Fei-Hung (Tak-Hing) who finds himself at odds with treacherous, two-faced villain and rival fighter Ko (Biao) when the latter attempts to frame our hero for murder. Despite the serious-sounding story line, most of *Magnificent Butcher* is devoted to nearly nonstop kung-fu of the slapstick kind. Helmer Ping, who went on to direct Jackie Chan in *Drunken Master* and Jet Li in *Tai Chi Master* (Tai Seng, DVD), keeps the consistently amusing action moving at a swift pace.

MALONE   (1987) **

D: Harley Cokliss. Burt Reynolds, Cliff Robertson, Cynthia Gibb, Scott Wilson, Lauren Hutton, Kenneth McMillan. 92 mins. (Orion)

One of Burt's single-word '80s titles—see also *Stick* (Universal) and *Heat* (Paramount)—that bombed both with critics and at the box office, *Malone* is essentially a limp, contemporized *Shane* revamp. Burt's a retired CIA assassin who stumbles into rich right-winger Robertson's Pacific Northwest turf and tangles with the latter and his small army of inept hired hoods. Wilson, in the Van Heflin role, plays a 'Nam-vet gas-station owner who refuses to sell his property to Robertson's goons; Gibb, as his daughter, serves as a distaff Brandon DeWilde stand-in. Wounded in a shoot-out, Burt gets to spend about half the movie on his back before recovering in time to embark on the expected one-man rampage in the flick's predictably fiery finale. He largely limits his emoting to some occasional grunting and eye shifting here but scores enough close-ups to satisfy fans of his famous hairpiece.

MANCHURIAN AVENGER (1985) **½

D: Ed Warnick. Bobby Kim, Lella Hee, Bill ("Superfoot") Wallace, Michael Stuart. 87 mins. (HBO)

HANDS OF IRON, FEET OF STEEL. HE SMASHES BONES THAT NEVER HEAL. So reads the calling card of *Manchurian Avenger* Kim. And while it may not be as catchy as, say, HAVE GUN, WILL TRAVEL, you can't accuse Kim of violating any truth-in-advertising sanctions. In this chopsocky western, Bobby breaks enough bones to keep the staffs of *ER* and *Chicago Hope* busy for years. As laconic hero Joe, Kim helps a young couple battle the villainous Chang, a typical Asian gang boss of an unnamed sagebrush town circa 1880. Aided by Mexican outlaw Diego (Stuart), Joe delivers high-kicking death blows to a small army of six-gun goons, culminating in a feet-first showdown with Wallace's evil, multiethnic band of Old West martial artists, who, in full regalia, resemble a kung-fu version of the Village People. Kim himself has the distinction of being a dead ringer for Charles Bronson, albeit a compact (roughly 5-feet-2) Asian version. While he may lack the latter's thespian abilities—he emotes as if he's been trained by Sho Kosugi, with a little help from Stallone's vocal coach—he's got the pencil-line moustache down pat. And his movie's a lot better than his later atrocity *Kill Line* (see index).

EL MARIACHI   (1992) ***

D: Robert Rodriguez. Carlos Gallardo, Consuelo Gómez, Reinol Martinez, Peter Marquardt. Subtitled/dubbed. 81 mins. (Columbia/TriStar)

Initially lensed for $7,000—less than what it probably costs to feed and care for Arnold Schwarzenegger for a day—Rodriguez's celluloid debut (reportedly audiovisually sweetened to the tune of an additional $150,000 post-production dollars prior to its theatrical release) at once conforms to, spoofs, and transcends the type of Mexican-border actioner that used to play Times Square's Hollywood Twin and still proliferates on video via titles like 1999's *Border Wars* (Spectrum). (Walter Hill allotted the full-blown Tinseltown treatment to the genre with his 1987 Nick Nolte vehicle *Extreme Prejudice* [see index]). In *El Mariachi*, Rodriguez's simple mistaken-identity hook serves as an effective frame for a lively series of

violent misadventures. When hit men employed by double-crossing drug lord Marquardt mistake titular itinerant guitarist/singer Gallardo for pro assassin Martinez (who totes an arsenal-equipped guitar case), Gallardo finds refuge with foxy saloon owner Gómez. Our hero spends much of the film's running time running from the gringo crime lord's army of inefficient hirelings, ultimately developing considerable killer skills himself. *El Mariachi's* deft combo of bloody action, slapstick gallows wit, and visual style (including some brief nightmare sequences) results in a true genre treat that equals such earlier precocious indies as the Coen brothers' *Blood Simple,* Andy Anderson's *Positive I.D.* and Quentin Tarantino's *Reservoir Dogs* (see index).

MARKED FOR DEATH   (1990) ***

D: Dwight H. Little. Steven Seagal, Basil Wallace, Keith David, Tom Wright, Joanna Pacula, Al Israel. 94 mins. (Fox) DVD

Marked for Death (originally titled *Screwface*) sees violence-weary (yeah, sure) DEA agent Seagal attempt to act upon a priest's advice to "find a gentle self inside you" by retiring to his sister's house in a Chicago 'burb. Steve's newfound pacifism lasts roughly half a reel, ending abruptly when a posse of Rasta crack dealers led by Screwface (Wallace, in a menacing turn) shoot his young niece. Steve teams up with gung-ho African-American high school coach David and Jamaican undercover cop Wright to terminate Screwface and cronies' criminal careers. While *Marked for Death* may be slim in the credibility department, it's admirably thorough in its determination to cover all action/exploitation bases, offering plenty of kung-fu combat, bloody shoot-outs, eye-gougings, decapitations, lovingly lensed high-tech hardware worship, and even some dirty dancing, all set to a lively reggae soundtrack.

MARTIAL LAW:
THE SERIES

MARTIAL LAW   (1990) **

D: S. E. Cohen. Chad McQueen, Cynthia Rothrock, David Carradine, Andy McCutcheon. 88 mins. (Media, n.i.d.)

Hong Kong–trained five-time Women's Karate World Champ Rothrock is forced to play second nunchuck to McQueen in her maiden American B-movie showcase, a capably rendered but thoroughly routine urban-action caper. Chad's a hard-chopping cop (his nickname's "Martial Law") whose kid brother (McCutcheon) gets mixed up with L.A. crime boss Carradine. McQueen displays some fancy foot-and-fist work, if little of his late pop's charisma, while Carradine gets to dust off a few of his old *Kung Fu* moves (though his stunt double shoulders the more strenuous action chores). Cynthia, cast as Chad's fellow cop and token love interest, shows she can take her kicks as well as dish them out. No relation to the Sammo Hung teleseries or the 1993 Jeff Wincott vehicle *Martial Outlaw* (Republic).

MARTIAL LAW II: UNDERCOVER (1992) **½

D: Kurt Anderson. Cynthia Rothrock, Jeff Wincott, Billy Drago, Paul Johansson, Evan Lurie. 92 mins. (Universal)

Martial Law II: Undercover represents a significant improvement over the original. Cop Cynthia teams with a faster-footed Wincott to pursue the usual slew of wealthy drug lords, their martial arts minions, and corrupt-cop cohorts, steadily employed heavy Drago among them. While Wincott works from the outside, our heroine goes undercover as a barmaid at an upscale sleaze club to collar cruel dope czar Johansson. The plot serves as an adequate frame for another series of fairly spectacular fights, shoot-outs and chases—the only times Cynth departs from her otherwise unfailingly mild, pleasant demeanor. Cynth can also be seen in, among others, *Angel of Fury, China O'Brien, China O'Brien II, Lady Dragon, Lady Dragon 2* (all Imperial); *Fast Getaway, Rage and Honor, Rage and Honor 2* (all Columbia/TriStar); *Fast Getaway 2* (Artisan); *No Retreat, No Surrender II* (Forum); and *Undefeatable* (Fox).

MASK OF DEATH (1997) ***

D: David Mitchell. Lorenzo Lamas, Rae Dawn Chong, Billy Dee Williams, Conrad Dunn, Thomas Cavanaugh. 125 mins. (Dimension)

Lamas goes the dual-role route in what rates as his best vehicle to date, a direct-to-home-vid entry that's better than most big-screen action releases. Lorenzo begins the flick as Lyle Mason, brutal "American muscle for the Russian Mafia" (Soviet breakup be damned; we still can't trust them pesky Russkis), who's looking to score a potentially calamitous microchip from renegade mobster DiLeo (a colorful Dunn). When Lyle gets wasted in the spectacular opening action sequence, a facially wounded cop fitting his general description reluctantly agrees to undergo plastic surgery and pose undercover as Mason as part of an FBI sting engineered by agent Jeffreys (Williams). Lamas does a good job in making the temporary moral and behavioral transition to a cold-blooded killer who, like Laurence Fishburne in *Deep Cover* and Johnny Depp in *Donnie Brasco* (see index), starts losing track of his original mission, particularly when his criminal actions result in the violent deaths of several cops and innocent bystanders. Chong has a subordinate role as Lamas's former police partner who's not in on the scheme, while Cavanaugh enjoys a neat character turn as DiLeo's ginseng-addicted henchman.

MASTER OF THE FLYING GUILLOTINE (1975) ***

D: Jimmy Wang Yu. Jimmy Wang Yu, Kam Kang. 90 mins. (Sinister Cinema)

This intense, violent, and characteristically surreal Hong Kong period actioner recounts the titular hero's decapitating exploits. Be prepared to duck!

MAXIMUM FORCE (1992) **½

D: Joseph Merhi. Sam Jones, Sherrie Rose, Jason Lively, Richard Lynch, Mickey Rooney, John Saxon. 90 mins. (PM)

Maximum Force pits specially trained cops Jones, Rose, and Lively against vet supervillain Lynch and his henchhordes. Saxon supplies the expository glue as the trio's soon-to-retire leader, while Rooney, as a corrupt police chief, emotes in a limo, collects an easy check, and rides on. *Maximum Force* lacks magic and soul, but the action's well staged.

MAXIMUM RISK (1996) ***

D: Ringo Lam. Jean-Claude Van Damme, Natasha Henstridge, Jean-Hugues Anglade, Zach Grenier, Stéphane Audran, Paul Ben-Victor, David Hemblen. 101 mins. (Columbia/TriStar) DVD

Hong Kong action ace Lam—whose *City on Fire* (Tai Seng, DVD) purportedly provided a major inspiration for Tarantino's *Reservoir Dogs*—makes his stateside debut with this better-than-average Van Damme bashfest. As in *Double Impact,* J-C gets to play dual roles as twins separated at birth, though he doesn't land a chance to beat himself up in this one, as badder half Mikhail, a Russian Mafia–connected fugitive, gets wasted in the opening scene. As good-guy French cop Alain, Van Damme journeys from Nice to New York's not-so-nice Little Odessa enclave in Brighton Beach, Brooklyn, to untangle

the mystery surrounding his brother's demise. *Species'* alien man-eater Henstridge plays the late Mikhail's grieving squeeze, and it doesn't take her long to tumble for Alain as well, at one point chirping, "So you looked pretty comfortable with that gun stuck in that guy's neck today!" Dialogue, courtesy of Larry (*Gunfighter's Moon, Beyond the Law*) Ferguson, is not *Maximum Risk*'s strong point, but the film offers more plot than most J-C efforts, and director Lam doesn't stint in the action department, utilizing everything from careening cars to out-of-control chainsaws. Van Damme gives a subdued, almost humble (indeed, nearly *human*) perf, while Gallic stalwarts Audran (as his briefly seen mom) and *Killing Zoe* costar Anglade (as his French police partner) lend a touch of thespian pedigree. While some exteriors were shot in NYC and Philadelphia, Toronto, fast becoming America's Film Capital, again subs for the USA most of the way. No relation to Fred Olen Ray's propitiously timed sound-alike release, *Maximum Security* (New Horizons).

MEN OF WAR (1994) ***

D: Perry Lang. Dolph Lundgren, Charlotte Lewis, Anthony John Denison, Tim Guinee, Trevor Goddard, B. D. Wong, Don Harvey, Tiny ("Zeus") Lister, Tom Wright, Kevin Tighe, Aldo Sambrell. 102 mins. (Dimension)

Dogs of War Meets *The Magnificent Seven* in this unusually lively Lundgren vehicle, which sees the Swedish strongman contribute his finest emotive effort, even topping his triumphal character turn in *Johnny Mnemonic* (see index). Based on a script by John Sayles—who'd earlier borrowed from Kurosawa's *Seven Samurai* with his 1980 *Magnificent Seven*-in-Space opera, *Battle Beyond the Stars*—and the *Demon Knight* team of Ethan Rieff and Cyrus Voris, *Men of War* opens with guilt-driven ex-merc Dolph pacing Chicago's icy streets, so down and out that a flask has replaced a .45 in his shoulder holster. After some requisite initial reluctance, Lundgren, melted by military mentor Tighe's avuncular intervention, sets out to round up his old merc crew. Their mission? To "persuade" the primitive people on an obscure island off the Thailand coast to sell the rights to the isle's nitrous-rich bird droppings to a pair of smug, avaricious yuppies (including director Lang in a cameo). Swayed by the natives' courageous refusal and the eloquent arguments of their jive-English-speaking spokesman Wong, four of the seven mercs decide to stay and help the locals defend against an invasion now entrusted to Tighe and certifiable psycho Goddard (terrif in a role tailor-made for Vernon Wells). *Men of War* pretty much has it all: mass battles, mutilations, decapitations, exotic narcotics, romance, betrayal, despicable villains, internecine conflicts, and topless communal bathing scenes. Viewers looking for a straight-ahead actioner combining old-fashioned heroism with contempo carnage won't be disappointed. Avoid Louis Mourneau's similarly themed but seriously subpar *Soldier Boyz* (HBO), with Michael Dudikoff.

MEN WITH GUNS   (1997) ***1/2

D: John Sayles. Federico Luppi, Damián Alcazár, Tania Cruz, Damián Delgado, Dan Rivera González, Mandy Patinkin, Kathryn Grody. Subtitled. 128 mins. (Columbia/TriStar)

Writer, director, and editor Sayles follows his 1996 Texas-set storytelling triumph, *Lone Star* (see index) with the equally excellent, thematically reverberant *Men with Guns*. Luppi (*Cronos*) powers the picture via his award-worthy turn as Dr. Fuentes, an aging physician living a comfortably sheltered life in the capital of an unnamed Central American country (presumably El Salvador). The newly widowed doctor decides to forgo his usual vacation for a rural quest to reconnect with several medical students he'd encouraged to set up practices in impoverished Indian villages. Instead of the medical "legacy" he'd intended, he finds that his students have been systematically slaughtered, along with countless locals, by the titular death squads dispatched to keep the natives ignorant and in line. On his journey through a jungle hell, the hitherto naïve doctor receives a belated education of his own, taught by an army deserter, a worldly preteen native, a mute rape victim, a faithless priest, and a pair of American archaeologists. Especially chilling is a scene wherein Dr. Fuentes discovers that a student's medical instruments have been turned into tools of torture by pillaging soldiers.

Like *Lone Star*, Sayles's complex tale of degradation and redemption wrapped in adventure guise is a gem of pure storytelling pleasure. *Men with Guns* represents another step forward in Sayles's development as a novelist with a movie camera, avoiding the youthful didacticism and self-indulgence of some of his earlier works. While the title may mislead some into thinking it's a straight-up action flick, *Men with Guns* is unlikely to disappoint any video renter. Except for Yanks Patinkin and Grody's dialogue, the film is spoken in Spanish and Indian dialects.

MERCENARY   (1996) **1/2

D: Avi Nesher. Olivier Gruner, John Ritter, Robert Culp, Ed Lauter, Martin Kove, Michael Zelniker, Lara Harris. 105 mins. (PolyGram)

Ritter goes the macho action route in a ridiculously plotted but fun exercise in virtually nonstop carnage. Though second-billed under kickboxer Gruner, Ritter scores more dialogue as an electronics mogul whose wife (along with about two dozen extras) is killed during a "terrorist" raid on his manse. Ritter accompanies title merc Gruner and crew on an assault against Russki villain Kove at the latter's medieval-styled Afghani redoubt. Along the way, Ritter gets shot, stabbed, beaten within an inch, tortured by a killer Fido, and upchucks while hang-gliding (he's a vertigo sufferer), all of which was still probably preferable to acting opposite Joyce DeWitt. Followed by 1999's *Mercenary 2: Thick and Thin* (Touchstone).

MIAMI BLUES   (1990) ***1/2

D: George Armitage. Alec Baldwin, Fred Ward, Jennifer Jason Leigh, Nora Dunn, Charles Napier, José Peréz. 99 mins. (Orion)

Miami Blues is a raw, lively, darkly funny cop-versus-crazy caper directed by onetime Roger Corman apprentice George (*Vigilante Force*) Armitage, also responsible for the 1997 black comedy *Grosse Pointe Blank* (Touchstone, DVD). Baldwin contributes a dynamite perf as versatile psycho Junior Frenger, a lowlife who's equally adept at composing haikus, reeling off Al Pacino *Scarface* imitations, and killing irritating airport Krishnas with a simple hand grip. Ward and Leigh likewise excel as a toothless homicide cop and a naïve hooker, respectively. Beyond its able cast, *Miami Blues* further benefits from evocative location lensing and a perverse script based on Charles Willeford's noir novel. The flick even scores high in the gore department with its eyebrow-sewing and finger-chopping segments.

MIDNIGHT EXPRESS   (1978) ***

D: Alan Parker. Brad Davis, John Hurt, Irene Miracle. 120 mins. (Columbia/TriStar) DVD

Based on a true story, Parker's harrowing account of young smuggler Davis's nightmarish internment in a Turkish prison still packs a punch. Randy Quaid contributes a top turn as a fellow American inmate. Now available in a special "20th anniversary edition."

MIDNIGHT MURDERS (1991)***

D: Dick Lowry. Rod Steiger, Michael Gross, Gary Basaraba, Christopher Rich, Beth Fowler, Henderson Forsythe. 95 mins. (New Horizons)

Veteran TV-movie helmer Lowry imparts an adroit verité feel to this fact-based account, ably capturing North Dakota's drab expanses, a landscape that mirrors many of his characters' bleak interior lives. Steiger gives a chilling perf as right-wing extremist Gordon Kahl, a grim, schizophrenic self-made murderer/martyr who places his paranoid "principles" above his own family's welfare. After spending a year in Leavenworth for income-tax evasion, Kahl vents his festering hatred and frustration in an ill-advised backroads shoot-out that leaves two lawmen dead and his own subservient son seriously wounded. FBI agent Gross, sort of a poor man's Alan Alda, teams with courageous local deputy Basaraba to track a fugitive Kahl through an underground network that ultimately leads to an Arkansas farm and a final violent confrontation. New Horizons' 1995 video release proved timelier than anticipated, arriving in the wake of the Oklahoma City atrocity. *Midnight Murders* sheds light on the type of paranoid "victim" mind-set that infects terrorists of all stripes.

MIDNIGHT WITNESS (1993)***

D: Peter Foldy. Paul Johansson, Maxwell Caulfield, Karen Moncrief, Jan-Michael Vincent, Kelli Maroney, Virginia Mayo, Mark Pellegrino, Ellen Geer. 90 mins. (Academy, n.i.d.)

At least the second film to draw its premise directly from the Rodney King case—see also the C. Thomas Howell vehicle *To Protect and Serve* (see index)—*Midnight Witness* employs its videotaped police-brutality hook as a convenient intro to a more conventional chase plot. While bickering couple Johansson—who records cop Caulfield and cronies' fatal beating of a Latino drug dealer—and Moncrief make for dull protagonists, director/writer Foldy compensates with unexpected details that lend considerable authenticity to the sleazy, anxiety-fraught milieu in which our endangered duo suddenly find themselves immersed. Making said milieu more interesting than the couple trapped therein actually works to *Midnight*'s advantage. The pic likewise benefits from its full complement of colorful supporting characters, starting with oedipal wreck Caulfield and his mom (venerable Mayo, in a rare contempo role). Vincent contributes another strong character turn as a long-haired, crank-crazed lowlife who, with preggers wife (Maroney), gives our fleeing couple an ill-advised lift that ultimately implicates them in murder. *Midnight Witness* transcends its imitative premise to provide its share of low-budget thrills.

MILLER'S CROSSING (1990)***1/2

D: Joel Coen. Gabriel Byrne, Albert Finney, Marcia Gay Harden, John Turturro, Jon Polito, J. E. Pressman, Steve Buscemi. 115 mins. (Fox)

Miller's Crossing is a consistently compelling period gangster caper fueled by the Coen brothers' twisty, ultimately cyclical story line and solid script (even if it runs a bit thick with [oft invented] hard-boiled '30s slang and the occasional deliberate anachronism). Byrne, Finney, Turturro, and Polito all turn in convincing work as the major players in a multicross mob game. Coens crony Sam Raimi cameos as a "snickering gunman" in one of the film's many violent set pieces.

MILLIONAIRE'S EXPRESS (1986)***

D: Sammo Hung. Sammo Hung, Yuen Biao, Eric Tsang, Olivia Cheng Man-Ngar, Rosamund Kwan, Yukari Ôshima, Richard Norton, Cynthia Rothrock, Dick Wei. Subtitled/dubbed. 107 mins. (Tai Seng) DVD

Multitalented Hung directs and stars as a slippery-rogue-turned-unlikely-hero in this gala kung-fu/spaghetti-western comedy (a.k.a. *Shanghai Express,* no relation to the Sternberg classic [Universal]). The action centers on a remote Chinese town, where a fugitive Hung hopes to set up shop with his string of call girls. Meanwhile, a horde of multiethnic bandits—Aussie martial artist Norton and a young Rothrock among them—plan to halt and plunder the title train, carrying a wide array of wealthy riders, outside that selfsame town. Comedic threads and subplots abound—one of the best running riffs involves a pair of seemingly dignified rival martial arts masters and their rambunctious six-year-old sons—while Hung makes fun of everything from Leone westerns to Japanese samurai flicks. *Millionaire's Express* rates as a wild romp that, despite a few broad strokes, remains relentlessly entertaining throughout.

MINISTRY OF VENGEANCE (1989)**

D: Peter Maris. John Schneider, Ned Beatty, Yaphet Kotto, James Tolkan, George Kennedy, Appollonia Kotero. 93 mins. (Media, n.i.d.)

"He was a soldier who found religion in the hellhole of 'Nam! Now his wife and daughter have been brutally slain by terrorists! It's time for Rev. David Miller to swap his collar for an M-16 and establish his own…Ministry of Vengeance!" Ex–*Dukes of Hazzard* hero Schneider—previously seen serving a celluloid one-man-army hitch in 1986's execrable *Cocaine Wars* (Media)—stars as the mad-as-hell man of God who goes gunning for seasoned screen sadist Robert Miano and his terrorist lackeys. While *Ministry* delivers its fair share of action, Schneider is bland as the combative clergyman (sort of a Billy Grahambo) and the plot, with its multiple "crosses" and double crosses, ultimately stretches B-movie credibility to the breaking point. Appollonia fans, meanwhile, can find their idol on generous view in the 1990 actioner *Back to Back* (MGM/UA), the 1991 thriller *Black Magic Woman* (Trimark), and, of course, with mentor the Artist Formerly and Once Again Known as Prince in 1984's *Purple Rain* (Warner, DVD).

MISSING IN ACTION:
THE SERIES

MISSING IN ACTION   (1984) *

D: Joseph Zito. Chuck Norris, M. Emmet Walsh, Lenore Kasdorf. 101 mins. (MGM)

Chuck makes a major career move, abandoning his kung-fu Clint Eastwood–wannabe persona to become Rambo clone Colonel Braddock, an imitative tactic that succeeded in brightening his then-fading, since-revived media allure.

MISSING IN ACTION 2:
THE BEGINNING   (1985) *

D: Lance Hool. Chuck Norris, Soon Teck-Oh, Steven Williams, Bennett Ohta, Cosie Costa. 96 mins. (MGM)

A prequel to Chuck's *Missing in Action*, *MIA 2* chronicles Colonel Braddock's brutal stay in a Vietcong POW compound. The most imaginative sequence sees Chuck strung upside down with a bag over his head. What's in the bag? A hungry rat! Chuck saves his neck and simultaneously registers his low opinion of VC cuisine by biting the hapless rodent's head off! Chuck returns, sans rat, for more of the same in the series' overdue finale, 1988's *Braddock: Missing in Action III* (Media).

MISSION: IMPOSSIBLE   (1996) **½

D: Brian De Palma. Tom Cruise, Jon Voight, Emmanuelle Béart, Jean Reno, Ving Rhames, Kristin Scott Thomas, Vanessa Redgrave. 110 mins. (Paramount) DVD

Mission: Impossible (whose long-running TV-series predecessor was never a Phantom fave) is at its best when director De Palma goofs on the high-tech-spy genre. As an abandoned undercover op suspected of being a mole, Cruise grins a lot with seeming incomprehension (not surprisingly, given the convoluted plot) and performs both his major action scenes in a supine position. De Palma crafts a terrif ultraminimalist disc-retrieval sequence that's dependent on an upchucking CIA worker and is almost undone by an errant rat and a bead of sweat. The climactic train chase rates as another off-the-wall winner. *M:I* also contains stretches static enough to give the nearly motionless campfest *Spy Squad* (see index) a run for its inertia. Our short-statured hero receives able support from Voight as the *M:I* team leader, Redgrave as an ultracivilized villain, and Rhames (sporting his *Pulp Fiction* Marcellus look) as a renegade computer hacker. This is one megabudget movie that plays better on video, where you can freeze-frame and rewind to figure out what the hell is going on.

MR. MAJESTYK   (1974) ***

D: Richard Fleischer. Charles Bronson, Al Lettieri, Linda Cristal. 103 mins. (MGM)

Mobsters machine-gun Chuck's melons (among other atrocities), setting our hero off on a vengeance spree in a superior Elmore Leonard–scripted citrus-circuit variation on Bronson's *Death Wish* series.

MR. NICE GUY   (1997) **½

D: Sammo Hung. Jackie Chan, Richard Norton, Gabrielle Fitzpatrick. 87 mins. (New Line) DVD

A potentially fun premise—Jackie plays the titular chef on an Aussie TV show—receives disappointingly short shrift. The pic quickly degenerates into a filmlong series of repetitious chases and comic kung-fu showdowns when our hero winds up with a videotape that incriminates local drug lord Norton. Chan fans will want to tune in for the inventive action scenes, but the plot's satiric potential goes woefully unrealized.

MOBSTERS   (1991) **½

D: Michael Karbelnikoff. Christian Slater, Patrick Dempsey, Richard Grieco, Anthony Quinn, Lara Flynn Boyle, Michael Gambon, Costas Mandylor, F. Murray Abraham. 104 mins. (Universal)

The first MTV-styled gangster movie—unless you count Alan Parker's precocious preteen 1976 mob musical *Bugsy Malone* (Paramount)— *Mobsters* recycles roughly the same events chronicled in the superior early-'80s teleseries *The Gangster Chronicles*. Celluloid cover boys Slater, Dempsey, and Grieco replace *Chronicles*'s Michael Nouri, Brian Benben, and Joe Penny as Lucky Luciano, Meyer Lansky, and Bugsy Siegel, respectively, with Mandylor tossed in as Frank Costello. Our story finds the posturing partners-in-period-crime matching wits and muscle with reigning rival dons Faranzano, snarlingly interpreted by Gambon, and Masseria, lustily overplayed by Quinn, who spends most of his screen time shoveling pasta (though, in keeping with the MTV mood, he also resurrects a few rusty *Zorba* dance moves). Abraham cameos as Arnold Rothstein, while Nicholas Sadler enjoys a memorable nose-biting scene as Mad Dog Coll, and hulking genre heavy Robert (*Maniac Cop*) Z'dar proves he's just as scary without makeup. While *Mobsters* actually flirts with the facts at times, the pic packs all the authenticity of a Roaring '20s theme park, incorporating such creative anachronisms as Lansky's cry of "We'd be history!" On the upside, the movie crams in enough violence to require the gory expertise of horror-makeup-FX ace Tony Gardner and moves with sufficient speed to conceal its more egregious gaffes (like rewriting Coll's famous phone-booth execution).

MOONSHINE HIGHWAY (1996) ***

D: Andy Armstrong. Kyle MacLachlan, Randy Quaid, Jeremy Ratchford, Gary Farmer, Maria Del Mar. 96 mins. (Paramount)

An entertaining *Thunder Road*–styled (see index) action drama set in the South, circa 1957, *Moonshine Highway* chronicles booze runner MacLachlan's struggles with corrupt local sheriff Quaid, pesky federal revenuers, rival 'shiners (a cameoing David Cronenberg [!] among them), impatient squeeze Del Mar, who wants Kyle to quit the life, and mechanic Farmer, who's after our hero to take up legit stock-car racing. Filled with elaborate vehicular stunts, scored by a hot soundtrack composed of original instrumentals and vintage Sun Records rockabilly tunes, and boasting an authentic look and feel, *Moonshine Highway*, originally aired on Showtime cable, represents the type of A- product that's no longer deemed large enough to play in bijous but is well worth popping into your VCR.

THE MOST DANGEROUS GAME (1932) B&W ***

D: Ernest B. Schoedsack, Irving Pichel. Joel McCrea, Leslie Banks, Fay Wray. 78 mins. (Sinister Cinema) DVD

Mad hunter Banks ("Release the hounds!") sets out after human prey McCrea in one of the most imitated movies in genre history (John Woo's *Hard Target* is one of many

recent clones). The original—costarring premier screen screamer Wray—has lost little of its initial impact.

MOST WANTED (1997) **1/2

D: David Glenn Hogan. Keenen Ivory Wayans, Jon Voight, Jill Hennessy, Paul Sorvino, Eric Roberts, Robert Culp, Wolfgang Bodison, Simon Baker Denny. 99 mins. (Warner) DVD

Too routine for the big screen, where it proved anything but wanted during its brief theatrical run, *Most Wanted* is better suited to home-vid, where it plays like a relatively lavish, better-than-average B actioner with a seasoned name cast. The movie finds comedian Wayans, who also scripted, in a mostly mirthless mode as a fugitive military sniper set up to take the fall for the First Lady's assassination. Our hero enlists medico Hennessy to his cause, and the pair spend most of the pic gathering evidence while eluding evil army general Voight (employing a broad Southern accent and a full range of hammy tics). Former *I Spy* guy Culp turns up as a ruthless biochemical mogul, Sorvino is a quietly forceful CIA chief, and Roberts proves unusually subdued as the latter's assistant. Scripter Wayans springs few surprises but keeps the story moving at a brisk pace.

MOUNTAINS OF THE MOON (1990) ***1/2

D: Bob Rafelson. Patrick Bergin, Richard E. Grant, Fiona Shaw. 140 mins. (Artisan) DVD

Rafelson's excellent, sweeping, undeservedly obscure epic (barely released theatrically) chronicles 19th-century explorers Sir Richard Burton (Bergin) and John Speke's (Grant) quest for the source of the Nile and their adventure's less-than-amicable aftermath.

MOVING TARGET (1996) **1/2

D: Damian Lee. Michael Dudikoff, Billy Dee Williams, Michelle Johnson, Aaron Bess, Tom Harvey. 106 mins. (A-Pix) DVD

Ex–*American Ninja* Dudikoff scores what may be his best direct-to-home-vid vehicle (admittedly not saying much). As Sonny McClean, a bounty hunter caught in the crossfire between warring Russian Mafia factions, the Dudman gets to emote more than usual and, in the physical arena, proves he can get as good as he gives, absorbing innumerable beatings as the reels roll on. The Toronto-lensed pic relies on intrigue more than action and manages to maintain at least a watchable level throughout. Billy Dee drinks a lot as Sonny's veteran cop buddy. Johnson costars as Sonny's pregnant wife, who gets upset when hubby shoots it out with machine-gun-toting cyclists during one of her birthing classes. Hey, Little Miss Prima Donna, get with the program!

MS. .45 (1980) ***

D: Abel Ferrara. Zoe Tamerlis (Lund), Edward Singer, Jack Thibeau, Peter Yellen. 90 mins. (Image) DVD

It's a tribute to Zoe Lund's emotive abilities that she's able to wring so much expression from a pantomime role in which she barely utters word one. As mute garment-center seamstress Anna, the then-teenage actress plays a ready-made victim. Her turning point is not so much the opening-reel rape by a masked assailant, or the subsequent attack she suffers at the hands of a leather-jacketed mugger who loosens his gun grip during orgasm, allowing Anna to crush his skull with an iron, a symbolically feminine weapon. The real moment of truth arrives when our enigmatic heroine comes into possession of her late attacker's "male" weapon, the titular handgun, which both empowers

PHANTOM: How do *you* view the character of Anna?

LUND: I see her as a very humble sort of metaphor for rebellion. The film's sort of a rough gem. It struck a chord with the audience. It's not about women who've been raped, or deaf people, seamstresses—it's somehow a very broad metaphor. The producers at the time wanted me to ultimately locate the original rapist and off him. And that would've been irrelevant. It was the boss from the beginning, and at the end it's the boss that I murder, and that's that. That was what it was all about. Had it been that I locate the same guy and kill him, it would have been a movie of no consequence and I wouldn't have made it. At that time I had no particular aspiration to be an actress. It took me several weeks to decide if I wanted to do it. I decided to go for it, as long as it *wasn't* a *Death Wish*. The combination of the intelligence and yet the extreme simplicity of the situation seemed a whole vision. It works very well. It was very chancy because I do not speak. The script was minimal to begin with. Scenes were described by a small paragraph of text. The fact that I didn't have any lines was at once challenging and gave me a lot of freedom. In effect, I could write my part; my lines were my face. So I really wrote my part and had my own vision of the role.

PHANTOM: Did you have to get familiar with guns?

LUND: I had been familiar with guns. I'm good with guns. I was second place in an East Coast rifle competition some years before. And it was actually a .38—a .45 for some of the tight close-ups.

PHANTOM: Was there ever talk of a *Ms. .45* sequel?

LUND: There was some joking about it. There was actually even a scene shot, for the fun of it. I was shooting something I cowrote in Europe. We had all the equipment there, so for the hell of it we shot a scene in a big nightclub in Paris. There was a shot of me lying on the ground with people's feet around me. It was sort of a promotional thing to see if we could get interest in doing a sequel.

and enslaves her. Rather than embark on a focused vendetta, à la Bronson's more simplistically motivated *Death Wish* avenger, Paul Kersey, Anna wields her weapon at the expense of any random male who crosses her path. The only males she empathizes with are a neighbor's dog (!) and a depressed salesman who takes her gun and voluntarily uses it on himself. During the dynamic climactic Halloween party sequence, when Anna, dressed as a nun (shades of *Bad Lieutenant!*), initiates an all-out massacre, with her horny boss as the first victim, it's the earthiest of her distaff coworkers who, phallic knife strategically positioned at crotch level, penetrates her with lethal results. Ferrara specializes in morally complex stories and seemingly contradictory characters, like Anna, Christopher Walken's philanthropic drug mogul in *King of New York* and Harvey Keitel's utterly depraved yet "justice"-obsessed cop in the Ferrara/Lund collaboration *Bad Lieutenant* (see index). Ferrara has never been shy about sacrificing narrative integrity for a flashy action opportunity, which he does in *Ms. .45* during Anna's unlikely, stylized Sergio Leone–style circular showdown with a gang of lowlifes. Still, while *Ms. .45* contains its share of ragged edges, it's easy to see why this bold indie became an immediate and enduring cult hit. Mention should also be made of the excellent, adrenalizing music score that reaches its crescendo during the Halloween scene.

THE NAKED CAGE (1986) ***

D: Paul Nicholas. Shari Shattuck, Angel Tompkins, Lucinda Crosby, Christina Whitaker, Faith Minton, John Terlesky. (Media, n.i.d.)

Michelle (Shattuck) is a sweet, clean-cut blonde out for nothing more exciting than the occasional romp on her beloved mare, Misty. Unfortunately for Michelle, her lowlife ex-beau, Willie (Terlesky), has gotten himself mixed up with escaped con Rita (Whitaker), a mean gutter scum queen who talks a coked-up Will into helping her pull a heist at the very bank where our hapless heroine works. By the time the smoke clears, Willie's wasted, while Michelle, wrongly implicated in the crime, winds up in a wild femme pen that makes *The Snake Pit* look like Sunnybrook Farm. While not as hot as his *Chained Heat* (see index), where he had the incomparable Linda Blair and Sybil Danning to work with, Nicholas's *Naked Cage* ("Raw violence and hot rage explode behind bars!") supplies vicious catfights aplenty, gratuitous nudity, and more seething inmate unrest than you could shake a nightstick at. Toss in racial hostilities, brutal prison power struggles, and a lively climactic riot ("This used to be such a *nice* place," our corrupt lesbian warden Tompkins wistfully reminisces), and you have one of sleazedom's best broads-behind-bars flicks.

THE NAKED COUNTRY (1984) ***

D: Tim Burstall. John Stanton, Rebecca Gilling, Ivor Kants, Tommy Lewis. 90 mins. (Hemdale, n.i.d.)

Based on a Morris West novel and set in northern Queensland, Australia, in 1955, *The Naked Country* dramatizes the violent tragedies set in motion by multiple misunderstandings between newly arrived Aussies and their Aborigine neighbors. A subplot details rancher Stanton and wife Gilling's marital difficulties, leading to her brief fling with alcoholic lawman Kants. While conventionally structured, *Naked Country* avoids predictability and doesn't romanticize the Aborigines' own rather pragmatic approach to mysticism. The flick is well worth a look for anyone who enjoys movies like Cornel Wilde's *Naked Prey*, Nicolas Roeg's *Walkabout* (see index) or, for that matter, vintage American westerns.

NAKED LIES (1998) **½

D: Ralph Portillo. Shannon Tweed, Fernando Allende, Jay Baker, Michael Rose, Salvador Pineda, Hugo Stieglitz, Mineko Mori, Steven Bauer. 93 mins. (Columbia/TriStar)

Looking fairly fab and flab-free at 40, onetime reigning erotic-thriller queen Shannon (*No Contest*) Tweed opts to go the action route in *Naked Lies*, a reasonably stirring south-of-the-border-set sting-operation suspenser. Shan's a typically guilt-plagued DEA agent—she accidentally killed a kid during an L.A. drug bust two years earlier—working undercover at a Mexican casino, the better to get next to suave counterfeiting honcho Allende. (Indeed, Shan's lone shower scene is nearly ruined by her interior guilt-tripping, at least until a convenient break-in necessitates her hasty, semirevealing emergence from the stall.) An early gratuitous sex scene (not involving Shannon) slows the narrative thrust, but the pic picks up once our heroine begins her cat-and-mouse games with Allende, whom she eventually beds to earn his trust. Complicating the case is Shan's bitter relationship with her outside law-enforcement contact (Baker), a former lover who's yet to get over their affair. Baker scores the flick's most lyrical line when he guzzles from a bottle of booze after eavesdropping on Tweed's tryst with the villain. To wit: "When your microphone falls prey to foreplay, only alcohol will do." (Hey, we'll drink to that!)

THE NAKED PREY (1966) ***

D: Cornel Wilde. Cornel Wilde, Ken Gampu, Gert Van Den Bergh. 96 mins. (Paramount)

Former matinee idol Wilde does a commendable job both directing and starring (virtually sans dialogue) as a white man pursued by a band of hostile African tribesmen in an almost film-long chase. *Naked Prey* succeeds in generating suspense *and* in making its point.

NEVER SAY DIE (1994) **½

D: Yossi Wein. Frank Zagarino, Billy Drago, Jennifer Miller, Todd Jensen, Robin Smith, Ted Le Plat. 99 mins. (New Line)

Zagarino follows his robust robot-villain turn in the high-energy *Night Siege* (see index) with a more heroic role in this equally violent actioner lensed in South Africa. Director Wein takes his story all over the map, from Vietnam to a faux Jonestown called the Garden of Eden, ruled by the Reverend James (a former Special Forces killer, spiritedly interpreted by professional psycho Drago). FBI agent Roper (Jensen, of *Cyborg Cop* obscurity) leads an assault on Drago's redoubt, resulting in the first of several bloodbaths on view here. Boat mechanic Zagarino (who just happens to live nearby) joins the fray when he learns of Drago's involvement; he was the only survivor of a 'Nam team Drago was ordered to terminate to cover up an inadvertent My Lai–type massacre. While logic never looms large in Wein's pulpy exercise, he more than amply delivers in the action department.

NEW JACK CITY   (1991) **½

D: Mario Van Peebles. Wesley Snipes, Ice-T, Judd Nelson, Allen Payne, Chris Rock, Mario Van Peebles, Vanessa Williams. 97 mins. (Warner) DVD

Actor Van Peebles's directorial debut details undercover cops Ice-T and Nelson's strenuous efforts to bag uptown crack kingpin Snipes. While a solid B flick, *New Jack City* doesn't approach De Palma's *Scarface* remake (despite the inclusion of several clips from that masterful gangster epic) or Abel Ferrara's *King of New York*. But as rap actioners go, *NJC* represents a vast improvement over Rick Rubin's often risible amateur-night Run-D.M.C. vehicle, *Tougher Than Leather* (Columbia/TriStar).

THE NEWTON BOYS   (1998) ***

D: Richard Linklater. Matthew McConaughey, Ethan Hawke, Skeet Ulrich, Vincent D'Onofrio, Julianna Margulies, Dwight Yoakam, Bo Hopkins, Luke Askew. 122 mins. (20th Century Fox) DVD

It says something about the current state of multiplex affairs that a film as solidly entertaining as *The Newton Boys* could come and go with barely a whisper, despite an organic script, pedigreed indie director (Linklater, of *Dazed and Confused* fame), and high-profile Gen-X cast. The frequently miscast McConaughey (*Amistad, Contact*) lands a friendlier role here as the affable leader of four Texas brothers who gained enduring notoriety in the 1920s by becoming the most successful bank

robbers in American history. The Lone Star State–bred star receives able support from Hawke, Ulrich, and D'Onofrio as his similarly sticky-fingered siblings, while Yoakam, unforgettable as the loudmouthed murder-waiting-to-happen in Billy Bob Thornton's *Sling Blade*, proves equally adept here as the bro's' low-key nitro-expert crony. Margulies adds considerable appeal as McConaughey's understanding missus, while old pros Hopkins and Askew supply welcome sights as good cop/bad cop lawmen on the gang's trail. Relatively light on violence—the brothers never killed anyone during their heists—*The Newton Boys* rates high in the excitement and suspense departments. Linklater concludes the film with clips of two of the actual Newtons—by then well into their dotage—describing their escapades (on a Johnny Carson *Tonight Show* segment and in an indie documentary, respectively) over the end credits, a risky touch that works perfectly here.

NEXT OF KIN   (1989) **½

D: John Irvin. Patrick Swayze, Liam Neeson, Helen Hunt, Andreas Katsulas, Adam Baldwin, Michael J. Pollard. 108 mins. (Warner) DVD

Irwin's energetic hillbillies-versus-hoods yarn casts a convincing Swayze as a hick-turned-Windy-City-dick, while all-purpose screen ethnic Katsulas scores as a Chicago Mafia boss and former *Bonnie and Clyde* fugitive Pollard impresses (for a change) as a helpful flophouse operator. Dominating the pic, however, are then-newcomer Neeson as Swayze's vengeance-minded backwoods bro' and a hulking Baldwin as a brutal mob hit man. (Hunt fares less fortuitously as Patrick's big-city violinist wife, who's largely left to fiddle while Swayze burns.) While the flick admittedly clicks into total brain-lock at times and should have been sheared by a full reel, *Next of Kin* supplies enough cross-

cultural color and senseless violence to make it a solid big-budget B movie.

NIGHT VISION   (1997) **

D: Gil Bettman. Fred Williamson, Cynthia Rothrock, Robert Forster, Amanda Welles, Frank Pesce, Willie Gault. 95 mins. (Xenon)

Forster's last B movie before landing his career-resurrecting, Oscar-nominated role in Tarantino's *Jackie Brown* casts the charismatic thesp as the superior of booze-plagued Houston cycle cop Dakota Smith (Williamson, who's nothing if not gutsy here, in both senses of the word), who teams with high-kicking transferred-fuzz Rothrock to track a vicious serial killer called the Video Stalker. The result is a strictly routine late-'80s-styled direct-to-video throwback of interest solely to Hammer, Cynth, and Forster fans (in total, a not inconsiderable audience). The pic doesn't cast the Houston PD in a particularly brilliant light (when asked "Why haven't you caught this guy?" a ranking officer replies, "He's intelligent."). Producer Fred places too much emphasis on Dakota's alcohol rehab for a video best not seen sober. On the upside, no night-vision glasses were harmed—or, for that matter, employed—in the making of this motion picture.

NO CONTEST   (1994) ***

D: Paul Lynch. Shannon Tweed, Andrew Dice Clay, Robert Davi, Roddy Piper, Nicholas Campbell. 98 mins. (Columbia/TriStar)

After seeing his screen career plummet from the comparative heights of *The Adventures of Ford Fairlane* (Fox) to the abyss of Albert Pyun's *Brain Smasher...A Love Story* (Trimark) in less than half a decade, the Diceman reemerges triumphant with a chilling perf as a sadistic terrorist leader (complete with dryly timed one-liners) in Paul (*Cross Country*) Lynch's "*Die Hard*-at-a-Beauty-Contest" exercise. Dice and crew (Piper, in a rare villainous role, among them) commandeer the comely contestants at a Vegas beauty pageant with a plan to ransom one of the wenches, daughter of a super-rich senator against whom Clay also holds an intense personal grudge. After wiring his hostages with explosives, Dice and cronies start their countdown while hapless authorities keep an impotent vigil without. Unfortunately for our bad guys, one of their captives is the ever popular Tweed, who sheds her usual silky erotic-thriller bimbo persona to play a screen kickbox queen hired to host the contest. Shan soon assumes the Bruce Willis role, with walkie-talkie help from ex-agent Davi. *No Contest* represents one of those too rare B movies that blends all the essential ingredients, shakes to perfection, and pours out a video cocktail with a real kick. Avoid the uncredited sequel, *Face the Evil* (A-Pix).

NO RETREAT, NO SURRENDER:
THE SERIES

NO RETREAT, NO SURRENDER (1986) *

D: Corey Yuen. Kurt McKinney, J. W. Falls, Kathie Sileno, Jean-Claude Van Damme, Kim Tai-Chong, Kent Lipham. 85 mins. (New World)

No *Retreat*'s original print ads made it look like a fourth-rate *Rocky IV* rip-off (itself a third-rate *Rocky* rip-off), but this home-movie-level loser, (mis)directed by Hong Kong martial arts ace Yuen, has nothing so grandiose on its addled little mind. Instead, its story concerns the plight of teenage kung-fu hopeful McKinney, who runs away from his Seattle home after his karate-teacher dad (Tim Baker) tears up his cherished Bruce Lee poster. With the help of a break-dancing buddy (Falls), Kurt sets up his portable gym in

an abandoned garage, where Bruce Lee's ghost (Tai-Chong) treats him to a crash course in the latest full-contact karate techniques. This spirited training comes in handy during the pic's grand finale—the Full-Contact Karate Championship of the World, staged in what looks like a junior-high gym before a capacity crowd of dozens. Ruthless East Coast promoters (there must have been hundreds of dollars riding on this gala event) unleash a killer Russki (future star Van Damme), who wipes out the local pro talent but (natch) proves no match for the new, improved Kurt. Now, what *we* want to know is who put up the dough for this amateur-night fiasco? The Seattle Chamber of Commerce? Ruthless East Coast promoters? The ghost of Bruce Lee? Believe it or not, not one but two sequels followed in this cheapie's wake—1989's *No Retreat, No Surrender 2* (MCEG), also directed by Yuen, and 1991's *No Retreat, No Surrender 3: Blood Brothers* (Imperial).

NO WAY HOME (1997) ***1/2

D: Buddy Giovinazzo. Tim Roth, Deborah Kara Unger, James Russo, Saul Stein. 101 mins. (Artisan)

Gotham-bred auteur Giovinazzo first splattered upon the genre scene with his raw, gritty homemade horror/noir *Combat Shock* (see index). Buddy's back nearly a dozen years later with another Staten Island–set outing, this time with a topflight pro cast replacing *Combat Shock*'s largely amateur players, a tight, textured script, and an edgy but never gratuitously flashy cinematic style. Roth stars as a slow-witted but soulful ex-con newly released from prison. He takes temporary shelter in the home of his lowlife dope-dealing older bro' (a typically bellicose Russo) and his foxy, sympathetic spouse, a part-time strip-o-gram worker (Unger, of *Crash* fame). History begins to repeat itself, as the outwardly helpful

Russo drags his brother into his criminal intrigues, and the film details Roth's difficult identity search and painful descent into his own tragic past. Giovinazzo, who also scripted this powerful, ultimately violent drama, gradually peels the layers of gauze from Roth's (and our) eyes and creates some truly memorable tableaux along the way.

NOWHERE TO HIDE (1987) **1/2

D: Mario Azzopardi. Amy Madigan, Daniel Hugh Kelly, Robin MacEachern, Michael Ironside, John Colicos, Maury Chaykin. 90 mins. (Warner)

Madigan excels as a tough ex-marine mom on the run—with her six-year-old son—from the vicious gunmen who've just killed her hubby (Kelly). Seems her spouse had uncovered a crooked defense contractor's plot to peddle shoddy machinery to the marines—equipment that had already resulted in two fatal copter crashes. While predictable, *Nowhere to Hide* delivers some excitingly staged action, particularly when Amy teams up with laconic 'Nam vet/survivalist Ironside to take on a small army of bad guys.

NOWHERE TO RUN (1993) *1/2

D: Robert Harmon. Jean-Claude Van Damme, Rosanna Arquette, Kieran Culkin, Joss Ackland, Ted Levine. 94 mins. (Columbia/TriStar) DVD

Hot-ticket scripter Joe (*Basic Instinct, Showgirls*) Eszterhas is one of four credited writers whose combined efforts add up to naught but a lame rehash of *Shane* (Paramount). Van Damme plays good-hearted escaped con Sam (originally from Quebec, we're told, in the latest bid to explain J-C's persistent Belgian drawl), who rides to the rescue of widderwoman Arquette and her two young'uns, including Macauley's less cute little bro' Kieran—who'd yet to learn how to slap his hands to his cheeks and make a perfect *O* with his mouth—in the Brandon De Wilde part. Seems ruthless developers led by Ackland are trying to force Rosanna from her land. When Sam fails to take kindly to that notion, hired enforcer Levine (in the Jack Palance role) and goons seek to straighten him out. Beyond its utter absence of originality, *Nowhere to Run* rates as Van Damme's dullest vehicle since his futuristic fist-fest *Cyborg* (see index); J-C does little more than stare intently as the pic's parade of updated western clichés passes him by. For the record, Van Damme works in one trademark bare-butt shot. No relation to the 1989 David Carradine crime snoozer *Nowhere to Run* (MGM/UA).

ONCE A THIEF (1996) **

D: John Woo. Sandrine Holt, Ivan Sergei, Nicholas Lea, Robert Ito, Michael Wong, Alan Scarfe, Jennifer Dale. 99 mins. (A-Pix) DVD

Holt, Sergei, and Wong form a mixed Asian-Anglo team of highly trained Vancouver-based thieves in the employ of Wong's big-time Hong Kong gangster dad (Ito). Lame wisecracking dialogue, predictable plot turns, and dull romantic complications clutter this un-Woo-like made-for-TV entry, loosely drawn from his 1991 Hong Kong film of the same name (*Tai Seng*) and presented here in a "director's cut." For Woo completists only.

ONCE UPON A TIME IN CHINA:
THE SERIES

ONCE UPON A TIME IN CHINA (1991) ***½

D: Tsui Hark. Jet Li, Yuen Biao, Rosamund Kwan, Kent Cheng, Jacky Cheung. 112 mins. (Tai Seng) DVD

Like its Sam Peckinpah and Sergio Leone models, the debut entry in

Hark's historical-action series focuses on a way of life that's about to vanish. Here, instead of the rugged American West, we see an 1875 China beset by rapacious, technologically advanced foreigners eager to divide, conquer, and exploit that Far Eastern frontier. Hark's story centers on Li as martial arts ace Dr. Wong Fei Hung, a real-life Chinese hero earlier legendized in countless Hong Kong B flicks. Supplying Wong with both moral and martial support is his loyal band of "local militia," including portly Porky Lang (Cheng) and Westernized comic relief Buck Teeth Sol (Cheung). Wong has his lightning-fast hands full throughout the film's nearly two-hour running time, not only with the invading *gwilos* (foreign devils) but with local bureaucrats, obstructive police, a persistent band of lowlife extortionists, and faded-but-still-lethal rival Biao (who, were this a backdate spaghetti western, would have been played by Lee Van Cleef) bent upon besting our hero in mortal combat. Kwan provides marginal, exceedingly chaste romantic interest as the semi-Westernized Aunt Yee. Li emerges as both an appealing thesp and a dynamic martial arts wiz who employs feet, fists, poles, and even umbrellas to subdue his numerous foes. The film also offers a fascinating view of the incursive American soldiers, who spend most of their screentime guzzling wine and harmonizing (badly) on the "Battle Hymn of the Republic" (!). With its entertaining blend of action, comedy and history, *Once Upon a Time in China* presents the kind of sweeping escapist fare Hollywood rarely makes anymore. Li returns in the sequels *Once Upon A Time in China 2, Once Upon a Time in China III,* and *Once Upon a Time in China and America* (Tai Seng, DVD).

ONE WAY OUT (1995) ***

D: Kevin Lynn. Jack Gwaltney, Jeff Monahan, Annie Golden, Isabel Gillies, Michael Ironside, Robert Turano. 106 mins. (Arrow)

When decent, low-key Frank (Gwaltney) gets out of jail, he teams up with wild card Bobby (Monahan) and his stripper squeeze, Eve (Golden), and visits his slow-witted but appealing bro' Snooky (Turano). Frank learns that Snooky's boss (Ironside, in another effective arrogant-lowlife turn) has been ripping him off, so the group decides to return the favor. Naturally, the heist goes haywire, leading the motley gang to kidnap Snooky's fellow worker (Gillies) and head out on the road to inevitable tragedy. While the bare-bones plot offers little new, Lynn manages to create credible characters brought to life by an excellent cast; the group's adventures in many ways mirror some of the better low-budget road movies of the late '60s and early '70s, with the de rigueur '90s addition of copious gunplay. Lynn and crew also pull off the not inconsiderable trick of subbing rural New Jersey for nearly half the country, from Tennessee to Texas (!).

187 (1997) ***

D: Kevin Reynolds. Samuel L. Jackson, John Heard, Kelly Rowan, Clifton González González, Tony Plana. 119 mins. (Warner)

A solid exploitation pic in social-issue guise, scripted by a former teacher and directed by erstwhile Kevin Costner collaborator Reynolds, *187* features a charismatic Jackson as an NYC high school teacher who finds himself understandably disillusioned after suffering multiple stab wounds at the hands of a disgruntled gangbanger student. Jackson moves to California, where he's hired as a substitute at an equally unsavory L.A. high. A tad tamer than *Class of 1984* and *The Substitute* (see index), *187* (police code for "homicide") chronicles Jackson's descent into doubt, frustration, and ultimately vigilante violence.

OPEN FIRE   (1994) **½

D: Kurt Anderson. Jeff Wincott, Patrick Kilpatrick, Mimi Craven, Lee De Broux, Arthur Taxier. 93 mins. (Republic)

Poker-faced martial-arts ace Wincott, who fares far better in *The Killing Man* (see index), makes for a bland lead in this otherwise watchable *"Die Hard* in an Industrial Plant" entry. Chief villain Kilpatrick provides a welcome shot of badass charisma as a prison-sprung merc leader who threatens to nerve-gas Los Angeles. Anderson keeps his predictable but slickly staged story moving at a fast clip.

OPERATION CONDOR:
THE SERIES

OPERATION CONDOR
(1991) **½

D: Jackie Chan. Jackie Chan, Carol Cheng, Eva Cobo De Garcia, Shôko Ikeda, Alfred Bael Sanchez. Dubbed. 92 mins. (Touchstone) DVD

Operation Condor is a reedited, dubbed edition of 1991's *Armour of the Gods II: Operation Condor.* Jackie directs and coscripts (with Edward Tang) an overly broad comic adventure that borrows heavily from both *Raiders of the Lost Ark* and *Romancing the Stone.* Three disparate major babes (Cheng, De Garcia, Ikeda) join Jackie on a globe-hopping quest to retrieve a cache of Nazi gold buried in the African desert. There are three excellent action tableaux—the *Raiders*-inspired prologue, an involved motorcycle chase, and, best of all, a terrif scene set in a wind tunnel that allows our hero to showcase his fighting and physical-comedy skills. The filler, unfortunately, is fairly lame. Oddly, the flick scored a PG-13 rating despite flashes of nudity, double entendres, and even condom jokes. In the J.C. tradition, blown-stunt outtakes unspool under the end credits.

OPERATION CONDOR 2: THE ARMOUR OF THE GODS   (1987) ***

D: Jackie Chan. Jackie Chan, Alan Tam, Rosamund Kwan, Lola Forner. 75 mins. (Dimension)

Actually a *prequel* to *Operation Condor, Operation Condor 2: The Armour of the Gods* (originally titled simply *Armour of God*) represents Jackie's first foray into *Indiana Jones* territory. Actor/director Chan is a former rock singer turned adventurer (he even gets to belt out the closing theme song, "High Up on High," in typically aggressive if somewhat tortured English) who teams with Tam to rescue kidnapped former squeeze Kwan and claim the title treasure, a priceless set of mystical armor dating back to the Crusades. Fortunately, there's less emphasis on the convoluted plot than on Jackie's standard stock-in-trade—high-speed action comedy—as he braves, among other perils, snarling pit bulls, a sect of machine-gun-wielding martial arts monks, a quartet of cat-suited Amazonian kung-fu queens, angry island natives, and careening vehicles galore. Filming the Yugoslavia-lensed flick also precipitated the worst of Jackie's many serious stunt injuries: a fall from a snapped tree branch that cracked his skull and very nearly ended his life (a truly scary moment that's eerily included in the otherwise light-hearted outtakes that run under the closing credits). For the inside scoop on Jackie's wild and woolly on- and off-screen life, scope out Chan's self-directed documentary, *Jackie Chan: My Story* (WinStar).

ORIGINAL GANGSTAS   (1996) ***

D: Larry Cohen. Fred Williamson, Jim Brown, Pam Grier, Paul Winfield, Isabel Sanford, Richard Roundtree, Ron O'Neal, Robert Forster, Wings Hauser, Charles Napier, Christopher B. Duncan, Dru Down, Timothy Lewis. 98 mins. (Orion) DVD

Veteran writer/director Cohen, who helmed such seminal Fred ("the Hammer") Williamson vehicles as *Black Caesar* and sequel *Hell Up in Harlem,* rounds up several of the genre's prime usual suspects for a rousing, high-energy, straight-ahead urban actioner pitting yesterday's code-bound heroes against today's amoral gangbangers. Cohen and crew spring a real surprise by demonstrating there can be life in the "blaxploitation" genre without resorting to spoofery. Allegedly, a real-life return visit to a gang-plagued Gary, Indiana (which replaced Detroit as America's "Murder Capital"), by Williamson, who grew up there, sparked the project.

Here Fred essays the role of John Bookman, a former NFL star who journeys homeward to investigate the wounding of his grocer dad (Oscar Brown, Jr.) at the handguns of the present-day members of the Rebels, the very gang he'd founded decades before. Bookman Sr. had made the mistake of fingering the gang members who'd slain young basketball player Kenny (Lewis) in a drive-by. Kenny's absentee father, former boxer Trevor (Brown), also surfaces to comfort his understandably hostile ex-wife (Grier). When the efforts of police, represented by Forster, city officials (embodied by Napier and Hauser), and a mediating minister (Winfield) fail to facilitate justice, Fred, Jim, and Pam seek to incite internecine warfare among the Rebels and two other dominant gangs. Finally, though, our lead trio, joined by former *Shaft,* Roundtree, and ex-*Superfly* O'Neal, meet the lethal gangbangers in a bloody climactic showdown. Actual Gary and East Chicago, Indiana, locations add gritty authenticity. An excellent cast, including the mostly unknowns who portray the local gang kids, a mixed hip-hop and '70s-soul soundtrack (with an on-screen appearance by the Chi-Lites), plenty of promised action, and a serious subtext about the fate of urban wastelands like Gary contribute to an impressive package. The Orion cassette also contains three complete original rap videos keyed to the film.

OUT FOR JUSTICE (1991) **

D: John Flynn. Steven Seagal, William Forsythe, Jo Champra, Jerry Orbach, Gina Gershon, Jay Acovone. 91 mins. (Warner) DVD

Out for Justice is the only Seagal slayfest (so far) to open with a quote from Arthur Miller. But while the film (originally titled *The Price of Our Blood*) unfolds in Brooklyn, it's a pretty far distance from *A View from the Bridge*—though there *are* times when our hero appears bent on literalizing Thomas Wolfe's contention that only the dead know Brooklyn. Seagal goes the heavy-goomban route as a neighborhood-*paisan*-turned-lawman who's out to avenge the blatant murder of a fellow officer by psychotic crack-smoking "wiseguy wannabe" Forsythe. He also gets to display a few backdate Brando moves—there's even a femme character named Terry Malloy (!), Marlon's famous *On the Waterfront* moniker—when he expresses his Brooklyn xenophobia: Before buying dog food for his adopted pup, Seagal asks a clerk, "None of this is from Jersey, right? 'Cause I don't want no radioactive stuff."

OUT ON BAIL (1989) ***

D: Gordon Hessler. Robert Ginty, Kathy Shower, Tom Badal, Sydney Lassick. 102 mins. (TWE, n.i.d.)

One of B-star Ginty's best action vehicles casts our hero as a purposeful stranger in a corrupt small town. Character thesp Lassick's turn as a worse-than-shady lawyer supplies a highlight. Sadistic sheriff Badal doubles as the pic's coscripter.

OVER THE TOP (1987) **

D: Menahem Golan. Sylvester Stallone, Robert Loggia, David Mendenhall, Susan Blakely, Rick Zumwalt. 94 mins. (Warner)

A sort of *"Rocky Versus Kramer,"* *Over the Top* stars Sly as Lincoln

---

PAM GRIER: *FOXY AS SHE WANTS TO BE*

As Told to The Phantom

Once revered as the genre screen's reigning black action queen at the height of the '70s "blaxploitation" craze for her work in pics like Coffy *and* Foxy Brown, *actress Pam Grier later made a successful transition to supporting roles in films ranging from John Carpenter's* Escape from L.A. *and Tim Burton's* Mars Attacks! *to Larry Cohen's* Original Gangstas. *Pam has since served as the focus of film fests devoted to her work and returned to star status in the title role in Quentin Tarantino's* Jackie Brown.

PHANTOM: Have you trained [in martial arts]?

GRIER: Yes, I studied it when I was a teenager. I studied with one of the local Denver police sergeants who was a black belt in karate and aikido. And, being an air-force brat, they taught it at school also. I apply it to my work and I apply it to my art; it kind of extends your facets.

PHANTOM: But you didn't know at that time you'd be using it on-screen.

GRIER: Oh no, never. I thought I'd be using it at med school!

PHANTOM: How did you get into films to begin with?

GRIER: I always wanted to be in films, but my mother started me toward the medical field to be a doctor. There wasn't a film school in Colorado. I was working, putting myself through school, and I decided to take a sabbatical, so I went to Los Angeles and *met* some actors. And that just changed my whole life. The sense of family they had, and being honest with their emotions without being neurotic—in most of society you're taught not to show your emotions—don't cry, don't kiss your mom in public, don't hold hands, so many backward things that make us unsure about ourselves in relationships with people. I just liked the *truth* of the actor. Some people would say, "What truth? Actors are *pretending*." Any actor who's false, the audience will know it and so will the actor. But it's a sense of truth they bring to a role, and I really loved that. Things that I didn't have in school. I was geared toward science, math, and chemistry, for premed, and I just didn't get anything rewarding from it. But when I met these actors and they were talking about human behavior and sensitivity, I had missed a lot of that, and I just kind of guided myself into that field. My first job was with Roger Corman— *The Big Doll House.* I remember going in there and running into Jonathan Demme, Jonathan Kaplan—I think Martin Scorsese was hanging out also in the offices—bearded wonders in all these plaid shirts and khaki pants.

PHANTOM: A lot of people came out of that era and that group.

GRIER: Gale Ann Hurd, the producer, who produced *The Abyss.* I learned a lot from so many people.

PHANTOM: How do you feel now about Roger Corman?

GRIER: He makes films the way he sees them, on a budget that he knows is appropriate, bare-bones, no false overheads—you can learn from him. I love him. He was just terrific for me.

PHANTOM: Some people I've talked to have some resentment, in terms of the money, that he exploited them.

GRIER: You have to remember he was taking the risks, too. They know they'll get a chance if they work with him, so they just give up a little. If they hit it big, they don't have to work with him anymore. They can basically write their own ticket with any other company. It's a trade-off. His experience and expertise and a chance to learn and be in the business and really hone your skills, and you're not paying him, he's still paying you—even though it may be minimum. Whether he's exploiting people or not, he's still taking the risk.

PHANTOM: You don't mind having a supporting role in a big movie?

GRIER: Oh, no, not at all, because of the work and what you can do with it. I've been fortunate to be able to work with Gene Hackman in *The Package*, Jason Robards in *Something Wicked This Way Comes*, Burt Lancaster in *Rocket Gibraltar*. Our piece was cut out, but I got to work with one of my idols. And Charles Durning in *Stand Alone*. So I've been really fortunate to get to work with mainstream actors. Generally, that's not the thing; you're kind of cornered—you'll do black pictures, you won't do any others.

PHANTOM: How do you react to the term "blaxploitation"?

GRIER: Many of us have completely denounced that term. All we wanted to do with the films was show our own culture. Many of us did well. We got a lot of people in the unions, a lot of people began their internships and apprenticeships through these projects, so basically there are more pros than cons. The only exploitation was the fact that, yes, there was violence and killing—but that's in any movie. They're not gonna call Sylvester Stallone's exploitation films. It caught on with people who didn't know what they were talking about. You never heard Samuel Arkoff, who produced them, call them "black exploitation" movies. Or Roger Corman. They gave me the biggest break of my career, which is to become a filmmaker, to be part of the cast, part of the writing. I just learned so much from the other side, which today you can't learn unless you go to a film school because you can't get on the lot.

Hawk, a trucker, arm wrestler, and errant dad who's sent to drive estranged 12-year-old son, Mike (Mendenhall), cross-country to visit his ailing mom (Blakely). At first the kid, a military-academy prig, regards his primitive pop with a less-than-loving attitude. ("There's more to life than just muscles," Junior huffily opines.) But the boy soon changes his tune as Sly leads him on a merry descent down the evolutionary scale, introducing him to the joys of junk food, truck driving, and arm wrestling, while Giorgio Moroder's snappy synthesizer rhythms lend their musical approval. It's at Vegas's international arm-wrestling gala that *Over the Top* reaches its high-concept peak, as Hawk matches blood, sweat, and 'ceps with a succession of macho throwbacks hulking enough to make Sly look like Danny DeVito, if not Dr. Ruth. The arm-wrestling scenes are lensed in *Raging Bull*–styled slo mo (!) while the soundtrack swells with anguished bellows not unlike those of bull elephants in musk. *Over the Top* represents a radical, risky departure from the typical Sly vehicle—a tale calculated to warm your heart and tug at your hamstrings (a strong stomach also helps)—and one that flopped miserably at the old B.O. (though Sly reportedly came out some 12 million of Cannon's dollars to the good). Stallone later tanked going the comic route with *Oscar* (Columbia/TriStar) and *Stop! Or My Mom Will Shoot* (Universal), though earned some respect with his overweight, partially deaf sheriff turn in 1997's *Cop Land* (Miramax, DVD).

THE PACKAGE (1989) ***½

D: Andrew Davis. Gene Hackman, Joanna Cassidy, Tommy Lee Jones, John Heard, Dennis Franz, Pam Grier, Thalmus Rasulala. 108 mins. (Orion) DVD

Despite drawing sixth billing, Pam Grier gets run over (off-screen) after what amounts to a mere cameo as an army lieutenant. The movie's worth seeing anyhow: *The Package* is a sturdy, fast-paced action thriller featuring top work by Pam's fellow cast members Hackman (who even reprises a condensed version of his famous *French Connection* car chase), Cassidy, Jones, and the late Rasulala.

PATRIOT GAMES (1992) ***

D: Phillip Noyce. Harrison Ford, Anne Archer, Patrick Bergin, Richard Harris, Thora Birch. 116 mins. (Paramount) DVD

Patriot Games loses points for its cheap exploitation of the Irish struggle but otherwise shapes up as a solid B actioner lensed on an A budget and highlighted by computer-driven high-tech detective work. Director Noyce, who first made a name via his seagoing psycho chiller, *Dead Calm* (see index), again utilizes his cinematic nautical skills for *Games*'s climactic boat chase. Ford comes through with another of his patented hesitant-hero perfs; long-suffering Archer (*Fatal Attraction*) looks convincingly pained about her endangered screen family's fate; and the pair's plucky patriotic daughter (Birch) regrets only that she has but one spleen to give for her country. Like *The Silence of the Lambs* before it, *Patriot Games* doubtless boosted sales of night-vision glasses. Ford also displays his two-fisted mettle as government agent Jack Ryan in the lively 1994 Tom Clancy–based caper *Clear and Present Danger* (Paramount, DVD) and as an embattled prez in *Air Force One* (Warner, DVD).

PENITENTIARY:
THE SERIES

PENITENTIARY (1979) ***

D: Jamaa Fanaka. Leon Isaac Kennedy, Thommy Pollard, Hazel Spears, Chuck Mitchell. 99 mins. (Unicorn, n.i.d.)

Fanaka's bid to revive the flagging lads-in-leg-irons genre is a fast-paced, funny, funky mix of realism and exploitation focusing on framed con Kennedy's efforts to box his way out of stir. Fanaka's knowing script and nearly verité direction combine to make this one of the best. Kennedy is convincing as Sugar Ray Leonard look-alike Too Sweet, as are Floyd Chatman as his elderly mentor, Seldom Seen, and Badja Djola as bullying nemesis Half Dead. The pic's casually candid treatment of inmate homosexuality remains one of its strongest suits. Fanaka failed to recapture the magic with 1982's *Penitentiary II* (MGM/UA) but fared somewhat better with 1987's *Penitentiary III* (Warner), wherein a caged Kennedy receives an unexpected assist from pro midget wrestler the Haiti Kid as a mutant killer dwarf called the Midnight Thud.

THE PERFECT WEAPON (1991) **½

D: Mark DiSalle. Jeff Speakman, John Dye, Mako, James Hong, Professor Toru Tanaka, Dante Basco, Mariska Hargitay. 84 mins. (Paramount)

The Perfect Weapon's theatrical tag line ("No gun. No knife. No equal.") was a bit of a cheat—Jeff wields two knives at film's end and more than meets his match in Harold "Oddjob" Sakata successor Tanaka—but the film itself shapes up as a steady if steadfastly formulaic flying-feet-and-fists fest. The pic traces young Speakman's progress from troubled teen to karate king under the guidance of Korean mentor Mako. When the latter is killed by L.A. Korean

THE BEST OF MALES-IN-JAIL MOVIES

BRUTE FORCE (1947) B&W***½
D: Jules Dassin. Burt Lancaster, Hume Cronyn, Charles Bickford, Yvonne De Carlo. 98 mins. (Kino) DVD
Vicious guard captain Cronyn makes life miserable for tough-guy Burt and fellow cons in Dassin's excellent, hard-hitting prison drama, scripted by Richard Brooks.

COOL HAND LUKE (1967)***½
D: Stuart Rosenberg. Paul Newman, George Kennedy, Strother Martin. 127 mins. (Warner) DVD
Newman's chain-gang rebel without a pause lifts the spirits of his downtrodden fellows in Rosenberg's powerful drama. Martin supplies scene-stealing support as the warden who bemoans his and Paul's "failure to communicate."

ESCAPE FROM ALCATRAZ (1979)***
D: Don Siegel. Clint Eastwood, Patrick McGoohan, Roberts Blossom. 112 mins. (Paramount) DVD
Clint toplines as a con bent on busting out of the seemingly escape-proof title facility in an essentially old-fashioned but suspenseful rehash of the once-popular male-jailbreak genre.

THE GLASS HOUSE (1972)***
D: Tom Gries. Alan Alda, Clu Gulager, Vic Morrow. 92 mins. (Anchor Bay)
For a made-for-TV movie starring Alan Alda, this Truman Capote–scripted prison drama is a surprisingly gritty affair, featuring an especially strong turn by the late Morrow as a behind-bars bully.

I AM A FUGITIVE FROM A CHAIN GANG (1932) B&W***½
D: Mervyn LeRoy. Paul Muni, Glenda Farrell, Preston Foster. 93 mins. (MGM)
Muni dominates the proceedings in LeRoy's classic fact-based account of a wrongly accused inmate who goes on the run. The final fade-out remains one of the screen's most indelible moments.

THE JERICHO MILE (1979)***
D: Michael Mann. Peter Strauss, Roger E. Mosley, Brian Dennehy. 97 mins. (New Line)
Michael (*Miami Vice*) Mann directs an unusually edgy TV prison movie starring Strauss as a lifer training for an Olympics berth against a backdrop of racially motivated inmate unrest.

LOCK-UP (1989)***
D: John Flynn. Sylvester Stallone, Donald Sutherland, Sonny Landham. 115 mins. (Artisan) DVD
Sly finds himself in stir and at the mercy of sadistic warden Sutherland. Not as compelling as Tom Selleck's jailhouse adventures in the then-contemporary *An Innocent Man* but a better-than-average biceps-behind-bars caper in its own right.

PAPILLON (1973)***
D: Franklin J. Schaffner. Steve McQueen, Dustin Hoffman, Victor Jory. 151 mins. (Fox) DVD
Devil's Island prisoners McQueen and Hoffman experience over two and a half

hours of living hell, with hardships, cruelties, and deprivations galore—and *you are there!*

RIOT IN CELL BLOCK 11   (1954) B&W***

D: Don Siegel. Neville Brand, Emile Meyer, Frank Faylen. 80 mins. (Republic)

Thesps Brand, Meyer, Faylen, and Leo Gordon prove they're not just pretty faces in a hard-hitting account of a prison riot that's more realistic than most. Noir/action ace Siegel supplies the tough-guy direction.

Mafia godfather Hong and henchman Tanaka, Jeff draws upon his Kenpo code to achieve vengeance with honor. As an actor, the stoic Speakman lacks Seagal's mean edge and Van Damme's Belgian accent. On the plus side, Speakman projects a tad more charisma than French kung-fu contender Olivier Gruner, while managing the difficult feat of keeping his derriere-garde Don Johnson *Miami Vice* stubble at uniform length all movie long.

PICASSO TRIGGER   (1988) **

D: Andy Sidaris. Steve Bond, Dona Speir, Hope Marie Carlton, Roberta Vasquez, John Aprea, Harold Diamond, Guich Koock. 98 mins. (Warner)

Picasso Trigger continues the saga of crooked-shooting superstud Rowdy Abilene. The original Rowdy, Ronn Moss, is replaced by former soap star Steve (no relation to James) Bond, but two-fisted, large-breasted ex-Playmates Speir and Carlton reprise their earlier roles as undercover—or more precisely, uncovered—agents Donna and Taryn, two gals who'll jump into the nearest Jacuzzi at the drop of a halter. (Fully seven ladies of the Playmate persuasion appear here in all.) The high-concept title refers both to an exotic breed of Hawaiian fish and to archvillain Aprea, who employs "Picasso Trigger" as his underworld code name and who instigates an involved assassination outbreak that whips our sundry heroes and heroines into action. *Picasso Trigger* offers sufficient infusions of wanton sex, sense-

less violence, and sun-soaked sleaze to please the Sidarises' fans.

PLATO'S RUN   (1996) **

D: James Becket. Gary Busey, Roy Scheider, Steven Bauer, Jeff Speakman, Tiani Warden. 96 mins. (Artisan)

Three old merc buds (Busey, Bauer, Speakman) get embroiled in a Cuban escape caper that's really a cover for a Miami power grab engineered by minefield enthusiast Scheider. Busey handles most of the action scenes by his lonesome in this largely dull outing; the Three Direct-to-Video-Teers team up only for the climactic battle with Scheider and goons. On the Weight Watchers front, Bauer's slimmed down almost to his svelte *Scarface* form, and Busey maintains a consistent flab level, but Speakman goes all puffy here, though he must have managed to perform his own stunts since the end credits list no fewer than three stunt doubles for Gary, one for Steve, and none for Jeff. "Cuban" villain Horacio ("So I choot him") Le Don copped our Worst Accent of 1996 honors.

POINT BLANK   (1967) ***1/2

D: John Boorman. Lee Marvin, Angie Dickinson, Keenan Wynn. 92 mins. (MGM)

Boorman, working from Donald E. Westlake's novel, crafts a lean, mean precursor to today's spate of postmodern action noirs, with Marvin in fine form as a relentless avenger. West-

lake's novel also served as the basis for the middling 1999 Mel Gibson vehicle *Payback* (Paramount, DVD).

POINT BLANK   (1998) *1/2

D: Matt Earl Beesley. Mickey Rourke, Kevin Gage, Danny Trejo, Frederic Forrest, Michael Wright, James Gammon. 90 mins. (Sterling) DVD

A lot of good actors and Mickey Rourke are wasted in this aggressively brain-dead, Fort Worth–set *"Die Hard in a Shopping Mall." Point Blank* involves a volatile band of escaped cons who commandeer said mall and commit all manner of mayhem while holding helpless authorities, including a wry Forrest, at bay. The scum soon rue their decision and the day when ex-merc O'Rourke, brother of criminal leader Gage (late of *Heat*), pulls a predictable Bruce Willis routine. Still bulked-up from his *Double Team* turn, a stone-faced Mick conserves his thespian energy while his stunt double provides the impressive ninja flips.

POINT BREAK   (1991) ***

D: Kathryn Bigelow. Keanu Reeves, Patrick Swayze, Gary Busey, Lori Petty. 117 mins. (Fox)

Reeves and a hyper Busey team up as FBI agents on the trail of the "Ex-Presidents," a quartet of slick stickup artists who wear Reagan, Carter, LBJ, and Nixon masks (Ford continues to get no respect) while taking off area banks. Keanu goes undercover as a surf dude in a bid to cuff the culprits, led by Swayze as a pseudo-Zen hang-tenner named Bodhi (the same Buddhist-derived moniker, you'll recall, owned by the glowing alien beachball in the 1987 Brooksfilms bomb *Solarbabies*). While learning his watery ropes, our hero not only male-bonds with the bank robbers but tumbles for tough, sexy surferette Petty. And he still finds time to get shot, bashed by surf Nazis, bitten by attack dogs, and beaten up by a naked lady (!). Kathryn (*Near Dark, Strange Days*) Bigelow's surf-gangster caper may be short on logic, but it more than compensates with adrenalizing action.

POINT OF IMPACT   (1993) **½

D: Bob Misiorowski. Michael Pare, Barbara Carrera, Michael Ironside, Lehua Reid, Ian Yule, Michael McGovern. 97 mins. In R and unrated editions. (Trimark)

Pare again proves himself an amiable, low-key lead in this fairly well done action/suspenser lensed in lush South Florida locales. After a botched bust results in the deaths of five fellow customs agents, Pare is tossed from the force. Suspecting boss Yule of being behind the blown operation, our hero hires on as bodyguard to foxy Carrera, wife of a volatile Cuban gangster (an excellent Ironside), who has long-standing links with Yule. While there's more emphasis on eros than action—indeed, in the unrated edition Pare, Carrera, and their respective body doubles may set a new homevid record for gratuitous sex scenes (a kidnap attempt set in a crowded distaff locker room adds another imaginative exploitation touch)—*Point of Impact* maintains interest throughout.

P.O.W.: THE ESCAPE   (1986) *½

D: Gideon Amir. David Carradine, Charles Floyd, Steve James, Mako. 90 mins. (Media, n.i.d.)

Carradine's Colonel ("Everybody Goes Home!") Cooper copters down into a secret VC camp to spring a group of POW's and simultaneously deliver a "loud message to Hanoi." Dave's bravery swiftly results in his own incarceration. Things look bleak until cruel Cong camp commander Mako confesses that *he'd* like to cut out too—to Miami Beach, no less—so the two

form an uneasy alliance as they lead the POW's on a wild escape through VC territory. Along the way, Dave single-handedly slaughters the usual slew of Asian extras (even dispatching a few via his patented kung-fu footwork) while wearing not only the requisite Rambo headband but an American flag over his shoulder! Afterward Dave joins the rescued GI's in a spirited rendition of "Proud Mary," then informs them that Jimi Hendrix was once a member of the 101st Airborne—"a Screaming Eagle all the way." So there was no irony in Jimi's feedback-driven Woodstock rendition of the "Star Spangled Banner" after all; geez, it took the '80s to clue us we'd gotten the '60s all wrong.

PRAY FOR DEATH   (1985) ***

D: Gordon Hessler. Shô Kosugi, James Booth, Donna Kei Benz, Michael Constantine, Robert Ito, Kane Kosugi, Shane Kosugi. 92 mins. (Artisan)

Shô portrays a Japanese businessman (and closet ninja, natch) who, accompanied by screen wife Benz and real-life sons Kane and Shane, relocates to Houston in search of "success." At first Shô is hesitant about the move. "American cities are so violent!" he protests. To which wife Donna Kei counters, "You've been watching too many movies" (like this one). Sure enough, faster than you can say "land of the free," Shô and family run afoul of a gang of vicious hoods led by Limehouse, interpreted with sadistic flair by Brit thesp Booth (once a supporting player in A pics like *Zulu*), who also penned the script. Limehouse and cronies are looking for a priceless necklace they think Shô has discovered in his newly purchased restaurant and will stop at the proverbial nothing to get their slimy hands on same. They illustrate that contention by killing Shô's wife and snatching son Shane. The cops, as always, prove incapable of redressing these wrongs, so Shô dons his ninja threads

and heads out to "redefine revenge." *Pray for Death* may not be a great advertisement for life in these United States, but its predictable plot barrels along at a brisk clip, the action scenes (including a kiddie kung-fu set-to between young Kane and some preteen toughs) are excitingly mounted, and Booth makes for a memorable screen villain. Withal, *PFD* ranks as Kosugi's best.

PRIME CUT   (1972) ***

D: Michael Ritchie. Lee Marvin, Gene Hackman, Angel Tompkins, Sissy Spacek. 88 mins. (Key)

Marvin is a troubleshooter for an Irish Chicago mob being cheated by Kansas City slaughterhouse owner and all-around malefactor Hackman in a sleazy, irreverent A film with a B-movie soul. Director Ritchie kicks the proceedings off to a fast, offbeat start, though he can't quite sustain the idiosyncratic feel for the duration. *Prime Cut*'s still well worth seeing, though, for the tough male leads, young Spacek as one of Hackman's white-slaver victims, bursts of bloody action, and Ritchie's skewed cinematic view.

THE PRINCIPAL   (1987) **

D: Christopher Cain. James Belushi, Louis Gossett, Jr., Rae Dawn Chong, Michael Wright, J. J. Cohen, Esai Morales. 110 mins. (Columbia/TriStar)

That Jim Belushi sure is one whale of a brawlin', beer-swillin', hog-ridin' macho stud educator! When high school teach Jim screws up, punitive school authorities appoint him head of the town's toughest facility, Brandell. There—despite indifference, rampant crime, and armed threats posed by teenage drug lord Wright—Jim takes it into his head to set these kids on the right track. On hand to help is Gossett, as head of Brandell's security. Hollywood to the core, *The Principal* compromises its own modest ambitions at every potentially exciting turn—from Belushi's ill-timed wisecracks to multiple product plugs to filler footage filmed solely for later insertion into the pic's inevitable rock-video promo.

THE PRODIGAL SON   (1982)***

D: Sammo Hung. Yuen Biao, Lam Ching Ying, Sammo Hung. Subtitled/dubbed. 100 mins. (Tai Seng) DVD

In Hung's excellent 1982 period martial arts epic, Yuen Biao takes the title role as a spoiled rich kid conned into thinking he's a kung-fu ace (he ultimately learns otherwise—the hard way), but the flick belongs to the late Ying, who portrays a cross-dressing, frequently falsetto-voiced, tough-as-nails, asthmatic martial-arts-champ-cum-Peking Opera performer (you know the type). Biao, meanwhile, teams with Occidental kickbox queen Cynthia Rothrock, as a prosecutor-turned-vigilante and a tough cop, respectively, in the recommended, hard-edged 1986 actioner *Righting Wrongs* (Tai Seng).

THE PROFESSIONAL: GOLGO 13 (1990)**1/2

D: Osamu Dezaki. Animated. Subtitled/dubbed. 95 mins. (Streamline Pictures)

Dezaki's frantic, full-scale adaptation of Takao Saito's adult-oriented graphic novels tracks the ultraviolent adventures of professional assassin Duke Togo (a.k.a. "Golgo 13") on missions that take him from Malibu to Sicily and leave in their wake a trail of heartbroken babes and mangled bodies (occasionally in the same package). Your Phantom ultimately wearied of *The Professional*'s conventional plotting and relentlessly cold, humorless tone. But *animé* buffs will enjoy Dezaki's wild visual style, a painstakingly cinematic approach that at once simulates live

action and makes inventive use of animation techniques (e.g., subbing comic-book panels for conventional freeze-frames). Carl Macek's dubbed edition is solidly straightforward, with only scattered lapses into awkward translations (e.g., lovestruck gal to emotionless Duke: "I waited so long for you to pull my trigger, lovingly and softly.") If Bruce Willis actioners like *Die Hard* and *The Last Boy Scout* had gone the animation route, they'd probably look a lot like *The Professional*. No relation to Luc Besson's 1994 *The Professional* (Columbia/TriStar, DVD), with Jean Reno, Natalie Portman, and Gary Oldman.

PULP FICTION   (1994)****

D: Quentin Tarantino. John Travolta, Samuel L. Jackson, Uma Thurman, Bruce Willis, Tim Roth, Amanda Plummer, Ving Rhames, Christopher Walken, Harvey Keitel, Peter Greene. 154 mins. (Miramax) DVD

With his brilliant *Pulp Fiction*, Tarantino solidified his position as an Orson Welles for the '90s. Q.T.'s acting skills may not match O.W.'s, but in all other areas—from sheer writing and directorial talent to savvy self-promotion—he's every bit the maestro's equal. (He's even, like Welles, resorted to self-parody, satirizing *Pulp Fiction* on the network sitcom *All American Girl*.) The academically trained Orson often brought high culture to the masses (though he usually proved more popular with buffs and critics), while the vid-store-schooled Tarantino specializes in polishing B-movie riffs to a high, heady gloss and has scored pretty much across the board, with buffs, critics, and mass auds alike. (Of course, Welles also had considerable success mining Tarantino's turf with the pulp-novel-drawn *Lady from Shanghai* and the recently reconstructed nightmare noir *Touch of Evil*.) Tarantino excels at offering an edgier variation on the ZAZ (*Naked Gun*) Team's *MAD* magazine "Scenes We'd

Like to See"–inspired approach, so even if you caught *Pulp Fiction* during its lengthy bijou run, the film's video incarnation offers fresh rewards. You may have missed some of Tarantino's film homages—e.g., the B&W rear projection seen during boxer Willis's cab flight after winning a fight he'd sworn to throw. It's the type of visual gimmick, thoughtfully employed here, that Oliver Stone bludgeoned to death (reportedly along with Tarantino's original script) in his bloated, sledgehammer "satire" *Natural Born Killers* (see index).

Featuring an excellent script (written with Roger Avary, of the recommended *Killing Zoe*) and indelible perfs by a great cast—especially Travolta and Jackson as motormouthed hit men, Thurman as a modern-day moll, Rhames as her ultra-tough gangsta beau, Walken as a solemn 'Nam vet, Keitel as a mob troubleshooter, and the aforementioned Willis—*Pulp Fiction* shapes up as one of the swiftest, most intricate genre movies ever made. And the soundtrack, kicking off with Dick Dale's instrumental surf classic "Miserlou," is well worth owning too. 1998's *Plump Fiction* (Rhino Video), starring Tommy Davidson and Julie Brown, sends up Tarantino in particular and the "buzz"-driven indie-film biz in general.

PURGATORY   (1989)**

D: Ami Artzi. Tanya Roberts, Julie Pop, Harold Orlandini, Rufus Swart. (New Star, n.i.d.)

In *Purgatory* ("The Women's Prison That's One Step From Hell!"), former *Charlie's Angel*/screen *Sheena* Roberts and newcomer Pop topline as a pair of Peace Corp volunteers stationed in a mythical African nation. No sooner do the opening credits end than martial law is declared and all foreigners are advised to leave. Tanya takes the news in stride ("So much for the Peace Corps!") but proves less adaptable when she and Ms. Pop are tossed into the titular hoosegow on trumped-up drug charges. In fact, over the first 80 minutes or so, Tanya gives every indication of not being tough enough to hold her own in this demanding genre. Not only does she go to whining and weeping at the drop of a truncheon, but she proves exceedingly discreet in the gratuitous-nudity department, shows zero enthusiasm for her "work detail" chores as a loaned-out hooker at a local hotel, and even performs her token upchuck scene with a decided lack of passion. Fortunately, she finally snaps to in the actional final reel of this otherwise low-energy female *Midnight Express* manqué by leading the inevitable inmate breakout and forcefully settling the score with the prison's predictably sadistic authorities. While *Purgatory* may not constitute a major career move for Tanya, it's definitely a step up for the memorably monikered Skip Schoolnik, who'd earlier directed the hideous *Hide and Go Shriek* (New Star) but who scores an executive producer credit here. No relation to the 1999 allegorical western *Purgatory* (Warner), starring Sam Shepard and Eric Roberts.

THE QUEST   (1996) **¹/₂

D: Jean-Claude Van Damme. Jean-Claude Van Damme, Roger Moore, James Remar, Aki Aleong, Louis Mandylor. 95 mins. (Universal) DVD

Van Damme's directorial debut—J-C and kickboxing mentor Frank Dux share story credit—is an unabashed bid to return to old-fashioned adventure entertainment, a goal the Muscles from Brussels falls short of reaching, due largely to an overly simpleminded script (even for him). The pic opens somewhere around present day, with J-C, in theatrical old-man makeup, reminiscing in an NYC bar (with time out for the nonagenarian to beat up a couple of thugs). We flash back to 1925, when Van Damme, on stilts and in clown makeup (!), "entertains" on the teeming streets to help feed a small army of orphans. A run-in with local mobster Mandylor lands our hero literally at sea, where he's eventually befriended by civilized pirate/former James Bond Moore. A few plot twists later, J-C and American boxing champ Remar are entered into a brutal international martial arts free-for-all, where the story stops for an eventually numbing succession of exotic bouts. While *The Quest* never quite transcends its routine B-movie soul, director Van Damme at least fills the screen with lush locales, vivid colors, and panoramic sweep. The flick failed to bag the crossover swag that his *Sudden Death* (see index) managed to snag, but committed J-C fans won't find it a drag.

QUICK   (1993) **¹/₂

D: Rick King. Teri Polo, Jeff Fahey, Martin Donovan, Robert Davi, Tia Carrere. 99 mins. (Academy, n.i.d.)

Quick has a lot going for it but, unlike assassin Polo's aim, just misses the mark. The flick kicks off to a bright start: In the opening-credit sequence, a disguised Polo, on her way to a Beverly Hills hit assignment, cruises through an ever changing L.A.scape while appropriate ethnic songs play on her car radio. But her character, like corrupt-cop beau Fahey, philosophical big-time speed dealer Davi, and fugitive accountant/embezzler Donovan, is too malleable to the whims of the story line to carry much credibility. Still, for all its rampant illogic and myriad off-key details (such as making Davi's henchmen total buffoons), *Quick* manages to entertain almost in spite of itself.

RAGE OF HONOR   (1987) *¹/₂

D: Gordon Hessler. Shô Kosugi, Lewis Van Bergen, Robin Evans, Gerry Gibson, Chip Lucia, Richard Wiley. 92 mins. (Media, n.i.d.)

Rage of Honor is nothing if not a one-man Shô. In addition to personally designing all the "special weapons" on view, an out-of-control Kosugi shows Arnie, Sly, and Chuck what mass destruction's really all about as he single-handedly slays or maims a small army of Arizona drug dealers. Then, when a colleague is killed, Shô decides to get *serious*. With what seems like a single back-flip, he lands in Argentina, where he wipes out a *large* army of South American drug dealers *and* half a native tribe that happens to get in his way. But it's not over yet— CIA choppers ostensibly sent to rescue Shô actually contain deadly ninjas bent on eliminating our hero. He annihilates 'em to a man (and a chopper), all the while delivering even the most innocuous dialogue with feral intensity. (He may be the only actor extant who can make "I cannot go on a date with you" sound like a death threat.) Tune in next time, when enemy forces hit him with a 50-meg nuke warhead and Shô is momentarily dazed!

RAPID FIRE   (1992) ***

D: Dwight H. Little. Brandon Lee, Powers Boothe, Nick Mancuso, Kate Hodge, Raymond J. Barry, Tzi Ma. 95 mins. (Fox)

After appearing in such unworthy items as *Laser Mission* (Turner) and *Showdown in Little Tokyo* (see index), the late Brandon Lee landed his first sturdy stateside vehicle with Dwight (*Getting Even*) Little's *Rapid Fire*. Lee toplines as college student Jake Lo, a combo sketch artist/kung-fu wiz unwittingly embroiled in a four-way war among Chinese smack suppliers, Chicago Mafiosi, corrupt FBI agents, and Windy City cops headed by Boothe and Lee's eventual screen squeeze (Hodge). While the peripatetic plot's not exactly a paragon of logic, straying from Tiananmen Square to Thailand, L.A., and some of Chicago's meaner streets, *Rapid Fire* amply delivers in the all-important mindless-action department. The flick features three major shoot-outs, a high body count on both sides of the law, and several stunning kung-fu set-tos wherein director Little even works in a few John Woo–type moves, particularly during a spectacular stick-fight/third-rail ballet atop a Chicago El track. Director Little is so determined to keep viewers awake that he even interrupts Hodge and Lee's requisite slo-mo love scene with bursts of story-advancing violence. Lee handles his role with impressive aplomb, taking some hard hits while displaying a strong knack for droll humor.

RAVEN (1996) **1/2

D: Russell Solberg. Burt Reynolds, Matt Battaglia, Krista Allen, Richard Gant, David Ackroyd. 93 mins. (New Line) DVD

A pre–*Boogie Nights* Burt, in his baddest role since his crazed-cracker turn in *The Maddening* (see index), plays a ruthless merc who risks life, limb, and hairpiece to retrieve a valuable nuclear decoder from Bosnian forces. Burt and a battle-weary Battaglia are the only team members to survive the risky mission. Matt quits the game, assumes a new identity and settles in with fetching senatorial aide Allen, but a merciless Burt tracks him down and assembles a new killer crew to wage a terrorist campaign against the corrupt government honchos who initially betrayed him. Director Solberg, whose narrow-cast previous credits consist of two obscure Cory (Son of Bob) Eubanks actioners, *Payback* and *Forced to Kill* (see index), keeps his literally explosive narrative moving at a swift-enough pace to satisfy action addicts and Burt buffs alike. Reynolds returns, as a hard-case mountain man, in 1999's *The Hunter's Moon* (Monarch, DVD).

RAW DEAL (1986) **

D: John Irvin. Arnold Schwarzenegger, Kathryn Harrold, Darren McGavin. 106 mins. (HBO) DVD

A rn takes on the Mafia in an improbable slaughterfest that peaks early when Schwarzenegger, as your typical Austrian-accented Southern sheriff, has a cake tossed at him by his inebriated wife, Blanche Baker. Quips our hero: "You shouldn't drink und bake!" The film falls apart when Arnie's mechanized monomania muscles in. Possibly due to an undetected circuitry malfunction, he obsessively repeats shticks from earlier flicks—donning his leather-bar threads, complete with gun and grenade accessories, à la *Commando*; driving a truck, *Terminator*-style, through a local hood hangout, etc.—before losing *all* control, at which point he systematically wastes most of the cast. Thus depleted of supporting characters, *Raw Deal* has little choice but to end. No relation to Anthony Mann's superior 1948 noir, *Raw Deal* (see index).

THE RAZOR:
THE SERIES

THE RAZOR: SWORD OF DEATH (1972) ***1/2

D: Kenji Misumi. Shintarô Katsu, Yukiji Asaoka, Mari Atsumi, Ko Nishimura. Subtitled. 90 mins. (AnimEigo)

L one Wolf and Cub helmer Kenji also handles directorial chores on this choice entry in the samurai "Jap-sploitation" sweepstakes. A portly Katsu (*Zatoichi*), who also produced, stars as Hanzo, an honest cop, lightning-swift swordsman, and unlikely self-styled stud who goes against a corrupt chief constable's orders and investigates an escaped criminal. "Assisted" by three bumbling minions (sort of a samurai Three Stooges), Hanzo puts his ratiocinative powers, deadly blade, and legendary procreative organ to daunting use. Big on both self- and other-torture, Hanzo comes across as a medieval blend of James Bond, Clint Eastwood's Dirty Harry, and Charles Bronson's Paul Kersey. Samurai buffs and cross-

cultural action fans of all stripes will want to scope out this winner. Anim-Eigo followed with *The Razor: Sword of Justice* and *The Razor: Who's Got the Gold?*

RED HEAT (1985) **

D: Robert Collector. Linda Blair, Sylvia Kristel, Sue Kiel, William Ostrander. 105 mins. (Vestron, n.i.d.)

N o relation to the Schwarzenegger vehicle of the same name, *this Red Heat* stars chronic celluloid recidivist Blair as an American kidnapped by Commies while visiting her soldier fiancé (Ostrander) in Germany. By the second reel, poor Linda's in the can again—this time an East German joint dominated by mean queen con Kristel, of *Emmanuelle* fame. From that point on, Linda is run through the usual gamut of indignities and perversions—rape, deprivation, physical abuse. *Red Heat* does offer one creative moment amid the yawns when—in a witty *Exorcist* nod—Linda gets pea soup thrown in *her* face, courtesy of a hostile fellow inmate.

RED HEAT (1988) ***

D: Walter Hill. Arnold Schwarzenegger, James Belushi, Peter Boyle, Ed O'Ross, Laurence Fishburne, Gina Gershon. 106 mins. (Artisan) DVD

A rn is cast as rock-bodied Russki cop Ivan "Iron Jaw" Danko in what ranks as the first official glasnost genre movie. After an opening duke-out set in a coed Russian steel-mill gym, wherein Arn performs his first major nearly nude scene since *The Terminator,* and a subsequent Moscow-set shoot-out, our pec-heavy hero hops a jet to Chicago to join jokey American cop Belushi in a violent, high-energy search for Soviet-émigré psycho killer and drug dealer Viktor Rosta (a neat, nasty turn by O'Ross). While ultimately predictable,

Red Heat offers a number of fresh variations on the standard mismatched-cops clichés; Arn even shows a sensitive side when he expresses concern re the plight of the parakeet he left behind in Moscow. With its nonstop action, culminating in a high-speed bus chase through the Windy City streets ("This is all too Russian for me!" Belushi moans), *Red Heat* rates as a reliable item for action buffs.

RED LION (A.K.A. *AKAGE*) (1969) ***1/2

D: Okamoto Kihachi. Toshirô Mifune, Iwashita Shima, Takahashi Etsushi, Terada Minori, Otowa Nobuku. Subtitled. 111 mins. (AnimEigo)

Mifune gets to display his comic gifts more than his swordsman skills as an illiterate, combat-ready peasant who serves as an emissary to his own hometown during Japan's "World Renewal" period in 1868. As the impulsive, enthusiastic Gonzo, Mifune is only too happy to return as the bearer of glad tidings re an era in which peasant life will improve dramatically, land taxes will be halved, and the forces of local corruption expelled. What he doesn't realize is that the whole deal's an elaborate setup and that he's actually a stooge for imperial forces less interested in liberating peasants than in expanding their own power base. Much of this rousing Toshiro showcase concentrates on Gonzo's bid to settle old scores, reunite with former squeeze Shima (forced into prostitution during Gonzo's decadelong absence), and rally the locals to prepare for the coming changes.

RED SCORPION (1989) **1/2

D: Joseph Zito. Dolph Lundgren, M. Emmet Walsh, Al White, T. P. McKenna, Brion James. 102 mins. (SGE) DVD

Lundgren stars as Nikolai, a "perfect killing machine" sent by his Soviet superiors to assassinate a troublesome African rebel leader. As expected, Dolph eventually sees the errors of his Commie ways and decides to throw his considerable weight behind the outmanned, outgunned freedom fighters' cause. Lundgren is wisely given only a few lines to grunt; expository chores are instead handled by rebel lieutenant Kalunda (White) and foulmouthed Yank journalist Dewey (Walsh). Dolph does get to display his true talents, however, by doffing his shirt midway through the third reel. Whether being tortured by Cuban interrogators, menaced by desert scorpions, tattooed by friendly bushmen, or paying back his former employers via a varied array of automatic weapons, our hulking hero manages to keep it off most of the rest of the way. Followed by the related-in-name-only *Red Scorpion 2* (Universal), with Matt McColm.

RED SUN RISING (1994) **1/2

D: Francis Megahy. Don ("the Dragon") Wilson, Terry Farrell, Michael Ironside, Mako, Edward Albert, Soon-Teck Oh, James Lew, Stoney Jackson. 96 mins. (Imperial)

Don's a Kyoto cop sent to L.A. to retrieve errant gangster Oh and his "death touch" assassin partner, Lew, who descend upon the Big Enchilada in hopes of sparking—and subsequently supplying the weapons for—an all-out street war between the Chicano "Malitos" and the black "Icemen." *Red Sun Rising* benefits from several energetic action set pieces—Don scores an "Executive in Charge of Fight Action" (!) credit—and cross-genre horror touches. Withal, *Red Sun Rising* rates as a busy if oft brainless action package; those searching for wisdom can tune out after the pic's opening quote, from 17th-century Japanese mystic Miyamoto Musashi's *Book of Five Rings*: "Today is victory over yourself of yesterday."

REMO WILLIAMS: THE NONSERIES

REMO WILLIAMS: THE ADVENTURE BEGINS... (1985) **1/2

D: Guy Hamilton. Fred Ward, Joel Grey, Kate Mulgrew, Wilford Brimley. 121 mins. (HBO)

Ward makes for a refreshingly unglamorous hero, while Asian mentor Grey turns in a credible Pat Morita imitation in a flawed but mostly fun *Indiana Jones* wannabe that failed to attract enough attention to attain film-franchisehood. Action set pieces include a punch-up atop the Statue of Liberty (shades of Hitchcock's *Saboteur!*) and a chase through an army weapons-testing site.

RENEGADES (1989) ***

D: Jack Sholder. Kiefer Sutherland, Lou Diamond Phillips, Jamie Gertz. 105 mins. (Universal) DVD

Undercover cop Sutherland and Native American Phillips team up to nail mutual enemies in Jack (*Alone in the Dark*, *The Hidden*) Sholder's entertaining, high-energy mismatched-partners caper.

THE REPLACEMENT KILLERS (1998) *1/2

D: Antoine Fuqua. Chow Yun-Fat, Mira Sorvino, Michael Rooker, Jürgen Prochnow, Clifton González González, Patrick Kilpatrick. 88 mins. (Columbia/TriStar) DVD

Mira Sorvino proves she's no Cynthia Rothrock, while Chow Yun-Fat shows that, sans the right surroundings, he's no Chow Yun-Fat. In this unflaggingly limp, low-impact attempt to replicate a standard Hong Kong actioner, the erstwhile H.K. icon plays a marksman pressured into performing three designated hits to pay off a debt to a States-based Chinese gangster. When his final target turns out to be the seven-year-old son of cop Rooker, our hero balks and goes on the run with gun-wielding forger Sorvino. Several dull shoot-outs ensue in a soulless, thrill-free yawner that feels far longer than its professed 88-minute running time. Yun-Fat fares at least somewhat better in 1999's *The Corruptor* (New Line).

RESERVOIR DOGS   (1992) ***½

D: Quentin Tarantino. Harvey Keitel, Tim Roth, Lawrence Tierney, Michael Madsen, Chris Penn, Steve Buscemi. 105 mins. (Artisan) DVD

Dark wit, knockout ensemble acting, abrupt and senseless violence, and a tight, lean story line encased in a carefully fractured structure combine to make Tarantino's directorial debut an intense experience. A deceptively casual opening set in a roadside diner introduces the major characters—a crew of contempo desperadoes headed by vet thesp Tierney (accurately described by one of the group as resembling comicdom's "the Thing") and screen offspring Penn. The father-son duo have hired a half dozen pros, with literally colorful aliases ("Mr. White," "Mr. Pink," etc.), to execute a precision diamond heist. When the caper goes awry, the surviving thieves try to sort out what went wrong and why. Mounting distrust, conflicting moral codes, and macho frictions soon have the pack of mongrel mobsters at one another's throats. The brisk, inventive dialogue—which ranges from paranoid musings to a discussion of action icon Pam Grier's merits (!)—is expertly delivered by the all-male cast, which includes code-bound Keitel (Mr. White), anxious iconoclast Buscemi (Mr. Pink), trigger-happy sadist Madsen (Mr. Blonde), and a badly wounded Roth (Mr. Orange) as the principal miscreants. A fictitious (we hope) radio show hosted by a monotoned deejay (deadpan comic Steven Wright) and devoted to spinning nothing but '70s

pop schlock tunes supplies an appropriately maddening musical counterpoint. Self-conscious homages to Sam Peckinpah and Stanley Kubrick distract from the film's reality (though we liked longago screen Dillinger Tierney's description of a fellow hood as being "dead as Dillinger") while a few incidents merely discussed in the pic would have been better dramatized.

RETREAT OF THE GODFATHER (1991) ***

D: Chan Chi Hwa. Ko Chung Shiung, Dee Wai, Long Shiao Hwa, Kim Kong, Lin Wen, Wu Ma. 90 mins. (SYS International/Tapeworm)

This excellent 1980s urban-gangster entry pits three renegade exhenchmen against a brace of warring Hong Kong Mafia factions. While Hwa doesn't scale John Woo's celluloid heights, there's no lack of elaborate gunplay, acrobatic martial arts displays, intense melodrama, and scattered comic moments. In the Jackie Chan tradition, *Retreat of the Godfather* concludes with outtakes—ranging from blown lines to painfully botched stunts—screening under the end-credits crawl.

RETURN TO SAVAGE BEACH (1998) **½

D: Andy Sidaris. Julie Strain, Julie K. Smith, Shae Marks, Rodrigo Obregón, Marcus Bagwell, Christian Letelier, Gerald Okamura. 90 mins. (Monarch)

A loose sequel to Sidaris's *Savage Beach*, *Return* reopens the original case and puts the LETHAL team, headed by bodacious Strain, Smith, and Marks, on the trail of a gang out to cop a cache of stolen gold buried by Japanese soldiers in the Philippines during World War II. Okamura, meanwhile, scores his own action vehicle with the martial arts opus *Demon Master* (Screen Pix).

THE RIVER WILD   (1994) ***

D: Curtis Hanson. Meryl Streep, Kevin Bacon, David Straithairn, Joseph Mazzello, John C. Reilly, Benjamin Bratt, Buffy. 112 mins. (Universal) DVD

Meryl ("the Body") Streep, a.k.a. "the Muscles from Basking Ridge, New Jersey," bulks up, adds a steely ocular glint, and kicks butt bigtime in her first all-out action role. (She could even contend with Kathleen Kinmont as "the next female Arnold Schwarzenegger," though, after his preggers turn in the B.O. dud *Junior*, Arn can legitimately claim that title himself.) Meryl's a Boston-based history teacher who returns to her Wild West roots when she takes young son (Mazzello) and wimpy architect hubby (Straithairn) on a white-water-rafting jaunt along the Idaho/Canadian border. Trouble ensues when thieves Bacon and Reilly commandeer her raft and force her to guide them through dangerous rapids in a bid to escape after a quarter-mil bank heist. Though dissed by most mainstream critics, *The River Wild* shapes up as a fairly entertaining suspenser that will leave Meryl fans' knuckles as white as the water. The flick further benefits from Jerry Goldsmith's rousing score, a strong psycho perf by Bacon, and strenuous heroics not only by Meryl but by family dog Maggie (played by professional pooch Buffy).

RIVERBEND   (1989) **½

D: Sam Firstenberg. Steve James, Margaret Avery, Tony Frank, Julius Tennon, Alex Morris, Vanessa Tate. 106 mins. (Paramount)

Set in 1966, *Riverbend* stars the late, great Steve James as Major Sam Quinton, who, with two fellow black officers, escapes from a skedded court martial—he'd refused orders to slaughter innocent women and children in 'Nam—near Riverbend, Georgia, a redneck burg ruled by racist, sociopathic sheriff Jake (Frank). After falling for widow Avery, Steve stays on to train local blacks to fight back against the lawman's reign of terror. The situation eventually escalates into an armed showdown between Steve's ragtag troops and a small army of state militia. Sam (*Avenging Force*) Firstenberg's low-budget indie can't decide whether it's an earnest civil-rights drama or a flat-out action flick. James is his usual charismatic self as the morally tormented Major Q., though his considerable kung-fu skills are utilized in only two major fight scenes here. Despite a few glaring glitches—such as a scene wherein Steve's distinctive voice is blatantly looped by a different actor (!)—*Riverbend* is worth a look for James's fans.

THE ROCK   (1996) **¹/₂

D: Michael Bay. Sean Connery, Nicolas Cage, Ed Harris, Michael Biehn, William Forsythe, David Morse, Tony Todd, John C. McGinley. 136 mins. (Hollywood Pictures) DVD

Reasonably entertaining in spite of its multiple excesses, *The Rock* shapes up as a typically ridiculous blockbuster actioner with an incongruously self-important edge, mostly supplied by Harris's character, a deranged, self-righteous general who invades a tourist-packed Alcatraz and threatens to nerve-gas San Francisco if the government doesn't own up to abandoning its "black" (illegal) ops in various foreign wars. Despite their expressed indignation, Harris and his renegade military cohorts exhibit few qualms about slaughtering those fellow servicemen guarding a bio-warfare munitions dump they raid for its high-tech machinery. Cage, who's much better than the material here, plays a lab-bound chemical-weapons FBI expert forced to bond with long-imprisoned Brit ex-spy Connery, recruited because he's the only inmate ever to escape the titular facility. Connery's also apparently an ex-hippie who sired a daughter with a woman picked up at a backdate Led Zeppelin

concert (though his character would have been close to 40 at the time). An otherwise insignificant character, the daughter was obviously written in to offer an excuse for a totally extraneous 20-minute vehicular-chase sequence that pads the flick almost beyond endurance. On the upside, *The Rock* does deliver on the mega-action level and also arrives as a fine Tony Todd showcase; the erstwhile Candyman, cast as Harris's looniest minion, makes the most of his modest screen time, managing to convey true madness and menace. A horrific nerve-gas meltdown provides another fleeting highlight.

ROCKY IV   (1985) *

D: Sylvester Stallone. Sylvester Stallone, Talia Shire, Dolph Lundgren, Brigitte Nielsen, Carl Weathers, Burt Young. (Fox) DVD

ROLLING THUNDER   (1977) **¹/₂

D: John Flynn. William Devane, Tommy Lee Jones, Linda Haynes, James Best. 99 mins. (Vestron, n.i.d.)

Flynn's seminal 'Nam-vets-bring-the-war-back-home actioner benefits from a strong cast—particularly Devane as the alienated returnee whose family's massacre gives him a reason to live—and helped launch a long-lived action subgenre.

ROLLING VENGEANCE   (1987) **¹/₂

D: Steven H. Stern. Don Michael Paul, Lawrence Dane, Ned Beatty, Lisa Howard, Michael Kirby. 90 mins. (Charter, n.i.d.)

We don't know about you, but The Phantom had been waiting a long time for *the* definitive monster-truck movie, a flick that would put those

---

THE RAP ON *ROCKY*

Y'all know Rocky, of fistic fame,
Now bashin' Commies is his new game.
Ivan Drago's the name of the Russian contender
Who's out to prove he's no pretender.
This Great Red Hope's a mountain of a man,
Makes Arnold S. look like Peter Pan.
And when the monster Commie creams Apollo Creed
Rocky vows to avenge that evil deed.
Rock goes into training, gets into shape
So he and Ive can go at it, ape to ape.
When the big bout unfolds in Moscow town
The homies scream for Rocky to go down.
But Rock's so brave and devoid of fear
That even the Russians stand and cheer.
Rock smacks that Russki upside the head
Till our arrogant Commie's more dead than Red.
Now Rocky may seem stupid, but he's really Sly
'Cause on the bottom line he keeps an eagle eye.
So Rock socks it to us, blow by blow.
He can't speak good English, but he rakes in the dough.
But now we've suffered through Rockys 1 through 4
The Phantom's got a request for Mr. Balboa:
Hang 'em up, Sly, we can't take it no mo-a!

macho Bigfoot and King Kong machines to more creative use than hauling giant prop six-packs around a dirt track on ESPN late-night monster-truck rallies. Well, we have seen the future of monster-truck movies, and its name is *Rolling Vengeance*. The pic kicks off to slow start with several dull scenes detailing young trucker Paul's family life. But when said family gets totaled in a series of violent road "accidents" engineered by evil go-go-bar owner Beatty (in greaseball hairstyle and black-leather threads) and his five dim-witted sons, *Rolling Vengeance* switches into high gear, turning into a *Death Wish* on Wheels as Don squashes the opposition (and everything else in his sizable path) in lovingly lensed detail. *Rolling Vengeance* may be short on subtlety and logic, but it's long on authentic monster-truck thrills.

RONIN (1998) ***

D: John Frankenheimer. Robert De Niro, Natascha McElhone, Jean Reno, Stellan Skarsgard, Jonathan Pryce, Sean Bean, Skip Sudduth. 120 mins. (MGM) DVD

While he doesn't recapture the emotional intensity of true originals like *The Manchurian Candidate* and *Seconds* (see index), Frankenheimer skillfully transforms what could have been pure convoluted potboiler material into a mostly breathless nonstop thriller. De Niro, who'd earlier displayed his simultaneously energetic and world-weary action-noir chops in Michael Mann's *Heat*, receives serious thespian competition from fellow mercs Jean (*The Professional*) Reno and Stellan (*Insomnia*) Skarsgard as a team (along with newcomer Sudduth) recruited by presumed Irish terrorist McElhone and her shadowy contact Pryce to retrieve a classic McGuffin, a mysterious, ever elusive briefcase that's in feverish demand by a host of dangerous international factions. The early reels proceed as a more or less straight-

forward, hard-boiled caper as our "heroes" and their enemies crash, burn, and shoot up the narrow streets of a gritty, frequently rainy nocturnal Paris and a chilly pre-Christmas Nice (both rendered with striking visual impact). The plot thickens as treachery and betrayals rapidly multiply, infecting our protagonists with well-earned distrust and paranoia. While the characters remain superficial—their charisma comes from the perfs, not the script—and the film runs on roughly a reel too long, *Ronin* isn't likely to disappoint devotees of intense action thrillers. An assassination set during an ice show provides a classic Frankenheimer set piece, while a scene wherein a seriously wounded De Niro supervises his own surgery, shown not only in extreme close-up but through a mirror to boot, may well rate as 1998's most teeth-gritting, seat-squirming sequence.

THE ROOKIE (1990) **1/2

D: Clint Eastwood. Clint Eastwood, Charlie Sheen, Raul Julia, Sonia Braga, Tom Skerritt, Lara Flynn Boyle, Pepe Serna. 121 mins. (Warner)

Sort of a "The Rook, The Thief, His Lover, and Her Uzi," *The Rookie* offers a mismatched-cops plot containing little that's new, with street-hardened vet Clint breaking in "virgin" Sheen, a would-be butt-kicking rich kid. The duo go after German chop-shop honcho Julia and his mean-tempered, machine-gun-toting squeeze (Braga). The pace picks up considerably once Clint gets copnapped by Raul and raped (!) by Sonia, a scene, involving handcuffs, razor blades, and videotape, that rates as the ultimate in unsafe sex. Charlie, meanwhile, proves his mettle by pistol-whipping an entire barful of lowlifes before burning the joint to the ground. The final reels, reeking more of James Bond than Dirty Harry, culminate in an elaborate airport shoot-out worthy of *Die Hard 2*.

ROSEWOOD (1997) ***

D: John Singleton. Ving Rhames, Jon Voight, Don Cheadle, Loren Dean, Bruce McGill, Esther Rolle, Michael Rooker. 135 mins. (Warner) DVD

John (*Boyz 'N the Hood, Higher Learning* [both Columbia/TriStar]) Singleton brings scope, sweep, suspense, and powerful human drama—along with some largely unnecessary Hollywood-oid fictional elements—to his account of a previously obscure American atrocity. In 1923 North Central Florida, a bogus racist rumor led a white mob from the nearby trash town of Sumner to attack and ultimately destroy the somewhat more prosperous African-American village of Rosewood. Singleton and scripter Gregory Poirier cover the genocidal outbreak from start to aftermath, and most of the basic info presented is rooted in truth, from black piano teacher Cheadle's one-man stand against the armed rabble to the nocturnal escape of several of Rosewood's women and children. The introduction of gunslinging, horse-riding World War I vet Mr. Mann (Rhames) is pure fantasy, however, and detracts from the pic's verisimilitude.

ROYAL WARRIORS (1986) ***

D: David Chung. Michelle Yeoh, Michael Wong, Henry Sanada. Subtitled/dubbed. 85 mins. (Tai Seng) DVD

An entry in the Asian action queen's popular *In the Line of Duty* policewoman series, *Royal Warriors* casts Yeoh as a no-nonsense Hong Kong cop who teams with her romantically inclined partner (Wong) and visiting Japanese detective (Sanada) to battle superviolent (and virtually invincible) terrorists. While sporting its share of credible character development, the accent is firmly on action, from an opening skyjack sequence to a grueling climactic battle on a deserted construction site.

RUMBLE IN THE BRONX (1995)***

D: Stanley Tong. Jackie Chan, Anita Mui,
Françoise Yip, Bill Tung, Mark Akerstream,
Gavin Cross, Morgan Lam, Kris Lord. 98 mins.
(New Line) DVD

After failing to chop his way into American hearts in lower-budgeted '80s efforts like *The Big Brawl* and *The Protector,* international martial arts star Chan scored his first stateside hit with *Rumble in the Bronx.* Jackie toplines as Hong Kong tourist Keung, a lightly sketched average Joe (or at least average Jackie—Keung also happens to be a former martial arts champ) who comes to America to attend the wedding of his uncle (Tung). When said uncle sells his Bronx supermarket, the kindly Keung hangs on to lend a helping hand (and eventually flying feet) to new owner Mui. This being, after all, a Jackie Chan movie, it's not long before Keung gets into an extended tangle with a gang of local toughs, headed by late stunt ace Akerstream. The Bronx of Chan and director Stanley Tong bears scant resemblance to the actual NYC borough (not too surprising, considering the film was lensed in Vancouver). This is a South Bronx where the major crimes are mob-engineered diamond heists and the rowdy antics of overaged, multiethnic motorcycle gangs. The sundry factions collide when a gang member (Cross) makes off with the mobsters' gems, prompting the heavies to persecute the gang. Jackie calls a truce with his former adversaries and sides with them against the organized criminals' superior forces. A creaky subplot involves Chan's amateur social work duties with fetching deb Yip and her irritating wheelchair-bound little bro' (Lam).

Fortunately, as in Chan's previous and subsequent outings, breakneck action remains *Rumble*'s real raison d'être, and Jackie dishes it out in generous doses. In addition to the clever, balletic, and often comedic fighting, highlights include a lengthy climactic

---

JACKIE CHAN'S MASTER PLAN

As Told to The Phantom

The Phantom met with the charismatic, ever kinetic Jackie Chan just prior to Rumble's *wide stateside release.*

PHANTOM: I remember when *The Protector* came out.

CHAN: Doesn't work. Even in Asia, it doesn't work. I think every director want to change me. Like Jimmy Glickenhaus. When I saw his movies, I liked them—with all the stunts and what he did. Then he comes to me: "Jackie, I want to make you like Clint Eastwood. You must act like Eastwood. Tough. You are New York police." Then I think, *"I'm* New York police?! What about my English?" Every day on the set I just practice my English: "New Yawk. I come from New Yawk. New *Yawk.*" He's a good director, but he choose the wrong part for me. So back in Hong Kong, I make my own films. I'm more comfortable. I control everything by myself. When I'm filming in America, it's two minutes on the set, back to the motor home. I do nothing.

PHANTOM: When you have somebody else direct, do you still direct with them?

CHAN: When they do something wrong, I tell them. If not, let them go. I don't want always Jackie Chan–style movie; I want to try something new. I have total control at the end—the editing myself, music, I control everything— that's the most important part. A lot of directors, they're not doing editing, they're wrong. In editing you know more the rhythm, the tempo, the whole movie.

PHANTOM: Is the Bronx very famous in Hong Kong?

CHAN: No. In Hong Kong we have a different title—*Trouble Area.* But in North America, everybody knows the Bronx. I believe you can see I put Bronx more prettier.

PHANTOM: Definitely!

CHAN: More colorful. When casting, everybody choose a lot of black people for me. I said no. I just want one or two black people. I want Italian guy, Chinese guy, American guy: everybody in the same place. The movie may be called *Rumble in the Bronx,* but I want to say, "Good people, bad people are everywhere. Not only Bronx." That's my message. I want to say to the audience, like after the fighting scene, "We could have tea together, not fight next time."

PHANTOM: In your scenes with Françoise Yip, you don't go too far.

CHAN: That's part of my rules. I cannot have those things in the movie. Too many fans. When I kiss somebody, the whole theater—everybody says, "No!" A girl suicide in front of my office—drinking a poison. Even my private life very secret. Cannot let those fans know. Before John Lennon got killed, I thought, never happen to me. A girl came to slap me in front of a thousand people. After slap me, she's smiling, then just slowly walk away. For three years, every year she come into Hong Kong to slap me. There's a bunch of crazy people out there. It makes me very worried. So cannot fooling around, cannot going to the disco, cannot fighting on the street, cannot do something wrong. Also, no blood from one punch. When I'm making a movie, I'm very careful. Maybe I'm on first unit, I'm not on second unit; when they bring back the film in editing, I look: "How can you do that? Retake the shot—no blood." I hate violence. But I like action. It's a dilemma.

PHANTOM: What do you think of John Woo's films, which *are* violent?

CHAN: I think everybody have own personality. I cannot criticize them. I don't know what are they really thinking. I watch—not John Woo, but some other movies—they're really violent. I hate them. How can they do that? Too disgusting. Maybe they think *my* movies disgusting.

PHANTOM: Do you think there'll come a point when you'll cut back on the stunts? You only have one body, and you want to stay active as an actor and filmmaker.

CHAN: No, I'll continue. Sometimes people ask me, "Why are you doing this stunt? Too hard." I'm doing this stunt for myself, not for you. Don't worry about me. When I design all the choreography and fighting stunts, I know how far I can go. I have a limit. I know what I'm doing; I'm not stupid. Maybe twenty years ago, I was *very* stupid.

PHANTOM: You've had some serious injuries.

CHAN: Yes. I fractured my skull, almost died, in Yugoslavia [on *Armor of God*]. I broke my ankle, you see in the movie [*Rumble*]. Used to it. I believe there's a lot of American movie stuntmen get hurt—they just don't show it. They just care about the actor. So when stuntman get hurt, nobody knows. I know stuntmen, so I know a lot of people get hurt. In my movies, I show my stuntmen get hurt. That's what we do in the movies. I appreciate all the stunt guys and people work with me. It's not only me, I show everybody. But I even get one cut and newspaper: "Oh! Jackie Chan get hurt! Oh! Jackie Chan get hurt again!" Small things, they write, "He's in coma for three hours!" It makes me very mad.

PHANTOM: Do you think it's difficult for an Asian actor to be an action star in America?

CHAN: Yeah, because we are not used to speak English. They're not used to dubbing. American movies are dubbed in Asia. Even I sing the song for *Beauty and the Beast*—Cantonese version, Mandarin version. We have American version at American theater for the North American people to look at. Some theaters is for Cantonese. Then in Mandarin, for Taiwan, mainland China. But American audience, they not accept something dubbed.

PHANTOM: The real fans like to see it subtitled. But in mall theaters, they don't like subtitles either.

CHAN: For the American version [of *Rumble*], I get rid of the subtitles, so they can concentrate on my action and my acting. I want to be an actor. Action-star life very short. If you can be an actor, your life more long.

PHANTOM: Like what Stallone and Schwarzenegger are doing.

CHAN: Yes. I think Schwarzenegger is very clever. He's from action star to *Kindergarten Cop*, *Twins*—very clever.

PHANTOM: You had something of an image change with *Crime Story*.

CHAN: Originally, it's a real story. A rich man got kidnapped twice in Hong Kong. I act like a serious policeman. I want to try something new. I got the

(continued)

chase scene that ultimately features an outsized Hovercraft plowing down an ersatz midtown Manhattan with a flotilla of wildly careering cop cars in crazed pursuit. (And Jackie, of course, all over the place.) New Line boldly launched *Rumble* (which had earlier enjoyed a less heralded Chinatown run in a slightly different version) on some 1,800 screens nationwide. *Rumble*'s broad comedy strokes, partial dubbing, cardboard characterizations, and paucity of lethal violence didn't deter American mall moviegoers used to a more demolitions-driven brand of action fare—at one point, *Rumble* and John Woo's *Broken Arrow* ranked at the top of the B.O. charts for an unprecedented Hong Kong one-two punch—and paved the way for a spate of big-screen Jackie actioners that produced decent (if diminishing) returns until the triumph of *Rush Hour* (New Line), where Chan found his ideal partner in motormouthed comic Chris Tucker.

RUN LOLA RUN (1999) ***

D: Tom Tykwer. Franka Potente, Moritz Bleibtreu, Herbert Knaup, Armin Rohde, Joachim Król. 81 mins. (Columbia/TriStar) DVD

Teutonic auteur Tykwer's somewhat overhyped (at Sundance and other buzzhappy fests) but conceptually clever, consistently entertaining, and swiftly paced indie is structured as a cerebral (the film opens with a T. S. Eliot quote) video game brought to relentlessly kinetic screen life. When her criminal gofer beau, Manni (Bleibtreu), loses a bag containing 100,000 ill-gotten marks—since snatched by an enterprising bum (Król)—Lola (Potente) has 20 minutes to score an equal sum and deliver it to Manni before the latter gets whacked by his brutal employer. Writer/director Tykwer literally runs Lola through a series of ever changing scenarios, demonstrat-

Golden Harvest Award from Taiwan—Best Acting. Some people, they don't like it—too serious.

PHANTOM: Bruce Lee was right on the verge of being a superstar here when he died. What did you think of the film *Dragon: The Bruce Lee Story*?

CHAN: Because I worked with Bruce Lee, I know a lot of stories, but I don't like *Dragon*. Stories are not right—not real. It doesn't work in Asia. In Asia everybody knows what happened. Even my name at that time "Second Bruce Lee, Jackie Chan." I like Bruce Lee, but I wanted to get rid of the Bruce Lee shadow. I don't want my whole life learn from him. So where he kick high, I kick low—totally opposite. He's a superhero; I'm not a superhero. I look at Steven Seagal, who always push people away—okay, I'm not doing him. Van Damme, he always open his legs; I'm not doing him. I have my own style.

PHANTOM: What techniques do you specialize in?

CHAN: I learned southern style and northern style—both styles. After that, I learned karate, tae kwando. I put everything in the movies that I learned. And always something new—roller blades, skateboards.

PHANTOM: Who are some of the people you like to watch?

CHAN: I like Buster Keaton. Marlon Brando. But now Marlon Brando is out. I learn from Dustin Hoffman, Al Pacino. I like Stallone. Also I can learn from Steven Spielberg, George Lucas, James Cameron. I think they are geniuses. And Quentin Tarantino. When I saw Fred Astaire dancing to the piano, coming back with the light pole, sit down on the sofa. Good for me fighting. Now I'm fighting with a refrigerator, sofa—I use every prop.

PHANTOM: Who do you think is a good fighter or a good athlete? Van Damme?

CHAN: Oh, there's too many. That depends who's famous. If Van Damme's famous, everybody thinks Van Damme's a good fighter. What I know is there are many, many good fighters. Chuck Norris. Muhammad Ali. Sugar Ray Leonard. Everybody have a different technique. Very hard to say who is the best. Maybe if I fight with Van Damme, he can knock me down for one second. But on the street, he cannot chase me. Because I run faster than him, climb up buildings faster. Different people have a different-type technique. Like Steven Seagal—nobody can go near to him. But he cannot chase somebody.

ing how a random move can radically alter the ultimate outcome of the "game." As Lola races the clock, Tykwer wrings genuine suspense through intense crosscutting between his hyperactive heroine's maneuvers and her frightened, waiting beau, who enacts wild, panic-driven schemes of his own.

Tykwer adds a number of other neat touches. We get rapid flashback montages of several peripheral characters Lola encounters during her frantic sprints through city streets, office buildings, and back alleys, while Lola herself comes equipped with a superhuman,

literally glass-shattering screaming ability that rivals Meg Tilly's in Abel Ferrara's *Body Snatchers* and Alan Bates's in *The Shout*. Tykwer also incorporates snippets of video-game-styled animation and sets the action to a pulsing Euro technopop soundtrack which he cocomposed (joining John Carpenter as one of the few auteurs who write their own music scores). Actress Potente turns in riveting work in the title role; with her intensely expressive face, dyed-red hair, and tight lime-green jeans, she instantly joins the expanding ranks of the Euro indie screen's unforgettable

power women (e.g., *Razor Blade Smile*'s Eileen Daly). With its inherent video-game sensibility and approach, *Run Lola Run* plays just as well on video as it does on the big screen.

RUNAWAY TRAIN (1985) ***¹/₂

D: Andrei Konchalovsky. Jon Voight, Eric Roberts, Rebecca De Mornay, John P. Ryan, Kyle T. Heffner, Kenneth McMillan, T. K. Carter. 112 mins. (MGM) DVD

Based on a vintage screenplay by Akira (*Seven Samurai*) Kurosawa, *Runaway Train* is an exciting actioner with a high-budget body and a B-movie soul. Voight gives a rousing, primal performance as supercon Manny Manheim, who, accompanied by young Buck (Roberts), busts out of Alaska's max-security Stonehaven Prison and unwisely boards the title train. Hot on the pair's frozen heels are Ryan, the meanest movie warden since Strother Martin in *Cool Hand Luke*, and a team of anxious railway employees tracking the train's chaotic path via an elaborate computer hookup. Minus the cusswords and computers, *Runaway Train* could pass for a classic '50s adventure flick—a jolting, emotionally intense thriller.

RUSH (1991) **¹/₂

D: Lili Fini Zanuck. Jason Patric, Jennifer Jason Leigh, Sam Elliott, Max Perlich, Greg Allman. 120 mins. (MGM)

Rush charts undercover cops Patric and Leigh's growing addiction both to controlled substances and the junkie/narc lifestyle in 1975 Texas. The flick rates as a credible but rarely riveting exercise in retro dope porn, replete with "penetration" shots of needles entering veins in extreme close-up. Beyond scoring the cogent point that drug prohibition seems to work about as well as its anti-alcohol counterpart, *Rush* offers little insight into our protagonists' lives as paid pincushions.

Aside from a brief highway hallucination, *Rush* likewise lacks the visual flair of the psychedelic cinema of yore (e.g., *The Trip*) and fails to match the action, sleaze, or suspense quotients generated by more up-front exploitation pics.

SATAN'S SADISTS   (1969) **¹/₂

D: Al Adamson. Russ Tamblyn, Scott Brady, Kent Taylor. 86 mins. (Super)

"Satan's Sadists are helling it like it is, baby!" asserts the trailer for this tale of a "rebellion of human garbage!" (Oh, why won't human garbage just stay in its place?) If you like vintage trash, you won't want to miss a single hour of Adamson's vision of Harley hell or even so much as *one* of Tamblyn's bad teeth shown in extreme close-up and living off-color. Adamson failed to recapture the magic with his mostly woeful distaff variation, *Angels' Wild Women* (Super).

SAVAGE BEACH   (1989) ***

D: Andy Sidaris. Dona Speir, Hope Marie Carlton, Rodrigo Obregón, John Aprea, Michael Shane, Eric Chen. 94 mins. (Columbia/TriStar)

Savage Beach sees Speir and Carlton reprise their roles as busty blond government agents. This time out, our bosom buddies find themselves in the middle of a three-way scramble for a gold fortune buried on a remote Pacific atoll by Japanese soldiers during World War II and still guarded by a semi-senile self-styled samurai with a bad makeup job. Violently competing for the cache are good-guy naval officers Aprea and Bruce Penhall, mercenaries led by Chen, and hot-blooded revolutionaries Obregón and Terry Wiegel (who gets to deliver the deathless line "Your every move inspires a passion in me!"). While the pic boasts its share of gratuitous nudity and double-entendre dialogue, *Savage Beach* packs in more genuine suspense than most Sidaris efforts.

SCARFACE   (1983) ****

D: Brian De Palma. Al Pacino, Michelle Pfeiffer, Steven Bauer, Robert Loggia, Harris Yulin, Mary Elizabeth Mastrantonio. 170 mins. (Universal) DVD

For The Phantom's moolah, De Palma's *Scarface* is the best crime movie ever made, and one of the best flicks of any kind. Pacino turns in his finest work (and that's going some) as the Freedom Flotilla refugee who becomes an eager student of Yankee capitalism. Add vivid cinematography, exotic South Florida locations, top supporting perfs, inspired dialogue, and sharp wit, and you have one of Hollywood's all-time winners. The final shoot-out even tops *The Wild Bunch*'s. This is one case where a "remake" blows away its original model, Howard Hawks's 1932 Al Capone–based fable, *Scarface* (Universal), though comparisons between the two are as irrelevant as they are unfair.

SET IT OFF   (1996) **¹/₂

D: F. Gary Gray. Jada Pinkett, Queen Latifah, Vivica A. Fox, John C. McGinley, Kimberly Elise, Blair Underwood. 123 mins. (New Line) DVD

A mix of the genuinely compelling and the woefully contrived, F. Gary (*Friday, The Negotiator*) Gray's *Set It Off* sifts out as a "Girlz 'N the Hood" Meets *Thelma & Louise* detailing how four L.A. ghetto gals decide to become big-time bank robbers. After her sweet turn in *The Nutty Professor* and raucous role in *A Low Down Dirty Shame* (Touchstone), an appealing Pinkett continues to demonstrate her range, this time as a working woman whose brother is wrongfully gunned down by McGinley (who's not, to the pic's credit, portrayed as a knee-jerk racist cop). Fox plays an unfairly fired teller who possesses the inside knowledge to plan the heists, while Latifah contributes strong work as a lesbian "'hood rat" (though Elise seems a tad too naïve as a single mom who

reluctantly joins the group), and Underwood manages to be sympathetic in a tricky role as a corporate banker "buppie" who courts Pinkett and gives her a taste of the good life. Rapper/deejay Dr. Dre cameos as a local gun dealer.

SHADOW OF THE WOLF   (1993) **¹/₂

D: Jacques Dorfmann. Lou Diamond Phillips, Toshirô Mifune, Jennifer Tilly, Donald Sutherland. 108 mins. (Columbia/TriStar)

All-purpose ethnic thesp Phillips *is* Agaguk, rebellious son of Eskimo chief Mifune, who, against Dad's wishes, takes off tundra-ward with mate Tilly after killing a deserving white man. While not up there with the 1960 Anthony Quinn Eskimo adventure *The Savage Innocents* (n/a), *Shadow of the Wolf* isn't the campy clunker many mainstream critics made it out to be. The flick mushes along at a brisk-enough pace, Sutherland is solemnly effective as Phillips's pursuer, and the icy location lensing makes *Shadow* a natural for deep-summer home-viewing.

SHADOWMAN   (1973) ***

D: Georges Franju. Gert Frobe, Gayle Hunnicutt, Josephine Chaplin, Jacques Champreux. Dubbed. 90 mins. (Cult Video, n.i.d.)

Franju's playful caper is an updated ode to the cliffhangers of yore, with the masked title villain, abetted by henchwoman Hunnicutt, out to steal the legendary treasure of the Knights Templar in contempo France. Lensed in vivid cartoon colors, *Shadowman* costars former *Goldfinger* Frobe as the determined Parisian police chief who aids hero Champreux (who also scripted) and squeeze Chaplin in defeating the disguised evildoers. Despite some uneven dubbing, *Shadowman* shapes up as an entertaining fantasy adventure.

SHAFT:
THE SERIES

SHAFT (1971) ***

D: Gordon Parks. Richard Roundtree, Moses Gunn, Charles Cioffi, Christopher St. John, Antonio Fargas. 100 mins. (MGM)

Roundtree plays a superslick, Apple-based P.I. hired by Harlem crime kingpin Gunn to rescue the latter's kidnapped daughter in the first—and best—of a trio of "blaxploitation" adventures, juiced by Isaac Hayes's justly famous score. One of the genre's true pioneers, *Shaft* set the tone and standards by which future urban actioners would be judged. Followed by *Shaft's Big Score* (1972) and 1973's *Shaft in Africa* (both MGM).

SHAKEDOWN (1988) ***

D: James Glickenhaus. Peter Weller, Sam Elliott, Patricia Charbonneau, Blanche Baker, Antonio Fargas, Richard Brooks. 96 mins. (Universal) DVD

Weller is a public defender about to go yupscale until his would-be final client—crack dealer and accused cop-killer Brooks (in a skilled performance)—leads him into a web of police corruption. The situation likewise edges him into an uneasy alliance with shaggy maverick plainclothes cop Elliott, who spends much of his time in the balcony of 42nd Street's (now sadly Disneyfied) New Amsterdam Theater. More than anything else, *Shakedown* is a kinetic homage to Gotham's legendary Deuce, and director Glickenhaus makes extensive, inventive use of that formerly notorious stretch of NYC real estate in crafting the film's central action sequence. (He also works in plugs for his own earlier Deuce perennials, *The Soldier* and *The Exterminator*—titles seen plastered across 42nd Street marquees!) Toss in strenuous stunts (including a frenetic Coney Island roller-coaster chase), copious gunplay, plus cameos by the late cult thesps Paul Bartel (as a judge) and Shirley (*Honeymoon Killers, Frankenhooker*) Stoler, and you have a taut B actioner that ranks among the best.

SHANGHAI TRIAD (1995) ***1/2

D: Zhang Yimou. Gong Li, Li Boatian, Li Xuejian. 108 mins. (Columbia/TriStar)

Zhang (*Raise the Red Lantern*) Yimou's darkly lyrical, supremely atmospheric crime drama chronicles a young country boy's immersion in the gang-dominated demimonde of 1930s Shanghai, where treachery is as much an art form as it is a way of life.

SHARKY'S MACHINE (1981) ***

D: Burt Reynolds. Burt Reynolds, Rachel Ward, Vittorio Gassman. 122 mins. (Warner) DVD

One of Burt's (who doubles as director) better *policiers, Sharky's Machine* comes packed with noise, violence, and action and features a fine, slimy perf by professional sleazeball extraordinaire Henry Silva, cast here as a coke-crazed assassin our hero's determined to eliminate.

SHOWDOWN IN LITTLE TOKYO (1991) *1/2

D: Mark L. Lester. Dolph Lundgren, Brandon Lee, Carey-Hiroyuki Tagawa, Tia Carrere. 76 mins. (Warner) DVD

Dolph portrays a Japanophile LAPD cop partnered with half-Nipponese but otherwise All-American Valley Boy Lee. Together, they trash hordes of disposable henchmen employed by a sadistic Tagawa, the self-same Yakuza chief who'd slain Dolph's parents decades earlier. In the course of this predictable caper, Dolph also rescues and beds (or, more accurately, futons) fetching Yakuza victim Carrere, shows off his 'ceps, pecs, and new kung-fu moves, and, in one memorable moment, literally leaps over a speeding car in a single bound (!). A few novel touches occasionally relieve the tedium, among them female sumo wrestlers, a sex-and-decapitation scene, and Yakuza minions so tough they'd sooner snap their own necks (!) than squeal to the cops.

SILENT HUNTER (1995) **1/2

D: Fred Williamson. Miles O'Keeffe, Peter Colvey, Lynne Adams, Jason Cavalier, Sabine Karsenti, Fred Williamson. 97 mins. (New Line)

Actor Fred takes a backseat to director Williamson in a violent actioner with a *Cliffhanger* hook. The pic opens in Miami's South Beach. Unarmed cop O'Keeffe survives an assault by a trio of psycho siblings (brothers Colvey and Cavalier and lesbian sis Adams) that claims the lives of his wife and young daughter. Two years later a recovering O'Keeffe, now living in cold, mountainous climes, encounters the same trio, bolstered by three additional henchmen (to help hike the body count), on a wild kill spree and gets an op for some belated revenge. Unlike some of Williamson's messier movies—e.g., his 1987 camp classic, *The Messenger* (Orion)—*Silent Hunter* is a crisply assembled, highly watchable affair. On-screen, the older, wiser, fatter former footballer eschews a sex scene for himself and limits his athletic antics to a couple of brief sprints, a snowmobile jaunt, and a tense moment where he rolls over the hood of an ice-covered car.

SONATINE (1993) ****

D: Takeshi Kitano. "Beat" Takeshi, Tetsu Watanabe, Aya Kokumai. Subtitled. 94 mins. (Miramax)

In this earlier entry from Takeshi (*Fireworks*) Kitano, Japan's Emperor of All Media directs, writes, edits, and toplines as a calm, ruthless but world-weary Yakuza soldier. As the film opens, Kitano and several of his men are assigned to establish peace between warring Okinawan outfits with Tokyo ties. Following a bloody barroom shoot-out, Kitano and four fellow survivors lie low at a beach hideaway, where they pass the time playing games, pulling pranks, staging amateur Kabuki shows (!), and bonding in a gruff guy way. Kitano is clearly sick of the Yakuza lifestyle but knows that death offers the only honorable exit. *Sonatine* echoes everything from Marlon Brando's *One-Eyed Jacks*, Tarantino's *Reservoir Dogs* and its Hong Kong antecedent, Ringo Lam's *City on Fire*, to John Woo, Sam Peckinpah, and even, in one scene, Richard Lester's *A Hard Day's Night*, while still emerging as a completely singular film that's bloody, funny, and at times oddly serene. In late '99 WinStar issued two highly recommended earlier Kitano outings, 1989's *Boiling Point* and 1990's *Violent Cop* (DVD).

SOUL HUSTLER   (1976) ***

D: Burt Topper. Fabian, Casey Kasem, Larry Bishop, Nai Bonet. 91 mins. (Artisan)

Fabian's fab as a sleazy hustler who becomes a singing evangelist in longtime AIP helmer Topper's entertaining action exploitationer designed to cash in on Marjoe Gortner's then-current celebrity. Deejay Kasem plays Fabe's shrewd manager.

SOUL VENGEANCE   (1975) ***

D: Jamaa Fanaka. Mario Monte, Reatha Gray, Stan Kamber. 90 mins. (Xenon)

Originally titled *Welcome Home, Brother Charles, Penitentiary* auteur Fanaka's film debut defies description but demands the awed attention of serious Fanaka fans and

action addicts who like their genre fare laced with the surreal and the bizarre. The infamous phallic strangulation scene alone must be seen to be disbelieved.

SOUTHERN COMFORT (1981) ***

D: Walter Hill. Keith Carradine, Powers Boothe, Fred Ward. 105 mins. (Embassy, n.i.d.)

Ragin' Cajuns wage guerrilla warfare against green Yankee national guardsmen in a remote bayou. Not very credible and *Two Thousand Maniacs!* offered a better variation on the same basic situation, but good performances, steady pacing, and an authentic Cajun soundtrack make Hill's Louisiana-set mini-'Nam replay work on a visceral level.

THE SPECIALIST   (1994) **

D: Luis Llosa. Sylvester Stallone, Sharon Stone, James Woods, Eric Roberts, Rod Steiger. 110 mins. (Warner) DVD

Stone meets Stallone (though not for several reels) in Llosa's largely risible Miami-set bombfest. Sharon hires Sly to blow up her parents' killers—Roberts among them—many years after the fact. ("I'm told you can control your explosions," she deadpans.) Sly at first demurs, until he learns that his hated ex-CIA demolitions-explosives partner (Woods, who easily steals what show there is here) is working for the thugs' boss and Roberts's dad, veteran drug lord Joe Leon (Steiger, whose pronunciation of "essplosives esspert" alone should have netted him an Oscar nod). Exotic South Beach scenery, elaborate explosions, and Elvis the Cat's turn as Sly's adopted stray supply other fleeting highlights, while former *Creature from the Black Lagoon* gill-suit inhabitant Ricou Browning scores a "Marine Coordinator" credit. Stone and

Stallone's then-much-hyped shower sequence rates as a fairly grotty affair, with a self-conscious Sly sporting the sort of lumpy, translucent-looking skin that made your Phantom glad he misspends his leisure time on the couch rather than at the gym. Feline-film fans, meanwhile, can also catch Elvis the Cat in *That Darn Cat* (Disney) and *Assassins* (also with Sly, see index).

SPEED:
THE SERIES

SPEED   (1994) ***

D: Jan De Bont. Keanu Reeves, Sandra Bullock, Dennis Hopper, Jeff Daniels, Robert DoQui. 119 mins. (Fox) DVD

In De Bont's surprise box-office smash, demolition ace and all-around Boy Scout Reeves, with the help of volunteer driver Bullock, must keep a bomb-rigged bus from dipping below 50 MPH to avoid an explosion, the evil handiwork of Hopper, in an almost too-patented madman turn. (A parallel scene, involving a tripwired computer, surfaces in the B.O. dud *Blown Away* [MGM].) The pacing stays true to the title; spectacular crashes and stupid bus tricks abound; and the pic gets by without mounting a mega body count. Followed by the much maligned sequel, *Speed 2: Cruise Control* (Fox, DVD), wherein madman Willem Dafoe supplies the villainy, again at Sandra's expense.

THE SPOOK WHO SAT BY THE DOOR   (1973) **1/2

D: Ivan Dixon. Lawrence Cook, Paula Lawrence, Janet League. 102 mins. (Xenon)

Actor Dixon directs a subversive, if sometimes shaky, tale, based on the novel of the same name, about a token black CIA trainee (Cook) who uses his expertise to organize an urban-guerrilla (or "gorilla," as original cassette supplier Video City's box had it!) movement. With music by Herbie Hancock. Xenon also has the ambitious O. C. Smith-scored "blaxploitation" rarity *The Bus Is Coming*.

STAND ALONE   (1985) **

D: Alan Beattie. Charles Durning, Pam Grier, James Keach, Bert Remsen, Barbara Sammeth, Luis Contreras. 90 mins. (New World)

Bye-bye, Sly—say hi to the screen's most improbable Rambo of the '80s, as chunky Durning dons combat fatigues, digs out his trusty M-16, and shows the neighborhood drug scum who's boss. That's what unfolds in *Stand Alone*, when World War II vet Durning avenges the murder of an old army buddy by single-handedly confronting a contingent of vicious pushers responsible for the misdeed. While Charles may be a tad over his fighting weight, he *is* three years younger than Bronson and demonstrates his military mettle in this emptyheaded urban-action quickie. Pam Grier is also along for the ride.

THE STAR CHAMBER   (1983) ***

D: Peter Hyams. Michael Douglas, Yaphet Kotto, Hal Holbrook. 109 mins. (Fox)

Fed-up judge Douglas joins a clandestine band of his peers who hire a hit man to dispatch guilty but unconvicted criminals. Kotto steals the show as the phlegmatic but unstoppable cop who investigates the group's illicit activities in what rates as one of the era's better vigilante fantasies.

THE STEEL HELMET   (1951) B&W ****

D: Sam Fuller. Gene Evans, Robert Hutton, James Edwards, Steve Brodie. 84 mins. (Burbank)

Sam Fuller's Korean War–set masterwork presents an ultragritty look at combat, as experienced by one of the offbeat auteur's greatest characters, Evans's grizzled, battle-weary Sergeant Zack. By our lights, the best modern war movie ever made.

STEELE JUSTICE   (1987) **

D: Robert Boris. Martin Kove, Sela Ward, Ronny Cox, Bernie Casey, Joseph Campanella, Soon-Teck Oh. 96 mins. (Starmaker)

Character thesp Kove requisitions the Rambo headband as yet another vengeful Viet vet—"You don't recruit John Steele. You unleash him!"—who wages a one-man jihad against L.A.'s notorious Vietnamese Mafia. This strictly routine affair is elevated solely by Soon-Teck Oh's perf as oily villain General Kwan and a flashback in which Steele narrowly escapes death via a rat with a grenade strapped to its back (!), perhaps a vengeful relative of the rodent that had its head bitten off by Chuck Norris in *Missing in Action II*.

STONE COLD   (1991) ***1/2

D: Craig R. Baxley. Brian Bosworth, Lance Henriksen, William Forsythe, Arabella Holzbog, Sam McMurray. 91 mins. (Columbia/TriStar)

Boz stars as Joe Huff, an Alabama undercover cop coaxed by the FBI into infiltrating (under the alias John Stone) the Brotherhood, an ambitious biker organization whose members spend their time committing major crimes, battling their Mafia competitors, and assassinating obstructive public officials with impunity (and automatic weapons). Director Baxley (*Action Jackson*) employs this basic hook to cook up a series of spectacular, ever escalating action set pieces, ranging from bike chases to a wholesale slaughter sequence pitting Brotherhood hit men against a national-guard unit. *Stone Cold* benefits immensely from a taut script, evocative Mississippi/Florida Panhandle location lensing, and a top supporting cast. Among the latter, Henriksen, as gang leader "Chains," turns in his best screen-scuzz work since *Johnny Handsome*, while Forsythe scores as a trigger-happy psycho biker, Holzbog impresses as Henriksen's abused squeeze, and McMurray contributes a winning bit as a health-phobic FBI agent. As for the Boz, he wisely plays it straight as a largely humorless hunk who relies more on action than on words and saves his most romantic moments for his pet lizard. With its breakneck pace and relentless emphasis on murder, mutilation, berserko biker rituals (including a ceremonial cremation), gratuitous nudity, and pure authentic sleaze, *Stone Cold* stacks up as the best biker flick to surface since Tom (*Billy Jack*) Laughlin's *Born Losers* (see index) back in 1967.

STRAIGHT TIME   (1978) ***

D: Ulu Grosbard. Dustin Hoffman, Theresa Russell, Gary Busey, Harry Dean Stanton. 114 mins. (Warner)

Dusty gets tough as a paroled con who tries to adjust to a civilian world that has no use for him in an effective blend of social commentary and exploitation, featuring strong supporting turns by Stanton and Busey as a pair of criminal cohorts. The flick's jewel-robbery sequence conveys the erotic excitement of a finely timed heist better than any film in memory. A wimpy Dustin is forced to go primitive to protect his turf and slutty mate Susan George from a band of barbaric locals in Sam Peckinpah's harsh transplanted western *Straw Dogs* (Anchor Bay, DVD).

THE STREET FIGHTER:
THE SERIES

THE STREET FIGHTER
(1974) ***

D: Shigehiro Ozawa. Sonny Chiba,
Gerald Yamada, Shirley
Nakajima. Dubbed. 91 mins.
(New Line)

Sonny Chiba fans (and we know
you're out there, we can hear you
tearing out windpipes) had reason to
rejoice when New Line released the
Japanese chopsocky champ's kick-ass
classic in its original, uncut form. The
film was formerly out only in a heavily
eviscerated 75-minute version from
CBS/Fox. The new tape's available in a
pan-and-scan version, or you can see
the infamous X-ray shot of a skull being
splintered by one of Chiba's firmer
chops in a "collector's letter-boxed edition." (No relation to the 1994 Van
Damme video-game adaptation *Street
Fighter* [Universal, DVD]). New Line
likewise issued three Sonny sequels:
Return of the Street Fighter, *Sister
Street Fighter*, and *The Street Fighter's
Last Revenge*. You can also sight Sonny
in several other titles not covered else-
where in this tome: *Assassin* (CBS/
Fox); *The Bodyguard* (Media); *Dragon
Princess* and *Karate Warriors* (both
IUD); *Hunter in the Dark*, *Immortal
Combat* (A-Pix); *Killing Machine*
(Prism); *Kowloon Assignment* (Media);
Roaring Fire (HBO); *Shogun's Ninja*
(Media); *Terror Beneath the Sea*
(DVT); and *Virus* (Media).

STREET HUNTER   (1990) **½

D: John A. Gallagher. Steve James,
Reb Brown, Valerie Pettiford, John
Leguizamo, Frank Vincent, Richard
Panebianco, Tom Wright. 95 mins.
(Columbia/TriStar)

The late, great Steve James landed
his own action vehicle (which he
also coscripted) with this NYC-set

COLICO CAT: The late, great Steve James takes aim with his way-cool Colico gun
in scene from John Gallagher's urban actioner *Street Hunter.*
Courtesy of John Gallagher

slayfest. Steve lends his considerable
martial arts skills and characteristic
brand of low-key charisma as ex-cop/
current bounty hunter Logan Blade,
a contempo Clint Eastwood type
who lives in a van and travels with his
trusty pooch partner, a killer pinscher
named Munch. The plot places Blade in
the center of a raging drug war being
waged between local Mafiosi and a
Latino gang, the Diablos, led by Angel
(future comic star Leguizamo). In an
imaginative cross-genre twist, Angel
hires psycho mercenary Colonel Walsh
(beefcake vet Brown, in a rare bad-
guy role) to train his henchmen in the
art of guerrilla warfare, though it soon
develops that the paranoid paramili-
tarist harbors mad schemes of his own.
Street Hunter benefits from vivid
Gotham location lensing, including a
scene shot in the Lower East Side's
late, lamented fleapit Variety Photo-
Plays. Folkie Richie Havens cameos as
club owner Daze. On the downside,
Street Hunter, while mostly effective
scene by scene, rambles in spots and
fails to build to a sufficiently rousing climax. Still, it's a must for Steve James
fans.

STREET KNIGHT   (1993) **½

D: Albert Magnoli. Jeff Speakman,
Christopher Neame, Jennifer Gatti, Richard
Coca, Bernie Casey, Richard Allen, Ramon
Franco. 88 mins. (Warner)

Kenpo karate ace Speakman, looking a bit bulked-up from his previous showcase, *Perfect Weapon* (see
index), portrays Jake Barrett, a barrio-
based garage owner and ex-cop haunted
by a past hostage incident that resulted
in a young girl's death. Jake finds himself literally in the middle of a tense
truce between formerly warring black
and Latino street gangs who threaten to
resume armed hostilities after several
of their members are brutally slain.
What Jake and gang leaders 8 Ball
(Allen) and Cisco (Franco) don't know
(but we do) is that the killings are being
perpetrated—under the direction of
unlikely, Brit-accented, Shakespeare-
quoting leader Neame—by a band of
corrupt-cops-turned-criminals looking
to create a smokescreen for their own
illicit activities. Our tight-jeaned hero
proves as quick with a .45 as he does
with his fists and feet in this adequate
vehicle.

STRIKING DISTANCE (1993) **

D: Rowdy Herrington. Bruce Willis, Sarah Jessica Parker, Dennis Farina, Tom Sizemore, Robert Pastorelli, Brion James. 102 mins. (Columbia/TriStar) DVD

Striking Distance looks like it began as *"Die Hard* on a Boat" till someone realized Steven Seagal had beaten Bruce to that high-water concept with 1992's *Under Siege* (see index). Instead, the flick emerges (or, more often, *submerges*) as a convoluted serial-killer mystery that resorts to the underhanded ploy of resurrecting a presumed-dead character as the perp and the dull device of using last-reel flashbacks to explain the unlikely plot machinations, whose gears grind louder than Bruce's high-powered boat.

THE SUBSTITUTE:
THE SERIES

THE SUBSTITUTE (1996) ***

D: Robert Mandel. Tom Berenger, Diane Venora, Ernie Hudson, Glenn Plummer, William Forsythe, Cliff De Young, Marc Anthony, Luis Guzmán. 114 mins. (Artisan) DVD

Sort of a "To Sir, With Live Ammo," The Substitute—scripted by Roy (*Street Trash*) Frumkes, Rocco Simonelli, and Alan (*Children Shouldn't Play With Dead Things*) Ormsby—shapes up as an agreeably explosive actioner peppered with perverse one-liners and offbeat wit. Berenger plays it typically stoic as a no-nonsense merc who goes undercover at a crime-plagued (to put it mildly) Miami high school where unruly drug pushers have beaten up Tom's teacher squeeze, Venora (later leading to one of the most physically uncomfortable erotic encounters we've witnessed in a while). Tom soon determines that seemingly progressive principal Hudson is actually one of the dope ring's criminal masterminds. (At least he's a hands-on educator, even to the point of helping his under-

lings stack bags of crack and smack in the school basement!) Tom recruits several merc friends (including the ever reliable Forsythe) to stage a climactic raid on the school that sends bullets and bodies flying with equal abandon. To soften the proceedings a mite, several scenes depict Tom attempting to reach out to some of his more receptive teen charges, regaling them with tactical tales from his Vietnam days. Among the supporting thesps, Plummer stands out as an honest teacher, while De Young contributes an amusing bit as a cowardly, health-conscious criminal go-between. (We also liked the notion of ruthless mercenaries who come equipped with their own "Greatest Hits" video demo reels!) For action fans, *The Substitute* delivers the real goods. The series continues with *The Substitute 2: School's Out* and *The Substitute 3: Winner Takes All* (Artisan, DVD), with Treat Williams in the Berenger role.

SUDDEN DEATH (1995) ***

D: Peter Hyams. Jean-Claude Van Damme, Powers Boothe, Whittni Wright, Raymond J. Barry, Dorian Harewood, Ross Malinger. 111 mins. (Universal) DVD

While not big in the originality department (even the title's been used at least thrice before), Sudden Death, a *"Die Hard* in a Hockey Rink," rates as a superior Van Damme vehicle. Divorced fire marshal J-C, haunted by his failure to save a child's life during his firefighting days, takes his young son and daughter to the Stanley Cup final the same night extortionists, led by ex-CIA op Boothe, kidnap a visiting vice president (Barry), rig the arena with explosives, and demand the immediate transfer of $1.7 billion in international assets frozen by the government. J-C's daughter (Wright) winds up as one of the hostages, so our hero, impatient with agent Harewood's wait-and-see approach, takes matters into his own hands. Highlights include J-C's lengthy kitchen-set battle with a femme killer

dressed as the Pittsburgh Penguin mascot (!), a better-than-average death-by-chicken-bone scene, and a groaning plot contrivance that puts Van Damme (a former semipro goalie, we'd been earlier informed) in the Pittsburgh net with the game on the line. The action's as nonstop as it is mindless, and *Sudden Death* stacks up as a pure B movie with an A budget that delivers on its promise.

SUGAR HILL (1994) ***

D: Leon Ichaso. Wesley Snipes, Michael Wright, Theresa Randle, Clarence Williams III, Abe Vigoda, Ernie Hudson, Joe Dallesandro. 123 mins. (Fox)

Misperceived as an urban-action flick by audiences and many mainstream critics, Sugar Hill is more a dysfunctional-family drama unfolding against the backdrop of the contempo Harlem heroin trade. Better realized than Brian De Palma's similarly plotted *Carlito's Way* (Universal)—both pics harken back to the Warner gangster fables of the '30s—*Sugar Hill* focuses on dealer brothers Snipes, who wants out of the rackets and the 'hood alike, and Wright, who can't cope without his younger bro'. Harlem's ever changing streetscape emerges more as a living organism than a mere location here, serving as something of a visual chorus to the dramatic proceedings. An eventual descent into operatic melodrama (à la *Godfather 3*) and a rather ludicrous "happy" epilogue weaken the pic's overall impact. But director Ichaso, who earlier helmed the gritty made-for-cable psycho thriller *The Fear Inside* (see index), shapes most of his material with a sure hand.

SUPERCOP: POLICE STORY III (1992/1996) ***1/2

D: Tong Kwai Lai. Jackie Chan, Michelle Khan (Yeoh), Maggie Cheung. Dubbed. 96 mins. (Miramax) DVD

Supercop's standard but swiftly paced story line offers a variation on the mismatched-partners formula. Undercover ace Chan's pairing with Cantonese cop Khan allows for a multitude of cross-cultural riffs in a Hong Kong–versus–mainland China vein. (It may also have represented something of a peace gesture on Jackie's part at the time, with Hong Kong's 1997 reabsorption into mainland China then fast approaching.) To get the goods on a major smack trafficker, Chan assumes an underworld identity and infiltrates the gang's inner ranks. Khan, posing as Chan's sister, joins our hero for a virtually nonstop spate of chases, shoot-outs, and, of course, the intricately choreographed martial arts displays that have elevated Chan to international action-star status. Chan doesn't neglect his trademark comedy elements either. One particularly funny scene finds the undercover Chan, accompanied by three of his newfound criminal cronies, forced to visit his fictional mainland "family," including his H.K. police superior, who poses in drag as our hero's elderly mom. An ill-timed encounter with girlfriend Cheung at a Malaysian resort likewise leads to comic complications. Boasting a reported $10 mil budget, *Supercop* hops literally all over Asia, making primo use of its authentic locations, while the usual outtakes run under the end credits. *Supercop* enjoyed a belated 1996 wide release here to cash in on *Rumble in the Bronx*'s relative box-office success.

SUPERFLY:
THE SERIES

SUPERFLY   (1972) ***1/2

D: Gordon Parks, Jr. Ron O'Neal, Carl Lee, Sheila Frazier, Julius W. Harris, Charles McGregor. 96 mins. (Warner)

O'Neal is first-rate as a midlevel uptown-NYC coke dealer whose crimes pale beside those perpetrated by local police and politicians. The pic has a knowing, accurate POV, though not an especially popular one with many mainstream critics of the day (shocked outcries re the movie's "amorality" abounded). McGregor, also strong in *Superfly* scripter Philip Fenty's *The Baron* (see index), lends memorable support as doomed addict Freddie, while Curtis Mayfield composes and performs one of *the* classic film scores of *any* genre, producing such crossover hits as the title theme and "Freddie's Dead." O'Neal returned in (and directed) 1973's *Superfly T.N.T.* (Paramount), while Nathan Purdee assumed the titular role in the seriously belated (and supremely unnecessary) 1990 sequel, *The Return of Superfly* (Trimark).

SURVIVING THE GAME   (1994) **1/2

D: Ernest Dickerson. Ice-T, Rutger Hauer, Gary Busey, Charles S. Dutton, F. Murray Abraham, John C. McGinley, William McNamara, Jeff Corey. 96 mins. (New Line) DVD

Longtime Spike Lee cinematographer Dickerson fashions one of the more watchable of the many *Most Dangerous Game* rip-offs to surface over the last few years. As in *Hard Target,* a pair of professional "promoters" (Hauer and Dutton in place of Lance Henriksen and Arnold Vosloo) lead a group of wealthy sportsmen (Busey, McGinley, Abraham, and the latter's reluctant son, McNamara) in a wilderness hunt for a transplanted urban homeless man (T in the Van Damme part). Hauer and Busey lend charisma to their villainous roles, while Ice-T is credible as their sour, relentlessly pragmatic prey, who uses guile more than brawn to foil his foes. (The flick gets our Most Innovative Weapon of 1994 Award when T defeats asthmatic hunter McGinley using only secondhand cigarette smoke [!].) A "trophy" room crowded with Mason jars housing severed human heads adds a visceral visual touch. Octagenarian Corey, in his filmic farewell, delivers a deft opening cameo as the Iceman's doomed street companion.

SWEETHEART!   (1985)
B&W/COLOR***

D: Donald Brittain. Maury Chaykin, Gary Reineke, R. H. Thomson, Sean McCann. 115 mins. (Videosmiths, n.i.d.)

Chaykin stars as Hal Banks, a real-life American union thug who journeyed north to rule the Canadian waterfront with a variety of skull-crunching methods. Produced by the National Film Board of Canada, this *Untouchables*-type exposé blends brutal drama with B&W flashbacks and documentary inserts. The full title on the tape itself reads *Canada's Sweetheart: The Saga of Hal C. Banks*.

SWEET SWEETBACK'S
BAADASSSS SONG   (1971) ***

D: Melvin Van Peebles. Melvin Van Peebles, Rhetta Hughes, Simon Chuckster, John Amos. 97 mins. (Xenon)

Quadruple-threat writer, director, composer, and star Van Peebles offers an offbeat, mostly effective one-man mix of earnestness, rebellion, and exploitation that tracks the adventures of a professional stud who runs afoul of racist cops. Sweetback's bizarre "duel" with a butch distaff biker stacks up as one of many highlights on view. A promised sequel has yet to arrive.

TAI CHI II   (1995) ***

D: David Wu. Young Shun Wu, Darren Shalavi, Lin Tung, Ya Sung. Subtitled/dubbed. 90 mins. (Tai Seng) DVD

A captivating kung fu historical epic set in the early days of the 20th century, *Tai Chi II* charts the martial and romantic adventures of charismatic thesp Wu as amiable young "Jackie" (the Western name he eagerly adopts). At first apolitical, Jackie increasingly sides with his Westernized squeeze, Rose, and her radical friends to defeat evil opium importers led by a brutal Brit thug (Shalavi). Highlights include an extended fight on roller skates, several encounters with a foe-turned-eventual-friend known only as "Great Kick of the North," and multiple exhibitions of Jackie's "braid stance," where he uses his traditional braid to whip his enemies into submission.

TANGO & CASH   (1989) **

D: Andrei Konchalovsky. Sylvester Stallone, Kurt Russell, Teri Hatcher, Jack Palance, Brion James, James Hong. 98 mins. (Warner) DVD

Overkill antics ultimately bury what begins as a promising buddy actioner. Russell impresses in his drag scenes, though, where he looks almost as incongruous as Sly does in rimless glasses. Worth a look for Palance's villainous turn, but director Konchalovsky did better with *Runaway Train* (see index).

TERMINAL ISLAND   (1973) ***1/2

D: Stephanie Rothman. Don Marshall, Phyllis Davis, Tom Selleck, Roger Mosley, Barbara Leigh, Sean Kenney. 88 mins. (Continental, n.i.d.)

Rothman fashions a fun trash allegory: To save taxpayers money, convicted criminals are exiled to a barren isle off the Pacific coast, where they form factions and fight for control. The pic blends black humor, social satire, extreme violence, and genuine suspense. Selleck enjoys one of his better early roles as a humane medico wrongly assigned to the site. The 1991 Irene Cara vehicle *Caged in Paradiso* (Trimark) recycles the plot with far less success, while John Carpenter's more

enjoyable *Escape from New York* and *Escape from L.A.* (see index) contain similar *Terminal Island* echoes.

TERROR SQUAD   (1987) ***

D: Peter Maris. Chuck Connors, Bill Calvert, Jill Sanders, Kavi Raz, Ken Foree. 90 mins. (Forum, n.i.d.)

Terror Squad is the first film to dramatize a Libyan invasion of Kokomo, Indiana (!). After failing to blow up the local nuke power plant, a quartet of Qaddafi fanatics blast their way through the bustling Kokomo streets in an orgy of nonstop destruction. (For a low-budget flick, *Terror Squad* boasts an impressive array of exploding cars and toppling water towers.) In pursuit of the villains is police chief Connors, clad in a vintage Brooklyn Dodgers jacket. (Chuck played one game for the Bums back in 1949.) The Libyans eventually hole up with several teenage hostages in a high school detention hall for a Chuck Norris Meets John Hughes denouement. While *Terror Squad* owes much to both *Red Dawn* and *Invasion U.S.A.*, it's far superior to either, a trashy, tense, relentlessly kinetic treat for hard-core action fans that should have put Kokomo on the B-movie map.

THIEF   (1981) ***

D: Michael Mann. James Caan, Tuesday Weld, James Belushi, Willie Nelson. 126 mins. (MGM/UA) DVD

Miami Vice auteur Mann brings urgency to a timeworn plot about a burglar, intensely played by Caan, and his desperate bid for one last score and a subsequent "normal" life. Robert Prosky makes for a properly repulsive villain. No relation to the 1952 dialogue-free gimmick spy flick *The Thief* (Englewood) or the highly recommended 1998 Russian import of the same name (Columbia/TriStar).

THUNDER ROAD   (1958) B&W ***

D: Arthur Ripley. Robert Mitchum, Gene Barry, Jacques Aubuchon, Keely Smith, James Mitchum. 92 mins. (MGM/UA)

At the height of his big-time mainstream-movie stardom, Robert Mitchum took time out to topline in this low-budgeter—an evocative, fast-paced moonshine movie that went on to become an enduring cult fave. Our story, which Mitchum also concocted (he likewise penned—and sings—the pic's "Whippoorwill" theme song), involves bootleg driver Bob's efforts to (a) stop powerful villain Aubuchon from muscling in on his turf and (b) keep his own younger brother—played by Bob's real-life *son* Jim Mitchum—from following in his criminal footsteps (or, in this case, tire tracks). Bob handles the role with his customary cool, Barry is solid as Mitchum's tough but fair revenue-agent nemesis, while zombielike chanteuse Smith supplies some laid-back love interest and also croons a tune or two. Beyond its kinetically choreographed high-speed car chases, *Thunder Road* offers low-key insights into the 'shiners' furtive but unashamed lifestyle. For an even funkier example of 'shine cinema, scope out Ron Ormond's *White Lightnin' Road* (Nashville Cinema).

THUNDERBOLT AND LIGHTFOOT (1974) ***1/2

D: Michael Cimino. Clint Eastwood, Jeff Bridges, George Kennedy, Geoffrey Lewis, Catherine Bach, Gary Busey. 114 mins. (MGM)

Cimino actually stays on track (and possibly even within budget) with this tough, immensely entertaining buddy caper teaming taciturn Clint with reckless young motormouth Bridges. Kennedy contributes a key turn as a convincingly unpleasant ex-crony of

Clint's in this deft mix of action, suspense, character study, and lowlife Americana.

THUNDERHEART (1992) ***

D: Michael Apted. Val Kilmer, Sam Shepard, Graham Greene. 118 mins. (Columbia/TriStar) DVD

Apted's suspenseful policier teams Shepard and part Native American Kilmer as FBI agents with conflicting agendas who investigate killings on a Western reservation. Greene lends solid support, as does Chief Ted Thin Elk as Kilmer's unofficial spiritual advisor.

TIGER CLAWS (1991) **1/2

D: Kelly Markin. Cynthia Rothrock, Jalal Merhi, Bolo Yeung, Billy Pickels. 93 mins. (Universal)

Tiger Claws offers a psycho twist on the chop-and-sock genre. Frequent screen villain Yeung (Bloodsport) plays the dread "Death Dealer," a serial killer who employs the arcane "tiger claws" technique to eliminate rival martial arts champs—including Pickels, kung-fu's answer to Captain Lou Albano, who specializes in dancing on broken glass (attention, Denny Terio!). NYC fuzz Cynthia partners with suspended cop Merhi, sporting an Eastern accent and a Steven Seagal–styled ponytail, to put the blocks to Bolo. While Cynthia and Jalal may not remind viewers of Meryl Streep and Jack Nicholson, both leads project a natural awkwardness that actually adds to their credibility and helps make them a highly watchable duo. The sawed-off, bulked-up Bolo emerges as an excellent adversary (though his evil cackle needs work). Even more impressive are the nearly nonstop bouts (especially Rothrock's rout of a poolroom full of overmatched toughs), involving a wide array of fighting styles and set to a peppy, percussive synth score. Beyond a few exterior shots, Toronto once again subs for Manhattan.

TIGRERO: A FILM THAT WAS NEVER MADE (1994) ***1/2

D: Mika Kaurismaki. Samuel Fuller, Jim Jarmusch, the Karaja tribespeople. 75 mins. (Arrow)

Then-octogenarian movie maverick Sam (Shock Corridor) Fuller, who gave a great perf playing a manic vampire-hunter in Larry Cohen's sequel A Return to Salem's Lot (see index), does an equally wonderful job playing himself in Mika (Condition Red) Kaurismaki's semidocumentary Tigrero. This loose, off-the-cuff Fuller showcase tracks Sam and idiosyncratic fellow director Jim Jarmusch to the Brazilian forest where, back in 1954, Fuller had scouted and lensed locations for a proposed adventure film, the eponymous Tigrero. (Tigrero was to have starred John Wayne, Ava Gardner, and Tyrone Power but was ultimately canceled by Fox boss Darryl F. Zanuck due to prohibitive insurance costs.) Fuller screens his original footage for the local Karaja Indians, several of whom remember his earlier visit, while Kaurismaki's camera captures their emotional responses. The raspy, zesty Fuller and the self-contained Jarmusch (with a voice that's a cross between Lee Marvin and William Hurt)—affectionate polar opposites, personality-wise—project a terrific offbeat chemistry. Fuller's anecdotal case history of the ill-fated Tigrero, a look at the lifestyles of the resilient Karaja, and clips from Shock Corridor showing where Fuller inserted bits of his otherwise doomed footage furnish further highlights.

TO PROTECT AND SERVE (1992) **1/2

D: Eric Weston. C. Thomas Howell, Lezlie Dean, Richard Romanus, Joe Cortese. 93 mins. (Artisan)

With a title taken from the police credo, To Protect and Serve became the first flick to capitalize consciously on the Rodney King case (the better-known Unlawful Entry was as unwitting as it was prescient in its depiction of a similar incident). Here the lethal clubbing of a Latino thief by an integrated team of corrupt cops is stripped of any racial angle but works to fuel a plot that finds the guilty officers being offed one by one by an unknown assassin. Investigating the incidents are ex–Brat Packer Howell (who also associate-produced) and his fellow fuzz/former squeeze Dean, whose stabs at reconciliation supply this not-bad policier with an emotional subplot. The pic starts strong, with several vicious slayings—including an S&M-flavored one recalling Ken Russell's Crimes of Passion (see index)—before drifting into more formulaic turf. Award yourself a free six-pack if you correctly identified the TV clip of an aged Mickey Rooney as a scene from another Artisan release, Silent Night, Deadly Night V: The Toy Maker.

TOMORROW NEVER DIES (1997) **1/2

D: Roger Spottiswoode. Pierce Brosnan, Michelle Yeoh, Jonathan Pryce, Teri Hatcher, Judi Dench, Desmond Llewelyn, Joe Don Baker, Vincent Schiavelli. 119 mins. (Warner) DVD

One of James Bond's more far-fetched and less impressive recent adventures, dealing with the suave secret agent's efforts to defeat Rupert Murdoch–like mad media mogul Pryce, Tomorrow remains well worth catching for international action starlet Yeoh's contributions, some neatly executed action set pieces, and a raft of colorful character-actor cameos. Followed by The World Is Not Enough (2000, Warner, DVD). All 17 previous films featuring Ian Fleming's indomitable and enduring icon are also available on

VHS (with many on DVD), though titles are routinely put on moratorium, then reissued following the ebb and flow of Bond's big-screen release patterns.

TONGS: AN AMERICAN NIGHTMARE (1988) ***1/2

D: Philip Chan. Simon Yam, Tan, Anthony Leung, Christopher O'Conner, Ouitan Han. Subtitled. 89 mins. (Academy, n.i.d.)

Former Young Lord, Last Poet, newscaster, and deejay Felipe Luciano receives an "original script" credit, while "screenplay" honors go to Stacey Asip, for this excellent indie, a Chinatown twist on the old *Scarface* story. (The on-screen credits give the pic's full title as *Tongs: A Chinatown Story*.) Immigrant brothers, Hong Kong star Yam and the monomonikered Tan, follow separate paths in NYC's Chinatown, with Yam scheming and killing his way to the top of the local drug trade. Director Chan gets a lot out of a low budget, in terms of authenticity, performances, well-staged action scenes, and overall sweep.

TOP OF THE HEAP (1972) ***1/2

D: Christopher St. John. Christopher St. John, Paula Kelly, Florence St. Peter, Leonard Kuras, Patrick McVey, Almeria Quinn. 83 mins. (Unicorn, n.i.d.)

Though sold as a "blaxploitation" film, *Shaft* alum St. John's one-man wonder—he wrote, produced, directed, and stars—is an ambitious and highly original work. Our story picks up Washington, D.C., cop George Lattimer (St. John) at a crisis point. A 12-year veteran repeatedly passed over for promotion, George can no longer cope with his job, his alienated wife (St. Peter), troubled teen daughter (Quinn), unstable mistress (Kelly), his mother's recent death, and his own thwarted

ambitions. Writer/director St. John punctuates his narrative with George's hyperactive fantasy life, where, among other imaginary excursions, the cop envisions himself as the first black astronaut (complete with simulated lunar landing) *and* as an actor portraying the selfsame astronaut in a movie version. Basically decent but frustrated and self-obsessed, George begins blithely ignoring the real dangers his profession poses, even, after apprehending an armed perp, discovering he'd forgotten to load his own gun (!). One especially brilliant, uncomfortable sequence details George's visit with retired cop McVey, whose sobering observations on the subject of old age further depress our tortured hero. From its opening scene, where George helps break up a demonstration whose warring factions—college protestors and hardhats—both revile him (as a cop and a black, respectively)—to his domestic morass, his grudging friendship with his unambitious white partner (Kuras), and his alternately poignant, funny, and bizarre daydreams, *Top of the Heap* consistently defies expectations.

TRACKED (1997) *1/2

D: Ken Russell. Bryan Brown, Dean Cain, Tia Carrere, Richard Chevolleau. 92 mins. (Artisan)

It's hard to believe that the creative force behind such richly loopy classics as *The Devils* and *Lair of the White Worm* (see index) could be reduced to helming a dog-eared, made-for-cable *Most Dangerous Game* rip-off, but credits don't lie, and there's Ken Russell's name all over this snoozer, from director, to coscripter, to your full-blown "A Ken Russell Film" banner. That last, at one time much anticipated label hadn't graced a film since 1991, when Ken directed two efforts, the made-for-cable *Prisoner of Honor*, a dramatization of the famed French Dreyfus case, and the controversial

theatrical release *Whore* (Trimark). Even the most scrutinizing Russell-phile would be hard put to find any of the oft trippy maestro's touches here, except, perhaps, in Carrere's awful high-camp performance (but she may well have brought along that baggage herself).

Our recycled story stars TV's *Lois & Clark: The New Adventures of Superman* stud Cain as a two-fisted prisoner in an unorthodox pen run by Fido-obsessed Aussie émigré Cap Brown (Bryan Brown). Our hero's assigned to an inmate canine-training corps, where he's befriended by undercover op Chevolleau, who, with outside contact Carrere, is trying to determine why so many of Brown's charges are ending up as human Alpo. We can't blame Russell for wanting to work, but it is a tad surprising to see how faint an imprint an auteur of such extreme idiosyncracy can leave even on a project as hack as this. Retitled *Dogboys* for later TV airings.

TRESPASS (1992) ***

D: Walter Hill. Bill Paxton, William Sadler, Ice-T, Ice Cube, Art Evans. 101 mins. (Universal) DVD

While Paxton emotes with his usual edgy aplomb, Hill's urban *Treasure of the Sierra Madre* update (formerly *Looters*, a title scrapped following the L.A. riots) belongs to gangsta rappers Ice-T and Ice Cube. As fractious fellow members of the same ghetto gang, Mr. Cube and Mr. T supply *Trespass* with much of its building tension. Their increasingly antagonistic relationship thwarts their efforts to eliminate intruders Paxton and Sadler, two white firefighters scouring an abandoned East St. Louis factory for a decades-old stash of stolen gold. Like such similarly claustrophobic actioners as *Enemy Territory* and John Carpenter's *Assault on Precinct 13* (see index), *Trespass* tracks the attempts of our outnumbered protagonists—whose own disintegrating partnership parallels the enemy Icemen's—to escape the heavily armed gang with their lives and loot intact. The always welcome Art (*White of the Eye, Die Hard 2*) Evans, as a homeless man caught between the warring factions, also joins in the scramble for the precious booty. John Huston's original classic *The Treasure of the Sierra Madre*, with an unforgettable Bogie as everyone's fave paranoid, Fred C. Dobbs, is also available (MGM).

TRUE LIES   (1994) *

D: James Cameron. Arnold Schwarzenegger, Jamie Lee Curtis, Tom Arnold, Bill Paxton, Art Malik, Tia Carrere. 130 mins. (Fox) DVD

In this grotty, mean-spirited, mainstream $120-mil juggernaut—even more of an entertainment dud than the media-lambasted *Last Action Hero* (see index)—Schwarzenegger, a suave James Bond–ian superspy in drab computer-salesman drag, runs his femmy screen spouse (the normally feisty Curtis) through a series of humiliations and acts of emotional terrorism, finally forcing her to pose as a whore and perform a "comic" bump-and-grind routine for her disguised hubby's entertainment. All this because Arn suspects she's been carrying on with braggadocious used-car salesman Paxton (in an equally humiliating role). A film with a lesser pedigree would have gotten critically creamed by the PC Police for the rampant misogyny and blatant racism (in the form of Malik and his fellow Arab-terrorist caricatures) on view here. But mainstream critics must have thought they owed Arn one for their savaging of *Last Action Hero* the previous summer. *True Lies*'s retro grotesqueries might have been easier to take if the film worked on the action and suspense levels, but here too the flick comes up surprisingly lame.

TRUE ROMANCE   (1993) ****

D: Tony Scott. Christian Slater, Patricia Arquette, Dennis Hopper, Gary Oldman, Brad Pitt, Christopher Walken. In R and unrated editions. 121 mins. (Warner) DVD

Scott's Tarantino-scripted B-movie homage shapes up as the ultimate film-nerd fantasy. Slater stars as a Detroit movie maniac who turns badass hero by killing pimp Oldman for the love of ditsy hooker Arquette. After lighting out for Tinseltown in a vintage purple Caddy convertible with a cache of stolen coke, the pair soon find themselves embroiled in a criminal web involving cops, Mafiosi, and sleazy Hollywood producers (pardon our redundancy). Tarantino's determinedly outrageous scenario includes bows to Japanese chop champ Sonny Chiba and Hong Kong action auteur John Woo, while heretofore mainstream auteur Tony (*Top Gun*) Scott yields top thespic turns from Oldman, Walken, Hopper, Chris Penn, Bronson Pinchot, and a perennially stoned Pitt (mellowing out after his energetic psycho turn in *Kalifornia* [see index]). The best line, though, belongs to Slater, who describes his thirst for travel thusly: "I always wanted to see what TV looked like in other countries." The video's available in two versions, the R-rated, 119-minute theatrical release and a "more bang for your buck" 121-minute "unrated director's cut."

TRUTH OR CONSEQUENCES, N.M. (1997) **½

D: Kiefer Sutherland. Vincent Gallo, Mykelti Williamson, Kiefer Sutherland, Kevin Pollak, Kim Dickens, Grace Phillips, Rod Steiger, John C. McGinley. 101 mins. (Columbia/TriStar) DVD

What starts out in familiar Tarantino territory veers into contempo spaghetti-western turf in Sutherland's ultraviolent caper. Kiefer costars as the craziest of a quartet of clumsy drug thieves whose bullet-driven outburst leaves several federal agents dead. With outlaw lovers Gallo and Dickens and partner Williamson, Kiefer commandeers a yuppie couple's (Pollak, Phillips) Winnebago for a wild odyssey that leads to a three-way showdown among our antiheroes, federal agents, and mob assassins sent by Mafioso Steiger. Although a box blurb lauds Kiefer's "solid directing bow," Sutherland had earlier helmed the 1993 cable-TV feature *Last Light* (Trimark). His psycho-a-go-go-styled work here rivals his crazed-guidance-counselor turn in Matthew Bright's *Freeway* (see index). Utah subs for New Mexico and other Southwest locales. Sometime actor Cory (Son of Bob) Eubanks returns to his humbler stunt roots here, while Rachel Sutherland scores an unusual troika of production credits—as a costumer, grip, and assistant to the assistant property master (!).

UNDER FIRE   (1983) ***

D: Roger Spottiswoode. Nick Nolte, Gene Hackman, Joanna Cassidy. 128 mins. (Artisan)

Photojournalist Nolte gets personally involved in exposing a corrupt Central American dictatorship in a compelling action drama (scripted by Ron [*Blaze, Tin Cup*] Shelton) helped by Hackman as an investigative reporter and Ed Harris as a cold-blooded American mercenary. Oliver Stone's similarly themed 1986 *Salvador* (Artisan), with James Woods, is also recommended.

UNDER SIEGE:
THE SERIES

UNDER SIEGE   (1992) **½

D: Andy Davis. Steven Seagal, Tommy Lee Jones, Gary Busey, Erika Eleniak, Patrick O'Neal. 100 mins. (Warner) DVD

Seagal tends to alternate between good stupid three-word actioners

(*Marked for Death, Fire Down Below*) and bad stupid three-word actioners (*Hard to Kill, Out for Justice*); unfortunately, *Under Siege* (his first *two*-word title) leans in the latter, leeward direction. Our story unfolds aboard the soon-to-be-decommissioned battleship *Missouri,* where Seagal labors as the ship's soon-to-retire cook. When a polyglot team of equal-opportunity terrorists led by ex-CIA assassin Jones and turncoat naval officer Busey kill kindly captain O'Neal and capture the crew, it's up to our jowly hero to save the ship, day, and, this being a nuclear-armed vessel, world as well. In a series of unimaginative strategems, Seagal, sonically uplinked to government bigwigs in D.C., takes out the terrorists one by one, using explosives, automatic weapons, knives, and his ever dependable fists and feet. Steve also receives an assist from a (rather retro) former *Playboy* Playmate (Eleniak) lured aboard the troubled ship under false pretenses. An over-the-top Jones and Busey (who performs a decidedly grotty drag routine) furnish most of the fun here.

UNDER SIEGE 2: DARK TERRITORY (1995) ***

D: Geoff Murphy. Steven Seagal, Eric Bogosian, Katherine Heigl, Morris Chestnut, Everett McGill, Nick Mancuso, Peter Greene, Lincoln Kilpatrick. 98 mins. (Warner) DVD

While this "Die Hard on a Train" variation springs few true surprises, the flick scores as an adrenalizing actioner bolstered by a great group of bad guys, led by a sardonic Bogosian as yet another government employee gone bad. Bogosian's small army of ruthless goons in turn includes the always welcome Peter (*Clean, Shaven*) Greene, Lincoln (*Death Warrant*) Kilpatrick, and Everett (*Quest for Fire*) McGill. As our story opens, Bogosian commandeers a train, takes 200 passengers hostage, and threatens to nuke

select sectors of the world via computer-satellite control if his monetary demands aren't met. Unfortunately for Eric, former agency operative Seagal's aboard that selfsame train, accompanying his niece (Heigl) on a cross-country jaunt. With assistance from porter Chestnut, Seagal picks off the bad guys one by one. With its large-scale villainy and high-tech James Bond–ian sweep, *Under Siege 2* delivers more bang for the video buck than any of Seagal's previous efforts.

UNDERWORLD, U.S.A. (1961) B&W ***½

D: Sam Fuller. Cliff Robertson, Dolores Dorn, Beatrice Kay. 99 mins. (Columbia/TriStar)

Robertson infiltrates the syndicate to avenge his father's murder in a rough, tough, wonderfully lurid Fuller pulpfest. One of Sam's best, with a top supporting cast of veteran screen villains, including Robert Emhardt, Richard Rust, and Paul Dubov.

UNHOLY ROLLERS (1972) ***

D: Vernon Zimmerman. Claudia Jennings, Louis Quinn, Betty Anne Rees. 88 mins. (HBO)

Late, great Playmate-turned-action-starlet Jennings overcomes all obstacles, from vicious rivals to domestic woes, in her relentless pursuit of roller-derby glory in this funky, funny lowlife odyssey. Inspirational, and one of Claudia's best showcases as a female Rocky of the rink. Couchside Claudia buffs can also catch the curvaceous heroine in the futuristic *Death Sport* (Warner), with Big Bill Smith in David Cronenberg's *Fast Company* (Admit One), the swamp-set *Gator Bait* (Paramount), the adrenalizing Southwest-set crime-spree caper *The Great Texas Dynamite Chase* (Warner), Stephanie Rothman's B-film feminist comedy *Group Marriage* (Cinema Group), the sober-minded Viet-vet

drama *Jud* (Prism), *The Love Machine* (Columbia/TriStar), the redneck romp *Moonshine County Express* (Warner), the horrific *Sisters of Death* (VCI), *The Stepmother* (Academy), and Mark L. Lester's energetic *Truck-Stop Women* (Vestron), with C.J. in classic form as a two-fisted business bimbo at a roadside cathouse.

UTU: THE UNRATED DIRECTOR'S CUT (1983/1988) ***

D: Geoff Murphy. Anzac Wallace, Bruno Lawrence, Wi Kuki Kaa, Tim Elliott, Kelly Johnson. 122 mins. (Kino)

Combining the action and sweep of a vintage John Ford western with an alternately harsh and satiric revisionist edge, Murphy's *Utu* represents a reel treat for action buffs. Set during New Zealand's Maori Indian rebellions of the 1870s and based on actual incidents, the film charts the violent exploits of Te Wheke (Wallace), a Brit-employed army scout who returns to his Maori warrior roots with a literal vengeance—*utu* is the Maori word for "ritualized revenge"—after seeing his village massacred by his white saddlemates. Murphy presents a complex canvas that avoids glamorizing any of the participants in the bloody conflicts. Kino's wide-screen "unrated director's cut" restores 14 minutes of footage excised from the Kiwi western's original stateside theatrical release. Murphy has gone on to helm such comparatively routine Hollywood genre fare as *Freejack* and the Seagal sequel *Under Siege 2: Dark Territory* (see index).

VICE SQUAD (1982) **½

D: Gary A. Sherman. Wings Hauser, Season Hubley, Gary Swanson. 97 mins. (Embassy, n.i.d.)

The incomparable Hauser's totally over-the-top, marvelously vile performance as a psychotic pimp on a filmlong kill spree is the only reason to see this otherwise mediocre actioner—but it's more than reason enough.

THE VIKING SAGAS (1995) **¹/₂

D: Michael Chapman. Ralf Moeller, Ingibjörg Stefándóttir, Sven-Ole Thorsen. 83 mins. (New Line)

Cinematographer Chapman (*Raging Bull*, *The Fugitive*) helms what appears to have been a severely edited coproduction sporting a simple story line about hero Moeller (late of *Universal Soldier*) seeking violent Viking justice in medieval Iceland with the help of a fabled "ghost sword." One highlight sees Moeller's dying warrior dad wrap his own intestines around a rock (!), a rite dubbed "taking the walk," while severed heads and limbs go the airborne route with merry abandon during the many battle scenes that pass for good, clean Viking fun. The best line belongs to a more cautionary warrior, who reminds our hero, "Killing isn't *everything.*" For more Norse mayhem, scope out Richard Fleischer's 1958 *The Vikings* (MGM), with Kirk Douglas, Tony Curtis, Ernest Borgnine, and Janet Leigh, and Cameron Mitchell in Mario Bava's 1965 *Knives of the Avenger* (a.k.a. *Viking Massacre*), available from Sinister Cinema. Hammer's 1966 *The Viking Queen* (Anchor Bay, DVD) actually unfolds in first-century Britain, with nary a Viking in sight.

VIPER (1988) **¹/₂

D: Peter Maris. Linda Purl, Jeff Kober, Chris Robinson, James Tolkan, Ken Foree. 94 mins. (Fries, n.i.d.)

Rebellious CIA agent Robinson (who broke into showbiz by designing the title monster for the 1959 Roger Corman quickie *The Beast from Haunted Cave*) seeks to expose a murderous Indianapolis mock-terrorist plot actually hatched by U.S.-government creeps. When Robinson is eliminated, plucky widow Purl eludes and ultimately defeats the villains. With Tolkan in another of his patented (to say nothing of male-patterned) bald-headed baddie roles, Maris regular Foree, and "Puppy Purl" as "the Dog."

WALKABOUT (1971) ***

D: Nicolas Roeg. Jenny Agutter, Lucien John, David Gumpilil, John Meillon, Peter Carver. 100 mins. (Home Vision) DVD

The first reasonably wide-release film to bring the wonders and dangers of the Australian outback to international eyes, Nicolas (*Don't Look Now*) Roeg's nature-versus-civilization meditation, drawn from James Vance Marshall's novel, retains its visual grandeur (Roeg doubles as cinematographer) and much of its deceptively simple story line's elemental power. A deranged Aussie dad (Meillon) blows his brains out in the desert, leaving adolescent daughter Agutter and young son John to fend for themselves. The largely hapless white kids receive a huge assist from teenage Aborigine Gumpilil, currently wandering the terrain as part of a coming-of-age ritual, or "walkabout." Glad for the company and happy to help out, Gumpilil connects with six-year-old John but can't quite penetrate Agutter's emotional veil, a situation that leads to eventual tragedy. The film's final moments punch Roeg's message home with haunting poignancy. On the downside, Roeg's reliance on then-popular "arty" techniques, especially his excessive freeze-frame use, lend *Walkabout* a sometimes mannered look, and his decision *not* to translate Gumpilil's language, while obviously intentional, makes the character more cryptic than necessary. In the guise of celebrating unselfconscious "innocence," the camera's '70s-styled (as opposed to '90s-styled) prurience likewise grows grating after several reels.

WALKING TALL:
THE SERIES

WALKING TALL (1973) ***

D: Phil Karlson. Joe Don Baker, Elizabeth Hartman, Noah Beery, Jr. 126 mins. (Rhino) DVD

Baker wields a baseball bat with bone-cracking aplomb as corruption-fighting sheriff Buford Pusser in Karlson's solid, fact-based bashfest. Bo Svenson inherits the bat for the sequels, *Walking Tall: Part 2* and *Walking Tall: The Final Chapter* (both Artisan), while Brian Dennehy performs similar chores in the made-for-TV version, *A Real American Hero* (Video Treasures).

WANTED: DEAD OR ALIVE (1986) **¹/₂

D: Gary Sherman. Rutger Hauer, Gene Simmons, Mel Harris, Robert Guillaume. 104 mins. (Starmaker)

Hauer toplines as the bounty-hunting, harmonica-tooting great-grandson of Josh Randall (Steve McQueen) from the original *Wanted: Dead or Alive* teleseries. (How's *that* for high concept?) Hauer's hot on the trail of sneering terrorist Simmons (still the Kiss crooner's finest B-pic perf to date) whose initial act of violence entails blowing up 138 *Rambo* fans (!) at an L.A. bijou. *Wanted: Dead or Alive* is a tongue-in-cheek action outing that chronicles Rut's desperate race against time *and* a double-dealing pack of slimy CIA types who are using him as bait. Despite its occasionally meandering pace, *Wanted*'s well worth a look.

WAR PARTY (1989) ***

D: Franc Roddam. Kevin Dillon, Billy Wirth, Tim Sampson, M. Emmet Walsh, Jimmy Ray Weeks. 99 mins. (HBO)

A solid action movie in serious-issue guise, *War Party* sees a modern cavalry-versus-Indians battle reenactment open up old wounds and spill new blood as the simulation explodes into real racial violence. Dillon, Wirth, and Sampson are Native American fugitives who become the objects of a prolonged postbattle manhunt. Not as crazed as *Johnny Firecloud* (see index) but engrossing in its own right.

THE WHITE DAWN (1974) ***

D: Philip Kaufman. Warren Oates, Louis Gossett, Jr., Timothy Bottoms. 110 mins. (Paramount)

Oates, Gossett, and Bottoms are a trio of lost whalers rescued by Eskimos in the 1890s. Kaufman's Arctic account shapes up as a consistently compelling, underrated if ultimately downbeat adventure fable.

WHITE LINE FEVER (1975) ***

D: Jonathan Kaplan. Jan-Michael Vincent, Kay Lenz, Slim Pickens, L. Q. Jones. 89 mins. (Columbia/TriStar)

Kaplan crafts one of the earliest and best trucker-vengeance movies, with young Vincent as the angry diesel driver who takes on the forces of corruption.

WHO AM I? (1998) ***

D: Jackie Chan, Benny Chan. Jackie Chan, Michelle Ferre, Mirai Yamamoto, Ron Smorczak, Ed Nelson. 108 mins. (Columbia/TriStar) DVD

In the globe-hopping *Who Am I?* Jackie plays the lone, amnesic survivor of a crack top-secret commando team sabotaged by a renegade CIA agent (Smorczak) and his evil corporate cohort (former Roger Corman thesp and long-time *Peyton Place* regular Nelson). The action shifts from South Africa—where our temporarily clueless hero happily goes native with a friendly local tribe—to Rotterdam, where, with the help of foxy

undercover agent Ferre, he gets to lay vengeful hands (and feet) on the two malefactors and their steady supply of thugs. (As Jackie explains to the chief villains, "I may have amnesia, but I'm not stupid!") As with most Chan adventures, plot takes a backseat to pure, often comic action, and *Who Am I?* delivers the stunt goods on a grand scale. In addition to the usual breathless escapes and chases, the movie includes a showstopping skyscraper rooftop fight between Jackie and two martial arts mavens who are nearly (though not quite) his equal, one of the most heart-pounding sequences to be found in Chan's voluminous celluloid canon; Jackie concludes the segment with a jaw-dropping slide down the building's entire length. Along the way, Chan also gets to dust off a few of his beloved "Drunken Master" moves, save an endangered poodle (!), and exhibit a bit of high-speed "car-fu." As in most of Chan's movies, stunt outtakes from the shoot unspool under the closing credits.

WILD AT HEART (1990) ***

D: David Lynch. Nicolas Cage, Laura Dern, Willem Dafoe, Diane Ladd, Isabella Rossellini, Harry Dean Stanton, Crispin Glover. 125 mins. (Media, n.i.d.)

Lynch stirs another cauldron of low-life lust, familial betrayals, kinky power games, and abrupt and senseless violence. While those by-now familiar elements don't jell nearly as well here as they did in his peerless *Blue Velvet* (see index), the movie's not without its over-the-top merits. Cage is relatively restrained as a self-styled Elvis manqué, while Dern delivers another impressive *Blue Velvet*–styled crying jag as his lovestruck squeeze. Dafoe and Glover supply trademark geekoid turns; Ladd kicks in with her most memorable perf since *Wild Angels;* and there are welcome cameos by Rossellini, Calvin (*The Beast Must Die*) Lockhart, the late Jack (*Eraserhead*) Nance, and even the Good Witch of the North (!), of *Wizard*

of Oz fame (a flick that provides *Wild* with its central metaphor). Effective brain-bashing and decapitation scenes likewise offer fleeting highlights. While it was inevitable that the wildly overhyped David be lynched by a few heartless critics, *Wild at Heart* still proffers more offbeat entertainment value than most mainstream releases.

WILD GEESE:
THE SERIES

THE WILD GEESE (1978) ***

D: Andrew V. McLaglen. Richard Burton, Roger Moore, Richard Harris, Jeff Corey, Stewart Granger. 132 mins. (Fox)

Burton stars as the leader of the titular mercenary team, out to rescue an imperiled African ruler, in Andrew V. McLaglen's rousing, if overlong, pulp actioner, rivaled only by John Irvin's *Dogs of War* (MGM) as the best mainstream merc movie ever made. Followed by two less galvanizing sequels, *Wild Geese 2* (MGM/UA) and *Codename: Wild Geese* (Anchor Bay).

THE YOUNG AMERICANS (1993) ***

D: Danny Cannon. Harvey Keitel, Iain Glen, Viggo Mortensen, John Wood, Terence Rigby, Keith Allen, Craig Kelly, Thandie Newton. 108 mins. (Artisan)

Harv stars as a Yank DEA agent brought in to assist Brit police in solving the identically staged executions of several high-profile local crime figures. Keitel's convinced the killings are the work of peripatetic American drug mogul Mortensen, whose M.O. involves recruiting aimless, expendable youths to serve as his personal hit squad. When young Kelly sees his best friend slashed and his father slain by Mortensen's minions, he agrees to go undercover to get Harv the hard evidence he needs to pinch the perps. As in other recent Brit crime dramas, like the Peter Medak duo *The Krays* (Paramount) and *Let Him Have It* (see index), *The Young Americans* has a broader sociological sweep than most of its stateside counterparts (though *Sugar Hill* rates as an exception). John Boorman's *The General* (Columbia/TriStar, DVD), John Mackenzie's *The Long Good Friday* (Video Treasures, DVD), and Neil Jordan's *Mona Lisa* (Anchor Bay) are also worth scoping out.

ZULU (1964) ***½

D: Cy Endfield. Stanley Baker, Jack Hawkins, Michael Caine. 139 mins. (New Line) DVD

Endfield's sweeping account of out-numbered Brit troops' filmlong fight against attacking Zulu warriors stands tall as one of the best battle films of all time. Richard Burton handles narration chores. The 1979 prequel, *Zulu Dawn,* on the defunct TWE label, rates as a video rarity.

Planet of the Tapes:
SCIENCE FICTION & FANTASY

"Only four points less than human—I wonder what it's like."
—curious clicker, CREATION OF THE HUMANOIDS

THE ABYSS: SPECIAL EDITION (1989/1993) ***

D: James Cameron. Ed Harris, Mary Elizabeth Mastrantonio, Michael Biehn, Todd Graff, John Bedford Lloyd, Chris Elliott. 167 mins. (Fox) DVD

The Abyss: Special Edition restores some 27 minutes of footage trimmed from the 1989 theatrical release of Cameron's undersea epic. Some of the additions lend greater texture to scripter Cameron's characterizations and strengthen the central conciliatory romance between divorce-bound diver Harris and engineer Mastrantonio. Weirdly enough, the major block of restored footage—elaborate climactic FX set pieces featuring thousand-foot tidal waves—represents some of the megabudgeted movie's most expensive sequences, millions of bucks' worth of shooting that originally ended up on the cutting-room floor! Unlike the restored version of *Blade Runner,* which transformed an excellent film into a masterpiece, *The Abyss*'s belated alterations exert a more schizophrenic influence. The already strong subaqueous salvage mission gains suspense, but the "Close Encounters of the Wet Kind" overlay (*The Abyss* first arrived near the end of Hollywood's We Have Met the Aliens and They Like Us cycle), while fun to watch, seems more far-fetched than ever. Double ditto for the dizzying profusion of last-reel miracles, a veritable orgy of "feel-good" plot resolutions that undermine the flick's better, starker instincts. The 140-minute version is also available.

THE ADVENTURES OF BARON MUNCHAUSEN (1989) ***

D: Terry Gilliam. John Neville, Eric Idle, Sarah Polley, Oliver Reed, Charles McKeown, Robin Williams, Jonathan Pryce, Uma Thurman. 126 mins. (Columbia/TriStar) DVD

Another gala Gilliam exercise in visual overkill, à la his earlier *Brazil,* this over-the-top version of tall-tale teller Baron M.'s fanciful escapades occasionally wanders off the mark but furnishes its fair share of surreal spectacle and offbeat wit. The film further benefits from several deft star cameos, especially the usually unbearable Williams's wild turn as the King of the Moon. Though overly broad and excessive in spots, *Munchausen* makes for rousing entertainment and represents a marked improvement over Josef von Baky's 1943 German version, *The Fabulous Baron Munchausen* (Video City, n.i.d.). Karel Zeman's 1961 semiani-mated Czech version, *Fabulous Adventures of Baron Munchausen,* was released via Vestron, while Englewood Entertainment has Zeman's *Fabulous World of Jules Verne.*

THE ADVENTURES OF BUCKAROO BANZAI ACROSS THE EIGHTH DIMENSION (1984) ***1/2

D: W. D. Richter. Peter Weller, John Lithgow, Ellen Barkin, Jeff Goldblum, Christopher Lloyd, Clancy Brown. 103 mins. (Vestron, n.i.d.)

Buckaroo Banzai features a title hero (Weller) who lives out the American Everyboy's wildest dreams. Not only is he a neurosurgeon, a martial artist, an "astounding jet car" driver, and a rock star, but he's even got his own comic book chronicling his ongoing exploits! Throw in blond love interest Penny Priddy (Barkin) and a gang of loyal sidemen ("those hard-rocking scientists, the Hong Kong Cavaliers"), and you've got a hero who makes Flash Gordon look like a chartered accountant.

Lithgow gives a truly demented perf as Mussolini-esque mad scientist Dr. Emilio Lizardo, a loony in league with Eighth Dimension aliens. The FX are flashy, the tempo's swift, and Earl Mac Rauch's (later responsible for the ill-advised John Belushi bio *Wired,* on Artisan) twisty script never lapses into the predictable or mundane. This imaginative study in sustained weirdness—largely misunderstood and/or overlooked during its initial release, later a cult icon complete with its own fan club and websites—definitely deserves your viewing attention. Richter also helmed the lamentable time-travel fable *Late for Dinner* (Columbia/Tri-Star).

SUPERMAN:
THE SERIES

THE ADVENTURES OF SUPERMAN (1948) B&W ***

D: Spencer G. Bennet, Thomas Carr. Kirk Alyn, Noel Neill, Tommy Bond, Carol Forman, Pierre Watkin, Charles King. 230 mins. (Warner)

A surreal combo of film, cartoon (the Man of Steel's flights are rendered via expert but obvious animation), and radio, this generally stirring chapter play toplines an unbilled (!) Alyn as the comic-book Christ figure. Kirk is backed by tiny but feisty Neill as Lois Lane—she reprised the role on the George Reeves–starred *Superman* teleseries—and former Little Rascal Bond, who plays cub reporter Jimmy Olson in brash wiseacre style. The 15-chapter serial is strongest in its early installments, detailing (albeit with the aid of copious stock footage) the destruction of Krypton and young Supe's formative years with his adoptive parents, the kindly Kents. Especially moving is the scene wherein Ma Kent sends a now-grown Clark off to right the world's wrongs: "Here's a uniform I made for you out of the blankets you were wrapped in when we found

you. It's a strange kind of cloth that resists both fire and acid. I hope it will protect you always." Our unflappable hero replies: "Well, thank you, Mother!" Equally riveting are the chapters introducing Clark to Metropolis and Superman to the world. Our story sinks a bit with the appearance of the notorious Spider Lady (Forman), who, abetted by her seemingly inexhaustible supply of devoted henchmen in fedoras and pencil-line moustaches, endlessly battles the Man of Steel for possession of the precious "reducer ray." The latter, by the way, is *not* a high-tech dietary device but a powerful weapon, which, in the wrong hands, could well spell the end of civilization-as-we-know-it. Still, there are enough plot twists, feats of derring-do, doses of campy dialogue ("How thoughtful of you," Lois chides Clark, "to be so considerate of yourself!"), and general cliffhanging to keep Superman fans and serial buffs happy.

ATOM MAN VS. SUPERMAN (1950) B&W ***

D: Spencer G. Bennet. Kirk Alyn, Noel Neill, Lyle Talbot, Tommy Bond, Pierre Watkin, Don Harvey. 250 mins. (Warner)

A lyn reprises his Man of Steel role to take on archvillain Lex Luthor (played by a chrome-domed Talbot) and his alter ego, the foreign-accented Atom Man, replete with glittering white frightmask. Like its forebear, the sequel alternates between live action and animation (in Supe's more acrobatic aerial sequences), moves at a brisk if occasionally redundant clip, and brings back beloved *Daily Planet* personnel Lois Lane (Neill), Jimmy Olson (Bond), and gruff editor Perry White (Watkin). Our fave episodes deal with our hero's banishment to the "Empty Doom," a nebulous netherworld where Superman exists only in superimposition and which prompts

many of the serial's sharpest exchanges. To wit:

ATOM MAN:
Before you depart for an eternity of aimless wandering into the Empty Doom, what have you to say?

SUPERMAN:
I'll be back!

With this release, Warner wisely included the opening credits preceding each chapter, rectifying an *Adventures of Superman* omission that had riled many hard-core cliffhanger fans.

SUPERMAN AND THE MOLE MEN (1951) B&W ***

D: Lee Sholem. George Reeves, Phyllis Coates, Jeff Corey, Walter Reed, Billy Curtis. 58 mins. (Warner)

G eorge Reeves assumes the Man of Steel role in this surprisingly liberal plea for the rights of Mole Men the world over, directed in faster-than-a-speeding-bullet style by infamous quickie king Lee ("Roll 'Em") Sholem. While it may not be much in the FX department—the mini-E.T.'s (led by erstwhile *Terror of Tiny Town* star Curtis) wield a sophisticated cosmic weapon since identified by experts as an earthly vacuum cleaner (!)—*SATMM* shapes up as a winning low-budget fable that led to Reeves's long-running Supe teleseries. Four volumes of *TV's Best Adventures of Superman* are on video (Warner), along with *Superman: The Lost Episodes* (Video Dimensions, DVD), Fleischer Studios' 17 Supe cartoons (*Superman: The Complete Collection,* via Video Dimensions; some also turn up in WinStar Entertainment's *Cartoon Crazys* series) and the full-length animated feature *Superman: The Last Son of Krypton* (Warner). All four of Warner's lavish screen epics with Christopher Reeve in the title role—*Superman: The Movie, Superman 2, Superman 3,* and *Superman 4: The*

Quest for Peace—are, of course, also available (Warner), as is the 1984 Faye Dunaway/Helen Slater–starrer *Supergirl* (Artisan). Camp followers should scope out the off-the-wall Indian "Bollywood" import *Superman: The Hindi Version* (Video Screams).

AKIRA (1988) ***

D: Katsuhiro Ôtomo. Animated. 124 mins. (MGM)

Akira is the film most responsible for popularizing the *animé* genre in the West. At $7 million, animator Ôtomo's film adaptation of his best-selling graphic novel represented the most expensive animated feature ever produced in Japan until *Ghost in the Shell*'s (see index) emergence in 1994. The animation is so complexly cinematic, incorporating more than 2,000 individual shots, that it's easy at times for viewers to forget they're not watching a live-action movie. Like many Japanese films, ranging from *Godzilla* to *Akira Kurosawa's Dreams* (Warner), *Akira* is another attempt—albeit in a high-tech, rock-'n'-roll, comic-book format—to grapple with the atomic destruction of Hiroshima and Nagasaki and their lingering fallout, both literal and figurative. (See also the more somber, directly autobiographical *animé Barefoot Gen* [Orion, DVD].) Our story is set in the "Neo Tokyo" of 2019 A.D., where teen biker gangs clash in the shadows of megalopolitan skyscrapers risen from the ashes of World War III. A gang member stumbles upon secret government ESP experiments and soon develops awesome powers, as well as suffering elaborately animated hallucinations. Also involved in the intertwining action are manipulative bureaucrats, military officials, and a band of revolutionaries out to topple Japan's postnuke regime. Though *Akira*'s story line occasionally grows repetitive over the film's 124-minute span, the graphics are rarely less than hypnotic.

ALIEN:
THE SERIES

ALIEN (1979) ***1/2

D: Ridley Scott. Sigourney Weaver, Tom Skerritt, Harry Dean Stanton, Yaphet Kotto, John Hurt, Veronica Cartwright, Ian Holm. 116 mins. (FoxVideo) DVD

The plot may have been lifted from the '50s B fave *It! The Terror from Beyond Space* (MGM), but director Scott and scripter Dan (*Dark Star*) O'Bannon add impressive sci-fi frills galore—from the elaborate spaceship set to the slimy FX and ever mutating monster (designed by H. R. Giger)—and know how to deliver the chills. Jerry Goldsmith's score adds immeasurably to the tension. Hurt's postprandial encounter of the gross kind ranks as one of the scream screen's deservedly legendary scenes, while scantily clad heroine Weaver's climactic battle with the slime critter has become one of the most imitated.

ALIENS (1986) ***1/2

D: James Cameron. Sigourney Weaver, Michael Biehn, Carrie Henn, Paul Reiser, Lance Henriksen, Jenette Goldstein. 137 mins. (Fox) DVD

Aliens is one sequel that actually surpasses the original, at least in terms of sheer spectacle and carnage. In the capable hands of *The Terminator* director/producer team of James Cameron and Gale Ann Hurd, with a sizable assist from FX ace Stan Winston, *Aliens* hurtles headlong into a high-tech nightmare. Weaver again proves tough as nails (and we don't mean the kind you polish), though she also reveals a softer, maternal side when she adopts young space-colony alien-massacre survivor Henn. Biehn contributes a crisp stint as a resourceful, determinedly PC marine corporal, as do Reiser as an evil space yuppie and Henriksen as the crew's token android. On the downside, *Aliens*

features too much macho cliché-swapping and dumb-grunt dialogue among the gun-happy space marines (though we did appreciate Goldstein's turn as tough-gal Private Vasquez; she's as close to a female-vintage Stallone as *we'd* ever want to see). Sig, meanwhile, gets to don T-shirt and panties, in not one but two scenes, though they're not nearly as brief as the scanties she wore during the original *Alien*'s climax. Equally important, the sequel's changing-sex-roles and motherhood-is-powerful subtexts—much ballyhooed at the time of the pic's initial release—are sufficiently superficial so as not to get in the way of the nearly nonstop action. Also available in a 1999 "special edition."

ALIEN 3 (1992) **

D: David Fincher. Sigourney Weaver, Charles Dance, Charles S. Dutton, Paul McGann, Brian Glover, Lance Henriksen. 115 mins. (Fox) DVD

So: Does alien-fighter Weaver get down to her trademark panties during this mostly sober-minded sequel? As it turns out, that key query is answered early on when, in her very first full-body shot, Sig is pulled unconscious from her peripatetic space pod wearing—you guessed it—her patented black bikini briefs. Unfortunately for Sig, though, this Ripley reprise finds companions Carrie Henn and space marine Michael Biehn dead on arrival and android Henriksen seriously short-circuited when their craft lands on stark prison planet Fury 161. One traveler who *does* make the flight is the dreaded "Bitch" alien, who soon sets her sights on the cons and their keepers. *Alien* hasn't been exactly what you'd call a cheery series from the get-go, but David (*Se7en*) Fincher's *3* is easily the coldest, murkiest, most downbeat of the lot. Your sentimental old Phantom prefers up-tempo orgies of destruction, like *The Road Warrior* and the original *Terminator;* life on Fury 161 is so unremittingly grim we had to wonder why its inhabitants would fight so hard to preserve it. Still, *Alien 3* comes through in the action and chills departments via the expected all-out FX-driven last-reel battle 'twixt voracious alien and unarmed humans.

ALIEN RESURRECTION (1997)***

D: Jean-Pierre Jeunet. Sigourney Weaver, Winona Ryder, Ron Perlman, Dominique Pinon, Michael Wincott, Dan Hedaya, Brad Dourif. 108 mins. (Fox) DVD

Under French genre auteur Jean-Pierre (*City of Lost Children*) Jeunet's imaginative supervision, the Ridley Scott–spawned *Alien* franchise rebounds with this actionful, thematically enriched series entry. Weaver's resilient Ripley is back, via the miracle of cloning, some 200 years after her official "death." Trouble is, her alien "offspring" is also along for the ride, and it's multiplying at an alarming rate. Jeunet keeps his typically claustrophobic tale moving as Weaver, Ryder, macho man Perlman, and other assorted humans (and humanoids) seek to elude the critters' clutches. The pic also extends the maternal themes established in *Aliens*, with Ripley, who'd served as an unwitting incubator for the beast, increasingly torn between self-preservation and a motherly drive to protect her misbegotten "baby." An ever eccentric Dourif stands out as a wayward scientist, while the expected high-tech FX expertise helps drive this unusually thought-provoking thrill ride home.

ALIEN INTRUDER (1993)**½

D: Ricardo Jacques Gale. Billy Dee Williams, Maxwell Caulfield, Tracy Scoggins, Richard Cody, Stephen Davies, Jeff Conaway. 94 mins. (PM)

A cheap but engrossing mix of *Alien, Dark Star,* and *Total Recall,*

Alien Intruder opens with spaceman Conaway slaughtering his crew over the favors of mysterious femme fatale Scoggins, an alien virus in seductress form. Williams recruits a quartet of convicts from the "New Alcatraz" (complete with laser bars) to accompany him on a dangerous fact-finding mission to the "G Sector," the dead-space zone where Conaway killed his cohorts before blowing his own brains out. For entertainment, the four volunteers—led by Caulfield (whose character's named Nick Mancuso [!] after the Canadian thesp)—enjoy their own individual virtual-reality porn booths, where they install themselves into steamy replays of such famous flicks as *High Noon, Casablanca,* and *The Wild One;* the flight proceeds more or less smoothly until the selfsame Scoggins begins infiltrating their Hollywoodoid reveries. The ship's interior resembles a Home Depot outlet and the exterior space visuals are sub–*Dark Star,* but the acting, characterizations, and interweaving fantasies make this improbably plotted pulp odyssey compelling all the way.

ALIEN NATION (1988)**½

D: Graham Baker. James Caan, Mandy Patinkin, Terence Stamp, Kevin Major Howard, Leslie Bevis, Peter Jason. 89 mins. (Fox)

Alien Nation posits that a slave saucer carrying a quarter mil genetically engineered E.T. workers landed near L.A. in 1988. The human-like aliens, labeled Newcomers, were quickly integrated into that city, where presumably they wouldn't stand out too much. Three years later, bigoted human cop Caan sees his partner slain by a lowlife "slag" (as the aliens are pejoratively referred to), then volunteers to accept the first Newcomer LAPD detective (Patinkin) as his new sidekick, the better to help him zero in on the killer E.T.s' whereabouts. Essentially a retread of Jack Sholder's superior *The*

Hidden (see index), *Alien Nation*—produced by *Aliens* producer Gale Ann Hurd—stacks up as a fairly standard mismatched-cops caper with an alien overlay, though Rockne O'Bannon's script supplies enough inventive riffs to keep the flick afloat, at least in the early going. We learn, among other things, that Newcomers own two hearts, get high on sour milk (in the most disgusto sour-milk scene since Buddy Giovinazzo's *Combat Shock*), play their own weird sports, and—in an Ellis Island replay—bear stupid Anglo names (e.g., Sam Francisco, Rudyard Kipling) handed out by contemptuous immigration authorities. Despite the film's inexorable slide into increasingly contrived and predictable schticks, the above bits—along with Caan's and Patinkin's lively work—make *Alien Nation* worth a look. The film spawned a successful teleseries, with Gary Graham and Eric Pierpont replacing Caan and Patinkin; the TV movie *Alien Nation: Dark Horizon* is also available via Fox.

Other alien-oriented titles out there include Kevin Lindenmuth's 1997 trilogy, *Alien Agenda: Out of the Darkness* (Tapeworm), starring Debbie Rochon; the Frank Zagarino-starred *Alien Chaser* (A-Pix, DVD); Luigi Cozzi's *Alien Contamination* (Regal); Fred Olen Ray's *Alien Dead* (Academy); Don Dohler's *The Alien Factor* and the prolific Albert Pyun's *Alien from L.A.* (both Media); *Alien Predators* (Video Treasures); *Alien Prey* (Cinema Group); *Alien Private Eye, Alien Seed,* starring Erik Estrada, and *Alien Space Avenger* (all AIP); *Alien Species* (Dead Alive); *Alien Terminator* (New Horizons); *Alien Warrior* (Vestron); *Alien Women* (a.k.a. *The Love Factor,* Sinister Cinema), Fred Olen Ray's *Alienator* (Prism); the TV movie *The Aliens Are Coming* (Goodtimes); *Amanda and the Alien* (Republic); *Invasion Earth: The Aliens Are Here* (New World); and the docudrama *Aliens from Spaceship Earth* (Video Gems), with Donovan.

THE ALLIGATOR PEOPLE (1959) B&W ***

D: Roy Del Ruth. Beverly Garland, George Macready, Lon Chaney, Jr., Richard Crane, Frieda Inescourt, Bruce Bennett. 74 mins. (Fox)

Feisty femme and premier screamer Garland finds that hubby Crane has been turned into a human-alligator hybrid at a bayou-set lab in Del Ruth's entertainingly far-fetched 1959 creature feature undermined only by some unusually dumb makeup FX. Chaney gives his all as the hook-handed gator-hater who gets to deliver the deathless threat "I'll kill you, Alligator Man—just like I'd kill any four-legged gator!"

ALPHAVILLE (1965) B&W ***

D: Jean-Luc Godard. Eddie Constantine, Anna Karina, Akim Tamiroff. 100 mins. (Home Vision) DVD

Jean-Luc looks into the future and sees a pulp-noir world dominated by alienating machinery. Godard's offbeat effort ranges from funny and perceptive to slow and pretentious, but its hommage-gone-wild style has been mega-influential. Home Vision offers the film in clean, digitally remastered form.

ALTERED STATES (1980) ***

D: Ken Russell. William Hurt, Blair Brown, Bob Balaban. 102 mins. (Warner) DVD

Strong hallucinatory imagery and intense performances elevate this loopy sci-fi/monster fable, more Ken Russell than Paddy Chayefsky (who penned the original novel), about scientist Hurt, whose isolation-tank tinkering causes him to regress to a killer-simian state.

ANDROID (1982) ***

D: Aaron Lipstadt. Klaus Kinski, Don Opper, Brie Howard. 80 mins. (JEF Films)

Android is a playful sci-fi flick about a Pinocchio-like, pop-culture-influenced android (Opper, who also coscripted), the human object of his newfound affections (foxy fugitive Howard), and his cruel creator (the late, great Kinski). The instrumental theme, "Sergio Leone," is also a winner.

THE ANDROMEDA STRAIN (1971) ***

D: Robert Wise. James Olson, David Wayne, Arthur Hill. 130 mins. (Universal) DVD

The Day the Earth Stood Still director Wise crafts a suspenseful, if somewhat overlong, screen version of Michael Crichton's novel chronicling scientists' painstaking efforts to prevent an alien microbe from destroying the world.

THE ANGRY RED PLANET (1959) **½

D: Ib Melchior. Gerald Mohr, Nora Hayden, Les Tremayne, Jack Kruschen. 84 mins. (HBO)

Auteur Melchior's otherwise standard astronauts-march-through-Mars plot is greatly enhanced by lurid color photography, "negative" effects (brought to you by the wonders of "Cinemagic"), and an array of imaginative Martian creatures. Beware the Crab-Rat-Spider!

ARCADE (1993) **½

D: Albert Pyun. Megan Ward, Peter Billingsley, John DeLancie, Sharon Farrell, Seth Green, Norbert Weisser. 85 mins. (Paramount)

Prolific but largely-underachieving B auteur Pyun assembles a flick that's as much about adolescent anxieties as it is about video-game virtual-reality graphics (themselves imaginatively executed on a modest budget). Ward plays an alienated teen whose journey through the seemingly supernaturally evil title game leads to psychodramatic confrontations with her suicidal mom (Farrell), among other primal traumas. Arcade is at least more thoughtful than Super Mario Bros. (Hollywood Pictures), Mortal Kombat, and sequel Mortal Kombat: Annihilation (both Universal, DVD).

ARMAGEDDON (1998) **

D: Michael Bay. Bruce Willis, Ben Affleck, Billy Bob Thornton, Liv Tyler, Will Patton, Steve Buscemi. 151 mins. (Buena Vista) DVD

While infinitely more rock 'n' roll than its summer-'98 McBlockbuster counterpart, Deep Impact (see index), Armageddon hurtles along as a relentlessly shallow mélange of MTV quick cuts, cosmic CGI FX, and push-button emotions, a long movie with a short attention span. Beyond the special effects, Armageddon's only discernible pluses are a cameo by increasingly ubiquitous cult thesp Udo (Blade) Kier (as a NASA shrink), a reference to Olga's House of Pain (!), and the antics of the always galvanizing Buscemi, especially during his "space dementia" phase.

THE ARRIVAL:
THE SERIES

THE ARRIVAL (1996) ***

D: David Twohy. Charlie Sheen, Lindsay Crouse, Ron Silver, Teri Polo, Richard Schiff, Leon Rippy, Tony T. Johnson. 109 mins. (Artisan) DVD

Scripter David (The Fugitive, Alien 3) Twohy's directorial debut arrives as a cross between Close Encounters of the Third Kind and 1957's Quatermass 2 (see index). Like Richard Dreyfuss in Close Encounters, Sheen, a professional sky-listener, becomes obsessed when he records a 42-second sonic blip he's positive emanated from a planet some 14-plus light-years away. While not as FX-driven as some of its bigger-budgeted counterparts, *The Arrival* more than compensates with suspense, inventive aliens, and one of the most elaborate descending-bathtub disaster scenes ever captured on celluloid. A Mexico-set centerpiece unfolds during a "Day of the Dead" celebration, adding a measure of gaudy gothic atmosphere to those sequences. Followed by the lame direct-to-video *Arrival II* (Artisan), aired on cable TV as *The Second Arrival*.

AT THE EARTH'S CORE (1976) **½

D: Kevin Connor. Doug McClure, Peter Cushing, Caroline Munro. 90 mins. (Warner, Video Treasures)

Connor helms a fun Edgar Rice Burroughs adaptation featuring McClure and Cushing as intrepid Victorians who burrow their way to the title destination, where they encounter prehistoric monsters, subterranean primitives, and the always welcome Munro. For more retro fun, see George Pal's 1961 *Atlantis, the Lost Continent* (MGM), an entertainingly tacky pulp sci-fi fantasy chronicling captured fisherman Anthony Hall's misadventures on the mythical titular landmass.

ATLAS (1960) ***

D: Roger Corman. Michael Forest, Barboura Morris, Frank Wolff. 80 mins. (Sinister Cinema)

Corman attempts the Herculean task of fashioning a sword-and-sandal spectacular with a skinny hero, a skinnier budget, and a cast of dozens. Fortunately, Charles B. (*Little Shop of Horrors*) Griffith's witty script and Morris's appealing presence help save the day.

THE ATOMIC CAFE (1982) B&W/COLOR ***

D: Kevin Rafferty, Pierce Rafferty, Jayne Loader. 92 mins. (HBO)

This ace montage of clips assembled from '40s and '50s news and propaganda films offering utterly useless and latently lethal misinformation re our then-new Atomic Age rates as the last word on a (we hope) closed topic.

ATOMIC DOG (1998) *

D: Brian Trenchard-Smith. Daniel Hugh Kelly, Isabella Hoffman, Cindy Pickett, Micah Gardener, Katie Stewart, Eryl Hayes. 86 mins. (Paramount)

Paramount's box art (the best thing connected with this canine clinker) suggests that *Atomic Dog* is an exercise in retro sci-fi camp, but this dog-eared dud proves all too leadenly earnest. The exceedingly brain-dead plot posits that a pooch abandoned in a faulty nuke power plant turns into the rabid title character and bedevils a dull 'burb family. Aussie auteur Trenchard-Smith (*Leprechaun 3*) keeps his two-decade-long flat-line career intact with his amazingly primer-level direction: In one scene, actors are actually seen standing in place, on their marks, awaiting their "Action!" call—the first time we can recall witnessing that elementary cinematic gaffe since Roger Corman's *Gunslinger*. For a truly fun, demented entry in the Domesticated Pets Turned Atomic Terrors subgenre, try Greydon (*Forbidden Dance*) Clark's *Uninvited* (New Star), featuring an irradiated mutant killer kitty that attacks Clu Gulager, George Kennedy, and a boatful of bikini babes. Now, *that's* entertainment!

ATOMIC SUBMARINE (1959) B&W ***

D: Spencer G. Bennet. Arthur Franz, Dick Foran, Brett Halsey, Bob Steele, Joi Lansing, Brett Halsey, Tom Conway, Paul Dubov. 72 mins. (Sinister Cinema) DVD

Producer Alex Gordon stocks his low-budget but admirably earnest alien encounter with many of his (and our) fave old-time thesps. Aside from its nostalgia value, the pic generates genuine suspense and features a neatly lensed sequence that finds four crewmembers, led by Franz, aboard an atmospheric subaqueous alien craft ruled by a high-handed cyclopean creature. Memorable dialogue likewise abounds, as when officer Dubov notes with alarm (and in refreshingly nontechno lingo), "A mass of jelly-like stuff came out of the thing and caught our torpedo!" Franz and the alien enjoy the best exchange, however. To wit:

ALIEN:
It may interest you to know I have visited hundreds of other worlds and, of all of them, your Earth seems the most suitable.

FRANZ:
Swell!

Other relevant backdate atomic titles include the nuclear-kidnap caper *Atomic City* (Paramount), the Mickey Rooney radiation comedy *The Atomic Kid* (Republic), and the time-twisted suspenser *The Atomic Man* (Sinister Cinema).

ATTACK OF THE CRAB MONSTERS (1957) B&W ***

D: Roger Corman. Richard Garland, Pamela Duncan, Russell Johnson, Leslie Bradley, Mel Welles, Ed Nelson. 68 mins. (Sinister Cinema)

In this classic Corman cheapie, people-eating, brain-absorbing giant atomic land crabs plague a scientific party seeking to determine the fate of an earlier expedition that disappeared without a trace on a remote Pacific atoll. While seriously hampered by the usual budgetary constraints, Charles B. (*Little Shop of Horrors*) Griffith's script is really quite ahead of its time, positing intriguing sci-fi concepts galore. Corman manages to camouflage Bronson Canyon and the California shoreline as the South Pacific with far more credibility here than he did when he subbed those same locales for ancient Scandinavia in *The Saga of the Viking Women and Their Journey to the Waters of the Great Sea Serpent* (n/a). An earnest cast that includes future *Gilligan's Island* regular Johnson (testing the waters, as it were) helps bring urgency and conviction even in the face of some of the cheesiest critters ever to hie to the Griffith Park hills. To say nothing of the hungriest: As scientist Bradley puts it, "Rather than our receiving radio signals, they would prefer to receive us in that great common stomach of theirs." To which marine biologist and lone femme Duncan replies, scarcely missing a beat, "Well, I guess it's about time I fixed us some food."

> ## TRAGIC OBSERVATION DEPARTMENT
> "Once they were men. Now they're land crabs."
> —*Attack of the Crab Monsters*

ATTACK OF THE GIANT LEECHES (1959) B&W **

D: Bernard Kowalski. Ken Clark, Yvette Vickers, Bruno VeSota. 62 mins. (Sinister Cinema)

Scripted by actor Leo Gordon, this is one of AIP's less inspired quickies, with the title monsters—inert props manipulated by semisubmerged extras (!)—terrorizing Florida swamp trash. Worth catching for *Attack of the 50 Foot Woman* alum (and current songstress) Vickers's provocative turn as fat-man VeSota's slutty, two-timing wife.

BARB WIRE (1996) **

D: David Hogan. Pamela Anderson Lee, Temuera Morrison, Victoria Rowell, Jack Noseworthy, Steve Railsback, Xander Berkeley, Udo Kier, Clint Howard, Nicholas Worth. In R and unrated editions. 109 mins. (PolyGram) DVD

It's "Play It Again, Pam" time in this loud, empty, futuristic *Casablanca* wannabe, set in 2017 Steel Harbor and based on the Dark Horse Comic created by Chris Warner. Instead of owning Rick's, Pam's an exotic dancer and professional hit person, a Bogie with boobs who hangs at the headbanger club Hammerhead. Ex-beau Morrison is the patriotic rebel an embittered Barb is persuaded to aid in his and new squeeze Rowell's fight against "congressional directorate" forces, Nazi-esque government fascists headed by a sadistic Railsback, who revels in overseeing neural/virtual torture sessions. Berkeley scores best as the Claude Rains corrupt cop stand-in, while Kier manages some deft Peter Lorre–like moves as Barb's aide-de-camp, and a thrashing heavy-metal soundtrack replaces Dooley Wilson's vocal and piano stylings. But despite all its audiovisual Sturm und Drang, *Barb Wire* shapes up as a crashing bore. Pam fans can also catch her in *Naked Souls* (WarnerVision), *Raw Justice* (Republic), and *Snapdragon* (Prism), as well as *Baywatch the Movie: Forgotten Paradise* (Artisan) and, of course, the infamous Pam and Tommy Lee amateur erotic video.

BARBARELLA (1968) ***

D: Roger Vadim. Jane Fonda, David Hemmings, John Phillip Law, Anita Pallenberg, Milo O'Shea. 98 mins. (Paramount) DVD

From Jane's opening antigravitational striptease to her chaste tryst with blind angel Law to an eye-patched dominatrix bit by former Keith Richards squeeze Pallenberg, Vadim's adaptation of the famed French comic—set in a psychedelic 41st century—supplies a plethora of visual and verbal fun. In fact, this may be Ms. F.'s sexiest turn (outside of her '80s workout tapes), though Jane can be feisty when the situation calls, as when she commands Anita, "Decrucify the angel or I'll melt your face!" Jane also worked under then-hubby Vadim—who, according to actress Barbara Leigh, "was a real charmer but, being French, didn't wear underpants"—in *Circle of Love* (JEF), *The Game Is Over* (Media), and *Spirits of the Dead* (see index).

THE BARBARIANS (1987) *1/2

D: Ruggero Deodato. David Paul, Peter Paul, Richard Lynch, Eve La Rue, Virginia Bryant, Michael Berryman. 88 mins. (Media, n.i.d.)

The defunct Cannon Group's aggressively stupid "Hercules in the Valley of the Road Warriors"–type adventure begins brightly enough with a strenuous pitched battle between the forces of the evil Kadar (Lynch) and the beleaguered, peace-seeking, nomadic "Ragnicks." Two of the captured Ragnicks are twin boys who grow up (though none of the other characters seem to age) to become the Barbarian Brothers, played by real-life megabicepped twins David and Peter Paul. *The Barbarians* starts its rapid celluloid slide as soon as our boneheaded bodybuilders—who come equipped with Bronx accents (!)—enter the picture and set out on a peripatetic (and largely pathetic) quest to reunite with the surviving Ragnicks. The pic's tongue-in-cheek tone fails to salvage the proceedings, though La Rue offers some visual relief as a curvaceous fugitive the boys meet on the road, and Berryman surfaces long enough to show off his shiny dome. The Barb Bros., meanwhile, return in *Double Trouble, Twin Sitters* (both Columbia/TriStar); *Ghost Writer* (Prism); and their best effort, *Think Big* (Media).

BATMAN: MASK OF THE PHANTASM (1993) ***

D: Eric Radomski, Bruce W. Timm. Animated. Voice cast: Kevin Conroy, Dana Delany, Mark Hamill, Hart Bochner. 76 mins. (Warner) DVD

Drawn from the animated tele-series, *Batman: Mask of the Phantasm* emerges as a far purer *Dark Knight* tale than those bloated, megabudgeted live-action *Batman* epics—*Batman, Batman Returns, Batman Forever,* and *Batman & Robin* (all Fox, DVD). Our story finds Batman/Bruce Wayne (voiced by Conroy) investigating the slayings of several veteran mobsters at the metallic hands of a costumed assassin called "the Phantasm." *Batman's* assorted animators employ an impressive cinematic style that, in certain long shots, looks almost like live action. Overhead angles, pans, B&W sequences, and other devices lend the feature mood and shading, while the kinetic action scenes add further juice. Voice-over chores are adroitly handled, not only by the leads but by such familiar supporting thesps as Abe Vigoda, Dick Miller, John P. Ryan (as the doomed gangsters), and Efrem Zimbalist, Jr., as Bruce's faithful retainer, Alfred. *Batman*-iacs can also avail themselves of the generally amusing 1966 TV-based feature *Batman: The Movie* (Paramount), with Adam West and Burt Ward as Batman and Robin, along with Penguin Burgess Meredith, Joker Cesar Romero, Riddler Frank Gorshin, and Cat-Woman Lee Meriwether; the animated *Adventures of Batman & Robin Vols. 1–4* and *Super Powers: Batman* (Warner); and the compilation film *Batman and Robin and Other Super Heroes* (Media). The hilarious 1940s *Batman* serials (Goodtimes) are on moratorium, as of this writing. Other popular animated features include *Batman and Mr. Freeze: Sub-Zero, The Batman and Superman Movie,* and *Batman Beyond* (all Warner).

BATTLE BENEATH THE EARTH (1968) **1/2

D: Montgomery Tully. Kerwin Matthews, Peter Arne, Viviane Ventura. 112 mins. (MGM)

Red Chinese forces attempt to tunnel through the earth with their super laser drill (!) and only Kerwin can stop them in this dumb but fun late-arriving Commie-menace campfest released the same year as *The Bamboo Saucer* (Republic), wherein American and Russian scientific teams, led by Dan Duryea (in his filmic farewell) and Lois Nettleton, respectively, race each other and rival Chinese forces to find the title vehicle.

BATTLE BEYOND THE STARS (1980) ***

D: Jimmy T. Murakami. Richard Thomas, George Peppard, Sybil Danning. 105 mins. (Vestron, n.i.d.)

John Sayles's in-joke-laden script plus a top cast of B-movie vets lift this postmodern, Roger Corman–produced space western well above most of its low-budget ilk, even if it does steal shamelessly from *Star Wars* and *The Magnificent Seven* (with a buxom Danning in the Horst Buchholz role).

THE BEASTMASTER:
THE SERIES

THE BEASTMASTER (1982) **1/2

D: Don Coscarelli. Marc Singer, Tanya Roberts, Rip Torn. 118 mins. (MGM)

Phantasm series auteur Coscarelli tackles the sword-and-sandal genre with hero Singer stalking evil sorcerer Torn and courting slave bimbo Roberts in a standard effort that at least lightened unemployment lines for Hollywood's animal wranglers. Events grow more surreal in the belated 1991 sequel, *Beastmaster 2: Through the Portal of Time* (Republic), where villain Wings Hauser (in another energetic turn in a lost cause) time-trips to modern L.A. to lay hands on a portable nuclear detonator; genre faves Robert Z'dar and Michael Berryman turn up in cameos. Tony Todd and David Warner lend their thespian talents to the Singer-starred 1995 entry *Beastmaster III: The Eye of Braxus* (Universal).

BEAUTY AND THE BEAST (1946) B&W ***1/2

D: Jean Cocteau. Jean Marais, Josette Day, Marcel André. 93 mins. (Home Vision) DVD

Cocteau's classic reinterpretation of this venerable fable unfolds in dream time, offers unforgettable black-and-white imagery, and rates as must viewing for fantasy-film fans. Late *Carnival of Souls* auteur Herk Harvey cited the film as a major influence. Other available *Beauty and the Beast* versions include the 1963 American remake, with Mark Damon and Joyce Taylor (MGM), the famed animated Disney musical, and the modern-day televariation with Linda Hamilton and Ron Perlman (Republic).

BEGINNING OF THE END (1957) B&W ***

D: Bert I. Gordon. Peter Graves, Peggie Castle, Morris Ankrum, Thomas Browne Henry. 73 mins. (Rhino)

Gordon's insect "stretcher" stands up as one of Mr. B.I.G.'s better sci-fi outings. When giant locusts eat the populace of a small Illinois town, the trouble's traced to scientist Graves's experiments in veggie enhancement, resulting in titanic tomatoes, Brobdingnagian berries, and, as an unintended side effect, said outsized insects. The rear-projection FX seem primitive by today's standards (and even '50s big-budget standards) but have their moments, and the grasshoppers rack up a sizable human body count on their way to the Windy City. No relation to 1947's *The Beginning or the End* (n/a), a fact-based but jingoistic account of the birth of the A-bomb.

BEYOND THE TIME BARRIER (1960) B&W ***

D: Edgar G. Ulmer. Robert Clarke, Darlene Tompkins, Vladimir Sokoloff. 75 mins. (Sinister Cinema)

Ulmer's cheap but entertaining sci-fi quickie, lensed back-to-back with the same auteur's less successful *Amazing Transparent Man* (Sinister Cinema), stars Robert *(Hideous Sun Demon)* Clarke as a time-traveling pilot.

BIG TROUBLE IN LITTLE CHINA (1986) ***

D: John Carpenter. Kurt Russell, Kim Cattrall, Dennis Dun, Victor Wong, James Hong, Kate Burton. 99 mins. (Fox)

Russell plays trucker Jack Burton, an all-American noir jerk who witnesses the airport abduction of his Chinese pal Dun's bride-to-be, the emerald-eyed Suzee Pai. The ensuing chase leads our heroes to a subterranean Chinatown crawling with ornery kung-fu demons (superfluously equipped with machine guns) and ruled by the ancient evil spirit Lo Pan (veteran genre thesp Hong), a cross between Fu Manchu and Howard Hughes. Carpenter directs his stoned pulp adventure in high, throwaway style, sending up everything from chopsocky cheapies to high-tech extravaganzas like *Raiders of the Lost Ark*. The action is alternately violent and absurdist (and nothing if not nonstop), while the characters exchange more clichés than you could, well, shake a stick at. At times *Big Trouble* plays more broadly than it might have (Russell's Duke Wayne impersonation grows stale pretty pronto, pilgrim) and revels too much in its own lay-it-on-thick shtick. The flick's Hong Kong film referencing was ahead of its time but hasn't kept the pic from becoming a fixture on many Asian cineastes' permanent dis list, for what they deem its ill-informed treatment of its subject matter.

BLACK FRIDAY (1940) B&W **1/2

D: Arthur Lubin. Boris Karloff, Bela Lugosi, Stanley Ridges, Anne Nagel, Anne Gwynne. 70 mins. (Universal)

One of several period films to cast Karloff as a scientist with a penchant for bizarre experiments, this brain-exchange epic sees Boris portray a condemned doc, who, on his way to the chair, entrusts his secret journal to a reporter. In the ensuing filmlong flashback, B.K. receives an unexpected opportunity to test a pet cerebral theory when he saves the life of a dying friend, English-lit prof Ridges, by implanting part of an injured gangster's brain. A typically miscast Lugosi surfaces as a doomed hood. Nightclub chanteuse Nagel and her Art Deco–bedecked Manhattan digs furnish a bit of sex appeal, and Karloff does what he can with his unlikely role, but overall *Black Friday* shapes up as a basically botched operation. (Universal flacks, meanwhile, claimed Bela had been hypnotized before enacting his claustrophobic death scene.) Universal's Poverty Row competitor Monogram managed to squeeze far more campy fun from an almost identical premise in its inspiredly brain-damaged 1942 cheapie *The Man With Two Lives* (Sinister Cinema). Boris plays a kindly mad scientist seeking to perfect an anti-aging serum, with dire side effects, in 1940's *Before I Hang* (Columbia/TriStar), an intriguing, if ultimately compromised, sci-fi chiller; a dead doc brought back to life to wreak vengeance on the jurors who'd sentenced him to die in 1939's middling *The Man They Could Not Hang* (Goodtimes); and a neurosurgeon who switches patients' personalities and brains in the superior 1936 Brit entry *The Man Who Lived Again* (Sinister Cinema), a.k.a. *The Man Who Changed His Mind*.

BLACK ORPHEUS (1959) ***1/2

D: Marcel Camus. Breno Mello, Marpessa Dawn, Léa Garcia. 103 mins. (Home Vision) DVD

Camus's Brazil-set retelling of the Orpheus-Eurydice legend offers an exciting score, stunning color photography, and the ever alluring Dawn (later a dance critic for *The Village Voice*) in her only starring role. Now available in a digitally remastered, letter-boxed, subtitled edition.

BLACK SCORPION: THE SERIES

BLACK SCORPION (1995) **

D: Jonathan Winfrey. Joan Severance, Bruce Abbott, Garrett Morris, Rick Rossovich, Casey Siemaszko. 92 mins. (New Horizons)

Severance stars as Darcy Walker, a disgruntled "Angel City" police officer who dons revealing leather threads and takes the law into her own hands after her ex-cop pop (Rossovich) is cold-bloodedly gunned down by the city's spaced-out district attorney. Seems the D.A., unbeknownst even to himself, is a member of an army of asthmatics hooked on mind-controlling inhalers (!) supplied by a costumed supervillain called "the Breathtaker" (Siemaszko). While brave, shapely Joan does her costume proud, *Black Scorpion*, despite a smattering of amusing moments, doesn't quite cut it. Severance returns in *Black Scorpion 2* (New Horizons), which, if little else, at least matches the standards set by the original *BS*, and paved the way for a syndicated tele-series.

BLADE RUNNER: THE DIRECTOR'S CUT (1982/1992) ***1/2

D: Ridley Scott. Harrison Ford, Rutger Hauer, Sean Young, Darryl Hannah, Joanna Cassidy, Edward James Olmos, Brion James, William Sanderson, Joe Turkel. 117 mins. (Warner) DVD

Scott's original cut of his hypnotic 1982 adaptation of Philip K. Dick's *Do Androids Dream of Electric Sheep?*—which received a limited 1992 theatrical rerelease—represents a case of addition by subtraction: Scott deletes android-hunter Ford's voice-overs, a semi-idyllic ending, and, oddly enough, the gorier aspects of the eye-gouging scene wherein angry "replicant" Hauer terminates his soulless creator, Tyrell (Turkel). The film's other elements remain intact and as spellbinding as ever, highlighted by Vangelis's droning, fever-dream synthesizer score, Douglas Trumbull's spectacular FX, and Lawrence G. Paul's elaborately hallucinatory set designs: 2019 L.A.'s dark, rainy hellscape is still the scariest we've ever seen west of the Jersey Turnpike. *Blade Runner*'s central theme, involving human Ford and his replicant targets' parallel identity crises, has lost none of its power. The perfs are first-rate, from Ford to replicants Hauer, Cassidy, James, and especially Young. Even the normally vacuous Hannah, as a punkette replicant with a talent for ninja flips, turns in effective work here.

THE BLOB (1958) ***

D: Irwin Yeaworth, Jr. Steven McQueen, Aneta Corseaut, Olin Howlin, Earl Rowe, Vince Barbi. 85 mins. (Columbia/TriStar)

"Steven" McQueen (in his screen debut; he followed with the terrif indie *The Great St. Louis Bank Robbery* [see index]) and a gang of geeky teens take on an amorphous mass of killer Jell-O from outer space. From its Mexi-flavored theme song, "Beware of the Blob" (composed by a mysteriously uncredited Burt Bacharach) to its vintage array of flashy land yachts, *The Blob* shapes up as *the* quintessential late-'50s monster movie. The gaudy color, lightly self-mocking tone, and memorable title creature likewise add to the fun. The scene wherein the Blob invades the local bijou's Midnight Spook Show (the feature is John Parker's experimental fright flick *Daughter of Horror*) provides a special treat for B-movie buffs. Though some of the pic's expository portions move almost as slowly as the Blob itself, *The Blob* remains a must for the uninitiated and a musty delight for the rest. Director Yeaworth had earlier specialized in Christian propaganda films; his *Flaming Teen-Age* (see index) is a compelling example. The feeble *Son of Blob* (a.k.a. *Beware! The Blob*) (Video Gems), directed by future "J.R." Larry Hagman, followed in 1972.

THE BLOB (1988) ***1/2

D: Chuck Russell. Kevin Dillon, Shawnee Smith, Donovan Leitch, Jeffrey DeMunn, Candy Clark, Joe Seneca. 92 mins. (Columbia/TriStar)

Even hard-core *Blob*-ophiles will agree that, as fright flicks go, the original *Blob* was more iconic than classic, the celluloid equivalent of a novelty record like *The Purple People Eater* (itself the basis for a weak 1988 sci-fi comedy with Ned Beatty [Video Treasures]). Visceral chills did not rank high among *The Blob*'s quirky virtues. Not so Russell's new, improved FXplicit edition. While sticking—quite literally at times—to the original story line, Russell's remake injects the shock-movie juice its model largely lacked. *This* Blob, from its initial on-screen appearance to its last-reel rampage, benefits mightily from high-tech FX and disgusto gore galore. Like David Cronenberg's fresh *The Fly* revamp, *The Blob* never wallows in synthetic nostalgia but accurately updates its source material. The pic views the 1980s as a replay of the '50s, stripped of the latter's innocence (though ignorance and stupidity run more rampant than ever, with typically aggressive '80s abandon). Where reassuring authority figures supplied the solution in the first *Blob,* they constitute a major part of the problem here. The main characters are likewise reinvented. Dillon, as a local cycle rebel, adds a stronger outlaw note to the original McQueen role. And heroine Smith, while every bit as fetching as Aneta Corseaut, is far more active as the high school cheerleader who displays *mucho* grit and valor under fire (or, more often, slime).

THE BLOOD OF HEROES (1989) ***

D: David Peoples. Rutger Hauer, Joan Chen, Vincent D'Onofrio, Delroy Lindo, Anna Katarina, Max Fairchild. 91 mins. (HBO)

Blade Runner scripter Peoples's directorial debut (originally titled *Salute of the Juggler*) is a postnuke duke-out that follows a team of wandering "juggers," elaborately scarred athletes (they look like they were made over by the "ugly expert" from John Waters's *Desperate Living*) who play a primitive sort of nuclear winter sport that combines the rudiments of football and hockey while multiplying the violence quotient of both. The minimal plot involves aspiring jugger Chen, who joins Rutger's roving band for a climactic match against a killer pro team led by Fairchild. Despite *Blood*'s derivative setting and story line—the flick lifts liberally from *Mad Max Beyond Thunderdome, Rollerball, Rocky, The Running Man, Solarbabies,* and even ESPN extreme trash-sports events—and risible dialogue that occasionally flirts with high-camp disaster (e.g., "I never hurt anyone except to put a dog's skull on a stick!"), the pic's unrelieved intensity ultimately carries the day.

BOMBSHELL (1997)**½

D: Paul Wynne. Henry Thomas, Frank Whaley, Madchen Amick, Pamela Gidley, Brion James, Victoria Jackson. 95 mins. (Trimark)

With *Bombshell,* writer/director Wynne crafts a slick sci-fi thriller with a serious core. Set in 2011, *Bombshell* stars erstwhile *E.T.* kid Thomas as a young scientific wiz whose tissue-regenerating, cancer-fighting "nano engine" design is being rushed into production by greedy Nanolab corporate head James, a move that seriously irks coworker Whaley. After a mysterious encounter with a masked terrorist, Thomas awakes to find his kidney's been replaced by a latently lethal device. When his medico squeeze (Amick) is kidnapped by the unknown terrorist, our hero is forced to race against time to save both their lives—and possibly a significant portion of the rest of the planet's as well. *Bombshell* sports a modest but effective production design that convincingly propels us a few years into the future, maintains a subtly melancholy tone, and wrings a fair amount of tension from its story line.

A BOY AND HIS DOG (1975)***

D: L. Q. Jones. Don Johnson, Susanne Benton, Jason Robards, Alvy Moore, Helene Winston, Charles McGraw. 87 mins. (First Run Features) DVD

Drawn from Harlan Ellison's blackly comic fable of the same name and directed in deadpan style by actor/auteur Jones, *A Boy and His Dog* casts Johnson as an opportunistic postnuke survivor who gets by with more than a little help from his (frequently foulmouthed) canine best friend, Tiger (voiced by Tim McIntyre, Alan Freed in *American Hot Wax*). Don's wasteland wanderings eventually lead him to an underground totalitarian community modeled in the image of vintage Topeka, Kansas (!), a happy-face dystopia ruled by folksy fascist Robards and enforced by killer farmer robots. Don's troubles escalate when he's taken captive by the mostly sterile postholocaust hayseeds, who press him into service as an in-house stud. First Run's reissue (*Boy* was originally out on the defunct Media label) ably illustrates why this irreverent subterranean romp (which once played 42nd Street under the bogus title *Psycho Boy and His Killer Dog* [!]) enjoyed a long life as a midnight-movie staple.

BRAIN DEAD (1990)****

D: Adam Simon. Bill Pullman, Bud Cort, Bill Paxton, Patricia Charbonneau, George Kennedy, Nicholas Pryor. 84 mins. (MGM)

Your Phantom's admittedly a sucker for surreal shockers, especially when they involve deranged brain experiments. (We wouldn't go so far as to say we've never met a deranged brain-experiment movie we didn't like, but that wouldn't be *too* far off the mark.) Simon's *Brain Dead* represents a welcome addition to this cerebral subgenre. Updated from a previously unfilmed script (originally titled *Paranoid*) by the late, great scare scribe Charles Beaumont, who wrote many of *The Twilight Zone's* best episodes, *Brain Dead* stars future *ID4* prez Pullman as neurologist Rex Martin, a scientist so in love with his work that he talks to the preserved, jar-encased brains that line his lab. Martin's troubles begin when corporate creep Paxton enlists him to retrieve a vital mathematical formula buried in the addled cerebrum of paranoid genius Cort (in a memorably over-the-top turn). No sooner does our hero start consorting with Cort than he too descends into total paranoid lunacy. Or does he? Only sinister shrink Pryor seems to know for sure, and he may be jiving too. Aside from conscious nods to *Re-Animator*—Martin is a graduate of H. P. Lovecraft's infamous "Miskatonic" med school—and the notorious nympho-ward scene from Sam Fuller's *Shock Corridor, Brain Dead* wisely plays its mad material straight. Add graphic brain-surgery close-ups, a cameo by the legendary George Kennedy as a craven corporate head, and inventive nightmare imagery, and you have one of the '90s' freshest frightfests, guaranteed to keep adventurous viewers both guessing and gasping. Director Simon—whose main claim to fame is as a fleeting opening-reel audio in-joke in Robert Altman's *The Player*—deserves credit for recognizing the brilliance of Beaumont's script and bringing it to hallucinatory screen life.

BRAINSCAN (1994)**

D: John Flynn. Edward Furlong, Amy Hargreaves, Frank Langella, T. Ryder Smith. 96 mins. (Buena Vista)

Brainscan uses the same video-game-from-hell hook as the lower-budgeted *Arcade* (see index) while introducing "the Trickster," whom producers vainly hoped would prove a grisly gold mine in a Freddy Krueger vein. As interpreted by Shakespearean stage thesp Smith, with special makeup FX by Steve Johnson, "the Trickster" more closely resembles Sammi Curr (Tony Fields), the dead headbanger avenger in Charles Martin Smith's wittier 1986 scare satire, *Trick or Treat* (see index). In *Brainscan* the villainous Trickster hails from the eponymous video game alienated teen Furlong finds advertised in *Fangoria* mag and which propels him into a neighborhood slay spree that may or may not be real. *Brainscan* tries to play it both ways, as a supernatural suspenser *and* a hallucinatory VR tease, ultimately falling short on both counts.

BRAINSTORM (1983) **1/2

D: Douglas Trumbull. Christopher Walken, Natalie Wood, Louise Fletcher, Cliff Robertson. 106 mins. (MGM) DVD

In this early venture into virtual reality, scientists Walken and Fletcher design a headset capable of tapping into the sensations felt by other people. A pretty horrifying idea, all right, but not much is done with it here. Fastforward to the FX scenes, which, under *2001* FX-ace-turned-director Trumbull's supervision, are truly first-rate. The film was nearly jettisoned after costar Wood's drowning death halted production. Not to be confused with the twisty 1965 B&W Jeffrey Hunter thriller, *Brainstorm* (n/a).

BREEDERS (1997) **1/2

D: Paul Matthews. Todd Jensen, Samantha Janus, Oliver Tobias, Kadamba Simmons, Nigel Harrison, Clifton Lloyd-Bryan. 92 mins. (A-Pix) DVD

The Matthews clan—director Paul, producer Elizabeth, and editor Peter H., who'd earlier contributed the flat *Bigfoot*-styled clinker *Grim* (A-Pix, DVD)—returns with this livelier account of a randy alien invader who, like those much beloved *Humanoids from the Deep* (see index), is here on a mission to mate with human females. He picks the right spot to land, at an all-femme college, where handsome art prof Jensen and blond student-squeeze Janus are among the first to discover the large, toothy terror's presence in the school basement. While derivative, *Breeders* generates its share of scares and suspense, backed by comparatively beefed-up production values.

THE BROTHER FROM ANOTHER PLANET (1984) ***

D: John Sayles. Joe Morton, Dee Dee Bridgewater, Ren Woods, Steve James, Maggie Renzi, John Sayles, Tom Wright. 104 mins. (Key)

The prolific Sayles's socially conscious sci-fi comedy/drama could easily have drifted into a series of "E.T. Goes to the Ghetto" riffs. But Sayles's generally crisp scripting and Morton's winning performance as the speechless title alien make this a witty, low-key exercise for sci-fi fans and mainstreamers alike. The late, great Steve James turns in top work as Odell the bartender, while Sayles cameos as an extraterrestrial bounty hunter.

CARNOSAUR:
THE SERIES

CARNOSAUR (1993) **1/2

D: Adam Simon. Diane Ladd, Rafael Sbarge, Jennifer Runyon, Harrison Page, Ned Bellamy, Clint Howard. 82 mins. (New Horizons)

While not up there with his brilliant *Brain Dead*—to which the auteur pays not-so-humble homage via on-screen TV clips and by reviving the "Eunice Corp." handle—Simon's *Carnosaur* at least offers a refreshingly sick alternative to Spielberg's sticky *Jurassic Park* (Universal, DVD). Sort of a *Jurassic Park* Meets *The Unborn*, *Carnosaur* stars Ladd (Laura Dern's real-life mom) as a secretive genetic genius who plans to replace mankind with dinosaurs by injecting dino DNA into pregnant women. Doses of dark wit and a downbeat ending further separate *Carnosaur* from its mega-successful model. Like a pesky pterodactyl buzzing a lumbering T rex, Corman's B flick opened just ahead of or right behind *JP* in many American theatrical markets and beat Spielberg's *Jurassic* juggernaut into vid stores by a month or more.

CARNOSAUR 2 (1994) **1/2

D: Louis Mourneau. John Savage, Cliff De Young, Rick Dean, Ryan Thomas Johnson, Arabella Holzbog, Don Stroud. 83 mins. (New Horizons)

Producer Corman's *Carnosaur 2* actually owes far more of a debt to Ridley Scott's frequently Roger-raided *Alien* than to its predecessor: Members of a coed repair crew under the command of deceitful military officer De Young find themselves trapped between tiny dinos and a leaky nuclear-waste repository in a remote Nevada outpost. Our protagonists must prevent a potentially apocalyptic meltdown, all the while eluding the hatched dinosaur eggs that have been gestating in the subterranean facility. As in *Alien*, a more imposing dinosaur mom turns up to protect her endangered young. John Buechler handles the FX chores with minimalist aplomb, while director Mourneau actually wrings more tension from his underground nuclear-bunker dramatics than he does from the marauding monsters.

CARNOSAUR III: PRIMAL SPECIES (1996) **

D: Jonathan Winfrey. Scott Valentine, Janet Gunn, Rick Dean, Rodger Halston, Anthony Peck, Terri J. Vaughn, Stephen Lee, Cyril O'Reilly. 82 mins. (New Horizons)

You can't accuse *Carnosaur III* of being overly plotted; this life-in-the-fast-food-chain follow-up consists of a series of bloody wipeouts. A terrorist team destroys a military escort and captures the wrong cargo—three living, breathing, hungry dinosaurs, who in turn devour the terrorist team *and* a squad of port police. Commando leader Valentine, cold-fish scientist Gunn, wisecracking soldier Dean, and a handful of others next take on the rampaging dinos in a docked ship's infrastructure, with disastrous results for nearly all involved. The filmmakers, who lose sight of the *Carnosaur* series original *Jurassic Park*–rip-off roots, save most of their creativity for the end-credit crawl, where *Carnosaur* and *Carnosaur 2* helmers Simon and Mourneau receive "Carnosaur Wranglers" credit.

CHERRY 2000 (1988) **

D: Steve De Jarnatt. Melanie Griffith, David Andrews, Ben Johnson, Tim Thomerson, Harry Carey, Jr., Pamela Gidley, Michael C. Gwynne. 93 mins. (Orion)

Director De Jarnatt pegs his futuristic farce to an updated version of a time-honored Tinseltown formula: Boy (Andrews) meets android, boy loses android, boy hires tough distaff "tracker" (Griffith) to lead him into a perilous wasteland in search of a suitable robotic replacement. Unfortunately, *Cherry 2000* abandons its better instincts early on and skids into tired, tongue-in-cheek *Road Warrior*–wannabe territory. De Jarnatt went on to helm the truly brilliant *Miracle Mile* (see index) but hasn't hardly been heard from since.

CIRCUITRY MAN:
THE SERIES

CIRCUITRY MAN II: PLUGHEAD REWIRED (1994) **1/2

D: Steven and Robert Lovy. Vernon Wells, Deborah Shelton, Jim Metzler, Paul Wilson, Dennis Christopher, Traci Lords, Nicholas Worth, Buck Flower. 97 mins. (Columbia/TriStar)

Like their original 1990 *Circuitry Man* (Columbia/TriStar), the Lovy brothers' sequel shapes up as an uneven mix of bright concepts and self-indulgent slapstick. In our polluted future, humans share subterranean space with "biosynthetic" androids; several competing teams head toward the surface South American penal colony of "Brazilamerica," home of biosynthetic brain fiend Plughead (Wells, reprising his original role). Metzler takes top acting honors as a biosynth programmed for chivalry and romance, while the ever popular Lords appears as Shelton's mother (!). A third installment, *Circuitry Man III: I Plug New York,* was announced but has yet to materialize.

CITY OF LOST CHILDREN (1995) ***1/2

D: Marc Caro, Jean-Pierre Jeunet. Ron Perlman, Daniel Emilfork, Judith Vittet, Dominique Pinon, Jean-Claude Dreyfus, Mireille Mossé. Subtitled. 112 mins. (Columbia/TriStar) DVD

French filmmakers Caro and Jeunet—the same darkly whimsical Parisian pair responsible for the 1992 cult cannibal comedy *Delicatessen* (see index)—scale even greater heights here. *City*'s surreal story line centers on twisted scientist Krank (Emilfork, sort of a Euro art-house Michael Berryman, whose credits range from Fellini films to fright flicks like *The Devil's Nightmare*). Off the coast of a grim, fog-enshrouded port city, Krank shares a haunted castle–like rig with his bizarre creations—six cloned assistants (all played by facile, rubber-faced Pinon), the diminutive "Miss Bismuth" (Mossé), and "Irvin," a disembodied brain voiced by Jean-Louis Trintignant. Krank, it seems, suffers from a serious ailment: His utter inability to dream is causing him to age prematurely; his counterplan involves dispatching his creepy cadre of one-eyed henchman to kidnap local children, the better that Krank might commandeer their dreams. When a group of armed cyclopes snatch Denree (Joseph Lucien), the adoptive little brother of circus strongman/ex-sailor "One" (Perlman), One eventually enlists the aid of a gang of light-fingered orphans who steal for their precarious survival.

In the course of their quest, the hulking One and the petite Miette (Vittet) encounter not only Krank and crew but evil Siamese twins called "the Octopus" (Genevieve Brunet, Odile Mallet), an underwater amnesiac dubbed "the Diver" (Pinon again, in his seventh role), and Marcello, the flea trainer (Dreyfus), who provides our embattled protagonists with an unexpected assist that leads to one of Caro and Jeunet's trademark Rube Goldberg–styled visual jokes. The tandem combine elaborate live-action cartoon imagery with a story that's endlessly inventive, funny, and poignant (though never cloying), all realized with technological resources that early French cinemagician Georges Méliès—whose spirit the filmmakers in many ways embody—probably couldn't even have dreamed of. The film also benefits from frequent David Lynch composer Angelo Badalamenti's evocative score, as well as excellent physical performances from all involved, particularly the flamboyant Emilfork, the enchanting Vittet, the strapping but sensitive Perlman (who speaks his spare dialogue in phonetic French), and the incredible Pinon, whose six clones are often seen interacting within the same frame.

CLASH OF THE TITANS   (1981) **

D: Desmond Davis. Harry Hamlin, Laurence Olivier, Judi Bowker, Ursula Andress, Burgess Meredith, Maggie Smith, Claire Bloom. 118 mins. (MGM)

It's a god-eat-god world as ancient Greek deities squabble over the course of earthly events. Tony thespian cameos and Ray Harryhausen's spectacular FX supply this otherwise overblown exercise in comic-book mythology with its main raison d'être.

CLASS OF 1999:
THE SERIES

CLASS OF 1999   (1990) ***

D: Mark L. Lester. Malcolm McDowell, Stacy Keach, John P. Ryan, Pam Grier, Bradley Gregg, Traci Lin, Patrick Kilpatrick. 98 mins. (Vestron, n.i.d.)

Lester's futuristic follow-up to his alarmist high school psycho romp *Class of 1984* (see index) finds America's urban centers under siege by marauding youth gangs. In a bid to establish order at Seattle's embattled Kennedy High, principal McDowell hires crazed albino scientist Keach (wearing alienoid contact lenses) and his trio of armed android teachers (Ryan, Kilpatrick, and an ever fierce and fetching Grier). Trouble is, the teachers are reconverted military robots, and it doesn't take long for some serious glitches to kick in. When student Gregg and principal's daughter Lin learn the truth re their terminating teachers, they persuade warring gangs the Blackhearts and the Razorheads to stop using their Uzis on each other and turn them instead on their common foes. As Gregg puts it in a rousing rallying cry, "I'm going in there to waste some teachers! Are you with me?" *Class of 1999* is a fast, funny, ultraviolent sci-fi actioner that surrounds its neat central conceit with high-energy shootouts, chases, and gore. Sasha Mitchell assumes the disciplinary role in the

weak 1993 sequel, *Class of 1999 II: The Substitute* (Trimark).

A CLOCKWORK ORANGE   (1971) ***

D: Stanley Kubrick. Malcolm McDowell, Patrick Magee, Adrienne Corri, Steven Berkoff, David Prowse. 137 mins. (Warner) DVD

Kubrick's then-controversial dystopian satire, based on Anthony Burgess's none-too-subtle novel, has never been one of The Phantom's faves but does rate as an undeniably slick, violent, over-the-top affair featuring more than its share of indelible scenes.

THE CLONUS HORROR   (1978) ***

D: Robert Fiveson. Tim Donnelly, Dick Sargent, Peter Graves, Paulette Breen, Keenan Wynn, Lurene Tuttle. 90 mins. (Lightning, n.i.d.)

The Clonus Horror (a.k.a. *Parts: The Clonus Horror*) deals with a political/corporate plot that gradually unravels due to an errant can of Milwaukee beer (!). Beyond that, we can say no more without subtracting from this sci-fi sleeper's considerable suspense. (Even Lightning's video cover copy gives too much away.) Suffice it to say that *The Clonus Horror* is an excellent, intense chiller that demonstrates how a solid story line, a tight script, taut direction, and good performances (from Donnelly in the lead to vets Graves, Sargent, Wynn, and Tuttle in key cameos) can overcome a low budget.

CLOSE ENCOUNTERS OF THE THIRD KIND: THE SPECIAL EDITION (1977) ***

D: Steven Spielberg. Richard Dreyfuss, Teri Garr, François Truffaut. 132 mins. (Columbia/TriStar)

Spielberg crafts a suspenseful tale of alien visitation capped by a spectac-

ular spaceship sequence. French auteur Truffaut appears as a scientist on the case, while *Star Wars*' John Williams handles the rousing score chores. The special edition, issued in 1980, is three minutes *shorter* than the original theatrical release due to some editorial tightening in the final reels. A new "special edition" (137 minutes) was introduced in 1998.

COLOSSUS: THE FORBIN PROJECT (1970) ***

D: Joseph Sargent. Eric Braeden, Susan Clark, William Schallert. 100 mins. (Universal)

American and Soviet supercomputers link up, find love, and seek to control their obstructive human creators in Sargent's witty, chilling, and prescient parable about science amok. Colossus itself makes for a memorably arrogant villain.

COMA   (1978) ***

D: Michael Crichton. Genevieve Bujold, Michael Douglas, Elizabeth Ashley, Richard Widmark, Rip Torn. 113 mins. (MGM) DVD

Petite but brave Bujold takes on male-chauvinist hospital authorities—screen vet Widmark among them—in a bid to solve a sinister mystery involving several suddenly comatose patients in Crichton's engrossing mainstream sci-fi thriller.

COMMUNION   (1989) *½

D: Philippe Mora. Christopher Walken, Lindsay Crouse, Frances Sternhagen, Andreas Katsulas, Joel Carlson. 103 mins. (MCEG/Virgin)

If you buy the notion (which many obviously have) that altruistic aliens conveniently showed up to help struggling novelist Whitley Streiber over a writer's block by presenting him with a socko idea for a "nonfiction" best-seller, then you may have a better time with *Communion* than we did. In Mora's film version of Streiber's book—coproduced and scripted by Streiber—our nominal hero, as interpreted (with wavering accent) by Walken, comes across as a terminally narcissistic, self-indulgent, puerile, and generally unappealing jerk. And while the alien episodes described on-screen are dull enough to smack of authenticity, they failed to convince yours truly that they were ever more than fanciful projections of Streiber's own outsized ego. On the plus side, Mora supplies several visually deft moments, and Eric Clapton's moody theme music works well enough. But Streiber's meandering encounters of the self-aggrandizing kind offer little beyond several uninvolving insights re Whit's own none-too-fascinating self.

THE COMPANION (1994) ***

D: Gary Fleder. Kathryn Harrold, Bruce Greenwood, Talia Balsam, Joely Fisher, Brion James, James Karen. 94 mins. (Universal)

In the near future, romance novelist Gillian (Harrold) orders a low-level android named Jeffrey (Greenwood) to accompany her during a rustic writing stint. When Jeffrey suggests she bump up his abilities by linking him to her computer, Gillian not only acquiesces but continues to boost his power until he acquires a mind of his own—which is when our heroine's troubles begin. Something of a cross between *Creation of the Humanoids*, a cybernetic *Collector* (Columbia/TriStar), and *Making Mr. Right* (HBO), *The Companion* avoids becoming purely formulaic by focusing on the believable bond that develops between the initially altruistic android and his at-first skeptical, soon smitten owner. Director Fleder went on to helm the generally insufferable Tarantino-esque turkey *Things to Do in Denver When You're Dead* (Touchstone) and the somewhat better serial-killer thriller *Kiss the Girls* (see index).

CONAN THE BARBARIAN (1982) **

D: John Milius. Arnold Schwarzenegger, Sandahl Bergman, James Earl Jones, Max von Sydow. 129 mins. (Universal) DVD

The pic that put Arnold the Austrian on the relatively big-time movie map: Arnie brings his early anvil acting style and bloodied broadsword to the screen as the celluloid incarnation of Robert E. Howard's pulp hero. Arn returned to Conanland in Richard Fleischer's inferior sequel, *Conan the Destroyer* (Universal), with Wilt Chamberlain and Grace Jones, and contributed a contractual cameo in Fleischer's campy Howard-drawn *Red Sonja* (MGM), where Brigitte Nielsen put the *broad* in *broadsword* by battling a returning Sandahl Bergman.

CONGO (1995) *½

D: Frank Marshall. Dylan Walsh, Laura Linney, Ernie Hudson, Tim Curry, Grant Heston, Joe Don Baker. 109 mins. (Paramount) DVD

Not over-the-top enough to make it as pure pulp, nor sufficiently witty to operate as low camp—and way too lame to work as a straight-ahead adventure—*Congo* emerges as an assembly-line product manufactured by a team of high-ticket hacks, from original author Michael Crichton to slumming scripter John Patrick (*Moonstruck*) Shanley to producer-turned-director Frank (*Arachnophobia*) Marshall. Rather than using actual apes (see Barbet Schroeder's documentary *Koko: A Talking Gorilla* [Warner] to scope out what real gorillas are capable of, quite likely including making better movies than this), Paramount opts for synthetic simians and animatronic apes designed by makeup-FX ace Stan Winston (who performs identical chores for 1999's *Instinct* [Touchstone, DVD]). Our story involves primate-language scientist Walsh, who wants to return his "talking chimp" Amy (the only live authentic

pongid on view) to the wilds of Central Africa, where, as fate and the filmmakers would have it, lies the lost city of Venga, the very spot where workers in the employ of corporate villain Baker located diamonds valuable in developing new laser technology. Perfs here range from bland (Walsh, Linney) to hammy (Curry, sounding like a cross between Bela Lugosi and Pee-wee Herman, and Hudson, sporting an ersatz Brit accent). More incredibly, considering the budget, the production looks inexcusably rushed and shoddy. Sam Raimi superstar Bruce (*Evil Dead*) Campbell wisely makes an ultra-early exit.

CONTACT (1997) **½

D: Robert Zemeckis. Jodie Foster, Matthew McConaughey, James Woods, John Hurt, Tom Skerritt, William Fichtner, David Morse, Angela Bassett, Jake Busey. 150 mins. (Warner) DVD

Drawn from the late Carl Sagan's novel, *Contact* suffers from unaffecting lead characters, pat plot progression in the early stages, and an initial reluctance to cut to the chase. Foster and McConaughey are both vaguely offputting as the maverick skylistener and the New Agey religious pundit, respectively, who will ultimately represent opposing takes on Foster's major discovery—a strong signal sent from space and instructions on how to build a device to transport a single Earth traveler there (shades of *This Island Earth*'s Interociter!). Political infighting first puts Jodie's boss, a conniving, PR-savvy Skerritt, in the driver's seat, but further complications lead to our heroine being singled out to pilot the fabled flight. It's at that late-arriving point that *Contact* really heats up, and Foster's magical, FX-driven journey is, by itself, well worth the price of a rental. *Forrest Gump* (Paramount) auteur Zemeckis's creepy, unauthorized integration of unrelated Bill Clinton clips into his fictional narrative brings us another mindless step closer to entering Huxley's *Brave New World*. Withal, *Contact* is an unwieldy but ultimately worthwhile mix of the thrilling, the thought-provoking, the predictable, and the downright dull (not, we suppose, unlike life itself).

THE CORPORATION   (1996) ***

D: Andrew Stevens. Ian Ziering, Katherine Kelly Lang, Dee Wallace Stone, Andrew Stevens, Marc Riffon, Larry Manetti. 81 mins. (New Horizons)

It's *The Firm* Meets *The Stepford Wives* in actor/auteur Stevens's generally compelling sci-fi-tinged thriller. Interactive-video-game designer wiz Ziering and grad-student spouse (Lang) are lured to Las Vegas, where Ziering accepts a high-paying gig with a sinister corporation. Under evil CEO Stevens's supervision, the company has been stealing duped subjects' sensory responses, "digital-audio reproduction of brain waves," to make their games the video equivalent of *Brave New World*'s famed "feelies." Lang, Ziering, and the latter's slacker-hacker pal (Riffon) gradually uncover the conspiracy. Stone (of *The Howling* fame) gets to show some range as the brainwashed, sexually abused wife of doomed exec Manetti, while Andrew's mom, Stella Stevens, contributes a cameo. The company's "Eroticom" games supply a convenient excuse to insert several gratuitous sex scenes, while Ziering and Lang do the deed at regular intervals sans VR excuses.

THE COSMIC MAN   (1959) B&W ***

D: Herbert Greene. John Carradine, Bruce Bennett, Angela Greene, Paul Langton, Scotty Morrow. 72 mins. (Rhino)

Carradine turns in stellar work as the titular alien, a benign E.T. who beams down to our humble planet in a kind of intergalactic golfball (!) to carry out a minor scientific mission. Physicist Bennett (playing a character obviously inspired by Robert Oppenheimer), local widow Greene, and her wheelchair-bound young son (Morrow) seek to communicate with the mysterious visitor (glimpsed only in negative), while military forces represented by Langton adopt a more suspicious stance. While *The Cosmic Man* lacks high-tech FX, its simple moral message is entertainingly delivered with a minimum of padding.

THE COSMIC MONSTERS   (1958) B&W **1/2

D: Gilbert Gunn. Forrest Tucker, Gaby André, Alec Mango, Martin Benson. 75 mins. (Englewood)

Adapted from the BBC-TV serial *The Strange World of Planet X*, based on René Ray's novel, *Cosmic Monsters* stars a distracted, chain-smoking Tucker as a Yank scientist, part of a Britain-based team whose experiments accidentally perforate the ionosphere, causing an increase in cosmic rays that turn locals loco and insects outsized and aggressive. Tucker, French scientist André (initially the brunt of much blunt sexist banter, excessive even for its unenlightened day), and mysterious Planet X emissary Benson attempt to halt the bugs' attacks on the populace. It's fairly static going in the early reels, but the film picks up with the insects' appearance and incorporates a few genuine shocks, despite the generally shoddy matte FX.

THE CRAWLING EYE   (1958) B&W ***

D: Quentin Lawrence. Forrest Tucker, Janet Munro, Laurence Payne. 85 mins. (Englewood)

The second and better of Tucker's Brit chillers (original companion feature to *Cosmic Monsters*) envisions an invasion of outsized alien eyeballs (!) who emerge from a radioactive cloud to terminate alpine earthlings. Some classic, if low-budget, monster-movie imagery makes the eyeballs' assault worth the wait.

THE CRAZIES   (1973) ***1/2

D: George Romero. Lane Carroll, W. G. McMillan, Harold Wayne Jones, Lloyd Hollar, Lynn Lowry, Richard Liberty. 103 mins. (Anchor Bay)

Romero's *The Crazies* (a.k.a. *Code Name: Trixie*) recycles many *Night of the Living Dead* elements but manages to put a fresh, prescient spin on its superficially similar crazed-citizens-amok story line. When an insanity-inducing virus seeps into the water supply of rural Evans City, Pennsylvania, protective-suited soldiers commandeer the town in a bid to contain the menace. Five survivors, led by ex–Green Beret McMillan, battle confused, trigger-happy GI's and their own advancing dementia, while on-site scientists grope for answers and clueless authorities prove more concerned with concocting eventual cover-up scenarios. *The Crazies* scores as both a straight-ahead, verité-styled terror tale and a lacerating Vietnam-inspired parable that's only gained in power over the ensuing decades.

CREATION OF THE HUMANOIDS (1962) ****

D: Wesley E. Barry. Don Megowan, Erica Elliott, Don Doolittle, Dudley Manlove. 78 mins. (Sinister Cinema)

Part ontological meditation, part then-contempo civil-rights parable (and oft cited as Andy Warhol's avowed fave film), this 1962 postnuke epic pits the Klan-like Order of Flesh and Blood, led by Craigus (B vet Megowan), against a horde of well-meaning, chrome-domed automata (called "clickers" by their bigoted human overseers). When Craigus learns that his own sister is "in rapport" with a clicker named Pax, he vows to home-wreck their happy relationship. At one point, the terminally logical Pax breaks out in a fit of mechanical laughter. "It's the humor circuit," he explains, "it's much harder to control than the pain." Barry's low-key direction, Ted Rich's garish, precocious pop-art sets, and Jay (*The Killer Shrews, Panic in Year Zero!*) Simms's genuinely witty script—to say nothing of Dr. Louis M. Zabner's "special eye effects"—should leave vid viewers with a wry smile too.

CREATURE FROM THE BLACK LAGOON: THE SERIES

CREATURE FROM THE BLACK LAGOON (1954) B&W***

D: Jack Arnold. Richard Carlson, Julie Adams, Richard Denning. 79 mins. (Universal) DVD

Justifiably one of the '50s' most popular misunderstood-monster fables, *Creature* chronicles the femme-starved Gill-Man (played by pro swimmer Ricou Browning underwater and former dancer Ben Chapman topside) and his lethal misadventures among a largely hostile humankind. Originally shown in 3-D, the film spawned two lesser but entertaining sequels—*The Creature Walks Among Us,* with *This Island Earth* duo Jeff Morrow and Rex Reason, and *Revenge of the Creature* (both Universal), starring John Agar—plus a Dave Edmunds rock song.

CRITTERS: THE SERIES

CRITTERS (1986)**

D: Stephen Herek. Dee Wallace Stone, M. Emmet Walsh, Billy "Green" Bush, Scott Grimes, Terence Mann. 86 mins. (Columbia/TriStar)

Critters is a pastiche of shameless lifts not only from *Gremlins, The*

Terminator, and *The Brother from Another Planet* but from such already secondhand sci-fi fare as *Ghoulies* (which itself spawned three sequels, *Ghoulies 2, Ghoulies 3: Ghoulies Go to College,* from Vestron, and *Ghoulies 4,* from Columbia/TriStar). To his credit, director/coscripter Herek manages to shake his artificial ingredients with sufficient energy to bring the proceedings to a watchable level. Followed by three lamer sequels—*Critters 2: The Main Course, Critters 3* (golden boy Leonardo DiCaprio's screen debut), and *Critters 4* (all Columbia/TriStar).

THE CROW: THE SERIES

THE CROW (1994)**1/2

D: Alex Proyas. Brandon Lee, Ernie Hudson, Michael Wincott, David Patrick Kelly, Rochelle Davis, Tony Todd, Bai Ling, Jon Polito. 100 mins. (Buena Vista) DVD

Music-vid vet Proyas's dark, portentous, ponderously downbeat screen translation (coscripted by splatterpunk novelist David J. Schow) of James O'Barr's comic-book creation represents an extreme example of style over substance, with much audiovisual

headbanger Sturm und Drang masking a thin, cliché-saddled, ultimately suspenseless vengeance plot. Grotty echoes of Lee's own accidental on-set shooting death abound in the late star's portrayal of resurrected rocker Eric Draven, who, in one scene, not only bites a fired bullet but swallows it to boot. Perhaps not surprisingly, Lee's tragic demise not only failed to kill *The Crow* but lent the finished film a major publicity boost that helped it net some $50 mil in domestic B.O. revenue alone. The Buena Vista video extends that trend by following the feature with the documentary short *Brandon Lee: The Last Interview.* Among the pic's pluses, Wincott, with his broken-glass voice, lends some flair to his lead-villain role, while the ever reliable Todd makes for a sturdy henchman.

THE CROW: CITY OF ANGELS (1996)*1/2

D: Tim Pope. Vincent Perez, Mia Kirshner, Richard Brooks, Iggy Pop, Vincent Castellanos, Thomas Jane, Thuy Trang, Ian Dury. 86 mins. (Miramax) DVD

This highly regurgitative sequel delivers more portentous boredom drawn from James O'Barr's graphic

---

TONY TODD ON THE DEATH OF BRANDON LEE
As Told to The Phantom

• •

We were working mainly through the nights, so we'd go to work at five-thirty and go past five-thirty in the morning, sometimes till ten-thirty or eleven, night after night after night. And we had a director doing basically his first film, and Brandon trying to duck and dodge any association with his father....To me it was totally a fluke. It was one of those stupid things. There were two guns—one was being used on a second-unit shot; they were under pressure. Somehow the chamber didn't get completely checked. A little piece of wadding got reloaded; then the last thing that went wrong was that instead of aiming off to the side, the gun was aimed at his abdomen. Then another freak thing was that it hit a major artery....It was a tiny, tiny piece of wadding. It was so *odd.*

novel series. Spanish thesp Perez, late of the lively period adventure *Queen Margot* (Miramax), replaces the late Brandon Lee in the nondimensional title role. Best Credit honors go to "Crow Crucifixion Scene Puppet by Animated Engineering." The running time's padded by a 6:13 end-credit crawl. Followed by 1999's direct-to-video *The Crow: Stairway to Heaven* (PolyGram), with Mark Dacascos in the title role.

CUBE (1998) ***

D: Vincenzo Natali. Maurice Dean Wint, David Hewlett, Nicole de Boer, Nicky Guadagno, Andrew Miller. 89 mins. (Trimark) DVD

Sort of a "Six Characters in Search of an Exit," debuting Canadian director Natali's exercise in Pirandellian gore sci-fi finds a half-dozen disparate (and increasingly desperate) citizens inexplicably, inextricably stuck inside an elaborately booby-trapped cube, with no clues about how they got there or how they might get out. The sealed sextet include pragmatic but tightly wound cop Quentin (Wint), recessive teen mathematical genius Leaven (de Boer), paranoid New Agey femme physician Holloway (Guadagno), and Worth (Hewlett), a technician who eventually fesses up to having constructed the mysterious cube's outer shell. Clearly a metaphor for "the System," Natali's *Cube* sometimes lacks the infernal logic and precision of his ingeniously designed, multiroomed set, ultimately degenerating into standard slasher histrionics. (*Cube* probably would have fared better as an hourlong *Twilight Zone* episode.) A solid cast works hard to lend credibility to their roles and their shared, legitimately scary predicament, though, and *Cube* delivers enough shock value and intensity to make it worth a visit. Barely released theatrically, *Cube* went on to become a surprise homevid smash.

DICED AND CUBED: Soon-to-be-sliced victim Julian Richings looks in vain for a way out of Vincenzo Natali's *Cube*.
Courtesy of Trimark Home Video

CYBER TRACKER:
THE SERIES

CYBER TRACKER (1994) **½

D: Richard Pepin. Don "the Dragon" Wilson, Richard Norton, Stacie Foster, John Aprea, Joseph Ruskin, Abby Dalton, Steve Burton, Jim Maniaci. 91 mins. (Imperial) DVD

Homevid kickbox heroes Wilson and Norton find themselves on opposite sides of the law in Pepin's reasonably punchy low-budget *Terminator/RoboCop* clone. Aprea makes for a smooth heavy, while Dalton, though a long way from her *Saga of the Viking Women and Their Journey to the Waters of the Great Sea Serpent* prime, looks almost spookily well preserved (if not always quite *alive*) here. Our fave touch is the Dragon's femme-voiced computer, Agnes, who can be programmed for inebriation (!), supplying our lonely hero with a reliable late-night drinking companion. Followed by *Cyber Tracker 2* (PM). Other available *Cyber* titles include *Cyber Bandits* (Columbia/Tri-Star), *Cyber Ninja* (Fox Lorber), *Cyber Seeker* (Gigo), *Cyberstalker* (Stardance),

Cyber Vengeance, and Fred Olen Ray's *Cyber Zone* (New Horizons).

CYBORG:
THE SERIES

CYBORG (1989)½*

D: Albert Pyun. Jean-Claude Van Damme, Deborah Richter, Vincent Klyn, Alex Daniels, Dayle Haddon. 86 mins. (Cannon) DVD

The Phantom would have bet his last simolean that no auteur could fashion a *Road Warrior* rip-off lamer than Albert Pyun's 1987 yawner *Radioactive Dreams* (Artisan). But *Cyborg*, under the supervision of that selfsame auteur, manages to meet that mighty challenge, with ennui to spare. Van Damme stars as a Mad Max stand-in named Gibson (now, *that's* original!), while Haddon handles the title role of Pearl Prophet, a mechanized miss who hires our high-kicking hero to lead her through your standard low-budget futuristic wasteland. Their ultimate destination is exotic Atlanta (!), where the "world's last doctors" are working on a cure for a rampaging plague that's destroyed most of the planet's populace. Standing in their way is hulking villain Fender Tremolo (Klyn) and his band of head-banger heavies, whose losing battles with a nearly comatose Jean-Claude consume most of this moronic grunt-a-thon's seemingly interminable running time. Followed by the largely lame *Cyborg 2* (Vidmark), with Jack Palance as a villainous hologram. No relation to the startlingly routine *American Cyborg* (Cannon) or the David Bradley snooze-fests *Cyborg Cop* (Trimark) and *Cyborg Soldier* (New Line).

THE CYCLOPS (1957) B&W **

D: Bert I. Gordon. James Craig, Gloria Talbott, Lon Chaney, Jr., Tom Drake. 75 mins. (IVE, n.i.d.)

Mr. B.I.G. strikes again, this time with an enormous one-eyed atomic mutant amok in a back-lot Mexico. Not as good as the same "stretchers 'n' shrinkers" specialist's *Amazing Colossal Man* but a good bet for Talbott fans.

DAMNATION ALLEY (1977) **

D: Jack Smight. George Peppard, Jan-Michael Vincent, Dominique Sanda. 91 mins. (Key, n.i.d.)

Smight's fairly awful adaptation of Roger Zelazny's postnuke novel about five survivors who traverse the American wasteland in an armored van is occasionally abetted by some chilling FX, especially the outsized desert cockroaches.

DARK BREED (1995) ***

D: Richard Pepin. Jack Scalia, Lance LeGault, Donna W. Scott, Robin Curtis, Jonathan Banks. 104 mins. (PM)

PM presents one of its slickest, largest-looking productions with

this engrossing *Alien* variation that mixes extraterrestrial world-conquest plans with government conspiracies and cover-ups, along with the usual PM quota of chases, mass auto wreckage, high-body-count shoot-outs with exotic weaponry, effective gore-and-mutation FX, an obligatory alien-springs-from-an-abdomen scene, an action sequence that lends new meaning to cable (or, more accurately, satellite-dish) surfing, a feminist subtext, *and* a love story.

DARK CITY (1998) **1/2

D: Alex Proyas. Rufus Sewell, Kiefer Sutherland, Jennifer Connelly, William Hurt, Richard O'Brien, Ian Richardson. 100 mins. (Warner) DVD

Alex *(The Crow)* Proyas's *Dark City* features a similar look and many of the same themes as coscripter Lem Dobbs's 1991 *Kafka* (Paramount), directed by Steve *(Out of Sight)* Soderbergh, and yields equally mixed results. Here a race of pale, bald aliens (led by *Rocky Horror Picture Show* alum and cowriter O'Brien) inhabiting dead earthlings plays elaborate mind games with the unwitting populace of the titular metropolis—a city plunged into perpetual night—with the traitorous aid of eccentric renegade scientist Sutherland. Hero Sewell is on to the scheme but seems a hopeless match for the E.T.s' superior brainpower. He eventually enlists the aid of lawman Hurt, who, like Sewell and everyone else in the city, can never be certain of anything, even their own identities and memories. A mix of the intriguing and the unsatisfyingly underrealized, *Dark City* falls far short of attaining *Blade Runner* status but, with its striking designs and superior FX, is worth a look for sci-fi noir fans. No relation to Albert Magnoli's *Dark Planet* (A-Pix, DVD), a decent, if derivative, space-travel tale with Paul Mercurio and Michael York.

DARK STAR (1974) ****

D: John Carpenter. Brian Narelle, Dan O'Bannon, Cal Kuniholm, Dre Pahich. 95 mins. (VCI) DVD

In addition to its other virtues, Carpenter's *Dark Star,* which began life as a USC student project, has to be the best-*looking* $60,000 sci-fi feature ever lensed. This witty, often brilliant satire starts as a *2001* takeoff but swiftly soars into totally original terrain. *Dark Star* is a scout ship whose 20-year mission involves searching out and destroying unstable planets approaching a nova state. Aboard are four crew members (Pahich, Narelle, Kuniholm, and O'Bannon, who also coscripted), the ship's late commander (stashed in a cryogenic tank, where his brain is occasionally activated), a vicious alien "pet" (actually a hyperactive beachball [!] with clawed feet and a voracious appetite), a nagging computer, and a prim, Franklin Pangborn–type voice-equipped thermonuclear device that's just itching to explode. The space jockeys' chief enemy, however, is relentless, overwhelming, utterly stultifying *boredom;* anyone who's ever worked too long in the same office will instantly identify with the crew's comically desperate attempts to alleviate same. *Dark Star* remains Carpenter's most profound celluloid statement.

DARKMAN:
THE SERIES

DARKMAN (1990) ***

D: Sam Raimi. Liam Neeson, Frances McDormand, Colin Friels, Larry Drake, Nelson Mashita. 95 mins. (Universal) DVD

Raimi's original *Darkman* plays like a live-action sci-fi-slanted comic strip blending superhero antics with *Phantom of the Opera*–type elements. (The pic also echoes 1932's *Dr. X* [see index], with its synthetic-skin experiments, and *The Hunchback of Notre*

Dame, when Darkman briefly rests among a group of rooftop gargoyles.) Our story finds scientist Neeson a near-fatal victim of Donald Trump–like real-estate mogul Friels, his brutal enforcer Drake (*L.A. Law, Dr. Giggles*), and a team of gun-wielding goons (Sam's real-life bro' Theodore Raimi among them). After returning as the horribly scarred title hulk, Neeson's Darkman assembles a makeshift lab, where, drawing upon his liquid-skin expertise, he duplicates the faces of his enemies, the better to infiltrate their ranks and wreak gleeful revenge. Our hero's own biodegradable flesh, meanwhile, allows him only short stretches of superficial normality, which he uses to resume his relationship with squeeze McDormand, a lawyer in Friels's employ. Raimi enlivens his otherwise predictable action plot with his patented brand of black humor (e.g., villain Drake's extensive severed-finger collection), wacky violence (including a memorable squished-head scene), and off-the-cuff quips (heroine McDormand to bullying Friels, "If you're not going to kill me, I have things to do."). He also succeeds in exposing the oft infantile rage that roils beneath the avenging Darkman's righteous surface; our unstable hero's severely diminished coping skills are dramatically demonstrated during a hallucinatory carnival sequence that sees him violently abuse a surly game-booth operator who refuses to surrender a fluffy pink elephant (!). Look for frequent Raimi thesp Bruce Campbell and director John Landis in silent split-second cameos.

DARKMAN II: THE RETURN OF DURANT   (1995) ***

D: Bradford May. Arnold Vosloo, Larry Drake, Kim Delaney, Renee O'Connor, Jesse Collins, Lawrence Dane. 92 mins. (Universal) DVD

Arnold (*The Mummy*) Vosloo ably fills Liam Neeson's shoes (and synthetic skin) in May's belated but satisfying follow-up. Our disfigured hero again finds himself up against arch-villain Durant (a returning Drake), who, though seemingly dispatched in the original, resurfaces with a new crew of criminal cronies, his trusty finger-chopping cigar cutter, and a scheme to produce superweapons for sale to a right-wing senator and his skinhead minions. Followed by *Darkman III: Die Darkman Die* (Universal), likewise with Vosloo in the lead.

THE DAY OF THE TRIFFIDS (1963) ***

D: Steve Sekely. Howard Keel, Nicole Maurey, Janette Scott. 95 mins. (Media)

Carnivorous plants from outer space cause an outbreak of mass blindness as they stalk their human prey. Keel and friends frantically work to reverse the situation. Probably the classiest of all killer-plant movies, despite Keel's testy outburst, "What we need is a weed-killer!"

THE DAY THE EARTH CAUGHT FIRE (1961) B&W ***

D: Val Guest. Edward Judd, Janet Munro, Leo McKern. 99 mins. (HBO)

Vet sci-fi helmer Guest crafts a bleak Brit doomsday vision that emphasizes human reactions to an impending catastrophe triggered by nuclear recklessness. Engrossing all the way, with one of the most memorable fade-outs in genre-film history. You'll need a cold one after watching this.

THE DAY THE EARTH STOOD STILL (1951) B&W ***1/2

D: Robert Wise. Michael Rennie, Patricia Neal, Sam Jaffe. 92 mins. (Fox)

Day still stands tall as one of celluloid sci-fidom's early greats. Rennie is an interplanetary peacenik sworn to warn foolhardy earthlings to cease their nuclear follies. His 8-foot robot, Gort, is on hand to supply the metal muscle in one of the McCarthy era's few liberal-minded sci-fi movies. *New York Times* critic Bosley Crowther was less than impressed by Gort, however. Boz wrote in his original review, "We've seen better monsters in theatre audiences on 42nd Street." Which is almost as memorable a remark as "Klaatu barada nikto."

DEAD MAN WALKING (1988) ***

D: Gregory Brown. Wings Hauser, Jeffrey Combs, Brion James, Pamela Ludwig, Sy Richardson. 90 mins. (Republic)

Director Brown, responsible for the over-the-top 1990 mind-control movie *Street Asylum* (see index), also fashioned this earlier, equally depraved effort featuring three of *Asylum's* thesps—James, Richardson, and the ever energetic Hauser as a terminally ill "Zero Man" in the postplague America of 1997. Brown successfully blends subversive satire with well-staged action and a thoroughly degenerate ambience. Hauser and Combs form an entertaining team as the doomed bounty hunter and mild-mannered chauffeur, respectively, out to rescue snatched heiress Ludwig from madman James's demented clutches. Incidental highlights include a Russian-roulette variation played with chainsaws (!), a human-torch nightclub act, and several witty one-liners: e.g., when a gun goes off at the "Cafe Death," Wings casually remarks to Combs, "Don't worry, it's not our table." Brown has enjoyed two other film careers, as soft-core erotic-thriller specialist Gregory Hippolyte (his real moniker) and as cutting-edge hard-core porn auteur Gregory Dark, of "the Dark Brothers" notoriety (e.g., *New Wave Hookers*).

DEADLOCK: THE SERIES

DEADLOCK (1991) ***

D: Lewis Teague. Rutger Hauer, Mimi Rogers, Joan Chen, James Remar, Stephen Tobolowsky, Grand L. Bush. 103 mins. (Fox)

Blood of Heroes teammates Hauer and Chen reunite in a fun, fast-moving, futuristic chase film. *Deadlock* casts a beefy, oddly passive Rut, burdened with an unflattering hairstyle and dorky wardrobe, as an electronics genius/jewel thief incarcerated at the experimental "Camp Holiday" prison after being betrayed (and shot three times) by criminal partners Chen and Remar. Hauer is electronically "wed" (hence the film's TV title, *Wedlock*) to fellow inmate Mimi via a wired neck brace set to explode should they attempt an escape. *Deadlock* offers a deft mix of action, sci-fi, and wit, with Hauer especially effective as a wussed-out victim who braces his faltering spirits by chanting the private mantra, "I'm not gonna get killed today." Chen again impresses as a cheerfully amoral, eccentric killer, while Tobolowsky makes for a memorable villain. *Deadlock* also contains two of the best exploding-head shots seen outside a *Scanners* movie. Followed by *Deadlock 2* (Evergreen), with Esai Morales in the lead.

THE DEADLY MANTIS (1957) B&W **1/2

D: Nathan Juran. Craig Stevens, Alix Talton, William Hopper, Donald Randolph, Pat Conway. 78 mins. (Universal)

Juran's *Them!*-inspired big-bug opus opens as a "Deadly *Dull* Mantis": Several minutes of a "Mr. Radar and You"–styled educational short unspool before our promised prehistoric insect even awakes. (Indeed, antique stock footage abounds here, from grainy scrambling Eskimos to Defense Department scenes of our air force in action.) Our story proper involves an archetypal '50s foursome—the Real Man (fearless officer Stevens, in his pre–*Peter Gunn* days), the Nominal Career Woman Who Secretly Pines for a Real Man (Talton), the Sexless Scientist (Hopper), and the Massive External Threat (the predatory title creature as your basic Commie-menace stand-in). The flick's final scene neatly puts each of our period icons in his, her, and its proper place. A few effective monster-amok sequences add some juice, while the cast emotes with dogged enthusiasm in the face of overwhelming clichés. Far scarier as a social document than as a horror pic, *The Deadly Mantis* makes an ideal warm-up for Joe Dante's *Matinee* (see index).

DEATH MACHINE (1995) **1/2

D: Stephen Norrington. Brad Dourif, Ely Pouget, William Hootkins, John Sharian, Martin McDougall, Andreas Wisniewski. 99 mins. (Trimark) DVD

While weakened by too many in-jokes (one character's named Scott Ridley) and references to (and outright steals from) numerous other genre films, veteran FX ace Stephen (*Aliens, Gorillas in the Mist*) Norrington's *Death Machine* proceeds with sufficient verve and wit to qualify it as a more-than-merely-watchable sci-fi entry. Providing much of the flick's propulsion is a typically over-the-top Dourif, resident deranged dweeb techno-genius at the evil weapons-manufacturing CHAANK Corp. When rumors of CHAANK's more insidious experiments—including the creation of an indestructible cybersoldier (a hook earlier used in the Van Damme vehicle *Universal Soldier*)—leak to the public, three members of the Humanist Alliance resistance movement decide to invade CHAANK's HQ. Their timing proves unfortunate when Dourif, rejected by unrequited love object and CHAANK exec Pouget, picks that moment to unleash his homemade "Warbeast," an ungainly killing machine resembling a stripped-down Terminator. Few other thesps could lend Brad's idiosyncratic conviction to lines like, "You're *making* me kill you for a *stupid* reason!"

DEATH RACE 2000 (1975) ***1/2

D: Paul Bartel. David Carradine, Simone Griffeth, Sylvester Stallone. 80 mins. (New Horizons) DVD

Cult actor/auteur Bartel's promising premise—futuristic car wars, where death-dealing drivers try to rack up pedestrians in a kind of human demolition derby—boasts more than its fair share of clever strokes. One of Sly's more intelligible early roles casts him as tough-guy driver Machine Gun Joe Viterbo. Don't miss! Followed by *Death Sport* (Warner, DVD), with Carradine and Claudia Jennings.

DEATH WARMED UP (1985) ***

D: David Blyth. Gary Day, Michael Hurst, Margaret Umbers, David Letch, Bruno Lawrence. 83 mins. (Vestron)

A longtime late, lamented 42nd Street perennial, *Death Warmed Up* is a fun, perverse, New Wave–style, New Zealand–lensed zombie outing in a *Re-Animator* vein. Day is the loose-screwed Dr. Archer ("Trust me!") Howell, head living-dead doc at the isolated TransCranial Applications hosp. On to his island redoubt come two young couples led by Hurst, whom the bonkers brain surgeon had hypnotized into killing his own parents some seven years before. A prolonged bloody show-down—replete with eye-arresting subterranean motorcycle chases—ensues between the youths and Howell's undead minions.

DEATH WATCH   (1980) **

D: Bertrand Tavernier. Romy Schneider, Harvey Keitel, Harry Dean Stanton, Max von Sydow. 117 mins. (HBO)

Keitel plays a journalist with a camera lens implanted in his brain who, in a nearly disease-free future, records a terminally ill Schneider's final days for a morbid TV audience. Tavernier's downbeat fable loses its focus along the way, ending up as a maudlin soaper rather than a sharp media satire.

DEEP IMPACT   (1998) *½

D: Mimi Leder. Tea Leoni, Morgan Freeman, Robert Duvall, Elijah Wood, Vanessa Redgrave, Maximilian Schell, Denise Crosby. 120 mins. (Paramount) DVD

A thoroughly empty, surprisingly clumsy—considering the credited contributions of hitherto able scripters Bruce Joel (*Jacob's Ladder*) Rubin and Michael (*The Player*) Tolkin—doomsday thriller, *Deep Impact* represents Mimi (daughter of Paul) Leder's second technically adept but otherwise dull epic (see also *The Peacemaker* [Universal/Dreamworks, DVD]). The climactic FX provide the pic with its only plus, but these, while stirring, enjoy relatively brief screen time (certainly compared with the product placements, wherein a certain nutrient drink receives intermittent exposure throughout this long, long film). The filmmakers permit themselves a fleeting in-joke via a Times Square marquee sporting the 1993 title *Fire in the Sky*, briefly glimpsed not once but twice in a pair of NYC cutaways.

DELUGE   (1933) B&W ***

D: Felix E. Feist. Peggy Shannon, Sidney Blackmer, Lois Wilson, Fred Kohler, Edward Van Sloan. Subtitled. 59 mins. (Englewood)

Long thought lost, a print of the granddad of disaster films was discovered by none other than *Famous Monsters of Filmland* founder Forry Ackerman in an Italo film vault in 1981, and it's that Italian-dubbed, English-subtitled edition that Englewood intros to homevid. The tape's running time clocks in at nine minutes less than the film's official length; a viewing suggests that the missing footage hails from the opening reels, since the setup for the solar eclipse that causes worldwide flooding receives exceedingly short shrift. FX ace Ned (*Things to Come*) Mann designed the pic's depiction of the destruction of New York. And while his combo of miniatures and rear-screen projection fail to convey much verisimilitude today, they still pack a surreal power as Gotham landmarks topple, crumble, and tumble on extras fleeing in the foreground. Working from S. Fowler Wright's novel, *Deluge* scripters John Goodrich and Warren B. Duff dispense with the Armageddon elements fairly swiftly, concentrating instead on the disaster's immediate aftermath.

After believing he's lost his wife, Helen (Wilson), and two children in the floods, distraught lawyer Martin (Blackmer, much later of *Rosemary's Baby* fame) hies to the Westchester wilderness, where he lives as a landlocked modern Robinson Crusoe until fetching swim-champ survivor Claire (Shannon) shows up at his makeshift doorstep after escaping the clutches of forest brute Jepson (Kohler). Inexorably, Martin and Helen form (in Kurt Vonnegut's phrase) a "nation of two" while warding off Jepson's gang of armed renegades until civilization gradually returns. *Deluge*'s focus on survival and reconstruction is very much in keeping with its Depression-era zeitgeist. The film carries more time-capsule curio than dramatic value but is well worth watching on that level. Mann's FX, meanwhile, were endlessly recycled in future B flicks and serials.

DEMOLITION MAN   (1993) **½

D: Marco Brambilla. Sylvester Stallone, Wesley Snipes, Sandra Bullock, Nigel Hawthorne, Denis Leary, Rob Schneider, Benjamin Bratt. 115 mins. (Warner) DVD

Demolition Man sees cryogenically iced lawman Sly defrosted in the 21st century to fight already thawed maniac Snipes. Femme cop Bullock lends tremendous appeal to her early, attention-getting role as an enthusiastic student of the previous century's violent culture stranded in a strictly PC society where serious crime is virtually nonexistent and ever-polite, brain-fried citizens mindlessly sing along with the commercial jingles of the distant past. *Demolition Man* rates as an essentially soulless but actionful and fitfully amusing bastardized hybrid of Verhoevian satire and futuristic crunchfest. The basic concept was recycled to far more inventive effect in Mike Myers's comedy *Austin Powers: International Man of Mystery* (see index).

THE DEMOLITIONIST   (1995) **½

D: Robert Kurtzman. Nicole Eggert, Bruce Abbott, Susan Tyrrell, Richard Grieco, Heather Langenkamp, Peter Jason, Tom Savini. 100 mins. (A-Pix) DVD

An initially entertaining, over-the-top distaff *RoboCop* rip-off/spoof, *The Demolitionist*—Eggert's answer to fellow *Baywatch* babe Pamela Anderson Lee's *Barb Wire* (see index)—runs out of comedic fuel long before its black-leather-clad bionic heroine's trusty motorcyle but still supplies enough satiric juice to justify a look. Best here is the opening electrocution scene, where condemned crime czar Grieco turns the tables (or, more accurately, the electric chairs) on warden Reggie (*Phantasm*) Bannister. Tyrrell's in fine form as election-obsessed Mayor Grimbaum, while erstwhile Freddie Krueger prey Langenkamp plays a vapid telejournalist (pardon our redundancy).

DEMON SEED   (1977) ***

D: Donald Cammell. Julie Christie, Fritz Weaver, Gerrit Graham. 97 mins. (MGM)

A horny, power-crazed HAL clone (voiced by Robert Vaughn) has the hots for Christie in this claustrophobic but generally compelling cautionary tale re the dangers of computer rape. Maverick auteur Cammell went on to helm the excellent hallucinatory 1988 thriller *White of the Eye* and 1997's *Wild Side* (Evergreen), before committing suicide shortly after the latter's completion.

DESTINATION MOON   (1950) ***

D: Irving Pichel. John Archer, Warner Anderson, Tom Powers. 91 mins. (Englewood)

P roducer George Pal and coscripter Robert A. (*Stranger in a Strange Land*) Heinlein lend an air of scientific accuracy to this fun tale of man's first lunar landing, the *2001* of its day.

DISTURBING BEHAVIOR
(1998) **¹/₂

D: David Nutter. James Marsden, Katie Holmes, Nick Stahl, Bruce Greenwood, William Sadler, Steven Railsback. 84 mins. (MGM) DVD

D istilled from a rather vast vat of previous mind-control pics—*A Clockwork Orange, Invasion of the Body Snatchers, The Stepford Wives, The Class of 1999, Massacre at Central High, Seconds,* and even the sound-alike *Strange Behavior,* to cite a few—David (*Trancers 5*) Nutter's *Disturbing Behavior* represents at least a semisatisfying crazed-teens B-movie brew. The opening scene sets the tone: A "clean" jock flies into a hormonal rage during a lovers'-lane make-out session that goes

"too far," snapping a "slut's" neck and shooting an intervening deputy. High school rebel Stahl witnesses the incident and an immediate cover-up perpetrated by local top cop Railsback. Stahl voices his suspicions of a wider conspiracy to teen newcomer Marsden, more than hinting that Cradle Bay (actually Vancouver) may not qualify as the "ideal" town it's advertised to be. The school's ruled by the robotic "Blue Ribbon" jocks and their scrubbed squeezes, who spend their spare time grooving to Wayne Newton tunes (!) at the local Yogurt Shoppe. It soon transpires that area parents are voluntarily entrusting their offspring to mad scientist Greenwood and his "weekend enlightenment seminars," and Stahl may be next. *Disturbing Behavior* delivers the genre goods for its targeted teen-horror audience with far less smarm than Robert Rodriguez's *Invasion of the Body Snatchers* variation *The Faculty* (see index), scripted by Kevin Williamson.

DR. CYCLOPS   (1940) ***

D: Ernest Schoedsack. Albert Dekker, Thomas Coley, Janice Logan, Victor Killian, Charles Halton. 76 mins. (Universal)

S choedsack, of *King Kong* fame, fashions a lively pulp update of the cyclops legend in one of the first films to use atomic energy as a destructive scientific hook. Dekker hams it up *con mucho gusto* as a demented scientist who shrinks unwanted guests at his remote South American jungle hideaway. The film is further abetted by its rich Technicolor lensing.

DR. X   (1932) **¹/₂

D: Michael Curtiz. Lionel Atwill, Fay Wray, Lee Tracy, Preston Foster. 77 mins. (MGM)

A weird if uneven mix of effective sci-fi horror, creaky haunted-house doings, and tiresome comic "relief" supplied by nominal hero Tracy

(essentially reprising his wisecracking-reporter role from Broadway's *Front Page*), *Dr. X* is highlighted by elaborate lab sets, Curtiz's deft direction, and an early two-strip Technicolor process. A graphic demonstration of the wonders of "synthetic flesh" supplies a memorable moment, as does young Foster's turn as a demented precursor to *Re-Animator*'s Herbert West. Premier screamer Wray gives her lungs a full airing as the daughter of head doc Atwill.

DONOVAN'S BRAIN   (1953)
B&W ***

D: Felix Feist. Lew Ayres, Gene Evans, Nancy Davis. 85 mins. (MGM)

C urt Siodmak's cerebral story, lensed later both as *The Brain* (Sinister Cinema) and, with a Nostradamus twist, as W. Lee Wilder's unforgettable *Man Without a Body* (n/a), finds scientist Ayres controlled by a dead power-broker's brain. Future First Lady Davis plays the dame in the case.

DRAGONHEART   (1996) **¹/₂

D: Rob Cohen. Dennis Quaid, Sean Connery (voice only), David Thewlis, Pete Postlethwaite, Julie Christie. 103 mins. (Universal) DVD

I n a high-concept career move, *Dragon: The Bruce Lee Story* director Rob Cohen graduates to *Dragon-HEART*, which, if little else, should at least lend resonance to his résumé. A bouncy Quaid, as an itinerant dragon-slayer in tenth-century England, shares screen time with Draco, an impressively executed dragon (voiced by Connery, with little regard for subtlety); the natural foes team up to take on snotty, sadistic sovereign Thewlis (in another largely thankless role—see also *The Island of Dr. Moreau*). *Dragonheart* basically shapes up as *Rodan* Meets *Braveheart* and is intermittently enjoyable on that level. This is another of those lavish "family films" that, like *The Lost World: Jurassic Park* and 1999's *The Mummy* (both Universal), escaped an R rating (it's PG-13) so as not to damage its B.O. potential, despite the presence of copious battleground gore. Filmed in Slovakia, where it possibly could have almost happened.

DREAMSCAPE (1984) ***

D: Joseph Ruben. Dennis Quaid, Max von Sydow, Eddie Albert, Kate Capshaw, Christopher Plummer, David Patrick Kelly. 99 mins. (HBO)

Though marred by occasionally glib treatment, *Dreamscape* posits a fascinating premise. Psychic Quaid enters guilt-plagued President Albert's recurrent postnuke nightmare to save him from paranormal assassin Kelly. The film's surreal centerpiece is an extended nightmare sequence that sees contempo FX techniques applied with uncommon skill and imagination.

DUNE (1984) **1/2

D: David Lynch. Kyle MacLachlan, Francesca Annis, Jose Ferrer, Sting, Max von Sydow. 137 mins. (Universal) DVD

Lynch opted for an "Alan Smithee" credit to disassociate himself from the "long" TV version of his oft incoherent adaptation of Frank Herbert's cult novel. The flick is not without its fans, though.

EARTH VS. THE FLYING SAUCERS (1956) B&W ***

D: Fred F. Sears. Hugh Marlowe, Joan Taylor, Donald Curtis, Morris Ankrum. 82 mins. (Goodtimes)

One of the best of the decade's E.T.-paranoia pics, *Earth* comes complete with the saucer-zapping of Washington, D.C., alien brainwashing, faceless robot hordes on the march, and excellent FX work by Ray Harryhausen. More important, it contains the seeds of Ed Wood's soon-to-be-unleashed *Plan 9 from Outer Space* (see index).

EARTH VS. THE SPIDER (1958) B&W **1/2

D: Bert I. Gordon. Ed Kemmer, June Kenney, Gene Persson, Gene Roth, Sally Fraser. 73 mins. (Columbia/TriStar)

The horrific handiwork of Bert I. ("Mr. B.I.G.") Gordon—who, in typical AIP fashion, manages to work in plugs for his then-recent *Amazing Colossal Man* and *Attack of the Puppet People*—*Earth vs. the Spider* features Kenney and Persson as a wholesome teen couple who run afoul of the titular arachnid. Nice-guy science teacher Ed (*Space Patrol*) Kemmer and local authorities led by Gene (*She Demons*) Roth kill the creature and store its carcass in the high school gym, where it's unwittingly reanimated by a live rock-band rehearsal (!). The rest is a relatively standard monster rampage/rescue effort as our teens find themselves trapped in a local cave (actually Carlsbad Caverns) with the reawakened insect. Gordon incorporates few plot surprises and the superimposed spider is rarely convincing, but there are a couple of surprisingly graphic shock moments.

EDWARD SCISSORHANDS (1990) **

D: Tim Burton. Johnny Depp, Winona Ryder, Dianne Wiest, Anthony Michael Hall, Alan Arkin, Kathy Baker, Vincent Price. 100 mins. (Fox)

Price appears (in a trio of brief flashbacks) as an eccentric elderly inventor who resides in what resembles a gothic theme park overlooking a tacky, color-coordinated planned community, where he creates the title character—an androgynous android played by Depp with sad-eyed unsubtlety—but expires before fitting him with humanoid hands. After happening upon the strange youth, Avon Lady Wiest whisks him down to 'burbtown. With his flair for creative hairstyling and shrub sculpting, Edward is at first treated as a welcome novelty act, and even lusted after by nabe nympho Baker, before a predictable chain of misunderstandings engineered by teen bully Hall lands him on the outs with the locals. Employing a framework reminiscent of Rob Reiner's similarly overrated *The Princess Bride* (Columbia/TriStar), Burton's Christmas fable shapes up as a tame affair padded with lazy, condescending satire that rarely rises above a self-consciously skewed sitcom level. Burton also tosses in some prefab poignancy, via Edward's doomed relationship with teen airhead Ryder, and a contrived *Frankenstein*-styled climax.

ELECTRA (1995) ***

D: Julian Grant. Shannon Tweed, Joe Tab, Sten Erik, Katie Griffin, Lara Daans, Dyanne DiMarco. 85 mins. (New Horizons)

As the New Horizons box explains, "When his leatherclad super agents can't force Billy into giving up his secret [to the art of physical regeneration], Roach recruits Billy's sexy stepmother, Lorna, into his perverse oedipal plan." The Billy in question (Tab) is a superpowered teen whose secret, implanted by his late scientist dad, can only be extracted via intimate sexual contact. When the aforementioned leather-clad killer bimbettes of cybervillain Roach (Erik) fail in their efforts to drain our teen hero of his precious bodily fluids, stepmom Lorna (Tweed) dons her trusty B&D regalia and goes for the gusto. *Electra* rates as one of the first stateside B videos to ooze with Hong Kong genre influences. The flick features everything from semi-nude ninja flips and kung-fu catfights staged in midair to laser-ray battles, cheap virtual-reality FX, and even exploding hamsters (!). For weird plotting, over-the-top thesping, and brain-damaged dialogue galore, *Electra* is tough to beat.

BOAST OF THE MILLENNIUM

"I've got billions of gigs' worth of information, Billy, from the sexual records of Sigmund Freud to the strategic commands of Attila the Hun!"

—*cybervillain Sten Erik,*
Electra

ENEMY MINE   (1985) ***

D: Wolfgang Petersen. Dennis Quaid, Louis Gossett, Jr., Brion James, Richard Marcus, Carolyn McCormick, Bumper Robinson. 108 mins. (Fox)

Despite its occasional static stretches, lapses in logic, and descents into dumb dialogue, Petersen's space opera is an entertaining exercise in high-tech sci-fi pulp. Gossett gives a winning performance as the hermaphroditic Drac Jeriba, an alien fighter pilot downed on a barren asteroid who's forced to cooperate with his similarly stranded human counterpart, Willis Davidge (Quaid). After a period of mutual hostility, the pair forge a survival bond that gradually grows into a genuine friendship. *Enemy Mine* essentially unfolds as a well-crafted B movie (its reputed then-lavish $33 million budget doesn't show on-screen, the Industrial Light and Magic crew's cosmic FX notwithstanding). The alien sets and skyscapes are imaginatively rendered, though, and a run-in with a gang of interplanetary slave-traders (who look more like fugitives from a vintage

Roger Corman biker flick) supplies solid action.

ESCAPE FROM NEW YORK: DIRECTOR'S SPECIAL EDITION (1981) ***

D: John Carpenter. Kurt Russell, Lee Van Cleef, Ernest Borgnine, Donald Pleasence, Harry Dean Stanton, Adrienne Barbeau. 106/133 mins. (total) (Paramount) DVD

Carpenter fashions a bleak but exciting futuristic exercise in Big Apple–phobia that finds tripwired con Russell out to free kidnapped president Pleasence from lowlifes surviving in the sprawling penal colony that is Manhattan 1997. New Line's digitally remastered, letter-boxed version offers previously unseen footage, the original theatrical trailer, and an exclusive interview with auteur Carpenter.

ESCAPE FROM L.A.   (1996) ***

D: John Carpenter. Kurt Russell, Stacy Keach, Steve Buscemi, Peter Fonda, George Corraface, Cliff Robertson, Valeria Golino, A. J. Langer, Pam Grier. 101 mins. (Paramount) DVD

The sequel is set in the wake of a quake-leveled L.A. of A.D. 2013 during a repressive administration headed by fundamentalist president Robertson, who's moved the capital to Lynchburg, Virginia (!) while designating the now water-surrounded City of Angels a dumping ground for "immoral" citizens. (Those so convicted can choose between a life of L.A. savagery or immediate electrocution.) When Robertson's dissident daughter, Utopia (Langer), teams up with self-styled revolutionary Cuervo Jones (Corraface) and makes off with the key to a civilization-ending weapon, government stooges Keach and Forbes force Snake Plissken (Russell) to enter the L.A. jungle, retrieve the device, and terminate Utopia. To ensure his cooperation, the pair inject Snake

with a virus that will prove fatal unless an antidote is administered within ten hours. As is apparent from the above description, *Escape from L.A.* is less a sequel than a transplanted remake of *Escape from New York*. Rife with El Lay and industry in-jokes (along with cryptic references to an "Escape from Cleveland" caper), *Escape* hurtles along at breakneck speed as Snake slithers his way through L.A.'s variegated human vermin. Genre buffs will especially enjoy Carpenter's culty casting: Fonda as an aging surfer waiting for the big tsunami due to crest over Melrose Avenue, the always welcome Grier as a two-fisted transsexual (!), Bruce Campbell as the cosmetology-crazed "Surgeon General of Beverly Hills," Paul Bartel as a congressman, and Robert Carradine as a skinhead. Golino, as a fetching survivor, and the busy Buscemi, as Cuervo's top spy, are likewise in the fast-moving mix. Lavish FX—including the digital destruction of L.A.—help propel the story along without overwhelming it.

EVENT HORIZON   (1997) ***

D: Paul Anderson. Laurence Fishburne, Sam Neill, Kathleen Quinlan, Joely Richardson, Richard T. Jones, Jack Noseworthy, Jason Isaacs, Sean Pertwee. 97 mins. (Paramount) DVD

The year is 2047. A small rescue crew is dispatched to locate the mysteriously vanished exploratory vehicle *Event Horizon*. Much to their eventual dismay, they find it—and that's when all alien hell breaks loose: The E.T.-tampered ship now possesses the ability to conjure horrific hallucinations that force the earthlings to experience their worst fears, and self-destruct in the process. Lifting its central idea from Andrei Tarkovsky's Soviet sci-fi epic *Solaris* (Fox Lorber), *Event Horizon* takes a straight-ahead fright-film approach and largely succeeds on that level.

EXCALIBUR (1981) ***

D: John Boorman. Nicol Williamson, Helen Mirren, Nigel Terry. 141 mins. (Warner) DVD

Boorman translates the Arthurian legends into a crowd-pleasing FX orgy while retaining an effective medieval atmosphere and an often off-beat point of view. A top Brit cast also helps. Superior to *Sword of the Valiant* (MGM), where even the presence of Peter Cushing and Sean Connery can't quite counteract the casting of Miles O'Keeffe as Sir Gawain. *Merlin* (Hallmark), *Merlin and the Sword* (Vestron), and the animated *Sword in the Stone* (Disney) offer further variations. Fantasy-film fans of a medieval bent may also want to try *Ladyhawke* (Warner) and *Labyrinth* (Nelson).

eXistenZ (1999) ***

D: David Cronenberg. Jennifer Jason Leigh, Jude Law, Ian Holm, Willem Dafoe, Don McKellar, Cullum Keith Bennie, Sarah Polley, Christopher Eccleston. 98 mins. (Dimension) DVD

Writer/director Cronenberg returns to his *Videodrome* concerns with this somewhat lighter-veined goof on virtual-reality games. Stripped of the millennial L.A. glitz of Kathryn Bigelow's somewhat similarly themed *Strange Days* (see index) and the puerile excesses of *The Matrix* (Warner, DVD), this low-glam, quintessentially Canadian production opens with a rag-tag group of VR enthusiasts who gather to test "Game Pod Goddess" Leigh's latest creation, the eponymous eXistenZ. The game has barely begun when reality terrorists attempt to assassinate our heroine with the aid of a "gristle gun," a typically icky Cronenberg-ian invention that fires not your conventional bullets but human teeth (!). Or is all this part of the game? (The oft uttered operative on-screen advice here is "Trust no one.") In either case, Leigh flees the scene with VR publicity flack Law. This

being a Cronenberg film, the game pod is not your usual sleek techno device but a living-blob organism that's plugged directly into the player's cortex via an "umby cord" that fits into a "bioport," a synthetic spinal aperture that's literally drilled into the participant's body. When Leigh learns that Law's a "virtual virgin," she takes him to a remote gas station, where pump jockey Dafoe fits the initiate with the necessary artificial orifice. As it happens, however, Dafoe is unmasked as a traitor to the VR cause and has equipped Law with an imperfect implant. Leigh and Law continue their virtual adventures, even as *her* pod turns sickly. As in many of his previous pics (e.g., *Shivers*, *The Fly*), Cronenberg deconstructs nothing less than the human organism, accentuating its multiple appetites, treacheries, and frailties. Trouble is, the game itself isn't much *fun* (which is probably the point—another game's entitled Hit by a Car [!]), with its emphasis on paranoia-driven escapades, with characters frequently inquiring, "Are we still in the game?" Cronenberg's treading water—or, more accurately, viscera—here, but its very themes make *eXistenZ* an extremely video-friendly viewing experience. Frequent Cronenberg composer Howard (*Naked Lunch*) Shore contributes an excellent, subtly ominous score.

THE FACULTY (1998) **

D: Robert Rodriguez. Jordana Brewster, Clea DuVall, Laura Harris, Josh Hartnett, Shawn Hatosy, Elijah Wood, Salma Hayek, Famke Janssen, Piper Laurie, Chris McDonald, Bebe Neuwirth, Robert Patrick, Jon Stewart. 104 mins. (Dimension) DVD

When tiny alien slime critters take over the bodies of several teachers at a local high school, a disparate band of adolescent outsiders seeks to expose and destroy the menace in Rodriguez's dumbed-down, teen-targeted *Invasion of the Body Snatchers* update. Far scarier than the E.T. threat

is the film's view, one shared by numerous other entries in the late-'90s high school movie glut, of its young characters as sour, sarcastic, selfish sitcom brats possessed of scant innocence but vast ignorance. As in *Disturbing Behavior* (see index) and others of its darkly "comic" ilk, parental units are either absent or blindly intrusive without being helpful—basically older, busier, even more insensitive and self-absorbed versions of the teen protags themselves; most teachers and authority figures, likewise largely depicted as sadistic bullies or useless obstacles, see the kids as necessary nuisances at best. Here, as in the *Scream* flicks, the media have replaced family and school as the source of knowledge—though not, as even these kids realize, necessarily trustworthy knowledge. Thus we're again treated to endless references to other films, primarily the above-cited *Body Snatchers*, proffered by the pop-culture-savvy but experience-starved teens. While the postmodern approach worked fairly well in the monster hits *Scream* and *Scream 2*, here *Scream* writer Kevin Williamson, scripting from a story credited to David Wechter and Bruce Kimmel, seems content to recycle what have fast become clichés in a pic that yields few thrills, dark yoks, or true surprises (thought the prolific KNB team supplies some imaginative FX). Late-night telehost Stewart is unexpectedly deft as a science teacher, one of the film's few sympathetic adults, while portly pop-cult cyberguru Harry Knowles (of aintitcool.com fame) cameos as a fellow instructor.

FAHRENHEIT 451 (1966) ***

D: François Truffaut. Julie Christie, Oskar Werner, Anton Diffring. 111 mins. (Universal) DVD

Truffaut's adaptation of Ray Bradbury's vision of a future dystopia where books are banned and literacy is illegal makes for deliberately paced but ultimately rewarding viewing.

THE FANTASTIC PLANET (1973) ***

D: Rene Laloux. Animated. Subtitled. 84 mins. (Anchor Bay) DVD

Laloux's adventure, coscripted by fellow illustrator Roland Topor from the Stefan Wul novel *Oms en Serie,* chronicles the conflicts that arise between the "Traags," a dominant race of physical and intellectual alien giants, and the diminutive, oppressed, human-like "Oms." In Laloux's futuristic world, "tame" Oms are adopted as pets for Traag children, while their "wild" counterparts are cruelly hunted and killed. When a juvenile Om dubbed "Terr" escapes from his Traag masters, the act sets in motion a series of incidents that ultimately turns the tide in the tiny Oms' favor. Laloux's charming, satiric, and profoundly eerie antiwar parable unfolds against a colorful, richly rendered alienoid landscape, while his core moral message remains as eternal as it is universal. *The Fantastic Planet*'s restored, subtitled edition enjoyed a select 1999 theatrical release.

FANTASTIC VOYAGE (1966) ***

D: Richard Fleischer. Raquel Welch, Stephen Boyd, Edmond O'Brien, Donald Pleasence. 100 mins. (Fox)

Raquel and pals shrink and swim through an endangered VIP's bloodstream in what remains one of genredom's unlikeliest story lines. What's even more amazing is the fact that, abetted by imaginative FX, it actually works.

FIEND WITHOUT A FACE (1958) B&W ***

D: Arthur Crabtree. Marshall Thompson, Kim Parker, Terence Kilburn. 74 mins. (Republic)

One of the era's better brainsucker quickies, *Fiend* features Thompson as an earnest hero out to foil floating, cerebrum-starved intruders. Not as hot as the same year's *The Brain from Planet Arous* (Englewood) but close enough.

THE FIFTH ELEMENT (1997) **

D: Luc Besson. Bruce Willis, Gary Oldman, Milla Jovovich, Chris Tucker, Luke Perry, Brion James. 125 mins. (Columbia/TriStar) DVD

In prepublicity for this bloated summer-'97 "blockbuster," director Luc *(The Professional)* Besson stated that he'd had the plot and look of *The Fifth Element* festering in his brain since age 13, and after catching this jejune exercise in comic cosmic overkill, we believe him. Willis, clad in a variety of futuristic T-shirts, is an airborne NYC cabbie whose life changes forever when femme "messiah" Milla crashes into his conveyence. In a hook established in the pic's effective 1914 Egypt-set prologue (shades of *Stargate*), the otherworldly Milla is supposed to know the whereabouts of a set of mystical stones that will enable their owner to rule the universe. Villain Oldman, in a Hitler-ian 'do and lisping Southern accent, is determined to get his greedy hands on same. *The Fifth Element* begins unraveling in earnest once our principal players—joined by irritating media motormouth/drag personality Tucker, as sort of a high-decibel postmillennial Oprah-cum-RuPaul—relocate to an elaborate resort planet. Impressive sets, costumes, alien designs, and scattered amusing moments aren't enough to salvage this ultimately wayward flight.

THE FINAL COUNTDOWN (1980) **1/2

D: Don Taylor. Kirk Douglas, Martin Sheen, Katharine Ross. 104 mins. (Vestron)

While this time-warp adventure sometimes plays like a bloated *Twilight Zone* episode, good performances and a '50s-style earnestness transform a potentially ludicrous fable about a nuke carrier whirled back to 1941 Pearl Harbor into fairly diverting sci-fi fare.

FIRE IN THE SKY (1993) **1/2

D: Robert Lieberman. D. B. Sweeney, Robert Patrick, James Garner, Craig Sheffer, Henry Thomas, Peter Berg. 107 mins. (Paramount)

Based on a "true" incident, this alien-abduction tale dramatizes the traumas of five lumberjacks who see a flying saucer flatten their friend Travis (Sweeney) near Snowflake, Arizona. Suspicion—in the accusatory form of state investigator Garner—falls on the five survivors, especially Travis's best bud, Patrick, and surly drifter Sheffer. Unnecessary flashbacks, dull exposition, and bogus stabs at suspense prevent *Fire* from ever catching same, though the pic's payoff sequence makes the trip worthwhile: Travis's gross encounter with the aliens boasts a legit nightmare quality as our hapless human captive undergoes terrifying medical treatments. No relation to the made-for-TV movie of the same title (n/a).

FIST OF THE NORTH STAR (1991) **

D: Toyoo Ashida. Animated. 100 mins. (Streamline Pictures) DVD

Adapted from a graphic-novel series by artist Tetsuo Hara and writer Barunson, *Fist of the North Star* is an animated postapocalyptic splatterfest in a sub-*Akira* vein. The plot follows martial artist Ken, a devotee of the "North Star" school of combat, through a series of superviolent encounters with various *Road Warrior*–esque rivals, including reps of the "Southern Cross" fighting style. An ecology-minded subplot, tied to young femme Lynn, charts the progress of the first flower to bloom in the postnuke wasteland. *Fist*'s chief appeal lies in its often spectacularly rendered martial arts showdowns, complete with bone breakings, head crushings, and blood and gore galore. On the downside, *Fist* sports a comic-book story line that's at once simplistic, convoluted, and deeply rooted in Japanese mystic martial arts arcana. The American release also suffers from generally uninspired, one-note dubbing, though late thesp Jeff Corey deftly handles his vocal chores as venerable teacher Ryuken.

FIST OF THE NORTH STAR (1995) **½

D: Tony Randel. Gary Daniels, Costas Mandylor, Chris Penn, Malcolm McDowell, Melvin Van Peebles, Downtown Julie Brown, Isako Washio, Clint Howard, Tracey Walter. 90 mins. (BMG) DVD

The *Hellbound: Hellraiser 2* team of director Tony Randel and scripter Peter Atkins does a decent job of translating the feel of the original *anime* feature to live action, adding welcome horror elements and atmospheric visuals. Reluctant hero Daniels comes to the aid of a Paradise Valley populace oppressed by Mandylor's brutal hordes in a water-depleted future. Martial arts action of the bursting-bladders and exploding-heads schools dominate, and devotees of the genre should enjoy.

FLASH GORDON (1980) **½

D: Mike Hodges. Sam J. Jones, Melody Anderson, Max von Sydow. 111 mins. (Universal) DVD

This lighthearted revamp of the comic-strip cliffhanger wisely declines to play its recycled material straight, and the results are fairly entertaining. The original Buster Crabbe–starred serials are also available—*Flash Gordon* (also in a shortened, feature-length version titled *Flash Gordon: Rocketship*), *Flash Gordon's Trip to Mars,* and *Flash Gordon Conquers*

the Universe (Questar)—along with Crabbe's *Buck Rogers* (UAV). Also out are two volumes of the 1950s teleseries *Flash Gordon* and the animated *Flash Gordon: Marooned on Mongo: The Animated Movie* (Artisan). Eight volumes of the *Buck Rogers* TV series are also on tape, along with episodes of the later series *Buck Rogers in the 25th Century* (Universal).

FLATLINERS (1990) ***

D: Joel Schumacher. Kiefer Sutherland, Kevin Bacon, Julia Roberts, William Baldwin, Oliver Platt. 111 mins. (Columbia/TriStar) DVD

Sort of a science-based variation on *Carnival of Souls,* *Flatliners* focuses on five med-school students, led by Sutherland, who dabble in temporary, self-induced death in order to (a) unlock the secrets of the afterlife, (b) score a segment on *60 Minutes,* and (c) "upstage the [expletive deleted] baby boomers" (no wimpy LSD trips for this crowd!). Director Schumacher successfully avoids stock shocks and cheap laughs here, steering the flick into authentically surreal primal-fear terrortory as our flatliners are forced to confront specters from their pasts, who subject them to hallucinatory guilt trips of horrific proportions. Schumacher's penchant for stylized rock-vid gothic visuals supports and intensifies his essentially serious story line. He also gets good perfs from his ensemble cast—an ambitious Sutherland, compassionate Bacon, repressed Roberts, womanizing Baldwin, and voyeuristic Platt—who, in the spirit of collegiate competition, strive to see who can stay dead the longest. While *Flatliners* isn't quite a movie to die for—the film spends too much time dealing with Kiefer's karmic debt, squanders several ripe fright opportunities, and treats the death trips themselves a bit too lightly—the film emerges as a rare contempo example of entertaining moral sci-fi.

THE FLY: THE SERIES

THE FLY (1958) ***

D: Kurt Neumann. Vincent Price, David Hedison, Patricia Owens. 94 mins. (Key)

Neumann's original is no match for the Cronenberg remake but still rates as superior '50s sci-fright fare, with that unforgettable transformation scene ("Help meeee…") that even Cronenberg didn't try to top. As scientist Hedison at one point remarks, "It would almost be funny, if life weren't so sacred!" Followed by 1959's mediocre *Return of the Fly* (Fox) and 1965's *Curse of the Fly* (n/a).

THE FLY (1986) ***½

D: David Cronenberg. Jeff Goldblum, Geena Davis, John Getz, Joy Boushel. 100 mins. (Fox)

While creatively changing characters and locales, Cronenberg manages to stick to the first *Fly's* essence. Goldblum is excellent as benignly awkward scientist Seth Brundle, who drunkenly spills the secret of his teleportation machine to journalist Davis. It's also after downing too much champagne that Seth decides to take his premature and ultimately disastrous teleportation trip. (Moral: If you drink, don't teleport.) What transpires after that is well worth seeing for yourself. Suffice it to say that Cronenberg succeeds in fashioning a *Fly* that's by turns funny, poignant, repulsive, and intense. As he's done before and since, D.C. plunges us into some pretty primal territory, exploiting deep-seated fears of illness, aging, and other bodily treacheries; Seth's gradual transformation is like unto Shakespeare's famed seven stages of man, reduced to maybe two or three stages and not limited to man. We've gotta hand it to him (Cronenberg, not Shakespeare)—it's not every filmmaker who can work out his rawest phobias on-screen and entertain the rest of us in the process. FX-ace-turned-director Chris Walas fails to recapture the magic in 1989's *The Fly II* (Fox); despite some vivid gore and makeup effects, that *Fly*'s buzz (actually more of a *Godzilla*-esque roar) proved worse than its sting.

FORBIDDEN PLANET (1956) ***1/2

D: Fred McLeod Wilcox. Walter Pidgeon, Anne Francis, Leslie Nielsen, Warren Stevens, Jack Kelly. 98 mins. (MGM) DVD

An exotic Francis, a serious Nielsen, a winning Robby the Robot, spectacular sets, original Krell music, and Pidgeon's rampaging id add up to a sci-fi classic, loosely based on Shakespeare's *The Tempest.* Available in a remastered, letter-boxed edition.

FORBIDDEN QUEST (1992) B&W ***

D: Peter Delpeut. Joseph O'Connor, Roy Ward. 75 mins. (Kino)

For this lyrical exercise in icy whimsy, Dutch filmmaker/archivist Delpeut reedits authentic turn-of-the-century polar-expedition footage (from more than a dozen different journeys and sources) to form a new fictional narrative. In 1941 a documentarian (Ward, heard but never seen) discovers a lone survivor (O'Connor) of a doomed 1905 Antarctic expedition, whom he interviews in his Ireland cottage. Delpeut cuts between the found footage and his interviewee's often colorful verbal account of the tragic voyage. Much of the footage, of roughly 1905–1913 vintage, is fascinating in its own right, as the medium's earliest verité pioneers capture hitherto unseen sights, ranging from shipboard routines to encounters with Eskimos to the bleak beauty of the polar terrain itself. Delpeut likewise assembled the equally evocative silent-film montage *Lyrical Nitrate* (Kino).

FORTRESS (1993) ***

D: Stuart Gordon. Christopher Lambert, Loryn Locklin, Kurtwood Smith, Tom Towles, Jeffrey Combs, Lincoln Kilpatrick, Vernon Wells. 91 mins. (Trimark) DVD

With *Fortress*, cult auteur Stuart (*Re-Animator*) Gordon crafts a high-tech prison pic with darkly comic undertones, sort of a macho version of *The Handmaid's Tale* (see index). Lambert and Locklin violate the law of our future fascistic land when the latter becomes pregnant with her second child. Both husband and wife are tossed into separate sectors of the same titular lockup, 30 stories of subterranean hell monitored by warden Smith and talking scanning devices headed by Zed-10 (voiced by Gordon's real-life actress wife, Carolyn Purdy-Gordon). Lambert must cope not only with hostile cell mates Towles and Wells but with laser bars, dream-detection devices, virtual-reality torture machines, and a personal "intestinator," an anti-escape intestinal implant capable of inducing everything from transient pain to instant obliteration. Locklin, meanwhile, becomes the involuntary object of prison director Smith's voyeuristic lusts. Director Gordon goes against the genre grain here: While most dystopian films are dark and loud, *Fortress* is bright, both visually and mentally, and relatively low on the decibel meter. Gordon doesn't stint on gimmickry or gore, but the emphasis is ultimately on the story's human rather

Filmmakers in Focus!

STUART GORDON: THE FORCE BEHIND *FORTRESS*

As Told to The Phantom

PHANTOM: **Could you tell us about the genesis of *Fortress*?**

GORDON: **It was a script that originally had been written for Arnold Schwarzenegger, but Arnold decided not to do it. Fox put it into turn-around, and it was picked up by an Australian company called Village Roadshow. They decided to do it with a much smaller budget and contacted me because of my background in low-budget films. I came in and had some ideas about the script. The main character, Brennick, was written like Arnold, so you didn't have to worry about him at all. It seemed important to me that this guy be much more an everyman, so the audience could relate to him and put themselves in his shoes, going to this incredibly horrific prison. A little bit later I got a call from Christopher Lambert saying he had read the script and would I be interested in talking about him starring in the movie. That idea really appealed to me a great deal.**

PHANTOM: **Lambert doesn't come off as a superman.**

GORDON: **He's a wonderful actor. A lot of these leading-men types, especially the action stars, do not want to portray themselves being afraid. They think it's gonna make them look weak. Whereas Lambert realizes that being a hero is doing something even though you *are* afraid.**

PHANTOM: **Loryn Locklin's character also depends on her wiles.**

GORDON: **We did not want another damsel in distress. In the original, she was not in prison with her husband. The whole thing about the babies was something that was added after I got onboard. Originally, I think his crime was he had broken a robot. To me it was important, the idea of a husband**

(continued)

and wife working to save each other. It gave the film a lot of heart, and a romantic quality.

PHANTOM: What kind of shooting schedule did you have?

GORDON: Forty-five days. Lambert had gone to the Cannes Film Festival and came back with money to make the movie. It was one of those things where we had to have the film finished within a year. From that point on, it was like a race. Because of all the special effects and everything that had to be built and designed, preparation was very, very quick. We got the go-ahead in June and started shooting the beginning of October. Normally a movie like this would have six months to a year's preparation.

PHANTOM: The fortress itself is pretty complex.

GORDON: What we did before we started, we visited some of the new prisons that have been built in California. We modeled the fortress after a super-maximum-security prison in Northern California called Pelican Bay, where they send the worst two percent of the prison population. It's brand-new, very futuristic-looking, with a lot of electronic-surveillance equipment—one of the scariest places I've ever been. We had to sign a release saying that we understood that if we were taken hostage, they would not try to rescue us. We had to wear stabproof vests. Then they told us, "They always go for your eyes anyway" [!].

As it turns out, it was one of the safest places I've ever been. You start feeling sorry for them after about five minutes. They keep them in their cells for about twenty-two and a half hours every day. It really is a place where they kind of break them down. And it's very quiet. Most prisons are very noisy places, but there you can hear a pin drop. There's less interaction between the guards and the prisoners and more reliance on electronics, computers, and so forth. So we just kind of took that to its logical conclusion, with one person running the whole prison. [The actors] interviewed a lot of prisoners. Lambert was actually locked in a cell for a while.

PHANTOM: Was the idea of the intestinator in the original script?

GORDON: No, that was something that was added. Again, all of the technology in the movie is based on reality. They do have things like this—tracking devices on prisoners' wrists, which don't emit pain, but if they attempt to escape, a loud-pitched noise registers on their equipment. You find out when you research that the weirdest stuff you can dream up actually exists.

PHANTOM: What about the fortress itself?

GORDON: In actuality, there are supposed to be eleven cell blocks stacked on top of each other. We built one, which was four stories tall. It was the largest set ever built in Australia.

PHANTOM: It also supplies a lot of stunt opportunities.

GORDON: Both Christopher and Vernon [Wells] did their own stunt work, almost entirely. The only time Lambert and I got into a fight was when he got angry with me when I didn't want him to stand in front of that truck in the end with the flamethrower when it was coming at him. We shot that scene very early on. I said to Chris, "It's going to be very hard for me to finish the movie if you get run over by a truck." Eventually we compromised—the stunt guy did the first take, and he did the second take. And the second take was the one we ended up using.

than techno elements, touching on themes earlier explored in such kindred celluloid spirits as *Blade Runner* and the ever visionary *Creation of the Humanoids* (see index). Lambert brings vulnerability to his role, while Smith is excellent as the emotionally conflicted, artificially "enhanced" warden. While *Fortress* obviously lacks the budget of a *Terminator 2* or *Total Recall*, the movie more than compensates with wit, suspense, and Gordon's trademark subversive stamp.

4D MAN (1959) ***

D: Irwin S. Yeaworth, Jr. Robert Lansing, Lee Meriwether, James Congdon. 85 mins. (New World)

The Blob director Yeaworth assembles a solid low-budget sci-fi thriller about scientist Lansing, whose matter-transposing experiments enable him to walk through walls. In promos for the original film, producer Jack H. Harris offered a million bucks to any moviegoers who could prove they could duplicate Lansing's feat. Many broken bones undoubtedly ensued, but as far as we know, Harris held on to the jack.

FREEJACK (1992) **

D: Geoff Murphy. Emilio Estevez, Mick Jagger, Anthony Hopkins, Rene Russo, David Johanssen, Jonathan Banks, Amanda Plummer, Esai Morales. 108 mins. (Warner)

Lots of A stars, elaborate action, and high-tech FX service a strictly B script in *Freejack*. The title refers to racer Estevez, who's transported from an imminently fatal crash into the year 2009, where his brain-erased body will house the mind of a newly dead VIP via an "electronic transplant." The crafty Emilio escapes freejack hunter Jagger's instant-lobotomy ray (!), and the film-long chase is on. Emilio's mad dash through an ozone-depleted future NYC reunites him with squeeze Russo, now a high-powered exec at Hopkins's McCandless Corp. (which, we're informed, "owns everything"). Emilio also encounters foulmouthed, shotgun-wielding nun Plummer, veteran screen sadist Banks, and ex-partner Johanssen. Clichés and logical lapses abound, though we do learn that *vino* hasn't been around since "the ten-year depression." (Talk about your no-wine situations.)

FROM BEYOND   (1986) ***

D: Stuart Gordon. Jeffrey Combs, Barbara Crampton, Ted Sorel, Ken Foree, Carolyn Purdy-Gordon. 85 mins. (Vestron, n.i.d.)

Director/coscripter Gordon's second H. P. Lovecraft–based outing toplines *Re-Animator* alum Combs as Dr. Crawford Tillinghast, victim of perverted pineal-gland experiments perpetrated by mad medico Dr. Pretorius (Sorel). Crampton again costars, this time as the svelte blond shrink who—along with cop Foree—battles slimy, ill-tempered fourth-dimension demons conjured by Pretorius's sinister "Resonator." While it lacks some of *Re-Animator*'s sheer shock value, *From Beyond* packs plenty of punch in its own right, mixing elements of the original *Alien, The Tingler,* and even *The Brainiac* with typically twisted Lovecraft-ian lunacy and the director's own wild style.

FUTURE FORCE   (1989) ***

D: David A. Prior. David Carradine, Anna Rapagna, Robert Tessier, Dawn Wildsmith, William Zipp. 84 mins. (AIP)

"You have committed a crime. You are presumed guilty until proven innocent. You have the right to die. If you choose to relinquish that right, you will be placed under arrest and imprisoned." So recites future bounty hunter Carradine in this lively, low-budget *RoboCop* rip-off. As in *Robo-Cop,* an American city entrusts its law-enforcement operations to a civilian corporation's hired mercenaries. Corruption in the latter's ranks causes top cop Carradine to split from the group, making him and nosy newsperson Rapagna the targets of a violent film-long chase. Despite the pic's paltry production values—the budget allows for only one high-tech element, a laser-shooting mechanical hand (sort of a "RoboGlove") that D.C. makes frequent use of—director Prior's bizarre action tableaux, Carradine's casual thesping, and the script's sly satire make *Future Force* a fun outing. It also marks late Native American actor Tessier's final film appearance. No relation to *Future Fear* (New Horizons) or *Futuresport* (Columbia/TriStar).

FUTURE SHOCK   (1993) **1/2

D: Francis "Oley" Sassone, Matt Reeves, Eric Parkinson. Bill Paxton, Vivian Schilling, Martin Kove, Scott Thompson, Brion James, Sam Clay, Sydney Lassick, James Karen. In PG-13 and unrated editions. 97 mins. (Hemdale, n.i.d.)

A wildly uneven anthology loosely linked by shrink Kove's fear-confrontation therapy sessions, *Future Shock* shifts radically in tone and quality from episode to episode. (It may also hold the distinction of being the first vid issued in unrated and PG-13 editions.) A precredits, virtual-reality-themed lab sequence (cut from the PG-13 version)—wherein coldhearted scientists, abetted by former *Playboy* Playmate and Andy Sidaris regular Julie Strain, fry a dim-witted volunteer subject's brain—is played for splatstick humor. The initial episode (directed, like the prologue, by Parkinson) is written by and stars Schilling (who performed identical tasks for the promising 1991 fright indie *Soultaker* [AIP]) as a phobic lass left home alone by businessman hubby James. After she catches a few *Return of the Living Dead* clips on TV, a chance encounter with Lassick's dog propels Viv into a vivid wolfpack-attack fantasy. Paxton shows up as a roommate from hell in Episode 2, where he's typically strong as the mega-obnoxious tenant of wimpy morgue attendant Thompson (of *Kids in the Hall* fame). Best of the bunch is Episode 3, another tale of phobias run amok, written and directed by Reeves, who opts for a subtler and ultimately funnier approach to a life-after-death story line.

FUTUREWORLD: SEE WESTWORLD: THE SERIES

THE GAMMA PEOPLE   (1956) B&W **1/2

D: John Gilling. Paul Douglas, Eva Bartok, Leslie Phillips. 79 mins. (Goodtimes)

The offbeat tone and cast manage to transform this Poverty Row polemic about Commie brainwashers and their zombie-making machinery into a fairly engrossing item. The lumbering, middle-aged Douglas makes for an unusual '50s sci-fi hero.

GATTACA   (1997) ***

D: Andrew Niccol. Ethan Hawke, Uma Thurman, Alan Arkin, Jude Law, Loren Dean, Ernest Borgnine, Gore Vidal. 112 mins. (Columbia/TriStar) DVD

Refreshingly free of contempo "attitude," future *Truman Show* (Paramount) scripter Niccol's earnest meditation on the nature of personal identity and destiny proved too quiet a genre film to make much of a big-screen splash. A futuristic story sporting the look and feel of a quality midbudget '60s/'70s sci-fi film (e.g., *Charly* [Fox], *Logan's Run* [MGM]), *Gattaca* stars Hawke as a self-styled "degenerate," a mere mortal in a high-tech world in which only genetically engineered humans (like his own younger brother) are geared for success. It's "genoist" victim Hawkes's all-consuming obsession to transcend his societally imposed limitations and qualify for an exploratory trip to a distant planet with the Gattaca Aerospace Corporation; that assignment remains a possibility only so long as he can perpetrate an elaborate hoax by switching identities with vanished genetic superior Law (a willing participant in the scheme) and escape the authorities' ever vigilant notice. While thinner in theme, texture, and satirical thrust than its obvious literary model, Aldous Huxley's increasingly prophetic 1932 novel, *Brave New World* (itself translated into a disappointing 1998 USA Network telemovie [n/a]), *Gattaca* boasts low-key intensity, shaded perfs, and cool, clean set designs (a concert performed by a 12-fingered pianist supplies another neat touch) that make it a modest winner, especially for speculative-cinema fans who don't list giant alien insects as a nonnegotiable viewing requirement. Look for octogenarian Ernest Borgnine and writer Gore Vidal in supporting roles.

GHOST IN THE MACHINE (1993) **¹/₂

D: Rachel Talalay. Karen Allen, Chris Mulkey, Will Horneff, Ted Marcoux. 93 mins. (Fox)

Combining elements of *The Lawnmower Man, Pulse,* and *Shocker,* Talalay's *Ghost* sees the evil soul of computer wiz/serial killer Marcoux infiltrate a far-reaching database, whence the fiend torments intended victim Allen by killing her boss, her dog, and her credit rating. Karen's initially surly teen-hacker son, Horneff, and outlaw techno genius Mulkey team up to battle the rampaging cyberpsycho. *Ghost* offers its share of effective (if predictable) jolts, further bolstered by lots of flashy computer-generated FX.

GHOST IN THE SHELL (1995) ***

D: Mamoru Oshii. Animated. Dubbed. 81 mins. (Manga Entertainment) DVD

Boasting the biggest budget ever afforded an *animé* feature—a record previously held by the pioneering *Akira* (see index)—Oshii's *Ghost* supplies a sensory feast of dizzying high-tech imagery and exotic music. Drawn from cyberpunk artist Masamune Shirow's manga of the same name, *Ghost in the Shell* unfolds in 2029, when an Asian bloc headed by Japan dominates a post–World War III and IV world. Semicybernetic femme agent and "ghost hacker" Kusanagi heads a security team searching for an ace computer terrorist known only as "Puppet Master," a mysterious "virtual entity" created by a rival agency. The nature of personal identity gradually emerges as *Ghost's* primary theme. When Puppet Master, like the talking thermonuclear device in John Carpenter's *Dark Star,* decides that it's an independent life form unto itself, one "born in a sea of information," it demands both political asylum and a physical body. The Puppet Master's pronouncements lead heroine Kusanagi to question the nature of her own identity. Ontological explorations aside, most of *Ghost* is given over to actionful battles between the competing security agencies, along with elaborately animated virtual-reality displays and visual odes to Kusanagi's flawlessly sculpted, frequently naked cyberbody. While the uninitiated may deem the English-dubbed *Ghost's* arcane intrigues difficult to follow at times, the film's sheer visual and aural dazzle more than compensate for the plot complications.

YOUR OFFICIAL GODZILLA CHECKLIST
(in chronological order)

* *

Gigantis, the Fire Monster (a.k.a. *Godzilla Raids Again*) (1959, Goodtimes)

King Kong vs. Godzilla (1962, Goodtimes)

Godzilla vs. Mothra (1964, Simitar) DVD

Godzilla vs. Monster Zero (1965, Simitar) DVD

Ghidrah, the Three-Headed Monster (1965, Anchor Bay)

Godzilla vs. the Sea Monster (1966, DVT)

Son of Godzilla (1968, Anchor Bay)

Destroy All Monsters (1968, A.D. Vision)

Godzilla's Revenge (1969, Simitar) DVD

Godzilla vs. Gigan (1971, Anchor Bay)

Godzilla vs. the Smog Monster (1972, Orion)

Godzilla vs. Megalon (1973, Anchor Bay)

Godzilla vs. Mechagodzilla (a.k.a. *Godzilla vs. the Cosmic Monster*) (1974, Anchor Bay)

Terror of Mechagodzilla (1975, Simitar) DVD

Godzilla 1985 (1985, Anchor Bay)

Godzilla vs. Biollante (1989, HBO)

Godzilla vs. King Ghidora (1991, Columbia/TriStar)

Godzilla vs. Mothra (a.k.a. *Godzilla and Mothra: The Battle for Earth*) (1992, Columbia/TriStar)

Godzilla vs. Space Godzilla (1994, Columbia/TriStar)

Godzilla vs. Destoroyah (1995, Columbia/TriStar)

GLEN AND RANDA (1971)***

D: Jim McBride. Steven Curry, Shelley Plimpton, Gary Goodrow. 94 mins. (VCI)

A generally unsung indie sci-fi fable about postnuke nomads, this early effort by Jim (*The Big Easy, Blood Ties*) McBride is a perverse, mostly effective mix of earnestness and satire. High points include the wanderers' decelerated rendition of the Stones' "Time Is on My Side" (learned from an antique phonograph in need of new batteries) and Goodrow's turn as the Magician, the last "civilized" man. Occasional descents into pretentiousness constitute the flick's only major flaw.

GODZILLA, KING OF THE MONSTERS (A.K.A. *GOJIRA*) (1956) B&W ***

D: Inishiro Honda. Raymond Burr, Takashi Shimura. 80 mins. (Paramount) DVD

Though Burr's American-lensed inserts as an intrepid reporter cheapen it a mite, Honda's original B&W *Godzilla*, unlike many of the sequels and the soulless 1998 Hollywood remake (Columbia/TriStar, DVD), is a serious-minded sci-fi fable about nuclear energy run amok.

GREYSTOKE: THE LEGEND OF TARZAN, LORD OF THE APES (1984) ***

D: Hugh Hudson. Christopher Lambert, Ralph Richardson, Andie MacDowell, Ian Holm. 130 mins. (Warner)

Hugh (*Chariots of Fire*) Hudson crafts a superior *Tarzan* remake, featuring fine supporting work by actual chimps and their costumed human stand-ins. Richardson's not bad either as the jungle wildman's doddering grandfather, while Lambert, in the title role, lends conviction to his struggles to conform to Scottish upper-crust customs, and Rick Baker earns kudos for his

---

GODZILLA CONFIDENTIAL!
EVERYTHING YOU ALWAYS WANTED TO KNOW ABOUT THE BIG G BUT WERE (UNDERSTANDABLY) AFRAID TO ASK

BY ANY OTHER NAME DEPARTMENT

The working title for the original 1954 *Godzilla* was the decidedly less catchy *Big Monster from 20,000 Miles Beneath the Sea,* an obvious lift from Toho Studios' immediate American monster-movie model (and international box-office hit), 1953's *Beast from 20,000 Fathoms.* The ultimate Japanese title, *Gojira,* is a combination of *gorilla* and *kujira* (Japanese for "whale").

GELTZILLA

Production costs on the original *Godzilla* ran to approximately 60 million yen (roughly $900,000 in Yankee dollars), three times the cost of the average Japanese movie and nearly twice as much as Akira Kurosawa's critically acclaimed *The Seven Samurai.* The film earned some 152 million yen during its initial domestic run.

GODZILLA, AMERICAN STYLE

The dubbed, reedited 1956 American version, *Godzilla, King of the Monsters,* also proved a monster hit in Japan, where it played under the title *Monster King Godzilla.* Besides Raymond Burr, other American thesps to appear in Japanese *kaiju eiga* ("monster movies") include the late Nick Adams (*Monster Zero*), Myron Healey (*Varan, the Unbelievable*), and Russ Tamblyn (*War of the Gargantuas*).

THE MAN IN THE GRAY RUBBER SUIT

Stuntmen Katsumi Tezuka and Haruo Nakajima took turns inside Toho's rubber Godzilla suit (which, contrary to popular belief, was painted charcoal gray, not green) in the original B&W production. Something of a Method stuntman, Nakajima prepped for his "suitmation" role by studying bear behavior at a local zoo; he won the unenviable job of donning the dinosaur armor for an additional 11 Godzilla features, through 1971's *Godzilla vs. Gigan,* and also put in screen time as fellow Toho monsters Mothra and Rodan.

MORE ROAR THAN YOUR AVERAGE 'SAUR

According to David Kalat, author of the definitive and highly recommended Big G tome *A Critical History and Filmography of Toho's Godzilla Series* (McFarland & Co.), classical composer Akira Ifukube, who wrote many Godzilla scores, created the monster star's distinctive roar "by rubbing a leather glove across a contrabass and applying an echo to that recording."

TAKEI'S TACKY START

Future *Star Trek*ker George (Mr. Sulu) Takei received his first showbiz break as the sole Japanese-American on the otherwise all-Anglo dubbing crew for *Gigantis* and later *Godzilla* imports, joining such voice-over vets as Daws (Yogi Bear) Butler and Paul (Boris Badenov) Frees, both of whom supplied the voices for several different Japanese characters within the same film.

(continued)

excellent ape-makeup effects. Tarzan fans can also find Edgar Rice Burroughs's celebrated apeman in the original Elmo Lincoln silents *Tarzan of the Apes* and *The Adventures of Tarzan* (Grapevine Video), Johnny Weissmuller–starred *Tarzan the Apeman, Tarzan and His Mate, Tarzan Escapes, Tarzan Finds a Son, Tarzan's New York Adventure,* and *Tarzan's Secret Treasure* (all MGM); *Tarzan the Fearless* with Buster Crabbe, *Tarzan's Revenge* with Glen Morris, *Tarzan and the Green Goddess* with Bruce (Herman Brix) Bennett, and *Tarzan and the Trappers* with Gordon Scott (all Sinister Cinema); John and Bo Derek's legendary *Tarzan, the Ape Man* (MGM) with Miles O'Keeffe, along with the mostly silent 15-chapter 1929 serial, *Tarzan the Tiger* (Facets), and the 1998 dud *Tarzan and the Lost City* (Warner, DVD).

THE H-MAN   (1958) ***

D: Inoshiro Honda. Kenji Shara, Yumi Shirakowa, Akihiko Hirata. 79 mins. (Columbia/TriStar)

Japanese monster-movie specialist Honda helms a weird sci-fi noir, lensed in color with strong FX, involving a peripatetic pool of toxic liquid bent on dissolving Tokyo residents. Other worthwhile vintage Japanese sci-fi efforts that don't rely on Godzilla and gang include Honda's Yeti adventure *Half Human* (Rhino), *The Human Vapor* (Prism), and Hajaime Sato's compellingly bizarre *Body Snatcher from Hell* (Sinister Cinema).

HABITAT   (1996) ***

D: Rene Daalder. Alice Krige, Balthazar Getty, Tchecky Kayro, Laura Harris, Kenneth Welsh, Brad Austin. 103 mins. (A-Pix) DVD

After a two-decade directorial hiatus, cinematographer Daalder, who helmed the oft imitated 1976 cult fave *Massacre at Central High* (see index), returns with another twisted high school fable, this one with bizarre Cronenbergian overtones. Set "Sometime in the Near Future," after the ozone layer has been drastically depleted, *Habitat* stars young Getty as a sensitive transfer student plagued by school bully Austin and boxing coach Welsh, and smitten by the latter's daughter (Harris). If our hero's school situation rates as strained, his home life is downright *strange.* Getty's scientist dad (Kayro) has already transmuted himself into a floating stream of yellow-and-green atoms (!), while his house, with the approval of New Agey, econut mom (Krige), is turning into a mini–rain forest, complete with overflowing killer vegetation. Scripter/director Daalder's offbeat sci-fi-thriller-cum-social-parable loses a bit of its focus via a last-reel descent into carnivorous flora-and-fauna attack motifs, but this U.S., French-Canadian, and Dutch coproduction definitely sports a tone and ambience all its own.

THE HANDMAID'S TALE   (1990) ***

D: Volker Schlondorff. Natasha Richardson, Robert Duvall, Faye Dunaway, Aidan Quinn, Elizabeth McGovern, Victoria Tennant, Traci Lind. 109 mins. (HBO)

Sort of a thinking woman's *The Stepford Wives,* Schlondorff's adaptation of Margaret Atwood's sci-fi allegory takes a bleakly witty peek into a war-torn, sexist, fundamentalist future USA (rechristened the Republic of Gilead), a nation so polluted that all but 1 percent of its female population has been rendered sterile. Richardson finds herself among the "fortunate" few, so instead of being classified as "livestock" (!), she gets to serve as the surrogate wife of right-wing security chief Duvall, a situation that's not always to the liking of his barren spouse (Dunaway). Also in the picture are secretly dissident guard Quinn, lesbian rebel McGovern (in a fine, feisty turn) and brainwasher/wicked-warden stand-in Tennant. Much of Harold Pinter's script plays like a superior chicks-in-chains flick, one of many reasons why *The Handmaid's Tale* is not to be missed, whether you're a mister or a ms.

THE HARVEST   (1992) **

D: David Marconi. Miguel Ferrer, Leilani Sarelle, Harvey Fierstein, Henry Silva, John Anthony Denison, Tim Thomerson, Matt Clark. 97 mins. (Columbia/TriStar)

Sort of a *Brain Dead* variation, only with kidneys subbing for brains, *The Harvest* stars Ferrer as a blocked, Prozac-taking screenwriter who, at strident agent Fierstein's urging, holes up in a mythical Central American country in a desperate bid to get a grip on his elusive script. Ferrer is later beaten by unidentified thugs and wakes up minus a kidney—a sacrifice to the international organs black market—but with a great hook for his stalled screenplay. *The Harvest* ambitiously bleeds reality with fantasy but does so at such a torpid pace that The Phantom's attention span vanished nearly as quickly as Miguel's kidney.

HEAVY METAL   (1981) ***

D: Gerald Potterton. Animated. Based on original art and stories by Richard Corben, Angus McKie, Dan O'Bannon, Thomas

Warkentin, Berni Wrightston. Voices: Jackie Burroughs, John Candy, Joe Flaherty, Eugene Levy, Alice Playten, Harold Ramis, John Vernon, Zal Yanovsky. Featuring songs by Black Sabbath, Blue Oyster Cult, Cheap Trick, Devo, Donald Fagen, Don Felder, Grand Funk Railroad, Sammy Hagar, Journey, Nazareth, Stevie Nicks, Riggs & Trust. 90 mins. (Columbia/TriStar) DVD

With *animé*'s rising popularity, the animated anthology *Heavy Metal* seems more in the zeitgeist today than it did during its initial release nearly two decades ago. In the intervening years, Potterton's headbanger hit has acquired a multigenerational youth-cult following. In our current era of MTV-fostered cultural simultaneity—where almost no rock-'n'-roll fashion ever goes *completely* out of style—even *Heavy Metal*'s digitally remastered music tracks, featuring such sonic giants as Black Sabbath, Blue Oyster Cult, Devo, and Grand Funk Railroad, sound less old than eternal. *Heavy Metal*'s testosterone-fueled fantasies—exotic erotic interludes showcasing buxom space sirens and sweeping scenes of violent cosmic combat consume much of the running time—likewise remain as timeless as ever. The anthology's disparate stories are linked, à la *2001*'s floating Monolith, by a peripatetic green meteorite—dubbed "the Loch-nar" and containing (we're told) "the sum of all evils"—that alights in different eras and places to cast its destructive spell. *Heavy Metal*'s aggressive antics should score with nostalgia buffs, *animé* fans, and antsy adolescents of all ages. Ralph Bakshi's 1981 animated cult musical, *American Pop* (Columbia/TriStar), is also available.

HELL COMES TO FROGTOWN (1988) **½

D: Donald G. Jackson. Roddy Piper, Sandahl Bergman, Rory Calhoun, William Smith. 88 mins. (New World, Starmaker)

The brains behind *Demon Lover* (Unicorn), *Roller Blade* (New

World), *Roller Blade Warriors: Taken by Force* (Raedon), and *The Rollerblade Seven* (York) hits his creative zenith with the imaginatively titled *Hell Comes to Frogtown*. Hell is Sam Hell (Piper), a potent male selected by the femme powers-that-be (headed by Bergman) to help repopulate a barren postapocalyptic America. But first he must rescue a gaggle of gals held captive at the title site: a dangerous redoubt ruled by one King Toady and his race of mutant frog-people (!). Aiding Rowdy Roddy in his quest is ex-action stalwart Calhoun; opposing him is fave B-movie bad guy Smith. Followed by *Return to Frog Town* (York) and *Toad Warriors*.

THE HELLSTROM CHRONICLE (1971) **½

D: Walon Green. Lawrence Pressman, Lots of Bugs. 90 mins. (Columbia/TriStar)

Paranoiac entomologist Dr. Hellstrom (Pressman) hosts what's essentially a nature documentary on the wide world of insects. A surprise "head-movie" hit in its day and a precursor of 1996's more balletic bug study *Microcosmos* (Buena Vista), the film managed to cop an Oscar for Best Feature Documentary.

HERCULES   (1959) **

D: Pietro Francisci. Steve Reeves, Sylvia Koscina, Fabrizio Mioni. 107 mins. (VidAmerica, Moore Video)

The Italo flick that launched a thousand sword-and-sandal cheapies and sent hordes of acting hopefuls knuckle-running to the nearest gym retains an impressive fan base today. Reeves's less-than-vaunted thespian rep gains in value on video, at least compared with Lou Ferrigno's interpretation of the role in *Hercules* and *Hercules 2* (MGM), to say nothing of Arnold Schwarzenegger's early stab at the part in *Hercules in New York* (see index).

VidAmerica issued the uncut versions of both *Hercules* and *Hercules Unchained*. Insatiable Steve addicts can also catch their hero in *Athena, Goliath and the Barbarians* (MGM); *The Avenger, The Giant of Marathon, Last Glory of Troy* (Sinister Cinema); *Last Days of Pompeii* (Goodtimes); *Morgan the Pirate, Thief of Baghdad* (Embassy); and *Pirates of the Seven Seas* (Lightning). Sinister Cinema and Something Weird Video both carry a wide selection of sword-and-sandal titles, including the immortal Jayne Mansfield/Mickey Hargitay matchup *Loves of Hercules*. Episodes from the Kevin Sorbo *Hercules* TV series and spin-offs are also available (Universal, DVD).

HERCULES IN THE HAUNTED WORLD   (1961) **½

D: Mario Bava. Reg Park, Christopher Lee, Leonora Ruffo. 83 mins. (Sinister Cinema)

Gothic-horror master Bava lends some eerily surreal touches that help hoist this Herc entry well above the level of most of its cardboard competition. And while Reg Park may be no Steve Reeves, Christopher Lee *is* Christopher Lee.

THE HIDDEN   (1987) ***

D: Jack Sholder. Michael Nouri, Kyle MacLachlan, Ed O'Ross, Clu Gulager, Claudia Christian, William Boyett. 98 mins. (Anchor Bay)

Sholder's *The Hidden* recycles elements from such varied sources as *Lethal Weapon, The Terminator, Night of the Creeps, The Brain from Planet Arous,* and even comicdom's *J'onn J'onzz, Martian Manhunter,* yet manages to emerge as an entertaining (and itself since-much-imitated) sci-fi actioner with an eccentric tone all its own. Our story involves ace LAPD dick Nouri, spacey "FBI agent" MacLach-

lan, and their mutual search for a series of random maniacs partial to loud music and fast Ferraris and who enjoy stealing and killing to get their hands on same. (Sounds like your typical Hollywood personality profile to us.) As it quickly turns out, the assorted psychos—who include a fat guy with gastritis, a zaftig stripper, and a dog (!)—are merely serving as the hosts for your basic amoral alien slime-creature who uses them till their bodies give out, then moves on to his next victim, relay-race-style. Lending texture to this lively filmlong chase—which features a prolonged police massacre to rival *The Terminator, The Hitcher,* and *Ninja 3: The Domination* (MGM)—is the gradual bond that develops between human cop Nouri and his cosmic counterpart, MacLachlan (though they never get as seriously involved as a couple as *Lethal Weapon's* Danny Glover and Mel Gibson). Avoid the dull 1993 sequel, *The Hidden 2* (New Line).

HIGHLANDER:
THE SERIES

HIGHLANDER   (1986) *

D: Russell Mulcahy. Christopher Lambert, Roxanne Hart, Sean Connery, Clancy Brown. 111 mins. (HBO) DVD

One thing you can't accuse Mulcahy's *Highlander* of is typecasting. This mindless but hugely popular heavy-metal sword-and-sorcery saga and pioneer in the "duh, whatever" school of filmmaking stars French thesp Lambert as Connor McLeod, a remarkably spry 568-year-old Scotsman posing as an American antiques dealer. Connor understandably owns one of the oddest accents ever heard on-screen. (As a member of New York's Finest pithily puts it, "You talk funny!") But it's no odder than the one sported by costar Connery, a Scot cast here as Connor's Yoda-like Spanish-Egyptian (!) mentor, Ramirez. Seems that Chris and Sean are

fellow Immortals—mysterious warriors destined to spend their lengthy, even interminable, lives decapitating others of their ilk. (Why? you ask. Well, Chris puts that very query to Sean as the latter instructs him in the tricks of their arcane trade. "Who knows?" comes Sean's reasoned reply.) While *Highlander* lifts liberally from *The Terminator, Conan, The Empire Strikes Back, Rocky,* and *Chariots of Fire,* our fave moment is its touching *Elvira Madigan* steal: Sean and Chris's slo-mo sylvan romp is almost worth the price of a rental. Sean and Chris reunite in Mulcahy's *Highlander 2: The Quickening* and the "alternative" edition *Highlander 2: The Renegade Version* (both Republic, DVD), a director's cut featuring an additional 19 minutes of footage. *Highlander: The Final Dimension* in an "Exclusive Director's Cut with Steamy New Scenes" (Touchstone, DVD), *Highlander: The Gathering,* a feature culled from episodes of the popular teleseries, and individual TV episodes are also available (both Republic).

HOLOGRAM MAN   (1995) ***

D: Richard Pepin. Joe Lara, Evan Lurie, William Sanderson, Michael Nouri, Arabella Holzbog, Tiny "Zeus" Lister, Jr., John Amos, Joseph Campanella, Nicholas Worth. 96 mins. (PM)

Taking its cue from *Demolition Man,* with additional steals from *Robocop* and *Speed, Hologram Man* casts younger, taller Stallone clone Lurie—who also receives story, coscreenplay, and associate-producer credits—as Slash Gallagher, a self-styled revolutionary whose merry band has been busily reducing the police population of a near-future Los Angeles. À la *Robocop's* Detroit, the city's now run by a ruthless corporation (CAL Corp.), headed by Nouri, and encased in a transparent "biodome" necessitated by a depleted ozone layer. When dedicated cop Lara takes Lurie alive, the latter is electronically "reduced" to hologram status and sealed in a computerized chamber. Five years later corrupt computer op Sanderson uses Lurie's token parole hearing to sabotage the system, free the homicidal hologram, and set the stage for another 80 or so minutes of abrupt and senseless high-tech violence. *Hologram Man* shakes and bakes its lifted riffs into a satisfying sci-fi/action mix.

HUMANOIDS FROM THE DEEP (1997) ***

D: Jeff Yonis. Robert Carradine, Emma Samms, Mark Rolston, Justin Walker, Danielle Weeks, Clint Howard, Kaz Garas, Bert Remsen. 84 mins. (New Horizons)

The busy Roger Corman Celluloid Recycling Plant spits out a winner with Yonis's crowd-pleasing remake of Barbara (*Bury Me an Angel*) Peeters's 1980 killer-fish fable, *Humanoids from the Deep* (Warner, DVD). After an opening decapitation tableau, the scene shifts to small-town Harbor Shores, where young protesters monitor the illicit activities of local "Rogeman Pharmaceuticals" polluters led by Rolston. Ex-*Nerd* series regular Robert (Youngest Son of John) Carradine is allied with the polluters (though he openly disapproves of their tactics), causing domestic friction with daughter Weeks. When several locals turn into bloody fishbait, scientist Samms clues Carradine to the dread secret behind the savage slayings—five crazed mutant "amphibious soldiers" created by a military experiment gone awry. The genetic fiends are devouring local males but temporarily sparing the lives of their female captives, the better to impregnate them and spawn a new litter of monsters. Capably acted and swiftly paced, *Humanoids* amply delivers the gory goods, from *Jaws*-like subaqueous slaughterfests to *Alien*-styled birthing scenes.

HYPER SPACE (1989/1997) **1/2

D: David Huey. Richard Norton, Lynn-Holly Johnson, Don Stroud, Ron O'Neal, James Van Patten, Rebecca Cruz. 90 mins. (Screen Pix)

In *Hyper Space,* originally titled *Black Forest: Rage in Space* and sporting a 1989 copyright, six crewmembers aboard a nuclear-waste-disposal ship awake to discover their computer's malfunctioned; fuel levels are so low, a return trip to Earth will now take 22 years. One lucky crewperson can shave that travel time by two decades by going solo in an attached escape shuttle. Former *Superfly* O'Neal wins that honor but gets his guts eaten by his own ornery alien pet (!) prior to takeoff. Sneaky captain Van Patten, rough-trade android Stroud, and pilot Cruz fight to take O'Neal's place, while hero Norton and computer programmer (and ex–*Ice Castles* ingenue/Sonja Henie for the '70s) Johnson try in vain to maintain order. Director Huey and scripter Robert Dominguez wring a fair amount of suspense from their character-driven exercise in sci-fi minimalism. Wrestlers Big John Studd and Professor Toru Tanaka cameo as belligerent androids in a couple of largely pointless flashbacks.

I COME IN PEACE (1990) **

D: Craig R. Baxley. Dolph Lundgren, Brian Benben, Betsy Brantley, Matthias Hues. 93 mins. (Media, n.i.d.)

The ultimate "high"-concept movie, *I Come in Peace* exposes the threat posed by killer drug-dealers from outer space (!). As soon as humongous heavy-metal alien Hues crash-lands in Houston, he gets right down to business, ripping off a heroin stash from a yuppie crime syndicate called "the White Boys" and zapping the opposition with CD-shaped, throat-slitting boomerang devices. Our galactic lowlife proceeds to force-feed unwary earthlings with the stolen smack, the better to build up

their endorphins, which he then violently extracts from their brains for resale back on his home turf. In pursuit of the evil E.T. are maverick beefcake cop Lundgren and his straitlaced FBI partner (a pre–*Dream On* Benben). The on-screen participants are in no way abetted by a leaden, cliché-laden script ("Bring the space gun and we're outta here!") but some high-energy action set pieces and unintentional laughs raise *ICIP*'s entertainment level a mite.

I MARRIED A MONSTER FROM OUTER SPACE (1958) B&W ***1/2

D: Gene Fowler, Jr. Tom Tryon, Gloria Talbott, Ken Lynch. 78 mins. (Paramount)

Fowler's faintly homophobic horror tale centers on ugly aliens who commandeer earthmen's bodies and turn them from their wives. Future best-selling novelist Tom (*The Other*) Tryon stars as the distracted honeymooner who wantonly neglects spouse Talbott. Ex-wrestler Slapsy Maxie Rosenbloom is a suspicious barkeep at the roadhouse where our E.T. boys hang. Compelling all the way. Remade as a surprisingly deft 1999 TV movie (Paramount).

ICEMAN (1984) ***1/2

D: Fred Schepisi. Timothy Hutton, John Lone, Lindsay Crouse, Josef Sommer, David Straithairn. 101 mins. (Universal)

Iceman is an excellent, original, often moving story about a revivified 40,000-year-old Eskimo at the mercy of a modern American scientific team. John (*The Last Emperor*) Lone is tops as the titular Neanderthal whose attempts to make sense of his puzzling predicament prompt him to undertake a personal religious quest. The film is further abetted by a haunting score (including Lone and sympathetic scientist Hutton's unique a cappella rendition of Neil Young's "Heart of Gold") and Aussie auteur Schepisi's sure-handed direction.

IDAHO TRANSFER   (1971) ***

D: Peter Fonda. Kelley Bonham, Keith Carradine, Kevin Hearst, Caroline Hildebrand. 90 mins. (MPI, n.i.d.)

Idaho Transfer is a minimalist ecological allegory offering a novel story line and skillful, if economy-minded, execution. The title refers to a secret time machine that transports a group of youthful volunteers (including Carradine, the only experienced thesp among an otherwise nonprofessional but capable cast) 56 years into a resource-depleted future. The precise nature of the planet's corroded condition is hinted at rather than explicitly explained, until an ironic punch line drives the movie's message home. While occasionally too taciturn and understated, *Idaho Transfer* is well worth scoping out. The vid version comes complete with a new intro, wherein auteur Fonda delivers a brief account of the film's aims and troubled history.

IMPULSE: THE COLLECTOR'S EDITION   (1984) ***

D: Graham Baker. Tim Matheson, Meg Tilly, Hume Cronyn. 95 mins. (Anchor Bay) DVD

Toxic waste in the local milk supply makes hitherto normal townsfolk misbehave on a grand scale—like killing local kids—in a pic that doesn't fully exploit its promising premise but provides enough honestly perverse tableaux to qualify as worthwhile offbeat sci-fright fare. Anchor Bay presents the film in a remastered wide-screen edition. No relation to the 1974 William Shatner sleazefest (see index) or the 1990 Theresa Russell thriller of the same name (Warner).

THE INCREDIBLE SHRINKING MAN (1957) B&W ****

D: Jack Arnold. Grant Williams, Randy Stuart, April Kent. 81 mins. (Universal)

One of the best sci-fi fables ever lensed, Arnold's tale (scripted by frequent *Twilight Zone* contributor Richard Matheson) of the titular atomic mutant's (Williams) gradual descent into being and nothingness fully retains its irony and power. Williams turns in ace work, particularly during his 4-foot phase, when he rejects his unwanted celebrity status, runs away from his "normal" wife and home, and takes up with a female circus midget (!). Grant's troubles *really* begin when his once manageable cat attacks him and escalate when he's forced to battle a "giant" spider over a moldy morsel of rat-trap cheese. A cogent comment on the plight of the "little man" in an increasingly technocratic world and a haunting take on the human condition itself, *The Incredible Shrinking Man* is brilliant all the way.

INDEPENDENCE DAY   (1996) **1/2

D: Roland Emmerich. Will Smith, Bill Pullman, Jeff Goldblum, Mary McDonnell, Judd Hirsch, Margaret Colin, Randy Quaid, Robert Loggia, James Rebhorn, Harvey Fierstein, Harry Connick, Jr. 145 mins. (Fox)

Independence Day earned its status as *the* cinematic thrill ride of summer '96 with its deft bonding of honestly adrenalizing alien-battle FX with a shamelessly populist plot, utterly free of postmodern touches or even basic irony, that recalls both the patriotic sci-fi flicks of the '50s (specifically *War of the Worlds*) and the page-turning, heart-palping sci-fi pulp mags of yore. Add TV-miniseries-styled soapy subplots and you have a mass crowd-pleaser that covers all the bases. Having the U.S. president (Pullman) portrayed as an ex–Gulf War air ace who leads a polyglot squadron of ragtag fighter pilots (including appealing

crackpot crop-duster Quaid) culled from the planet's alien-decimated ranks represents a stroke of pure pulp genius. While more a marketing triumph than a classic genre film, *Independence Day* registered big-time with national auds, and it's easy to see why.

THE INDESTRUCTIBLE MAN (1956) B&W **1/2

D: Jack Pollexfen. Lon Chaney, Jr., Marian Carr, Casey Adams (Max Showalter). (Goodtimes, Sinister Cinema) DVD

Chaney is an electrically revived killer, sort of an updated, down-and-out version of his *Man Made Monster* character, who embarks on a low-budget, high-voltage vengeance spree in a simpleminded but oddly compelling artifact from the 1950s' Poverty Row ranks.

THE INVADER   (1997) **1/2

D: Mark Rosman. Sean Young, Ben Cross, Daniel Baldwin, Nick Mancuso. 97 mins. (Artisan)

A New Agey variation on *The Terminator*, Rosman's made-for-cable *The Invader* stars Young as a hitherto infertile Washington State schoolteacher whose life changes dramatically when she's kissed and instantly impregnated (!) by mysterious title stranger Cross, whose own embattled species teeters on the brink of extinction. The odd couple is relentlessly pursued by evil extraterrestrial Mancuso, posing as an earthbound bounty hunter on Ben's trail, and Sean's own state-trooper ex-beau, played by one of the dorkier Baldwin brothers (Daniel). While the premise may be less than fresh, Rosman (who also scripted) and his sympathetic leads imbue the tale with enough human (and alien) emotion to lend a considerable degree of unexpected texture. No relation to 1991's *Invader* (Trimark).

INVADERS FROM MARS
(1953) ***1/2

D: William Cameron Menzies. Arthur Franz,
Jimmy Hunt, Helena Carter. 78 mins.
(Englewood) DVD

Martian Commie creeps commandeer the brains of local authority
figures, suck unsuspecting citizens into
the sandpits, and otherwise terrorize
embattled youngster Hunt in Menzies's
wonderfully febrile paranoid parable
from the darkest heart of the McCarthy
era. Tobe Hooper and crew fail to
recapture the magic in the farcical 1986
revamp, *Invaders from Mars* (Media,
DVD), despite memorable turns by
Louise Fletcher, as a dictatorial teacher
fond of munching on live frogs, and
James Karen, who eschews the frogs but
chews the scenery as a gung-ho general
("Marines have no qualms about killing
Martians!").

INVASION OF THE BEE GIRLS
(1973) ***

D: Denis Sanders. William Smith, Victoria
Vetri, Cliff Osmond, Anitra Ford. 85 mins.
(MGM)

Insectoid women in housewife guise
sap guys of their precious bodily fluids and lives alike as part of an alien plot.
Big Bill Smith investigates. It's as good
as it sounds, due to Nicholas (*The Seven
Percent Solution*) Meyer's witty script,
which sends up the Swingin' '70s.

INVASION OF THE BODY
SNATCHERS (1956) B&W ****

D: Don Siegel. Kevin McCarthy, Dana Wynter,
Carolyn Jones. 80 mins. (Republic) DVD

The ultimate McCarthy-esque Com-
mie-menace-as-sci-fi movie, based
on the Jack Finney novella, can also be
seen as an anticonformity exercise *and*
comes equipped with a more existential
self-versus-other subtext as pods from
outer space replicate our friends and

neighbors, recasting them as bland,
brainwashed slaves. Hero McCarthy's
desperate cry of "They're here already!"
will echo forever through the halls of
celluloid history. Philip Kaufman's 1978
remake (MGM, DVD) retains the original's basic story line while satirizing
'70s New Age trends. See also Abel
Ferrara's *Body Snatchers* (below).

BODY SNATCHERS (1994) ***

D: Abel Ferrara. Gabrielle Anwar, Billy Wirth,
Meg Tilly, Terry Kinney, Forest Whitaker,
R. Lee Ermey, Christine Elise, Reilly Murphy.
87 mins. (Warner) DVD

While freely lifting from both Don
Siegel's original and Philip
Kaufman's remake, Ferrara eschews
the former's Commie-fear approach
and the latter's New Age spoofery.
Instead, the confrontational filmmaker
and scripter Nicholas St. John hone the
tale down to its quintessential universal

nightmare elements, delivering a jolting, no-frills fright flick that's closer in
spirit to George Romero's *Living Dead*
exercises than it is to the earlier *Snatchers*. Ferrara's version focuses on already
alienated teen Anwar, who's forced to
deal with a new stepmother (Tilly) and
little brother (Murphy) while living on a
faceless Southeastern military base. In
one of the flick's scariest scenes, Anwar
is warned of impending danger by a
crazed soldier hiding in a lightless gas-
station rest room. The sense of menace
mounts when medical officer Whitaker,
in a brief but vivid perf, nervously
expresses his still-vague fears about the
soldiers' behavioral changes to Anwar's
EPA-worker dad (Kinney). When the
pods begin striking closer to home, they
do so sans the marginal rationality that
informed the first two films. The imper-
sonal nature of the pods' assault intensifies *Body*'s nightmare quality. The
literally explosive ending is in keeping
with the movie's military theme. Fer-

Filmmakers in Focus!

READY, WILLING AND ABEL
ABEL FERRARA ON *BODY SNATCHERS*

As Told to The Phantom

PHANTOM: **Several people received script or story credits on *Body Snatchers*,
including Larry Cohen, Stuart Gordon, and Dennis Paoli. What was the
film's genesis?**

FERRARA: They had the typical process going. When I decided to make it, I just
tossed what they had and Nicky [longtime collaborator Nicholas St. John]
wrote it.

PHANTOM: **You take the story in a different direction than the first two versions.**

FERRARA: We locked on to the original book, a novella by Jack Finney that was
serialized in the early fifties. It's quite an extraordinary piece, so we kind
of used that as our source material. The military bit was a whole new setting. That was kind of there when I got involved. Under intense analysis,
it really works against the story because to say someone is not themselves,
you gotta know them. So to place your characters in a foreign setting kind
of works against it. But I don't know, something about the military gives
you something else too.

As for the aliens, in Finney's piece their attitude really was, they came

(continued)

out and said, "We're gonna bring you the good news. We're gonna show you a way to a greater future." It's not like they're trying to hide. "You'll wake up to a better tomorrow. Trust me—I'm not gonna let you down. Let's go." But then there's that fear, that holding on to one's self. There's two ways of looking at it. In the original book, the aliens' attitude was, "What are you holding on to, man? You've taken this planet and you're destroying it. You, as the human race, are destroying the world you live in. We're gonna show you a different way. Okay, you don't get it, you're aggressive; as a human, you're holding on to your individuality." In the original book, the aliens just took off and split, basically saying, "Okay, guys, *you* live here and drink the water. Sayonara, homey, we'll go somewhere else!"

PHANTOM: That's not an ending any of the film versions used.

FERRARA: No. I like ending with the possibility of destruction. That's our genre, right? In this film, we kill everybody on the planet. You can't top that.

PHANTOM: You kept the pod scream from the 1978 version.

FERRARA: That was the last shot in the Kaufman picture. We saw both those movies 500 times and took the best parts of them, and that, to me, was a killer. Especially when Meg [Tilly] lets out that scream. She's awesome!

PHANTOM: Are you generally happy about the way *Body Snatchers* turned out?

FERRARA: I like the movie. We put a lot of energy into it. It was made in the tradition of the way Siegel made his film. There are things in Siegel's movie that aren't one hundred percent, but it's a dynamite movie. It's a funny premise. You've gotta give that guy [Finney] credit for coming up with it. As much as I respect Siegel and his movie, he had something to work with; that film did not just spring out of the air.

rara manages to bring a fresh perspective to a project that would have seemed, on the surface, doomed to redundancy.

INVISIBLE INVADERS   (1959)
B&W ***

D: Edward L. Cahn. John Agar, Jean Byron, John Carradine, Robert Hutton. 67 mins. (MGM)

Prolific Poverty Row auteur Cahn's cheap but often genuinely chilling *Night of the Living Dead* precursor sees invisible aliens with low auditory-pain thresholds commandeer earthly cadavers for the usual sinister purposes. Heroes Agar and Hutton ride their trusty sound truck (!) to the rescue. An iconic B cast and risibly improvised FX add to the retro fun.

THE INVISIBLE MAN:
THE SERIES

THE INVISIBLE MAN   (1933)
B&W ***

D: James Whale. Claude Rains, Gloria Stuart, Una O'Connor. 71 mins. (Universal)

Director James (*Frankenstein*) Whale and an intense Rains as the man who loses his visibility and his mind (in that order) combine to bring H. G. Wells's darkly comic sci-fright fable to entertaining life. Followed by direct sequels *The Invisible Man Returns,* with a spirited Vincent Price, *Invisible Agent,* with Jon Hall as a transparent Nazi-fighter, and *The Invisible Man's Revenge* (all Universal), with Hall and John Carradine; *The Invisible Terror,* the German *Invisible Dr. Mabuse,* and *The Invisible Avenger,* a 1958 quickie

based on *The Shadow* radio show (Sinister Cinema); *The Invisible Boy* (MGM), with Richard Eyer and *Forbidden Planet*'s Robby the Robot; Fred Olen Ray's farce *Invisible Mom* (New Horizons) and 1997 follow-up *Invisible Dad* (A-Pix); Jess Franco's *The Invisible Dead* (Wizard); *The Invisible Maniac* (Republic); 1976's *The Invisible Strangler,* with Robert Foxworth (TWE); *Invisible: The Chronicles of Benjamin Knight* (Paramount); and Edward Sutherland's amusing 1940 farce, *The Invisible Woman* (Universal), with John Barrymore and Virginia Bruce.

THE INVISIBLE RAY   (1936)
B&W ***

D: Lambert Hillyer. Boris Karloff, Bela Lugosi, Frances Drake. 81 mins. (Universal)

This early sci-fi effort reteams Boris and Bela, fresh from their *Raven* and *Black Cat* successes, with Boris as a scientist whose radium experiments give him a lethal touch and disintegrating mind. We would have preferred Bela in the demented-doc role, but this is still a strong, if downbeat, sci-fi chiller.

IRON WARRIOR   (1987) *

D: Al Bradley. Miles O'Keeffe, Savina Gersak, Tim Lane, Elizabeth Kaza. 82 mins. (Media)

This sequel to the 1982 Thorne EMI release *Ator, the Fighting Eagle* (no relation to Ajax, the Foaming Cleanser) finds O'Keeffe reprising his role as the hunky Ator, he of the rippling pecs and wooden personality. Here he's pitted against the skull-masked title villain and evil sorceress Kaza (who resembles Phyllis Diller in a bright red fright wig), united in their determination to thwart Ator's attempts to restore shapely princess Gersak to the throne of Dragmoor. This deadly dull dud comes to fleeting life only during Ator's snappy repartee with the princess. To wit:

PRINCESS:
These dark powers are
taking over my kingdom.

ATOR:
So I noticed.

To say nothing of:

PRINCESS:
What if they kill you?

ATOR:
Then I'd be dead.

ISLAND OF LOST SOULS (1933) B&W ****

D: Erle C. Kenton. Charles Laughton, Richard Arlen, Leila Hyams, Kathleen Burke, Bela Lugosi, Arthur Hohl. 71 mins. (Universal)

In Kenton's perverse, disturbing adaptation of H. G. Wells's *The Island of Dr. Moreau,* Laughton delivers a peak performance as the impatient, whip-wielding, megalomaniacal genius who accelerates the process of evolution to transform animals into "manimals," or as Bela puts it, "part men, part beast—*things!*" Laughton especially shines during his scenes with sexy panther girl Lota ("I'll burn *all* the animal out of her!"), played by Burke, a dental aide who'd won Paramount's national panther-girl contest (actress Gail Patrick was a runner-up). Bela makes the most of his scant screen time as the "Sayer of the Law" ("Are we not men?"—later anthemized by Devo), while the obscure Hans Steinke as "Ouran" is an unforgettable figure. (Also reportedly among the manimals are Alan Ladd, Buster Crabbe, Randolph Scott, and stunt ace Joe Bonomo.) Despite a fine cast, the bland 1977 remake, *The Island of Dr. Moreau* (Warner), captures none of the original's magic, which pulses with the rhythm and precision of a recurrent nightmare—a major reason, along with its cross-species sexuality and vivisection motifs, why it was banned in many countries (it wasn't screened in England until 1958!).

THE ISLAND OF DR. MOREAU (1996) *1/2

D: John Frankenheimer. Marlon Brando, Val Kilmer, David Thewlis, Fairuza Balk, Temuera Morrison, Ron Perlman. 95 mins. (New Line) DVD

This ill-advised celluloid albatross (or dodo at the very least) got off on the wrong foot right from day two, when original helmer Richard (*Dust Devil*) Stanley received his walking papers from New Line. (He reportedly clandestinely visited the set by dressing as one of Moreau's manimals [!]). Not even so skilled a helmer-for-hire as John (*The Manchurian Candidate, Seconds*) Frankenheimer could spin celluloid gold from the dross he'd inherited—a revamp that squanders even the most elementary components of the original—so *Moreau* more or less went its own zany way until the weary director at last called it a day.

Brando, entering late and exiting early, indulges his two-ton whimsy to the max, playing the mad scientist as a cross between Alfred Hitchcock and Queen Victoria, while mewing his lines through a Bugs Bunny–esque prosthetic overbite and wearing white robes, headdress, powder, and, in one memorable scene, an ice bucket (!). A sulky Kilmer—who insisted on switching his role from the hero (taken instead by a clueless Thewlis) to Montgomery, Moreau's smirky, drug-addled accomplice in medical crime—labors shamelessly to wrestle the limelight from Marlon. Brando bonds with several of his manimals, including a diminutive thingie (who, as a *Village Voice* critic astutely pointed out, bears at least a passing resemblance to director Elia Kazan) with whom he performs piano duets. Marlon also delivers an impromptu musical lecture on the joys of Gershwin to several of his understandably stunned beastie boys. After Moreau's untimely passing well before the movie's climax, Kilmer gains an additional measure of on-screen revenge

by resorting to mimicking Marlon's mincing delivery. Sultry Balk comes across best, though she's no match for Kathleen Burke's original panther woman.

As for plot, all *Moreau*'s creative forces could come up with was to arm the manimals with automatic weapons and let them have at one another. And why hire Ron Perlman (as the Sayer of the Law) if you're going to hide him under layers of Ron Perlman makeup? Nice trailer, though.

ISLAND OF TERROR (1967) ***

D: Terence Fisher. Peter Cushing, Edward Judd, Carole Gray, Niall MacGinnis. 90 mins. (Universal)

On a remote isle off the Irish coast, researchers working on a cancer cure inadvertently create a horde of crawling, green, tortoiselike man-eating tumors, with amoebalike reproductive abilities and long, rectractable phallic protuberances (you know the type). Not to worry, though, because intrepid scientific investigator Cushing's on the case and there's no way he won't get to the bottom of it even *after* half his arm's chopped off and many of the island's residents have turned into tumor snacks. Reminiscent of a scaled-down Professor Quatermass caper, *Island of Terror* is a highly entertaining, straight-ahead sci-fi/horror hybrid that more than delivers on its titular promise.

ISLAND OF THE BURNING DOOMED (1967) **1/2

D: Terence Fisher. Peter Cushing, Christopher Lee, Patrick Allen. 94 mins. (New Star, n.i.d.)

The ever excellent Cushing and Lee head a crisp (and crisped) Brit cast plagued by a heat wave created by unfriendly aliens. The freeze-framed opening credits offer some relief. Also released as *Night of the Big Heat.*

IT CAME FROM BENEATH THE SEA (1955) B&W ***

D: Robert Gordon. Kenneth Tobey, Faith Domergue, Donald Curtis. 80 mins. (Goodtimes)

The budget allowed for only five tentacles, but FX ace Ray Harryhausen's giant radiation-spawned octopus supplies its fair share of scares as it attacks San Francisco. Former Howard Hughes protégée Domergue offers riveting distaff diversion.

IT CAME FROM OUTER SPACE (1953) B&W ***

D: Jack Arnold. Richard Carlson, Barbara Rush, Charles Drake. 81 mins. (Goodtimes)

Originally lensed in 3-D, Jack (*The Incredible Shrinking Man*) Arnold's alien-visitation tale relies more on atmosphere and mood than on cheap chills to weave its cinematic spell. A useless, belated made-for-cable sequel, *It Came from Outer Space II* (Universal), followed in 1996.

IT CONQUERED THE WORLD (1956) B&W ***

D: Roger Corman. Peter Graves, Lee Van Cleef, Beverly Garland, Sally Fraser, Charles B. Griffith, Dick Miller, Jonathan Haze. 68 mins. (Columbia/TriStar)

This classic Corman quickie features several essential '50s B sci-fi elements: a bland but stalwart hero (Graves); a tunnel-visioned scientist (an intense Van Cleef) led astray by manipulative aliens; a feisty heroine (the ever formidable Garland); decidedly superfluous comic relief (supplied by Roger regulars Miller and Haze); and, surely not least, the unforgettable carrot creature from Venus (designed by Paul Blaisdell). Van Cleef makes the mistake of guiding the violent Venusian visitor to Earth, where it dispatches flying "bat mites" to transform the locals into obe-

dient slaves. This swiftly paced paranoid parable was remade by the infamous Larry Buchanan a decade later as *Zontar, the Thing from Venus* (Sinister Cinema), starring John Agar and later the subject of an inspired *SCTV* parody.

IT! THE TERROR FROM BEYOND SPACE (1958) B&W ***

D: Edward L. Cahn. Marshall Thompson, Shawn Smith, Kim Spalding, Ann Doran. 69 mins. (MGM)

A hungry, rubber-suited alien stowaway (played by erstwhile sagebrush star Ray Corrigan) chomps its way through an unwary crew in Cahn's low-budget but atmospheric *Alien* precursor, a film that's won a considerable boomer-based cult following over the decades.

IT'S ALIVE:
THE SERIES

IT'S ALIVE (1974) ***

D: Larry Cohen. John P. Ryan, Sharon Farrell, Andrew Duggan. 91 mins. (Warner)

Cohen's breakthrough mutant-baby movie blames faulty fertility pharmaceuticals for causing normal couple Ryan and Farrell to procreate the title creature. Cohen again employs a fright format to deal with serious issues while still delivering the genre goods in this recommended chiller. He continues the theme in the worthwhile sequels *It Lives Again* (1978) and the somewhat goofier but effective *It's Alive III: Island of the Alive* (1988), starring a scenery-chewing Michael Moriarty (also Warner).

JASON AND THE ARGONAUTS (1963) ***

D: Don Chaffey. Todd Armstrong, Gary Raymond, Nancy Kovack, Honor Blackman. 104 mins. (Columbia/TriStar) DVD

FX genius Ray Harryhausen's creatures highlight this Saturday-matinee version of the title characters' search for the Golden Fleece. Bernard Herrmann contributes an appropriately stirring score.

JOHNNY MNEMONIC (1995) ***

D: Robert Longo. Keanu Reeves, Dolph Lundgren, "Beat" Takeshi Kitano, Ice-T, Dina Meyer, Henry Rollins, Udo Kier. 98 mins. (Columbia/TriStar) DVD

While flawed, cyberpunk writer William Gibson's screen adaptation of his own short story, directed by artist Longo, offers more entertainment value than its mostly negative notices would indicate. True, Reeves is pretty bad in a role ideally suited for Don ("the Dragon") Wilson, who'd be less likely to try to wrench thespic "moments" from his one-dimensional part. As for the story line, *Johnny Mnemonic* employs a serviceable cybernetic variation of a hook earlier used by John Carpenter in *Escape from New York:* Here Reeves is a 21st-century cybercourier who wants out but agrees to make a final delivery—even though he knows he lacks the requisite cranial storage capacity and that the resultant electronic seepage will kill him if he doesn't have the data removed within 24 hours. (His mental-messenger duties, we learn, have already cost him most of his long-term memory.) Unbeknownst to our hero, the data contains a cure for widespread NAS (nerve attenuation syndrome), a form of "information sickness," making him the target for competing factions ranging from Yakuza assassins (led by Japanese actor/auteur Kitano, wielding a decapitating ninja laser) to self-styled religious maniac Lundgren (in one of his better turns). Johnny receives head-saving help from self-appointed femme bodyguard (and NAS sufferer) Meyer, rebel leader Ice-T (lending his usual sour charisma to the role), a resistance movement physician (punk rocker Rollins), and even a dolphin that happens to be a satellite-communications expert (!). Unlike the irritatingly tongue-in-cheek *Tank Girl* (see index), *Johnny Mnemonic* spins its wild sci-fi-pulp plot with a straight (at times positively blank) face and furnishes its share of fun along the way.

JOURNEY TO THE CENTER OF THE EARTH (1959) **½

D: Henry Levin. James Mason, Arlene Dahl, Pat Boone. 132 mins. (Playhouse)

Levin's fairly lavish, well-crafted screen version of Jules Verne's inner-Earth exploration adventure proved too long and wholesome for yours truly's taste. Boone, along for the trip, represents another major minus, though Bernard Herrmann's bottom-heavy score offers considerable aural compensation.

JOURNEY TO THE CENTER OF TIME (1967) **½

D: David L. Hewitt. Scott Brady, Gigi Perreau, Anthony Eisley, Poupee Gamin. 82 mins. (Englewood)

Scott, Gigi, and Tony time-trip 5,000 years into the future, where they encounter imminent nuclear annihilation and unforgettable chrome-domed, cleavage-driven alien Gamin (her only known screen appearance, sadly enough) in what may be the best effort of opticals-expert-turned-Poverty Row auteur Hewitt (*The Mighty Gorga*). With timeless lines like "Okay, see you the day before yesterday!"

JOURNEY TO THE FAR SIDE OF THE SUN (1969) **½

D: Robert Parrish. Roy Thinnes, Lynn Loring, Herbert Lom. 99 mins. (Universal) DVD

Space explorers hie to the title site, where they discover a hitherto hidden planet in a well-done sci-fi outing with a memorable twist ending. The film inspired the teleseries of the same name.

KILLERS FROM SPACE (1954) B&W **½

D: W. Lee Wilder. Peter Graves, Barbara Bestar, James Seay. 71 mins. (Rhino)

Popeyed E.T.'s kidnap scientist Graves and try to scare him with insect and wildlife stock footage. Pretty persuasive sci-fi from Billy Wilder's less prominent brother, the brains behind *Man Without a Body* (n/a) and *Phantom from Space* (see index).

KRONOS (1957) B&W ***

D: Kurt Neumann. Jeff Morrow, Barbara Lawrence, John Emery. 78 mins. (Englewood)

Despite its dependence on stock footage, cheap FX, and other cost-cutting measures, this earnest account of an energy-sucking mechanical colossus that arrives from outer space to stalk the Mexican countryside rates as a prime example of fun '50s genre filmmaking.

KURT VONNEGUT'S HARRISON BERGERON (1994) ***

D: Bruce Pittman. Sean Astin, Miranda De Pencier, Christopher Plummer. 99 mins. (Republic)

Director Bruce (*Hello Mary Lou: Prom Night II*) Pittman and scripter Arthur Crimm do a trim job of adapting and expanding Vonnegut's fable, which originally preemed on Showtime cable, about a future America where systematic "dumbing down" has become government policy. Buck Henry, Howie Mandel, and *SCTV* alums Eugene Levy and Andrea Martin contribute cameos.

THE LAND UNKNOWN (1957) B&W ***

D: Virgil Vogel. Jock Mahoney, Shawn Smith, William Reynolds, Henry Brandon, Phil Harvey, Douglas Kennedy. 78 mins. (Universal)

A quartet of Antarctic explorers—naval men Mahoney, Reynolds, Harvey, and blond *Oceanic Press* reporter Smith—crash-land their chopper in a temperate polar volcano where prehistoric dinosaurs roam. They also encounter a previous visitor (a strapping, bearded Brandon) who's gone native and can control the outsized local wildlife with the aid of his trusty seashell horn (it even plays subtle jazz riffs!). With its fanciful matte-painting, stock-footage, and live-action mix, this atmospheric pic plays more surreally than originally intended—though Mahoney's femme-directed sentiments root the film firmly in the '50s. To wit: "Although I know basically women consist mostly of water, a few pinches of salt and metals thrown in, you have a very unsalt-like, nonmetallic effect on me."

LAST EXIT TO EARTH (1997) **

D: Katt Shea. Kim Greist, Costas Mandylor, Amy Hathaway, David Groh, Michael Cudlitz. 80 mins. (New Horizons)

Dance of the Damned auteur Katt Shea—the subject of an early '90s NYC Museum of Modern Art retro (she even got a dinner!)—lands back in the Corman stable with *Last Exit to Earth*. Set in 2500 A.D. "after the Great Feminine Revolution," the pic posits a world ruled by women who've been splicing the "aggression genes" from male babies since the 23rd century. Most of the remaining males—infertile to a man—serve as pretty-boy "poodles" groomed to pamper and pleasure empowered females. With the planetary sperm count at zero and cloning techniques still unperfected, scientist Greist leads a select crew to invade a male-inhabited time-warp-trapped repair ship and bring the hopefully potent boys back home. *Last Exit to Earth* boasts some witty, if underdeveloped, ideas and gags—an enclosed lab crowded with male scientific subjects sports a DO NOT FEED sign, while most of the women are accompanied by symbolic pet cats that they're forever stroking. The flick also features some choice dialogue, as when Greist describes the sexual mores of yore to her daughter, who replies, "In other words, Mother, sex is supposed to be dirty." Says Mom, "If it's done properly." Unfortunately, Katt and crew undermine what could have been a fun satiric fable by incorporating jarringly callous mood-killing violence. Former actress Katt cameos as "Surgeon Athena."

THE LAST MAN ON EARTH (1964) B&W **1/2

D: Sidney Salkow. Vincent Price, Franca Bettoia, Emma Danieli, Giacomo Rossi-Stuart. 86 mins. (Sinister Cinema)

Salkow's Italo-lensed film, based on the Richard Matheson novel *I Am Legend* (later filmed as *Omega Man*), features Price as the sole survivor of an unstoppable plague that's transformed most of the world's population into living-dead bloodsucking mutants. Price, as the title character, has the task of driving his hearselike station wagon through an unnamed city, staking his daily quota of vampires, and tossing their bodies into a burning pit (a thankless job, to be sure, but no one else is around to do it). We also see him pass many long, dull nights arranging his garlic collection (to ward off the vampires), listening to old records, and watching home movies that, while a cut below your average *America's Funniest Home Videos* segment, nonetheless launch our hero into prolonged bouts of hysteria, which Price delivers with his customary aplomb. The pic picks up

when Vincent flashes back to the plague's beginnings, scenes brimming with authentically grim imagery. An uneven mix of the good, the bad (some atrocious dubbing), and the static, *The Last Man on Earth* is well worth a look, both for its intermittent originality and its striking similarity, thematically and visually, to George Romero's legendary *Night of the Living Dead*, which surfaced just four years later. A megabuck Hollywood remake, with Arnold Schwarzenegger, was long rumored but came to naught.

THE LAWNMOWER MAN:
THE SERIES

THE LAWNMOWER MAN (1992) **1/2

D: Brit Leonard. Pierce Brosnan, Jeff Fahey, Geoffrey Lewis, Jenny Wright, Jeremy Slate, Mark Bringleson. In R and unrated "Director's Cut" editions. 108 mins. (New Line) DVD

Marginally drawn from a Stephen King short story (he had his name removed from the title), *The Lawnmower Man* stars Brosnan as a virtual-reality genius who, à la the 1968 sci-fi fable *Charly* (Fox), artificially induces some much needed smarts in local landscaper Fahey. Unlike Cliff Robertson's Charly, who enjoyed a more gradual ascent up the evolutionary scale (one that even embraced a brief biker phase!), Jeff leaps from moron to self-styled deity. Once he glitches big-time after Pierce's evil employers tinker with his experiments, we're treated to a telekinetic revenge spree, flashy demolecularization murders, and a climactic power duel between Brosnan and his rambunctious creation. Fahey does reasonably well in a role tailor-made for Brad Dourif, while Wright impresses as a randy neighbor. While the movie touches on the theme of abusive authority figures, ranging from 'burb bad dads to corporate Big Brothers, the

computer-driven FX constitute nearly the whole show here; fortunately, they're knockout enough to justify the film. There's nothing on view to justify the 1996 sequel, *Lawnmower Man 2: Jobe's War* (New Line), an unwaveringly feeble fable set in your standard-issue dystopian faux–*Blade Runner* future L.A., where "awesome" and "cool" have somehow survived as the adolescent adjectives of choice.

LEGEND (1986) *

D: Ridley Scott. Tom Cruise, Mia Sara, Tim Curry, David Bennent, Alice Playten, Billy Barty. 89 mins. (Universal)

Reportedly, Universal execs repeatedly delayed the theatrical release of Scott's *Legend* while frantic film editors hacked the two-hour opus down to 89 minutes. Even in that truncated state, *Legend* manages to pack in more boredom per frame than most flicks. Our story unfolds long ago (though not in a galaxy far away) in an enchanted forest where feathers, leaves, and what looks like lint are all the time swirling about. (*Legend* is also a leading contender for the *Robot Monster* Memorial Award for Most Extensive Use of a Bubble Machine.) As we open, Princess Lily (Sara), a sprightly waif, glides through the expensive scenery for a rendezvous with young Jack (Cruise), the local unicorn keeper. Meanwhile, back in hell, the subterranean Lord of Darkness (Curry) decides he's had enough of this insufferable sweetness and so dispatches hit goblin Barty to off one of the "ugly, one-horned mules." Once this is accomplished, the surviving unicorn silently informs Jack (Mr. Ed's voice would have come in handy here) that he must do battle with the L of D himself in order to restore the world's balance of darkness and light. As *Legend* limps along, we're further treated to elaborate but wasted FX work and irritating elves who supply slapstick low-comedy relief of a sort unseen on-screen since Fuzzy

St. John's heyday. If Tinkerbell had a nightmare, it would probably look a lot like *Legend*.

LENSMAN (1990) ***

D: Y. Kawajiri, K. Hirokawa. Animated. 107 mins. (Streamline)

Adapted from the sci-fi novels of E. E. ("Doc") Smith, *Lensman* chronicles the adventures of teen hero Kim Kinnison, who's recruited into the elite ranks of the "Lensmen," space warriors with scanner-equipped hands. Aided by hulking pal Buskirk, petite Galactic Patrolperson Chris, flying alien Wurzel, and cosmic club emcee Bill, Kim faces the evil forces of the planet Boskone in a series of visually spectacular confrontations. While the *Star Wars*–styled story line and characters may be little more than amiably serviceable, the pyrotechnic animation more than carries the day.

LEVIATHAN (1989) **

D: George P. Cosmatos. Peter Weller, Richard Crenna, Amanda Pays, Daniel Stern, Ernie Hudson, Meg Foster. 98 mins. (MGM) DVD

If *Alien* didn't already exist, *Leviathan*, with its able cast, fast pace, flashy production values, and state-of-the-art creature (courtesy of FX craftsman Stan Winston), would stack up as a fairly shipshape sci-fi chiller. Unfortunately for Cosmatos and crew, *Alien* does, so *Leviathan* doesn't. The plot emerges as a peg-by-peg steal: Crenna and Weller head a deep-sea mining expedition financed by the corporate creeps at Tri-Oceanic. A parasitic mutant incubates in the crew's token screw-up "Sixpack" (Stern) before springing forth, fully formed and famished, to claim other cast members one by one. Even *Leviathan*'s tag line ("Imagine being trapped…where no one can hear you") echoes *Alien*'s "In

space, no one can hear you scream." To his credit, then-frequent Stallone helmer Cosmatos lays out the waterlogged clichés with unswerving competence. Other, less seaworthy underwater alien efforts include *DeepStar Six* (Artisan) and *Lords of the Deep* (MGM).

LIFEFORM (1996) ***

D: Mark H. Baker. Cotter Smith, Deidre O'Connell, Robert Wisdom, Robert Philippe, Raoul O'Connell, Leland Orser. 90 mins. (Artisan)

As low-budget *Alien* rip-offs go, *Lifeform* rates among the better ones—an admirably earnest, no-nonsense, old-fashioned (in a positive sense) sci-fi thriller that travels in a tense straight line from the desert discovery of a mysteriously returned Martian probe to the lab-set escape of an alien stowaway on a sinister mission. Scientists Smith and O'Connell and a platoon of young soldiers are all that stand in the way of the cryptic E.T.'s freedom. Director Baker yields exciting results from what could have been a stock situation. The acting's crisp, the dialogue free of wisecracks and artificial "attitude," and the creature itself is a neat invention. A surprise, downbeat ending completes *Lifeform*'s satisfying package.

LIFEPOD (1993) **1/2

D: Ron Silver. Robert Loggia, Ron Silver, Stan Shaw, Jessica Tuck, Kelli Williams, Adam Storke, CCH Pounder, Ed Gale. 100 mins. (Cabin Fever)

On its own, thesp Silver's directorial debut rates as okay made-for-cable sci-fi fare. As a futuristic variation on Hitchcock's *Lifeboat* (Fox), however, it's not even in the same ocean, let alone league. While Silver and his scripters admirably acknowledge their source material in the opening credits, they're not up to equaling the admit-

tedly formidable challenge of matching Hitch's 1944 masterpiece. Since it's set in space, in a sealed escape pod separated from its doomed mother ship, *Lifepod* proceeds sans the original's great hook of having its characters board the craft one at a time. And while *Lifepod* boasts a better-than-adequate cast, none of the assembled actors project the offbeat charisma of a Tallulah Bankhead, Walter Slezak, or William Bendix (the Ernest Borgnine of his day). But the chief breakdown lies in a functional but bare-bones script stripped of *Lifeboat*'s playfulness and poetry, drawn from John Steinbeck's original story. *Lifepod*'s one inspired addition is the character of "Toolie" (Gale), a dwarf who, like all lifepod mechanics, has literally cut off his right arm and replaced it with a sort of high-tech Swiss Army limb to land his job, one he understandably takes very seriously. *Lifepod* also borrows liberally from *Alien*, while Cabin Fever's box art is an outright rip-off of *Alien*'s original ad campaign.

THE LIFT (1985) ***

D: Dick Maas. Huub Stapel, Willeka van Ammelrooy, Josine Van Dalsum, Hans Veerman. 95 mins. (Media, n.i.d.)

A Dutch import written and directed by Maas, *The Lift* is a sardonic sci-fi thriller about a killer elevator and the stubborn young repairman (Stapel) who's determined to defeat it. *The Lift* has a lot going for it—a laconically effective performance by Stapel, well-sketched supporting characters, deadpan humor mixed with moments of genuine suspense, and the most skeptical view of our machine-run world since Chaplin's *Modern Times*. Weak science and occasionally slack pacing prevent *The Lift* from reaching the top fright-flick floor, but this video is definitely worth a look. Maas followed with the middling 1988 action thriller *Amsterdamned* (Vestron).

LIGHT YEARS (1986) **½

D: Rene Laloux. Voice cast: Glenn Close, Christopher Plummer, Jennifer Grey, John Shea, Earl Hyman, Terrence Mann. 83 mins. (Trimark)

French animator Laloux, of *Fantastic Planet* (see index) fame, fashions another whimsical sci-fi feature, "presented" and "adapted" by Isaac Asimov. The slight story line concerns a New Agey society threatened by an army of Darth Vader–like androids, and the efforts of young hero Sylvain to reverse the deadly invasion. Laloux's parable warns of the dangers of unchecked technology, as the robot hordes turn out to be the creation of a synthetic brain that's grown independent from—and more powerful than—its creators. Aiding Sylvain in his mission are a breed of Boschian mutant outcasts, the tragic results of ill-advised genetic-engineering experiments. If you enjoy the genre in general, and *Fantastic Planet* in particular, you'll want to scope out *Light Years*.

LIGHTBLAST (1984) **½

D: Enzo Q. Castellari. Erik Estrada, Mike Pritchard. 89 mins. (Lightning, n.i.d.)

A sinister scientist is terrorizing San Francisco with his flesh-disintegrating mobile laser cannon. Erik rides to the rescue. *Lightblast* didn't do much to further Estrada's comeback bid at the time, but it's pretty entertaining sci-fi pulp, with lots of hot face-melting close-ups.

LINK (1986)0 *

D: Richard Franklin. Terence Stamp, Elisabeth Shue, Steven Pinner, Richard Garnett. 103 mins. (HBO)

Avowed Hitchcock clone Franklin's misguided chimp-monster movie is an insult to simian and homo-sap home-viewers alike. First he cites pongid authority Jane Goodall's research in a bid to make this monkey business sound more credible, then he casts an orangutan in the leading psycho-chimp role (!). Even beyond its despicable bid to drag chimps down to our level, *Link* is a turgid mess whose own low-camp detours fail to provide enough unintended laughs to save it.

LIQUID SKY (1983) ***½

D: Slava Tsukerman. Anne Carlisle, Paula E. Sheppard, Otto Von Wernherr. 112 mins. (WinterTainment) DVD

Pint-sized aliens invade NYC's East Village, where they live off the orgasms (!) of narcissistic downtown poseurs in this highly original and idiosyncratic (if somewhat overlong) sci-fi satire/enduring cult fave from Russian émigré Tsukerman. Star Carlisle later wrote the novelization. Lilliputian lesbian Paula E. Sheppard is the selfsame Paula Sheppard who played the unforgettable *Bad Seed*–type role in Alfred Sole's *Alice, Sweet Alice* (see index).

LORD OF THE FLIES (1963) B&W ***

D: Peter Brook. James Aubrey, Tom Chapin, Hugh Edwards. 90 mins. (Top, Hallmark)

Island-stranded Brit schoolboys degenerate into savagery in Peter Brook's moody B&W screen translation of William Golding's symbol-rich novel, which remains several cuts above the more explicit 1990 remake (Columbia/TriStar).

THE LOST CONTINENT (1951) B&W **½

D: Sam Newfield. Cesar Romero, Hillary Brooke, Hugh Beaumont, John Hoyt, Acquanetta, Sid Melton. 86 mins. (Sinister Cinema)

A fun Lippert Pictures back-lot cheapie that used to air endlessly on NYC TV stations in the '50s, *The Lost Continent* tracks a mountain search for a missing atomic rocket that takes an earnest B cast (including one-time Universal "Jungle Woman" Acquanetta) through lots of dinosaur-infested stock footage. Lippert regular Melton supplies the obligatory comic relief. Sinister's vid version includes the green tint that originally coated part of the theatrical print's final reel.

THE LOST CONTINENT (1968) ***

D: Michael Carreras. Eric Porter, Hildegarde Knef, Suzanna Leigh, Tony Beckley, Nigel Stock. 98 mins. (Anchor Bay) DVD

Drawn from Dennis Wheatley's novel *Unchartered Seas*, Carreras's *Lost Continent* represents another bizarre winner from Anchor Bay's Hammer Collection. What begins as a moral fable about doomed passengers aboard a mysterious tramp steamer ultimately mutates into a high-seas adventure tale, then a monster movie when our survivors arrive at the title landmass, one populated by giant mollusks, killer weeds, and the hostile descendants of a shipwrecked Spanish crew. Shifting color designs add to the film's surreal quality.

LOST HORIZON (1937) B&W ***

D: Frank Capra. Ronald Colman, Jane Wyatt, John Howard, Sam Jaffe, Edward Everett Horton. 132 mins. (Columbia/TriStar) DVD

While not quite the flawless masterpiece many have proclaimed it, *Lost Horizon* certainly ranks as quality offbeat entertainment, with Jaffe especially impressive as the high lama. Still photos serve as narrative bridges over those brief segments missing from the original print; the audio track is intact.

THE LOST WORLD (1925)
B&W ***1/2

D: Harry O. Hoyt. Bessie Love, Lloyd Hughes, Lewis Stone, Wallace Beery, Arthur Hoyt, Margaret McWade, Bull Montana. 63/90 mins. (Milestone Film & Video) DVD

The dedicated archivists at Milestone, who'd earlier brought us the spectacular 1927 semidocumentary *Chang*, perform a valuable service in transferring the Lumivision laser disc edition of *The Lost World* to video. Only 63 of the film's original 125 minutes survive, and Milestone uses the only existing 35-millimeter print for its transfer. Since *The Lost World* was originally trimmed in 1930, only five years after its much heralded debut, for a sound-era rerelease, the story retains its narrative flow even in truncated form (though many entire scenes are missing). Drawn from Sir Arthur Conan Doyle's story, the film charts the expedition of aggressive explorer Professor Challenger (Beery) into the Amazon jungle, a journey whose purpose is to prove the existence of a preserved prehistoric enclave where dinosaurs roam (and frequently do battle). Romantic complications, interpersonal frictions, and jungle perils provide a compelling backdrop, but the show belongs to future *King Kong* creator and protean FX pioneer Willis O'Brien's amazing menagerie of prehistoric critters, beasts realistic enough to prompt *The New York Times* critic to write, "monsters of the ancient world or of a new world… were extraordinarily lifelike. If fakes, they were masterpieces." (*If*?!) The pic's pièce de résistance, like *King Kong*'s, involves transporting one of the gargantuan beasts—in this case a nonviolent (but inadvertently destructive) brontosaurus—to civilization. The bronto's unplanned tour of London brims with spectacular imagery. Milestone follows the shortened feature with rare stills and background info covering much of the missing material, and it's

only then that the viewer realizes how much more epic the original film was. R. J. Miller composed the excellent modern score, while restoration credit goes to the International Museum of Photography at the George Eastman House.

THE LOST WORLD (1960) ***

D: Irwin Allen. Michael Rennie, Claude Rains, Jill St. John, Fernando Lamas, David Hedison, Richard Haydn. 98 mins. (Fox)

While Disaster Master Allen's 1960 version of Conan Doyle's 1912 novel may pale beside the more ambitious 1925 silent, the pic still boasts plenty of pluses—lush color photography, a full complement of giant lizards, outsized spiders, fright-wigged cannibals, and foxy native babes, along with an ever endangered all-star cast. The latter includes Rennie, Rains, Lamas (who looks mahvelous), and St. John (no scenery slouch herself). The ending's a bit of a cheat, though, with Allen and crew no doubt thinking sequel. Timothy Bond directed a pair of made-for-cable revamps, 1992's *The Lost World* and 1993's *Return to the Lost World* (both Worldvision).

THE MACHINE (1994) ***1/2

D: Francois Dupeyron. Gerard Depardieu, Nathalie Baye, Didier Boundon, Natalia Woerner, Erwan Baynaud. 96 mins. (PolyGram)

An excellent, genuinely disturbing horror/sci-fi thriller that predates John Woo's *Face/Off*, *The Machine* opens with an eerie flash-forward showing a sullen, twitchy boy (Baynaud) watching a slasher movie on TV while his solicitous mom (Baye) tries in vain to communicate with him. We cut to 18 months earlier. The boy's obsessive criminal-psychologist dad (Depardieu) has perfected a device that can trans-

plant cerebral matter and identity from one body to another. In a bid to better understand his subjects, Depardieu convinces captive serial-killer Boundon to volunteer for an experiment where they will temporarily switch bodies. Unfortunately for G.D., the killer uses the op to escape, assuming Depardieu's identity and life while the scientist's trapped in the fugitive's body, events that ultimately circle back to the opening scene. Director Dupeyron, drawing from Rene Belletto's source material, uses this potentially pulpy premise to explore the nature of personal identity while never stinting on the terror and suspense.

MAD MAX:
THE SERIES

MAD MAX (1980) ***

D: George Miller. Mel Gibson, Joanne Samuel, Hugh Keays-Byrne. 93 mins. (Artisan) DVD

The original "Thunder from Down Under" introduced Gibson as a futuristic maverick motorcycle cop out to rid an already ruined Australia of its myriad road vermin. The American vid release is dubbed by American actors (!). The series would really hit its stride with *The Road Warrior* before stalling out with *Mad Max Beyond Thunderdome*.

THE ROAD WARRIOR (1981) ****

D: George Miller. Mel Gibson, Bruce Spence, Vernon Wells, Virginia Hay. 94 mins. (Warner) DVD

Simply one of the greatest genre movies of all time, ranking right up there with *The Terminator*, Miller's transplanted postnuke western (originally titled *Mad Max 2*) brilliantly blends and reinvents the best elements of that all-but-defunct genre and has itself become one of the most imitated films ever. All would-be action auteurs should study *Road Warrior*'s kinetic climax, where creative editing, not budget, makes the difference. Also available in a 1999 "special edition."

MAD MAX BEYOND THUNDERDOME   (1985) **

D: George Miller, George Ogilvie. Mel Gibson, Tina Turner, Angelo Rossitto, Helen Buday, Rod Zuanic, Angry Anderson, Frank Thring. 106 mins. (Warner) DVD

There's a not-so-thin line between taking a tongue-in-cheek approach and resorting to broad self-parody. Miller's *Mad Max Beyond Thunderdome* sinks below said line right from reel 1 and wallows therein the rest of the way. In the third installment of Miller's postnuke saga, Max (Gibson) straggles off the fast track that the wonderfully kinetic *Road Warrior* traveled and wanders into Bartertown, a post-holocaust hellhole presided over by one Auntie Entity (oy!), ear-splittingly interpreted by Turner, who's embroiled in a power struggle with a dwarf/giant tandem named Master and Blaster (double oy!). After duking it out with the latter, Max heads desertward, where he's soon adopted by a juvenile *Lord of the Flies*–type tribe. Not only are these kids afflicted with a collective (and infinitely irritating) case of echolalia, but they talk in a bastardized version of the pidgin English spoken in the postnuke novel *Riddley Walker*. (They're also given to screeching a garbled variation on the "What is the law?" chant from *Island of Lost Souls*.) Much expensive, high-decibel milling ensues before the climactic battle arrives; alas, it too is but a pale shadow of *The Road Warrior*'s stirring, thrill-a-nanosecond finale. The late great Angelo Rossitto—Bela Lugosi's henchdwarf in several 1940s cheapies—plays Master, the nominal brains behind Bartertown.

THE MAGIC SWORD   (1962) ***

D: Bert I. Gordon. Basil Rathbone, Gary Lockwood, Estelle Winwood, Anne Helm. 80 mins. (MGM)

One of Mr. B.I.G.'s better productions, starring Lockwood as Saint George, features a top veteran cast, improved FX, and a wisely brief running time. Look for legendary *Plan 9* actress/telehorror hostess Vampira in a bit part.

MAN FACING SOUTHEAST (1986) ***

D: Eliseo Subiela. Lorenzo Quinteros, Hugo Soto, Inez Vernengo. 105 mins. (New World, n.i.d.)

A low-key allegory in a *Brother from Another Planet* vein, *Man* involves the mysterious, Christ-like Rantes (Soto), who turns up at a Beunos Aires mental institution claiming he's from outer space. Auteur Subiela, who also scripted, hedges his bets by hinting that Rantes really *is* a literal alien while ultimately skirting the issue. Still, *Man Facing Southeast* shapes up as a quietly ironic if downbeat exploration of identity, belief systems, and society's inability to cope with the outsider.

MAN MADE MONSTER   (1941) B&W ***

D: George Waggner. Lionel Atwill, Lon Chaney, Jr., Anne Nagel, Frank Albertson, Samuel S. Hinds. 59 mins. (Universal)

Like the luckless Ted (David Bruce) in *The Mad Ghoul* (see index), Chaney, as sideshow "Electric Man" Dan McCormick, is less a hero or monster than a passive victim. The lone survivor of an electrical accident, Dan is invited by kindly scientist Dr. Lawrence (Hinds) to stay at his poshly appointed digs, where the good doc will oversee his recovery. Hinds's loony partner (an inspiredly over-the-top Atwill) has

other plans for Dan, transforming him into a walking electrode with a lethal touch. Less than two years past what would forever remain his shining celluloid moment, *Of Mice and Men*, Chaney resorts to recycling many of his Lenny moves. Nagel makes for an intelligent heroine, though Albertson's frequently annoying as her wiseacre reporter suitor. Evidence of the era's knee-jerk racism surfaces not in the movie proper but in the end credits, when Hinds's cook—a middle-aged character named Wong, played by Chester Gan—is listed in the cast as "Chinese Boy" (!).

THE MAN WHO COULD WORK MIRACLES   (1937) B&W ***½

D: Lothar Mendes. Roland Young, Ralph Richardson, Joan Gardner. 82 mins. (Home Vision)

Young is an ordinary haberdashery worker who discovers he possesses special powers in this popular and memorably bizarre Brit adaptation of H. G. Wells's famous fantasy. The film features fright fave George Zucco as an unflappable butler, Ernest Thesiger as an idealistic loony, and a young George Sanders typecast as the god "Indifference," plus neat FX courtesy of Ned (*Deluge*) Mann.

THE MAN WHO FELL TO EARTH (1976) ***

D: Nicolas Roeg. David Bowie, Candy Clark, Rip Torn, Buck Henry. 118/138 mins. (Columbia/TriStar) DVD

Roeg's icy but compelling adaptation of Walter Tevis's novel combines satire with sci-fi in tracking alien Bowie's climb up the American corporate ladder. Bowie makes for a convincing E.T., while Torn and Henry lend quirky support. Available in two versions, including one that restores 20 minutes missing from the theatrical release.

MAN'S BEST FRIEND   (1993) ***

D: John Lafia. Ally Sheedy, Lance Henriksen, Frederic Lehne, Robert Costanzo, Max. 87 mins. (New Line)

Lafia's suspensefully structured hellhound horror wisely dispenses with the usual pseudoscientific preliminaries, plunging us directly into the action as idiotic TV reporter (pardon our redundancy) Sheedy dognaps supermutt Max (a Tibetan mastiff, to be precise) from a vivisection lab. Giving chase is the canine's crazed creator (the ever intense Henriksen), who knows the million-dollar Fido is timed to go psycho within hours of his escape. Scarier and wittier than *Zoltan: Hound of Dracula* (Republic) (a.k.a. *Dracula's Dog*) or *Cujo* (Warner)—to say nothing of *Devil Dog: The Hound of Hell* (Vestron), *Monster Dog* (TWE), with Alice Cooper, *The Pack* (Vestron), *Revenge* (United), with John Carradine and the dog god Caninus (!), the 3-D *Rotweiler: Dogs of Hell* (Media), or even the Diane Keaton/Danny DeVito–voiced pooches in *Look Who's Talking Now* (Columbia/Tri-Star)—*Man's Best Friend* comes highly recommended here. For the record, Max's final fatality tally: seven humans, one cat, a parrot, and a fire hydrant.

FU MANCHU:
THE SERIES

THE MASK OF FU MANCHU   (1932) B&W ***

D: Charles Brabin. Boris Karloff, Lewis Stone, Myrna Loy, Karen Morley, Charles Starrett, Jean Hersholt. 67 mins. (MGM)

Sax Rohmer's "Yellow Peril" *par excellence* Fu (Karloff) races Neyland Smith (Stone) and fellow Brits for the lost tomb of Genghis Khan—not occupied by John Wayne, alas, else we might have been treated to a repeat of Genghis Duke's immortal line from *The Conqueror:* "I would greet you properly, but I am bereft of spit"—in this aggressively racist campfest. The infamous "Torture of the Bells" rates as one undeniable highlight as does the bloodthirsty Fu and randy daughter Loy's debate re to which purposes studly young hero (and future "Durango Kid" B-western star) Starrett might best be put. The movie climaxes in a veritable orgy of ethnic cleansing. Several later Christopher Lee Fu outings are also out there, including *The Castle of Fu Manchu* (HHT) and sequel *Kiss and Kill* (Moore Video), *The Brides of Fu Manchu, The Face of Fu Manchu,* and *The Vengeance of Fu Manchu* (all Warner).

MASTER OF THE WORLD (1961) ***

D: William Witney. Vincent Price, Charles Bronson, Mary Webster. 104 mins. (Warner)

Price is a militant 19th-century pacifist who roams the skies in his airborne sub, bombing battleships and other military targets in this engaging AIP adaptation of Jules Verne's *Robur the Conqueror.* No relation to the 1987 Dolph Lundgren action-figure dud *Masters of the Universe* (Warner).

METAMORPHOSIS   (1990) **½

D: "G. L. Eastman" (Luigi Monetefiori). Gene Le Brock, Catherine Baranov, Harry Cason, David Wicker, Stephen Brown, Laura Gemser. 96 mins. (Imperial, n.i.d.)

No relation to Franz Kafka's famous cockroach fable of the same name, *this Metamorphosis* is a modest, Italo-financed, Virginia-lensed tale about a maverick scientist (Le Brock) whose genetic experiments go too far. When academic bureaucrats threaten to cut off his funding, our hero seeks to avoid that painful fate by using himself as a guinea pig, a decision that straightaway sends him speeding down the mutation trail and evolutionary scale. *Metamorphosis* may sport a less-than-original plot and title, but this polished regional indie emerges as fairly sturdy B-movie fare. No relation either to 1993's low-budget *Alien* clone, *Metamorphosis—The Alien Factor* (Vidmark).

METROPOLIS   (1926) B&W/COLORIZED ***½

D: Fritz Lang. Brigitte Helm, Alfred Abel, Gustav Froehlich. 115 mins. (Sinister Cinema) DVD

The original version of Lang's spectacular vision of a future machine age on the brink of an apocalyptic class war is in the public domain and available on several labels. Vestron released the colorized 1984 *Metropolis,* recut (down to 87 minutes) and scored by Giorgio Moroder.

MIMIC   (1997) ***

D: Guillermo Del Toro. Mira Sorvino, Jeremy Northam, Alexander Goodwin, Giancarlo Giannini, Charles S. Dutton, Josh Brolin, Alix Koromzay, F. Murray Abraham. 105 mins. (Dimension) DVD

Mexican director Del Toro first drew viewers' attention and earned considerable acclaim (including the Cannes Festival Critics' Award) with his 1993 debut feature, *Cronos* (see index). With his encore film, *Mimic,* Del Toro delivers an extremely dark, unrelievedly intense insect-fear fable. Sorvino plays a scientist whose ingenious genetic-engineering prowess seemingly saves an endangered NYC from a plague that claimed the lives of scores of children, a disease carried by rampaging roaches. She accomplishes this miracle by creating a predatory species, called the Judas breed, programmed to eradicate the carriers, then self-destruct within six months. Three years later she learns that the breed (designed by Rob Bottin) has developed a way to survive, assuming the rough form of its human predators, and now poses a threat even greater than the original roach menace. Most of *Mimic* unfolds in the depths of the Delancey Street subway station (painstakingly recreated on Toronto soundstages by production designer Carol Spier, drawing on Internet photos of an actual abandoned station built in 1904), where Sorvino, fellow-scientist hubby Northam, assistant Brolin, earthy transit cop Dutton, kindly old shoe repairman Giannini and his autistic grandson Goodwin, wage a terrifying subterranean war against the relentless creatures and look to eliminate the Judas breed's lone fertile male. Del Toro and cinematographer Dan Laustsen lens that slimy struggle in densely layered patterns of dark and light (or dark and darker), effectively preying on audience fears of the unseen. (You'll definitely want a shower after this one.) The mean streets above, with weather worthy of *Blade Runner*'s meteorologist, aren't much more inviting than the hellscape below. Scripted by Del Toro and Matthew Robbins from Donald A. Wollheim's short story, *Mimic* is a straight-ahead scarefest that delivers the gory goods.

MIRACLE MILE (1989)****

D: Steve De Jarnatt. Anthony Edwards, Mare Winningham, Denise Crosby, Mykel T. Williamson, Robert DoQui, Brian Thompson, John Agar. 87 mins. (HBO)

Life appears to be looking up for lonely young Harry (future *ER* heartthrob Edwards) when he meets kindred spirit Julie (Winningham). Serious trouble soon ensues, however, when Harry accidentally overhears classified info re an impending nuclear war, leaving little time for romance to bloom, let alone mushroom. In fact, Harry spends most of the movie playing an atomic Paul Revere, alerting L.A.'s nocturnal denizens to the terminal danger that may await them. Auteur De Jarnatt, late of the interesting postnuke misfire *Cherry*

Filmmakers in Focus!

GUILLERMO DEL TORO ON *MIMIC*

As Told to The Phantom

PHANTOM: Was New York the setting in the original short story?

DEL TORO: To be absolutely honest, the original short story was four pages or something like that—really short—and I read it two and a half years ago, but I believe it was *not* set in New York. As far as my memory goes, it was set Anywhere, USA. An urban setting but not New York City.

PHANTOM: So was that your idea, to set it there?

DEL TORO: Well, the thing I felt, it was—you know that phrase, "Only in New York"? Well, that's what set it up for me. I felt it was the only place larger-than-life enough to accommodate any sort of creature that I could create.

PHANTOM: And the film itself was actually shot in Toronto?

DEL TORO: It was shot in Toronto. We had, I would say, about two days of second unit during the blizzard in New York. We needed some shots in the blizzard, so we had second unit pick up a couple of shots. It was real snow.

PHANTOM: It was almost kind of a *Blade Runner* look.

DEL TORO: No, that's the real city! I wanted the city to feel desolated and sort of medieval. And many of these angles give you almost an apocalyptic feeling.

PHANTOM: It's hellish aboveground, and below it's tremendously claustrophobic.

DEL TORO: The general idea of the movie, the feeling of the streets, the feeling of everything was to make it sort of a claustrophobic feeling like a medieval fairy tale. We tried to evoke the feeling of a dark forest, of medieval structures and architecture. One of the reasons we shot some of the streets in a studio was because the studio streets are more narrow and claustrophobic.

PHANTOM: The insects themselves, were they mostly animatronic or digital?

DEL TORO: A combination of both. We constructed around a dozen ranging from seven, eight inches tall all the way to six feet tall—very, very complex robotics. We had a minimum of six to twelve operators per puppet. Then on top of that we had some computer-generated images, some CGI effects. We tried to follow textures, forms, and colors of nature and to treat the creatures and effects in the same casual manner, you might say, as you treat any other image in the movie. We didn't showcase them like most movies where you go, "Oh, that's an effect." What we did is we created the best creatures possible and then put them in the shadows, used them in long shots, sometimes put water on the lens to make an image a little more flawed; sometimes we got most of the creature out of focus, just the head or the claw in focus, and what that gives you is a sense of "mistakes" that occur in real life when you're shooting an animal.

PHANTOM: The lighting is so dense. It must have taken a while to shoot.

DEL TORO: It took a while to shoot also because we wanted, with everything from the production design to the lighting, to make a hyperreal New York.

> Not a New York that exists but a New York the way I see it. The way someone coming from the outside sees New York, sort of this gloomy, dark, imposing gothic city.
>
> **PHANTOM:** In *Cronos* there was also an insect that played a pivotal role.
>
> **DEL TORO:** Well, I think they are beautifully designed creatures. And I think that they are perfect villains. If anything, I want to come across about them in the movie the fact that they are ruthless killing machines, absolutely efficient and precise, and they don't care if you're old, young, if you're a woman, if you're white, black, whatever—they don't care if you're a mammal. They are the Grim Reaper.
>
> **PHANTOM:** The scary element here, too, is that this breed mimics us.
>
> **DEL TORO:** Yeah, the thing is the Judas breed prey on their own species, then betray their creators. Because nature decides she won't let them die.
>
> **PHANTOM:** It had some dark humor in it too.
>
> **DEL TORO:** Yes, I try to weave in some dark humor in everything I do. I think *Mimic* has some pretty humorous moments in the middle of the darkness, especially in the character of Charles Dutton, which basically brings the perspective of the man-in-the-street to the movie, brings a regular fellow into the matter. All the others are pretty special characters—an autistic kid, a shoeshine guy, two scientists. Dutton is basically all of us; he is the audience. I like the humor to come out not of a "ha-ha" situation but to come out of tension. So when he asks a question like, "What the hell was *that*!" people get release because that's exactly what *they* were thinking.

2000 (see index), succeeds in crafting a tense, fast-paced, blackly comic, at times poignant and ultimately devastating thriller, the scariest Armageddon movie to surface since Lynn Littman's ultra-bleak 1983 *Testament* (Paramount) and the Brit telemovie *Threads* (World). An unglamorous Edwards and Winningham lend credibility to their characters, while Williamson (now Mykelti, of *Forrest Gump* fame), Crosby, DoQui, Schwarzenegger clone Thompson, and the one-and-only John Agar (in his first grandfatherly role) all supply solid support. One of the last entries in the Cold War–doomsday genre, *Miracle Mile* rates as one of the best.

THE MOLE PEOPLE   (1956) B&W ***

D: Virgil Vogel. John Agar, Hugh Beaumont, Cynthia Patrick, Alan Napier, Nestor Paiva. 78 mins. (Universal)

A laid-back Agar, bland Beaumont (of Ward Cleaver fame), and nervous Nestor Paiva discover a subterranean Sumerian civilization where underground albinos play court politics, sacrifice excess inhabitants in the fires of Ishtar (*not* the burning celluloid from Elaine May's 1987 megadud of the same name), and bully the hapless title creatures into submission. Agar helps raise collective mole-people consciousness while finding time to romance "dark one" Patrick, a blue-eyed wench who plays a mean three-stringed lute. This thematically rich flick would have worked even better had the studio sprung for classier mole makeup, rather than adopting the same penny-pinching approach that sank Fox's 1959 mutant romp *The Alligator People*. Like many sci-fiers of the era, *The Mole People* also opens with a boring short, hosted by Dr. Frank Baxter, but at least it's briefer than *The Deadly Mantis*'s yawn-inducing military sermon.

MONKEY BOY   (A.K.A. *CHIMERA*) (1990) ***

D: Lawrence Gordon Clark. John Lynch, Christine Kavanagh, Kenneth Cranham. 104 mins. (Prism)

The title and video box make it look like a simian variation on *Child's Play*, but this Brit import is closer in spirit to a vintage Professor Quatermass caper. Though not quite in the latter's class, the movie, based on Stephen Gallagher's novel *Chimera* (also the film's original title), is a bloody but earnest sci-fi thriller that effectively mixes pathos with chills. *Monkey Boy* begins with a lab massacre that rapidly runs the body count to an impressive nine as the genetically engineered title mutant, earmarked for live vivisection, flees his cell with vengeance in mind. Like *Watchers* and sequels (see index), the plot follows several factions as they pursue the mutant, including its creators, the police, and the conscience-stricken scientist who arranged for the creature's escape. Lynch, as the boyfriend of a lab victim, is equally determined to expose the unnatural experiments that hatched the monster. While *MB*'s components may be familiar, director Clark and scripter Gallagher keep the film consistently engrossing.

MONKEY SHINES: AN EXPERIMENT IN FEAR   (1988) **

D: George A. Romero. Jason Beghe, John Pankow, Kate McNeil, Joyce Van Patten, Christine Forest, John Tucci. 115 mins. (Orion) DVD

In the less-than-grand tradition of *Link* and *In the Shadow of Kilimanjaro* (Artisan), featuring 90,000—count 'em—90,000 killer baboons, comes *Monkey Shines,* yet another misbegotten bid to exploit our lower primate cousins. Our story concerns quadriplegic Allan Mann (Beghe) and his furry companion, Ella (Boo), a talented capuchin monkey who serves as Allan's live-in helpmate. Unbeknownst to Allan, friendly neighborhood mad scientist Pankow has surreptitiously injected the simian servant with human brain-juice serum that not only augments Ella's intelligence but makes her a ready receptor for Allan's darkest thoughts—thoughts Ella interprets as violent commands. Not the most promising premise ever to scamper down the scare-pic pike, and not even as proven a fright-meister as Romero can yield real chills from this uninspired situation. At the same time, *Monkey Shines* does proffer sights previously unseen on-screen. It's the first flick, for instance, that tries to wring gut-wrenching suspense from a climactic showdown whose vital components are a motionless quadriplegic, an equally stationary voice-controlled computer, a half-dead scientist shot through with enough barbiturates to "bring down King Kong," and a cute little hyperactive capuchin monkey running amok with a straight razor (!).

THE MONOLITH MONSTERS (1957) B&W **1/2

D: John Sherwood. Grant Williams, Lola Albright, Trevor Bardette, Les Tremayne, William Flaherty, Richard Cutting. 77 mins. (Universal)

Based on a story cowritten by ace sci-fi director Jack (*The Incredible Shrinking Man*) Arnold, *The Monolith Monsters* supplies its share of atmosphere in the early going as geologist Williams, teacher Albright, and newspaper editor Tremayne trace several desert deaths to the presence of strange black rocks that, like Joe Dante's future *Gremlins,* multiply when wet. The mouthy script ultimately turns *Monolith* into a major yak-a-thon, however, replete with homilies, analogies, and scientific theorizing galore. And even at heights reaching 30 feet or more, brainless shambling rock formations qualify as unlikely candidates for world domination. (Then again, we've been wrong before.) No relation to

the mediocre 1993 alien-possession tale *Monolith* (Universal), with Bill Paxton.

THE MONSTER AND THE GIRL (1941) B&W ***

D: Stuart Heisler. Ellen Drew, Robert Paige, Paul Lukas, Joseph Calleia, George Zucco, Rod Cameron, Marc Lawrence. 65 mins. (Foothill Video)

A somewhat sanitized road-show exploitation plot collides with mad-scientist melodramatics in this earnestly off-the-wall quickie boasting a relatively name cast. An innocent Phillip Terry stands trial for murder, framed by the gang who scammed his sister (Drew) into prostitution. After going the death-row route, Terry's brain is transplanted, by handy doc Zucco, into the body of a gorilla, enabling Terry to get his revenge against the gangsters. Thug Lawrence sums up their collective response: "I don't *wanna* get mangled!"

MONSTER ON THE CAMPUS (1958) B&W **1/2

D: Jack Arnold. Arthur Franz, Joanna Moore, Troy Donahue, Judson Pratt, Ross Elliott. 76 mins. (Universal)

MOTC casts Franz as an academia-based scientist obsessed with returning to man's primal roots. When a dead prehistoric fish drips on student Donahue's dog, the mutt goes briefly berserk. Over squeeze Moore's understandable objections, Franz injects himself with the fluid and reverts to a murderous simian state, leaving outsized hand- and footprints at the campus slay sites. Local cops fail at first to nail the culprit, even after fingerprinting the entire football team (!). Franz adds his sentiments to the decade's cinematic sexist canon when he categorizes temporarily unconscious assistant Moore as "a female in the perfect state—defenseless and silent." And that's *before* his transformation!

THE MYSTERIANS (1959) ***

D: Inoshiro Honda. Kenji Sahara, Yumi Shirakawa, Momoka Kochi. 85 mins. (Video Treasures)

This wonderfully lurid, high-decibel invasion staged by the horny, manic Mysterians from the planet Mysteroid (where else?) is arguably director Honda's liveliest Godzilla-less Toho terrorfest.

MYSTERIOUS ISLAND (1961) ***

D: Cy Endfield. Gary Merrill, Michael Craig, Michael Callan, Joan Greenwood, Herbert Lom. 101 mins. (Columbia/TriStar)

Merrill, Craig, and Callan are fugitive Union POW's who escape by balloon to the title isle, where they encounter Lom's Captain Nemo along with some of FX ace Ray Harryhausen's menacing creations in a loose but fun adaptation of the Jules Verne story. Bernard Herrmann contributes the stirring score.

NAKED LUNCH (1991) **1/2

D: David Cronenberg. Peter Weller, Judy Davis, Ian Holm, Julian Sands, Roy Scheider. 117 mins. (Fox)

Cronenberg's uneven but undeniably bold translation of the "unfilmable" William Burroughs novel chronicles the misadventures of Burroughs alter ego William Lee (author Weller) in the "Interzone," a blend of seedy '50s Morocco and a hallucinatory world of paranoid delusions. Cronenberg's meditation on madness and the creative process is greatly abetted by Howard Shore's cool-jazz score.

THE NAVIGATOR (1988) ***

D: Vincent Ward. Bruce Lyons, Hamish McFarlane, Marshall Napier, Chris

Haywood, Noel Appleby, Sarah Pierse. 92 mins. (Orion)

Ward's sometimes slow but intriguing time-travel tale finds a band of plague-haunted medieval villagers emerging in contempo New Zealand. Director Ward eschews a flip, rock-'n'-roll treatment in favor of an earnest, lyrical approach embellished by a somber visual style.

NEO-TOKYO   (1993) **1/2

D: Rin Taro, Yoshiaki Kawajiri, Katsuhiro Otomo. Animated. 50 mins. (Central Park Media)

Neo-Tokyo incorporates a trio of shorts from three different animators. Both Taro's "Labyrinth," a vaguely ominous Alice Through the Looking Glass variation, and Kawajiri's "Running Man," a visually hypnotic, neon-bright run around a futuristic racetrack, are longer on style than substance. Only Otomo—responsible for the animé cult classic Akira—manages to fuse excellent panoramic animation with a strong story line. His "Order to Stop Construction" recounts the misadventures of Tokyo "salary man" Sugioka, sent to shut down a cost-inefficient construction project in an unstable Third World country. The initially confident human emissary soon learns that he's no match for the site's tightly wound robot foreman, sort of a mechanized Captain Queeg. Funny, pointed, and spectacularly drawn, "Order" represents Neo-Tokyo's lone crossover segment.

THE NEST   (1988) **

D: Terence H. Winkless. Robert Lansing, Lisa Langlois, Franc Luz, Terri Treas, Stephen Davies. 88 mins. (MGM)

It's "Days of Slime and Roaches" time as seasoned celluloid exterminator Lansing—who'd previously battled outsized ants in Empire of the Ants (Embassy) and radioactive crabs in Island Claws (Vestron)—contends here with a special breed of rampaging roaches genetically engineered to destroy their more common bug brethren, then conveniently die out. Well, needless to say, die out they don't; in fact, they downright flourish (shades of Mimic). The Nest breaks little new bug-movie ground, though there's a clever montage depicting a restaurant roach massacre, set to the strains of "La Cucaracha," and some suitably sickening makeup FX. The flick also deserves credit for coming up with 1988's best (if most cryptic) tag line: "Why is the cheese moving?" The answer, alas, is not as intriguing as the question.

THE NEXT VOICE YOU HEAR (1950) B&W **1/2

D: William Wellman. James Whitmore, Nancy Davis, Jeff Corey, Lillian Bronson, Art Baker. 83 mins. (MGM)

God commandeers Earth's radio airwaves (!) to tell us all to lighten up a little. The movie cheats by never letting us hear the actual broadcasts (Whitmore is always getting to the nearest radio a moment too late). A bizarre Cold War paranoia piece, tinged with optimistic hysteria, Voice makes a fine companion for 1952's similarly themed Red Planet Mars (MGM), wherein scientist Peter Graves discovers that messages seemingly transmitted from Mars are actually direct communiques from God, which leads to a religious revival in Russia (!).

NIGHT OF THE COMET   (1984) ***

D: Thom Eberhardt. Catherine Mary Stewart, Kelli Maroney, Robert Beltran, John Achom, Mary Woronov, Geoffrey Lewis. 94 mins. (Fox)

A kind of The World, the Flesh, and the Brain-Damaged, Eberhardt's Night of the Comet imagines an Earth seemingly stripped of all "civilized" human life but for three San Berdoo deadheads—Val Gal sisters Stewart and Maroney and trucker Beltran— who soon find themselves imperiled by mad scientists (led by the always welcome Woronov), marauding punks, and the usual flesh-eating zombies (who are, unfortunately, underutilized here). While Comet doesn't quite attain top cult-movie rank—it indulges in too many mood-ruining wisecracks and lensward winks—the flick does take a perverse idea and, if not exactly runs, at least jogs briskly with it.

NIGHT SIEGE: PROJECT SHADOWCHASER 2   (1995) ***

D: John Eyres. Frank Zagarino, Bryan Genesse, Beth Toussaint, Todd Jensen. 97 mins. (New Line)

It's The Terminator Meets "Die Hard in a Nuclear Power Plant," with kickboxer Genesse (as a "drunken janitor"), scientist Toussaint, and her young son sharing the Bruce Willis role. When bulked-up, white-haired android Zagarino and his human terrorist squad slaughter dozens of plant workers, it's up to our heroic trio to save the day while local authorities and ruthless military brass keep vigil outside. Director Eyres lends his derivative but kinetic, well-acted, tautly paced sci-fi actioner a large look.

NIGHTFALL   (1988) **1/2

D: Paul Mayersberg. David Birney, Sarah Douglas, Alexis Kanner, Andra Millian, Starr Andreeff. 82 mins. (MGM)

A fairly compelling parable penned by prolific sci-fi scribe Isaac Asimov, Nightfall unfolds at an unspecified place and time—from the characters' tonsorial, sartorial, and New Agey styles, our guess would be Santa Cruz, circa 1973—on a planet illuminated by three suns that are gradually growing dark. Attempting to cope with the impending disaster are a burned-out scientist (Birney) and a blind religious zealot (Kanner) who's trying to exploit the drastic situation to augment his own power. Sort of a "My Three Suns," *Nightfall* works reasonably well as a sci-fi pulp version of a grade-B Greek myth. The mostly unknown thesps lend intensity to what's essentially a film-long science-versus-religion debate ("Nature" is likewise represented, in the form of sensuous "desert woman" Millian) and a talky one at that. *Nightfall* actually plays better on video, where its low-budget lack of action and FX are a lot less conspicuous than they were on the big screen.

NO ESCAPE   (1994) ***1/2

D: Martin Campbell. Ray Liotta, Lance Henriksen, Stuart Wilson, Kevin Dillon, Kevin J. O'Connor, Michael Lerner. 118 mins. (HBO) DVD

Despite its obvious high-tech *Escape from New York/Terminal Island/Fortress* roots and barbarous *Road Warrior* trappings, *No Escape* is much closer in spirit to *The Great Escape* and other POW epics of yore. (There are no female characters, and even the male-bonding rituals are relatively restrained.) Liotta plays a guilt-driven ex-military man who flees Warden Lerner's futuristic prison and ends up on an island torn by warring ex-inmates—Wilson's savage hordes and Henriksen's outnumbered civilized contingent. Director Campbell supplies well-staged wide-scale action galore and, except for the perennially wise-cracking Wilson, the thesps maintain an old-fashioned (in the best sense) earnestness throughout. For whatever reason—its generic B title, bad timing, or lack of star value—*No Escape* failed to score a bijou following.

NOT OF THIS EARTH   (1957) B&W ***

D: Roger Corman. Beverly Garland, Paul Birch, Morgan Jones, William Roerick,

Jonathan Haze, Dick Miller. 67 mins. (Allied Artists)

A prime example of Corman's ability to make a low budget work in his favor, *Not of This Earth* also benefits greatly from frequent AIP scribes Mark Hanna and Charles B. Griffith's compact but creepy script, as well as Garland's turn as the increasingly curious nurse hired to look after sunglassed secret alien Birch, newly beamed down from the planet Davana. The simple act of removing those ominous shades threw major scares into audiences of the day. Ditto for the voice-overs employed when Birch and endangered distaff alien Anne Carroll communicate telepathically while outwardly ignoring each other. The ever waiting furnace, next to the fridge housing a human blood supply, in Birch's sinister basement also kept viewers on edge without costing Rog a proverbial red cent.

NOT OF THIS EARTH   (1988) *1/2

D: Jim Wynorski. Traci Lords, Arthur Roberts, Lenny Juliano, Ace Mask, Kelli Maroney. 80 mins. (MGM)

Much B-video ballyhoo accompanied the casting of former under-age porn starlet Lords in the Garland role in the first of Roger's remakes. As it turns out, Traci's not what's wrong with this picture. While no match for the formidable Garland as the feisty nurse who uncovers an alien vampire's plot for world conquest, Traci acquits herself quite adequately here, as does Roberts as the unemotional E.T. who likes to zap his victims with his glowing radioactive eyes. What's wrong here is the flick's campy, soulless fan-boy script and direction, ingredients that thoroughly trample the original's charms.

NOT OF THIS EARTH   (1996) ***

D: Terence A. Winkless. Michael York, Parker Stevenson, Elizabeth Barondes, Richard

Belzer, Mason Adams, Bob McFarland. 88 mins. (New Horizons)

Exec producer Corman's second recycling gets it right, preserving the pulp dignity of the original while embellishing the story line with low-budget but effective FX, courtesy of Media Magic and John Carl Buechler, among others. Erstwhile Brit star York represents an improvement over Paul Birch, communicating his stranger-in-a-strange land status with appropriately spaced-out speech and body tics. While no Beverly Garland (a one-of-a-kind in any case), Barondes registers well as the increasingly suspicious nurse hired to attend to the weird Mr. Johnson's unusual plasma needs, even tossing in a gratuitous shower scene. Belzer easily outsleazes Jonathan Haze's chauffeur character, and revamping Dick Miller's vacuum salesman as a door-to-door religious zealot represents a clever stroke. Indeed, Charles Philip Moore's light rewrite attests to the strength of Hanna and Griffith's original script, with HIV fears smoothly subbing for the veiled Commie-invasion threat that supplied the context for the original (and so many other '50s sci-fi frightfests). The ending packed more punch in the original—it was shot more dramatically and was also far less of a cliché than it seems today—but overall this *Earth* rates as an urgent, swiftly paced scare pic that helps erase the bad taste left by the 1988 desecration. Recidivist Roger reworks the story yet again, in a gender-reversed variation with Athena Massey as the space vamp, in the 1997 dud *Star Portal* (New Horizons).

THE OMEGA MAN   (1971) ***

D: Boris Sagal. Charlton Heston, Rosalind Cash, Anthony Zerbe. 98 mins. (Warner)

The second screen adaptation of Richard Matheson's *I Am Legend*

CORMAN ON STRONG: Alien vampire Michael York shields sensitive ears in producer Roger Corman's superior 1996 remake of his 1957 sci-fi winner *Not of This Earth. Courtesy of Concorde–New Horizons Corp.*

sequences and dumbed-down dramatics. It's up to newly estranged scientific couple Hoffman and Russo, with assists from wisecracking aide Spacey and straight-arrow army officer Gooding, to locate and isolate an escaped monkey who's spreading a deadly African virus across the country. Much of the action unfolds in and around an infected California town that evil military honcho Sutherland wants to nuke off the face of the map, a move opposed by conscience-stricken general Freeman. The flick's tag line—"Try to remain calm"—doesn't exactly stack up with "Be afraid…Be very afraid" or "In space, no one can hear you scream," but Petersen and crew try hard to alarm and entertain, tasks at which they mostly succeed.

OUTLAND   (1981) ★★★

D: Peter Hyams. Sean Connery, Peter Boyle, Frances Sternhagen. 109 mins. (Warner) DVD

Peter *(The Relic)* Hyams assembles a bleak but effective *High Noon* variation that shifts the action from the Wild West to a grim mining settlement in space. Connery is especially convincing in the updated Gary Cooper role, while Sternhagen lends excellent support.

PANDORA AND THE FLYING DUTCHMAN   (1951) ★★★

D: Albert Lewin. James Mason, Ava Gardner, Nigel Patrick, Sheila Sim, Harold Warrender, Mario Cabre. 123 mins. (Kino)

In his supernatural romantic fantasy, producer-director-scripter Lewin updates the legend of the Flying Dutchman, relocating it to an expatriate Anglo enclave in a little Spanish coastal town circa 1930. Mason casts an eerie, weary shadow as the erstwhile Dutch sea captain (clad in contempo garb and with no trace of a Netherlands accent) doomed to wander the seas for eternity for having murdered his wife some 300 years

stars Heston as a plague survivor battling contaminated hordes in a futuristic L.A. While the pic itself's an improvement, Chuck's no match for Vincent Price in the earlier adaptation *The Last Man on Earth* (see index). No relation to the Albert Pyun dud *Omega Doom* (Columbia/TriStar), with Rutger Hauer.

OUTBREAK   (1995) ★★★

D: Wolfgang Petersen. Dustin Hoffman, Rene Russo, Morgan Freeman, Cuba Gooding, Jr., Patrick Dempsey, Donald Sutherland, Kevin Spacey. 128 mins. (Warner) DVD

Petersen's large-scale entry in the killer-virus genre shapes up as a somewhat schizy mix of exciting action before; only the love of a woman willing to die for him can set him free from his solitary sentence and grant him the death he so desperately desires. A radiant Ava—a capricious American cabaret singer who's adored by racing driver Patrick and matador Cabre—seems a highly unlikely candidate for the job. As the reels roll on, however, Mason and Gardner find their fates becoming increasingly intertwined. Lewin's tale is a mostly melancholy, even downright downbeat affair that benefits from superior perfs, rich Technicolor location lensing (by Jack Cardiff), and a bittersweet ambience. Particularly striking from a genre standpoint are those sequences depicting Mason afloat on his ghost boat, complete with phantom crew. Though slow sailing at times, *Pandora* is well worth the ride.

PANIC IN YEAR ZERO! (1962) B&W ***¹⁄₂

D: Ray Milland. Ray Milland, Jean Hagen, Frankie Avalon, Mary Mitchell, Joan Freeman, Richard Garland, Dick Bakalyan, Rex Holman. 92 mins. (Orion)

Panic in Year Zero!, directed by Milland from a sharp script cowritten by Jay (*Creation of the Humanoids, The Killer Shrews*) Simms, shapes up as a surprisingly gritty postnuke survival story released theatrically at the height of 1962's Cuban missile crisis, a period vividly recalled in Joe Dante's *Matinee* (see index). Milland also enjoys starring honors, as a vacationing middle-class dad forced into sometimes brutal resourcefulness when A-bombs pelt the California coast. Milland leads his postnuclear family unit—wife Hagen, son Avalon, and daughter Mitchell—past traffic-choked roads, raging chaos, and a trio of thugs headed by peerless screen punk Bakalyan. Relentlessly unsentimental, *Panic* generates considerable tension as Milland and clan are compelled to make snap moral decisions that challenge their own sense of decency.

PAST PERFECT (1998) **¹⁄₂

D: Jonathan Heap. Eric Roberts, Nick Mancuso, Saul Rubinek, Laurie Holden, Matt Hildreth. 92 mins. (Artisan)

A far-fetched but fairly entertaining sci-fi/action tale, *Past Perfect* stars Mancuso as a vigilante from the future who, accompanied by rotund statistician Rubinek, journeys to our time to terminate a quartet of violent youths whom contempo lawman Roberts and partner Holden have been tracking. Standard shoot-outs and chases abound, but *Past Perfect* incorporates a couple of neat elements—the time travelers devolve from their present age to infancy before they die, and the opening credits run over a sobering montage of bullets being manufactured along an assembly line. On the downside, the pic has the temerity to rip off *Maniac Cop*'s tag line when Roberts snarls at a cornered killer, "You have the right to remain silent…forever."

THE PHANTOM (1996) **

D: Simon Wincer. Billy Zane, Kristy Swanson, Treat Williams, Catherine Zeta Jones, James Remar, Patrick McGoohan, Carey Hiroyuki-Tagawa, Casey Siemaszko, Samantha Eggar. 100 mins. (Paramount) DVD

Lee Falk's venerable syndicated comic-strip hero's long journey to the big screen ended in considerable disappointment. Despite its pedigree (Joe Dante's among the pic's many executive producers), able cast, polished production values, terrif late-'30s props, and vivid cartoon colors, *The Phantom* never really ignites. Reminiscent of 1991's *The Rocketeer* (see index), which benefitted from a sharper script than the one Jeffrey Boam word-processed here, *The Phantom* lacks the necessary cinemagic to bring Falk's "Ghost Who Walks" to rousing screen life. One highlight features a variation on the famed spiked-binoculars scene

from *Horrors of the Black Museum* (see index), but the movie's exciting moments are woefully few and far between. Paramount marketeers went all out with their home-video promotions, though; the hologram-styled lenticular box rates as a keeper, and we likewise thank them for the cool key chain and Phantom ring.

PHANTOM FROM SPACE (1953) B&W **¹⁄₂

D: W. Lee Wilder. Harry Landers, Rudolph Anders, Noreen Nash. 72 mins. (Goodtimes)

Okay, so nothing much really *happens*—an invisible alien runs around an observatory—but the ensemble cast's admirable enthusiasm got *this* Phantom caught up in the nonaction. And *Phantom* represents one of the least risible efforts of Billy Wilder's brothers, scripter Myles and director W. Lee.

THE PHANTOM PLANET (1961) B&W **¹⁄₂

D: William Marshall. Dean Fredericks, Coleen Gray, Anthony Dexter. 82 mins. (Englewood)

Fredericks is an astronaut who undergoes cut-rate Gulliver-type experiences in space in an earnest B sci-fier whose ideas frequently exceed its budget. Silent-film star Francis X. Bushman returns to the screen as the planet's alien honcho.

THE PHILADELPHIA EXPERIMENT:
THE SERIES

THE PHILADELPHIA EXPERIMENT (1984) **¹⁄₂

D: Stewart Raffill. Michael Pare, Nancy Allen, Bobby DiCicco. 102 mins. (HBO)

Raffill's convoluted time-warp tale alternates between the admirably complex and the merely illogical, but World War II sailors Pare and DiCicco's jaunt from 1943 to 1984 is, in the end, a trip worth taking.

THE PHILADELPHIA EXPERIMENT 2 (1993) **1/2

D: Stephen Cornwell. Brad Johnson, Marjean Holden, Gerrit Graham, Cyril O'Reilly, James Greene. 98 mins. (Trimark)

Cornwell's belated time-travel sequel posits the existence of a parallel reality wherein the Nazis—having nuked Washington, D.C., in 1943 with a stealth bomber stolen from the future—have controlled America for 50 years. It's up to survivor Johnson (in the original Pare role) and anti-Nazi guerrillas to reverse history, a scheme opposed by villain Graham. The sequel loses points for its narrow focus and slow, at times almost comatose pace, but it balances these defects with an effectively somber mood.

PI (1998) B&W ***1/2

D: Darren Aronofsky. Sean Gullette, Mark Margolies, Ben Schenkman, Samia Shoaib, Pamela Hart, Ajay Naidu. 85 mins. (Artisan) DVD

With its jittery intensity, ultra-grainy black-and-white cinematography, and pervasive air of ever escalating paranoia, *Pi* plays like a refugee from filmdom's Golden Age of Anxiety, the early-to-mid-'60s, when moviegoers squirmed to the likes of John Frankenheimer's *Seconds* (see index) and Arthur Penn's *Mickey One* (Facets Video). Gullette stars as a reclusive mathematical genius who may be close to discovering the numerical equivalent of the secret of the universe, a discovery that's made him the target of rival factions ranging from corporate villains to Hasidic mystics. Working on a reported $60,000 budget, debuting writer/director Aronof-

sky truly works miracles in creating a mini-gem that scores both as a cerebral puzzle and a pulse-racing thriller, excitingly lensed on authentic Manhattan (mostly Chinatown) locations.

PIRANHA: THE SERIES

PIRANHA (1995) **1/2

D: Scott Levy. William Katt, Alexandra Paul, Darleen Carr, Soleil Moon Frye, James Karen, Mila Kunis, Monte Markham, Lincoln Kilpatrick. 81 mins. (New Horizons) DVD

Director Levy and crew look to put the *ick* in *ichthyological* in a relatively pointless but undeniably bloody revamp of Joe Dante's recommended 1978 original, *Piranha* (Warner, DVD), itself followed by James Cameron's directorial debut, *Piranha 2: The Spawning* (Nelson). Though based on the same John Sayles script, Levy's version plays the story line, about genetically enhanced piranha on the loose at a remote resort, a bit more straight-faced. If you've been longing to see former *Punky Brewster*, Frye, chewed to bits by the titular fish, *Piranha* may well be your only chance.

PLANET OF BLOOD (1966) **1/2

D: Curtis Harrington. John Saxon, Basil Rathbone, Dennis Hopper. 81 mins. (Sinister Cinema)

Originally titled *Queen of Blood*, this was Val Lewton–inspired auteur Harrington's second teaming (after *Night Tide*) with actor Hopper, cast here as a member of a spaceship crew that brings an E.T. vampire aboard. The recycled FX (lifted from a Roger Corman–leased Russian sci-fi flick, *Niebo Zowlet*) look fine but fatally delay the start of what might otherwise have been an interesting story line. Florence

Marly makes for an inventive vampire, though.

PLANET OF THE APES: THE SERIES

PLANET OF THE APES (1968) ***1/2

D: Franklin J. Schaffner. Charlton Heston, Kim Hunter, Roddy McDowall, Maurice Evans. 112 mins. (Fox) DVD

The debut adaptation—Rod Serling was among the scripters—of novelist Pierre Boulle's vision of a simian dystopia, wherein apes achieve primate supremacy over humans, remains the series' best and one of the greatest sci-fi epics of its era. The film's final-twist image has attained deserved classic status. Available in a remastered "30th anniversary edition," in wide-screen and full-frame formats. The "making-of" documentary *Behind the Planet of the Apes* (Fox) is also recommended.

BENEATH THE PLANET OF THE APES (1970) ***

D: Ted Post. James Franciscus, Kim Hunter, Charlton Heston. 95 mins. (Fox)

The sci-fi simian series' first sequel shapes up as an effectively wacko affair, stolen by hymn-singing, H-bomb-worshipping mutants. Repeat after us: "Glory be to the Bomb/And to the Holy Fallout..."

ESCAPE FROM THE PLANET OF THE APES (1971) ***

D: Don Taylor. Roddy McDowall, Kim Hunter, Ricardo Montalban. 98 mins. (Fox)

Brainy chimps McDowall and Hunter experience severe culture shock and fur-raising adventures when they travel back in time to a human-dominated Earth. The third *Apes* installment rates as another winner.

CONQUEST OF THE PLANET OF THE APES (1972) ***

D: J. Lee Thompson. Roddy McDowall, Don Murray, Ricardo Montalban, Natalie Trundy. 87 mins. (Fox)

Despite a faint made-for-TV feel, Part 4 of the *Apes* series supplies sufficient action as thinking chimp McDowall leads his fellow primates against their human oppressors.

BATTLE FOR THE PLANET OF THE APES (1973) **½

D: J. Lee Thompson. Roddy McDowall, Natalie Trundy, John Huston. 86 mins. (Fox)

The last and least *Apes* entry stresses action over ideas as humanoid mutants seek to topple the ruling chimp elite. Still fun for the celluloid simian series' fans.

POISON (1990) B&W/COLOR **½

D: Todd Haynes. Edith Meeks, Larry Maxwell, Susan Norman. 85 mins. (Fox Lorber)

Haynes's interesting if overrated indie received considerable publicity when reactionaries complained about its NEA funding, but the film isn't nearly as outrageous as the resultant hype. Haynes's intercutting of three short films—"Hero," "Horror," and "Homo"—seems more willed than inspired, and the tone remains too distant and occasionally pretentious to register full impact. The B&W "Horror" segment has its moments, though: A pointed '50s-styled sci-fi parody, it sees a scientist isolate, extract, and accidentally ingest the vital components of the human sex drive, a move that eventually transforms him into the frothing, scabrous "Leper Sex Killer" (!). Haynes returned with 1995's intriguing "envi-ronmental illness" inquiry *Safe* (Columbia/TriStar) and 1998's 1970s-set glam-rock examination *Velvet Goldmine* (Buena Vista).

PREDATOR:
THE SERIES

PREDATOR (1987) **½

D: John McTiernan. Arnold Schwarzenegger, Carl Weathers, Elpidio Carillo, Bill Duke, Sonny Landham, R. G. Armstrong. 107 mins. (Fox) DVD

Arnie toplines as "Dutch," macho leader of a wild and crazy mercenary band who land in a Central American jungle to stage a hostage-rescue mission with the dubious aid of CIA op and fellow Nautilus mutant Weathers. A high-concept combo of the action and alien-amok genres, *Predator* finds our heroes completing their violent guerrilla assignment with the usual consummate ease, only to wind up on the other end of the chase, targets of an outsized, laser-equipped E.T. (time-shared by tall Kevin Peter Hall, also seen as the far wimpier Bigfoot in *Harry and the Hendersons* [Universal], and a young Jean-Claude Van Damme) on an earthly hunting vacation (a riff earlier employed in *Without Warning*, from Video Screams). The extremely predictable but reasonably engaging proceedings ultimately narrow down to a toe-to-toe showdown between Arnie and the alien. (No contest.)

PREDATOR 2 (1990) **½

D: Stephen Hopkins. Danny Glover, Gary Busey, Ruben Blades, Maria Conchita Alonso, Bill Paxton, Robert Davi, Calvin Lockhart, Morton Downey, Jr., Kevin Peter Hall. 108 mins. (Fox)

Despite the Mighty Arnie's absence, the virtually all-star sequel stacks up as a serviceable sci-fi actioner that offers up less suspense but a higher body count than the original. An alien hunter drawn to human heat and violence again wends his way earthward, this time forsaking the Central American jungle in favor of a 1997 L.A. that, like *RoboCop*'s Detroit, is an open battlefield occupied by rival drug syndicates, in this case of the Jamaican and Colombian persuasions. Cop Glover's protracted climactic battle with the insatiable alien (played by returnee Hall) doesn't quite live up to Arnold's bout with the original predator, but he does deliver a rousing roundhouse to the jaw of Morton Downey, Jr., typecast here as a scuzzbucket telejournalist.

PROGENY (1998) ***

D: Brian Yuzna. Arnold Vosloo, Jillian McWhirter, Brad Dourif, Lindsay Crouse, Wilford Brimley, Don Calfa. 90 mins. (Sterling)

Hitherto infertile E.R. doc Vosloo and wife McWhirter are thrilled when they learn she's pregnant—until they discover the fetus she's carrying is a result of alien insemination. Or is it? Not at all the simple E.T.-amok chiller its packaging suggests, *Progeny* has more disturbing notions on its twisted little brain. That shouldn't be too surprising, considering that the film was spawned by the fertile minds of writer Stuart (*Re-Animator*) Gordon and director Brian (*The Dentist*) Yuzna. Unlike most of the pair's separate and collaborative creations, *Progeny* proceeds sans a sardonic, satiric overlay, playing its unsettling material totally straight, and it's the story's note of growing ambiguity that makes the film all the more powerful. Vosloo is intense as the overworked physician who may harbor mental problems beyond work stress, while the always welcome Dourif typically gives his all as an obsessive alien "expert" who rallies to the couple's cause. *Progeny* is structured to provide plenty of shocks and carnage as the silvery, tentacled, obsidian-eyed aliens execute their real or imagined schemes.

PROJECT X   (1987) ***

D: Jonathan Kaplan. Matthew Broderick, Helen Hunt, Bill Sadler, Johnny Ray McGhee, Dick Miller, Willie, Karanja, Okko, Luke. 108 mins. (Fox)

A fun if formulaic fantasy, *Project X* toplines Broderick as Jimmy Garrett, a grounded airman assigned to work with chimps at a Florida-based air force flight-simulation program. Our hero forms a close attachment to young Virgil (vividly interpreted by simian thesp Willie), a literate chimp dumped from sign-language experiments conducted by psych student Hunt. When Jimmy learns of the sinister fates awaiting the chimps, he enlists Hunt's aid in staging a maverick rescue mission. The pongid performers and their off-screen trainers do a fine job here, and Kaplan treats his subject matter with admirable respect. (He also pays homage to his own B-movie roots by casting Roger Corman vet Miller in a cameo and, in a neat nod to Ed Wood, naming a minor character Dr. Criswell.) The flick's negative take re the air force's callous attitudes supplies a welcome change from knee-jerk flag-wavers of that gung-ho era like *Top Gun* (though *Project X* does have its own fleeting "Top Chimp" moments). No relation to 1968's futuristic sci-fier *Project X* (n/a).

PULSE   (1988) ***

D: Paul Golding. Cliff De Young, Roxanne Hart, Joey Lawrence, Matthew Lawrence, Charles Tyner, Myron Healey. 91 mins. (Columbia/TriStar)

Something of an earnest sci-fi revamp of Buster Keaton's anarchic *Electric House*, *Pulse* pits a modern 'burb family—dad De Young, stepmom Hart, and son Joey Lawrence—against their hith-

erto normal abode's suddenly subversive electrical wiring. At first only young Lawrence—with an assist from "paranoid" electrician Tyner (who resembles Freddy Krueger sans scar tissue)—is on to the arcane scheme. But when TVs, washer-dryers, and heating systems start openly revolting, our imperiled nuclear unit realizes what they're up against. *Pulse* doesn't do full justice to its genuinely unnerving premise—its occasionally slack pacing, made-for-TV feel, and general lack of juice keep the electric chaos too low-voltage at times—but the pic supplies enough honest jolts to give sci-fright seekers a charge.

THE PUPPET MASTERS (1994) ***

D: Stuart Orme. Donald Sutherland, Eric Thal, Julie Warren, Keith David, Will Patton, Yaphet Kotto. 109 mins. (Buena Vista)

Orme's *Puppet Masters* plays like a modernized '50s sci-fi flick, in the best sense. Drawn from Robert Heinlein's 1951 novel of the same name, *The Puppet Masters* sports virtually the same plot as Jack Finney's original *Invasion of the Body Snatchers* novella. The filmmakers further emphasize that connection by casting Sutherland, late of Philip Kaufman's 1979 *Invasion of the Body Snatchers* remake, in the lead. While the story line is similar, *The Puppet Masters*, like Britain's Nigel Kneale–adapted *Quatermass* series, takes a tense, straight-line approach, with no time out for subplots or frills. Here the aliens—resembling higher-tech (they're 60 percent brain) variations on Roger Corman's bat-mite creatures from *It Conquered the World*—strike right in reel 1, "riding the backs" of small-town Ambrose, Iowa, residents. Assisted by his government-agent son, Thal, fellow agent David, and scientists Warren and Patton, no-nonsense investigator Sutherland races against time to contain the

aliens' rapid spread and find a way to destroy them while saving their involuntary human hosts.

QUATERMASS:
THE SERIES

THE QUATERMASS XPERIMENT (1956) B&W ***

D: Val Guest. Brian Donlevy, Margia Dean, Jack Warner. 78 mins. (MGM)

An authoritative Donlevy, as Professor Quatermass, deals harshly with a mutated astronaut in this tense, no-nonsense British entry in Nigel Kneale's popular *Quatermass* sci-fi series, originally released stateside as *The Creeping Unknown*. *First Man into Space* (Rhino), *Night of the Blood Beast* (Sinister Cinema), and the more recent *Mutant Species* (Artisan) sport similar story lines, less adroitly handled.

QUATERMASS 2 (1957) B&W ***

D: Val Guest. Brian Donlevy, Michael Ripper, Bryan Forbes. 85 mins. (Anchor Bay) DVD

Released in the U.S. as *Enemy from Space*, the second big-screen installment in the Quatermass series finds the dogged Professor Q. (a returning Donlevy) battling blob monsters, brainwashed zombies, and alien invaders in a low-budget but adrenalizing roller-coaster ride. Anchor Bay also has the tense Quatermass-like 1956 inner-earth invasion pic *X the Unknown*.

QUATERMASS AND THE PIT (1968) ***½

D: Roy Ward Baker. Andrew Keir, Barbara Shelley, James Donald, Julian Glover. 98 mins. (Anchor Bay) DVD

The third and best of Kneale's *Quatermass* adventures to reach the big screen, *Quatermass and the Pit* (better known stateside as *Five Million Years to Earth*) casts Keir as the intrepid Professor Q., who's called in to investigate an exceedingly strange discovery at a London underground station. Hostile military man Glover insists that the odd object is an arcane Nazi weapon, buried since World War II, but Keir, along with fellow scientists Donald and Shelley, uncovers a far more sinister explanation. The less the uninitiated viewer knows going in, the better, since scripter Kneale and director Baker unravel the mystery in truly inventive fashion. Tobe Hooper's *Lifeforce* later lifted whole chunks from this twisty shocker, but the original's still the greatest. Sinister Cinema, meanwhile, carries the complete 1958 BBC-miniseries version of the tale, likewise titled *Quatermass and the Pit*.

THE QUATERMASS CONCLUSION (1980) **½

D: Piers Haggard. John Mills, Simon MacCorkindale, Barbara Kellerman. 105 mins. (HBO)

Mills assumes the Quatermass mantle in a cost-efficient but interesting tale, originally produced for British TV, about a ray from outer space that paralyzes the planet's youth (an early MTV satellite beam?).

QUEST FOR FIRE (1981) ****

D: Jean-Jacques Annaud. Everett McGill, Rae Dawn Chong, Ron Perlman, Nameer El Kadi. 97 mins. (Fox)

A trio of prehistoric tribesmen—sort of an earnest Stone Age Stooges—set off for parts unknown in search of the title element. Along the way, they encounter hungry cannibals, hostile apemen, giant mastodons (who are at least willing to negotiate), and Chong as

HIT PIT: Professor Q. (Andrew Keir) and scientific ally James Donald inspect underground Martian grasshopper in the alien insect classic *Quatermass and the Pit* (a.k.a. *Five Million Years to Earth*).
Courtesy of Anchor Bay Entertainment

a stray member of a more advanced tribe. While we weren't too impressed with Anthony Burgess's minimal linguistic contributions, the gestural thesping (Desmond Morris, of *The Naked Ape* fame, served as a consultant here) is first-rate, the action exciting, and the story at once funny, rousing, and poignant. Unfairly ignored during its initial theatrical release, *Quest*, in its cable-TV and video afterlife, has since gained the audience support it has long merited. Other cave faves include the 1940 video rarity *One Million B.C.* (Hal Roach Video) and the 1966 Hammer gruntfest *One Million Years B.C.* (Fox),

featuring Raquel Welch and her pelt bikini.

THE QUIET EARTH (1985) **

D: Geoff Murphy. Bruno Lawrence, Alison Routledge, Peter Smith. 91 mins. (Fox)

Murphy's New Zealand–set reworking of *The World, the Flesh and the Devil* (n/a), replete with racial angle, stars Lawrence as a doomsday survivor who discovers he's not alone in the world after all. Spectacular visual effects help compensate for some predictable plot turns.

RABID (1977) ***

D: David Cronenberg. Marilyn Chambers, Frank Moore, Joe Silver. 91 mins. (Warner)

Ex-porn starlet Chambers is an accident victim whose real troubles begin when she enters a research hospital, where she's subjected to experimental surgery, develops the titular condition, and subsequently spreads it through Montreal. Much graphic sexual/medical madness ensues in a film that's somewhat basic by Cronenberg's later standards but still stacks up as good, sick fun. Marilyn's genre-movie career, meanwhile, went generally downhill from here, with appearances in, among others, *Angel of H.E.A.T.* (Vestron), *Bikini Bistro* (Arrow), and *Party Incorporated* (Video Treasures).

RATBOY (1986) *

D: Sondra Locke. Sondra Locke, Robert Townsend, Christopher Hewett, Larry Hankin, Gerrit Graham, Louie Anderson. 105 mins. (Warner)

Clint Eastwood must have liked former squeeze and later litigant Locke a *lot* at one time to lend a helping hand to this embarrassing "cult"-movie manqué. (On second thought, maybe *not*.) The plot finds hopeless schemer Locke (who also directed) running into the title anomaly, an unexplained hybrid between rat and boy who, in his ubiquitous shades, resembles a younger Bob Dylan on a *terrible* day. With the help of her "comic"-relief brothers, Sondra runs Ratboy through the L.A. wringer in a bid for fame and fortune. Warning: The brain cells you save may be your own.

RE-ANIMATOR (1985) ***1/2

D: Stuart Gordon. Jeffrey Combs, Bruce Abbott, Barbara Crampton, Robert

Sampson, David Gale, Carolyn Purdy-Gordon. In R and unrated editions. 88 mins. (Vestron) DVD

Re-Animator focuses on some grisly fun and games going on at the Miskatonic, Massachusetts, Med School morgue, where precocious mad scientist Herbert West (Combs) is perfecting a secret serum to reanimate the dead. To this end, he recruits fellow med student Daniel Kane (Abbott) and a number of soon-to-be-lively cadavers. Director Gordon, basing his loopy gorefest on a venerable H. P. Lovecraft story, keeps the demented action moving at a brisk pace. To learn why a murdered, revivified, and then lobotomized (!) med-school dean delivers his naked blond daughter (Crampton) to the decapitated-but-still-living head of a lascivious brain surgeon—well, you'll just have to see for yourself.

REJUVENATOR (1988) **1/2

D: Brian Thomas Jones. Vivian Lanko, John MacKay, Jessica Dublin. 85 mins. (Sony)

No relation to *Re-Animator*, *Rejuvenator*—or *Rejuvenatrix*, as the title credits have it—involves a rich, geriatric actress (Dublin) who's funding a scientist (MacKay) working on a human brain-juice serum that reverses the aging process. Unfortunately, if not unexpectedly, there are serious side effects, as when our rejuvenated heroine (now played by Lanko) runs out of juice and transmogrifies into a screeching disfigured hag, replete with pulsating face—a condition that prompts her to remove and devour the gray matter of those hapless victims who cross her voracious path. While not exactly big in the originality department—the enjoyably campy bug-lady romp *Evil Spawn* (Camp Video) sports virtually the same *Wasp Woman*–inspired plot—*Rejuvenator* succeeds as a deadpan, gorified

re-creation of a typical '50s sci-fi/horror cheapie.

REMOTE CONTROL (1988) ***

D: Jeff Lieberman. Kevin Dillon, Deborah Goodrich, Christopher Wynne, Frank Beddar, Jennifer Tilly, Bert Remsen. 88 mins. (Avid)

An *Invasion of the Body Snatchers* for the video generation, *Remote Control* is a witty, high-concept sci-fi satire. Dillon toplines as a vid-store clerk who notices that a new arrival—ostensibly a campy '50s sci-fi flick titled *Remote Control* (itself an expert send-up of that vanished genre)—is having a bizarre effect on viewers, turning them into murderous brainwashed alien slaves. The chase is soon on as Kev, abetted by Goodrich and vid-store owner Wynne, races against time to destroy the alien cassettes before *they* destroy us video-addicted earthlings. The crisp performances, fast-paced direction, funny futuristic set and wardrobe designs, and consistently clever script conspire to make *Remote Control* a winner. Lieberman also directed the superior rainy-night-in-Georgia-set killer-sandworm romp *Squirm* and the trippy terror tale *Blue Sunshine* (both Vestron).

REPTILICUS (1962) **1/2

D: Sid Pink. Carl Ottosen, Ann Smyrner, Mimi Heinrich, Asbjorn Andersen, Marla Behrens, Bent Mejding. 81 mins. (Orion)

Attempting to do for Copenhagen what *Godzilla* did for Tokyo, *Gorgo* did for London, and *The Beast from 20,000 Fathoms* did for Wall Street and Coney Island, then-expat American auteur Pink contributes this energetically destructive, if narratively clichéd, dinosaur romp. It's a slow buildup from oil driller Mejding's discovery of a living giant-reptile tail to the beast's eventual regeneration under scientist Andersen's care at the Denmark Aquarium. Director Pink interrupts the proceedings for a lengthy Copenhagen travelog (!), as initially gruff American officer Ottosen and blond Smyrner cruise the Danish capital's scenic streets before partaking of the pleasures of the famed Tivoli Gardens, where a local chanteuse croons the ditty "Tivoli Nights." Once the monster awakes, however, Reptilicus proves he can hold his own with the global creature competition, leveling much of the city, chomping on citizens, and spewing animated green-yellow flames at his military attackers—scenes decently executed on a limited budget. (Particularly impressive is a panicked citizenry's flight across a bridge, an exodus that sends several cyclers crashing helplessly into the waters below.) The movie concludes on a typically open-ended note, but no sequel proved forthcoming. *Reptilicus,* shot in gloriously preserved Pathé-Color, is the type of monster flick you can watch with the sound off and not miss much.

SWAMP THING:
THE SERIES

THE RETURN OF SWAMP THING (1989) **½

D: Jim Wynorski. Dick Durock, Heather Locklear, Louis Jourdan, Sarah Douglas, Daniel Taylor, Ace Mask. 88 mins. (Columbia/TriStar)

The film's comic-book plot—involving Dr. Arcane's (Jourdan) loony lab experiments in creative genetic mutation—serves as a suitable frame for a fast-paced series of mock confrontations twixt good and evil. In addition to representing a marked improvement over Wes Craven's rather leaden 1982 original, *Swamp Thing* (Columbia/TriStar), *Return* is also the first flick to pose the thought-provoking query "Why aren't men more like plants?"

THE ROAD WARRIOR: SEE MAD MAX: THE SERIES

ROBOCOP:
THE SERIES

ROBOCOP (1987) ****

D: Paul Verhoeven. Peter Weller, Nancy Allen, Ronny Cox, Kurtwood Smith, Miguel Ferrer, Robert DoQui. 103 mins. (Orion) DVD

This brilliantly subversive movie amply delivers on both the action and lampoon levels, weaving abrupt and senseless violence into Dutch-émigré director Verhoeven's deadpan dissection of America's corporate lusts, trashy sitcom culture, and pandemic greed for power, speed, and general *bigness*—in cars, guns, and bank accounts. As the title character, Weller plays a Detroit lawman-turned-cyborg who comes equipped with a snappy machine-pistol, an acute identity crisis, a baby-food diet (!), and a gait that should be registered with Monty Python's Ministry of Silly Walks. Allen supplies solid backup as Robo's partner, while Smith makes for a memorably scurvy villain. Cox and Ferrer are appropriately slimy as a pair of competing corporate creeps. A must for action, sci-fi, and satire fans alike.

ROBOCOP 2 (1990) **

D: Irvin Kershner. Peter Weller, Nancy Allen, Dan O'Herlihy, Belinda Bauer, Tom Noonan, Gabriel Damon, John Glover. 118 mins. (Orion) DVD

When last we left RoboCop Weller, he was assuring his critically wounded partner, Allen (who'd absorbed at least nine bullets, by our count), that she too could be bionically repaired. ("They can fix you. They can fix anything.") We therefore assumed that Nancy's robotic resurrection would play a role in *RoboCop 2*. Instead, the incident is completely ignored—Nancy's seen fully restored and back

on the force, sans explanation, as the sequel opens. Plot continuity isn't the only ingredient missing from Kershner's pedestrian retread of Verhoeven's brilliant original. Gone too are Verhoeven's finely tuned anarchic vision and cutting anti-corporate satire, replaced by mostly mindless comic-book overkill. That's not to say that *RoboCop 2* is entirely devoid of inventive touches: Drug czar Noonan's preteen partner, Damon, is a neat variation on your standard adult evilmonger; Glover contributes a funny cameo as a pitchman for "MagnaVolt," a lethal car-security device; and a contortionist's violin rendition of Steppenwolf's "Born to Be Wild" (!) during a TV telethon to save Detroit supplies a moment yours truly will long remember.

ROBOCOP 3 (1993) ***

D: Fred Dekker. Robert John Burke, Nancy Allen, Rip Torn, John Castle, Remy Ryan, Jill Hennessy, CCH Pounder, Mako, Robert DoQui. 105 mins. (Orion) DVD

Panned by most mainstream critics, Fred (*Night of the Creeps*) Dekker's *RoboCop 3*, while falling well short of Verhoeven's original, represents a vast improvement over *RoboCop 2*. Dekker takes the concept in a fresh direction, fashioning what plays like the live-action equivalent of an *anime* feature. A Japanese firm, working with the omnivorous Omni Products Corp., plans to redevelop Detroit's downtrodden Delta City and hires mega-armed mercenaries to clear the area of its impoverished inhabitants. Freedom fighters headed by Pounder and aided by cute, orphaned computer-wiz Ryan enlist RoboCop (Burke, replacing Weller) to join their struggle. Proceeding at a breakneck pace, *RoboCop 3* offers gunfights, pitched battles between Robo and bionic ninjas, high-speed car chases (including one wherein Robo commandeers a purple pimpmobile to pursue evildoers), and even aerial sequences when Robo straps on a jet pack designed by sympathetic scientist Hennessy. Torn turns in amusing work as Omni's cowardly CEO. Phil Tippett's excellent stop-motion animation FX bring the overtly cartoonish fantasy to full escapist life.

ROBOMAN   (1975) ***

D: Jack Gold. Joseph Bova, Elliott Gould, Trevor Howard, Ed Grover, James Noble, John Lehne. 93 mins. (ACE, n.i.d.)

The obscure ACE Video label receives an official Phantom Untruth-in-Advertising citation for its extravagantly misleading box art and copy: a skeletal *Terminator* clone pointing a gun, beneath the title *Roboman: The Kill Machine with the Megaton Mind* (!). Actually, *RoboMan,* produced by future mainstream mogul Barry (*Wag the Dog*) Levinson, rates as a highly original, low-key sci-fi "thriller"—shot in 1975 under the title *Who?* but unreleased until 1982—that uses Cold War intrigues and robotic technology as an excuse to explore the nature of individual identity. Stage thesp and onetime NYC kid-show host Joseph ("Uncle Joe") Bova puts his considerable mime talents to good use as Lucas Martino, an American scientist rescued by Russian agents from a near-fatal car crash. After his obliterated face is fitted with a metal mask, Bova is returned to the West, where he's relentlessly hounded by suspicious FBI agent Gould. Though light on action and occasionally sketchy, *RoboMan* makes for suspenseful viewing.

ROBOT CARNIVAL   (1990) ***

D: Atsuko Fukushima, Hiroyuki Kitakubo, Hiroyuki Kitazume, Mao Lamdao, Kouji Morimoto, Takashi Nakamura, Hidetoshi Ohmori, Katsuhiro Otomo, Yasuomi Umetsu. Dubbed. 91 mins. (Streamline)

Nine noted Japanese animators contribute a total of seven robot-themed shorts—some dubbed, others with music and sound-FX tracks only—to this compilation, ranging from Morimoto's robotic Frankenstein variation, "Franken's Gears," to Lamdo's mood piece "Cloud," to Ohmori's futuristic war cartoon, "Deprive." The individual pieces are framed by Kasuhiro (*Akira*) Otomo's opening and closing sequences. Umetsu fashions *Robot Carnival*'s most thoughtful segment, "Presence," a pointed, poignant fable about a Brit inventor and his secret creation, a fetching femdroid with a will and dreams of her own, while Kita scores with his satiric, 19th-century-Japan–set "Tale of Two Robots." *Animé* buffs should find *Robot Carnival* a super sampler of then-state-of-the-art animation styles.

ROBOTJOX:
THE SERIES

ROBOTJOX   (1990) ***

D: Stuart Gordon. Gary Graham, Anne-Marie Johnson, Paul Koslo, Robert Sampson, Hilary Mason, Carolyn Purdy-Gordon. 84 mins. (Columbia/TriStar)

Gordon's sci-fi entry takes place in yet another polluted postnuke future, where a burnt-out Russia (here redubbed "the Confederation") and America settle their differences via robotic gladiatorial matches. Amiable Graham (of TV's *Alien Nation*), sort of a B-movie Kevin Costner (as was Kev himself a few years back when he answered casting calls for flicks like *Shadows Run Black* and *Sizzle Beach, U.S.A.* [both Troma]), is a giant-robot pilot who accidentally squashes several hundred spectators (*oops*) during a bout with cackling Russki robofoe Koslo. Gary decides to quit before a skedded rematch, much to the delight of upcoming femme fighter Johnson, the genetically engineered "GenJock" designated to take our hero's place. While the movie, recycling riffs from such earlier sci-fi sports fare as *Death Race 2000, Rollerball, The Running Man,* and *RoboCop,* fails to represent the *Re-Animator* auteur at his subversive best, *RobotJox* still stacks up as a lively outing peppered with his patented deadpan wit. Followed by Albert Band's uninspired 1993 sequel, *Robot Wars* (Paramount).

THE ROCKETEER   (1991) ***

D: Joe Johnston. Bill Campbell, Jennifer Connelly, Alan Arkin, Timothy Dalton, Paul Sorvino, Terry O'Quinn. 108 mins. (Disney) DVD

The Rocketeer rates as the only major mainstream movie in recent memory to feature an extended tribute to Rondo Hatton, the late, great '40s fear-film icon. Called "Lothar" here and played by Tiny Ron, the character's a dead ringer for Rondo, even down to his trademark chapeau, a prop that supplies *The Rocketeer* with one of its better running gags. Unlike the original, though, this Rondo doppelgänger is *all* makeup, with facial prosthetics credited to FX ace Rick Baker. While the Rondo/Lothar villain represents one of *The Rocketeer*'s neatest touches—W. C. Fields, portrayed by actor Bob Leeman, also puts in a cameo—the rest of Johnston's 1938-set sci-fi-tinged pulp adventure isn't half bad either. Campbell captures the naïve quality of the cliffhanger heroes of yore as young Cliff Secord, a racing pilot who happens upon a jet pack invented by Howard Hughes (*The Stepfather*'s O'Quinn). Nazi spy, swashbuckler star, and all-around Errol Flynn stand-in Neville Sinclair (slickly interpreted by Dalton) harbors evil designs on the jet pack and hires local hoods led by Sorvino to wrest the device from young Cliff. (Sorvino also delivers the movie's most memorable—if somewhat oxymoronic—line: "I may not make an honest buck, but I'm one hundred percent American!") Based on Dave Stevens's graphic novel, *The Rocketeer* avoids the bloated overindulgences of a *Batman* or a *Dick Tracy* and unfolds sans the smarmy tone that mars some of Indiana Jones's adventures. Spectacular aerial sequences provide additional pluses.

ROCKETSHIP X-M (1950) B&W ***

D: Kurt Neumann. Lloyd Bridges, Osa Massen, Hugh O'Brian. 77 mins. (Englewood)

Lunar-bound voyagers take a wrong turn and land on Mars in Neumann's fun '50s sci-fi pioneer. The Englewood edition also contains trailers for other era sci-fi films.

ROLLERBALL (1975) **1/2

D: Norman Jewison. James Caan, Maud Adams, John Houseman. 123 mins. (MGM/UA) DVD

An occasionally portentous but effectively brutal look at the future gladiators who play the lethal title sport, *Rollerball* has since been topped by the similarly themed Rutger Hauer actioner *Blood of Heroes* (see index). Avoid the 1999 made-for-cable rip-off *Futuresport* (New Line, DVD), with Dean Cain and Wesley Snipes.

ROUJIN-Z (1995) ***

D: Hiroyuki Kitakubo. Animated. Dubbed. 80 mins. (Software Sculptors) DVD

In *Roujin-Z*, written by *Akira* creator Katsuhiro Otomo, ailing elderly home-care patient Takazawa is conscripted into testing the Z-001, an elaborate computerized bed—a combo cybernurse, entertainment center, and medical monitoring machine—designed to care for all geriatric needs, thus freeing younger folk from tending to such unpleasant chores. In typically surreal style, the nearly comatose Takazawa's brain waves intersect with the bed's computer network, transforming the device into an ungainly, outsized, rampaging robot guided by the spirit of Takazawa's late wife. While medical authorities seek to effect a cover-up, and police prove helpless in stopping the amok machine, young nurse Haruko and her hospital-worker pals, aided by three super-annuated computer hackers, rally to Takazawa's cause. While *Roujin-Z* scores cogent points re the theme of technological "efficiency" versus human compassion—and health care for the aged is a major issue in Japan, which sports a sizable elderly population—the story's padded with a surfeit of predictable geriatric jokes, clichéd corporate intrigues, and the oft tedious juvenile antics of Hiruko's friends, particularly Maeda (voiced by Adam Henderson), the only male in the group, who comes on like a loudmouthed leftover from an '80s frat-house farce. *Animé* mavens will enjoy *Roujin-Z's* relatively lavish production values and Kitakubo's strikingly cinematic visual approach.

RUNAWAY (1984) **

D: Michael Crichton. Tom Selleck, Cynthia Rhodes, Gene Simmons, Joey Cramer, Kirstie Alley, Stan Shaw. 100 mins. (Columbia/TriStar, Goodtimes)

A lowbrow, medium-budget exercise in high-tech paranoia, *Runaway* plays like a glossy update of a vintage serial as runaway-robot tracker Selleck dons his "electro-magnetic suit" to destroy a rabid robot, dodges heat-seeking minimissiles fired from villain Simmons's silver handgun, and even dines at a robotic sushi bar. For all its flaws, *Runaway* offers a number of improbable images at once endearing and enduring, as when a cute little automated "household helper" with a serious Clint Eastwood complex scoots about a 'burb home blasting its owners with a .357 Magnum (!). In the end, though, there's too much Tom and not enough inspired high-tech tomfoolery.

THE RUNNING MAN (1987) ***1/2

D: Paul Michael Glaser. Arnold Schwarzenegger, Maria Conchita Alonso, Richard Dawson, Yaphet Kotto, Jim Brown, Jesse Ventura, Erland Van Lidth, Mick Fleetwood, Dweezil Zappa. 101 mins. (Vestron) DVD

"Get me the Justice Department—Entertainment Division!" So demands an angry Dawson, who, in a bit of high-concept typecasting, portrays the repulsive sleazoid host of futuristic police-state America's most popular TV show, the titular *Running Man*, a sort of *Beat the Clock* Meets *The Most Dangerous Game*. Schwarzenegger is the unlucky contestant, a framed ex-flyer who's forced to flee a lethal lineup of professional "stalkers" (since-ascendant Minnesota governor Ventura, Brown, Professor Toru Tanaka, and an opera-singing Van Lidth) in a bid to claim the game's grand prize: trial by jury (!). Based on the Richard Bachman (Stephen King) novel depicting the ultimate merger of government and show-biz, and borrowing liberally from *Blade Runner*, *Rollerball*, and *The Tenth Victim*, *The Running Man* is a sometimes sophomoric but generally fun and scarily prescient dystopian slaughter-fest. The flick succeeds in sending up game shows, pro wrestling, and official duplicity while still filling the screen with enough chainsaws, shoot-outs, and exploding heads to hold hard-core genre fans' attention. On the downside, Arn delivers his by-now formulaic one-liners more stiffly than ever and meets his thespian match in Alonso—for sustained unintelligibility, their exchanges rival Stallone and Brigitte Nielsen's in *Cobra* (though Sly managed *without* an accent).

SATURN 3 (1980) **½

D: Stanley Donen. Kirk Douglas, Farrah Fawcett, Harvey Keitel, Douglas Lambert. 88 mins. (Fox) DVD

A dubbed (!) Keitel and companion—horny Hector the pinheaded robot (who prefigures *The Terminator*)—make life miserable for Kirk and Farrah at their previously paradisiacal space hideaway in a pic that has enough sci-fi gimmickry and cosmic camp value to make it worth a look and listen.

SCANNERS:
THE SERIES

SCANNERS (1981) ***

D: David Cronenberg. Jennifer O'Neill, Stephen Lack, Patrick McGoohan, Lawrence Dane, Charles Shamata. 102 mins. (Nelson, n.i.d.)

C ronenberg virtually invented the popular, oft-imitated and -sequelized exploding-heads genre with this typically over-the-top terror tale wherein telekinetic rivals wage a gory mind-control war. *Scanners* arrived as a real shocker in its day and still rates as the best of the series, which carried on without D.C.'s cerebral involvement.

SCANNERS II: THE NEW ORDER (1991) **½

D: Christian Duguay. David Hewlett, Deborah Raffin, Yvan Ponton, Isabelle Mejias, Tom Butler. 104 mins. (Fox)

H ewlett plays a young med student whose telekinetic powers (caused by a toxic pregnancy drug) remain undiscovered until his move to a stressful big city. Since those leftover "scanners" quartered at the Morse Institute are either raving psychos or burned-out veggies, the evil Dr. Morse (Butler) and his power-crazed cop cohort, Forrester (Ponton), look to recruit David's "virgin mind" to their corrupt cause (i.e., control of the city). While more formulaic than Cronenberg's original, Duguay's sequel offers intermittent suspense, a decent amount of wanton violence, and competent perfs, particularly by Hewlett and Mejias as his non-scanner squeeze. True, there's only one legit exploding head shot on view, but it's one of the better ones we've seen.

SCANNERS III: THE TAKEOVER (1992) ***

D: Christian Duguay. Steve Parrish, Liliana Komorowska, Valerie Valois. 101 mins. (Republic)

D uguay's second *Scanners* sequel blends black humor, sci-fi, action, telekinetic showdowns, and, of course, the requisite exploding heads without which no *Scanners* movie could be deemed complete (here we get four, compared with *II*'s lonely one) in a lively grue brew that demonstrates Canadians (at least French Canadians) *can* concoct flavorful fright flicks when they put their minds, or exploding heads, to it. The wit—such as ego-inflated scanner Komorowska's playful telekinetic interference with a bland TV talk show—is welcome but never intrusive, and the pic operates just as ably on a straight-ahead thriller level.

SCANNER COP (1993) ***

D: Pierre David. Daniel Quinn, Darlanne Fluegel, Richard Lynch, Richard Grove, Hilary Shepard, Mark Rolston, Gary Hudson, Cyndi Pass, Luca Bercovici, Brion James. 94 mins. (Republic)

S ort of a *Maniac Cop* in reverse, the L.A.-set *Scanner Cop* finds vengeful demented neurologist Lynch and his distaff henchpsychic, Shepard, abducting normally law-abiding citizens and programming them to hallucinate their worst fears at the sight of a police uniform or badge. This, unsurprisingly, leads to the sudden extinction of several local officers. Scanner Quinn (who resembles a younger Brad Dourif), adopted years earlier by current LAPD top cop Grove, is a rookie patrolman who reluctantly taps in to his telepathic powers to help track down the culprits. When Quinn quits taking his daily dose of Ephemerol—scanners' answer to Prozac—he's able to retrieve vital info from the perps' brains; he's simultaneously subjected to attacks of sensory overload that push him to the precipice of incipient psychosis. Lynch and Shepard are in fine villainous form here, while foxy Pass puts in an intense appearance as one of Lynch's cerebral-dry-cleaning victims. The exploding-head count is a modest two, but both, courtesy of low-budget FX vet John Carl Buechler, are fairly spectacular eruptions that succeed in expanding the detonating-dome horizon.

SCANNERS: THE SHOWDOWN (1994) ***

D: Steve Barnett. Daniel Quinn, Patrick Kilpatrick, Khrystine Haje, Stephen Mendell, Brenda Swanson, Robert Forster, Jewel Shepard. 95 mins. (Republic)

T he fifth installment in the David Cronenberg–created *Scanners* series—or the second in producer Pierre David's *Scanner Cop* series, take your pick—*Scanners: The Showdown* serves up more of the same brand of abrupt and senseless telekinetic violence *Scanners* fans have come to know and love. Quinn reprises his role as scanner cop Staziak, who needs all his special powers to take on vengeance-bent scanner Kilpatrick. Kilpatrick prefers to cook and melt his victims (John Carl Buechler again supplies the cheap but gaudy gore FX) and runs up a sizable body count en route to his ultimate encounter with Quinn. Though there's only one skull-burst scene, it's a strong one.

SCREAMERS (1996) ***

D: Christian Duguay. Peter Weller, Jennifer Rubin, Roy Dupuis, Andy Lauer, Charles Powell, Michael Caloz, Liliana Komorowska. 107 mins. (Columbia/TriStar) DVD

Direct-to-video *Scanners* specialist Duguay graduates to the big screen with this engrossing pulp sci-fi adventure. A complicated setup finds Colonel Hendricksson (Weller) heading embattled Alliance troops trapped on an isolated, radiation-plagued mining planet, circa 2078. Weller and crew have been locked in a ceaseless war with equally weary forces in the corporate employ of the New Economic Bloc. To balance the military scales a mite, the outnumbered Alliance fighters use mobile subterranean decapitating (!) attack units (the titular "screamers") who slice and dice all living things not equipped with Alliance bio-I.D. tags. Trouble is, the screamers have found a way to increase their mental capacity *and* assume new forms unknown to their own creators. This presents a problem for Weller, who, accompanied by high-tech marksman Ace (Lauer), embarks on a trek across the planet's poisoned surface to answer a peace-talk plea sent by stranded NEB troops. On their journey, Hendricksson and Ace encounter an outwardly harmless, teddy bear-clutching orphan (Caloz), suspicious NEB soldiers Becker (Dupuis) and Ross (Powell), fetching black marketeer Jessica (Rubin), and, of course, ever mutating screamers galore. Weller, who'd earlier brought dignity to his bionic *RoboCop* character, lends quiet authority, even solemnity, to his role as the decent but emotionally decimated Hendricksson. While *Screamers* is derivative in spots—little of its stated source material, Philip K. Dick's short story "Second Variety," survives—Duguay and scripters Dan (*Total Recall*) O'Bannon and Miguel Tejada-Flores generate bleak tension and an omnipresent air of heightened paranoia throughout.

Filmmakers in Focus!
DIRECTOR CHRISTIAN DUGUAY ON *SCREAMERS*
As Told to The Phantom

● ●

The script was presented to me in 1993, and I actually passed on it the first time, for several reasons. I thought it was not Dan O'Bannon's best stuff. My feeling was the script was one he had used before, in *Total Recall*, *Alien*, and all that; it felt to me a bit *déjà vu*. Also it was a bit of a reaction because I had started with horror films and I got a bit categorized for that.

The producer is a friend, Tom Berry, and he said, "Please, read between the lines; there are things that are interesting." I reread it and reread it and found out that yes, there were things in there. The premise of these evolving little creations that these guys made to protect themselves is an interesting one. Not knowing how they evolve and what they're gonna become and introducing the whole sense of paranoia between these guys. The connection that Peter [Weller] and I had was really good. I was warned at the beginning that Peter can be hands-on and he wants things to go his way. But there was a great communion between both of us.

I'm an ex-DP [director of photography]; when I go on the set, I know which tool to use. I do all my camera work, every single frame you see in the film. I operate all the cameras, from the remote cam to the handheld to the steadicam. But I've been doing this for twenty-five years; I don't even *compose* the image, it's just direct intuition. The real work between the actors and the director is the blocking—how you're gonna block the scene, what it says, does it link with the scene that was before, are we telling the audience here what needs to be told, and are we also adding, within all the personalities of the characters, more colors as the film evolves. After that, the director makes sure that visually he'll be interesting; if he needs to pump visually or pull back to let the performance live....I couldn't look at it through a little television set, I've got to be there with them [the actors], feel them, be behind them, feel that shudder, go through that lens and kick in that film, so I know whether it's gonna go in or not. At the beginning they said, "Well, maybe he's going to be more of a technical director." But every single actor came out of this saying it's a real experience. We go on set, the actors feel that I'm with them, and it's a dance; we choreograph together and just go for a dance. It's very exciting.

SECONDS (1966) B&W ****

D: John Frankenheimer. Rock Hudson, Salome Jens, John Randolph, Will Geer, Jeff Corey, Richard Anderson, Murray Hamilton, Karl Swenson, Khigh Deisho. 106 mins. (Paramount)

Though blasted by many mainstream critics of the day and even booed at the 1966 Cannes Film Festival (!), *Seconds* ranks right up there with the same auteur's earlier masterpiece of pervasive paranoia, *The Manchurian Candidate* (see index). Lensed in sharp black and white, *Seconds* tells its tale of double disillusionment in jangly, deliberately disorienting style. Frankenheimer establishes the pic's nightmare tone right from the opening credits (brilliantly designed by Saul Bass) via ghostly, distorted, extreme close-ups of a floating face seen in various phases of surgical alteration. An antsy handheld camera (veteran James Wong Howe served as cinematographer) pursues heavily perspiring middle-aged banker

Arthur Hamilton (Randolph) through a rush-hour Grand Central Station, where a stranger hands him a slip of paper that will literally and irrevocably change his financially comfortable but spiritually empty life. A hallucinatory edge likewise informs subsequent scenes, as when Randolph hies to the meat-packing warehouse that serves as the sinister company's cruelly appropriate front. The company caters to a truly select fraternal order—like Hamilton, mostly white, middle-aged, Ivy League–greased power-elite types who, by their very presence there, offer silent witness to the inner sterility of their outwardly enviable lives. All are ready to pay handsomely to "die" and be reborn with fresh, more meaningful identities. Though split into two distinct acts, *Seconds* loses none of its drive or intensity once the action shifts to laid-back Malibu and Rock Hudson replaces Randolph in the Hamilton role. (The irony of casting a closeted gay actor in so extreme a dual-identity part won't be lost on contemporary viewers, as it doubtless wasn't on Rock himself.) Hudson gives one of his best performances as Hamilton's reinvented self, "artist" Tony Wilson. Among the supporting thesps, Geer is menacingly brilliant as the folksy old monster, sort of a cross between Colonel Sanders and Martin Borman, who runs the company. Anxiety-provoking actor Corey is perfect as the casually callous aide who informs Hamilton, "The question of death selection may be the most important decision of your life," while Jens lends appeal as the lady in Hamilton's new life, and Deigh, as a company shrink, virtually reprises his *Manchurian Candidate* brainwasher role. Paramount presents the European-release cut, one that restores two scenes missing from broadcast-TV airings we've seen—Hudson's self-conscious bacchanalian "romp" in a California wine vat with Jens and friends (featuring some discreet but then-taboo nudity) and his clandestine visit with the "widow"

(Frances Reid) he'd left behind in the wake of his surgical rebirth. Whether you're a newcomer or a devoted fan, you won't want to miss Paramount's edition of this unforgettable chiller.

THE SECRET ADVENTURES OF TOM THUMB (1993) ****

D: Dave Borthwick. Nick Upton, Deborah Collard, Frank Passingham, John Schofield. 61 mins. (Manga Entertainment) DVD

This multi-award-winning stop-motion feature from the Bristol-based "bolexbrothers" (a.k.a. animator Dave Borthwick) began life as a controversial ten-minute BBC short. In *Secret Adventures*, Borthwick reworks the Tom Thumb and Jack the Giant Killer myths within a surreal urban wasteland, where tiny Tom (looking vaguely like *Eraserhead*'s offspring in the David Lynch film) is snatched from his hapless dad (Upton) and mom (Collard) by a mysterious agent of the Laboratorium, where unspeakable experiments are being inflicted on a menagerie of fanciful creatures ranging from cowlike animals to living human hands (!). Tom helps an escaped insectoid critter perform mass euthanasia on the tortured beings, then wanders into a camp of fellow lilliputian sorts. There Jack, a lone warrior who targets dangerous local "giants" as his prey, takes Tom under his wing, even as Tom's now-widowed dad continues to search for his errant son. Unfolding like some sort of wild prenatal nightmare, *The Secret Adventures of Tom Thumb*, with its pixilated mix of animation and live action, sports a look and feel all its own, one painstakingly achieved by Borthwick and crew. *Adventures* conveys a haunting mood of melancholy, paranoia, dread, and innocence defiled. You don't have to be an animation fan to fall under the spell of Borthwick's visionary *Thumb*. For more eerie animation/live-action fare, scope out the equally surreal *Brothers Quay Collection* (Kino, DVD).

THE 7TH VOYAGE OF SINBAD (1958) ***

D: Nathan Juran. Kerwin Matthews, Kathryn Grant, Torin Thatcher. 87 mins. (Columbia/TriStar)

One of the most popular fantasy films ever made, this kiddie-matinee perennial is aided and abetted by the Harryhausen/Hermann FX/music team, plus fine work by Thatcher as an evil magician. Followed by 1974's *The Golden Voyage of Sinbad* (Columbia/TriStar).

THE SHADOW (1994) **

D: Russell Mulcahy. Alec Baldwin, Penelope Ann Miller, John Lone, Peter Boyle, Tim Curry, Jonathan Winters. 108 mins. (Universal) DVD

Director Mulcahy and crew resurrected Lamont Cranston—of pulp fiction, radio, and cliffhanger fame—in apparent hopes of creating a *Batman*-esque cash cow, but this uninspired rehash vanished from the nation's bijous faster than you could say "The Shadow knows." The low-concept plot finds Genghis Khan (Lone)—a character seen to far more entertaining advantage in *Bill & Ted's Excellent Adventure* (see index)—turning up in 1930s NYC hell-bent on building an atom bomb, the better to rule the world. Baldwin, as our mysterious superhero, sporadically grows a big nose, while many of his minions sport mood rings. The art direction clones *Batman* pretty closely, and the entire project, though less portentous than Tim Burton's on-screen *Dark Knight* epics, serves mostly to reaffirm the old Hollywood maxim that clouded minds think alike.

SHADOWZONE (1989) **1/2

D: J. S. Cardone. Louise Fletcher, David Beecroft, James Hong, Shawn Weatherly, Lu Leonard. 88 mins. (Paramount)

As low-budget sci-fi rip-offs go, *Shadowzone,* sort of a *The Thing* Meets *Alien* on *Elm Street,* is far from the worst. Despite its single subterranean lab set and dubious science, *Shadowzone* holds its own by building suspense via its earnest tone and sturdy thesping, particularly by Fletcher as a quietly crazed scientist. The unlikely story involves suspended-animation experiments that inadvertently allow a shape-shifting fourth-dimensional thingie access into our world. In time-honored B-movie tradition, the cost-effective creature can assume the form of rats, monkeys, and other inexpensive beings. The film includes the usual gore and requisite exploding-heads FX. No relation to the cable-TV juvenile-oriented horror series *Shadowzone: The Undead Express* (Evergreen), featuring a cameo by Wes Craven as a child psychologist (!).

SHE (1935) B&W ★★★★

D: Irving Pichel, Lansing C. Holden. Helen Gahagan, Randolph Scott, Helen Mack, Nigel Bruce, Gustav von Seyffertitz, Samuel S. Hinds, Noble Johnson. 95 mins. (Kino) DVD

King Kong coproducer Merian C. Cooper's gala adaptation of H. Rider Haggard's venerable 1887 fantasy/horror novel stars an unsaddled Scott as Leo Vincent, a British lad who accedes to the dying wish of his uncle (Hinds) to investigate a long-standing family legend about a magical flame, sequestered somewhere in the caves of icebound northern Russia, that grants immortality. Accompanied by scientist Bruce and newly orphaned wench Mack (late of *Son of Kong*), Randy locates a hidden civilization ruled by a forever-young "She Who Must Be Obeyed" (Gahagan), who believes Scott to be his own distant ancestor and her long-lost lover, whom she'd slain in a fit of jealousy some 500 years before. While brimming with passion, adventure, spectacle, and splendor—complete with awesome outsized sets, impressive special effects,

elaborate dance numbers, and a reported cast of 5,000 (!)—*She* registers equally well as a thought-provoking meditation on mortality. *She* also marks stage actress Gahagan's only screen appearance; she later served as a congresswoman until a late-'40s smear campaign engineered by Richard Nixon virtually killed her political career. Athlete extraordinaire Jim Thorpe cameos as Gahagan's Captain of the Guard, while von Seyffertitz is effective in a role tailor-made for John Carradine.

Lensed twice before in silent form (1919 [n/a], 1925 [Video Yesteryear]), *She* was remade by Hammer (Fox) in 1965—with Ursula Andress, Peter Cushing, and Christopher Lee, followed by the 1967 sequel, *Vengeance of She* (Anchor Bay), with Olinka Berova—and by Cannon in 1985 (Vestron), a schlocky edition starring Sandahl Bergman. Previously available only in 89-minute television prints, Kino's *She* represents the complete 95-minute cut and rates as an essential addition to any genre buff's home-vid library.

SHIVERS: DIRECTOR'S CUT (1975/1998) ★★★

D: David Cronenberg. Paul Hampton, Joe Silver, Lynn Lowry, Barbara Steele. 91 mins. (Avalanche) DVD

Cronenberg's feature-film debut—formerly available, in slightly truncated form, as *They Came from Within,* on the Vestron label—arrives via Avalanche in a director's cut (not letterboxed, unfortunately) that restores bits of missing footage and includes the original theatrical trailer. Sort of a "Night of the Living Ill," the flick depicts the visceral chaos that grips a suburban Montreal high-rise after a mad scientist experiments with a horny parasite. As fellow scientist Silver explains to resident condo medico Hampton, "So what he came up with to help our guts along is a parasite that's a combination of aphrodisiac and venereal disease that will hopefully turn

the world into one big beautiful mindless orgy." As might be expected, then-fledgling writer/director Cronenberg, who'd earlier lensed the short films "Stereo" and "Crimes of the Future" (both on the Nightmare label), has a frightful field day with his parasitic premise, as the critters wreak havoc migrating from floor to floor and host to host, turning the building's inhabitants into sex-crazed sickos, until only hero Hampton is left. Highlights include a bit where a victim upchucks his parasite from a high terrace onto a transparent umbrella below; sepulchral scream siren Barbara Steele's parasite-shared bathtub scene; and a pool-set finale that finds Hampton pursued by his rampaging patients. While borrowing elements from George Romero's *Night of the Living Dead* and *The Crazies* and employing an *Invasion of the Body Snatchers*–inspired ending, Cronenberg fashions a highly original horror film that sets forth several of the themes he continues to explore, with an ever widening range, in recent films like *Crash* and *eXistenZ.*

SILENT RUNNING (1971) ★★¹/₂

D: Douglas Trumbull. Bruce Dern, Cliff Potts, Ron Rifkin. 90 mins. (Universal) DVD

FX-ace-turned-auteur Trumbull's *Silent Running* is pretty much a one-man show as space-station survivor Dern, accompanied only by three diminutive, pre-R2D2 'droids, seeks to preserve Earth's last vegetation samples in this sometimes slow but generally engrossing ecological thriller.

SINBAD THE SAILOR (1947) ★★★

D: Richard Wallace. Douglas Fairbanks, Jr., Maureen O'Hara. 117 mins. (RKO)

Doug junior proves appropriately dashing as Sinbad in a lavish Technicolor spectacular further abetted by a top supporting cast that includes Walter Slezak and Anthony Quinn. Sinbad fans can also scope out the 1952 Soviet epic *Magic Voyage of Sinbad* (Sinister Cinema), which promised "1001 Chills and Delights"; the irreverent 1971 Hungarian *Sinbad* (Facets); 1977's *Sinbad and the Eye of the Tiger* (Columbia/TriStar), powered by Ray Harryhausen's FX; and the 1989 Lou Ferrigno campfest *Sinbad of the Seven Seas* (Warner).

SKEETER (1993) **

D: Clark Brandon. Tracy Griffith, Jim Youngs, Charles Napier, Michael J. Pollard, William Sanderson, Jay Robinson. 95 mins. (New Line)

Giant toxic mosquitos fly amok—a hook presciently lampooned in the "Mosquito!" segment of the so-so 1991 scare satire *Popcorn* (Columbia/TriStar) and later played straight in 1995's *Mosquito* (Hemdale)—in a defenseless Southwest in Brandon's inferior insect-fear fest. While Frank H. Isaac's mosquito models aren't much to look at, their POV shots supply some grisly fun, and Napier contributes a standout death scene as a skeeter victim. But *Skeeter,* despite its respectable running time, exhibits all the traits of an unfinished film.

SLAUGHTERHOUSE-FIVE (1972) ***

D: George Roy Hill. Michael Sacks, Valerie Perrine, Ron Leibman. 104 mins. (MCA/Universal) DVD

Hill helms a fairly faithful and effective adaptation of Kurt Vonnegut's time-and-space-hopping novel detailing the surreal misadventures of GI "Candide" Billy Pilgrim, winningly portrayed by Sacks.

SOLAR CRISIS (1992) *1/2

D: "Allen Smithee." Tim Matheson, Charlton Heston, Peter Boyle, Annabel Schofield, Corky Nemec, Jack Palance, Michael Berryman. 111 mins. (Trimark) DVD

"Allen Smithee"—the alias adopted by directors (in this case, Richard Sarafian), and occasionally scripters and producers who want to keep their names off celluloid turkeys—strikes again with this self-serious, unremittingly dull Japanese-financed (a reported $35 mil!)

ALLEN/ALLAN/ALAN SMITHEE'S GREATEST HITS

• •

Prolific auteur "Allen/Allan/Alan Smithee" first surfaced in 1967, when directors Don Siegel and Robert Totten both disavowed their contributions to the Richard Widmark western *Death of a Gunfighter* (Universal). The Directors Guild invented the pseudonym for use by any director, scripter, or producer who could present a cogent case for why their names should be omitted from films they'd worked on. (Director Jud Taylor alone has exercised this privilege at least three times!) The ultimate Smithee feat remains the Joe Ezsterhas–scripted dud *An Alan Smithee Film: Burn, Hollywood, Burn* (Touchstone), wherein director Arthur Hiller, most likely in a publicity ploy as lame as the movie itself, took an Alan Smithee credit. The following list represents most of the rest of Smithee's output to date. The filmmakers' real names (when known) are also included, as are video labels for those who might want to stage their own home Allen Smithee Film Fest.

Appointment with Fear (1985, IVE) D: Razmi Thomas
Bloodsucking Pharoahs in Pittsburgh (1990, Paramount)
D: Dean Tschetter
The Challenge (1970, TV movie, n/a)
City in Fear (1980, TV movie, Artisan) D: Jud Taylor
Dalton: Code of Vengeance (1986, TV movie, n/a)
Dune (1984, expanded TV version, n/a) D: David Lynch
Fade-In (1968, n/a) D: Jud Taylor
Fun and Games (1980, TV movie, n/a)
Ghost Fever (1987, Charter) D: Lee Madden
Gypsy Angels (1989, Trimark)
Hellraiser 4: Bloodline (1995, Paramount) D: Kevin Yagher
I Love N.Y. (1987, Magnum)
Joan Rivers & Friends Salute Heidi Abramowitz
(1985, TV special, Warner)
Let's Get Harry (1986, HBO) D: Stuart Rosenberg
The Long Ride (1998, Salt City) editor: unknown
Meet Joe Black (1998, airline edition) D: Martin Brest
Moonlight (1982, TV movie, n/a) D: Jackie Cooper, Rod Holcomb
Morgan Stewart's Coming Home (1987, HBO) D: Paul Aaron
Raging Angels (1995, Trimark)
Riviera (1987, n/a) D: John Frankenheimer
The Shrimp on the Barbie (1989, Media) D: Michael Gottlieb
Stitches (1985, Media) D: Rod Holcomb
Student Bodies (1981, Paramount) producer: Michael Ritchie
Sub Down (1997, Trimark) D: Greg Champion

sci-fi bomb, which may be the most expensive flick to skip bijous for a direct-to-home-vid bow. (The Whoopi Goldberg fiasco *Theodore Rex* is another contender for that dubious honor, as is the more successful Jean-Claude Van Damme adventure *Legionnaire* [see index], which did land a Euro theatrical release.) Adapted from a Japanese novel, *Solar Crisis* employs a story line similar to the equally deadly *Highlander* 2 about a solar flare that threatens to destroy Earth. Matheson pilots a spaceship that represents the planet's last hope, while Palance hams it up as a desert loony who delivers AWOL student Nemec ("I escaped from Bennington!") to his military granddad (Heston). Producers (who include FX ace Richard Edlund) at least saved a few bucks on Schofield's Sigourney Weaver–inspired T-shirt-and-panties ensemble. No relation to Boaz Davidson's lame 1994 *Road Warrior* rip-off, *Solar Force* (Hallmark).

SOLARBABIES (1986) 0*

D: Alan Johnson. Richard Jordan, Jami Gertz, Jason Patric, Lukas Haas, Charles Durning, James LeGros. 94 mins. (MGM)

[Mel] Brooksfilms's pathetic *Mad Max* rip-off hurtles us into a grim, totalitarian 42nd century, a time so bleak it could almost pass for the 1980s. In many ways, it's a *lot* like that benighted decade: The teens at the prisonlike Orphanage 43 use words like "awesome," cover local walls with graffiti, and even do beat-box imitations à la the Fat Boys. Working from a script that must have been scrawled in Crayola, *Solarbabies* follows a band of said teens who—accompanied by little Lukas Haas (who looks here like a Walter Keene painting come to frightening life) and his magical alien pal, Bodhi (a phosphorescent beachball)—escape sadistic orphanage overseer Jordan and make tracks for the desert. There they

encounter virtually every futuristic cliché under the celluloid sun, even wandering into an ersatz *Beyond Thunderdome* set, replete with Aussie-accented (!) lowlifes. *Solarbabies* may be lacking in originality, but it's rich in brain-dead dialogue, as when ingenue Gertz growls at an overly amorous punk, "Get out, you creature of filth!" Our sentiments exactly.

SOLARIS (1972)
B&W/COLOR **½

D: Andrei Tarkovsky. Donatas Banionis, Natalya Bondarchuk, Yuri Jarvet. 167 mins. (Fox Lorber) DVD

The restored edition of Tarkovsky's philosophical Soviet sci-fi epic, based on a Stanislaw Lem novel and lensed alternately in color and black and white, chronicles psychologist Kelvin's (Banionis) visit to a nearly abandoned space station overlooking an alien ocean. There the station's two surviving inhabitants, scientists Sartorious and Snouth, reveal that repeated bombardment with X rays has given said ocean the strange ability to materialize people from onlookers' pasts. Not immune to this mysterious process, Kelvin soon finds himself reunited with a willing but soulless replicant of his late wife, Hari (Bondarchuk), a suitably bizarre affair that dominates the film's second half and prompts the cynical Snouth to articulate the movie's ultimate message: "We don't want other worlds; we want mirrors." While the film conjures up comparisons to such past American pics as *Forbidden Planet, Dark Star, Journey to the Seventh Planet,* and *Blade Runner* (to say nothing of the works of Tolstoy and Dostoyevski, whom our screen scientists, being Russkis, are fond of quoting), *Solaris* ultimately emerges as fairly unique and original sci-fi fare. The endlessly recyclable Hari's refusal to disappear—she becomes more real, human, autonomous, and downright neurotic

with each "reincarnation"—arrives as a fresh concept, while an impressive romantic antigravity interlude suggests what it might be like to reside inside a Chagall painting. The trouble with *Solaris* is that, at 167 minutes, it's just too damn long. Slowing down the pace doesn't necessarily pump up a pic's profundity level, and it's only for the most patient of sci-fi buffs that we recommend this thoughtful but terminally windy tale. Fox Lorber also has Tarkovsky's 1979 sci-fi epic, *Stalker.*

SOLDIER (1998) ***

D: Paul Anderson. Kurt Russell, Jason Scott Lee, Connie Nielsen, Michael Chiklis, Gary Busey, Sean Pertwee. 99 mins. (Warner) DVD

Sort of a *"Universal Soldier* Meets *The Road Warrior* in Space," *Soldier* showcases a bulked-up, buttoned-down Russell as programmed fighting unit Todd, a character so mechanically macho and emotionally taciturn he makes the same thesp's Snake Plissken look like Mr. Rogers. In the early 21st century, Todd's breed of brainwashed soldier is deemed obsolete, a fate sealed when he loses a vicious hand-to-hand fight with one of his replacement models, an equally steroided Lee (looking about twice his *Dragon: The Bruce Lee Story* size). Todd's presumably dead body is dumped on a small waste-disposal planet secretly inhabited by a New Agey colony of spacecraft-crash survivors who teach our hero the rudiments of human emotions. Todd, in turn, uses his considerable combat expertise to protect them when Lee and a platoon of heavily armed cohorts attack the makeshift community. The performances take a distant backseat to the mayhem—even the normally intense Busey is relatively restrained as the leader of the new, not-so-improved troops, while Lee has little to do beyond his grunting and flexing chores—but *Soldier* ably fills the rousing action bill.

SOLO (1996) **½

D: Norberto Barba. Mario Van Peebles, William Sadler, Barry Corbin, Adrien Brody, Seidy Lopez, Jaime Gomez. 106 mins. (Columbia/TriStar)

Liberally lifting from *Universal Soldier*, among others, and based on the Robert Mason novel *Weapon, Solo* arrives as a sort of "RoboShane" Meets *"The Magnificent Seven* Minus Six," with a buff Van Peebles (who also co-exec-produced) cast as Solo, a bionic fighting machine abandoned after a thwarted U.S. commando-team assault on a Central American–rebel airstrip. When the injured Solo happens upon a village filled with soulful peasants imperiled by local rebels, he decides to join their side, using his programmed combat expertise to train them in the art of self-defense. Solo's genesis is related via flashback from the android's POV, where we learn he selected Michael Jordan as his basic body model (!). Meanwhile, back at the Pentagon, General Corbin assigns psycho commando Sadler and Solo's techno-nerd creator, Brody, the task of finding and, if necessary, eliminating the renegade combat unit. Though overlong and rife with ripe dialogue (e.g., Sadler to Solo: "You fought well for a flawed unit"), *Solo* manages to entertain most of the way, due in part to Mario's meditative work as the soul-searching machine. A clip from Columbia's *Earth vs. the Flying Saucers* puts in a cameo on a static-plagued TV.

SOMETHING WICKED THIS WAY COMES (1983) **½

D: Jack Clayton. Jason Robards, Jonathan Pryce, Diane Ladd, Pam Grier. 94 mins. (Anchor Bay) DVD

Self-conscious handling sometimes undermines this Bradbury fable about a sinister carnival that steals into a turn-of-the-century Middle American town. Bradbury buffs and Pam Grier fans will want to tune in. Bradbury also

adapts his own *The Wonderful Ice Cream Suit* (Buena Vista), a 1998 fantasy directed by Stuart *(Re-Animator)* Gordon.

SOYLENT GREEN (1973) ***

D: Richard Fleischer. Charlton Heston, Edward G. Robinson, Leigh Taylor-Young. 100 mins. (MGM/UA)

Fleischer's dystopian New York City–set sci-fi flick takes the era's you-are-what-you-eat credo to its outer limits. Robinson is particularly memorable in his filmic farewell, while a square-jawed Heston capably handles heroic chores.

SPACE RAGE (1986) **½

D: Conrad E. Palmisano. Michael Paré, Richard Farnsworth, John Laughlin. 78 mins. (Lightning, n.i.d.)

Paré stars as a brutal superthug who leads a violent breakout on a distant prison planet, prompting geriatric hero Farnsworth to don his black-leather battle fatigues, reach for his trusty shotgun, and creak into action in this derivative but undeniably lively sci-fi actioner. Only the straight-faced use of the line "It's *too* quiet, I don't like it" compelled us to subtract a half star from our rating.

SPARE PARTS (1979) **½

D: Rainer Erler. Jutta Speidel, Wolf Roth, Herbert Herrmann, Charlotte Kerr, Christopher Lindert, Tedi Altice. 108 mins. (Trimark)

Produced, directed, and scripted by German sci-fi auteur Erler under the original title *Flesh, Spare Parts*—lensed on location in Las Cruces, New Mexico, and New York, largely with dubbed Teutonic actors in American roles—is a far more ambitious undertaking than the lurid horror-vid box art

would indicate. *Spare Parts* opens with a honeymooning couple—spunky German lass Speidel and her American musician spouse, Herrmann—checking into a seedy Las Cruces motel, where Herrmann is kidnapped by a renegade ambulance, à la Larry Cohen's later *The Ambulance* (see index), and Speidel is relentlessly pursued by same. Speidel is rescued by trucker Roth, who decides to help her solve the mystery, ultimately leading to a sinister organs-for-sale operation. Both Speidel and Roth emerge as complex characters whose budding relationship supplies the film with one of its best motifs. Erler, who'd earlier helmed the Mexico-set sci-fi opus *Operation Ganymede* (n/a), also offers a unique outsider's view of American desert-and-trucker culture that's easily the equal of fellow Teuton Perry Adlon's better-known *Bagdad Cafe* (PolyGram). Though Erler commits a fatal narrative blunder that drains his story of tension just when it should be revving into high gear, *Spare Parts* remains well worth a look.

SPECIES:
THE SERIES

SPECIES (1995) ***

D: Roger Donaldson. Ben Kingsley, Michael Madsen, Alfred Molina, Forest Whitaker, Marg Helgenberger, Natasha Henstridge. 108 mins. (MGM) DVD

Featuring the foxiest space siren (Henstridge) seen on-screen since *Lifeforce*'s Mathilda May took her lengthy nude stroll through an alien-bedeviled London back in 1985, *Species* is a fun mutant-hunt thriller that runs out of steam only during its protracted climactic chase scene. A mumbling Kingsley looks grumpy throughout (like maybe he'd like to terminate his agent more than the monster) as the cold, unemotional scientist responsible for creating the menacing "Sil," which begins life as a human spiked with alien

DNA sent by "friendly" E.T.'s. While Ben's not at his best here, troubleshooter Madsen, behaviorist Helgenberger, scientist Molina, and especially neurotic "empath" Whitaker make for an enjoyably jerky investigative team. Scripter Dennis Feldman yields much mileage from Henstridge's ongoing culture shock as she grows to womanhood literally overnight and heads for Hollywood in search of a mate. (Bad news for the local stud population.) When Henstridge finds fatal (for them) fault with her intended partners, she's driven to commit ever more reckless acts. Fearfilm fans who don't make untoward demands on a flick that's out solely to entertain, not enlighten, should deem *Species* a viewer-friendly experience. 1998's *Species 2* (MGM, DVD) failed to recapture the magic.

SPECIMEN (1996) **

D: John Bradshaw. Mark Paul Gosselaar, Doug O'Keeffe, Ingrid Kalevaars, David Herman, David Jackson, Michelle Johnson. 85 mins. (A-Pix) DVD

Gosselaar is an orphaned youth with mysterious pyrokinetic abilities and an obsession with learning his unknown dad's I.D. When he lands a job as a grammar school coach, he discovers among his charges a withdrawn kid who shares his otherworldly traits. Originally aired on the USA Network, *Specimen* rates as fairly intriguing in the early going but ultimately degenerates into yet another lame, late-arriving *Terminator* clone.

SPHERE (1998) ***

D: Barry Levinson. Dustin Hoffman, Sharon Stone, Samuel L. Jackson, Peter Coyote, Liev Schreiber, Queen Latifah. 134 mins. (Warner) DVD

A mysterious alien prone to radical mood swings holds an A-List cast at bay in an inventive, suspenseful sci-fi

thriller that plays better on video (rewinding helps in some of the trickier spots) than it did on the big screen. Psychologist Hoffman, biochemist Stone, mathematician Jackson, and astrophysicist Schreiber are separately summoned by military op Coyote to explore a humongous alien craft found surrounded by coral in the South Seas. What follows is well worth keeping under wraps. Suffice it to say that, based on Michael Crichton's novel and directed by *Wag the Dog*'s Levinson with claustrophobic aplomb, the pic represents a rare instance where the FX, while copious and sometimes spectacular, serve the story line (divided into "chapters") rather than overwhelm it. Said story bears an uncanny resemblance to *Event Horizon* (see index) but boasts better dialogue, richer characters, and twistier concepts.

SSSSSSS (1973) ***

D: Bernard L. Kowalski. Strother Martin, Dirk Benedict, Heather Menzies, Richard B. Shull, Tim O'Connor, Jack Ging, Kathleen King, Reb Brown. 99 mins. (Universal)

Corman vet Kowalski's (*Attack of the Giant Leeches*) serpentine scarefest rates as a genuinely disturbing chiller. Martin wisely low-keys it as harddrinking herpetologist Dr. Stoner, a scientific loner whose tunnel-visioned efforts to merge snake (specifically a king cobra) with man transport him beyond moral concerns. Somewhat reminiscent of 1943's *The Mad Ghoul* (see index) in its theme of a single-minded scientist systematically destroying his own innocent, trusting assistant (Benedict) in the name of scientific gain, *Sssssss* uses a gradual buildup to yield max impact from its few but highly effective shock payoffs. Kowalski and scripter Hal Dresner unobtrusively weave a biblical Garden of Eden theme into their story line, when Benedict undergoes venom-induced religious visions and he and burgeoning squeeze Menzies (as Stoner's

daughter) partake of an idyllic (though chastely rendered) nude swim. Future B action stalwart Brown scores an early role as an arrogant college jock.

STAIRWAY TO HEAVEN (1946) B&W/COLOR ***1/2

D: Michael Powell, Emeric Pressburger. David Niven, Kim Hunter, Roger Livesy, Raymond Massey, Marius Goring, Richard Attenborough. 104 mins. (Columbia/TriStar)

In the Powell/Pressburger team's Brit fantasy fave (a.k.a. *A Matter of Life and Death*), Niven stars as a seemingly doomed RAF pilot who, due to a celestial oversight, survives his intended death long enough to fall in love with WAC nurse Hunter. To settle this otherworldly snafu, our hero agrees to plead his case in a heavenly court. The dual auteurs, who dubbed themselves "the Archers," sprinkle their supernatural romance with edgy political satire—including a bizarre (when witnessed today) battle of words on the subject of England versus America—and make dazzling use of glorious Technicolor for the earthly sequences and a stately monochromatic black-and-white tone for the heaven-set scenes. *Stairway to Heaven* is a one-of-a-kind viewing experience with appeal for classics buffs and genre fans alike.

STARGATE (1994) **1/2

D: Roland Emmerich. James Spader, Kurt Russell, Jaye Davidson, Viveca Lindfors, Alexis Cruz, Mili Avital, Leon Rippy, John Diehl. 119 mins. (Artisan) DVD

Reportedly radically reedited right before its theatrical release, future *ID4/Godzilla* auteur Emmerich's *Stargate* rates as a reel cosmic Cuisinart, lifting elements not only from earlier sci-fi spectaculars but from Egyptian epics like *Land of the Pharoahs*, Sam Fuller's *Steel Helmet,* and even the Gulf War's lethal remote-control pyrotechnics.

Spader's a spacy Egyptologist who cracks the code that enables him and a squad of soldiers led by an embittered Russell to visit a planet ruled by sun god Davidson; *The Crying Game* dragster flashes our heroes some megamean looks and hisses effectively in an electronically enhanced voice. Spader indulges in his usual fumbling, self-conscious tics, while a mostly silent Russell looks merely ticked off. Relentlessly ridiculous yet strangely compelling, *Stargate* is the type of unlikely entertainment that melts from your mind mere minutes after the end credits crawl. Now available in a "special edition" with additional footage. The 1997 pilot for the cable-TV series, *Stargate SG-I: Children of the Gods*, is also available.

STARLIGHT (1997) *

D: Jonathon Kay. Rae Dawn Chong, Willie Nelson, Billy Wirth, Alex Daikun, Deborah Wakeham, Jim Byrnes. 98 mins. (Monarch)

Chong, who's yet to recapture her *Quest for Fire* glory, is a New Agey alien, or "halfling," sent to Earth on some type of important but unforgivably boring mission. She meets a braided Willie Nelson, who shows off his glowing green eyes and croons a few soundtrack tunes. A hostile alien resembling a cross between *Terminator 2*'s Robert Patrick and a midcareer Jerry Lee Lewis shows up. The inaction is regularly interrupted by cheap but "uplifting" computer-generated FX. In short, *Starlight* is the type of late-night filler that makes one long for the Golden Age of Test Patterns.

STARMAN (1984) **1/2

D: John Carpenter. Jeff Bridges, Karen Allen, Charles Martin Smith. 115 mins. (Columbia/TriStar) DVD

Carpenter's cosmic-visitation parable gives Bridges a chance to

stretch as the spaced-out title character and ranks as a generally suspenseful, occasionally funny outing until the clichés get in the way.

STAR QUEST:
THE SERIES

STAR QUEST (1994) ***

D: Rick Jacobson. Steven Bauer, Emma Samms, Alan Rachins, Brenda Bakke, Cliff De Young, Ming-Na Wen, Gregory A. McKinney. 95 mins. (Cosmic Video/New Horizons)

No relation to 1989's dull, subpar *Star Quest* (Trimark), this *Star Quest* recycles a premise earlier seen in the 1967 campfest *The Doomsday Machine* (a.k.a. *Escape from Planet Earth*), and 1985's *Def-Con 4* (New World)—an isolated space crew witnesses from afar the destruction of Earth—but serves the story line better and incorporates a couple of effective twists. The squabbling international crew (including *Rocky Horror* sequel *Shock Treatment*'s De Young, sporting a French accent!) indulges in several power plays, mostly between sympathetic Russian Bakke and by-the-book Brit Samms. While some virtual-reality filler adds little to the proceedings, the cast and script manage to keep *Star Quest* afloat on the way to a surprise climax. Followed by 1999's *Star Quest II* (New Horizons).

STARSHIP TROOPERS (1997) **1/2

D: Paul Verhoeven. Casper Van Dien, Dina Meyer, Denise Richards, Jake Busey, Neil Patrick Harris, Patrick Muldoon, Michael Ironside, Clancy Brown. 129 mins. (Columbia/TriStar) DVD

Dutch-émigré auteur Verhoeven hit his (so far) American pop-cultural peak with 1987's *RoboCop*, a nearly seamless blend of over-the-top

pulp sci-fi and stinging, dead-on corporate/media satire (we'll still buy *that* for a dollar!). Three years later, he filtered a jacked-up Hollywood adaptation of Philip K. Dick's short story "We Can Remember It for You Wholesale" through his cheerfully acerbic European prism; the result was the generally felicitous Schwarzenegger vehicle/mind-trip combo *Total Recall*. Verhoeven's rep suffered a quiverful of critical arrows when he helmed the Joe Eszterhas–scripted *Showgirls*, a hilarious American rise-and-fall showbiz spoof that's since won its share of ardent supporters (yours truly among them). Alas, Verhoeven mostly coasts with *Starship Troopers*. His overlay of recycled *RoboCop* sarcasm does little to elevate Robert Heinlein's furiously jingoistic, Cold War–based exercise in buff military mindlessness, and much of the movie plays like *Mars Attacks!* minus most of the laughs. At core a hoary World War II–styled training film in high-tech futuristic mufti, *Starship Troopers* follows a handful of stereotypical, gender-mixed recruits—rich kid Van Dien, pilot-trainee squeeze Meyer, loyal Richards, and gung-ho Jake (Son of Gary) Busey—through their bootcamp paces en route to a lengthy, admittedly eye-popping (to say nothing of limb-chopping and brainsucking) battle royale between our brave space cadets and their ruthless outsized-insect foes. It's in these lengthy latter sequences that *Starship Troopers* earns its highest marks.

STAR TREK:
THE SERIES

STAR TREK—THE MOTION PICTURE (1979) **

D: Robert Wise. William Shatner, Leonard Nimoy, DeForest Kelley. 143 mins. (Paramount)

The cult sci-fi teleseries's long-delayed big-screen debut is pretty much an overlong, overblown yawn, in your Phantom's humble opinion, though no self-respecting Trekker would be without it. Paramount's video version restores additional footage cut from the original theatrical print.

STAR TREK II: THE WRATH OF KHAN (1982) **½

D: Nicholas Meyer. William Shatner, Ricardo Montalban, Leonard Nimoy. 113 mins. (Paramount)

A long-locked Montalban, as space villain Khan, provides obstacles galore for the *Enterprise* crew in an overlong but generally entertaining sequel to the slower-moving *Star Trek: The Movie.*

STAR TREK III: THE SEARCH FOR SPOCK (1984) **½

D: Leonard Nimoy. William Shatner, Christopher Lloyd, DeForest Kelley. 105 mins. (Paramount)

F eisty Klingons led by a flamboyant, pre–*Back to the Future* Lloyd complicate Captain Kirk and crew's titular mission in this moderately engaging sequel.

STAR TREK IV: THE VOYAGE HOME (1986) ***

D: Leonard Nimoy. William Shatner, Leonard Nimoy, Catherine Hicks, DeForest Kelley. 119 mins. (Paramount) DVD

K irk and crew beam down to contempo San Francisco in search of a pair of humpbacked whales who hold the key to Earth's future (!) in an arcanely plotted but fun sequel that yields much amusement from our heroes' collective case of culture shock. The pic provides its primary fun in detailing the displaced *Enterprisers'* efforts to cope with our "primitive, paranoid" culture. Spock, still recover-

ing from brain damage sustained in *Star Trek III,* is cleverly passed off as a '60s acid casualty (!)—he "took too much LDS," Kirk explains—while the Russki-accented Chekov (Walter Koenig) asks startled passersby for directions to a nearby naval base with "nuclear wessels." Director Nimoy employs a welcome light touch in steering the veteran crew through their time-warped mission.

STAR TREK V: THE FINAL FRONTIER (1989) ***

D: William Shatner. William Shatner, Leonard Nimoy, DeForest Kelley, Laurence Luckinbill, David Warner. 106 mins. (Paramount) DVD

W ith the series entering its geri-aTrek phase, director Shatner shepherds our aging *Enterprisers* through a cosmic shaggy-God story with a mature "We have met the deities and they are us" message. We especially enjoyed Spock's flying Reeboks and natal flashback, Uhura's (Nichelle Nichols) melodic Sally Rand–styled fan dance, and our earthlings' glasnost-esque reconciliation with an uncharacteristically apologetic Klingon crew.

STAR TREK VI: THE UNDISCOVERED COUNTRY (1991) **½

D: Nicholas Meyer. William Shatner, Leonard Nimoy, DeForest Kelley, Kim Cattrall, Christopher Plummer, David Warner. 109 mins. (Paramount) DVD

T he final entry to feature most of the original crew casts our aged heroes as the interplanetary equivalents of old Cold Warriors, who reluctantly agree to go where no *Enterprisers* have gone before—to talk peace with those barbarous Soviet stand-ins the Klingons, who've endangered their planet via a Chernobyl-type disaster.

The motormouthed script—cowritten by director Meyer from a story coconcocted by Nimoy—relies heavily on Shakespearean quotes, a practice that's particularly overindulged by Plummer's Klingon General Chang—"You've not experienced Shakespeare," he announces, "until you've read him in the original Klingon"—moving McCoy (Kelley) to complain, "I'd give real money if he'd shut up." (That's a sentiment we have no problem seconding.) *Star Trek VI* is lighter on spectacular FX than its immediate predecessors, though alien Rosana DeSoto's shape-shifting antics, an antigravity gore scene, and a sequence that sees Kirk literally fight himself (à la Van Damme in *Double Impact)* add some spice. B-movie buffs will appreciate brief appearances by kung-fu queen Shakti and literal screen giants John (*Dracula vs. Frankenstein)* Bloom and Matthias (*I Come in Peace)* Hues.

STAR TREK GENERATIONS (1994) **½

D: David Carson. William Shatner, Patrick Stewart, Malcolm McDowell, Jonathan Frakes, Whoopi Goldberg, James Doohan, Walter Koenig. 118 mins. (Paramount) DVD

B ald but proud Captain Picard (Stewart) bonds with skyrugged predecessor Captain Kirk (Shatner) in a large-scale but only intermittently compelling merger of *Star Treks* old and new. Scotty (Doohan) and Chekov (Koenig) turn up in cameos, but this show basically belongs to the *Next Generation* crew, who, with Kirk's aid, are out to stop villain Dr. Soran (McDowell) from destroying the universe in his selfish bid to return to a planet where fantasies come true. Android Data's (Spiner) virginal experiences handling his newly implanted human-emotion chips supply some initial fun but ultimately wear thin. (Where's Spock when we need him?) And for all its lavish high-tech embroidery, *Star Trek Gen-*

erations concludes with a prolonged clifftop fistfight right out of a cheapjack backdate B western.

STAR TREK: FIRST CONTACT (1996) ***

D: Jonathan Frakes. Patrick Stewart, Alice Krige, Jonathan Frakes, Brent Spiner. 110 mins. (Paramount) DVD

The *Next Generation* crew inherits *Star Trek*'s big-screen series in an exciting tale of time-travel travails and battles with the relentless alien Borg, led by seductive she-borg Krige. Crewmember Frakes displays a sure hand in his directorial debut. Followed by 1998's *Star Trek: Insurrection* (Paramount, DVD), likewise helmed by Frakes. Episodes of the original *Star Trek* teleseries, *Star Trek: The Next Generation*, *Star Trek: Deep Space Nine*, *Star Trek: The Animated Series*, several behind-the-scenes videos, and the 1999 theatrical documentary *Trekkies* are also available from Paramount.

STAR WARS:
THE SERIES

STAR WARS (1977) ***

D: George Lucas. Mark Hamill, Harrison Ford, Carrie Fisher, Alec Guinness. 121 mins. (Fox)

George Lucas weds high-tech FX with *Flash Gordon*–styled fantasy in a flick that revitalized the sci-fi genre, launched a mega-lucrative franchise, and established Harrison Ford as a new Hollywood hero. But you probably know that. Hamill's Luke Skywalker and crew return in 1980's high-energy, FX-laden *The Empire Strikes Back*, a sequel that, fueled by an expanded budget, outdazzles the original, and 1983's typically crowd-pleasing *Return of the Jedi*. Followed by 1999's *Star Wars Episode I: The Phantom Menace* (all Fox), which you've definitely heard of,

even if you *do* live a long time ago in a galaxy far, far away.

STEEL AND LACE (1990) ***

D: Ernest Farino. Clare Wren, Bruce Davison, Stacy Haiduk, David Naughton, Michael Cerveris, David L. Lander. 92 mins. (Fries, n.i.d.)

In limited theatrical release a few months prior to 1991's bigger-budgeted, far lamer *Eve of Destruction* (Columbia/TriStar), *Steel and Lace* rates as a solid B variation on a similar she-borg theme. Despondent rape victim Wren kills herself after her five young corporate-creep attackers are acquitted on all charges. Her scientist brother (Davison) recreates Clare in bionic form and programs her for revenge. One by one, the slimy yups eat gory android death, while detective Naughton and an ex-courtroom sketcher (the fetching Haiduk) investigate the slayings. Director Farino invests his formula plot with stylish visuals, authentic suspense, and well-developed characters. The pic also scores points re male aggression by gradually equating the vengeance-driven Davison with his vile targets.

THE STEPFORD WIVES:
THE SERIES

THE STEPFORD WIVES (1975) **½

D: Bryan Forbes. Katharine Ross, Paula Prentiss, Peter Masterson, Nanette Newman, Patrick O'Neal, Tina Louise, William Prince. 114 mins. (Anchor Bay) DVD

In Bryan (*King Rat*) Forbes's 1975 adaptation of Ira Levin's distaff-'droid novel, Ross and Prentiss take top thespian honors as a pair of recent reluctant émigrés to the "perfect" 'burb of Stepford, Connecticut, where the rest of the local femme population consists of airheaded, male-enslaved,

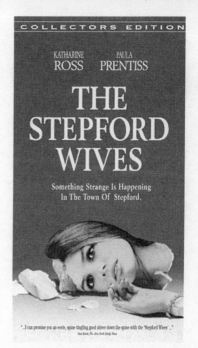

MS. STEP: Trouble lies ahead for urbanites investigating chauvinist 'burb conspiracy in *The Stepford Wives. Courtesy of Anchor Bay Entertainment*

happy-face drones. Despite a climate of raging indifference that escalates into open menace, the two seek to investigate the town's sinister secret. The downside to this otherwise chilling bedroom-community creepfest is its wildly uneven pacing—an ultra-leisurely buildup chased by an overly rapid-fire finale. *The Stepford Wives* still ranks as an essential companion to such identity-crisis-driven sci-fi classics as Don Siegel's original *Invasion of the Body Snatchers* and John Frankenheimer's *Seconds* (see index).

REVENGE OF THE STEPFORD WIVES (1980) ***

D: Robert Fuest. Sharon Gless, Don Johnson, Julie Kavner, Arthur Hill. 95 mins. (Goodtimes)

This surprisingly effective made-for-TV feature updates the fates of the bionic 'burb wives of big-screen fame.

Julie (Marge Simpson) Kavner turns in excellent work as a motormouthed victim of the ongoing Stepford conspiracy. The made-for-TV *Stepford Husbands* is out via Anchor Bay, but the inevitable *Stepford Children* remains unavailable as we go to press.

STEPPENWOLF (1974) **½

D: Fred Haines. Max von Sydow, Dominique Sanda, Pierre Clement. 105 mins. (Trimark)

Haines's screen translation is pretty ponderous for the most part and doesn't really capture the febrile flavor of Herman Hesse's novel, but the Magic Theater sequence has its share of hot hallucinatory tableaux.

STRANGE BEHAVIOR (1981) **½

D: Michael Laughlin. Michael Murphy, Louise Fletcher, Dan Shor. 98 mins. (Columbia/TriStar)

Although largely undeserving of its fleeting cult rep, this New Zealand–lensed, America-set sci-fi about brainwashed teens has enough going for it to make a rental worthwhile. Also out as *Dead Kids* on the Canadian IFS label. The briefly busy Laughlin also directed the 1983 semispoof *Strange Invaders* and the 1984 period thriller *Mesmerized* (both Vestron), with Jodie Foster and John Lithgow.

STRANGE DAYS (1995) ***

D: Kathryn Bigelow. Ralph Fiennes, Angela Bassett, Juliette Lewis, Tom Sizemore, Michael Wincott, Richard Edson, Vincent D'Onofrio, William Fichtner, Glenn Plummer. 145 mins. (Fox) DVD

A likely victim of its own overhype during its strangely disastrous theatrical run, *Strange Days* is well worth scoping out on video. Sort of a *Blow-Up* Meets a "Virtual-Reality *Peeping Tom*" on the eve of the millennium in 1999

THE BATTLE OF THE SEXES: GENRE MOVIE DIVISION

"Say, you're either too beautiful to be smart or too smart to be beautiful!"
—scientist George Nader to brainy ingenue Claudia Barrett, *Robot Monster* (1953)

"She doesn't have enough brains for a bimbo, or even a bimbette in training!"
—cohort to Tanya Roberts–smitten Andrew Stevens, *Night Eyes* (1990)

"I love bimbos!"
—Henry Silva, *Possessed by the Night* (1993)

"One stuck her face in the blade of an electric fan. Said she thought it was a vibrator."
—detective Joe Partridge, *The Hypnotic Eye* (1960)

"You're not too smart, are you? I like that in a man."
—femme fatale Kathleen Turner to lawyer William Hurt, *Body Heat* (1981)

"I have the highest regard for you—you're smart, you have courage, and you're all woman."
—American astronaut to distaff Martian scientist, *Cat-Women of the Moon* (1954)

"I'm not a lady. I'm an anthropologist."
—Barbara Anne Constable, *Lady Terminator* (1989)

"How could girls make a death ray capable of destroying Earth? And even if they could, how could they aim it?"
—male cosmonaut to crony, *Queen of Outer Space* (1958)

"I've never found a man I'd want to marry. The ones who'd make good family men are so dumb, I couldn't stand them. The ones I like are so worthless, I'd starve."
—smart dame, *Mad Youth* (1935)

"You women are changing the natural order of things. Men looking after children. Women competing for our jobs. Somebody had to do something."
—Arthur Hiller, *The Stepford Wives* (1975)

"Thou has done well to make the strange men captive. They came from the sea, as the Hairy Men once did. Ye were young and cannot remember."
—Druid princess Sandra, *Untamed Women* (1952)

L.A., *Strange Days* is at core a conventional but engrossing mystery embroidered with sci-fi gimmickry and armed with an edgy take on the state of the nation (or at least the state of L.A.). Ex-vice cop Fiennes is now an illegal VR-disc dealer, specializing in "reality" tapes for addicted "wireheads." Two violent story threads—the murder of influential rap star Jeriko One (Plummer) and the snuff-video rape/murder of Fiennes's hooker friend (Brigitte Bako)—gradually converge, while Fiennes simultaneously attempts to "rescue" rock chanteuse Lewis from paranoid music mogul Wincott's clutches. Aiding our hero are cop pal Sizemore and superwoman Bassett, who's not only beautiful but skilled in everything from hand-to-hand combat to stunt-driving. Despite its excesses and logical lapses, *Strange Days* stacks up as an entertaining, disturbing, visually and thematically ambitious exercise that rates with such previous Bigelow winners as *Near Dark* and *Blue Steel* (see index).

STRANGER FROM VENUS   (1954) B&W ***

D: Burt Balaban. Patricia Neal, Helmut Dantine, Derek Bond. 78 mins. (Englewood)

Sort of a roadshow *Day the Earth Stood Still* (it's even got Patricia Neal), this solid Brit sci-fier features Dantine as a cautionary visitor from the title planet. The film is also out as *Immediate Disaster* (Amvest).

STREET ASYLUM   (1990) ***

D: Gregory Brown. Wings Hauser, G. Gordon Liddy, Alex Cord, Sy Richardson, Roberta Vasquez, Brion James. 89 mins. (Magnum, n.i.d.)

Any flick that starts with G. Gordon Liddy strangling a dominatrix because she fails to inflict sufficient pain (!) runs a serious risk of peaking early, but Gregory (*Dead Man Walking*) Brown's *Street Asylum* manages to sustain this level of sleazy lunacy most of the way. In a rather extreme example of Tinseltown typecasting, Liddy plays a fanatical, ultra-right-wing bionic L.A. mayoral candidate who sponsors a psycho squad of killer cops who've been covertly wired to react with maximum violence. The normally over-the-top Wings wavers between rationality and madness as a newly transistorized recruit who gradually uncovers the sinister plot. While *Street Asylum* echoes *The Terminator* and *RoboCop*, the movie ultimately succeeds in charting its own perverse path through contempo SF-tinged action turf.

SUNRISE—A SONG OF TWO HUMANS   (1927) B&W ****

D: F. W. Murnau. Janet Gaynor, George O'Brien, Margaret Livingston, J. Farrell MacDonald. 110 mins. (Critics' Choice Video)

More recently on view as one of the films sunlight-starved bloodsucker Brad Pitt goes to see in *Interview with a Vampire*, Murnau's *Sunrise—a Song of Two Humans* rates as an unqualified fantasy classic. Winner of several of the first Academy Awards ever handed out, the Teutonic auteur's American debut unspools as an intense, magical fever dream that swings from potential tragedy to reverie to near-doom and casts an irresistible spell throughout. Future B-western star O'Brien plays a simple farmer misled by a "woman of the city" (Livingston) into attempting to drown his wife (Gaynor). Instead of (literally) tossing her over, a repentant O'Brien struggles to regain Gaynor's trust and love by joining her on a surreal journey through a city that's not only big but impossibly larger than life. While flash cards substitute for spoken dialogue, *Sunrise*, lensed at the dawn of the sound era, was released with a music-and-audio-effects soundtrack that remains intact here. *Sunrise* understandably entranced stateside audiences with its visual grandeur and universal story line, and has lost none of its power since.

SUSPECT DEVICE (1995) ***

D: Rick Jacobson. C. Thomas Howell, Stacey Travis, Jed Allen, Jonathan Fuller, John Beck, Marcus Aurelius. 90 mins. (New Horizons/Cosmic Video)

Howell, in his most paranoid role since *The Hitcher* (see index), is effective as the normal middle-class Joe (or C. Thomas) who unwittingly taps into a secret file on his office computer. Soon all his fellow workers are mercilessly machine-gunned, with Howell emerging as both the sole survivor of and chief suspect in the slaughter. He returns home to learn that his "wife" doesn't recognize him, his poker buddies have never heard of him, and that he's being relentlessly pursued by a team of government hit men, several of whom he dispatches using marksman and martial-arts skills he never knew he possessed. With sympathetic scientist Travis as his lone ally, Howell gradually closes in on the secret forces controlling him, only to discover more bad news. Despite its *Total Recall* echoes, *Suspect Device* gathers steam as it races along, leading to a surprise climax.

THE SWORD AND THE DRAGON (1956) **1/2

D: Alexander Plushko. Boris Andreyev, Andrei Abrikosov, Nathalie Medvedeva. 81 mins. (United/VCI, Sinister Cinema)

Those harboring fond, distant matinee memories of this Soviet spectacular detailing Russia's mythical struggle against the invading Tugar hordes may be disappointed with the video. For starters, this wide-screen epic (which boasts no fewer than 106,000—count 'em—106,000 extras) loses much of its grandeur on the home screen. (Letter-boxing might have helped.) Worse, the United edition adds a tacky, shot-on-video wraparound showing an American tyke reading the legend of 11th-century Russian hero Ilya Mouremetz (Andreyev) in a local library. Still intact, though, are such surreal sights as the wind demon, the giant Tugar emissary, the three-headed title dragon, and the immense human pyramid formed by the Tugar warriors. Voice-over ace Paul Frees, of *Rocky and Bullwinkle* fame, does a strong job dubbing the evil Tugar chieftain, Khalin. We recommend *The Sword and the Dragon* as a nostalgic treat for its patient fans and as a curiosity piece for adventurous viewers. The pic also served as the centerpiece of one of *Mystery Science Theater 3000*'s funniest episodes.

TANK GIRL (1995) *1/2

D: Rachel Talalay. Lori Petty, Ice-T, Naomi Watts, Malcolm McDowell, Jeff Kober. 104 mins. (MGM)

Petty is obnoxiousness personified in director Rachel (*Freddy's Dead*) Talalay and scripter Tedi (*Road Killers*) Sarafian's visually impressive, empty-headed adaptation of the comic-book series of the same name. Both Petty and the script are all wiseass, self-referential MTV pseudo-'tude, which makes for a long viewing experience for anyone

over 13. Talalay mixes in animated sequences that flash far more imagination than the live action, and *Tank Girl* probably would have worked better had it gone the Hollywood *animé* route. (As it was, it easily lived up to its name at the box office.)

TARANTULA (1955) B&W ***

D: Jack Arnold. John Agar, Mara Corday, Leo G. Carroll, Nestor Paiva, Ross Elliott, Clint Eastwood. 80 mins. (Universal)

A growth serum concocted by scientist Carroll gives rise to giant rabbits, rats, and, of course, the 100-foot title arachnid. The FX are superior to many '50s insect-fear films. Agar contributes his usual calm perf, while Carroll is convincingly distracted as the obsessed scientist, Corday screams with enthusiasm, and future *Mole People* fatality Paiva surfaces as a skeptical local sheriff. A deliberately paced buildup leads to some back-end haste, though the tarantula racks up a decent body count before young pilot Clint breaks out the napalm and sends the outsized insect to a fiery demise. The Southwest-desert locales add to the film's genuine sense of dread.

TARGET EARTH (1954) B&W ***

D: Sherman A. Rose. Kathleen Crowley, Richard Denning, Virginia Grey, Richard Reeves, Robert Roark, Whit Bissell. 75 mins. (VCI)

Target Earth opens on a starkly brilliant note. A morbidly inquisitive camera pokes about a boardinghouse room until it locates an unconscious young woman sprawled across a bed, an open bottle of sleeping pills resting beside her immobile hand. Moments later, the failed suicide awakes, groggy but alive, to a dead world. Produced by Herman Cohen from a script by Wyatt Ordung and soon-to-be AIP honcho James H. Nicholson, *Target Earth* fol-

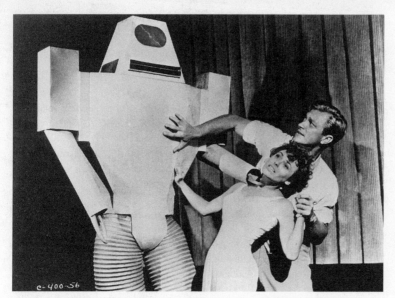

TARGET *PRACTICE:* Richard Denning and Kathleen Crowley encounter pushy codpieced invader in publicity still for *Target Earth.*
Courtesy of VCI Home Video

lows the young woman (Crowley) onto L.A. streets utterly empty save for the occasional terror-struck, open-eyed corpse. She literally runs into sales rep Denning, a mugging victim who likewise slept through what they determine must have been a mass evacuation from the city. The pair next encounter a rough-and-tumble couple (Reeves, Grey) guzzling champagne and partying on in a deserted club. The foursome join forces in a desperate bid to escape the unnamed danger surrounding them. The nature of the threat is gradually revealed to be an alien invasion of remote-controlled robots. From that point on, the action splits between our stranded citizens' desperate attempts to survive and the round-the-clock efforts of government scientists (led by the ever authoritative Bissell) to find an exploitable weakness in a captured robot before resorting to the nuclear annihilation of L.A. While *Target Earth* is a mixed bag, it boasts its share of low-budget pluses. The robots' initial appearance, as ominous shadows spreading across empty skyscrapers, is

an honestly chilling moment; unfortunately, the codpieced clankers lose much of their menace in the ensuing close-ups. The cheesy Pentagon and lab sets likewise lend the Mighty U.S.A. a Third World look. For the most part, though, Cohen and crew make their obvious lack of bucks work to their atmospheric advantage, creating a mood of overwhelming gloom and doom by plunging us into a big city stripped of its noise, clutter, and very pulse.

TEENAGE CAVEMAN (1958) B&W **½

D: Roger Corman. Robert Vaughn, Darrah Marshall, Frank De Kova. 66 mins. (Columbia/TriStar)

Vaughn makes for an overaged, decidedly preppy-looking Cro-Mag adolescent in a typically low-budget but cheesily entertaining saga of a prehistoric rebel lost in stock-footage land. With a memorable twist ending. (Director Corman still stubbornly refers to the film by its original title,

Prehistoric World, on those doubtless rare occasions when he's called upon to refer to it at all.)

TEKWAR: THE MOVIE (1994) **

D: William Shatner. Greg Evigan, Eugene Clark, Torri Higginson, William Shatner, Sheena Easton. 92 mins. (Universal)

Tekwar: The Movie is, of course, *Tekwar:* The Made-for-TV Movie, feature pilot for the teleseries drawn from Shatner's own sci-fi novels. In addition to directing, the erstwhile Captain Kirk, looking round, smug, and skyrugged to perfection, plays a government-agency head who, in a *Demolition Man* move, springs ex-lawman/ convicted killer Evigan (of TV's *B.J. and the Bear* fame) from cryogenic stir to help crush the burgeoning traffic in "teks," illegal 21st-century virtual-reality "drugs" (whose hallucinatory visual possibilities go underexploited here). *Tekwar* is a competently assembled but formulaic affair offering little in the way of thrills or surprises.

THE TENTH VICTIM (1965) ***

D: Elio Petri. Marcello Mastroianni, Ursula Andress, Elsa Martinelli. 92 mins. (Embassy, n.i.d.)

Ursula and Marcello hunt human prey—and ultimately each other— for professional legal sport in Petri's prescient (comic books are viewed as high art, for instance) Italo sci-fi fable. Ace huntress Andress's literally killer bra supplies a fashion high point.

TERMINAL VIRUS (1996) **

D: Dan Golden. James Brolin, Bryan Genesse, Kehli O'Byrne, Elena Sahagun, Richard Lynch, Susan Africa, Nikki Fritz. 74 mins. (New Horizons)

The germ of a good idea is quickly exterminated in Dan (*Naked*

Obsession) Golden's *Terminal Virus,* a largely brain-dead *Road Warriors* rip-off with an AIDS-inspired lethal-sex twist. In a future America wasted by nuclear war *and* a deadly sexually transmitted virus, the battle of the sexes has turned literal and lethal, with men and women occupying separate armed camps. The guys, led by the ever popular Lynch, are bad, while the gals are good. (And yes, they apparently still have silicone in our otherwise resource-depleted future.)

THE TERMINATOR:
THE SERIES

THE TERMINATOR   (1984) ****

D: James Cameron. Arnold Schwarzenegger, Linda Hamilton, Michael Biehn, Paul Winfield, Lance Henriksen, Dick Miller. 108 mins. (HBO) DVD

Quite possibly *the* greatest pure-genre movie of all time, Cameron's relentlessly kinetic roller-coaster ride neatly integrates nearly every necessary genre-film ingredient—from high-tech gadgetry and special effects to visceral bursts of abrupt and senseless violence. Though it's been ripped off endlessly and from every conceivable angle, *The Terminator* has yet to be duplicated. Schwarzenegger reportedly nixed the hero assignment (played by the wider-ranged, narrower-shouldered Biehn) in favor of the killer-cyborg role—a move that proves that not *all* of Arnold's brains are in his biceps. Hamilton is excellent as the endangered Sarah Connor, in whose salvation the fate of mankind lies, as are Winfield and Henriksen as a pair of beleaguered police officials. *The Terminator*'s story line has its roots in the Harlan Ellison–drawn *Outer Limits* episode "Demon with a Glass Hand" (Ellison receives an on-screen credit), while also bearing a strong resemblance to the 1967 B sci-fier *Cyborg 2087* (n/a), starring Michael Rennie.

TERMINATOR 2: JUDGMENT DAY (1991) ***

D: James Cameron. Arnold Schwarzenegger, Linda Hamilton, Edward Furlong, Robert Patrick, Earl Boen. 135 mins. (Artisan) DVD

In *T2,* Schwarzenegger's homicidal cyborg officially enters its *Godzilla* phase. Just as Japan's formerly no-nonsense atomic avenger later abandoned his human-destroying ways to protect mankind from alien threats like the ecologically unsound Smog Monster, so Arn's formerly unfeeling Terminator returns to the past to help a committed (figuratively and literally) Sarah Connor (reprised by a hard-bitten, bulked-up Hamilton) and her typical surly Hollywood-'burb brat son John (Furlong), the (maybe) future savior of our species. While Arnold experiences some initial difficulty in making the transition from pulverizer to protector (he goes through a stage where he merely maims his opponents instead of killing them), his rebirth as a "good" Terminator seriously reduces the sequel's body count. This regrettable slack is only partially taken up by shape-shifting authentic Terminator Patrick, while Arn spends most of his screen time playing high-tech Tin-Man to Furlong's gender-switched Dorothy. Arn's benign, Speilberg-ian transformation isn't the sequel's only flaw. *Terminator 2*'s lurching narrative constitutes a separate problem, and the pic's pace seriously falters between its then-much-heralded megabuck action scenes; the lean, mean, B-movie intensity that informed the original is replaced here by an irritating self-seriousness. Stan Winston's amazing liquid-metal FX, the film's hyper action set pieces, and what easily rates as the greatest nuclear nightmare sequence ever committed to celluloid make *Terminator 2* well worth seeing. Artisan's "special edition" features 15 minutes of additional theatrical footage and 60 minutes of behind-the-scenes material.

TERROR IS A MAN   (1959) B&W **1/2

D: Gerry DeLeon. Francis Lederer, Richard Derr, Greta Thyssen. 89 mins. (Sinister Cinema)

Terror rates as a pretty solid low-budget *Island of Lost Souls* variation, lensed in the Philippines and complete with a William Castle–like on-screen warning signal that buzzes before the "gruesome" scenes.

TESTAMENT   (1983) ***1/2

D: Lynne Littman. Jane Alexander, William Devane, Roxana Zal, Kevin Costner, Rebecca De Mornay. 90 mins. (Paramount)

An unremittingly grim look at the banality of nuclear annihilation as it affects a small Northern California town, *Testament*'s unsensationalized approach helps make it the most frightening treatment of the subject found on film, easily outdistancing *On the Beach* (Fox) or the widely hyped doomsday miniseries *The Day After* (Paramount).

TETSUO:
THE SERIES

TETSUO: THE IRON MAN   (1989) B&W **1/2

D: Shinya Tsukamoto. Shinya Tsukamoto, Tomoroh Taguchi, Kei Fujiwara. 67 mins. (Fox Lorber) DVD

Tsukamoto's *Tetsuo* stars the auteur himself as the ultimate cyberpunk. In the opening scene, Tsukamoto is seen inserting a pipe into a self-inflicted leg gash. Soon after, he's run down by a white-collar worker, or "salaryman" (Taguchi), who himself begins a gradual but violent transformation into a grotesque cyborg. Much screen time is devoted to charting how this transmogrification affects Taguchi's love life with his understandably surprised squeeze (Fujiwara). (Mostly adversely, we'd say, particularly after the character's procreative organ mutates into an angry power drill (!).) "Metal fetishist" Tsukamoto, meanwhile, who's likewise becoming a literal metal man, discovers he can communicate telepathically with Taguchi. The two "iron men" eventually square off in a demented showdown that roughly approximates what a Godzilla movie might look like were it directed by vintage Sam Raimi. Tsukamoto's wild celluloid style borrows not only from Raimi and Godzilla, but from Davids Lynch and Cronenberg, samurai movies, punk rock, "manga" comics, and *animé* epics like *Akira*. While the two are essentially inseparable, Tsukamoto's dizzying B&W cinematic technique tops his tunnel-visioned content. *Anime* fans will enjoy this sustained live-action technotrash fever dream, but the uninitiated may find Tsukamoto's nearly dialogue-free flight of metal fancy too esoteric and repetitious for their tastes. Followed by 1991's equally over-the-top *Tetsuo II: Body Hammer* (Manga Entertainment, DVD). Tsukamoto resurfaced in 1995 with the recommended *Tokyo Fist* (Manga, DVD), a boxing film sufficiently extreme to make *Raging Bull* look like *Bambi*.

T-FORCE   (1994) ***

D: Richard Pepin. Jack Scalia, Erin Gray, Evan Lurie, Bobby Johnston, Deron McBee, Jennifer MacDonald, Vernon Wells. 97 mins. (PM)

Prolific PM auteur Pepin, whose earlier action entries have varied wildly in quality, proceeds here from a winning cast and script (by Jacobsen Hart). The opening scene is strictly business as usual, with frequent screen villain Wells leading 30 armed henchpersons on a fairly ambitiously choreographed slaughter spree through a high-rise office building in 2007 L.A. The violence further escalates when the cyborgian "Terminal Force" shows up to blow away the bad guys. Unfortunately for them, their self-

appointed leader, Adam (Lurie), takes it upon himself to explode a chopper filled with innocent hostages, leading mayor Gray to order the law-enforcement androids' immediate disassembly, at which point the pic crosses into more original, compelling turf. Lurie and mechanical cohorts McBee and MacDonald rebel, while obedient android Johnston volunteers to help human cop Scalia track the kill-happy cybernauts. Soon the robot-hating Scalia—who packs a *Sledge Hammer!*-styled handgun big enough to give Dirty Harry a raging case of barrel envy—and the ever helpful Johnston bond big-time while the body count rises around them. Despite obvious debts to *Blade Runner, The Terminator, RoboCop,* and even *Creation of the Humanoids, T-Force* offers textured characterizations, credible dialogue, a wealth of clever near-futuristic details, and a tone that's witty rather than wiseass.

THEM!   (1954) B&W ***½

D: Gordon Douglas. Edmund Gwenn, James Arness, Joan Weldon, James Whitmore. 94 mins. (Warner)

Still the best giant-insect movie ever made, with dad/daughter scientists Gwenn and Weldon, assisted by lawmen Arness and Whitmore, tracking atom-spawned ants from the New Mexican desert to the L.A. sewer system. Fess (Davy Crockett) Parker has a neat bit as an incredulous pilot.

THEY LIVE   (1988) ***

D: John Carpenter. Roddy Piper, Keith David, Meg Foster, Buck Flower, Peter Jason, Raymond St. Jacques, John Goff. 97 mins. (Universal) DVD

Carpenter's *They Live* boasts a brilliant premise in an updated *Invasion of the Body Snatchers* vein: Seems the American media's secretly being run by manipulative aliens from outer

space. (That would at least account for Kathy Lee and Regis.) Itinerant construction worker Nada (Piper) stumbles upon this cosmic conspiracy after donning a pair of truth-seeking sunglasses (!) that reveal the skeletal visages hidden behind the human masks worn by the E.T. powers-that-be—faces as ugly as the aliens' rapacious instincts. The shades also detect subliminal *1984*-esque messages—e.g., "Obey," "Consume," "Submit"—posted on billboards and TV screens. These scenes play like a politicized update of the old 3-D hallucination *The Mask* (only instead of floating skulls, Roddy sees corporate heads). The aliens' mission is to keep the general populace "asleep, selfish, sedate" while they—a race of corporate raiders assisted by greedy human collaborators—plunder our planet of its natural resources. Our now enlightened hero connects with a band of earthly resistance fighters, and the battle is on in earnest. *They Live* is well worth watching for its more imaginative components and a message that's even truer today than it was back in '88.

THE THIEF OF BAGDAD   (1940) ***

D: Michael Powell, Ludwig Berger, Tim Whelan. Sabu, Conrad Veidt, Rex Ingram, June Duprez. 106 mins. (Embassy)

Sabu, with more than a little help from his genie (Ingram), goes one on one with wicked conjuror Veidt in what still ranks as one of the most spectacular fantasies ever lensed. Doug Fairbanks' silent version, filmed in black and white, is also on cassette (Kino).

THE THING (FROM ANOTHER WORLD)   (1951) B&W ***½

D: Christian Nyby. Kenneth Tobey, Margaret Sheridan, Robert Cornthwaite. 87 mins. (Turner)

According to star Tobey, Howard Hawks did indeed direct this seminal sci-fi tale (official credit went to film editor Nyby), which offers overlapping dialogue, nail-biting suspense, and future *Gunsmoke* icon James Arness as the hostile Veg-Man from another world.

THE THING   (1982) ***½

D: John Carpenter. Kurt Russell, Wilford Brimley, T. K. Carter. 108 mins. (Universal) DVD

Scaremaster Carpenter injects tension, juice, and gore galore into his expanded, over-the-top reworking of the 1951 sci-fi classic, about a voracious alien loose at a remote Antarctic military base, and crafts one of the few remakes that equals the original's impact.

THINGS TO COME   (1936) B&W **½

D: William Cameron Menzies. Raymond Massey, Ralph Richardson, Margaretta Scott, Cedric Hardwicke. 92 mins. (Englewood) DVD

Future *Invaders from Mars* auteur Menzies adapts H. G. Wells's futuristic fable (Wells also scripted), which finds "benign" high-flying fascist Massey imposing order on a chaotic postholocaust world. The spectacular sets and Ned Mann's effects make *Things* a visual treat. Other early sci-fi efforts now available on tape include *F.P.1 Doesn't Answer* (Sinister Cinema) and *Transatlantic Tunnel* (Moore Video).

THIS IS NOT A TEST   (1962) B&W **½

D: Frederic Gadette. Seamon Glass, Mary Morlas, Thayer Roberts. 80 mins. (Sinister Cinema)

This truly bizarre desert-set cheapie stars Glass as a harried hardheaded state trooper who tries to warn singularly uncooperative motorists of an impending atomic attack. He later goes postal over an oxygen-stealing poodle. The ending's a minor classic.

THIS ISLAND EARTH (1955) ***

D: Joseph Newman. Rex Reason, Faith Domergue, Jeff Morrow. 86 mins. (Universal) DVD

A levelheaded earth scientist (played by the aptly named Rex Reason) constructs a mysterious machine (the immortal "interociter") that ultimately leads him and scientist Domergue to the endangered planet of Metaluna, where they encounter big-headed alien Morrow and his humanoid insects. While the *MST3K* crew successfully skewered the flick in its big-screen incarnation, *Mystery Science Theater 3000: The Movie* (see index), *TII* survives as a fine '50s sci-fi film in its own right.

THX 1138   (1971) ***

D: George Lucas. Robert Duvall, Donald Pleasence, Maggie McOmie. 88 mins. (Warner)

Aided by Duvall's turn as an unlikely hero, future industry giant Lucas's low-budget debut holds up as a bleakly effective vision of a future police state. Duvall's climactic race against the cash register is nothing short of brilliant.

TICKS   (1993) ***

D: Tony Randel. Rosalind Allen, Ami Dolenz, Seth Green, Virginia Keehne, Peter Scolari, Clint Howard. 85 mins. (Republic)

Giant toxic ticks crawl amok in Northern California in this lean, tightly plotted chiller. Director Randel wisely lets us get to know the film's characters before placing them in the anticipated danger. Green, as a neurotic but likable teen, and Ribeiro, as a slightly older South Central youth, are two of several troubled adolescents taken on a "therapeutic" rural field trip by New Agey therapists Scolari and Allen. Herbal steroids used by local marijuana growers have pumped up the native tick population to deadly proportions. Our group soon finds itself endangered by both the pesky critters and a pair of deranged 'Nam-vet pot harvesters. Credible dialogue, legit suspense, an overlay of dark humor, and modest but effective FX work make *Ticks* a rousing creepfest for fans of updated takes on the bug movies of yore.

THE TIME MACHINE (1960) ***½

D: George Pal. Rod Taylor, Yvette Mimieux, Alan Young, Sebastian Cabot. 103 mins. (MGM)

Pal's pleasingly pulpy adaptation of H. G. Wells's seminal time-travel tale is supremely entertaining and, in its Morlock segment, effectively chilling. Then-teenage Yvette ("the shape of things to come," according to the pic's trailer) likewise impresses. A dull 1978 made-for-TV remake is also available (VCI). Taylor and Mimieux, joined by Jim Brown, reteamed for the lively 1968 Africa-set mercenary actioner *Dark of the Sun* (MGM).

THE TIME TRAVELERS (1964) **½

D: Ib Melchior. Preston Foster, Philip Carey, Merry Anders. 82 mins. (HBO, n.i.d.)

Foster leads a time-travel crew into the postnuke future, where hostile mutants abound, in this decidedly trippy tale. *Famous Monsters* founder Forry Ackerman cameos as a scientist. No relation to the 1966 Japan-set campfest of the same name (see index).

TIMEBOMB (1992)**½

D: Avi Nesher. Michael Biehn, Patsy Kensit, Richard Jordan, Robert Culp, Raymond St. Jacques. 95 mins. (MGM)

The Terminator Meets The Man-churian Candidate in Nesher's derivative but well-staged sci-fi actioner, wherein peaceful watchmaker Biehn learns he's actually the last survivor of a sinister scheme to transform Vietnam vets into remorseless superkillers. Kensit fills Linda Hamilton's shoes as a shrink shanghaied into serving as Biehn's eventual partner in escape. Highlights include a porn-theater-set shoot-out, hallucinatory FX work, and an earnest perf by sensitive, oft injured Biehn (the gals just love to lick his wounds).

TIMECOP (1994) ***

D: Peter Hyams. Jean-Claude Van Damme, Ron Silver, Mia Sara, Bruce McGill, Gloria Reuben, Scott Bellis. 99 mins. (Universal) DVD

J-C takes the title role of time-traveling lawman Max Walker, whose task it is to stop corrupt congressman Silver from committing past atrocities that will alter the future. Max also hopes to reverse the murder of wife Sara. While inconsistencies crop up in Mark Verheiden's otherwise solid script (based on the comic-book series by Verheiden and Mike Richardson), TimeCop works more often than not. One of its more playful conceits finds bad-guy Silver running into his past self (à la teens Bill and Ted in Bill & Ted's Excellent Adventure), encounters contentious enough to prompt Van Damme to command, "Stop arguing among yourself!"

THE TINGLER (1959)
B&W/COLOR****

D: William Castle. Vincent Price, Darryl Hickman, Patricia Cutts, Judith Evelyn, Philip Coolidge. 82 mins. (Columbia/TriStar) DVD

The Tingler features a truly sicko story line—a spinal-fear lobster can grow in your body and kill you if you don't yell it away—the screen's first LSD trip, undertaken by scientist Price ("The walls! The waaallls!"), a partial-color sequence showing bright crimson blood flowing from a faucet, and more screams per frame than any other horror pic on record. (For max effect, play at top volume; your neighbors will never forget you.) All that's missing is the original "Percept-O!" process that saw select theater seats wired to shock viewer butts during those strategic moments when the Tingler scurries through an on-screen bijou with a silents-only policy. (The film on view is the 1921 melodrama Tol'able David; Castle may have missed a bet by not choosing a fright film, like Nosferatu, instead.) Among the characters, Coolidge's bijou owner/undertaker easily rates as the creepiest, while Evelyn delivers what amounts to a silent-film performance as his deaf/mute wife. (For several years The Tingler was shown in its original Percept-O! format at the NYC retro house Film Forum 2.) Don't forget to scream for your lives!

TOMCAT: DANGEROUS DESIRES (1993) ***

D: Paul Donovan. Richard Grieco, Maryam D'Abo, Natalie Radford. 96 mins. (Republic)

Arguably the best cat-brain movie to surface since 1964's Atomic Brain (a.k.a. Monstrosity, Sinister Cinema), Tomcat features a hunky, athletic Grieco as a terminally ill youth transformed into a prowling, amoral fiend after receiving cerebral cat-enzyme injections (!) administered by infatuated femme scientist D'Abo. In no time, Grieco loses his fear of heights, performs—sans training or practice—as a professional music-video dancer, and generally becomes an insatiable stud. On the downside, the feline influence also turns him into quite the conscienceless cad, compelling him to kill all who would obstruct his relentless pursuit of sensual pleasure. Grieco obviously has fun with this showy role and, unlike the insectoid Jeff Goldblum in The Fly or the lycanthropic Jack Nicholson in Wolf, suffers nary a moment of remorse over his gleeful misdeeds. Though Republic pushed Tomcat as an "erotic thriller," it's much more a monster movie for the MTV Generation.

THE TOMMYKNOCKERS (1993) ***

D: John Power. Jimmy Smits, Marg Helgenberger, Traci Lords, Joanna Cassidy, E. G. Marshall, Cliff De Young. 120 mins. (Trimark) DVD

Blocked poet Smits is one of small-town Haven's last holdouts when a local "curse" exerts a strange influence on the citizenry, prompting several of their number to start suddenly inventing green machinery. (Indeed, The Tommyknockers may be the greenest movie ever made.) Smits impresses in his Kevin McCarthy–like resister role, while Marshall registers well as the senior cit who's the first to suspect that something's rotten in Haven. Ex-porn starlet Lords gets a lot of mileage out of her vanishing-lipstick tube.

TOTAL RECALL (1990) ***

D: Paul Verhoeven. Arnold Schwarzenegger, Sharon Stone, Rachel Ticotin, Michael Ironside, Ronny Cox. 113 mins. (Fox) DVD

Verhoeven steers a futuristic Arnold through an explosive filmlong maze ablaze with nonstop violence (including a bone-crunching kung-fu catfight segment), tricky mind games, and spectacular high-tech FX. Adapted from sci-fi scribe Philip K. Dick's "We Can Remember It for You Wholesale," Total Recall casts Arn as construction worker Doug Quaid, whose artificially induced Martian holiday leads to a twisty search for his own stolen identity and a sinister scheme hatched by corporate creep Cohaagen (RoboCop alum Cox). Along the way, Total Recall intros such fun concepts as VR vacations implanted directly into the brain, hologram tennis instructors, and robot-run taxis called "Johnnycabs." While this slick Arnie vehicle incorporates elements borrowed from such earlier films as *Westworld, Outland, Forbidden Planet, Aliens, The Running Man, RoboCop,* and *The Terminator* (replacing android Arn's infamous eye-extraction scene with a similarly disgusto sequence involving the muscled one's proboscis), director Verhoeven and three scripters—Dan (*Dark Star*) O'Bannon among them—add enough fresh fire to keep even these reheated riffs alive and cooking. Another plus is a dependable cast recruited mostly from the B-movie ranks (maybe because Arn pocketed such a prohibitive portion of the pic's budget), including a pre-star Stone as Arn's duplicitous spouse.

A TOWN HAS TURNED TO DUST (1998) **½

D: Rob Nilsson. Stephen Lang, Ron Perlman, Gabriel Olds, Judy Collins. 90 mins. (Bedford Entertainment)

A moody moral western (complete with grizzled settlers and vanquished Indians) cloaked in grim futuristic sci-fi mufti and scripted by late, great *Twilight Zone* creator Rod Serling back in 1958, *A Town Has Turned to Dust* unfolds in the bleak frontier town of Carbon, one of an ecologically ravaged Earth's few remaining outposts. When cruel, crude town boss Perlman leads a mob to lynch his young wife's Native American lover, tension mounts between Indian and white factions. Caught in the middle is ineffectual lawman Lang, who eventually finds the courage to challenge his employer (and former partner in crime) Perlman. Novice video journalist Olds, assigned to do a story on the decaying settlement, supplies the tale with its narrative glue. While overwhelmingly downbeat, *Town* is a well-written (not surprisingly), earnestly acted piece that rates as a

must for Serling completists and a fair bet for more general sci-fi fans.

TRANCERS:
THE SERIES

TRANCERS   (1985) **½

D: Charles Band. Tim Thomerson, Helen Hunt, Michael Stefani, Art La Fleur. 76 mins. (Vestron, n.i.d.)

*T*rancers (released theatrically as *Future Cop*) tells the highly derivative but fitfully entertaining tale of tough-guy "trooper" Jack Deth (Thomerson), a hard-boiled Dirty Harry type who ceaselessly battles malevolent mystic Whistler (Stefani) and his lobotomoid minions, called "trancers," in the ruins of a 23rd-century L.A. destroyed by "the Great Quake." When Whistler time-trips back to Angel City '85 to wipe out the ancestors of his future enemies—our Mr. Deth among them—Jack is quick to give pursuit. There he enlists the aid of innocent femme Leena (future A star Hunt) in his bid to rid the world of this once-and-future menace. Thomerson and Hunt return for the convoluted, mediocre 1991 sequel, *Trancers 2: The Return of Jack Deth,* while Thomerson goes it alone in *Trancers 3: Deth Lives, Trancers 4: Jack of Swords,* and *Trancers 5: Sudden Deth* (all Paramount).

TRON   (1982) **½

D: Steven Lisberger. Jeff Bridges, David Warner, Bruce Boxleitner. 96 mins (Disney) DVD

T he Disney folks miscalculated a mite by setting this pioneering videogame flick inside the game itself. Still, while the story's not much, the inventive graphics remain great fun to watch, especially with the sound turned down.

TWELVE MONKEYS   (1995) ***

D: Terry Gilliam. Bruce Willis, Madeleine Stowe, Brad Pitt, Christopher Plummer, Frank

Gorshin. 130 mins. (Universal) Collector's Edition DVD

T erry Gilliam's twisty time-travel thriller, inspired by Chris Marker's 1962 short "La Jetée" (Moore Video), represents a real treat for sci-fi fans. A bruised and abused Bruce toplines as a future courier sent back to the '90s to trace the origins of a killer virus that's set to annihilate the planet's population. While incarcerated in a present-day mental hospital, Bruce encounters Pitt, a schizy self-styled terrorist who may hold the key to Earth's destiny. Stowe is also in the mix as a scientist Bruce recruits to help him in his quest. While some deemed *Twelve Monkeys* too convoluted and downbeat for its own good, the flick is an undeniably gripping affair that will keep viewers guessing all the way.

20 MILLION MILES TO EARTH (1957) B&W ***

D: Nathan Juran. William Hopper, Joan Taylor, Frank Puglia, Thomas B. Henry. 82 mins. (Universal)

H opper toplines as an astronaut who crash-lands off the Italian coast following an ill-fated Venus probe. Trouble is, he didn't come back alone—a canister containing a tiny, bloblike Venusian lifeform also made the journey. When the creature (an "Ymir") grows to gargantuan proportions, Ray Harryhausen (who cameos as a zookeeper) kicks in with his trademark FX expertise, particularly during the scene that finds the now outsized Ymir locked in mortal combat with an elephant.

2001: A SPACE ODYSSEY   (1968) ***

D: Stanley Kubrick. Keir Dullea, Gary Lockwood, William Sylvester. 139 mins. (MGM) DVD

T he big screen remains the ideal venue for Kubrick's cosmic epic, still a highly (accent on *high*) original mix of interstellar light show and suspense, with an unforgettable performance by

HAL the singing computer. Peter Hyams's 1984 sequel, *2010* (MGM, DVD), highlighted by Arthur C. Clarke's earnest script and Richard Edlund's spectacular FX, runs out of rocket fuel following a bright start.

THE UNBORN:
THE SERIES

THE UNBORN (1991)**½

D: Rodman Flender. Brooke Adams, Jeff Hayenga, James Karen, Lisa Kudrow, K Callan. 84 mins. (Columbia/TriStar)

An updated variation on Larry Cohen's *It's Alive* killer-infant trilogy (with even deeper roots in *Rosemary's Baby*), *The Unborn* stars Adams as an infertile children's-book author who, with lawyer hubby Hayenga, consults miracle fertility expert Dr. Mayerling (Karen). Said visit soon leads to a series of creepy artificial-insemination procedures. Despite Doc Karen's assurance that "this is not a gothic novel," Brooke finds herself pregnant with your typical genetic mutant. Brooke, whose character already suffers from preexisting mental imbalances, delivers an intense perf as the understandably paranoid monster-mom-to-be. Callan supplies dark comic relief as Brooke's even nuttier mother: Upon observing her extravagantly preggers daughter smoking cigarettes and knocking back hard booze, K remarks, "Isn't that bad for the baby these days?" *The Unborn* is at its best when satirizing sinister medicos, slick media types, and pretentious New Agers, like the lesbian couple who ban fathers from their holistic birthing classes because they consider them "outsiders" (!). Director Flender returns with the dismal 1999 frightcom *Idle Hands* (Columbia/TriStar).

THE UNBORN II (1994)**

D: Rick Jacobson. Michele Greene, Scott Valentine, Robin Curtis, Leonard O. Turner, Michael James McDonald, Brittany Powell. 84 mins. (New Horizons)

An effective opening sequence sees femme assassin Curtis cold-bloodedly execute local kids and newborns. Turns out she's a victim of mad geneticist Karen's plot, outlined in the first flick, to produce brain-boosted but utterly amoral youths who would later apply their heightened cerebral powers to solving the planet's ecoproblems. Curtis meets resistance from single mom Greene (of *L.A. Law* fame), who's fiercely protective of her outsized six-month-old monster son, Joey, who, having devoured his own dad (!), is already responsible for his mom's widowhood. (He later adds baby-sitter Powell, her boyfriend, and a nosy social worker to his menu.) While slickly lensed and decently acted, particularly by Greene, *The Unborn II* springs few genuine surprises.

UNEARTHLY STRANGER (1963)
B&W ***

D: John Krish. John Neville, Gabriella Licudi, Philip Stone, Jean Marsh, Patrick Newell. 68 mins. (Sinister Cinema)

Sort of a gender-reversed Brit variation on *I Married a Monster from Outer Space, Unearthly Stranger* stars Neville as a space researcher concerned about a rash of fatal brain implosions suffered by several fellow scientists in such far-flung locales as the U.S. and Russia. Seems each of the victims had recently married spouses who'd subsequently vanished. That disclosure throws suspicion on Neville's new bride, the fetching but clearly strange Licudi, who sleeps with her eyes open, never blinks, and is impervious to 275-degree heat. The best line belongs to one of Neville's scientific colleagues, who volunteers, "Would you allow me to come to your house and, in your presence, anesthetize your wife?" A compact 68 minutes, *Unearthly Stranger* builds steady suspense as the evidence mounts against our hero's mysterious missus and culminates in a low-key but honestly chilling climax. One obvious glitch, though: While the script makes much of Gabriella's blinkless stare, the camera repeatedly catches her blinking with heedless abandon—in extreme close-up, no less. A little Scotch tape might have helped here, without seriously stretching the pic's tight budget.

UNIVERSAL SOLDIER:
THE SERIES

UNIVERSAL SOLDIER (1992)**

D: Roland Emmerich. Jean-Claude Van Damme, Dolph Lundgren, Ally Walker, Ed O'Ross. 102 mins. (Artisan) DVD

In Lundgren, Van Damme matches (half)wits with the worst actor he's faced since he played twins in *Double Impact*. Here Dolph and J-C portray a pair of scientifically revived army rivals who battle over feisty blond reporter Walker. For those who care, Jean-Claude bares his Belgian butt in loving close-up, and he and D.L. butt heads during the flick's fist-and-kick-crazed finale, one of several strong action scenes that help relieve the script's predictable tedium. Followed by the cheap direct-to-video sequels *Universal Soldier II* and *III;* J-C reprised the role in 1999's *Universal Soldier: The Return* (Columbia/TriStar).

UNKNOWN WORLD (1951)
B&W **½

D: Terrell O. Morse. Bruce Kellogg, Marilyn Nash, Victor Kilian. 73 mins. (Englewood)

Unknown World is a liberally bent sci-fi quickie about a group of scientists who bore into the earth to find a safe haven in the event of nuclear annihilation. Trouble is, after an entertaining start, the flick will bore you too. Still worth seeing for its historical value.

VIDEODROME (1983) ***½

D: David Cronenberg. James Woods, Debbie Harry, Sonja Smits. 87 mins. (Universal) DVD

David Cronenberg meets Marshall McLuhan when the ever twitchy Woods uncovers a mysterious S&M TV station that specializes in live torture broadcasts. Rampant paranoia, disturbing FX (e.g., the breathing Blondie TV), and a generally unwholesome atmosphere make *Videodrome* a one-of-a-kind viewing experience.

VILLAGE OF THE DAMNED (1960) B&W ***

D: Wolf Rilla. George Sanders, Barbara Shelley, John Phillips. 78 mins. (MGM)

Rilla adapts John Wyndham's novel *The Midwich Cuckoos* into a suspenseful sci-fi film about a dozen pregnant British women who give birth to blond alien offspring reminiscent of Hitler's Aryan youth. A rushed climax rates as *Village*'s only serious flaw. The 1961 sequel, *Children of the Damned* (MGM/UA), is also available.

VILLAGE OF THE DAMNED (1995) ***

D: John Carpenter. Christopher Reeve, Kirstie Alley, Linda Kozlowski, Michael Paré, Meredith Salenger, Mark Hamill, Buck Flower. 99 mins. (Universal) DVD

Carpenter shifts the action from seaside England to a contempo California coastal town, where the entire populace—pets and farm critters included—conks out during an early A.M. church barbecue. (One hapless soul, who dozes off on the grill [!], never wakes up.) Naturally, officious government types rush in and wild theories spread, especially when it's soon discovered that eight of the town's women—including a virgin (Salenger)—are mysteriously pregnant. Carpenter's best at milking those scenes more discreetly

handled in the original. He conveys the primal panic of childbirth with black humor and high-decibel horror when all the women deliver their alien spawn on the same chaotic night. Once the alien Aryan youngsters, via their superaccelerated development, achieve some measure of self-sufficiency, they waste no time in putting their evil plans into play, telekinetically punishing those adults who dare to stand in their way (a series of violent tableaux executed with typical Carpenter-ian panache.) If you watched the first film and idly wondered what John Carpenter might do with the same material, *Village* answers that question with dark wit, genuine scares, and state-of-the-art FX (by Industrial Light & Magic).

VIRTUAL COMBAT: THE SERIES

VIRTUAL COMBAT (1995) **½

D: Andrew Stevens. Don ("The Dragon") Wilson, Athena Massey, Loren Avedon, Ken McLeod, Turhan Bey, Stella Stevens. 97 mins. (A-Pix) DVD

Kickbox champ Wilson scores one of his better vehicles with a sci-fi actioner that borrows liberally from *Blade Runner* and *Demolition Man* while adding a few fresh twists of its own. Vet thesp Bey plays a sort of cyber-Frankenstein who's able to convert virtual-reality computer programs into living tissue and uses this arcane ability to create—what else?—a sex goddess (Massey) and a dominatrix "born" with whip in hand (!). Art Camacho deserves credit for choreographing the generally crisp fight scenes, while Stella (Mother of Andrew) Stevens appears as cop Wilson's computer-screen department link, and Rip Taylor cameos as a bald, mustachioed, effeminate Vegas hologram cybersex pitchman. Followed by *Virtual Combat 2* (A-Pix). Other additions to the virtual-video subgenre include the Michael Dudikoff dud *Vir-*

tual Assassin (1995, Turner); Julie Strain vehicle *Virtual Desire* (Triboro, DVD); Elizabeth (*Assault of the Killer Bimbos*) Kaitan comeback bid, *Virtual Encounters* (1996, Surrender); techno-erotica exercise *Virtual Seduction* (1995, New Horizons), with Jeff Fahey and Ami Dolenz; and Brett Leonard's big-budget, Denzel Washington–starred bomb, *Virtuosity* (1995, Paramount).

VOYAGE TO THE BOTTOM OF THE SEA (1961) ***

D: Irwin Allen. Walter Pidgeon, Peter Lorre, Barbara Eden, Frankie Avalon. 105 mins. (Fox)

An atomic sub races to extinguish a burning Van Allen radiation belt before it's too late. A fine cast and solid central story line make *Voyage* more fun than most of director Irwin ("Master of Disaster") Allen's efforts.

WAR OF THE WORLDS (1953) ***½

D: Byron Haskin. Gene Barry, Ann Robinson, Les Tremayne, Carolyn Jones. 85 mins. (Paramount) DVD

H. G. Wells's story and producer George Pal's magnificent FX make this a spellbinding—if occasionally corny (in the religion and love-story tangents)—example of '50s sci-fi filmmaking at its best. *Independence Day* lifted some of its best riffs from *War*.

WARGAMES (1983) ***

D: John Badham. Matthew Broderick, Ally Sheedy, Dabney Coleman. 110 mins. (MGM) DVD

With *WarGames*, Badham crafts an intriguing sci-fi thriller about a teen computer genius (Broderick) who unwittingly taps in to the Pentagon's nuke-defense network. While the film ultimately takes too many easy, crowd-pleasing turns, it still rates as entertaining fare and a far better bet than Marshall Brickman's similarly themed but insufferably smarmy *Manhattan Project* (HBO).

THE WASP WOMAN (1959)
B&W **¹/₂

D: Roger Corman. Susan Cabot, Anthony Eisley, Michael Marks. 66 mins. (Sinister Cinema)

Wasp Woman is not about a rampaging distaff white Anglo-Saxon Protestant; rather, it's a typically iconic, entertaining Corman cheapie about Cabot's ambitious cosmetics queen's addiction to a wasp-hormone-based beauty cream that transforms her into the titular creature. Remade as 1996's stingless *Wasp Woman* (New Horizons).

WATCHERS:
THE SERIES

WATCHERS (1988) **

D: Jon Hess. Corey Haim, Michael Ironside, Barbara Williams, Lala. 98 mins. (Artisan)

The original *Watchers* charts the adventures of teen Haim and his adopted dog, Lala, a canine genius who's also a fugitive from a government lab where vile military experiments are being conducted. Hot on our heroes' trail is the end result of one such experiment—the dread OXCOM 7 (that's "outside experimental combat mammal" to you), a feral mutant killing machine telepathically linked to our imperiled Fido. While *Watchers* is technically competent and engineers a neat twist involving ruthless OXCOM tracker Ironside, the pic is mostly a series of repetitious chase-and-slaughter scenes, with Haim, screen mom Williams, and the undeniably talented Lala striving to keep one step ahead of the creature while the latter eviscerates any number of hapless secondary charac-

ters. Followed by the slightly improved *Watchers II* (Artisan), less a sequel than a remake, the less successful *Watchers 3*, with Wings Hauser, and yet another remake, *Watchers Reborn* (both New Horizons), with Mark Hamill.

WAVELENGTH (1983) **¹/₂

D: Mike Gray. Robert Carradine, Cherie Currie, Keenan Wynn. 87 mins. (Embassy)

China Syndrome auteur Gray fashions a fairly good genre flick about a reclusive folk-rocker (Carradine) and a distaff drifter (fetching ex-Runaway Currie) who uncover undersized aliens being held subterranean captives by evil government officials (à la the alleged Roswell incident). Tangerine Dream supplies the score.

WAX, OR THE DISCOVERY OF TELEVISION AMONG THE BEES (1992) ***¹/₂

D: David Blair. David Blair, Meg Savlov, Florence Ormezzano, William S. Burroughs. 85 mins. (First Run Features)

In his thoroughly hypnotic, philosophical cyberdream, director Blair uses film, computer graphics, collage, and historical footage to backtrack to the origins of a single act of destruction while exploring such arcane concepts as supernormal photography, Cain and Abel's lasting legacy, and an inner-earth dimension shared by dead humans and thinking bees (!). There's no dialogue, but Blair provides a running linear narration (e.g., "I became a short poem in the language of Cain") while appearing on-screen as Jacob Maker, an Alamogordo, New Mexico, worker about to embark on a spiritual journey. This painstakingly assembled, grant-funded film features evocative location lensing amid New Mexico's eerie abandoned nuclear-test sites, Kansas's Garden of Eden, NYC, and upstate New York. Burroughs contributes a silent cameo as

Jacob's scientifically inclined grandfather. While not to every taste, *Wax* manages to be at once hallucinatory and serious without resorting to undue gravity or pretentiousness.

WESTWORLD:
THE SERIES

WESTWORLD (1973) ***

D: Michael Crichton. James Brolin, Richard Benjamin, Yul Brynner. 88 mins. (MGM) DVD

Costumed androids run wild in a Huxleyesque amusement park—sort of a mechanized *Fantasy Island*—in a fun flick that puts its one gimmick to consistently inventive use. Brynner impresses as an android version of his *Magnificent Seven* gunslinger.

FUTUREWORLD (1976) ***

D: Richard T. Heffron. Peter Fonda, Blythe Danner, Yul Brynner. 104 mins. (Warner)

Great St. Louis Bank Robbery (see index) scripter Heffron assembles a solid *Westworld* sequel. Fonda and Danner are journalists investigating what went "WORNG" at an android amusement park, only to uncover an insidious robot plot. Brynner briefly reprises his cyborg gunslinger role. The same basic story line is recycled with a gangster motif in 1998's *Gangster World* (Spectum)—later aired on cable TV as *The Outsider*.

WHEN WORLDS COLLIDE (1951) **¹/₂

D: Rudolph Maté. Barbara Rush, Richard Derr, John Hoyt. 81 mins. (Paramount)

Producer George Pal's paranoid parable about Earth's imminent collision with a runaway planet is strengthened by imaginative FX that succeed in balancing out a generally bland cast.

A TALE OF TWO (WICKED) CITIES

WICKED CITY (1992) ***

D: Peter Mak. Jacky Cheung, Leon Lai, Michelle Li. Subtitled/dubbed. 88 mins. (Fox Lorber) DVD

Hong Kong genre honcho Tsui Hark produced and coscripted this live-action adaptation of Hideyuki Kikuchi's popular Japanese comic strip. *Wicked City* chronicles the ongoing battle of H.K. cop Taki (Cheung) with invasive "Reptoids," a race of humanoid reptiles who feed off human greed. In a near-future Hong Kong, said Reptoids are distributing a steroidlike drug called "Happiness" (leading to lines like "Confiscate all the goddamned Happiness!"). Like Ridley Scott's precocious *Blade Runner*, director Mak's *Wicked City* is also a treatise on personal identity: Taki's own partner and best friend, Ken (Lai), is half Reptoid, as is onetime squeeze Li, while the flick's chief villain frequently points out that Reptoids are no more embodiments of pure evil than humans are of unadulterated good. Fortunately, the philosophizing takes a distant backseat to Mak's wild action sequences, flashy FX, surreal sexual encounters, and elaborate martial arts choreography.

WICKED CITY (1993) ***

D: Yoshiaki Kawajiri. Animated. Dubbed. 90 mins. (Streamline)

Kawajiri's visually sweeping *Wicked City* depicts a near-future Earth about to enter into a nonaggression-pact renewal with humanoid inhabitants of a parallel dimension dubbed the "Black World." Like many adults-only *anime* efforts, *Wicked City* blends comic-book action with erotic interludes, frequently grisly in nature, as when Taki shares an ill-advised tryst with an undercover Black World terrorist who transforms into a grotty spiderwoman, equipped with an updated set of *vagina dentata* (!). While *Wicked City* can be interpreted as an allegory re mighty modern Japan's dealings with an often economically envious West, the flick, like its live-action counterpart, is far more interested in furnishing sex, violence, romance, and sci-fi-tinged action than political philosophy.

WITHIN THE ROCK (1996) **1/2

D: Gary J. Tunnicliffe. Xander Berkeley, Caroline Barclay, Bradford Tatum, Calvin Levels, Earl Boen, Dale Dye. 91 mins. (A-Pix) DVD

This better-than-average *Alien* rip-off charts a space crew's efforts to shift the course of a fugitive moon before it collides with Earth. Making their time-pressured mission more difficult is the presence of an alien predator. Berkeley turns in an impressive perf as the casually corrupt crew chief who supplies scientist Barclay with constant grief and whose heedless greed results in the creature's (a slightly updated rubber-suit job) escape in the first place. While the space FX are fairly cheesy, *Within the Rock* is well paced and deftly scripted.

X: THE MAN WITH THE X-RAY EYES (1963) ***

D: Roger Corman. Ray Milland, Diana Van Der Vlis, John Hoyt, Harold J. Stone, Don Rickles. 79 mins. (Warner)

William Castle's *The Tingler* (1959) may have been the first official LSD movie, and Corman's *The Trip* (1967) the definitive acid-exploitation experience, but Rog's sci-fi foray often proves more harrowingly hallucinogenic than either of the above. Milland stars as a scientist who devises a formula enabling him to see through solid matter. The transformation is fun enough during its early *Immoral Mr. Teas*–type phase, where Ray employs his newfound ocular powers to penetrate femme wardrobes (!). But Ray soon starts seeing far more than he bargained for on his way to eventual madness and the film's unforgettable revival-meeting climax. *X*, which also contains Don Rickles's only major horror-movie contribution until 1992's *Innocent Blood,* is packed with surreal imagery worthy of frequent video replays. Radically reworked for 1999's Corman-produced juvenile comedy *The Kid with the X-Ray Eyes* (New Horizons).

ZARDOZ (1974) ***

D: John Boorman. Sean Connery, Charlotte Rampling, Sara Kestleman. 105 mins. (Key)

Boorman's visually expressive vision of a futuristic dystopia (called Vortex) stars Connery as Zed the Exterminator, a "primitive" exploited by a ruling class of sexless intellectuals. Boorman manages to make this ontological sci-fi satire consistently compelling.

ZERAM (1991) **1/2

D: Keita Amamiya. Yuko Moriyama, Yukihiro Hotaru, Kunihiko Ida. Dubbed. 92 mins. (Fox Lorber) DVD

A live-action *anime*-styled cross between *Aliens, Godzilla,* and the Korean camp classic *Infra-Man* (Sinister Cinema), with intentional comedy tossed into the mix, *Zeram* should please Asian-fantasy fans. Moriyama stars as a Sigourney Weaver–type alien-fighter who, with the aid of her male computer, "Bob," squares off against the title creature in a battle that rages over the course of a single night. In the gender-bending department, *Zeram* itself is presumably male, equipped with a phallic appendage and a Kabuki-mask female face but also capable of producing eggs that turn into mewling, puking minimonsters. (Go figure.)

Killer Thrillers
AND *FILMS FATALE*

"The head getting blown off, the hand getting blown off—
it's all really wonderful stuff."
—actor/producer Tom Poster on SMALL KILL

ABSOLUTE POWER (1997) ***

D: Clint Eastwood. Clint Eastwood, Gene Hackman, Ed Harris, Laura Linney, Scott Glenn, Judy Davis, E. G. Marshall, Dennis Haysbert, Penny Johnson. 121 mins. (Warner) DVD

In a crowded field, Hackman easily cops Sleaziest Screen President of 1997 honors via his portrayal of our nation's leader as a sadistic thug and whiny coward with a penchant for rough sex. Gentleman jewel thief Clint witnesses the prez's violent abuse—and Secret Servicemen Glenn and Haysbert's subsequent slaying—of the wife of tycoon Marshall, Hackman's very mentor. Clint vows to expose the churlish chief while still finding time to bond with his own long-estranged district-attorney daughter (Linney). Though thoroughly pulpy, bald on logic, and hampered by a static opening, Clint's second geriatric actioner with a White House hook in four years (see also *In the Line of Fire*) supplies its share of well-orchestrated thrills.

AFTER DARK, MY SWEET (1990) ***

D: James Foley. Jason Patric, Rachel Ward, Bruce Dern, George Dickerson. 114 mins. (Artisan) DVD

Based on the Jim Thompson novel, Foley's offbeat philosophical noir manages to capture the book's quirky, surreal quality, thanks to its deliberate pacing and parched Arizona landscapes. Patric gives a convincing perf as a punchy but intuitively savvy ex-boxer drawn into an ill-advised kidnap caper by a sleazy Dern (in the type of unbalanced-lowlife role at which he's long excelled) and foxy widow Ward. Modern-noir fans should enjoy.

ALBINO ALLIGATOR (1997) ***

D: Kevin Spacey. Matt Dillon, Faye Dunaway, Gary Sinise, Viggo Mortensen, William Fichtner, Skeet Ulrich, Joe Mantegna, M. Emmet Walsh. 94 mins. (Miramax) DVD

Actor Spacey's directorial debut is a solidly scripted (by Christian [Son of Fabian] Forte), excellently acted hostage caper that eschews Tarantino-esque moves and zeroes in on traditional, no-nonsense suspense. After a botched warehouse robbery that leaves three agents dead, three small-time crooks—leader Dillon, an injured Sinise, and sociopathic Fichtner (in another impressive heavy role; see also *Heat*, *Strange Days*, and *The Underneath*)—

hole up in a basement bar near the New Orleans docks. Their hostages include defiant owner Walsh, conciliatory barmaid Dunaway, teen Ulrich, and an initially mysterious Mortensen. While longer on words than action, *Albino Alligator* suffers no lack of intensity, and the showdown with lawmen led by Mantegna shakes out in unpredictable fashion. In a neat, wisely underplayed touch, events in the bar unfold under Bogie's unchanging countenance, in a poster for *Dead Reckoning*. *Albino Alligator* is the type of small but tense outing that adapts well to the small screen. No relation to the initially intriguing but less successful 1991 road noir *Alligator Eyes* (Academy).

THE AMAZING MR. X (A.K.A. *THE SPIRITUALIST*) (1948) B&W ***

D: Bernard Vorhaus. Turhan Bey, Lynn Bari, Cathy O'Donnell, Richard Carlson, Donald Curtis. 78 mins. (Sinister Cinema)

One of the ever exotic Bey's best roles casts him as a con-man clairvoyant who charms rich sisters Bari and O'Donnell, while Bari's beau, Carlson, seeks to expose him. A suprisingly moody thriller with a solid twist, *AMX* makes especially atmospheric use of its coastal California setting in several evocative nocturnal scenes.

AMNESIA   (1997) ***

D: Kurt Voss. Ally Sheedy, Sally Kirkland, John Savage, Nicholas Walker, Dara Tomanovich. 92 mins. (Peachtree)

Director Voss, who gave us the clever noirs *The Horseplayer* and *Baja* (see index), comes up with another modest, seriocomic winner. Small-town minister Walker is carrying on a torrid affair with foxy schoolteacher Tomanovich. The pair regularly meet at a remote motel, where love-starved manager/owner Kirkland eavesdrops on their trysts and develops a serious crush on the rev, who winds up as her amnesic sex prisoner. *Amnesia* springs far more surprises than most mainstream thrillers in recent memory.

AND THEN THERE WERE NONE (1945) B&W ***

D: René Clair. Barry Fitzgerald, Walter Huston, Judith Anderson, Roland Young. 97 mins. (VCI) DVD

The best of several versions of the Agatha Christie mystery, Clair's original offers humor, suspense, and top-notch ensemble playing by a seasoned cast. The 1975 remake, *Ten Little Indians* (Charter), with Elke Sommer, and the 1989 edition, *Ten Little Indians* (Cannon), with Donald Pleasence and Frank Stallone, are also available.

AND THEN YOU DIE   (1972) ***

D: René Clément. Robert Ryan, Jean-Louis Trintignant, Tisa Farrow, Aldo Ray. 95 mins. (Unicorn, n.i.d.)

French thriller ace Clément crafts a clever, if initially claustrophobic, caper that comes complete with a coherent central metaphor, with Trintignant

cast as a kidnapped crook playing elaborate cat-and-mouse games with captors Ryan, Ray, and their confederates. Other available Clément suspensers include *The Deadly Trap* (1971, Facets), *Forbidden Games* (1952, Embassy), *Joy House* (1964), *Rider on the Rain* (1969, both Monterey), *Wanted: Babysitter* (1975, Academy), and *Purple Noon* (1960, see index).

THE ANDERSON TAPES (1971) ***

D: Sidney Lumet. Sean Connery, Dyan Cannon, Martin Balsam. 98 mins. (Columbia/TriStar/Goodtimes)

Connery heads a criminal crew planning an elaborate heist in Lumet's suspenseful, intricately detailed, high-tech-driven caper. The excellent supporting cast includes Ralph Meeker and Christopher Walken (in his big-screen debut).

ANGEL BLUE   (1997) **

D: Steven Kovacs. Sam Bottoms, Lisa Eichhorn, Yeniffer Behrens, Marco Rodríguez, Karen Black. 91 mins. (Vanguard)

Resembling something of a Cabbage Patch Harrison Ford, Bottoms plays a happily married, middle-aged banker who unwisely responds to the adolescent advances of friend Rodríguez's fetching, infatuated teen daughter (Behrens) in an indie that straddles the line between earnestness and exploitation with only intermittent success. A subplot involving a junkyard stalker further thickens the unlikely plot. *Angel Blue* works best during its brief, illicit erotic interludes, especially a scene where writer/director Kovacs yields unintentionally risible sexual symbolism from ordinary bathroom fixtures. Karen Black cameos as a clueless social worker (pardon our redundancy).

ANGEL DUST   (1996) **½

D: Sogo Ishii. Kaho Minami, Takeshi Wakamatsu, Etsushi Toyokawa. Subtitled. 116 mins. (New Yorker)

Something of a Japanese *Silence of the Lambs* Meets *The Usual Suspects*, Ishii's *Angel Dust* charts the efforts of telepathic police psychologist Setsuko (Minami) to locate a serial killer who injects lethal poison into unsuspecting young femme subway riders. Setsuko believes the key to the killer's identity resides within the first victim, a since-deprogrammed (or "rebrainwashed," in the pic's parlance) member of the Ultimate Truth Church. The search leads Setsuko to her ex-lover, professional deprogrammer Rei (Wakamatsu), smug, sinister, control-freak head of the "Refreezing Psychorium." While the story line and underlying mind-control theme initially intrigue, Ishii ultimately demonstrates he's more interested in playing head games with the audience in what's at core an overly manipulative puzzle masquerading as a thriller.

ANGEL HEART   (1987) ***

D: Alan Parker. Mickey Rourke, Robert De Niro, Lisa Bonet, Charlotte Rampling, Brownie McGhee. In R and unrated editions. 115 mins. (Artisan) DVD

Set in the '50s, *Angel Heart* follows shamus Harry Angel (Rourke) on a shaggy-dog search for missing mystery man Johnny Favorite, a task commissioned by the sinister Louis Cyphers (a bearded De Niro). Corpses keep piling up in Harry's wake as he journeys to the voodoo dens of New Orleans, where he also takes up with Bonet for a bloody sex scene that raised hell with the MPAA. (The unrated video version restores several seconds of footage scissored from the theatrical release.) For most of the way, *Angel Heart* succeeds in serving up sufficient suspense. Unfortunately, it winds up being a tad too existential for its own good and compounds this misdemeanor by perpetrating the filmic felony of employing a cheap, clichéd climax. Still, the buildup alone makes *Angel Heart* worth a look.

ANGELS AND INSECTS (1995) ***

D: Philip Haas. Mark Rylance, Patsy Kensit, Kristin Scott Thomas, Jeremy Kemp, Douglas Henshall, Chris Larkin. 116 mins. (Evergreen)

Adapted from A. S. Byatt's short story "Morpho Eugenia" and lushly directed by Haas—who earlier helmed the Paul (*Smoke*) Auster–based fable *The Music of Chance* (see index)—*Angels and Insects* charts the odd 1860s England-set adventures of scientist Rylance. Rescued from a shipwreck on his return from years of fieldwork in the Amazon, Rylance is taken in by a wealthy family headed by Kemp, where he enlightens several young charges and their spinsterly governess (Thomas) in the ways of an ant colony that's thriving on the estate's expansive grounds. Our hero also courts and eventually weds daughter Kensit. Kensit, in turn, enjoys an unusually "close" relationship with her upper-class twit brother, Henshall, who resents Rylance's presence. Director Haas draws ominously ironic parallels between the insect and human worlds as Kensit starts popping out offspring at an alarming rate. (In one memorable early scene, Kensit panics when she's "attacked" by butterflies just as the laid-back Rylance proposes to her.) An unsettling, hypnotic blend of dark comedy and skewed drama, *Angels and Insects* earns its cult status.

APARTMENT ZERO (1988) ***1/2

D: Martin Donovan. Colin Firth, Hart Bochner, Dora Bryan, Liz Smith, James Teller. 114/124 mins. (Fox Lorber, Academy) DVD

Donovan's deadpan, Buenos Aires–set black comedy/thriller is a genuinely unsettling, admirably perverse, and ultimately grisly affair. The film chronicles the bizarre bond that forms between repressed, high-strung film nerd Adrian (Firth) and charismatic stranger Jack (Bochner). When Jack rents a room abandoned by Adrian's crazed, hospitalized mom, he immediately ingratiates himself not only with a hopelessly smitten Adrian but with the latter's neighbors, a mixed group of eccentrics who've long viewed the terminally aloof Adrian with suspicion and contempt. And while Adrian sees the handsome young Yank as a contempo James Dean, director Donovan lets us know early on that Jack's a secretly psychotic professional assassin. Donovan's film-savvy script blends elements from Roman Polanski's *The Tenant* with several David Lynch–type twists (there's even an on-screen reference to *Blue Velvet,* while Firth himself looks a bit like a Brit Eraserhead). Both Firth and Bochner turn in excellent work as the dueling roomates, whose relationship teems with tacit sexual tension and intense mutual emotional need. Director Donovan sheared some ten minutes from the original theatrical version for the Academy video release, footage since restored in the Fox Lorber reissue.

THE APOSTLE (1997) **1/2

D: Robert Duvall. Robert Duvall, Miranda Richardson, Farrah Fawcett, June Carter Cash, Todd Allen, Billy Bob Thornton. 134 mins. (Universal) DVD

It's easy enough to understand why actors relish the stretch possibilities of portraying flamboyant Pentecostal preachers, whether bogus (Steve Martin in *Leap of Faith,* from Paramount) or earnest (Duvall here), and R.D. certainly can't be accused of ignoring the role's potential (he wrote it, after all, and directed himself): The man gets downright funky and a half here. What's surprising is that a flick as simply structured and character-driven as *The Apos-*

tle would be so full of plot and motivational holes. Duvall does a great job re-creating a regional American Christian microcosmos (in Bayou Boutte, Louisiana) and capturing the communal feeling shared by his modest, ragtag flock; it's the chain of events that leads him there that requires a tad too much faith on the viewer's part. After "saving" a car-wreck victim, performing acts of kindness for his elderly mom (Cash, who's roughly the same age as the then-67-year-old Duvall), and holding imaginary pep talks with (an unseen) Jesus, Duvall loses it when he learns a local minister (Allen) is getting it on with his organist spouse (Fawcett). While Duvall admirably resists visualizing the old Redd Foxx joke about chasing a cheating preacher into a church and catching him by the organ, he *does* take a lethal baseball bat to the rival minister's head, an act that seems out of keeping even for R.D.'s admittedly emotional character. Still, Duvall largely succeeds in atoning for that key celluloid sin, putting on a one-man show that's sure to please the inventive actor's fans.

APT PUPIL (1998) ***

D: Bryan Singer. Ian McKellen, Brad Renfro, Bruce Davison, Elias Koteas, Joe Morton, Jan Triska, Heather McComb, David Schwimmer, James Karen. 111 mins. (Columbia/TriStar) DVD

While not as perverse as the French import *Baxter* (see index), Bryan (*The Usual Suspects*) Singer's examination of similar themes of good and evil, drawn from the Stephen King novella, yields its share of insights and suspense. McKellen, so excellent as James Whale in *Gods and Monsters,* equally impresses here as an elderly Nazi fugitive posing as a harmless naturalized American citizen in a California town, circa 1984. Enterprising high-schooler Renfro gets the goods on the reclusive war criminal, but instead of turning him in, Brad blackmails him into sharing intimate stories of his atrocity-driven past. Showing considerable promise as a Nazi-youth candidate, Renfro both learns from the old master and helps rekindle the latter's long-dormant desire to resume a more active evil lifestyle. Not surprisingly, the versatile McKellen easily steals his and Renfro's many scenes together, but Brad's believable in a white-bread-gone-bad sort of way. TV refugee Schwimmer turns in effective supporting work as Brad's overly intrusive guidance counselor, while frequent genre thesp Karen cameos as Renfro's wheelchair-bound grandfather. Director Singer creates a genuinely unwholesome, creepy ambience amid the sunny small-town mise en scène.

ARLINGTON ROAD (1999)***

D: Mark Pellington. Jeff Bridges, Tim Robbins, Joan Cusack, Hope Davis, Robert Gossett, Spencer Treat Clark, Mason Gamble. 117 mins. (Columbia/TriStar) DVD

Pellington's ingeniously plotted (by scripter Ehren Kruger) suspenser casts Bridges as Michael Faraday, a Reston, Virginia, academic who specializes in teaching classes on terrorism. Turns out that Mike's FBI-agent wife was killed in a botched raid on armed suspected separatists, which helps explain his ongoing obsession. Faraday's trying to get his life back together with his nine-year-old son (Clark) and grad-student squeeze (Davis) when he saves new neighbors the Langs' (Robbins, Cusack) son, severely injured in a suspicious "fireworks" accident. Mike's initially warm-and-fuzzy feelings freeze fast when he suspects Robbins of harboring a forged identity, secret past, and threatening future. While the normally excellent Bridges too often goes the overwrought route here, both Robbins and Cusack (with the usually comic actress playing against type) are chilling as our hero's neighbors from hell. Like

many contemporary films, *Arlington Road* also defies audience expectations, a trend, we suspect, that owes much of its inspiration to *The X-Files* (Fox, DVD), itself both a major reflection and minor instigator of our current conspiratorial climate. While it doesn't inhabit the paranoia pantheon occupied by such towering forebears as *The Manchurian Candidate* and *Seconds* (see index), *Arlington Road*'s admirably downbeat direction places it above most recent entries in the mainstream thriller genre.

THE ART OF DYING (1991)***

D: Wings Hauser. Wings Hauser, Kathleen Kinmont, Gary Werntz, Michael J. Pollard, Mitch Hara, Sydney Lassick, Sarah Douglas. 90 mins. (PM)

The ever energetic Hauser stars in and directs this extremely sleazy, generally gripping thriller about a snuff-movie maniac amok. Wings is a volatile LAPD dick investigating the murders of several young runaways and aspiring actors (male and female), victims of amateur "auteur" Werntz and his gay "talent scout" Hara. Director Hauser intercuts his own character's kinky affair with mysterious fox Kinmont with Werntz's literally lethal re-creations of gory tableaux from *The Deer Hunter*, 1983's *Scarface*, *The Godfather*, and *Psycho*. While the terminally twitchy Pollard is less than credible as a police psychiatrist, the 6-feet-6 Werntz is truly sinister as the deliberate, articulate, celluloid-obsessed serial killer.

THE ASPHALT JUNGLE (1950) B&W****

D: John Huston. Sterling Hayden, Jean Hagen, Sam Jaffe, Marilyn Monroe. 112 mins. (MGM)

Huston crafts one of the best heist films ever made, with a hard-boiled but soft-centered Hayden deter-

mined to better his life. Jaffe (as the quietly lecherous brains behind the operation) steals his scenes, while Monroe makes the most of her brief appearance.

AT CLOSE RANGE (1986)***

D: James Foley. Sean Penn, Christopher Walken, Mary Stuart Masterson. 115 mins. (Vestron/Video Treasures) DVD

Based on a true story, Foley's compelling descent into Sleaze Americana stars Penn as an aimless youth who unwisely hooks up with his lowlife dad, Walken, and his gang of thieving rednecks. The pic's pacing is sometimes slow but faithful to the rhythms of our seedy characters' dead-end lives—stretches of mundane time-killing punctuated by bursts of sudden violence. A deft effort all around.

ATLANTIC CITY (1980)****

D: Louis Malle. Burt Lancaster, Susan Sarandon, Kate Reid. 104 mins. (Paramount)

Aging petty crook Lancaster and restless waitress Sarandon go unexpectedly upscale in Malle's excellent, atmospheric caper. The best line in John Guare's standout script belongs to Burt, who, apropos the Atlantic Ocean, remarks: "That's nothing. You should have seen it thirty years ago."

BABY DOLL (1956) B&W***

D: Elia Kazan. Carroll Baker, Karl Malden, Eli Wallach. 115 mins. (Warner)

While no longer the shocker it was considered during its initial release, Kazan's Tennessee Williams adaptation still rates as an effectively eccentric character study of child bride Baker, brainless hubby Malden, and the egotistical business rival (an excellent Wallach) who covets Karl's property. The original crib-driven poster art remains a classic.

THE BABYSITTER (1995) **

D: Guy Ferland. Alicia Silverstone, Jeremy London, J. T. Walsh, Lee Garlington, Nicky Katt, George Segal. 90 mins. (Republic)

Not the babysitter-from-hell-type thriller its packaging suggests, *The Babysitter* instead shapes up as a quintessential 1970s-styled suburban fable. How '70s is it? It's so '70s it's not only drawn from a Robert Coover short story but also features George Segal, one of that era's reigning Hollywood angst icons. A pre-*Clueless* Silverstone plays the title character (a role tailor-made for the *very* young Barbara Hershey), a chastely foxy, blissfully oblivious nymphette who serves as the center of four diverse males' secret desires. While *The Babysitter* offers a scattering of insights into the male psyche, most of this meandering movie rehashes libidinous clichés as the guys' various fantasies converge in a real-life catastrophe. For the record, Alicia indulges in one discreet bathing scene.

BACKFIRE (1988) **½

D: Gilbert Cates. Karen Allen, Keith Carradine, Jeff Fahey, Bernie Casey, Dean Paul Martin, Dinah Manoff. 91 mins. (Trimark)

Rich 'Nam vet Fahey suffers from violent wartime flashbacks that are putting a considerable strain on his marriage to former poor girl Allen. When Jeff—after a night of particularly vivid hallucinations (including finding his bed filled with bloody, extracted eyeballs!)—slips into a catatonic state, the situation doesn't immediately improve for his less-than-compassionate better half. Further complications ensue when mysterious drifter Carradine wanders into Karen's chaotic life, which is being covertly observed by local sheriff Casey. While *Backfire* gets off to an almost fatally slow, meandering start, viewers who hang in for the long haul should find this well-acted thriller's inventive twists increasingly compelling. No rela-

tion to the 1994 firefighting farce *Backfire!* (A-Pix), with Robert Mitchum.

THE BAD AND THE BEAUTIFUL (1952) B&W ***½

D: Vincente Minnelli. Kirk Douglas, Lana Turner, Dick Powell. 118 mins. (MGM)

The *Player* of its day, Minnelli's witty inside-Tinseltown drama casts Kirk as an amoral producer who systematically alienates a topflight supporting cast, including Powell, Gloria Grahame, Barry Sullivan, and Gilbert Roland. The "Doom of the Cat-Men" sequence was partly based an RKO frightmeister Val (*Cat People*) Lewton's Hollywood experiences.

BAD COMPANY (1995) ***½

D: Damian Harris. Laurence Fishburne, Ellen Barkin, Frank Langella, Michael Murphy, Spalding Gray, Michael Beach. 108 mins. (Warner)

From its packaging, *Bad Company* would appear to be just another standard-issue mainstream suspenser, but director Harris has a deeper agenda, and he executes it with admirable precision. While his basic plot may be fairly routine, Harris employs it to draw us into an ultracool, emotionally detached world populated by amoral characters who, while spanning a wide gender, age, and ethnic spectrum, are uniformly lacking a serious human dimension—the ability to experience the slightest flicker of empathy—that serves as both professional virtue and fatal flaw. Ex-CIA op Fishburne joins a team of smoothly ruthless corporate enforcers run by fellow former government op Langella, who's in turn assisted by an equally viperous Barkin. It's Fishburne's apparent mission to bribe a debt-riddled judge into voting in favor of plaintiff Gray (in a quirky, petulant perf), whose pollutants have killed or deformed dozens of innocent kids. As various plots and counterplots unfold, it

becomes clear that there's no one to root for here (not, at least, until very late in the game). The thesps' tightly controlled perfs—Fishburne and Barkin continue to breathlessly conspire even during sex (!)—make *Bad Company* a viewing experience as compelling as it is chilling. No relation to Robert Benton's agreeably offbeat 1972 western of the same name (Paramount).

BAD DAY AT BLACK ROCK (1955) ***½

D: John Sturges. Spencer Tracy, Robert Ryan, Ernest Borgnine. 81 mins. (MGM)

One-armed World War II vet Tracy investigates a mysterious death in a beat-out desert hamlet. Director Sturges needs only 81 minutes to limn this taut account of an ugly small-town conspiracy and its aftermath. Reissued in 1997 in a wide-screen edition that does justice to its brilliant use of Cinemascope.

BADLANDS (1973) ***½

D: Terrence Malick. Martin Sheen, Sissy Spacek, Warren Oates. 95 mins. (Warner) DVD

Malick's moody, disturbingly deadpan fictionalized account of Charles Starkweather's psycho rampage stars Sheen as an alienated serial killer and Spacek as his loyal teenage girlfriend. The result is a truly scary experience that ranks right up there with Arch Hall, Jr.'s, Starkweather variation, *The Sadist* (see index). *Badlands* was reissued in 1999 in a remastered "25th anniversary edition."

BAJA (1995) ***

D: Kurt Voss. Molly Ringwald, Lance Henriksen, Michael A. Nickles, Donal Logue, Corbin Bernsen. 92 mins. (Republic)

Quirkmeister Voss scores with this relatively understated desert-set noir. When self-loathing loser Logue kills a drug pusher in a deal gone south, he and passive squeeze Ringwald take off for the title destination. On their trail is her ex-hubby, Nickles, still seeking a reconciliation, and hit man Henriksen, both sent, separately, by Molly's despicable dad (an almost unrecognizable Bernsen in an effective character turn). Where Voss succeeds is in charting the banality of the four chief characters' daily routines as they kill time in a run-down Baja burg while awaiting the inexorable collision of their separate fates. Henriksen is especially enjoyable as the mean but flaky assassin who likes his work but *loves* tequila (we'll drink to that!) and spends much of his downtime alternately wooing and threatening his estranged wife's answering machine. Actor Nickles went on to write and direct the moody meditation *Desert Winds* (see index).

BAT*'S ENTERTAINMENT!:* Chester Morris displays menacing mien in a scene from Roland West's visually inventive "old dark house" thriller, *The Bat Whispers. Courtesy of Milestone Film and Video, NYC*

THE BANKER (1989) **½

D: William Webb. Robert Forster, Duncan Regehr, Shanna Reed, Jeff Conaway, Leif Garrett, Richard Roundtree. 95 mins. (MCEG/Virgin, n.i.d.)

Killing well is the best revenge for The Banker (Regehr), a brain-fried financial wiz who spends his leisure hours zapping hapless hookers with his laser-sighted designer crossbow (!) in emulation of an obscure South American god. Hot on the misogynistic murderer's twisted trail is L.A. cop Forster, whose TV newsperson ex, Reed, has earned a berth on our villain's hit list by baiting him on the air. Director Webb imbues his basically stupid story line (sort of a "Deathstyles of the Rich and Famous") with enough flair and suspense to lift it to the watchable level, while Forster again adds credibility and human dimension to what could have been a clichéd role. Ex-*Shaft* Roundtree contributes a capable bit as Bob's harried boss.

THE BAT WHISPERS (1930) B&W ***

D: Roland West. Chester Morris, Una Merkel, Richard Tucker. 82 mins. (Milestone) DVD

Based on a play by Mary Roberts Rinehart and Avery Hopwood, *The Bat Whispers* is a superior mystery chiller that's especially strong on atmosphere. The film features some impressively surreal camera work that's unusually fluid for the normally static early-talkie era.

THE BEDROOM WINDOW (1987) ***

D: Curtis Hanson. Steve Guttenberg, Elizabeth McGovern, Isabelle Huppert, Paul Shenar, Frederick Coffin, Carl Lumbly. 112 mins. (Anchor Bay) DVD

Guttenberg is in bed with the boss's wife (Huppert) when he witnesses, via the titular aperture, a woman being brutally attacked on the street below. The latter escapes unharmed, but other victims around the city (Washington, D.C.) do not fare as fortunately. Will Steve risk his career by going to the cops, or will he foolishly investigate on his own? We think you know the answer. *The Bedroom Window* makes tense use of its premise before increasingly implausible plot complications begin to strain credulity. Still worth a look for its better stretches.

BEST SELLER (1987) **½

D: John Flynn. James Woods, Brian Dennehy, Victoria Tennant, Paul Shenar. 110 mins. (Orion)

Woods is a hyperactive hit man who wants blocked Joseph Wambaugh–like writer/cop Dennehy to collaborate on his story in order to wreak revenge on his former corporate employers, led by *Scarface*'s Shenar. A hit-and-miss affair scripted by the prolific Larry Cohen, *Best Seller* wavers between the contrived and the inspired; a visit with Woods's utterly normal suburban parents stands out as a sharp example of the latter. Director Flynn also does an ace job in choreographing the pic's climactic showdown.

BEWARE, MY LOVELY (1952) B&W ***1/2

D: Harry Horner. Robert Ryan, Ida Lupino, Taylor Holmes. 77 mins. (Republic)

Rob portrays a psychotic handyman, suffering from a severe inferiority complex, who's hired by unsuspecting widow Ida in small-town Middle America, circa 1918. Some genuinely tense cat-and-mouse games ensue as Ryan edges ever closer to a total homicidal breakdown in this unsung gem.

BEYOND SUSPICION (1994) **1/2

D: Paul Ziller. Jack Scalia, Stepfanie Kramer, Howard G. H. Dell, Franceso Ferrucci, Roger R. Cross, Mark Acheson. 98 mins. (Libra)

Veteran TV hunk Scalia stars as a corrupt killer cop who tumbles for photojournalist Kramer, initially unaware she's in possession of incriminating evidence that could put him away. While *Beyond* breaks no new ground, it's an unsentimental, tautly assembled addition to the bad-cop genre, and Scalia's convincingly creepy as the cop-turned-drug-cartel hit man.

THE BIG COMBO (1955) B&W ***

D: Joseph H. Lewis. Cornel Wilde, Jean Wallace, Brian Donlevy, Richard Conte, Lee Van Cleef. 89 mins. (Prism, n.i.d.)

Hard-bitten violence abounds when stubborn cop Wilde, aided by betrayed moll Wallace (then Cornel's real-life wife), takes on vicious hood Conte and his menacing minions. Though associated with bigger A films (like *Teahouse of the August Moon*) by that time, ace noir cinematographer John Alton took time out to team with *Gun Crazy* auteur Lewis on this A-project, fashioning some of his most inventive visuals to date.

THE BIG HEAT (1953) B&W ***

D: Fritz Lang. Glenn Ford, Gloria Grahame, Lee Marvin. 90 mins. (Columbia/TriStar)

The Big Heat offers gritty, hardboiled action, the incomparable Fritz Lang way, wherein a superior cast, direction, pacing, and mood more than compensate for a basically familiar story line.

THE BIG SLEEP (1946) B&W ***1/2

D: Howard Hawks. Humphrey Bogart, Lauren Bacall, Martha Vickers. 114 mins. (MGM)

Bogie and Bacall rejoin forces in Hawks's compelling adaptation (coscripted by William Faulkner) of Raymond Chandler's hard-boiled classic. Former B-western star Bob Steele turns in top supporting work as a sadistic hit man. A newly discovered version, with additional, previously unseen footage, received a limited retro-house big-screen rerelease in 1997 and is also available on video (MGM). Beware the computer-colorized version. Robert Mitchum and Sarah Miles took the Bogie and Bacall roles in Michael Winner's 1978 remake (Columbia/TriStar).

BITTER MOON (1992) ***1/2

D: Roman Polanski. Peter Coyote, Emmanuelle Seigner, Hugh Grant, Kristin Scott Thomas, Victor Banerjee. 139 mins. (New Line)

Director/coscripter Polanski (assisted by longtime collaborator Gerard Brach and John Brownjohn) crafts a witty, perverse fable, a battle of the sexes waged with doomsday machines. Wheelchair-bound novelist manqué Coyote regales an initially reluctant fellow passenger on an India-bound ship—uptight Brit Grant—with the flashback-related saga of his roller-coaster relationship with sexy Seigner (Roman's real-life wife). The couple experience every possible extreme—from uncontrolled passion to sado-masochistic violence to boredom and contempt—leaving Coyote barely alive to tell the tale. Polanski, who cameos as one of Coyote's former drinking buddies, springs constant surprises as he cuts back and forth between the present cruise and Coyote/Seigner's recent Parisian past. Polanski's *Love Story* for the '90s received a limited theatrical release, as did his 1994 adaptation of Ariel Dorfman's play *Death and the Maiden* (New Line), with Sigourney Weaver as an embittered torture victim who turns the tables on former tormentor Ben Kingsley.

BLACK DAY BLUE NIGHT (1995) ***

D: J. S. Cardone. Gil Bellows, Mia Sara, Michelle Forbes, J. T. Walsh, Tim Guinee, John Beck. 99 minutes. (Republic)

With *Black Day Blue Night*, veteran B auteur Cardone gets the roadkill formula right. Despite the presence of the usual set of American Southwest mise-en-scène clichés, credible characters and a textured story save the day, and Cardone refreshingly refrains from resorting to frequent bursts of abrupt and senseless violence to propel his tale along. Cardone returns with 1999's sometimes bumpy but worthwhile road noir *Outside Ozona* (Columbia/TriStar), with Robert Forster, Penelope Ann Miller, and David Paymer.

BLACK WATER (1989) ***

D: Nicolas Gessner. Julian Sands, Stacey Dash, Ned Beatty, Ed Lauter, Rod Steiger, Denise Crosby, Brian McNamara. 105 mins. (Academy, n.i.d.)

Often messy but rarely less than mesmerizing, vet helmer Gessner's (*Peking Blonde, The Little Girl Who Lives Down the Lane*) adaptation of the Hans Werner Kettenbach novel *Minnie* stars the ever capable Sands as a Brit tax attorney who witnesses a murder while on a solo fishing trip in rural Tennessee. The pic's frequently illogical thriller elements take a backseat to the prissy, initially resistant Sands's relationship with black teen hitcher Dash. *Black Water* (a.k.a. *Tennessee Nights*) gains further momentum after the innocent Sands (who's not at all your standard potboiler hero) winds up in the hands of the local law; here Gessner and crew capture the random Kafka-esque insanity of the System in an almost verité (and truly nightmarish) way as Sands finds himself buffeted by good cops, bad cops, hostile inmates, lawyers, and a screw-loose judge interpreted, with inspired flair, by a typically unshy Steiger. Though flawed, *Black Water* floats high above your standard direct-to-home-vid thriller fare. Johnny Cash cameos as himself, but his character's billed in the closing credits as simply "Country Singer."

BLINK (1994) **½

D: Michael Apted. Madeleine Stowe, Aidan Quinn, James Remar, Peter Friedman, Bruce A. Young, Laurie Metcalf. 106 mins. (New Line)

Stowe lends too abrasive an edge to her role as a blind musician given gradual sight via smitten doc Friedman's corneal-transplant operation. It's not long before our heroine sees a serial-killer suspect, but her virginal eyes are too untried to be totally trusted. Quinn is the equally corrosive cop assigned to the case; predictable interpersonal entanglements ensue, while the body count mounts. The inventive optical FX provide the only true points of interest in this otherwise padded, rambling Windy City–set thriller.

BLOOD AND CONCRETE: A LOVE STORY (1991) **

D: Jeffrey Reiner. Billy Zane, Jennifer Beals, Darren McGavin, James LeGros, Nicholas Worth, Mark Pellegrino. 97 mins. (Columbia/TriStar)

Reiner's contempo B thriller/black comedy tips its heavy hand early when protagonists Zane and Beals "meet cute" in a cemetery: Zane, an amiable lowlife bleeding profusely from a stab wound, literally stumbles over Beals, a career neurotic intent on slashing her wrists with a razor. The duo undertake an on-again, off-again liaison that's increasingly buried in the background while director Reiner focuses on the movie's self-conscious noir machinations. He also lifts a riff, involving an overweight, chopsticks-wielding informer, from Sam Fuller's infinitely superior 1953 noir, *Pickup on South Street* (see index). Reiner's characters rarely seem more than pawns of his will, although Pellegrino invests his gay strong-arm role with much scene-stealing energy. Beals is especially unappealing as the would-be kooky neurotic, who says re former beau LeGros, "He made the Marquis de Sade look like Pat Boone" (a Hobson's choice if ever there was one).

BLOOD AND WINE (1997) ***

D: Bob Rafelson. Jack Nicholson, Michael Caine, Stephen Dorff, Jennifer Lopez, Judy Davis, Harold Perrineau, Jr., Mike Starr. 101 mins. (Fox)

Amid the contempo clutter of cassette crime capers, Rafelson's *Blood and Wine* stands out on the strength of its atmospheric South Florida locales, emotional texture, and, above all, quality thesping. Nicholson as a failing wine-merchant-turned-jewel thief, Davis as his embittered wife, Dorff as his hostile stepson, and Lopez as his Cubana mistress all turn in strong work. But the show ultimately belongs to Caine as Nicholson's dying but dangerous Brit criminal cohort. With his "spray-painted" black hair and chronic coughing fits, Caine could have easily slipped into caricature; instead, he lends both edge and credibility to a perf that helps hoist the film above some of its rougher plot stretches. Rafelson and Nicholson previously worked together on the Monkees romp *Head* (see index), which Jack scripted; *Five Easy Pieces, The King of Marvin Gardens* (both Columbia/TriStar); *The Postman Always Rings Twice;* and the misstep *Man Trouble* (both Fox).

BLOOD SIMPLE (1984) ***

D: Joel Coen. John Getz, M. Emmet Walsh, Frances McDormand, Dan Hedaya, Samm-Art Williams. 97 mins. (Universal)

The Coen brothers helped jump-start the indie industry with their clever, twisty, cutting-edge noir, set in contempo Texas, a film that packs more surprises per reel than most of its 1940s/'50s models. Walsh is especially effective as one of noirdom's sleaziest sleuths.

BLOW OUT (1981) ***

D: Brian De Palma. John Travolta, Nancy Allen, John Lithgow. 108 mins. (Warner)

De Palma's blatant audio-verité rip-off of Antonioni's *Blowup* (MGM) is a pretty fair thriller in its own right—sans Antonioni's pretentious touches—with soundman Travolta tracking the source of a mysterious gunshot that turns up on one of his tapes.

THE BLUE DAHLIA (1946)
B&W ***1/2

D: George Marshall. Alan Ladd, Veronica Lake, William Bendix, Howard Da Silva, Doris Dowling, Tom Powers, Hugh Beaumont, Will Wright. 99 mins. (Universal)

Scripting from his own story, Raymond Chandler limns a slick, tight, satisfying noir crackling with dark, witty dialogue and further enhanced by director Marshall's atmospheric Deco-and-shadows-driven mise en scène. When returning serviceman Ladd, in one of his toughest taciturn turns, seeks to reunite with his party-girl wife (Dowling), a fight ensues, prompting Ladd to leave her to her current beau, gentleman gangster Da Silva (in a smooth, charismatic perf). Dowling soon turns up murdered; number-one suspect, Ladd, takes it on the lam in a quest to discover the real culprit, eventually linking up with a fetching Lake. Chandler keeps the guessing games going as several suspects emerge, including Ladd's erratic and volatile ex-service buddy Bendix, who's clearly operating sans a full deck but with a steel plate in his head. (Bendix, later of *The Life of Riley* fame, is one of three future big-time sitcom dads on view, along with serviceman Hugh [*Leave It to Beaver*] Beaumont and thug Frank [*Dobie Gillis*] Faylen.) Kino, meanwhile, has Fritz Lang's sound-alike 1953 mystery *The Blue Gardenia*, with Anne Bancroft imperiled by a slimy Raymond Burr. Ladd can also be seen at the top of his laconic form in *The Glass Key* and *This Gun for Hire* (both Universal).

BLUE STEEL (1990) ***

D: Kathryn Bigelow. Jamie Lee Curtis, Ron Silver, Clancy Brown, Elizabeth Pena, Louise Fletcher, Philip Bosco. 102 mins. (MGM)

Curtis, starring as one of your sexier NYPD rookies, blows away an armed robber her first night on the job. The thief's gun winds up in the hands of commodities trader Silver and soon triggers what we're forced to assume were his long-dormant psycho tendencies. The wacko Wall Streeter initiates a clandestine slaughter spree as the mysterious ".44 Magnum Killer." Former screen screamer Jamie Lee proves an able action thesp, Silver makes for an especially loathsome creep, and director Bigelow (with an assist from coscripter Eric Red) piles on the warped plot twists, including a scene wherein Jamie busts her own wife-beating dad (Bosco). If you can get past this kinetic gun-fetish flick's blatant disregard for even marginal credibility and accept wimpy Silver's transformation into a *Terminator*-type killing machine, you'll enjoy Bigelow's violent, stylish thriller.

BLUE VELVET (1986) ****

D: David Lynch. Kyle MacLachlan, Isabella Rossellini, Dennis Hopper, Laura Dern, Dean Stockwell, Hope Lange, Jack Nance, Brad Dourif. 120 mins. (Warner) DVD

From its brilliantly grotesque life-and-death-cycle opening, Lynch's *Blue Velvet* is an imaginatively bizarre, consistently unpredictable, blackly funny sleaze nightmare combining traces of his earlier cult fave *Eraserhead* with an offbeat thriller plot. With his nitrous-inhaling Frank Booth, Hopper creates one of the most indelible villains in screen history. And don't forget: "It's a sunny, woodsy day in Lumberton: Get those chainsaws out!"

BODY CHEMISTRY:
THE SERIES

BODY CHEMISTRY (1990) **

D: Kristine Peterson. Marc Singer, Mary Crosby, Lisa Pescia, David Kagen, Joseph Campanella. 84 mins. (MGM)

The mind of a scientist! The soul of a dominatrix! The body of a woman! That pretty much sums up Dr. Claire Archer, as impressively embodied by Pescia, cast in the Glenn Close role in exec-producer Roger Corman's nearly note-for-note *Fatal Attraction* clone. A scientist conducting sexual-aggression studies at the generically labeled "Neurological Institute," Claire soon sinks her kinky claws into coworker/Michael Douglas manqué Marc (*The Beastmaster*) Singer, who finds himself flagrantly cheating on his faithful house mouse of a spouse (Crosby in the Anne Archer part). While a tad more erotically explicit than its higher-priced model, *Body Chemistry* otherwise adds little in the way of variations. Followed nonetheless by three equally uninspired sequels: *Body Chemistry 2: Voice of a Stranger* (1992, Columbia/ TriStar), with a returning Pescia and Morton Downey, Jr. (!); *Body Chemistry 3: Point of Seduction*, with Morgan Fairchild; and *Body Chemistry 4: Full Exposure*, starring Shannon Tweed (both New Horizons).

BODY DOUBLE (1984) ***

D: Brian De Palma. Craig Wasson, Melanie Griffith, Gregg Henry. 109 mins. (Columbia/TriStar) DVD

De Palma's overtly voyeuristic version of Hitchcock's *Rear Window*, relocated to a contemporary porn-film milieu, stacks up as an entertainingly sleazy, satiric, and suspenseful exercise that transcends its imitative instincts. *Body Double* almost scales the heights of the same auteur's Hitch-inspired *Dressed to Kill* (Warner), with Michael Caine and Angie Dickinson.

BODY HEAT (1981) ***

D: Lawrence Kasdan. William Hurt, Kathleen Turner, Richard Crenna. 113 mins. (Warner) DVD

Femme fatale Turner recruits dim lawyer/lover Hurt to aid in her scheme to bump off sleazy hubby Crenna in Kasdan's modernized noir, executed with style and flair. Mickey Rourke stands out in an attention-getting supporting role as an ex-con mechanic.

BODY OF INFLUENCE:
THE SERIES

BODY OF INFLUENCE   (1993)*

D: Gregory Hippolyte. Nick Cassavetes, Sharon Whirry, Richard Roundtree, Sandahl Bergman, Don Swayze. 98 mins. In R and unrated editions. (Academy, n.i.d.)

The selfsame Gregory Hippolyte who gave us *Animal Instincts I* and *II* (Academy, n.i.d.) when the B.O. big-gie *Basic Instinct* (itself available, via Artisan, in an uncut "director's edition") came out on cassette links his fate here with a far less hotsy title: Madonna's risible literal killer-bod "thriller," *Body of Evidence* (MGM/UA). Pouty blonde Whirry, who'd so unimpressed in *Animal Instincts,* unwisely stretches here as a lust-driven femme fatale who lures hitherto virtuous shrink Cassavetes into her silky web of sex, death, and bad acting. As in *Animal Instincts,* soft-core kink alternates with dull stabs at suspense in a dud that lacks the earlier vid's marginal camp value. The rated version runs four minutes longer than the unrated. Go figure. Followed by *Body of Influence 2* (1996, A-Pix).

BOOGIE BOY   (1998) **½

D: Craig Hamann. Mark Dacascos, Jaimz Woolvett, Emily Lloyd, Frederic Forrest, Traci Lords, Joan Jett. 93 mins. (Sterling) DVD

Sterling's screener box copy for *Boogie Boy*—"From the Academy Award–winning writer of *Pulp Fiction*"— is a bit misleading, since the writer in question, Roger Avary, served solely in a producing capacity here. Still, *Boogie Boy* is not without its positive points.

The pic follows ex-con Dacascos (the B-video action star displays some legit acting chops here) and his relationship with former cell mate and current junkie Woolvett, who embroils our hero in a misguided drug deal that leaves several corpses in its wake. Earlier the same night, Dacascos lands a drumming gig with the band of femme singer Jerk (rocker Jett in an admirably low-glam role) but must first extricate himself from his criminal jam. *Boogie Boy* works best as a character study but probably wouldn't have scored even low-budget financing without the violent noir overlay, ultimately its weakest element. Although Avary didn't have a credited hand in the script, *Boogie Boy* features a smack sequence that mirrors a similar, more elaborate scene in the superior *Killing Zoe* (see index), which he wrote and directed. Underutilized erstwhile scream queen Linnea Quigley cameos in a fictional direct-to-video-within-the-direct-to-video segment.

BOXING HELENA   (1993) **½

D: Jennifer Lynch. Julian Sands, Sherilyn Fenn, Kurtwood Smith, Art Garfunkel, Bill Paxton. 107 mins. (Orion)

Despite its title, Jennifer (Daughter of David) Lynch's *Boxing Helena* is *not* a femme-slanted martial arts pic but something of a fuller-bodied update of 1963's *The Brain That Wouldn't Die* (see index). Repressed surgeon Sands can't turn haughty bimbo Fenn's head in his direction until a convenient car accident enables him to tend to his suddenly legless love object without fear of her walking out. To be on the safe side, he later removes her upper limbs to boot. Part instructional sex video, part extended sick joke, *Boxing Helena* is undone by an underdeveloped script full of muddled messages, an overly static visual approach, and the biggest cheat ending this side of *Sliver* (see index). Still, even half-baked ideas are better than none, and *Boxing Helena* is as thought-provoking as it is inarticu-

ACTOR JULIAN SANDS ON *BOXING HELENA*
As Told to The Phantom

When I was first given the script, I thought it was a very original and funny metaphor for all relationships. I didn't find anything gory, offensive, exploitive, or sadistic about it. I suppose just the idea of a woman in a box became interpreted as the theme and gave the impression of it being a pretty gory psycho film. At least it went for something, is how I feel about it. And for a first-time director who's written and directed something independently financed, I think that's something that deserves encouragement rather than derision, whether it's flawed or not.

My concept of the film is that it *wasn't* a dream, even though everybody tells me to the contrary. I think Jennifer Lynch would argue that it was immaterial whether it was reality or a dream; if it is immaterial, I would rather believe it was a true love story, not a dream love story.

[Later] I was in Cambodia doing a little drama/documentary about Cambodia's new democracy and the return of refugees....Today the most common sight and ailment in Cambodia is artificial limbs. Among the adult population there are so many amputees—arms, legs. Nobody was getting paid for the film, and any money it makes will go toward an artificial-limbs hospital in Cambodia. So there's some poetic justice for *Boxing Helena.*

late. Sands gives a great seriocomic perf as our confused antihero; the incredible shrinking Fenn is fine as Helena. Other cast members seem to flounder under Lynch's inexperienced direction—Paxton resorts to a Jim Morrison impersonation, while Smith relies on facial tics to add character to his thinly written role as Sands's fellow surgeon and a distracted Garfunkel looks like he's searching the set for Simon. Despite its advance notoriety, *Boxing Helena* lacked legs at the old B.O.; Orion pumped *mucho* bucks into flogging the "misunderstood" movie's video release.

THE BOYS CLUB   (1997) **½

D: John Fawcett. Chris Penn, Dominic Zamprogna, Stuart Stone, Devon Sawa, Nicholas Campbell. 92 mins. (A-Pix) DVD

Three 14-year-old Canadian kids find their lives seriously disrupted when wounded "cop" Penn takes refuge in their secret shack in this earnest, well-acted, but only semi-successful thriller. Penn proves sufficiently chilling as the fugitive who at first befriends but ultimately terrorizes the youths (of the three, only Zamprogna's character is adequately fleshed out). Sort of a teen-Tarantino take on a *Stand by Me* tale of adolescent friction and camaraderie, *The Boys Club* supplies enough suspense to make it watchable but lacks the necessary juice to boost it to the next rank.

BRAINWASH   (1983) ***

D: Bobby Roth. Yvette Mimieux, Christopher Allport, John Considine, Scott Marlowe, Danny Dayton, Denny Miller. 98 mins. (Media, n.i.d.)

Alternately monikered *Circle of Power* (its theatrical title), *Mystique*, and *Naked Weekend*, *Brainwash* is a simultaneously thought-provoking and thoroughly sadistic exposé of corporate Big Brotherhood, 1980s-style. Allegedly based on a real case, our story involves a sort of yuppie boot camp operated by the powers-that-be at the Mystique Corp., where company climbers are put through torturous paces—deprivation, physical abuse, sexual humiliation, and other bracing rites of passage—designed to sharpen their corporate killer instincts. Former screen sex kitten Mimieux—a long way from her *Time Machine* "shape of things to come" days—shines in an Ilsa-like turn as our corporate masochists' superbitch instructor. Among Yvette's victims are a balding Marlowe (an even longer way from his *Cool and the Crazy* '50s juvenile-delinquent days), former Steve Allen regular Dayton, and Allport as the group's token skeptic. Ex-*Tarzan* Miller lends additional muscle as Yvette's scary Schwarzenegger/Werner Erhard hybrid henchman, while male trainer Considine torments the ladies in attendance. *Brainwash* may be light on lethal violence, but it's high on anxiety; many of the on-screen "therapy" sessions are truly ugly to behold. While director Roth occasionally waxes pretentious here, for the most part his underseen sleeper works as a solid exploitation outing with a worthy message.

BREAKING POINT   (1994) **½

D: Paul Ziller. Gary Busey, Kim Cattrall, Darlanne Fluegel, Jeff Griggs, Blu Mankuma. 95 mins. (Republic)

A charismatic cast and taut pacing help put this cliché-strewn Seattle-set serial-killer thriller over the top. Busey's a frustrated cop temporarily disabled—by male stripper Jack the Ripper–type Griggs (dubbed "The Surgeon")—who enthusiastically trysts and more reluctantly partners with femme fuzz Fluegel while trying to regain the estranged affections of ex-wife Cattrall. Busey and Fluegel give strong perfs, while a copycat-killer subplot supplies a convenient excuse to pump up the body count.

A BRILLIANT DISGUISE   (1994) **

D: Nick Vallelonga. Lysette Anthony, Anthony John Denison, Corbin Bernsen, Gregory McKinney, Robert Shafer, Nick Vallelonga. 97 mins. (Prism)

Written and directed by actor Vallelonga, who also plays a supporting role, *A Brilliant Disguise* kicks off to a decent start as sportswriter Denison alienates his tight circle of jock-world friends when he takes up with Anthony, a painter afflicted with multiple personality disorder. The plot seems headed in a serial-killer *Sybil* direction before taking an even dumber twist that plunges the pic into pure camp, though Britcom vet Anthony impresses with her contortive, multi-voiced performance. *ABD* recycles several story elements earlier seen in *Save Me* (Columbia/TriStar), also starring Anthony.

BRILLIANT LIES   (1996) ***

D: Richard Franklin. Gia Carides, Anthony LaPaglia, Zoe Carides, Ray Barrett. 93 mins. (Peachtree)

A subject that might have received soap-opera or artificial-thriller treatment in an American movie enjoys more complex handling in this Aussie import. When foxy office worker Susy (Gia Carides) accuses coarse ex-employer Gary (LaPaglia, getting a chance to use his native Australian accent here) of sexual harassment, the charges bring out the worst in all involved. Based on David Williamson's play, *Brilliant Lies* spends considerable time exploring Susy's dysfunctional family members—her womanizing dad, passive lesbian sister (played by real-life sibling Zoe Carides), and Christian-oid brother—without reducing them to stereotypes. Flawlessly acted and continually surprising, the film's emphasis on human—rather than purely gender—power games represents a refreshing approach to a tricky topic.

BULLET TO BEIJING   (1995) **½

D: George Mihalka. Michael Caine, Jason Connery, Mia Sara, Michael Gambon, Michael Sarrazin, Len Prygunov, Burt Kwouk. 105 mins. (Paramount)

Consummate thesp Caine's cheerfully weary delivery carries the day in this otherwise routine post-Soviet breakup espionage caper originally aired on Showtime cable. After a three-decade absence, Caine reprises his role as Len Deighton's stoic Cold Warrior Harry Palmer, forced into early retirement by a Brit government that no longer requires his services. Harry receives a summons from Russki power broker Gambon, ostensibly to prevent North Korean interests from getting their hands on a killer virus called "Red Death." The mostly Siberia-set story sleds downhill once the increasingly convoluted plot machinations overcome Caine's charismatic presence. Of Caine's three big-screen Palmer capers, 1966's *Funeral in Berlin* (Paramount) and 1965's *The Ipcress File* (Universal) are available, while 1967's *Billion Dollar Brain* has yet to join the home-vid ranks.

BUTTERFLY KISS   (1995) *½

D: Michael Winterbottom. Amanda Plummer, Saskia Reeves. 90 mins. (First Run Features)

Unless you're aching to see a Brit-accented Amanda Plummer naked, save for tattoos, bruises, and chains (hey, dude, whatever curls your toes!), you may want to pass on this derivative serial-killer romp. An undeniably intense Amanda portrays a plainly daft overaged punk lesbian highway psycho who proves mysteriously irresistible to emotionally regressive petrol-station nonentity Reeves, who, though she disapproves of random violence, joins Amanda on her slay spree. The pair emerge as older, less credible variations on the antisocial distaff tandems on view in Rafael Zelinsky's *Fun* and Peter Jackson's infinitely superior *Heavenly Creatures* (see index). The Cranberries-flavored soundtrack supplies an auditory plus.

CAFE SOCIETY   (1995) **½

D: Raymond De Felitta. Frank Whaley, Peter Gallagher, Lara Flynn Boyle, Anna Thomson, David Patrick Kelly. 104 mins. (Columbia/TriStar)

Filmmaker De Felitta's feature debut is a deliberately stylized descent into Manhattan's high-glam nightclub demimonde of the early '50s. Whaley portrays Mickey Jelke, a real-life playboy set up to take the fall for an intricate call-girl-ring bust, a case that registered mega-headlines in its day, while frequent David Lynch regular Boyle plays the ambitious aspiring model who becomes Mickey's main squeeze and Gallagher is the ultimately reluctant undercover cop who helps engineer his demise. The film seems more concerned with period detail and atmosphere than drama and unfolds at a leisurely, at-times repetitive pace. Still, viewers interested in its exotic milieu will deem *Cafe Society* worth a look.

CALL NORTHSIDE 777   (1948) B&W ***½

D: Henry Hathaway. James Stewart, Richard Conte, Lee J. Cobb. 111 mins. (Fox)

Chicago reporter Stewart builds a case pointing to convicted killer Conte's innocence in Hathaway's excellent, fact-based suspenser. Authentic location lensing, steady pacing, and uniformly fine performances put *Northside* near the top of the celluloid crime-drama list.

CANVAS: THE FINE ART OF CRIME (1992) ***

D: Alain Zaloum. Gary Busey, John Rhys-Davies, Vittorio Rossi, Nick Cavaiola, Cary Lawrence. 94 mins. (Artisan)

Promising painter Rossi reluctantly agrees to aid in several art heists to cover loan-shark debts incurred by his screwed-up younger bro' Cavaiola, in a thriller highlighted by Busey's confidently quirky perf as a killer art dealer and Rhys-Davies's textured work as his number-one thief.

CAPE FEAR   (1991) ***

D: Martin Scorsese. Nick Nolte, Robert De Niro, Jessica Lange, Juliette Lewis, Joe Don Baker, Illeana Douglas. 128 mins. (Universal)

From the eerie title sequence fashioned by sometime director Saul (*Phase IV*) Bass and spouse, Elaine, to longtime Hammer horror helmer Freddie Francis's cinematography, Scorsese's remake of J. Lee Thompson's 1962 *Cape Fear* (Universal), drawn from the John D. MacDonald novel, sports a consistently dynamic look. The pic further benefits from a deeper script that puts a more perverse spin on the original's vengeance-driven story line (earlier aped by Joel Silver's inferior *Ricochet*, from HBO) and paints the victims of mad Max Cady (De Niro)—lawyer Nolte, illustrator wife (Lange), and alienated daughter (Lewis)—in a more neurotic light. While original Cady, Robert Mitchum (strong here in a supporting role as a local cop), ultimately made for a more credible crazy, De Niro's bulked-up, tattooed Travis Bickle variation also has his moments, especially in a bar scene with Nolte coworker Illeana (granddaughter of Melvyn) Douglas (who's excellent here) and a masterfully leering exchange with teenager Lewis. Baker likewise impresses as a dogged detective fond of quaffing Jim Beam and Pepto-Bismol cocktails (*feh*). On the downside, the film runs on too long, losing some of its tension shortly before its requisite watery windup. Scorsese also over-indulges his penchant for incorporating gratuitous religious imagery (e.g., Nolte's manual stigmata in the last reel). Still, while not as rich as a *Goodfellas* or *Raging Bull*, *Cape Fear* is a compelling Scorsese blend of senseless brutality and moral meditation.

CAPRICORN ONE   (1978) ***

D: Peter Hyams. Elliott Gould, James Brolin, Hal Holbrook, Sam Waterston. 123 mins. (Fox) DVD

Hyams applies rampaging '70s para-noia to the space program, with journalist Gould on the trail of a bogus launch. Brolin and Waterston are among the astronauts seeking to elude govern-ment assassins in this sturdy thriller.

CASUALTIES   (1997) **1/2

D: Alex Graves. Caroline Goodall, Mark Harmon, Michael Beach, Jon Gries, John Diehl. 85 mins. (Trimark)

Former leading man Harmon goes the creepy-assassin route in a lean thriller with a domestic-violence hook. Tormented by her maniac cop hubby, Gries, Goodall (late of *Disclosure* and *Cliffhanger*) finds a potential way out when she meets Harmon at her cooking class, only to discover he's an even bigger psycho than her brutal mate. Director Graves keeps his thriller ingredients sim-mering at an even boil and serves up the expected literal battle of the sexes at film's end. *Casualties* makes an apt sec-ond feature for a home-vid double bill with *In the Company of Men* (see index).

CELIA: CHILD OF TERROR
(1988) ***1/2

D: Ann Turner. Rebecca Smart, Nicholas Eadie, Maryanne Fahey, Victoria Longley. 102 mins. (Trylon, n.i.d.)

Turner's excellent offbeat Aussie outing resists easy genre place-ment. Much of the movie is a realistic account of a slightly eccentric nine-year-old girl (Smart) growing up in a 1957 Australia overrun by rabbits (real) and Reds (imagined). Celia herself is more tormented by her own monster-ridden nightmares and the waking whims of an insensitive dad who doesn't want her consorting with the Commies (or "ratbags," as he refers to them) next door. Strange touches include Celia and friends' amateur voodoo rituals, learned at a showing of the 1941 Mantan More-land fright flick *King of the Zombies* (!), and our young heroine's ultimately lethal campaign to save her endangered pet rabbit from meddling authorities. While it echoes such diverse films as *The Bad Seed, Lord of the Flies, Stand by Me*, and even the 1972 bad-hare-day horror *Night of the Lepus* (n/a), *Celia* is ultimately a highly original effort.

THE CHAMBER   (1996) **1/2

D: James Foley. Chris O'Donnell, Gene Hackman, Faye Dunaway, Robert Prosky, Bo Jackson. 113 mins. (Universal) DVD

James (*After Dark, My Sweet*) Foley's John Grisham adaptation empha-sizes drama over thrills as young iden-tity-crisis-driven attorney O'Donnell

attempts to save his long-imprisoned racist/killer granddad (Hackman) from the death penalty in Mississippi. Hack-man steals the show as the sour, unre-pentant Klansman finally forced to reevaluate the course of his violent, pointless life. Ex-athlete Jackson plays against type as a quiet, unassuming death-row guard. Hackman (65) and screen daughter Dunaway (55), mean-while, boast an even smaller real-life age gap than son Albert Brooks (49) and mom Debbie Reynolds (64) in *Mother*, though son Michael J. Fox (24) and dad Crispin Glover (21!) in *Back to the Future* may still hold the celluloid record in that department.

THE CHASE   (1946) B&W ***1/2

D: Arthur Ripley. Robert Cummings, Steve Cochran, Peter Lorre, Michele Morgan. 86 mins. (Sinister Cinema)

Venerable offbeat scripter Philip (*Johnny Guitar, Death Wish Club*) Yordan adapted this terrific, bizarre noir from a Cornel Woolrich tale. Drifter Cummings hires on as a chauf-feur for Florida gangsters Cochran and Lorre (who make a great upscale lowlife team), then runs off to Cuba with Cochran's squeeze (Morgan). Or does he? You'll want to hang on to find out. No relation to Arthur Penn's wonder-

---

10 COURTROOM CLASSICS ON CASSETTE
. . . .

Anatomy of a Murder (1959, Columbia/TriStar)
...And Justice for All (1979, Columbia/TriStar)
A Civil Action (1998, Touchstone)
Defenseless (1991, Artisan)
The Firm (1993, Paramount)
Music Box (1989, Artisan)
Reversal of Fortune (1990, Warner)
True Believer (1989, Columbia/TriStar)
The Verdict (1982, Fox)
Witness for the Prosecution (1957, Fox)

fully lurid 1966 Texas-set thriller, *The Chase* (Columbia/TriStar), with Jane Fonda, Robert Redford, and a mumbling Marlon Brando as a harried sheriff.

THE CHINA SYNDROME (1979) ***

D: James Bridges. Jane Fonda, Jack Lemmon, Michael Douglas. 123 mins. (Columbia/TriStar) DVD

It's Mondo Meltdown time as a nuclear reactor threatens to self-destruct in Bridges's urgent, suspenseful thriller, which benefitted from uncanny timing with Pennsylvania's Three Mile Island incident. Power-plant official Lemmon wrests top acting honors from younger thesps Fonda and Douglas (the latter also produced).

CHINATOWN (1974) ***

D: Roman Polanski. Jack Nicholson, Faye Dunaway, John Huston. 131 mins. (Paramount) DVD

Scripter Robert Towne and director Polanski's original, moody noir finds Jack and Faye in top form, while Polanski himself portrays moviedom's most memorable pint-sized hood since Elisha Cook, Jr.'s, "Wilmer" in *The Maltese Falcon* (MGM). Nicholson and Towne reteamed for the less inspired, belated sequel, *The Two Jakes* (see index).

CITY THAT NEVER SLEEPS (1953) B&W ***

D: John B. Auer. Gig Young, Mala Powers, Chill Wills, William Talman, Edward Arnold, Marie Windsor, Wally Cassel. 90 mins. (Republic)

An odd blend of the cornball and the honestly bizarre, *City* casts Young as a latently crooked cop whose biggest beef is that his designer wife (Windsor) makes too much money (!), so he takes up with poorer club entertainer Powers.

Chill Wills is the "Voice of Chicago" (the pic was lensed on location) on the soundtrack and mystically materializes in the flesh as Gig's mysterious new partner and surrogate conscience. Cassel adds another offbeat note as a professional "mechanical man" who performs robotic proto-break-dance routines in a nightclub window and who has trouble being human until he witnesses a murder committed by psycho Talman, who thinks Cassel's a literal dummy. (The premise was recycled in a *Twilight Zone* episode starring Harpo Marx and in the 1994 direct-to-video thriller *Flinch*, on Paramount.) Fans of surreal noir will want to tune in.

CLEAN, SHAVEN (1993) ****

D: Lodge Kerrigan. Peter Greene, Robert Albert, Megan Owen, Jennifer MacDonald, Molly Castelloe. 80 mins. (Fox Lorber)

In Kerrigan's brilliant *Clean, Shaven,* Greene turns in restrained but arduous work as Peter Winter—a rapidly deteriorating schizophrenic prone to outburts of sudden violence—on a desperate, inarticulate quest to connect with the young daughter (MacDonald) he hasn't seen since infancy. Greene conveys Winter's tormented state less through words or extravagant actions than through obsessive behavior—taping up mirrors and windows, curling into fetal positions, and ritualistically mutilating himself. (Warning: Watching Winter cut his hair, shave, and remove a secret "transmitter" from his fingernail requires *mucho* intestinal fortitude on the viewer's part.) Kerrigan painstakingly employs a fractured narrative and multilayered sound design to put us squarely inside his subject's disoriented senses with nearly virtual-reality immediacy and intensity, and he likewise locates wonderfully bleak New Brunswick landscapes to match Winter's hellish interior state. *Clean, Shaven* is extremely strong stuff, a grim

but unforgettable look at the world through believably tortured eyes. Fox Lorber thoughtfully issued the film in letter-box format.

COLD COMFORT (1989) ***

D: Vic Sarin. Maury Chaykin, Margaret Langrick, Paul Gross. 92 mins. (Republic)

Ubiquitous Canadian character thesp Chaykin, best remembered for blowing his brains out as the deranged army officer in Kevin Costner's *Dances with Wolves*, has an emotive field day as the sociopathic centerpiece of a three-character psychodrama that began life as a stage play. Chaykin "rescues" accident victim Gross (later of the TV sitcom *Due South*) and takes him home as a birthday present for his teenage daughter. This consistently sicko mini-suspenser rates as a worthy addition to the ranks of sleazy hostage thrillers.

THE COLD LIGHT OF DAY (1995) **½

D: Rudolf Van Den Berg. Richard E. Grant, Lynsey Baxter, Perdita Weeks, Simon Cadell, Thom Hoffman, James Laurenson. 101 mins. (PolyGram)

Grant stars as an ex-cop obsessed with trapping a child-slayer in a classier-than-usual, Eastern Europe–set serial-killer thriller adapted by director Van Den Berg and scripter Doug Magee from Friedrich Dürrenmatt's original source material. The title refers both to the time of day the crimes take place and the illumination Grant feels will reveal itself at the end of his investigative tunnel. Despite its post-Commie political subtext, crisp cinematography, and capable cast, *The Cold Light of Day* is basically your standard suspense fare and, while watchable, offers little in the way of truly fresh ideas.

THE COLLECTOR   (1965) ***

D: William Wyler. Terence Stamp, Samantha Eggar, Mona Washburne. 119 mins. (Columbia/TriStar)

Wyler crafts a suspenseful if overwhelmingly downbeat thriller, with Stamp strong in a role tailor-made for the late Rondo Hatton as the repressed wimp who imprisons hapless Eggar. The theme enjoyed a late-'90s resurgence in low-budget indie films like *Starved* (Spectrum) and *The Vicious Sweet* (Salt City).

THE COLONY   (1995) ***

D: Rob Hedden. John Ritter, Hal Linden, Mary Page Keller. 93 mins. (Universal) DVD

In scripter/director Hedden's Hell's Gated Community thriller, security-systems designer Ritter wins not only a contract from self-styled social engineer Linden but a lavish home in the latter's titular planned community. No sooner do Ritter, spouse Keller, and their two kids move in than they discover something seriously amiss—the Colony is a lot closer in spirit to Village of the Damned than to Our Town. The Colony's book of rules and regs is dictionary-thick with strictly enforced sicko ordinances, ranging from proper jogging attire to acceptable decibel levels for dogs. While Hedden's premise may have deserved edgier treatment, the pic's bland made-for-TV look, complete with commercial-friendly dissolves, and tube-bred cast actually help convey *The Colony's* numbing sterility and happy-face menace. No relation to the so-so 1997 sci-fier of the same name (Trimark), since retitled *The Advanced Guard.*

CONSPIRACY THEORY   (1997) **

D: Richard Donner. Mel Gibson, Julia Roberts, Patrick Stewart, Cylk Cozart. 135 mins. (Warner) DVD

Conspiracy Theory kicks off to a bright, precise start in a montage that sees crazed, conspiracy-obsessed cabbie Jerry Fletcher (Gibson) spin his wild, paranoid yarns to a succession of speechless passengers. Indeed, the flick exhibits considerable early promise as a dark comedy. But it doesn't take long for the initially tasty ingredients to dilute into a typically inorganic "event-movie" stew. Brian Helgeland's script plays like it was spit out of a state-of-the-art screenplay software program rich in thematic reverberance but poor in focus, credibility, and, most fatally, soul. Mel easily steals the show in a strenuously masochistic role, while Julia, as his reluctant Justice Department recruit, underplays it most of the way, and Stewart makes for an assembly-line agency-creep villain. A late-arriving on-screen *Manchurian Candidate* reference invites an unwise comparison that makes *Conspiracy Theory's* accomplishments seem all the paltrier.

THE CONVERSATION   (1974) ***½

D: Francis Ford Coppola. Gene Hackman, John Cazale, Frederic Forrest, Teri Garr. 114 mins. (Paramount) DVD

Hackman is perfect as an emotionally disconnected wiretapper drawn into an escalating mystery in Coppola's post-Watergate meditation on the professional creep mentality. The late Cazale turns in equally ace work as his loyal assistant.

COP   (1987) **½

D: James B. Harris. James Woods, Lesley Ann Warren, Charles Durning, Charles Haid, Randi Brooks. 110 mins. (Paramount)

Hyper hero Woods adds another intensely twitchy role to his résumé as a maniac cop obsessed with tracking down yet another of moviedom's misogynistic serial killers. *Cop* wavers between the genuinely riveting and the gratuitously contrived, but Woods and Durning (as his more level-headed partner) carry the day with their strong thespic teamwork. Warren has a tougher time trying to convince in the weakly written role of a "feminist" who's become the killer's target.

COPYCAT   (1995) **

D: Jon Amiel. Sigourney Weaver, Holly Hunter, Dermot Mulroney, William McNamara, Will Patton, Harry Connick, Jr., J. E. Freeman. 123 mins. (Warner) "Special Edition" DVD

This aptly titled terror tale finds up-and-coming serial-killer celeb McNamara seamlessly re-creating infamous atrocities committed by such Psycho Hall of Famers as the Boston Strangler, Ted Bundy, and Son of Sam. Serial-killer specialist and author Weaver—a helpless agoraphobe since nearly meeting her end at the hands and rope of currently incarcerated killer Connick, Jr. (legitimately repulsive in his limited screen time)—volunteers her housebound services to investigating Frisco cops Hunter and Mulroney. Even as McNamara apes his homicidal heroes to the letter, director Amiel and crew echo many a psycho thriller past, from giants like *The Silence of the Lambs* to obscurities like Wings Hauser's *The Art of Dying* (see index). Predictable, contrived, and lacking in basic genre logic, *Copycat* does offer a few new wrinkles in computer gore. While Weaver may be past her panty-flashing *Alien* prime, *Copycat* honors celluloid tradition by having death-row inmate Connick extend his long-distance assistance in exchange for an autographed pair of Sig's undies (!).

CORNERED   (1945) B&W ***

D: Edward Dmytryk. Dick Powell, Walter Slezak, Micheline Cheirel. 102 mins. (RKO)

Powell's at his hard-boiled best as a former air ace who takes off for

Buenos Aires in search of his wife's killers. Steve Martin borrowed bits from the flick for the climactic scenes in his clip-driven 1982 noir spoof, *Dead Men Don't Wear Plaid* (Universal).

CORRUPT (1983) ***

D: Roberto Faenza. Harvey Keitel, John Lydon, Nicole Garcia, Leonard Mann, Sylvia Sidney. 99 mins. (HBO)

Ex–Sex Pistol John (Johnny Rotten) Lydon is a masochistic nutcase who threatens to expose killer cop Keitel (doing a *Bad Lieutenant* warm-up) in an offbeat, suspenseful NYC-set thriller. The film has also surfaced on bargain labels as *Cop Killer* and *Order of Death*.

CRASH (1996) **½

D: David Cronenberg. Holly Hunter, James Spader, Rosanna Arquette, Elias Koteas, Deborah Kara Unger. In R and "controversial NC-17" editions. 100 mins. (New Line) DVD

Cars, of course, is an anagram for *scar*. And when visceral auteur Cronenberg hasn't been dealing cinematically with scars, he's been dealing with cars—in the one D.C. pic few clamor to see, the straight-ahead 1976 Canada-lensed racing drama *Fast Company* (Admit One), along with the announced Ferrari–focused *Red Cars*. *Crash*, then, with its blending of the twain, arrives as something of a natural. Drawn from J. G. Ballard's novel, *Crash* is a legitimately twisted study of a group of autoerotic crashaholics who need crushed chrome and burning leather in order to do the deed. Priapic TV softcore porn producer James (*A Fistful of Bimbos*) Ballard—an active Spader, making up for his impotent voyeur persona in *sex, lies & videotape*—is seduced into the scene after surviving an auto accident that claims the life of the other driver; squeeze Catherine

(Unger) gets turned on by Spader's new bruised condition. While recovering in hosp, our hero also encounters his victim's widow (Hunter), who's experiencing a similar sexual awakening and consummates same with Spader after the pair experience a near accident together. Spader, Hunter, and Unger soon convene with crash theoretician and prime practitioner Vaughn (Koteas)—who stages illicit reenactments of lethal celebrity crackups, with James Dean's blue-highway fatality his current attraction (he's got Jayne Mansfield's in the planning stages!)—and *his* car-maimed mate, Arquette. Much of the remaining screen time chronicles the characters' various carset couplings (and occasionally triplings) in erotic tableaux shocking not so much for their explicitness but for their fetishistic intimacy; these are folks whose most fervent collective libidinal wish is to be French-kissed by the jaws of death. As a cautionary fable, *Crash* would seem geared to a highly specialized (and, we hope, extremely limited) audience. Still, there's no denying that *Crash*—which copped a Cannes '96 Special Jury Prize for "originality, daring and audacity"—is nothing if not original, daring, and audacious, albeit in the same distanced way of Cronenberg's *Dead Ringers* and *Naked Lunch*. While *Crash* rates as essential viewing for D.C. devotees, the pic still made yours truly glad he goes Greyhound (a concept Cronenberg might well turn into a treatise on bestiality).

CRIMES OF PASSION (1984) ***

D: Ken Russell. Anthony Perkins, Kathleen Turner, John Laughlin. 101 mins. (Starmaker) DVD

Perkins plays a psycho street preacher and Turner is designer-by-day/hooker-by-night China ("B movies have always been my inspira-

tion") Blue in Russell's bright, headlong leap into Russ Meyer territory. This entertainingly absurdist psychosexual exploitation romp is available in two video versions, one restoring theatrically scissored sequences, including a scene wherein Turner helps cop Laughlin enjoy a more intimate relationship with his nightstick.

CRIMETIME (1996) **½

D: George Sluizer. Stephen Baldwin, Pete Postlethwaite, Sadie Frost, Geraldine Chaplin, Karen Black, James Faulkner, Phil Davis. 95 mins. (Trimark)

Dutch auteur Sluizer—late of brilliant *The Vanishing* (see index) and his own execrable American remake of same—returns to semi-form with this flawed but interesting Brit-set serial-killer/media-meditation combo. Postlethwaite portrays a TV repairman whose wife (an excellent Chaplin) is gradually going blind. In his spare time, Pete's also the notorious "Stocking Killer," a psycho who stabs his distaff victims, steals their stockings, *and* slices out their left eyes. He achieves a greater measure of vicarious notoriety when intense young American actor Baldwin is hired to reenact the heinous crimes on a popular tab-TV show, the eponymous *CrimeTime*. The killer, via phone, begins coaching the young thesp, who wants the slayings to continue so he can retain his high-profile role. Sort of a cross between *Natural Born Killers* and Bigas Luna's ocular fear fable *Anguish*, *Crimetime* definitely has its moments, as when Postlethwaite's glimpsed at home in front of his telly playing with his plate of excised eyeballs and ruefully repeating, "No one sees me." If *Crimetime* had arrived earlier in the game, it would have registered greater impact; by this time, we've been down this road too often (even the TV-show riff was used earlier in *Curdled* [Miramax] and the obscure indie *Naked Beneath the Water* [Lackadaisical Productions], among others, while Wes Craven employed a killer TV repairman [Mitch Pileggi] in *Shocker*). Karen Black, looking like she's been through a few laser lifts, is in fine form as *CrimeTime*'s programming head, while Sluizer cameos as a hack Hollywood director. Marianne Faithfull croons a pair of moody tunes of her own composition in a club-set, David Lynch–like opening sequence.

CRISS CROSS   (1949) B&W ***

D: Robert Siodmak. Burt Lancaster, Yvonne De Carlo, Dan Duryea. 98 mins. (Universal)

Good guy Burt and bad guy Dan play crooks in conflict while Yvonne's the willing dame caught in the middle in a flavorful caper flick brightened by an excellent cast that also includes a young Tony Curtis in his bigscreen debut. With exotic music supplied by Esy Morales and His Rumba Orchestra, and a rare meaty role for professional creep Percy Helton, cast here as Burt's sympathetic barkeep confidant. Remade in 1995 as *The Underneath* (see index).

CROSS COUNTRY   (1983) ***1/2

D: Paul Lynch. Richard Beymer, Nina Axelrod, Michael Ironside, Brent Carver. 95 mins. (Charter)

Twin Peaks freaks and David Lynch lovers should enjoy this kinky Canadian psychosexual thriller directed by Paul Lynch (no relation). Beymer (*Peaks*'s Benjamin Horne) stars as a high-strung ad exec suspected of slaying his sleazy mistress. He sets off on the title trip, accompanied by neurotic topless dancer Axelrod and her equally unstable musician friend (Carver), with crooked cop Ironside in hot pursuit. The characters are uniformly unsavory, with secret agendas and offbeat erotic predilections galore, in this taut, twisty, often vicious and intense odyssey. *Cross*

Country was originally intended as the first of a trilogy based on Herbert Kastle's crime novels, with Ironside's "Ed Roersch" as an ongoing linking character.

CROSSFIRE   (1947) B&W ***1/2

D: Edward Dmytryk. Robert Ryan, Robert Mitchum, Robert Young, Gloria Grahame. 86 mins. (Fox)

Two tough Bobs topline in a tense, terse noir about a manhunt for an anti-Semitic killer in one of the first Hollywood films to tackle a previously taboo theme. The Oscar-winning *Gentleman's Agreement* (Fox) explored the same topic in a less violent context.

THE CRUDE OASIS   (1995) **1/2

D: Alex Graves. Jennifer Taylor, Aaron Shields, Robert Peterson. 82 mins. (Paramount)

Containing echoes of *Carnival of Souls, Blue Velvet*, and *Safe*, producer, director, writer, and editor Graves's Kansas-set celluloid debut succeeds in creating a seductively dreamlike atmosphere but ultimately amounts to a filmlong tease. After a failed suicide attempt, depressed housewife Taylor—whose bland hubby (Peterson) is conducting a mysterious extramarital affair—literally finds the man of her melancholy dreams in laconic pump jockey Shields. Graves keeps us guessing in which direction he'll take his anxiety-fraught exercise in magical minimalism; running riffs include dangerous oil spills, radio reports of a missing woman who roughly fits our heroine's description, surreal landscapes, and visits to the titular roadside saloon the Crude Oasis, sort of a scaled-down version of *Blue Velvet*'s Slow Club. Ominous red herrings are ingeniously planted, but the pic's anti–punch line arrives as a disappointment.

THE CRUSH   (1993) ***

D: Alan Shapiro. Cary Elwes, Alicia Silverstone, Jennifer Rubin, Kurtwood Smith, Gwynyth Walsh, Matthew Walker. 89 mins. (Warner)

The Crush shapes up as both a fairly tense, relatively nonviolent suspenser and, in time-honored exploitation tradition, a legit *DOMD* (i.e., *Dirty Old Man's Delight*). Elwes stars as a not-so-dirty, not-too-old (28) journalist who rents a cottage in back of an opulent 'burb home, where he soon becomes the unwitting lust object of 14-year-old wacko Darien (Silverstone), a fetching blond nymphette in a Drew Barrymore mode. At first flattered by the bright, buxom teen's untoward attention, Nick offers only token resistance to what he views as a harmless flirtation at worst. Darien, in turn, demonstrates her affection by breaking into Nick's computer and polishing his copy. ("You have such a terrible time with the objective case," she seductively explains. "Your split infinitives put such a stress on your adverbs.") So adroit an editor is she that he's moved up the ladder at prestigious *People*-like *Peep* magazine (!). When Nick more emphatically rejects Darien's increasingly bold overtures, she resorts to more drastic reprisals, like siccing a nest of wasps on his new photographer squeeze (Rubin). Darien's affluent parents (Smith, Walsh), meanwhile, see no evil in their precocious offspring, even though an earlier "crush" ended up mysteriously deceased. Elwes is effective as the bemused writer forced to battle pressing deadlines and crazed Lolitas alike. Former *RoboCop* villain Smith adds a jovially sinister spin as Darien's dad, and Silverstone performs ably under the scrutiny of Shapiro's discreetly leering lens. As an entry in the Loony Lolita genre, one then-newly rejuvenated by Amy Fisher's real-life escapades, *The Crush* achieves its sleazy aims with deadpan wit and efficiency. For further research, scope out the three (!) available dramatizations of Amy Fisher's lowlife frolics: the Drew Barrymore–starred *Amy Fisher Story* (Anchor Bay), *Casualties of Love: The "Long Island Lolita" Story* (Columbia/TriStar), with Alyssa Milano, and *Lethal Lolita—Amy Fisher: My Story* (Turner), with Noelle Parker.

CRY DANGER   (1951) B&W ***1/2

D: Robert Parrish. Dick Powell, Rhonda Fleming, Richard Erdman, William Conrad, Regis Toomey. 79 mins. (Republic)

When con Powell is freed from stir, he doesn't have a nickel in his pocket; at film's finish, he walks away with 20 bucks. (So much for happy endings.) In between, Parrish's excellent noir takes us inside a California trailer park, Powell's base while he tries to nail villain Conrad for framing him, and follows our hero as he dodges dogged cop Toomey and romances sultry Fleming. At once trim, grim, wry, and realistic, *Cry Danger* represents one of the best of the noirs sprung from the Republic archives. Others of note include Joan Fontaine in *Born to Be Bad;* Olivia de Havilland as good/evil twins in Robert Siodmak's taut 1946 suspenser, *The Mirror;* the intermittently effective *Finger Man,* starring the ever sunny Frank Lovejoy; Joe Kane's entertaining *Hoodlum Empire,* with Brian Donlevy, Claire Trevor, and John Russell; *Make Haste to Live,* with Dorothy McGuire and Stephen McNally; Ida Lupino's corrupt-cops caper *Private Hell 36; The Scar* (a.k.a. *Hollow Triumph*), with Paul Henreid; Fritz Lang's ultimately disappointing *Secret Beyond the Door,* with Joan Bennett and Michael Redgrave; the overwrought Ben Hecht–scripted psycho ballet (!) thriller, *Spectre of the Rose;* and the hokey but watchable *When Gangland Strikes* (where, as The Phantomess points out, actor William Hudson addresses heroine Marjie Miller as "Joan" and "June" within the same scene!).

DADDY'S GIRL   (1996) **

D: Martin Kitrosser. William Katt, Michele Greene, Roxana Zal, Gabrielle Boni, Mimi Craven, Whip Hubley. 95 mins. (Artisan)

Young Boni plays red-haired Bad Seed Jody ("Sure are a lot of bad people in this neighborhood!") Mitchell in this item from Canadian producer Pierre David's (Fill in the Blanks) from Hell thriller factory. When the 11-year-old 'burb hellion perceives threats to her relationship with toy designer/adoptive dad Katt, she overturns tables, destroys flower gardens, poisons Grandma's prune juice (!), and eventually treats interlopers to a variety of violent demises. David and director Kitrosser employ nightmare fake-outs and cheap setups galore, separated by commercial-friendly dissolves.

DANGEROUS GAME   (1993) ***

D: Abel Ferrara. Harvey Keitel, Madonna, James Russo, Nancy Ferrara, Reilly Murphy. In R and unrated Original Director's Cut editions. 107 mins. (MGM)

Ferrara's showbiz psychodrama stars Keitel as a filmmaker directing Madonna and Russo in a fictional movie called *Mother of Mirrors.* In the film-within-a-film segments, an abusive Russo torments battered half Madonna for abandoning their heretofore open sex-and-drugs-drenched lifestyle in favor of a sudden religious fervor. Off-camera, the duo develop a similarly contentious relationship, one encouraged by ambitious director Keitel. Ferrara also focuses on the bicoastal Keitel's domestic life with wife (Nancy Ferrara, Abel's then-real-life spouse) and young son (Murphy). *Dangerous Game,* originally titled *Snake Eyes,* received a mostly negative critical response during its sparse theatrical run, but Ferrara's flick is nothing if not a daring one.

DARK OBSESSION   (1991) **1/2

D: Nick Broomfield. Gabriel Byrne, Amanda Donohue, Douglas Hodge, Sadie Frost, Michael Hordern, Ian Carmichael. 97 mins. (Kino)

Documentarian Nick (*Kurt and Courtney*) Broomfield's fiction-film debut is a well-crafted but mostly unexciting Brit thriller about vehicular homicide, upper-crust lust, and paranoia among the privileged set. Supplying the pic with its chief allure is Donohoe as Byrne's foxy fashion-designer wife. Amanda, who'd earlier impressed as the serpentine Lady Sylvia in Ken Russell's *Lair of the White Worm,* not only acts up a storm but exhibits her shapely form in several gratuitous sex scenes that burdened *Dark Obsession* with an undeserved NC-17 rating.

DARK ODYSSEY   (1957) B&W ***

D: Radley Metzger, William Kyriakis. Jeanne Jerrems, Athan Karras, David Hooks, Rosemary Torri, Edward Brazier. 85 mins. (First Run Features) DVD

Filmmaker Metzger is best known for his stylish forays into exotic erotica, but *Dark Odyssey* shows a different side of the soft-core auteur. Cowritten as well as codirected by Kyriakis, *Dark Odyssey* is closer in style and spirit to vintage John Cassavetes than it is to Metzger's own later work. Karras stars as a solemn young Greek sailor who jumps ship in NYC, with plans to slay the bounder who caused the death of his sister in their village back home. His slated vendetta is at least temporarily delayed when he meets friendly Greco-American gal Jerrems, who invites him to her family's Washington Heights home. What follows is a thoroughly engaging, alternately warm and edgy naturalistic drama that doubles as an evocative time-capsule portrait of 1950s NYC. *Dark Odyssey* virtually vanished after its brief initial bijou release, but First

Run salvages the pic from celluloid oblivion in this remastered director's cut that comes complete with the original theatrical trailer. Metzger's softcore erotic efforts include *The Alley Cats, Camille 2000, Carmen, Baby, The Lickerish Quartet, Little Mother, Score,* and *Therese & Isabelle* (all First Run).

THE DAY THE SUN TURNED COLD (1994) ***½

D: Yim Ho. Sigin Gowa, Tuo Zhong Hua, Ma Jingwu, Wei Zhi, Li Hu. 99 mins. (Kino)

Touted as "the first true film noir from Mainland China," *Day,* save for the sheerest of modern overlays, could as easily have unfolded in the 12th century. That's not to take anything away from Yim Ho's excellent familial mystery, which grips from the opening shot and doesn't let up until its ironically idyllic fade-out. Reportedly based on an actual case, *The Day the Sun Turned Cold* opens with young factory welder Hua approaching police captain Hu with an unusual accusation—that his mother (Gowa) poisoned his father (Jingwu) a decade earlier. Hua musters enough circumstantial evidence to persuade the world-weary, chain-smoking officer to accompany him to his mother's village to pursue a formal investigation. Ho pans effortlessly between the past and present in chronicling a case that points up housewife Gowa's paucity of options when she decides she prefers easygoing forest worker Zhi over her current spouse and father of her three kids. Complexities abound in a story that proceeds sans villains or heroes, with the nature of regret emerging as Ho's central theme.

DEAD CALM (1989) ***½

D: Phillip Noyce. Sam Neill, Nicole Kidman, Billy Zane. 97 mins. (Warner) DVD

Australian director Noyce—later of *Patriot Games* and *Clear and Pre-*

sent *Danger* fame—made his initial celluloid splash with a tense, expertly executed nautical nail-biter that sees Kidman menaced by psycho Zane in the temporary absence of mate Neill. DP Dean Semler's brilliant sea-tossed cinematography may have you reaching for the Dramamine.

DEAD HEART (1996) ***

D: Nick Parsons. Bryan Brown, Ernie Dingo, Angie Milliken, Gnarnayarrahe Waitaire, Aaron Pedersen. 103 mins. (Fox Lorber) DVD

In the tradition of Nicolas Roeg's *Walkabout* and Peter Weir's *The Last Wave* (see index), Parsons's *Dead Heart* powerfully dramatizes an ultimately tragic culture clash between encroaching Anglos and indigenous Aborigines. When a young mixed-breed impulsively chooses a sacred site as a trysting spot with a white schoolteacher's wife, a vengeful chain of events is set in motion, leading to the youth's murder and a double-bind situation for the local constable (Brown). Parsons's thoughtful script, like John Sayles's *Lone Star* (see index), employs a murder-mystery framework to explore touchy issues of ethnic and individual identity, with characters on both sides of the racial divide exploiting the incident to further their own individual agendas. James Bartle's cinematography vividly captures the exotic outback landscape, adding an eloquent visual dimension to Parsons's complex tale.

DEAD OF WINTER (1987) ***

D: Arthur Penn. Mary Steenburgen, Roddy McDowall, Jan Rubes, William Russ, Ken Pogue, Wayne Robson. 100 mins. (Fox)

Steenburgen stars in this nearly seamless, literal "chiller" (a loose reworking of the '40s B flick *My Name Is Julia Ross* [n/a]) as an out-of-work actress whose successful audition lands

her in a bizarre role indeed. She's taken by the seemingly meek Mr. Murray (McDowall) to the frozen upstate New York estate of wheelchair-bound shrink Dr. Lewis (Rubes), who explains that she's to fill in for a look-alike actress whose nervous breakdown has forced her to leave an in-progress film. Nothing is what it seems, natch, and Mary soon finds herself a prisoner of the sinister pair and a doomed pawn in an elaborate blackmail game. Penn lends further flair via striking wintry visuals that contribute greatly to the flick's frigid ambience.

DEAD ON (1993) **½

D: Ralph Hemecker. Matt McCoy, Shari Shattuck, Tracy Scoggins, David Ackroyd, Thomas Wagner. In R and unrated editions. 92 mins. (Orion)

Dead On is about lust, deceit, murder, and betrayal, but mostly it's about bathrooms. *Dead On* has more johns than Heidi Fleiss's phone book. The pic opens with a doorman apologizing for momentarily leaving his post for a bathroom break. At least seven subsequent scenes unfold in almost as many different bathrooms, from fancy mansion numbers to cramped airplane WC's. Not that *Dead On* is at all scatological; it just seems that director Hemecker (of TV's *Silk Stalkings* fame) and scripter April Wayne apparently couldn't think of other settings in which to further their plot. The latter is an openly acknowledged *Strangers on a Train* lift. Blond painter Shattuck can't stand her private-plane-flying attorney hubby (Ackroyd); pilot McCoy hates his super-rich bitch of an airline-owning wife (Scoggins). Shari suggests that they off each other's spouses. After several reels padded with "erotic" scenes between our murder-minded principals (the unrated version offers five minutes of additional footage), their scheme is put into action. The whole affair kept your Phantom reasonably entranced for the duration. We'd say more, but the bathroom beckons.

DEAD RINGERS (1988) ***

D: David Cronenberg. Jeremy Irons, Jeremy Irons, Genevieve Bujold, Heidi Von Palleske. 117 mins. (Media) DVD

I rons amazes as a set of seriously disturbed twin gynecologists, one of whom eventually resorts to using what amounts to torture devices as medical instruments (!). Cronenberg's perverse handling of a fact-based case makes for twisted but compelling viewing.

DEADBOLT (1992) ***

D: Douglas Jackson. Justine Bateman, Adam Baldwin, Michelle Scarabelli, Chris Mulkey, Cyndi Pass. 95 mins. (Columbia/TriStar)

S ort of a "Single White Male" mixed with Misery and The Collector (see index), Deadbolt is an oft contrived, illogical, and lazily motivated thriller that nonetheless manages to be authentically sick and gripping. Bateman plays a med student who ignores prissy former spouse Mulkey's advice and accepts stranger Baldwin into her life and condo. Baldwin is fairly strong in a Wings Hauser–esque part (especially during a scene in which he tricks Justine's ex into blowing his own brains out), while Bateman is convincingly frazzled as his eventual captive.

DEADLY VOYAGE (1996) ***1/2

D: John Mackenzie. Omar Epps, Joss Ackland, David Suchet, Sean Pertwee, Andrew Divoff. 92 mins. (HBO)

A trite generic title hides a terrific, fact-based seagoing suspenser that originally aired on HBO cable. An excellent Epps stars as Kingsley, a young Ghanian newlywed and father-to-be who dreams of relocating to New York. With seven cronies (and a stranger from Cameroon) who harbor similar desires, he stows away on a Russian-crewed ship headed for France, then the States. Shipping-company insurance agent Suchet is also along for the journey, ready to dock captain Ackland $45,000 each for any stowaways who manage to sneak onboard. When the nine hidden passengers are discovered at sea, ruthless first mate (Pertwee) and four crewmembers decide to execute them and dispose of the evidence. Director Mackenzie and scripter Stuart Urban (drawing from Kingsley's own account and a newspaper article by Nick Davis) lend shading to all the participants, including the villainous Pertwee. As Kingsley, Epps turns in strenuous dramatic and athletic work as he seeks to escape the armed crewmen through the bowels of the ship. Exec-produced by actor Danny Glover, Deadly Voyage powerfully conveys the uncertainty of a situation that's inexorably escalating into an unspeakable (and nearly unspoken) atrocity.

DECEIVER (1997) **1/2

D: Jonas and Joshua Pate. Tim Roth, Chris Penn, Michael Rooker, Renee Zellweger, Ellen Burstyn, Rosanna Arquette, Mark Damon, Michael Parks. 102 mins. (MGM)

T win auteurs Jonas and Joshua Pate, late of The Grave (see index), construct a noir psychodrama/puzzle, sort of a closet The Usual Suspects. Set primarily in a police interrogation room (with some exterior flashbacks) during a series of polygraph tests, Deceiver stars a shifty Roth as a rich, epileptic, but mentally nimble suspect in hooker Zellweger's murder. Roth's superior intellect enables him to get the upper hand in his constant verbal sparring with his interrogators, guileless gambling addict Penn and his smarter, secretly volatile partner (Rooker). Thanks to the Pates' flair for clever dialogue, Deceiver is fun to watch until its (perhaps inevitably) disappointing denouement. No relation to the 1991 Goldie Hawn dud Deceived (Touchstone).

DECONSTRUCTING SARAH (1994) **1/2

D: Craig R. Baxley. Sheila Kelley, Rachel Ticotin, A Martinez, Peter Andrews, Jenifer Lewis, Dwier Brown, Caroline Williams, Clyde Kusatsu. 92 mins. (Universal)

C raig R. (Stone Cold) Baxley's Deconstructing Sarah offers a solid twist on a clichéd "erotic thriller" premise. Kelley's high-powered ad exec with a self-destructive Mr. Goodbar complex that sees her assume a covert nocturnal identity and hang with lowlifes at a seedy bar called the Hell Hole. She keeps her secret safe from her concerned (to the point of intrusive) best friend, the straitlaced Ticotin. Trouble brews when a particularly scuzzy Hell Hole regular (Martinez) begins stalking and harassing Kelley, who eventually turns up missing. Ticotin's subsequent investigation into the matter ultimately uncovers a separate scandal. While competent in the plot and perfs departments, Deconstructing Sarah lacks the edge needed to make it memorable rather than merely watchable. No relation to Woody Allen's Deconstructing Harry (Miramax), nor have any plans been announced for a "When Deconstructing Harry Met Deconstructing Sarah."

DEEP CRIMSON (PROFUNDO CARMESÍ) (1997) ***1/2

D: Arturo Ripstein. Daniel Gimenez, Regina Orozco, Marisa Paredes, Patricia Reyes Espindola, Veronica Merchant. Subtitled. 109 mins. (New Yorker)

D rawing from the same real-life case that begat Leonard Kastle's 1970 cult fave The Honeymoon Killers (Video Treasures), veteran Mexican auteur and former Luis Buñuel associate Ripstein's Deep Crimson takes an equally harsh, repulsively compelling look at the media-dubbed "Lonely Hearts Killers." Gimenez stars as Nicolas, a pathetic, small-time Lothario, with a zealously guarded wig and a fake Castilian accent, who ekes out a sleazy living seducing and robbing lonely widows. When Nicolas attempts to set up crazy, fat Coral (Orozco) as his next victim, he discovers instead a match made in hell. Coral (who's hopelessly enamored of French film star Charles Boyer) dumps her two kids at a nearby nunnery and orchestrates Nicolas's romantic campaigns. Trouble is, Coral can't control her jealousy and winds up killing her client/lover's prospective marks. As the pair motor through rural Mexico, circa 1949, Ripstein offers an unblinking visual journal of a self-rationalizing depravity that's at once difficult and fascinating to behold. The killings are improvisational and brutal, and the victims' near-complicity in their own destruction adds another unsettling dimension. While the entire cast turns in worthy work, Orozco steals the show as the ungainly, ruthless, yet, when it comes to Nicolas, utterly lovesick sociopath.

DEEPLY DISTURBED (1995) ***

D: Lory-Michael Ringuette. Paula Matlin, Lory-Michael Ringuette, Derek James Yee, Ron Vincent, Frank X. Mur. 82 mins. (Loonic)

While it trods much the same mudcaked verité turf as other stark indies who've followed in the psychotic wake of *Henry: Portrait of a Serial Killer*—e.g., *Confessions of a Serial Killer* (New Horizons), *Jeffrey Dahmer: The Secret Life* (see index)—and not as adroitly as its model, *Deeply Disturbed* largely succeeds in tearing a chilling new page from the Cinematic Serial-Killer Casebook. As in *Henry*, a lethal oedipal wreck, Howard Wilson (somewhat tritely motivated but convincingly portrayed by Ringuette, who also produced, directed, scripted, and composed and performed the film's closing

theme, "A Fine World for Killers"), manages to abduct women (he also shoots the odd male who happens to tick him off), rape and imprison them in his small apartment in a relatively busy building, kill and bury them (in the same increasingly overpopulated spot) while initially escaping the scrutiny of the law. Unlike *Henry*, notable for its almost total absence of authority figures, *Deeply Disturbed* eventually involves two cops (Mur, Yee) who are actively investigating the disappearance of 'burb housewife Matlin. In some ways, Ringuette concocts an even scarier scenario than *Henry*'s in that said cops, while decent and dedicated, never question the investigative misstep that puts them in unwavering pursuit of the wrong man. On the downside, the film suffers from a couple of amateur performances in minor roles that, like their counterparts in otherwise brilliant indies like *Carnival of Souls*, stand out in still bolder relief when played against the effective pro thesps who dominate the cast (a common hazard of no-budget filmmaking). Ringuette also indulges in a few overly Freddy-esque one-liners—e.g., killer to fresh corpse: "Guess it's time you met Mom!" and "Can't live with 'em, gotta kill 'em"—but otherwise plays his grim tale admirably straight. Authentic West Coast locations contribute to the pic's gritty, determinedly mundane mise en scène. *Deeply Disturbed* also incorporates an appropriately bizarre clip from a vintage *Little King* cartoon, *A Dizzy Day*.

DESERT WINDS (1995) ***

D: Michael A. Nickles. Heather Graham, Michael A. Nickles, Jack Kehler, Grace Zabriskie, Monique Parent. 93 mins. (Vanguard)

Though better known for her high-profile roles as porn starlet "Rollergirl" in *Boogie Nights* (see index) and secret agent Felicity Shagwell in *Austin

Powers: The Spy Who Shagged Me* (New Line, DVD), Heather Graham (like Sandra Bullock) began her acting career working the genre and indie circuits. In one of her earliest vehicles, the haunting 1994 mood piece *Desert Winds,* Graham gives a terrifically appealing performance as Jackie, a soulful New Mexico teen who "meets" lonely Arizona native Eugene (writer/director Nickles) sight unseen, via an eerie wind tunnel that carries their voices over hundreds of miles. Young Jackie and the slightly older Eugene first exchange confidences and articulate their yearnings and dreams on the very night that Eugene takes off for what turns into a *Midnight Cowboy*–like lowlifestyle in Philadelphia; they reconnect seven years later, when he returns and *she's* about to leave. A surreal, long-distance love story, *Desert Winds* rates as a true original, an unpretentious, lyrical, and poignant exploration of the themes of destiny, perception, and the nature of intimacy.

DESPERATE (1947) B&W ***

D: Anthony Mann. Steve Brodie, Audrey Long, Raymond Burr, Douglas Fowley, William Tallman. 73 mins. (Kino)

Brodie is convincing as an honest citizen falsely implicated in a cop killing in this typically tight postwar outing by noir master Mann and cinematographer John Alton. Burr and future *Perry Mason* opponent Tallman are properly repellent as the principal thugs, while Fowley lends shading to his sleazy shamus role. An interlude set on a Minnesota farm adds exotic ethnic flavor.

THE DESPERATE HOURS (1955) B&W ***1/2

D: William Wyler. Humphrey Bogart, Fredric March, Martha Scott. 112 mins. (Paramount)

Bogie and escaped-con cronies hide out with a hapless 'burb family in

Wyler's taut *Father Knows Best* Goes Noir adaptation of Joseph Hayes's novel and play. Avoid Michael (*Heaven's Gate*) Cimino's redundant 1990 remake (MGM/UA), with Mickey Rourke in the Bogie role.

DETOUR (1945) B&W ***1/2

D: Edgar G. Ulmer. Tom Neal, Ann Savage, Claudia Drake. 69 mins. (Englewood)

Neal takes an iconic, paranoiac rear-projection cross-country ride with amoral destiny in Ulmer's ultracheap but utterly hypnotic noir, a film fully deserving of its cult status. It was less successfully remade in 1991 with Tom Neal, Jr., in the lead. Englewood has the definitive remastered edition.

DEVIL IN A BLUE DRESS (1995) ***

D: Carl Franklin. Denzel Washington, Tom Sizemore, Jennifer Beals, Don Cheadle, Maury Chaykin. 101 mins. (Columbia/TriStar) "Special Edition" DVD

Set in 1948 L.A., *Devil* stars an earnest Washington as Easy Rawlins, a transplanted Texan who, after losing his job, is desperate to meet the mortgage payments on his house. He's approached by white thug Sizemore to do a little digging on Beals. When Washington realizes he's in over his head, he reluctantly summons his borderline-psycho bud "Mouse" (Cheadle in a scene-stealing perf) from Houston to furnish some armed protection, a service the trigger-happy newcomer is all too happy to provide. No matter how deeply he's dragged into an ever widening conspiracy, Washington remains credible and focused, without transforming into a sudden superhero. In addition to fashioning a satisfyingly complicated mystery, Franklin succeeds in re-creating a specific time, place, and mind-set with remarkable yet unobtrusive precision.

THE DEVIL'S OWN (1997) ***

D: Alan J. Pakula. Harrison Ford, Brad Pitt, Margaret Colin, Ruben Blades, Treat Williams, George Hearn. 110 mins. (Columbia/TriStar) DVD

Widespread reports of a troubled set notwithstanding, *The Devil's Own* is a cohesive, reasonably textured thriller that doesn't skimp in the dramatic or action departments. Traumatized Irish assassin Pitt comes to America to realize his modest dream of scoring a few Sting missiles for the Cause. Sympathetic judge Hearn places Pitt with unsuspecting veteran cop Ford and family. The focus ultimately narrows down to Pitt and Ford's growing conflict, set in motion when Harrison gets wise to his mysterious lodger's lethal game. Ably scripted (*Pope of Greenwich Village* novelist Vincent Patrick's among the three credited scribes) and briskly helmed by Pakula, *The Devil's Own* shapes up as solid, traditional entertainment that delivers on its promise.

DIABOLIQUE (1955) B&W ***1/2

D: Henri-Georges Clouzot. Simone Signoret, Véra Clouzot, Paul Meurisse. 114 mins. (Home Vision) DVD

Clouzot's classic suspenser about an intricately plotted scheme hatched by a cruel headmaster's mistress (Signoret) and wife (Clouzot) has more tricks up its celluloid sleeve than many a Hitchcock flick. Beware the flaccid 1996 remake (Warner).

DISCLOSURE (1994) ***

D: Barry Levinson. Michael Douglas, Demi Moore, Donald Sutherland, Caroline Goodall, Dennis Miller, Dylan Baker, Roma Maffia. 129 mins. (Warner) DVD

Poor Mike just doesn't learn. After his *Fatal Attraction* tryst with Glenn Close led to a lethal conclusion—Mike survived but the rabbit

died—he tangled with icepick queen Sharon Stone in *Basic Instinct* (Artisan). This time out, our middle-aged male sex object suffers the indignity of being sexually harassed at the workplace by beautiful young power-mad ex-paramour Moore. Fortunately, Levinson's astute direction and Paul Attanasio's intricate script get the most out of Michael Crichton's unpromising premise and contrivance-strewn story line, resulting in a tense mainstream thriller. Though the body count holds firm at zero, a late-arriving virtual-reality riff adds an unexpected sci-fi dimension. Telesatirist Miller seems completely at home playing a smarmy, self-serving coworker. Mike returns for more middle-aged madness in the utterly lame *The Game* (PolyGram).

D.O.A. (1949) B&W ***

D: Rudolph Mate. Edmond O'Brien, Pamela Britton, Luther Adler, Neville Brande. 83 mins. (Sinister Cinema) DVD

Mate's mystery packs one of noirdom's greatest hooks: a poisoned O'Brien lives just long enough to track down his own murderer. Look for Beverly Garland (acting as "Beverly Campbell") in her screen debut. Avoid *Max Headroom* creators Rocky Morton and Annabel Jankel's soulless 1988 remake/update (Touchstone). Another uninspired version, *Color Me Dead* (Republic), starring Tom Tryon and Carolyn Jones, appeared in 1969.

DOG EAT DOG (1965) B&W ***

D: Gustav Gavrin. Jayne Mansfield, Cameron Mitchell, Dody Heath, Ivor Salter, Isa Miranda, Werner Peters. 84 mins. (Sinister Cinema)

Released shortly after the film version of Jean Genet's *The Balcony* (Mystic Fire Video) and sharing a similar world-as-whorehouse central metaphor, *Dog Eat Dog* offers the unforgettable combo of Mansfield (first glimpsed writhing orgasmically, to a rock-'n'-roll beat, atop a bed of thousand-dollar bills!) and Mitchell in a cheap but twisty tale of greed and betrayal detailing the above duo and cocrook Salter's filmlong squabble over the proceeds of a million-dollar heist. When the trio hole up in a would-be deserted bordello on an obscure Greek isle, they encounter several other avaricious interlopers, including a nutty German pimp, a sleazy nightclub manager and his sneaky sister, and a crazed ex-madam who's returned home "to die." *Dog Eat Dog* is a cheesy but admirably perverse B movie full of odd exchanges, bizarre behavior, and profound non sequiturs. A somewhat chunky, towel-clad Jayne supplies the pic's deepest philosophical sentiment, however, when she muses, "Right now I'd settle for fresh lipstick and panties in Teaneck, New Jersey!"

DOLORES CLAIBORNE   (1995)***

D: Taylor Hackford. Kathy Bates, Jennifer Jason Leigh, Christopher Plummer, Judy Parfitt, David Straithairn, Eric Bogosian, John C. Reilly. 132 mins. (Columbia/TriStar) DVD

Drawn from Stephen King's novel, *Dolores Claiborne* arrives as a cleverly woven if occasionally overly melodramatic dysfunctional-family mystery enhanced by director Hackford's clever but never intrusive visual touches. The story artfully explores suspected murderess Bates's one-on-one relationships with her wealthy, elderly employer/"victim" (a skillful Parfitt), embittered journalist daughter (Leigh), persecutive cop (Plummer), and, in frequent flashbacks, Bates's late hubby (Straithairn). (Bogosian scores little more than a cameo as Leigh's callous NYC magazine editor and ex-lover.) *Dolores Claiborne* dilutes its feminist case a mite by making Bates's lout of a spouse *so* blatantly despicable—a foulmouthed, thieving, child-molesting, wife-beating drunk—that *anyone* would be happy to knock him off.

While not a horror film, *Dolores Claiborne* contains several effective hallucinatory sequences (e.g., the lyrical eclipse scene wherein the major murder unfolds) that lend the movie added edge.

DON'T LOOK BACK   (1996)***

D: Geoff Murphy. Eric Stoltz, John Corbett, Josh Hamilton, Annabeth Gish, Amanda Plummer, Dwight Yoakam, Billy Bob Thornton, R. G. Armstrong, Peter Fonda. 91 mins. (HBO)

Scripted by the *One False Move* team of Tom Epperson and future star Billy Bob Thornton (the latter gives a chilling perf as a calmly ruthless drug-mogul killer), *Don't Look Back* doesn't quite hit *OFM*'s heights but plays out as a solid, character-driven contempo noir in its own right. Following an idyllic prologue set in 1976 Galveston, the pic picks up Texan-turned-L.A. junkie Stoltz, who stumbles onto a soured dope-deal-in-progress and makes off with a briefcase containing 200 G's. Stoltz decides to use the dough to set his wrecked life straight and returns to Galveston, where he reunites with boyhood pals Corbett and Hamilton. Employing much the same structure as *One False Move*, the flick cuts between Stoltz and friends' troubled Texas reunion and Thornton and crew's brutally thorough (and thoroughly brutal) L.A. search for the missing money and its elusive new owner, a search that ensures a violent showdown at trail's end. Strong performances, credible dialogue, and culty cameos by the likes of Plummer and Fonda add up to an entertaining package.

DOUBLE EXPOSURE   (1993)***

D: Claudia Hoover. Ron Perlman, Ian Buchanan, Jennifer Gatti, William R. Moses, James McEachin, Dedee Pfeiffer. 93 mins. (Prism)

Despite its generic title, Hoover's *Double Exposure* is an engrossing,

twisty mystery given an interesting, though never intrusive, femininist spin. Shady businessman Buchanan, suspecting young spouse Gatti of having an affair, hires amoral P.I. Perlman (who has troubles of his own) to whack her unidentified lover, setting in motion all manner of mayhem. Well-paced, crisply lensed, and credibly acted—particularly by Dedee (sister of Michelle) Pfeiffer as Gatti's best friend—*Double Exposure* should have no difficulty hooking suspense fans and may well be the first film in which Ron Perlman's vomit supplies police with a key clue (!). No relation to the 1982 Michael Callan–starred psycho romp of the same name (Vestron).

DOUBLE INDEMNITY   (1944) B&W ***½

D: Billy Wilder. Barbara Stanwyck, Fred MacMurray, Edward G. Robinson. 106 mins. (Universal) DVD

Directed by Wilder and coscripted by Raymond Chandler from James M. Cain's novel, this pedigreed noir about an elaborate insurance scam remains one of vintage Hollywood's hardest-boiled suspensers.

DOUBLE OBSESSION   (1993)**½

D: Eduardo Montes. Margaux Hemingway, Frederic Forrest, Maryam D'Abo, Scott Valentine, Beth Fisher, Jamie Horton. 88 mins. (Columbia/TriStar)

It's Mondo Margaux time as M.H. sinks her overbite into a full-blown psycho role reportedly based on a true story. Director Montes employs an at-times creatively fractured narrative style to depict Margaux's degeneration from her 1980s college days (at "Freudville University"!), where she develops an unhealthy obsession with roommate D'Abo, to her postgrad madness, which culminates in a murder spree and the kidnap/torture of D'Abo substitute Fisher. While Montes and a pair of fellow scripters don't entirely succeed with their quirky approach to the material, they at least dare to take *Double Obsession* beyond your standard made-for-cable "erotic thriller" formula, and Margaux gives nothing if not her all as the overbearing wacko.

DOUBLE THREAT   (1992) **¹/₂

D: David A. Prior. Sally Kirkland, Andrew Stevens, Sherrie Rose, Chick Vennera, Richard Lynch, Anthony Franciosa. 96 mins. (A.I.P./West Side, n.i.d.)

Double Threat is a twisty thriller that unfolds on and off a B-movie set, where second-rate thesp Stevens, his comeback-bound keeper, Kirkland (in a rare restrained turn), and her body double, Rose, comprise a tense off-screen triangle. Despite the movie's ultimate turn toward the contrived, *Double Threat*'s strong acting, crisp pacing, and neat but never overextended interplay between real and reel life make it worth a look.

DREAM LOVER   (1994) **¹/₂

D: Nicholas Kazan. James Spader, Madchen Amick, Bess Armstrong, Fredric Lehne, Larry Miller, Kathleen York, Irwin Keyes. In R and unrated editions. 103 mins. (PolyGram) DVD

Vet scripter Nicholas (son of Elia) Kazan's directorial debut at least sports an entirely different plot from Alan J. Pakula's lame 1986 Kristy McNichol thriller of the same name (MGM). Indeed, Kazan's loopy outing—replete with carnival nightmares, evil clowns, and, in Amick, the most elaborately artificial figure of feminine evil since Nicole Kidman in *Malice* (see index)—is more reminiscent of such off-the-wall 1980s Philip Yordan flicks as *Bloody Wednesday* and *Death Wish Club* (see index) than most slick mainstream contempo thrillers. *Dream Lover* may not make much sense, but at least it's not

predictable. Amick delivers the deathless line "A psychopath can still love somebody, can't they?" The "sexy unrated version" promises "5 minutes of un-cut, un-censored footage."

DUEL   (1971) ***

D: Steven Spielberg. Dennis Weaver. 90 mins. (Universal)

This trim made-for-TV thriller stars Weaver as a random motorist senselessly and relentlessly pursued by a killer truck. Spielberg's directorial debut remains one of his best and certainly least sentimental efforts.

THE EDGE   (1997) ***

D: Lee Tamahori. Anthony Hopkins, Alec Baldwin, Elle Macpherson, Harold Perrineau, L. Q. Jones, Bart the Bear. 122 mins. (Fox) DVD

While not on the level of his trickiest scripts (e.g., *House of Games, The Spanish Prisoner*), veteran playwright/scenarist David Mamet's alfresco fable yields its fair share of rewards. Hopkins scores another memorable role as an ultraresourceful tycoon equipped with an uncanny ability to retain all manner of facts, great and small. While on a Far North fashion shoot with supermodel spouse Macpherson, Hopkins, photographer Baldwin, and photo assistant Perrineau are stranded in the frigid wilderness after their small plane crashes. At first the three victims struggle for basic survival, with the unflappable Hopkins leading the way, but a more emotional competition develops between Hopkins and Baldwin, with Elle as the potential prize. In addition to the excellent leads, director Lee (*Once Were Warriors*) Tamahori extracts colorful perfs from young Perrineau, vet character actor L. Q. (*The Wild Bunch, Casino*) Jones, and fifth-billed Bart the Bear (assisted by four trainers, a bear double, three

stunt players, *and* an animatronic doppelgänger!). Bart failed to nail an Oscar nom for his strenuous contribution to this potent combo of drama and adventure.

EVE'S BAYOU   (1997) ***

D: Kasi Lemmons. Samuel L. Jackson, Lynn Whitfield, Debbi Morgan, Jurnee Smollett, Dianne Carroll, Lisa Nicole Carson, Vondie Curtis Hall, Branford Marsalis. 109 mins. (Trimark) DVD

Actress Lemmons (*Candyman, Hard Target*) makes an impressive scripting and directorial debut with this alternately elegiac and ominous domestic drama tinged with magic realism, voodoo elements, and a *Bad Seed* twist. Set in early-'60s small-town Louisiana and related from then-ten-year-old Eve's (Smollett) POV, the pic explores our young heroine's increasingly intricate relationships with her philandering physician father (Jackson), anxiety-prone mom (Whitfield), puberty-confused sister (Carson), and eccentric aunt (Morgan), a psychic counselor whose tragic past is littered with late husbands. The film takes a turn for the bizarre when Eve decides her dad's to blame for all her family's emotional woes and rather cold-bloodedly plots his comeuppance. Beautifully shot and creatively scored with choice Bobby "Blue" Bland, Etta James, and Curtis Mayfield cuts, *Eve's Bayou* boasts its pluses.

EVIL HAS A FACE   (1996) ***

D: Rob Fresco. Sean Young, William R. Moses, Joe Guzaldo, Brighton Hertford, Chelcie Ross, Morgan McCabe. 92 mins. (Universal)

Small Kill (see index) director Fresco writes and helms another superior endangered-tyke thriller, further bolstered by soulful work from erstwhile offbeat screen sex symbol Young. Sean plays a forensic sketch artist dispatched to *Fargo* country deep in rural Minnesota, not far from her own birthplace, where seven-year-old Hertford has escaped the clutches of an unknown abductor. When Young re-creates the face of Hertford's elusive captor, she discovers it's a dead ringer for her own late, abusive stepdad. Fresco builds suspense without sacrificing mood or credibility in a neatly arced story that delivers some good cheap damsel-in-distress thrills at film's end.

EXIT IN RED   (1997) *½

D: Yurek Bogayevicz. Mickey Rourke, Annabel Schofield, Carre Otis, Anthony Michael Hall. 96 mins. (Paramount)

Mickey Rourke's a Palm Springs shrink (yeah, right) with a portrait of Chief Tecumseh on his wall. He's also a self-confessed femme "addict," and the feeling's mutual in several unlikely instances. At one point, he blows part of former John Hughes towhead Hall's nose off. The sex scenes rate as erotic only if you succeed in blocking out Mick's half of the screen. Producer Steve Paul (who gave us the Jerry Lewis version of Kurt Vonnegut's *Slapstick of Another Kind* [Vestron]) keeps his hitless track record intact with this failed stab at Taranti*noir.*

EXOTICA   (1994) ***

D: Atom Egoyan. Bruce Greenwood, Elias Koteas, Mia Kirshner, Arsinee Khanjian, Don McKellar, Victor Garber. 104 mins. (Miramax) DVD

Mannered but oft ingenious Canadian auteur Egoyan crafts a satisfying exercise with *Exotica*. The title refers to the world's most genteel (hey, we *said* this was Canada) strip joint, where (admittedly foxy) nude lapdancers ritualistically gyrate to a techno Middle Eastern beat. (As Kirshner, sort of the young Mother Teresa of strip-

pers, puts it, "Not all of us have the luxury of deciding what to do with our lives.") Egoyan gradually acquaints us with several of the club's principals, personnel, and clientele alike, and chronicles, via a seemingly tangential narrative, their increasingly intertwined lives. Cleverly constructed, with some of the pithiest dialogue this side of *Pulp Fiction*, *Exotica* sees Egoyan hone his own idiosyncratic formula, one that had worked only intermittently in such interesting but flawed earlier efforts as *The Adjuster* (Orion) and *Speaking Parts* (Fox Lorber). Egoyan's Canadian telefeature *Calendar* (Kino), and early films *Family Viewing* (Fox Lorber) and *Next of Kin* (Connoisseur) are also out, while the auteur's acclaimed *The Sweet Hereafter* is available via New Line.

EXTREME MEASURES   (1996) **½

D: Michael Apted. Hugh Grant, Gene Hackman, Sarah Jessica Parker, David Morse, Bill Nunn. 118 mins. (Warner) DVD

Produced by supermodel Elizabeth Hurley as a vehicle for then-beleaguered beau Grant and drawn from Michael Palmer's novel, this medical "thriller" generates more anxiety than suspense and works far better as a moral fable than as a nail-biter. The story tracks dedicated E.R. doc Grant's perilous investigation of lethal spinal experiments conducted by respected surgeon Hackman (who puts in relatively scant screen time here) at the expense of several homeless men. The film incorporates some effectively horrific mediphobic elements—like Grant's temporary paralysis—but falls flat with its bursts of bogus violence, blind stabs at suspense, and a trip to a subterranean homeless enclave that plays like an urban *Island of Lost Souls.* Though more closely resembling a made-for-cable movie than a big-screen release, *Extreme Measures* drives home its share of cogent points. David Cronenberg cameos as a hospital lawyer.

EYE OF THE STORM   (1991) **½

D: Yuri Zeltser. Craig Sheffer, Dennis Hopper, Bradley Gregg, Lara Flynn Boyle. 98 mins. (Columbia/TriStar)

In this desert-set psycho noir, Sheffer operates a hellish motel that earlier served as the site of his parents' murder and his younger brother Gregg's blinding; he's been making unwary visitors pay for that decade-old atrocity ever since. Quarreling couple Hopper (in another of his patented lowlife-loony turns) and *Twin Peaks* alum Boyle unwisely wander into the Norman Bates–styled establishment. The pair's disruptive presence gradually precipitates a serious rift between unstable siblings Sheffer and Gregg. While *Eye* only partially succeeds in achieving its aims, it's a must for Hopper-heads.

EYES OF LAURA MARS (1978) ***

D: Irvin Kershner. Faye Dunaway, Tommy Lee Jones, Brad Dourif, Raul Julia. 103 mins. (Goodtimes)

What's basically a standard B-movie slasher tale (coscripted by frightmeister John Carpenter) receives glitzy mainstream treatment as fashion photographer Faye finds herself at the mercy of an eye-gouging psycho.

FATAL ATTRACTION   (1987) **

D: Adrian Lyne. Michael Douglas, Glenn Close, Anne Archer, Stuart Pankin, Fred Gwynne. 119 mins. (Paramount)

This fierce affirmation of traditional family values—an '80s *Psycho Meets Sex Madness* by Way of "Father Shoulda Known Better"—features Douglas as a model postyuppie family-guy and publishing lawyer whose ill-fated fling with predatory associate editor Close nearly causes him to lose it all. Basically a protracted soaper stocked with crowd-pleasing contrivances, *Fatal*

Attraction boasts "steamy sex" (Mike and Glenn get it on everywhere, most definitely including the kitchen sink), "unbearable suspense" (as Mike's car, career, daughter, wife, and rabbit are threatened, not necessarily in that order), *and* a climactic explosion of adrenalizing violence, replete with yet another *Terminator* lift. We're still looking forward to the inevitable sequel—*Fetal Attraction,* wherein Glenn's baby survives the final-reel ordeal and wreaks revenge on an older Mike and family some two decades hence. Viewers in search of an already existing variation can check out the Japanese edition, the notorious "suicide version," where Glenn cuts her own throat and Mike's busted for her murder.

FATHERS & SONS (1992) **

D: Paul Mones. Jeff Goldblum, Rory Cochrane, Rocky Carroll, Ellen Greene, Rosanna Arquette, John C. McGinley. 100 mins. (Columbia/TriStar)

An otherwise excellent Jersey Shore travelog—stretching from Long Branch to Belmar—is pretty much ruined by a story line that features Goldblum as a terminally irritating ex-director, Cochrane as his surly teen son, Arquette as an Asbury Park boardwalk fortune-teller, and a serial psycho called "the Shore Killer" who's authored a little red book that most of the characters spend time reading. Cochrane's scenes with his peers, including a '60s-styled drug segment, provide *Fathers & Sons* with its most believable moments.

FEAR (1988) **

D: Robert A. Ferretti. Cliff De Young, Kay Lenz, Frank Stallone, Robert Factor, Scott Schwartz. 96 mins. (Virgin Vision, n.i.d.)

Sly's talented brother Frank costars in this combo jailbreak/psycho rampage. Though prominently featured on the video box ("Frank Stallone Is Unchained!"), Frank apparently nixed the crazed 'Nam-vet role (taken instead by Factor) to avoid comparisons with his sibling's Rambo persona. A sly move on Frank's part, since in addition to avoiding going one-on-one with his younger bro', he gets to exit this movie, courtesy of a shotgun blast, earlier than most of his less fortunate thespian brethren. Still, Frank's fans won't be disappointed; the lesser-known Stallone is in fine, aggressive form as belligerent prison bully Armitage, one of a quartet of desperate cons who bust loose to terrorize a vacationing family unit led by Cliff and Kay. No relation to the 1996 Mark Wahlberg showcase (Universal, DVD), the 1990 Ally Sheedy nail-biter (Vestron), the 1980 Italo suspenser (Wizard), or the 1946 noir (Vestron) of the same name.

THE FEAR INSIDE (1992) ***

D: Leon Ichaso. Christine Lahti, Dylan McDermott, Jennifer Rubin, David Ackroyd. 100 mins. (Fox)

The Fear Inside is an effectively warped *Lady in a Cage* variation. Wired psychos McDermott and Rubin, posing as a brother/sister tandem, rent rooms in agoraphobic painter Lahti's spacious manse. Separated from fed-up hubby Ackroyd and (briefly) from her young son, Lahti is left home alone to cope with the quarreling killer couple. Director Ichaso, working mostly with a single set, manages to keep his film simultaneously claustrophobic and kinetic.

THE FENCING MASTER (1992) ***

D: Pedro Olea. Assumpta Serna, Omero Antonutti, Joaquim de Almeida. Subtitled. 88 mins. (New Yorker)

When a mysterious beauty (Serna) convinces an initially reluctant fencing master (Antonutti) to teach her his dueling secrets, a series of intrigues and murders is set in motion. Olea's romantic suspenser—based on Antonio Perez Reverte's eponymous novel—unfolds in 1860s Spain amidst an atmosphere of political upheaval and rampant mistrust. Handsomely lensed and plotted with the precision of an intricate duel, the film follows Antonutti as he seeks to absolve himself of suspicion in the slaying of his royal friend (Almeida, later of *Desperado*) and unmask the true culprit.

---

52 PICK-UP (1986) ***

D: John Frankenheimer. Roy Scheider, Ann-Margret, John Glover, Vanity, Robert Trebor, Clarence Williams III. 111 mins. (Video Treasures, Media)

Frankenheimer's utterly implausible but consistently tense and sleazy adaptation of Elmore Leonard's novel casts Scheider as a successful L.A. businessman whose casual fling with a porn-scene floozy embroils him in a harrowing blackmail scheme. Scheider is strong as the beleaguered blackmailee—ditto Ann-Margret as his imperiled wife—but the real show here belongs to three of the weirdest, sickest (to say nothing of clumsiest) villains ever seen on-screen, vividly brought to lowlife by Glover, Trebor, and Williams. Scheider's desperate cat-and-mouse maneuvers with this geeky trio are guaranteed to keep you glued.

FLESH AND BONE (1993) ***

D: Steve Kloves. Dennis Quaid, Meg Ryan, James Caan. 127 mins. (Paramount)

Peripatetic Texan Quaid is haunted by a violent past personified by his lowlife dad (Caan). Writer/director Kloves's leisurely paced thriller is longer on atmosphere than suspense, but the performances of Quaid, Ryan, and a chilling Caan make it worthwhile.

FLESHTONE (1994)***

D: Harry Hurwitz. Martin Kemp, Lise Cutter, Tim Thomerson, Graham Armitage, Suanne Braun. In R and unrated versions. 91 mins. (Prism)

Late indie auteur Hurwitz contributed his fair share of turkeys, from the John Carradine/Nai Bonet disco vampire fiasco, *Nocturna* (Media) to *Safari 3000* (MGM), over the decades. Even his past successes, like the quirky cult comedy *The Projectionist* and the oft hilarious all-star B-movie send-up *That's Adequate!* (see index), have mined a narrow showbiz-satire vein. All of which left us unprepared for *Fleshtone*. Here Hurwitz deftly scripts and directs a hauntingly offbeat mood piece that, abetted by a spare but evocative score, transcends its modest budget and misleading "erotic thriller" tag. Former Spandau Ballet rocker Martin (*The Krays*) Kemp plays a lonely L.A. painter who embarks on an elaborate phone-and-photo affair with mysterious Kansas City femme Cutter. His seemingly harmless long-distance liaison ultimately leads him into a sinister political conspiracy where he becomes both pawn and prime suspect in a gory murder case. Kemp and Cutter portray unusually specific and credible characters whose minor roles in the conspiracy keep them (and us) from ever discovering the true culprits. While this makes for an "unsatisfying" conclusion in a traditional sense, it's consistent with the pic's deliberately shadowy, darkly lyrical tone. Available in a "sizzling" unrated version and a merely "sexy" R-rated edition.

FRANTIC (1988)***1/2

D: Roman Polanski. Harrison Ford, Emmanuelle Seigner, Betty Buckley, John Mahoney, Jimmie Ray Weeks. 120 mins. (Warner) DVD

Polanski again proves a master of paranoia, perversity, and suspense as he runs tourist Ford through a nightmare Parisian sojourn. When wife Buckley vanishes from their hotel room, Ford heads out in a confused, labyrinthine pursuit that ultimately unites him with flaky femme drug-runner Seigner and embroils him in a network of elaborate international intrigues. Polanski expertly charts Ford's escalating loss of control and unerringly conveys the latter's stranger-in-a-strange-land sense of fear and desperation.

FROM HOLLYWOOD TO DEADWOOD (1990)**1/2

D: Rex Pickett. Scott Paulin, Jim Haynie, Barbara Schock. 96 mins. (Media, n.i.d.)

Paulin and Haynie are a pair of L.A. private eyes hired by sleazy film honchos to find the faded starlet (Schock) who walked out on their latest production. The trail eventually leads to Deadwood, North Dakota, where obsessed sleuth Paulin learns that all is not what it seems. *From Hollywood to Deadwood* benefits from solid acting, Pickett's appropriately low-key visual style, and a sincere narrative free of the pretensions that plague many postmodern noirs. Inserts from a fictional film-within-a-film, titled *Blue Stranger* and featuring actress Schock, provide neat, never overbearing parallels to the main story line.

FULL BODY MASSAGE (1995)**1/2

D: Nicolas Roeg. Mimi Rogers, Bryan Brown. 93 mins. (Paramount)

Roeg's *Full Body Massage* is not the erotic thriller its packaging suggests but an essentially two-character, one-set psychodrama that unfolds like a filmed play. Rogers, in varying degrees of nakedness throughout, portrays a California architect whose regular masseuse sends Brown in her stead. The two engage in a filmlong exchange, interrupted by occasional illustrative flashbacks and cutaways, with Brown's peripatetic New Ager proposing spiritual alternatives to Mimi's more pragmatic, materialistic approach to life. While reasonably well written (by Dan Gurskis) and ably performed, *Full Body Massage* lacks the probing perversity of Roeg's and Donald Cammell's classic closet encounter, *Performance*.

FUN (1994) B&W/COLOR***

D: Rafael Zelinsky. Renee Humphrey, Alicia Witt, William R. Moses, Leslie Hope, Ania Suli. 105 mins. (Spectrum)

Fun's story line uncannily echoes Peter Jackson's fact-based masterwork *Heavenly Creatures* (see index) and suffers a bit by comparison. While lacking *HC*'s bold, innovative approach, *Fun* offers a sturdy, disturbing portrait of a pair of troubled teens who develop an instant emotional and sexual bond and cement it with a random act of ritual murder. Director Zelinsky cuts between the present, with the since-separated girls in custody (segments lensed largely in B&W), and color flashbacks tracing their meeting, mating, and mutual murder of an elderly neighbor (Suli). In custody awaiting trial, the hostile but creative Hilary (Humphrey) and the flighty, fantasy-consumed Bonnie (Witt, who proclaims, "Fun is the only thing I believe in!") interact with resident social worker Hope and *Tomorrow*-magazine reporter Moses, who's there to kick-start the inevitable media-exploitation cycle that leads Bonnie to inquire, "Think Drew Barrymore will play me?" The dialogue-driven dramatics occasionally betray the film's stage roots (James Bosley scripts from his original play), while director Zelinsky's attempts to free the flick from same occasionally lead to gimmicky MTV-style moves, including a fast-motion montage right out of *A Clockwork Orange*. Unlike contemporary amoral-

FUN *AND GAMES:* Renee Humphrey and Alicia Witt plan lethal mischief in a lighter-hearted moment from Rafael Zelinsky's *Fun.*
Courtesy of Darrin Ramage

youth outings like *Kids* (Trimark), *Fun* avoids sweeping generational indictments, treating the destructive duo as individuals. What really makes *Fun* come alive, though, are the manipulative Humphrey and manic Witt's peerless performances.

FUNNY GAMES (1997) **

D: Michael Haneke. Susan Lothar, Ulrich Muhe, Arno Frisch, Frank Giering. Subtitled. 103 mins. (Fox Lorber) DVD

Sort of a postmodern *The Penthouse* (n/a) Meets *Man Bites Dog* (see index), Teutonic auteur Haneke's pretentious shocker subjects the viewer to a filmlong torture-and-humiliation session conducted by a pair of squeaky-clean youths (Frisch, Giering) at the expense of a vacationing middle-class family. Haneke seeks to make the audience an active participant in the smarmy aggressors' systematic destruction of husband Muhe, wife Lothar (in an undeniably powerful, harrowing perf), and their young son. While adroitly rendered, Haneke's dark "com-

edy"/thriller is neither as original nor provocative at it thinks it is.

F/X (1986) ***½

D: Robert Mandel. Bryan Brown, Brian Dennehy, Diane Venora, Jerry Orbach, Cliff De Young, Mason Adams. 106 mins. (HBO)

F/X is a true Hollywood rarity: an ultra-"high-concept" thriller that actually works. Brown toplines as Rollie Tyler, a special-effects ace whose credits include *Vermin from Venus, Planet of the Female Mummies,* and *I Dismember Mama.* (If you identified the last as the only real-movie title of the bunch, award yourself 10 points.) Tyler's approached by Justice Department agents De Young and Adams to stage the phony gangland-style slaying of mobster-turned-stoolie DeFranco (Orbach). The assignment takes a number of violent twists, and Tyler must resort to his bag of FX tricks to bring down the bad guys and save his own nonsynthetic skin. Fugitive, semiretired FX ace Brown and renegade ex-cop Dennehy reunite in Richard Franklin's

1991 *FX 2: The Deadly Art of Illusion* (Orion), a contrived but swiftly paced sequel buoyed by the stars' breezy thesping and the expected special-effects gimmicks.

THE GANGSTER (1947)
B&W ***½

D: Gordon Wiles. Barry Sullivan, Belita, Akim Tamiroff, John Ireland, Harry Morgan, Sheldon Leonard. 84 mins. (Fox)

This strange, highly stylized, nearly stage-bound *noir* stars Sullivan as an insecure, even borderline paranoid racketeer who's more concerned with explaining his worldview than with protecting his Neptune Beach, Brooklyn, turf from interlopers led by future sitcom mogul Leonard. Then again, *all* the characters—Sullivan's troubled singer/squeeze Belita, pressured merchant Tamiroff, pathetic gambling addict Ireland, and womanizing soda jerk Morgan—are bent on philosophizing at length. The obviously painted sets and indoor exteriors lend a note of visual surrealism to the offbeat proceedings, a highly recommended oddity that's strikingly out of step with the usually laconic hard-boiled crime capers of its era.

GANGSTER STORY (1960)
B&W ***

D: Walter Matthau. Walter Matthau, Carol Grace, Bruce McFarlan, Garrett Wallberg. 65 mins. (Goodtimes)

Walter Matthau isn't a name normally associated with the far fringes of indie filmmaking, but back in 1960 the then-only-semiknown actor starred in and directed this shoestring crime caper. Matthau's gritty B movie emerges as a cross between a West Coast *Blast of Silence* (n/a)—Allen Baron's funky, no-budget 1961 NYC-set noir—and a warm-up for his better-known bank-robber character in Don Siegel's *Charley Varrick* (see index). While neither as arty as *Blast* or as slick as *Varrick*, *Gangster Story* is a tough little B&W item that works more often than not. Following a memorable theme song called "The Itch for Scratch," thief/killer Jack Martin (Matthau) pulls off a smooth heist by posing as a Hollywood location scout (he even scores police cooperation!). Our cool, calculating antihero takes up with an equally cold companion, enigmatic librarian Grace (who bears a passing resemblance to *Carnival of Souls*'s Candace Hilligoss). The odd couple share a symbiotic but emotionally distant relationship that's threatened when hitherto-solo operator Martin agrees to work for organized-crime lord McFarlan. This offbeat footnote to Matthau's career holds up well, from its inventive handheld-camera work to its refusal to slacken its consistently cynical, unsentimental tone. With *Gangster Story*, Matthau joins the rarified ranks of one-shot auteurs who succeeded in their only try.

THE GLASS SHIELD   (1995) ***

D: Charles Burnett. Michael Boatman, Ice Cube, Lori Petty, Michael Ironside, M. Emmet Walsh, Elliott Gould, Linden Chiles. 110 mins. (Miramax)

Burnett, of *To Sleep with Anger* (Columbia/TriStar) fame, assembles an unsentimentalized account of the problems encountered by African-American rookie Boatman and femme Jewish cop Petty at an old-white-boy-run California police precinct. When black motorist Cube is set up to take the rap for a murder he didn't commit, Boatman and Petty, with a reluctant assist from older cop Chiles, uncover a long-standing pattern of corruption. Burnett resists turning *The Glass Shield* into a standard shoot-'em-up—the violence here is mostly verbal and attitudinal—or offering an easy, crowd-pleasing resolution. (Indeed, if

the pic has a weakness, it's its anticlimactic conclusion.) The three leads turn in worthy work, while Walsh contributes a croak scene straight out of the Robert Duvall School of Cinematic Death Throes.

GOLD COAST   (1997) ***

D: Peter Weller. David Caruso, Marg Helgenberger, Jeff Kober, Barry Primus, Wanda De Jesus, Richard Bradford, Rafael Báez, Melissa Raven. 109 mins. (Paramount)

Actor-turned-auteur Peter (*Robo-Cop*) Weller does a good job bringing Elmore Leonard's titular novel to the small screen in this made-for-Showtime caper. Ex–*NYPD Blue* star Caruso portrays a code-bound crook-cum-dolphin-trainer who surfaces to collect a minor debt from the troubled widow (Helgenberger) of a dead crime kingpin (Bradford). He learns that the lady's been banned from consorting with men for the rest of her life by a twisted will enforced by her late spouse's attorney (Primus) and a psychotic cowboy hit man (Kober). What follows is an entertaining series of cat-and-mouse games leading to (if you've seen other Leonard-based flicks) a not-unexpected denouement. The exotic South Florida location lensing, with stops in Miami Beach, Fort Lauderdale, and other sunny spots, provides an additional viewing plus.

THE GOOD SON   (1993) **½

D: Joseph Ruben. Macauley Culkin, Elijah Wood, Wendy Crewson, David Morse, Jacqueline Brookes. 87 mins. (Fox)

Several mainstream critics reacted with outrage when hitherto cuddly million-dollar towhead Culkin launched his Little Mac Attack in *The Good Son*. In point of fact, Mac was merely observing a venerable Tinseltown tradition, as

well as prepping for his filmic future. The image of a makeup-laden Mac starring in "Home Alone 26" at age 40 is, let's face it, a far from pretty one. Drew Barrymore proved hip to a similar career move at age eight or so when she graduated from her sweet kid-sis turn in *E.T.: The Extra-Terrestrial* to her pyromaniac part in *Firestarter*. Clint Howard, bigtimer Ron's on- and off-tube little bro' on *The Andy Griffith Show*, finds regular employment as a professional screen geek; Clint's twisted body of work will doubtless be studied by genre scholars long after brother Ron's become the merest of movie footnotes. The Phantom's only complaint re *The Good Son* is that it didn't turn out to be a better, more frightening flick. The high-concept pairing of *The Stepfather* director Ruben and killer-kid Culkin—who, in one scene, is even heard humming The Stepfather's signature tune, "Camptown Races" (!)—isn't much stronger than your average made-for-cable thriller, even if M.C. does say the *f* word.

THE GRAVE   (1995) **½

D: Jonas Pate. Craig Sheffer, Gabrielle Anwar, Josh Charles, Donal Logue, John Diehl, Anthony Michael Hall, Max Perlich, Keith David, Eric Roberts. 90 mins. (Republic)

Related in flashback, tall-tale style by an initially unidentified prison inmate, *The Grave* details the search for a treasure rumored to be buried in the title site. Convict brothers Sheffer and Charles break out of a North Carolina pen with the help of bribed guard Diehl. When Charles catches a bullet, Sheffer brings him to mortician Hall (the erstwhile John Hughes juve is excellent here) and briefly reunites with former squeeze Anwar. Hall and his lowlife buds Logue and Perlich cut themselves into the hunt, but that's only the beginning of the myriad plot twists that snake through this often clever thriller. Director Pate, who coscripted with twin brother, Josh, keeps his outlandish story moving at a steady, unpredictable pace, and if you ignore a few logical lapses and some strained stabs at Tarantino-esque exchanges, *The Grave* will likely hook you.

THE GREAT ST. LOUIS BANK ROBBERY   (1959) B&W ***½

D: Charles Guggenheim, John Stix. Steve McQueen, Crahan Denton, David Clarke, Molly McCarthy, James Dukas. 87 mins. (Ivy) DVD

Dismissed in the few film-reference guides in which it even receives a mention, this is an excellent, extremely hard-edged, verité-styled noir, reportedly based on an actual heist and lensed on a low budget in some of the titular city's grittier precincts. Future TV and film director Richard T. *(Futureworld, I Will Fight No More Forever)* Heffron populates his sharp script with textured characters who behave and talk like real people. While McQueen, billed above the title (the "Great," by the way, *doesn't* appear in the opening credits), more than holds his own in his second screen role (following *The Blob*), top acting honors go to vet character thesp Denton as John, the no-nonsense, 60ish career criminal who masterminds the caper. McQueen plays George, an expelled former college athlete who agrees to drive the getaway car at the urging of lowlife Gino (Clarke), whose sister (McCarthy) used to be George's squeeze. There's a coded but fairly obvious homoerotic link between John and his partner, Willie (Dukas), his former prison punk, who's growing too "old" and "fat" to hold John's attention. John hopes to replace him with George—even telling McCarthy that George is "too much of a man for a woman" (!). Tense, riveting, and way ahead of its time, *The Great St. Louis Bank Robbery* can take its honored place beside such enduring cult caper faves as *Blast of Silence,* Hubert Cornfield's *Plunder Road,* and Stanley Kubrick's *The Killing.*

THE GRIFTERS   (1990) **

D: Stephen Frears. Anjelica Huston, John Cusack, Annette Bening, Pat Hingle, J. T. Walsh, Henry Jones. 114 mins. (HBO) DVD

The third adaptation of a Jim Thompson novel to reach the screen in 1990 (along with *The Kill-Off* and *After Dark, My Sweet), The Grifters* centers on a decidedly offbeat mother-and-child reunion between seasoned racetrack scam artist Huston and small-time con man Cusack. Further complicating the picture is Cusack's conniving gal pal (Bening), who schemes to relieve Anjelica of her ill-gotten gains. The uniformly unsympathetic characters are unconvincingly updated from the earlier era they more comfortably inhabited in Thompson's novel, and the film further suffers from frequently smarmy, self-conscious touches on the part of director Frears *(My Beautiful Laundrette, The Hi-Lo Country).* Instead of building to a satisfying payoff, the story splinters to the point where the viewer becomes the ultimate mark.

GRIND   (1996) ***

D: Chris Kentis. Billy Crudup, Adrienne Shelly, Paul Schulze, Frank Vincent, Saul Stein, Amanda Peet. 96 mins. (Fox Lorber)

In an era of indie overhype, *Grind* was a victim of serious *under*buzz. While containing "criminal" components, this sharp collaboration between director, editor, and coscripter Kentis and writer/producer Laura Lau forgoes the contrived-caper route, opting instead for powerful human drama. When aspiring racer Eddie Dolan (Crudup) is released from stir after serving a term for a major vehicular violation, he accepts the invitation of his working-stiff older bro', Terry (Schulze), to stay at his Clifton, New Jersey, home with wife Janey (Shelly) and their infant daughter. Terry also helps Eddie land two paying gigs—one legit, in a treadmill factory where their dad (Vincent) is also employed, and another working a stolen-car insurance scam for local schemer Jack (Stein). After Eddie's put on the night shift, he gets to spend too much time at home with Janey, and their natural attraction eventually turns serious. Kentis and Lau present a refreshingly noncondescending portrait of (slightly stained) blue-collar Jersey life and extract outstanding perfs from their cast. If you go for gripping, emotion-driven stories, you won't want to miss *Grind.*

GROUND ZERO   (1987) ***

D: Michael Pattinson, Bruce Myles. Colin Friels, Jack Thompson, Donald Pleasence, Natalie Baye, Simon Chilvers. 109 mins. (Artisan)

This trim, exciting Aussie suspenser stars Friels as a cameraman who, via seemingly innocent home movies left by his late dad, stumbles on to a Down Under A-bomb scandal dating back to the early '50s, when Brit-sponsored atomic tests claimed the lives of several military personnel and untold numbers of Aborigines. A multiple winner at the 1987 Australian Film Institute Awards (though barely released in the U.S.), *Ground Zero* does an excellent job of using a pulp-thriller format to examine a legit issue. Fear-film fave Pleasence plays an embittered but resourceful test survivor who decides to aid Friels in his quest for the truth. Friels, meanwhile, virtually reprises his character, recast as a psycho-hunting reporter, in *Grievous Bodily Harm* (Fries, n.i.d.), a well-crafted but ultimately unsatisfying thriller.

A GUN, A CAR, A BLONDE (1997) B&W/COLOR**¹/₂

D: Stefani Ames. Jim Metzler, Billy Bob Thornton, Kay Lenz, John Ritter, Andrea Thompson, Victor Love. 101 mins. (Avalanche)

Sort of a road-show *Singing Detective* (Fox) sans the singing, coscripted (with director Ames) by frequent Billy Bob Thornton collaborator Tom (*One False Move*) Epperson, *A Gun, a Car, a Blonde* is a sincere, cleverly written but ultimately depresso outing. When New Agey pal Ritter suggests paralyzed tire magnate Metzler seek relief by indulging in "objectification therapy," the latter obligingly retreats into a B&W noir fantasy world. There he transforms into hard-boiled P.I. Rick Stone while recasting characters from his wheelchair-bound real life: Ritter becomes a bartender confidant, male nurse Love a sort of slim, black Sydney Greenstreet, parasitic sister Lenz a treacherous floozy, etc. (Thornton offers the most memorable work here in his dual role as Lenz's amiably lowlife boyfriend and, in the noir sphere, a corrupt cop.) It's hard to find fault with any of Epperson and Ames's elements, but it may be equally hard finding an audience for a flick whose main premise has been handled more adroitly before and whose melancholy tone isn't likely to satisfy modern-noir fans attracted by what turns out to be an ironic title.

THE HAND THAT ROCKS THE CRADLE (1992) **

D: Curtis Hanson. Rebecca De Mornay, Annabella Sciorra, Matt McCoy, Ernie Hudson, Madeline Zima. 110 mins. (Hollywood Pictures) DVD

Suspense specialist Hanson's awkwardly monikered psycho thriller is basically a rehash of William Friedkin's 1990 turkey, *The Guardian,* minus the latter's baby-eating monster druid tree. Hanson adopts a more down-to-earth approach for *his* nanny-from-hell histrionics: De Mornay plays Peyton, the widow of a wealthy obstetrician who kills himself after being fingered as a hands-on pervert by preggers patient Sciorra. Since Peyton subsequently suffers a miscarriage, a hysterectomy, and a severe financial setback as a direct result of said suicide, she sets out to settle the score. The end result is a laboriously contrived "thriller" leavened only by some agreeably grotesque touches and a plethora of unintentional laughs. Among the performers, Sciorra most impresses, especially during her on-screen asthma attacks, which come complete with *Exorcist*-like sound effects, while the late Bela Lugosi continues his busy posthumous career, following up his *Devil Bat* cameo in *Basket Case 3* with clips from *White Zombie,* which the demented Peyton screens for young Madeline in an admirable bid to broaden the white-bread 'burb tyke's cultural horizons. A climactic catfight between Annabella and Rebecca supplies another brief highlight. *Cradle* is campy enough to provide some fleeting entertainment value, but The Phantom, for one, really missed that baby-munching tree.

HARD CHOICES (1986) **¹/₂

D: Rick King. Gary McCleery, Margaret Klenck, John Sayles, Martin Donovan, J. T. Walsh, Spalding Gray. 90 mins. (Lorimar, n.i.d.)

Liberal lawyer Klenck falls for sensitive teenage con McCleery, springs him from jail, and leads him to a career opportunity as a drug-smuggling pilot. Future B director King keeps this loosely fact-inspired account relatively credible and low-key. John Sayles cameos as a drug dealer.

HARD EIGHT (1996) ***

D: Paul Thomas Anderson. Philip Baker Hall, John C. Reilly, Gwyneth Paltrow, Samuel L. Jackson. 101 mins. (Columbia/TriStar) DVD

Best known for his Richard Nixon portrayal in both the play and film versions of the one-man show *Secret Honor* (Artisan), Hall scores a high-profile role as a veteran, Zen-like Reno gambler who harbors a dark secret. For initially unknown reasons, Hall comes to young loser Reilly's rescue, virtually adopting him as a son as well as tutoring him in the professional-gambling trade. Trouble arises when Reilly links up with hostess/hooker Paltrow and escalates when the pair seek the dubious help of troublemaking casino security worker Jackson. The less the viewer knows about *Hard Eight* going in, the better; suffice it to say that the story line remains unpredictable throughout, while future *Boogie Nights* director Anderson ably captures the casino atmosphere and lifestyle.

THE HAWK (1993) **¹/₂

D: David Hayman. Helen Mirren, George Costigan, Rosemary Leach, Owen Teale, Melanie Hill. 84 mins. (Academy, n.i.d.)

In *The Hawk,* adapted by Peter Ransley from his novel, popular PBS *Prime Suspect* star Mirren gives a shaded perf as a lower-middle-class Brit homemaker with a history of mental instability. When an outbreak of particularly vicious serial killings, accompanied by rapes and eye-gougings, begins plaguing Helen's nabe, key clues point to her hubby (Costigan) as the probable perp, but our heroine has a hard time separating evidence from paranoia. After generating a fair amount of initial suspense, *The Hawk* ultimately falls short, though Mirren mavens will want to tune in to see their fave's typically inventive thesping.

HE WALKED BY NIGHT (1948) B&W ★★★

D: Alfred L. Werker, Anthony Mann. Richard Basehart, Scott Brady, Roy Roberts, Whit Bissell, Jack Webb. 79 mins. (Kino)

Cop Brady leads a manhunt through the L.A. sewer system, where elusive psycho killer Basehart's at bay. Werker (and uncredited codirector Mann) relate the suspenseful tale in a documentary style that emphasizes police methodology. Jack Webb, who has a small role here, later used the film as the basic model for his long-running *Dragnet* series.

HEART OF MIDNIGHT (1989) ★★½

D: Matthew Chapman. Jennifer Jason Leigh, Peter Coyote, Gale Mayron, Sam Schact, Frank Stallone, Brenda Vaccaro. 93 mins. (Virgin Vision, n.i.d.)

"Is this good or is this bad?" That rhetorical query, posed by one of *Heart of Midnight*'s unlikely characters, applies to the flick itself, a determinedly bizarre, wildly contrived, and consummately sleazy B thriller in a *Repulsion* Meets *Hardcore* vein. Leigh toplines as your typical mentally shaky virgin who decides to move into an abandoned sex club (!), inherited from her late, evil uncle, Fletcher (rhymes with *lecher*). After being raped by local lowlifes, Jen starts cracking up, suffering hideous audiovisual hallucinations. Mysterious stranger Coyote shows up to complicate matters further, while Sly's bro' Frank Stallone (in a then-rare clean-shaven role) plays the understandably confused cop assigned to the original rape case. Add a series of psycho murders, a cache of perverted videotapes, and a wealth of circular dialogue worthy of Ed Wood, and you have a cinematic oddity that, depending on your taste and tolerance, will either hold you spellbound with disbelief or send you howling from the couch.

HEAVENLY CREATURES (1994) B&W/COLOR ★★★½

D: Peter Jackson. Melanie Lynskey, Kate Winslet, Sarah Peirse, Diana Kent, Clive Merrison, Simon O'Connor. 99 mins. (Miramax)

Based on New Zealand's most infamous true-crime case—the murder of a 'burb mom by her teenage daughter and the latter's best friend in 1954—*Heavenly Creatures* gained greater notoriety by inadvertently "outing" one of the convicted killers as popular mystery novelist "Anne Perry" (Juliet Hulme). (Theatrical distributor Miramax later used that info as part of the film's promo campaign.) Former splatter satirist Peter (*Dead Alive, Meet the Feebles*) Jackson boldly employs FX-driven fantasy sequences, black-and-white segments, and even clips from *The Third Man* to enhance this bizarre story of an adolescent friendship so exclusive and intense that it impelled two middle-class high school girls to commit a brutal act of matricide. Lynskey and future *Titanic* star Winslet are phenomenal as the oft brooding, overweight Pauline, whose diary entries were later used as evidence against her, and the more sophisticated, whimsical (and tubercular) Juliet, respectively. Together the girls create their own mythology, a magical kingdom called Borovnia, peopled by a fictional royal family (along with singer Mario Lanza!), in which they revel in the emotional riches missing from their mundane daily lives. Jackson's composition and color schemes lend his film the look of kinetic period postcards, while the script—which earned an Academy Award nomination for Best Original Screenplay, by Jackson and frequent collaborator Frances Walsh—captures both the universality and extreme specificity of the girls' special bond, adolescent sapphic attraction, and shared fantasies. Their pointless, desperate crime comes across as more sad than sensational. Jackson followed,

thus far, with *The Frighteners* (see index) and the clever celluloid mockumentary *Forgotten Silver* (First Run Features).

HIDDEN OBSESSION (1993) ★★

D: John Stewart. Heather Thomas, Jan-Michael Vincent, Nick Celozzi, David Glasser. 92 mins. (Universal)

Jan-Michael exhibits his full range of acting chops here, turning from a sensitive but manly rural deputy (sort of an Iron Jan-Michael) to a raving misogynistic psycho. Thomas, as a newly divorced blond news anchor on a life-sorting vacation, helps trigger J-M's rad personality change but proves less adept at stretching herself, thesp-wise, especially during a lengthy inebriation sequence wherein she appears more comatose than crocked. An extremely cheap end-credit crawl features several obvious aliases of the sort normally associated with far worse flicks. In other endangered-journalist outings, Barbara (*I Dream of Jeannie*) Eden portrays a threatened TV reporter in *Lethal Charm* (Artisan), while ex-cop Tim Thomerson aids an imperiled cameraman in *Prime Time Murder* (Academy).

HIDER IN THE HOUSE (1990) ★★★

D: Matthew Patrick. Gary Busey, Mimi Rogers, Michael McKean. 109 mins. (Vestron)

Busey stars as a career sociopath who torched his parents' house (with them inside) while an abused teen. Now, two decades later, Gary hides in a secret room in a 'burb manse newly occupied by Rogers, stressed-out spouse (McKean, in a rare noncomedy role), and their two kids. At first, Busey's content to share vicariously in the family's domestic affairs. But he soon begins taking a more active role, killing off a nosy exterminator and covertly tipping Mimi off to hubby McKean's infidelities. While it doesn't scale the horrific heights of *Stepfather*, *Hider*, scripted by Lem (*Kafka*) Dobbs, overcomes its far-fetched premise via credible perfs by Rogers and Busey, who manages to evoke both sympathy and menace.

THE HITCH-HIKER (1953)
B&W ***

D: Ida Lupino. Edmond O'Brien, Frank Lovejoy, William Talman. 71 mins. (Kino)

Talman is truly terrifying as a homicidal hitcher in Lupino's tense, loosely fact-based psycho road noir, a forerunner to Robert Harmon's more flamboyant *The Hitcher* (see index) and a nerve-jangling ride in its own right. Director/actress Lupino scored another offbeat winner with the same year's *The Bigamist* (Kino), also starring noir fave O'Brien. For more bad-motoring thrills, see 1947's *The Devil Thumbs a Ride* (RKO), with supreme screen hard-case Lawrence Tierney as a ruthless thug who preys on highway motorists.

HITLER'S CHILDREN (1943)
B&W ***

D: Edward Dmytryk. Tim Holt, Bonita Granville, Otto Kruger. 83 mins. (Media, n.i.d.)

Dmytryk's then-shocking look at the Hitler Youth Movement still packs a punch as the pic chronicles young Holt's indoctrination into the Nazi fold. The even better *Tomorrow the World*, with Skip Homeier as a junior Nazi adopted by American parents, has yet to join the homevid ranks. Other period Hitler exposés include *Hitler's Henchmen* (Sinister Cinema) and *Hitler—Dead or Alive* (Goodtimes), wherein three Yank gangsters led by Ward Bond go gunning

ROAD WORRIERS: Anxious vacationers Frank Lovejoy and Edmund O'Brien are terrorized by highway psycho William Talman in Ida Lupino's 1953 noir *The Hitch-Hiker.*
© Kino International Corporation 1999

for Adolf (!) to collect on a million-dollar bounty.

HORSEPLAYER (1991) ***

D: Kurt Voss. Brad Dourif, Sammi Davis-Voss, M. K. Harris, Vic Tayback. 90 mins. (Republic)

Voss's minimalist but effective L.A.-set psycho fable stars the always welcome Dourif in another of his patented eccentric perfs. Here Brad plays a racetrack devotee, parolee, and (it's hinted) reformed maniac who also works for a heavily accented liquor-store owner (the late Tayback in his filmic farewell). Complications intrude upon Brad's voluntarily monastic lifestyle in the form of flip alkie artist Harris and his seductive sister, Davis-Voss. When Harris chooses Brad as the unwitting subject for a cycle of violent paintings, he sends sis Sammi to seduce the loose-screwed loner, the better to chart his habits and tics. Trouble is, once the art-hating Brad is lured out

of his strict, self-imposed routine, his attitude takes a decided turn for the worse. Sort of a deadpan, updated reverse variation on Roger Corman's *A Bucket of Blood*, *Horseplayer* is a neat, agreeably subversive celluloid jigsaw puzzle whose pieces fall into place in oft original patterns. Dourif excels as the reclusive ex-con, while Harris delivers a droll turn as the sarcastic, exploitive painter and Davis-Voss is fetchingly devious as Harris's sibling and uncredited "muse." The Pixies' soundtrack tunes add an appropriate note.

THE HOT SPOT (1990) **½

D: Dennis Hopper. Don Johnson, Virginia Madsen, Jennifer Connelly, Charles Martin Smith, Jack Nance. 130 mins. (Orion)

A chunky Johnson is a used-car salesman with a hidden agenda in a small Texas town. He soon gets involved with the boss's slutty, conniving spouse (Madsen), troubled teen Connelly, and assorted intrigues. Hopper's well-crafted noir makes good use of its heat metaphors and authentic locales, but *The Hot Spot* is frequently slack and ultimately lacking in climactic impact.

A HOUSE IN THE HILLS (1993) ***

D: Ken Wiederhorn. Michael Madsen, Helen Slater, Jeffrey Tambor, James Laurenson, Elyssa Davalos. 91 mins. (Artisan)

A tired premise—aspiring actress Slater house-sits a Hollywood manse, where she's held captive by intruder Madsen—yields surprisingly sharp results in a perverse, witty thriller directed/coscripted by the normally unimpressive Ken (*Meatballs 2*) Wiederhorn (who cameos as a newsman). In addition to Madsen's and Slater's charismatic turns, the flick features several unpredictable (if far-fetched) twists that hoist *House* well above the usual run of femme-slanted home-alone suspensers.

HOUSE OF GAMES (1987) ***1/2

D: David Mamet. Lindsay Crouse, Joe Mantegna, Lilia Skala, Ricky Jay. 102 mins. (HBO)

C rouse is a sheltered shrink who, despite having a book (*Driven: Obsession and Compulsion in Everyday Life*) on the best-seller list, feels frustrated about her inability to help her own patients in any concrete way. When a compulsive-gambler client tells her that his $25,000 debt to a local tough guy has marked him for death, she decides to do something about it. Soon she's entangled with professional con man Mantegna (in an Oscar-quality performance), who leads her through a maze of increasingly elaborate scams that force her to face the fact that she actually knows precious little re basic homo-sap psychology—especially her own. (She proves a quick study, though.) Mamet's nail-biting meditation explores the very core of human nature and also has a lot to say about "crime" and class.

THE HOUSEKEEPER (1986) ***

D: Ousama Rawi. Rita Tushingham, Ross Petty, Tom Kneebone, Shelly Peterson, Jessica Stern, Jackie Burroughs. 97 mins. (Lorimar, n.i.d.)

T ushingham toplines as Eunice, a recessive, phobic Brit hampered and haunted by her lifelong case of dyslexic illiteracy. Figuring that housekeeping is one occupation that won't betray her condition, she moves to the States (the low-budget pic was actually lensed in London and Toronto) and takes a live-in gig with a well-heeled doctor (Petty) and his family. We don't want to reveal more of this flawed but tense thriller's plot; suffice it to say that *The Housekeeper* would have been even more at home working for *The Stepfather*. Rita does an exceptional job as the loveless, telly-addicted loner, especially when she reminisces re her late mother's abuse and her dad's intervention: "He didn't like her hurting me. He thought it was *his* job." Beyond its basic psycho story line, *The Housekeeper*—based on Ruth Rendell's novel *A Judgment in Stone*—is laced with grim class ironies, sometimes playing like a B-movie *Upstairs, Downstairs* with a distaff Norman Bates as one of the downstairs "help."

I CAN'T SLEEP (1994) **1/2

D: Claire Denis. Katerina Golubeva, Richard Courcet, Alex Descas, Béatrice Dalle. 110 mins. (New Yorker)

M ost of Claire (*Chocolat*) Denis's superbly crafted feature charts the drudgery-driven daily lives and largely dashed dreams of several Parisian immigrants: Daiga (Golubeva), an independent Lithuanian looker who drives to Paris in hopes of launching an acting career; Theo (Courcet), a black musician determined to split the City of Lights with his toddler son and estranged wife (Dalle) for a simpler lifestyle in Martinique; and Camille (Descas), Theo's moody, gay drag-queen performer brother who, with his white lover, has been secretly pursuing a second vocation as the city's notorious "granny killer." While drawn from a real-life rash of senior-citizen slayings perped by just such a gay couple in 1980s Paris, this randomly violent thread radically detracts from the movie's main concerns. Worse, there's nothing in Camille's character or behavior that would persuade us to accept his sudden, unmotivated descent into monsterdom. We thought the French didn't have to stoop to cheap serial-killer tricks to get serious slice-of-life flicks in the can. Guess they're finally getting with the program.

I WENT DOWN (1997) ***

D: Paddy Breathnach. Brendan Gleeson, Peter McDonald, Tony Doyle, Antoine Byrne, Peter Caffrey, Joe Gallagher. 111 mins. (Artisan)

L ow-key young ex-con Kit (McDonald) and earthy, rotund gangster gofer Bunny (Gleeson) make for an appealing odd couple of crime. Kit and Bunny are sent by veteran mobster Tom French (Doyle) to locate and retrieve his vanished ex-partner, Grogan (Caffrey)—*or else*. Kit and Bunny's motor journey through a scenic Cork countryside evolves into an increasingly complicated comedy of errors, with Kit doing his best to keep the impulsive Bunny out of extracurricular mischief (like robbing convenience stores along the way) and focused on the task at hand. When they do recover the garrulous Grogan, they're forced to contend with his version of the "truth" re his and

Tom's contentious history. While *I Went Down* might have benefited from a bit of a trim, crime and comedy fans won't be disappointed by this clever Hibernian caper.

IN THE COMPANY OF MEN (1997) ***1/2

D: Neil LaBute. Aaron Eckhart, Stacy Edwards, Matt Malloy. 93 mins. (Columbia/TriStar) DVD

A 1997 Sundance-fest fave (and official Filmmakers' Trophy winner), debuting writer/director LaBute's clever morality tale fully lives up to its buzz. Chad (Eckhart) and Howard (Malloy), two midlevel Dilberts from hell, have both been rejected by their respective squeezes. ("Women," muses Chad, "they're all the same inside—meat, gristle, and hatred.") While killing time in an airport on their way to a six-week corporate assignment in scenic Fort Wayne, Indiana, an aggressive Chad suggests to his dweebier pal that they select a vulnerable woman whom they'll separately woo, win, and abandon in a bid to gain symbolic revenge on the entire opposite sex. Mover-and-shaker Chad finds their prospective mark in temp secretary Christine (Edwards), who more than meets their criteria—she's not only attractive and vulnerable but deaf to boot. From the opening and entr'acte jungle-jazz riffs (which sound like a duet for tom-toms and testosterone), to the clean, nearly verité lensing in blandly quintessential Middle-American locales, to the three leads' subtle work, *In the Company of Men* rarely hits a false note. The film ultimately has more to say about traditional struggles between hunter and prey than it does about the battle of the sexes. It may not be an ideal date video, but *In the Company of Men* rates as must viewing. LaBute followed with the dark-toned comedy *Your Friends and Neighbors* (see index).

THE INFORMANT (1998) ***

D: Jim McBride. Cary Elwes, Timothy Dalton, Anthony Brophy, Maria Lennon, Sean McGinley, Carian Fitzgerald. 106 mins. (Paramount)

While it doesn't scale the heights of John Ford's *The Informer* (Turner) or Jim Sheridan's *In the Name of the Father* (Universal), McBride's drama about reluctant-IRA-fighter-turned-even-more-reluctant-informer (or "tout") Sean McAnally (a convincingly tormented Brophy) succeeds in packing a punch. *The Informant* is set in Northern Ireland in 1983, a time when British soldiers and civilian inspectors—represented by a sympathetic Elwes and a gruff, tough, against-type Dalton, respectively—actively recruited participants on both sides of the Irish divide to snitch in return for suspended sentences and government protection. Scripter Nicholas Meyer, adapting Gerald Seymour's book *Field of Blood,* ably conveys young Sean's predicament as his former cronies, feisty spouse (Lennon), and even young son (Fitzgerald) turn against him. All four leads contribute top work—though Elwes, at times, seems a tad *too* noble—and the gray moral zone in which all are forced to reside is vividly re-created. Since this was originally a Showtime cable-TV movie, producers even manage to slip in a totally gratuitous sex scene between Cary and his foxy squeeze.

INSOMNIA (1997) ***

D: Erik Skjoldbjaerg. Stellan Skarsgård, Sverre Anker Ousdal, Bjørn Floberg, Gisken Armand. Subtitled. 95 mins. (Home Vision) DVD

A spellbinding noir set in Norway's relentlessly bright Land of the Midnight Sun, *Insomnia* stars international thesp Skarsgård as a Swedish inspector assigned to solve the mysterious murder of a teenage girl. Our story takes a radical turn when the already

unpopular cop accidentally kills his longtime partner and subsequently devotes more time to engineering an elaborate cover-up than attending to the original case. In addition to fashioning a twisty plot, director Skjoldbjaerg paints a unique visual landscape where the endless sunlight serves as a corollary to the glare of Skarsgård's own guilty conscience, a combo that robs him of sleep and makes his deceitful maneuvers seem all the more desperate. *Insomnia* rates as a tense treat for modern-thriller and mystery fans.

THE INTRUDER (1961) B&W ***1/2

D: Roger Corman. William Shatner, Frank Maxwell, Beverly Lansford, Leo Gordon. 80 mins. (Englewood)

A rare message movie from Roger Corman, *The Intruder* (a.k.a. *Shame, I Hate Your Guts!*) casts a young Shatner as an itinerant hatemonger who stirs up racial unrest in a small Southern town. Frequent *Twilight Zone* scribe Charles Beaumont scripted this intense civil-rights thriller and appears on-screen as a sympathetic high school teacher.

JACKIE BROWN (1997) ***

D: Quentin Tarantino. Pam Grier, Samuel L. Jackson, Robert De Niro, Robert Forster, Bridget Fonda, Michael Keaton, Chris Tucker, Michael Bowen, Sid Haig. 154 mins. (Miramax)

Tarantino, who seems to be coasting a mite here, makes some positive and negative choices in adapting Elmore Leonard's novel *Rum Punch* to the screen. In a high-concept decision, he recasts the white character of sympathetic, 44-year-old money-running stewardess Jackie Burke to the black (but otherwise unchanged) Jackie Brown, affording former "blaxploitation" queen and underrated actress Grier her best role in eons. In a somewhat less felicitous but relatively minor move, he shifts the action from Leonard's Florida home turf to Southern California. Some of his casting is positively uncanny—both De Niro, as oft dazed ex-con Louis, and especially Forster (in a career-reviving role), as world-weary bail bondsman Max, seem sprung to life literally intact from Leonard's pages. Jackson is, as always, excellent as pressured, motormouthed arms dealer Ordell, who needs Jackie to transport a considerable cash cache stashed in a Mexican bank. Trouble is, U.S. marshal Keaton and local lawman cohort Bowen have Jackie in their claws, and she's forced to make some hard choices to extricate herself from her double-bind situation. Tarantino also accomplishes the odd feat of assembling a long film from a short novel while simultaneously omitting some key celluloid-friendly scenes (most notably a subplot involving white supremacists) and slowing down the pace. The climactic, mall-set sting—somewhat confusing in both book *and* film—isn't milked for max suspense, and the wrap-up is surprisingly routine. Still, while not a great Leonard re-creation, *Jackie Brown* is a terrific actor's movie and easily rates as essential viewing on that level alone.

JOHNNY SKIDMARKS (1998) **½

D: John Raffo. Peter Gallagher, Frances McDormand, John Lithgow. 97 mins. (Columbia/TriStar)

A deft Gallagher stars as a cold-fish forensics photographer whose moonlighting gig as a blackmail-ring snapper lands him in big trubs in director/coscripter Raffo's intriguing but extremely gruesome and sadistic noir. Several lapses in genre logic also work to undermine the flick, but there's enough downbeat inventiveness and serious thematic explorations to keep the proceedings fairly compelling. *Fargo's* McDormand turns in a subdued perf as

an alcoholic divorcée with whom our damaged hero becomes entangled, while Lithgow saves his patented over-the-top moves for the final reel.

KALIFORNIA (1993) ***

D: Dominic Sena. Brad Pitt, Juliette Lewis, David Duchovny, Michelle Forbes, Sierra Pecheur, Gregory Mars Martin. In R and unrated editions. 117 mins. (PolyGram) DVD

A s a title, *Kalifornia* makes as little sense ("Killifornia" would be closer to it) as the pic's premise—that writer (future *X-Files* icon) Duchovny and photog Forbes would sooner share a ride in their Lincoln convertible with unstable redneck Pitt and pathetic squeeze Lewis than trade down for cheaper wheels. Petty logic aside, once veteran music-vid director Sena's feature debut gets rolling, it accelerates into a pretty fair serial-killer romp, with Pitt pulling out all the psycho stops.

KANSAS CITY CONFIDENTIAL (1952) B&W ***

D: Phil Karlson. John Payne, Coleen Gray, Preston Foster. 98 mins. (Goodtimes)

I ts title notwithstanding, nearly the entire film unfolds in Mexico (!), K.C. apparently having failed to measure up as a suitable celluloid-sin spot. Beyond that, noirmaster Karlson's caper is a tense, twisty, well-acted effort populated by such fine character mugs as Neville Brand, Jack Elam, and Lee Van Cleef.

THE KEEPER (1996) ***

D: Joe Brewster. Giancarlo Esposito, Regina Taylor, Isaach de Bankolé, Ron Brice, Victor Colicchio. 97 mins. (Kino)

E sposito plays Paul, a conscientious corrections officer at King's County House of Detention in Brooklyn. Paul's perils begin when he takes

pity on Haitian-immigrant prisoner Jean-Baptiste (Bankolé), an accused rapist our protagonist feels is innocent of that charge. After he rescues the ashamed inmate from a suicide attempt, Paul feels responsible for Jean-Baptiste, posting bail out of his own pocket and eventually sharing his modest Queens home with him. Paul regrets his generosity when he suspects his guest of using his charms (both of the personal and voodoo variety) to win over his schoolteacher wife, Angela (Taylor). Writer/director Brewster resists steering his organic, cleanly lensed, and impeccably performed pic in predictable directions, delivering instead a complex moral fable fueled by credible human emotions (a quality missing from so many contempo mainstream Hollywood films). Along the way, he grants us intimate peeks into the detention center's inner workings—where officers and inmates alike escape the usual stereotyping—a tour of some of Brooklyn's meaner streets, and an exotic Haitian-nightclub sequence.

KEY LARGO (1948) B&W ***½

D: John Huston. Humphrey Bogart, Edward G. Robinson, Lauren Bacall. 101 mins. (Fox)

J ohn Huston's sometimes mouthy but mostly masterful and ahead-of-its-time downbeat noir sees Edward G. (in top sneering form) and hoods put the squeeze on Bogie and Bacall at a storm-swept Florida Keys hotel.

KILL ME AGAIN (1989) ***

D: John Dahl. Joanne Whalley-Kilmer, Val Kilmer, Michael Madsen, Pat Mulligan, Bibi Besch. 94 mins. (MGM)

T hen-real-life husband and wife Kilmer and Whalley-Kilmer star as a down-and-out private dick and a bimbo femme fatale in Dahl's sturdy directorial debut. After Joanne and psycho partner Madsen rip off a mob courier for nearly a mil in hot bills, Joanne splits with the loot, her jilted beau in furious pursuit. Our antiheroine soon finds her way to Reno, where she hires a financially strapped Val to help her stage her own bogus murder. That's only the beginning of the complications in a deliberately paced but consistently absorbing tale that makes excellent use of the dusty glitter and surrounding expanse of its authentic Southwest locales.

THE KILLER ELITE   (1975) **1/2

D: Sam Peckinpah. James Caan, Robert Duvall, Arthur Hill, Bo Hopkins, Gig Young. 122 mins. (MGM) DVD

While not one of Peckinpah's pearls, *The Killer Elite* is still a serviceable big-budget B movie that finds rival soldiers of fortune Duvall and Caan at violent odds. It would have benefitted from a shorter running time and a bigger payoff. (Then again, so would most of us.)

THE KILLER INSIDE ME   (1976) **1/2

D: Burt Kennedy. Stacy Keach, Susan Tyrrell, Tisha Sterling, John Carradine. 99 mins. (Warner) DVD

Based on a book by cult noir novelist Jim Thompson, *The Killer Inside Me* features Keach at his psychotic best as a deputy sheriff suffering from homicidal impulses in Kennedy's occasionally cryptic adaptation. Keach fans might want to rent this with *The Ninth Configuration* (see index) for a "Spacy Stacy" demented double bill.

THE KILLERS   (1946) B&W ***1/2

D: Robert Siodmak. Burt Lancaster, Ava Gardner, Edmond O'Brien, Albert Dekker. 105 mins. (Universal)

Suspense master Siodmak's classic noir, based on an Ernest Heming-

way story (and with an uncredited script assist by John Huston), gave Lancaster his first major role, as a doomed ex-boxer targeted by ruthless hoods. Ronald Reagan, meanwhile, quit movies for politics after his rare turn as a screen heavy in Don Seigel's fair, if comparatively pale, 1964 remake, also titled *The Killers* (Universal), costarring Lee Marvin, John Cassavetes, and Angie Dickinson.

THE KILLING   (1956) B&W ****

D: Stanley Kubrick. Sterling Hayden, Coleen Gray, Marie Windsor. 83 mins. (MGM/UA) DVD

Kubrick crafts a classic, ahead-of-its-time caper flick, with Hayden and desperate cronies battling the odds to pull off a racetrack heist. Vince Edwards, Timothy Carey, James Edwards, and Elisha Cook, Jr., all contribute memorable supporting perfs.

THE KILLING GROUNDS (1998) **1/2

D: Kurt Anderson. Anthony Michael Hall, Cynthia Geary, Priscilla Barnes, Charles Rocket, Courtney Gains, Rodney A. Grant. 93 mins. (A-Pix) DVD

It's no *Treasure of the Sierra Madre,* wilderness *Reservoir Dogs,* or *A Simple Plan,* but direct-to-homevid vet Anderson's *The Killing Grounds* is sufficiently dark, tense, sadistic, and twisted to qualify as a reasonably compelling addition to the celluloid greed-fable ranks. An elaborate double cross gone awry results in the fatal deep-woods crash of a small plane carrying some $3 mil in stolen gold. Happening upon the cache are a quarreling couple (Barnes, Rocket), their Native American guide (Grant), and a backpacking secret player (Geary) in the caper. Their troubles begin when the original heist's seriously villainous masterminds— erstwhile John Hughes towhead Hall

and a gleefully psychotic, weasel-faced Gains—get wind of the doomed craft's whereabouts. At its best, *The Killing Grounds* plays like a mean, contempo spaghetti western. One breakthrough scene of sorts sees psycho Gains beat a man to death with his own prosthetic arm, upping a similarly pioneering moment from Ron Ormond's infamous 1968 sleaze/horror hybrid, *The Monster and the Stripper* (see index).

KILLING OBSESSION (1994) **1/2

D: Paul Leder. John Savage, John Saxon, Kimberly Chase, Bernard White, Hank Cheyne, Mitch Hara, Bobby DiCicco, Hyapatia Lee. 95 mins. (Triboro) DVD

On the scene—or at least the fringes—for over three decades, late exploitation auteur Paul (father of Mimi) Leder made a memorable debut with 1961's *The Rotten Apple,* available via Sinister Cinema as *Five Minutes to Love* (see index). Leder later achieved greater notoriety as a director whose credits included such snappily monikered madman movies as 1974's *I Dismember Mama* (Simitar) and 1984's *My Friends Need Killing* (n/a). The veteran helmer dramatically upped his output in the '90s, delivering direct-to-homevid epics like *Exiled in America* (Prism) and *Frame-Up* (Republic), both toplining Wings Hauser. (Leder long exhibited a propensity for working with the same thesps on different projects; in addition to Hauser, that lengthy list includes John Saxon, Greg Mullavey, Marilyn Hassett, Bobby DiCicco, Gary Werntz, Frances Fisher, and the late Dick Sargent. In both *The Baby Doll Murders* [Republic] and *Killing Obsession,* he even treats his cast to end-credit close-ups, à la the studio films of yore.)

With *Killing Obsession,* Leder returns to his frequent serial-killer concerns, assembling what shapes up as one of his more coherent, even compelling efforts, thanks partly to Savage's nearly autistic turn as Alan, a cross between Dustin Hoffman's Rain Man and Anthony Hopkins's Hannibal Lecter. We first encounter Alan, happily hallucinating dancing with and chastely romancing a bridal-gown-bedecked 11-year-old girl, prior to his release from the mental institution where he's been incarcerated since his mass-murder spree some 21 years earlier. Hospital head Saxon vehemently opposes the move and is proven right on Alan's very first night of freedom, when the career crazy slays an annoying desk clerk (Maurice Shrog) and an abusive pimp (DiCicco). The body count mounts as Alan, with the aid of the L.A. phone directory, conducts a methodical, *Terminator*-type search for "Annie Smith," the little girl seen in the opening scene, who's retained her status as a "symbol of purity" in Alan's warped mind. One "Annie Smith" turns out to be a professional drag queen (!), played by Mitch Hara, who manages to survive Savage's confused wrath. The real Annie, meanwhile, is now a 32-year-old fashion photog (Chase) who's as obsessed and haunted by Alan as he is by her. *Killing Obsession* is far from a great flick, but celluloid serial-killer scholars will want to tune in.

THE KILLING OF A CHINESE BOOKIE (1976) ***

D: John Cassavetes. Ben Gazzara, Timothy Agoglia Carey, Azizi Johari, Seymour Cassel, Morgan Woodward, Haji, Vince Barbi. 109 mins. (Touchstone) DVD

Cassavetes controls his self-indulgent impulses in this offbeat noir (some 17 minutes shorter than the original theatrical release, which probably helps). Gazzara is the proud owner of an oddball L.A. strip club, Crazy Horse West, that combines

contempo ecdysiast acts with anachronistic cabaret elements overseen by the melancholic "Mr. Sophistication" (Meade Roberts). Trouble ensues when our hero unwisely celebrates completing his final club payments by losing $23,000 at a Mafia-owned casino. To settle his debt, mobsters Woodward, Carey, and Cassel make Gazzara an offer he can neither refuse nor survive. Cassavetes's relatively simple story line plays equally well on the lyrical, visceral, visual (with California sunshine ever streaming through the windows of the darkened dens wherein Ben spends his days) and meditative levels. Russ Meyer regular Haji shows up as one of Gazzara's Crazy Horse gals.

THE KILL-OFF (1990) **½

D: Maggie Greenwald. Loretta Gross, Cathy Haase, Steven Monroe, Jordan Fox, Andrew Lee Barrett, William Russell, Jackson Sims. 100 mins. (Xenon)

The Kill-Off is a low-budget, downbeat, minimalist noir that's even less rock-'n'-roll (though more tinny sax) than the comparatively expansive Jim Thompson adaptation *After Dark, My Sweet* (see index). Our story, adapted by director Greenwald, unfolds in a seedy, burnt-out New Jersey beach town, where bedridden, poison-tongued phone gossip Gross causes no end of hassles for the local lowlifes, most of whom hold ongoing grudges against one another. A stripped-down *Blue Velvet* sans Lynch's surreal touches, *The Kill-Off* boasts authentically stark sets, believably beat-out thesps, and several slowly unfolding plot elements resourcefully united by film's end (changed from the novel). Other Jim Thompson screen translations include *Coup de Torchon* (New Yorker), *The Getaway*, *The Grifters*, and *The Killer Inside Me* (see index). Thompson also coscripted Stanley Kubrick's *The Killing* and *Paths of Glory*.

A KISS GOODNIGHT (1994) **½

D: Daniel Raskov. Al Corley, Paula Trickey, Mark Moses, Lawrence Tierney, Sydney Walsh, Brett Cullen, James Karen, Robert Wuhl. 88 mins. (Academy, n.i.d.)

A fairly compelling L.A.-set entry in the popular One-Night-Stand-from-Hell genre (see also 1977's *One Night Stand* [TWE], Talia Shire's 1995 *One Night Stand* [New Horizons], and Mike Figgis's 1997 *One Night Stand* [Warner]), *A Kiss Goodnight* stars an appealing Trickey as a foxy account exec whose ill-advised fling with psychotic lawyer Corley leads to a filmlong nightmare. Writer/director Raskov consistently keeps his erotic-thriller pot boiling well above room temp and gets convincing perfs from his cast, most notably endangered lead Trickey and Tierney as a hard-boiled cop. Comic actor Robert (*Arli$$*, *Batman Returns*) Wuhl contributes a mystifying cameo as a garage mechanic.

KISS ME DEADLY (1955) B&W ****

D: Robert Aldrich. Ralph Meeker, Albert Dekker, Paul Stewart, Cloris Leachman, Maxine Cooper. 108 mins. (MGM)

MGM presents a true treasure for noir fans with its *Kiss Me Deadly* reissue, which comes complete with the film's original trailer. Director Aldrich and scripter A. I. Bezzerides's bold reinvention of Mickey Spillane's Mike Hammer caper places the literally slaphappy sleuth (a nearly Cro-Mag Meeker) at the center of an ominous nuclear-conspiracy plot. The film ultimately offers a hyperparanoiac vision of a destructive new techno world that renders individual tough guys like Hammer helpless and obsolete. *Kiss* also featured one of the most shocking endings of its era; in this collector's edition, MGM follows that original ending with an 82-second alternate one that Aldrich reportedly preferred. Fortysomething years after its initial release, *Kiss Me Deadly* still packs a potent atomic punch.

KISS OF DEATH   (1995) ***½

D: Barbet Schroeder. David Caruso, Nicolas Cage, Samuel L. Jackson, Helen Hunt, Kathryn Erbe, Stanley Tucci, Michael Rapaport, Ving Rhames. 101 mins. (Fox)

Schroeder's *Kiss of Death* follows the plot of the original *Kiss of Death* (Fox, 1947), scripted by Ben Hecht and Charles Lederer from Eleanor Lipsky's story source, far more faithfully than another acknowledged remake—the terrif 1958 psycho western *The Fiend Who Walked the West* (n/a), starring future movie mogul Robert Evans in the title role. In addition, Richard (*Clockers*) Price's screenplay successfully updates the material and imbues it with a flavor and edge all its own. Though the original *Kiss* was also shot on NYC locations, Schroeder uses his actual locales to far more evocative advantage. Ex-*NYPD Blue* star Caruso offers a lower-keyed but still effective interpretation of Victor Mature's ex-con character, who's squeezed by both his former criminal cronies and the authorities' ever escalating demands. While Cage's perf as sociopathic thug Little Junior Brown lacks the impact of Richard Widmark's Tommy Udo—no fault of his own, since Widmark's timing couldn't be duplicated; he was the first psycho of his kind seen on-screen to that point—he wisely creates a more pent-up, literally asthmatic character who casually rationalizes his violent, often lethal outbursts. Price and Schroeder take a more cynical view of the law's motives, and Caruso, despite his past felonies, comes off as a more decent, code-bound, stand-up guy than any of the screen lawmen, with the possible exception of Jackson. *Kiss of Death* won't displace the original from its per-

manent niche as one of its era's most brutal noirs, but this taut, textured caper rates as the superior version of the vintage tale.

KISS THE GIRLS   (1997) ***

D: Gary Fleder. Morgan Freeman, Ashley Judd, Cary Elwes, Tony Goldwyn, Jay O. Sanders, Bill Nunn, Alex McArthur, Jeremy Piven. 117 mins. (Paramount) DVD

Director Fleder rebounds from his moribund *Things to Do in Denver When You're Dead* (Touchstone) with this at-times overly solemn but generally suspenseful serial-killer chiller drawn from James Patterson's novel. Sort of a *Se7en* Meets *The Collector*, *Kiss the Girls* benefits from a top cast, headed by ever reliable *Se7en* alum Freeman as a compassionate forensics psychologist determined to solve a baffling bicoastal case that includes his own niece among the victims. Judd turns in relatively tamped-down work as a fetching young kickboxing physician who escapes the masked killer's clutches and aids our hero in his complex investigation. There are a couple of scenes that defy motivational credibility, a common flaw in this popular subgenre, but *Kiss the Girls* offers enough shocks, suspense, and creepy flair to hoist it above most of the contempo serial-killer competition. No relation to the Aussie road noir *Kiss or Kill* (Universal).

KLUTE   (1971) ***

D: Alan J. Pakula. Jane Fonda, Donald Sutherland, Charles Cioffi, Roy Scheider. 114 mins. (Warner)

Jane's a sensitive, neurotic hooker being stalked by a buttoned-down psycho; Don's the earnest rube sheriff who comes to the big city to save her in an effective, textured thriller that's also sleazier than most mainstream fare of its era.

L.A. CONFIDENTIAL (1997) ***½

D: Curtis Hanson. Kevin Spacey, Russell Crowe, Kim Basinger, Guy Pearce, Danny DeVito, James Cromwell, David Strathairn, Jim Metzler, Matt McCoy. 136 mins. (Warner) DVD

Adapted from James Ellroy's novel, *L.A. Confidential* rates as superior, intricately plotted, superbly crafted pulp fare. Spacey, Crowe, and Pearce are all effective as three flawed cops who find their own reasons to investigate a crime wave that may be spreading from within their own ranks. Cromwell turns in award-worthy work as the wily precinct captain, while Basinger fares reasonably well in the far more rote role of a golden-hearted hooker in the employ of sleaze mogul Strathairn, who runs a call-girl service specializing in celeb look-alikes (Kim's his Veronica Lake model). Hollywood references abound. In one scene, "Hollywood cop" Spacey—official consultant on the fictional *Dragnet*-drawn TV show *Badge of Honor* (with frequent B lead Matt McCoy cast as a Jack Webb doppelgänger)—and scandal rag publisher/photog DeVito set up a pot bust near a theater where *When Worlds Collide* is preeming. Another key scene unfolds in a bar adjacent to a bijou where *The Bad and the Beautiful* is the current attraction. Brief clips from *The Blue Dahlia* and *Roman Holiday* are also on view. Lana Turner (portrayed by Brenda Bakke) puts in a cameo when cops Spacey and Pearce's path crosses with Johnny Stompanato, the real-life thug slain by Turner's teenage daughter in 1957; a self-righteous Pearce mistakes her for one of Strathairn's celeb sluts. Unfortunately, yours truly suffers from a chronic aural allergy to the era's cloying pop tunes, like "Accentuate the Positive" and "Wheel of Fortune," though they're cleverly integrated here. In a *New York Times* item, director Hanson accused Warner of mismarketing the flick, which, despite its considerable critical acclaim and crowd-pleasing elements, failed to rack up powerhouse numbers.

THE LADY FROM SHANGHAI (1948) B&W ***

D: Orson Welles. Rita Hayworth, Orson Welles, Everett Sloane. 87 mins. (Columbia/TriStar)

Welles's visually dizzying (see the climactic hall of mirrors scene) pulp thriller packs enough perverse touches (such as one character's all-consuming A-bomb paranoia) and charismatic perfs to camouflage the fact that the story line's fairly routine.

LADY IN A CAGE (1964) B&W ***½

D: Walter Grauman. Olivia de Havilland, James Caan, Joan Blondell. 93 mins. (Paramount)

Caan makes his film debut in this sleaze classic as the lowlife leader of a trio of thugs who torture hapless rich lady de Havilland, who archly observes, "You're one of the many bits of offal produced by the welfare state. You're what so many of my tax dollars go to the care and feeding of!" Second only to *Kitten with a Whip* (n/a) as the best A-level trash movie of 1964.

LADY KILLER (1997) **½

D: Terence H. Winkless. Ben Gazzara, Alex McArthur, Stephen Davis, Terri Treas, Rick Dean. 81 mins. (New Horizons)

Gazzara is excellent as a veteran, currently desk-bound cop conducting his own discreet investigation into a slate of femme slayings perped by the unknown "Piggy-Bank Killer," so named for his trademark M.O. of stuffing his victims with force-fed coins and placing pennies on their sightless eyes (did we mention he also

BEN THERE, DONE THAT: Ben Gazzara guns for errant psycho in derivative but lively serial-killer thriller *Lady Killer.*
Courtesy of Concorde–New Horizons Corp.

takes time to shear off their faces?). Unemployed actor Richard Darling (McArthur, who portrayed a truly chilling psycho in William Friedkin's *Rampage*) becomes a major suspect in the case, and it's his and Gazzara's edgy chemistry that helps hoist *Lady Killer* above the usual run of direct-to-homevid psycho *policiers. Lady Killer* effectively keeps the fiend's identity in doubt throughout and, in its own unwholesome way, conveys a more verité feel than bigger-budgeted serial-killer rivals like *Copycat* (see index) and *Jennifer 8* (Paramount). No relation to 1993's *Ladykiller* (Universal), with Mimi Rogers, or the pluralized *Ladykillers* (Prism), a made-for-TV male-strip-club thriller with Marilu Henner, Susan Blakely, and Lesley-Anne Downe.

LAST BREATH (1998) **

D: P. J. Posner. Luke Perry, Francie Swift, Gia Carides, Gary Basaraba, Jack Gilpin. 90 mins. (A-Pix) DVD

Married high school teacher Perry lusts after Realtor Carides because she sports a great set of lungs (!) and he wants them transplanted into

his dying wife (Swift) in a creepily effective but relentlessly downbeat medical soaper/thriller combo. As initially established, Perry's character would seem incapable of carrying out the elaborate murder scheme sketched here, while the fragile Swift also undergoes an unlikely change of heart (to say nothing of lungs). Still, fans of slick, literally sick thrillers and *ER* addicts might enjoy.

THE LAST DAYS OF FRANKIE THE FLY (1996) **½

D: Peter Markle. Dennis Hopper, Kiefer Sutherland, Daryl Hannah, Michael Madsen, Dayton Callie. 96 mins. (Cabin Fever)

Hopper scores a shiny showcase role as veteran mob gofer "Frankie the Fly" in an uneven but ultimately involving slice of L.A. lowlife intricately scripted by actor Callie, who doubles on-screen as a gang enforcer. Frankie gets in trouble when he covers for gambling addict/NYU film-school grad Joey (Sutherland), forced to direct low-level porn vids to pay off his debts to Mafioso honcho Sal (Madsen). The essentially decent, old-fashioned

Frankie also develops a major crush on junkie porn "starlet" Margaret (Hannah, stretching here in a variety of B&D outfits), who wants to be a serious actress. Frankie, meanwhile, in a scaled-down variation of the hoods in *Get Shorty* (see index), gets bitten by the movie bug and vows to write a script designed to show off Margaret's "talents." This alternately whimsical and brutal pic mostly succeeds in putting a fresh twist on the over-worked modern-noir genre and rates as a significant step up for veteran director Markle, whose less-than-glittering previous credits range from *Hot Dog: The Movie* to *Wagons East*.

THE LAST SEDUCTION (1994) ***1/2

D: John Dahl. Linda Fiorentino, Peter Berg, Bill Pullman, Bill Nunn, J. T. Walsh. 110 mins. (PolyGram) DVD

Fiorentino, who paid her dues in duds like *Vision Quest* and *Gotcha!*, finally gets her due via her icepick-sharp perf as the ultimate femme fatale. Linda didn't land an Oscar nod due to a much publicized technicality—that director Dahl's twisty modern noir debuted on cable TV before scoring big-screen venues, thus disqualifying it as a theatrical film. (A related fate befell Dahl's previous venture, the highly, if belatedly, acclaimed *Red Rock West*.) Supported by a tight script, atmospheric direction and a high-caliber cast, Linda shines as the errant spouse of drug-dealing doc Pullman, absconding with his ill-gotten gains and hiding out in a nondescript small town. Linda's too scam-addicted to simply hide out, however, and assuming a new identity, she embroils smitten local Berg in a fresh scheme that eventually loops back to her earlier exploits. Despite occasional *Body Heat* echoes, *The Last Seduction* shapes up as thoroughly arresting fare. The relentlessly politically incorrect Linda, who likes booze, cigarettes, and zipless sex, com-

pletely dominates the proceedings. Fiorentino returned for the "erotic thriller" dud *Jade* (Paramount).

LET HIM HAVE IT (1991) ***1/2

D: Peter Medak. Christopher Eccleston, Paul Reynolds, Tom Bell, Eileen Atkins, Clare Holman, Tom Courtenay. 115 mins. (New Line)

Based on an infamous case that took place in England in the early '50s, *Let Him Have It* stars Eccleston as a basically decent, slow-witted kid who falls in with a wild teen crowd of would-be toughs fond of aping American gangster movies. (One scene shows them going off to watch the Cagney classic *White Heat*.) When one of the other boys turns trigger-happy, it's Eccleston who winds up in the dock, facing execution for a killing he didn't commit. Director Medak not only transforms this real-life incident into a compelling suspense film but paints a vivid picture of lower-middle-class life in postwar England. Eccleston is haunting as the unlucky victim of British "justice," while Courtenay is quietly brilliant as his grief-stricken dad.

LIES (1983) ***

D: Ken and Jim Wheat. Ann Dusenberry, Gail Strickland, Bruce Davison, Clu Gulager, Terence Knox, Bert Remsen, Dick Miller. 98 mins. (Key)

The Wheats' stylish low-budget thriller bears a passing resemblance to *Dead of Winter* (which it predates): An actress (Dusenberry) is hired, under false pretenses, to impersonate a mental patient traumatized by the murder of her parents. It's all part of an elaborate inheritance scam, a plot hoary at heart but enlivened here by enough fresh twists, suspenseful pacing, and earnest performances by a more-than-capable cast to make it a minor homevideo winner. The elevator

scene alone is worth the price of a rental.

THE LIGHTSHIP (1985) **1/2

D: Jerzy Skolimowski. Robert Duvall, Klaus Maria Brandauer, Michael Lyndon, William Forsythe. 89 mins. (Fox)

Effete criminal Duvall (in an entertainingly idiosyncratic turn) and goons confront accused-coward captain Brandauer aboard the title vessel. *The Lightship*, based on a story by Siegfried Lenz, is less than profound as a morality play but fairly seaworthy as a '50s-style B thriller that happened to be filmed three decades later.

LITTLE FUGITIVE (1953) B&W ***

D: Ray Ashley, Morris Engel, Ruth Orkin. Richie Andrusco, Rickie Brewster, Winifred Cushing. 80 mins. (Kino) DVD

The debut feature film of still photographers Morris Engel and Ruth Orkin, this Brooklyn-set neorealist indie relates the odyssey of seven-year-old Joey (Andrusco), who's tricked into believing he fatally shot his older brother Lennie (Brewster) while mom Cushing was away. Joey flees to nearby Coney Island, and most of the movie charts his picaresque adventures at the famed amusement park. Andrusco brings a good deal of raw charm to his naturalistic perf, but the pic's real strength lies in Engel and Orkin's oft striking compositions, images that betray their still-photography roots. While the loose narrative runs out of steam a bit before reuniting our young hero with his fretful, regretful sibling, *Little Fugitive* works as a moving album of a flavorful period and place. Kino also released the Engel/Orkin team's more drama-driven feature *Lovers and Lollipops* (1955), with Gerald O'Loughlin and Lori March, and Engel's 1958 solo film, *Weddings and Babies*, starring Viveca Lindfors and John Myhers.

LIVING IN PERIL (1997) ***

D: Jack Ersgard. Rob Lowe, James Belushi, Dana Wheeler-Nicholson, Alex Meneses, Dean Stockwell, Richard Moll, Patrick Ersgard. 95 mins. (New Line)

It's no Polanski's *The Tenant,* but if you buy into extreme urban-terror tales that suspensefully up the paranoid ante, *Living In Peril* rates as a good bet. Lowe projects credible anxiety as an architect who drives from Seattle to a bullying L.A. on a temp assignment. He encounters trouble on the freeway when he locks horns with an obstreperous truck driver who runs him off the road. Next he rents an apartment where the irascible manager (Stockwell) won't help him, and the tenants—East German would-be stand-up comic (and coscripter) Ersgard, call-girl-next-door Meneses—won't leave him alone to get his work done. Abrasive, cigar-chewing client Belushi is unhappy with Lowe's architectural efforts, while back home Rob's pregnant wife's (Wheeler-Nicholson) shadowy ex is aggressively threatening her. Rob, too, receives phone threats; rats invade his lair; and a mysterious intruder in an S&M mask steals in one night and breaks his toe (!). Rob naturally suspects the offended trucker, but the situation may be graver than that. *Living in Peril* plays out its nightmare tale with considerable dark wit.

LIVING TO DIE (1990) **½

D: Wings Hauser. Wings Hauser, Darcy DeMoss, Asher Brauner, Arnold Vosloo. 84 mins. (PM)

Hauser makes his directorial debut with this fairly solid modern noir set in Las Vegas's neon jungle. Normally kinetic actor Wings contributes a relatively restrained turn here as an ex-cop who helps corrupt gaming commissioner Brauner cope with a lowlife attempting to blackmail him for a murder he didn't commit. The plot quickly thickens when shapely alleged slay victim DeMoss turns

up alive and well enough to seduce our hero. The pic's low budget occasionally hinders the proceedings, but auteur Hauser displays a deft visual sense, the story's gray tones make *Living to Die* more morally complex than most of its ilk, and a low-key musical score helps establish a quietly unnerving mood.

LONE STAR (1996) ***½

D: John Sayles. Kris Kristofferson, Chris Cooper, Elizabeth Pena, Matthew McConaughey, Frances McDormand, Ron Canada, Clifton James, Joe Morton. 137 mins. (Columbia/TriStar)

When human bones and a rusty badge are discovered in a shallow desert grave, the case of the mysterious 1957 disappearance of corrupt, bullying local sheriff Kristofferson is reopened. Scripter Sayles uses the mystery angle to etch a complex portrait of a multiethnic Texas town's interweaving intrigues over nearly 40 years. Director Sayles gets uniformly fine performances from his large, diverse ensemble cast, particularly Sayles regular Cooper as a low-key contempo lawman investigating the case, Canada as a black club-owner who played a central role in the original incident, and erstwhile *Brother from Another Planet* Morton as a military officer newly returned to his former hometown after a long, estranged absence. McDormand enjoys a brief but resonant bit as Cooper's boozing, football-addicted ex-wife; McConaughey plays Cooper's strong-willed deputy dad in several flashbacks. *Lone Star* offers what shapes up today as a reel rarity—137 minutes of pure storytelling pleasure.

LOST HIGHWAY (1997) **

D: David Lynch. Bill Pullman, Patricia Arquette, Balthazar Getty, Robert Blake, Robert Loggia, Gary Busey. 135 mins. (PolyGram)

Lynch and cowriter Barry Gifford, who took to the road with swifter

results in *Wild at Heart,* seem to be spinning their wheels with *Lost Highway.* Tedium subs for mood, pretentiousness for inspiration, and contrivance for surprise in too many stretches of this surreal nightmare noir with a *Jacob's Ladder* hook. Floating identities, intertwined destinies, sexual obsession, betrayal, and even snuff-moviemaking pave a twisted path best taken by Lynch completists and video rubberneckers. Blake turns in effectively quirky work as a grinning, pint-sized Grim Reaper with a camcorder, while the oddball supporting cast includes cameos by a wheelchair-bound Richard Pryor, mock-shock-rocker Marilyn Manson, John Waters regular Mink Stole, and the late Jack *(Eraserhead)* Nance. For more on Lynch, scope out the feature-length documentary *Pretty As a Picture: The Art of David Lynch* (Fox Lorber).

LOVE AND HUMAN REMAINS (1993) ***

D: Denys Arcand. Thomas Gibson, Ruth Marshall, Cameron Bancroft, Mia Kirshner, Joanne Vannicola, Matthew Ferguson, Rick Roberts. 100 mins. (Columbia/TriStar)

French-Canadian auteur Denys *(Jesus of Montreal)* Arcand's mostly riveting screen translation of scripter Brad Fraser's play *Unidentified Human Remains and the True Nature of Love* chronicles the intertwining destinies of a group of gay, straight, and bi thirty-something Canadians groping (often literally) for love, meaning, and the next bottle of beer. An unnecessary serial-killer angle constitutes the weakest element of Arcand's and Fraser's otherwise sharply written, directed, and performed black comedy.

LOVE, CHEAT & STEAL (1993) ***

D: William Curran. John Lithgow, Eric Roberts, Madchen Amick, Richard Edson, Donald Moffat, David Ackroyd, Dan O'Herlihy. 95 mins. (Columbia/TriStar)

With it's A– cast and derivative *sex, lies & videotape*–inspired title, *LC&S* would appear to be little more than a relatively high-end cable-TV time-killer. Instead, writer/director Curran's caper flaunts a hard edge, embodied by escaped con/killer Roberts, who fulfills a lovingly nurtured revenge scheme when he tracks down ex-spouse and partner in crime Amick, who set him up some seven years earlier. Now wed to respectable banker Lithgow (in a smart, restrained perf), Amick supplies Roberts and lowlife techno-expert sidekick Edson with an ideal heist opportunity. Lithgow, meanwhile, learns his bank is a holding tank for laundered Colombian coke money. *LC&S* offers incisive character studies without sacrificing pace and neatly resolves its converging plot threads.

LOVERS   (1991) **½

D: Vicente Aranda. Victoria Abril, Jorge Sanz, Maribel Verdú. Subtitled. 105 mins. (Worldvision)

Aranda's "true-life story" is an eroti-cized crime caper that garnered overrated reviews during its American art-house run. Sanz plays a recently discharged soldier who takes temporary leave of his betrothed—pretty but mundane maid Verdú—ostensibly to make his fortune in Madrid. Instead, he hooks up with landlady Abril, a sneaky seductress who introduces him to true passion while embroiling him in her illicit financial affairs. Unlike most American erotic thrillers, *Lovers,* while at times more explicit, decreases its celluloid sex content on the way to a bleak denouement.

M   (1931) B&W ***½

D: Fritz Lang. Peter Lorre, Ellen Widmann, Inga Landgut, Gustaf Gundgrens. 111 mins. (Home Vision) DVD

Lorre is at once pathetic and chilling in Lang's grimly brilliant story of a child murderer whose reckless rampage arouses the ire of Berlin's underworld, leading to an unforgettable "trial" sequence. Home Vision's definitive, digitally remastered edition restores 12 minutes of footage missing from *M*'s previous cassette incarnations. *M* was remade in 1951 (n/a), with David Wayne in the Lorre role, and "inspired" Ulli Lommel's 1973 *Tenderness of the Wolves* (Anchor Bay, DVD).

MADIGAN   (1968) ***

D: Don Siegel. Richard Widmark, Henry Fonda, Inger Stevens, Harry Guardino. 101 mins. (Universal) DVD

Widmark turns in strong work as a weary NYPD detective up against a cunning psycho (the late Steve Ihnat) in Siegel's gritty *policier,* evocatively shot on locations, and boasting a top supporting cast led by Fonda.

THE MANCHURIAN CANDIDATE (1962) B&W ****

D: John Frankenheimer. Frank Sinatra, Laurence Harvey, Janet Leigh, Angela Lansbury, James Gregory, Henry Silva, Khigh Dhiegh. 126 mins. (MGM/UA) DVD

Frankenheimer's blackly comic thriller, based on the Richard Condon novel, seems even more surreal, perverse, and brilliantly sick when measured against most slick but comparatively pale contemporary fare. Highlights include one of the screen's earliest all-out karate battles, between Sinatra (then a merely Middle-Aged Blue Eyes) and consummate movie villain Silva; a train scene wherein Frank and Leigh "meet weird," featuring one of the greatest non sequitur exchanges ever scripted; and, of course, the central premise itself, which finds oedipal wreck and bogus "war hero" Harvey operating as an unwitting assassin for the International Commie Conspiracy. ("His brain hasn't just been *washed,*" laughs jovial Pavlov Institute heavy Dhiegh, "it's been *dry-cleaned.*") Gregory and Lansbury also contribute key turns as a McCarthy-esque senator and his Machiavellian spouse, while Sinatra's final two words succinctly convey the film's ultimate message (and we couldn't agree with it more). The video version includes a 12-minute docu segment, in which Sinatra, Frankenheimer, and scripter George Axelrod discuss the making of the film.

MANHUNTER   (1986) ***½

D: Michael Mann. William Petersen, Kim Greist, Dennis Farina, Brian Cox, Joan Allen, Stephen Lang, Tom Noonan. 120 mins. (Warner)

Unlike many of the '80s spate of glossy, high-tech noirs (*To Live and Die in L.A.,* on Artisan, *8 Million Ways to Die,* on Fox, et al.), Mann's *Silence of the Lambs* precursor doesn't substitute style for substance but brings considerable visual flair to a complex story line (adapted from the Thomas Harris novel *Red Dragon*). Petersen is ex-FBI agent Will Graham, recovering from severe physical and psychic wounds inflicted by now incarcerated psycho Hannibal ("the Cannibal") Lecter (Cox, in the role Anthony Hopkins would later immortalize). When Graham is wooed from his idyllic Captiva, Florida, home and family to help fed Farina decipher clues left by a new serial killer, the former agent is forced to confront both the madman and the latent psychoses simmering within himself. *Manhunter* thus provides viewers with two levels of tension and explores both without resorting to sensationalism or pretentiousness. A chilly but memorable, brutal and disturbing thriller.

MASQUERADE   (1988) ***

D: Bob Swaim. Rob Lowe, Meg Tilly, Kim Cattrall, Doug Savant, John Glover, Dana Delany. 91 mins. (Fox)

Murder among the monied Hamptons set serves as the premise for a twisty mystery by erstwhile ex-expatriate auteur Bob *(La Balance)* Swaim, who manages to squeeze considerable suspense from potentially routine material. Glover contributes another memorable evil turn as Tilly's abusive stepdad.

MEPHISTO (1981) ***1/2

D: Istvan Szabo. Klaus Maria Brandauer, Krystyna Janda, Karin Boyd. Subtitled. 144 mins. (Republic)

Brandauer makes for a charismatic antihero as a vain actor who unwisely remains in a genocidal (and self-cannibalizing) Nazi Germany in order to improve his professional status in Szabo's brilliant and scary adaptation of the Klaus Mann novel.

MISBEGOTTEN (1998) **1/2

D: Mark L. Lester. Kevin Dillon, Nick Mancuso, Lysette Anthony. 97 mins. (Trimark)

Adapted by scripter Larry Cohen from James Gabriel Berman's novel, *Misbegotten* plays like an even grottier variation on Cohen's 1996 pregnancy thriller, *Invasion of Privacy* (Trimark). In that one, maniac Johnathon Schaech impregnates and imprisons hapless spouse Mili Avital. Here sexually dysfunctional killer Dillon murders and impersonates a sperm donor; his genetic contribution goes to artificially inseminate upscale art-gallery worker Anthony, wed to infertile yacht designer Mancuso. Donor Dillon proceeds to stalk celluloid hysteria-specialist Lysette in a bid to convince her to ditch Nick for him. While Cohen delved into serious political issues with *Invasion,* he steers his similar plot in a far pulpier direction here, with Dillon embarking on a rampage that results in a *Se7en*-styled decapitation scene and a wholesale police slaughter (where director Lester dusts off his action

chops), leading to a final twist involving a cynical medical deception. *Misbegotten* provides enough shocks and surprises to edify Cohen completists.

MISERY (1990) ***

D: Rob Reiner. James Caan, Kathy Bates, Frances Sternhagen, Lauren Bacall, Richard Farnsworth, Graham Jarvis, J. T. Walsh. 107 mins. (Columbia/TriStar) DVD

Reiner's clever but unobtrusive direction—we especially enjoyed a typing montage keyed to a Liberace medley (!), sort of the dark side of Jerry Lewis's old musical-typewriter routine—keeps the story in tight focus as deranged fan Bates rescues and cares for seriously injured romance author Caan at her secluded Colorado redoubt. When crazy fat Kathy learns that Caan has killed off her fave fictional character, Misery Chastain, in his latest book, her formerly worshipful attitude goes all "oogie" and she subjects the captive novelist to unending abuse. Especially horrifying is a scene wherein Kathy makes J.C. burn the lone copy of his latest manuscript, a serious non-Misery novel that K.B. deems offensive. Next she forces him to return Misery to "life" by writing a new installment and whacks his feet with a sledgehammer (!) to prevent him from shirking his work. (It was at this point that The Phantom deduced that the short-tempered, tunnel-visioned Kathy is less a stand-in for overly rabid fandom than for the publishing industry itself and, by extension, the mass media in general.) In any case, Bates is thoroughly believable as the fanatical femme, while Caan does a good job handling the strenuous physical chores his role demands. (Maybe it's all a belated celluloid karmic payback for his bad behavior in his film debut, *Lady in a Cage.*) Bacall, herself the target of latently lethal admirer Michael Biehn in 1981's *The Fan* (Paramount), appears as Caan's agent.

MOMMY: THE SERIES

MOMMY (1995) ***

D: Max Allan Collins. Patty McCormack, Rachel Lemieux, Jason Miller, Brinke Stevens, Majel Barrett, Sarah Jane Miller, Mickey Spillane. 89 mins. (M.A.C./Eagle) DVD

Writer Collins's directorial debut, an entry in the popular mad-mater subgenre, doesn't quite match John Waters's *Serial Mom* but scores well above such other recent efforts as *Mom* (Columbia/TriStar) and *Ed and His Dead Mother* (Fox). The *Bad Seed* of yore returns as a crazed mom with a normal (though understandably anxious) daughter, convincingly played by young Lemieux. Miller, who made his movie mark battling *The Exorcist's* Linda Blair, portrays a dogged local detective who suspects that Pat's behind the recent rash of lethal accidents plaguing Rachel's grade school. Veteran scream queen Stevens stretches in a fully clothed role as Patty's kindly younger sister and Rachel's empathetic aunt, while Spillane cameos as Pat's lawyer and long-time *Trek*ker Barrett appears as one of Pat's victims. *Mommy* registers more strongly as a dysfunctional-family melodrama with a deadpan darkly comic edge than as a straight-ahead thriller: Patty's actually more chilling when she's behaving "normally" than when she's killing.

MOMMY 2: MOMMY'S DAY (1996) **1/2

D: Max Allan Collins. Patty McCormack, Paul Petersen, Gary Sandy, Brinke Stevens, Rachel Lemieux, Mickey Spillane, Allen Dean Snyder, Michael Cornelison, Sarah Jane Miller. 89 mins. (Eagle) DVD

Collins serves up a fresh Patty Mac Attack, lensed, like the original, in the wilds of Muscatine, Iowa. The sequel sees convicted "Killer Mommy"

PATTY McCORMACK
Academy Award®-nominated star of *THE BAD SEED* returns as
mommy

Jason Miller
THE EXORCIST

Mickey Spillane
MIKE HAMMER

Majel Barrett
STAR TREK

Brinke Stevens
HAUNTING FEAR

Never let her tuck you in!

PAT'S ENTERTAINMENT!: Actress Patty McCormack goes full circle, from *The Bad Seed*'s psycho tyke to mad mater in Max Allan Collins's *Mommy* and sequel *Mommy 2: Mommy's Day. Courtesy of Max Allan Collins*

McCormack escape her court-ordered execution when she's wounded in a failed breakout bid. In the intervening year, physician Cornelison has convinced the courts to let Patty live in a halfway house as long as she agrees to accept a violence-controlling implant of his own design. Pat's also forbidden to speak with her beloved daughter (Lemieux), whom she nearly succeeded in strangling at the end of *Mommy*. Lemieux is now the ward of Pat's sister (Stevens), who's since married Petersen, a true-crime author who

made a mint writing a "Killer Mommy" book based on Pat's bloody exploits. When Pat violates her parole by clandestinely visiting with Lemieux, those standing in her way again start turning up dead. (There's even a death-by-word-processor sequence that yours truly could relate to, though ours proceeds at a slower pace.) Genre buffs may also want to scope out the soundtrack CD, where both Patty and Paul get to croon tunes ("If Life Was Fair" and "Little Ice Princess," respectively), while multithreat Collins

sings and handles keyboard chores on "Shockabilly," a ditty of his own composition.

MONIQUE (1979) *1/2

D: Jacques Scandelari. Florence Giorgetti, John Ferris, Barry Woloski, Sonia Petrovna, Todd Isaacson, Pierre Zimmer. 96 mins. (VCL/Media, n.i.d.)

Monique (Giorgetti, of *The Lacemaker* semi-fame) is a lonely 35-year-old trust funder and literary editor alive and unwell in NYC, where she's haunted by traumatic B&W flashbacks involving her mother's accidental shooting death some three decades earlier. Monique complains to her shrink that she wants a spouse and child. She marries an ambitious young artist who specializes in grotesque baby paintings. He's also gay. When Monique discovers this fact, she freaks out and embarks on a slay spree in Greenwich Village's gay bars and waterfront trysting sites (!). The film is supposedly based on an actual case, and the epilogue informs us that, after eight years of incarceration, the homicidal homophobe "now teaches yoga in a small city in the center of France." This ponderous Eurotrash slasher obscurity features a score by former disco kingpin Jacques Morali, the man who gave us the Village People.

MORTAL PASSIONS (1990) **

D: Andrew Lane. Zach Galligan, Krista Errickson, Michael Bowen, Luca Bercovici, David Warner, Sheila Kelley. 96 mins. (Fox)

Galligan is a rich young depressed wimp wed to conniving slut Errickson, who plots with lowlife beau Bercovici to zap Zach for his inheritance dough. Though far from credible, *Mortal Passions* is rarely less than watchable, largely due to several entertainingly bad performances and a script that leans as much on soap-opera histrionics as it does on noir conventions. The movie's ultimate message, meanwhile, is conveyed by golden-hearted bimbo Kelley, who sympathizes with the beleaguered Zach's potentially fatal plight: "No matter how bad things might be at home, no one expects to get killed for it."

MORTAL THOUGHTS   (1991)**¹/₂

D: Alan Rudolph. Demi Moore, Bruce Willis, Glenne Headly. 104 mins. (Columbia/TriStar) DVD

Lowlife crackhead Willis croons "Kung-Fu Fighting." Abused spouse Demi commits justifiable homicide. Cop Keitel investigates in what may be the best Bayonne-set movie ever made.

MOTHER'S BOYS   (1994)***

D: Yves Simoneau. Jamie Lee Curtis, Peter Gallagher, Joanne Whalley-Kilmer, Luke Edwards, Vanessa Redgrave, Joss Ackland. 96 mins. (Buena Vista) DVD

Simoneau's effective oedipal thriller relies more on emotional terrorism than on physical violence. Curtis turns in strong work as the lean, unbalanced ice queen who wants to reunite with ex-mate Gallagher, now involved with local teacher Whalley-Kilmer, and their three sons, most passionately eldest boy Edwards. Curtis adopts so alienating a style that even her own mom (Redgrave) dislikes her, while Jocko the Dog (played by a professional canine named John) also maintains an air of healthy suspicion. The pic veers into some fairly perverse turf with Curtis's methodical "seduction" of young Edwards—she even flashes him under the guise of showing him her cesarean scars (!)—and succeeds in building a general atmosphere of hysteria. *Mother's Boys'* combo of cheap suspense, raw emotions, and high camp make for an entertaining 96 minutes.

MURDER AT 1600 (1997)**¹/₂

D: Dwight Little. Wesley Snipes, Diane Lane, Alan Alda, Ronny Cox, Dennis Miller, Daniel Benzali, Harris Yulin. 107 mins. (Warner) DVD

When a fetching blond worker turns up dead at the titular address an hour after having sex with president Cox's playboy son, suspicion naturally points to a sensitive area. The fatality's timing—in the midst of a tense North Korean hostage situation—also raises eyebrows, hackles, and questions galore. Investigating D.C. cop Snipes (who comports himself with his usual highly watchable, low-key charisma) feels he's receiving less than the government's full cooperation. Ultimately, he and Secret Serviceperson Lane find themselves on the trail of a more sinister conspiracy, leading to the expected chase sequences and a climactic scene of presidential endangerment. While suffering from a serious credibility gap, *Murder* is reasonably entertaining most of the way, though we much prefer films wherein smarmmeister Dennis Miller's character gets killed—(e.g., *Never Talk to Strangers, The Net*)—and his mere wounding here arrived as a bit of a disappointment.

MURDER AT THE VANITIES   (1934) B&W***

D: Mitchell Leisen. Jack Oakie, Kitty Carlisle, Victor McLaglen, Toby Wing, Duke Ellington. 89 mins. (Universal)

McLaglen is a tough shamus on the trail of a backstage murderer in a stranger-than-usual all-star mystery, highlighted by musical numbers like "Ebony Rhapsody" and the one-of-a-kind "Sweet Marihuana." For more vintage backstage thrills, scope out William Wellman's surprisingly racy 1943 Gypsy Rose Lee–based mystery, *Lady of Burlesque* (Englewood).

MURDER BY CONTRACT   (1958) B&W***¹/₂

D: Irving Lerner. Vince Edwards, Phillip Pine, Herschel Bernardi. 81 mins. (Goodtimes)

Lerner's excellent, thoroughly offbeat low-budget noir casts Edwards as a self-made hit man who likes philosophizing even more than killing. Pine and Bernardi make for a memorable team of syndicate underlings assigned to chaperone Edwards as he preps for a major assassination. Filled with idiosyncratic dialogue and situations, *Murder* is the best of several B's—e.g., *City of Fear, The Scavengers* (both n/a)—toplining Edwards before he moved on to tube stardom as Ben Casey. The Goodtimes transfer quality is quite good, despite its LP mode, but don't read the box synopsis, which gives away the entire last reel (!).

MURDER, MY SWEET   (1944) B&W***

D: Edward Dmytryk. Dick Powell, Claire Trevor, Mike Mazurki. 95 mins. (Media/Critics' Choice)

Powell is a persuasive Philip Marlowe in Dmytryk's atmospheric adaptation of the Raymond Chandler novel *Farewell My Lovely*. The film was remade in 1975, under Chandler's original title, with Robert Mitchum as Marlowe (Artisan).

MURDER ONE   (1988)***

D: Graeme Campbell. Henry Thomas, James Wilder, Stephen Shellen, Errol Slue. 86 mins. (Nelson, n.i.d.)

Based on a true story, Campbell's *Murder One* stars an almost-grown Henry (*E.T.*) Thomas as a basically decent teen who unwisely tags along with his trashy escaped-con brothers (Wilder and Shellen), who embark on a series of mindless thrill killings that culminate in the massacre of an entire rural Georgia clan. (Several Georgia theaters refused to book the film during its brief theatrical release.) While director Campbell doesn't shed much light on the murderers' motivations, Wilder and Shellen turn in convincing work as the lowlife gunmen, as does Slue as a fellow escapee who wants no part of the slaughter but can't flee the killers' company. Thomas's character remains the murkiest of the quartet, functioning mostly as a passive witness to the brutal proceedings. Campbell directs his simple but suspenseful story in an admirably clean, lean style, and *Murder One* stacks up as a solid B thriller.

MURDERERS ARE AMONG US (1946) B&W ***

D: Wolfgang Staudte. Hildegard Knef, Ernst Wilhelm Borchert, Erna Sellmer, Arno Paulsen. Subtitled. 84 mins. (Kino)

The first German film to deal with national war guilt, *Murderers Are Among Us*, lensed (with the occasional expressionistic flourish) amid the ruins of postwar Berlin, effectively conveys a pervasive sense of social and moral disorientation. When a fetching Knef returns home from a concentration camp (apparently her late father had been targeted as a dissident), she finds her apartment has been rented to a wild-eyed lush (Borchert) who, it turns out, was a surgeon who'd served during the war but has since lost his faith. The pair agree to share the pad and help each other heal, a process that ultimately leads to romance. Borchert, meanwhile, encounters his former commander (Paulsen), now a fat-cat factory owner, who'd earlier ordered the Christmas Eve "liquidation" of more than 100 innocent Poles. While Paulsen seeks to embrace his former subordinate, Borchert plots to kill him for his unpunished war crimes. The film concludes with a truly memorable montage. *Murderers Are Among Us* didn't reach these shores until 1948.

THE MUSIC OF CHANCE (1993) ***

D: Philip Haas. James Spader, Mandy Patinkin, M. Emmet Walsh, Charles Durning, Joel Grey, Samantha Mathis, Christopher Penn. 98 mins. (Columbia/ TriStar)

Adapted by cowriter Belinda and director Philip Haas from Paul (*Smoke*) Auster's novel, *The Music of Chance* is an offbeat, oft brilliant, unpretentious fable marred only by a disappointing denouement. Patinkin is especially excellent as an ex-Boston fireman who picks up beat-up card shark Spader (in a role tailor-made for Steve Buscemi) and joins him for a marathon poker game with smug millionaire lottery winners Durning and Grey. The flick takes a drastic twist at game's conclusion and continues on an unpredictable course the rest of the way.

THE MYSTERY OF RAMPO B&W/COLOR (1994) ***½

D: Kazuyoshi Okuyama. Naoto Takenaka, Michiko Hada, Masahiro Motoki, Mikijiro Hira. 101 mins. (Evergreen)

The *Mystery of Rampo* (a.k.a. *Rampo*) is a complex self-referential fable drawn from an original story by Japanese mystery scribe Rampo Edogawa. When his latest novel is banned in 1930s Japan, Rampo (Takenaka) begins encountering in reality characters depicted in his doomed book, most notably a beautiful widow (Hada) acquitted of charges of killing her sickly husband. Frequently taking over for Rampo is his suave fictional alter ego, Detective Akechi (Motoki), who conducts the seduction the awkward, sheltered author cannot, even in his own fantasies. Under Okuyama's inspired direction, *The Mystery of Rampo* casts a fever-dream spell, complete with erotic tableaux that range from the romantically exotic to the

voyeuristically bizarre. Trippy visuals, animated sequences, a fictional B&W hack pulp cliffhanger film-within-a-film (called *The Phantom with 20 Faces*) and Rampo's own more grandly imagined version of same further add to the film's unique appeal.

THE NAKED CITY (1948) B&W ***

D: Jules Dassin. Barry Fitzgerald, Howard Duff, Don Taylor. 96 mins. (Kino) DVD

Dassin's NYC-set *policier* offers pioneering location lensing as head detective Fitzgerald leads his team through a twisty murder investigation. The film later spawned the long-running teleseries of the same name.

THE NAKED KISS (1964) B&W ***½

D: Sam Fuller. Constance Towers, Anthony Eisley, Virginia Grey, Patsy Kelly, Michael Dante, Edy Williams. 93 mins. (Home Vision) DVD

From its infamous opening scene, wherein a welching pimp receives a strenuous purse-whipping at the hands of a bald-headed hooker (!), to its unpredictable climax, *The Naked Kiss* represents maverick auteur Fuller at his most earnestly and artfully deranged. Our story takes the above-mentioned courtesan, Kelly (Towers), to the small town of Grantville in search of a fresh start. At first Kelly's future appears bright: She not only lands a job as a nurse working with handicapped kids, but she wins the affections of Grantville's wealthiest bachelor (Dante). Kelly's Middle-American Dream is violently shattered, however, when she discovers her rich, cultured beau is actually the burg's biggest sicko. Fuller keeps the twists coming through this mad morality melodrama. In addition to its other virtues, *The Naked Kiss* also marked the feature-film debut of irrepressible future Russ Meyer blond goddess Edy Williams, glimpsed briefly but memorably as a brunette (!) hooker named Hatrack ("There isn't a customer here who doesn't want to hang his fedora on her," madam Grey explains). For the record, Edy's first screen line is "Did I do something wrong?"

NAKED OBSESSION (1991) B&W/COLOR***

D: Dan Golden. William Katt, Rick Dean, Maria Ford, Elena Sahagun, Wendy MacDonald, Tommy Hinkley. In R and unrated editions. 93 mins. (Vestron, n.i.d.)

Director Golden goes for David Lynch–like lowlife lyricism and offbeat sleaze in this transcendent strip-club epic. Golden's raunchier-than-average low-budget thriller—which features the expected undraped femme flesh and some unexpectedly explicit rough-sex tableaux—casts Katt as a West Coast councilman with mayoral ambitions who gets, in rapid order, mugged while investigating a seedy urban quarter, befriended by philosophical wino Dean, and tempted by foxy ecdysiast Ford. Katt soon returns to the scene of the slime—partially to escape his nagging, driven, cold-fish spouse (MacDonald)—and finds himself implicated in a series of murders. While thoroughly implausible, *Naked Obsession* offers erotic scenes that are stronger than the norm, Dean impresses as the seemingly supernatural derelict, and B auteur Fred Olen Ray is convincing as the strip-club's oily emcee. The surreal touches include several black-and-white sequences (including an excellent near-death experience), a hot Angelo Badalamenti–esque soundtrack, and a memorable Kabuki-styled strip act performed before a literally captive audience.

STRIPPING THE LIGHT FANTASTIC REMEMBRANCES OF G-STRINGS PAST
Phantom's Top 10 Strip-Flick Picks

● ●

Dance of the Damned (1988, Virgin Vision)
Exotica (1994, Miramax)
Heart of Midnight (1989, Virgin Vision)
Lady of Burlesque (1943, Englewood)
The Monster and the Stripper (1968, Nashville Cinema)
Naked Obsession (see left)
Striporama (1954, Something Weird)
The Stripper (1963, Fox)
Stripteaser (1995, New Horizons)
Teaserama (1955, Something Weird)

THE NARROW MARGIN (1952) B&W ***1/2

D: Richard Fleischer. Charles McGraw, Marie Windsor, Jacqueline White. 70 mins. (RKO)

Fleischer's tough, twisty, seamless suspenser doesn't squander a second of celluloid as hard-boiled cop McGraw escorts gun-moll-turned-government-witness Windsor on a cross-country train ride. Much superior to Peter Hyams's slick but pointless 1990 remake, *The Narrow Margin* (Artisan, DVD), with Gene Hackman and Anne Archer.

THE NEIGHBOR (1993) **

D: Rodney Gibbons. Linda Kozlowski, Ron Lea, Rod Steiger, Frances Bay, Bruce Boa, Jane Wheeler. 93 mins. (Academy, n.i.d.)

The Neighbor adds a sick twist to the endangered-family genre; instead of a nutzoid nanny (see *Hand That Rocks the Cradle, Midnight's Child, My Daughter's Keeper* [Artisan], et al.), *The Neighbor* gives us an obsessed obstetrician (Steiger). Seems Rod thinks that Kozlowski is a dead ringer for his late mater, who died in childbirth a half century earlier, causing a then-12-year-old

Rod to kill his newborn brother. When he learns new neighbor Linda K. is pregnant, he does his doctorly best to terminate her fetus. More unpleasant than suspenseful, this Vermont-set, Canadian-produced effort performs its shock chores with a certain professional, if rarely exciting, efficiency, though a subdued Steiger sounds more like Jimmy Stewart than his old mega-decibel self here.

THE NET (1995) ***

D: Irwin Winkler. Sandra Bullock, Jeremy Northam, Dennis Miller. 114 mins. (Columbia/TriStar) DVD

Former NYC indie actress Sandra *(Who Shot Patakango?, Me and the Mob)* Bullock's dominant perf keeps Winkler's thriller humming over its stretched-out running time. When hermetic hacker Sandra unwittingly taps into a nationwide computer-terrorist campaign, she's forced to take it on the lam while suave but vicious Brit hit man Northam and corporate coconspirators erase her legal identity and chase her from California to the Yucatán and back. While mavens maintain that *The Net* credits computers with powers they don't possess, here that high-tech poetic license makes for exciting viewing—at least until an over-load of pursuit clichés (including a consummately cornball carousel sequence) threaten to boot the pic into terminal default. A computer chorus that echoes the "one of us" wedding-banquet chant from *Freaks* represents a first, though. *The Net* also spawned the poorly received 1998 teleseries of the same name.

NEVER TAKE CANDY FROM A STRANGER (1960) B&W ***1/2

D: Cyril Frankel. Owen Watford, Patrick Allen, Felix Aylmer, Niall MacGinnis, Alison Leggett, Bill Nagy, Janina Fay. 81 mins. (Sinister Cinema)

Blasted by Brit critics who assumed that the Hammer imprimatur automatically signaled an exploitation pic, the taut, crisply scripted *Never Take Candy from a Stranger,* adapted from Roger Garis's play *The Pony Cart,* never received the theatrical exposure it deserved. When English high school principal Allen and spouse Watford relocate to a small, insular Canadian city, their nine-year-old daughter (Fay) and a young friend are coaxed into dancing nude (off-camera) by a senile pervert (Aylmer) with a serious Lewis Carroll complex. Trouble is, the perv in question is also the town's leading citizen and economic provider. His wheeler-dealer son (Nagy) attempts to squelch the incident—one of many such offenses previously suffered in silence by the dependent local citizenry—but Allen and Watford insist on taking the case to trial, despite the risk of social ostracism and intensified trauma for young Fay, whose testimony is the defense's only weapon. *Never* packs several genres into one film— riveting courtroom thriller, absorbing social drama, and, in its final reels, creepy chiller as the zombielike molester pursues the two girls through the woods. The performances, from young

Fay to Aylmer's pathetic deviate, are uniformly excellent, as is frequent Hammer director Freddie Francis's cinematography, pristinely preserved in Sinister Cinema's mint, letter-boxed print.

NEVER TALK TO STRANGERS (1995) ***

D: Peter Hall. Rebecca De Mornay, Antonio Banderas, Dennis Miller, Len Cariou, Harry Dean Stanton. 86 mins. (Columbia/TriStar) DVD

Mostly dismissed as a routine damsel-in-distress exercise, *Never Talk to Strangers* shapes up as a modest but unpredictable thriller. De Mornay, who also exec-produced, portrays Sarah Taylor, a Manhattan psychologist who's been in emotional cold storage since the disappearance of her (unseen) fiancé. She spends much of her work-day interrogating accused serial killer Stanton, who claims to suffer from MPD (multiple personality disorder). Sarah's not in the mood, then, when she's first approached in a supermarket by swingin' "surveillance consultant" Tony (Banderas), but eventually she surrenders to his charms. When an unknown perp begins harassing her— sending dead flowers, killing her cat (the usual screen-psycho tricks)—sus-picion points to Tony. Other possible suspects include Stanton (via his outside attorney), Sarah's creepy traveling-salesman dad (Cariou), and obnoxious upstairs neighbor Miller, who describes himself as "Sisyphus with a hard-on" and spouts philosophical *bon mots* like "People are only animals with beepers." The pic's final, radical twist straddles the line between clever and contrived, but you can't accuse *Never* of going in predictable directions. Hall's almost dignified direction and Pino Donaggio's strong score furnish further pluses. Toronto and Budapest (!) are less successful at subbing for downtown NYC.

NIAGARA (1953) ***

D: Henry Hathaway. Joseph Cotten, Marilyn Monroe, Jean Peters. 89 mins. (Fox)

A murder-minded Marilyn seeks to eliminate neurotic hubby Cotten. Hathaway's trim thriller makes inspired use of authentic Niagara Falls locations. The blond icon also costars, with Barbara Stanwyck and Robert Ryan, in Fritz Lang's atmospheric 1953 mood piece *Clash by Night* (Turner), drawn from Clifford Odets's play, and as an unbalanced baby-sitter in Roy Ward Baker's ahead-of-its-time thriller *Don't Bother to Knock* (1952, Fox), featuring Richard Widmark and Anne Bancroft.

NIAGARA, NIAGARA (1997) ***

D: Bob Gosse. Robin Tunney, Henry Thomas, Michael Parks, John MacKay, Candy Clark, Stephen Lang. 96 mins. (Artisan)

Tunney turns in standout work as a troubled Tourette's-syndrome sufferer, and it's her strenuous performance that elevates *Niagara, Niagara* above the rest of the contempo young-criminal-couple-on-the-run pack. Tunney and erstwhile *ET* towhead Thomas "meet cute" while separately shoplifting at an upstate New York department store. Our seriously unstable heroine decides she has to lay hands on a black Barbie doll (!) and convinces Thomas to abandon his grumpy dad (MacKay) and join her in her quest, with Toronto their ultimate destination. Along the way, the self-medicating, Jack Daniel's–guzzling gal and her clueless but obliging partner rob a pharmacy when the nutzoid owner (Lang) won't fill her prescriptions. Thomas is wounded in the incident, but the pair find shelter at the farm of lonely rural oddball Parks— where Robin's tragic condition kicks in big-time. Viewers who savor truly brave performances—and Tunney's rivals Dustin Hoffman's *Rain Man* (MGM) and Peter Greene's in *Clean, Shaven* (see index)—will warrant *Niagara, Nia-*

gara well worth a look. For a more irreverent take on the subject, scope out mock-rockers Feo Y Loco's demented ditty "Tourette's Syndrome Blues."

NIGHT AND THE CITY (1950) B&W ***

D: Jules Dassin. Richard Widmark, Gene Tierney, Googie Withers, Francis L. Sullivan, Hugh Marlowe, Herbert Lom, Stanislaus Zbysko, Mike Mazurki. 95 mins. (Fox)

NIGHT AND THE CITY (1992) **1/2

D: Irwin Winkler. Robert De Niro, Jessica Lange, Cliff Gorman, Jack Warden, Alan King. 104 mins. (Fox)

While following roughly the same story line, drawn from Gerald Kersh's novel (the remake's adapted by prolific novelist/scripter Richard Price), the two simultaneously video-released versions are as different as, if not day and night, then certainly dusk and dawn. De Niro offers a jokier spin on Widmark's desperate petty hustler Harry Fabian, and a mostly daylit contempo NYC provides a sharp contrast to the original's B&W nocturnal-London setting. The shift from a wrestling to a boxing milieu is a sensible alteration, and Warden is a better thesp than his Tor Johnson–like counterpart, Zbysko, in the pivotal retired-warrior role. Neither film is without its flaws, but both are worth watching, especially back-to-back.

NIGHT EYES: THE SERIES

NIGHT EYES (1990) *1/2

D: Jag Mundhra. Tanya Roberts, Andrew Stevens, Warwick Sims, Karen Elise Baldwin, Cooper Huckabee, Chick Vennera. 95 mins. (Prism, n.i.d.)

Ex–*Charlie's Angel*, screen *Sheena*, and sometime erotic-thriller star-

let Roberts sluts it up as the estranged wife of an obnoxious rock star who hires the "Night Eyes" security firm to catch and record Tanya in an adulterous act. Guard Stevens soon falls prey to Tanya's anything-but-hidden charms, however, and becomes an unwitting pawn in her deceitful game. *Night Eyes* moves with all the urgency of a somnambulistic made-for-TV movie as director Mundhra turns the flick into a virtual Tanya travelog. Viewers in search of a tense suspenser in a low-budget *Body Heat* vein are thus advised to shun *Night Eyes;* Tanya fans, on the other hand, will have a field day slo-moing through this feature-length tribute to their femme fave's most discernible talents. Followed by *Night Eyes 2* and *Night Eyes 3*, with Shannon Tweed replacing Tanya, and *Night Eyes 4: Fatal Passion* (all Prism), with Paula Barbieri.

NIGHTMARE (1991) ***

D: John Pasquin. Victoria Principal, Paul Sorvino, Danielle Harris, Jonathan Banks, Gregg Henry. 84 mins. (New Horizons)

Surprisingly intense for a PG-13-rated telemovie, the generically misnomered *Nightmare* casts Principal as the tormented mom of a young girl (Harris, of *Halloween IV* and *V* fame) who's abducted, molested, and nearly slain by local psycho Banks. When the system proves predictably lax, letting the clearly bonkers Banks out on bail, Victoria and Danielle find themselves stalked and harassed. Sympathetic but judicially handcuffed cop Sorvino is ineffective, so Principal takes it upon herself to turn the tables on Banks. *Nightmare* generates true tension while scoring cogent points re situational ethics and is far superior to its Sally Fields–starred big-screen near-clone *Eye for an Eye* (Paramount).

NIGHT MOVES (1975) ***

D: Arthur Penn. Gene Hackman, Susan Clark, Jennifer Warren. 100 mins. (Warner)

Penn's dense, textured noir features a strong performance by Hackman as a private eye on a missing-person case. Look for a teenage Melanie Griffith (she's hard to miss) in a memorable swim scene.

THE NIGHT OF THE HUNTER (1955) B&W ***1/2

D: Charles Laughton. Robert Mitchum, Shelley Winters, Lillian Gish. 93 mins. (MGM) DVD

Charles Laughton's lone directorial assignment left him batting 1.000. A moody, idiosyncratic thriller, *Night* teems with indelible imagery, while Mitchum turns in truly scary work as a psychopathic self-styled preacher on the track of stolen bank loot. Remade as a TV movie (n/a), with Richard Chamberlain in the Mitchum role.

THE NINTH CONFIGURATION (1979) ***

D: William Peter Blatty. Stacy Keach, Scott Wilson, Ed Flanders, Jason Miller, Neville Brand. 115 mins. (New World, Starmaker)

Produced, directed, and scripted (from his own novel) by William Peter (*The Exorcist*) Blatty, this surreal exercise (originally titled *Twinkle, Twinkle, Killer Kane*) casts Keach as Kane, a shrink ostensibly sent to separate the men from the *meshuggeners* at a remote gothic castle in the Pacific Northwest that's been converted into a sort of military playpen for real and/or imagined 'Nam mental casualties. Only problem is, Kane may be the looniest of the lot. *The Ninth Configuration* is a wildly uneven mix of free-form Freudian vaudeville—at its best, its non sequitur exchanges play like a *One Flew*

Over the Cuckoo's Nest script-doctored by Bill Griffith's Zippy the Pinhead—broad satire lifted from some bad college play, remedial theological probings, and at its core, an intriguing tug-of-war between Keach and off-balance ex-astronaut Wilson. Despite its flaws, Blatty's one-man movie offers enough black humor, offbeat dramaturgy, and celluloid surprises to earn its long-standing cult status.

NO MERCY   (1986) ***1/2

D: Richard Pearce. Richard Gere, Kim Basinger, Jeroen Krabbe, George Dzundza, William Atherton, Ray Sharkey. 105 mins. (Columbia/TriStar) DVD

A truly intense *policier, No Mercy* stars Gere as a tough Chicago cop who ventures into the seamy depths of New Orleans's Algiers district in search of his partner's killer, creepily interpreted by Krabbe, who lists disembowelment with a serrated knife as his preferred method of murder. Basinger is effective as the Cajun blonde sought by both Krabbe and Gere. No relation to the pretentious NYC-set indie kidnap caper *Mercy* (A-Pix). Gere also turns in impressive work as an amoral cop in Mike Figgis's *Internal Affairs* (Paramount, DVD).

NO WAY OUT   (1987) ***

D: Roger Donaldson. Kevin Costner, Gene Hackman, Sean Young, Will Patton, George Dzundza, Howard Duff. 118 mins. (HBO)

N aval commander Costner's tryst with Young, mistress of desperate defense secretary Hackman, leads him into a labyrinth of mounting danger in a gripping thriller—drawn from Kenneth Fearing's novel *The Big Clock,* previously filmed in 1948 (Universal)—weakened only by a contrived denouement. Patton's a standout as Hackman's high-strung, power-crazed homosexual assistant.

NO WAY TO TREAT A LADY (1968) ***

D: Jack Smight. Rod Steiger, George Segal, Lee Remick. 108 mins. (Paramount)

S teiger provides Peter Sellers and Jerry Lewis with some thespian competition by playing a misogynistic madman who employs a multitude of accents and disguises to carry out his murderous misdeeds. Segal likewise impresses as the neurotic but relentless detective dogging Rod's bloody trail.

NORMAL LIFE   (1996) ***

D: John McNaughton. Luke Perry, Ashley Judd, Jim True, Kate Walsh, Edmund Wyson, Tom Towles. 108 mins. (New Line)

A fter helming the low-impact mainstream Hollywood dramedy *Mad Dog and Glory* (Universal), Chicago-based director John (*Henry: Portrait of a Serial Killer*) McNaughton returns to his grittier Illinois roots with this grimly effective crime story "inspired by actual events." Employing a semi-flashback structure, *Normal Life* charts the doomed relationship between laconic loner cop Perry (in what's easily his best big-screen role to date) and flamingly nutzoid squeeze Judd (of *Heat, Double Jeopardy,* and *A Time to Kill* fame), who exhibits more mood swings than a hyperactive pendulum. When Luke loses his law-enforcement job, the pair find themselves plunged into a deep financial abyss. Perry extracts them from same by using his police training to pull off a string of successful suburban bank heists that nonetheless lead to inevitable disaster. Not at all a "hip," flip, postmodern caper flick, *Normal Life* boasts much the same verité flavor McNaughton brought to *Henry,* transplanted to a clean, bland 'burbscape. While it doesn't pack *Henry's* punch or shock value, *Normal Life* is in many ways an equally difficult film to watch as McNaughton offers an almost *too*-intimate portrait of this sad, troubled, ultimately dangerous duo. The

director aggressively campaigned for and secured a token '96 theatrical release for *Normal Life.* If you missed it on the big screen, it's well worth checking out on homevid. *Henry's* screen partner, Towles, has a small but poignant role as Perry's sickly pop.

OBSESSED   (1988) ***

D: Robin Spry. Saul Rubinek, Kerrie Keane, Daniel Pilon, Alan Thicke, Colleen Dewhurst. 100 mins. (New Star, n.i.d.)

W hen Yank motorist Rubinek kills a Canadian kid in a hit-and-run accident, the latter's distraught mom (Keane) and divorced dad (Pilon) seek to extradite the driver to stand trial in Canada. A legal technicality provides a thorny obstacle, so Keane devises a more elaborate scheme to extract, if not justice, then at least revenge. This subtly shaded thriller, something of a forerunner of *The Crossing Guard* (Touchstone), manages to avoid easy TV-movie morality in working out its plot permutations. Culprit Rubinek may be a coward, but he's not a stock villain, while the sympathetic Keane may well be in the throes of a dangerous psychotic state. The three principals handle their roles with deft finesse; Dewhurst as a judge and Thicke as a sleazy lawyer likewise impress. *Obsessed* also offers the best all-out male-versus-female punch-up (a Great White North specialty, it seems) we've seen since fat villain Maury Chaykin and a pregnant Terri Austin went at it in Canada's 1986 *Terminator* rip-off *The Vindicator* (see index).

ON DANGEROUS GROUND   (1951) B&W ***1/2

D: Nicholas Ray. Robert Ryan, Ida Lupino, Ward Bond, Ed Begley, Cleo Moore, Charles Kemper. 82 mins. (Republic)

R ay's lean, offbeat noir meditation reverses many of the genre's traditional gender conventions as depressed basket-case cop Ryan, investigating a murder in frigid upstate New York, finds new meaning and resolve via Lupino's blind but strong and independent character. This austere entry takes risks that reflect its multi-tiered title and easily rates as one of the era's best. Hugo Haas icon Moore receives one of her more upscale screen credits here.

ON THE WATERFRONT   (1954)
B&W ****

D: Elia Kazan. Marlon Brando, Eva Marie Saint, Lee J. Cobb, Karl Malden, Rod Steiger. 108 mins. (Columbia/TriStar)

When Cobb's mobsters muscle in on union men, Marlon vows to take it out of their skulls. Brilliant acting, dialogue (by Budd Schulberg), and direction make *Waterfront* a definite contender for Best Mainstream American Movie Ever Made honors.

ONE FALSE MOVE
(1992) ***1/2

D: Carl Franklin. Bill Paxton, Cynda Williams, Jim Metzler, Billy Bob Thornton, Michael Beach, Earl Billings. 105 mins. (Columbia/TriStar) DVD

One False Move springs from a complex, organic script (by actor Thornton and Tom Epperson) given life by director Franklin. After a bloody L.A. drug rip-off leaves six people dead, murderous redneck Ray (Thornton), black psycho Pluto (Beach), and Ray's passive mulatto squeeze, Fantasia (Williams), head for Ray and Fantasia's hometown of Star City, Arkansas, where gung-ho lawman "Hurricane" Dixon (Paxton) eagerly awaits them. Joining Dixon, in a reverse *Beverly Hills Cop* move, are LAPD detectives Metzler and Billings. Franklin crosscuts between the killers' bloody progress and the law enforcers' preparations for their expected arrival.

Paxton turns in finely tuned, textured work in a role that demands a radical character change roughly halfway through. The supporting players likewise emote sans false notes, with Thornton and Beach convincingly scary, and Williams credibly desperate as their confused cohort. *One False Move* also dares to dig beneath the surface to examine subtle racial issues along with the well-rounded characters' individual dilemmas. The authentic locations add another exotic touch.

OUT OF SIGHT   (1998) ***

D: Steven Soderbergh. George Clooney, Jennifer Lopez, Ving Rhames, Don Cheadle, Michael Keaton, Albert Brooks, Dennis Farina, Nancy Allen, Steve Zahn, Luis Guzmán. 102 mins. (Universal) Collector's Edition DVD

The best Elmore Leonard adaptation to reach the big screen since Barry Sonnenfeld's *Get Shorty* (see index), Soderbergh's lively caper film splits its time between sunny South Florida (mostly Miami and environs) and a deep-frozen Detroit. The normally smarmy Clooney (*Batman and Robin, One Fine Day*) turns in charismatic work as a charming thief who, with confederate Rhames, breaks out of a Belle Glades pen, taking the nation's foxiest U.S. marshal, Lopez, temporary hostage. The pair's mutual but complex attraction begins while sharing the claustrophic trunk (!) of a getaway car (mis)handled by perennial petty-criminal screw-up Zahn (a brilliant turn by the *SubUrbia* alum). A scheme to rob the manse of recently released insider-trading mogul Brooks (effectively playing against type and bravely appearing sans his hairpiece) with the "help" of devious ex-con Cheadle (excellent as ever) hits the expected Leonard-esque snags as not-so-well-laid plans dissolve into utter chaos. While many of the moves will be familiar to longtime Leonard fans, Soderbergh

crafts a tricky, textured, immensely entertaining crime film laced with dry wit and juicy characterizations. Our only real criticism involves starlet Lopez's odd reluctance to showcase her much publicized, justly famous jutting butt, arguably international filmdom's best since Brigitte Bardot's, highlighted here only briefly in one throwaway moment.

OUT OF THE BLUE   (1980) **1/2

D: Dennis Hopper. Dennis Hopper, Linda Manz, Sharon Farrell, Raymond Burr. 94 mins. (Anchor Bay) DVD

Punkette Manz, obstructed by her junkie mom (Farrell) and drunken ex-con/biker dad (Hopper), searches for the meaninglessness of life in Hopper's downbeat look at West Coast white-trash angst. A more mature Manz more recently resurfaced in Harmony Korine's Midwest-set white-trash-fest *Gummo* (New Line).

OUT OF THE DARK   (1988) **1/2

D: Michael Schroeder. Karen Black, Bud Cort, Cameron Dye, Geoffrey Lewis, Starr Andreeff, Paul Bartel, Divine, Tab Hunter. 89 mins. (Columbia/TriStar)

Schroeder's semisatiric psycho romp features Andreeff as a new recruit at a phone-sex service (operated by a relatively subdued Black) where fellow workers are being eliminated one by one by a candy-colored clown called Bobo. The hoary story line is somewhat enlivened by Schroeder's tongue-in-cheek tone and a top genre cast—besides Andreeff and Black, Bartel (who also exec-produced and manages to sneak in a plug for his weak frightcom *Mortuary Academy*), Lewis and Cort have significant roles, while Lainie Kazan and the *Polyester* team of Tab Hunter and the late, great Divine (cast here as a hard-boiled LAPD dick!) contribute brief but fun cameos.

PAINT IT BLACK   (1989) ***

D: Tim Hunter. Rick Rossovich, Doug Savant, Julie Carmen, Jason Bernard, Sally Kirkland, Martin Landau. 101 mins. (Vestron, n.i.d.)

Director Hunter follows his funky *River's Edge* with this effective art-world thriller. Savant plays a dilettante psycho out to "protect" artist Rossovich from being victimized by philistines like agents Landau and Kirkland in a B+ flick that achieves more than many of its megabudget A counterparts. A clifftop climax constitutes an especially clever highlight. Hunter strikes out with his 1997 youth-noir yawner, *The Maker* (Artisan).

THE PAPERBOY   (1994) **1/2

D: Douglas Jackson. Alexandra Paul, Marc Marut, William Katt, Brigid Tierney, Krista Errickson, Frances Bay. 93 mins. (Republic)

While lacking a prepubescent marquee name like *The Good Son's* Macauley Culkin, *The Paperboy* is a thoroughly predictable but well-wrought and shamelessly sadistic killer-kid romp. Young Marut's psycho tyke is a formerly abused (by his late Christian mom), currently neglected (by his oft absent dad) 12-year-old (who looks more like 15) who gloms on to happy-face divorcée Paul and her young daughter (Tierney), luring them to his nabe by suffocating Paul's elderly mater with a plastic bag. When Marut's desperate attempts to become part of Paul's little clan meet with rejection, he sets out to eliminate all whom he perceives as standing in his way, though he spares the life of Peaches the dog (played by pro canine Frelin). The pic ends with all the pieces in place for a sequel that has yet to arrive.

PAPER MASK   (1991) ***

D: Christopher Morahan. Paul McGann, Amanda Donohoe, Frederick Treves, Barbara Leigh-Hunt. 105 mins. (Academy, n.i.d.)

Ambitious Brit medical aide Matthew (McGann) filches a dead doc's identity and wins a ward appointment at a distant hospital, where unsuspecting nurse Donohoe not only helps him over the health-care humps but soon becomes his lover. *Paper Mask* begins as a drama but takes a sudden lurch into thriller turf when Matthew's inexperience leads to a patient's death. From that point on, our initially idealistic hero turns ruthless in his attempts to cover up his misdeed and protect his new upscale status. While *Paper Mask,* adapted by Richard Collee from his novel, resorts to contrivance to keep its plot wheels spinning, the movie generates genuine suspense. The film also presents a picture of British-hospital life that's neither glamorized nor sensationalized, though its portrait of self-forgiving killer medics surely will make viewers want to hang on to their health insurance (to say nothing of their health).

THE PARALLAX VIEW   (1974) ***

D: Alan J. Pakula. Warren Beatty, Paula Prentiss, William Daniels. 102 mins. (Paramount) DVD

While *The Paranoid View* may have made for an apter title, Pakula's elaborate political thriller abundantly delivers the nail-biting goods as Bernstein/Woodward-styled journalist Beatty uncovers a sinister assassination agency and a conspiracy of epic proportions. Conspiracy flicks worth avoiding include *Executive Action* (Warner) and *November Men* (Troma).

PATH TO PARADISE   (1997) ***

D: Leslie Libman, Larry Williams. Peter Gallagher, Ned Eisenberg, Marcia Gay Harden, Mike Starr. 95 mins. (HBO)

Originally aired on HBO cable, *Path to Paradise* painstakingly re-creates the events leading to the 1993 World Trade Center bombing and the tragedy's immediate aftermath. Scripter Ned Curren and dual directors Libman and Williams manage to put a human face on the Muslim terrorists without sympathizing with them. The film depicts how, despite several screw-ups and the presence of a paid FBI informer (played by Eisenberg), said terrorists succeeded in accomplishing their lethal mission while authorities essentially chased their own tails. Buoyed by a topflight cast, including Gallagher and Harden as FBI agents monitoring the eventual bombers, authentic NYC and gritty Jersey City location lensing, and an excellent Eastern-flavored score, the swiftly paced *Path to Paradise* lets the facts speak, all too painfully, for themselves.

A PERFECT MURDER   (1998) **1/2

D: Andrew Davis. Michael Douglas, Gwyneth Paltrow, Viggo Mortensen, David Suchet, Sarita Choudhury, Constance Towers. 105 mins. (Warner) Special Edition DVD

Loosely updated by Patrick Smith Kelly from Frederic Knott's play *Dial M for Murder* (filmed by Alfred Hitchcock in 1954), *A Perfect Murder* is at once more active and less suspenseful than Hitch's version. Douglas trots out his by-now tired slick middle-aged rich-guy moves, while Paltrow plays his blond trophy wife with conviction if not stunning charisma and Mortensen is appropriately edgy as the latter's artist/ex-con lover. Though better known as an action director, Davis (*The Fugitive, Under Siege*) wrings a reasonable amount of tension from his retooled tale and offers an atmospheric view of his NYC and outer-borough locations. Warner later issued an alternative edition of the film, with a different ending.

PERFECT STRANGERS   (1984) ***

D: Larry Cohen. Anne Carlisle, Brad Rijn, John Woerhle. 91 mins. (Embassy, n.i.d.)

A killer seeks to eliminate the two-year-old witness to his crime, only to become romantically involved with the tot's mom—played by *Liquid Sky's* Carlisle—in Cohen's suspenseful B precursor to the mainstream hit *Witness* (Paramount).

PERFORMANCE (1970) ***1/2

D: Nicolas Roeg, Donald Cammell. Mick Jagger, James Fox, Anita Pallenberg. 105 mins. (Warner)

Reclusive rock star Jagger and cheap hood Fox play stoned mind games in this wittily perverse closet thriller and enduring cult fave, codirected by Roeg and the late Donald *(White of the Eye)* Cammell.

PHANTOM KILLER (1942) B&W **

D: William Beaudine. Dick Purcell, Joan Woodbury, Mantan Moreland. 61 mins. (Sinister Cinema)

William ("One-Take") Beaudine's routine PRC mystery cheapie is distinguished solely by inventive comic Moreland's bravura efforts to transcend racial stereotyping of the most demeaning and, in this case, convoluted sort. No relation to the dull but evocatively titled 1945 backstage murder mystery *Phantom of 42nd Street* (Sinister Cinema), with *Reefer Madness* alum Dave O'Brien.

PHOENIX (1998) ***

D: Danny Cannon. Ray Liotta, Anjelica Huston, Anthony LaPaglia, Brittany Murphy, Daniel Baldwin, Jeremy Piven, Giancarlo Esposito, Tom Noonan. 107 mins. (Artisan) DVD

For yours truly's moolah, actor Liotta is worth watching in just about any film, and it's his potent performance that powers Danny *(The Young Americans, Judge Dredd)* Cannon's *Phoenix.* Liotta (who also coproduced) plays a basically decent Arizona cop whose compulsive gambling has landed him in serious hock to local loan shark Esposito. That life-

endangering debt prompts our pressured hero to join corrupt cohorts LaPaglia, Baldwin, and a more reluctant Piven (who's secretly in league with Internal Affairs) to rip off Esposito's digs. Director Cannon wisely allots considerable screen time to Liotta's complex, conflicted character, a guy who'll literally bet on racing raindrops, get hung up on the illogical plot machinations of *King Kong* (!), and who prefers weathered barmaid Huston over her seductive young daughter, Murphy. The supporting perfs are fine down the line, with tall Tom Noonan especially impressive as a literate, lisping enforcer.

PICKUP ON SOUTH STREET (1953) B&W ***1/2

D: Sam Fuller. Richard Widmark, Jean Peters, Thelma Ritter. 80 mins. (Fox)

Pickpocket Widmark proves patriotic at heart when he unwittingly filches top-secret microfilm. Fuller's febrile, brutal, blistering noir features standout work both by Widmark and Ritter (who earned a Best Supporting Actress Oscar nom) as his down-and-out South Street pal. One of noirdom's—and Fuller's—best.

THE PLAYER (1992) ****

D: Robert Altman. Tim Robbins, Greta Scacchi, Peter Gallagher, Vincent D'Onofrio, Lyle Lovett, Sydney Pollack, Whoopi Goldberg, Fred Ward, Brion James. 123 mins. (New Line) Special Edition DVD

Altman's satiric thriller rates as the first film to realize John Waters's long-avowed dream of casting major celebs as extras, including the ubiquitous Karen Black and late action icon Steve James. Perennial B-screen heavy Brion James stretches in a rare straight role as a solemn studio head, while Richard E. *(Warlock)* Grant and Dean *(Blue Velvet)* Stockwell shine as a hustling screenwriter/agent tandem. Star Robbins contributes his first bizarre bathing scene

since his icy immersion in *Jacob's Ladder,* and Tod Browning's *Freaks* receives a neat homage, in a thoroughly brilliant flick buffs won't want to miss.

PLUNDER ROAD (1957) B&W ***1/2

D: Hubert Cornfield. Gene Raymond, Jeanne Cooper, Wayne Morris, Elisha Cook, Jr., Steven Ritch. 76 mins. (Republic)

A realistic, no-nonsense heist caper, with a story by actor Ritch, *Plunder Road* shapes up as the *Detour* of the '50s as a band of sympathetic thieves pit old-fashioned guile against modern police technology. (As one character puts it, "Science is against you.") Enacted by a stellar cast, *Plunder Road* is easily the best of the B's produced under 20th Century Fox's brief-lived low-budget Regal Pictures wing. A must for fans of the era's unsung gems.

POISON IVY:
THE SERIES

POISON IVY (1992) **1/2

D: Katt Shea. Drew Barrymore, Sara Gilbert, Tom Skerritt, Cheryl Ladd. 95 mins. In R and unrated editions. (New Line) DVD

As free-spirited punkette Ivy, Barrymore plots to replace plain-Jane rich-girl friend Gilbert's sickly mom (Ladd, in a drippy role) in the heart, bed, and bankbook of her ex-souse TV-exec spouse (Skerritt). While auteur Shea's lensing is often lyrical, her story falls somewhere between a domestic-sleaze thriller and an edgy coming-of-age drama. Barrymore establishes her psycho credentials early on when she bashes in a dying dog's head; in the main, though, Shea chooses nuanced menace over cheap chills. *Poison Ivy* lacks both the gleeful exploitation quotient of the similarly themed 1969 Brit fave *Baby Love* (Nelson) and the bittersweet violence of Shea's own *Dance of the Damned* (see index), but its shaded approach supplies a welcome change of pace. Anne Goursaud's *Poison Ivy II: Lily* (1995, New Line, DVD) is an otherwise unrelated, fairly excruciating Alyssa Milano showcase shoehorned into the series. The franchise receives a bit of a boost in the hands of helmer Kurt Voss, who brings a sense of fun to 1997's *Poison Ivy: The New Seduction* (New Line, DVD), goofing on the genre with neat visual and soundtrack touches while still maintaining some level of suspense and finding room for the de rigueur erotic interludes.

POSITIVE I.D.   (1987) ***

D: Andy Anderson. Stephanie Rascoe, John Davies, Steve Fromholz, Laura Lane. 96 mins. (Universal)

From its triple-tiered title to its nearly flawless execution, Anderson's Texas-lensed, self-financed *Positive I.D.* rates as an indie gem. Fort Worth housewife/rape victim Rasco partially sheds her overburdened self by embarking on a double life. By day, she's a part-time Realtor and depressive suburban mother, wed to wimpy hubby Davies; by night, a bimboized regular at a downtown lowlife bar. At first it appears that Stephanie seeks only temporary escape, but it turns out she has a far better laid plan in mind. Less a standard thriller than a complex but unpretentious meditation on the nature of personal identity, Anderson's slickly mounted opus rarely telegraphs its next move but cleverly toys with audience expectations on its way to a satisfying climax. Anderson earlier directed the sci-fi indie *Interface* (Vestron).

PRESSURE POINT   (1962) B&W ***

D: Hubert Cornfield. Sidney Poitier, Bobby Darin, Peter Falk, Carl Benton Reid, Yvette Vickers, Richard Bakalyan. 91 mins. (MGM)

As a vehicle for greaser icon Dick (*The Cool and the Crazy*)

Bakalyan, *Pressure Point* disappoints. Though he does appear on the vid's cover, the quintessential screen juvenile delinquent's participation here is limited to a speechless cameo, during a flashback sequence, as American Nazi Darin's partner in sadistic crime. (Bakalyan later played Darin's neighborhood pal in sketches seen on the late singer's network variety show.) On all other fronts, this Stanley Kramer production rates as a then-daring, still-intense showdown between shrink Poitier and racist sociopath Darin. Look for genre fave Yvette (*Attack of the 50 Foot Woman*) Vickers in a brief bit as a "Drunken Woman."

PRETTY POISON   (1968) ***½

D: Noel Black. Anthony Perkins, Tuesday Weld, Beverly Garland, John Randolph, Dick O'Neill. 89 mins. (Wood Knapp, n.i.d.)

The title of Black's perverse high-concept thriller refers both to cheerleader Weld and the prismatic pollutants produced by the glass factory where pyromaniac outpatient Perkins works. When relatively harmless loony Tony hooks up with the genuinely unhinged Tuesday, *he's* the one who's in for a surprise as she gradually reveals her true psychotic colors. We can say no more without telling too much, except to add that Tony, Tues, and ex-horror ingenue Garland all turn in top work in this low-key but ingenious cult fave. The cassette itself rates as a video rarity.

PREY OF THE CHAMELEON (1991) **½

D: Fleming Fuller. Daphne Zuniga, James Wilder, Alexandra Paul, Don Harvey. 91 mins. (Prism)

A reworking of Jack Sholder's *The Hidden* sans the sci-fi elements, *Prey* stars Zuniga as a serial killer who

adopts the identity of her latest victim. The pic's most interesting twist arrives when she falls for drifter Wilder, then robs banks and blows away victims in (rather unconvincing) male guise. While it doesn't fully exploit its strong premise, *Prey* rates as one of the better direct-to-video psycho outings.

THE PRIVATE FILES OF J. EDGAR HOOVER   (1977) ***

D: Larry Cohen. Broderick Crawford, Dan Dailey, Rip Torn, Michael Parks. 112 mins. (HBO)

Cohen's deadpan bio focuses on the conflicts between the obsessive FBI head (a growling Crawford) and such soon-to-be-late enemies as JFK, Bobby Kennedy, and Martin Luther King, Jr. The result is perverse political sleaze and a good job all around.

PRONTO   (1997) ***

D: Jim McBride. Peter Falk, Glenne Headly, James LeGros, Sergio Castellitto, Walter Olkewicz, Luis Guzmán, Glenn Plummer. 100 mins. (Paramount)

Falk lends his usual shuffling, mumbling charisma to his role as a beleaguered Miami Beach bookie on the run (or, more often, trot) from local mobsters who've just learned of his long-standing larcenous ways in McBride's Elmore Leonard adaptation. Falk hides out in an Italian villa, where he's joined by squeeze Headly, Stetson-topped, Magnum-toting federal agent LeGros, and the Sicilian hit man (Castellitto) who failed to nail him back in the States. While laced with Leonard's trademark wry wit, the accent here is on the increasingly intricate cat-and-mouse games played out among the various rival factions. LeGros is especially winning as the fed whose affection for Falk gradually persuades him to shift from adversary to ally. Terrific location lensing, in South

Florida (including a scene in the legendary Miami Beach eatery Wolfie's Celebrity Corner) and Corfu, adds further visual flavor to the tale, which originally aired on Showtime cable.

PUBLIC ACCESS   (1993) **

D: Bryan Singer. Ron Marquette, Dina Brooks, Burt Williams, Larry Maxwell, Charles Cavanaugh. 90 mins. (Triboro) DVD

Director Singer's tune-up for *The Usual Suspects* takes a promising premise and ruins it via an overly opaque approach. Marquette stars as Whiley Pritcher, a cryptic stranger (sort of a cathode Keyser Soze) who buses into the small town of Brewster, buys time on the local public-access station, and poses the question "What's wrong with Brewster?" That seemingly innocuous query provokes an array of volatile responses that stokes escalating frictions among the local citizenry. The basic idea of a political variation on *The Stepfather*—a right-wing creep in continuous search for the "perfect" town—is a potentially strong one. But Singer makes Marquette's character so difficult to read that there's little impact when his vague plans are finally revealed.

THE PUBLIC EYE   (1992) ***

D: Howard Franklin. Joe Pesci, Barbara Hershey, Stanley Tucci, Jerry Adler, Jared Harris. 99 mins. (Universal)

Obviously inspired by the real-life exploits of freelance photog Weegee (Arthur Fellig), *The Public Eye* neatly weaves the details of Weegee's nocturnal NYC world into a World War II Mafia/black-market thriller plot that bends but doesn't quite break credulity. Pesci is magnetic as sawed-off solo shutterbug Leon "Bernzy" Bernstein (a.k.a. "the Great Bernzini"), who haunts Manhattan's nightspots and crime scenes in obsessive pursuit of his gritty "art." While the movie's a mite

stylized at times, Pesci's intense, earthy perf keeps the action from freezing into a series of period stills. For a more verité portrait, scope out the documentary *The Real Weegee* (Sherman Price). The real Weegee also goes the *Immoral Mr. Teas* route in the 1961 "nudie-cutie" *The Imp-Probable Mr. Weegee* (Something Weird).

A PURE FORMALITY   (1994) **½

D: Guiseppe Tornatore. Gerard Depardieu, Roman Polanski. Subtitled. 107 mins. (Columbia/TriStar)

Cinema Paradiso auteur Tornatore cowrites and directs an essentially two-character confrontation that plays like a cerebral, two-reels-too-long *Twilight Zone* episode. Depardieu stars as Onoff, an acclaimed but hermetic, depressed novelist who's detained at a regional Euro police station for his failure to produce an I.D. (Protests Dep: "It's like a Hollywood B movie!") A superb Polanksi portrays the inspector who grills Onoff (for most of the film's running time) on suspicion of murder. Cryptic flashbacks combine with fictional literary discussions—Polanski's inspector is a major fan of Onoff's work, though he grows increasingly repulsed by the man himself—in a circular story line that leads to a potentially powerful climax. Viewers willing to endure needless repetition should find enough rewards in the consistently sharp acting and often incisive dialogue to hang on for the entire grueling session.

PURPLE NOON   (1960) ***½

D: René Clement. Alain Delon, Maurice Ronet, Maria Laforet, Frank Latimore, Ave Ninchi. 118 mins. (Miramax)

Adapted from Patricia Highsmith's novel *The Talented Mr. Ripley*, *Purple Noon* stars Delon as a poor but ambitious youth who embarks on an elaborate stolen-identity scam that

requires every ounce of resourcefulness and ruthlessness he possesses. Delon (later in frequent, highly publicized trouble for his off-screen criminal associations, ties that preceded his acting career), Ronet as his antagonistic "mentor," and Laforet as the latter's underappreciated spouse all turn in top work. Henri Decae supplies the alluring sand-and-surf-swept cinematography, on view in all its wide-screen glory.

QUICKSAND   (1950) B&W ***

D: Irving Pichel. Mickey Rooney, Jeanne Cagney, Peter Lorre, Barbara Bates, Taylor Holmes, Wally Cassell, Art Smith. 79 mins. (Englewood)

Quicksand casts Rooney as a decent but impulsive auto mechanic. When Mick finds himself 20 bucks short for a hot date with flashy frill Cagney, he "borrows" a bill from his Scrooge-like boss's (Smith) till, a petty theft that snowballs into an inadvertent crime spree. Though Bates is a bit much as the good girl unrequitedly in love with Rooney, Mick himself's in top form as the little guy who can't catch a break. Cagney's convincing as the opportunistic dame with a jones for mink, and a terrifically sleazy Lorre steals his scenes as a conniving arcade owner. (Coin-op devotees will get off on the antique pinball and related games on view.) Evocatively lensed in and around the then-honky-tonk Santa Monica Pier, *Quicksand* is a neatly scripted, taut little noir marred only by a somewhat anticlimactic denouement.

RAGE   (1972) ***

D: George C. Scott. George C. Scott, Martin Sheen, Richard Basehart. 100 mins. (Warner)

When authorities initiate a cover-up re his young son's death from radiation poisoning, contaminated Wyoming rancher Scott embarks on a filmlong vengeance spree. Scott doubles as director on this tense, satisfyingly exploitive approach to a serious issue.

RAILROADED (1947) B&W ***

D: Anthony Mann. John Ireland, Sheila Ryan, Hugh Beaumont, Jane Randolph, Keefe Brasselle. 71 mins. (Kino) DVD

Ireland turns in strong work as a sleazy killer who locks horns with cop Beaumont (in his pre–Ward Cleaver days), who's trying to protect target Ryan, in another sturdy second-feature *policier* enhanced by the director Mann/cinematographer John Alton tandem's visual magic.

RAISING CAIN (1992) **½

D: Brian De Palma. John Lithgow, John Lithgow, John Lithgow, John Lithgow, John Lithgow, Lolita Davidovich, Frances Sternhagen, Steven Bauer, Mel Harris. 95 mins. (Universal) DVD

It's Mondo Lithgow time! After his Anthony Hopkins/Hannibal Lecter impersonation in the dud *Ricochet* (HBO, DVD), future *3rd Rock from the Sun* telestar Lithgow plays fully five loonies here: child psychologist Carter Nix; his own sinister brother, Cain; their sadistic Norwegian behavioral-scientist dad; a juvenile alter ego named Josh; and, in his first drag perf since *The World According to Garp* (Warner), the domineering Margo. While Lithgow gives each part his all, our fave moment arrives when Dad tells evil son, "Shut up and finish your drink!" Alas, *Raising Cain* is less a coherent black-comedy thriller than a succession of cheap fright tricks that hit and miss in roughly equal measure. Some scenes are terrific, such as a long tracking shot that follows shrink Sternhagen as she delivers a mobile, breathlessly verbose analysis of the senior Dr. Nix. Others are calculatingly sick, as when Bauer's terminal-cancer-patient wife suffers a cardiac arrest upon seeing her spouse making out with doc Davidovich (!). The best

MANN AT HIS BEST: Tough mug John Ireland plays it rough with Sheila Ryan in Anthony Mann's hard-boiled *Railroaded.*
© Kino International Corporation

shock arrives last, lending the film the feel of a 95-minute setup for a 2-second punch line. (At least it's a *good* one.)

RAMPAGE (1987/1992) ***

D: William Friedkin. Michael Biehn, Alex McArthur, Nicholas Campbell, Deborah Van Valkenburgh, Royce Applegate. 92 mins. (Paramount)

After five years in legal limbo, Friedkin's serious-minded 1987 serial-killer probe finally reached screens in October 1992. One reason for the film's eventual unveiling may well have been

its peripheral but uncanny parallels to the then-current Jeffrey Dahmer case. Real-life allusions aside, *Rampage* rates as a quality flick that's more interested in exploring the legal ramifications of homicidal madness and the scars senseless slayings inflict on their victims' surviving family members than it is in supplying conventional suspense or vicarious chills. That's not to say *Rampage* doesn't boast its share of brutal moments. Friedkin conveys considerable terror in those tableaux depicting otherwise ineffectual psycho McArthur's murder-and-mutilation sprees. The sequence that sees stunned cops uncover

McArthur's satanic basement shrine, strewn with human body parts, is especially strong and unsettling. Much of the movie, based on William P. Wood's novel, deals with the struggle of Stockton, California, assistant D.A. Biehn to reconcile his own liberal views with his mandate to win a death-penalty conviction for the killer. Further complicating Biehn's involvement is his recent, wrenching decision to pull the plug on his own brain-dead young daughter. All the principals contribute convincing work in this grim but compelling exercise, with Applegate particularly unforgettable as a broken survivor whose wife and young son were among McArthur's victims. While not quite as visceral as John McNaughton's squirm-provoking *Henry*, *Rampage* amply dramatizes the ordinary individual's helplessness in the face of unbridled sociopathic aggression.

RANSOM (1996) **¹/₂

D: Ron Howard. Mel Gibson, Rene Russo, Gary Sinise, Lili Taylor, Liev Schreiber, Brawley Nolte. 120 mins. (Touchstone) DVD

A pumped-up, rock-'n'-roll remake of the rather obscure 1956 Glenn Ford–starrer of the same name (n/a), *Ransom* charts self-made airline mogul Mel's efforts to nail the lowlifes, led by rogue cop Sinise (in a convincingly sinister turn), who've kidnapped his young son (Nolte). *Ransom* would have worked better with less contrivance, a shorter running time, and a lower forced intensity level (as would most of us). One odd scene has Sinise, via cell phone, explain the plot and philosophy of *The Time Machine* to an impatient Mel.

RAVAGE (1997) ***

D: Ronnie Sortor. Mark Brazeale, Dan Rowland, Dina Harris, Frank Alexander. 85 mins. (Salt City)

With *Ravage*, Missouri-based auteur Sortor does an impressive job assembling a blistering, almost Hong Kong–styled action/psycho thriller on a home-movie budget. Brazeale stars as a criminal psychologist bent on avenging the senseless slaughter of his two daughters at the knife of sociopath Rowland. A video-surveillance clip places the murderer's whereabouts in Chicago, where he leads a ragged cult of random killers. Sortor tosses in a clever hook that further complicates the case. While some of the thesps betray limited range, Alexander as a Chicago undercover cop (he also boasts several behind-the-scenes credits, including stunts), turns in solid work, while Rowland is terrifically brutal in dual roles. *Ravage* is the type of rare, rough gem that gives the "outlaw video" indie genre the good name it so rarely deserves. We also liked the closing credit: "Extra Special Thanks to Dan Rowland for sacrificing his Memorial Day weekend."

RAW DEAL (1948) B&W ***

D: Anthony Mann. Dennis O'Keefe, Claire Trevor, Marsha Hunt, Raymond Burr, John Ireland. 79 mins. (Kino)

O'Keefe escapes from stir and goes after the sadistic sleazeball who framed him (a masterfully repulsive Burr). O'Keefe's competing affections for dames Trevor and Hunt further complicate the case in another noir fever dream from the team of Anthony Mann and cinematographer John Alton.

RED ROCK WEST (1992) ***¹/₂

D: John Dahl. Nicolas Cage, Dennis Hopper, Lara Flynn Boyle, J. T. Walsh, Timothy Carhart, Dwight Yoakam. 98 mins. (Columbia/TriStar) DVD

Director Dahl follows his sharp 1989 desert noir, *Kill Me Again* (see index), with an even better entry in the same subgenre. An updated *Detour* Meets *Blood Simple*, *Red Rock West* casts Cage as a decent, if somewhat dim-witted, drifter whose earnest search for gainful employment leads him into a chain of ever escalating criminal activities, initially sparked by a case of mistaken identity. Hopper invests his by now patented loony-killer role with admirable energy, while Walsh is subtly menacing as a sneaky sheriff and Boyle lends a hard edge to her portrayal of Walsh's endangered wife. Scattered regional screenings and cable-TV exposure preceded the pic's vid release. Dahl followed with the unfortunately forgettable *Unforgettable* (MGM).

REFLECTIONS IN THE DARK (1994) **¹/₂

D: Jon Purdy. Mimi Rogers, Billy Zane, John Terry, Kurt Fuller, Lee Garlington. 83 mins. (New Horizons)

Writer/director Purdy, creator of the fun pulp gangster caper *Dillinger and Capone* (see index), aims higher here but, despite his film's interesting structure, falls short of the mark. *Reflections* opens with Rogers—who seems to specialize in playing resentful crazies, like her swinger-turned-fundamentalist-fanatic in Michael Tolkin's *The Rapture* (Columbia/Tri-Star) and her suicidal heroine in Mark Malone's *Bulletproof Heart* (Republic)—on death row awaiting imminent execution for the confessed killing of hubby Terry on their seventh anniversary (lending new rad-feminist meaning to the term "seven-year itch"). She relates her sorry story to guard Zane, who, we learn, volunteered for the assignment since becoming something of a fan of the celebrated killer; in flashbacks, we witness the events leading to her sexistential crime. Trouble is, Mimi, her smarmy spouse, and their friends Fuller and Garlington are such unbearably smug characters that strapping *all* of them into an electric couch and pulling the switch would have been a more crowd-pleasing resolution.

RELENTLESS:
THE SERIES

RELENTLESS (1989) **½

D: William Lustig. Judd Nelson, Robert Loggia, Leo Rossi, Meg Foster, Angel Tompkins, Buck Flower. 92 mins. (Columbia/TriStar)

For *Relentless*, director Lustig lines up an A– cast that includes Loggia, Foster, and former Brat Packer Nelson as a murderous nutjob. The real star here, though, is Rossi, sort of a B-movie Joe Mantegna (who's since become a B-movie mainstay himself), as newly promoted LAPD dick Sam Dietz, a transplanted New Yorker impatient with partner Loggia's laid-back approach to Judd's seemingly random rampage. It's Rossi's charisma that hoists *Relentless* a notch above the usual run of psycho-amok flicks.

RELENTLESS 3 (1993) ***

D: James Lemmo. Leo Rossi, William Forsythe, Signy Coleman, Tom Bower, Robert Costanzo. 84 mins. (New Line)

Rossi returns as detective Sam Dietz in what rates as the *Relentless* series's best entry to date. (The lame *Relentless 2*, on Columbia/TriStar, is well worth avoiding.) What could have been just another low-budget *Silence of the Lambs* knockoff (replete with your requisite disgusto autopsy sequence) is elevated by Rossi's credibly human perf (any screen cop who confesses, "I *hate* sports metaphors" scores points in our book), a controlled, quirky turn by celluloid psycho extraordinaire Forsythe as the latest in a long line of Ed Gein–inspired maniacs, and the Lemmo-penned script's admirable avoidance of stereotypes and clichés. On the downside, the flick has a foreshortened feel that leaves a few key plot queries unanswered.

RELENTLESS 4 (1994) ***

D: Oley Sassone. Leo Rossi, Famke Janssen, Colleen Coffey, Ken Lerner, Christopher Pettiet. 91 mins. (New Line)

Rossi, who coproduced, and caustic partner Coffey pursue a serial killer fond of subjecting his victims to death rituals drawn from different religions. Said victims are all former patients of foxy shrink Janssen. Rossi's naturalistic style keeps a subplot about his widowed character's strained relationship with surly teen son Pettiet from turning maudlin. Suspense, selective splatter, an effective near-death sequence, and a credible cast make *Relentless 4* (*Relentless IV: Ashes to Ashes* per the on-screen credits) a modest winner.

ROAD HOUSE (1948) B&W ***

D: Jean Negulesco. Ida Lupino, Cornel Wilde, Richard Widmark, Celeste Holm, O. Z. Whitehead, Ian MacDonald. 95 mins. (Fox)

Lupino's appealing as a tough, sandpaper-voiced chanteuse, sort of a femme Tom Waits, who works in Widmark's title establishment. Trouble ensues when Ida spurns R.W.'s advances in favor of underling Wilde. Widmark, fresh from his *Kiss of Death* crazed-killer triumph, goes psycho in the final two reels. The pic's tart dialogue and smoky atmosphere (the cast consumes enough cigarettes to make watching this carcinogenic noir potentially hazardous to the viewer's health) contribute to the dark-toned fun.

ROAD-KILL U.S.A. (1994) **½

D: Tony Elwood. Andrew Porter, Sean Bridgers, Deanna Perry. 93 mins. (AIP)

In this Charleston, North Carolina–lensed indie, hitchhiking college student Bridgers unwisely accepts a ride from philosophical redneck psycho Porter (well cast in a role tailor-made for Wings Hauser or Gary Busey) and his pathetic (though more lethal) squeeze (Perry). Like Brad Pitt in the similarly themed *Kalifornia* (see index), Porter has a rather aimless agenda, with no particular place to go or planned victims (who range across the entire age and gender map) on tap. What Porter's character brings to the roadkill table is a fondness for particularly nasty slay techniques, such as using a shard of broken glass to slice a former crony's olfactory breathing apparati, inducing slow, tortured suffocation. The pic's most consciously bizarre sequence sees the trio pick up a party clown—in full costume and makeup (!)—whose car's conked out en route to a local kiddie gig; turns out he's an obnoxious, foulmouthed transplanted Long Islander who performs an impromptu Joe Pesci *GoodFellas* impersonation—Porter dispatches him with particular relish, first shooting him, then slitting his throat. While not in *Kalifornia*'s league, this derivative but well-executed indie isn't likely to leave potential renters either bored *or* enlightened.

THE SADIST (1963) B&W ***½

D: James Landis. Arch Hall, Jr., Helen Hovey, Don Russell, Marilyn Manning. 95 mins. (Rhino) DVD

Arch Hall, Jr., unlikely star of such legendary camp turkeys as *Eegah!*, *The Nasty Rabbit*, and *Wild Guitar* (all Rhino), actually once toplined in a *good* low-budget flick. *The Sadist* casts him as a gun-toting maniac loosely based on Charles Starkweather. Mean Arch and dim-witted squeeze Manning terrorize a trio of lost schoolteachers derailed at a desert garage en route to an L.A. Dodgers game. *The Sadist*, which unfolds virtually in "real" time, is a truly tense, well-crafted sleazoid suspenser that successfully plays with audience expectations and delivers some genuine shocks. Lensed in evocative black-and-white, *The Sadist* can take its place with such equally perverse early-'60s sickies as *Lady in a Cage* and *Kitten with a Whip*.

SCAM   (1993) ***

D: John Flynn. Christopher Walken, Lorraine Bracco, Martin Donovan, Miguel Ferrer. 102 mins. (Fox)

Expert acting, especially by Bracco, lifts *Scam* above the standard run of direct-to-video caper flicks. Adapted by Craig Smith from his novel *Ladystinger*, *Scam* casts Bracco as a small-time Miami con artist partnered with a sleazy Ferrer. Walken coerces the petty grifter into playing for higher stakes—piles of Jamaican drug money embezzled by crooked computer hacker Donovan. Walken and Bracco's burgeoning relationship takes precedence over the usual chases and shoot-outs, and, one fairly graphic decapitation scene aside, director Flynn adopts a low-key approach to the oft scenic proceedings.

SCARLET STREET   (1945) B&W ***

D: Fritz Lang. Edward G. Robinson, Joan Bennett, Dan Duryea. 95 mins. (Sinister Cinema)

A repressed Robinson is led astray by bad girl Bennett and lowlife male cohort (played to oily perfection by Duryea) in Fritz Lang's classic noir outing, based on Jean Renoir's 1931 *La Chienne*. Also available in a colorized edition.

SCORPION SPRING   (1997) **

D: Brian Cox. Alfred Molina, Ruben Blades, Patrick McGaw, Esai Morales, Kevin Tighe, Matthew McConaughey, Angel Aviles, Richard Edson, John Doe. 89 mins. (New Line)

Scorpion Spring, directed by actor Cox, represents an especially annoying flick, since it gets off to a bright-enough start to keep you hanging on

before taking a typically tired turn into Tarantino-manqué territory. Rejected Gen-X New York native McGaw, tooling around the Arizona desert in your typical vintage convertible, picks up Molina, a stranded French actor (!) with an expired visa, and their early scenes together supply a good deal of amusement. Trouble rears its sneering head in the form of screwdriver-killer Morales, a border low-life who's using his "sister" (Aviles) as a drug mule *and* forcing her to hook on the side. It all collapses in a welter of obnoxious roadkill clichés that insult both the viewer's intelligence and the pic's own initial integrity. Molina, though, is excellent throughout as the hedonistic, self-serving Frenchman. X rocker Doe cameos as a deputy, while McConaughey has a small criminal role.

SEA OF LOVE   (1989) ***

D: Harold Becker. Al Pacino, Ellen Barkin, John Goodman. 112 mins. (Universal) DVD

After his gay undercover turn in *Cruising* (Warner), cop Pacino braves the unattached-hetero scene in a bid to bag a serial killer who's preying on single men, with a sexy Barkin emerging as a prime suspect. Look for Michael (*Henry*) Rooker in a small but pivotal role.

SECOND CHANCE   (1953) ***

D: Rudolph Maté. Robert Mitchum, Linda Darnell, Jack Palance. 82 mins. (Media)

Tough guy Mitchum tries to shield mob target Darnell in Mexico. The standard story line receives a boost from a top cast (which also includes Palance) and authentic locations. Originally shown in 3-D.

SERIAL KILLER   (1995) **

D: Pierre David. Kim Delaney, Gary Hudson, Tobin Bell, Pam Grier, Marco Rodriguez,

Lyman Ward, Cyndi Pass, Andrew Prine. 94 mins. (Republic)

A creepy perf by Bell as the dead-eyed "Picasso Killer" plus an appearance by the always welcome Grier (albeit in a bland police-chief role) comprise the sole distinguishing characteristics of this otherwise typical Delaney-in-distress affair from Pierre David's Canadian canned-thriller factory. There are some creatively grisly touches—as when Bell leaves two surgically excised eyeballs next to a pair of glasses (!)—but this formulaic *Silence of the Lambs* clone is otherwise equally bald on surprises and suspense.

SE7EN   (1995) ***

D: David Fincher. Brad Pitt, Morgan Freeman, Gwyneth Paltrow, Richard Roundtree, R. Lee Ermey, John C. McGinley, Kevin Spacey. 127 mins. (New Line) DVD

Veteran cop Somerset (a calmly authoritative Freeman), only days away from retirement, teams with gung-ho young transferee Mills (a twitchy Pitt) to track a preternaturally patient madman who keys his slayings to the seven deadly sins. The determined detectives' background research leads to two rarities in recent American cinema—lengthy library-set scenes and literary allusions (largely to Dunne and Chaucer)—as well as a surfeit of more typical disgusto slay-scene and autopsy imagery, with expert makeup FX courtesy of Rob (*The Thing*) Bottin. (A scene in which an authentic-looking "corpse" springs to spastic life may well go down as the celluloid horror highlight of 1995.) Though written and played with an admirable thoroughness—the film's one-week time span neatly frames the "seven" motif—it's in the lensing itself that *Se7en* makes its lasting cinematic mark. (Even the seven-deadly-sins hook was earlier used in Jean Brismee's 1971 Euro fright film, *The Devil's Nightmare* [Image/Redemption]). Shot in nearly sepialike tones, where stark whites collide with dull beiges and greens while shadows sprout everywhere, *Se7en* presents a view of a modern metropolis as a Dantean inferno, without resorting to exaggerated dystopian sets. The Stan Brakhage–styled opening and closing credits further fuel this feel-bad film's all-encompassing visual air of urban decay and despair (a theme often double-stated in the dialogue), while prolific composer Howard (*Ed Wood*, *Naked Lunch*) Shore again contributes a flawlessly atmospheric score.

SEVEN DAYS TO NOON (1950) B&W ***

D: John Boulting. Barry Jones, Olive Sloane, Andre Morell. 93 mins. (Sinister Cinema)

Guilt-ridden scientist Jones threatens to explode an A-bomb in London if his demands for a nuclear ban aren't met in this tense, change-of-pace thriller from the Boulting brothers, normally associated with classic Brit comedies.

THE SEVENTH FLOOR (1993) *

D: Ian Barry. Brooke Shields, Masaya Kato, Linda Cropper, Craig Pearce. 99 mins. (A-Pix) DVD

Director Barry and "actor" Kato (cast as a closet psycho) team up with former starlet manqué Shields for this dull Down Under blunder. Brooke's the widow of a fast-lane exec who knew too much about a sleazy corporate conspiracy hatched by office ice queen Cropper. Our heroine takes up with computer genius Kato, who eventually moves into her seventh-floor loft, where she becomes his virtual prisoner. If possible, *The Seventh Floor* is even worse than director Barry and costar Kato's earlier *Crime Broker* (A-Pix, DVD), since Kato shows no thespic improvement, Barry exhibits just as little directorial flair, and Shields is a far droopier presence than *Crime*

Broker's talented Jacqueline Bisset, who's also thoughtful enough to please her fans by flashing some skin and modeling several wigs.

sex, lies & videotape (1989) ***

D: Steven Soderbergh. James Spader, Andie MacDowell, Peter Gallagher, Laura San Giacomo. 101 mins. (Columbia/TriStar) Special Edition DVD

Soderbergh's overrated but still compelling and original exercise in video voyeurism launched the screen careers of several new thesps and helped pave the way for today's ongoing indie-film boom.

SEXUAL INTENT (1994) ***

D: Kurt Mac Carley. Gary Hudson, Sarah Hill, Erica Howard, Christine Sholle, Michelle Brin. 88 mins. (Columbia/TriStar)

Not the run-of-the-mill "erotic thriller" the misleading box art implies, director/scripter Carley's *Sexual Intent* is actually an engrossing, serious-minded, supposedly reality-based case study of the so-called Sweetheart Scammer. Hudson, a veteran of hack erotic thrillers, is quite convincing as a sociopathic chameleon who seduces and fleeces femme victims, ranging from easy prey, like his young stripper squeeze (Sholle), to true challenges, like sophisticated shrink Howard. When one of his marks decides to strike back, her vengeance quest is handled with unusual credibility, and it's fun to see

the smug con man slowly crumble under her relentless campaign. *Sexual Intent* deftly blends dramatic and exploitation elements in a satisfying mix.

SHOCK CORRIDOR (1963) B&W/COLOR ****

D: Sam Fuller. Peter Breck, Constance Towers, Gene Evans, James Best, Hari Rhodes, Larry Tucker. 101 mins. (Home Vision) DVD

Pulitzer Prize–obsessed reporter Breck feigns insanity and poses as a mental patient the better to discover who killed Sloane in the kitchen. Many of the inmates become polar opposites of their former sane selves—nuclear physicist Evans is reduced to mental six-year-old status, civil-rights pioneer Rhodes delivers racist harangues—in a self-contained black hole that gradually sucks Breck of his rationality (marginal to begin with). Fuller's ahead-of-its-time (and quite possibly out-of-its-mind) filmic fever dream may well rate as the maverick auteur's signature work in a career crammed with unforgettable films.

SHOWGIRL MURDERS (1995) **1/2

D: Gene Hertel. Maria Ford, Matt Preston, Jeff Douglas, Samantha Carter, Bob McFarland, Kevin Alber, Nikki Fritz. 84 mins. (New Horizons)

Then-reigning Roger Corman B queen Ford toplines as a femme fatale in this *Postman Always Rings Twice* Meets *Body Heat* at a Strip Club. Fugitive Maria goes undercover at a dead-end bar owned by Douglas and his boozy, guilt-driven wife (Carter). Our enterprising antiheroine wastes no time transforming the sleepy dive into a wildly lucrative strip joint she redubs "Pandora's Boxxx." Between frequent down-and-dirty dance sets—with "Principal Dances Performed, Themed and

Costumed by Maria Ford"—Maria uses her wiles to convince Douglas to murder his spouse. Also in the picture are inept hit man Alber, blackmailer/DEA agent McFarland, nightmare sequences, a quickie clip from *Bram Stoker's Burial of the Rats,* and a pivotal tune recycled from 1990's *Naked Obsession.* Frequent Fred Olen Ray player Fritz joins Ford for a spirited Eve-and-Lilith specialty number.

THE SILENT PARTNER
(1978) ***

D: Daryl Duke. Elliott Gould, Christopher Plummer, Susannah York. 103 mins. (Vestron)

Bank teller Gould matches wits with sadistic robber Plummer (in one of his best roles) in a sly, suspenseful sleeper lensed in Toronto. Duke also directed the excellent country-and-western-themed *Payday* (HBO), with Rip Torn as a doomed C&W star.

A SIMPLE PLAN   (1998) ***1/2

D: Sam Raimi. Bill Paxton, Billy Bob Thornton, Bridget Fonda, Brent Briscoe, Gary Cole. 121 mins. (Paramount) DVD

A *Simple Plan* presents a cogent case for letting novelists adapt their own work to the screen: Scott B. Smith crafts a nearly flawless script from his novel of the same name, brought to vivid life by erstwhile *Evil Dead* auteur Sam Raimi—abandoning his usual pyrotechnic style to fit Smith's more austere material—and an ace cast headed by Paxton as seemingly well-adjusted working stiff Hank; Thornton as his slow-witted but often instinctively insightful older brother, Jacob; and Fonda as Sarah, Paxton's increasingly scheming wife. The characters' troubles begin when Hank, Jacob, and the latter's crude buddy and unemployed "town drunk," Lou (Briscoe) stumble upon a crashed private plane containing

a stash of more than $4 million in presumably illegal cash—or, as Lou puts it, "the American dream in a gym bag." Initially resistant to the idea of copping the loot, Hank quickly revises his outlook and devises the titular scheme: He'll hold on to the bread until spring; if the coast looks clear, they'll divvy it up in an even three-way split and leave town. Naturally, the coast grows inclement indeed, clouded with rampant mistrust and crowded with unanticipated corpses. Writer Smith's inventive plotting and character development result in several unexpected twists as the film's four major players find more spiritual erosion than material fortune in their tortured futures. Smith, Raimi, and cinematographer Alar Kivilo fully exploit the story's wintry, *Fargo*-like setting but, unlike the Coen brothers in that tongue-in-bloody-cheek classic, play their violent tale totally straight, encouraging an audience complicity that compels viewers to question their own sense of situational ethics. Like director Raimi, prolific composer Danny Elfman chooses moody understatement over Sturm und Drang suspense stings. The similarly themed *Route 9* (Sterling), less psychologically complex but consistently absorbing, also rates a look.

SINGLE WHITE FEMALE
(1992) ***

D: Barbet Schroeder. Bridget Fonda, Jennifer Jason Leigh, Steven Weber, Peter Friedman. 107 mins. (Columbia/TriStar) DVD

Schroeder's upscale slasher tale is basically a distaff variation on Martin Donovan's more perverse *Apartment Zero* (see index). Leigh adds another impressive unstable role to her résumé (see also *Miami Blues, Heart of Midnight, Rush*) as the roommate from hell who apes and eventually seeks to control enviable Manhattan career babe Fonda. Highlights include a bit by Ken (*The Thing*) Tobey, a grisly spiked-heel

murder, and a claustrophobic elevator-set catfight. *Single White Female* stacks up as Schroeder's scariest film since his documentary *Idi Amin Dada* (Warner).

SISTER MY SISTER   (1994) ***

D: Nancy Meckler. Julie Walters, Joely Richardson, Jodhi May, Sophie Thursfield. 98 mins. (A-Pix) DVD

Sort of a sisterly variation on Peter Jackson's *Heavenly Creatures,* this fact-based story opens with a *Stepfather*-like postslaughter scene, then backtracks to chronicle the crime's genesis. Richardson and May are throughly credible as the lonely, sheltered young Parisian siblings who lead ultraminimalist lives as maids (and, eventually, lovers) in the employ of tyrannical widow Walters and her own sheltered twentysomething daughter (Thursfield). At once a strong character study and class-warfare fable, *Sister My Sister* succeeds in drawing viewers into the foursome's claustrophobic world. Director Meckler and scripter Wendy Kesselman eschew *Heavenly Creatures*'s boldly surreal approach in favor of a straightforward, PBS-styled account, with few attempts to lend this Brit production a Gallic flavor. Though more sad than suspenseful, the film's muted treatment makes the sisters' final violent outburst seem all the more brutal.

SLAMDANCE   (1987) **1/2

D: Wayne Wang. Tom Hulce, Mary Elizabeth Mastrantonio, Virginia Madsen, Harry Dean Stanton, Don Opper, Adam Ant. 99 mins. (Key)

Slammed by most critics of the day, *Slamdance* is a flawed but involving L.A.-set thriller starring Hulce (*Amadeus*) as a freelance cartoonist embroiled in the murder of an ex-flame, victim of a political-scandal cover-up. Hulce conducts his own, often inept investigation while trying to forge a reconciliation with ex-wife Mastrantonio. *Slamdance* is burdened by padded footage, an overbearing patina of El Lay glitz, and director Wang's (*Chan Is Missing*) fondness for clichéd rock-vid visuals, but there is a story underneath it all, and not a bad one at that. Wang went on to direct, among others, *The Joy Luck Club*, *Smoke* (both Touchstone), and *Chinese Box* (Trimark).

SLAUGHTER OF THE INNOCENTS (1993) **

D: James Glickenhaus. Scott Glenn, Jesse Cameron-Glickenhaus, Sheryl Tousey, Darlanne Fluegel. 104 mins. (Universal)

Any similarity between Jim (*The Exterminator, Shakedown*) Glickenhaus's *Slaughter of the Innocents* and *The Silence of the Lambs* is purely intentional. Beyond the sound-alike title, *Slaughter* casts *Silence*'s FBI field boss Glenn as—you guessed it—an FBI field boss. While he's also partnered with a younger femme agent (Tousey, in place of Jodie Foster), Glenn receives most of his major assists from his own preteen computer-genius son (!), sporting the worst wardrobe seen outside a KrissKross video and played, in a rather blatantly nepotistic move, by Glickenhaus's real-life offspring Cameron-Glickenhaus. While creatively grisly touches abound in the Utah-set manhunt for a religious-crackpot child-killer, young Jesse's Culkin-esque intrusions place an increasingly burdensome strain on viewer tolerance as the reels roll on.

SLEEPING WITH THE ENEMY (1991) **½

D: Joseph Ruben. Julia Roberts, Patrick Bergin, Kevin Anderson, Elizabeth Lawrence, Kyle Secor. 98 mins. (Fox)

The *Stepfather* auteur Ruben's domestic thriller, sort of a *Step-husband*, lacks the perverse chills of his earlier work. In the ever escalating psycho sweepstakes, mad hubby Bergin, who doesn't inflict so much as a single fatality all film long, isn't fit to carry Hannibal ("the Cannibal") Lecter's face restraint. Roberts did get our nod for Best Reverse Drag Performance of 1991, though, when, as Bergin's fugitive wife, she dons a male wig and moustache (!) to visit her blind mother (Lawrence) in a nearby nursing home, easily the highlight of this watchable but completely contrived pseudoshocker.

SLING BLADE   (1996) ***½

D: Billy Bob Thornton. Billy Bob Thornton, Dwight Yoakam, John Ritter, J. T. Walsh, Natalie Canerday, Lucas Black, James Hampton, Robert Duvall. 135 mins. (Miramax) DVD

Actor/auteur Thornton's uphill climb with *Sling Blade*—which began screen life as a 25-minute short titled *Some Folks Call It a Sling Blade* (Vanguard), starring Thornton, Walsh, and Molly Ringwald and directed by George Hickenlooper—led to several Academy Award noms and a Best Adapted Screenplay Oscar for the Arkansas-born B-movie and cable-TV vet. In what rates as the kindest, gentlest psycho-killer movie we're likely to see, Thornton creates and inhabits an indelible character in soulful, slow-witted social reject Karl Childers. After spending 25 years in a mental hospital for the childhood murders of his mom and her lover, Karl returns to his birthplace, lands a handyman job at a local garage, and is eventually "adopted" by fatherless kid Black and his kindly mom (Canerday). What's wrong with this domestic picture is the loud, abusive presence of Canerday's no-account construction-worker beau, Doyle (country crooner Yoakam), whose violent, boorish behavior increasingly offends Karl and terrorizes his surrogate family. Thornton receives strong support from Yoakam, young Black, Canerday, and especially Ritter (in an against-type turn, to put it mildly, as Canerday's gay, New Agey convenience-store boss and best friend). Walsh puts in showy wraparound appearances as a garrulous serial killer/fellow inmate. Duvall is largely unrecognizable in an eye-blink cameo as Karl's dad. *Dead Man* director Jim Jarmusch also shows up, as a fast-food vendor, in an early scene. In addition to his on-screen brilliance, scripter/director Thornton does a fine job conveying the atmosphere and rhythms of Southern small-town life. *Sling Blade*'s only serious flaw lies in its elongated running time. While the film works scene by scene, there's a major lag about halfway through, where Thornton's deliberately static camera and overly detailed observations, no matter how dead-on, stall his story's forward drive. (A budding romance with a "slow" store clerk could have been dropped or at least shortened.) Still, *Sling Blade* represents a legit triumph of indie filmmaking, and the obviously determined Thornton fully deserves the accolades he's received.

THE WIT AND WISDOM OF KARL CHILDERS
"There were these two fellas standin' on a bridge goin' to the bathroom. One fella says the water's cold; other fella says the water's deep. I believe one fella come from Arkansas. Get it?"
—*Billy Bob Thornton*, **Sling Blade**

SLIVER   (1993) **

D: Philip Noyce. Sharon Stone, William Baldwin, Tom Berenger, Martin Landau. 106 mins. (Paramount)

Sort of a shallow, high-tech *Peeping Tom*, *Sliver* stars Stone as (like *Fatal Attraction*'s Glenn Close before her) an unusually well-heeled book editor. Unbeknownst to Stone, the "horror high-rise" she's just moved into served as the site of several murders. The troubled building is owned by a dedicated voyeur (Baldwin)—a Norman Bates for the '90s, complete with an active libido—whose ubiquitous video cameras covertly record his tenants' not-so-private lives. Stone finds herself irresistibly drawn to the overtly creepy Baldwin, even once his "secret" obsession casts him as the leading suspect in a fresh outbreak of in-house homicides. Baldwin's master-control room, with its blinking bank of multiple monitors flashing the intimate details of his tenants' lives, ranks as *Sliver*'s strongest riff. Unfortunately, the script, by *Basic Instinct*'s Joe Eszterhas, cops out when it comes to Stone's wavering complicity in Baldwin's addictive, godlike games. Worse, the flick is irredeemably done in by the biggest cheat ending seen onscreen since *The Temp* and Jennifer Lynch's *Boxing Helena*. (Several endings were apparently tested; we would have preferred one wherein Stone shot herself, then Glenn Close.)

SMALL KILL (1993) ***

D: Rob Fresco. Gary Burghoff, Jason Miller, Fred Carpenter, Donnie Kehr, Rebecca Ferrati, Tom Poster. 86 mins. (VCI)

*S*mall Kill is a raw, edgy showcase for the considerable screen-psycho talents of diminutive Burghoff (former *M°A°S°H* regular Radar). As Fleck, a busy schizophrenic, bisexual transvestite fortune-teller, kidnapper, child-murderer, and would-be drug lord (you know the type), Burghoff easily purloins the pic. The movie opens with a super-gory drug-related shoot-out (special makeup FX by Brian Holt), wherein cop Kehr bails out endangered partner (and coscripter) Carpenter (who resembles Al Pacino's undercover character in *Serpico*). Police captain Christopher Cooke reassigns the tandem to investigate a rash of frequently fatal kidnappings. The seemingly separate cases

---

Filmmakers in Focus!

ACTOR/PRODUCER TOM POSTER ON *SMALL KILL*

As Told to The Phantom

Tom Poster is nothing if not a cinematic jack-of-all-trades. In addition to coproducing and costarring in Small Kill, *he's worked as an actor* (Transylvania Twist, Yesterday's Target), *stuntman* (Watchers II), *and FX sculptor* (Masque of the Red Death).

PHANTOM: How did *Small Kill* evolve?

POSTER: *Small Kill*, which I looked at as a cross between a Steven Seagal film and *The Silence of the Lambs*, was in a state of flux for approximately three years. Originally, the film was going to be shot in North Carolina. Then they were going to shoot it in New York City. Eventually, it ended up happening on Long Island. Money was being raised every day the film was being shot, a bit over thirty days in all. We didn't know if we'd have enough to finish.

PHANTOM: Was Gary Burghoff involved from the beginning?

POSTER: Gary came into it early through [actor/coproducer] Fred Carpenter. At first Jonathan Barnes, the banker I play, was also Esmarelda [Fleck's elderly fortune-teller drag persona in the finished film]. Then when Gary Burghoff got ahold of the script, because of his desperate need to try to change his image as Mr. Good Guy "Radar," he said, "Hey, I wanna do that. Let's make this part of Fleck's character." Which was okay with me. If I was producing a film and I had a choice between myself and Tom Berenger, I'd go with Berenger!

PHANTOM: When did Jason Miller come aboard?

POSTER: I was doing *Inherit the Wind* at the Scranton Public Theater with Jason, who's very much involved with that and the Pennsylvania Summer Theater Festival. After we finished the play, I said, "Jason, how would you like a little role in this film? If you work on it, I'll get some of the actors from the Scranton Public Theater small roles in the film and some of the profits would go to the theater."

PHANTOM: He also received fairly prominent billing.

POSTER: For a very small role. There were creative differences between myself and the company; I would have done things a lot differently. I would have liked to have seen his role expanded.

PHANTOM: Were there any problems with Burghoff's provision that he direct his own scenes?

POSTER: No. The only problem was that he thinks on a big-budget scale, and we were making a very, very low-budget film [$650,000]. When you work for years and years in that system, shooting *M°A°S°H*—they don't think about money. Everything you could ever imagine is *there*. Snap your fingers and you've got it. So when he's directing and he's thinking on that level—it's difficult. You don't have the time or the ability to get some of the things he wants. The pen that I stab Fred with at the end of the film— originally the prop department had just a regular pen. And Gary just went off. He saw the pen as an important item. He actually put out his own money and bought a $350 pen!

PHANTOM: The pen received a prominent close-up in the bank scene.

POSTER: We shot that whole bank scene, and when we went to the screening room it was all out of focus. And that was the last day of shooting! So we had to actually go back about a month later and reshoot, without the original director [Rob Fresco] and without Gary Burghoff, who wasn't around at all. There was such pressure. We were shooting with tail ends of film, counting down, "We've got a hundred feet left." Everyone who worked on that film, from grips on up, worked twenty hours a day. And everybody had their hearts in it.

PHANTOM: That gory shoot-out in the beginning must have taken some time.

POSTER: The head getting blown off, the hand getting blown off—it's all really wonderful stuff. Brian Holt, who'd worked on *The Abyss*, put a lot of time into it. He even put his own money into buying some of the materials he wanted. I'm a sculptor, so I sculpted some of the gunshot wounds. Brian also created a wonderful cataract eye for the old geezer who finds the kid's shoe, but we had difficulty with the lighting that night, so you don't really see it too well.

PHANTOM: You knew something about low budgets going in—you'd earlier worked for Roger Corman.

POSTER: Yes, I did quite a few things over at Corman's Concorde Pictures. I did a lot of the makeup on *Masque of the Red Death*, with Patrick Macnee. The stunt coordinator recognized me from a stunt class we were both in at UCLA, so I wound up doing horseback riding in the film. I also did a film there called *Overexposed*. Larry Brand, the director, asked me if I'd like to play a role in the film. I read the script and the role I thought I'd be really good for was the detective, but *he* was going to play that role. So there was a girl who was actually supposed to play the role of Angie, [soap star] Catherine Oxenberg's assistant. When she backed out, I said I'd do it as a gay guy. I have all her mail. I come up to her and say, "Missives from the masses!" I look at her and go, "Honey, I hope you got some good mail today 'cause I sure did last night." That's an improv line; it wasn't in the script. I didn't make the line up. There was a gay guy who lived next door to me. Every time I went to my mailbox, this guy would run out and get his mail too and he would say that. So I stole it from that guy. I also did *Watchers II*. I'm the monster. That was an interesting experience because I was not only the monster but involved in making part of the monster's costume.

PHANTOM: What happened to Gary Burghoff's $350 pen?

POSTER: He gave it to the production company. I still have it!

converge in Burghoff, who turns out to be something of a one-transvestite crime wave. A low-budgeter that garnered mostly upbeat reviews when it unspooled at various film markets and fests, *Small Kill*, lensed in authentic Long Island locales, combines a gritty, verité look with the same sort of febrile tone that informs Larry Cohen's *God Told Me To* and Jonathan Demme's *The Silence of the Lambs*. Occasional story flaws keep *Small Kill* from scaling the latters' heights, but this is an unsettling item genre buffs won't want to miss. Sec- ond-billed Jason (*The Exorcist*) Miller shows up only in a brief wino cameo, looking fat and awful (we hope it's more of Holt's makeup FX). Former New York *Daily News* "People Page" columnist Tom Poster, Sr., plays a doomed cop, while his coproducer son portrays a creepy banker. Actors Miller and Carpenter reteamed for the semisuccessful 1994 Long Island–set thriller *Murdered Innocence* (Columbia/TriStar).

SORRY, WRONG NUMBER (1948)
B&W ***

D: Anatole Litvak. Barbara Stanwyck, Burt Lancaster, Wendell Corey. 89 mins. (Paramount)

Barb's tour-de-force perf as a woman who overhears conspirators planning her murder earned the intense actress a deserved Oscar nomination in a film adapted by Lucille Fletcher from her radio play, which originally featured Agnes Moorehead as the endangered femme.

THE SPANISH PRISONER
(1997) ***

D: David Mamet. Campbell Scott, Rebecca Pidgeon, Ben Gazzara, Felicity Huffman, Ricky Jay, Steve Martin. 112 mins. (Columbia/TriStar) DVD

Veteran playwright Mamet's exceedingly tricky script runs unlikely hero Scott—and the viewer—through the ultra-paranoid wringer. Seems independent contractor Scott's devised a formula (referred to simply as "the Process") that's certain to reap huge windfall profits for the corporation he works for. But boss Gazzara's refusal to guarantee Scott a specific cut of the loot sends him into a tizzy of uncertainty. Rival corporate interests, meanwhile, will stop at nothing, even murder, to wrest the secret from its naïve inventor, and Scott's soon embroiled in a wrenching game of Who(m) Do You Trust? Outwardly friendly investor Martin? Best friend/company lawyer Jay? Loyal, romantically inclined office assistant Pidgeon? FBI agent Huffman? Mamet keeps Scott and the rest of us guessing even as the stakes continue to mount. As in the best of Mamet's previous work, the writer explores the very nature of individual belief systems, the duplicitous power of words (especially the cliché-addicted Pidgeon's), and the boundaries of acceptable behavior, all neatly woven into a genre plot. Look for Jonathan Katz (Mamet's real-life Boston neighbor), of Comedy Central's *Dr. Katz: Professional Therapist* fame, in an attorney cameo.

SPECIAL EFFECTS   (1984) ***

D: Larry Cohen. Eric Bogosian, Zoe Tamerlis, Brad Rijn, Kevin O'Connor, Bill Oland. 103 mins. (Embassy, n.i.d.)

An ironic meditation on our American mediacracy, *Special Effects* stars Bogosian as Christopher Neville, a perverse, Michael Cimino–like director who's on the outs with Hollywood after blowing $30 mil on an unfinished film. The unpopular auteur attempts to repair his shattered outsized ego by starting work on a sinister cinema verité project involving a real-life murder that he himself sets in motion. *Special Effects* takes an opposite approach to the conceptually similar *F/X* (see index) by incorporating no special effects at all—a strategy that's at once witty and, perhaps as important, money-saving.

SPLIT SECOND   (1953) B&W ***

D: Dick Powell. Stephen McNally, Alexis Smith, Jan Sterling, Richard Egan. 85 mins. (RKO)

Actor Powell directs a bizarre noir, with McNally cast as an escaped con holding hostages in a Southwest atomic-test area. *Split Second* features a great ending, followed by a deep-thought epilogue. No relation to the lame 1992 Rutger Hauer horror flick of the same name (HBO).

STARK FEAR   (1961) B&W ***

D: Ned Hockman. Beverly Garland, Skip Homeier, Kenneth Tobey, Hannah Stone, Paul Scovil. 84 mins. (Sinister Cinema)

This regional rarity rates as one of the strangest flicks we've ever witnessed (which is admittedly going some). Sort of a *Sleeping with the Enemy* in reverse, *Stark Fear* sees sadistic hubby Homeier repeatedly abuse, then summarily abandon spouse Garland. The normally feisty Bev—earlier the scourge of screen monsters ranging from the Venusian veg creature in *It Conquered the World* to white-eyed alien vampire Paul Birch in *Not of This Earth*—spends the rest of the flick desperately searching for the psychotic, sexist lout. Even after she's raped in a graveyard by Skip's cloddish best friend while her errant mate secretly (and gleefully) looks on, Bev remains bent on regaining his "affections." When Bev spurns the more civilized advances of successful oilman Kenneth (*The Thing*) Tobey, a friend is moved to understate: "Sometimes I wonder about you." Beyond its skewed psychology and casting, *Stark Fear*, lensed in and around Oklahoma City and financed with local dough, sports many an odd cinematic touch. Sex, for example, is represented not by the expected oil-rig action but by an out-of-focus camera roving over an abstract painting (!). (We also get to see an authentic Native American "stomp dance" and several evocative O.C. tourist sites.) *Stark Fear* is either itself a candidate for a psychiatrist's couch or a brilliant screen treatise on neuroses run wild. Either way, it comes highly recommended here.

THE STEPFATHER:
THE SERIES

THE STEPFATHER   (1987) ***½

D: Joseph Ruben. Terry O'Quinn, Shelley Hack, Jill Schoelen, Stephen Shellen, Charles Lanyer. 89 mins. (Columbia/TriStar)

Another cogent case of talent (particularly mystery writer Donald E. Westlake's tight, ingenious script) accomplishing what a megabudget in the hands of Hollywood hacks cannot, *The Stepfather* is a sardonic, unerringly suspenseful B thriller. O'Quinn is unforgettable as an all-American, middle-class maniac driven to violence first by his real, then by his adopted, families' failure to live up to his scrambled Ward Cleaver standards. Hack and Schoelen are likewise effective as the lonely widow and suspicious daughter, respectively, whom O'Quinn embraces. In another neat touch, O'Quinn works as a suburban real estate agent ("selling the American dream," he terms it), and the action unfolds against a backdrop of painfully mundane normality. A subplot involving a previous murder victim's justice-seeking brother (Shellen) is artfully integrated into the main story line.

STEPFATHER II: MAKE ROOM FOR DADDY   (1989) **½

D: Dwight Little. Terry O'Quinn, Meg Foster, Caroline Williams, Jonathan Brandis, Henry Brown. 86 mins. (HBO)

After somehow surviving the multiple gunshot-and-stab wounds that put an end to his pseudo-patriarchal peccadilloes in *The Stepfather*, O'Quinn turns up alive and sick in a Seattle mental hospital, promptly bludgeons his way out of same, and heads south to L.A. (where, presumably, his erratic behavior will attract less attention).

Terry resumes his apple-pie life-style by renting new suburban digs, posing as a family counselor (!), and eliminating potential rivals and spies with a variety of blunt instruments and sharp one-liners. On its own, *Stepfather II* rates as a fairly slick, witty psycho pic; unfortunately, it was already done nearly note for note (and with a clever subplot that's absent here) in *The Stepfather*. O'Quinn's brilliant Happy Face from Hell perf makes this otherwise staggeringly redundant "sequel" worth a look. The O'Quinn-less *Stepfather 3: Father's Day* (Trimark) rates as a total waste of time and tape.

THE STRANGER (1987) **¹/₂

D: Adolfo Aristarain. Bonnie Bedelia, Peter Riegert, Barry Primus, Julio De Grazia, David Spielberg. 93 mins. (Columbia/TriStar)

The Stranger stars Bedelia as a massacre witness suffering from amnesia. Riegert is her gambling-addicted shrink, while Primus plays the hard-working California cop who's usually a step behind the action, and De Grazia, who resembles a reincarnated Akim Tamiroff, makes for an effective lead heavy. *The Stranger* has its slack stretches, but it's a good-looking film, lensed in rich primary colors, and features one truly socko plot twist. No relation to the classic 1946 Orson Welles thriller *The Stranger* (Congress).

STRANGER ON THE THIRD FLOOR (1940) B&W ***

D: Boris Ingster. Peter Lorre, John Maguire, Margaret Tallichet, Elisha Cook, Jr. 64 mins. (RKO, n.i.d.)

Director Ingster assembles a bizarre, febrile B flick, featuring a fine *Caligari*-esque hallucinatory sequence and a memorably offbeat perf by Lorre as a reclusive immigrant.

STRANGERS KISS (1984) **¹/₂

D: Matthew Chapman. Peter Coyote, Victoria Tennant, Blaine Novak. 94 mins. (HBO)

Chapman's interesting, if occasionally pretentious, behind-the-scenes fringe-Hollywood story is drawn from (uncredited) director Stanley Kubrick's experiences working on his low-budget feature *Killer's Kiss*, with Coyote starring as Stanley's on-screen stand-in.

STREETS (1990) **

D: Katt Shea Ruben. Christina Applegate, David Mendenhall, Eb Lottimer, Starr Andreeff, Patrick Richwood, Mel Costelo, Kay Lenz. 83 mins. (MGM)

Another lyrical sleazefest from Katt Shea Ruben (director, coscripter) and then-hubby, Andy Ruben (producer, coscripter), *Streets* tells the story of 'burb boy Sy (Mendenhall), street girl Dawn (Applegate, then of TV's *Married…with Children* fame), and the psycho motorcycle cop (Lottimer) who's busily killing off the pic's secondary characters with a customized shotgun while searching for witness Dawn. Between brutal slayings, the Rubens take us on an extended, if none too enlightening, tour of Venice, California's mean streets and beaches, where discarded teens hustle to survive. Mendenhall and Applegate (whom a street crony refers to as an "old-fashioned girl" because she prefers heroin to coke!) turn in decent work, but loony law officer Lottimer leans a tad too heavily on Schwarzenegger's *The Terminator* and Rutger Hauer's *The Hitcher* for thespian inspiration. Phantom fave Andreeff contributes a fleeting cameo as a mounted policewoman. Remade (very poorly) as 1997's *Rumble in the Streets* (New Horizons).

STRIPPED TO KILL:
THE SERIES

STRIPPED TO KILL II: LIVE GIRLS (1989) **

D: Katt Shea Ruben. Maria Ford, Eb Lottimer, Karen Mayo Chandler, Birke Tan, Marjean Holden, Debra Lamb. 82 mins. (MGM)

Katt Shea Ruben follows her genre-establishing 1987 *Stripped to Kill* (MGM) with this equally uneven sequel. Neurotic ecdysiast Shady (Ford) is plagued by nightmares in which she slashes her fellow strippers at L.A.'s lowlife Paragon Club. The situation worsens when said strippers do indeed start turning up dead. Fortunately for Shady, equally neurotic cop

Decker (Lottimer)—who owns a plastic leg and a biofeedback machine—refuses to finger our heroine as the culprit. Instead, the pair embark on a rather lackluster love affair while Decker closes in on the real killer. With its emphasis on grisly razor murders and stylized but largely dark-themed strip acts, the film threatens at times to verge on the, well, almost unsavory. Worse, the Rubens, working under cost-conscious exec-producer Roger Corman, craft a flick that's as underlit as it is underdressed, and intensely claustrophobic into the bargain.

STRIPTEASER (1995) ***

D: Dan Golden. Maria Ford, Rick Dean, Lance August, Nikki Fritz, R. A. Mihailoff. In R and unrated editions. 82 mins. (New Horizons)

Sort of an updated, strip-club-set knockoff of Roger Corman's 1957 Dick Miller showcase, *Rock All Night* (see index), *Stripteaser* sees psycho Dean, at first feigning blindness, hold several hostages at a late-night L.A. strip joint called Zipper's Clown Palace. Dean gives an over-the-top, in-your-face perf as an articulate, self-aware sicko who, it develops, has been following foxy ecdysiast Ford as an alternative to the planned suicide he obviously richly deserves. As in *Naked Obsession*, Golden again proves a master at assembling tense erotic tableaux with a heady S&M flavor, where the stakes are life, sex, and death.

SUDDEN FEAR (1952) B&W ***1/2

D: David Miller. Joan Crawford, Jack Palance, Gloria Grahame, Bruce Bennett, Virginia Huston, Touch Connors. 110 mins. (Kino) DVD

Joan enjoys a thespian field day in Miller's excellent suspenser, drawn from the Edna Sherry novel. Though a fabulously wealthy heiress *and* a mega-

---

successful playwright, lonely Joan suffers the misfortune of falling for the ultimate Mr. Wrong, outwardly charming, inwardly churning actor manqué Palance. In the opening scene, the two "meet bitter" when Joan, over her subordinates' objections, rejects Jack for the leading-man role in her new Broadway play, citing his lack of erotic charisma. Jack soon makes a mockery of Joan's judgment when he intercepts her aboard a Gotham-to-Frisco train, where he determinedly woos and wins her in the course of their cross-country ride (and rarely has celluloid train travel seemed as romantic as it's rendered here). After the pair wed, Jack begins to hatch his sinister schemes, schemes that grow more complicated when his con-girl ex (Grahame) shows up in San Fran, forcing Jack to cut her into his plans to off his happy spouse and collect her inheritance. Joan's shining moment arrives when she hears an inadvertently recorded conversation detailing Jack and Gloria's killer conspiracy. For what seems like minutes, she mimes every conceivable expression of horror, shock, incredulity, and terror as her world crumbles underfoot. She recovers quickly enough, however, to concoct a clever counterstrategy of her own. *Sudden Fear* received considerable recognition in its time, netting Oscar noms for Crawford, Palance, and cinematographer Charles Lang. Reportedly Joan and

Jack's antipathy proved all too real, with the Method-trained Palance providing the studio-styled Crawford with no end of on-set annoyance. Joan had the last laugh when she opted for a 48 percent share of the pic's profits over her standard $200 grand salary and *Sudden Fear* made a major box office impact.

SUDDENLY (1954) B&W ***

D: Lewis Allen. Frank Sinatra, Sterling Hayden, James Gleason, Nancy Gates. 77 mins. (Sinister Cinema) DVD

Sinatra enjoys one of his finest roles as an icy assassin out to off the prez. With henchmen Paul Frees and Christopher Dark, he holds a typical American family hostage and boldly debunks our cherished democratic ideals while calmly setting up his high-powered rifle. Sinatra reportedly sought to suppress the film in the wake of the Kennedy assassination.

SUNSET BOULEVARD (1950) B&W ***1/2

D: Billy Wilder. Gloria Swanson, William Holden, Erich von Stroheim. 100 mins. (Paramount)

Wilder's classic dark dramedy (he also receives costory credit) detailing delusional Hollywood has-been Norma Desmond's descent into

JOANNIE GOT HER GUN: A vengeful Crawford gives it her best shot in top-notch suspenser *Sudden Fear.*
© Kino International Corporation 1999

tightly wired Wes, stunned by Larry's rejection and his own wife's and son's growing alienation, begins losing it big-time, an emotional descent that hits bottom during a climactic deer-hunting trip. While slowly paced in spots, *Sure Fire* rings true with authentic dialogue, sharply etched characterizations, and an eerie atmosphere that makes the pic impossible to forget. World Artists presents *Sure Fire* in a letter-boxed format that preserves Jost's painterly approach to the medium. Earlier Jost films currently available on homevid include *All the Vermeers in New York* (World Artists), *Angel City, Bell Diamond, Chameleon, Last Chants for a Slow Dance, Plain Talk and Common Sense, Rembrandt Laughing, Slow Moves, Speaking Directly, Stagefright,* and *Uncommon Senses* (all via Facets).

SUTURE   (1993) B&W ***

D: Scott McGehee, David Siegel. Dennis Haysbert, Mel Harris, Michael Harris, Sab Shimono, David Graf, Dina Merrill. 96 mins. (Hallmark)

Co-exec-produced by Steven Soderbergh, lensed in B&W, and sporting the look and feel of an offbeat mid-'60s thriller (e.g., *Seconds, Lady in a Cage*) crossed with a feature-length *Twilight Zone* episode, *Suture* hinges its entire premise on a case of mistaken identity between two nearly "identical" brothers—one, Vincent Towers (*Horseplayer*'s Michael Harris), rich and a suspected patricidal killer, the other, Clay Arlington (Haysbert), poor and long-lost. The script and direction—McGehee and Siegel share equal screen credit for both—steer us through a fairly entertaining suspenser, an idiosyncratic mix of the surreal and mundane. Where the filmmakers play with audience expectations, however, is in the casting: Harris is white; "identical" brother Haysbert is black; even beyond pigmentation, they share absolutely no resemblance in height, weight, or

madness netted three Oscars and remains as fresh and cynical as it was a half century ago. Von Stroheim's a standout as Gloria's loyal chauffeur, while Buster Keaton and Cecil B. DeMille supply cameos.

SURE FIRE   (1993) ***

D: Jon Jost. Tom Blair, Kristi Hager, Robert Ernst, Kate Dezina, Phillip R. Brown. 86 mins. (World Artists)

Indie auteur Jost has been making features and shorts for decades, but

Sure Fire is one of the few to receive even a token theatrical release. Employing an idiosyncratic visual style somewhat reminiscent of Lars von Trier's *Zentropa* and making the most of his naturally awesome Utah locales, Jost assembles a compelling treatise on the theme of "winning" versus "losing." Tunnel-visioned middle-aged real-estate entrepreneur Wes (Blair, excellent in a role tailor-made for Bruce Dern) tries to hire his lifelong "loser" friend Larry (Ernst), whose family ranch is going under, to take care of his business's more menial details. The features—the effect is akin to casting *Twins*'s Arnold Schwarzenegger and Danny DeVito in a "serious" film. Your tolerance for this filmlong visual irony will likely determine whether or not you enjoy the ride.

SVENGALI (1931) B&W ***

D: Archie Mayo. John Barrymore, Marian Marsh, Donald Crisp. 82 mins. (Sinister Cinema)

Barrymore gives an intense perf as the hypnotic artist who mesmerizes young singer Marsh in a production further enhanced by bizarre sets and effects. Remade in 1954, with Donald Wolfit and Hildegarde Neff, and in a 1983 made-for-TV version, with Peter O'Toole and Jodie Foster, both likewise titled simply *Svengali* (Sinister Cinema, IVE, respectively).

SWEET KILLING (1993) **

D: Eddy Matalon. Anthony Higgins, F. Murray Abraham, Leslie Hope, Andrea Fereol, Michael Ironside. 87 mins. (Paramount)

Burb banker Higgins employs techniques culled from his favorite comic book to waste his boorish wife, then takes up with hip designer Hope, who pouts, "I don't want to go to the suburbs; I want to have fun!" Cop Ironside, suspecting the truth, sends mysterious informer Abraham to trap Higgins. Drawn from the Angus Hall novel *Qualthrough*, *Sweet Killing* has a potentially fun black-comic plot, but it gets snuffed by scripter/director Matalon's literal-minded approach. You can tell the flick was lensed in Canada by all the ostentatiously placed American flags.

SWITCHBACK (1997) **

D: Jeb Stuart. Danny Glover, Dennis Quaid, Jared Leto, R. Lee Ermey, Ted Levine, William Fichtner. 121 mins. (Paramount) DVD

Vet scripter Stuart's directorial debut rambles along as a fitfully watchable but utterly pointless serial-killer/train-thriller combo. Glover works hard as a folksy, motormouthed suspected psycho who gives a harrowing ride to young hitcher Leto, while Quaid contributes a curiously flatline turn as an obsessed FBI agent who has a personal stake in the case. Ermey injects considerably more life into one of his more prominent recent roles as an election-year sheriff stumped by the slayings. The climactic Colorado-set train sequence is almost worth the price of a rental all by its lonesome.

TAILS YOU LIVE, HEADS YOU'RE DEAD (1995) **1/2

D: Tim Matheson. Corbin Bernsen, Ted McGinley, Tim Matheson, Maria Del Mar, Jeff Pustil, John White. 91 mins. (Paramount)

Erstwhile *Animal House* lothario "Stratton" Matheson doubles as director and costar of this edgier-than-usual made-for-TV serial-killer caper, based on the Bill Pronzini short story "Liar's Dice." Bernsen plays a maniac who informs family man McGinley that he's about to become his 13th murder victim, but not before he teases and tortures him. After Bernsen pulls a series of dirty tricks and the local police prove typically useless, McGinley hires ex-military-investigator-turned-P.I. Matheson. Matheson's stripped-down thriller—free of the multiple plot encumbrances that frequently burden many of the pic's lavish Hollywood counterparts—works pretty well most of the way, but an elaborately illogical climax complete with a cheap nightmare fakeout fadeout detracts a mite.

THE TAKING OF PELHAM ONE TWO THREE (1974) ***

D: Joseph Sargent. Walter Matthau, Robert Shaw, Martin Balsam. 104 mins. (Fox)

Shaw leads a criminal quartet who ransom a subway train for a million bucks; city officials actually campaign to get it back. Matthau's excellent as the weary cop on the case in Sargent's tense thriller, one leavened with welcome cynical wit.

TALL, DARK AND DEADLY (1995) ***

D: Kenneth Fink. Kim Delaney, Jack Scalia, Todd Allen, Gina Mastrogiacomo, Ely Pouget. 88 mins. (Paramount)

This surprisingly taut, tense, and vicious psycho-killer thriller stars Delaney as a mechanically inventive Houston architect who, after splitting up with nice guy Allen, makes the mistake of bedding titular heavy Scalia. Trouble brews when Scalia begins invading Kim's privacy, and our heroine's problems escalate drastically from there. Delaney gets to play a Sigourney Weaver–esque femme who, while victimized both by Scalia and authorities who've fingered her as a murder suspect, is smart and feisty without resorting to martial arts moves. Scalia is utterly convincing as Kim's possessive pursuer. On the shelf, this may resemble routine "erotic thriller" fodder, but *Tall, Dark and Deadly* can hold its own with most major theatrical thriller fare.

TARGET (1985) **1/2

D: Arthur Penn. Gene Hackman, Matt Dillon, Gayle Hunnicutt, Josef Sommer, Victoria Fyodorova, Guy Boyd. 117 mins. (Fox)

In *Target*, Hackman gets to act out the middle-aged American everydad's wildest fantasy: When wife Hunnicutt is kidnapped during a solo Parisian vacation, Gene shocks surly son Dillon by transforming from a dull Dallas businessman into an international superspy. (Seems that Gene is really an ex-CIA agent.) When he and his wide-eyed offspring hit Europe, Gene goes into action with a vengeance, leading said son through an involved maze of East-West intrigues past and present. *Target* is a contrived, often ridiculous, but fairly engrossing thriller, with Hackman in typically fine form. On-screen wife Hunnicutt lands one of the era's least inspiring femme roles here, spending most of her screen time bound, gagged, and trip-wired to a pile of explosives.

TARGETS (1968) ***1/2

D: Peter Bogdanovich. Boris Karloff, Tim Kelly, Nancy Hsueh, Peter Bogdanovich, James Brown, Sandy Baron. 91 mins. (Paramount)

Bogdanovich's first complete feature—he'd previously worked on a couple of Roger Corman's cut-and-paste jobs—pits aged horror-film star Byron Orlok (Karloff, in his last good role) against an all-too-real monster, a colorless but lethal psycho sniper loose at a local drive-in. Bogdanovich's best film (along with the similarly bijou-related *Last Picture Show* [Fox]), deservedly became an instant cult fave with its pointed mix of seriousness and exploitation.

A TASTE FOR KILLING (1992) **1/2

D: Lou Antonio. Michael Biehn, Jason Bateman, Henry Thomas, Helen Cates, Blue Deckert. 87 mins. (Universal)

Texas wildcatter Biehn embroils rich kids Bateman and Thomas in murder, with blackmail his ultimate goal. The film draws a deft personality parallel between the bonkers Biehn and the amoral Bateman, with sensitive ex-*E.T.* tyke Thomas occupying the story's moral

center. Though slow at times, *A Taste for Killing* achieves most of its modest aims.

TAXI DRIVER (1976) ***1/2

D: Martin Scorsese. Robert De Niro, Jodie Foster, Cybill Shepherd, Harvey Keitel. 113 mins. (Columbia/TriStar) DVD

Scorsese's scorching portrayal of solipsistic psycho Travis Bickle (De Niro) remains a film that's impossible to forget: celluloid sprinkled with angel dust. Keitel contributes a deft cameo as the precocious Foster's Lower East Side pimp. Now available in a new, remastered edition, complete with cast-and-crew interviews in both VHS and DVD formats.

THE TEMP (1993) **

D: Tom Holland. Timothy Hutton, Lara Flynn Boyle, Faye Dunaway. 99 mins. (Paramount)

Big trubs at Mrs. Appleby's Cookie Corp.: Not only has the Portland, Oregon, firm just been taken over by heavyweight NYC interests, endangering CEO Dunaway's future ("I've had more knives stuck in me than Julius Caesar!"), but exec Hutton is still recovering from a paranoiac condition that led to a separation from his wife and young son. Seemingly riding to the rescue is titular temporary worker Boyle, who's both a biz wiz and a physical wow. Unfortunately for boss Hutton and cohorts, Boyle harbors a hidden agenda that bodes ill for all concerned. Kevin Falls's appropriately cookie-cutter script has the scheming temp implement her planned rise rung by rung, arranging everything from transfers to lethal "accidents" for uncooperative associates. Hutton gradually grows wise to Boyle's wiles, but who can take the word of a recovering paranoid? Veteran horror helmer Holland employs his well-honed thriller skills to keep the formulaic action fairly compelling in the early going. Ultimately, though, the

script attempts to keep the suspense alive long after Boyle's antics should be obvious to everyone on-screen. Worse, *The Temp* wraps with a limp, let's-get-this-over-with climax. On the upside, the flick finds gory new uses for an ordinary office paper-shredder, incorporates an insect-oriented homage to *The Silence of the Lambs*, and features what may be the most creative poisoned-cookie scene since 1987's *Flowers in the Attic* (see index).

THE TENANT (1976) ***1/2

D: Roman Polanski. Roman Polanski, Isabelle Adjani, Melvyn Douglas, Shelley Winters, Jo Van Fleet, Bernard Fresson. 126 mins. (Paramount)

Polanski's brilliantly perverse exercise in urban paranoia, adapted from Roland Topor's novel, deserves every bit of its vaunted cult rep. Polanski shines in three departments here—as coscripter, director, and most of all, actor, in the lead role of a hapless office worker whose ill-advised move into a creepy Paris apartment house triggers his gradual breakdown.

THEY MADE ME A FUGITIVE (1947) B&W ***1/2

D: Cavalcanti. Trevor Howard, Sally Gray, Griffith Jones, Rene Ray, Mary Marrall, Vida Hope. 96 mins. (Kino)

With *They Made Me a Fugitive* (released in the U.S. as *I Became a Criminal*, in a 78-minute edition), *Dead of Night* contributor Cavalcanti fashions a flavorful, edgy caper that rates at the top of the period Brit crime-drama list. Based on Jackson Budd's novel *A Convict Has Escaped* (adapted by *Wizard of Oz* scripter Noel Langley), *Fugitive* casts Howard as Clem, a bored, adrift ex-RAF pilot who, in search of excitement, unwisely hooks up with a colorful (indeed nearly Dickensian) band of Soho gangsters ruled by the mock-suave, explosively sadistic Narcy (short for Narcissus), memorably interpreted by Jones. When Clem balks at the mob's proposed drug dealing, Narcy arranges a heist that leads to Clem's arrest and conviction. Our anti-hero escapes and begins a suspenseful underground odyssey back to the gang and his budding squeeze, nightclub performer Gray. Cavalcanti adopts a verité approach to his tale, one brought to evocative visual life by ace cinematographer Otto (*Alfie*) Heller, as he steers us through Soho's seedy clubs, pubs, and back alleys (the gang uses a coffin shop as its front!), as well as London's outlying areas, when Clem catches a nocturnal ride with a suspicious trucker and invades the 'burb home of a woman who wants him to murder her husband. Like the best of its contemporary American counterparts, *Fugitive* depicts a postwar world where amorality is on the rise and trust is at a minimum. Withal, *They Made Me a Fugitive* stands tall as a tough, unsentimental, unrelentingly intense affair no noir fan will want to miss.

MANN'S MEN: Undercover agent Dennis O'Keefe spies on enforcer Charles McGraw in atmospheric moment from noir master Anthony Mann's *T-Men*.
© Kino International Corporation

THE THIEF   (1952) B&W **

D: Russell Rouse. Ray Milland, Rita Gam, Martin Gabel. 85 mins. (Englewood, VCI)

This gimmick spy movie, made without dialogue, casts Milland as a regretful nuclear physicist who passes secret documents to the Russkis. The novelty value wears thin pretty quickly, though the flick is not without its fans.

THE THIRD MAN   (1949) B&W ***

D: Carol Reed. Orson Welles, Joseph Cotten, Alida Valli. 104 mins. (Home Vision) DVD

Welles turns in indelible work as cad-about-town Harry Lime in Carol Reed's effective (if somewhat overrated) postwar Vienna-set mystery, the movie that put zithers on the soundtrack map. Clips from the film play an important role in Peter Jackson's *Heavenly Creatures*.

T-MEN   (1947) B&W ***½

D: Anthony Mann. Dennis O'Keefe, June Lockhart, Alfred Ryder, Charles McGraw, Wallace Ford. 96 mins. (Kino) DVD

Treasury Department agent O'Keefe attempts to thwart a counterfeit ring in this terse, shadow-enriched *Dragnet*-styled semidocumentary caper. Ace direction from Mann, along with John Alton's B&W cinematography, make the film a lot more exciting than it might have been in lesser hands, as the pair evince a real feel for the criminal lifestyle and its atmospheric locales: shady bars, sweaty steambaths, dingy warehouses, secret gambling dens, and nocturnal back alleys galore. Perennial movie mug McGraw gives one of his hardest-boiled perfs as the funny-money mob's remorseless enforcer, while Wallace (*Freaks*) Ford is a standout as "Schemer," a Chinese-herb-chewing gang associate set up for a fall by heroes O'Keefe and Ryder.

TOUCH OF EVIL   (1958) B&W ****

D: Orson Welles. Charlton Heston, Janet Leigh, Orson Welles, Marlene Dietrich, Akim Tamiroff, Joseph Calleia. 108 mins. (Universal)

Tijuana hoods commanded by Tamiroff hold police detective Heston's better half (Leigh) hostage while corrupt cop Welles tries to cover up his own multiple misdeeds. *Citizen Kane* (Turner) notwithstanding, Welles's nightmare noir, complete with crazed camera angles and a genuinely paranoiac aura, may be his best all-around film. Universal carries the complete 108-minute version, not the shorter one seen during the movie's initial theatrical release. A "director's cut" edition, with a rescored opening and changes made in accordance with the late director's posthumously discovered notes, made the revival- and art-house rounds in 1998–99.

TOWN WITHOUT PITY (1961) B&W***

D: Gottfried Reinhardt. Kirk Douglas, Christine Kaufmann, E. G. Marshall, Robert Blake, Richard Jaeckel, Frank Sutton, Barbara Rutting. 105 mins. (MGM)

One of several Douglas films dealing with the theme of military morality—see also Stanley Kubrick's *Paths of Glory* (MGM) and George Seaton's *The Hook* (n/a)—*Town Without Pity* casts Kirk as a defense attorney assigned to represent four GI's (led by Sutton, *Gomer Pyle*'s future topkick) who raped teenager Kaufmann outside her small German hometown. Drawn from Manfred Gregor's novel *The Verdict, Town* depicts Kaufmann's gradual disintegration in the crucible of other characters' agendas, military officials and locals alike. Lensed on location, this bleak, then-controversial courtroom drama retains its tension as Kirk battles both the town and himself in carrying out a distasteful mission to tilt the truth in his scuzzy clients' favor. A strong tolerance for Gene Pitney's title song is required, as we hear it roughly 101 times in nearly as many arrangements.

TRANSGRESSION (1994)***

D: Michael P. DiPaolo. Molly Jackson, Marc St. Camille, Julio Rodriguez, Morris Miller, Sharon Ana Sposta. 82 mins. (Masque Cinema/Chiaroscuro)

Veteran videomaker DiPaolo makes an impressive (16-millimeter) feature-film debut with *Transgression*, a low-budget but highly professional cross between *The Silence of the Lambs* and a José Mojica (Coffin Joe) Marins–styled morality play in thriller guise. One of the auteur's real-life jobs entailed videotaping confessions for the Brooklyn District Attorney's Office, an experience he puts to chilling use here. The film opens on death row, where telejournalist-turned-murderess Jack-son casually informs us, "I killed three men and found God." DiPaolo backtracks to Jackson's interactions with depraved serial killer/shrink St. Camille. Despite the efforts of her older-cop boyfriend (Rodriguez), Jackson is captured by the black-hooded maniac, who's determined to turn her into not another fatality but his successor in the psycho trade. A complex tale that generates little sympathy for Jackson even in her journalistic stage, *Transgression* creates a genuinely unsettling aura while largely dispensing with gratuitous gore and conventional suspense. Making DiPaolo's pic even more remarkable is the fact that it was shot, in NYC and upstate New York in 12 days, and took only six months in all, from story treatment to finished product. A quartet of DiPaolo's earlier, late-'80s video features are available—*Bought & Sold, Brutal Ardor, Requiem for a Whore,* and the documentary *Where No Sun Shines* (Chiaroscuro).

TROJAN EDDIE (1996)***

D: Gillies MacKinnon. Stephen Rea, Richard Harris, Brendan Gleeson, Sean McGinley, Angeline Ball. 105 mins. (Peachtree)

Set against the grim backdrop of Irish gypsy "traveler" life, *Trojan Eddie* features standout performances by leads Rea and Harris. Rea plays a likable, low-level lackey who's happiest when merrily spieling at local "auctions" set up to sell gangster Harris's stolen goods. Against overwhelming odds, Rea's "Trojan Eddie" (nicknamed not for the famous condom brand but for the Trojan van he drives) provides for his young daughters, copes with an intrusive ex-wife, and tries to maintain some semblance of a behavioral code within a cutthroat environment. Harris is equally arresting as a snarling, oft paranoid crime boss whose marriage to a local beauty young enough to be his granddaughter ends in humiliation, betrayal, and revenge. Billy Roche's textured script and director MacKinnon's gritty location lensing add to this indie import's impact. Mike Newell's 1992 *Into the West* (Touchstone) offers a more whimsical take on a "traveler" family, while Jack N. Green's 1996 *Traveller* (Evergreen), with Bill Paxton and Mark Wahlberg, presents a portrait of Irish-American "traveler" life.

TURBULENCE (1997)**½

D: Robert Butler. Ray Liotta, Lauren Holly, Hector Elizondo, Ben Cross, Brendan Gleeson, Rachel Ticotin. 103 mins. (HBO) DVD

Liotta, in his looniest turn since *Unlawful Entry* (see index), has a lot of infectious fun as a psycho loose aboard an unpiloted airliner on Christmas Eve. In an airborne Sandra (*Speed*) Bullock role, flight attendant Holly has to fend off an ultraviolent Ray while trying to follow crisis-center pilot Cross's instructions re how to steer the plane through a severe storm and land at LAX. Director Butler and crew make creative use of the plane's claustrophobic (and holiday-ornament-festooned) interior and refrain from overcrowding the unlikely story line with such excess baggage as character development or dramatic subplots. *Turbulence* crashed and burned with critics and audiences alike during its bijou flight but supplies its share of over-the-top pulpy fun on a slow video night.

THE TURNING (1993)**

D: L. A. Puopolo. Michael Dolan, Tess Harper, Karen Allen, Raymond Barry, Gillian Anderson. 93 mins. (Leo Films) DVD

Scully gets nekkid...and you are there! That's pretty much the sole reason this 1993 indie found a belated video release, for a scene wherein *X-Filer* Anderson, in her film debut, briefly bares her seemingly non-silicone-enhanced breasts. Gillian enjoys a secondary role as the waitress / former squeeze of prodigal son Dolan, a neurotic neo-Nazi (pardon our redundancy) who returns to his Virginia small-town roots when he hears of his parents' (Harper, Barry) impending divorce. Though admirably earnest, much of Puopolo's psychological drama betrays its stage origins (Chris Ceraso's *Home Fires Burning*) via static scenes, ripe dialogue, and self-conscious thesping. Scully lovers will doubtless want to fast-forward to her topless bit.

12 ANGRY MEN   (1957) B&W ****

D: Sidney Lumet. Henry Fonda, Lee J. Cobb, Martin Balsam, E. G. Marshall, Ed Begley. (MGM)

Director Lumet, working from a Reginald Rose script, assembles an intense, thoroughly mesmerizing drama about an all-male jury with conflicting views re a seemingly open-and-shut murder case. Worthy of repeat viewings. Remade as a cable-TV movie with Jack Lemmon, George C. Scott, and Ossie Davis. Our dream cast for the next remake? Arnold Schwarzenegger, Sly Stallone, Charles Bronson, Chuck Norris, Steven Seagal, Sonny Chiba, Dolph Lundgren, Don ("the Dragon") Wilson, Jean-Claude Van Damme (as twins), and Jackie Chan (ditto).

TWILIGHT'S LAST GLEAMING
(1977) ** 1/2

D: Robert Aldrich. Burt Lancaster, Richard Widmark, Melvyn Douglas, Charles Durning, Paul Winfield, William Smith. 146 mins. (Key)

As in *Seven Days in May* (Warner), Burt again plays a mad military man, this time out to end nuclear proliferation by commandeering a nuke silo, in Aldrich's far-fetched but watchable pulp thriller. B-action fave Big Bill Smith is one of Burt's henchmen but doesn't make it past reel 1.

TWIN PEAKS: FIRE WALK WITH ME
(1992) ***

D: David Lynch. Sheryl Lee, Moira Kelly, Ray Wise, Chris Isaak, Kyle MacLachlan. 134 mins. (New Line)

Although we've long admired most of David Lynch's celluloid ouevre—from the rad *Eraserhead* to the brilliant *Blue Velvet*—The Phantom scarcely qualifies as a freak for *Peaks*, a show that reeked more of desperation than inspiration as the weeks wore on, so we weren't expecting much of the feature incarnation, *Twin Peaks: Fire Walk with Me*. But the film proved a happy revelation. Strip away the FBI characters (including Lynch himself as a deaf bureau chief) and the mannered absurdist fat that bloats the running time to an unwieldy, filled-with-star-cameos 134 minutes, and you have a core story that's as strange, haunting, and hypnotic as anything Lynch has ever done. It's the only authentic tale *Twin Peaks* ever had to tell and makes the rest look like hours of pointless tease—the story of tortured Laura Palmer (Lee), her dysfunctional family, and the terrors lurking behind the title site's small-town façade. While Lynch recycles riffs lifted from earlier works, here the surrealism, given voice by Angelo Badalamenti's evocative score, weaves a powerful spell. Lee proffers a moving performance as the troubled teen who can't find salvation in the love local good guy James Marshall offers, instead seeking temporary relief in drugs and sleazoid sex. Wise is equally excellent as her incestuous, violent dad, as is Kelly as her shy best friend. The Keystone FBI buildup represents potentially funny material in an *On the Air* (Lynch's short-lived cable-TV comedy show) vein but doesn't belong here, where it clutters and nearly snuffs out what's otherwise a genuinely potent work. If you have the time, watch the entire tape, then fast-forward past the first half hour or so, to the "One Year Later" title, rewatch from that point on, and see if you agree.

2 DAYS IN THE VALLEY   (1996) ***

D: John Herzfeld. James Spader, Danny Aiello, Eric Stoltz, Teri Hatcher, Jeff Daniels, Paul Mazursky, Marsha Mason, Greg Cruttwell, Glenne Headly, Charlize Theron, Keith Carradine, Louise Fletcher, Austin Pendleton, Lawrence Tierney. 105 mins. (HBO) DVD

A derivative but diverting trip into well-worn Tarantino territory, writer/director Herzfeld's *2 Days in the Valley* is sort of a stripped-down *Pulp Fiction* that even recruits *PF* player Stoltz. (*Reservoir Dogs* thesp Tierney also enjoys a one-line cameo, reacting to an unseen catfight between Hatcher and Theron with a pensive "Maybe that's how they make love in Tarzana.") Spader turns in menacing work as Lee, a cold-blooded killer who fails in his bid to eliminate "loser" partner Dosmo (Aiello), leading the latter to hide out in the Valley digs of suffering (physically at least; he's just had kidney-stone surgery) artist Cruttwell. Cruttwell's loyal, neglected assistant (Headly), suicidal ex-TV director (Mazursky, undoubtedly tube vet Herzfeld's most autobiographical character), his dog (Coby), and Cruttwell's half-sister/nurse (Mason) also wind up at the site. *2 Days* lacks the texture of Tarantino's best work but employs enough fresh spins (and views its own contrivances with an unpretentious wink) to make it well worth a look for dark-crime/comedy fans.

THE TWO JAKES   (1990) ** 1/2

D: Jack Nicholson. Jack Nicholson, Harvey Keitel, Meg Tilly, Eli Wallach, Madeleine Stowe, Ruben Blades, David Keith. 137 mins. (Paramount) DVD

In his long-delayed *Chinatown* sequel, scripter Robert Towne explores private dick Nicholson's inability to escape his past (set forth in the original *China-town*). Seems that's a condition not unknown to Towne too, since here, as in his soporific *Tequila Sunrise* (Warner), which he also directed, the screenwriter replays the same basic situation seen in his film debut, the 1960 Roger Corman quickie *The Last Woman on Earth* (Sinister Cinema), in which Towne also costarred (under the *nom de thesp* Edward Wain) as the second-to-last man on earth. Each film finds a lone professional experiencing a love/hate relationship with an unsavory employer or former friend while lusting after the latter's squeeze. In *Last Woman*, it's Towne himself as a lawyer involved with mobster Antony Carbone and mistress Betsy Jones-Moreland; in the pretentious, self-indulgent *Tequila Sunrise*, it's DEA agent Mel Gibson, drug czar Raul Julia, and Michelle Pfeiffer; here it's Nicholson, murderous real estate mogul Keitel, and Meg Tilly. *The Two Jakes*, while a notch below *Chinatown*, rates as the best of the above-cited trio, with a fat Jack huffing and puffing his way through a tangled web of deceit to arrive at an existential conclusion. The film would have probably played better, though, had Jack's search been shaved by two or three reels.

TWO-MOON JUNCTION (1988) **½

D: Zalman King. Sherilyn Fenn, Richard Tyson, Louise Fletcher, Burl Ives, Martin Hewitt, Millie Perkins. 104 mins. (Columbia/TriStar)

Actor/auteur King, homevideo's reigning "erotic thriller" king, scripted and directed this steamy, trend-setting pic designed primarily for the distaff and couples market. Our story concerns Alabama belle Fenn, who tumbles for hunky traveling carnystud Tyson, thereby endangering her impending marriage to rich frat boy Hewitt. The result is sort of a *Dirty*

Dancing sans the dancing, or a "Last Tango in Tuscaloosa," as Fenn lives out femme fantasies with wild man Tyson, while her reproving grandmother (Fletcher) and the local sheriff (Ives) seek to discourage the trashy tryst. Cameos by Herve *(Fantasy Island)* Villechaize and Screamin' Jay Hawkins, in their only screen teaming, further bolster *Two-Moon Junction*. Followed by 1993's *Return to Two-Moon Junction* (Trimark). King likewise launched the prolific *Red Shoe Diaries* series, totaling (thus far) ten entries (all via Republic).

THE UNDERNEATH (1995) ***

D: Steven Soderbergh. Peter Gallagher, Alison Elliott, William Fichtner, Elisabeth Shue, Paul Dooley, Adam Trese, Joe Don Baker, Shelley Duval. 99 mins. (Universal) DVD

While not on a par with Barbet Schroeder and Richard Price's *Kiss of Death* revamp (see index), Soderbergh's laid-back update of Robert Siodmak's 1949 noir *Criss Cross* (see index) holds interest most of the way. Soderbergh goes back to the original source material (Don Tracy's novel) but spends more time exploring the theme of responsibility as ironic anti-hero Gallagher returns to the hometown, family, squeeze (Elliott), and debts he'd earlier abandoned and soon drifts back into his old illicit ways. Gallagher makes for a more passive character than Burt Lancaster, but Fichtner is impressive in the original Dan Duryea gangster role. While Soderbergh comes up a bit short in the critical heist scene and aftermath, *The Underneath* is well worth a look for noir fans.

UNDERTOW (1995) ***

D: Eric Red. Lou Diamond Phillips, Mia Sara, Charles Dance. 90 mins. (Republic)

Directed by Eric *(The Hitcher, Cohen and Tate)* and coscripted

with Kathryn *(Strange Days)* Bigelow—the pair's previous collaborations include such solid genre fare as *Near Dark* and *Blue Steel*—*Undertow* offers an extreme variation on an elemental Boy Meets Man to Fight Over Girl story line, sort of a landlocked Yank version of Roman Polanski's *Knife in the Water*. Phillips plays a young drifter unfortunate enough to crash his wheels near the remote self-built rural redoubt of nutzoid survivalist Dance and his girl/wife Sara. A hurricane hits while the paranoid, weapons-crazed Dance extends his minimal hospitality, and the guys wind up fighting both the elements and each other. While flawed by a seemingly obligatory rush of last-reel overkill climaxes very much in a *Hitcher* vein, *Undertow* generates genuine tension along the way and features a bravura perf by a crazy-eyed Dance as the intense backwoods wacko.

THE UNDERWORLD STORY (1950) B&W ***

D: Cy Endfield. Dan Duryea, Gale Storm, Herbert Marshall, Mary Anderson, Michael O'Shea, Howard Da Silva. 90 mins. (Fox)

This misnomered murder tale (originally titled *The Whipped*) actually involves a scandalous slaying in a wealthy New England village, where exiled callous newsman Duryea exploits the tragedy to further his own ends. While well crafted, *The Underworld Story*—much of it a second-rate precursor to Billy Wilder's brilliant media meditation *Ace in the Hole* (a.k.a. *The Big Carnival*) (n/a)—is likely to disappoint hard-core noir hounds who rent or buy the tape on the basis of its title and cast. Among the latter, Da Silva is great as a perennially amused mob boss (an ahead-of-its-time character), while Roland Winters contributes a swift bit as a cynical celebrity lawyer.

UNION STATION   (1950) B&W ***

D: Rudolph Maté. William Holden, Nancy Olson, Barry Fitzgerald. 80 mins. (Kartes, n.i.d.)

Director Maté sets this gripping, excitingly lensed noir in L.A.'s famed train depot; Holden portrays a determined plainclothes cop hunting for the crazed kidnapper who's snatched a rich man's blind daughter.

UNLAWFUL ENTRY   (1992) ***

D: Jonathan Kaplan. Kurt Russell, Ray Liotta, Madeleine Stowe, Roger E. Mosley. 107 mins. (Fox)

Psycho fuzz Liotta decides that happily married lust object Stowe is nothing but a lowdown cop-teaser, so he campaigns to ruin hubby Russell's credit rating. Events grow considerably more drastic from there in a flick that leans less on logic than on crowd-pleasing thrills. The most inspirational dialogue belongs to the loony Liotta, when he tells a terrified Stowe: "I don't have to be a cop. I could do something different. Something *clean.*" (!) A cheap cat scare is supplied by a professional feline named Merv, who shares top thespic honors here with vet character actor Dick Miller, long a fave among grads of Roger Corman's Auteur Academy, from Kaplan to Joe Dante.

THE USUAL SUSPECTS   (1995) **½

D: Bryan Singer. Gabriel Byrne, Chazz Palminteri, Kevin Spacey, Kevin Pollak, Stephen Baldwin, Benicio Del Toro, Pete Postlethwaite. 105 mins. (PolyGram) DVD

Singer's highly overrated descent into Tarantino-esque trippy-crime turf is a cleverly woven but ultimately pointless tangle of false leads, red herrings, and outright lies. The pic opens in the aftermath of a seaside slaughter that results in 27 charred corpses. Special agent Palminteri interrogates survivor Spacey, a partially crippled petty thief, who backtracks to the crime's origins when five disparate suspected offenders are rounded up to participate in the same lineup. The crew—Spacey, ex-cop Byrne, antsy felon Pollak, and the heist team of Baldwin and Del Toro—concoct a caper while sharing the same holding cell. All roads ultimately lead to real or imagined Turkish kingpin Keyser Soze, sort of a Freddy Krueger of crime. Postlethwaite is memorable as Soze lieutenant Kobayashi, while Del Toro gives a wonderfully idiosyncratic perf, Paul Bartel cameos as a drug courier, and Peter Greene appears as a fence. *The Usual Suspects* will either hook you completely or leave you coldly admiring it from afar.

U-TURN   (1997) ***

D: Oliver Stone. Sean Penn, Jennifer Lopez, Nick Nolte, Powers Boothe, Claire Danes, Joaquin Phoenix, Billy Bob Thornton, Jon Voight, Julie Hagerty, Bo Hopkins. 125 mins. (Columbia/TriStar) DVD

Your Phantom hasn't been a major fan of Oliver Stone's Self-Important Cinema (e.g., *JFK, The Doors, Natural Born Killers*) over the years, but the Stoneman helms a winner with *U-Turn.* Proceeding from John (*Cold Around the Heart*) Ridley's novel *Stray Dogs* (he also scripted), Stone steers us through an ultrablack comedy that takes modern noir clichés to their darkly hilarious extremes. Penn portrays Bobby Cooper, a career loser who's on a bad streak even for *him.* In serious hock to, and on the run from, Russian Vegas mobsters who've already snipped two fingers off his left hand, Bobby's luck worsens when his vintage "1964½" orange Mustang convertible breaks down outside the parched desert town of Superior, Arizona. Entrusting the showcase car to filth-and-grease-caked mechanic Darryl (an excellent Thornton), Penn unwisely heads for town, where a series of spiraling disasters await. Cleverly plotted, with a deadpan absurdist tone, *U-Turn* handily achieves its merrily nihilistic aims.

THE VANISHING   (1988) ***½

D: George Sluizer. Bernard-Pierre Donnadieu, Johanna Ter Steege, Gene Bervoets. 107 mins. (Fox Lorber) DVD

Sluizer's suspenser employs a highly inventive but never pretentious or confusing narrative structure to investigate the rest-stop disappearance of the distaff half of a Dutch couple vacationing in the South of France. To say much more would be to risk ruining the many unsettling surprises *The Vanishing* holds in store. Suffice it to say that Donnadieu makes for one of the most laidback sociopaths in screen history, while the film itself sports an ending that, in its own idiosyncratic way, even outdoes *Henry*'s climax. Sluizer's brilliant exercise in subtle but consummately sadistic audience torture is not to be missed by anyone who can take the tension. Avoid Sluizer's own soulless Hollywood remake (Fox).

VOYAGE   (1993) ***½

D: John Mackenzie. Rutger Hauer, Eric Roberts, Karen Allen, Connie Nielsen. 86 mins. (Fox)

Roman Polanski's *Knife in the Water* Meets Phillip Noyce's *Dead Calm* in John (*Deadly Voyage*) Mackenzie's expertly shaded seagoing suspenser. Although it's a bit hard to swallow Rut—cast here as a semi-flabby 38-year-old ex-high-school diving champ currently slowed by a heart condition—being the same age as a buff Roberts (off-screen he's 12 years Eric's senior), the rest of this gripping character study arrives nearly free of flaws. Couple Hauer and Allen have resolved to chuck their staid stateside existence to rehab their newly purchased Malta manse. Running into a clearly psycho Roberts and his unhinged younger squeeze, Nielsen, at a high school reunion, Rut unwisely invites the pair to share his planned sail. Tension mounts as Roberts seeks to compete with Hauer, comes on to Allen (with whom he'd had a distant teenage fling), and generally makes their shipboard arrangement increasingly intolerable. The characters remain believable throughout, while a violent finale delivers the promised genre goods.

WHERE SLEEPING DOGS LIE (1992) **½

D: Charles Finch. Dylan McDermott, Tom Sizemore, Sharon Stone, Mary Woronov. 92 mins. (Columbia/TriStar)

When struggling writer and part-time realtor McDermott is evicted from his L.A. pad, he moves into one of his own unsold properties, where everyone (including cheerfully morbid tourist Woronov) but our hero seems to know a family massacre had been committed some years before by a still-free serial killer. At the urging of aggressive lit agent and lover Stone, the dim McDermott decides to write a nonfiction thriller about the unsolved case. Enter the bland, polite, enigmatic Sizemore, who signs on as a temporary tenant and turns out to be you-know-who. An initially gripping exercise in the popular "get to know your psycho" subgenre slips through director Finch's fingers due to torpid pacing and stalled suspense.

WHISPERS IN THE DARK (1992) ***

D: Christopher Crowe. Annabella Sciorra, Jamey Sheridan, Alan Alda, Jill Clayburgh, John Leguizamo, Deborah Unger. 103 mins. (Paramount)

Ludicrous as an earnest thriller, Whispers works quite nicely if viewed as a paranoiac black comedy.

Passive shrink Sciorra is surrounded on all sides by madness and violence that ultimately wipes out nearly everyone she knows. Leguizamo and the zaftig Unger are fun as two of Annabella's flamboyantly pervo patients. The ever annoying Clayburgh's violent encounter with a full wine bottle represents another highlight, as does Alda's against-type turn. For an entire "Night of the Evil Alda" bill, pick up the 1972 obscurity *To Kill a Clown* (Video Treasures), wherein the usually PC Bob plays a lame 'Nam vet who tortures a vacationing couple on a remote New England isle.

WHITE HEAT (1949) B&W ****

D: Raoul Walsh. James Cagney, Virginia Mayo, Edmond O'Brien, Steve Cochran, Margaret Wycherly. 114 mins. (Fox)

Cagney's nothing short of brilliant as migraine-plagued killer Cody Jarrett in an intense noir that also portends Hollywood's later psycho craze. An absolute must for buffs and film lovers of every stripe, this is a movie that never grows old. Beware the colorized version.

WHITE OF THE EYE (1988) ***

D: Donald Cammell. Cathy Moriarty, David Keith, Alan Rosenberg, Art Evans, Marty Hayashi, William Schilling. 111 mins. (Paramount)

Cammell crafts a bold, bizarre and truly sicko psycho-killer thriller in a quasi–*Blue Velvet* vein. The action unfolds in small-town Arizona, where Bronx refugee Moriarty trades in her lowlife beau (Rosenberg) for the possibly homicidal Keith. Auteur Cammell employs decidedly unconventional methods, ranging from the hallucinatory to the deliberately mundane, in relating his often terrifying tale. His creative camera work and complex flashback structure succeed more often than

not, while the principals turn in solid work, with Evans a standout as a cagey Tucson detective. Even occasional stretches of self-indulgence and several less-than-credible plot twists fail to strip this surreal anti-ode to American Romance of its intensity, power, and primal rage.

WILD HORSES (CABALLOS SALVAJES) (1995) ***

D: Marcelo Piñeyro. Hector Alterio, Leonardo Sbaraglia, Cecilia Dopazo, Federico Luppi. Subtitled. 122 mins. (New Yorker)

When an elderly man (Alterio) on a mysterious mission robs a Buenos Aires bank and embroils a yuppie employee (Sbaraglia) in his escape, the stage is set for an alternately satiric and romantic road odyssey through rural Argentina. The unlikely fugitives become national media heroes as they evade the law, pursuing journalists, and vengeful thugs in the corrupt bank's employ. Piñeyro's evocatively lensed adventure suffers from some overly lyrical indulgences, but solid thesping by the likable leads and a genuinely engaging story ultimately carry the day.

WILD SIDE (1995) **½

D: Franklyn Brauner. Christopher Walken, Joan Chen, Steven Bauer, Anne Heche. In R and unrated editions. 96 mins. (Hallmark)

Cowritten (with wife China Kong) and directed by Donald (*White of the Eye*) Cammell—who had his directorial credit removed—*Wild Side* lives up to its title, at least in the acting department, with Walken, as money-laundering mogul Bruno Buckingham, scaling way over the top, cooking up a multimillion-dollar scam while finding time to dally with his wife (Chen, who associate-produced), *her* bi-lover (Heche, *and* his reluctant driver (Bauer, recycling his Manny bit from *Scarface*). Walken muses, "Women! With 'em, without 'em, who could live?", but a secondary character comes closer to capturing the pic's core: "Gender is irrelevant. This is California." Cammell committed suicide soon after the film's reported postproduction mutilation.

WILD THINGS   (1998) ***

D: John McNaughton. Matt Dillon, Neve Campbell, Kevin Bacon, Theresa Russell, Denise Richards, Bill Murray. 108 mins. (Columbia/TriStar) DVD

High school guidance counselor Dillon encounters female trouble galore, in the form of two pulchritudinous students, "swamp trash" Campbell and upscale Richards, in director John (Henry) McNaughton's relentlessly clever, delightfully seamy, steamy South Florida noir. A much publicized (before and during the pic's theatrical release) ménage à trois among Matt, Neve, and Denise is more teasing than shocking, though Kevin, as an obsessed cop on the case, briefly bares his bacon in a gratuitous shower scene. (He also exec-produced; full-frontal flash rights were probably part of the deal.) Murray's a hoot as Matt's skid-row whiplash lawyer.

THE WINDOW   (1949) B&W ***

D: Ted Tetzlaff. Bobby Driscoll, Barbara Hale, Arthur Kennedy. 73 mins. (Fox Hills, n.i.d.)

Driscoll stars as a young boy who can't convince his incredulous parents (Hale, Kennedy) that he's actually witnessed a murder in this tight, effective B noir. The recommended 1970 Brit thriller Sudden Terror (Magnetic) sports a similar hook.

WINTER KILLS   (1979) ***

D: William Richert. Jeff Bridges, John Huston, Anthony Perkins. 97 mins. (Columbia/TriStar)

Bridges is a sort of slacker Bobby Kennedy stand-in who uncovers an involved plot behind his president-brother's assassination in Richert's adaptation of novelist Richard (Prizzi's Honor) Condon's black comedy/thriller. Huston and Perkins are particular standouts.

WITNESS   (1985) ***

D: Peter Weir. Harrison Ford, Kelly McGillis, Alexander Godunov. 112 mins. (Paramount) DVD

Aussie auteur Weir inspired an entire celluloid subgenre dealing with displaced cops (e.g., A Stranger Among Us, from Hollywood Pictures) with this suspenser about Ford going undercover in Amish country to protect young murder witness Lukas Haas.

A WOMAN OBSESSED   (1989) **

D: Chuck Vincent. Linda Blair, Ruth Raymond (Georgina Spelvin), Gregory Patrick, Troy Donahue. 103 mins. (Academy, n.i.d.)

No relation to the 1959 Susan Hayward film of the same name (n/a), this Woman Obsessed again finds Linda Blair entrusted to Chuck Vincent's slack directorial care (see also Bedroom Eyes II, from Trimark). Here Linda is cast in a role that parallels her famed Exorcist turn, as she's slowly poisoned by her hapless lawyer-hubby's mad mom (ex-porn starlet Spelvin); she spends half the flick in a sickbed before being slaughtered (in slo mo, no less). While often static, this undeniably perverse and totally tasteless oedipal sickie sadly ranks among the better examples of Linda's relatively recent output.

WOMAN OF DESIRE   (1993) *1/2

D: Robert Ginty. Bo Derek, Jeff Fahey, Steven Bauer, Robert Mitchum. 97 mins. (Trimark)

Erstwhile B action star Robert (The Exterminator, Out on Bail) Ginty writes and directs a dull "erotic" thriller that's sure to bore all but the most devoted Bo-in-the-buff buffs. For the record, the Bodacious One plays the widow of a newly drowned Carib-island honcho (Bauer), whose twin (also Bauer) accuses Fahey of the crime. A somnolent Mitchum plays Jeff's cagey attorney. Not as inept as Bo's Ghosts Can't Do It (Columbia/TriStar)—which, obscure though it may be, already inspired the low-budget Ghosts Can Do It (Atlas)—but even more yawn-inducing, unless you crave to watch Jeff and Bo do it on the back of a motorcycle (unfortunately, not in motion at the time).

THE YAKUZA   (1975) ***

D: Sydney Pollack. Robert Mitchum, Takakura Ken, Brian Keith. 112 mins. (Warner)

Before Michael Douglas and Andy Garcia in Black Rain (Paramount) and Sean Connery and Wesley Snipes in Rising Sun (Fox), hard-boiled Bob Mitchum went head-to-head with Japanese miscreants in Pollack's exotic noir, cracklingly written by near-future Taxi Driver scripter Paul Schrader. No relation to American Yakuza (Columbia/TriStar), with Viggo Mortensen.

ZENTROPA   (1991) COLOR/B&W ***

D: Lars von Trier. Jean-Marc Barr, Barbara Sukowa, Udo Kier, Eddie Constantine, Jørgen Reenberg. Subtitled. 112 mins. (Touchstone)

Unlike his relentlessly grim, sepia-toned metaphysical-psycho debut, The Element of Crime (Home Vision)—a film more original than watchable—Dutch director Trier's second effort, Zentropa, is not only a visually arresting but a highly entertaining postwar noir nightmare. Here Trier's unique style serves to support rather than distract from his offbeat but conventionally structured story line (cowritten with Niels Vorsel). Barr stars as Leo Kessler, a German-American pacifist who, in late 1945, journeys to occupied Frankfurt, where he finds work as a sleeping-car conductor on the Zentropa railway. He also meets sultry Kat Hartmann (Sukowa), whose father (Reenberg) owns the railroad in question. A dinner invitation soon involves the idealistic Leo not only with Kat and her war-dispirited dad but with her cynical homosexual brother (Kier), local priest (Erik Mork), American

officer (Eddie *[Alphaville]* Constantine), and several unrepentant Nazi guerrillas known as "Werewolves" (earlier the subject of the Sam Fuller film *Verboten!*, from Image). Like a Danish David Lynch, Trier blends satire, surrealism, and straightforward narrative. An omniscient but unseen Max von Sydow (as God, we presume) supplies a resonant voice-over that moves the story forward. Like the later, more widely hyped *Pleasantville, Zentropa* uses color and B&W, often within the same frame, as well as

superimposition, rear projection, and other creatively distortive techniques. (One especially striking segment contrasts bright-red blood with a B&W background in a way that tops a similar scene earlier seen in the William Castle classic *The Tingler*.) Like the eponymous railway, *Zentropa* proceeds slowly at times, even threatening, on occasion, to grind to a halt. But this haunting thriller, laced with unforgettable imagery, remains an experience adventurous viewers won't want to miss.

CUTTING-EDGE COMEDIES

"I think she does everything most people wish their mother would do for them."
—John Waters on *SERIAL MOM*

ABBOTT AND COSTELLO GO TO MARS   (1953) B&W ***

D: Charles Lamont. Bud Abbott, Lou Costello, Robert Paige, Mari Blanchard, Martha Hyer, Horace McMahon, Jack Kruschen, Joe Kirk, Anita Ekberg. 77 mins. (Universal)

A&C's surreal space caper makes an excellent candidate for time-capsule preservation for future anthropologists studying 1950s American pop culture. The boys accidentally launch themselves in a Mars-bound rocket that, after an inspired detour through NYC's Lincoln Tunnel (!), lands near New Orleans during Mardi Gras. In a thoroughly bizarre sequence, it takes A&C a couple of reels before they realize the costumed celebrants aren't Martians. Escaped cons McMahon (future star of TV's *Naked City*) and Kruschen stow away for our heroes' second takeoff, which propels them to an all-femme Venus, where queen Blanchard reluctantly accepts Costello as king. (Ekberg can be glimpsed as a Venusian palace guard.) All four guys are unceremoniously booted off the planet after Blanchard treats her subjects to a muscleman slide show that clues them in to how *real* men should look (!). She also casts a curse on any subject who kisses any of the interlopers, leading to one fairly sicko sight gag. Alternately (sometimes even simultaneously) hackneyed and weird, *A&C Go to Mars* has enough offbeat crossover appeal to entertain nonfans as well as A&C addicts. Most of the team's feature films, along with episodes of their much beloved early 1950s TV show, have joined the homevid ranks.

THE ABSENT-MINDED PROFESSOR (1961) ***

D: Robert Stevenson. Fred MacMurray, Nancy Olson, Keenan Wynn, Tommy Kirk. 97 mins. (Disney)

Titular prof MacMurray stumbles upon an antigravity gas. Though dated, this quintessential Disney comedy is fully capable of inducing fits of hopeless nostalgia in unregenerate members of the Flubber Generation. MacMurray returns in 1963's *Son of Flubber* (Disney). Joe Dante and crew brilliantly send up Disney's family comedies of the era with the "The Shook-Up Shopping Cart" segment in *Matinee*. The more scatologically minded, quintessentially '90s remake, *Flubber* (Touchstone), with the ubiquitous Robin Williams, is also out there.

ACTING ON IMPULSE   (1993) **1/2

D: Sam Irvin. Linda Fiorentino, C. Thomas Howell, Nancy Allen, Tom Wright, Isaac Hayes, Paul Bartel, Adam Ant, Patrick Bachau. 94 mins. (Academy, n.i.d.)

Irvin's second feature film represents a decided improvement over his ham-handed black-comedy debut, *Guilty as Charged* (1991, Columbia/TriStar)—as least for its first 80 or so minutes. A spirited, hard-drinking "scream queen" (a pre–*Last Seduction* Fiorentino) flees a low-budget fright-flick set, leaving producer Bachau's dead body in her wake (and with a rabid, possibly homicidal fan in hot pursuit). After randomly checking in to a Northern California hotel where a pharmaceutical convention's being held, Linda takes up with straight-arrow young suit Howell and his equally uptight femme counterpart (Allen). The trio's ensuing adventures supply a good deal of credible anarchic fun as Linda lends an air of spontaneity and excitement to the squares' lives, but Irvin and his scripters blow it with a contrived, violent climax. *Acting on Impulse* still rates a look, though, both for its unpredictable early reels, which incorporate some deft behind-the-scenes B-screen observations, and a nonstop parade of quirky cameos by the likes of, among others, *Happy Days'* Donnie (now simply "Don") Most, Zelda (*Poltergeist*) Rubinstein, Mary Woronov, Cassandra (Elvira) Peterson, Miles O'Keeffe, and even legit scream queen Brinke Stevens. Irvin returns with the sci-fi/western comedies *Oblivion* and *Backlash: Oblivion 2* (Full Moon).

THE ADDAMS FAMILY:
THE SERIES

THE ADDAMS FAMILY   (1991)***

D: Barry Sonnenfeld. Raul Julia, Anjelica Huston, Christopher Lloyd, Dan Hedaya, Christina Ricci, Jimmy Workman. 102 mins. (Paramount)

Sonnenfeld's big-screen adaptation of Charles Addams's cartoon-turned-sitcom-hit shouldn't disappoint the Family's fans. The skeletal plot—shyster Hedaya tries to foist a phony Fester on the clan in a bid to bag their bucks—serves as an adequate frame for a series of gags ranging from the cute to the creaky to the legitimately sick and surreal, as when young Wednesday (Ricci) persuades brother Pugsley (Workman) to strap himself into a live electric chair for a game of "Is There a God?" (!). The expected high-tech FX help expand the slapstick possibilities, allowing hyper living hand "Thing" to enjoy a more active role, while the elaborate, imaginative sets, especially the Addams manse's full-blown basement sea, contribute a major visual plus.

ADDAMS FAMILY VALUES (1993)***

D: Barry Sonnenfeld. Anjelica Huston, Raul Julia, Christopher Lloyd, Joan Cusack, Christina Ricci, Carol Kane, Jimmy Workman. 93 mins. (Paramount)

Director Sonnenfeld's series settles into a comfortable sitcom groove

with an episodic affair focusing on two main story threads—gold-digging nanny Cusack's marital abduction of wealthy but virginal bachelor Fester (an excellent Lloyd) and sibs Wednesday (Ricci) and Pugsley's (Workman) misadventures at an upscale summer camp, an exile prompted by the pair's efforts to eliminate their moustachioed infant bro', "Pubert." Episodes from the original teleseries are also available on tape.

THE ADVENTURES OF PRISCILLA, QUEEN OF THE DESERT   (1994)***

D: Stephan Elliott. Terence Stamp, Hugo Weaving, Guy Pearce. 102 mins. (PolyGram) DVD

Aussie drag queens Weaving and Pearce (later of *L.A. Confidential*) and transsexual Stamp (in a grand stretch) get their gender-bending act together and take it on the outback road in Elliott's amusing odyssey, a must for all but the most extreme ABBA-phobes.

AFTER HOURS   (1985)**1/2

D: Martin Scorsese. Griffin Dunne, Rosanna Arquette, John Heard, Teri Garr, Verna Bloom. 97 mins. (Warner)

A disastrous date leads a lost Dunne into the bowels of a SoHo hell. Scorsese's heady farce features offbeat detours galore and a top supporting cast that includes Linda Fiorentino and Catherine O'Hara, even if it ultimately has nowhere to go. Scripter Joseph Minion returned with the equally offbeat, hit-and-miss 1992 road odyssey *Motorama* (Columbia/TriStar).

AIRPLANE!   (1980)***1/2

D: Jim Abrahams, David Zucker, Jerry Zucker. Robert Hays, Julie Hagerty, Peter Graves, Lloyd Bridges. 88 mins. (Paramount)

This oft brilliant, anything-goes parody of air-disaster flicks, peppered

with star cameos, rates as the ultimate *MAD*-magazine strip come to celluloid life. The pic put the ZAZ Team on the movie map and remains thoroughly deserving of its vaunted comic rep. Not so the ZAZ-less *Airplane II: The Sequel* (Paramount).

THE ALARMIST   (1998)***

D: Evan Dunsky. David Arquette, Stanley Tucci, Kate Capshaw, Mary McCormack, Hoke Howell. 93 mins. (Columbia/TriStar) DVD

Fans of extremely dark comedy will want to scope out *The Alarmist*, adapted from Keith Reddin's play *Life During Wartime*. An appealing Arquette plays Tommy Hudler, an eager young home-security-systems salesman newly employed by Heinrich (an excellent Tucci). Tommy seems to be on his way up the company and personal ladder when he lands a sale and a lover (Capshaw) on his very first assignment. Our modern-day Candide's skies darken, however, when he discovers some secrets about Tucci's worse-than-shady business practices. While not every element works (e.g., a totally unnecessary flash-card epilogue), *The Alarmist* can't be accused of moving in predictable directions.

AMAZON WOMEN ON THE MOON (1987)***

D: John Landis, Joe Dante, Robert K. Weiss, Peter Horton, Carl Gottlieb. Carrie Fisher, Griffin Dunne, Rosanna Arquette, Steve Guttenberg, Steve Allen, Steve Forrest, Sybil Danning, Ed Begley, Jr., Lou Jacobi. 85 mins. (Universal) DVD

Fashioned by five directors and featuring "Lots of Actors," *Amazon Women on the Moon* is a mostly on-target spoof of vintage brain-damaged TV programming, from Leonard Nimoy's *In Search Of…* to late-night B-movie fests. Among the best bits here are an *Invisible Man* takeoff (a riff earlier "seen" in the Hong Kong comedy *Winners and Sinners,* on Tai Seng); a generic *el cheapo* '50s sci-fi flick; and the Dante-directed *Damaged Lives/Sex Madness* send-up, "Reckless Youth," starring Carrie Fisher and Paul Bartel. The once-in-a-lifetime cast includes Danning (as the Amazon queen), Henry Silva, Robert Colbert, Mike Mazurki, Joey (Brother of John) Travolta, William (*Blacula*) Marshall (as the captain of a crew of video pirates), and Russ Meyer as a shady vid-store clerk.

THE AMBULANCE
(1990/1993) ***

D: Larry Cohen. Eric Roberts, James Earl Jones, Red Buttons, Megan Gallagher, Janine Turner, Eric Braeden. 95 mins. (Columbia/TriStar)

The *Ambulance* involves comic-book artist Roberts, who witnesses a diabetic woman (Turner) being whisked away by the title conveyence. Turner's subsequent failure to turn up at any known NYC hospital arouses the excitable artist's suspicions. While Eric succeeds, with the help of feisty tabloid reporter Buttons, in accumulating evidence of a malevolent medical conspiracy, he can't convince high-strung NYPD detective Jones that foul play's indeed afoot. Cohen's intriguing premise, somewhat reminiscent of *Coma* and *Spare Parts* (see index), might have been better served by a less comedic, more sci-fi/thriller-oriented approach. On the upside, scripter Cohen infuses his story with several unpredictable twists, sharply observed details, and memorable lines (e.g., mad medico Braeden to involuntary patient: "I just like to touch human skin through a surgical glove, that's all.") The pic's ultimate punch line cleverly puts all that's gone before in a shaggy-doc story mode, and Cohen's healthy skepticism re our native health system simmers beneath the farcical surface.

...AND GOD SPOKE   (1994) **½

D: Arthur Borman. Michael Riley, Stephen Rappaport, Soupy Sales, Eve Plumb, Lou Ferrigno. 82 mins. (Artisan)

...A nd God Spoke chronicles the misadventures of low-level moviemakers Riley and Rappaport as they blow their first big budget on an ill-fated biblical epic titled *...And God Spoke.* While most of director Borman's targets are less than fresh and his film rarely scales the heights of Harry Hurwitz's more outrageous celluloid send-up, *That's Adequate!*—let alone Rob Reiner's brilliant heavy-metal mockumentary, *This Is Spinal Tap*—his cheerful satire scores a number of honest yoks and features former kid-show host Sales (as Moses!), along with erstwhile Hulk/Hercules Ferrigno and onetime *Brady Bunch*er Plumb.

ANDY KAUFMAN'S SOUND STAGE
(1983) ****

D: Dick Carter. Andy Kaufman, Elayne Boosler, James Bradley. 59 mins. (Lightning, n.i.d.)

The late conceptual comic, subject of the biopic *Man on the Moon*, explodes the TV talk-show format with mock-sincere brilliance as life imitates artlessness and vice versa in a winner worthy of repeat viewings.

ANDY WARHOL'S BAD
(1977) ***

D: Jed Johnson. Carroll Baker, Perry King, Susan Tyrrell. 100 mins. (Embassy, n.i.d.)

Camp icon Carroll (*Harlow, Baby Doll*) Baker is all business as a Queens housewife who uses her electrolysis practice as a front for a freelance assassination operation in a genuinely sick, frequently funny excursion into John Waters territory, further aided by authentic borough locales.

THE APE WOMAN
(1964) B&W ***

D: Marco Ferreri. Ugo Tognazzi, Annie Girardot, Achille Majeroni. Dubbed. 92 mins. (Something Weird)

Tognazzi, later of *La Cage aux Folles*, plays Antonio, a two-bit Italo roadshow "impresario." Antonio shows topless-African "educational" slides at a Catholic home for the poor, where he encounters title character Maria (Girardot), an innocent orphan girl covered with hair. He convinces her to work as a "phenomenon" at a homemade jungle exhibit he constructs; they later graduate to a Parisian strip club, where they re-create her jungle "capture" at his hands. Meantime, Maria tumbles for the manipulative Antonio, and he marries her to keep her from returning to the home. When she becomes pregnant in Paris, Antonio, on a local doctor's recommendation, votes for an abortion, but Maria refuses and Antonio accedes to her wishes. Not only is the baby born normal, but Maria's hirsute condition is cured during her hospital stay, spelling potential financial ruin for the family. In Something Weird's dubbed version, the one that played in most venues beyond Italy, the film shifts from the fabulistic to the neorealistic as the reels roll on. Ferreri filmed a radically different ending exhibited at Italian theaters, wherein Maria and her infant die in childbirth and Antonio tours with their mummified bodies to pay off his debts (!). "Neither [version] has a happy ending," the late filmmaker explained to yours truly in 1996. "In that [the first] one, the guy has to work for the rest of his life!" Other Ferreri films available on homevid include *Bye-Bye Monkey, Don't Touch the White Woman, Seeking Asylum,* with Roberto Benigni, and the Charles Bukowski–based *Tales of Ordinary Madness* (all Image/Vanguard, DVD), starring Ben Gazzara; the cult fave *La Grande Bouffe* (Water Bearer), *El Cochecito,* and *L'Udienza* (both Facets).

ARSENIC AND OLD LACE (1944) B&W***

D: Frank Capra. Cary Grant, Priscilla Lane, Raymond Massey, Peter Lorre. 118 mins. (Fox)

The usually sunny Capra exhibits a darker comedic side with his wonderfully acted adaptation of Joseph Kesselring's sardonic play about a weirdo family led by a pair of geriatric euthanasia enthusiasts. Massey replaced Boris Karloff, who'd costarred in the Broadway play.

ATTACK OF THE 50 FOOT WOMAN (1994) **½

D: Christopher Guest. Daryl Hannah, Daniel Baldwin, William Windom. 90 mins. (HBO)

While the concept might have better benefitted from an over-the-top ZAZ Team/*Naked Gun* approach (and a funnier actress than Hannah), Guest's deadpan, stretched-sketch reworking of Nathan Hertz's 1958 camp classic of the same name (Key) at least reaches most of its modest comedic goals. Guest goes for chuckles over guffaws by running the quintessentially '50s plot through a mock '90s politically correct wringer and incorporating a plethora of accessible in-jokes (e.g., a truck emblazoned with ARKOFF & CORMAN INDUSTRIAL MOVERS and a nod to the giant-hypo scene from *The Amazing Colossal Man*).

ATTACK OF THE 60 FOOT CENTERFOLD (1995) **½

D: Fred Olen Ray. J. J. North, John LaZar, Ted Monte, Raelyn Saalman, Tammy Parks, Tim Abell, Jay Richardson, Russ Tamblyn, Tommy Kirk, Ross Hagen, Stanley Livingston, Michelle Bauer, George Stover. 84 mins. (New Horizons)

Attack is arguably indefatigable low-budget auteur Ray's finest filmic moment since his *Hollywood Chainsaw*

Hookers (see index). Some gags work (particularly the evocative mock-'50s opening-credits sequence), while LaZar (*Beyond the Valley of the Dolls*'s Z-Man) is fine as the scientist who reluctantly entrusts "aging" model Angel Grace (North) with an overly generous supply of experimental rejuvenating serum. Tamblyn, of *West Side Story*, *Satan's Sadists*, and *Twin Peaks* fame, onetime Disney towhead Kirk, and Livingston (whose career has ranged from *My Three Sons* to Paul Bartel's *Private Parts*) supply serviceable comic cameos. (You can also spot Forry Ackerman as a Bela Lugosi statue.) If you've half a mind to kick back with a dumb but genial T&A-laced time-waster, you could do worse than *Attack*. Ray strikes again with *Bikini Drive-In* (Arrow).

AUSTIN POWERS:
THE SERIES

AUSTIN POWERS: INTERNATIONAL MAN OF MYSTERY (1997) ***

D: Jay Roach. Mike Myers, Elizabeth Hurley, Michael York, Mimi Rogers. 89 mins. (New Line) DVD

Former *SNL* regular/*Wayne's World* mastermind Myers scored a surprise smash with his mostly smashing send-up of "hip" and "happening" spy flicks of the late '60s and introduced indelible screen characters with the bucktoothed, terminally randy Austin and his hopelessly out-of-it archnemesis, Dr. Evil (also Myers). The series doesn't flag with the equally popular 1999 sequel, *Austin Powers: The Spy Who Shagged Me* (New Line, DVD).

BABE:
THE SERIES

BABE (1995) ***

D: Chris Noonan. James Cromwell, Magda Szubanski. 91 mins. (Universal) DVD

An orphaned pig finds a new home with farmer Cromwell and his barnyard denizens in Noonan's disarming, refreshingly unsappy talking-animal fable, adapted from Dick King-Smith's book "The Sheep-Pig." Followed by the equally enchanting, if commercially underachieving, *Babe: Pig in the City* (Universal).

BACK TO THE BEACH (1987) **½

D: Lyndall Hobbs. Frankie Avalon, Annette Funicello, Connie Stevens. 92 mins. (Paramount)

Middle-aged "stressed-out car salesman" Frankie and Stepford-like wife, Annette, return to their sandy roots in this systematic deconstruction of the early-'60s beach-party mythos. Pee-wee Herman's unique interpretation of the the Trashmen's "Surfin' Bird" supplies an indelible highlight.

BACK TO THE FUTURE:
THE SERIES

BACK TO THE FUTURE (1985) ***½

D: Robert Zemeckis. Michael J. Fox, Christopher Lloyd, Crispin Glover, Lea Thompson, Claudia Wells. 116 mins. (Universal)

Back to the Future won yours truly over on the strength of its vintage-movie nostalgia value alone. When young Marty McFly (Fox) rewinds to 1955, we see his hometown's two broken-down bijous—since converted into a porn house and a church, respectively—restored to their former glory. (One advertises *Cattle Queen of Montana*, starring Ronald Reagan.) When Marty prepares to fast-forward to the present, his time machine (a souped-up DeLorean) passes through the '50s bijou and emerges from the '80s church! Beyond its fun bijou byplay, *Back to the Future* is a bright fantasy brimming with playful temporal conceits and clever pop-cultural comparisons between the '50s and the '80s.

BACK TO THE FUTURE II (1989) **

D: Robert Zemeckis. Michael J. Fox, Christopher Lloyd, Lea Thompson, Thomas F. Wilson, Joe Flaherty. 107 mins. (Universal)

*B*TTF II stacks up as a slick, busy, but mostly soulless affair that substitutes surface intricacy for genuine ingenuity, artificial frenzy for authentic energy. The sequel picks up where the original left off, with neighborhood mad scientist Lloyd and apparently eternal adolescent Fox zooming into a future awash with blatant high-tech product plugs, a scene that mixes soft satire with hard sell as the camera lavishes much loving attention on the brand names in question. Once the commercials are over, Chris and Mike crisscross between the past of *Back I* while also finding time to enter a disastrous "alternate reality" that cops much of its inspiration (and we use the term loosely) from Frank Capra's darkly cheery chestnut *It's a Wonderful Life* (20th Century Fox). It's here that *Back II* descends into the sort of broad sitcom antics the original largely avoided. Fox's transvestite interlude is unlikely to cause Ed Wood's *Glen or Glenda* to lose any serious beauty sleep.

BACK TO THE FUTURE III
(1990) **½

D: Robert Zemeckis. Michael J. Fox, Christopher Lloyd, Mary Steenburgen, Thomas F. Wilson, Lea Thompson. 118 mins. (Fox)

*D*irector Zemeckis knows how to craft an adrenalizing chase scene, and we also appreciated his by-now obligatory nods to B-movie nostalgia; one scene is staged at a 1955 drive-in (where *Tarantula* and *Revenge of the Creature* share a double bill). Lloyd maintains a high level of comic energy

as obsessive inventor Doc Brown, while old-timers Harry Carey, Jr., Pat Buttram, and Dub Taylor contribute crusty coot cameos during the Wild West–set centerpiece. Though *III* represents an improvement over *II*, we ultimately felt crushed under the sheer weight of producer Steven Spielberg's anvil whimsy.

BAD TASTE (1988) ***

D: Peter Jackson. Peter Jackson, Pete O'Herne, Mike Minett, Terry Potter, Craig Smith. 90 mins. (Magnum)

*A*lien zombies in the employ of ruthless fast-food franchisers from outer space invade rural New Zealand in a bid to turn earthlings into cosmic comestibles in Jackson's debut outing, filmed over several years on an invisible budget. Wise to the E.T.s' gustatory scheme are four unlikely macho commandos who engage the unfriendly aliens in an ultraviolent filmlong battle. While some of the satiric jabs are, at this late date, nearly as clichéd as their targets, and a few N.Z. references will be lost on most American viewers, Jackson's minimalist, mock-offensive splatter spoof survives as a mostly fun romp in a Sam Raimi–meets–John Waters vein, crammed with cartoon gore galore.

BARFLY (1987) ***

D: Barbet Schroeder. Mickey Rourke, Faye Dunaway, Alice Krige, Jack Nance, J. C. Quinn, Frank Stallone. 99 mins. (Warner)

*C*harles Bukowski's script, a deft distillation of several autobiographical short stories, takes the viewer through a few barhopping days (make that *daze*) in the life of C.B.'s fictional alter ego, writer/drunk (not necessarily in that order) Henry Chinaski. This laidback (occasionally passed-out) but consistently funny slice of lowlife is cleverly, unobtrusively framed by an identical opening and closing L.A.-tavern travelog, set to a jukebox rendition of

Booker T.'s "Hip Hug-Her," that succinctly underscores the cyclical nature of Henry's barfly continuum. Personified by a swaggering and staggering Rourke (Dennis Hopper must have been otherwise engaged), Henry drinks, writes, fights continuously with beefy barkeep Stallone, drinks, has an *affair de liqueur* with femme lush Dunaway, gets pursued by private dick Nance, is wooed by slumming publisher Krige, and drinks. Rourke mutters many memorable Bukowski lines (though the actor's inflection unfortunately alters from scene to scene) and is himself summed up by a fellow wino who observes, "He hates help." *Barfly* makes for fluid video viewing—there's even a lively barroom catfight 'twixt Dunaway and Krige—preferably accompanied by a half-pint of cheap whiskey and a couple of brews. Schroeder's two-volume verité work *The Charles Bukowski Tapes* is also out (Lagoon Video), as is *Bukowski at Bellevue: Spring 1970* (Black Sparrow). Mystic Fire Video, meanwhile, carries an impressive lineup of Beat-themed tapes.

BARTON FINK (1991) ***½

D: Joel Coen. John Turturro, John Goodman, Judy Davis, Michael Lerner, John Mahoney, Jon Polito, Steve Buscemi. 116 mins. (Fox)

*J*oel and Ethan Coen's idiosyncratic vintage-Tinseltown satire depicts a private Hollywood hell inhabited by a neurotic New York playwright of limited range (Turturro, as a character obviously based on Clifford Odets) who moves West at the lucrative behest of crass movie mogul Lerner (in a brilliant turn). Holed up with his typewriter in a sinister, rotting hotel, Fink suffers a paralyzing attack of writer's block while trying to script a Wallace Beery wrestling picture. Commiseration appears in the fat form of fellow hotel resident Goodman, a philosophical salesman with a full flask and empty homily ever at the ready. Mahoney and Davis excel as a sold-out Southern novelist based on William Faulkner and his more-than-helpful secretary/mistress. Unfortunately, *Barton Fink* takes a wrong turn in its latter reels, one from which it never fully recovers. Still, the rest is so eccentrically brilliant that we recommend the flick sans reservations.

BASKET CASE:
THE SERIES

BASKET CASE: THE SPECIAL EDITION   (1982/1999) ***1/2

D: Frank Henenlotter. Kevin Van Hentenryck, Terri Susan Smith, Beverly Bonner, Robert Vogel, Diana Browne. 91 mins. (Something Weird) DVD

The tireless genre archivists at Something Weird not only return Henenlotter's darkly comic fright fable to the homevid ranks but present the film in a digitally remastered version that removes most of the murk that clouded its original release on the defunct Media label. *Basket Case* tells the heartwarming tale of young naïf Duane (Van Hentenryck) and his mutant, basket-dwelling Siamese-twin brother, Belial, who descend upon NYC to wreak vengeance against the quack doctors who'd forcibly separated them years earlier. While the pic may have lost some of its initial shock value, *Basket Case*'s exploration of (decidedly bizarre) sibling love-hate relationships and its insights re the nature of individual identity hold up quite nicely, as do its inventive splatter moments. *Basket Case* also gains greatly in nostalgia value via its loving look at a vintage, since-vanished 42nd Street, captured here in all its authentic seedy glory. Brief outtakes follow the feature in SWV's restored edition. Despite some wackily effective bits—like Belial's romance with female mutant Eve—the 1990 sequel, *Basket Case 2*, largely spins its wheels until its over-the-top final reels. The pace picks up with 1992's *Basket Case 3* (both SGE, n.i.d.), which sees

the Bradley boys, along with freaks-rights activist Granny Ruth (jazz chanteuse Annie Ross) and a whole fleet of freaks, journey to Georgia, where a kindly doctor (Dan Biggers) oversees mutant Eve's pregnancy—with frightfully funny results.

BAXTER   (1991) ***

D: Jérôme Boivin. Lise Delamare, Jean Mercure, Jacques Spiesser, Catherine Ferrán, François Driancourt. Subtitled. 82 mins. (Fox Lorber)

A Machiavellian mutt plots to improve his lot (usually with dire consequences for his various "masters") until he meets more than his match in burgeoning young Hitler-obsessed sociopath Driancourt. Boivin's perverse, highly original black comedy, ingeniously related from Baxter's POV (sort of a canine version of Camus's *L'Étranger*), doesn't present a precise antithesis of your typical faithful-Fido film; it's subtler and less predictable than that. In fact, Baxter's calculating quest for survival is ultimately far less frightening than kid Driancourt's willing descent into incipient psychosis. For more deviant doings in a canine vein, scope out *Marquis* (see index), a barnyard French Revolution satire in puppet form that casts Sade as a horny dog (!).

BEAN   (1997) ***

D: Mel Smith. Rowan Atkinson, Peter MacNicol, Pamela Reed. 92 mins. (PolyGram) DVD

Gifted comic Atkinson's titular one-man wrecking crew's big-screen debut doesn't quite match the impact of his short sketches, but enough of the latter are on view to make *Bean* a consistently amusing, occasionally hilarious experience. Several Atkinson teleshowcases, like *The Best Bits of Mr. Bean* (DVD) and the *Black Adder* series, are available on the BBC Video label.

BEAT THE DEVIL   (1954) ***

D: John Huston. Humphrey Bogart, Jennifer Jones, Gina Lollobrigida. 89 mins. (Columbia/TriStar) DVD

Director Huston/scripter Truman Capote's collaboration flopped in its time, but their laid-back meditation on human greed has since become an enduring cult fave. As always, Peter Lorre's a treat in a sinister supporting role, and the film is blessed with a top-drawer ensemble cast.

BEAVIS AND BUTT-HEAD DO AMERICA   (1996) ***1/2

D: Mike Judge. Voice cast: Mike Judge, Robert Stack, Cloris Leachman, Eric Bogosian, Richard Linklater, Tim Guinee. 82 mins. (Paramount) DVD

It took some three decades for the American underground cartoon tradition to break through commercially on the big screen. Ralph Bakshi's 1972 R. Crumb–based *Fritz the Cat* (Warner, n.i.d.) stirred more controversy—both for its uninhibited erotic antics and its mangling of Crumb's vision—than bucks at the box office, while Terry Zwigoff's acclaimed 1995 documentary profile *Crumb* (New Line), focused more on the cartoonist's mega-dysfunctional family than on his pioneering artwork. When second-generation subterranean animator Mike Judge's *Beavis and Butt-head* scored big-time on MTV, the series likewise generated dissent, largely among those mainstream critics who didn't get the joke, judging the show as an exercise in cultural puerility rather than a meandering but dead-on satire of same, much as they initially did with Matt Groening's equally accurate crossover telehit *The Simpsons*. (Viewers, fortunately, *did* get the joke, and *B&B* creator Mike Judge later landed the spinoff series *King of the Hill*.) The good news here is that the animated brain-dead teens lose none of their subversive edge in their debut theatrical pratfall. The simple story line, scripted by Judge and Joe Stillman, parallels Tim Burton's *Pee-wee's Big Adventure* (see index), with a stolen TV replacing Pee-wee's purloined bike as the impetus for a cross-country odyssey. The flick opens with a clever shared dream, where an overgrown Butt-head plays King Kong (à la Eddie Murphy in *The Nutty Professor*) to an outsized Beavis's Godzilla. The boys rudely awaken to discover their TV, their very life-support system and link to the "outside" world, mysteriously missing. Following a terrif *Shaft*-styled opening-credits sequence (with music by original *Shaft*man, later *South Park* regular Isaac Hayes), the despairing duo's search for a replacement ultimately leads to our heroes becoming the effortlessly elusive targets of a national law-enforcement manhunt. As in *Pee-wee's Big Adventure,* the plot here serves as a loose frame for a host of inventive comic set pieces as B&B blithely barrel their way through a world of senseless adult agendas they don't even care to comprehend. Highlights include the boys' Vegas sojourn, their destruction of the Hoover Dam, a ride with a busful of nuns, and a desert detour wherein they meet their absentee dads (former Mötley Crüe roadies!) and undergo heavy-metal-flavored near-death hallucinations as their passive existences flash before their eyes. Beavis, meanwhile, jacked on sugar cubes (sans LSD) and "No Drowz" caffeine pills, lands not one but two opportunities to do his classic "Cornholio" routine.

Among the voice cast, Cloris Leachman is in top form as a kindly old lady, while Robert Stack reprises his basic Elliot Ness persona as a government agent with a penchant for ordering "full cavity searches." In one of the flick's most subversive moments, subordinates show Stack a film detailing the lethal test results of a toxic virus on unwitting American army "volunteers." Steams Stack: "Jesus Jumped-up Christ! If this were to fall into the wrong hands…"

Judge thus paraphrases another influential, oft anarchic cartoonist, Walt (Pogo) Kelly: *We have met the wrong hands, and they are ours.* Judge, meanwhile, contributes his own multiple vocal talents, as the nasal, snickering Butt-head and speed-babbling Beavis, as well as the boys' blustering secret-pervert high school principal and a New Agey teacher who croons a hilarious plea for tolerance titled "Lesbian Seagull" (reprised in the closing credits by Engelbert Humperdinck!).

BEDAZZLED (1967) ***

D: Stanley Donen. Peter Cook, Dudley Moore, Eleanor Bron. 107 mins. (Fox)

Donen directs the Cook-Moore team, then at the height of their comic powers, through an irreverent *Faust* update that sees Moore make an unholy (and unwise) bargain with deadpan devil Cook. The pair earlier joined forces with Peter Sellers for Bryan Forbes's wildly funny 1966 Victorian farce, *The Wrong Box* (Columbia/TriStar).

BEETLEJUICE (1988) **½

D: Tim Burton. Michael Keaton, Geena Davis, Winona Ryder, Alec Baldwin. 92 mins. (Warner) DVD

Keaton steals the show as a wisecracking supernatural "bio-exorcist" hired by ghosts Davis and Baldwin to terrorize their erstwhile home's obnoxious new tenants (including always welcome *SCTV* alum Catherine O'Hara) in Tim Burton's uneven, FX-laden frightcom.

BETRAYAL (1983) ***½

D: David Jones. Jeremy Irons, Patricia Hodge, Ben Kingsley. 95 mins. (Fox)

Harold Pinter's witty script charts an extramarital affair in reverse chronological order, beginning with the breakup and tracking back to the beginning. Kingsley is excellent as Hodge's supposedly cuckolded hubby.

THE BIG CRIMEWAVE (1987) ***

D: John Paisz. John Paisz, Darrel Baran, Eva Kovacs. 80 mins. (Cinema Group, n.i.d.)

From Winnipeg's windy wastelands comes deft low-budget comic actor/auteur John Paisz, whose 1987 feature, *Crimewave,* received the homevid title *The Big Crimewave* (with *The Big* clumsily superimposed over the existing title credits) doubtless to differentiate it from the Sam Raimi/Coen brothers' 1985 comedy of the same name (New Line). A nearly expressionless Paisz takes the silent starring role of spacy young would-be screenwriter Steven Penny. Steven's struggles are narrated by his lone fan, Kim (Kovacs), ten-year-old daughter of the couple who own the Winnipeg home where Steven rents an upstairs garage garret. Kim deems Steven irresistibly exotic and resolves to help her nerdy idol break into the world of "big-time color crime moviemaking." Paisz relates Steven's dubious progress with an unremittingly deadpan tone. Highlights include dramatized excerpts from our hero's abortive scripts, which Paisz uses to satirize Canadian mundanity (pardon our redundancy), Elvis imitators, killer Amway reps, greedy "self-help" gurus, Steven's own self-mythologizing, and the myriad ways in which life imitates artlessness in a vicarious, media-mad culture. Paisz even works in a last-reel rush of mock-sordid sex, brutality, and exploding heads as Steven's film career finally takes off in earnest. Despite its occasional echoes of Scorsese's *King of Comedy, The Big Crimewave,* lensed in "TotalColor and Select-O-Sound," emerges as an immensely enjoyable underground comedy that establishes Paisz—like fellow Manitoban moviemaker Guy Maddin—as a legit original.

THE BIG SQUEEZE (1996) ***

D: Marcus De Leon. Lara Flynn Boyle, Peter Dobson, Danny Nucci, Luca Bercovici, Teresa Dispina, Sam Vlahos. 107 mins. (BMG)

Debuting auteur De Leon assembles a cheerful scam comedy buoyed by fine perfs from Boyle as a frustrated barmaid, frequent B actor (and filmmaker) Bercovici (*The Granny, Rockula*) as her religious-minded ex–baseball player spouse, Dobson (*The Frighteners*) as a hustling drifter, and Nucci as a softhearted gardener. When Bercovici refuses to part with a $130,000 injury-settlement check, Boyle accepts Dobson's underhanded help in tricking the stubborn Christian into donating it to a local church where a horticultural "miracle" is in progress. De Leon and cast manage to make the unlikely plot play out almost credibly while avoiding an attack of the cutes. The flick's further abetted by ex-Devo front man Mark Mothersbaugh's '60s-flavored score, with frequent help from Tommy James and the Shondells' immortal psychedelic/bubblegum mantra "Crimson and Clover."

BILL & TED:
THE SERIES

BILL & TED'S EXCELLENT ADVENTURE (1989) ***

D: Stephen Herek. Keanu Reeves, Alex Winter, George Carlin, Bernie Casey. 90 mins. (Columbia/TriStar)

Dim-bulbed San Dimas dudes Reeves and Winter journey through time to collect famous historical figures for a class project in a witty, highly original send-up of contemporary American mores. While the 1991 sequel, *Bill & Ted's Bogus Journey* (Orion), lacks some of the original's subversive edge, the tiny-brained teens' descent into hell offers a number of hilarious highlights, including memorable work by William Sadler as

"Death" and a great Tina Turner impersonation by Pam Grier.

BIMBO MOVIE BASH! (1997) **½

D: David Parker, Mike Mendez. Adrienne Barbeau, Shannon Tweed, Morgan Fairchild, Julie Strain, Linnea Quigley, Elizabeth Kaitan, Brinke Stevens, Michelle Bauer, Bill Maher. 82 mins. (Cult Video)

Bimbo Movie Bash! may well rank as the ultimate scream-queen/bimbo extravaganza, wherein Parker and Mendez remix scenes from more than 15 previous pics to concoct a tasty video-bimbo stew. Modestly self-described as "the *Independence Day* of Bimbo Movies!," *Bimbo Movie Bash!* employs a loose space-bimbo-invasion framework to incorporate clips featuring such illustrious B-screen teases as Linnea (*Sorority Babes in the Slimeball Bowl-A-Rama*) Quigley and Brinke (*Slave Girls from Beyond Infinity*) Stevens, along with the ubiquitous Michelle Bauer and Julie Strain. As a genre sampler, *Bimbo Movie Bash!* supplies its share of retro-viewing fun.

BLOOD & DONUTS (1995) ***

D: Holly Dale. Gordon Currie, Justin Louis, Helene Clarkson, Fiona Reid, Frank Moore, David Cronenberg. 89 mins. (Artisan)

A kinder, gentler vampire comedy from up Canada way, *Blood & Donuts* stars Currie as Boya, a bloodsucker whose depression over the 1969 moon landing leads him to crawl into a golf bag (!), whence he emerges a quarter century later. The disoriented Boya retrieves his belongings from a nearby graveyard, rents a room in a run-down Toronto nabe, and hangs at an all-night donut shop. There he (at first unwittingly) serves to facilitate a romance between waitress Clarkson (on whom he initially has his own designs) and a comic immigrant cabbie (Louis in an amusing turn). Boya, meanwhile, is

plagued by his last femme conquest (Reid), who resents him for not vampirizing her 26 years earlier to save her from her subsequent life of aging and drudgery. An effective Cronenberg cameos as a local crime lord. Light on violence and gore FX, *Blood & Donuts* shapes up as a compelling mix of low-key sitcom and *Dance of the Damned*–type doomed romanticism. In the Creative Credits Department, the flick ends with a "Filmed on location in Toronto, Canada [and] Sea of Tranquility, The Moon" credit. Guns N' Roses's Nash the Slash composed the hooky score for a soundtrack that's also liberally sprinkled with '50s oldies.

BLOODBATH AT THE HOUSE OF DEATH (1985) **½

D: Ray Cameron. Vincent Price, Kenny Everett, Pamela Stephenson, Gareth Hunt. 92 mins. (Video Treasures)

Our story finds a team of inept scientists investigating the former site of a bloody massacre. Trying to scare them away is an equally incompetent coven of dotty devil-worshippers headed by a testy Price (who delivers a fine high-camp performance). Unfortunately, while this Brit horror spoof showcasing comic Everett features some flashes of wit, the hit-and-miss script too often sacrifices satire for cheap jokes that have become almost as clichéd as the scare-movie conventions they seek to mock. There are some high points, though—specifically a killer teddy bear and a bright send-up of *Alien*'s infamous upset-stomach scene.

BLOOD HOOK (1986) **½

D: James Mallon. Mark Jacobs, Lisa Todd, Patrick Danz, Sarah Hauser. 85 mins. (Troma)

"This ain't no Japanese monster movie," insists a character in *Blood Hook,* and we have to agree with him there. Fact is, future *Mystery Science Theater 3000* producer Mallon's *Blood Hook* is less a horror flick than a deadpan comedy of (mostly ill) manners. The pic follows a band of five young folks and a typically crass family of Ugly American vacationers ("Katharine Hepburn never put up with what *I* have to," ditsy Mom moans re slob Dad) into the turbulent waters of Muskie, Wisconsin, where an unknown maniac has been baiting the title implement for human prey. There are a number of inspired encounters between the innocent interlopers and several local eccentrics, including a paranoid 'Nam vet who's convinced the murders are part of a larger conspiracy. Todd is especially deft as the psychobabbling squeeze of Jacobs, the unlikely hero who finally succeeds—via an inventive musical hook—in unmasking the killer. Fairly sparse on gore save for one victim-gutting scene, *Blood Hook* is fun most of the way, running out of creative steam only during its protracted last-reel punch line.

BLOOD SALVAGE   (1990) ***

D: Tucker Johnston. John Saxon, Lori Birdsong, Ray Walston, Danny Nelson, Christian Hesler, Ralph Pruitt Vaughn. 91 mins. (Magnum, n.i.d.)

An entertaining splatter spoof in a *Texas Chainsaw Massacre* Meets *Motel Hell* vein, *Blood Salvage* gives us a twisted backwoods clan—patriarch Nelson, misogynistic psycho Hesler, and Lenny-like halfwit Vaughn—who operate a human chop shop with an auto-salvage front, selling live organs to shady sawbones Ray (*My Favorite Martian*) Walston. When the Bible-quoting Nelson develops an affection for wheelchair-bound teen beauty-queen aspirant Birdsong, he arranges a highway mishap that brings Lori's family (including B vet Saxon as her hapless dad) to his humble digs. Soon it's up to the feisty Lori, whose para-

lyzed legs miraculously heal, to nix the sick hicks. High points of this agreeably demented gore-cliché send-up include a tour of the clan's barely living victims (Elvis among them!), an able cast, and Bill Johnson's appropriately disgusto makeup FX. Look for heavyweight Evander Holyfield (who also coproduced!) in a carnival-boxer cameo.

BLOODSUCKERS FROM OUTER SPACE   (1984) **½

D: Glenn Coburn. Thom Meyer, Laura Ellis, Pat Paulsen, Billie Keller. 79 mins. (Lorimar, n.i.d.)

Seems that formerly fine, upstanding Texas farm folk are transforming into brainwashed bloodsuckers, and only freelance photog Meyer and main squeeze Ellis can save mankind. Question is: Should they bother? Coburn's crude but frequently funny creature comedy poses this and other probing queries while taking broad satiric aim at ornery rednecks, lazy lawmen, spaced-out scientists, and mad military brass. Guest star Paulsen literally phones in his cameo as our imperiled nation's distracted chief exec.

BOB ROBERTS   (1992) **½

D: Tim Robbins. Tim Robbins, Alan Rickman, Giancarlo Esposito, Ray Wise. 102 mins. (Artisan)

Robbins's political satire, wherein Tim takes the title role of a folksinging, right-wing demagogue, is a wavy blend of sophistication, naïvete, and desperate plot resolutions. Still, *Bob Roberts* has its witty, scary, and dead-on moments. Spike Lee regular Esposito is especially good as a muckraking gadfly who haunts Bob's corrupt trail, while such real-life Robbins cronies as (off-screen squeeze) Susan Sarandon, John Cusack, James Spader, and Fred Ward contribute cameos. Warren Beatty takes an edgier approach

with his 1998 kamikaze campaign-trail comedy, *Bulworth* (20th Century Fox).

BODY MELT   (1993) ***

D: Philip Brophy. Gerard Kennedy, Andrew Daddo, Ian Smith, Vince Gil, Regina Gailgalas. 82 mins. (Prism, n.i.d.)

Under his modestly monikered "Dumb Films" banner, Brophy directs, coscripts, and composes the quirky synth score for a comic splatterfest in the tradition of New Zealand neighbor Peter Jackson's *Bad Taste* and *Dead Alive* (see index). In *Body Melt*, several residents of the stark Melbourne 'burb of "Homesville" become the unwitting subjects of vile biochemical experiments when they ingest free vitamin samples that arrive in the mail. While small amounts cause users to hallucinate, stronger dosages result in bodily meltdowns, explosions, and other crowd-pleasing atrocities, all gleefully rendered by Brophy's busy FX crew. Brophy and his crisp Aussie cast maintain an appropriately deadpan tone throughout. Gore buffs looking to relax with a solid, dependable people-melting movie could certainly do worse than this one.

BOOGIE NIGHTS   (1997) ***½

D: Paul Thomas Anderson. Mark Wahlberg, Julianne Moore, Burt Reynolds, Don Cheadle, John C. Reilly, William H. Macy, Heather Graham, Nicole Parker, Philip Seymour Hoffman, Robert Ridgely, Ricky Jay, Alfred Molina, Luis Guzmán. 155 mins. (New Line) Special Edition DVD

Then-twentysomething auteur Anderson follows his impressive *Hard Eight* (see index) with the truly remarkable *Boogie Nights* (or *Hard Thirteen*, as some industry wags dubbed it). The son of the late Ernie Anderson—better known as legendary Cleveland TV horror host "Ghoulardi" (to whom this "Ghoulardi Production" is dedicated)—

must have done his homework and then some to capture so accurately and vividly the late-'70s/early-'80s California hard-core porn milieu. Anderson depicts the assembled smut performers as vapid, barely articulate but emotionally needy orphans who form their own adoptive family. Egotistical, only marginally talented director Jack Horner (Reynolds) plays father figure to his core group of "actors," while seasoned porn pro Amber Waves (Moore) performs surrogate-mother chores. Monstrously endowed teen loser Eddie (a deft Wahlberg, who later takes on the alias Dirk Diggler) flees his own ugly nuclear-family unit to join Jack's porn posse. Like the title character and crew in *Ed Wood,* these motley wannabes support one another's extravagant delusions; Anderson etches their multiple personal and career ups and downs (and ins and outs) with flawless precision, extracting, along the way, indelible work from an ensemble cast that truly (and often literally) rises to the occasion.

Anderson also tackles the changing nature of the porn biz—chiefly, the pivotal switch from film to videotape—along with the influence of '80s glam drugs like coke and crystal meth, professional rivalries and jealousies, and contemporary tastes (or tastelessness) in cars, clothes, and music (disco, unfortunately but inevitably, dominates). The film-savvy auteur sprinkles his tale with in-jokes—director Robert Downey, Sr., cameos as a recording-studio manager, while Cheadle's character is named Buck Swope, a nod to Downey's breakthrough 1969 celluloid satire, *Putney Swope*—guaranteed to score with buffs without interrupting the narrative flow. And, observing genre-film tradition, Anderson doesn't show "the monster"—Dirk's prodigious privates—until virtually the final shot in the film. *Boogie Nights* is a boffo accomplishment, re-creating a specific time and scene as well as any film we've ever seen. And watching is infinitely preferable to being there.

BOY! WHAT A GIRL! (1946) B&W***

D: Arthur Leonard. Tim Moore, Duke Williams, Elwood Smith. 70 mins. (DVT)

Underrated comic Moore (Kingfish on TV's *Amos and Andy*) goes the drag route in this swiftly paced black indie comedy. Fine perfs, an honestly funny plot, and hot musical numbers make this one a winner.

BRAIN DAMAGE (1988) ***1/2

D: Frank Henenlotter. Rick Herbst, Gordon MacDonald, Jennifer Lowry, Theo Barnes, Lucille Saint-Peter. 89 mins. (Paramount)

The brains behind *Basket Case* scores another bull's-eye with this literally "mind-blowing" tale about a boy and his parasite. The latter, a deceptively cute minimonster named Aylmer (distinctively voiced by longtime TV horror host and "Cool Ghoul" Zacherley), supplies human host Herbst with hallucinogenic "juice" in exchange for live human brains—a deal that results in a rash of empty-headed bodies turning up in downtown Gotham (more than usual, we mean). Less an antidrug film (as it's been interpreted by some) than a meditation on addictions of *all* kinds and the subsequent surrender of personal autonomy they invariably entail, *Brain Damage* succeeds equally on the black-humor, the visceral-shock, and the cerebral level.

BRAZIL (1985) ***1/2

D: Terry Gilliam. Jonathan Pryce, Robert De Niro, Michael Palin, Katherine Helmond, Kim Greist, Bob Hoskins. 131 mins. (Universal) DVD

Ex-*Python*ite Gilliam's suitably grotesque *1984* takeoff stars Pryce as Sam Lowry, a daydreaming clerk trapped in a future dystopia ruled by crazed bureaucrats and malfunctioning machines, both of which serve as frequent targets of mysterious terrorist attacks. Sam leads a life of relentless, usually arbitrary harassment, perpetrated by everyone from vengeful repairmen to his meddlesome mom. While the central idea may not be the freshest, Gilliam's treatment (with major assists from coscripters Tom Stoppard and Charles McKeown) is consistently inventive and further bolstered by a top-notch cast. Gilliam's original director's-cut edition enjoyed a select 1998 theatrical release, after controversial unauthorized cuts marred its initial run.

BREAST MEN (1997) ***

D: Lawrence O'Neil. David Schwimmer, Chris Cooper, Emily Procter, Louise Fletcher, Matt Frewer, Terry O'Quinn, Lisa Marie, John Stockwell. 95 mins. (HBO)

Loosely based on the exploits of a pioneering pair of breast-implant surgeons, *Breast Men* builds an ironic, perceptive account of the silicone industry's rise and semidemise. Ably scripted by actor Stockwell (who doubles on-screen as an upscale strip-club owner), this made-for-cable winner traces nerdy inventor Dr. Saunders (*Friends* alum Schwimmer) and medical mentor Dr. Larson (*Lone Star*'s Cooper) from their early-'60s struggles to burgeoning surgical success to an eventual and extremely bitter falling-out. Like *Boogie Nights, Breast Men* paints an accurate picture of the eras in which it unfolds, placing its main emphasis on Saunders's fate as he becomes a boozing, coke-snorting Implant Surgeon to the Stars, a self- (and shelf-) destructive trend that ultimately dissolves his marriage to longtime nurse/partner Procter. Lisa Marie appears as one of Saunders's (literally) biggest successes, while ex-*Stepfather* O'Quinn portrays the class-action attorney who nails the docs' silicone supplier and curtails their careers. "David Schwimmer's Age Prosthetics" earn not one but two separate end-credit nods.

BUFFALO '66 (1998) ***1/2

D: Vincent Gallo. Vincent Gallo, Christina Ricci, Anjelica Huston, Ben Gazzara, Mickey Rourke, Jan-Michael Vincent. 112 mins. (Universal) DVD

With *Buffalo '66*, multitalented multihyphenate actor, artist, composer, auteur, and "Ugly Chic" fashion model Gallo coscripts, directs, and stars in a thoroughly original lowlife-affirming odyssey. Gallo plays Billy Brown, a lifelong loser newly sprung from an upstate pen, who impulsively "kidnaps" equally clueless tapdance student Layla (Ricci) and forces her to pose as his wife in a bid to impress his extravagantly dysfunctional and supremely disinterested parents. Following Billy and Layla's ultrasurreal visit with the former's alternately surly and lecherous ex-crooner dad (Gazzara) and football-obsessed mom (Huston), *Buffalo '66* (the title refers to Billy's birthplace and date) turns into a bizarre hybrid of *Taxi Driver* and *It Happened One Night*, with Billy nurturing a crazy plot to whack a former Buffalo Bills field-goal kicker he blames for ruining his life and Layla deciding she's fallen in love with the emotionally needy loony. Director Gallo yields unforgettable perfs from his entire cast (including himself), with Gazzara and Huston striking especially haunting and sadly funny chords as Billy's weirdo progenitors. Rourke scores a rare choice role as a tough local bookie, while erstwhile golden boy/ later B-action mainstay Vincent surfaces as an amiable bowling-alley operator, one of Billy's few local supporters. Filmmaker Gallo deftly employs a number of inventive visual techniques, from multiscreen images to slo mo, which lend his mundane landscape an otherworldly quality.

CANNIBAL! THE MUSICAL (1996) ***1/2

D: Trey Parker. Trey Parker, Ian Hardin, Matt Stone, Jon Hegel, Jason McHugh, Dian Bachar, Teddy Walters. 105 mins. (Troma)

Writer, director, lyricist, composer, star, and future *South Park* cocreator Parker was a University of Colorado student when he devised this catchy low-budget account of inept 1870s trail guide Alfred Packer, who was eventually convicted of cannibalism after the disappearance of the five prospectors who'd unwisely hired him to lead them to gold and glory. (A straightforward version, *The Legend of Alfred Packer*, was produced in 1980.) Parker's rendition of this famed real-life frontier tragedy is a consistently funny, oft brilliant deadpan comedy, complete with cartoon gore, seven bouncy original tunes (including "Let's Build a Snowman" and "Hang the Bastard"), biting lyrics, and even a couple of full-fledged *Oklahoma!*-styled production numbers. (Veteran experi-

TREY CHIC: Future *South Park* cocreator Trey Parker cut his directorial teeth on his cheerfully tasteless cult treat *Cannibal! The Musical.*
© *Troma Entertainment, Inc.*

mental auteur Stan Brakhage, no doubt teaching at U.C. at the time, cameos as one of the unlucky prospectors' dads.) For more tasteless cannibal comedy, see Antonia Bird's underrated American frontier-set fable *Ravenous* (Fox).

CANNIBAL WOMEN IN THE AVOCADO JUNGLE OF DEATH (1988) ***

D: J. F. Lawton. Adrienne Barbeau, Shannon Tweed, Bill Maher, Karen Mistal, Barry Primus. 90 mins. (Paramount) DVD

*P*retty *Woman* scripter Lawton's 1991 feminist-themed *Cannibal Women in the Avocado Jungle of Death* is a wacky outing (which Lawton directed under the alias "J. D. Athens") that sends up everything from *Heart of Darkness* to *Raiders of the Lost Ark* within a bimbo-movie context. *Cannibal Women* toplines "erotic thriller" refugee Tweed as a no-nonsense professor out to stop the man-eating "Piranha Women"—led by renegade feminist Barbeau (as "Dr. Kurtz")—while a pre–*Politically Incorrect* Maher serves as her inept jungle guide and Mistal plays her bimbo sidekick, Bunny. *Cannibal Women* still rates as the best entry in the field it created—the sophisticated bimbo flick.

CARO DIARIO (1994) ***

D: Nanni Moretti. Nanni Moretti, Renato Carpentieri, Antonio Neiwiller, Jennifer Beals. Subtitled. 100 mins. (New Line)

*C*omic Italo auteur Moretti (*Palombella Rossa*) rides his Vespa through Rome, goes island-hopping in the Mediterranean, and otherwise indulges his oft amusing sense of whimsy in this Continental variation on a Ross (*Sherman's March*) McElwee–styled exercise in light autobiographical verité. Moretti's abiding obsessions include *Flashdance*'s Jennifer Beals (who cameos as herself) and, in a negative vein, John McNaugh-

ton's *Henry: Portrait of a Serial Killer,* which our hero catches at a Rome cinema—several *Henry* clips are seen— then broods over the positive reviews it's garnered. (Indeed, *Caro Diario*'s funniest scene is a fantasy sequence wherein Moretti tortures a guilt-torn film critic by forcing him to listen to his own critiques—now, *that's* scary!) Moretti's luckless quest for medical assistance in treating a skin rash results in a far more frightening segment, though the flick concludes on an upbeat note.

CARRY ON NURSE (1959) B&W **1/2

D: Gerald Thomas. Kenneth Connor, Kenneth Williams, Charles Hawtrey. 86 mins. (HBO)

*T*he flick that kicked off the extremely popular and prolific Brit *Carry On* series sets the tone (broad) and level (low) for the sequels to come. Fans of Benny Hill–styled comedy should enjoy. Movies Unlimited carries many of the subsequent *Carry On* entries.

CAR WASH (1976) ***

D: Michael A. Schultz. George Carlin, Franklin Ajaye, Sully Boyer. 97 mins. (Universal) DVD

*M*usic plays a major role in Schultz's sometimes broad but often on-target, inventive, and overwhelmingly popular low-budget romp. Richard Pryor has a neat bit as a flashy Reverend Ike–like preacher.

CHOPPER CHICKS IN ZOMBIETOWN (1989) ***

D: Dan Hoskins. Jamie Rose, Catherine Carlen, Don Calfa. 86 mins. (Columbia/TriStar)

*F*oxy motorcycle mamas save a small town from mad mortician Calfa ("I'm not doing this for science. I'm just mean.") in a fun biker/black-comedy/

horror hybrid. Says one resigned local resident: "Nobody ever gets out of here. You go to school here, get married, inbreed, and die." Look for former MTV veejay Martha Quinn as a cranky pregnant woman.

A CHRISTMAS STORY (1983) ***

D: Bob Clark. Peter Billingsley, Darren McGavin, Melinda Dillon. 95 mins. (MGM) DVD

*P*orky's auteur Clark attempts a successful change of pace with a made-for-TV, Midwest-set holiday tale, about one boy's determined quest to snare a Red Ryder BB rifle, faithfully adapted from a story by late writer and monologist Jean Shepherd, who also supplies the first-person narration. For additional edgy Christmas comedy fare, scope out 1995's *Reckless* (Hallmark), with Mia Farrow and Scott Glenn, and 1988's *Scrooged* (Paramount), with Bill Murray as a callous, self-important network-TV head.

CITIZEN COHN (1992) ***1/2

D: Frank Pierson. James Woods, Joe Don Baker, Pat Hingle, Lee Grant, Ed Flanders. 112 mins. (HBO)

*T*he ever hyper Woods proves an ideal choice to portray the late, unlamented lead in this American Successpool Story originally aired on HBO cable. Woods injects sly wit into his interpretation of McCarthy hatchet man, J. Edgar Hoover crony, and megarich attorney Roy Cohn as an avaricious sleazeball who seemed to thrive on the hostility his amoral antics aroused. The mock–*Citizen Kane* format—the bio's related in flashbacks from Cohn's deathbed while a toy frog subs for Orson's snow shaker—supplies a deft frame for this spirited profile in sewage. Hingle is a standout as Hoover, but the best line belongs to Flanders as Joseph Welch, who, in phantom form, visits a lingering Roy's bedside to deliver the following request: "Mr. Cohn, have you no sense of mortality, sir, at long last? Will you not rid us of your presence? We need the room."

CLERKS   (1994) B&W ***

D: Kevin Smith. Brian O'Halloran, Jeff Anderson, Marilyn Ghigliotti, Jason Mewes, Lisa Spoonauer, Kevin Smith. 92 mins. (Miramax) DVD

Longer on wit than execution, Smith's dark-comedy debut gives us a disastrous day in the life of Dante Hicks (O'Halloran), a convenience-store clerk in scenic Highlands, New Jersey. Among the figures in the 22-year-old Dante's underachieving existence are his determinedly obnoxious video-store-clerk bud (Anderson), loyal current squeeze (Ghigliotti), ex-girlfriend (Spoonauer), parking-lot drug dealer/gangsta manqué (Mewes) and his laconic sidekick, Silent Bob (director Smith, who, despite his heft, executes an energetic breakdance), plus a variety of mostly annoying customers. In some ways reminiscent of early John Waters works like *Multiple Maniacs, Clerks* is buoyed by dialogue that's simultaneously bright and credible. (One running riff has the assorted characters telling Dante things he'd really rather not have to know—like girlfriend Ghigliotti's extensive history as a freelance fellatrix!) *Clerks* is occasionally burdened by amateurish perfs from some of the movie's secondary characters; a few apparently one-take physical bits also fall flat. But Smith's $27,000 debut is not only a promising start but a very funny work in its own right. Soul Asylum, Alice in Chains, and Bad Religion are among the groups who contribute to the high-energy soundtrack. Smith followed with the lamentable *Mallrats* (Universal, DVD), the far sharper *Chasing Amy* (Touchstone), and the "controversial" *Dogma* (2000, Columbia/TriStar, DVD).

CLOSE TO EDEN   (1992) ***

D: Nikita Mikhalkov. Badema, Bayaertu, Vladimir Gostukhin, Baoyinhexige. Subtitled. 109 mins. (Paramount)

Mikhalkov's shaggy-Mongol story offers a fascinating, gently comedic look at a rural Manchurian family who befriend homesick Russian road worker Gostukhin. A Sly Stallone *Cobra* poster plays a pivotal part in the proceedings. Guess there's just no escaping.

COLD FEVER   (1995) ***

D: Fridrik Thor Fridrickson. Masatoshi Nagase, Lili Taylor, Fisher Stevens. 85 mins. (Fox Lorber)

Young Japanese "salaryman" Nagase undertakes a reluctant odyssey through distant Iceland to honor his late parents in Fridrickson's consistently amusing and insightful ice-bound road comedy. Taylor and Stevens cameo as a neurotic American couple our hero encounters along the way.

COMBINATION PLATTER   (1993) ***

D: Tony Chan. Jeff Lau, Colleen O'Brien, Lester Chan. 84 mins. (Arrow)

Then-24-year-old auteur Tony Chan fashions an excellent low-key, low-budget look at a cross section of characters at a Chinese restaurant in Queens, focusing on immigrant waiter Lau's uninspired romance with local girl O'Brien.

THE COMEDY OF TERRORS (1964) ***

D: Jacques Tourneur. Vincent Price, Peter Lorre, Boris Karloff, Basil Rathbone, Joe E. Brown, Joyce Jamison. 84 mins. (Orion)

The Comedy of Terrors may be broad and uneven at times, but what other flick can you name that gathers Price, Lorre, Karloff, Rathbone, and Joe E. Brown under the same celluloid roof? (Answer: None.) And despite its occasional comedic slumps, *Comedy* contains several priceless (though not Vincent-less) scenes. Impoverished undertakers Price and Lorre drum up business by reducing the local New England populace, including Rathbone as a wealthy eccentric who refuses to die. Price drunkenly reels off bowdlerized Poe, while Rathbone recites passages from *Macbeth,* graveyard attendant Brown croons Irish tunes, and Karloff passes out in his soup. A short, fat, unflappable Lorre is the real comic treasure here, however. He manages to be funny even when he blows his lines. When Price accidentally steps on his fingers, Lorre blurts, "My foot!" Then, realizing his error, he calmly amends, "*Your* foot! My *fingers!*" Seems like odd turf for Val Lewton protégé Tourneur (*Cat People, Curse of the Demon*)—who reportedly wasn't too keen on the assignment himself—but this quirky, Richard Matheson–scripted mirthfest works more often than not.

THE COMIC   (1969) **1/2

D: Carl Reiner. Dick Van Dyke, Michele Lee, Mickey Rooney. 96 mins. (Columbia/TriStar)

Reiner's seriocomic chronicle of a composite silent-film comedian, energetically interpreted by Van Dyke, shapes up as an oddball mix of inspired mirth and embarrassing dramatics. A must for silent-comedy buffs, though (the films-within-the-film are a highlight). Rooney plays Dick's Ben Turpin–based sidekick, "Cockeye."

CONEHEADS   (1993) ***

D: Steven Barron. Dan Aykroyd, Jane Curtin, Michael McKean. 86 mins. (Paramount)

Aliens Aykroyd and Curtin adapt to North Jersey life in a consistently funny expansion of the *Saturday Night*

Live skit series, peopled with top comic supporting thesps, including Michael McKean, Dave Thomas (as the alien leader), David Spade, and Chris Rock.

COOLEY HIGH   (1975) ***

D: Michael A. Schultz. Glynn Turman, Lawrence Hilton-Jacobs, Garrett Morris. 107 mins. (Orion) DVD

Something of an edgier, inner-city *American Graffiti* (Universal, DVD), *Cooley High* shapes up as an episodic but mostly winning affair featuring top work by Turman as a beleaguered student. *Cooley High* also makes creative use of a great '60s Motown soundtrack, before the latter became a Hollywood audio cliché.

COTTON COMES TO HARLEM (1970) ***

D: Ossie Davis. Raymond St. Jacques, Godfrey Cambridge, Calvin Lockhart, Redd Foxx. 97 mins. (MGM)

Director Davis achieves a deft blend of action and comedy as tough cops St. Jacques and Cambridge look into larcenous preacher Lockhart's bogus back-to-Africa campaign. Based on the novel by Chester Himes and followed by *Come Back, Charleston Blue* (n/a).

CRACKING UP   (1983) **1/2

D: Jerry Lewis. Jerry Lewis, Herb Edelman, Foster Brooks, Milton Berle, Sammy Davis, Jr. 87 mins. (Warner)

Cracking Up (a.k.a. *Smorgasbord*) represents Jerry, if not at his best, then surely at his most unfettered. The pic consists of a series of frequently surreal slapstick set pieces linked to chronic loser Warren Nefrin's (Lewis) sessions with shrink Edelman. All the traditional Jerry trademarks are here: a big-band soundtrack, comic cameos by the likes of Milton Berle (as a nymphomaniac!) and Sammy Davis, Jr. (as "himself"), and

multiple product tie-ins. Jerry also plays shamelessly to the French (who awarded him a Legion of Honor medal some years back), from a "Title Song Sung by Marcel Marceau" credit to an extended French flashback that's easily the flick's weakest sequence. Some of the better conceptual sight gags are reminiscent of Ernie Kovacs's early TV work, but *Cracking Up* is closer in spirit to *Never Give a Sucker an Even Break* (see index), W. C. Fields's final and most wildly idiosyncratic outing. If you've ever wondered what the "mature" Jerry would do with *total* creative freedom, *Cracking Up* supplies the answer.

CRIMES AND MISDEMEANORS (1989) ****

D: Woody Allen. Woody Allen, Mia Farrow, Alan Alda, Martin Landau, Anjelica Huston, Sam Waterston, Claire Bloom, Jerry Orbach. 104 mins. (Orion) DVD

Allen's best movie to date is a simultaneously serious and very funny meditation on the irony of life's myriad injustices, dramatized here by a top cast, including Woody himself as a hapless documentary filmmaker whose unflattering portrait of self-important TV "pioneer" Alda provides the film with one of several standout scenes. Huston's murder, handled with chilling understatement, supplies a genuine jolt. If the Woodman never made another movie, this seamless masterpiece would ensure his reputation as one of the sharpest social observers of his day. All of Allen's features—even the "early, funny" ones—are available on cassette.

CRY-BABY   (1990) ***

D: John Waters. Johnny Depp, Amy Locane, Susan Tyrrell, Polly Bergen, Iggy Pop, Ricki Lake, Traci Lords, Kim McGuire. 86 mins. (Universal)

Set in 1954, at the very dawn of juvenile delinquency and rock 'n' roll,

Cry-Baby chronicles a little-known chapter in Baltimore's War Between the Squares and the Drapes. The latter, an enclave of transplanted rockin' rednecks, are led by Depp as Cry-Baby Walker ("What a sad and silly name for a young man," sighs an on-screen judge), who tumbles for Square-cum-closet-Drape Locane. Their cross-class *Romeo and Juliet* romance sets off a series of satiric rumbles, with Square honcho and Amy's intended beau, Stephen (Son of Norman) Mailer, leading his crew-cut troops against a Drape clan that includes a patriarchal Pop, foxy Lords, the always welcome Tyrrell, pudgy future trash-TV queen Lake ("She's pregnant," says Cry-Baby, "but she can fight like a man!"), and "Hatchet-Face" McGuire, who resembles a young female Rodney Dangerfield French-kissed by a chainsaw. With *Cry-Baby*, Waters also moves closer to achieving his avowed aim of casting a film where even the extras are played by stars: such past and present notables as Polly Bergen, Willem Dafoe, Joe Dallesandro, Patty Hearst, Joey Heatherton, Troy Donahue, David Nelson, and longtime Waters regulars Mary Vivian Pearce and Mink Stole all put in cameos here.

DAZED AND CONFUSED   (1993) ***

D: Richard Linklater. Jason London, Rory Cochrane, Wiley Wiggins, Sasha Jenson, Milla Jovovich. 103 mins. (Universal) DVD

Richard (*Slacker*) Linklater presents a sharp kinetic snapshot of high school life in 1976 Texas, where coming of age doesn't necessarily lead to the getting of wisdom. Wiggins is appealing as the story's framing character, a freshman initiated into full high-schoolerhood via a nightlong rite of passage following the school year's final day. Credible supporting perfs, particularly by Cochrane as a hard-core stoner, bring Linklater's "Texas Graffiti" to life. The butt-kicking '70s soundtrack offers a potent rebuttal to *Reservoir Dogs*'s purposely pale score drawn from the same era.

DEAD ALIVE (1992)***

D: Peter Jackson. Timothy Balme, Diana Penalver, Elizabeth Moody, Ian Watkin, Forrest J Ackerman. In R and unrated editions. 97 mins. (Trimark) DVD

Future *Heavenly Creatures* auteur Jackson's *Dead Alive* (originally titled *Brain Dead*) may well be *the* goriest frightcom ever committed to celluloid. Jackson's frantic tale, set in 1957, gets off to a relatively sedate start. After fending off offended natives played by the real-life Fijian Rugby Team (!), a New Zealand zoo official unwisely captures a vicious "Sumatran Rat Monkey" in the wilds of King Kong's mythical stomping ground, Skull Island. Once the caged critter sinks its teeth into nerd Lionel's (Balme) overbearing mom (Moody), the pic's pace and body count pick up considerably. Lionel soon has his hands (and basement) full of cannibalistic zombies—former neighbors all—who seriously threaten his burgeoning romance with lovely Spanish lass Paquita (Penalver), who reports early on: "Your mother ate my dog!" When Lionel's crude, avaricious, inheritance-seeking uncle Les (Watkin) hosts a populous party at Lionel's zombie-infested home, the scene and screen are set for a nonstop gore orgy that pulls out all the splatter stops. While vastly superior to such similarly themed family cannibal romps as *Rabid Grannies* (Media) and *Flesh-Eating Mothers* (Academy), *Dead Alive* falls a notch short of matching the bloody mirth of Sam Raimi's *Evil Dead 2* or Stuart Gordon's *Re-Animator* (though it easily outgrosses both). If a black comedy awash in wall-to-wall blood and ceiling-to-floor gore is just what you're hankering for, *Dead Alive* fills the bill like no other flick before. The R version runs a full 12 minutes shorter than the unrated.

FAME AND GORY: Diana Penalver takes a reluctant stab at splatter stardom in Peter Jackson's ultimate zombie-gore epic *Dead Alive* (a.k.a. *Brain Dead*).
Courtesy of Trimark Home Video

DEADLY ADVICE (1993)**1/2

D: Mandie Fletcher. Jane Horrocks, Brenda Fricker, Imelda Staunton, Jonathan Pryce, Edward Woodward, Billie Whitelaw, Hywel Bennett, Jonathan Hyde, Sir John Mills, Eleanor Bron. 91 mins. (Evergreen)

Frequent Mike Leigh starlet Jane (*Life Is Sweet*) Horrocks, more recently known for her showcase *Little Voice* (Buena Vista), plays a timid miss urged to murder her domineering mom (Fricker) by a quintet of conjured killers, including Mills as Jack the Ripper. Horrocks's initial criminal act inevitably leads to further cover-up killings. Fletcher's stab at classic Brit black comedy is compromised by underdrawn characters, lapses in comic logic, and a bet-hedging flashback that puts too leadenly "real" a spin on what should have been a frothier, funnier affair. Committed Anglophiles may find enough entertainment value in the

PETER JACKSON ON *DEAD ALIVE*

As Told to The Phantom

PHANTOM: *Dead Alive* may be the gore movie to end *all* gore movies. Was that your intent from the outset?

JACKSON: *Dead Alive* was made because I was a fan of those sorts of movies. I love *Re-Animator*, I love the *Evil Dead* films. If it hadn't been for those films being made, *Dead Alive* probably wouldn't have existed. You don't want to do a rip-off of *Evil Dead* or *Re-Animator*. You want it to have its own identity. It's a responsibility of anybody who tackles an over-the-top gory zombie movie—you've got to look at what the gore quotient is and try and top it.

PHANTOM: How did you stage the lawnmower scene?

JACKSON: We had two or three cameras going during some of that stuff. I think the one group of people that need the biggest congratulations are the zombie extras. They were twenty or twenty-five very brave people. We had the lawnmower—it wasn't, obviously, a real lawnmower, it was this fake fiberglass thing we had made that had these hoses that were connected to a huge pump that was in turn connected to this massive forty-four-gallon drum of fake blood that was maple syrup with food coloring. We'd sort of tested this thing with water and we'd seen the water spurting out, yet we didn't know what it was going to do to the syrup—we hadn't done it with human beings before. My only instruction really to the extras was to be as brave as they possibly could and to throw themselves against the mower till we yelled, "Cut."

PHANTOM: You also have the initially reluctant heroine, Diana Penalver, eventually taking charge.

JACKSON: I didn't want to make a film where the female characters just sit around and scream and get terrified. Diana absolutely *hated* horror films. The first special-effects scene we did with Diana is where she's cutting through a zombie hand with a pair of nail scissors. She's cutting through the wrist of a zombie that's clamped around Lionel's throat. It was just a rubber band with some blood tubes in it. She was chopping away and the blood was spurting in a very realistic way, and I'm thinking, "Great, this is looking good." And then when I yelled "Cut!" I looked up at her and she was crying. But she got used to it after a while.

PHANTOM: How did you manage to work Forry [*Famous Monsters*] Ackerman into a New Zealand film?

JACKSON: Forry came out to do a science-fiction convention about six months before we started shooting. I thought, "There's gotta be some way I can get Forry into my movie." We have the sequence at the zoo, where I knew I was going to need cutaways and reaction shots. I grabbed my Bolex, took Forry to the zoo, and I just positioned him for reaction shots. When Mum hits the rat monkey with her handbag and squashes its head with the heel of her shoe, there's a shot of a tourist taking a photo. That's Forry.

PHANTOM: How would you like audiences to regard *Dead Alive*?

JACKSON: *Dawn of the Dead* I think of as the zombies in the shopping mall. And *Re-Animator* is the zombies in the medical laboratory. And *Evil Dead* is obviously the zombies in the cabin. I hope people think of *Dead Alive* as the one with the guy with the zombie mother in the 1950s.

DEAD MAN (1996) B&W ***1/2

D: Jim Jarmusch. Johnny Depp, Gary Farmer, Lance Henriksen, Michael Wincott, Mili Avital, Robert Mitchum, Gabriel Byrne, John Hurt, Alfred Molina, Eugene Byrd, Billy Bob Thornton, Iggy Pop, Jared Harris, Crispin Glover. 121 mins. (Buena Vista)

From its opening quotation from Henri Michaux—"It is preferable not to travel with a dead man"—to its grimly elegaic fade-out, Jarmusch's Old West–set *Dead Man* takes the form of a filmlong death trip. A very effective Depp stars as William Blake, a Cleveland-bred Candide who's as good as dead as soon as he boards a train headed West. A crazed coal man (an under-control Glover) delivers the news in the film's first burst of dialogue: When Depp informs the illiterate train worker of his plans to find employment, the coal man calmly insists, "You're just as likely to find your own grave." Blake reaches his destination literally at the end of the line, the town of Machine— a muddy, smoky patch of industrial hell in a wasteland wandered by cryptic solipsistic crackpots—only to discover his promised job's been taken. On his first night in town, he tumbles for prostitute Avital; in the morning her jilted beau (Byrne), son of Blake's would-be employer (Mitchum), shows up to kill her; Blake reflexively shoots him in self-defense. Mitchum hires a trio of eccentric bounty hunters (Henriksen, Wincott, Byrd) to terminate Blake, and the chase is on. Our confused hero finds an unlikely friend in an educated Native American (Farmer) who insists on believing his new bud is *the* William Blake, Brit poet of yore, but not even the loyal Farmer can prevent Blake from meeting his fate.

Jarmusch's extremely dark comedic

vision of the Old West as a cold, bleak inferno is greatly abetted by Robby Muller's painterly black-and-white photography, Neil Young's haunting electric and acoustic guitar score, and a once-in-a-lifetime cast that even includes punk rocker Iggy Pop (as a trapper in pioneer drag!). We also recommended Jarmusch's debut *Stranger Than Paradise, Down by Law* (both Fox), with Roberto Benigni, and *Mystery Train* (Orion).

DEATH BECOMES HER (1992) ***

D: Robert Zemeckis. Meryl Streep, Goldie Hawn, Bruce Willis, Isabella Rosellini, Ian Ogilvy, Michelle Johnson. 104 mins. (MGM) DVD

A Z-video concept gets the Hollywood megabuck treatment, with surprisingly felicitous results, as clever dialogue, dark wit, swift pacing, and goofy splatstick FX bring this dueling-dead-bimbos (Streep, Hawn) comedy to often riotous life. Even Bruce Willis is funny. The film won a well-deserved Best Visual Effects Oscar.

THE DELI (1997) ***

D: John Gallagher. Mike Starr, Judith Malina, Gretchen Mol, Matt Keeslar, Brian Vincent, Ice-T, Frank Vincent, Tony Sirico, Burt Young. 95 mins. (Golden Monkey Pictures) DVD

T he Deli rates as a tasty slice-of-life comedy in the tradition of *Clerks* and *Smoke*, lensed largely in New Rochelle, New York. Veteran character actor Starr takes center stage as deli owner Johnny Amico, a stand-up guy with one major flaw: an uncontrollable itch for gambling and an uncanny knack for placing bad bets (make that *two* major flaws). Director/coscripter Gallagher's swiftly paced pic follows Johnny over the course of a single week as he tries to stall creditors while scraping together enough bread to pay off local bookie Vincent. Johnny's juggling act intensifies when the number his mom (Malina) thinks he's been playing for her comes up an unexpected winner; our beleaguered hero has to produce an additional $12 grand or face eternal maternal disgrace. Like *Smoke* and the follow-up, *Blue in the Face* (Miramax), *The Deli* benefits from a host of offbeat star cameos by the likes of rappers Ice-T and Heavy D, comic Jerry Stiller, singer David (Buster Poindexter) Johansen, Heather *(Welcome to the Dollhouse)* Matarazzo, and Burt *(Rocky)* Young (as a local Mafia capo).

DELICATESSEN (1991) ***

D: Jean-Pierre Jeunet, Marc Caro. Dominique Pinon, Marie Laure Dougnac, Jean-Claude Dreyfus, Ticky Holgado, Howard Vernon. Subtitled. 95 mins. (Paramount)

C aro and Jeunet's dark postapocalyptic farce deserves to take its rightful place among such quality cannibal comedies as *Spider Baby, Motel Hell,* and *Terror at Red Wolf Inn.* Sort of a Jacques Tati Meets *Eraserhead* by Way of Terry Gilliam (who, in fact, "presents" the film), *Delicatessen* sees ex-clown Pinon unwisely sign on as a handyman at the title site, a more-than-suspicious butcher shop/apartment house overseen by gruff proprietor Dreyfus. ("I'm a butcher," he informs our unwary applicant, "but I don't mince words.") Pinon eventually discovers that transients at Jean-Claude's establishment ultimately end up, figuratively and literally, in the soup. The humor, ranging from traditional sight gags to the downright deranged, is brought to life by an excellent comic cast, from the menacing Dreyfus, to Dougnac as his myopic daughter, to the rubber-faced Pinon. From its opening trash-can tableau to its lyrical rooftop *aubade* at film's end, *Delicatessen* rates as an uncompromisingly quirky black comedy that offers a tasty alternative to Hollywood's often bland fare.

DESPERATE LIVING (1977) ***1/2

D: John Waters. Mink Stole, Jean Hill, Edith Massey, Liz Renay, Mary Vivian Pearce, Susan Lowe. 90 mins. (Cinema Group, n.i.d.)

L ate Waters regular Massey enjoys her finest filmic hour here as the imposing Queen Carlotta of Mortville, a memorable patch of living hell located not far from Baltimore. It's in Mortville that hysterical housewife Stole and her more sensible two-ton maid (Hill) find themselves trapped after fleeing a murder rap. Despite Divine's conspicuous absence (he/she was off pursuing a theatrical/disco-diva career at the time), *Desperate Living* ranks as one of Waters's sickest, truest, and funniest trash romps. "Transsexual" Susan Lowe's immortal line "Will you ever be able to *love* my operation?" wins The Phantom's Ed Wood *Glen or Glenda* Memorial Award for Distinguished Screenwriting.

THE DEVIL'S SON-IN-LAW (1977) ***

D: Cliff Roquemore. Rudy Ray Moore, Jimmy Lynch, Leroy and Skillet, Ebony Wright, G. Tito Shaw, Wildman Steve. 95 mins. (Xenon)

R edoubtable "blaxploitation"-parody pioneer Rudy Ray Moore— who cut his comedic teeth recording raunchy party LP's in a Redd Foxx *Laff of the Party* vein and still works primarily as a stand-up comic—was busily spoofing that urban genre as early as 1975, when he introduced *Dolemite*, a mock-macho hero (played by Rudy Ray himself) in a Richard *(Shaft)* Roundtree/Jim Brown vein. Rudy Ray reprised his Dolemite persona in the farcical follow-ups *The Human Tornado* (a.k.a. *Dolemite 2: The Human Tornado*) and *Disco Godfather* (both

Xenon, DVD), movies that mixed Moore's lady-killing antics with slapstick kung-fu work and superheroics of the most outrageous sort. Rudy, who often coproduced and contributed to the story lines, could be counted on to work in some of his stand-up shticks, most notably his patented rhyming routines. (It was, for the record, Rudy Ray Moore—*not* Benjamin Franklin—who first coined the famous phrase "*Romance without finance is a damned nuisance.*") Rudy's best effort, however—the supernatural spoof *The Devil's Son-in-Law*—sees Moore drop his Dolemite character to play kung-fu-trained comic Petey Wheatstraw (presumably in honor of the late, great blues singer of the same name), hence the pic's alternate title, *Petey Wheatstraw: The Devil's Son-in-Law.* We know from reel 1 that Petey is not your average dude: Not only is he born at roughly age seven (!), but he beats up the doctor who tries to treat him to the traditional postpartum spanking. Our story fast-forwards to the present, when Petey has become a stand-up superstar. Rival comics Leroy and Skillet (as themselves) will literally kill to keep Petey from competing with their own planned stage extravaganza—one funded by local Caucasian hoods led by the menacing Mr. White—which leads to a churchfront massacre that counts Petey among the fatalities. (Mixing realistically rendered screen violence with wacky comedy has long been a Rudy Ray trademark.) A dapper devil (Shaw) intervenes and makes the expired Petey an offer he can't refuse—life, success, and magic powers in return for marrying Lucifer's ugly daughter (!). It's at this point that this offbeat farce really begins to heat up. Moore's comedy-concert cassette, *Rawer Than Raw,* a.k.a. *Rude,* the compilation tape *The Legend of Dolemite,* and *Shaolin Dolemite* (to which Rudy Ray contributes a cameo) are also out via Xenon. Moore also costars with Yaphet Kotto in 1977's *Monkey Hustle* (Orion).

THE DISAPPEARANCE OF KEVIN JOHNSON (1995) ***

D: Francis Megahy. Pierce Brosnan, James Coburn, Dudley Moore, Kari Wuhrer. 105 mins. (Columbia/TriStar)

Megahy's mockumentary is an odd bird indeed, an utterly deadpan send-up of Hollywood *and* earnest, in-your-face Brit documentaries devoted to same, with a specific nod to verité specialist Nick (*Heidi Fleiss: Hollywood Madam, Kurt & Courtney*) Broomfield. Brosnan, Coburn, and Moore (as themselves) appear as the token celebs who describe their encounters with the shadowy titular con artist, a reportedly charming British would-be producer whose elaborate scams have led to his mysterious disappearance. Megahy avoids cheap shots in concocting a mock thriller that's so compelling on the suspense level that *KJ* continually threatens to fly its humor coop. Performed with precision accuracy—erstwhile MTV veejay Wuhrer is especially convincing as a candidly self-deluded Hollywood hooker—*Disappearance* is a consistently distantly amusing whodunit (and withwhom).

THE DISCREET CHARM OF THE BOURGEOISIE (1972) ***1/2

D: Luis Buñuel. Stéphane Audran, Fernando Rey, Jean-Pierre Cassel. 100 mins. (Corinth)

Approaching 70 himself here, Buñuel still enjoyed thumbing his nose at middle-aged upper-middle-class hypocrites, by this time a generation his junior. The results are as savage as ever. Many other Buñuel classics—like *Belle de Jour* (Touchstone) and *The Exterminating Angel* (Hen's Tooth), a fable that finds emotionally paralyzed guests unable to leave a dinner party—are available on video and DVD.

DR. GOLDFOOT AND THE BIKINI MACHINE (1965) **1/2

D: Norman Taurog. Vincent Price, Frankie Avalon, Dwayne Hickman, Susan Hart, Jack Mullaney, Fred Clark. 90 mins. (Orion)

Sporting the glossy cardboard look of a then-contempo Jerry Lewis movie (and directed by frequent Martin and Lewis helmer Taurog), *Dr. Goldfoot* is an amiably brain-dead blend of secondrate Jerry-atric slapstick, James Bond spoofery, and incongruous AIP horror elements. (Dr. G.'s bumbling assistant, Igor—played by a decidedly unsinister Mullaney—has been resurrected from the dead, while Price equips his robotic bikini babes with poison-tipped, spring-bladed opera glasses, à la *Horrors of the Black Museum,* to eliminate potential rivals, and the pic includes an elaborate *Pit and the Pendulum* parody.) The script's central conceit sees the greedy Dr. G. (a pained-looking Price) dispatch his bionic bimbos to marry and murder a dozen of the world's wealthiest men. (One of the odder gags involves Goldfoot's rejection of a newly assembled femme robot for being too butch; a better one places live, spying eyes in a Walter Keane painting [!].) It's *Dr. Goldfoot*'s very awkwardness that makes it as watchable as it is. Followed by *Dr. Goldfoot and the Girl Bombs* (n/a).

DR. STRANGELOVE, OR: HOW I LEARNED TO STOP WORRYING AND LOVE THE BOMB (1964) B&W ****

D: Stanley Kubrick. Peter Sellers, Sterling Hayden, George C. Scott. 93 mins. (Columbia/TriStar) DVD

Director Kubrick and coscripter Terry Southern's brilliant, oft uproarious doomsday collaboration, drawn from the straightforward novel *Red Alert,* may be the best black comedy ever made—certainly the last word re the end of the world. Sellers is terrific in three radically different roles, including the title maniac. The same year's *Fail-Safe* (Goodtimes) presents a more sobering interpretation of a similar apocalyptic scenario.

DON'T BE A MENACE TO SOUTH CENTRAL WHILE DRINKING YOUR JUICE IN THE HOOD   (1995) ***1/2

D: Paris Barclay. Shawn Wayans, Marlon Wayans, Tracy Cherelle Jones, Chris Spencer, Lahmard Tate, Antonio Fargas, La Wanda Page, Suli McCullough. 88 mins. (Miramax) DVD

Written by Shawn and Marlon Wayans (who also co-exec-produced), along with Phil Beauman, *Don't Be a Menace* sends up the entire catalog of 'hood-flick clichés. Shawn plays straight man Ashtray, returned to the 'hood by his upscale mom to learn the ways of adulthood from his dad (Tate), who, Tray informs us, "is only a couple of years older than me." For further education, Tray hooks up with his cousin Loc Dog (Marlon) for a series of consistently clever misadventures. Older bro' (and coproducer) Keenen Ivory Wayans supplies eye-blink cameos and three more Wayans siblings (Kim, Craig, Damien) appear, while Fargas plays "Old School," a middle-aged ghetto survivor whose mom (Page) won't let him leave the porch (!). Jones, as super-fertile femme Dashiki; Spencer, as a Muslim with a secret penchant for white wenches; and McCullough, as wheel-chair-bound "Crazy Legs," lend able comic support.

DRACULA, FATHER AND SON (1976) ***

D: Edouard Molinaro. Christopher Lee, Bernard Ménez, Marie-Helene Breillat, Catherine Breillat, Jean-Claude Daupin, Anna Gael. Dubbed. 96 mins. (Water Bearer)

Future *La Cage aux Folles* auteur Molinaro's debut feature is a clever

vampire comedy with a standout turn by Lee that subtly spoofs his horrific Hammer persona. The pic opens in 1784 Transylvania with Drac selecting a mortal woman to bear him a son, Ferdinand, a failure from the outset. (As a testy Drac snaps at his rambunctious, then-five-year-old offspring, "Ferdinand, drink your blood and go to bed!") In the 20th century, Communists (using a hammer and sickle as a cross) evict the toothy tenants from their traditional Transylvanian home. Dracula *père* becomes a successful vampire-film star in London (transforming, in effect, into Christopher Lee), while hopeless, good-hearted Dracula *fils* (Menez, who resembles a goofier Euro Jeff Daniels) leads an impoverished existence in Paris, where, incapable of drinking from live human necks, he subsists on small animals and fresh morgue residents. He also suffers the ultimate vampire humiliation when, caught in the act of raiding a plasma bank, he's forced to *give* blood (!) to make restitution. Father and son reunite in Paris, happily at first, but their relationship strains when both tumble for the same ad-agency femme (Breillat), with radically different intentions.

Working from Claude Klotz's book, Molinaro and coscripters Jean-Marie Poire (*The Visitors*) and Alain Goddard concoct a tasty blend of physical, character-, and culture-clash comedy, complete with a more serious father-son subtext and the occasional in-joke (a doctoral thesis penned by a "Professor Polanski"). Water Bearer releases a (reasonably adroitly) dubbed edition (with Lee, crucially, supplying his own voice) that's entertaining from beginning to end.

DRUGSTORE COWBOY   (1989) ***

D: Gus Van Sant. Matt Dillon, Kelly Lynch, James LeGros. 100 mins. (Artisan) DVD

Dillon and Lynch celebrate the petty-thief/junkie lowlifestyle in Van Sant's gritty, nearly verité, darkly

comic account adapted from James Fogle's unpublished jailhouse memoir, featuring strong turns by supporting thesps LeGros, James Remar, and Max Perlich.

EARTH GIRLS ARE EASY   (1989) ***

D: Julien Temple. Geena Davis, Jeff Goldblum, Julie Brown, Charles Rocket, Jim Carrey, Damon Wayans, Michael McKean. 100 mins. (Vestron) DVD

Julie (*Shakes the Clown*) Brown coscripts and serves as a Val-gal version of a Greek chorus in a bright, live-action cartoon detailing the earthly misadventures of a trio of party-animal aliens who happen to be covered with brightly colored fur. Goldblum and future *In Living Color* mainstays and megastars Wayans and Carrey are in fine form as the fun-loving E.T.'s. *Earth* is a better pop musical than the similarly themed Pia Zadora vehicle, *Voyage of the Rock Aliens* (Prism), though Brown's since topped herself with the brilliant Madonna parody *Medusa: Dare to Be Truthful* (Columbia/TriStar).

EATING RAOUL   (1982) ***

D: Paul Bartel. Paul Bartel, Mary Woronov, Robert Beltran. 83 mins. (Fox)

The enterprising Mr. and Mrs. Bland (Bartel, Woronov) slay and rob local swingers to finance their planned restaurant. Beltran, as the eponymous Raoul, plays a burglar who complicates the Blands' scam in director Bartel's satiric bad-taste romp, coscripted by Richard (*Lemora*) Blackburn.

ED WOOD   (1994) B&W ***

D: Tim Burton. Johnny Depp, Martin Landau, Sarah Jessica Parker. 124 mins. (Buena Vista)

Tim Burton's epic tribute to the transvestite auteur and *Plan 9 from*

Outer Space creator, lensed in glorious black and white, may be uneven as comedy or biography but succeeded in making its subject the household name he long deserved to be. Landau won a well-earned Oscar for his interpretation of an aged Bela Lugosi.

ELVIRA, MISTRESS OF THE DARK (1988) **1/2

D: James Signorelli. Elvira (Cassandra Peterson), W. Morgan Sheppard, Daniel Greene. 96 mins. (Starmaker)

Wisecracking, cleavage-driven Cassandra (Elvira) Peterson—heavy-metal monsterdom's answer to Mae West—supplies the main attraction in a hit-and-miss comedy vehicle tailored to showcase the TV horror hostess's sizable talents. Elvira's admirers can also catch their fave in *Acting on Impulse* (see index), *Balboa* (Vestron), *Echo Park* (Barr Films), *Pee-wee's Big Adventure* (see index), the sketch collection *Uncensored* (WesternWorld), and 1975's *Working Girls* (VCI), wherein a young Cassandra performs a striptease number.

ELVIS MEETS NIXON (1997) ***1/2

D: Allan Arkush. Rick Peters, Bob Gunton, Richard Beymer, Curtis Armstrong, Alyson Court, Gabriel Hogan, Jackie Burroughs. 103 mins. (Avalanche)

According to *Elvis Meets Nixon*, a few days before Christmas 1970, a bored, frustrated Elvis Presley (an excellent Peters)—armed only with a credit card, a $20 bill, a customized scepter, a cache of the prescription drugs that would eventually help kill him, and a Colt .45 holstered in his gaudy purple suit (oh yeah, and a loaded derringer in his boot!)—fled Graceland for a series of solo flights that eventually landed him in Washington for a bizarre summit with Nixon (a dead-on Gunton). Former Roger Corman apprentice Arkush (*Rock*

'n' Roll High School) and producer/writer Allen Rosen craft a brilliant, dead-pan chronicle of the King's peripatetic journey. Highlights include a confrontation in a black-ghetto donut shop, a detour to a hippie-packed Sunset Strip record store (where the sheltered rock legend is shocked to find even his latest album stocked in the oldies section), and the climactic Pres-meet-Prez encounter, which includes the two luminaries harmonizing on "My Wild Irish Rose." Erstwhile tele-pundit Dick Cavett supplies the wraparound, while Arkush also incorporates commentary from guest celebs Wayne Newton, Edwin Newman, Tony Curtis, Graham Nash, and even "Deep Throat" (glimpsed only from behind). What makes *Elvis Meets Nixon* all the more jaw-dropping is the fact that it is indeed at least loosely drawn from a true incident; the end credits roll over an actual photograph of the American legends' meeting. Originally produced for Showtime cable, *Elvis Meets Nixon* is unpredictable, consistently funny, and frighteningly insightful re American culture then and now (two increasingly simultaneous time frames). Dan Hedaya plays Nixon in the 1999 comedy *Dick,* while Harvey Keitel gets to don the Elvis garb in 1999's *Finding Graceland* (both Columbia/TriStar, DVD).

EVIL ED (1996) **1/2

D: Anders Jacobsson. Johan Rudebeck, Per Lofberg, Olof Rhodin, Camela Leierth. 88 mins. (A-Pix) DVD

A Swedish spoof of American splatter movies, *Evil Ed* opens on a high note as a beleaguered gore-film editor freaks out, destroys reels of celluloid, and eats a grenade. To replace the late cutter, resident mogul Sam Campbell (Lofberg) dispatches mild-mannered Ed (Rudebeck) to an isolated house to complete editing chores on a fictional fright-franchise series entitled *Loose Limbs.* It's not long before Ed, like the editor who'd preceded him,

loses his head and returns the favor at the expense of several unwary visitors. Jacobsson's fitfully amusing spoof runs out of ideas a few reels in; its irreverent referencing of *Blue Velvet, Night of the Living Dead, Taxi Driver,* and generic slasher flicks supplies little new in the way of satiric thrusts (though presumably it played fresher on its home turf). FX end credits include "dr. wrench foot-effect by Kaj Steveman" and "mcdone's head explotion [*sic*] and mel's teeth-effect" by Joakim Lindman.

FARGO (1996) ***1/2

D: Joel Coen. Frances McDormand, William H. Macy, Steve Buscemi, Harve Presnell, Peter Stormare. 97 mins. (PolyGram) DVD

The Coen bros.' best film since *Barton Fink* chronicles an amateur kidnap scheme (reportedly loosely drawn from a real case) gone disastrously haywire and features a supremely entertaining perf by McDormand (wife of director/coscripter Joel Coen) as a deceptively persistent (and very pregnant) local cop who puts the brain in arctic Brainard, Minnesota. Macy is perfectly cast as the beleaguered Twin Cities car salesman who hatches the fog-noggined plan, while Buscemi scores a role worthy of his skills as the wild-card criminal Macy treks to neighboring Fargo, North Dakota, to recruit, Stormare lends dark humor as Buscemi's literally silent partner, and Presnell is amusingly overbearing as Macy's white-collar macho father-in-law. McDormand circles the chaotic situation with a cheerful relentlessness throughout. The Coens' seamless blend of thriller, black comedy, and regional anthropology is a joy to watch and hear. The brothers return with *The Big Lebowski* (PolyGram, DVD), which, while it doesn't scale *Fargo's* dizzying heights, offers its share of rewards, including Jeff Bridges's winning performance as a middle-aged stoner.

FEAR AND LOATHING IN LAS VEGAS (1998) **½

D. Terry Gilliam. Johnny Depp, Benicio Del Toro, Gary Busey, Ellen Barkin, Christina Ricci, Mark Harmon. 119 mins. (Universal) DVD

Gilliam's screen translation of Hunter Thompson's hallucinogen-fueled farewell to the hope and ecstatic abandon of the '60s shapes up as a singular blend of the strikingly good, self-indulgently bad, and determinedly ugly. With a nod to *Rolling Stone* artist and Thompson chronicler Ralph Steadman's trippy sketches, Gilliam and FX ace Rob Bottin succeed in painting an utterly convincing canvas that accurately outsurreals any previous attempts to re-create the acid experience on film. Unfortunately, the flamboyant visuals frequently dominate to the point of drowning out Thompson's more cogent, coherent observations (heard briefly in voice-over) re the slide from the promise of the '60s into the sellout of the '70s.

Like Bill Murray in 1980's utterly execrable Thompson-based turkey, *Where the Buffalo Roam* (Universal), Depp faithfully mimics Thompson's totally offputting vocal inflections, an auditory irritation readers *don't* have to endure when perusing H.T.'s highly recommended book. A grotesquely (and pointlessly) self-fattened Del Toro goes unwatchably over the top as Depp's partner-in-self-induced paralysis, his attorney/alter ego Dr. Gonzo (a role played by Peter Boyle in *Buffalo*). And both actors' penchant for in-your-fish-lens mugging is worse than redundant with the visual-overkill-crazed Gilliam at the helm. Las Vegas, then (1971) and now, proves an easy but undeniably rich locale to represent the trashiest of America's culture of joyless excess, and Gilliam spins the town like a psychedelic top. Several well- and lesser-known thesps contribute cameos; in addition to Busey (as a highway trooper), Ricci (as a Barbra Streisand–

obsessed teen "artist"), and Barkin (as a waitress), Cameron Diaz, Harry Dean Stanton, Jenette Goldstein, Tim Thomerson, and the Red Hot Chili Peppers' Flea all plunge into the mix, while 1956's *The Black Scorpion* makes a background TV appearance (there's also a funny mock B&W teen "educational" short shown at a Vegas law-enforcement convention our stoned protags attend). It's easy to see why *Fear* flopped miserably at the old B.O.; it needed to establish a stronger cultural context, beyond a mid-'60s San Francisco flashback and a few era rock anthems on the soundtrack, to convey its message to contempo audiences. Still, Gilliam's visual genius makes *Fear and Loathing* a homevid trip worth taking.

THE FEARLESS VAMPIRE KILLERS, OR PARDON ME, BUT YOUR TEETH ARE IN MY NECK (1967) ***

D: Roman Polanski. Roman Polanski, Jack MacGowran, Sharon Tate, Alfie Bass, Ferdy Mayne, Iain Quarrier. 111 mins. (MGM)

This director's cut of Polanski's bloodsucker romp incorporates some 20 minutes of footage missing from the version that played theatrically during the pic's initial stateside release. Director/coscripter Polanski (with frequent screen collaborator Gerard Brach) telegraphs his irreverent intentions right from the get-go, when he transforms the famous MGM lion into a vampire (!) and features an opening credit reading "Fangs by Dr. Ludwig Von Krankheit." Polanski costars as Alfred, earnest but thoroughly inept young assistant to obsessed, oft befuddled vampire-hunter Professor Abronsius, a Van Helsing wannabe brought to inventive eccentric life by Irish thesp MacGowran (who would later team with Donald Pleasence in Polanski's black comedy *Cul-de-sac* [Facets] and surface in *The Exorcist*). The pair stum-

ble upon a remote mountain village, where they encounter innkeeper Shagal (Bass) and his bath-addicted daughter, Sarah (Tate). Alfred and the professor's travels eventually land them within the walls of a local castle belonging to Count Von Krolock (portrayed, with regal menace, by Mayne), his gay son, Quarrier, antisocial hunchback Terry Downes, and assorted bloodsucking guests. While *The Fearless Vampire Killers* occasionally suffers from Polanski's penchant for overly broad bits (e.g., some of the gay and Jewish jokes) and exaggerated sight gags (including the ill-advised use of fast-motion photography), the restored version steers the action along at a statelier pace that enhances its frequent stretches of wry deadpan humor.

FEELING MINNESOTA (1996) ***

D: Steven Baigelman. Keanu Reeves, Vincent D'Onofrio, Cameron Diaz, Dan Aykroyd, Delroy Lindo, Courtney Love, Tuesday Weld. 95 mins. (New Line) DVD

While reminiscent of the Coen brothers' *Fargo* and Matthew Bright's *Freeway* (see index), debuting auteur Baigelman's low-life black comedy springs enough surprises to overcome its occasional contrivances. As long-estranged brothers, Reeves and D'Onofrio exchange more slaps and punches than you'll see at a Three Stooges marathon. The duo unwisely reunite when, at mom Weld's behest, ex-con Reeves shows up at older bro' D'Onofrio's wedding to extremely reluctant bride Diaz, a thief forced into the marriage by D'Onofrio's gangster employer (Lindo). Diaz promptly runs off with Reeves, but it's a long, bumpy ride between there and Happily-Ever-Afterville. The three leads all turn in arduous physical perfs, with D'Onofrio especially good as a crooked slob with an unerring instinct for making the wrong moves. A tubby Aykroyd plays a corrupt cop, while Kurt Cobain's merry widow, Love, late of *The People vs. Larry Flynt* (Columbia/TriStar) and Nick Broomfield's unflattering doc *Kurt & Courtney* (BMG), makes the most of her brief waitress role. Unlike *Fargo,* where locating real snow proved a major production problem, *Feeling Minnesota* forgoes a deep-winter setting for a more moderate Midwestern season.

FEMALE TROUBLE (1974) ***½

D: John Waters. Divine, David Lochary, Mink Stole, Edith Massey. 95 mins. (Cinema Group)

Waters's Divine comedy toplines the tubby transvestite as troubled teen Dawn Davenport, who runs away from home after a traumatic Christmas squabble (over an absent pair of promised cha-cha heels!) with her exasperated parents. We follow Dawn through an unwise sexual encounter with a foulmouthed slob (also, in a high-concept move, played by Divine, sans drag), an unhappy marriage to a hetero hairdresser, an abortive criminal career, and a brief, ill-fated fling as a media-fabricated "superstar." The result is a typically, often brilliantly sick sleaze opera that deftly mocks the media, effete Warhol-esque poseurs, trust-fund *artistes,* and sundry other seamy aspects of our trash culture.

A FISH CALLED WANDA (1988) ***

D: Charles Crichton. John Cleese, Jamie Lee Curtis, Kevin Kline. 108 mins. (Fox) DVD

Veteran Brit comedy director Crichton crafts an occasionally precious but more often fun farce detailing uptight attorney Cleese's misadventures with thieves Curtis, Kline, and a stuttering Michael Palin. The cast reunites for 1996's *Fierce Creatures* (Universal, DVD).

THE 5,000 FINGERS OF DR. T. (1953) ***

D: Roy Rowland. Hans Conried, Tommy Rettig, Peter Lind Hayes, Mary Healy, Henry Kulky. 88 mins. (Fox)

The only expressionist Hollywood musicomedy scripted by Dr. Seuss (!), this 1953 bizarrity stars Tommy (*Lassie*) Rettig as a hapless youth tormented by his tyrannical piano teacher, flamboyantly interpreted by Conried. A kind of kiddie-matinee edition of *Dante's Inferno,* most of the pic is an extended nightmare sequence that finds young Tom a prisoner at the "Happy Fingers Institute," where Dr. T. plans to install him and 499 other unlucky lads at a giant, wraparound piano at which they'll "practice 24 hours a day, 365 days a year." Help arrives in the form of plumber Hayes (who prefers to identify himself as an "independent contractor"), who assists Tom and his brainwashed mom, Healy (Hayes's real-life wife and longtime showbiz partner). *5,000 Fingers* offers campy humor, deranged ditties, much fancy (and often effete) footwork, and some of the most surrealistic sets seen on celluloid since Caligari last unlocked his cabinet. Highlights include a tour of Dr. T.'s basement penal colony and a hooded dungeonmaster's dirgelike ode to the grim joys of "ankle chains and nooses of the finest rope."

FLESH (1968) ***

D: Paul Morrissey. Joe Dallesandro, Geraldine Smith, Patti D'Arbanville. 90 mins. (Image) DVD

Morrissey's picaresque gutter trilogy—*Flesh,* 1970's *Trash,* and 1972's *Heat* (also Image, DVD)—follows charismatic junkie Dallesandro and friends on their zany underground rounds in fairly sharp if peripatetic social satires, with *Trash* standing out as the best of the three.

FLESH GORDON: COLLECTOR'S EDITION (1972) **½

D: Mike Light. Jason Williams, Suzanne Fields, John Hoyt. 90 mins. (Hen's Tooth)

This soft-core sex satire of *Flash Gordon* is pretty broad most of the way, but stop-motion FX ace David Allen fashions several memorable creatures. The flick's flashes of wit and flesh have earned it a loyal cult following. Followed by 1993's *Flesh Gordon 2: Flesh Gordon Meets the Cosmic Cheerleaders* (New Horizons).

FOUR ROOMS (1995) *

D: Allison Anders, Alexandre Rockwell, Robert Rodriguez, Quentin Tarantino. Tim Roth, Antonio Banderas, Madonna, Quentin Tarantino, Bruce Willis, Jennifer Beals, Sammi Davis, Lili Taylor. 98 mins. (Miramax) DVD

A quartet of Hollywood's then-hottest young auteurs get their actor buds to cavort for the cameras in a hotel-set anthology that arrives, after a whirlwind theatrical flame-out, as an unmitigated artistic, comedic, and financial flop. Roth in particular may want to confiscate all copies of this tongue-in-cheek, finger-in-nose, head-up-butt romp. No doubt cued by Quentin's (as a Hollywood impresario) on-screen homage to Jerry Lewis's *The Bellboy,* Roth wins the Sammy Petrillo Award for the most aggressive Jer-styled antics seen on-screen since Jonathan Haze went Lewis loony in Roger Corman's original *Little Shop of Horrors.* On the other hand, *Four Rooms* exhibits many of the same leering, mugging antiqualities of such awful but, in some quarters, now-beloved '60s B comedies as *Promises! Promises!, Three Nuts in Search of a Bolt* (Simitar), and *The Unkissed Bride* (New World). That being the case, we'd advise the morbidly curious to wait another couple of decades before checking in to *Four Rooms.* Who knows? By then it may even seem funny.

FRANKENHOOKER (1990) ***½

D: Frank Henenlotter. James Lorinz, Patty Mullen, Louise Lasser, Shirley Stoler, Zacherley. 89 mins. (SGE) DVD

The ultimate 42nd Street movie, Gotham-based auteur Frank (*Basket Case*) Henenlotter's gender-bending variation on the Frankenstein story chronicles the mad misadventures of young Jeffrey Franken (Lorinz), a New Jersey Electric employee, med-school dropout, and amateur "bioelectric technician." When his plump fiancée, Elizabeth Shelley (Mullen), literally loses her head in a Ho-ho-kus, New Jersey, power-mower mishap (!), our hero resolves to reattach her painstakingly preserved dome to a new, improved body. Following a self-administered trepanning treatment, Jeffrey gets the bright idea to shop for the requisite replacement parts among Manhattan's thriving prostitute population. That's only the start of the sick, witty fun that unfolds in this highly inspired outing, wherein Henenlotter again stretches genre conventions to explore such weighty issues as male objectification of women, amoral science, and intemperate controlled-substance use. Highlights include an impressive high-tech lab sequence that belies the pic's low budget, the resultant Frankenhooker's hilarious last-reel rampage, and a scene that gives us fully nine exploding hookers ("Oh, the humanity!" a repentant Jeffrey laments). Lead Lorinz turns in an inventive perf as the eccentric Jersey-accented scientist, while Mullen is a model of slutty menace as Frankenhooker. Cameos by horror host Zacherley as a TV weatherman, Stoler as a beefy butch barmaid, and Lasser as Jeffrey's bemused mom likewise add to the dark merriment. Employing a bright, cartoonlike look that recalls Carl Reiner's Steve Martin spoof *The Man with Two Brains*, *Frankenhooker* plays like a live-action underground comic book, adopting an unwaveringly cheerful tone while spinning its subversive tale.

FREAKED (1993) **½

D: Tom Stern, Alex Winter. Alex Winter, Randy Quaid, William Sadler, Megan Ward, Michael Stoyanov, Bobcat Goldthwait, Mr. T, Brooke Shields, Morgan Fairchild, Keanu Reeves. 79 mins. (Fox)

Before scoring big-time as Bill in *Bill & Ted's Excellent Adventure* and *Bill & Ted's Bogus Journey*, Alex Winter was an NYU Film School student who, with partner Tom Stern, wrote, directed, and acted in several anarchic comedy shorts, some of which were eventually aired on MTV and collected in the video anthology *Squeal of Death*. Winter wielded his newfound Tinseltown clout to get this surreal feature-length farce off

---

Freakmakers in Focus!

FX COORDINATOR THOMAS C. RAINONE ON *FREAKED*

As Told to The Phantom

● ●

"They [directors Winter and Stern] called me in right about the time I was wrapping up *Honey, I Blew Up the Kid*. We pretty much decided in the beginning how the work should be delegated based on who had certain strengths for certain characters. You always hire multiple shops so the work can be done quicker. That includes specialty-FX shops. When Toad inhales the bunny, that was a computer-generated shot by Pacific Data Images.

"Screaming Mad George pretty much designed all the actual freaks. From the initial drawings, there were test makeups done. They do what's known as a 'maquette,' a small clay sculpture that's shown for the director's approval. Then you put the actor in a head-and-body cast and sculpt exactly what you had on the maquette directly on the cast. It's molded in silicon—the original clay is destroyed in that process—you pour your polyfoam in, pull it out, and you have appliances that are trimmed and put on the actor's face."

Casting actors who could handle long shoots in full freak makeup posed a serious challenge.

"One of the things I went over with the casting director was, I said, 'Look, if any of these people have any allergies, are claustrophobic or react in weird ways under heat, do not cast them.' 'Cause these actors will say anything to score a part. For a while I was a little concerned about Keanu Reeves as the dog-faced boy. There was a big problem about how his makeup should look. It looked like a dog, and it was kind of silly 'cause you really couldn't tell it was Keanu. I was insisting on an *Island of Lost Souls*/Jack Pierce approach. [FX ace] Tony Gardner blocked the hair directly on Keanu's skin and added a slight dog-nose appliance. Keanu's a Method actor, so he was always Ortiz the Dawg Boy in his makeup. It must have been hot as hell in there, but he wouldn't even take off his gloves. He had to totally be that character or nothing!

"Alex was an unbelievable trouper because when he wasn't shooting, he had to direct in that makeup. It took four hours to apply, so he would wind up wearing it all night. Robert [Freddy Krueger] Englund will sometimes wear it overnight, 'cause it saves time, but Alex wore it up to four days in a row! At one point, his face broke out severely. Luckily, a dermatologist in Houston came up with a prescription that cured it overnight." [Rainone himself put in a silent on-screen cameo, sans makeup.] "In the 'Heavy Petting Zoo' sequence, that's me making out with the goat."

the ground. Related within a mock TV-talk-show flashback format, *Freaked* opens with shadow-cloaked celebrity Ricky Coogin (Winter) telling his weird tale of woe to hostess Shields and her live studio audience. The shallow teen idol's troubles begin when he agrees to rep a toxic pesticide for the sinister EES (Everything Except Shoes) Corp. in the Third World nation of Santa Flan, where he, sidekick Stoyanov, and visiting protester Ward wind up in the clutches of flamboyant entrepreneur Quaid, who uses said pesticide to turn our protagonists into new exhibits for his seedy theme park, "Freek Land." (Other mutant performers include Mr. T as a bearded lady [!], Bobcat Goldthwait as "Sock Man," and an unbilled Keanu Reeves as "Ortiz, the Dawg Boy.") The rest is a string of hit-and-miss bits, including a parody of *The Great Escape*, as our victims seek to turn the tables on the callous Quaid and his creepy corporate backers led by Sadler. While *Freaked* (originally *Hideous Mutant Freakz*) doesn't pack sufficient yoks to fill its relatively abbreviated running time, there are enough inventive riffs to make the flick—which received little more than a token theatrical release—well worth a look on video.

FREEWAY (1996) ***

D: Matthew Bright. Reese Witherspoon, Kiefer Sutherland, Dan Hedaya, Amanda Plummer, Bokeem Woodbine, Brooke Shields, Michael T. Weiss, Sydney Lassick. 102 mins. (Republic) DVD

Writer/director Bright continues his obsession with simultaneously innocent, victimized, and violently vengeful teenage girls—e.g., *Dark Angel: The Ascent* and *Guncrazy* (see index)—with this darkly clever "Little Red Riding Hood" Meets *Natural Born Killers* (Oliver Stone receives a co-executive-producer credit) scored by ex–Oingo Boingo front man turned megamovie composer Danny Elfman. Following an animated opening-credits

---

Filmmakers in Focus!

WRITER/DIRECTOR MATTHEW BRIGHT ON *FREEWAY*

As Told to The Phantom

PHANTOM: How did you get to direct *Freeway*?

BRIGHT: I'd given the script to Richard Rutowski. He's a close friend of Oliver Stone's. He gave two scripts of mine to Oliver, and Oliver said, "Clearly this writer should be directing it." They were professional enough to kind of get that. The directions are there in the script—which makes other directors nuts. That's a reason I've never gotten along with them so well. The mediocre ones.

PHANTOM: They feel it's a threat?

BRIGHT: Oh, yeah, they just don't want anyone else doing it. But they said this guy should be directing it. It's an edgy, out-there script. I'd never done anything before, directing-wise. The actors were really scared of coming in. They wanted someone to say, "This is okay." They don't want to look ridiculous. With Oliver's involvement, it's like the actors were able to feel a little better, to have Oliver say, "Yeah, you should do this."

PHANTOM: Did you get everyone you wanted?

BRIGHT: I got everyone I wanted. But I didn't know who I was gonna get for the lead guy. It's a thankless part; actors want to look good, especially movie stars. Here the character's the biggest dork in the world. You know how we got Kiefer Sutherland? Oliver was making *Nixon*. I didn't know Oliver at all at the time, I'd only met him once or twice. So he called us to the set of *Nixon*. We went through a million labyrinthine sets, and we suddenly were in the Oval Office. And we're sitting there, me and Kiefer, we haven't spoken yet. It looks *exactly* like the Oval Office. Oliver suddenly walks in like the president of the United States, sits down, and he's such a commanding presence; in the Oval Office, he looks positively presidential. I think it was basically the power of the presidency that pushed Kiefer over the edge. And then he got to the set, wondering, "What the hell am I doing here?"

PHANTOM: Were you intimidated at all by directing?

BRIGHT: Well, I was *respectful*, that it was a big job and I didn't try to bite off more than I could chew. I knew enough not to try to be a wiseass, in terms of trying to outdo Kurosawa and Scorsese and all those guys, 'cause I just don't have the chops. And I didn't have the time anyway, even if I did have the technical chops.

PHANTOM: How was Brooke Shields to work with?

BRIGHT: I loved her. What were those creatures called in *Blade Runner*?

PHANTOM: Replicants?

BRIGHT: She's a replicant. She's perfect. She looks like the Statue of Liberty. A lot of people think she's an idiot, 'cause she's serene. All you have to do is watch *Pretty Baby* to know something's in there.

PHANTOM: In three of your produced scripts—*Guncrazy*, *Dark Angel*, and *Freeway*—there's an adolescent girl who's a victim but kicks butt too.

BRIGHT: It's very strange. In about ninety percent of my stuff, the protagonist is an adolescent girl. I have to work to keep my male characters from being like ciphers, real zeroes to bounce off of. I haven't been able to figure it out.

sequence, *Freeway* details the trashy teen travails of modern Red Vanessa (Witherspoon), whose journey to Grandma's Stockton, California, trailer home begins after her hooker mom (Plummer) and crack-smoking stepdad (Weiss) get pinched by local L.A. fuzz. Bidding adieu to "fiancé" Woodbine and accepting his handgun as a going-away gift, Vanessa takes to the freeway. When her car breaks down, she's offered a ride by "professional counselor" Bob Wolverton (Sutherland), at which point her troubles begin in earnest. Bright's cheerfully grotesque indictment of our ineffectual-to-vicious judicial, law-enforcement, and penal systems runs Vanessa through the wringer (though she usually gives as good as she gets) before circling back to the Little Red motif. Bright's funky fable further benefits from an excellent, quirky cast, particularly the ever eccentric Plummer. Bright followed in 1999 with *Freeway 2: Confessions of a Trickbaby* (Full Moon, DVD), starring Natasha Lyonne and Vincent Gallo.

THE FRESHMAN   (1990) ***

D: Andrew Bergman. Marlon Brando, Matthew Broderick, Maximilian Schell, Bruno Kirby. 102 mins. (Columbia/TriStar) DVD

Naïve film student Broderick finds himself married to the mob in Bergman's offbeat farce. Highlights include Brando's mumbling Don Corleone reprise and Bert Parks's sparkling rendition of Dylan's "Maggie's Farm" (!).

THE FRIGHTENERS   (1996) ***

D: Peter Jackson. Michael J. Fox, Trini Alvarado, Peter Dobson, John Astin, Jeffrey Combs, Dee Wallace Stone, Jake Busey, R. Lee Ermey. 109 mins. (Universal) DVD

A slow, convoluted opening keeps Peter (*Heavenly Creatures*) Jackson's large-scale return to his low-budget *Bad Taste/Dead Alive* roots spinning its wheels before roaring into a high-gear *Poltergeist*-ian FX-fest. Fox plays a phony ghostbuster, assisted by three actual poltergeists (Astin, Chi McBride, Jim Fyfe), who discovers that a ghostly serial killer is claiming lives by the dozens. When Fox finds himself at the scene of several of these supernatural slayings, the finger of suspicion points to him. He learns that newly widowed doctor (and eventual love interest) Alvarado has been selected as the next victim (a number visible only to Fox glows on the targets' foreheads). In the film's climactic FX showdown, Fox chooses to "die," the better to do battle with the psycho spirit. While leads Fox and Alvarado are only adequate, Combs is terrific as a paranoid, hemorrhoidal, paranormal FBI investigator, sort of a Fox Mulder on bad drugs and a rubber inner tube. The virtually nonstop FX are nothing if not inventive—Rick Baker designed John Astin's "Judge" makeup—while the ubiquitous Danny Elfman composes an appropriately hyperactive score.

THE FULL MONTY   (1997) ***

D: Paul Cattaneo. Robert Carlyle, Tom Wilkinson, Mark Addy, Lesley Sharp. 95 mins. (Fox) DVD

Six unemployed steel laborers willing to bare their working-class willies in hopes of netting a few bob dance, bond, get cold feet, and ultimately go on with the show in a Brit comedy that displays more heart than crotch. While not worthy of a Best Picture nom, *The Full Monty* rates as an amusing, well-acted if at core formulaic affair. Subtitles would be helpful, as would censor bars, at least for the less appealing bods on view.

BY ANY OTHER NAME DEPARTMENT

According to a *Sunday Times of London* item, *The Full Monty* was one of several Anglo films to receive more imaginative monikers for their Asian releases, translated into Mandarin as *Six Naked Pigs* (!) and into Cantonese as *Six Stripped Warriors. As Good As It Gets*, in Cantonese, became *Mr. Cat Poop. Fargo* joined the Cantonese movie menu as *Mysterious Murder in Snowy Cream* (yum), while *The English Patient* was recast as *Do Not Ask Me Who I Am, Ever.* (And we mean that!)

FUNNY BONES   (1995) ***1/2

D: Peter Chelsom. Oliver Platt, Jerry Lewis, Leslie Caron, Lee Evans, Richard Griffiths, Oliver Reed, Ian McNeice, William Hootkins, Ticky Holgado, Ruta Lee. 128 mins. (Buena Vista)

Brit helmer Chelsom follows his quirky, critically acclaimed 1991 debut, *Hear My Song* (Paramount), with this highly original, oft brilliant meditation on the nature of comedy. Platt plays the terminally unfunny son of comic legend Lewis (in another of his deft semiautobiographical cameos). After bombing big-time in Vegas, Platt disappears, dons a disguise, and returns to his roots, the seaside carny town of Blackpool, England, in hopes of finding fresh material and reinventing himself. There he encounters a family of eccentric performers and a hitherto unknown legacy left behind by dad Lewis. Chelsom filters charm, meta-slapstick, sick gags, and bittersweet drama through an idiosyncratic, phenomenological prism, resulting in a movie that glows with subtle universal truths. If *Funny Bones* has a flaw, it's that Chelsom takes on too many themes and tangents to sort out in two hours. Still, you have to admire his ambition—even if his films' self-effacing quality has prevented him from becoming more of a media darling. Chelsom followed with 1999's *The Mighty* (Miramax).

FUNNYMAN   (1994) ***

D: Simon Sprackling. Tim James, Christopher Lee, Benny Young, Ingrid Lacey, Pauline Black, Matthew Devitt. 89 mins. (Arrow)

Britain hasn't been known as a breeding ground for the brand of indie live-action gore cartoons that have proliferated stateside, but Sprackling's agreeably anarchic *Funnyman* may help change that perception. With an antagonist who falls somewhere between Freddy Krueger and *Leprechaun*, *Funnyman* projects much of the same anything-goes spirit as Peter Jackson's early

comedic bloodlettings, *Bad Taste* and *Dead Alive*. *Funnyman* opens with a cryptic Lee losing a card game and forfeiting his house to rock-'n'-roll mogul Young, who promptly visits the site with wife (Lacey), daughter, and young son. Waiting to inflict lethal mischief on the brood is the titular demon, clad in classic joker regalia. Only a brain-fried Young is left alive when his rocker-manqué brother (Devitt) arrives, accompanied by a crew of hitchhikers he picked up on the way, including a ditsy distaff birdwatcher, a New Agey type, a macho man, and a femme Jamaican psychic (Black), the only one who realizes at once that something's seriously amiss. In a series of set pieces, *Funnyman* trades on the assembled visitors' various vanities and weaknesses to trap and dispatch them, capping each atrocity with a one-liner or a wink at the camera. Highlights include a lethal Punch and Judy puppet show, a grotty strip-club sequence, a Sergio Leone shoot-out spoof, and a mock rock concert. Lensed in bright cartoon colors, sporting strictly joke-shop gore, and animated by James's bouncy interpretation of the evil title elf, *Funnyman* rates as a surprisingly fresh, cheerfully cheeky entry that's both a wisecracking frightcom and an often witty spoof of same.

GET SHORTY   (1995) ***1/2

D: Barry Sonnenfeld. John Travolta, Gene Hackman, Rene Russo, Danny DeVito, Delroy Lindo, David Paymer, James Gandolfini. 105 mins. (MGM) DVD

Miami mob enforcer Travolta catches the movie bug big-time and hooks up with schlock mogul Hackman (whose fictional credits include *Slime Creature III* and *I Married a Ghoul from Outer Space*) in Sonnenfeld's hugely entertaining Elmore Leonard–based combo of crime comedy and Hollywood satire. Look for unbilled cameos by Penny Marshall (as a director), Harvey Keitel (as himself),

big-screen clips from *Touch of Evil*, and a still from *Highway to Hell*.

GETTING IN   (1994) **1/2

D: Doug Liman. Kristy Swanson, Steven Mailer, Dave Chappelle, Andrew McCarthy, Len Cariou, Christine Baranski. 94 mins. (Trimark)

Lensed at Duke University, in Durham, North Carolina, under the original title *The Student Body*, *Getting In* earns at least a passing grade as a sporadically pointed black comedy in a *Heathers* vein. When would-be med student Mailer only places sixth on the waiting list for Johns Hopkins—where several generations of his forebears made their medical bones—he attempts to persuade those ahead of him to remove themselves from his path. Among the latter are Mailer's soon-to-be love object Swanson and ambitious self-made maniac McCarthy, who puts Mailer's half-baked scheme to more murderous use. Liman's too-often bland effort ignores some prime opportunities to skewer a richly deserving American medical industry, but some legitimately sicko sight gags add a compensatory edge. Liman followed with *Swingers* (Touchstone) and the higher-profiled and very funny 1999 teen ensemble comedy *Go* (Columbia/TriStar).

GHOSTBUSTERS:
THE SERIES

GHOSTBUSTERS   (1984) ***1/2

D: Ivan Reitman. Bill Murray, Sigourney Weaver, Dan Aykroyd, Harold Ramis, Ernie Hudson. 107 mins. (Columbia/TriStar) DVD

Reitman directs a clever script brought to life by a top comedy cast as self-styled poltergeist-fighters Murray, Aykroyd, Ramis, and Hudson plunge Fun City into supernatural chaos. Reitman's *Ghostbusters 2* (Columbia/

TriStar, DVD), an ectoplasmic exercise in supernatural Apple-phobia, finds the spook-battling foursome up against a river of slime spawned by NYC's collective bad vibes (!). While not as spirited as the original, the sequel still supplies a fair amount of fright-farce fun. Both films' antecedent, the 1940 Bob Hope vehicle *The Ghost Breakers* (Universal), furnishes more chills than might be expected when Bob investigates strange happenings in a Caribbean mansion.

THE GIG   (1985) ***½

D: Frank Gilroy. Wayne Rogers, Cleavon Little, Andrew Duncan. 95 mins. (Lorimar)

Writer/director Gilroy takes a group of hitherto-amateur middle-aged musicians through their first pro job at a second-rate Catskills resort in a top-notch comedy/drama highlighted by excellent perfs. Little is especially good as the one professional hired to replace an ailing band member. *The Gig* is a perceptive, low-budget gem that never strains for impact.

THE GIRL CAN'T HELP IT   (1956) ***

D: Frank Tashlin. Jayne Mansfield, Tom Ewell, Edmond O'Brien. 99 mins. (Fox)

Ewell plays a boozy, has-been agent ordered by gangster O'Brien to transform buxom blond lust object Mansfield into a rock star. Tashlin's broad but undeniably iconic comedy features lively numbers by Little Richard, Gene Vincent, the Platters, and Fats Domino.

GIRLFRIENDS   (1993) ***

D: Mark Bosko, Wayne A. Harold. Nina Angeloff, Lori Scarlett, Mark Andreyko, Sara Showman, Ian MacLennan, Mark Wilt. 80 mins. (Riot Pictures)

Ohio-based codirectors Bosko and Harold (the latter can also take credit for the hip script) graduate from their *Killer Nerd* (Tempe) concerns with this fresh descent into vintage John Waters territory. *Girlfriends* is *not* your standard-issue Zit Zombies from Junior High amateur-night special. Bosko and Harold get the All-American Trash mind-set and lowlifestyle down to a literal T with their tale of two lesbians whose lust for beer, rent money, and the occasional dinner out drives them to kill a series of "loud fat men with big wallets." Butchy Wanda (Angeloff)—still bitter re her brief, bullet-halted marriage to an abusive cracker (glimpsed in a hilarious B&W flashback)—is the trigger woman, while more romantic femme (and closet Patrick Swayze fan!) Pearle (Scarlett) supplies the bait. Less screen time is devoted to chronicling the duo's crimes than to charting their mostly harmonious relationship. One scene finds the pair peer-pressured by an earnest member (Showman) of a local lesbian support group who feels they should become more "involved." Wanda and Pearle agree to attend an amateur play about a 'burb homemaker's sapphic awakening and subsequent breakup with her distraught hubby; her onstage description of the wonders of motherhood prompts Pearle to become consumed with the idea of maternity. The couple lure a virginal nerd to serve as the surrogate dad, an arrangement that lasts less than a night, with dire consequences for the nerd. In another wickedly funny scene, the decidedly non-PC Wanda—who's not above turning tricks despite her hatred of men (then again, she hates nearly everybody, including most other lesbians)—plays dominatrix to a creepy lawyer (pardon our redundancy), portrayed by MacLennan, who turns out to be a local serial killer. Their face-off rings of no small psychological truth in a lethal sequence that ends with a terrif shock cut to Pearle giving birth. Angeloff and Scarlett, recruited from local Cleveland-area theater groups, hit just the right notes as the odd couple, skirting stereotypes and caricatures to emerge as believable and, in Pearle's case, even likable characters, while MacLennan is simultaneously understated and appropriately repulsive as the demented attorney. Bosko and Harold likewise avoid fashioning what might be interpreted as an anti-sapphic screed, since the lesbians fare no worse than rest of *Girlfriends*'s brain-damaged characters. Don't be put off by the pic's amateurish opening scene (which the filmmakers might have been better off excising); the pic picks up immediately thereafter, emerging as a sharp comedy of bad manners. On the Riot Pictures video, the feature's followed by a brief documentary about the making of the film. No relation to 1978's *Girlfriends* (Warner) or 1990's weak killer-bimbo romp, *Girlfriend from Hell* (Artisan).

THE GODS MUST BE CRAZY (1984) ***

D: Jamie Uys. Marius Weyers, Sandra Prinsloo, Nixau. 109 mins. (Playhouse)

South African auteur Uys's comic culture-clash fable would have worked better sans the slapstick interludes, but the pic still scores its share of satiric points and features a winning perf by thesp Nixau as a tribesman on an unusual quest. Uys slips a mite with his even broader 1989 sequel *The Gods Must Be Crazy 2* (Columbia/ TriStar).

DE PALMA DOUBLE BILL

GREETINGS   (1968) ***

D: Brian De Palma. Robert De Niro, Jonathan Warden, Gerrit Graham, Richard Hamilton, Allen Garfield, Megan McCormick. 88 mins. (Trimark)

HI, MOM! (1970) ***½

D: Brian De Palma. Robert De Niro, Allen Garfield, Lara Parker, Jennifer Salt. 87 mins. (Facets)

De Palma started his directorial career in a Robert Downey, Sr., mode, lensing two semiunderground comedies featuring future megastar De Niro, who plays an aspiring filmmaker in each. In *Greetings,* De Palma takes mostly accurate satiric aim at such then-topical targets as hard-core conspiracy freaks (represented by Graham), the draft (whence comes the title), the porn-movie biz (in the credibly repulsive person of Garfield), and other late-'60s concerns. De Niro returns in the even funnier *Hi, Mom!*—also out on the Canadian GWN label under the more fanciful handle *Confessions of a Peeping Tom* (!)—highlighted by the hilarious liberal-bashing audience-participation play-within-a-film *Be Black, Baby!* For another excellent artifact of the era—a pic so ahead of its time that it wasn't released until 1989 (!)—see Michael Roemer's deadpan B&W comedy *The Plot Against Harry* (New Yorker); Roemer had earlier helmed the highly recommended 1964 civil-rights-era African-American drama *Nothing but a Man* (New Yorker).

GREMLINS:
THE SERIES

GREMLINS (1984) **½

D: Joe Dante. Zach Galligan, Phoebe Cates, Hoyt Axton, Dick Miller, Scott Brady, Jackie Joseph, Keye Luke. 106 mins. (Warner) DVD

Director Dante crafts a gala creature comedy that's as schizoid as its title thingies—a flick that alternately trashes and wallows in mall-American pop culture. While there are inspired moments and a memorable supporting cast of B-movie vets, Dante and producer Steven Speilberg want to have their cake, eat it, and regurgitate on the audience too. In that sense, the film's ahead of its time. In 1990's *Gremlins 2: The New Batch,* Dante moves the action to NYC in a mostly fun sequel that benefits greatly from Christopher Lee's wryly sinister turn as amoral geneticist Dr. Catheter.

GROUNDHOG DAY (1993) ***

D: Harold Ramis. Bill Murray, Andie MacDowell, Chris Elliott. 103 mins. (Columbia/TriStar) DVD

Cynical journalist Murray finds himself trapped in a *Twilight Zone*–type time warp that compels him to repeat the same day until he gets it right. Ramis's comedy works best in its edgy early reels before slipping a mite too far into sentimentality.

HAIRSPRAY (1988) ***½

D: John Waters. Ricki Lake, Divine, Jerry Stiller, Sonny Bono, Debbie Harry, Pia Zadora. 91 mins. (Columbia/TriStar)

While Waters eschews his customary gross-out tableaux in his debut crossover movie, *Hairspray* still succeeeds as a lively, satiric, and—most vital of all—subversive send-up of the early-'60s teen scene and the brain-damaged beehived "hairhoppers" who populated same. Lake—who looks like she really *could* have been Divine's daughter, had such a fate been biologically possible—stars as Tracy Turnblad, a fat girl who dances her way into the hearts of thousands on *The Corny Collins Show,* a Baltimore B-TV version of Dick Clark's *Bandstand.* Conflict ensues when Ricki's sudden popularity incurs the wrath of slender blond rival Amber Von Tussle (Colleen Fitzpatrick) and her scheming parents (Bono, Harry). Ricki not only triumphs but, with the aid of deejay Motormouth Maybell (ably interpreted by R&B singer Ruth Brown), uses her celebrity to further the cause of integration. In addition to Waters's off-the-wall comedy, *Hairspray* offers an uptempo array of choice period rock tunes. The late Divine is in fine form, as usual, in a dual role as Ricki's supportive mom *and* as racist TV-station owner Arvin Hodgepile. Pia Z. contributes a neat cameo as a raven-tressed beatnik chick (she even recites some of Allen Ginsberg's *Howl!*), and Waters himself turns up as a hypno-happy shrink.

HAPPINESS (1998) **½

D: Todd Solondz. Jane Adams, Elizabeth Ashley, Dylan Baker, Lara Flynn Boyle, Ben Gazzara, Jared Harris, Philip Seymour Hoffman, Louise Lasser, Jon Lovitz, Camryn Manheim, Rufus Read, Cynthia Stevenson. 139 mins. (Trimark) DVD

With *Happiness*—his first film after his highly recommended *Welcome to the Dollhouse* (Columbia/TriStar)—writer/director Solondz wants to have his cake, regurgitate on it, and have *you* eat it too. His overhyped, controversial dark comedy plunges us into a pervert-packed Jersey 'burb as might have been imagined by Krafft-Ebing. The characters are linked by their separate but equally futile search for the titular state, with most pursuing paths better not taken. At the film's core are a trio of sisters—hopelessly naïve plain Jane Adams, moderately successful but emotionally vapid hack writer Boyle, and initially happily married housewife Stevenson, whose bland therapist hubby (Baker, in a subtly scary turn) becomes a not-so-secret pedophile, drugging and sodomizing his oldest son's (Read) young friends. Also in the unhappy mix are a terminally bored Gazzara and flamingly neurotic Lasser as the siblings' newly divorced parents, Hoffman as Boyle's nerdy secret-stalker neighbor, Harris as a thieving Russian cabdriver who has a brief fling with Adams, and Lovitz as Adams' rejected would-be beau. While Solondz incorporates undeniably brilliant bits into his canvas of mundane carnal depravity, he relies too often on arbitrary shock tactics that undercut the flick's flashes of more honest wit. Sort of a cerebral *There's Something About Mary* (Fox), *Happiness* repeatedly opts for easy gross-out tableaux over genuinely subversive satire.

A HARD DAY'S NIGHT (1964) B&W ***

D: Richard Lester. The Beatles, Wilfrid Brambell, Norman Rossington. 90 mins. (Fox Lorber) DVD

Despite an overdose of "cute," Lester's classy Brit equivalent of a vintage Sam Katzman youth-trend quickie remains fun, occasionally clever, and packed with classic Fab Four tunes. Lester's wild and crazy 1965 James Bond spoof, *Help!* (Fox Lorber, DVD), has dated a mite over the intervening decades but still sports enough classic numbers and mirthfully quirky moments to make it worth a return trip. The Beatles' animated feature, *Yellow Submarine,* is also available (DVD).

HEAD (1968) **1/2

D: Bob Rafelson. The Monkees (Mickey Dolenz, Davy Jones, Michael Nesmith, Peter Tork), Victor Mature, Annette Funicello, Teri Garr, Jack Nicholson, Vito Scotti. 86 mins. (Rhino) DVD

The Monkees run amok on a movie set in a Jack Nicholson–coscripted romp that supplies more in the way of vanished pop-cultural artifacts than genuine laughs. Still, *Head* offers a fascinating view of the '60s as they never were—and the giant Victor Mature surely represents one of Hollywood's highest concepts yet. Other highlights include psychedelic graphics, Nehru jackets, clips from Karloff/Lugosi's *The Raven,* and sprightly tunes delivered by diminutive Davy Jones, the Dudley Moore of the group.

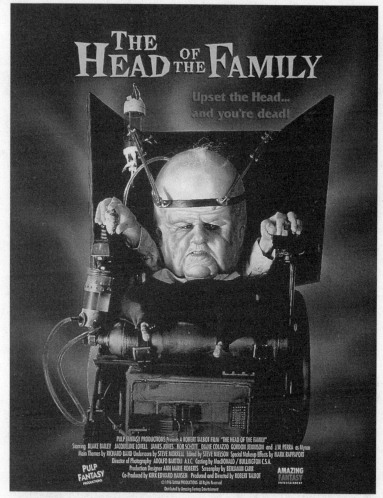

HEAD *GAMES:* Brainy bad guy Myron Stackpool (J. W. Perra) plots his next sinister move in ad art for Full Moon's black comedy *The Head of the Family. Courtesy of Full Moon Studios*

THE HEAD OF THE FAMILY (1996) ***

D: Robert Talbot. Blake Bailey, Jacqueline Lovell, James Jones, Bob Schott, Diane Colazzo, Gordon Jennison, J. W. Perra. 82 mins. (Amazing Fantasy Entertainment/ Full Moon) DVD

Diner operator Lance (Bailey) is having a torrid (and talkative) affair with Loretta (Lovell), who happens to be the wife of local biker gangster Howard (Jennison). Lance's troubles worsen when Howard decides to extort him, offering his dubious "protection" in return for a piece of the proceeds. Our hero stumbles on a potential solution to his problems when he learns that hermetic Myron Stackpool (Perra)—a huge, brainy head atop a tiny, wheelchairbound body—and his weird siblings (Jones, Schott, Colazzo) have been kidnapping and lobotomizing (!) unwary travelers. Lance arranges for Howard to become one of their subjects, then blackmails the bizarre clan, a scheme that leads to dire consequences for most of the pic's principals. With *Head of the Family,* producer/director Talbot, working from Benjamin Carr's original script, assembles a decidedly offbeat, deftly acted frightcom. The droll, articulate Myron is a terrif creation who orchestrates the flick's hands-down highlight— a Marat/Sade–an basement production of *Joan of Arc* performed by several of his lobotomy victims (!). Scripter Carr also penned the generally amusing Full Moon mini-monster romps *Creeps, Hideous!*, and *Mystery Monsters!* (DVD).

HENRY FOOL   (1998) **¹/₂

D: Hal Hartley. Thomas Jay Ryan, James Urbaniak, Parker Posey. 137 mins. (Columbia/TriStar)

Indie auteur Hartley's *Henry Fool* emerges as a frustrating mélange of serious themes, exceedingly sharp, insightful dialogue, and a gritty, specific Queens mise en scène undermined by a penchant for ill-earned "shocks," dead-end detours, and a padded running time. Ryan is fine as Henry Fool, an irresponsible, beer-swilling, self-styled literary "genius" who persuades recessive geek Simon Grim (Urbaniak) to record his own *pensées*. The latter goes on to become a trendy outre punk-lit sensation, while his self-imposed mentor sinks into a life of domestic misery with Urbaniak's sister (ubiquitous indie queen Posey). Hartley's too smart to lens an uninteresting film, and *Henry Fool* is no exception, but less funk, more focus would have made for a sharper work. Other available Hartleys: *The Unbelievable Truth* (Trimark), *Trust* (Republic), *Surviving Desire* (Fox Lorber), *Simple Men, Amateur,* and *Flirt* (all Columbia/TriStar).

HOLLYWOOD CHAINSAW HOOKERS (1988) ***

D: Fred Olen Ray. Gunnar Hansen, Linnea Quigley, Jay Richardson, Dawn Wildsmith, Michelle Bauer. 90 mins. (Camp Video)

Prolific auteur Ray's indefatigability pays off with a *good* campy T&A

gore comedy. Though Ray resorts to the hoary narrative device of relating his tale from yet another mock hard-boiled private eye's POV (well played by Richardson), we *do* get the promised gang of chainsaw-toting tarts ("They Charge an Arm and a Leg!") who kill for the love of their crazed Egyptian cult leader (rather woodenly interpreted by former "Leatherface" Hansen). In fact, there's more comedy than gore in this postmodern ode to splatter pioneer H. G. (*Blood Feast*) Lewis, much of it supplied by the ever lovely Linnea, who not only solidifies her niche as a gutter-flick Goldie Hawn but dances topless during a lengthy club scene. In sum, if you like the title, you'll doubtless dig the movie too.

HOLLYWOOD HARRY   (1985) **¹/₂

D: Robert Forster. Robert Forster, Shannon Wilcox, Kathrine Forster, Joe Spinell. 96 mins. (Media, n.i.d.)

Hollywood Harry recounts the misadventures of a down-and-out private dick (Forster, who also produced and directed) who spends his time scarfing cold pizza, guzzling Jim Beam, and quoting Arnold Toynbee (!). Harry's lowlife is irrevocably altered, however, when his runaway teen niece (played by Bob's real-life daughter Kathrine) turns up at his doorstep. *Hollywood Harry* mixes overly broad bits and in-jokes with genuinely affecting, expertly scripted scenes delineating the growing rapport between the secretly soft-boiled Harry and his hitherto neglected niece. Both Forsters turn in winning work, as does Spinell as Harry's equally inept partner.

HOLLYWOOD SHUFFLE   (1987) ***

D: Robert Townsend. Robert Townsend, Anne-Marie Johnson, Damon Wayans, Lisa Mende, Franklin Ajaye. 80 mins. (Virgin Vision, n.i.d.)

Townsend's one-man movie—he produced, directed, starred, coscripted, and raised the hundred

grand it took to make this surprisingly slick-looking flick—is a sometimes brilliant look at the schizy life of struggling black actor Bobby Taylor (Townsend), who tries to keep his menial job at the Winky Dinky Dog fast-food joint while auditioning for a demeaning role as a stereotypical street hood in Tinseltown Pictures's *Jivetime Jimmy's Revenge.* Townsend's pointed yet amiable satire also benefits from some fine ensemble work by the Hollywood Shuffle Players.

HOMEGROWN   (1998) **¹/₂

D: Stephen Gyllenhaal. Billy Bob Thornton, Hank Azaria, Kelly Lynch, Ryan Phillippe, Jon Bon Jovi, Judge Reinhold, John Lithgow, Jamie Lee Curtis, Jon Tenney, Ted Danson, Matt Clark. 101 mins. (Columbia/TriStar) DVD

Three lowly grass growers (Thornton, Azaria, Phillippe) find themselves in sudden possession of a potentially lucrative crop in Stephen (*Certain Fury, Paris Trout*) Gyllenhaal's uneven exercise in black-comic marijuana noir. When their mysterious employer (Lithgow) is murdered before their eyes, our stoned Three Stooges, with accomplice Lynch, try to parlay the situation into an ill-gotten windfall. Instead, they run afoul of the law, the Mafia, Lithgow's killers, and their own rampant paranoia. On the upside, Thornton and Azaria lend credibility to their roles, some of the dialogue rings true, and Gyllenhaal and coscripter Nicholas (Son of Elia) Kazan present a seemingly accurate portrait of the Pacific Northwest dope business and culture. But *Homegrown* falls short of its larger ambition to be a *Treasure of the Sierra Madre* for the toke set.

HOUSEWIFE   (A.K.A. *BONE*) (1972) ***

D: Larry Cohen. Andrew Duggan, Yaphet Kotto, Joyce Van Patten, Jeannie Berlin. 96 mins. (New World, n.i.d.)

Cohen's directorial debut stars Duggan and Van Patten as a middle-aged Beverly Hills couple whose posh pad is invaded by black thief "Bone" (Kotto, in a nuanced turn). A perverse treatise on identity and stereotyping, Cohen's farce takes its first twist when Kotto sends cashless used-car honcho Duggan to the bank for a hefty withdrawal, while he holds housewife Van Patten hostage. Duggan soon determines he'd rather keep the dough and let his naggy spouse go (a plot hook later employed in the better-known *Ruthless People*) and winds up in an offbeat tryst with professional shoplifter Berlin. Meanwhile, back at the manse, Kotto and Van Patten discover that, despite their ethnic and gender differences, they may have more in common than they'd originally imagined. First and foremost a writer's movie (almost a filmed play at times), *Housewife* suffers from some awkward staging but rates as a must for black-comedy fans.

HOW TO GET REVENGE!
(1989) **1/2

D: Bob Logan. Linda Blair. 45 mins. (Starmaster, n.i.d.)

Directed by Logan, who later helmed Linda's *Exorcist* spoof, *Repossessed* (see index), *How to Get Revenge!* opens with a memorable disclaimer: "The following program is presented for ENTERTAINMENT PURPOSES ONLY. It is intended as a humorous exercise for mature audiences. The producers expressly condemn the actual use of any of the following material." That out of the way, Linda proceeds to interview various real-life vengeance experts—mostly cops and private dicks—who supply surprisingly vile schemes involving everything from phone and postal harassment to marriage wrecking. Indeed, the tape's disclaimer notwithstanding, the scams dramatized herein are far more useful than humorous.

I'M GONNA GIT YOU SUCKA
(1988) ***

D: Keenen Ivory Wayans. Keenen Ivory Wayans, Bernie Casey, Antonio Fargas, Jim Brown, Isaac Hayes, Jan'et Dubois, Damon Wayans, Steve James, John Vernon, Clarence Williams III. 89 mins. (MGM)

Wayans's "blaxploitation" parody boasts a powerful all-star lineup that includes Brown and Hayes (looking convincingly out of shape) as retired tough guys Hammer and Slammer; Fargas, who deftly reprises his patented pimp role; urban-action stalwart Casey; Vernon as token honky heavy Mr. Big; and the late, great Steve James as terminally out-of-sync chopsocky champ Kung-Fu Joe. Wayans doubles as *Sucka*'s decidedly unmacho hero, a returning GI clerk-typist who's continually being rescued by his far fiercer mom (Dubois), while younger brother Damon scores as a Mr. Big henchman who suffers nonstop abuse at the hands of both the good guys and his own evil employers. Though Wayans's sometimes sketchy script and occasionally ill-timed direction keep the flick from soaring to max satiric heights, *Sucka* provides its share of honest laughs.

INNOCENT BLOOD   (1992) **1/2

D: John Landis. Anne Parillaud, Robert Loggia, Anthony LaPaglia, Don Rickles. 112 mins. (Warner) DVD

Sort of a Mafia-vampire variation on his earlier *American Werewolf in London*, Landis's bloodsucker romp pits sexy she-vamp Anne (*La Femme Nikita*) Parillaud against a crew of Pittsburgh wiseguys whom our heroine affectionately refers to as "my food." The mob-gobbling gal has the authorities baffled until she teams up with undercover cop LaPaglia to stop crazed capo Loggia, whose necking session with Anne has transformed him from a monstrous Mafioso into a *bloodsuck-*

ing monstrous Mafioso. The assembled thesps look like they had a good time with this one—though none more than Loggia, who attacks his fangster role with relish (to say nothing of ham). Rickles turns in credible work as Loggia's nervous attorney-turned-vampire; his sun-driven meltdown provides the pic with one of its primo FX set pieces (courtesy of makeup maven Steve Johnson). Landis also peppers *Innocent Blood* with offbeat cameos, including bits by *Famous Monsters* founder Forry Ackerman, directors Dario Argento, Sam Raimi, Michael Ritchie, and Frank Oz (in a particularly funny bit), *Night of the Living Dead* FX ace Tom Savini, and scream queen Linnea Quigley (who gives her pipes a high-decibel airing). Buffs will also appreciate clips from *Beast from 20,000 Fathoms, Dracula, Horror of Dracula, Phantom of the Rue Morgue,* and *Strangers on a Train.* Several effective cheap scares and disgusto images (especially during an autopsy sequence) dot the movie. *Innocent Blood* is the type of frightcom that goes in one eye and out the other but supplies fair gory fun while it lasts.

IRMA VEP   (1996)
B&W/COLOR***

D: Olivier Assayas. Maggie Cheung, Jean-Pierre Leaud, Lou Castel. 96 mins. (Fox Lorber) DVD

French auteur Assayas's ultra-inside cinema satire loses a bit in the transatlantic translation, both literally, when the Euro cast members speak English (former Godard/Truffaut hero Leaud especially needs subtitles), and figuratively, since the satire spins on an intimate knowledge of Gallic celluloid history, debates, and concerns. Leaud plays a largely washed-up director who decides to remake and update Louis Feuillade's iconic 1915 silent serial *Les Vampires* (Water Bearer), in France a sacrosanct pop-cultural milestone that's about as remake-friendly as Griffith's *Birth of a Nation* would be Stateside. In a perverse move, Leaud decides to cast the quintessentially Parisian character of Irma Vep (an anagram for *vampire*, but you already figured that out)—a femme-fatale cabaret performer who doubles as the latex-clad leader of a gang of anarchic cat burglars—with Asian action starlet Maggie (*Heroic Trio*) Cheung (playing herself). The production's already stuck in serious chaos when Maggie arrives, with the confused and constantly bickering crew at the mercy of the flaky Leaud, himself on the verge of a nervous breakdown. One of the better digressions sees Maggie interviewed on the set by a populist cinephile who promotes John Woo and Jean-Claude Van Damme over his homeland's dessicated, introspective "intellectual" auteurs but can't get an uncomfortable Maggie to agree with him. (Another, painfully bored character complains she's seen every movie in town, "even the new Seagal.") Vet Euro thesp Castel supplies amusement as another aging has-been who's hired to replace Leaud once his breakdown kicks in in earnest. (Termite note: For a film so steeped in cinematic minutiae, there's an odd continuity error, when Castel drains the same glass of beer twice. Unless that's one of Assayas's more obscure in-jokes.) Die-hard buffs and Cheung fans will want to tune in.

IT CAME FROM HOLLYWOOD (1982) ***

D: Malcolm Leo, Andrew Solt. Dan Aykroyd, John Candy, Gilda Radner. 80 mins. (Paramount)

Scripter Dana Olson's camp-crazed compilation film offers choice excerpts from scores of bad movies, including an Ed Wood segment hosted by the late John Candy. A must for celluloid-turkey buffs.

IT CAME FROM SOMEWHERE ELSE (1988) B&W/COLOR***

D: Howard Hassler. William VanArsdale, Robert Buckley, Al Johnson, Donald Aldrich, George Carlson, Richard Speeter, Larry Sutin. 90 mins. (Platinum)

Any vid that advertises itself as "Absolutely the Worst Film Ever Made" is a sure bet to pique your Phantom's curiosity and skepticism. As it turns out, *It Came from Somewhere Else* is far from the worst. In fact, this Minnesota-made obscurity shapes up as a very funny deadpan send-up of inept '50s sci-fi cheapies, contemporary horror/exploitation excesses, and small-town banality. Director Hassler, lensing mostly in black and white, achieves admirable verisimilitude in relating his entertainingly off-the-wall tale about a wave of alien-engineered spontaneous combustions that begin eliminating the largely brain-dead inhabitants of Grand Bosh, Minnesota. Among the town's odder residents are a hapless '50s sitcom-inspired couple—the perpetually grinning Mr. Buckner (Speeter) and his spouse (played by an actor in drag); a slew of obnoxious teens; and several aggressively indifferent authority figures—corrupt mayor Carlson, Von Daniken–influenced government researcher Sutin, useless lawmen VanArsdale and Aldrich, and geekoid, chain-smoking doctor Buckley, who's cheerfully spreading terminal cancer among Grand Bosh's populace via his beloved X-ray machine (!). The film integrates clever takeoffs on everything from Ed Wood's *Plan 9* to kung-fu movies to *Fail-Safe*, while intermittently switching to color for equally witty spoofs of early-'60s nudies and '80s gore orgies. More impressively, the filmmakers avoid the self-consciousness that often pervades low-budget regional parodies and never halt their story's forward momentum for the sake of a throwaway joke. *It Came from Somewhere Else* is one entry in the overcrowded genre-parody field that's well worth searching out.

JACK FROST (1997) **½

D: Michael Cooney. Chris Allport, Stephen Mendel, F. William Parker, Eileen Seeley, Rob LaBelle, Zack Eginton, Scott MacDonald. 89 mins. (A-Pix) DVD

An unpromising premise receives unexpectedly fun treatment in this Colorado-lensed indie. A secret genetic experiment performed on about-to-be-executed serial killer Jack Frost (MacDonald) goes seriously awry when the latter makes an attempted break. Though he's soon incinerated by an exploding prison van, Jack's genetic material merges with a handy snowbank that's later molded into a primitive snowman. Like a frigid variation on *The H-Man*, Jack not only lives but can melt and regroup at will. He sets out to fulfill his vow of vengeance against original arresting officer Allport, sheriff of the *Fargo*-like alpine hamlet of Snomonton, Colorado. Writer/director Cooney maintains a deadpan tone as the frozen fiend has his way with an assortment of brain-locked locals in a series of clever slay set pieces. *Jack Frost* runs on about a reel too long, but fans of quirky fright spoofs like *Monster in the Closet* and *Bloodsuckers from Outer Space* (see index) should deem *Jack* worthy of an overnight winter rental.

JAN SVANKMAJER: ALCHEMIST OF THE SURREAL (1989) ***

D: Jan Svankmajer. Live/animated. 75 mins. (Kino)

Svankmajer's featurettes combine live action with a full range of animation techniques to tell blackly comic parables that are never gross but always grotesque. Best among the shorts collected here are "Coffin Nails," a Punch and Judy variation performed by two puppets and one live guinea pig (!); "Jabberwocky," a simultaneously scary and lyrical Lewis Carroll salute; and an innovative rendition of Poe's "The Fall of the House of Usher," an animated tour of the decaying title abode, accompanied by a reading of Edgar Allan's actual story, that manages to be eerier than most dramatized feature versions of that venerable fear fable. While Svankmajer's shorts share similarities with such disparate talents as Buster Keaton, Ernie Kovacs, Franz Kafka, Terry Gilliam, David Lynch, and Luis Buñuel, the Czech animator's darkly ironic imagination and eclectic approach rate as truly unique. Svankmajer's full-length *Alice* (First Run), *Conspirators of Pleasure,* and *Faust* (both Kino) are also available.

JOHNNY STECCHINO   (1992) ***

D: Roberto Benigni. Roberto Benigni, Nicoletta Braschi, Paolo Bonacelli, Franco Volpi. 100 mins. (New Line)

Benigni directs, coscripts, and plays dual roles, as a school-bus driver and his Mafioso look-alike, in this quirky farce. Few comics can work so many escalating variations on what at first seem like throwaway riffs—herein involving bananas, kissing, and faked manual palsy, among others—as Benigni, whose sneaky comedic logic operates to often hilariously subversive, though rarely mean-spirited, effect.

KENTUCKY FRIED MOVIE (1977) ***

D: John Landis. Donald Sutherland, Bill Bixby, Evan Kim, Tony Dow. 85 mins. (Video Treasures)

Landis and the ZAZ Team (in their pre-*Airplane!* days) apply the *Groove Tube* (Hen's Tooth) approach to this bright anthology of movie parodies. Similar sketch-oriented celluloid satires include Peter Winograd's *Flicks*

(Media), and Ira Miller's *Loose Shoes,* a.k.a. *Coming Attractions* (Key), while *The Jet Benny Show* (United) and *Tunnelvision* (Hen's Tooth) tackle TV.

KIDS IN THE HALL: BRAIN CANDY (1996) ***1/2

D: Kelly Makin. David Foley, Bruce McCullough, Kevin McDonald, Mark McKinney, Scott Thompson. 88 mins. (Paramount)

The creators and stars of the long-running eponymous Comedy Central teleseries deliver an oft brilliant Huxley-esque fable about brain-dead consumerism, corporate greed, Prozac mania, and the (mostly depressing) quality of modern life. When financially strapped pharmaceutical giant Roritor's egomaniacal head, Don (McKinney), puts the squeeze on his R&D teams, scientist Chris (McDonald) prematurely announces that his new antidepressant, which locks the subject's brain in to its happiest memory and sustains that mood indefinitely, is ready for an unsuspecting public. Roritor marketing head Cisco (McCullough) dubs the resultant product "Gleemonex." In no time, Gleemonex becomes the nation's most popular drug, even putting crack out of business, while Chris is revered as a hero—until some unanticipated side effects kick in. The *Kids* quintet each play several different roles, of both genders and all ages, and do so with such unobtrusive ease that you really believe you're watching a cast of dozens. Their satiric skewering of our contempo culture is both deadpan and dead-on, with Chris's accurately inane appearance on the fictional *Nina Bedford Show,* a "straight" 'burb guy's (Thompson) acceptance of his homosexuality (complete with musical production number), and re-creations of the Gleemonex addicts' hilarious "happiest" memories supply a few of the flick's many highlights. Look for Janeane Garofalo in a nearly invisible cameo.

KILLER CONDOM (KONDOM DES GRAUENS)   (1996) **1/2

D: Martin Walz. Udo Samel, Peter Lohmeyer, Iris Berben, Marc Richter, Leonard Lansink. Subtitled. 108 mins. (Troma)

A homicidal prophylactic—autonomous *vagina dentata* described as a "cross between a giant worm, a jellyfish, and a piranha" (ouch)—feasts on the phallic population of Manhattan's sleazy Hotel Quickie in Walz's German-language, English-subtitled black comedy, based on a Rolf Konig comic book. Samel stars as your typical gay, hard-boiled, mega-endowed Sicilian-born NYC cop determined to end the toothed condom's bloody reign of terror. Though it ultimately bites off more than it can chew, thematically speaking, *Killer Condom* has more on its mind than your typical homegrown Troma splatstick outing. Part gore-movie spoof in a Teutonic John Waters vein (with a requisite *Psycho* shower-scene send-up), part broad political satire, *Killer Condom* is, in the end, nothing less than a plea for tolerance, generously lubricated with outrageous gags, kinky erotica, and literally splashy special effects. Swiss creature designer H. R. *(Alien, Species)* Giger scores a "Creative Consultant" credit, while *Necromantik* auteur Jorg Buttgereit handles the special effects.

THE KING OF COMEDY (1983) ****

D: Martin Scorsese. Robert De Niro, Jerry Lewis, Sandra Bernhard. 109 mins. (Columbia/TriStar)

Scorsese's brilliant, prescient, initially misunderstood (it was the lowest-grossing major-studio release of 1983) media satire about would-be comic Rupert Pupkin (De Niro) hits nary a false note and features great perfs by leads De Niro, Lewis, and Bernhard.

KING OF HEARTS   (1966) **½

D: Philippe De Broca. Alan Bates, Genevieve Bujold, Pierre Brasseur. 102 mins. (Fox)

Scottish soldier Bates wanders into an abandoned French village appropriated by escaped mental patients. De Broca's World War I–set fable wavers between the satiric and the sentimental and has been seen at least twice by virtually everyone who came of age in the late '60s. For a different take on a similar situation, see Sam Fuller's *The Big Red One* (Warner).

LITTLE MURDERS   (1971) ***

D: Alan Arkin. Elliott Gould, Marcia Rodd, Vincent Gardenia. 110 mins. (Fox)

Arkin cameos as a nerve-shattered NYC homicide detective and handles directorial chores on the film version of Jules Feiffer's theatrical black comedy about urban paranoia and domestic emotional violence. You probably won't see clips from this one turning up in any "I Love N.Y." campaigns.

THE LITTLE SHOP OF HORRORS (1960) B&W ***

D: Roger Corman. Jonathan Haze, Jackie Joseph, Mel Welles. 70 mins. (Rhino) DVD

Haze (doing an ersatz Jerry Lewis impersonation) stars as the ill-fated Seymour, a skid-row floral worker enslaved by his flesh-eating plant, Audrey Junior (voiced by scripter Charles B. Griffith, who also doubles as an on-screen crook), in the original Roger Corman celluloid "sick joke" that inspired the hit off-Broadway musical and lavish Hollywood remake of the same name.

LITTLE SHOP OF HORRORS (1986) ***

D: Frank Oz. Rick Moranis, Ellen Greene, Steve Martin. 88 mins. (Warner) Special Edition DVD

Fueled by a solid doo-wop score (by Howard Ashman and Alan Menken), Oz's screen version of the off-Broadway musical based on Corman's 1960 frightcom moves along at a bouncy clip, while Steve Martin and Bill Murray contribute top cameos as a sadistic dentist and his gleefully masochistic patient, respectively. The Four Tops' Levi Stubbs provides the voice of the man-eating plant (herein dubbed Audrey II).

LIVING IN OBLIVION   (1995) ***

D: Tom DiCillo. Steve Buscemi, Catherine Keener, Dermot Mulroney, James LeGros. 92 mins. (Columbia/TriStar)

NYC-based auteur DiCillo crafts a very funny, unobtrusively twisty comedy about the triumphs and (more often) travails of low-budget indie filmmaking. Buscemi, as nervous novice director Nick, heads a fine ensemble cast in a flick that captures the extreme insularity, anxiety, and excitement of a shoestring shoot where problems are long and time and money short. LeGros turns in witty work as a self-styled Hollywood "maverick"—a character reportedly based on Brad Pitt, star of DiCillo's *Johnny Suede* (Paramount)—who desires to dabble in cutting-edge indie films but whose ego can't be contained by the claustrophobic set. While insider references abound, *Living in Oblivion* is exceedingly viewer-friendly, and DiCillo deserves credit for keeping his film as low-key and character-driven as it is satiric.

LOBSTER MAN FROM MARS (1989) **½

D: Stanley Sheff. Tony Curtis, Deborah Foreman, Patrick Macnee. 84 mins. (Artisan)

While not quite as top-shelf a send-up as *Amazon Women on the Moon* or *Night of the Creeps*, Sheff's monster-movie spoof (with a central riff lifted from *The Producers*) is well worth catching for its memorable cast alone, from Curtis to Billy Barty, Bobby (Boris) Pickett, and Patrick (*The Avengers*) Macnee, along with nods to such '50s faves as *Plan 9 from Outer Space*, *Robot Monster*, and Roger Corman's *It Conquered the World*.

LOST IN AMERICA   (1985) ****

D: Albert Brooks. Albert Brooks, Julie Hagerty, Garry Marshall. 91 mins. (Warner)

The best of Brooks's bright cinematic satires finds our hero and spouse Hagerty, accompanied by their $100,000 "nest egg," on a quest to discover America. A classic Las Vegas layover jump-starts the duo on a downward spiral that lands them in the working-class wilds of Stafford, Arizona. *Lost* is aces all the way, with a sharp cameo by comedy producer Marshall as a bemused casino owner. Other recommended Brooks romps include his 1978 mockumentary debut, *Real Life* (Paramount), 1981's *Modern Romance* (Columbia/TriStar), with a hilarious film-within-a-film segment starring George Kennedy, and 1991's *Defending Your Life* (Warner), with Meryl Streep and Rip Torn.

LOVE AND DEATH ON LONG ISLAND   (1997) ***½

D: Richard Kwietniowski. John Hurt, Jason Priestley, Fiona Loewi, Maury Chaykin. 93 mins. (Universal)

Working from Gilbert Adair's novel, writer/director Kwietniowski crafts an engagingly oddball tale of unrequited love. Veteran Brit thesp John (*The Elephant Man*) Hurt is nothing short of brilliant as Giles De'ath, a stodgy but secretly soulful (and thoroughly out-of-it) academic author whose absentmindedness accidentally lands him in a local bijou where *Hot-pants College II* is the current attraction. There, the lonely, long-closeted gay widower develops a deep crush on one of the on-screen actors, sensitive hunk Ronnie Bostock (winningly portrayed by *Beverly Hills 90210* stud Priestley). Giles feeds his growing obsession by renting all of Ronnie's movies (fictional epics like *Skidmarks* and *Tex Mex*) on video and assembling a scrapbook of teen-zine clippings. The bemused Britisher ultimately decides to vacation in Bostock's hometown of Chesterton, Long Island, where, via a calculated encounter with Ronnie's girlfriend, Audrey (Loewi), he gains access to his newfound love object's life. Hurt turns in Oscar-worthy work in a charmingly quirky showcase full of fresh fish-out-of-water comic riffs and moments of touching drama. (We're also treated to hilariously dead-on clips from Ronnie's imaginary B-movie oeuvre.) Kwietniowski pulls off a true coup in presenting a completely believable London and an accurate Long Island (with Nova Scotia effectively subbing for the latter) and yields flawless perfs from his supporting cast, especially busy character actor Chaykin as a Long Island luncheonette owner. Though peppered with well-earned poignant tableaux, this loose, transplanted *Death in Venice* update remains resolutely upbeat throughout. We know that, while Giles's impossible dream can never reach complete fulfillment, both he and Ronnie gain in emotional strength as a result of their offbeat encounter.

LOVE AT FIRST BITE   (1979) ***

D: Stan Dragoti. George Hamilton, Susan St. James, Richard Benjamin, Dick Shawn. 96 mins. (Orion)

Former leading-man stiff Hamilton made a surprising comeback as a campy comedian in a lively vampire romp that sees an uprooted Dracula attempt to cope with life in the Big Apple.

THE LOVED ONE   (1965) B&W ***

D: Tony Richardson. Robert Morse, Jonathan Winters, Rod Steiger. 118 mins. (MGM)

While taking wild liberties with Evelyn Waugh's caustic novel, Richardson and top-shelf scripters Terry Southern and Christopher Isherwood assemble a bizarre, all-star black comedy about the L.A. funeral biz that boasts its own macabre virtues and features memorable work by Steiger as mortician Mr. Joyboy.

LUNATICS: A LOVE STORY (1992) **1/2

D: Josh Becker. Ted Raimi, Deborah Foreman, Bruce Campbell. 87 mins. (Columbia/TriStar)

Dedicated followers of the Sam Raimi/Bruce Campbell genre orbit might want to scope out this black comedy, produced by Raimi and Campbell (who doubles on-screen as a Hollywood heel), written and directed by Raimi protégé Becker, and toplining Sam's bro' Ted in a Woody Allen-esque turn as a bespectacled agoraphobe bugged by wild hallucinations. Becker's offbeat romance unites Ted with disaster-prone femme Foreman. Best here are Ted's paranoid fantasies, which find him dogged by a persistent rap group, rabid surgeons, and a giant spider that's escaped from his own brain (!).

LUST IN THE DUST   (1985) **1/2

D: Paul Bartel. Tab Hunter, Divine, Lainie Kazan. 85 mins. (New World, n.i.d.)

Director Bartel gathers a colorful cast, including Kazan, Cesar Romero, Henry Silva, and Woody Strode, for his amiably lewd lampoon of vintage American and '60s-era spaghetti westerns.

THE MAGIC CHRISTIAN   (1969) ***

D: Joseph McGrath. Peter Sellers, Raquel Welch, Ringo Starr. 93 mins. (Republic)

A great comedic cast, including Roman Polanski and Monty Python-ites John Cleese and the late Graham Chapman, and lively score (by Badfinger) bring Terry Southern's greed-themed novella to bright, quirky screen life.

MAN BITES DOG   (1992) B&W ***

D: Rémy Belvaux. Benoît Poelvoorde, Remy Belvaux, André Bonzel, Jenny Drye, Malou Madou. Subtitled. 95 mins. Uncut director's version (NC-17) and unrated edited version (Fox Lorber).

"Movie Bites Audience" might be a more fitting title for this brilliantly rendered but exceedingly raw and brutal Belgian satire. A no-budget B&W mockumentary hatched by on-screen principals Belvaux, Poelvoorde, and Bonzel, *Man Bites Dog* sends up the vicarious blood lust exploited by "reality TV" shows. The anarchic flick chronicles the lethal misadventures of a naïve docu-film crew (Belvaux, Bonzel, Jean-Marc Chenut) who follow garrulous, philosophical killer Ben (cocreator Poelvoorde in a charismatic turn) on his rounds as he shoots, strangles, and otherwise dispatches a wide variety of victims, including postmen, pensioners, and even small children. The passive crewmembers eventually become active accomplices, while Ben reciprocates by using some of his stolen lucre to buy film stock for his impoverished biographers (!). Along the way we meet the motormouthed maniac's mother and grandparents—comparatively normal shopkeepers enacted by Poelvoorde's real-life relatives—and other figures from Ben's off-duty life. *Man Bites Dog*'s idiosyncratic blend of deadpan wit and verité violence won't be (to put it mildly) everyone's cup of black comedy. There are wrenching stretches where it's easy to forget the filmmakers' ironic intent—until Ben's absurdist bravado or a crewman's gaffe returns us to the pic's irreverent roots. But adventurous viewers should find these then-twentysomething auteurs' bold foray into literally cutting-edge satire as unforgettable as it is unsettling.

THE MAN WITH TWO BRAINS (1983) ****

D: Carl Reiner. Steve Martin, Kathleen Turner, David Warner, Merv Griffin. 90 mins. (Warner) DVD

Reiner and Martin pool their brains and talents to create a deft sci-fi movie spoof that also has some pointed things to say re the stalemate between the sexes. Lensed in bright cartoon colors, *Man* features an inspired performance by Martin as the desperate scientist torn between cruel spouse Turner's tempting body and the disembodied brain (voiced by Sissy Spacek) he *really* loves.

MARQUIS (1990) ***

D: Henri Xhonneux. François Marthouret, Isabelle Canet-Wolfe. 88 mins. (First Run Features)

In *Marquis,* loosely drawn from Sade's *Justine,* Sade is depicted as a dog who holds lengthy philosophical discussions with his perpetually erect "manhood" (or, perhaps more accurately, *doghood*), Justine is a cow with human breasts and udders, and other Bastille personnel are represented by hens, roosters, and rats, all played by live actors in elaborate masks. There's even a pork-trafficking pig who, in a brief splatter sequence, cuts off his own leg to satisfy angry creditors (!). The overall effect is like watching an extremely perverse, determinedly raunchy rendition of Sade's final prison days on the eve of the French Revolution as depicted by the Muppets. (Not too surprising, since director Xhonneux and scripter/art director Roland

Topor had earlier lent their whimsical talents to the long-running French kiddie TV series *Telechat.*) While *Marquis,* which combines occasional claymation sequences with the bestial live action, definitely doesn't fall into your wholesome family-entertainment category, the film provides bawdy, imaginative fun.

MARS ATTACKS! (1996) **½

D: Tim Burton. Jack Nicholson, Danny DeVito, Glenn Close, Rod Steiger, Martin Short, Jim Brown, Pam Grier, Tom Jones. 106 mins. (Warner) DVD

Based on the infamous, wonderfully lurid 1962 bubble-gum-card set, *Mars Attacks!* takes us into live-action cartoon territory as our nation's invaded by hordes of diminutive Martians sporting big brains and bad 'tudes. The result is a mixed bag of inspired alien anarchy and tired slapstick. Nicholson, in dual roles, is fun as an oily U.S. president, less so as a Vegas-cowboy gambling czar, while Short is more consistently amusing as a leering aide seduced, in the pic's funniest sequence, by a Martian disguised as an earthly glam slut (Burton's then-off-screen squeeze Lisa Marie, later on view as slinky B-movie diva Vampira in the same auteur's *Ed Wood*). Crooner Tom Jones stretches as himself, while erstwhile "blaxploitation" heavyweights Brown and Grier enjoy solid roles as an estranged couple.

THE MASK (1994) ***

D: Charles Russell. Jim Carrey, Peter Riegert, Peter Greene, Amy Yasbeck, Richard Jeni, Cameron Diaz. 100 mins. (New Line) DVD

When dweeb bank-worker Carrey—establishing himself here as a Jerry Lewis (or at least Charlie Callas) for the '90s and launching his ascent up the big-time comedy ladder—plucks the lost title adornment from a polluted urban river, he soon learns that it's his ticket to a new identity and wild lifestyle

as a green-faced, zoot-suited superhero with killer dance moves and a flair for belting out old Desi Arnaz tunes (!). The elastic Carrey is nearly upstaged by his faithful Fido, Milo, who helps him out of numerous scrapes with both the law (represented by a hard-nosed Riegert) and villainous nightclub owner Greene. Though *The Mask,* adapted from the comic-book series of the same name, lacks a strong story line, Carrey's crazed antics, a lively vintage score, Diaz's ultrafoxy presence, and a dazzling array of spectacular comic FX easily compensate for the drab plot and only occasionally witty dialogue.

MATINEE (1993) ***½

D: Joe Dante. John Goodman, Cathy Moriarty, Simon Fenton, Omri Katz, James Villemaire, Jesse White. 99 mins. (Universal) DVD

Matinee rates as an excellent evocation of the Cuban missile crisis, William Castle–inspired gimmick flicks, and other fun stuff from 1962. *Matinee* unfolds in Key West, where 15-year-old navy brat and fright-film buff Gene Loomis (Fenton) feels the encroaching crisis more keenly than most. Not only is he a scant 90 miles from Cuba, but his dad's stationed on one of the ships blockading the island's ports. Arriving in the nick to exploit and alleviate the tense situation is flamboyant B-movie showman Larry Woolsey (ebulliently interpreted by Goodman), accompanied by downscale starlet and current squeeze Ruth Corday (Moriarty), a pair of professional shills (Dante perennial Dick Miller and moonlighting auteur John Sayles), and a print of *Mant!,* an insect-mutation romp lensed in "Atomo-Vision" and "Rumble-Rama." While Woolsey preps the local bijou for a test screening of his latest creation, Gene and friends try to conduct typical teen intrigues under the threat of possible imminent annihilation. Director Dante and scripters Jerico and Charlie Haas rarely hit a false note in fleshing out their potentially fragile conceit. For once, the on-screen teens aren't obnoxious little lustbuckets but relatively credible kids (though Villemaire's would-be lyrical leather-jacketed rebel stretches it a mite), while the B&W *Mant!* parody, featuring uncredited appearances by '50s stalwarts Kevin McCarthy, William Schallert, and Robert Cornthwaite, emerges as the sharpest celluloid schlock satire to surface since *Amazon Women on the Moon* (to which Dante also contributed). *Matinee* even boasts its share of poignant moments, as well as some keenly written and delivered paeans to the medium's magic. Indeed, movie magic, an elusive quality missing from a majority of mainstream pics, is a commodity *Matinee* has in spades.

ME AND THE MOB   (1994) ***

D: Frank Rainone. James Lorinz, Tony Darrow, Sandra Bullock, Frank Gio, Richard Bright, John Costelloe, Stephen Lee. 85 mins. (Arrow)

Originally lensed back in '92 under the working title *Who Do I Gotta Kill?*, *Me and the Mob* is a modest, mostly amusing showcase for deadpan comic actor James (*Frankenhooker*) Lorinz, sort of a younger Steven Wright on caffeine. Lorinz, who coscripted (with Rocco Simonelli and director Rainone), plays a struggling author who takes the advice of his gruff agent (a deft Lee) to do a "real-life crime story" by hooking up with his mobster uncle Tony (Darrow). Unfortunately for our hero, Uncle Tony envisions a more active mob role for him. What follows is a lightly plotted series of set pieces—some of them very funny, as when Jimmy's girlfriend, Lori (the since-ascendant Bullock), breaks up with him while simultaneously making passionate love. *GoodFellas* alum Darrow and several other familiar faces from NYC's celluloid Italian Connection provide adroit perfs as assorted mobsters. A master of offbeat comic timing, Lorinz is likewise in top form here, delivering his patented distracted asides and side-of-the-mouth

soliloquies as fate and the mob bounce him from one sticky situation to the next. Look for Steve Buscemi in an uncredited cameo as a paranoid conspiracy nut.

MEET THE APPLEGATES   (1991) ***

D: Michael Lehman. Ed Begley, Jr., Stockard Channing, Dabney Coleman. 90 mins. (Media)

Amazon insects mutate into a typical American family in Michael (*Heathers*) Lehman's underrated eco-comedy, released theatrically as simply *The Applegates*. Coleman impresses as a humanoid insect in drag, while Kevin Yagher contributes some excellent makeup FX.

MEET THE FEEBLES   (1989) ***1/2

D: Peter Jackson. 94 mins. (MTI)

Jackson's outrageous exercise in brutal whimsy—coscripted by Fran Walsh, Stephen Sinclair, and Danny Mul-

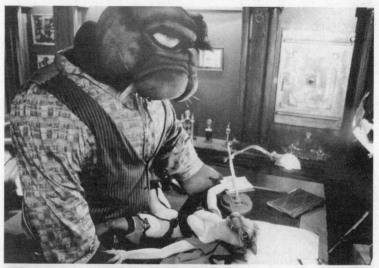

PUPPETS BEHAVING BADLY: Puppets act up on a grand scale in typically surreal scenes from Peter Jackson's madcap media satire *Meet the Feebles*. *Courtesy of Darrin Ramage*

heron—takes us behind the scenes at the popular TV show *The Feebles Variety Hour,* an extravaganza populated by a sprawling menagerie of exotic, often neurotic creatures. Our central story follows shy young hedgehog Robert, newly hired as a *Feebles* chorus boy, as he makes his scandalized way through the cast and crew's sundry backstage intrigues. Major plot threads include the fading relationship between star diva Heidi—"a gorgeous hunk of hippohood"—and *Feebles* founder Bletch, a gruff walrus who runs a lucrative heroin racket on the side; the travails of alcoholic host Harry, a sex-crazed rabbit who believes he's contracted a terminal venereal disease; lumbering Sid the elephant's ongoing paternity-suit troubles with a chicken he's impregnated (!); and the nightmarish 'Nam flashbacks of Wynyard, the show's strung-out knife thrower. The press is represented by a literal fly on the wall whose preferred pursuits include muckraking and coprophagia. While Robert woos beautiful poodle Lucille and receives advice from kindly centipede stage manager Ben, most of the other characters indulge their various vices. Heidi ultimately goes into breakdown overdrive, leading to a mass-slaughter sequence that unfolds during a *Feebles Hour* broadcast. Highlights include a puppet-cast *Deer Hunter* send-up, puppet porn films, and clever musical numbers, including "Garden of Love" and an ode to sodomy (!). The puppets themselves (nine puppeteers and two supervisors receive credit) are wonderfully expressive creations. When added mobility is called for, actors substitute by wearing life-sized puppet outfits (coscripter Mulheron plays Heidi in several scenes), a budget-minded move that's executed so seamlessly viewers may not even notice it at first. The versatile Jackson also performs camera-operator and puppet-maker chores. *Meet the Feebles* closes with the disclaimer "The producers wish to advise that no puppets were killed or hurt during the production of this film."

MEN IN BLACK   (1997) ***

D: Barry Sonnenfeld. Tommy Lee Jones, Will Smith, Linda Fiorentino, Vincent D'Onofrio, Rip Torn, Tony Shalhoub, Carel Struycken. 98 mins. (Universal) DVD

Deadpan veteran alien-tracker Jones and incredulous new recruit Smith make for an effective comic team in a film that doesn't rely strictly on instant-grat one-liners and FX gimmickry (though it boasts plenty of both). Sonnenfeld (*Addams Family Values, Get Shorty*) gives some set pieces room to breathe (e.g., Smith's government-testing scene). The pic posits that there are at least 1,500 known aliens, ranging from criminals to upstanding cits to talking dogs (!) and even celebrities (Sly Stallone, Newt Gingrich, Dennis Rodman, and Al Roker, to cite four), secretly living among us, with the majority ensconced in NYC. The central plot thread follows our Ray-Banned heroes' efforts to halt Earth's latest intergalactic menace, an ambitious outsized insect uncomfortably inhabiting a dead redneck's ill-fitting bod. D'Onofrio contributes a strenuous physical perf in that contortive part. Medical examiner Fiorentino (in a surprisingly secondary role) eventually joins the team in a race against time to prevent the planet's imminent annihilation, a pursuit that culminates in a showdown at the site of the 1964 New York World's Fair. The thesping, score (by the ubiquitous Danny Elfman), and FX (by Rick Baker) are all top-drawer. Former New York Mets outfielder Bernard Gilkey scores a close-up in a cameo, while Carel (Lurch) Struycken lands a slightly larger role as an endangered alien.

MIDNIGHT COWBOY   (1969) ****

D: John Schlesinger. Dustin Hoffman, Jon Voight, Sylvia Miles. 113 mins. (MGM) DVD

Director Schlesinger and scripter Waldo Salt craft a brilliant, offbeat, seriocomic tale about transplanted Texan Voight and Deuce lowlife Hoffman's unlikely bonding. Indelible perfs and evocative Times Square lensing add to the film's lasting power.

MISTRESS   (1992) ***

D: Barry Primus. Robert Wuhl, Martin Landau, Robert De Niro, Danny Aiello, Eli Wallach, Christopher Walken. 112 mins. (Artisan) DVD

While not as sardonic as Robert Altman's *The Player* (see index), actor-turned-auteur Primus's shaggy Hollywood story offers *mucho* bitter entertainment in its own right. Wuhl plays a struggling instructional-video director whose long-finished script about a suicidal artist falls into the hands of desperate indie producer Landau, who lines up three potential investors—De Niro, Aiello, and Wallach—all of whom insist their current mistresses have major on-screen roles in the project. Anyone into Inside-Tinseltown Tales, Fringe Division, will want to tune in.

MODERN TIMES   (1936) B&W ***1/2

D: Charlie Chaplin. Charlie Chaplin, Paulette Goddard, Henry Bergman. 89 mins. (Fox)

Chaplin's satire may be anachronistically silent most of the way, but his technology-amok message was not only timely but prophetic—and, of course, enduringly funny. Most of the Little Tramp's features are available on tape, while Kino Video has issued several Chaplin shorts collections.

MONDO TRASHO   (1969) B&W ***

D: John Waters. Divine, Mink Stole, Mary Vivian Pearce. 95 mins. (Cinema Group)

Lensed in black and white, sans dialogue (but with an extensive, brilliantly edited music track that actively comments on the on-screen action), Waters's minimalist maiden feature chronicles a typically disastrous day in the life of troubled transvestite Divine. Her woes begin when she accidentally runs down a blond bimbo whose unconscious body she's forced to tote with her through the remainder of the movie. Divine's travels take her to a thrift shop, a mental ward, a church (for a pivotal epiphany), and a quack surgeon's medical abattoir. It's a tribute to Waters's talent that he manages to wring 95 comically compelling minutes out of such sheer material. If you're curious to see what Waters was doing during his mock *Scorpio Rising* period, *Mondo Trasho* will fill you in.

THE MONSTER (1994) ****

D: Roberto Benigni. Roberto Benigni, Michel Blanc, Nicoletta Braschi, Dominique Lavanant, Jean-Claude Brialy, Franco Mesolini. Subtitled. 111 mins. (Columbia/TriStar) DVD

Italo comic genius Benigni tops his hilarious gangster farce *Johnny Stecchino* with this mistaken-identity serial-killer romp. The razor-thin (and -sharp) actor/auteur again proves a master of the delayed punch line and spiraling slapstick set piece. Benigni stars as Loris, a petty thief fingered as a sex-crazed psycho who's claimed the lives (and various body parts) of 18 women. To catch the presumed killer in the act, fetching policewoman Jessica (Braschi, who's very funny in her own right) agrees to share his rooms and rent and does everything in her considerable power to rouse his self-incriminatory lusts, flaunting her body at every conceivable opportunity in every sort of contortive pose, while a confused but gentlemanly Loris stalwartly resists her charms. Also on the scene are an obsessed police shrink, a language professor who's tutoring Loris in Chinese (he hopes to land an honest gig at a Chinese import-export outfit), and a landlord bent on evicting him. Benigni ingeniously weaves and builds his gags as he goes along, achieving some exquis-

ite, cheerfully sicko payoffs. He later hit the critical big time with his controversial *Life Is Beautiful* (Miramax, DVD).

MONSTER IN THE CLOSET (1986) ***

D: Bob Dahlin. Donald Grant, Denise DuBarry, Henry Gibson, Stella Stevens, Howard Duff, Paul Dooley, John Carradine, Jesse White, Paul Walker. 87 mins. (Troma) DVD

Dahlin's *Monster in the Closet* amiably spoofs the entire array of ripe '50s creature-feature clichés while retaining much of the same charm that informed those low-budget fright faves of yore. A once-in-a-lifetime lineup of B-movie greats—in parts ranging from eye-blink cameos (Stevens, Dooley, Carradine, White) to more substantial roles (Gibson as an Einstein-ian scientist, Claude Akins as a bullheaded small-town sheriff)—contributes mightily to the fun. Grant and DuBarry add appeal as the eager young reporter and prim biology teacher, respectively, out to foil the mysterious title monster (one of your better man-in-a-gray-rubber-suit creations), while young Walker gives a winning performance as a mechanical prodigy dubbed the Professor. Withal, *Monster* is a small-scale but entertaining and affectionate send-up.

CLOSET *ENCOUNTERS:* Scientist Henry Gibson attempts to communicate with the *Monster in the Closet,* Bob Dahlin's affectionate send-up of tacky '50s fear-fests. © *Troma Entertainment, Inc.*

MONTY PYTHON'S LIFE OF BRIAN (1979) ***1/2

D: Terry Jones. Graham Chapman, John Cleese, Eric Idle, Michael Palin, Terry Jones, Terry Gilliam. 94 mins. (Paramount) DVD

The Pythons' inspired satire of political factionalism, set within an irreverent religious framework, rates as one of the Brit bad boys' best, a comedy packed with brilliant invention. Other available Python romps include 1972's *And Now for Something Completely Different* (Columbia/TriStar), a collection of bits drawn from their hit Brit teleseries, including "The Lumberjack Song" and the classic "Dead Parrot" sketch; 1975's *Monty Python and the Holy Grail* (Columbia/TriStar), where the Pythons rewrite Arthurian legend; 1983's *Monty Python's The Meaning of Life* (Universal); the 1982 live-sketch collection, *Monty Python Live at the Hollywood Bowl* (Paramount); Terry Gilliam's 1981 *Time Bandits* (Paramount); and several volumes of their classic original teleseries (A&E, DVD).

THE MOUSE THAT ROARED (1959) ***

D: Jack Arnold. Peter Sellers, Jean Seberg, Leo McKern. 83 mins. (Columbia/TriStar)

The film, directed by Jack (*The Incredible Shrinking Man*) Arnold, that introduced Sellers's comic gifts to a wide stateside audience sees the late funnyman play several roles in a sharp satire—drawn from Leonard Wibberley's novel—about a tiny, financially strapped principality that declares war on the U.S.

MOVERS AND SHAKERS (1985) ***

D: William Asher. Charles Grodin, Tyne Daly, Walter Matthau, Vincent Gardenia, Gilda Radner, Bill Macy. 80 mins. (MGM)

A modest but at-times brilliant Hollywood lampoon, directed by *Beach Party* auteur Asher and scripted by Grodin, stars the future talk-show host as a bemused screenwriter hired to make a meaningful movie out of a sensational but utterly useless property. (The film was reportedly based on actual attempts to adapt Gay Talese's *Thy Neighbor's Wife* to the screen.) Sharp characterizations abound, with Matthau, as a beleaguered studio exec, a particular standout here.

MULTIPLE MANIACS (1970) B&W ***1/2

D: John Waters. Divine, David Lochary, Mink Stole, Mary Vivian Pearce, Cookie Mueller, Edith Massey. 90 mins. (Cinema Group)

Waters's first talkie feature, shot in black and white, is one of his wildest and most wonderfully hostile works. Divine and Lochary run a traveling freak show, Lady Divine's Cavalcade of Perversions, offering local lower-middle-class suckers such shocking sights as a junkie going cold turkey before their very eyes while a professional "puke-eater" does *his* thing in an adjacent ring. The show, though, is just a ruse for Divine to rob, abuse, and occasionally kill the assembled spectators. And that's only the start of the fun. Divine harangues beau Lochary for his mysterious alleged role in the Sharon Tate killing, has a mystical anal/lesbian epiphany with Mink Stole in a local church, and finally embarks on an all-out murder spree, wherein Waters spoofs the gamut of traditional monster-movie clichés. A brilliant display of pointed bad taste.

MURDER, HE SAYS (1945) B&W ***

D: George Marshall. Fred MacMurray, Helen Walker, Marjorie Main, Jean Heather, Porter Hall, Peter Whitney, Barbara Pepper. 93 mins. (Universal)

A hillbilly variation on the popular lethal laughfest *Arsenic and Old Lace,* released the previous year, this oft surreal farce casts Fred in the strenuous slapstick role of a bemused city-slicker pollster who unwisely calls upon the ramshackle manse of the violent Fleagle clan, headed by whip-wielding matriarch Main, of "Ma Kettle" fame. Fred soon becomes a pawn in a frantic search for hidden bank loot stashed in the house by since-jailed outlaw Bonnie Fleagle (Pepper). Furious physical humor mixes with off-the-wall conceptual wit as our story twists and turns in ever wilder directions. Future heavy Whitney turns in top comic work as Main's dim-witted twin sons.

MYSTERY SCIENCE THEATER 3000: THE MOVIE (1996) ***

D: Jim Mallon. Mike Nelson, Trace Beaulieu, Kevin Murphy, Jim Mallon. 74 mins. (Universal) DVD

Much trepidation ensued among genre fans when it was first announced that TV's *MST3K* crew would be skewering the 1955 sci-fi classic *This Island Earth* in their big-screen debut. True, that film stands forehead and shoulders above most *MST* targets, but as it turns out, the choice, if not ideal, wasn't a bad one. The *MST*ites felt they needed a movie technically slick enough to accompany the newly lensed wraparound footage and familiar enough not to alienate potential viewers with only a marginal interest in bad flicks. Despite its relatively lavish $2 mil budget, *Mystery Science Theater 3000: The Movie* doesn't rate among the elite of the teleshow's 1,000-plus (!) episodes, but it was still a lot funnier than almost any other theatrical offering to come out in '96. On the downside, most of the wit seems front-loaded here, which may have more to do with the comic possibilities of *Earth*'s plodding opening reels. Mike, Crow, and Tom Servo are especially merciless during *Earth* star Rex Reason and "wormy" hero-worshipping assistant Robert Nichols's attempts to construct Metalunan scientist Jeff Morrow's "inter-rociter," a triangular interstellar television. Further along, *Earth* becomes fairly intense in its own right, making it harder for the boy and 'bots in the front row to compete and encouraging them to resort to more scatalogical humor than they did on the TV show. Rhino, meanwhile, continues to issue select TV episodes on tape.

THE NAKED GUN: THE SERIES

THE NAKED GUN: FROM THE FILES OF POLICE SQUAD! (1988) ***1/2

D: David Zucker. Leslie Nielsen, Priscilla Presley, George Kennedy. 85 mins. (Paramount)

The ZAZ guys send up the entire catalog of TV-cop clichés in a rapid-fire parody that also includes what may be the funniest baseball sequence in movie history. With 1991's *Naked Gun 2¹/2: The Smell of Fear*, the team sustains its heady level of comic excellence in a sequel that's nearly as funny as its model, and maintain quality control in 1994's *Naked Gun 33¹/3: The Final Insult* (both Paramount), with Nielsen having a typically frenzied field day as intrepid LAPD dick Frank Drebin. Other ZAZ projects worth scoping out include the 1991 *Top Gun* spoof, *Hot Shots* (Fox), the nearly seamless 1986 farce *Ruthless People* (Touchstone), and the 1984 Elvis-movie/spy-romp combo *Top Secret!* (Paramount).

NATIONAL LAMPOON'S ANIMAL HOUSE (1978) **1/2

D: John Landis. John Belushi, Tim Matheson, Donald Sutherland. 109 mins. (Universal) DVD Special Edition

Landis's boisterous account of a frat house from hell, circa 1962, hits and misses in roughly equal measure but became a monster smash. Other

amusing *National Lampoon* outings include 1997's *National Lampoon's The Don's Analyst* (Paramount), 1983's *National Lampoon's Vacation* and 1985's lesser but still fitfully effective *National Lampoon's European Vacation* (both Warner, DVD), the Julie Brown coscripted anthology *National Lampoon's Attack of the 5'2" Woman* (Paramount), and the *Lethal Weapon* takeoff *National Lampoon's Loaded Weapon 1* (New Line).

NATURAL BORN KILLERS (1994) *

D: Oliver Stone. Woody Harrelson, Juliette Lewis, Robert Downey, Jr., Tommy Lee Jones, Tom Sizemore, Rodney Dangerfield. 119 mins. (Warner)

Woody Allen once remarked, "All movies should be preserved—except for *Porky's*." The Phantom would humbly add *Natural Born Killers* to the Woodman's short list. Mediamad spree killers Harrelson and Lewis attain heroic status under crazed telewhore Downey's direction (a portrait based on high-profile Aussie-bred tab-TV hack Steve Dunleavy). Reportedly disowned by Quentin Tarantino, who receives only a "story" credit after his original script was run through the Stone shredder, *NBK* is a bloated, self-indulgent, unforgivably interminable exercise in sledgehammer "satire" that's more audience-insulting than honestly subversive or outrageous. As for its vaunted "style," *NBK* may be the physically *ugliest* film yours truly's ever seen, a two-hour trail of visual vomit.

NETWORK (1976) ***1/2

D: Sidney Lumet. William Holden, Faye Dunaway, Peter Finch. 120 mins. (MGM) DVD

Twisted TV anchorman Finch gets mad as hell in writer Paddy Chayefsky's razor-sharp satire of a ratings-obsessed network. Dunaway is equally memorable as an overachieving

exec. For an ideal, telehell double bill, see also director Elia Kazan and scripter Budd Schulberg's even more prescient 1957 collaboration, *A Face in the Crowd* (Warner), which presents an atonce chilling and bitingly satiric portrait of two-bit country singer Andy Griffith's rise to media-demagogue status.

NEVER GIVE A SUCKER AN EVEN BREAK (1941) B&W ***1/2

D: Eddie Cline. W. C. Fields, Gloria Jean, Franklin Pangborn. 71 mins. (Universal)

Fields's final full-fledged feature film finds him at his wildest, weirdest, and frequently funniest in an affectionately unflinching self-portrayal as a tipsy movie personality trying to peddle a script to prissy studio exec Pangborn. Zany set pieces abound. Of course, you can't go wrong with any of Fields's features, especially the brilliant *Bank Dick* (1940), the still-biting *It's a Gift* (1934), the sublime *Man on the Flying Trapeze* (1935), and the wacky, circus-set *You Can't Cheat an Honest Man* (1939) (all Universal). Most of W.C.'s other features and timeless shorts are likewise available.

A NIGHT AT THE OPERA (1935) B&W ****

D: Sam Wood. The Marx Brothers, Margaret Dumont, Allan Jones. 92 mins. (MGM)

Groucho, Chico, and Harpo take highbrows down a few pegs in what's arguably the boys' finest film, from the justly famous stateroom scene to the final operatic anarchy. More Marxist mayhem available on cassette: *Animal Crackers* (1930), *The Cocoanuts* (1929), *Duck Soup* (1933), *Horse Feathers* (1932), *Monkey Business* (1931) (all Universal); *At the Circus* (1939), *The Big Store* (1941), *A Day at the Races* (1937), *Go West* (1940) (all MGM); *A Night in Casablanca* (1946) (IUD); *Room Service* (1938) (HHT); *Love Happy* (1949); and

Groucho's solo vehicle *Copacabana* (1947) (Republic), costarring the ever vivacious Carmen Miranda.

NIGHT OF THE CREEPS   (1986)***

D: Fred Dekker. Jason Lively, Jill Whitlow, Tom Atkins, Bruce Solomon, Dick Miller. 89 mins. (HBO)

While lifting wittily and openly from flicks as diverse as *Animal House, Plan 9,* and *Night of the Living Dead,* director Dekker fills this fast-paced, freewheeling fright farce with axe maniacs, frat-house zombies (complete with obligatory exploding heads), and even killer slugs from outer space. The result is a thoroughly crazed collage whose full-tilt overkill approach makes for great, grisly fun. Besides topliners Lively and Whitlow as a pair of embattled collegiates, the cast includes Roger Corman icon Miller, Solomon (the lovesick cop from TV's *Mary Hartmann*), and Atkins as a hard-boiled lawman extraordinaire. ("The good news is your dates are here," he informs a gaggle of sorority sisters. "The bad news is they're dead.")

NOTHING SACRED   (1937)***1/2

D: William A. Wellman. Carole Lombard, Fredric March, Walter Connolly. 75 mins. (Kino) Special Edition DVD

Lombard feigns terminal illness for an NYC lark orchestrated by headline-hunting reporter March in Wellman's savvy media satire. Remade in 1954 as the Dean Martin/Jerry Lewis vehicle *Living It Up* (n/a).

THE NUTTY PROFESSOR
(1963)***1/2

D: Jerry Lewis. Jerry Lewis, Stella Stevens, Del Moore. 107 mins. (Paramount)

Jerry's undisputed masterwork casts him as a geeky scientist whose magic potion transforms him into his smooth but evil other half—Dean Martin clone (!) Buddy Love. A higher concept you'll never find. You don't have to be French to enjoy this inspired synthesis of Lewis's best riffs, characters, and themes. Other recommended Jerry romps include: *The Bellboy* (1960), *Cinderfella* (1960), *The Errand Boy* (1961), *The Patsy* (1964) (all Artisan); *The Delicate Delinquent* (1957), *The Disorderly Orderly* (1964), *The Family Jewels* (1965), *The Geisha Boy* (1958), *The Ladies' Man* (1961) (all Paramount); and *The Big Mouth* (1967) (Columbia/TriStar). Of the many Martin-and-Lewis vehicles on tape, our fave is their final teaming, 1956's *Hollywood or Bust* (Paramount), a road comedy laced with clever songs, great comic bits, and even a tinge of magic realism; Lewis is particularly funny as what may be the screen's first full-fledged film-nerd character.

THE NUTTY PROFESSOR   (1996)***

D: Tom Shadyac. Eddie Murphy, Jada Pinkett, Dave Chappelle, Larry Miller, James Coburn. 96 mins. (Columbia/TriStar) DVD

Director Shadyac and four screen-writers accomplish the tricky feat of recasting and updating a pure Jerry Lewis vehicle as an equally pure Eddie Murphy showcase. The movie's sweeping opening sight gag—with thousands of hamsters running, leaping, and even flying amok on a college campus—captures the feel of a classic early-'60s Lewis comedy. Murphy shines as obese, socially recessive science prof Sherman Klump, making him a hugely likable figure while saving his brasher routines for Sherman's chemically induced badder half—manic, testosterone-fueled narcissist Buddy Love. Murphy stretches still further when he impersonates four additional members of the Klump clan—his fat, flatulent dad, cooing mom, crude brother, and, best of all, his feisty, semisenile grandmother. Pinkett projects a Stella Stevens-esque sweet-ness as Sherman's grad-student love object. *The Nutty Professor* (mis)shapes up as a witty, at times touching fable about personal identity and self-esteem. Murphy pays further homage to the Lewis tradition by following the film with a series of (very funny) outtakes.

PARENTS   (1989)**1/2

D: Bob Balaban. Randy Quaid, Mary Beth Hurt, Brian Madorsky, Sandy Dennis. 82 mins. (Vestron) DVD

Slow pacing and a sometimes thin script hamper Balaban's black comedy about a seriously disturbed 1950s family unit, but the flick comes through with its share of creatively sicko tableaux.

PECKER   (1998)***

D: John Waters. Edward Furlong, Christina Ricci, Lili Taylor, Martha Plimpton, Mary Kay Place, Brendan Sexton III, Mink Stole, Patty Hearst. 86 mins. (New Line) Special Edition DVD

Despite its mock-provocative title, John Waters's *Pecker* rates as a relatively low-key satire contrasting the proud-slob ethos of working-class Baltimore with the self-centered "sophistication" of Manhattan's downtown art snobs. Furlong takes the title role of Pecker, so named because he "pecks at his food" (okay), a teenage amateur photographer whose funky slice-of-lowlife snapshots capture the fancy of NYC agent Taylor. Pecker's resultant rise engenders resentment among his family and friends, including laundromat-worker squeeze Ricci, until he hits on a plan to turn the tables on the NYC media set. While Waters's good-natured romp is a long way from such grungy bad-taste classics as *Pink Flamingos* and *Desperate Living,* there are enough moments of rude mirth, involving everything from bizarre strip clubs to amorous rats, to engage his fans and sufficient crossover appeal to hook comedy lovers of all stripes. Waters is at his best here when he operates as sort of an alien anthropologist, observing and dramatizing such odd earthly customs as "teabagging" and "claw-machine" worship.

PEE-WEE'S BIG ADVENTURE (1985) ***¹/₂

D: Tim Burton. Paul Reubens, Elizabeth Daily, Mark Holton. 92 mins. (Warner)

Reubens devises a perfect plot—a cross-country quest for a stolen customized bike—for his Pee-wee persona and, aided by director Burton, crafts his comic vehicle with nearly flawless precision. Trucker "Large Marge" supplied the single scariest movie moment of 1985. Followed by the even weirder, if less successful, *Big Top Pee-wee* (Paramount). Several volumes of the cult teleseries *Pee-wee's Playhouse* are likewise on cassette.

PENN & TELLER GET KILLED (1989) ***

D: Arthur Penn. Penn Jillette, Teller, Caitlin Clarke, David Patrick Kelly. 89 mins. (Warner)

The postmodern black-"magicomedy" duo are pursued by a rabid fan in a loosely formatted, deadpan adventure that leaves plenty of opportunity for the self-styled "Bad Boys of Magic" to perform some of their better shticks. The Bee Gees' "I Started a Joke" supplies an appropriate musical coda.

PENNIES FROM HEAVEN (1981) **¹/₂

D: Herbert Ross. Steve Martin, Bernadette Peters, Christopher Walken. 107 mins. (MGM)

A self-conscious seriocomic antimusical, set in the Depression '30s and based on Dennis Potter's BBC series of the same name, *Pennies* casts Martin as an itinerant sheet-music salesman making the lowlife rounds. Walken, as a pimp, performs his (thus far) only on-screen striptease. The pic bombed with audiences expecting a typical Martin romp but has since found a friendlier cult niche on video. Potter's acclaimed BBC series *The Singing Detective* (BBC Video) has also joined the home-vid ranks.

THE PENTAGON WARS (1998) ***

D: Richard Benjamin. Kelsey Grammer, Cary Elwes, Viola Davis, Olympia Dukakis, Richard Benjamin, John C. McGinley, Tom Wright, Clifton Powell. 104 mins. (HBO)

Adapted (by producer Martyn Burke and frequent former *Spy*-magazine writer Jamie Malanowski) from Colonel James G. Burton's nonfiction book of the same name, *The Pentagon Wars* offers a darkly comic chronicle of the disastrous development of "the Bradley Fighting Vehicle." Under the supervision of a corrupt, self-aggrandizing general (a sputtering Grammer), 17 years and $14 billion went into making a tank/troop transport vehicle that tests proved to be an incendiary death trap. Elwes is excellent as the bemused Burton, who finds his attempts to subject the Bradley to fair tests stonewalled at every turn and is forced to resort to extreme measures to expose the defective equipment. If anything, *The Pentagon Wars*, set in 1983–1986, would seem to treat its sobering topic a tad *too* lightly; Grammer and lackeys' actions come closer to treason than mere self-aggrandizement and greed. Benjamin's crisp direction—he also appears on-screen as secretary of defense Casper Weinberger—builds the increasingly incredulous Burton's case at a steady pace, while a neat opening-credits tank-testing-through-the-ages montage, using rare B&W archival military footage, effectively sets the pic's tone.

PINK FLAMINGOS: 25TH ANNIVERSARY EDITION (1972) **¹/₂

D: John Waters. Divine, David Lochary, Mary Vivian Pearce, Edith Massey, Mink Stole. 95 mins./108 mins. total (Lightning) DVD

Waters's most infamous film also ranks as The Phantom's least fave. Here many of the gross-outs seem a tad too calculated and get in the way of Waters's deeper wit. Still, there are many hilarious moments on view as an upstart pervo couple (Lochary, Stole) attempt to wrest Filthiest Person in the World honors from Divine's tenacious grip. The incomparable Edith Massey receives her first major Waters role as Divine's brain-damaged mother, the unforgettable Egg Lady, a cheerful unfortunate who spends her screen time in a crib, demanding, eating, and paying lyrical tribute to ova of every kind. *Pink Flamingos* also contains the first—possibly *only*—screen scene of authentic coprophagia, courtesy of Divine and a passing poodle.

POLYESTER (1981) ***

D: John Waters. Divine, Tab Hunter, Edith Massey, Stiv Bators. 86 mins. (HBO)

In Waters's twisted Douglas Sirk Meets William Castle satire, Divine is just that as Francine Fishpaw, a harried housewife/misunderstood mom who seeks relief from her stultifying life in the arms of hunky Tod Tomorrow (Hunter, in his first *low*-camp role). Massey scores again as Cuddles, a molasses-witted heiress and Francine's best friend. Unfortunately, the vid version doesn't come equipped with the all-important Odorama scratch-'n'-sniff card; fortunately, the laser-disc edition *does*.

POWWOW HIGHWAY (1989) ***1/2

D: Jonathan Wacks. A Martinez, Gary Farmer, Amanda Wyss. 90 mins. (Cannon)

Farmer, a Native American naïf with a mystical bent, and Martinez, his embittered activist friend, undertake a modern-day quest through a racist Southwest in Wacks's highly original, underrated blend of action, comedy, and drama, the best unreleased movie of 1989.

THE PRESIDENT'S ANALYST (1967) ***

D: Theodore J. Flicker. James Coburn, Godfrey Cambridge, Severn Darden. 104 mins. (Paramount)

Coburn, in the title role, is privy to inside info that lands him in no end of trouble in Flicker's clever exercise in '60s pop paranoia. The late Cambridge lends able comic support.

PRISONERS OF INERTIA (1989) ***

D: J. Noyes Scher. Amanda Plummer, Christopher Rich, John C. McGinley, Gary Keats, Mark Boone Junior. 92 mins. (Studio, n.i.d.)

An entertaining low-budget shaggy day-in-the-life story, *Prisoners* follows West Village couple Rich and Plummer's thwarted attempts to buy brunch, a quest that ultimately leads them to disastrous misadventures in Hoboken, New Jersey, and upstate New York. Director/writer Scher achieves his modest aims, delivering fine deadpan fun.

PRIZZI'S HONOR (1985) ***1/2

D: John Huston. Jack Nicholson, Kathleen Turner, Anjelica Huston, Robert Loggia, William Hickey. 130 mins. (Vestron) DVD

Hit persons Nicholson and Turner learn the hard way that love and business make a bad mix in John Huston's fast and funny black farce, adapted from Richard Condon's novel.

THE PRODUCERS (1967) ***1/2

D: Mel Brooks. Zero Mostel, Gene Wilder, Kenneth Mars, Dick Shawn. 88 mins. (Columbia/TriStar)

The Producers still rates as Brooks's most original and perverse comedy, with top work turned in by Mostel as a seedy producer, Wilder as his nerdy partner-in-slime, Mars as a sentimental Nazi playwright, and Shawn as an eccentric hipster.

THE PROJECTIONIST (1971) ***

D: Harry Hurwitz. Chuck McCann, Ina Balin, Rodney Dangerfield. 85 mins. (Vestron, n.i.d.)

Hurwitz assembles a more-hit-than-miss exercise in cinematic whimsy detailing projectionist McCann's drab real life and rich reel life, where he assumes the guise of superhero Captain Flash and battles villain "the Bat," played by Dangerfield (in his film debut), who doubles as Chuck's cranky bijou-manager boss. Several deft film parodies, plus trailers for imaginary movies like *The Terrible World of Tomorrow*, highlight this clever indie.

PTERODACTYL WOMAN FROM BEVERLY HILLS (1995) **1/2

D: Philippe Mora. Beverly D'Angelo, Brad Wilson, Brion James, Moon Zappa, Stephen McHattie, Aron Eisenberg, Sharon Martin, Ruta Lee. 97 mins. (Troma)

An uneven mix of social satire and genre spoof, *Pterodactyl* has its soaring moments; at other times, Mora is definitely less. When paleontologist Wilson violates sacred turf, angry generic-native shaman "Salvador Dalí" (James, who's quite amusing in the role) casts a curse that causes Wilson's spouse (D'Angelo) to transmute into the title character. Back in Beverly Hills, Bev shocks friends and neighbors with her intermittent transformations, while her newfound flying habits arouse the suspicions of government agent McHattie (doing a fair Robert Stack imitation). Bev seeks help from TV trash-show hostess friend Zappa and New Agey guru James (in his second role) but also finds that her prehistoric status is not without its liberating aspects. While Mora exhausts his inspiration before he runs out of reels, he imbues the flick with a fair amount of infectious fun.

PUTNEY SWOPE (1969) B&W ***

D: Robert Downey, Sr. Arnold Johnson, Antonio Fargas, Stanley Gottlieb. 84 mins. (Columbia/TriStar)

Subterranean satirist Downey's best and most gleefully subversive feature chronicles a black takeover of a Madison Avenue ad agency in a scattershot but oft hilarious send-up populated by a memorably eccentric cast.

QUICK CHANGE (1990) ***

D: Bill Murray, Howard Franklin. Bill Murray, Geena Davis, Randy Quaid. 89 mins. (Warner)

Murray, Davis, and Quaid are crooks who attempt to escape NYC and encounter more problems than the law in a clever caper flick based on Jay Cronley's novel. Bob Elliott, of Bob and Ray fame, supplies an adroit cameo as a befuddled, bragadocious bank guard.

THE REAL BLONDE (1998) ***

D: Tom DiCillo. Matthew Modine, Catherine Keener, Daryl Hannah, Maxwell Caulfield, Elizabeth Berkley, Denis Leary, Marlo Thomas, Bridgette Wilson, Buck Henry, Christopher Lloyd, Kathleen Turner. 107 mins. (Paramount) DVD

NYC-based auteur DiCillo doesn't quite scale the gently loopy heights of his inside-the-indie-film-biz delight *Living in Oblivion* (see index), but he comes close enough. *The Real Blonde* follows underachieving aspiring actor Joe (an appealing Modine), who, at age 35, owns a threadbare résumé. He splits his time attending unpromising auditions and working as a tuxed waiter for upscale caterer Lloyd (in an amusingly prissy turn, sort of a low-key Franklin Pangborn for the '90s). Joe's squeeze, Mary (Keener), spends *her* days as a high-fashion makeup artist for airheaded models (like former *Showgirls* bimbo Berkley) on campaigns for such trendy products as a high-ticketed perfume called "Depression" (!). In her off-hours she attends self-defense classes run by a subtly sadistic Leary and visits her leering shrink (a very funny Henry). Caulfield receives a respite from his usual B-video thriller assignments (and gets to employ his natural Brit accent) as Joe's outgoing, femme-obsessed fellow actor pal and rival, who's just scored a low-status but high-paying gig playing handsome cad Dirk Drake on the TV soap opera *Passion Crest.* Even the normally irritating Hannah is credible here as the veteran soap star with whom Caulfield initiates an ill-advised affair. The cameo-studded cast also includes Thomas (as a fashion photographer) and Turner (as an abrasive casting agent). Writer/director DiCillo's unerring ear for ironic yet human-sounding dialogue, flawless sense of story structure, verité Manhattan locales and engaging characters add up to a treat that's certifiably real, even if his blondes aren't.

RED DESERT PENITENTIARY (1985) ***

D: George Sluizer. James Michael Taylor, Cathryn Bissell, Will Rose, Jim Wortham, Giovanni Korporaal. 104 mins. (Continental, n.i.d.)

Much hype accompanied the theatrical release of Belgian auteur George Sluizer's big-budget Hollywood remake of his 1989 Euro sleeper *The Vanishing* (see index). But *The Vanishing* isn't Sluizer's first American flick. That distinction belongs to *Red Desert Penitentiary.* The Phantom walked in during the middle of a Cannes Market screening of *RDP* back in '87 and couldn't make your proverbial heads or tails of it; fortunately, we later found a bargain-bin previewed copy of the elusive cassette and finally watched it all the way through—which is more than we can say for Continental's copywriter. The video-box synopsis makes *Red Desert Penitentiary* sound like a rip-roaring, knee-slapping B-movie spoof. While it does unfold during a fictional B-flick shoot near Sweetwater, Texas, Sluizer has more than mere spoofery on his mind. *RDP* at first focuses on second-rate low-budget Clint Eastwood wannabe Dan McMan (well played by Taylor), debuting starlet Myrna (Bissell), young-squirt screenwriter Chet (Wortham), and Polish director Mickey (Korporaal). Sluizer's early satiric scenes, when the characters schmooze, bicker, and rehearse, are barely a centimeter away from pure verité; indeed, some moments are *so* low-key that the pic threatens to disappear. Our story radically shifts gears when former imprisoned innocent James Gagan (Rose)—on whose life story the film-within-a-film is based—shows up on the set to complain about the script's myriad inaccuracies. The movie abruptly stops for a lengthy, thoroughly absurdist flashback resembling Kafka's *The Trial,* and director/scripter Sluizer never quite doubles back to the film's first half. In the end, *Red Desert Penitentiary* is an elaborate put-on that poses the same central question as *The Vanishing*: How much undeserved punishment can a body volunteer for and endure (let alone enjoy)? *Red Desert Penitentiary* is original and quite funny, in its own surreal, idiosyncratic, audience-baiting way. As the lighter side of *The Vanishing, RDP* definitely rates a look.

RENTED LIPS (1988) ***

D: Robert Downey. Martin Mull, Dick Shawn, Robert Downey, Jr., Jennifer Tilly, June Lockhart, Edy Williams, Shelley Berman, Kenneth Mars. 82 mins. (IVE, Avid)

Underground jester Downey's take-off on low-budget filmmaking finds the idiosyncratic auteur in inspired, off-the-wall comic form. Mull takes center stage as an earnest, hopelessly naïve director manqué who agrees, with cinematographer Shawn, to lens a Nazi-themed smut flick if he can use the same cast and facilities to realize his own celluloid vision: an educational musical called *Indian Farming Techniques* (!). Downey is particularly adept at exposing actors' and directors' desperate foibles (Downey Junior is very funny as a pretentious porn stud) and at exploring the often bizarre bonds that link seemingly disparate human tandems, like Mull's obsessive attachment to bubbleheaded would-be performer Tilly. Mars, as a sleazoid evangelist, also adds to the merriment. *Rented Lips* is a bumpy ride but one that vintage-Downey lovers won't want to miss.

REPO MAN (1984) ***

D: Alex Cox. Emilio Estevez, Harry Dean Stanton, Vonetta McGee. 92 mins. (Universal)

Cox's surreal cult fave ranges from broad to brilliant as punk teen Estevez joins the ranks of a determined breed of car repossessors led by a crusty Stanton, who sums up his credo thusly: "Ordinary people—I hate 'em!"

REPOSSESSED (1990) **½

D: Bob Logan. Linda Blair, Leslie Nielsen, Ned Beatty. 89 mins. (Artisan)

Writer/director Logan aims for *Airplane!*-level laughs and mostly misses, but it's great fun to see Linda B. reprise her notorious *Exorcist* role, this time as a 'burb housewife who becomes possessed while watching televangelist Beatty.

THE ROCKY HORROR PICTURE SHOW: SPECIAL EDITION (1975) ***

D: Jim Sharman. Tim Curry, Susan Sarandon, Barry Bostwick, Richard O'Brien. 105 mins. (Fox)

Infamous transvestite Dr. Frank N. Furter (Curry) educates squares Brad (Bostwick) and Janet (Sarandon) to the joys of horror and depravity in Sharman's ultimate rock-cult musical, featuring such timeless tunes as "Time Warp" and "Damnit Janet." Sharman's 1981 semi-follow-up, *Shock Treatment* (Fox), failed to match the latter's success but, with its TV-directed satire and lively rock score (courtesy of *Rocky Horror* returnee Richard O'Brien), boasts its share of subversive virtues.

SCHIZOPOLIS (1997) ***

D: Steven Soderbergh. Steven Soderbergh, Betsy Brantley, David Jensen, Eddie Jemison, Mike Malone. 96 mins. (Fox Lorber)

Part deconstructionist Godard-ian spoof, part on-screen nervous breakdown—with a dash of vintage Robert Downey–esque antics tossed in for good measure—*Schizopolis* is a bold, funny satire of modern American life. Soderbergh's primary targets are corporate culture (if that's not oxymoronic), self-help gurus, filmmaking, and the elasticity and degradation of language in our times. The *sex, lies & videotape/Kafka* auteur even takes the lead role of everycipher Fletcher Munson, sort of a Dilbert with an edge who works (or, more often, loafs) as a low-rung corporate slug for a self-help mogul whose philosophy is called "Eventualism." Fletcher resides in an anonymous 'burb with his bored wife (Brantley) and their young daughter. The couple frequently address each other in Coneheads-like shorthand (e.g., upon arriving home, Fletcher calls out, "Generic greeting"). Actor Soderbergh, who displays a legit comic gift

TROMATIC EXPERIENCE: Rick Gianasi and Susan Byun prepare to take on evildoers in Troma's cross-cultural comedy *Sgt. Kabukiman N.Y.P.D.* © Troma Entertainment, Inc.

here, doubles as a drab dentist who has the hots for Fletcher's wife *and* as an Italian-speaking stranger in whose arms said wife finds solace. Another thread follows Fletcher's newly fired cohort, Mr. Nameless Numberman (Jemison), while still another, a film within the film, tracks an exterminator (Jensen) who speaks in random words ("whale basket sneeze" is a typical pronouncement) and is lured into a different film midway through by yuppie-couple producers. There's lots more, but as the vid box puts it: "Warning: All attempts at synopsizing the film have ended in failure and hospitalization." Suffice it to say that this self-produced, highly polished vanity production scores more often than not on a surreal

but accessible satiric level. For a comic corporate-confinement double bill, scope out *Beavis and Butt-head* creator Mike Judge's witty 1999 live-action debut, *Office Space* (Fox, DVD).

THE SECRET CINEMA (1966) B&W ***1/2

D: Paul Bartel. Amy Vane, Gordon Felio, Connie Elison. 37 mins. (Rhino)

Bartel's film debut is a wonderfully paranoiac featurette about a young woman (Vane) whose life is being secretly filmed, then screened at the title bijou for the general amusement of relatives, friends, and strangers alike. Bartel later remade the short as a Steven

Spielberg's *Amazing Stories* episode but lost the original's subversive quality somewhere along the way. *The Secret Cinema* prefigured the late-'90s slate of such similarly themed evil-TV features as *The Truman Show, Pleasantville,* and Ron Howard's *EDtv* (Universal, DVD).

SGT. KABUKIMAN N.Y.P.D. (1990/1996) **1/2

D: Lloyd Kaufman and Michael Herz. Rick Gianasi, Susan Byun, Bill Weeden, Brick Bronsky, Larry Robinson. 104 mins. (Troma) Special Edition DVD

Troma's *Sgt. Kabukiman N.Y.P.D.* lends credence to the venerable adage that if you work a formula long enough, you may one day get it half right. Eliminating some (though by no means all) of the sloppiness that informed earlier oozefests like the *Toxic Avenger* and *Class of Nuke 'Em High* series, Tromauteurs Kaufman and Herz assemble an off-the-wall superhero spoof that hits almost as often as it misses. The unlikely story line sees bumbling NYPD dick Harry Griswold (Gianasi) transform, courtesy of a visiting Kabuki troupe, into a chopsticks-wielding, sushi-scarfing superhero chosen to fulfill an ancient Japanese prophecy and prevent the rise of "the evil one," who's taken the form of ruthless NYC real estate mogul Reginald Stuart (Weeden). Amidst the expected bodily effluvia-driven slapstick, gross-out gags, fat jokes, and cheerfully cheesy FX, *Sgt. Kabukiman* offers some legitimately funny sequences. The pic further benefits from veteran low-budget thesp Gianasi's likable, physically adept perf as the hapless title character, given decent support here from a better-than-average Troma cast. While *Sgt. Kabukiman* may win few new converts, committed Troma fans (and we know you're out there, we can hear you retching) should deem the flick just their cup of celluloid slime.

SERIAL MOM (1994) ***

D: John Waters. Kathleen Turner, Sam Waterston, Ricki Lake, Matthew Lillard, Mink Stole, Suzanne Somers, Patsy Grady Adams. 93 mins. (Columbia/TriStar) DVD

Set in a contempo Baltimore 'burb a slight step up from that on view in his 1981 Divine/Tab Hunter Odorama romance, *Polyester,* Waters's *Serial Mom* stars Turner as a happy-face housewife whose mounting collection of pet peeves finally drives her off the deep end, resulting in a weekend murder spree that claims the lives of neighbors, a local educator, and even a complete stranger who returned a tape to her son's (Lillard) video store without remembering to rewind (!). The result is a consistently funny addition to Waters's ouevre. While Turner hits the right balance between *Stepford* cheeri-ness and black rage, the rest of her family—bland dentist hubby (Waterston), chubby daughter (Lake), and horror-addicted son (Lillard)—lack the idiosyncratic zest former J.W. regulars like the late, great Divine, Edith Massey, and David Lochary brought to the table (and we're not talking manners). Mink Stole is aboard, however, as harassed neighbor Dottie Hinkle, frequent victim of Turner's obscene phone calls, while vet set director Vince Peranio and resident "ugly expert" Van Smith lend the film and players a subtly hideous look. Susan *(Desperate Living)* Lowe and Mary Vivian Pearce contribute cameos, as do several of Waters's more recent celebrity acquisitions, including Suzanne Somers, Traci Lords, Patty Hearst, and Joan Rivers. The "money shot" arrives when K.T. sneezes big-time on a baby's face during a church

---

Filmmakers in Focus!

JOHN WATERS STILL RUNS DEEP

As Told to The Phantom

PHANTOM: Do you think the image of the American Mom has deteriorated?

WATERS: I think I'm trying to build it back up. I love the *Serial Mom* character; I think she's really the heroine of this movie. I think she does everything most people *wish* their mother would do for them. I used to have teachers who'd say what's the matter with me. And my parents would just be worried. They wouldn't go in and say, "Oh, you idiot!" Which is basically what Kathleen does, only she kills them.

PHANTOM: Was *Serial Mom* the first project you wanted to do after *Cry-Baby?*

WATERS: No, I wrote this other one for Paramount called *Glamor Puss.* They paid me and everything. I liked the script. It was about a movie star that comes to Baltimore and goes crazy. And they liked it too, but *Soapdish* had just come out and had done not badly but not great. And that's the way they think: "We don't wanna do another behind-the-scenes showbiz thing when one just came out and didn't do so well." Of course, *The Player* came out right after that and was nominated for an Oscar. So you never know; a lot of times things like that affect decisions in Hollywood.

PHANTOM: Was Kathleen Turner your first choice?

WATERS: Kathleen Turner I've always liked from the beginning. The very fact that she'd made the Ken Russell movie [*Crimes of Passion*], I thought here's a movie star that takes chances. And she really had fun making this

(continued)

movie. She's an ultimate pro, and to watch her work for me was really fun. Just look at her face in the scene where she hears the verdict. She looks so insane.

PHANTOM: Would you say she's up there with Carroll Baker in *Bad*?

WATERS: I love Carroll Baker. I even have her novel. I have the Complete Books of Carroll Baker—she has three, an autobiography, a travel book about Africa, and the novel. And *Baby Doll*'s the whole reason I ever made movies in the first place. Because of the relentless Catholicism—telling us we would burn in hell if we saw this movie, and that's the movie they went the most berserk about. Actually, it's a pretty good movie. It's Tennessee Williams, for God's sake. Nobody goes to hell for liking Tennessee Williams! I think that's an automatic ticket to heaven, even for serial killers!

PHANTOM: One scene we liked a lot in *Serial Mom* was the *Annie* sequence.

WATERS: I was really happy too, because we got to murder a song ["Tomorrow"]. Which I had never done before. I'd have to think it's a pretty strong song, though, to want to murder it. I'm respectful of that song for its cloying, anxiety-provoking melody. So I'm not saying I *hate* that song at all. I never pick subjects I truly hate, because if I really hate it, I'm disinterested. That song is *worthy* of many beatings with a leg of lamb.

PHANTOM: Speaking of creative props, you still have the same set director.

WATERS: Vincent Peranio. The first thing he did for me he made "Lobstora" for *Multiple Maniacs* and that's his legs sticking out; he was inside it. He did the entire production design for *Serial Mom*. Same with Van Smith, who did the costumes from the very beginning, and Pat Moran, who's worked with me with casting.

PHANTOM: The ugliness is subtler in *Serial Mom*.

WATERS: Vincent I think did a great job because the house I think is scary in its own perfectness. I told him it wasn't the kind that had to immediately get a laugh; like in *Polyester*, you open the door and everybody roared. In this it had to be more subtle but at the same time I think it made it scarier and creepier, that pastel perfection.

PHANTOM: You would just want to get out of there.

WATERS: Yeah. But I think most people would want to get *in* there. Most people wanna live in a house like that. I don't think it's an *ugly* house; I don't think it's like the house in *Polyester*. I would *cry* if I had to live in the house in *Polyester*; I would merely *sob* in the one in *Serial Mom*.

PHANTOM: Do you still spend most of your time in Baltimore?

WATERS: Oh, yeah, I love it there, are you kidding? Most importantly, I like to write there. I love to make my movies there, but it's even more important to me that that's where I think 'em up. 'Cause I can drive around neighborhoods and go places that give me the ideas. For me to get the ideas, I have to be around people that pay to see movies, people who live in America like normal people. I don't know many people like that, so I always think it's good to listen to what they're saying and spy on 'em.

service. (But since Turner's such a devoted mom herself, wouldn't her sense of empathy lead to her own immediate suicide? Just asking.) *Serial Mom*'s at its best when Waters taps into his patented brand of one-of-a-kind weirdness. The extended tableaux involving the doomed video-renter rep-resents a prime example. We experience the illicit joys of verité-styled voyeurism as we watch Mrs. Jenson (Adams) sing along with her newly rented *Annie* video while her loyal dog, in loving close-up, treats her bare feet to an elaborate tongue massage. K.T. puts an abrupt, gory end to Mrs. J.'s Sunday-afternoon reverie with the aid of a lethal leg of lamb. For Mrs. Jenson, there will be no more "Tomorrow"s. Waters honors many of his cinematic influences and faves via clips from Herschell Gordon Lewis's "*Citizen Kane* of Gore" (per young Lillard) *Blood Feast*, Joan Crawford's axe-whacking scene from *Strait-Jacket*, a Leatherface moment from *Texas Chainsaw Massacre*, and even cleavage-crowded frames from Doris Wishman's deathless Chesty Morgan vehicle, *Double Agent 73*.

THE SEVEN-PER-CENT SOLUTION (1976) ***

D: Herbert Ross. Nicol Williamson, Alan Arkin, Vanessa Redgrave, Robert Duvall. 113 mins. (Universal) DVD

A stoned but stolid Sherlock Holmes (Williamson) and Watson (a deadpan Duvall) encounter Sigmund Freud (Arkin) in scripter Nicholas Meyer's witty, highly original romp. The title refers to Sherlock's preferred cocaine mix.

SEX AND ZEN (1993) **1/2

D: Michael Mak. Lawrence Ng, Amy Yip, Kent Cheng. 99 mins. (Tai Seng)

A dapted from Li Yu's Ming Dynasty novel *The Carnal Praying Mat*, Mak's wacky slapstick tragicomedy—sort of a John Woo Meets Doris Wishman—details randy young scholar Ng's relentless NC-17-level quest for carnal knowledge. Said quest takes many bizarre turns, with our hero ultimately opting for a horse-organ transplant (!), leading to all manner of madcap situations, including a brief encounter with the ill-fated equine's widow (!!). One Phantom caveat: Watch, enjoy, but *don't* try this at home. Followed by *Sex and Zen II* (Tai Seng).

SHAKES THE CLOWN (1991) ***½

D: Bob Goldthwait. Bobcat Goldthwait, Julie Brown, Paul Dooley, Adam Sandler, Blake Clark, Tom Kenny, Robin Williams. 83 mins. (Columbia/TriStar)

Comic Goldthwait reportedly scripted *Shakes* soon after starring in the 1988 talking-horse dud *Hot to Trot* (Warner), convinced he could write and direct a funnier film. *Shakes* proved him correct. *Shakes* takes a bleakly hilarious look at the clown subculture in Palukaville, USA, where said clowns, like *Roger Rabbit*'s 'toons, live by their own codes and inhabit their own demimonde. When not working kid parties and similar functions, the clowns drown their sorrows at the Twisted Balloon, where they booze, schmooze, gossip, backstab, and otherwise behave like most other showbiz groups. As the alcoholic Shakes, Bobcat copes not only with his drinking problem but with nonclown squeeze Brown and the ambitious Binky (Kenny), an evil clown who murders beloved rent-a-clown mogul Dooley. *Shakes*'s thin, traditional action-comedy story line serves as a convenient frame for Goldthwait's quirky bits. We learn, for example, that even basically good-natured clowns can't resist occasional mime bashing (!). ("You only pick on us 'cause we're *artists,*" whines one aggrieved victim.) At the same time, even relatively macho "party clowns" like Shakes and cronies quake when faced with redneck rodeo clowns. Goldthwait, Brown, Dooley, Florence Henderson (stretching as a clown groupie/Shakes conquest!), and a first-rate ensemble cast—including the since-ascendant Sandler as Shakes's best pal, Dink—bring auteur Goldthwait's script to oft hilarious life, while Williams contributes a deft uncredited

cameo as an effetely sadistic mime teacher who finds particular joy in humiliating Shakes. Crammed with inventive sight gags, clever one-liners, and deadpan satire, *Shakes the Clown* rates as a true original.

SHALLOW GRAVE (1994) ***

D: Danny Boyle. Kerry Fox, Ewan McGregor, Christopher Eccleston. 94 mins. (PolyGram) DVD

Blackly comic complications ensue when a trio of Edinburgh yuppies—doctor Fox, journalist McGregor, and chartered accountant Eccleston—trip over a suitcase full of stolen loot in a sardonic tale ably scripted by John Hodge and helmed by debuting director Boyle. While echoing everything from the Coen brothers' *Blood Simple* to dead-body comedies like Hitchcock's *The Trouble with Harry, Shallow Grave* locks on to a tone all its own. Among other innovations, Boyle and Hodge make imaginative use of screen violence; their characters inflict brutal damage while limiting their arsenal mostly to common household instruments, both sharp and blunt. The flat where most of the action unfolds also plays almost a living role here; the viewer eventually feels so familiar with the place that even minor prop additions, like McGregor's drum set, take on disproportionate (usually ominous) significance. Boyle and Hodge achieved permanent outre fame with their follow-up cult hit *Trainspotting* (Touchstone).

SHE DONE HIM WRONG (1933) B&W ***

D: Lowell Sherman. Mae West, Cary Grant, Gilbert Roland. 66 mins. (Universal)

The Divine Miss M adapts her cheerfully smutty Broadway hit *Diamond Lil* to the screen in what may be her purest movie vehicle. Mae mani-

acs can also find their frisky femme fave in *Belle of the Nineties* (1934, DVD), *Every Day's a Holiday* (1937), *Go West Young Man* (1936), *Goin' to Town* (1935), *I'm No Angel* (1933), *Klondike Annie* (1936), opposite W. C. Fields in *My Little Chickadee* (1940), *Night After Night* (1932) (all Universal), the grotty 1970 campfest *Myra Breckinridge* (Fox), and her own hip-shaking, jaw-dropping *Sextette* (Media, 1978).

SHERLOCK, JR. (1924) B&W ****

D: Buster Keaton. Buster Keaton, Kathryn McGuire, Ward Crane, Joseph Keaton. 45 mins. (Kino)

Keaton directs and stars in a pioneering exercise in comic surrealism as projectionist Buster enters the movie he's screening. The device has since been employed by everyone from Woody Allen (*The Purple Rose of Cairo*) to Arnold Schwarzenegger (*The Last Action Hero*) but rarely with such felicitous results. Most of Keaton's classic features (and we're not referring to his Great Stone Face) have joined the video ranks, while Kino has compiled an impressive array of his inventive short films.

A SHOCK TO THE SYSTEM (1990) ***

D: Jan Egleson. Michael Caine, Elizabeth McGovern, Peter Riegert, Swoosie Kurtz. 91 mins. (HBO)

Shock shapes up as a black comedy reminiscent of the classic Boulting brothers' Brit satires of the '50s and '60s. Formerly passive ad exec Caine discovers that murder can serve as a better instrument than loyalty or ability for corporate advancement. The idea is sounder than the execution as the pic is occasionally hampered by Boston-based helmer Egleson's static direction, but Caine's witty performance and a solid script make *Shock* worth watching.

SHORT CUTS   (1993) ***½

D: Robert Altman. Andie MacDowell, Jack Lemmon, Bruce Davison, Julianne Moore, Matthew Modine. 189 mins. (Columbia/TriStar)

Oft erratic auteur Altman is right on the money with his multilayered, tragicomic blending of several Raymond Carver stories, brought to vivid life by an all-star ensemble cast that also includes Tim Robbins, Fred Ward, and Jennifer Jason Leigh.

SITTING DUCKS   (1980) ***

D: Henry Jaglom. Zack Norman, Michael Emil, Patrice Townsend, Richard Romanus. 88 mins. (Media, n.i.d.)

Oft annoyingly self-indulgent auteur Jaglom—normally an acquired taste at best—fashions what may be his most purely entertaining film, a skewed caper comedy featuring standout teamwork by a blithe Norman and ragingly neurotic Emil as a pair of impulsive, inept crooks.

SIX-STRING SAMURAI   (1998) ***

D: Lance Mungia. Jeffrey Falcon, Justin McGuire, Stephane Gauger, John Sakisian. 91 mins. (Manga) DVD

Director/coscripter Mungia sets his kinetic send-up—a fun low-budget rock-'n'-roll *Road Warrior* spoof with echoes of Japan's *Lone Wolf and Cub* samurai series—in a postnuke USA. Seems the Russkis won the final war back in 1957 and have since controlled the ruins of what was America, save for a sole haven of freedom, Lost Vegas, ruled by King Elvis (!). Forty years later, several guitar-slinging contenders travel the perilous, gang-infested wasteland in hopes of claiming the vacant throne as their own. Our story focuses on one particularly determined Presley wannabe, the tuxedoed,

bespectacled Buddy (Falcon), sort of an ersatz Elvis Costello with Toshiro Mifune fighting skills, and the initially speechless urchin "the Kid" (McGuire, doing a deft impersonation of *Road Warrior*'s Feral Kid). Along the way, the duo encounter a "Windmill God," the Cleaver family (a clan of cheerful all-American cannibals), and even Death himself, in the form of a faceless heavy-metal rocker (Gauger). Filmmaker Mungia wisely adopts an utterly deadpan tone while putting his heroes through their outrageous paces. A buoyant rockabilly soundtrack, much of it by Russian-born rockers "the Red Elvises" (who also cameo on-screen), supplies just the right note to keep this finger-snapping spoof rocking at a steady pace.

SNAKES   (1974) ***

D: Arthur A. Names. Les Tremayne, Janet Wood, Bebe Kelly, Marvin Kaplan. 83 mins. (GWN)

Helmed by *Lemora* assistant director Art Names, *Snakes* is one of the very few films to employ serpents and John Philip Sousa (!) as its main themes. B-movie vet Tremayne (of *Angry Red Planet* and *The Slime People* fame) gives a bravura perf as eccentric, Sousa-loving Snakey Bender, serpent supplier to a Geekville, USA–type town apparently infected with a mutant strain of Swinging '70s–itis. Seems the local schoolmarm (Kelly) is unnaturally attracted to Snakey's slithering critters, while the obese brother-and-sister shopkeepers down the street are equally smitten with *her*, and Snakey's best bud, Bert, is about to marry a sex-mad go-go dancer (Wood), threatening an end to the pals' traditional Wednesday night booze-and-Sousa parties. Director Names delivers a fun, twisted send-up of small-town life and also wrings genuine yoks from Snakey and his serpentine friends' inevitable last-reel revenge spree. Like *Lemora*,

Snakes has sported several different titles, including *Fangs* (Gemstone) and *Holy Wednesday* (Liberty).

SOME LIKE IT HOT   (1959) B&W ***½

D: Billy Wilder. Jack Lemmon, Marilyn Monroe, Tony Curtis. 119 mins. (MGM)

Wilder taps such top talents as Lemmon, Monroe, Curtis, and Joe E. Brown (who supplies one of the screen's most memorable sign-off lines) for his classic Roaring '20s-set romp, arguably the best major-studio drag comedy ever made, *Tootsie* (Columbia / TriStar) notwithstanding.

SONS OF THE DESERT   (1933) B&W ****

D: William A. Seiter. Stan Laurel, Oliver Hardy, Mae Busch, Charlie Chase. 69 mins. (Nostalgia Merchant, Video Treasures)

Stan and Ollie sneak off to a lodge convention without the wives being any the wiser—or so they think. The national Laurel and Hardy fan club took its name from the title of this quintessential L&H romp, one of the boys' absolute best. Most of Laurel and Hardy's features and many of their sound and silent shorts are on video on a variety of labels, though their availability fluctuates. Movies Unlimited remains a top source for L&H cassettes.

SPACE TRUCKERS   (1997) **½

D: Stuart Gordon. Dennis Hopper, Stephen Dorff, Debi Mazar, Charles Dance, George Wendt, Vernon Wells, Barbara Crampton. 97 mins. (Sterling) DVD

Originally intended as a theatrical release (the pic received some Euro-bijou play), Gordon's *Space Truckers* preemed instead on cable TV ahead of its home-vid debut. While not peak Gordon, the flick measures up as a mostly fun exercise in fast-paced space camp. A winning Hopper, appealingly Brooklyn-ese Mazar, and largely bland Dorff take the title roles as a trio of drivers unwittingly on their way to deliver a small army of mechanical warriors (designed by veteran FX ace Screaming Mad George) to a potentially doomed Earth. Gordon's blend of space slapstick, corporate satire, and sci-fi carnage further benefits from *Re-Animator* cinematographer Mac Ahlberg's sharp lensing and cartoonish sets, include some clever sky-highway neon signage.

HERE'S LOOKING AT YOU, SID: Drooling imbecile Sid Haig and homicidal sis Jill Banner play prominent members of the demented Merrye clan in Jack Hill's cult cannibal comedy *Spider Baby.*
Courtesy of Johnny Legend

SPIDER BABY   (1964) B&W ***

D: Jack Hill. Lon Chaney, Jr., Carol Ohmart, Quinn Redeker, Beverly Washburn, Jill Banner, Sid Haig, Mantan Moreland, Karl Schanzer. 81 mins. (Something Weird) DVD

Firmly rooted in the celluloid "sick joke" tradition of Roger Corman's *Little Shop of Horrors* and *Bucket of Blood, Spider Baby* (a.k.a. *The Maddest Story Ever Told*) boasts a script and direction by onetime Corman underling Hill, who went on to helm such '70s sleaze classics as *The Big Bird Cage* and *Switchblade Sisters* (see index). (The Corman connection also extends to the score, by former Roger regular Ronald Stein; in an even scarier move, star Chaney croaks the theme song [!].) Embracing such outre themes as retardation, cannibalism, and dysfunctional-family values, *Spider Baby* unfolds like a combo Krafft-Ebing/William Castle variation on the then-popular *Addams Family* teleseries. Chaney, in one of his better later roles, portrays Bruno, chauffeur and guardian of the last of the Merrye family, a clan whose members suffer from a regressive syndrome that sinks them further into savage infantilism the older they get. Young Virginia (Banner) is fond of playing "spider," slicing, dicing, and dining on unsuspect-ing visitors to the Merrye Manse, while sister Elizabeth (Washburn) exhibits a similar homicidal streak. Their chrome-domed older bro, Ralph (Haig), has already been reduced to drooling-imbecile status, and "Uncle Ned" is now a largely unseen thing-in-the-basement. The Merrye Bunch's bizarre lifestyle becomes seriously endangered by the arrival of distant, untainted relatives Redeker, Ohmart, and their sleazy shyster Schanzer.

Cheesy production values, frequent day-for-night lighting confusion, erratic acting, and an uneven script betray *Spider Baby*'s invisible budget and quickie shooting sked. Still, what the flick lacks in sharp focus, it more than compensates for with sheer, unadulterated weirdness. Barely screened theatrically back in '64, *Spider Baby* was later dusted off, dressed up in a new mint print, and taken, by genre archivist Johnny Legend, on a city-by-city national tour. Legend's vid version includes fun coverage of the pic's official belated 1994 premiere at L.A.'s fabled Nu-Art Theater, with many of the flick's participants on hand to record their reactions.

SPIKE OF BENSONHURST (1988) ***

D: Paul Morrissey. Sasha Mitchell, Ernest Borgnine, Anne DeSalvo, Sylvia Miles, Talisa Soto. 91 mins. (MCEG/Virgin, n.i.d.)

One of the best barely released movies of 1988, Morrissey's comedy of street manners sees ambitious but tunnel-visioned young pugilist Mitchell, exiled from his native Benson-hurt after a run-in with local mob boss Borgnine, relocate to a nearby Hispanic nabe to prepare for his triumphant return. Morrissey crams his Brooklyn canvas with finely observed details and gets uniformly funny, unforced perfs from his cast. The late stand-up comic Rick Aviles impresses as a Nuyorican boxer and Spike's eventual pal, while Antonia Rey is wonderful as Aviles's upwardly mobile mom.

SPY HARD (1996) **½

D: Rick Friedberg. Leslie Nielsen, Nicollette Sheridan, Andy Griffith, Charles Durning, Marcia Gay Harden, Barry Bostwick, John Ales. 81 mins. (Buena Vista) DVD

Nielsen resorts to his familiar shtick as a simultaneously intrepid and inept lawman, this time as a government secret agent out to stop General Rancor (an over-the-top Griffith) from destroying the world. The nonstop gags range from antique to fresh (particularly in several recent film-parody segments) and manage to hit at least as often as they miss. Weird Al Yankovic's opening-theme video (complete with exploding-head finale) supplies a highlight, and there are cameos by, among others, Mr. T, Robert Culp, Hulk Hogan, Roger Clinton, Fabio, Michael Berryman, and even geeky Fred Olen Ray refugee Eddie Deezen.

STILL CRAZY (1998) ***½

D: Brian Gibson. Stephen Rea, Billy Connelly, Jimmy Nail, Timothy Spall, Bill Nighy, Janet Aubrey, Helena Bergstrom, Bruce Robinson. 97 mins. (Columbia/TriStar) DVD

Brimming with honest wit, earned pathos, and dead-on accuracy, *Still Crazy* arrives as a genuine audiovisual treat. The film charts the rocky Euro reunion tour of surviving (some barely) members of a fictional '70s Brit glam-rock band called Strange Fruit. Eschewing the broader (though admittedly hilarious) approach of Rob Reiner's *This Is Spinal Tap*, Gibson, working from Dick Clement and Ian La Frenais's nearly seamless script, presents the ragged but musically competent and occasionally inspired rockers as believably flawed, ultimately endearing flesh-and-blood characters. A top cast—including Rea as a calm keyboardist (who'd been working as a condom vendor!), Nighy as the addled lead

singer (a study in stately ruin), and Spall as an earthy drummer dodging imaginary taxmen—brings unwavering credibility to their roles, while Foreigner's Mick Jones and Squeeze's Chris Difford compose the Fruits' authentic-sounding original songs. One scene that sees the band finally come together in a humble Amsterdam nightclub captures with admirable, subtle, and exciting detail the exhilaration of communing and connecting with an appreciative audience.

STUART SAVES HIS FAMILY (1995) **½

D: Harold Ramis. Al Franken, Laura San Giacomo, Vincent D'Onofrio, Harris Yulin, Shirley Knight. 95 mins. (Paramount)

For some reason, *Stuart Saves His Family*, the big-screen incarnation of Al Franken's squishy all-purpose public-access Twelve-Step guru Stuart Smalley, bombed beyond all pessimism at the B.O., taking in next to nothing during its abortive bijou run—news grim enough to set Stuart off on a big-time tears and Fig Newtons jag. (Only fellow *Saturday Night Live* alum *It's Pat!* did worse, folding its gender-bent tent after a few disastrous test screenings.) The good news for Stu rooters is that *Stuart Saves His Family*, sort of a Frank Capra comedy for the '90s, scores considerable laughs and insights in its first half. Here the alternately melioristic and simpering Stuart, fired from his Windy City TV gig, returns to his Minneapolis home, where he makes it his extremely thankless job to help his bullying alkie dad (Yulin), negative overweight mom (Knight), freeloader bro' (D'Onofrio), and fat, thrice-divorced sister (Lesley Boone), a commitment that leads to much authentic mirth. It's only toward film's end that Franken and *SCTV* vet director Ramis lose their satirical grip, turning a tad *too* Smalley-esque for comfort.

Still, if you enjoy Franken's TV character, you should find amusement in this feature-length visit to a Smalley planet as well.

THE STUFF (1985) ***

D: Larry Cohen. Michael Moriarty, Andrea Marcovicci, Garrett Morris, Paul Sorvino, Scott Bloom, Danny Aiello. 93 mins. (New World, n.i.d.)

Cohen mainstay Moriarty stars as ex-FBI-agent-cum-industrial-spy "Moe" Rutherford. It's Rutherford's task to uncover the secret formula of "the Stuff," the cocaine of junk-food desserts, a killer product that's turning the nation into an army of crazed addicts (dubbed "Stuffies"). Along the way, Moe enlists the aid of publicity whiz Nicole (Marcovicci), deposed cookie king Chocolate Chip Charlie (Morris), right-wing paramilitary lunatic Colonel Spears (Sorvino), and Jason (Bloom), a kid who's seen his entire family succumb to the Stuff's seductive but lethal allure. The able topliners are complemented by cameos from Brooke Adams, Abe Vigoda, Clara ("Where's the Stuff?") Peller, and Patrick O'Neal. Cohen's blackly comic attack on America's cult of instant-grat consumerism and gluttony springs a wealth of perverse surprises.

subUrbia (1997) ***

D: Richard Linklater. Jayce Barton, Amie Carey, Parker Posey, Steve Zahn. 121 mins. (Warner)

Richard (*Dazed and Confused*) Linklater's adaptation of Eric Bogosian's play follows a group of small-town youths over the course of a pivotal night. First-rate ensemble acting further hoists a trenchant mix of wit and drama that would ring true in any era. Carey's a particular standout as an animated teenette with big-time dreams.

SULLIVAN'S TRAVELS   (1941)
B&W ***½

D: Preston Sturges. Joel McCrea, Veronica Lake, William Demarest. 91 mins. (Universal)

Sturges's classic Hollywood satire casts McCrea as a naïvely idealistic director who sets out to discover the "real" America, with oft disastrous results, in a film whose tone ranges from cheerfully satiric to harrowing to poignant. Universal has accorded the deluxe "collector's edition" treatment to most of Sturges's features.

MONDO MADDIN: GUY MOVIES

TALES FROM THE GIMLI HOSPITAL (1988) B&W ***

D: Guy Maddin. Kyle McCulloch, Michael Gottli. 72 mins. (Kino)

Related in flashback fashion, Maddin's inventively demented Manitoba-set debut feature unfolds circa 1920, when a smallpox outbreak consigns two victims—the alienated Einar the Lonely (McCulloch, who doubles as this $22,000 epic's assistant director) and the portly, affable Gunnar (Gottli)—to the title facility, a grim, primitive hosp brightened only by the unlikely presence of three fetching young nurses. When Gunnar wins the Gimli nurses' affections via his spirited accounts of several arcane Icelandic sagas (!), friend Einar becomes increasingly envious, causing an irreparable rift to grow between the twain. That's more or less the plot, or at least the situation, but auteur Maddin's bleak comic magic lies more in the telling than the tale. Lensed in stark black and white, with an air of mock Bergman-esque gloom, *Tales* stacks up as a consistently deranged, blackly funny, utterly deadpan farce that, while stylistically reminiscent of David Lynch's *Eraserhead* and Luis Buñuel's surreal early shorts, manages to score high marks in the originality department as

A TURN FOR THE NURSE: Gimli gals await fresh patients in Guy Maddin's Manitoba-set tragicomedy *Tales From the Gimli Hospital.*
© Kino International Corporation 1999

well. Especially impressive are a nightmare sequence that's nearly the equal of its counterpart in Ed Wood's *Glen or Glenda* and a terminally grotesque climactic fight scene (an example of Manitoban/Icelandic "Glima" wrestling) that rages between our sickly antagonists. Kino's cassette also contains the earlier Maddin short "The Dead Father," wherein a mourning young man devours his newly deceased dad.

ARCHANGEL: A TRAGEDY OF THE GREAT WAR   (1990) B&W ***

D: Guy Maddin. Kyle McCulloch, Kathy Marykuca, Ari Cohen. 82 mins. (Facets)

In *Archangel*, Maddin again pays meticulous attention to lampooning early cinematic styles, painstakingly recreating the look and sound of a late-1920s part-talkie. Our story, set in Hun-ravaged Russia circa 1917, involves Lieutenant John Boles (played not by the late thespian of the same name but by a returning McCulloch), a valorous Canadian soldier who, when not aiding his embattled Russian allies in the trenches, spends his time searching for his late love, Iris, a quest sometimes slowed but never completely halted by his ampu-

tated leg. Also central to Maddin's mock melodrama are jaunty American aviator Philbin (Cohen) and brave, beautiful, ever enigmatic Veronkha (Marykuca). By the time *Archangel* reaches its final reel, all three of our earnest protagonists are suffering from terminal amnesia (!). Maddin pokes fun at virtually every period propaganda, romantic, and combat cliché, capturing the iconography of that distant age with tireless precision via flash cards, ponderous voice-overs, deliberately unsynched dialogue, and hyperbolic imagery. (One scene even sees a mortally wounded Russian soldier employ his own disgorged intestines to strangle a baby-killing Bolshevik [!].) Anyone looking for an affectionate skewering of the brand of antique flicks they sat through in college film courses or at retro theaters should deem *Archangel* a subversive treat.

CAREFUL   (1993) ***

D: Guy Maddin. Kyle McCulloch, Paul Cox, Jackie Burroughs. 100 mins. (Kino)

With *Careful*, Maddin inches ever closer to the modern world, graduating to full-talkie and two-strip color status. Maddin sets his quintessentially Canadian comedy in the mythical Tolzbad, an alpine village so avalanche-prone that the slightest sneeze can wreak icy havoc. ("Hold your horses" and "Put a lid on it" are among the hamlet's most oft echoed caveats.) This leads its citizenry to exercise extreme caution—even domestic animals have their vocal cords severed (!)—but simultaneously encourages abnormal passions and desperate acts of lethal hysteria. A typical tableau finds a grown son feverishly ogling his bathing mater while she warns, "Better put your name on your new toothbrush before some accident happens." Complete with celeb cameos by Canadian thesp Burroughs (as a butler-academy teacher) and director Cox (as a long-sequestered nobleman), *Careful* rates as Maddin's funniest, most lavish effort to date.

TALES FROM THE HOOD
(1995) ***

D: Rusty Cundieff. Clarence Williams III, Rusty Cundieff, Rosalind Cash, Corbin Bernsen, Art Evans, David Allen Grier, Wings Hauser.
98 mins. (HBO) DVD

The wraparound ("Welcome to My Mortuary") for this creative creep-fest from Rusty (*Fear of a Black Hat,* on Fox) Cundieff offers a seemingly demented mortician (an excellent Williams) who lures a trio of violent home-boys to his undertaker digs on the pretext of having a stash of drugs to sell. Instead he treats the impatient kids to a quartet of moral fables cloaked in terror-tale garb, involving racist cops ("Rogue Cop Revelation"), abusive parents ("Boys Do Get Bruised"), belated slave revenge ("KKK Comeuppance") and a *Clockwork Orange*–type brain-washing experiment ("Hardcore Convert"). Cundieff, who coscripts and plays a supporting role as a concerned teacher in "Boys Do Get Bruised," makes his social points without stinting on either edgy laughs or legit scares.

Filmmakers in Focus!
GUY MADDIN: MADMAN OF MANITOBA
As Told to The Phantom

In all three of his feature films, Guy Maddin—named, he claims, after erstwhile American B star Guy Madison—makes extensive use of the celluloid techniques of the late-'20s part-talkie period. While directors of the era may have found said techniques cumbersome, Maddin views them in a different light.

"It actually gave filmmakers *more* options," asserts the Manitoban auteur, who goes "straight to the old B&W movies when I go to a video store" and cites F. W. (*Nosferatu*) Murnau and Erich von Stroheim among his fave directors. "You could use silent film if the story called for pantomime. And then you could have the actor open his mouth and words would come out. The kind of melodrama I'm interested in doing lends itself perfectly to that style. It's a style that still has plenty of potential but was discontinued for economic reasons."

One element that distinguishes *Archangel*—which Maddin would like to be remembered as "the first amnesic picture directed by an amnesic"—from other films, old and new, was the use of actual on-set hypnosis. Universal Pictures flacks maintained that Bela Lugosi had been hypnotized for his death scene in 1940's *Black Friday*, but that proved a mere publicity stunt. Not so with *Archangel*. Says Maddin: "A couple of actors performed while under hypnosis. Kyle McCulloch, the lead actor, not only insisted on being hypnotized for the last scene but underwent posthypnotic suggestion so he would have no recollection of ever having done the scene."

Maddin encountered resistance when *Tales from the Gimli Hospital* first opened on his home turf. "One morning I bought a paper," he recalls, "with a headline about the town of Gimli being in an uproar." The mayor, says Maddin, even went on record to assure the rest of the world that "the people of Gimli don't wear fish guts in their hair."

Maddin likewise sets *Careful* in "sort of a vague cinematic past" to explore the theme of caution. "I thought the theme was very Canadian. Even in our praise of something that thrills us, the highest compliment is 'pretty good.' And when we *don't* like something, we usually say it's 'pretty good,' because we don't want to hurt anyone either." As for Canadians' view of their image here, Maddin opines, "I think they're scared they're seen as Americans' geeky cousins."

Careful, budgeted at nearly $1 million, is not only the director's most expensive film but the first one lensed in color. Maddin toyed with shooting in B&W, then colorizing the film, but economic restraint ultimately prevailed. "I didn't want to go too fast into contemporary films," he confesses. "*Careful* gave me the perfect excuse to proceed with caution myself."

MONDO JUZO

TAMPOPO (1986) ***

D: Juzo Itami. Ken Watanabe, Tsutomu Yamazaki, Nobuko Miyamoto. Subtitled.
114 mins. (Republic) DVD

Laconic truck-drivin' macho man Watanabe helps a struggling widow make a go of her ailing noodle joint (!) in Itami's offbeat, movie-hip comedy of gustatory manners.

A TAXING WOMAN (1987) ***½

D: Juzo Itami. Nobuko Miyamoto, Tsutomu Yamazaki. Subtitled 127 mins. (Fox Lorber) DVD

Itami follows his innovative contemporary noodle western with this equally inventive comedy. Miyamoto brings a kind of nagging charm to her perf as a mega-persistent Japanese Revenue Service agent on the trail of a tricky tax cheat. She resurfaces for more sophisticated mirth in *A Taxing Woman's Return* (1988, New Yorker). Itami's *The Funeral* (1985, Republic) and *Minbo—Or the Gentle Art of Japanese Extortion* (1992, Hallmark) are also available. The filmmaker later jumped to his death after news of an extramarital affair appeared in the Japanese media.

TEENAGE CATGIRLS IN HEAT (1993) ***

D: Scott Perry. Gary Graves, Carrie Vanston, Dave Cox, Tina Martorell, Joy Gohring, Leslie Mitchell. 84 mins. (Troma)

You can't always judge a Troma flick by looking at its title, but the Gotham-based outfit's loopy low-budgeter, *Teenage Catgirls in Heat*, happily lives up to its madcap moniker. In Perry's Austin-lensed send-up, a cost-efficient cat statuette (the Egyptian "Icon of Keshra") telepathically commands local felines to voluntarily surrender all nine lives so they can (a) transform into the shapely titular critters; (b) mate with and terminate human males; and (c) pave the way for "the Great Litter." Professional cat-tracker Graves and pal Cox look to save their own skins and put a stop to the supernatural-kitty conspiracy. A pivotal plot thread finds young Cox falling head over paws for former feline turned major babe Cleo (Vanston). With its witty script—the sight of suicidal cat dummies hurling themselves off roofs provides a funny running

CAT'S ENTERTAINMENT!: Foxy feline harbors secret agenda in publicity still for Troma's *Teenage Catgirls in Heat.*
© *Troma Entertainment, Inc.*

gag—appealing perfs, and a half dozen seminaked catgirls, this sandpaper-tongue-in-cheek outing makes for a fun romp.

TEENAGE MUTANT NINJA TURTLES: THE SERIES

TEENAGE MUTANT NINJA TURTLES (1990) **½

D: Steve Barron. Judith Hoag, Elias Koteas, James Saito. 93 mins. (Artisan) DVD

The big-screen debut of those wildly overhyped Teenage Mutant Ninja Turtles, of cartoon, comics, and video-game fame, pits the tortoise foursome—Leonardo, Donatello, Michelangelo, and Raphael, along with their Zen rodent ninja master, Splinter—against the sinister Foot Clan, a collection of light-fingered youths under the command of Shredder (Saito), a Fagin-like Japanese villain clad in full warlord regalia. Fetching TV reporter Hoag and arrested adult figure Koteas join our half-shell heroes in what shapes up as a mostly fun outing marred by occasionally murky lensing and some dull stretches. Best here are the imaginatively choreographed ninja battles, several flashbacks explaining the *TMNT*'s unlikely origins, and a number of alternately boisterous and touching scenes that supply rare insight into adolescent-mutant-ninja-turtle-bonding rituals. We were less thrilled by the pic's blatant self-promotion and multiple product tie-ins. Followed by the less successful *Teenage Mutant Turtles II: The Secret of the Ooze* and *Teenage Mutant Ninja Turtles 3* (both New Line).

THAT'S ADEQUATE! (1989) ***

D: Harry Hurwitz. James Coco, Tony Randall, Bruce Willis, Peter Riegert, Robert Downey, Jr., Renee Taylor. 82 mins. (Southgate, n.i.d.)

Employing a *This Is Spinal Tap*–type mockumentary format to present an illustrated history of the fictional schlock studio Adequate Pictures, *That's Adequate!* stars Randall as our tour guide through Adequate's archives, while the late Coco plays the company's crude founding father. The pic further benefits from cameos by the likes of Professor Irwin Corey, Susan Dey, TV talk-show legend Joe Franklin, Richard Lewis, Brother Theodore, Robert Townsend, and even Bruce Willis (as a thesp who specializes in animal roles!). *That's Adequate!* is a hit-and-miss affair, but when it scores, it yields some genuine gems. Highlights include Adequate's rip-off of Chaplin's *The Gold Rush*, a "Barry the Talking Gorilla" series, Robert Vaughn as Hitler, and a "We Are the World" take-off featuring a horde of ego-crazed stand-up comics. The best bit, though, involves Adequate's Three Stooges clones, the Three Morons, who take the Stooges' violent slapstick to its natural conclusion.

THIS IS SPINAL TAP (1984) ****

D: Rob Reiner. Christopher Guest, Michael McKean, Rob Reiner, Harry Shearer. 93 mins. (New Line) DVD

Easily the funniest rock-'n'-roll satire ever filmed, Reiner's mockumentary profile of the fictitious title group ("one of England's loudest bands") never hits a false note. The Stonehenge production number is

one of many highlights, while bandmates Guest, McKean, and Shearer are excellent. Director Reiner struggled mightily—even financing a *Spinal Tap* demo reel—to get this offbeat gem produced, but his efforts have since been well rewarded. Followed by the 1992 direct-to-video sequel, *The Return of Spinal Tap*.

¡THREE AMIGOS! (1986) ***

D: John Landis. Steve Martin, Chevy Chase, Martin Short, Patrice Martinez. 105 mins. (HBO) DVD

The comic troika of Martin, Chase, and Short carry the day as three unemployed silent-movie cowboys on a misunderstood mission to an outlaw-plagued Mexican village in Landis's erratic but often funny *Magnificent Seven* parody.

TO DIE FOR (1995) ***1/2

D: Gus Van Sant. Nicole Kidman, Matt Dillon, Joaquin Phoenix, Illeana Douglas, Dan Hedaya, Kurtwood Smith, Buck Henry. 106 mins. (Columbia/TriStar) DVD

After his pretentious *My Own Private Idaho* and disastrous *Even Cowgirls Get the Blues* (both Columbia/TriStar), director Van Sant returns to the semi-verité approach of *Drugstore Cowboy* and comes up with a winner with this cheerfully dark comedy. Buck Henry, who appears on-screen as a cranky teacher, skillfully adapts Joyce Maynard's novel, very loosely based on a real-life case, about ambitious bubblehead Kidman's blindly ruthless efforts to attain TV stardom. While working as a local public-access weatherperson, Kidman decides her amiable-slob hubby (Dillon) is standing in her way—in reality, she has no "way" for Dillon to stand in—and enlists dim, lovestruck local teen Phoenix to help her do him in. Van Sant and Henry's inspired use of fic-

tional TV and video footage lend an added edge of scary credibility to their Barbie Doll from Hell tale, and the performers, from Kidman on down, are uniformly excellent.

TREES LOUNGE (1996) ***

D: Steve Buscemi. Steve Buscemi, Chloe Sevigny, William Baldwin, Anthony LaPaglia. 94 mins. (Artisan) DVD

Set in the wilds of Nassau County, Long Island, *Trees Lounge* stars debuting director Buscemi as Tommy, an amiable but terminally aimless dude waging a likely losing battle with a barfly future. Tommy drives an ice cream truck and drifts into an ill-advised flirtation with local teen Sevigny, but the lure of the titular local watering hole gradually becomes the strongest magnet in his clueless life. Buscemi humanizes his potentially trite material by creating specific, believable characters. Along the way, he makes evocative use of his Long Island locations and concludes his cautionary tale with a memorable fade-out.

TREMORS: THE SERIES

TREMORS (1989) **1/2

D: Ron Underwood. Fred Ward, Kevin Bacon, Finn Carter, Michael Gross. 96 mins. (Universal) DVD

Handymen Fred and Kevin lead an oddball band of embattled Southwest desert dwellers in a struggle against outsized killer slugs (dubbed "graboids") in Underwood's amusing spoof of vintage monster-movie clichés. Coscripter S. S. Wilson takes the directorial reins for 1995's *Tremors 2: Aftershocks* (Universal, DVD), wherein a returning Ward and Gross resume their fight with the persistent fiends in a generally effective Mexico-set follow-up.

TROMEO & JULIET (1996) **1/2

D: Lloyd Kaufman. Jane Jensen, Will Keenan, Debbie Rochon, Maximillian Shaun, Lemmy. In R and unrated editions. 102 mins. (Troma Team) DVD

As might be expected, those jejune jokesters at Troma take considerable poetic licentiousness in updating Shakespeare's tragic tale of adolescent love and familial conflict to a present-day NYC slob-and-bimbo scene. Director Kaufman and coscripter James Gunn do best when sticking with a straight-ahead burlesque approach that sees Tromeo (an effective Keenan) and Juliet (an appealing Jensen) drift in and out of the Bard's original dialogue, yielding some genuinely funny results. (When, for example, Juliet sighs, "Parting is such sweet sorrow," Tromeo avers with an enthusiastic "Totally sucks!") Elsewhere on the upside, Motorhead's Lemmy impresses as the flick's Falstaffian narrator, while Rochon gives a charismatic perf as Juliet's lesbian lady-in-waiting. Alas, the filmmakers, apparently suffering from a sort of Troma Team Tourette's Syndrome, too often resort to some extremely old tricks, tossing the usual stale scatological gags, splatstick shticks, and self-referential riffs into the mix. At one point an enraged Tromeo uses a weighty edition of *The Yale Shakespeare* to pound an abusive Pop Capulet (Shaun) into temporary submission, a moment that pretty much sums up Troma's appropriation of Old Will's work. Still, there are enough anarchic laughs here to make *Tromeo & Juliet* a must for bad-taste buffs.

THE TUNE (1992) ***1/2

D: Bill Plympton. Animated. 72 mins. (Triboro) DVD

Plympton's self-financed feature debut not only brims with the animator's unique brand of off-the-wall whimsy but offers a host of clever songs composed by singer Maureen McElheron, who formerly fronted a C&W band in which Plympton played pedal-steel guitar. Our story finds struggling songwriter Del (voiced by Daniel Neiden) at a loss to please his soulless boss, Mr. Mega (Marty Nelson), and salvage his romance with Mega employee Didi (McElheron). In an *Alice in Wonderland*–type twist, a wrong turn on a freeway leads Del into a series of surreal adventures involving, among others, a canine Elvis imitator (who sings "Dig My 'Do"), a proboscisless cabbie ("No Nose Blues"), a sadistic bellhop ("Lovesick Hotel"), a dance-entranced surf couple ("Dance All Day"), and a psychobabbling behemoth dubbed "The Wise One." Plympton's fable and McElheron's musical contributions serve as able frames for a succession of rapid-fire sight gags and surreal riffs filtered through the animator's darkly cheerful POV. Plympton even pauses to pay brief homage to Danny Antonucci's groundbreaking 1987 gore-toon *Lupo the Butcher*. Plympton can be forgiven for padding *The Tune* with his previous short "When Push Comes to Shove," repeated here in its entirety (much to Del and Didi's expressed confusion). Light but perverse and always inventive, *The Tune* rates as a sure bet for animaniacs.

TWILIGHT OF THE COCKROACHES (1987) ***

D: Hiroaki Yoshida. Setsuko Karasumaru, Kaoru Kobayashi. Subtitled. 105 mins. (Streamline)

Sort of a *Watership Down* of the cockroach kingdom and the obvious inspiration for the 1996 Stateside comedy *Joe's Apartment* (MGM), *Twilight of the Cockroaches* combines live actors with animated insects and relates its strange narrative mostly from the latter's inch-high POV. As our parable opens, a colony of talking cockroaches are enjoying a carefree existence in the home of lonely slob Saito (Kobayashi), where they're free to frolic, socialize, stage food fights, and even operate their own makeshift TV station (!). That cushy situation comes to an abrupt end when Saito takes up with femme neighbor Karasumaru, a fanatical neatnik who declares all-out war on the indigenous roach population. While Yoshida's premise is clearly satiric, he plays his story fairly straight, "humanizing" the embattled insects to serve as stand-ins for the "Other" of the viewer's choice. The central plot thread deals with young roachette Naomi's romantic involvement with her beau, Ichiro, and her subsequent infatuation with Hans, an officer in a neighboring tribe of roach warriors. The individual roaches' plights become secondary to simple survival, however, once the humans' genocidal campaign gets under way. *Twilight* is most effective in its roach-eye view of humans as noisy, capricious, ultimately vicious giants armed with an insurmountable array of chemical weapons. Yoshida manages the Herculean task of placing audience sympathy squarely with the endangered insects, a trend later given gala mainstream treatment in such animated 'plex hits as *Antz* (Artisan) and *A Bug's Life* (Touchstone).

UFORIA (1980) ***1/2

D: John Binder. Cindy Williams, Fred Ward, Harry Dean Stanton, Beverly Hope Atkinson, Harry Carey, Jr. 100 mins. (Universal)

It took nearly five years for Binder's low-key comedy about California UFO nuts to reach the screen, but it was well worth the wait. Williams stars as Arlene, an intense if unconscious checkout gal with a fetish for UFO's and a burgeoning belief that one is about to land in a nearby desert. Into her lonely life rides Sheldon (expertly played by Ward), a rhinestone-cowboy manqué who hooks up with phony evangelist Brother Bud (Stanton). Arlene's saucer-mania soon attracts a following of fellow wackos, from freelance futurists to New Age Jesus freaks, as well as Brother Bud's ever avaricious attention. *UFOria* is basically a comic meditation on beliefs, the universal need to own a set of same, and the loony lengths to which said need can take people who don't have a hell of a lot of earthly options. As Brother Bud puts it, "Everybody ought to believe in somethin'. I believe I'll have another drink." To which The Phantom can only add a heartfelt "Amen."

USED CARS   (1980) ***

D: Robert Zemeckis. Kurt Russell, Jack Warden, Gerrit Graham, Deborah Harmon. 113 mins. (Columbia/TriStar)

Warden, in a dual role, plays rival used-car pitchmen brothers in a frenetic early effort by the team of Bob Gale (coscripter) and Zemeckis (coscripter, director), of *Back to the Future* and *Who Framed Roger Rabbit?* fame. Graham turns in top work as Russell's superstitious cohort, while *SCTV*'s Joe Flaherty stands out as a casually corrupt attorney, and Al (Grampa Munster) Lewis cameos as an impatient judge.

VEGAS IN SPACE   (1993) **1/2

D: Phillip R. Ford. Doris Fish, Ramona Fischer, Ginger Quest, Lori Naslund. 85 mins. (Troma)

Billed as "the First All Drag Sci-Fi Musical Ever!," Ford's campy romp—about a trio of spacemen forced to switch sexes to investigate skulduggery on a "babes-only" planet—partially compensates with tacky, retro charm what it lacks in incisive satirical wit. The eye-curdling costumes, mile-high hairdos, and papier-mâché sets are enough to make *Queen of Outer Space*'s Zsa Zsa Gabor and her space cadettes turn green—with envy, nausea, or a combi-

nation thereof. Tunes like "Love Theme from *Vegas in Space*" and "Walk This Way" add to the amusement.

THE VISITORS   (1993) ***

D: Jean-Marie Poiré. Jean Reno, Christian Clavier, Marie-Anne Chazel. Subtitled. 106 mins. (Miramax)

Reportedly the most lucrative French comedy ever made, Poire's time-travel tale exerts a somewhat schizy effect. The opening, set in 1123, is consumed largely by broad slapstick—sort of a *Monty Python and the Holy Grail* with chain-mail wit. The pic gets much funnier once nobleman Reno and serf Clavier land in present-day France, where the story moves in a class-satire direction, striking a better balance between the blunt physical humor and sharp social commentary. Best of all, you don't have to be French to get the jokes.

VOLERE VOLARE   (1992) ***

D: Maurizio Nichetti. Maurizio Nichetti, Angela Finocchiaro, Mariella Valentini, Patrizio Roversi. Subtitled. 92 mins. (New Line)

Nichetti, often dubbed (or subtitled) "the Italian Woody Allen," follows his playful, media-bent neorealist parody *The Icicle Thief* (Fox Lorber) with the equally wacky *Volere Volare (I Want to Fly)*. The diminutive, mustachioed comic auteur again takes the lead role, this time as Maurizio, an eccentric audio expert who specializes in fashioning sound FX for vintage cartoons. *Volere Volare* chronicles our oddball hero's unlikely romance/professional partnership with Martina (Finocchiaro), who labors as a sort of freelance "social worker" for obscure sexual fetishists. Her clients—who contribute some of the flick's wittiest moments—range from a secretly infantile academic to a wealthy couple who take turns

mourning at each other's mock funerals (!). *Volere Volare* veers into more openly surreal territory when Maurizio begins metamorphosing into a cartoon character, à la Gabriel Byrne in Ralph Bakshi's far inferior semianimated dud *Cool World* (Paramount). Some of Nichetti's shticks—as when he dubs a porn film with cartoon sound FX—are as original as they are hilarious; at other times, his on-screen persona remains irritatingly ill defined, a pawn of writer Nichetti's random comic inspirations. Nichetti's comedies may lack the overall precision of Allen's best work, but he succeeds often enough here to make *Volere Volare* an offbeat treat.

WAG THE DOG   (1997) ***

D: Barry Levinson. Robert De Niro, Dustin Hoffman, Woody Harrelson, Anne Heche, Denis Leary, Willie Nelson, Andrea Martin. 96 mins. (New Line) DVD

During its theatrical run, Levinson's *Wag the Dog* benefitted mightily from its incredibly timely reflection of White House spin-doctoring on the Bill Clinton/Paula Jones/Monica Lewinsky affair(s)—though its satiric notions re behind-the-scenes media manipulation and image tinkering haven't really seemed all that far-fetched since the Gulf War (if not well before). In the film, a presidential sex scandal inspires White House spin doc De Niro to enlist Hollywood producer Hoffman (doing a dead-on impersonation of controversial real-life producer Robert Evans) to help him fabricate a burgeoning "war" between the U.S. and Albania. (Albanian-American Jim Belushi even gets into the act via a patriotic national-TV spot.) Levinson, who lensed the film on a relatively modest $15 million budget in a whirlwind 29 shooting days, and scripter David Mamet (working from Hilary Henkin's novel) succeed best in depicting the devious inner workings of the De Niro/Hoffman team's technology-driven propaganda machine. The pic takes a radical dip when a mugging Harrelson shows up as the psycho soldier the Pentagon picks to portray an invented war "hero"; the film's hitherto surgically precise scalpel is suddenly replaced by a chainsaw. Still, for most of its running time, *Wag the Dog*, while not quite as outrageous as it thinks it is, emerges as a savvy, sometimes scathing take on a reality that, to paraphrase *Invasion of the Body Snatchers*'s Kevin McCarthy, is here already.

WAITING FOR GUFFMAN (1997) ***½

D: Christopher Guest. Christopher Guest, Parker Posey, Fred Willard, Eugene Levy, Catherine O'Hara, Bob Balaban. 84 mins. (Warner)

The *This Is Spinal Tap* of regional theater, *Waiting for Guffman* is a consistently funny, sometimes raw, but never mean-spirited mockumentary chronicling the staging of fictional Blaine, Missouri's ("the Stool Capital of America"), susquentennial theatrical pageant, *Red, White and Blaine*. *Spinal Tap*–per Guest directs, coscripts, and stars as the indomitable Corky St. Clair, an earnest, effeminate, low-level NYC theater refugee hired to create the show. Corky, whose previous credits include a theatrical mounting of the movie *Backdraft* that resulted in an incinerated theater (!), recruits such dubious local "talents" as married, extroverted travel agents Willard and O'Hara, "comic" dentist Levy (who coscripted), and Dairy Queen ingenue Posey. In the face of envious musical director Balaban, klutzy cast members, a gung-ho but penurious city council, and his own copious shortcomings, Corky battles on, determined to bring the show to dazzling fruition. The McGuffin is supplied by the elusive Guffman, an NYC talent scout who's promised to be in attendance at the show's high-school-gym premiere. We're in the hands of some very skilled

and seasoned comic vets here, and they don't let us down: *Waiting for Guffman* hits the heights of the best *SCTV* specials, like the 1980s Capra Christmas send-up *It's a Wonderful Film*. The comic vignettes build to the show's opening night, and Guest and crew nail it to perfection with a first act burdened by a missing cast member, a lazy-eyed Levy's myopic mistakes, and a pervasive anxiety re the absent Guffman. According to *Entertainment Weekly*, Guest and crew shot over 58 hours of improv in assembling the film. Their efforts bear oft hilarious fruit: *Waiting for Guffman* rates as a true comic gem.

WATERMELON MAN (1970) ***

D: Melvin Van Peebles. Godfrey Cambridge, Estelle Parsons, Howard Caine. 97 mins. (Columbia/TriStar)

Cambridge is a white suburbanite who turns black overnight in Van Peebles's pointed racial satire. Not quite as out-there as the earnest *Black Like Me* (VCI) but pretty funny in its own right.

WEAPONS OF MASS DISTRACTION (1997) ***

D: Stephen Surjik. Ben Kingsley, Gabriel Byrne, Mimi Rogers, Jeffrey Tambor, Illeana Douglas, Paul Mazursky, Chris Mulkey, R. Lee Ermey, Tom Wright. 105 mins. (HBO)

A battle to buy an NFL team causes a long-raging war between egomaniacal international media moguls Kingsley and Byrne to escalate to near-nuclear proportions in a satire scripted by vet Larry (*Tootsie, The Wrong Box*) Gelbart. Employing characters obviously based on (but carefully compositized) Rupert Murdoch and Ted Turner, *Weapons* builds with the precision of a vintage Laurel and Hardy "Tit for Tat" routine. When their rivalry heats up, the strategy turns intensely

personal, with both power brokers dragging increasingly rotten skeletons— from Byrne's secret penile-implant operation to Kingsley's faked Holocaust past—to light. A clever parallel thread tracks two of the pair's typical victims (Douglas, Mulkey), a downwardly mobile Tucson, Arizona, working-class consumer couple who have no clue whose distant fingers are pulling the strings of their unexamined yo-yo lives. The only flaw in Gelbart's surgical vivisection of our contempo mainstream tab-trash culture is that he increasingly flirts with forgetting to be funny—a direction Joe Dante's *The Second Civil War* (HBO) also takes. *Weapons* originally aired on HBO cable, a venue that renders this biting-the-hand-that-feeds-it attack somewhat contextually toothless.

WEST IS WEST (1988) ***

D: David Rathod. Ashutosh Gowariker, Heidi Carpenter, Pearl Padamsee. 80 mins. (Milestone)

According to Milestone's box copy, writer/director Rathod spent time in India working with that nation's late, great movie maestro Satyajit Ray. Rathod embraces more modest aims than his mentor, and mostly achieves them with this low-key, slice-of-life comedy about Indian college hopeful Vhikram (Gowariker in an appealing, unforced performance) and his credible misadventures in San Francisco's seedy Mission District. When his plans to stay with a middle-class 'burb family fall through, our displaced hero finds lodgings and work manning the night desk of an Indian-run skid-row hotel. He spends the rest of his time evading immigration authorities and bonding with punkette movie-theater worker Carpenter. Part of the film was lensed at the Beale Theater, where George Romero's *Living Dead* trilogy forms the current program (Carpenter also mentions an upcoming bill of *Basket Case* and *Slumber Party Massacre*). Rathod pokes gentle fun at both American and Indian cultures, the latter via a mock musical number of the sort that are still de rigueur in Indian cinema. Cuts from contempo Indian pop artists Sheila Chandra and Jai Uttal enliven the soundtrack.

WHERE'S POPPA? (1970) ***

D: Carl Reiner. George Segal, Ruth Gordon, Ron Leibman. 84 mins. (Fox)

Reiner's raunchy comedy—scripted by Robert Klane from his own novel, *Going Ape*—plays like a filmlong sick joke as lawyer/oedipal wreck Segal attempts to cope with senile mom Gordon (in a show-stealing perf) and sundry courtroom insanities.

WICKED STEPMOTHER (1989) **1/2

D: Larry Cohen. Bette Davis, Barbara Carrera, Lionel Stander, Colleen Camp. 90 mins. (MGM)

Cohen's oft bizarre, ultimately uneven black comedy about modern-day witchery is worth catching for a wizened but still supremely acerbic Bette, in what proved to be her final film role. Bette walked off the set, never to return, causing Cohen no end of woes and greatly contributing to the film's subsequent awkward plot machinations.

WISE BLOOD (1979) ***1/2

D: John Huston. Brad Dourif, Ned Beatty, Amy Wright. 106 mins. (Universal)

Huston expertly captures the elusive, grotesque essence of Flannery O'Connor's black-comic novel about a self-made evangelist (a powerful Dourif) and his brain-damaged disciple. The film flopped at the box office, but it's a one-of-a-kind winner that's not to be missed.

WISE GUYS (1986) ***

D: Brian De Palma. Danny DeVito, Joe Piscopo, Ray Sharkey, Harvey Keitel, Dan Hedaya. 100 mins. (Fox)

De Palma returns to his NYC dark-comedy roots (e.g., *Greetings, Hi, Mom!*) with an amusing account of bumbling low-rung Mafia employees DeVito and Piscopo, who chance upon a stash of mob cash. Wrestling promoter Captain Lou Albano gives an unexpectedly expert perf as a violent thug.

THE WITCHES (1990) ***

D: Nicolas Roeg. Anjelica Huston, Mai Zetterling, Jasen Fisher, Rowan Atkinson. 92 mins. (Warner)

Quirky Brit auteur Roeg and late Muppet-master Jim Henson join creative forces for an edgy children's fable, based on a Roald Dahl story, about endangered tykes stranded at a witches' convention.

THE WITCHES OF EASTWICK (1987) **1/2

D: George Miller. Jack Nicholson, Cher, Susan Sarandon, Michelle Pfeiffer. 118 mins. (Warner) DVD

Not all of it works, but *Road Warrior* helmer Miller's screen translation of John Updike's oft smarmy farce is worth watching for Nicholson's sardonic perf as a satanic satyr. Cher, Sarandon, and Pfeiffer also impress as his three upper-middle-class victims/tormentors.

THE WIZARD OF OZ (1939) ***1/2

D: Victor Fleming. Judy Garland, Bert Lahr, Jack Haley, Ray Bolger. 101 mins. (MGM) DVD

L. Frank Baum's weird, fertile fable gets the grand-scale Hollywood

treatment, complete with surreal imagery, memorable characters, and music galore. MGM's restored "50th anniversary edition" offers many extras; even more can be found in the gala DVD version.

YOUNG FRANKENSTEIN (1974) ****

D: Mel Brooks. Gene Wilder, Madeline Kahn, Peter Boyle, Marty Feldman, Cloris Leachman. 105 mins. (Fox) DVD

Wilder essays the title role ("That's *Fronkensteen*") while Boyle plays the misunderstood monster in Brooks's superbright send-up of backdate chiller clichés, still the funniest fright-film parody ever made. Audiovisual "extras" abound in Fox's VHS and DVD "25½ anniversary" edition.

THE YOUNG POISONER'S HANDBOOK (1995) **1/2

D: Benjamin Rose. Hugh O'Conor, Antony Sher, Ruth Sheen. 99 mins. (Cabin Fever)

Benjamin (*Paperhouse*) Rose's extremely dark comedy, based on an actual case, traces laid-back teenage sociopath O'Conor's murderous misadventures in the toxic slow-death trade. The pic's best stretch details the killer's relationship with voyeuristic shrink Sher.

YOU'RE A BIG BOY NOW (1966) ***

D: Francis Ford Coppola. Peter Kastner, Elizabeth Hartman, Rip Torn, Geraldine Page. 96 mins. (Warner)

Coppola's quirky coming-of-age comedy casts Kastner as an innocent youth adrift in the wilds of darkest Manhattan, where he falls into the clutches of neurotic actress Hartman.

The top supporting cast includes Torn and Page as Kastner's eccentric parents, along with Julie Harris, Michael Dunn, Karen Black, Tony Bill, and Dolph Sweet.

YOUR FRIENDS AND NEIGHBORS (1998) ★★★

D: Neil LaBute. Jason Patric, Ben Stiller, Catherine Keener, Nastassja Kinski, Amy Brenneman, Aaron Eckhart. 100 mins. (PolyGram) DVD

Sort of a "Six Characters in Search of an Orgasm," LaBute's follow-up to his *In the Company of Men* (see index) lacks the purity and sense of completion that hoisted his brilliant debut effort but offers enough insights and sharp, uncomfortable exchanges to make it worth a look and listen. *Company* concerned a triangle among a testosterone-fueled corporate climber (Eckhart), his passive jerk friend, and the deaf woman both men conspire to seduce and abandon. Returning thesp Eckhart (who put on considerable poundage) assumes the passive-jerk role here, while Patric plays the brute—a proudly amoral macho medico—and Stiller completes the male troika as an irritating, overly analytical college acting teacher. As the film unfolds, Stiller makes a play for Eckhart's recessive writer wife (Brenneman), while Stiller's spouse (Keener) goes the lesbian route with art-museum worker Kinski, and Patric does what he can to stir up trouble with everyone he comes in contact with. As in *Company*, LaBute offers a dim portrait of male "friendship," male-female relationships, female-female relationships, and even onanistic relationships when Eckhart's character discovers that not only can't he please everybody, he can't even please himself.

ZOMBIE AND THE GHOST TRAIN (1991) ★★★

D: Mika Kaurismaki. Silu Seppala. Subtitled. 88 mins. (First Run)

Despite its title, 1991's *Zombie and the Ghost Train* is not a horror film but an alternately funny and wrenching portrait of a likable loser on a fast track to oblivion. Writer/director Kaurismaki charts the misadventures of the eponymous young "Zombie" (a winning Seppala), a Finnish-army deserter, bass player with a second-rate Scandinavian country-western band, and increasingly full-time alcoholic. The titular "Ghost Train" is a mysterious rock group that sporadically appears as a harbinger of Zombie's rapidly approaching doom. Kaurismaki infuses his potentially downbeat tale with enough life-affirming color, charm, humor, and humanity to make *Zombie and the Ghost Train* a rewarding and memorable experience.

Best of the Worst:
100 CAMP CLASSICS

"Can you prove that it didn't happen?"
—Criswell, *PLAN 9 FROM OUTER SPACE*

ASSAULT OF THE REBEL GIRLS
(1959) B&W ***

D: Barry Mahon. Errol Flynn, Beverly
Aadland, John McKay. 66 mins. (Fox Hills,
n.i.d.)

Shortly before his death, a dissipated
Errol Flynn agreed to "present,"
narrate, and sporadically appear in this
mud-stuck vehicle for his teenage
flame, Aadland. *Cuban Rebel Girls*
(retitled *Assault of the Rebel Girls* for its
vid release) is an incredibly shoddy
quickie featuring Flynn as himself
(though currently on assignment as a
roving Hearst reporter!) and Bev as a
blond bimbo who joins Castro's guerrillas to be near her mercenary boyfriend
(Mahon mainstay McKay). Applying the
same docu-schlock approach that
informed his highly recommended
Rocket Attack, U.S.A. (1961, Sony),
Mahon uses stock and newsreel footage
intercut with static "dramatic" scenes
shot in murky black and white to craft
his pro-Castro tract. (He wasn't doing
Fidel any favors.) Flynn looks wan and
embarrassed, while Bev enthusiastically
mouths lines like "I don't even know
who these Batista and Castro guys are!"
A prime example of artlessness imitat-
ing life, this campy curiosity piece definitely rates a look.

THE ASTOUNDING SHE MONSTER
(1958) B&W ***

D: Ronnie Ashcroft. Robert Clarke, Kenne
Duncan, Marilyn Harvey, Jeanne Tatum,
Shirley Kilpatrick, Ewing Brown. 77 mins.
(Englewood)

Apparently still recovering from his
self-produced *Hideous Sun Demon*
(Englewood), Clarke stars in this fun,
extremely cost-conscious clinker as an
isolated geologist whose rural California
cabin is invaded by two mugs (Brown
and Ed Wood vet Duncan), their socialite kidnap victim (Harvey), and the shim-
mering, irradiated, spandex-wrapped
titular creature (Kilpatrick), who comes
equipped with a lethal touch. The
shapely alien makes short work of the
bad guys before she's done in by a homemade acid bomb of hero Clarke's invention. Clarke and Harvey discover on her
late person a small, crumpled scrap of
paper containing a long-winded peace
message (in English, no less) explaining
that the ASM was actually a friendly
emissary sent by the exalted "Master
of Council of Planets, Telos Galaxy."
Clarke and Harvey express the fervent
hope that the next galactic gal will
exhibit sharper social skills. Longtime
Ed Wood cinematographer William C.
Thompson lensed this backyard epic.

ATTACK OF THE BEAST
CREATURES   (1985) ***

D: Michael Stanley. Robert Nolfi, Robert
Lengye, Julia Rust. 82 mins. (WesternWorld,
n.i.d.)

This hilarious obscurity pits a band
of rowboat-wreck survivors against
a horde of singularly unterrifying doll
people with stiff limbs and painted-on
eyes. During the major titular assault,
the creatures are literally *thrown* at the
hapless (and hopelessly amateur) actors
by off-screen crew members! "There
must be hundreds of them!" one soon-
to-be victim shrieks. (The Phantom's
freeze-framed critter count ran to
exactly 18.) Lensed in the sparse wilds
of surburban Connecticut and set in
1920, apparently to give the costume
designer a chance to show off, *Attack of
the Beast Creatures* stacks up as a solid
camp item.

BERETTA'S ISLAND   (1994) ***

D: Michael Preece. Franco Columbu,
Elizabeth Kaitan, Ken Kercheval, Van
Quattro, Arnold Schwarzenegger. 97 mins.
(Artisan)

On January 26, 1994, vid stores
rolled out the industrial-strength

red carpet for Arnold Schwarzenegger's *Last Action Hero* (see index). To boost consumer interest, Sega Genesis and Super Nintendo both intro'd *Last Action Hero* video games the same day—reportedly the first such simultaneous release in homevid history. A then-new but totally obscure Arnold flick also arrived on that date when Live (now Artisan) debuted *Beretta's Island,* starring Arn's onetime *Pumping Iron* pal and ex–Mr. World, Mr. Olympia, and Mr. Universe, Franco Columbu. Arn's cameo proves to be but one of many negative virtues on display here, as *Beretta's Island* emerges as a camp classic of the first rank. Columbu himself—who'd earlier essayed small roles as the short terminator in a *Terminator* flashback, a fighter in *Last Man Standing* (Academy), and a Mafia chief in the Genoa-lensed sleazefest *Desperate Crimes* (AIP)—resembles a genetic invention right out of *Twins* (Universal): Schwarzenegger musculature on a Danny DeVito bod (sort of a *Least Action Hero*). The short-statured would-be action icon also struggles more mightily with the English language than Arn ever did.

Cutting to the chase, *Beretta's Island* doesn't keep Arnold addicts in undue suspense: He shows up right after the opening credits for a roughly three-minute workout scene with Columbu, himself cast as a retired Interpol agent eager to return to his true loves—bodybuilding and wine-making. After the pair pump iron and trade scintillating dialogue (see above), Arn unceremoniously departs and Franco re-ups with Interpol in a bid to rid his native Sardinia of controlled substances. But first he and American agent Elizabeth (*Assault of the Killer Bimbos*) Kaitan fly to Las Vegas for a totally meaningless two-minute shoot-out that does nothing to advance the plot but succeeds in setting the pic's brain-damaged tone: Preece's direction is so inept that the legs of a supposedly dead Vegas bad guy can be seen conspicuously twitching (!).

Back in Sardinia, Columbu, who produced and cowrote this terminally stalled vehicle, spends most of his time touting the spot's tourist virtues, even halting the aimless action long enough to sing and dance at a local street fest. Luckily for our distracted hero, chief villain Quattro has a nasty habit of killing his own henchmen, thereby reducing Columbu's workload. The pic's professional thesps, including Kaitan and former *Dallas* regular Kercheval, look hopelessly lost around Columbu, who proves himself a master of the inappropriate response. In short, *Beretta's Island* approaches such inspiredly awful action yarns as Fred Williamson's *Foxtrap* and *The Messenger* and Duke Mitchell's legendary homemade Mafia-movie *mess*terpiece, *The Executioner* (see index).

TURNER TWIN BILL

BLACK DEVIL DOLL FROM HELL (1984) ***

D: Chester Novell Turner. Shirley Latanya Jones, Rickey Roach, Marie Sainviilus, Chester Tankersley, Rev. Ovie Dunson. 70 mins. (Hollywood Home Theater)

TALES FROM THE QUADEAD ZONE (1987) **1/2

D: Chester Novell Turner. Shirley L. Jones, Keefe L. Turner, Larry Jones, Lawrence R. Jones, John W. Jones. 61 mins. (BC Video)

During the vid industry's early, product-hungry days, enterprising, St. Louis–based homemade-horror maven Chester Novell Turner managed to move at least two of his garage-video wonders into a surprising number of stores. Of the twain, Chet's debut, *Black Devil Doll from Hell,* remains the more groundbreaking and earthshaking. This camcorder-shot oddity, discordantly scored on a Casio keyboard, opens with seven—count 'em—seven minutes of credits (fully 10 percent of the total running time!) before swinging into the heart-tugging tale of virginal church lady Jones and her unexpectedly torrid affair with a black Jerry Mahoney dummy (!) discovered in a religious thrift shop. Said dummy, outfitted with a dreadlocks wig, comes to life of its own volition to enlighten Shirl re the errors of her previously chaste ways. Following a series of ludicrous love scenes, our diminutive devil doll abruptly decides to take a powder, leaving Shirley to her own devices (batteries not included). Shirl, understandably despondent over her dummy's desertion, tries to muddle through by pairing off with a couple of normal flesh-and-blood-type guys, only to learn that they're no substitute for the real thing. Shirl eventually recovers the doll, who'd apparently walked back to the same thrift shop. Unfortunately, this time he's mad as hell and not about to take it anymore, which leads to an appropriately horrific climax. While this ultra-amateur exercise—minimalist enough to make Nick Philips's notorious *Crazy Fat Ethel II* (see index) look, if not like *Citizen Kane,* then at least like *The Killer Shrews*—may not shape up as what you (or even we) would categorize as *entertainment,* it's unlike anything we'd ever seen—at least until the emergence of *Tales from the Quadead Zone.*

Like *Black Devil Doll, Tales*—"Edited, Written, Produced & Directed" by the determined Mr. T.—kicks off with a similar Casio track, accompanied by a scary rap number. Shirley L. Jones is also back, this time as the loving mom of an invisible ghost tyke named Bobby, to whom she reads aloud from a mysterious tome titled (you guessed it) *Tales from the Quadead Zone.* Employing an integrated cast, Turner's first tale—titled "Food For…?"—concerns a redneck family of eight that has food enough only for four. Instead of simply splitting the morsels eight ways (now, isn't *that* a dull idea!), one quick-thinking family member instead decides to shoot four of his relatives, thereby supplying our tale with its requisite "ironic" twist. The killer's sentenced to death in the "state gas chair," while surviving relations live "high on the hog in a government witness program" (!). As Shirl herself puts it, "That was a strange tale, wasn't it, Bobby?"

In Tale 2, "The Brothers," a resentful sibling kidnaps his hated older brother's body from a local funeral home, dresses the corpse in a clown suit while delivering an angry diatribe ("Oh, what a rotten childhood I had!"), and winds up paying the ultimate price for his unfraternal behavior. We won't risk spoiling the surprise by revealing the high-concept third story here; suffice it to say that, in terms of irony and punch, it's easily the equal of the two preceding it. We *will* say that the absence of the gripping erotic elements that help make *Black Devil Doll* the unforgettable experience it is keeps *Quadead Zone* from reaching the same dizzying homemade horror heights.

BLACKENSTEIN (1973) ***

D: William Levey. John Hart, Ivory Stone, Liz Renay, Roosevelt Jackson, Joe DeSue. 87 mins. (Xenon)

Blackenstein (redundantly subtitled *The Black Frankenstein*) employs a simple *Frankenstein*-derived story line that finds female black doctor Stone joining medical mentor Dr. Stein (Hart, of TV's *Hawkeye* fame, seen here sporting white hair and a blue [!] moustache). At Hart's bidding, Stone talks her human-torso 'Nam-vet beau, Eddie (DeSue), into letting the acclaimed medico restore his lost limbs. (As our heroine puts it, "Yes, Eddie, Dr. Stein just won the Nobel Peace Prize for solving the DNA genetic code!"). Cutting to the skinny, the operation is a success but trouble soon ensues. When Stone spurns helper Jackson's romantic advances, the latter spitefully spikes Eddie's DNA juice, causing the patient to sprout a square Afro (!) and a mean temper. After tearing an arm off the sadistic hospital attendant who earlier tormented him, Eddie-cum-Blackenstein turns his murderous attention to several total strangers. He drops by the home of future John Waters superstar Liz *(Desperate Living)* Renay, startlingly coiffed in a blond beehive wig (indeed, the pic's hairstylist exhibits more imagination than anyone else involved), slays her poodle and boyfriend, then devours her intestines. Several additional killings follow before the monster meets a predictable fate. Highlights include Lou Frohman's lush, old-fashioned, inspiredly inappropriate score and lots of what look like ketchup-soaked sausages subbing for human innards. Director Levey lived on to helm *The Happy Hooker Goes to Washington* (Cannon), *Monaco Forever* (VCII, with a young Van Damme in his only gay role), *Slumber Party '57* (MGM), with a young Debra Winger, and *Skatetown, USA* (n/a).

BLOOD FREAK (1971) ***1/2

D: Steve Hawkes, Brad Grinter. Steve Hawkes, Dana Culliver, Randy Grinter, Jr., Tina Anderson, Heather Hughes. 86 mins. (Regal, n.i.d.)

The world's first (and thus far only) cautionary Christian anti-drug gore movie (!), this Jimmy Swaggart Meets H. G. Lewis affair stars Hawkes (who also coproduced) as Herschell, a dim-witted, hog-ridin' Elvis manqué who meets a typical Scripture-quoting miniskirted gal named Angel. Angel's wild and crazy sister, Ann—who, along with her geekoid friends, is "heavy into the drug scene"—soon leads Hersh down the path to perdition (which, we believe, is just south of Tampa). To make a bizarre story short, our hero is addicted to some sort of superpot, gets a job at a local poultry ranch, eats a capon laced with experimental preservatives, and transmogrifies into a rampaging turkey-monster (!) who feeds off the blood of his fellow substance abusers. The entire beyond-brain-damaged tale, meanwhile, is narrated by a Bible-spouting, sub-Criswell-ian sleazeball who delivers a disquisition re the hazards of drug pollution—while chain-smoking and eventually falling into an uncontrollable coughing fit! *Blood Freak* is either the craziest display of misguided sincerity or the most subversive deadpan put-on ever committed to celluloid.

MARJOE GORTNER'S GREATEST HIT

BOBBIE JO AND THE OUTLAW (1976) ***

D: Mark L. Lester. Lynda Carter, Marjoe Gortner, Jesse Vint. 89 mins. (Artisan)

Marjoe (the name's a combo of "Mary" and "Joseph") Gortner is the charismatic preacher whose performance in the eponymous 1972 documentary *Marjoe* (Columbia/TriStar) proved so popular that it launched him on a Tinseltown career. That career has now spanned over two decades, from 1974's critically massacred *Earthquake* (Univeral) to a small role in 1995's *Wild Bill* (MGM). In between, the lanky, fair-haired, sharp-featured ex-evangelist has interpreted so many memorable characters that choosing a single "greatest"

poses a formidable challenge indeed. Some would doubtless opt for his heroic roles in *Viva Knievel!* (Warner) or *Star Crash* (Charter). Others might argue on behalf of his obsessed-lobotomist turn in *Hellhole* or his deranged-geneticist bit in 1989's *American Ninja 3* (see index). Worthy perfs all, but for yours truly's money, none of the above come close to matching Marjoe's work in Lester's 1976 trash classic, *Bobbie Jo and the Outlaw,* a film that Gortner—actually billed above the title (!)—and costar Lynda (*Wonder Woman*) Carter positively carried (uphill all the way).

As titular outlaw Lyle Wheeler, Marjoe fancies himself the literal reincarnation of Billy the Kid and so quits his gig as a professional quick-draw specialist to pursue a life of violent crime. Our anti-hero next employs his persuasive powers to enlist restless carhop Carter to his criminal cause. Marjoe's big emotive moment arrives when, under the influence of peyote, he flashes back to reenact Billy's battle with Pat Garrett and posse ("Ow! I'm shot!"). Lynda likewise displays her range by strumming a guitar, singing, and contributing several topless scenes. While a notch or two below Arthur Penn's *Bonnie and Clyde, Bobbie Jo and the Outlaw* holds up well in the action and camp departments alike.

BORN AMERICAN (1986) *½

D: Renny Harlin. Mike Norris, Thalmus Rasulala, Steve Durham, David Coburn, Albert Salmi. 96 mins. (Video Treasures)

This feature-length demo reel from since-ascendant Scandinavian-born Hollywood action big shot Harlin—reportedly banned in the very Finland in which it was filmed—stars Mike (Son of Chuck) Norris as Savoy Brown (no relation to the erstwhile Brit blues band of the same name), one of three vacationing American party animals who, on a drunken lark, cross the border onto Russki turf. There, after staging a few innocent pranks—they kill a local priest,

incinerate a village, and knock off a dozen or so Russian soldiers—our boys are captured, tortured by a KGB sadist (a G. Gordon Liddy look-alike), and tossed into a correctional hellhole that makes the Gulag Archipelago resemble a Beverly Hills country club (actually, so far we've successfully avoided both). Once inside, Mike not only gets to display some fancy kung-fu footwork but proves he's every bit the actor his old man is. The weirdest preglasnost Red-baiting pulp movie to surface since John Milius's madcap *Red Dawn* (MGM), *Born American*—lifting liberally and mindlessly from such diverse sources as *The Deer Hunter* and *Mad Max Beyond Thunderdome*—achieves a brain-dead incoherence that borders on the downright surreal.

THE BRAIN THAT WOULDN'T DIE (1963) B&W ***

D: Joseph Green. Herb Evers, Virginia Leith, Adele Lamont. 81 mins. (Rhino)

Lensed in '59, this one lingered on the shelf long enough for lead Evers to change his name to Jason. He plays a ruthless brain surgeon who seeks to graft his fiancée's severed head onto a stripper's body while the dread Thing in the Closet (interpreted by famed "Jewish Giant" Eddie Carmel) watches and waits. (Head to Thing: "I'm only a head. And you're whatever you are. Together we're strong.") Rhino's uncut edition restores Evers's assistant's prolonged death scene and some choice views of the Thing. *Brain* later served as the centerpiece of one of *Mystery Science Theater 3000*'s funniest episodes.

THE BRAINIAC (1961) B&W ***

D: Chano Urueta. Abel Salazar, Ariadne Welter, Mauricio Garcés, Rosa María Gallardo. 75 mins. (Sinister Cinema)

This Mexican monster-movie masterpiece stars Salazar as an Inquisition victim who, prior to being burned at the stake, vows vengeance the next time the Great Comet lights up the night sky, some 300 years thence. True to his word, he materializes from a papier-mâché meteorite that bounces to Earth circa 1961. Our title fiend now boasts two distinct, if ill-explained personas: the suave, urbane Baron Batallas, and the bent-beaked, forked-tongued, cerebrum-sucking Brainiac. In addition to sporting what may well be the scream screen's first pulsating inflatable head (okay, so it's a cheap rubber mask hooked up to an air pump—there's more to life than special effects), the Brainiac can perform an impressive array of perverse party tricks: He can turn invisible at will, hypnotize via a pair of glowing eyes, and (his pièce de résistance) slurp the very brains out of his prey's skulls—*without* using a straw. All of which he proceeds to do, while simultaneously ducking a team of nosy scientists and dogged detectives, at a bloody bash staged for his killers' unwary descendants. And he *still* finds time for some indiscriminate between-slaughter snacking, munching on the brains of earlier victims from a colander stashed in his dining room cabinet! *The Brainiac* stands inflatable-head-and-shoulders above most of his bad-fright-flick brethren, Mexican and Anglo alike. Inveterate Mexican-monster-movie fans, meanwhile, are referred to Rhino Video and Sinister Cinema, both of which stock an impressive array of south-of-the-border B faves of '50s and '60s vintage.

RAT*'S ENTERTAINMENT!:* Rat queen Adrienne Barbeau (top right) rules in producer Roger Corman's camp-enriched adaptation of the Bram Stroker-based tale *Burial of the Rats.*
Courtesy of Concorde–New Horizons Corp.

BRAM STOKER'S BURIAL OF THE RATS (1995) **1/2

D: Dan Golden. Adrienne Barbeau, Maria Ford, Kevin Alber, Olga Kabo. 77 mins. (Cosmic Video/New Horizons)

Purportedly based on a Stoker short story, Dan (*Naked Obsession*) Golden's inspiredly brain-dead, Russia-lensed campfest stars Alber as young Bram himself. As our unlikely story opens, Bram and his dad are touring Eastern Europe when our hero's taken captive by self-described "Queen of Vermin" (!) Barbeau and her half-naked tribe of ravishing "rat-women." Bram and bodacious rat-lady Madeleine (ubiquitous Corman B queen Ford) soon tumble for each other. Barbeau, in turn, spares Bram a death sentence when she discovers his phrase-turning abilities and decides to keep him on as a chronicler of her exploits, which consist mostly of planning man-killing rat-women raids on local strongholds of male power. ("You shall have a proper tablet," Barbeau informs the grateful novice scribe, "and your lifestyle shall improve.") Part *Willard*-esque rat-gore antics, part sepulchral period strip show, *Burial* adds up to an all-camp exercise that supplies its share of flesh and fun. For further authenticity, veteran scream queens Linnea Quigley and Nikki Fritz put in split-second cameos as two of Adrienne's minions.

BROADWAY JUNGLE (1955) B&W ***

D: Phil Tucker. Norman Wright, George Robeleto, Bruno Metza. 60 mins. (Something Weird)

Phil (Robot Monster) Tucker's jaw-dropping abomination opens with a close-up of a HOLLYWOOD BOULE-VARD street sign, followed by a title card reading—what else?—Broadway Jungle (!). We're next treated to establishing shots of famous Hollywood-studio exteriors, accompanied by a droning narrator's profile of "Hollywood con man" Fletcher Mathering (Wright), an overweight Z-movie mogul manqué wearing a fake paintbrush beard. Broadway Jungle's "plot" alternates between Fletcher's efforts to launch a movie and a mobster's attempts to terminate chief backer and rival hood "Georgie Boy" (Robeleto). Plot, however, is not what Broadway Jungle is about. Broadway Jungle is about (often hilariously) unsynched bad dialogue, camera angles from hell, wipes and dissolves unseen since the silent era—withal, a celluloid bottomless pit that looks slow even in fast-forward. Nearly an entire reel is devoted to a mute hit man's (Metza, best known as "Manny" in the Ed Wood–scripted The Violent Years, though his surname's listed as Metsa there) interminable pursuit of Georgie Boy down seedy L.A. alleys, with the two characters rarely sharing the same frame. (At one point a dog on the street can be seen spontaneously joining the chase!) And that's the pic's most exciting sequence! Throughout Broadway Jungle, lensed in grainy black and white, footage simply accumulates, each scene more awkward, tortured, and meaningless than the last, until

Tucker mercifully ran out of film, chutzpah, or both. Broadway Jungle fully lives up to host Johnny Legend's promise of "a cinematic black hole that knows no bounds."

C.C. AND COMPANY (1970) **

D: Seymour Robbie. Joe Namath, Ann-Margret, William Smith. 88 mins. (MGM)

Joe Namath is aimless biker C.C. Ann-Margret keeps him company. Camp fans will watch with dropping jaws as Joe's abortive screen career gets sacked before their very eyes. Fans of genre faves Big Bill Smith and Sid Haig will want to tune in.

A CERTAIN SACRIFICE (1979/1985) **

D: Stephen Jon Lewicki. Jeremy Pattnosh, Madonna, Carl Kurtz. 60 mins. (Virgin, n.i.d.)

Originally lensed in Super 8 and transferred to video in 1985—the Virgin Video cassette carries a disclaimer warning viewers of the tape's inferior audiovisual quality—Lewicki's awful, pretentious student film is of interest solely for its early glimpse of future superstar Madonna. Here the monomonikered diva goes topless twice (once in a mild S&M sequence), indulges in an extended crying jag, and enjoys a big dramatic scene that's almost totally obliterated by the glitchy soundtrack (not necessarily a bad thing). Only Madonna curiosity-seekers and confirmed masochists need apply.

THE CHILDREN (1980) **1/2

D: Max Kalmanowicz. Martin Shakar, Gale Garnett, Gil Rogers, Jesse Abrams. 89 mins. (Vestron)

This one's got to be the sickest entry in genredom's short-lived let's-kill-the-kids craze. A nuke-plant leak transforms local schoolchildren into

parent-disintegrating mutants with black fingernails and a lethal touch. The only way to croak 'em, as sheriff Gil (apparently no relation to Mr.) Rogers keeps shouting, is to "cut off their hands! Cut off their hands!" The Children may not hold out much hope for the nuclear family's future, but it plays pretty funny most of the way. Heroine Garnett is best remembered for her rendition of the upbeat ditty "We'll Sing in the Sunshine," but the Ramones' "Beat on the Brat" would have made for more appropriate background music here.

THE COBRA (1968) ***

D: Mario Sequí. Dana Andrews, Anita Ekberg, Peter Martell, Elisa Montes, Jesus Fuente, Peter Dane. 93 mins. (Vestron, n.i.d.)

One of The Phantom's all-time fave Cold-War-Paranoia-Meets-International-Opium-Menace movies, The Cobra casts Andrews as an antidrug honcho bent on preventing the elusive title villain's planned importation of 150 pounds of opium. Dana describes the cache as being nothing less than a "time bomb from Peking to destroy the youth of America." To halt the spread of the "dreadful social leprosy" the drug represents, he speeds off to Istanbul to recruit discredited narc and falsely labeled "drunken traitor" Martell. Dana warns Pete of the dangers involved in undertaking so sordid an emprise, citing the drastically diminished life spans of those agents previously assigned to the case, the latest of whom is "now dead, shot by a dum-dum" (whether that's meant to describe the bullet employed or the assassin's mental acuity isn't clear). In any case, seeing as how his girl has already been rubbed out by a Cobra hit man, Pete wastes little time establishing himself as one immoderately mean mother. Cornering the assassin, he snarls, "Your first mistake was blasting the only person I ever really cared for" and offers in return for his cooperation not a reprieve but "one shot of snow." Tension continues to mount until Pete finally poses a tripartite question much on everyone's mind: "Why are you working for Ulriga, what do the black chrysanthemums mean, and what do you know about the Cobra?" In an even more revealing sequence, we learn of opium's ability to effect a "total obliteration of the will" when the Cobra's Red Chinese allies stage a test demonstration for a temporarily captive Andrews, summoning opium-addled slave Anita Ekberg, who utters an emotionless "Yes, master" to the Commies' every command. Quips Andrews, "Very clever, these Chinese."

THE CRAWLERS   (1990/1993) ***

D: Martin Newlin. Jason Saucier, Mary Sellers, Bubba Reeves, Chelsi Stahr, Edy Eby. 94 mins. (Columbia/TriStar)

Lensed in Alaska under the auspices of Italo gore auteur Joe (*The Grim Reaper*) D'Amato's Filmirage banner, *The Crawlers* opens with petite heroine Sellers returning via bus to her Northwest hometown, only to find it overrun not just by bad actors but by radioactive killer-tree roots spawned by toxic waste from the local nuke power plant, whose employees make Homer Simpson seem a paragon of safety. The pic's verité-looking, veg-like supporting thesps deliver their lines in phonetic-sounding monotones, while the tree-root attacks convey all the menace of Bela's dysfunctional prop octopus in Ed Wood's *Bride of the Monster*. Indeed, *The Crawlers* plays like a low-budget spoof à la the Minnesota-shot Super 8 *It Came from Somewhere Else* (see index), except that helmer Newlin and crew (who include appropriately named assistant cameraman Larry Plant) are deadly serious here. Then again, maybe we're being hypercritical and should instead heed Sellers's on-screen advice to her dim little bro'—to wit: "Just shut up and play with your carnivorous plant."

CRAZY FAT ETHEL II   (1985) ***

D: Nick Philips (Steve Millard). Priscilla Alden, Michael Flood, Jane Lambert. 60 mins. (Incredibly Strange Filmworks)

In Philips's seriously belated sequel to his bizarre, no-budget 1974 psycho romp, *Criminally Insane* (Incredibly Strange Filmworks), obese actress Alden reprises her gorging, gouging Crazy Fat Ethel character. *Crazy Fat Ethel II* shamelessly recycles the "good parts" from the 16-millimeter *Criminally Insane* within a new shot-on-video wraparound updating Ethel's stuff-'n'-snuff lifestyle. The result is a technically shoddy but utterly compelling chronicle. With its almost frighteningly verité look and alarmingly low level of alpha-wave activity, *Crazy Fat Ethel II* plays like a deranged homemade hybrid of the horror and documentary genres. The pic sees a long-institutionalized Ethel (sort of a Lizzie Borden on Thorazine) released to a halfway house—a move dictated by drastic state-budget cuts—operated by elderly Hope Bartholomew, whose oft repeated motto is "Let's never give up hope." Our hefty heroine, older but no wiser nor any less compulsive when it comes to food (as it does with numbing regularity), experiences numerous violent flashbacks from *Criminally Insane* while leisurely embarking on a new slaughter spree. As Hope puts it, "Ethel refused to take her medicine, and there was a terrible scene." Terrible scenes abound in this demented exercise, but there's no denying that Alden has underground star power to spare; whether viewed wreaking vengeance on all who would stand between her and her refrigerator or simply glaring at a perceived enemy, Priscilla's largely negative charisma dominates every scene. We also recommend *Death Nurse* (1987, ISF), with Alden as bogus nurse Edith Mortley.

THE CREEPING TERROR   (1964) B&W ***

D: Argyle Nelson. Vic Savage, Shannon O'Neill, William Thourlby. 75 mins. (United, n.i.d.)

"Broadlooms from Outer Space" would have been a more fitting title for this celluloid scam about the misadventures of what appear to be a pair of animated alien rugs, which land near Lake Tahoe for the purpose of picnicking on unsuspecting earthlings. Though the title creatures—leaf-covered carpets thrown over crawling extras—perambulate at an agonizingly languid pace, they have no trouble vacuuming up victims at a fishing pier, a hootenanny, and a local twist soirée. *The Creeping Terror* was shot on a reputed budget of $5,000 (little of which shows on-screen) by director Nelson, who, under the *nom de thesp* Vic Savage, doubles as the movie's leading man (and strikes out in both roles). In the tradition of the Tor Johnson showcase *The Beast of Yucca Flats* (1961, Something Weird), an off-screen narrator paraphrases the unheard exchanges uttered by the on-screen actors. After an army sergeant sees his entire platoon devoured by one of the ravenous rugs, the solemn voice-over informs us, "The sergeant, a shaken man, returned babbling about what had happened." *The Creeping Terror* may not be *the* worst movie of all time, but it comes close enough to merit your home-viewing attention.

THE CROSS AND THE SWITCHBLADE   (1972) **½

D: Don Murray. Pat Boone, Erik Estrada, Jackie Giroux, Jo-Ann Robinson, Dino DeFilippi. 105 mins. (United/Vanguard, n.i.d.)

For those who disapprove of the late-'90s heavy-metal, leather-boy Boone and pine for the patriotic, squeaky-clean Christianoid of yore, this backdate celluloid sermon may be just the tonic. Directed by actor Don Murray (who'd earlier portrayed Dr. Norman Vincent Peale in 1964's *One Man's Way* [n/a]) and based on the true story of humble country preacher David Wilkerson (earnestly interpreted by Pat), the pic dramatizes the Rev's efforts to convert two warring overaged street gangs, the black Bishops and the Latino Mau Maus, to a kinder, gentler lifestyle. Estrada, in his big-screen debut, appears in the crucial role of Mau Mau warlord Nicky Cruz, a hard-case who violently rejects Pat's offer of spiritual guidance, even as his fellow gang members gradually come around to the Rev's way of thinking. In fact, Erik actually scores more screen time than Pat and manages to make the most of it, not only by modeling his BVD's in one pivotal scene but by emoting with considerable intensity, as when he asserts, "I *like* to hate people!" Erik has no trouble winning audience sympathy, especially when he experiences nightmares of Pat Boone grinning at him. The pic culminates in a youth rally, where Pat summons "all the beboppers and jitterbuggers and everybody, every gang member and junkie in New York." But the rumble the Bishops and Mau Maus have agreed to stage in order to disrupt the event is abruptly terminated when, in the midst of Pat's sermon, Erik finally sees the light and decides to devote his life to church work (!). Estrada runs the entire gamut of adolescent emotions in a perf that would have done erstwhile sensitive Dead End Kid Billy Halop proud. Erik returns in the same label's equally inspirational *Ballad of Billie Blue,* costarring comic Marty Allen. Christian-camp aficionados should also scope out the ultraminimalist holy-roller howler *Man of Steel* (Something Weird).

CURSE OF THE ALPHA STONE (1972/1985) **1/2

D: Stewart Malleson. Jim Scotlin, Sandy Carty, Lowell Simon. 90 mins. (United, n.i.d.)

This obscurity chronicles the quest of one young visionary (Scotlin) to achieve better living through alchemy. Our hero first succeeds in turning metal into what looks like egg yolks. In its liquid form, however, this uncontrolled substance works as a powerful aphrodisiac, providing a perfect excuse for some soft-core "erotic" episodes. Though poor in every other department, *Curse* is rich in unintentional mirth, as when a shrink points to a straight-back chair and instructs his understandably confused patient to "lie down on the couch." (Guess the set designers neglected to read the script— not that we blame them.) Or when a gay subject becomes so virulently "straight" that he runs out and abducts a female mannequin (!). Hard-core bad-movie buffs may want to sift through long stretches of dross to extract *Stone's* gems of cinematic insipidity, but all others are advised to keep one finger firmly poised over the fast-forward control.

DANCE MACABRE (1991) **1/2

D: Greydon Clark. Robert Englund, Michelle Zeitlin, Marianna Moen. 97 mins. (Columbia/TriStar)

Lensed in Leningrad by veteran B auteur Greydon (*Satan's Cheerleaders*) Clark, *Dance* casts once and future Freddy Krueger, Englund, in dual roles as a bearded choreographer and, in drag (!), as an elderly ballet teacher at a dance academy where students are vanishing at an alarming rate. Rebellious American dancer Zeitlin ("This ballet stuff suffocates me!") gradually uncovers the truth re her fellow terpsichoreans' mysterious disappearance in this *Psycho*-Meets-*Suspiria*–styled chiller. While pretty dim-witted as a straight-ahead horror outing, *Dance Macabre* offers its fair share of campy antics in the time-honored Clark tradition (he also gave us, among others, *Forbidden Dance*, on Columbia/TriStar, arguably the most unforgettable Lambada movie ever

made). Highlights include Zeitlin's spirited go-go/ballet sequence, lots of leggy lasses in leotards, and, of course, Englund's fake-femme turn, wherein he comes across as something of a taller version of *Poltergeist* psychic Zelda Rubinstein, a performance that's well worth the price of a rental.

DAVID ISN'T DEAD ANYMORE! (1990) **

D: Ken Ward. Rhonda Joy, Steadman Stahl, Elvin Thomas, Ken Ward. 90 mins. (JWK, n.i.d.)

Camcorded in the bars and apartments of Miami, Key Largo, and Homestead, Florida, Ward's homemade voodoo video recalls the no-budget triumph *Black Devil Doll from Hell.* Social scientist Joy returns home from Haiti extolling that island nation's "anthropogical" [*sic*] wonders, especially the reanimating abilities of voodoo priest Pierre La Tue (Thomas). When Rhonda's lowlife beau, David (Stahl), transforms from a stumbling drunk to a stiff (big diff) after he accidentally asphyxiates himself, Rhonda calls on Pierre to help her turn Dave from a corpse to a zombie. The ritual's a success, but Dave proves a real ingrate; his first move is to eat Rhonda's Persian cat, Morris, thus eliminating the pic's most polished performer, before gore-slaughtering several of their mutual friends. Not to worry, though; seems the entire tawdry tale is a product of Rhonda's nocturnal imagination. Or is it? We'll probably never know for sure, since (we hope) a "David Still Isn't Dead Anymore!" isn't in the works.

THE DEAD TALK BACK (1957) B&W **

D: Merle S. Gould. Aldo Farnese, Carla Faryll, April Lynn, Wesley La Violette, Paul Barry. 70 mins. (Sinister Cinema)

Produced, written, and directed by one Merle S. Gould (whose only other listed credit, *The Body Is a Shell*, is the same film), this theatrically unreleased stiff plays like a 1930s Poverty Row spook-show clinker. The flick follows two LAPD dicks as they attempt to solve the crossbow murder of a young model at a local boardinghouse. One boarder happens to be the inventive Mr. Krasner (Farnese), who's built a radio designed to communicate with the deceased. Dr. K. eagerly volunteers to help ferret out the killer by going directly to the source—i.e., the late victim herself. Gould fails grandly in every filmmaking capacity: Director Gould uses so many overhead shots that the camera seems stuck to the ceiling, while scripter Gould serves up lines like "He's a friendless sort of man" and "Oh, shut up, you potentate of righteousness!" According to a narrator, incidentally, *The Dead Talk Back* is "based on a true incident taken from a recent psychic research file." Can you prove that it *didn't* happen?

DEVIL MONSTER (1946) B&W **½

D: S. Edward Graham, supervised by Adrian Weiss. Barry Norton, Blanche Mehaffey, J. Barton. 60 mins. (Sinister Cinema)

A small crew of bad actors led by heartthrob Norton sets sail for the Pacific in search of a missing seaman. Along the way, they see lots and *lots* of stock footage, from octopus battles to bare-breasted Polynesian dancing girls—the latter providing this entertainingly pathetic outing with its main raison d'être. Norton's gee-whiz voice-over moves our story forward but never for very long before Adrian (Son of Louis, Brother of George) Weiss, who also edited, cues up the library music and trots out more travel footage, whence also appears the decidedly unterrifying title creature. One brave sailor actually leaps into the stock footage to do superimposed battle with

the beast (!). Eat your heart out, Industrial Light & Magic!

THE DIVINE ENFORCER (1991) ***½

D: Robert Rundle. Michael Foley, Erik Estrada, Jan-Michael Vincent, Judy Landers, Don Stroud, Jim Brown, Robert Z'dar. 90 mins. (Prism, n.i.d.)

Boasting a once-in-a-lifetime B-movie cast (let us pray), *Divine Enforcer* is a clergical variation on *Death Wish* crossed with a bargain-basement *Silence of the Lambs*. As our story opens, the mysterious Father Daniel (Foley) reports to an L.A. rectory inhabited by Monsignor Estrada, fellow priest Vincent ("Dear God, grant me a transfer!"), and their cleanliness-obsessed blond housekeeper Landers (then of late-night phone-date "infomercial" fame)—a spiritual trio whose combined alpha-wave output registers barely above flatline. Father Daniel, meanwhile, is a self-appointed angel of death ("God forgives, but I don't!") who milks the confessional for hot tips on local criminal activities (!). After wiping out dozens of area drug dealers—a desperate Brown and screen heavy Z'dar among them—with a collection of cruciform knives and ninja stars, plus a pearl-handled .45, our white-collar hero (who's also blessed with second sight) goes into hypnotic trances to zero in telepathically on "the Vampire of Los Angeles," a bloodsucking serial killer (played by an over-the-top Stroud) who not only slays his female victims but uses their preserved skulls as cereal bowls.

Beyond bordering on bad taste, director Rundle's direct-to-home-vid horror show offers terrible action staging—after saying to a cop, "Let me walk you to the door," Estrada trips over his own robe (!), a gaffe the filmmakers apparently hoped would escape the eyes of inattentive couch potatoes—memorably atrocious act-

ing, and a final fade-out suggestion that Father Daniel may be God Himself (!). For bad-movie buffs, *The Divine Enforcer* represents not only 90 minutes well wasted but an outright religious experience.

THE EXECUTIONER (1978) ****

D: Dominic Miceli (Duke Mitchell). Duke Mitchell, Lorenzo Dodo, Vic Caesar, John Strong. 84 mins. (Video Gems, n.i.d.)

Back in 1952, the imitation Dean Martin and Jerry Lewis team of Duke Mitchell and Sammy Petrillo starred in the fright comedy *Bela Lugosi Meets a Brooklyn Gorilla* (Englewood). Jerry Lewis, one of the many who were unamused by the flick, threatened to sue Petrillo even deeper into oblivion should he mimic Jer again. Duke and Sammy eventually went their separate ways, with Duke pursuing a lounge-singer career and also turning up in an occasional film role (such as an overage juvenile delinquent in Hugo Haas's *Paradise Alley* [n/a]), while Sammy starred in Doris Wishman's awful 1974 soft-core sex farce, *Keyholes Are for Peeping* (Something Weird) and still works clubs as a comic. Nearly three decades after his *Brooklyn Gorilla* daze, Mitchell returned to write, direct, and star (under his real name, Dominic Miceli) as an emotional Mafia hit man in *The Executioner,* a hilariously inept *Godfather* wannabe featuring many of Duke's trademark tunes (including our personal fave, "Rigatone, Mostacciolo, and Spaghet," as well as the moving philosophical ballad "One Hundred Years from Today"), clumsily staged action scenes, and monologues like they just don't make anymore (and, in fact, *never* did), such as Duke's tearful tribute to the Italian Woman. *The Executioner* is one video the serious bad-movie buff cannot afford to miss. And we bet you can't watch it just once. Duke followed with the almost equally amazing *Gone with the Pope,* discovered by director/preservationist William Lustig but not yet available to the public.

FIREBALL JUNGLE (1969) ***

D: Joseph G. Prieto. John Russell, Lon Chaney, Jr., Alan Mixon, Randy Kirby, Nancy Donohue. 94 mins. (Sinister Cinema)

This Tampa-lensed indie details the nefarious efforts of colorfully monikered mobster Nero Sagittarius (Russell) to dominate the local track scene. Along the way, we witness lots of stock-car footage (accent on *stock*), and several appearances by distracted junkyard owner Chaney, who swills beer, talks to his dog in an indeterminate foreign accent ("This could be *good* junkyard!"), and burns up real good when the hoods set fire to his ramshackle establishment. *Fireball Jungle* really rolls into high gear when it tries to be now, hip, and with-it, Swingin' '60s–style. For one key scene, the action shifts

to the "Have-a-Joint Cafe," where local hipsters bliss out to the musical stylings of the "LSD for Lunch Bunch" (!), who sound about as psychedelic as the Brady Bunch. Best of all, though, is a nearby nightclub that comes equipped with a "Throne Room," where patrons park their posteriors on toilet-designed bar stools (!). And what happening 1969 youth flick could be considered complete without its very own Tiny Tim imitator, sporting an outsized prosthetic proboscis and harmonizing with a howling poodle? Certainly not *Fireball Jungle,* the type of pic you'll want to watch again and again, if only to make sure you really saw what you think you did.

FLAME OF ARABY (1951) ***

D: Charles Lamont. Maureen O'Hara, Jeff Chandler, Maxwell Reed, Susan Cabot, Lon Chaney, Jr., Buddy Baer, Richard Egan, Royal Dano. 77 mins. (Universal)

Fresh on the heels of playing Princess Marjan in *Bagdad* (Universal), red-haired Hibernian heroine O'Hara again goes the exotic route as Princess Tanya in this entertaining ultra-Hollywood Technicolor camp costumer. When her late ruler dad's evil cousin (Reed) takes over Tunisia, Maureen is forced to choose between bearded brother "corsair lords" Chaney and Baer (and no coarser lords are you likely to find). She refuses to marry either man until a Bedouin comes along. That fellow arrives in the form of handsome, headstrong nomad Tamerlaine (Chandler), who's in O'Hara's parts in search of a prize stallion he wants to trap and tame. *Flame*'s corsairs carry on like seagoing bikers; their drunken bash supplies a highlight, further spiced by future *Sorority Girl/Wasp Woman* Cabot's low-cut turn as a fiery corsair wench. A spanking scene, ripe dialogue, and stirring horseback action provide additional moments of merit. Maureen, meanwhile, proves prophetic when she utters the line "Were it necessary, I would ride unclad through the streets to reach my beloved father." She got her chance four years later as the titular lead in *Lady Godiva* (Universal). Universal also unearths Arthur Lubin's 1943 Arabian adventure, *Ali Baba and the Forty Thieves,* wherein the matchless Maria Montez and a heroic Jon Hall take the leads in another fun Technicolor trip to the beloved back-lot Bagdad of yore. While still grossly underrepresented on tape, Montez can also be seen in *Arabian Nights* (Universal).

FOR YOUR HEIGHT ONLY (1979) ***

D: Raymond Jury. Weng Wang. No other credits available. (Image) DVD

One flick The Phantom never thought would surface on relatively mainstream homevid was the fabled Filipino kung-fu fest *For Your Height Only,* starring the world's smallest martial artist, 3-foot 6-inch Weng

Wang (a.k.a. "Agent 00"). While the pic's simpleminded storyline serves as only the flimsiest framework for our hero's derring-do, it must be said that Weng acquits himself quite handily with his flying feet, furious fists, and wide array of bargain-basement James Bond–type gadgets. The chief trick for the diminutive Double W is getting his victims to the ground, where he then experiences little difficulty in smacking and kicking the living bejaysus out of them. Indeed, Weng is not only proficient but downright sadistic, grinning gleefully as he slaughters scores of unusually helpless villains. He's a mite less convincing in the romance department, particularly during an odd homage to Cary Grant and Eva Marie Saint's train compartment kiss from Hitchcock's *North by Northwest*. His thespian range is likewise limited; we'd place Weng well above Dolph Lundgren but a tad below Chuck Norris and Jean-Claude Van Damme. The vid's remedial American dubbing adds an unnecessary layer of would-be comic overkill to what's already a tongue-in-cheek cross between *Terror of Tiny Town* (Sinister Cinema) and an *el cheapo* Bond rip-off.

FOXTRAP (1986) **

D: Fred Williamson. Fred Williamson, Chris Connelly, Arlene Golonka, Donna Owen. 89 mins. (MGM)

Williamson stars as freelance enforcer Tom Fox ("He takes the jobs nobody wants…and gets the results nobody expects!"). We know Fox is a hard-case whose rep precedes him when two teens attempting to steal his unattended wheels are scared off by the mere sight of his foreboding license plate, reading simply but eloquently, DA FOX (!). Nothing if not a one-man show, *Foxtrap* is, according to its typo-plagued credits, "directed, produced an [sic] from a story" by Fred. The nonaction kicks off in L.A., where Fred is hired by

rich sleazeball Connelly—we know he's a lowlife because he guzzles Colt 45 from a can while Fred delicately sips Drambuie from a snifter—to find his "missing daughter." Fred next turns up in Cannes, where between frequent sartorial changes—*Foxtrap*'s primarily an 89-minute showcase for Fred's admittedly extensive wardrobe—he generously hands out plugs for other, better films, from *Mishima* to *The Purple Rose of Cairo*. After a brief detour to Rome for another Drambuie, Fred heads back to L.A., where he unveils the last of his threads and dispatches a small army of malefactors without so much as wrinkling them (his threads, not the malefactors). *Foxtrap* comes recommended for camp lovers, Fred fanatics, and *GQ* subscribers only.

FRANKENSTEIN MEETS THE SPACE MONSTER (1965) B&W ***

D: Robert Gaffney. James Karen, Nancy Marshall, Marilyn Hanold, Lou Cutell, Robert Reilly, Bruce Glover. 78 mins. (Prism, n.i.d.)

After a cheesily effective shock opening—stark credits unfolding against a silhouette of the titular space monster, Mull—*Frankenstein Meets the Space Monster* begins a filmlong plummet that takes us through yards of stock footage, aimless filler, bad acting, and Puerto Rican locales that, while undeniably authentic, add little to the intended atmosphere of alien menace. Quirky novelist, academic, and movie maven George Garrett, along with collaborators R.H.W. Dillard and John Rodenbeck, penned the original screenplay as an affectionate send-up of low-end fright flicks; while subsequently rewritten, the script retains its initial loopy tone. Martian "princess" Hanold (an *Ernie Kovacs Show* regular); Cutell as her effete, chromedomed right-hand eunuch, Dr. Nadir; and Glover as their bemused lieutenant supply the film with its most inspired moments, offsetting future supermar-

ket pitchman Karen's bland hero, Marshall's whiny ingenue, and Reilly's stumbling portrayal of "Frankenstein," a disfigured android astronaut named Frank.

GAME OF SURVIVAL (1989) **1/2

D: Armand Gazarian. Nikki Hill, Cindy Coatman, Roosevelt Miller, Jr. 85 mins. (Raedon, n.i.d.)

An entertainingly awful *Terminator*/ *Highlander* hybrid that's equally lacking in talent and budget, *Game of Survival* finds a group of lizard-faced, synthesizer-voiced aliens sentencing seven of the galaxy's toughest warriors to duke it out to the death on the streets of contempo L.A. The dumb-as-trees E.T.'s—who resemble sort of an Out-of-This-World Wrestling Federation council—watch from afar as our young underdog hero, Zane (Hill), enlists the aid of Earth lovely Cindy (Coatman) in battling such formidable foes as a clubwielding dwarf, a punkoid Asian alien, and muscle-bound space bully "Skullblaster" (Miller). *Game*'s inane, poorly postsynched dialogue, clumsily staged punch-ups, and tunnel-visioned sincerity should supply hardy bad-video buffs with many a mirthful moment. Hill returns in the equally brain-locked but far less enchanting *Alien Private Eye* (Raedon, n.i.d.).

GANG JUSTICE (1994) **1/2

D: Richard W. Park. Erik Estrada, Jonathan Gorman, Joon B. Kim, Nicole Rio, Angel Dashek. 92 mins. (AIP)

Beyond his Mexican soap-opera and late-night telepsychic chores, the indefatigable Erik Estrada has found his way into several strange, primarily direct-to-video projects that have stretched his thespic range mightily, mayhaps even to the breaking point. In addition to roles in such deathless fare as *Alien Seed* (AIP) and *Night of the*

Wilding (PM), Erik's portrayed a retired biker in *The Last Riders,* an international supervillain in Andy Sidaris's *Guns* (see index), and a priest seduced by a possessed nun (scream queen Michelle Bauer) in *Spirits* (Trimark). Here Estrada appears in his weirdest vehicle to date, a tale of sibling rivalry between Anglo and Chinese stepbrothers Gorman and Kim. Though billed above the title, Erik scores less than five minutes' screen time, bits apparently culled from a one-day, one-set shoot. A Chinese-produced and -financed effort lensed in Vancouver with a mostly Cauc cast, *Gang Justice* was obviously intended for Far Eastern export. That contention's confirmed early on when a block of Chinese dialogue goes unsubtitled, while James S. Lee's alternately Asian-flavored and aggressively American score supplies another giveaway.

The script, meanwhile, penned by director Richard W. Park and Simon Blake Hong, betrays occasionally radical ignorance of the American vernacular and its nuances, as when Erik, remarried here to the Chinese mother of put-upon protagonist Kim, says to his spouse, "But what about your son? He is an Oriental boy having to grow up in a predominantly white society!" Worse than merely awkward is an exchange between Kim's Anglo girlfriend, Angel (Dashek), and her politico father, who fears the arrangement might foster ill will among his constituents. Responds Angel, "But Dad, not only are your constituents Caucasian, there are niggers and spics." This in a speech protesting racism! Even the actors look stunned by the line. Woefully bald on action, *Gang Justice* ultimately narrows down to a social drama/ethnic soap opera replete with the type of tragic ending that's far more common in Hong Kong than Hollywood genre product. As for Erik, while his name appears atop AIP's print ads, his face is nowhere to be seen—he and the rest of the cast are replaced by a group shot of posed models in gang

gear who have nothing to do with the movie (!). Director Park returned in 1996 with *American Chinatown* (Home Video Films), starring Robert Z'dar.

THE GLOVE   (1978) **¹⁄₂

D: Ross Hagen. John Saxon, Rosey Grier, Joanna Cassidy. 93 mins. (Media, n.i.d.)

Not a Michael Jackson bio, *The Glove* is instead a hilariously inept action oddity, (mis)directed by frequent on-screen villain Hagen (who went on to helm several other, less inspired B pics), pitting a bounty hunter (Saxon) against an assailant (Grier) equipped with a steel riot glove. With cameos by Jack Carter, Joan Blondell, Keenan Wynn, and Aldo Ray. Also out on a bargain label as *The Glove: Lethal Terminator.*

GNAW: FOOD OF THE GODS PART 2 (1989) **¹⁄₂

D: Damian Lee. Paul Coufos, Lisa Schrage, Colin Fox, Frank Moore, Real Andrews, Jackie Burroughs. 91 mins. (Avid)

Lee's decade-late sequel to Bert I. Gordon's *Food of the Gods* (Artisan) bears even less resemblance to its H. G. Wells source material than the original did, but this Canadian-lensed campfest isn't entirely bereft of bad-movie virtues. For starters, *Gnaw* is the type of flick that, after carefully establishing its alleged Empire State setting via close-ups of New York license plates, blithely shows us a phone booth bearing a sign reading "Appels locaux" (!). The off-the-wall plot finds academic scientist Coufos discovering a miraculous growth serum, which prompts his overexcited assistant to gush, "This is the food of the gods!" and envision a utopian future filled with "Big cows! Big fish! Big…pigs!" Said serum is instead consumed by several unsuspecting lab rats, with the expected tragic results. Highlights include the enhanced

rodents' assault on a synchronized swim meet, a subplot involving an Amazing Colossal Brat, and one of the unlikeliest sex scenes we've ever seen on-screen. Lovers of bad rat-monster movies should eat this one up.

GROTESQUE   (1988) **¹⁄₂

D: Joseph Tornatore. Linda Blair, Tab Hunter, Donna Wilkes, Brad Wilson, Guy Stockwell, Charles Dierkop, Robert Z'dar. 80 mins. (Media, n.i.d.)

It would take The Phantom several pages to do justice to this aptly titled terror turkey, which is either a high-concept put-on (doubtful) or one of the most flamboyantly awful movies ever made (probable). The irrepressible Linda Blair (who also receives a coproducing credit) toplines as a Los Angelena who takes her depressed friend Wilkes (*Angel*) for a "quiet weekend" at her folks' secluded woodland hideaway. That planned idyll soon goes awry when a bunch of psycho punkers—hulking *Maniac Cop* Z'dar among them—slaughter Linda B.'s family, including her semiretired horror-movie makeup-FX-expert dad, and severely provoke her previously unseen adopted mutant brother (!). Enter her avenging plastic-surgeon uncle (screen legend Tab Hunter) for the final reels, where *Grotesque* truly lives up to its name. Even though Tab and Linda don't play any scenes together and Linda threatens to take her customary on-screen shower but somehow never gets around to it, *Grotesque* rates as a must for camp buffs.

GYMKATA   (1985) **¹⁄₂

D: Robert Clouse. Kurt Thomas, Tetchie Agbayani, Richard Norton, Conan Lee, Buck Kartalian, Edward Bell. 90 mins. (MGM)

Gymkata refers to an arcane combo of gymnastics and karate, of which young Jonathan Cabot (former

Olympian Thomas) is the world champ. Government agents pack him off to the primitive principality of Parmistan—the kind of back-lot mythical kingdom that proliferated in B movies past—to participate in the Game, sort of a free-wheeling Splatter Olympics that few contestants have ever survived. If young Kurt wins, he stands to gain not only the hand of the beautiful Princess Rubali (the fetching Agbayani) but permission from the Khan (wizened Mel Brooks look-alike Kartalian) to set up the first "Star Wars early-warning system" in a Parmistani mountain range! So much for plot. The real action begins with Kurt's arrival in Parmistan (which, judging by the extras, has to be the Bad Teeth Capital of the World—and Kurt knocks out a few more before he's through). There he learns the Game's been rigged by the Khan's treacherous advisor, Zamir (since-ascendant Aussie kickboxer and frequent Jackie Chan foil Norton). Kurt runs the course while alternately dodging and dispatching Zamir's evil minions and, in the movie's most memorable sequence, high-kicks his way through the Village of Crazies, a booby-trapped booby hatch populated by hooded, scythe-wielding lunatics. As an actor, Thomas makes for a great gymnast, but his lack of thespian talent never gets in the way of the action, and there's more than enough of the latter here to satisfy martial arts camp addicts.

GYPSY ANGELS   (1980/1994) ***

D: "Alan Smithee." Vanna White, Glen Bricknell, Tige Andrews, Richard Roundtree, Lyle Waggoner, Greg Mullavey. 93 mins. (Trimark)

"Alan Smithee" is the traditional pseudonym adopted by Directors Guild members who wish to remove their real monikers from movies they've worked on. Vanna White is TV's blond, cleavage-driven *Wheel of Fortune* letter flipper. These two media heavyweights pool their talents for the direct-to-

home-vid turkey *Gypsy Angels,* which marks Vanna's star debut and her only celluloid exposure of any kind beyond her brief bit in the 1981 slasher dud *Graduation Day* (Columbia/TriStar). And while this obviously troubled 1980-copyrighted air adventure may have crashed at takeoff, Vanna's fans can't fault their fave femme for lack of trying: in *Gypsy Angels* Vanna laughs, cries, loves, dances, and even takes her top off.

Employing a clumsy flashback framework, *Gypsy Angels* recounts the redneck romance that develops between Atlanta stripper Vanna and an itinerant divorce-lawyer-turned-stunt-pilot played by a singularly unappealing Bicknell (Jim Varney's "Ernest" would have been a better choice). The pair "meet cute" when Bicknell drags Vanna from a fiery car crash. Our heroine is at first resistant to the sky guy's advances. "You got a mouse in your pocket? What's this 'we' stuff?" she quips. Not exactly vintage Mae West material, perhaps, but about as witty as *Gypsy Angels* gets. (In the course of another strange exchange, Vanna, who's white, angrily addresses an unruly redneck as "honky" [!].) Anyhow, Glen and Vanna tiff over the latter's strip act—though she chastely keeps her halter and G-string on—leading our heroine to declaim, "I am one fine stripper. Real kinky. Know what I mean?" (Wait a minute, that's Ernest's line!) The pair repair their incipient rift via a topless alfresco tryst that ranks among the shortest "erotic" interludes in direct-to-home-vid history. Soon they're married by lecherous Vegas preacher Reverend Tyrone Knott (*Carol Burnett Show* vet Waggoner), but their honeymoon's cut short when Glen crashes during a Reno air show and wanders from the site with severe amnesia, only to be brought around by doctor Richard (*Shaft*) Roundtree in time to reunite with White and fulfill his lifelong dream of flying upside down. For blindly devoted Vanna fans, this *Vanna*ty production, lensed largely in authentic St.

Joe, Missouri, locations, rates as a reel no-brainer.

HELLBOUND   (1994) **½

D: Aaron Norris. Chuck Norris, Calvin Levels, Sheree J. Wilson, Christopher Neame, David Robb. 95 mins. (Cannon)

When Rabbi Schindler has his heart torn out on Chicago's Polanski Street, the brutal incident triggers a chain of events that ultimately lead to Chuck Norris kickboxing with the devil (!). Actually, the demon in question is a mere satanic emissary named Prosatanos (Neame). This ambitious (if unlikely) tale opens in 1186 A.D. when King Richard (Robb) and his Crusaders succeed in sealing the Freddy-voiced fiend in a cave-set crypt. Said crypt is opened by a pair of treasure-hungry Arabs in 1951, but it takes Prosatanos four-plus decades to retrieve all nine pieces of the broken unholy scepter he needs to implement his evil plans. The hapless rabbi's Windy City demise puts local cop Chuck and his dreadlocked partner (Levels) on the case, which takes them to Israel, where the demon is posing as an archaeologist. Up to this point, the peripatetic pic—which even manages a side trip to Northern Italy—more or less gets by on sheer incongruity. Things bog down in Israel, alas, with Chuck and Cal running through several *Lethal Weapon*–styled stupid cop tricks and even finding time to reform a junior pickpocket. The final showdown between Chuck and Neame packs more of a conceptual punch than a literal wallop and doesn't rate inclusion in vet fight coordinator Benny ("The Jet") Urquidez's career-highlights reel (see *Wheels on Meals* for The Jet at his best).

Though son Mike is nowhere in sight, Chuck's bro' Aaron handles directorial chores while one Eric Norris serves as stunt coordinator. *Hellbound*, billed as a "Direct-to-Video Theatrical Feature" (whatever the hell that is), is positioned between Chuck's image-change movies, *Sidekicks* (Columbia/TriStar), where he befriends an asthmatic kid, and *Top Dog* (Artisan), where he partners with a pooch, à la Tom Hanks in *Turner and Hooch* (Touchstone). All this, and a successful teleseries and vid spin-off *Walker, Texas Ranger: Deadly Reunion* [Warner]), too. You can't accuse Chuck of standing still, though some may wonder why he's still standing.

HERCULES IN NEW YORK (1970) *½

D: Arthur A. Seidelman. Arnold Strong (Schwarzenegger), Arnold Stang, James Karen, Taina Elg. 93 mins. (MPI)

Former screen Hercules Steve Reeves may have made an inauspicious debut when he first removed his shirt in Ed Wood's *Jail Bait* back in 1954, but that flick fairly shines next to Arnold Schwarzenegger's maiden movie. Formerly available on the Unicorn label, in a slightly shortened version (thank Zeus for small favors!) retitled *Hercules Goes Bananas*, *Hercules in New York* made its gala reappearance (amid much media fanfare) in a complete, 93-minute edition timed by MPI to coincide with the home-vid release of the Arnold blockbuster *Terminator 2: Judgment Day*. A sort of "Jerkules," Schwarzenegger costars—with another, less awesome Arnold (Stang)—under the *nom de screen* "Arnold Strong" and was lucky enough to have his lines looped by an anonymous voice-over ace who sounds like a leftover from Steve Reeves's post-dub days. As produced and written by Aubrey Wisberg, *HINY* is not only atrocious on every level, but—with its broad gags, awkward reaction shots, and tin-eared remedial dialogue—hopelessly dated, even by 1970 standards. The film represented Wisberg's first American script credit since 1957's *The Women of Pitcairn Island* (he'd earlier penned the much maligned Jack Benny vehicle

The Horn Blows at Midnight). Apparently no one informed Wisberg that the sword-and-sandal genre had peaked a good half decade before and had been spoofed as early as 1962 via the irreverently postdubbed *My Son, the Hero* (n/a).

Here Wisberg's slender story line sees Herc hightail it to Earth after angering his deity dad, Zeus, who brands the muscle-bound upstart an "offensive puppy." After being lost at sea (in more ways than one), Arn surfaces on our shores, where, in short order, he's befriended by pretzel vendor Stang, studied by college prof Karen, and conscripted by local hoods into the pro wrestling ranks. Arn also finds time to visit an automat, beat up a guy in a threadbare bear suit, and, in the movie's money shot, drive a chariot through the streets of Times Square.

HIT THE DUTCHMAN (1992) ***

D: Menahem Golan. Bruce Nozick, Sally Kirkland, Will Kemp, Eddie Bowz, Jack Conley, Jennifer Miller. 119 mins. In R and unrated editions. (Trimark)

Working from a script that sounds written by someone (one Joel Goldman, to be precise) for whom English is a second language at best, former Cannon mogul Golan takes the directorial reins himself to fashion a wonderfully clunky gangster saga complete with a *Godfather*-inspired synthesizer score, totally inappropriate James Bond–styled gimmickry (we especially liked the exploding-spaghetti trick), a mega-Schwarzenegger-esque body count, and a bizarrely accented cast delivering some of the most convoluted dialogue this side of Ed Wood. Lensed in Russia but set in Prohibition-era New York, *Hit* purports to dramatize yet again the rise and fall of Dutch Schultz. As Schultz, Nozick looks a lot like *The Gangster Chronicles*'s Brian (*Dream On*) Benben but sounds more like Jerry Lewis. Dutch and pal Joe Noe (Bowz)

cozy up to Legs Diamond (Kemp), while Dutch seduces Legs's squeeze, club chanteuse Frances Ireland (Miller), leading, in the unrated edition, to some gratuitous sex and brief frontal nudity on Nozick's part. Easily copping top acting honors is professional eccentric Kirkland, wonderfully miscast as Dutch's Yiddish mom (!) and wielding an accent thick enough to make Molly Goldberg sound like a D.A.R. dowager already. Sally's bid to travel the Shelley Winters route eventually finds her chug-a-lugging mugs of bootleg whisky and going into partnership with Legs (!). Scripter Goldman inserts not one but two virtually back-to-back homages to Sergio Leone's *The Good, the Bad and the Ugly:* After gunning down former cohort "Fatty" Abbadabba (not to be confused with Schultz's *Billy Bathgate* bookkeeper, "Abbadabba" Berman), Dutch snarls, "If you're gonna shoot, then shoot, don't talk." A moment later, he takes out another mobster while advising, "If you're gonna shoot, don't ask questions." Withal, *Hit the Dutchman* may well be the most entertaining bad mobster movie since Duke Mitchell's *The Executioner* (see index).

THE HOWLING: NEW MOON RISING (1995) *

D: Clive Turner. Clive Turner, Ernest Kester, Elizabeth Shé, John Ramsden, John Huff, Jacqueline Armitage. 92 mins. (New Line)

Talk about your one-man shows: Clive Turner, creative force behind the seventh and weakest entry in this fright-film franchise, wears more hats here than a saloonful of cowboys. In addition to writing, directing, producing, and costarring, Turner scores supervising editor, postproduction supervisor, and even accountant (!) credits (Clive Turner CPA). Less a horror flick than a feature-length salute to the dubious grandeur of Yucca Valley, California's tourist-driven Pioneer Town and its attendant cracker culture, this mind-bending vanity production also toplines Turner as a long-haired, middle-aged faux cowboy Aussie drifter, sort of a skid-row Paul Hogan, who eventually becomes the chief suspect when a rash of lupine killings breaks out around the P-Town Saloon. Turner casts real-life Pioneer Town people as their own inimitable selves, focusing on the folksy interplay that makes daily life around those parts such a source of unending fun and even pausing for several original C&W songs (e.g., "Prescription Beer") performed by locals Harriet (who also takes an "On-site Catering" credit) and "Pappy" Allen. Two bad actors playing a cop (Ramsden) and a priest (Huff) put in sporadic appearances to talk about werewolves and segue into a few fairly gory Romania-set flashbacks. The slayings in the film proper are shot through red filters that render the scenes visually indecipherable. As the celluloid mutant spawn of some sort of lowlife deal from hell involving Clive (probably in his CPA capacity), Pioneer Town's powers-that-be, and the current *Howling* brand-name copyright holders, though, *The Howling: New Moon Rising* is not without out a certain morbid fascination. The flick ends with the disclaimer "The events depicted in this motion picture are fictitious. The characters depicted in Pioneer Town are real." Now, *that's* scary!

THE INCREDIBLY STRANGE CREATURES WHO STOPPED LIVING AND BECAME MIXED-UP ZOMBIES (1964) ***

D: Ray Dennis Steckler. Cash Flagg (Ray Dennis Steckler), Carolyn Brandt, Atlas King. 81 mins. (Incredibly Strange Filmworks)

Video has rescued Steckler's legendary Las Vegas–lensed hallucination (billed as the "First Rock'n'Roll Monster Movie") from the ranks of the

World's Worst Movies, where it had been unfairly relegated, to the creative-camp arena to which it more properly belongs. Steckler's simple tale of a carefree slacker (played by Ray under his screen alias, Cash Flagg) who falls under the sinister spell of evil sideshow fortune-teller Estrella is rendered compelling by the amateur but likable performances—particularly that of King as Ray's heavily accented Greek bud—authentically aimless action, evocative amusement-park cinematography, tacky production numbers, and a wild extended-nightmare sequence that serves as the film's centerpiece. Incredibly Strange Filmworks stocks a lengthy list of additional Steckler titles.

INFRA-MAN (1976) ***½

D: Hua-Shan. Li Hsiu-hsien, Wang Hsieh, Terry Liu. 92 mins. (Prism)

This totally surreal, off-the-wall juvenile superhero saga from Hong Kong features a wide assortment of demons, monsters, kung-fu set-tos, and giant plush toys from hell. At its best, *Infra-Man* plays like a vintage American serial on hallucinogenic drugs.

INVASION, U.S.A. (1952) B&W ***

D: Alfred E. Green. Gerald Mohr, Peggie Castle, Dan O'Herlihy, Phyllis Coates, Robert Bice, Noel Neill. 74 mins. (Sinister Cinema)

This notorious anti-Commie screen screed sees mysterious stranger O'Herlihy, using naught but a snifter of brandy, mass-hypnotize a cross section of Manhattan bar patrons into experiencing a shared vision of a Russki invasion. At first the customers—who include newscaster Mohr and California industrialist Bice—watch the collective hallucination unfold on the tavern TV. But it's not long before all are personally involved in the widespread panic

as stock-footage atom bombs fly and enemy troops disguised as American soldiers infiltrate our cities, shoot our bosses, violate our womenfolk, and generally make mock of our democratic ideals. Our fave moment arrives when rescuers sifting through the rubble of an A-bombed NYC discover bartender Tom Kennedy beneath a pile of bricks, his lifeless hand still bravely clutching his cocktail shaker (!). (Our type of patriot.) Look for both of George (Superman) Reeves's Lois Lanes, Coates and Neill.

JUNGLE JIM DOUBLE FEATURE

JUNGLE JIM (1948) B&W ***

D: William Berke. Johnny Weissmuller, Virginia Grey, George Reeves, Rick Vallin, Skipper, Caw-Caw. 73 mins. (Goodtimes)

The original *Jungle Jim* sets the tone for schlock-movie producer Sam Katzman's decidedly surreal series. A filmic font of vast misinformation, the pic presents us with an Africa populated by stock-footage beasties and ersatz Polynesians (!) in fright wigs and sarongs. Our story involves a search for a polio cure conducted by Grey, an able scientist but tragically "misguided" femme—she wears glasses, "dresses like a man," and has a "man's job"—who believes a drug used by the dread human-sacrificing "devil doctors cult" may hold the answer. Grey enlists Jungle Jim and his trusty turbaned guide, Kolu (Vallin), to lead her through miles of treacherous stock footage, with the notorious "Temple of Zimbalu" as the safari's ultimate destination. Complicating their quest is the disruptive presence of charming ne'er-do-well George (Superman) Reeves (in a rakish perf), who's more interested in treasure than medicine. Since stock footage from earlier documentaries comprises most of Jungle Jim's neighborhood, our story's forward momentum is regularly halted for forays into the rear-projection bush. Jim's battles with the local wildlife are especially torturous, employing poorly matched footage, obvious stunt doubles, and singularly unconvincing toy animals. Other plot stoppers include comic-"relief" bits with Jim's pet crow, Caw-Caw, and pooch, Skipper—one scene, consisting solely of Skipper reacting to a stock-footage orangutan's antics (and orangs are no more native to Africa than Polynesians are) alone consumes over three minutes of screen time—swimming interludes wherein the shirtless Weissmuller demonstrates he should have spent less time in the jungle and more in the gym, and a creatively choreographed native-girl dance number that so arouses uptight scientist Grey's feminine envy that she promptly dons a bathing suit and executes a heedless headlong swan dive into dangerous jungle waters, where hero Jim saves her from a prop alligator equipped with a rubber tentacle (!).

SAVAGE MUTINY (1953) B&W ***

D: Spencer Bennet. Johnny Weissmuller, Angela Stevens, Tamba. 71 mins. (Goodtimes)

While 1948's *Jungle Jim* established the Weissmuller-series's retro ground rules, 1953's *Savage Mutiny* stacks up as our fave entry. Jim, now accompanied by Tamba "the Talented Chimp" (with whom he shares a rather testy relationship), is asked to assist in "Jungle Project X"—the first Anglo-American atom-bomb test in Africa. It's Jim's job to convince the Tulonga tribe (more Polynesians) to abandon their blast-site island for the safety of the mainland. When the Tulongans see their former home blown sky high in a billowing mushroom cloud (actually old Bikini Island footage), they promptly fall to their knees and worship the Bomb. Way to go, Jungle J! Other recommended *Jungle Jim* entries issued

by Goodtimes include *Cannibal Attack* and *Fury in the Congo*.

THE KILLER SHREWS (1959) B&W ***

D: Ray Kellogg. James Best, Ingrid Goude, Ken Curtis, Gordon McLendon, Baruch Lumet. 70 mins. (Sinister Cinema)

A one-of-a-kind monster cheapie, produced by right-wing radio magnate McLendon (who also costars as killer-shrew maven Dr. Radford Bane), *The Killer Shrews* finds unlucky island inhabitants menaced by dogs wearing phony shrew fangs (!). Replete with insulting retro racial stereotyping, bad acting, and a powerful climactic scene that sees our protagonists duckwalk to freedom while wearing empty trash barrels (cries one would-be escapee, "The shrews ate my shoes!"), *The Killer Shrews* is a camp-movie must. Its original cofeature, another McLendon Radio Pictures special, *The Giant Gila Monster* (Sinister Cinema), isn't as good/bad as *Shrews* but does include two unforgettable songs sung by teen hero Don Sullivan.

LADY TERMINATOR (1988) ***

D: Jalil Jackson (H. Tjut Djalil). Barbara Anne Constable, Christopher J. Hart, Claudia Angelique Rademaker, Adam Stardust. 92 mins. (Midnight, Studio Entertainment, n.i.d.)

This far-out, Far Eastern import, cast with badly dubbed American and Asian actors, kicks off as an exploration of the "legend of the South Sea Queen," a notorious femme fatale who liked to do in her mates while doing the deed, *vagina dentata*–style (!). Somehow, we abruptly cut to a century or so later, when young Constable, your typical scientist in hot pants, investigates the legend anew and soon finds herself stricken with the queen's curse, a development that bodes ill for the local male

populace. It was at this point that *Lady*'s producers apparently decided to scrap their original story line and remake *The Terminator* instead. They equip our afflicted heroine (who's been rendered invincible, we're told, by that selfsame curse) with leather threads and a machine gun and set about lensing unwaveringly inept nearly frame-by-frame re-creations of *The Terminator*'s money scenes: the disco shoot-out, the police-precinct massacre, even the infamous eye-gouging sequence. None of this makes any sense, of course, but what's even weirder is how this surreal rip-off—obviously intended for overseas audiences—ever landed a Stateside theatrical release in the first place. *Lady Terminator* is well worth seeking out.

LIFEFORCE (1985) **1/2

D: Tobe Hooper. Steve Railsback, Peter Firth, Mathilda May, Frank Finlay, Patrick Stewart, Michael Gothard. 100 mins. (Anchor Bay) DVD

Despite its ample budget, elaborate FX, and London Symphony Orchestra soundtrack, Hooper's *Lifeforce* is a laughably inept throwback to the '50s' cheesiest sci-fi cheapies. The pic begins on a promising note when a captive alien, imaginatively dubbed Space Girl (the genuinely alluring May in the most authentic Vampira imitation we've ever witnessed), walks around naked, showing off her big extraterrestrial breasts and turning unsuspecting citizens into mad, desiccated ghouls. Astronaut Railsback and Brit investigator Firth search for the elusive, energy-draining alien, while, in a scene reminiscent of 1968's far superior *Quatermass and the Pit* (a.k.a. *Five Million Years to Earth*, see index), London's crazed space-vampire victims riot amok in a cannibalistic frenzy. *Lifeforce*'s ludicrous, clinker-ridden dialogue, solemnly delivered by a straight-faced, mostly British cast, will have you howling from reel 1.

THE MANIPULATOR (1971) ***

D: Yabo Yablonsky. Mickey Rooney, Luana Anders, Keenan Wynn. 91 mins. (Vestron, n.i.d.)

Originally titled *B. J. Lang Presents,* this truly mind-melting exercise in celluloid excess was never released theatrically (small wonder). Rooney is on screen nearly every frame as deranged has-been director B. J. Lang. The bonkers B.J. repairs nightly to an abandoned movie set, where he engages in animated discourse with imaginary actors and technicians. Soon Rooney's being mocked by a chalk-white naked fat couple (!) who dance among the props while a tormented Mick screams out the lyrics to "Chattanooga Choo-Choo!" (!!). Next, Mick the Sick rolls out live actress Anders, whom he keeps strapped in a wheelchair. After spoon-feeding her applesauce, he poses as an effeminate makeup person, replete with lipstick and eye shadow. The versatile Mick then dons his Cyrano de Bergerac nose, plumed hat, and sword and commands the bound Luana to enact the Roxanne role. Later our sawed-off Cyrano discovers that a drunk (Wynn in an ill-advised cameo) has stumbled on to his secret set and runs him through with his rapier. Luana, meanwhile, attempts an escape but winds up in a frozen-meat locker where tuxedoed chamber musicians stage an impromptu concert (!).

An intensely incoherent meditation on the movie medium written and directed by Yabo Yablonsky—who went on to pen such immortal works as the Jack Palance caper *Portrait of a Hitman* (WesternWorld) and Ernie Pintoff's all-star *Jaguar Lives* (TWE), with John Huston, Capucine, Christopher Lee, Woody Strode, Donald Pleasence, and Barbara Bach—*The Manipulator* incorporates all those wonderful self-indulgent devices, gimmicks, and tricks beloved by bad filmmakers of the period: crazed camera angles, fuzzed focus, red and blue filters, speeded-up slapstick sequences,

and lots of strobe effects and slo mo. (To give Yabo his due, though, we should point out that the pic does contain laughing-furniture imagery that predates, by some 16 years, a similar scene in Sam Raimi's *Evil Dead 2*). Between Yabo's behind-the-scenes artistry and Mick's tour-de-farce perf, *The Manipulator* makes 91 minutes feel like a lifetime. Hard-core bad-movie buffs won't want to miss a single frame.

MANOS, THE HANDS OF FATE (1966) ***

D: Hal P. Warren. Tom Neyman, Diane Mahree, John Reynolds. 74 mins. (Sinister Cinema)

Looking for *the* worst movie of all time? *Manos* may well be it: a San Antonio–lensed satanist saga with basically one set, no talent, a story line that's neither to be believed nor missed, plus the timeless ditties "The Way" and "Baby Do a Thing with Me." *Viva Torgo!*

McBAIN (1991) **½

D: James Glickenhaus. Christopher Walken, Maria Conchita Alonso, Michael Ironside, Steve James, Chick Vennera. 102 mins. (SGE)

As the eponymous McBain, construction worker Walken heads a quintet of reunited middle-aged 'Nam vets, the type of dim but blithely confident guys who shoot first and philosophize later. Following a retro *Rambo*-esque opening, our heroes stage a solo invasion of Colombia to aid embattled revolutionary leader Alonso, sister of their slain former comrade Vennera, in her fight against a corrupt, oppressive government. Auteur Glickenhaus, who gave us the swift urban thriller *Shakedown* (see index), herein fashions what's essentially an expensive action cartoon highlighted by several effective battle scenes and aerial

sequences. The cornball acting and dialogue—as when Alonso greets Walken's dramatic airborne arrival with a cry of "The rebel army awaits your orders, sir!"—frequently push *McBain* to the edge of self-parody. As an earnest adventure, the flick's a flop, but *McBain*'s combo of campy antics and elaborate action tableaux supplies a fair measure of mindless fun.

THE MONSTER AND THE STRIPPER (1968) ***

D: Ron Ormond. Titania, Sleepy LaBeef, Georgette Dante, June Ormond, Vic Naro (Ron Ormond), Tim Ormond. 91 mins. (Nashville Cinema)

Originally released as *The Exotic Ones,* magician, mesmerist, and auteur Ron (*Mesa of Lost Women*) Ormond's New Orleans–set sleaze/horror hybrid stars still-active rockabilly legend LaBeef and monomonikered ecdysiast Titania in a crazed campfest that, among other firsts, sees a character beaten to death with his own arm nearly two decades before David Winters employed a similar stunt in *Deadly Prey* (AIP). (Sorry to be the one to break it to you, D.W., but facts are facts, and we might as well face 'em.) *The Monster and the Stripper* represented a rad departure for Ormond, who'd cut his directorial teeth helming Lash LaRue westerns before moving on to C&W actioners like *40 Acre Feud, The Girl from Tobacco Row,* and *White Lightnin' Road* (also available from Nashville Cinema), and it's a must for serious backdate trash collectors.

After an opening travelog extols the virtues of New Orleans's nightlife, Ormond takes us into a strip club owned by sleazeball Vic Naro (Ormond himself), a drug-smuggling gangster in shades and one of the worst wigs in screen history. Several mild but bizarre strip acts and musical numbers (including a requisite boring harmonica duet) play out before we cut to the chase—

and the bayou—where backwoods boy Tim (Ormond's son Tim, who proves one of the pic's more personable thesps) helps a low-budget bayou safari of three capture "the Swamp Thing." In a *Mighty Joe Young*–type move, the high-haired, bucktoothed (though oddly laid-back, at least between killing sprees) monster (LaBeef) is exhibited onstage, where he's subjected to several more acts, including contortionist Titania's flame-eating number and then-60ish June Ormond's parody of Sally Rand's infamous fan dance. The monster action heats up near film's end when, in the midst of a backstage catfight, the lumbering LaBeef offs Titania and filmmaker Ormond, leaving the latter's head looking, in the words of a local cop, "like a squashed watermelon." The Ormonds neglected to lens an ending, substituting instead a cheesy newspaper headline stating SWAMP MONSTER ESCAPES (!). No self-respecting camp devotee can afford to leave this amazing epic off his, her, or its must-see list.

THE MUMMY AND THE CURSE OF THE JACKAL   (1969) ***

D: Oliver Drake. Anthony Eisley, Martina Pons, John Carradine, Saul Goldsmith. 86 mins. (Academy, n.i.d.)

This riveting abomination can proudly take its place among the worst movies ever made. The film, in fact, was never actually completed, and the video version looks like it was assembled by stitching together every last bit of available footage (one explanation why entire scenes unfold in long shot). Eisley turns into a "werejackal" when he awakens female mummy Pons (who experiences little difficulty adjusting to her tacky new lifestyle as a downscale Vegas bimbo), thus invoking the title curse and prompting the murderous return of a male mummy (wordlessly interpreted by Goldsmith). Highlights include the mummy/werejackal "rampage" through the streets of

Vegas, where onlookers openly stare into the camera and grin at the "monsters'" antics.

NIGHT OF THE BLOODY APES (1968) ***

D: René Cardona, Sr. Armando Silvestre, José Elías Moreno, Carlos López Moctezuma, Norma Lazareno. Dubbed. 81 mins. (MPI, n.i.d.)

A classically awful wrestling/monster movie created by the father-and-son schlock team of René Cardona, Sr. and Jr., *Night of the Bloody Apes* sports a deranged plot and great dubbed dialogue. (Doctor to detective: "Maybe you have been watching on your television too many pictures of terror!") A demented doc transplants the heart of a man in a gorilla suit into his dying son, who in turn transforms into a muscle-bound ape-man with a taste for rape and murder. (Hence, the terror picture's admirably blunt Mexican title, *Horror y Sexo*). The literally in-depth surgical and eye-gouging FX, shown in extreme close-up, were apparently inserted by the flick's American distribs. Of the assembled thesps, Lazareno, as the lady wrestler in the case, makes the deepest impression, largely via her many and sundry gratuitous shower scenes. But why, we want to know, does the son still revert to a simian state after his ape heart is replaced by a woman's? That eternal conundrum aside, *Night of the Bloody Apes* rates as a reel anti-classic.

NIGHT TRAIN TO TERROR (1985) ***

D: John Carr, Jay Schlossberg-Cohen, Phillip Marshak, Tom McGowan, Greg Tallas. John Phillip Law, Cameron Mitchell, Marc Lawrence, Charles Moll, Meredith Haze, Ferdy Mayne. 93 mins. (Prism) DVD

Human vivisections! Nazi massacres! Exploding eyeballs! Full-

frontal lobotomies! Suicide cults! Kung-fu set-tos! Break-dancing! Cameron Mitchell! If one movie would seem to have it all, it would be the Philip Yordan–scripted *Night Train to Terror*. As the pic opens, a bad white-bread rock band break-dances through the title train performing the pic's unforgettable theme song, "Everybody's Got Somethin' to Do," while God and Satan discuss situational ethics in the compartment next door. The flick quickly derails, however, when Satan decides to illustrate his points by narrating a trio of tales—unrelated sequences, actually—from three earlier Yordan epics: *Death Wish Club* (Regal), *The Nightmare Never Ends* (Simitar), and an unfinished project featuring John Phillip Law. The result, as one might imagine, is an unholy, if weirdly entertaining, mess. (That the pic's wraparound participants felt less than proud of their contributions is evidenced by the end credits, where the thesp portraying Satan is billed as "Lu Cifer," while the actor [Mayne] playing God is listed as "Himself" [!].) The movie's most memorable moment depicts a zombielike doctor, his forehead bisected by a fresh lobotomy scar, wandering a hospital corridor, wielding a scalpel, and muttering, "I've gotta get to Surgery!"

ZSA ZSA VA-VOOM: A GABOR DOUBLE BILL

THE PEOPLE VS. ZSA ZSA GABOR (1991) ***

60 mins. (Tri-Coast Video)

For Zsa-Zsa devotees and cathode-courtroom junkies, there's only one video certain to satisfy both those cravings: Tri-Coast Video's verité exercise *The People vs. Zsa Zsa Gabor*. While Judge Judy may be nowhere in sight, the tape features 60 minutes of head-shaking highlights from Zsa Zsa's notorious 1989 assault case. Thrill as a battered cop relives the trauma of being slapped by an enraged Ms. Double Z, then stay tuned to hear the defendant's colorful version of the same incident (though a translator, or at least subtitles, would have been helpful at times). The video was issued in SP and LP (middle-speed) editions, with the former doing greater justice to Zsa Zsa's eye-assaulting wardrobe.

QUEEN OF OUTER SPACE
(1958) ***

D: Edward Bernds. Zsa Zsa Gabor, Eric Fleming, Dave Willock, Paul Birch, Laurie Mitchell. 80 mins. (Fox)

Zsa Zsa's unforgettable Venusian vehicle depicts the problems encountered by a typically cocky crew of American cosmonauts commanded by Fleming (*Rawhide*) when they run afoul of power-mad space ruler Yllana (Mitchell). Rebel leader Zsa Zsa, sporting the latest in high-profile, low-cleavage cosmic fashions *and* the only Hungarian accent on Venus, eventually allies with the good guys to bring the evil Yllana to justice. Lensed in lurid Deluxe Color, *Queen* not only features one of Zsa Zsa's most powerful screen turns but recycles sets and props from *Forbidden Planet, Flight to Mars,* and *World Without End.* Amen.

PLAN 9 FROM OUTER SPACE
(1956) B&W ****

D: Ed Wood. Bela Lugosi, Tor Johnson, Vampira, Gregory Walcott, Mona McKinnon, Lyle Talbot, Tom Keene. 78 mins. (Englewood) DVD

The movie that made Ed Wood a household name—if, at first, only in the oddest of households—holds unchallenged claim as the most enriching, entertaining bad movie ever made. You probably know the story: A

ACTOR CONRAD BROOKS ON *ED WOOD*
As Told to The Phantom

To Ed, growing up, going to movies, these were his heroes—Bela Lugosi and people like Lyle Talbot and Tom Tyler and Tom Keene. Ed was always loyal to these people. When Ed Wood wrote a script, he'd put in the actor he had in mind to play each character. He felt that he owed them something. He said, "They brought a lot of enjoyment to my life; I want to return something good to them."

He'd not only look out after the people who'd one time had names, but he'd also give a lot of new players a break. Like Tor Johnson was playing bit parts, but Ed Wood gave him the costarring role in *Bride of the Monster* and *Plan 9 from Outer Space.* He gave Steve Reeves, in *Jail Bait,* his first real role. And Steve Reeves went on and did *Hercules* and, I understand, made a lot of money.

[*Plan 9*] was a union film. Everybody got the minimum. It was shot on thirty-five-millimeter; everybody got paid. You had Bill Thompson, one of the finest movie photographers; he'd photographed pictures back in the twenties. Of course, they crucified it for how bad it was and all that. Sure it was bad, but listen—people like it! I make personal appearances at colleges and different places, and everybody loves it. They're laughing, having a great time. There's a little bit of Ed Wood in all of us.

---

trio of aliens—the dignified if short-tempered Eros (announcer Dudley Manlove, who later distinguished himself as one of *Creation of the Humanoids*'s leading clickers); Tana (future TV writer Joanna Lee); and the Ruler (nonactor transsexual wannabe John Breckenridge, who resorts to reading from his script on-screen)—invade California and institute the title scheme, which involves turning the massive Johnson, slinky Vampira, and aged Bela into (barely) living dead. Trouble was, Bela died in earnest shortly before shooting and had to be replaced by Mrs. Wood's chiropractor, Tom Mason, who was something less than a Lugosi look-alike. Add amateur acting, cardboard sets, toy flying saucers, Ed's trademark confusion of day and night, and circular dialogue that can only be described as truly out of this world, and you have what's rightfully become *the* camp-classic king.

ED WOOD'S GREATEST HITS

GLEN OR GLENDA (1953)
B&W ***½

D: Ed Wood. Bela Lugosi. "Daniel Davis" (Ed Wood), Dolores Fuller, Lyle Talbot, Timothy Farrell. 67 mins. (Rhino, Englewood)

Ed's debut feature (a.k.a. *I Changed My Sex* and *I Led Two Lives*) began life as a documentary but ended as a mélange of badly staged vignettes intercut with largely unrelated stock footage. Ed himself, under the *nom de thesp* Daniel Davis, plays the title role(s) of he-guy transvestite Glen/Glenda, whose fiancée (Ed's then-real-life squeeze, Fuller) can't understand his burning desire to don her angora sweaters. As "The Spirit," Bela sits on a threadbare throne and babbles stream-of-consciousness soliloquies not always related to the dramatic action at hand. (To wit: "Man's constant groping of things unknown brings to light many startling things!") Beyond crafting one of Z-moviedom's most memorable nightmare sequences (supplemented by borrowed soft-core S&M stag-film clips), Ed distinguishes himself as a master of movie montage, if not of narrative filmmaking, since fully 18 of *Glen or Glenda*'s 67 minutes are composed of stock footage.

JAIL BAIT (1954) B&W ***

D: Ed Wood. Timothy Farrell, Lyle Talbot, Dolores Fuller, Clancy Malone, Herbert Rawlinson, Steve Reeves. 70 mins. (Englewood)

Originally titled *The Hidden Face*, *Jail Bait* (the title refers to handguns, not underaged girls) actually flirts with mediocrity, though it still boasts plenty of unsteady thesping (especially from lead Malone, Ed's real-life delivery boy!) and Ed's patented circular dialogue, which at one point prompts exasperated hood Farrell to bark, "What do I have to do? Repeat myself all night?!" Among its other distinctions, Ed's low-budget noir also features Steve Reeves's screen debut as an LAPD dick who gets to flaunt his fabled physique. As an astute *Variety* reviewer remarked in 1954, little of *Jail Bait*'s reputed $21,000 budget shows on-screen.

THE VIOLENT YEARS (1956) B&W ***1/2

D: Fritz Eichorn. Jean Moorehead, Timothy Farrell, Glenn Corbett, I. Stanford Jolley. 75 mins. (Englewood, Rhino)

Ed wrote but didn't direct this wild tale about a quartet of crazy-for-kicks teen chicks who hold up gas stations, molest stray males, and generally ignore civilization's rules of decorum. The gals, hired by Commie lowlifes to trash the local high school, end up shooting it out with the fuzz, prompting one mortally wounded femme to observe, "It ain't supposed to be…this way." The girls' philosophy is best summed up, however, by gang leader Moorehead's oft repeated rhetorical query, "So *what*?" Judge Jolley's windy climactic ruling shows off Ed's writing talents as pointedly as anything in the auteur's entire ouevre.

THE BRIDE AND THE BEAST (1958) B&W **1/2

D: Adrian Weiss. Lance Fuller, Charlotte Austin, Johnny Roth, Steve Calvert. 78 mins. (Admit One)

The *Bride and the Beast* is a girl-gorilla romance Ed scripted for director Adrian Weiss, whose brother George had launched Ed's career by producing *Glen or Glenda* some five years earlier. *Bride* gets off to a promising start, with newlyweds Austin and her Great White Hunter hubby (Fuller) exchanging some classic Wooden dialogue while driving to the latter's estate. There, Charlotte, clad (natch) in a stunning angora sweater, meets Lance's secret pet—a gorilla named Spanky (!). When Charlotte and Spanky experience nothing less than love at first fright, Lance puts an abrupt end to their budding involvement by summarily shooting the lovesick simian. In a bid to board the then-hot Bridey Murphy/reincarnation bandwagon, a hypnotist is called in to regress Charlotte to her past life as—what else?—a girl gorilla (which, according to the mesmerist, explains Charlotte's "fixation for furlike materials. Basically," he further illuminates, "we're all animals.") Our honeymooners next embark on an African safari, where *Bride* hopelessly bogs down in long stretches of antique jungle stock footage.

BRIDE OF THE MONSTER (1956) B&W ***

D: Ed Wood. Bela Lugosi, Tor Johnson, Loretta King, Tony McCoy, Harvey B. Dunne, Paul Marcos. 69 mins. (Englewood)

Bela's only true starring role in an Ed Wood movie finds the Hungarian thesp at his hammiest as the mad Dr. Vornoff, a fugitive Russki scientist who's laboring, with the dubious help of his mute, moronic minion, Lobo (Johnson), to create a race of "superbeinks of unthinkable strength and size" in the basement lab of his secret redoubt. *Bride* was financed by an Arizona rancher who insisted that his scrawny, uncharismatic son (McCoy) play the hero. *Bride* features some of Ed's most inspired touches: Bela turns into a "superman" by donning a pair of platform shoes, then does battle with an immobile prop octopus left over from 1948's *Wake of the Red Witch*. Ed's main triumph here, though, is making what looks, sounds, and plays like an authentic 1942 Monogram horror movie in 1955.

NIGHT OF THE GHOULS (1959) B&W ***1/2

D: Ed Wood. Kenne Duncan, Duke Moore, Tor Johnson, Criswell, Valda Hansen, Paul Marcos, Don Nagel. 79 mins. (Englewood)

As is usually the case with Wood's work, it's not the plot but the bizarre execution that supplies *Ghouls*—a semisequel to *Bride of the Monster*—with its *el cheapo* charm. The ever flamboyant Criswell narrates from a customized coffin. Duncan portrays phony spiritualist Dr. Acula, a role originally designed with the late Lugosi in mind; Moore is the intrepid detective investigating a series of mysterious murders at the doc's old, dark lair; and Tor reprises his trademark role as the lumbering, dim-witted Lobo. Also along for the rocky ride are Marcos as comic-relief cop Kelton, sultry Hansen as the White Ghost, Vampira stand-in Jeannie Stevens as the Black Ghost, and Ed himself in a silent cameo as a corpse (!). While *Ghouls* proceeds sans *Plan 9*'s crazed energy, it still delivers its share of Wood-en thrills. Most memorable is

Dr. Acula's bogus séance, where floating trumpets (on visible strings) offer sour serenades; white-sheeted extras creak across the room; a "spirit guide" appears as a disembodied head wearing a pith helmet; and cadavers rise from their caskets to proffer business advice to the living. (As one weary shade puts it, "The task of spanning the everlasting is *so* tiring.")

THE SINISTER URGE (1961)
B&W ***½

D: Ed Wood. Kenne Duncan, Duke Moore, Dino Fantini, Jean Fontaine, Harvey B. Dunn. 75 mins. (Sinister Cinema)

Cops Duncan and Moore pursue a "smut-picture-racket" hit man (Fantini) terrorizing the city. Ed obviously saw himself in the character of stag-moviemaker Johnny Ryde (Carl Anthony), a talented but unlucky auteur who coulda been a contender if he'd just caught a few breaks. Cop Duncan takes a harder line: "Show me a crime, and I'll show you a picture that could've caused it." Top acting honors go to Wood regular Dunn as concerned taxpayer Mr. Romaine. The porn-film-within-a-film (including several blondes and a whip-wielding Mexican thesp in black leotards) and a lakeside undercover drag scene provide other highlights.

ORGY OF THE DEAD (1965) ***

D: A. C. Stephen (Stephen Apostoloff). Criswell, Fawn Silver, William Bates, Pat Barringer. 82 mins. (Rhino)

With this R-rated extravaganza lensed in "Astravision and Sexicolor," scripter Ed locates the fine line separating Eros from Thanatos and promptly trips over it. Hapless writer Bob and girlfriend Shirley (Wood-enly interpreted by coproducer Bates and Barringer, respectively) stumble upon a remote graveyard where Criswell, as the Master of the Dead, presides over a

"dance of the dead"—i.e., several strip acts performed by an exotic succession of ecdysiasts. Many classic Ed Wood touches are here in abundance: inspired dialogue (e.g., Bob to Shirley: "Your puritan upbringing may hold you back from my monsters, but it hasn't affected your art of kissing"); constant confusion between day and night; and camera work that harks back to the celluloid Stone Age. Special kudos go to choreographer Marc Desmond, particularly for his inventive work on Texas Starr's "Cat Dance."

ED EPHEMERA
"I'm always ready, willing and, I hate to use the word *able*, but for the lack of a better word, able."
—*sultry gal Fluff to local lothario Wimpy,*
Class Reunion

Following his glory daze, Ed found dubious further refuge in the skin-flick trade, scripting (under the alias Akdov Tilmeg) the soft-core cave-babe romp *One Million AC/DC* (1968), writing and directing 1971's *Necromania* (both Something Weird), penning 1971's *Class Reunion* and 1972's *Pleasure Unlimited* (both Private Screenings), coscripting *The Beach Bunnies* (1973) and *The Snow Bunnies* (1976), appearing in *Fugitive Girls* (1971), *Love Feast* (1970, all Something Weird), and 1970's *The Sensuous Wife* (Private Screenings). Something Weird also has *Take It Out in Trade: The Outtakes*, silent bits from an otherwise "lost" erotic caper, written and directed by Ed, who cameos as a drag queen. Conrad Brooks's compilation *Hellborn* features clips from Ed's abortive eponymous 1952 crime film, along with a short, "Mystery in Shadows," written and directed by Brooks. Several Ed-related documentaries are also available (see our "Phantom 'B'wards" section).

PLAYGIRL KILLER (1968) ***

D: Erick Santamaria. William Kerwin, Jean Christopher, Neil Sedaka. 85 mins. (New World, n.i.d.)

Former H. G. Lewis mainstay Thomas (*Blood Feast*) Wood, emoting under his real name William Kerwin, carries the day in this unofficial variation on Lewis's *Color Me Blood Red* (Something Weird) as a temperamental artist who murders his female models when their involuntary movements disrupt his creative concentration (!). Sedaka, collecting a (probably small) check between comebacks, is also on hand and at the ivories to lend a lighter note to the turgid proceedings. Also released as *Decoy for Terror*.

PREHISTORIC WOMEN (1950) **½

D: Greg Tallas. Allan Nixon, Lauretta Luez, Joan Shawlee. 74 mins. (Rhino)

Engor (Nixon) and Tigri (Luez) share primitive love when not battling 9-foot jungle bully Gwadi in this alternately dull and entertainingly inept Stone Age epic related mostly via voice-over. Not as good/bad as *Untamed Women*, let alone *Wild Women of Wongo* (see index), but worth a look for caveman-camp completists.

RAW FORCE (1981) ***

D: Edward Murphy. Cameron Mitchell, Hope Holiday, Geoff Binney, Julian Kressner, John Dresden, Vic Diaz, Ralph Lombardi. 86 mins. (Media, n.i.d.)

Murphy's deliciously stupid outing opens with a cross section of top-heavy bimbos, macho meatheads, and assorted morons—including members of the Burbank Karate Club (!)—setting sail on a Far East–bound party boat operated by avaricious tour agent Holiday and cranky captain Mitchell. Shipboard hijinks abound until the trashy tub cruises too near infamous Warriors

Island, a "Potter's Field of Kung-Fu," where a cabal of cannibalistic monks ("Female flesh gives them the power to raise the dead," we learn) led by vet Filipino villain Diaz trade jade with ex-Nazi Lombardi in exchange for tasty mainland maidens. The bad guys soon steal aboard the pleasure boat with wholesale slaughter in mind. Following the on-board bloodbath, a few survivors wash up on the dread isle, only to be cornered by the flesh-famished monks, who beseech the heavens to raise their kung-fu dead. "Oh, sacred masters of the sky, instill our fighting cadavers with kicking, slashing strength to execute righteous slaughter! Show us bloodshed like it used to be!" (Ah, the good old days!) And that's barely scratching the surface of this backdate campfest.

Beyond its brain-drained plot machinations, *Raw Force* features inspired dialogue, creative background overdubs (use your headphones for this one), and Holiday and the late Mitchell's bizarre comic rapport. (After a ship survivor gets sliced and diced by a samurai stiff, Hope is moved to weep, "He was one of my passengers—a *paying* passenger!") The flick culminates with an inexplicably confident "To Be Continued" notice, a promise that, at this late date, seems destined to remain sadly unfulfilled.

REBEL (1970) **

D: Robert Allan Schnitzer. Sylvester Stallone, Anthony Page, Rebecca Grimes, Roy White. 80 mins. (Paragon, American)

Maybe Sly's just one of those naturally funny guys whose comic talents are actually hampered by the constraints a formal comedy context (e.g., *Oscar*) can impose. He's certainly risible enough in his first legit starring role, the 1973 obscurity *Rebel* (a.k.a. *No Place to Hide*). In Schnitzer's 1969-set message movie, Sly plays Jerry Savage, a left-wing urban terrorist (talk about your rad image changes!) out to bomb a mid-

town Manhattan tiger-cage manufacturer. While Sly turns in another of his patented simian perfs, he does show a more sensitive side when he dons a rainbow-colored poncho and courts flower child Grimes. Like Sly's future Rambo persona, Jerry's a philosophical sort. "I think it's good to escape from thought," he announces at one point, a statement but a short leap from Rambo's "I think the mind is the best weapon." *Rebel* is also out as *A Man Called Rainbo* (Monarch), wherein several self-styled wits redubbed the original soundtrack, à la Woody Allen's *What's Up, Tiger Lily?* But the original *Rebel* supplies enough curio value in its own right to make additional embellishments unnecessary. Look for the video—featuring an unflattering close-up of Sly's face and left armpit—at a bargain bin near you.

GUEST REVIEW

ROBOT MONSTER (1953) B&W/3-D****

D: Phil Tucker. George Nader, Gregory Moffett, Claudia Barrett, Selena Royle, John Mylong. 63 mins. (Rhino)

Notwithstanding the visual appeal of the hilarious Ro-Man monster padding about in a furry gorilla suit with a fishbowl for a helmet, it is impossible to view *Robot Monster* without being struck by its childlike, and therefore all the more poignant, homage to and metaphor for the post–World War II holocaust reality. The often befuddled Ro-Man shows us the blank face of the banality of evil as, receiving instructions from his outer-space führer (Great Guidance) via a rickety TV awash in soap bubbles, he sets about his mission to destroy the last eight people left on earth. "Wouldn't it be nicer if we could live in peace with each other?" rhetorically asks the main resistance fighter (Mylong), who, not surprisingly, has a refugee's East European accent. But in this post-Armageddon world, annihila-

tion seems inevitable. "For you humans"—read Jews, dissidents, or, within a Cold War context, wretched survivors—"there is no escape," parrots Ro-man, who, mindlessly reflecting the sadistic concerns of his Mengele-like master, holds out the cheery promise of a "painless death." "We must die," concurs the patriarch of the clan, which has already been barricaded behind barbed wire and whose furtive life resembles a stark Anne Frank–type existence. The story is told from a child's point of view within the framework of a nightmare. It is stripped down and movingly ludicrous in places, but it is an allegory nonetheless, a moral fable through which is distilled the sadness and horror of the contemporary world. The seriousness of filmmaker (and World War II veteran) Tucker's intent was borne out by his reported suicide attempt following the scathingly negative reviews that greeted the film's humble release. Luckily, Tucker lived to create such other important works as *Broadway Jungle, Dance Hall Racket, Pachuco,* and *The Cape Canaveral Monsters.*

Back to you, Phantom.

—Nancy Naglin (a.k.a. The Phantomess)

(You didn't mention it's in 3-D! —The Phantom)

ROBO VAMPIRE (1993) **1/2

D: Joe Livingstone. Harry Myles, Joe Browne, Nick Norman, Diana Byrne. Dubbed. 90 mins. (Magnum)

À la the camp-classic import *Lady Terminator* (see index), several no-name Anglo actors (who are just as badly dubbed as their Asian counterparts) populate this loopy, Hong Kong–lensed cheapie, which mixes your standard hopping vampires with a *RoboCop* hook, martial arts action, meaningless firefights, a gratuitous eye-gouging incident, and a convoluted drug-smuggling plot. Highlights include a wedding scene between a distaff Anglo ghost (naked

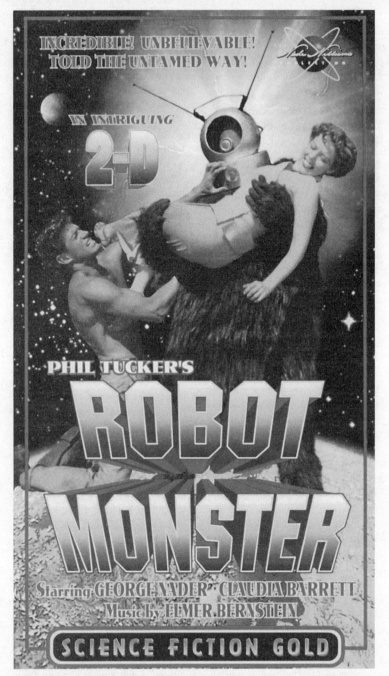

INCREDIBLE! UNBELIEVABLE! TOLD THE UNTAMED WAY!

IN INTRIGUING

2-D

PHIL TUCKER'S

ROBOT MONSTER

Starring GEORGE NADER · CLAUDIA BARRETT
Music by ELMER BERNSTEIN

SCIENCE FICTION GOLD

FALL OF THE RO-MAN EMPIRE: Furry, fish-bowled invader Ro-man briefly has his way with hapless humans in Englewood's box art for Phil Tucker's *Robot Monster. Courtesy of Englewood Entertainment/Wade Williams Distribution*

under her diaphanous gown) and a dead Chinese vampire in an unexplained gorilla mask. *Robo Vampire* easily cops all-time Most Obvious Use of a Stunt

Double honors when a blond female Cauc leaps through a window and flies out the other side as an Asian male in a long *gray* wig (!).

RUN...IF YOU CAN! (1987) ***

D: Virginia Lively Stone. Martin Landau, Yvette Nipar, Jerry Van Dyke, Phillip Pine. 92 mins. (Today, n.i.d.)

Run...If You Can! apparently represented something of an ill-advised comeback bid for producer/director Stone, who, with late spouse Andrew Stone, brought several quality B+ genre flicks, from the kidnap caper *Cry Terror* to the seagoing slaughterfest *The Decks Ran Red* (both n/a), to 1950s screens. Lensed during goredom's '80s cycle of psycho pics with snuff-movie themes, *Run* focuses on Kim Page (Nipar), a perky coed who agrees to house-sit an L.A. manse that happens to be situated in a nabe plagued by a depraved serial killer. Kim's troubles begin when a late-night TV broadcast of *Of Human Bondage* is interrupted by videotaped scenes of the rampaging sex maniac perpetrating his horrific deeds. At first our heroine sees nothing amiss, casually remarking to fellow student Jill: "I saw an old Leslie Howard last night on the late show. He stuffed a girl's body in a big plastic sack." To which Jill sagely points out, "Leslie Howard? He was dead long before they invented plastic sacks!" When the vile broadcasts persist, Kim goes to cops Landau (then in a busy career slump that included roles in such Z-level fare as *Access Code, Death Blow, Real Bullets,* and *Sweet Revenge*) and Jerry (Brother of Dick) Van Dyke. They naturally refuse to believe her story, until a police technician (Pine) determines that Kim's satellite dish could indeed be picking up "freak transmissions." "It's like an anomaly," Landau explains to less brainy partner Van Dyke. In addition to its inspiredly dumb dialogue and stupid plot—which relies on frequent character miscommunications to keep it stumbling more or less forward— *Run* is so surreally out-of-sync that it seems likely postproduction chores were never completed.

RUNNING DELILAH   (1993) **½

D: Richard Franklin. Kim Cattrall, Billy Zane, François Guéteray, Yorgo Voyagis, Diana Rigg. 85 mins. (Anchor Bay)

Run *RoboCop* and *La Femme Nikita/Point of No Return* through the network-TV wringer, and you get this entertainingly inane affair. Foxy Cattrall's an offed undercover operative robotically reborn at the insistence of smitten fellow agent Zane. While our revitalized heroine bemoans the loss of her identity, normality, and physicality (only her original head, neck, and left arm remain unchanged), in no time she's an expert martial artist, sharpshooter, linguist, concert-quality pianist, and (in the pic's neatest touch) an ace blues guitarist (!). Kim returns to the field with partner Zane, relocating to Paris to nab the big-time arms dealer who'd ordered her assassination in reel 1. Perennial Hitchcock manqué Franklin does a reasonable job handling the story's nominal suspense; Cattrall and Zane are fun to watch as they work to overcome the techno obstacles preventing the consummation of their mutual affections; and the final "erotic" interlude rates as a camp classic. Ex-Avenger Rigg contributes a mostly desk-bound cameo as our odd couple's agency superior.

SATAN'S CHEERLEADERS (1977) **½

D: Greydon Clark. John Ireland, Yvonne DeCarlo, Jack Kruschen. 92 mins. (United)

Clark's witless jiggle chiller offers a veteran cast and enough unintended laughs to qualify it as decent six-pack video fare. John Carradine cameos as an irascible hobo, while peripatetic auteur/actor Clark went on to dabble in "blaxploitation" pics, like *The Bad Bunch* and *Black Shampoo* (both United), before making a major career move with the femme-oriented actioner *Angels Brigade* (Vestron), where he worked with such heavyweights as Jack Palance, Peter Lawford, Jim Backus, and Arthur Godfrey.

SHOWGIRLS   (1995) ***

D: Paul Verhoeven. Elizabeth Berkley, Kyle MacLachlan, Gina Gershon, Robert Davi, Glenn Plummer, Alan Rachins, Gina Ravera, Lin Tucci, William Shockley. 131 mins. (MGM)

Dutch émigré auteur Verhoeven applies his *RoboCop* satiric edge to American showbiz mythology. This mostly misunderstood "Beyond the Valley of the Lapdancers"–styled spoof, scripted by overpaid "erotic thriller" machine Joe Eszterhas, sends up the entire catalog of clichés celebrated in such '60s camp classics as *The Oscar* (Embassy) and *Valley of the Dolls* (Fox). (Though *Showgirls* probably would have worked even better had it been cast with drag queens. Where are Patrick Swayze, Wesley Snipes, and John Leguizamo when we need them?) Verhoeven's G-strings-to-riches tale follows transient Nomi (a perennially pouting Berkley, whose ability to project pure stupidity is nothing short of scary), who hitches to Vegas from unspecified points East, where she loses first her luggage, then her lunch, before being rescued by kindly backstage costumer Molly (Ravera). Nomi pays her showbiz dues the hard way, lap-dancing at a sleazy Davi's lowlife Cheetah Club while hanging with the likes of tonnage-driven comic Henrietta Bazoom (Tucci), sort of a foulmouthed Totie Fields. Our heroine's "saved" from the lap-dancing life when a bitchy, bisexual, cigar-smoking, coke-snorting white-trash glitter-dance queen named Cristal (a campy Gershon) takes Nomi under her wing. Cristal persuades her entertainment-director beau, Zack (a zombielike MacLachlan), to let Nomi try out for a chorus role in her new extravaganza, where she's run through the wringer by self-confessed choreographer "prick" Tony (Rachins). After a brief but tumultuous affair with dreadlocked musician James (Plummer), Nomi dances her way to the top of the Vegas heap only to discover it's a lonely world up there. She gets to let off a bit of emotional steam by demonstrating her hitherto unmentioned kickboxing skills at the expense of evil rock star Andrew Carver (Shockley), who'd earlier led a brutal gang rape and assault on a helpless Molly. Whether Eszterhas's script was as hip as Verhoeven's handling—the pair previously collaborated on the largely laughless B.O. biggie *Basic Instinct*—remains open to debate, but the final results qualify for prime hoothood either way. In *Showgirls*, no cliché, no matter how worn or obvious, is merely presented when it can be telegraphed and double-stated. *Showgirls* may not do for ice what *Last Tango in Paris* did for butter, but by video's end it's a good bet there won't be a dry eye (or lap) in the room.

SLASHER IN THE HOUSE   (1981) **

D: Netie Pena. Jake Steinfeld, Peter De Paula, Charles Hoyes. 85 mins. (New Pacific)

Before attaining immortality as a cathode aerobics instructor, Jake (Body by Jake) Steinfeld landed this dubious—and uncommonly messy—slasher vehicle: In the very first scene, lumbering, T-shirt-clad Jake, cast as an escaped mental patient, strangles a beer-guzzling motorist, liberally spraying the camera lens with suds. Then, after commandeering his victim's car, Jake runs over the first little old lady he sees, splattering his windshield with gallons of ultrafake plasma. Our fave moment, though, arrives when Jake tells a *mime* in full white facial makeup, "Make a sound and I'll kill the girl" (!). Atrocious acting, inane dialogue, primitive postdubbing, and confused camera work (the script contains repeated references to Valium) combine to make *Slasher* (a.k.a. *Home Sweet Home*) a one-of-a-kind experience. Who'd've guessed Jake would go on to become one of TV's greatest sitcom stars? Wait, that's *Sein*feld. Never mind.

THE SLIME PEOPLE (1962) B&W***

D: Robert Hutton. Robert Hutton, Les Tremayne, Susan Hart, Robert Burton. 76 mins. (Rhino)

Vet B thesp Hutton decided he could make a movie every bit as slick as W. Lee Wilder's *Man Without a Body* (in which he'd recently appeared) or fellow thesp Robert Clarke's *Hideous Sun Demon*. The result is this low-budget tale, lensed largely in an L.A. warehouse, about subterranean atomic mutants. To further highlight his own comparative emotive aplomb, Hutton hired a klutzy cast (with the exception of ubiquitous '50s B-movie trooper Tremayne) who fail to establish a working relationship with the camera. Highlights include a neat precredits visual intro to the title creatures and the following words to live by: "When I'm sitting here with you, I don't even *think* about slime people." Watch it with someone you love, and maybe you won't either.

SONNY BOY (1990) ***½

D: Robert Martin Carroll. David Carradine, Paul L. Smith, Brad Dourif, Michael Griffin, Alexandra Powers, Savina Gersak, Conrad Janis. 98 mins. (Media, n.i.d.)

Sonny Boy opens in the white-trash town of Harmony, New Mexico, in 1970. Local lowlife Dourif blows away a vacationing couple and steals their car. Unbeknownst to Brad, there's a baby in the backseat. When he delivers the wheels to desert fence, killer, and painter (!) Smith, Smith's eccentric better half adopts the infant. It's at this point that *Sonny Boy* turns exceedingly strange indeed. Smith's wife is played by David Carradine in drag! The other characters all regard D.C. as an authentic femme, even though he, in long hair and tattered dresses, often speaks in his normal baritone. There are further surreal antics on view in this legendary

wall-to-wall jaw-dropper. Smith, Carradine, Dourif, and pal Sydney Lassick (continuing his career as sort of an edgy Marvin Kaplan) raise their hapless ward as a career geek, removing his tongue, keeping him in a cage, and feeding him live chickens. Seventeen years later ("Mother" Carradine now sports a smart gray coif more appropriate to "her" age), Smith & Co. unleash the flesh-eating adolescent Sonny Boy (Griffin) to eliminate their various enemies. We also learn, via Sonny Boy's voice-overs, that our teen geek is really an innately sensitive lad, who feels transformed after eating a priest ("the first time I'd tasted the blood of a good man"!). When the townsfolk eventually grow tired of Sonny Boy and clan, they storm Smith's desert redoubt en masse, only to encounter the wrath of Smith's handy home howitzer. That's barely scratching the surface of this fascinating atrocity. We also watch idyllic moments between the speechless Sonny Boy and free-spirited town teenette Powers; a cameo by Euro B starlet Gersak as a feisty femme with terrible teeth; and a monkey-tongue transplant (!) performed by drunken doc Janis. Withal, *Sonny Boy* is a vision of wasteland Americana that plays like a misguided union between Percy (*Bagdad Cafe*) Adlon and Ruggero (*Cannibal Holocaust*) Deodato, edited with a chainsaw.

SPACE PROBE TAURUS (1964) **½

D: Leonard Katzman. Jim Brown, Francine York, Baynes Barron, Russ Bender. 72 mins. (Sinister Cinema)

Also available under its original *Space Monster* handle from Something Weird Video, this static, claustrophobic, ultracheap, but meditative and at times drearily engaging sci-fier charts the space flight of a three-man, one-woman crew. Commander Brown is grumpy over femme scientist York's presence and crewman Barron's flip,

cynical attitude. Virtually nothing happens until two of the crew board an adrift craft, where they're confronted by a stunned, helmeted, dumb-looking alien who wiggles his extruded tongue in rude fashion, then, apparently not satisfied with delivering this sound taunting, physically attacks the two. After dispatching the impolite E.T. with a bullet, the pair return to their own ship, where virtually nothing else happens until their craft lands in monster-infested alien waters (actually a fish tank). One of the crew gives his life so that the others may continue their own humdrum existences. This entry in Heavy Eyelid Cinema, originally an AIP-TV production, makes for great hypnogagia-inducing late-night viewing.

SPY SQUAD (A.K.A. *CAPTURE THAT CAPSULE*) (1961) B&W***

D: Will Zens. Richard Miller, Dick O'Neill, Richard Jordahl, Pat Bradley. 75 mins. (Something Weird)

In his liner notes for this long-submerged Cold War turkey, Johnny Legend refers to the flick's "mind-boggling none-ness." And *Spy Squad*—which your Phantom had taped off a late-night TV airing about a decade back and kept ever since for occasional use as a video sleeping aid—may indeed rate as *the* nothingest movie ever made. Romance? Thrills? Sleaze? Suspense? Action? Drama? Simple sense? These are all qualities *Spy Squad* lacks in abundance. The assembled thesps, ranging from dull and geeky to downright ugly, seem selected out of some central casting from hell, while auteur Zens works hard to lens them from the most unflattering angles he can divine. Our story, such as it is, involves a government sting designed to net a handful of West Coast Commies. The latter retrieve a nose cone from a deliberately downed missile; instead of containing important classified info, though, it conceals a secret tracking device that allows our alert agents to follow the bumbling Reds to their secret leader's lair. For several reels we see the Keystone Commies lose (once to a demented little towhead looking for his lost snake, Slinky) and regain the capsule while the agents doggedly follow their progress. The Reds relate to one another almost entirely via garbled insults (e.g., "You're talking through that hole in your head rather than with your brain"), while the agents pass their time exchanging *Dragnet*-styled mundanities about the weather, cars, and their wives' shopping habits. While we miss the vintage Crazy Eddie ads and Craftmatic pitches that punctuated our old commercial broadcast tape, we can say with assurety that *Spy Squad* has lost none of its sedative powers over the years and is even more effective when observed in its uninterrupted entirety. (In fact, the film's final two spoken words are "sleep" and "sleep.") Zens, meanwhile, went on to craft a whole raft of future snoozers, including Vince Edwards and Robert Tessier in *The Fix* (1984) and future Cold-Warrior congressman Robert Dornan (!) in the military exercise *The Starfighters* (1963) (both World), not one but *two* Marty Robbins movies, *Hell On Wheels* (1967) (Acorn), costarring John Ashley and Gigi Perreau, and *The Road to Nashville* (1967) (script only, VCI), with Doodles Weaver and Johnny Cash, plus *Hot Summer in Barefoot County* (1974), *To the Shores of Hell* (1965), and *Trucker's Woman* (1983) (all from Paragon, n.i.d.). More than enough, in short, to stage your own Will Zens Home Film Fest. Just don't forget to set the alarm.

STREETS OF DEATH   (1987) **½

D: Jeff Hathcock. Tommy Kirk, Larry Thomas, Lawrence Scott, Susanne Smith, Simon DeSoto. 90 mins. (Video Features/AEC, n.i.d.)

Two film-school creeps posing as documentarians are actually making snuff movies on the side (for extra credit, maybe?). More or less to the rescue comes former kid-star Kirk, replete with too-tight sports jacket and seriously receding hairline. Tommy, whose career had been in terminal decline since his glory days at Disney (see *Mars Needs Women* and *Mother Goose a Go-Go*), hits rock bottom in this pathetic shot-on-video "thriller" that looks as if it were designed for the late-night public-access circuit. Kirk completists will want to tune in.

I WAS A TEENAGE ADOLESCENT: Coed awaits millionaire guidance counselor Richard Horian's help from the selfsame Horian's one-man camp *mess*terpiece *Student Confidential.*
© Troma Entertainment, Inc.

STUDENT CONFIDENTIAL (1987) ***

D: Richard Horian. Produced by Richard Horian. Written by Richard Horian. Edited by Richard Horian. Music composed and performed by Richard Horian. Starring Richard Horian. With Eric Douglas, Marlon Jackson, Susan Scott, Elizabeth Singer, Ronee Blakley. 95 mins. (Troma)

Richard Horian's one-man vanity production chronicles the solemn misadventures of Michael Drake, Millionaire Guidance Counselor (he quit big biz, we're told, to do something useful with his life) as he attempts to steer a quartet of troubled teens (Kirk's son Eric Douglas and Michael's brother Marlon Jackson among them) through the turbulent waters of adolescence. Complicating matters is Mike's unsympathetic bimbo of a wife (who considers our bearded hero something of a stiff) and his own efforts to make himself a more "feeling" person. Director Horian treats thesp Horian—a practitioner of the bulging-eyes-and-wild-grimace approach to acting—to any number of extreme close-ups, while scripter Horian contributes dialogue worthy of no less a genius than Ed Wood.

SWORD OF HEAVEN (1985) **1/2

D: Byron Meyers. Tadashi Yamashita, Mel Novak, Gerry Gibson, Joe Randazzo, Mika, Bill ("Superfoot") Wallace. 87 mins. (TWE, n.i.d.)

Yamashita toplines as a Japanese cop on loan to the LAPD. In the course of events, he happens upon the title weapon, a glowing sword that, according to the pic's original tag line, "fell from the heavens to create a hell on earth!" some 400 years back. Our hero proceeds to wield it against a band of mercenaries in the employ of a homicide (and homicidal) cop who moonlights as the overseer of a widespread murder-extortion ring. Sword's first half is actually pretty entertaining, in its own idiosyncratically stupid way. There's a greasy, undersized pimp named Cain apparently written into the script (it took fully four talents all told to word-process Sword's senseless scenario) to showcase the invisible thespian talents of one Joe Randazzo. (The film's producer happens to be one Joseph P. Randazzo.) Joe's emotive highlight arrives when he pushes a wheelchair-bound nun off a cliff for the high crime of getting in his way! Yamashita's no slouch in the bad-acting department either, especially when, sans explanation, he plays a bar scene in undercover drag. T.Y. barely speaks English, and his reading of the Mark Twain–lifted line, "Reports of my death have been greatly exaggerated," ranks among B-moviedom's more memorable deliveries. While Sword runs out of this sort of brain-damaged inspiration before it runs out of reels, it's worth a look for those in the mood for kung-fu camp.

TANYA'S ISLAND (1981) **1/2

D: Alfred Sole. Vanity, Richard Sargent. 82 mins. (Simitar)

Alice, Sweet Alice auteur Sole's rock-vid-styled feature stars Vanity, then operating under her "D. D. Winters" handle, as a model who indulges in a filmlong daydream that finds her and her abusive painter beau (Sargent) cavorting about the title isle. There, the pair's paradisical fantasy world soon shatters when a squabble leads our Minnesota starlet to split from her mate, don designer cave-girl garb, and befriend a local ape/human hybrid who exhibits much of the chivalry and sensitivity missing from her so-called "civilized" suitor. This inspires the jealous Sargent to go primitive with a vengeance, the better to battle his simian rival for Vanity's hand (to speak only of her hand).

As a film, Tanya's Island is a fairly excruciating (if often risible) affair sorely lacking in the profundity to which it apparently aspired. As a Vanity travelog, however, TI rates as a real freeze-frame special: Seems our free-spirited ingenue can't go more than 30 seconds without doffing her duds to shower, swim, mount horses, or simply frolic free of society's sartorial constraints. If you want to see all of Vanity, Tanya's Island is the tape for you. For those in need of further inducements, the pic also incorporates clips from Mighty Joe Young.

TEENAGERS FROM OUTER SPACE (1959) B&W ***

D: Tom Graeff. David Love, Dawn Anderson, Bryant Grant, Tom Lockyear, Harvey B. Dunn. 86 mins. (Sinister Cinema)

Graeff's oft-debunked $20,000 space oddity actually sports a pretty decent plot that prefigures the likes of such later sci-fi hits as The Terminator, The Hidden, and Brother from Another Planet. When the powers-that-be on a distant planet select Earth as a breeding ground for beastly herds of fast-growing "gargons," sensitive alien teen Derek (Love) flees his flying saucer to warn unsuspecting Earthlings of the impending disaster. Derek is in turn pursued by Thor, a ray-gun-wielding extraterrestrial hit man in a Terminator mode. Derek finds Ed Wood regular Dunn, tumbles for his fetching granddaughter (Anderson), and sets about saving the planet while Thor and a sample gargon pile up the body count. One-shot auteur Graeff exhibits a knack for swift pacing but is sabotaged by his own hilariously awful dialogue and shaky thesps (who labor under the additional handicap of being poorly postsynched). Still, Teenagers will keep you both involved and in stitches, a rare and admirable combo.

THREE THE HARD WAY (1974) **1/2

D: Gordon Parks, Jr. Jim Brown, Fred Williamson, Jim Kelly, Jay Robinson, Sheila Frazier. 93 mins. (Xenon)

In this highly profitable "all-star" martial arts epic, Jim, Fred, and the other Jim join forces to stop madman Robinson's racist scheme to eliminate the African-American population by pumping a secret antiblack serum into the water supply. (Huh?) The trio regrouped and added Richard *(Shaft)* Roundtree to the team in director Williamson's even campier *One Down, Two to Go!* (Rhino).

THE TIME TRAVELERS (1966) **½

D: Robert Dunham. Dan Yuma (Robert Dunham), Margot Patton, Linda Purl, Tuffy. 60 mins. (Yuma)

Starring under the celluloid alias Dan Yuma, expat racer-turned-auteur Dunham, who later appeared in Toho's *The Green Slime* (MGM), writes, directs, and edits this bizarre amateur obscurity about a vacation-bound space engineer who leaves his Tokyo home to find the world devoid of people and activity. He returns to discover spouse Patton, young daughter (future B-movie and video stalwart Purl) and dachshund Tuffy likewise among the missing. At first he assumes it's some sort of prank, calling out, with Ed Wood–worthy verbal aplomb, "If this is your idea of some vacation-type joke, then it isn't funny." Our hero then spends roughly half the film wandering around his deserted house talking to himself. Scripter Dunham comes up with the only imaginable situation more boring than the one we're already in when Dunham meets his doppelgänger. The latter turns out to be an alien, who injects our hero with a serum and buries him alive in his own backyard (!). The story turns out to be a nightmare, followed by another expected twist, capped by "THE END?" In capable hands, the germ of Dunham's plot might have made for a decent *Twilight Zone* episode. Fans of ultraminimalist home-movie sci-fi may want to tune in. Others may want to drop out after the memorable opening

acknowledgment: "Exterior and interior locations compliments of Mrs. Shibata."

TIMES SQUARE (1980) **½

D: Alan Moyle. Tim Curry, Trini Alvarado, Herbert Berghof. 111 mins. (HBO, n.i.d.)

Times Square is an at-times fascinatingly grotesque and extravagantly abysmal rock-runaway fable set in a glamorized, pre-Disneyfied Times Square and boasting a decibel level guaranteed to shock your mind. (THE SCREENWRITER WAS REPORTEDLY INTO PRIMAL-SCREAM THERAPY!). Pair this with the equally unbearable *Can't Stop the Music* (also HBO), the legendary Village People vehicle, for a home-vid one-two punch that's sure to make you nostalgic for the '90s.

THE UNEARTHLY (1957) B&W ***

D: Brooke L. Peters. John Carradine, Allison Hayes, Myron Healey, Tor Johnson. 73 mins. (Rhino)

Carradine plays a crazed scientist who's a long way from perfecting your typical exotic glandular experiments. (Quoth the trailer: "What this gland does to this blonde when it's electrolated into her body is an experience in horror that is *almost* unbelievable!") Posing as a sanitarium shrink, Long John lures several potential victims, including B-movie hero Healey and statuesque Hayes *(Attack of the 50 Foot Woman)* to his isolated lair. It's Tor, though, in a rare speaking role, who sums it up best with his terse directive "Time for go to bed!"

UNTAMED MISTRESS (1958) ***

D: Ron Ormond. Allan Nixon, Jacqueline Fontaine, Byron Keith, John Martin, Cliff Taylor, Carol Varga. 70 mins. (Nashville Cinema)

Ormond's backyard-safari epic features topless action, lots of mismatched stock jungle footage, and a gala gathering-of-the-gorillas climax that finds nearly every Z-movie ape suit extant, including the albino White Pongo, on elegant display. The movie's girl-gorilla "forbidden love" theme echoes the Ed Wood–scripted *Bride and the Beast* (n/a), lensed by Adrian (brother of George) Weiss the same year, but *Untamed Mistress* stacks up as a far funnier outing. The plot—fashioned by Ormond, vet scenarist Orville Hampton, and one Paul L. Peil (who also scores a "Mr. Ormond's Assistant" credit)—defies coherent synopsis, since it spins on footage from an entirely different movie concerning an Indian safari. Suffice it to say that Great White Hunter Nixon, emoting with a strong New England accent, leads a quartet that includes buxom white native wild girl Velda (Fontaine) through a Dark Continent now populated by actual Africans (albeit from unrelated documentaries). What they discover is well worth 70 minutes of your time. Arthur Trevenning Harris, M.D., served as "Technical Director," in case you were wondering.

VILLAGE OF THE GIANTS (1965) ***

D: Bert I. Gordon. Tommy Kirk, Ronny Howard, Beau Bridges, Joy Harmon, Johnny Crawford, Joseph Turkel. 82 mins. (Embassy, n.i.d.)

A loose-screwed revamp of H. G. Wells's *Food of the Gods*, Gordon's stunningly stupid tale tells the shocking story of teen troublemakers who, led by young Bridges, eat a magic growth drug called "Goo," sprout to Brobdingnagian proportions, and terrorize the hick town of Hainesville, California, mostly by playing their radios too loud and not watching where they're dancing. Gordon's Goliaths A-Go-Go extravaganza is one of those rare junk gems that has it all: one of filmdom's first major mud-wrestling scenes; music by Freddy Cannon and the

Beau Brummels; go-go gals galore; a pair of giant dancing ducks (!); lots of hip dialogue (e.g., "Dig that nitty-gritty!"); and a lineup that includes Johnny (*The Rifleman*) Crawford, Disney dropout Kirk, and future Oscar-winning director Howard as an 11-year-old genius named Genius.

THE VINDICATOR   (1985) **¹/₂

D: Jean-Claude Lord. Terri Austin, Richard Cox, David McIlwraith, Maury Chaykin, Pam Grier. 92 mins. (Key)

Another blatant *Terminator* takeoff that also incorporates components from such vintage cheapies as *Frankenstein Meets the Space Monster* (see index) and *The Colossus of New York* (n/a), Canada's *The Vindicator* (formerly *Frankenstein '88*) chronicles the misadventures of handsome researcher Carl Lehman (McIlwraith), who blows up in a lab accident at shady ARC Industries. In a hook that prefigures *RoboCop*, sinister scientist Randolph Whyte (Cox) implants Carl's brain and what remains of his face into an armored, computerized space suit that's programmed to kill. A dumb move on his part, since Carl promptly employs his new superpowers to track down and terminate the villains. Despite its modern overlay (corporate conspiracy, gratuitous nudity, R-rated language, and explicit violence), *The Vindicator* is essentially old-fashioned, generally enjoyable sci-fi-camp fare. Highlights include Grier's macho perf as a professional psycho-hunter (appropriately named Hunter), a prolonged fistfight between a pregnant woman (Austin) and an overweight wimp (Chaykin), and deathless lines like "I reprogrammed myself in the computer room—I don't have to kill anymore!"

THE VINEYARD   (1989) ***

D: James Hong, Bill Rice. James Hong, Karen Witter, Michael Wong. 95 mins. (Starmaker)

While veteran character thesp Hong has appeared, often in villainous roles, in scores of movies ranging in budget from A to Z, he received top billing in only one. Not so coincidentally, *The Vineyard* is also the only film he (co-)directed (he also coscripted). The result is an invigoratingly awful camp classic. Hong toplines as Dr. Po, an evil old winemaker who specializes in marketing an elite brand of rejuvenating *vino* brewed from (what else?) human flesh and virgin blood. To succeed at this reverse-transubstantiative process, Po lures unsuspecting victims to his island redoubt via promises of instant movie stardom. Most of the young hopefuls who accept his dubious offer end up buried alive and cultivated for eventual fermentation. Hong establishes Dr. Po's cruel nature early on. After he catches his mistress doing the deed with one of his henchmen, he barks out the following string of memorable commands: "Castrate him!" "Kill the eunuch!" "Take *her* down to the dungeon!" In short, a typically busy day at the old Po château. Hong tosses all manner of crowd-pleasing elements into his horror-film brew: a cellar filled with chained seminude nubiles, some disgusto bug-regurgitation scenes, lots of kung-fu action, and cheesy aging FX. Hong may have been trying to emulate the wacky action of such superior Hong Kong fright fare as *Mr. Vampire* or *Kung-Fu Zombie* (Tai Seng), but what he wound up with is home-brewed schlock of the lowest order, a pic that bad-movie buffs and Hong fans won't want to miss.

WILD WOMEN OF WONGO (1958) ***

D: James Wolcott. Ed Fury, Adrienne Barbeau, Jean Hawkshaw. 78 mins. (Camp)

Big trubs in Wongo: Seems that the wild women of same have lost their male counterparts in a sneak attack per-petrated by the local ape-men. Their village, set on the sands of primordial Coral Gables, is deserted, so there's naught to do but hie to the neighboring land of Goona. As luck would have it, the Goona guys (who include Steve Reeves wannabe Fury) are all hunks—vast improvements over the Wongo lunks. The rest, as they say, is prehistory. While *Wild Women of Wongo*—a classic nudist-camp-type romp *without* the nudity—may not be the *worst* flick ever made, it comes close enough to earn your scrutiny. The head Wongo woman's climactic battle with a plastic Crocodile God—which fully rivals Bela Lugosi's legendary struggle with a rubber octopus in Ed Wood's *Bride of the Monster*—is a scene you'll want to watch again and again.

WOMEN OF THE PREHISTORIC PLANET   (1966) ***

D: Arthur Pierce. Wendell Corey, Keith Larsen, John Agar, Paul Gilbert, Merry Anders, Irene Tsu. 87 mins. (Englewood)

Our adventure concerns a starship crew staffed by such B-movie stalwarts as Corey, Larsen, Anders, and the ever popular John Agar. As we open, said crew is headed home after 6 months—approximately 30 Earth years, we're told—spent in deep space. And obviously in deep thought, too. To wit:

> CREWMAN
> (musing aloud):
> Imagine what would happen if
> a married guy came home after
> five years and found his wife
> was an old woman.

> COHORT
> (following reflective pause):
> That's why married men can't qualify
> for cosmic expeditions!

Following an unexpected bout with "cosmic gas" (it couldn't have been something they ate—even the food's synthetic), they crash-land on a "stinking nowhere planet," where they trek through miles of cardboard jungle sets and monster-infested stock footage in search of a missing passenger, the lovely young Linda (Hsu). *Women* is rife with memorable lines and performances. As Commander King, Corey comes across like a legit space case, delivering his lines as though mumbling distractedly to himself (an especially bizarre effect when he's shouting, as the script frequently calls for him to do, if only to keep his fellow actors awake). There's even a stand-up (or float-up) comic aboard, who tosses off quips like "I've been on a diet for seven days and all I've lost is a week." Flute-playing planet native Robert Ito and his pal Chico the Dancing Chimp supply a musical highlight. *Women of the Prehistoric Planet* stacks up as ideal late-night video fare. The first half provides a plethora of unintended laughs; the second acts as a safe, gentle sedative guaranteed to put you under for at least a solid eight.

ALL NEW and IN COLOR
Released by REALART Pictures

WOMEN OF THE PREHISTORIC PLANET

BOTHER FROM ANOTHER PLANET: Cosmic chaos rages in poster art for Arthur Pierce's 1966 space oddity *Women of the Prehistoric Planet*.
Courtesy of Englewood Entertainment/Wade Williams Distribution

That's Exploitainment!
EXPLOITATION FAVES

"Man, you're crazy!"
—arresting officer, *MANIAC*

AROUSED   (1966) B&W ***

D: Anton Holden. Janine Lenon, Steve Hollister, Fleurette Carter, Joanna Mills, Tony Palladino, Ted Gelanza. 78 mins. (Something Weird)

Like many of its '60s "sexploitation" peers, *Aroused* is far less an exercise in erotica than an extremely dark, gritty, downbeat psycho noir. *Aroused* chronicles dedicated cop Hollister's pursuit of an unknown serial killer who's busily reducing NYC's hooker population. Our less-than-shining hero unwittingly entrusts his own wife to the maniac (who hears mocking voice-overs from his abused childhood when he kills), then gets it on with the prostitute he had been assigned to protect. *Aroused* features necrophiliac elements, a *Psycho*-inspired shower scene, a lengthy castration sequence, period Times Square footage, and a cyclical ending, all rendered in a deadly serious tone. The movie's only flaw is its penchant for painfully padded scenes that undermine its suspense. Well acted and directed, *Aroused* plays like a gutter harbinger of more recent slicked-up, big-budget erotic thrillers, like *Basic Instinct* and *Consenting Adults* (Hollywood).

THE AROUSERS   (1970) **½

D: Curtis Hanson. Tab Hunter, Nadyne Turney, Isabell Jewell, Roberta Collins, Sandy Kenyon. 90 mins. (Embassy, n.i.d.)

Hunter's failed comeback bid (released theatrically as *Sweet Kill*) casts him as a Venice, California, high school gym teacher who inadvertently kills a woman who tries to interest him in sex. This fuels our femme-fearing hero's already strong necrophiliac tendencies, and Tab embarks on an all-out misogynistic murder-and-sex spree. Pretty thin in the suspense department—though the same can't be said of Tab, who looks fairly flabby for a 39-year-old phys-ed teacher—*The Arousers* is of interest to Tab watchers who wonder what their idol was up to a decade before John Waters rescued him from oblivion via a key role in *Polyester*. The pic's kinky candor represents another plus; *The Arousers* would make a fine companion feature for the same era's *Carnal Knowledge* (Columbia/TriStar). Hanson earned greater later fame as the director of big-time suspensers like *L.A. Confidential* (see index).

THE BEAST THAT KILLED WOMEN (1965) **½

D: Barry Mahon. Starring "Miami Beach's Most Lovely Nudists." 60 mins. (Something Weird)

For this nudie romp, prolific sleazemeister Barry (*Cuban Rebel Girls, Pagan Island*) Mahon employs the unique hook of having a Florida nudist colony's fun and games—the usual volleyball and exotic-dancing-around-the-campfire action—interrupted by an escaped gorilla with an attitude. Mahon manages to stretch this unpromising situation into 60 credulity-defying minutes that only the most jaded of viewers are likely to forget.

LARRY BUCHANAN CONFIDENTIAL!

BEYOND THE DOORS   (1983) ***

D: Larry Buchanan. Gregory Allen Chatman, Riba Meryl, Bryan Wolf, Sandy Kenyon, Susanne Barnes, Stuart Lancaster. 117 mins. (Unicorn, n.i.d.)

Texas-based exploitation auteur Larry (*Naughty Dallas, Zontar*) Buchanan's pic posits the theory that the '60s' three "Pied Pipers of Rock"—Jimi Hendrix, Janis Joplin, and Jim Morrison—were the victims of a government plot carried out by a CIA assassin (Kenyon). While Larry's story line may be less than convincing, several of the backstage scenes featuring deft impersonators Chatman (Jimi), Meryl (Janis), and Wolf (Jim) do smack of a certain laid-back, spaced-out verisimilitude. (Particularly effective is a brief segment chronicling Janis and Jimi's imagined maiden meeting.) Ditto goes for much of the music, which succeeds in approximating, though rarely equaling, the distinctive styles of those late rock icons. *Beyond* serves as a valuable video companion piece to Oliver Stone's better-known, less-engaging Morrison bio, *The Doors* (Columbia/TriStar). Buchanan earlier helmed the conspiracy exploitation exposé *Hughes and Harlow: Angels in Hell* (1977, USA), a look at the torrid affair that transpired twixt Howard Hughes and Jean Harlow.

GOODNIGHT, SWEET MARILYN (1976/1989) **

D: Larry Buchanan. Misty Rowe, Jeremy Slate, Paula Lane, Terence Locke, Patch Mackenzie. 105 mins. (Studio, n.i.d.)

Buchanan's tabloid approach to exploitation cinema (or "tabsploitation") worked better in *Beyond the Doors* than in this pastiche of the auteur's 1976 *Goodbye, Norma Jean* and newer inserts pushing the theory that Marilyn Monroe was done in by a confidant named Mesquite (Slate) to "save" her from homicidal CIA spooks. The latter are bent on preventing a planned press conference, where Marilyn threatens to spill the beans re her involvement with Jack and Bobby Kennedy and their Mafia links. Rowe plays a teenaged Norma Jean Baker, who survives a series of rejections, personal and professional ("No contract player on this lot ever shows their lower

teeth the way you do!" one intemperate mogul heatedly informs her), rapes, suicide attempts, and any number of trashy traumas to launch her unique screen career. While tacky, the Norma Jean scenes prove fairly compelling and are definitely superior to the flat, static wraparound segments that relate the earlier footage in flashback form (though Lane turns in decent work as the more mature M.M.). Unlike *Beyond the Doors*, the original songs clogging *Goodnight, Sweet Marilyn*'s soundtrack are uniformly awful.

BEYOND THE VALLEY OF THE DOLLS (1970) ****

D: Russ Meyer. Dolly Read, John LaZar, Cynthia Meyers, Marcia McBroom, Charles Napier, David Gurian, Michael Blodgett, Edy Williams. 109 mins. (Fox)

For the sheer power of its lowlife-affirming vision, *Faster, Pussycat! Kill! Kill!* rates as the Russ Meyer movie your Phantom would want with him were he stranded on a desert isle. Running a close second is the deservedly vaunted nonsequel *Beyond the Valley of the Dolls*. Scripted by none other than Roger Ebert from a story he coconcocted with Meyer, *Beyond* bids the viewer to "come with the gentle people" on a cross-country odyssey to Hollywood Hell. Like the Jackie Susann campfest *Valley of the Dolls* (Fox), *Beyond* crams its mock-cautionary cinematic canvas with harrowing portraits, presented in Bosch-ian detail, of bright young lives ruined by their sudden immersion in showbiz decadence. Some—the lucky ones—are pulled back from the brink with only moments to spare; for others, violent death is the only way out. Several timeless performances mark *Beyond*: McBroom and ex-Playmates Read and Meyers as femme rock combo the Carrie Nations; future best-selling novelist Blodgett as callous gigolo Lance Rock; Williams as anything-goes gal Ashley St. Ives; LaZar

as the ever eloquent Z-Man Barzell; and, of course, the Strawberry Alarm Clock as themselves.

BIKERS, BLONDES & BLOOD! (1993) B&W/COLOR***

Compiled by Johnny Legend. 92 mins. (Something Weird)

Your Phantom has long harbored a soft spot for sleazy trailer tapes, and in *Bikers, Blondes & Blood* Johnny Legend has assembled a fun, high-concept one, alternating biker previews (e.g., *Satan's Sadists*), with blonde vehicles (Jayne Mansfield's *Single Room Furnished*) and blood-and-gorefests (*I Drink Your Blood*). Our fave is the Jungle Jim entry *Captive Girl*, where even the brief trailer teems with phony stunts and mismatched footage. An excellent party tape for beer blasts and intimate get-togethers alike. Both Something Weird and Sinister Cinema carry scores of excellent trailer compilations spanning the genre spectrum.

BLAZE STARR: THE ORIGINAL (1960) **½

D: Doris Wishman. Blaze Starr. 73 mins. (Blaze)

This is actually a retitling of *Blaze Starr Goes Nudist* (now, there's a leap!), one of many exercises in nudist-camp camp fashioned by exploitation legend Wishman. Ecdysiast Starr—whose real-life tryst with politico Earl Long was immortalized in the Paul Newman vehicle *Blaze* (Touchstone)—plays her own buxom self, only here she's a film starlet who's so famous and adored that she can't find a moment's peace. Clearly, there's naught for Blaze to do but hie to the nearest nudist camp, where she not only discovers tranquillity among the cellulite, beach balls, and accordions but falls in love with the only guy in camp who keeps his shorts on (!). While crammed with Ms. Wishman's trademark technical gaffes, the flick fails to reach the truly lunatic heights of her sublimely ridiculous *Nude on the Moon* (see index). Starr-gazers will want to take a gander.

BLONDE IN BONDAGE   (1957)
B&W***

D: Robert Brandt. Mark Miller, Lars Ekborg, Anita Thallaug, Brijitta Ander, Dagny Helander. 78 mins. (Sinister Cinema)

Jaunty but decent American reporter Miller, on assignment in Sweden, gets involved with smack-addicted blond songstress Thallaug (who repeatedly croons a ditty called "The Shock Around the Clock") and her seedy, dope-dealing manager/Svengali (Ekborg), in this largely Swedish-cast but English-language-lensed obscurity. Despite his film's title and topic, director Brandt opts for an earnest, nonexploitative tone in charting Miller's self-appointed rescue mission and even minimizes potential romantic entanglements between hero and victim. In a lighter running riff, playing to stateside notions re those Swingin' Swedes, Miller is ogled and pursued by virtually every shapely native femme he encounters, including an ultimately helpful sister act. A climactic funhouse chase/shoot-out sequence, while sub-Hitchcock-ian, is executed with considerable flair and suspense on an obviously threadbare budget. Authentic Scandinavian locations add to *Blonde's* verité flavor.

BUMMER   (1972)**1/2

D: William A. Castleman. Kipp Whitman, Connie Strickland, Dennis Burkley, Carol Speed. 90 mins. (Magnum, n.i.d.)

While sometimes static, *Bummer* (originally *Groupies*) is a fairly engrossing and credible account of the trials of an ambitious second-rate L.A. rock band, generically monikered "the Group." *Bummer* is best in its unglamorous verité details; its exploitation elements—especially future *Mary Hartman, Mary Hartman* regular Burkley's over-the-top turn as the fat, misogynistic maniac of the group—seem shoehorned in. Still, *Bummer* is well worth a look. Producer/writer David F. Friedman cameos as a sheriff, while Speed, of *Abby* (n/a) fame, costars as one of the groupies.

CAREER BED   (1969)***

D: Joel Reed. Lisa Duran, Honey Hunter, James David, Merle Miller. 79 mins. (Something Weird)

Reed directed this NYC-set cheapie about a stage mother from hell, and it's a lot funnier than his alleged "cult classic" *Bloodsucking Freaks* (Troma, also briefly available on the Magnum label under the fanciful handle *The Heritage of Caligula—An Orgy of Sick Minds* [!]). Actress Hunter delivers the best nasal shrew performance seen on-screen since Jean Fontaine held forth as smut-racket czarina Gloria Henderson in Ed Wood's *The Sinister Urge* (both likely graduates of the Shelley Winters Overacting Academy). The "erotic" content is typically minimal, but the motormouthed script more than compensates with its detailed delineation of several extravagantly unpleasant relationships, the only kind that exist in this film. As Honey puts it, "*Love!*? Don't invent words."

CHAINED FOR LIFE   (1951)
B&W**1/2

D: Harry L. Fraser. Daisy and Violet Hilton, Allan Jenkins. 75 mins. (Rhino)

Real-life Siamese twins Daisy and Violet Hilton—later the subject of a gala, if short-lived, Broadway musical—go on trial for a murder only one of them committed, posing a thorny ethical/legal problem for the most sophisticated of judicial minds. Don't miss the twins' musical duet, "Never Say You'll Never Fall in Love." For a fascinating verité look at the Hiltons and their sideshow brethren, scope out Ari Roussimoff's 1999 documentary *Freaks Uncensored! A Human Sideshow* (Bohemia).

THE COCAINE FIENDS   (1936)
B&W***

D: William A. O'Connor. Noel Madison, Lois January, Sheila Manners. 58 mins. (Sinister Cinema)

Originally titled *The Pace That Kills* and based on a 1928 silent bearing the same name (n/a), this feature-length cocaine condemnation lacks the wacky energy of a *Reefer Madness* (see index) but depicts enough down-and-dirty doings at the notorious Dead Rat Cafe to make it a must for vintage-sleaze buffs.

THE SCALI TRILOGY

THE DEVIL'S SLEEP   (1951)
B&W***1/2

D: W. Merle Connell. Lita Grey Chaplin, Timothy Farrell, William Thomason, Tracy Lynne, George Eiferman. 72 mins. (Sinister Cinema)

Late, great Ed Wood regular Farrell is best remembered for lending his acting skills, resonant baritone, and pencil-line moustache to such Wood-en wonders as *Glen or Glenda* (as the shrink/narrator), *Jail Bait* (as a vicious hood), and the Ed-scripted *The Violent Years* (as a dogged detective). Farrell also appeared in a trio of Poverty Row quickies informally known as the Scali Trilogy, since Tim portrayed the same cheerfully cynical racketeer, Umberto Scali, in all three—*Dance Hall Racket, Pin-Down Girls,* and this one. Here, Farrell/Scali runs a gym (it looks like the same one that served as the main set in *Pin-Down Girls*) for "fat society dames" who supplement their rigorous toe-touching tasks by munching on "goofballs" and "bennies." (Though the pic was advertised as an exposé of the "sleeping pill" racket, Scali mostly peddles speed—but, hey, we're not in the quibble biz here.) Honest cop Thomason and juvenile-court judge Lita Grey Chaplin (briefly Charlie's real-life wife) suspect Scali's also behind a recent teenage-crime wave. But our antihero temporarily derails the judge off the case by blackmailing her with naked pix of her daughter (Lynne) snapped during a wild, bennies-and-booze-fueled pool party. With the help of authentic 1948 Mr. America, Eiferman (whose thesping, as it was in *Pin-Down Girls*, is raw enough to make Schwarzenegger look like Laurence Olivier), however, Scali and his scurvy crew are ultimately brought to Z-movie justice.

Fun all the way, *The Devil's Sleep* features several brief flashes of femme flesh—though many of the clips were obviously snipped, either by ardent censors or randy projectionists, from Sinister Cinema's master print—flubbed lines, and cost-efficient camera work by regular Ed Wood cinematographer William C. Thompson. Sinister's jumpy print adds to the air of grindhouse authenticity.

PIN-DOWN GIRLS (1951) B&W ***

D: Robert C. Derteno. Timothy Farrell, Peaches Page, Clara Mortensen, Rita Martinez, Don Ferrar. 81 mins. (Sinister Cinema)

Farrell returns as sleazeball Scali, a moustachioed jack-of-all-rackets who runs a bookie operation, peddles pills, procures for a local cathouse, dopes horses, and—most central to our story—promotes up-and-coming lady wrestlers like bosomy blond bombshell Peaches Page. Produced by the ubiquitous George Weiss and lensed by William C. Thompson, *Pin-Down Girls* (a.k.a. *Racket Girls*) is structured around two prolonged stretches of actual mat footage, principally of then-

world champ Mortensen and Mexican Canvas Queen Martinez (who also put in brief thespian cameos), plus lots of jiggle shots of Peaches doing her road work and her fellow femme gym rats going through their bending-and-stretching paces. A simple plot eventually materializes when Scali draws heat from a rival racketeer (imaginatively monikered Mr. Big!), testifies against him in the world's smallest courtroom (even tinier than the one viewed in Ed Wood's *The Violent Years*), and eventually pays the ultimate gangland price. Director Derteno (*Gun Girls*) lacks Wood's flair, but Farrell, his hardworking femmes, and Ferrar as his diminutive minion Joe the Jockey make this cheesecake epic worth watching.

DANCE HALL RACKET (1953) B&W ***

D: Phil Tucker. Lenny Bruce, Honey Bruce, Timothy Farrell, Sally Marr. 60 mins. (Something Weird)

A would-be shocking exposé produced by the infamous George (*Glen or Glenda*) Weiss and directed by the one and only Phil (*Robot Monster*) Tucker, this exploitation oddity stars Lenny Bruce (who also scripted) as a switchblade-wielding bouncer (whose chief duty seems to be murdering dissatisfied customers!) at Scali's Dance Emporium, a waterfront clip joint operated by ubiquitous smooth-talking slimebag Umberto Scali (Farrell). Also in the cast are Lenny's then-wife, ecdysiast Honey Bruce, and mom, ex-vaudevillian Sally Marr. As an actor, Bruce makes like a psychotic Leo Gorcey ("Big deal—I killed a guy," he sneers. "That makes me a *criminal*?"), while his script is, by turns, functional, funny, and downright strange. (E.g., a mugging comic in a porkpie hat wanders in and out of the movie doing an anachronistic El Brendel imitation!) Highlights include fleeting nudity and Marr's extremely gratuitous Charleston

number. You can also catch Lenny, in more characteristic modes, in the docusalutes *Lenny Bruce* (Video Yesteryear) and *The Lenny Bruce Performance Film* (Vestron), which includes the classic animated sketch "Thank You, Masked Man." Bob Fosse's *Lenny* bio, with Dustin Hoffman in the lead, is also available (Fox). The earlier, low-budget biography *Dirtymouth* (1965) has yet to surface on homevid.

FASTER, PUSSYCAT! KILL! KILL! (1966) B&W ****

D: Russ Meyer. Tura Satana, Haji, Lori Williams, Stuart Lancaster, Susan Bernard, Mickey Foxx. 83 mins. (RM)

Meyer's breast-driven desert noir finds three crazy-for-kicks go-go chicks, headed by the incomparable Satana, embarking on a wild crime spree that includes murder, kidnapping, theft, and wanton exposure of seemingly limitless cleavage. Our top-heavy trio eventually tangles with a troika of mostly hapless males—including a lecherous old-timer (Lancaster) and his moronic stud of a son—in a perverse cat-and-mouse game that leads to a violent denouement. The dense, double-entendre-enriched script escalates the battle of the sexes to a wonderfully grotty war of attrition. *Faster, Pussycat! Kill! Kill!* shapes up as *the* definitive Meyer movie, an intensely crazed fable guaranteed to keep you on the edge of disbelief. The film has more recently become a mainstay at big-screen retro-fests. Most of Meyer's movies are available on his own label, RM Films.

THE FIEND OF DOPE ISLAND (1961) B&W **1/2

D: Nate Watt. Bruce Bennett, Robert Bray, Tania Velia, Ralph Rodriguez. 76 mins. (Something Weird)

Former Tarzan (under his real name, Herman Brix) Bennett

coscripts and plays against type as Charlie Davis, the lash-happy tyrant of the titular isle, where he overacts and employs his trusty whip to keep his marijuana-harvesting native workers in line. Yugoslavian sexpot Velia impresses as singer/dancer Glory La Verne, whom Charlie's imported to his little slice of Caribbean hell to serve as his private entertainer. (Bennett even gets to pound a conga drum in one of several odd musical numbers.) Bland cohort (and future *Lassie* dad) Bray, who at one point labels Charlie's product "the assassin of youth," is a secret undercover op out to sabotage Charlie's ambitious operation. Lensed on location in often washed-out black and white, *The Fiend of Dope Island* (a.k.a. *Whiplash*) suffers from a dearth of action sequences but includes a topless scene for the stunning Velia and furnishes enough sleaze to please backdate-exploitation buffs. SWV fleshes out the tape with some hot schlock trailers, including *Smoke and Flesh* and *Her Private Hell,* as well as *Fiend*'s original theatrical trailer.

TWO BY RUE

FIVE MINUTES TO LOVE (1963) B&W ***

D: John Hayes. Paul Leder, Rue McClanahan, King Moody, Will Gregory, Gail Gordon. 85 mins. (Sinister Cinema)

Most viewers know actress Rue McClanahan as the perennially randy member of TV's *The Golden Girls.* As it turns out, Rue began her career establishing a similar image in a pair of oddball early-'60s "sexploitationers," *Five Minutes to Love* (a.k.a. *The Rotten Apple, It Only Takes Five Minutes*) and *Hollywood After Dark* (a.k.a. *Walk the Angry Beach*). Less a sleaze outing than a bad ersatz existential (or "sexistential," if you will) Beat play committed to film, *Five* unfolds almost

entirely in a junkyard that serves, much like the whorehouse in Jean Genet's *The Balcony* (Mystic Fire), as an obvious metaphor for our debased society in particular and the human condition in general. Rue plays the dumb but enigmatic Poochie, a nihilistic tart who turns tricks in said junkyard, operated by the singularly unpleasant Harry (future auteur Leder), a motormouthed misanthrope who openly abuses all around him, including the hulking Blowhard (Moody), sort of an *Of Mice and Men*'s Lenny on drugs. The minimal action serves mainly as a frame for endless pretentious palaver. Our antihero, Harry, sets the talkative tone early on when he describes a recent wrecked arrival to his vehicular scrap heap thusly: "The dame was smashed up. The car was smashed up. Payments were smashed up. The dough was smashed up. The radio was smashed up. The heater was smashed up. The kid was killed in the backseat and the dog was cut in two." *Five Minutes to Love* may be the mouthiest exploitation pic ever produced; we can only imagine the language it must have provoked from those enraged grindhouse hounds who paid good money to see it.

HOLLYWOOD AFTER DARK (1961) B&W **½

D: John Hayes. Anthony Vorno, Rue McClanahan, Paul Bruce. 74 mins. (Sinister Cinema)

Hayes's *Hollywood After Dark* is another grim, though less ambitious, sexploitationer. This one opens with a shot of the famous Hollywood sign, then pans down to—you guessed it—another junkyard (!). Here future sexy senior Rue actually flashes a bit of skin as a burlesque ecdysiast who adopts an "artistic" approach to her trade. Rue again takes up with a junkyard philosopher (Vorno), who eventually agrees to join in an ill-advised heist planned by Rue's crooked club-owner boss. Fol-

lowing the inevitable last-reel tragedy, the pic closes with another shot of the Hollywood sign: irony like they don't hardly make anymore. While *Hollywood* lacks *Five*'s penchant for purple outbursts, it includes its share of cynical pronouncements, like the following fable angrily delivered by Vorno: "I knew a girl once who used to stand on the corner of Hollywood and Vine. She was a young actress from Dayton, Ohio. She thought if she just stood still, on that corner, long enough, something would happen to her. Something did. She got hungry. Soon the sun went down. She got cold. Then she couldn't keep her eyes open she got so sleepy. So she went home and went to bed. That's all."

FLESHPOT ON 42ND STREET (1971) ***

D: Andy Milligan. Diana Lewis, Lynn Flanagan, Bob Walters. 78 mins. (Something Weird)

Fleshpot may well rate as late, oft benighted Staten Island auteur Milligan's best celluloid effort. Now, that may not sound like much of a recommendation re a man who made no-budget movies directly commissioned for 42nd Street, but this funky Deuce drama is well worth watching for its own modest merits. Less a sexploitation film—the R-level erotic content is pretty tame for its era and venue—than a verité look at street hustlers, *Fleshpot* (SWV's print sports the title *The Girls of 42nd Street*) follows young part-time hooker Dusty (Lewis) on her rounds as she deserts her older, working-stiff boyfriend, rooms with aging transvestite Cherry Lane (Flanagan), and briefly takes up with Staten Island nice guy Bob (Walters—better known as future hard-core star Harry Reems). Milligan's camera catches Dusty, Cherry, overweight sibling sluts the Simmons sisters, and other Deuce denizens as they schmooze, squabble, and hustle in their natural habitats—the bars, cafeterias, and sidewalks of Times Square.

Some of Milligan's patented klutzy touches occasionally intrude: Dusty's burgeoning, surprisingly idyllic affair with Bob ends abruptly when a car runs him over (!), prompting Dusty's return to 42nd Street (talk about your "Deuce ex machinas"). Nor can Andy resist plugging a pair of his own rather execrable fright titles when, in one scene, Cherry promises Dusty, "We'll take in the double horror bill at the Lyric—*Torture Dungeon* and *Bloodthirsty Butchers.*" In the main, though, Milligan exhibits some legit proficiency in capturing the rhythms, speech, and ambience of the street he knew best. If *Fleshpot* were produced today, it would probably play the downtown art-house circuit. Come to think of it, it probably would have back in '71 too, if the Andy responsible had been Warhol rather than Milligan. Fortunately, SWV's letter-boxed video has saved *Fleshpot* for posterity.

FREE, WHITE AND 21   (1963) B&W ***

D: Larry Buchanan. Frederick O'Neal, Annalena Lund, George Edgely, Johnny Hicks, George Russell. 104 mins. (All Seasons, n.i.d.)

Despite its original ultra-sleazy ad campaign, Buchanan's civil-rights *Rashomon* makes for consistently compelling courtroom drama, if static filmmaking. *Car 54* regular O'Neal is excellent as a black Dallas businessman accused of raping neurotic Swedish freedom rider Lund. The prosecutor's and defense attorney's closing arguments are directed at the viewers, who then have three minutes of on-screen clock-ticking to reach their verdict. The William Castle–style gimmick aside, *Free, White and 21* represents Buchanan's most serious and credible film.

GIRL IN TROUBLE (1963) B&W ***

D: Lee Beale. Tammy Clark, Ray Menard, Martin Smith, Bettina Johnson. 77 mins. (Sinister Cinema)

Triple-threat writer, producer, and director Beale takes us on a virtually verité tour of New Orleans as seen through the eyes of small-town refugee Clark in one of the era's more engaging road-to-ruin-and-redemption exploitationers. Clark is appealing as the shapely naïf who, believing she's killed the lecherous driver who answered her hitchhiking plea, hides out in some of the Big Easy's lower-glam precincts, where her largely lateral career moves take her from Bucket O Chicken waitress to lingerie model to party girl to stripper. Beale somehow keeps his street odyssey from turning overly downbeat, despite a rape and a suicide attempt. More shockingly, though, given the genre, he totally muffs Clark's lone topless moment, which sneaks up on even the most focused couchside voyeur (let's hear it for freeze-frames!). Still, *Girl in Trouble* rates as a good bet for fans of sincere regional exploitation fare.

GROSS ENCOUNTERS

GIRL ON A CHAIN GANG   (1965) B&W **1/2

D: Jerry Gross. Julie Ange, William Watson, Arlene Sue Farber. R. K. Charles. 96 mins. (Something Weird)

TEENAGE MOTHER   (1966) **1/2

D: Jerry Gross. Julie Ange, Arlene Sue Farber, Frederick Riccio, Howard Le May, Fred Willard. 78 mins. (Sinister Cinema)

Enterprising producer Jerry (*I Drink Your Blood*) Gross claims writing, producing, and directing credits for both of these unsavory slices of small-town life. An example of the short-lived civil-rights exploitation-pic craze (scope out T. V. Mikels's superior *The Black Klansman* [Unicorn] and Larry Buchanan's *Free, White and 21* [see index]), *Girl on a Chain Gang* sees a trio of postgrad freedom riders subjected to prolonged Southern inhospitality courtesy of cigar- (and scenery-) chewing redneck sheriff Watson and two knuckle-walking deputies. Most of this B&W opus is a massive talk-a-thon (or, more accurately, drawl-a-thon) with our minibrained minions of the law verbally and physically abusing their Yankee captives for nigh on an hour. After eventually murdering the two males—one black, one white—the sheriff rapes distaff activist Ange, has her convicted on prostitution charges and sentenced to a stretch on an all-male chain gang (!). Unfortunately, auteur Gross gives this pivotal section of his story inexplicably short shrift—in fact, much of our heroine's potentially suspenseful escape scene unfolds off-camera (!)—wrapping up the movie with a breathless economy absent from the earlier reels.

Actress Ange doesn't escape for long, as it turns out. She resurfaces, this time as a Swedish sex-education teacher (!) assigned to a narrow-minded small-town high school, in Gross's misnomered companion feature, *Teenage Mother*. Our central plot thread involves Farber (seen as the village slut in *Girl on a Chain Gang*), an unhappy high-schooler who fakes pregnancy to shake up her non*sympatico* parents and altar-shy beau (Le May). Arlene eventually hooks up with a reefer-puffing hood (Riccio), who takes her to a drive-in to catch—what else?—*Girl on a Chain Gang*! (Not only does Gross thus plug his own film, but he even puts his name above the title on the drive-in marquee, which further advertises the B&W *Chain Gang* as being in "Widescreen and Color.") This results in what may be a B-movie first: Arlene, as the high-schooler, watches herself on-screen as an entirely different character. While Gross doubtless deserves credit for such heady conceptual fourth-wall breakthroughs, both movies' merits lie mostly in their considerable camp value. Scenarist Gross exhibits a definite flair for memorable dialogue. A doctor in *Chain Gang* comments, "There's people dyin' today who never died before," while in *Teenage Mother,* Arlene asks another sawbones, "You mean I'm not pregnant? Not even a little bit?" Gross also employs the ancient exploitation-pic practice of inserting a separate sex-education short into the feature. In *Teenage Mother,* it's a fairly grisly live-birth featurette tailor-made for your fast-forward control. Future Madison Avenue jingle wiz Steve Karmen composes lively scores for both Gross features, while *Teenage Mother* marks the screen debut of future *Fernwood 2-Night* cohost Fred Willard, seen here as a high school baseball coach.

HELP WANTED FEMALE (1968) B&W ***

D: Harold Perkins. Sebastian Gregory, Inga Olsen. 71 mins. (Something Weird)

One of the odder entries in the '60s exploitation field, *Help Wanted Female* opens with karate-trained hooker JoJo—who operates "JoJo's Kung-Fu" (though "JoJo's Dojo" might have carried more snap)—clobbering and robbing a traveling salesman after posing as a sex-starved runaway 'burb housewife. Our core story concerns JoJo's lesbian roomie and fellow floozy Luana (Olsen), who visits steady trick Mr. Gregory—the famous (?) Sebastian Gregory as "himself" (actually actor Jack Vorno)—a pipe-smoking Hef manqué who pops LSD cubes while watching Luana strip. In his hallucinatory reverie, Mr. G. calmly recounts a flashback about a former squeeze who murdered an innocent model for kicks and recruited our hero into helping dispose of the body. ("I never regretted any-

thing so much in my whole life," he compassionately understates.) Gregory in turn kills said squeeze, takes the corpse out for a day at the beach (!), and later chops her up and stores the pieces in the fridge. Back in the present, Luana attempts to elude the confessed killer's clutches, leading to a fight between JoJo and Gregory, who admits, "I don't have any technique, I just fight dirty." This lighthearted black comedy threads in and out of dreams and fantasies on its way to a final twist. Ample nudity, a great sleazy instrumental track, and memorable dialogue add to the trippy spectacle. Bits of footage are missing from Something Weird's print, but *Help Wanted Female* remains a must for serious celluloid-sleaze scholars and camp followers alike.

HOLLYWOOD UNCENSORED (1987) **1/2

D: James Forsher. Hosted by Douglas Fairbanks, Jr., Peter Fonda. With Mamie Van Doren, Martin Scorsese, Carroll Baker, Eli Wallach. 77 mins. (IVE)

A spotty survey of Hollywood's ever mutating censorship policies, from the pre–Hays era to the late '80s, this compilation tape may be of more interest to buffs than to casual viewers. Highlights include brief clips from such candid pre-Code fare as *Party Girl, Baby Face* (with a gold-digging Barbara Stanwyck), Dwain Esper's immortal *Love Life of a Gorilla* (a.k.a. *Forbidden Adventure*), and choice verboten moments from the original *King Kong.* Fairbanks and Fonda make for adequate but less-than-riveting hosts. In the interview segments, Scorsese scores best with his illustrated discussion of Michael Powell's *Peeping Tom,* and Van Doren, seen here reminiscing re such Albert Zugsmith sleazoid specials as *Girls Town* and *High School Confidential,* is always welcome on the Phantom's tube. Otherwise, selective fast-forwarding is advised.

IMPULSE (1974) **1/2

D: William Grefe. William Shatner, Jennifer Bishop, Ruth Roman, Kim Nicholas, Harold Sakata, Bill Kerwin. 85 mins. (IVE, n.i.d.)

Beyond his Captain Kirk persona, Shatner has long had a rep as a thesp with a broad tolerance for offbeat roles, ranging from the bold (the white-supremacist hatemonger in Roger Corman's *The Intruder*) to the downright bizarre (as the star of 1966's *Incubus,* the first and thus far only film spoken entirely in Esperanto!). *Impulse* (a.k.a. *Want a Ride, Little Girl?*) finds Bill working under the (mis)direction of vet Florida-based schlockmeister William (*Death Curse of Tartu*) Grefe in what may well be the actor's sleaziest turn, as psychotic con man Matt Stone (presumably no relation to the *South Park* cocreator of the same name).

The flick opens with a B&W 1945-set prologue that sees a juvenile Matt traumatized by the sight of his drunken mom being molested by an equally inebriated sailor (H. G. Lewis regular Kerwin) whom the kid winds up gutting with a souvenir samurai sword. Cut to the present, where a grown Matt, clad in an eye-assaulting array of classic '70s polyester leisure wear, strangles his girlfriend, then targets sexy widow Bishop as his next victim. While both Jen and her friend Julia (Roman) fall for Matt's dubious charms, our maniac encounters stubborn resistance from Bishop's resentful 12-year-old daughter (Nicholas), especially after she witnesses Matt's killing of blackmailer "Karate Pete" (played, with customary panache, by "Oddjob" Sakata). Of course, no one believes the tightly wired tyke's tale till it's nearly too late. *Impulse*'s unremittingly seedy ambience sustains interest even when its plot machinations gratingly grind on. Shatner looks convincingly unhealthy as the psychotic Stone, and a creepy chase through a cadaver-strewn funeral parlor provides another highlight. No relation to the mediocre Theresa Russell noir vehicle *Impulse* (Warner) or the sci-fi film of the same name (see index).

LASH OF THE PENITENTES (1937) B&W **1/2

D: Harry Revier, Roland C. Price. Jose Swickard, Marie de Forest, William Marcos. 35 mins. (Sinister Cinema)

*L*ash is the first film—"photographed at the risk of the cameramen's lives"—to expose the bizarre rites of the titular fanatics, who espouse self- (and other-) flagellation, crucifixions, and, in this pic, fleeting nudity. More fun than 1988's treatment of the same subject, *The Penitent* (Avid). This 35-minute version is apparently all that remains of the original feature.

THE LONELY SEX (1959) B&W ***

D: Richard Hilliard. Karl Light, Jean Evans, Leon Benedict, Richard Nicholls. 59 mins. (Sinister Cinema)

*T*he Lonely Sex tracks parallel perverts—"respectable" Mr. Wyler (Benedict), a bearded boarder at the abode of shrink Dr. Greene (Nicholls), and a tortured figure known only as "the Man" (Light), an abject loser who lives alone in a woodland shack, where he gets worked up listening to breathy lipstick commercials (!) and fiery evangelists on his radio. Hilliard's bleak, ultraminimalist (characters frequently interact before simple black backdrops) morality melodrama exposes the unctuous Mr. Wyler as a sleazy voyeur who likes to peek into a local strip joint's dressing room (where, unlike in many "skin flicks" of the era, we actually witness a few R-level flashes of undraped femme flesh). Wyler's also prone to pestering Dr. Greene's daughter Annabelle (Evans) by "accidentally" entering her room at every available opportunity.

Annabelle is also unlucky enough to get kidnapped by "the Man," who, after locking her in his shack, decides to visit her father to seek professional help (!). Hilliard went on to direct a higher-profiled cast, including Dick Van Patten, Sylvia Miles, and James Farentino, in 1963's *Psychomania* (Something Weird).

DWAIN ESPER:
THAT'S EXPLOITAINMENT!

MANIAC (1934) B&W ***1/2

D: Dwain Esper. Bill Woods, Horace Carpenter, Theo Ramsey, Phyllis Diller, Ted Edwards. 51 mins. (Kino) DVD

NARCOTIC (1933) B&W ***

D: Dwain Esper. Harry Cording, Joan Dix, Patricia Farley, Jean Lacey, J. Stuart Blackton. 57 mins. (Kino) DVD

*E*xploitation-pic pioneer Dwain Esper contributed a number of tarnished treasures to the American trash-movie trove, from dope exposés like 1937's *Marihuana: The Weed With Roots in Hell* to such shocking shorts as *How to Undress for Your Husband.* Many bad-movie buffs see Esper as the 1930s answer to Ed Wood when it came to combining the inspiredly bizarre with the technically inept. Dwain and Ed even shared the same Poverty Row photographer, William C. Thompson, who owns the unique distinction of lensing Esper's *Maniac* in 1934 and Wood's *Plan 9 from Outer Space* some two decades later. *Maniac* remains Dwain's most enduring contribution to our bad-cinema archives. Scripted by Esper's better (if not necessarily more competent) half, Hildegarde Stadie, *Maniac* opens in the basement lab of one Dr. Meierschultz (Carpenter), a demented medico who dreams of raising the dead. His equally addled assistant, Don Maxwell (Woods)—a hammy vaudevillian/professional impersonator on the

lam from his ex-wife—decides to knock off the doc and assume his identity (complete with specs-and-beard disguise). Maxwell is soon visited by hellacious visions (actually borrowed clips from the silent *Dante's Inferno*) and quickly degenerates into the title fiend. *Maniac* is rife with memorable sequences, including one wherein a psychotic patient (Edwards) transmogrifies into the "orangutan murderer from Poe's *Murders in the Rue Morge*" (!). Throw in literal and figurative catfights, brief nudity, and a scene that sees the mad Maxwell devour a cat's eye, and you have one of the strangest sustained hallucinations ever to flicker before grindhouse audiences' disbelieving orbs. As an arresting officer notes at film's end, "Man, you're crazy." Kino's digitally mastered tape includes *Maniac*'s original trailer, a mini-trip and a half in its own right.

Narcotic further reinforces Esper's rep as the Depression era's Ed Wood. The film purports to dramatize "the astounding biography of Dr. William G. Davies. With his captivating speeches, from wagon and tent, he made his notorious cure-all 'Tiger Fat' one of the best-known of all quack-medicine names." According to exploitation expert Bret Wood's liner notes, Davies (Cording)—portrayed on-screen as a promising physician gone to gradual ruin with the help of a philosophical opium-puffing Chinese bud (played by a Cauc actor in bad makeup)—was actually Hildegarde Esper's "opium-addicted snake-oil salesman" uncle. While Davies's descent, randomly interrupted by the director's trademark stock-footage (stock *mileage* might be closer to it) shock shots (including a brief cesarean birth), supplies its share of exploitainment, the flick's hands-down highlight is a last-reel dope party depicting the "weird and revolting behavior" of Davies and his degenerate friends, who sample from a drug buffet that includes opium, cocaine, heroin, and marijuana. The

IF YOU SHOW IT, THEY WILL COME: Vintage grindhouse staff anticipates onslaught of satisfied customers at showing of Dwain Esper's *Narcotic*.
© Kino International Corporation 1999

sequence dares to show verboten "penetration" shots of needles entering users' arms. *Narcotic*'s conclusion prefigures *Psycho*'s ending some three decades later.

MOM AND DAD (1944)
B&W ***

D: William Beaudine. Hardie Albright, Lois Austin. 97 mins. (Something Weird)

Exploitation king Kroger Babb produced and William ("One-Take") Beaudine directed this infamous roadshow perennial—a "Vital Educational Production Appealing to All True Americans"—that opens with a "Star-Spangled Banner" sing-along (!) before telling the timeworn tale of a good gal (Austin) whose lone illicit fling leads to lifelong misery. *Mom and Dad* is best remembered, though, for its lengthy childbirth inserts, "shocking" enough to keep the pic on the road-show and grindhouse circuits for nearly two decades. There's even an on-screen intermission so that live "noted hygien-

ist" Mr. Elliott Forbes could pitch the rubes a facts-of-life-type pamphlet.

NAUGHTY DALLAS (1964) **½

D: Larry Buchanan. Toni Shannon. 78 mins. (Something Weird)

Naughty Dallas traces exotic-dancer hopeful and all-around sweet young thang Shannon's odyssey from a humdrum small town to the big city, where she hankers to become a strip star and own "a pink French poodle to keep me company." Toni's arrival supplies director Buchanan with a convenient excuse to shoot lots of local strippers and bad "blue" comics, including a risqué "Mother Goose" drag act obviously patterned after Jonathan Winters's Maude Frickett character. The moment of truth arrives when our heroine struts her stuff in an "amatuer" [*sic*] strip contest, an honestly hilarious scene culminating in a dressing-room crying jag followed by an onstage pie fight (!). This important historical document offers a fascinating inside

look at Camelot Culture at its lowest end.

NUDE ON THE MOON
(1962) ***½

D: Doris Wishman. Marietta, William Mayer, Lester Brown, Pat Reilly, Ira Magee. 83 mins. (Something Weird)

Working in the overwhelmingly male-dominated grindhouse domain and often employing male aliases, Queens-bred exploitation-film legend Doris Wishman began her career crafting no-budget nudies like *Hideout in the Sun* and risqué B&W exposés like 1966's *Another Day, Another Man* (SWV). After these creaky genres sadly wheezed their last, Ms. Wishman went on to dabble in such diverse fare as intentional sex comedy (*Double Agent 73, Keyholes Are for Peeping*), bizarre noir (*The Amazing Transplant*), and horror (*A Night to Dismember*, on MPI). Few of her other efforts quite hit the heights of *Nude on the Moon*.

From its poignant (and oft repeated) "Moon Doll" theme—composed by Doris's very own niece Judith J. Kushner and movingly crooned by Ralph Young, of Sandler and Young fame— *Nude on the Moon* rates as a truly spellbinding celluloid atrocity. Our story concerns a brilliant young scientist who conveniently inherits 3 million smackers, "enough to build a rocket" (apparently out of some backdate Cape Canaveral stock footage) and "go to the moon." On their way to their secret launch site, our hero and his older mentor drive past a bijou that just happens to be showing an earlier undressed Wishman epic, *Hideout in the Sun*, at which point the elder partner confesses he'd sacrificed some much needed rest by catching the flick the night before, further asserting, "It was well worth it!" After surviving a singularly unstressful G-force experience, our celestial voyagers—now wearing smart green and red leotard-like space suits that would be more at home in a Greenwich Village Halloween parade—land on a "section of the moon that's never been seen before." Coincidentally, the area's a lunar ringer for Homestead, Florida's Coral Castle (earlier on view in the infamous cave-babe campfest *The Wild Women of Wongo* [see index]). Here our intrepid earthlings encounter a colony of lunar nudists sporting pipe-cleaner-styled antennae (!) and very little else. We won't ruin the many head-shaking surprises the pic has in store by revealing more here. Suffice it to say that if cellulitic space bimbos, airheaded heroes, loose talk, and tight panties are your Z-movie meat, you won't want to miss a single agonizing moment. Something Weird has virtually cornered the market in Doris Wishman movies.

OLGA'S GIRLS:
THE SERIES

OLGA'S GIRLS (1964) B&W***

D: Joseph P. Mawra. Audrey Campbell, Rickey Bell, Ava Denning, Darlene Bennett, Jean Laloni, Ann Pepper. 70 mins. (First Run)

From 1964 through 1966, rare indeed were the days when an *Olga* movie wasn't enjoying an extended run at a Deuce grindhouse, starting with *White Slaves of Chinatown* (Something Weird) and progressing (and we use the word loosely) through *Olga's Girls*, *Olga's House of Shame*, *Olga's Dance Hall Girls*, and *Olga's Massage Parlor*. Produced by onetime Ed Wood mentor George (*Glen or Glenda*) Weiss and starring a Mary Woronov–esque Audrey Campbell as sadistic Commie madam/drug pusher Olga, the *Olga* flicks, while tame by today's standards, earned a rep as the ultimate "nudie roughies" of their era. *Olga's Girls* unspools sans dialogue, its scant story line nudged forward by alternating narrators—Olga herself (sporting the

surname Saglo, changed from *White Slaves*'s Petroff) and announcer Perry Peters, whose oddly formal, even stately, narration attaches great significance to Olga and her hapless charges' mini-intrigues. In detailing her dealings with "syndicate man" Johnny Gordon, a.k.a. "the Pimp," we're informed, "This dickering for white flesh went on for some time." Peters also proffers such educational nuggets as "narcotics wholesalers must get their supplies from headquarters, either in Moscow or Peiping" (!). The lone major plot development involves one girl's attempts to break from Olga and start her own, more benign house. (Per Peters: "It was a good feeling to know that, even for prostitutes, life could have its better moments.") The "money scenes" unfold in Olga's notorious "Den of Persuasion," where, with the aid of several homemade torture devices and a rather redundantly labeled "Cage of Confinement," our antiheroine routinely torments her naughty girls before sending them off for "nice, warm showers." *Olga's Girls* descends into Grand Guignol territory with a dismemberment in silhouette (not a dance piece, despite the accompanying classical-music lifts) and a tongue-removal moment, though nothing graphic enough to have given then-contempo gore pioneer H. G. (*Blood Feast*) Lewis any sleepless nightmares. Olga's misdeeds fail to match the fanciful atrocities later committed by the infamous Ilsa (Dyanne Thorne) in her painful cult faves, *Ilsa, the Wicked Warden*; *Ilsa, Harem Keeper of the Oil Sheiks*; *Ilsa, She Wolf of the S.S.* (CIC); and *Ilsa, the Tigress of Siberia* (American), but the latter transpired in a more permissive age.

PAGAN ISLAND (1960) B&W**½

D: Barry Mahon. Edward Dew, Nani Maka. 60 mins. (Something Weird)

An entry in "Johnny Legend's Untamed Video" line, intro'd by

GIRLS JUST WANNA HAVE PUN(ISHMENT): Cruel Olga (center) rules in box art for the S&M sequel *Olga's Dance Hall Girls.* Courtesy of Something Weird Video

the Legend himself and his "Pagan Island Girls," *Pagan Island* finds prolific auteur Mahon up to his usual ultra-minimalist tricks. Here, surviving seaman Dew (*not* the obscure 1940s B-western hero of the same name) washes ashore on a Pacific atoll (actually Florida, with underwater scenes lensed at Miami's Seaquarium) inhabited by semitopless white women who speak in pidgin English and worship a grotty Sea God. Our hero plots to save the comely Ms. Maka from a fatal "marriage" to said sea deity, while assuring her fellow femmes he means no harm. To wit: "Don't worry, I'm not gonna hurt your Sea God. Hand me a rock." Ungainly choreography, a requisite round of "Kiss? What is *kiss*?," a giant clam, and an unhappy ending supply other highlights. *Pagan Island* is no *Wild Women of Wongo* (then again, what *is*?), but fans of the latter should find room in their hearts and viewing skeds for the former as well. SWV's tape follows the shortish feature with trailers for, among other attractions, the wild-youth obscurities *Teen-age Gang Debs* (1966) and *You've Ruined Me, Eddie!* (1958).

PLEASE DON'T TOUCH ME (1959) **½

D: Vittorio Di Naro (Ron Ormond). Al ("Lash") LaRue, Ruth Blair, Viki Caron, Larry Wallace, Ormond McGill (Ron Ormond). 67 mins. (Nashville Cinema)

Written and directed by Ormond (who doubles on-screen as hypnotist Ormond McGill) under the *nom de cinema* Vittorio Di Naro, *Please Don't Touch Me* opens with a rather low-energy assault on a redheaded wench (Caron) by a guy in a yachting cap, a scene scored by the familiar flamenco theme earlier heard in Ed Wood's *Jailbait* and Ormond's own *Mesa of Lost Women* (Englewood). Our barely begun story is summarily interrupted by almost 15 minutes of Mondo footage. A dramatized, narrated (by the ubiquitous Ormond) history of hypnotism takes us briefly to an ancient Egyptian "sleep temple" where primitive mesmerism is performed on a nearly naked nubile. (Ormond, re hypnotism, with qualified enthusiasm: "The results obtained literally border on the nearly miraculous.") Stock footage of self-punishing Filipino "flagellantes," a Borneo "fakir" who washes his face with broken beer bottles (!), and some particularly disgusto surgical footage follow before we return to our redhead, who, years after the opening attack, is not so happily married to a guy named Bill (Wallace). Vague memories of her alleged rape have turned Viki frigid. ("I haven't been feeling myself lately," she repeatedly explains. Then again, who's fault is *that*?) At the urging of her meddlesome mom (producer June Ormond), Viki visits a psychiatrist played by none other than the late S&M-tinged B-western icon Lash ("King of the Bullwhip") LaRue (!). Lash brings in hypnotist McGill, who gets Viki to relive and relieve herself of her past traumas. A Jack I. Gray, meanwhile, scores on-screen credit for designing the pic's "hypnotism machines." In addition to its tacky '50s mise-en-scène (in garish color), *PDTM* features some of the choicest exchanges and non sequiturs heard this side of an Ed Wood epic. When the curvaceous Viki flounces about in a skimpy negligé, hubby Bill confesses, "It sure does give me ideas!" To which Viki replies, "Would you like me to make you a sandwich?"

REEFER MADNESS (1936) B&W ***½

D: Louis Gasnier. Dorothy Short, Dave O'Brien, Kenneth Craig, Lillian Miles, Thelma White. 66 mins. (Kino) DVD

Before the advent of video, the film that put early exploitation movies on the contemporary camp map, theatrically revived by New Line Cinema in the '70s, enjoyed a wider cult audience than all its sleaze-bijou brethren combined. Gasnier's fast-paced anti-tea party, encouraged by ambitious DEA honcho Harry J. Anslinger (then embroiled in a fierce publicity war with image-obsessed law-enforcement rival, nascent FBI head J. Edgar Hoover), relates how a foursome of pot pushers infiltrate a local high school hangout, stage wild jitterbug, make-out, and marijuana soirées, and ruin the young lives of what could have been the future leaders of our land. Highlights include B thesp O'Brien's manic portrayal of a hard-core addict ("Faster! Play faster!"), a sensational trial sequence, and the one-toke-over-the-line grass bashes themselves. Though homevideo's ongoing exploitation explosion—made possible by archivists like Sinister Cinema, Something Weird, Rhino, and Kino—has placed *Reefer Madness* in a wider context, the pic still holds up as one of the most absurdly entertaining of its kind.

HIGH TODAY, GONE TOMORROW: Soon-to-be-turned-on teen Kenneth Craig enjoys the local dope ring's rapt attention in Kino's remastered anti-grass classic *Reefer Madness*.
© Kino International Corporation 1999

THE ROAD TO RUIN (1933) B&W ***

D: Melville Shyer, Mrs. Wallace Reid. Helen Foster, Nell O'Day, Glen Boles, Bobby Quirk. 68 mins. (Sinister Cinema)

"Eve, do you let boys kiss you?" That seemingly innocent query, posed by Eve's (O'Day) friend Ann (Foster), steers our heroines toward the titular destination in this remake of the 1928 silent of the same name. Both were produced (and this one "codirected") by Mrs. Wallace Reid—the enterprising widow of matinee-idol-turned-morphine-fatality Wallace Reid—who kicked off her long-lived exploitation-flick career with 1923's evocatively titled *Human Wreckage* (n/a). Actually, in *Road to Ruin* our gals get to have a pretty high time of it for several reels—smoking, drinking, partaking of strip crap games and naked pool parties, and generally slutting it up to their hearts' content. When punishment time at last arrives, it does so with merciless alacrity, as Ann gets busted and branded a "sex delinquent," learns she's pregnant, has an abortion, and dies. Friend Eve escapes with naught but a curable social disease, in one of the era's livelier wages-of-sin romps.

ROSELAND (1970) ***

D: Frederic Hobbs. E. Kerrigan Prescott, Christopher Brooks, Peggy Browne, Max Alter. 85 mins. (Something Weird)

One of four film oddities helmed by Hobbs—1969's *Troika* (n/a), the 1972 supernatural rock outing *Alabama's Ghost* (Artisan), and the mind-boggling *Godmonster of Indian Flats* (Something Weird) are the others—this "psychedelic fable" charts the lighthearted spiritual/sexual odyssey of Adam, a bearded space case likably embodied by Prescott. *Roseland* opens with our burned-out hero in the dubious care of one of underground moviedom's most beloved clichés, a crazy shrink (Alter), who torments him with everything from loud Beethoven organ solos to high-decibel disquisitions re Adam's disordered psyche. Adam soon escapes to the "real" world, where he works as a burlesque-house cashier, mimes his own grotty ecdysiast act, enjoys Fellini-esque sylvan romps with naked hippie nymphs, and otherwise indulges his libidinal whimsy. Back in captivity, Adam has a lengthy philosophical discussion with a black painter claiming to be Hieronymous Bosch while a ragged band of derelict musicians serenade them. It's in the musical arena (soundtrack by San Francisco's Loading Zone) that *Roseland* offers its major cultural contributions, particularly during an *Ed Sullivan Show*–set fantasy production number, replete with mock Busby Berkeley choreography, wherein our hero warbles an upbeat ode about the vagaries of modern love—a scene that must be seen and heard repeatedly to be disbelieved. *Warning:* If you're easily offended by lots of pre-Bunetics hippie nudity, you may want to keep a nimble fast-forward finger at the ready.

SATAN'S BED (1965) B&W **1/2

D: Marshall Smith, Tamijian. Yoko Ono, Val Avery, Glen Nielson, Gene Wesson. 72 mins. (Something Weird)

Beyond the novelty of seeing Yoko Ono cast as an innocent imported bridegroom who doesn't speak English (unfortunately, she sings briefly), *Satan's Bed* is a bore. It's actually two *different* bores—a low-energy unfinished feature titled *Judas City* (with Yoko), padded with unrelated inserts fashioned by the sleaze team of Roberta and the late Michael Findlay (later of *Snuff* infamy) about a trio of junkies who run around the suburbs (mostly sans dialogue) raping, roughing up, and ripping off unsuspecting housewives, the last of whom unceremoniously shoots all three of them. Ono completists will want to tune in.

SECRET FILE: HOLLYWOOD (1962) B&W **1/2

D: Ralph Cushman. Robert Clarke, Francine York, Syd Mason, Maralu Gray. 85 mins. (Loonic)

It's Follow the Bouncing Boom time! Yes, this cheesy sleaze indie sets the all-time celluloid record for Most Visible Boom Mike Shots in a single film. It follows our hero, Robert (*Hideous Sun Demon*) Clarke—an ex-shamus (his license was revoked after his involvement in a "beatnik club" shoot-out, itself a scene that cops Most Bullfight Posters in a Single Set honors) now working for the titular scandal rag—everywhere he goes. Ed Wood addicts, meanwhile, will immediately recognize snatches of the *Plan 9* theme on the soundtrack, while Bob and Ray buffs can detect the strains of the Hawaiian instrumental that intro'd the radio duo's "Wayside Doctor" playing incessantly during the gala Hollywood party scene. In short, this vintage cheapie, while a tad on the static side, has something for everyone.

THE SEVENTH COMMANDMENT (1960) B&W ***

D: Irvin Berwick. Jonathan Kidd, Lyn Statten, Frank Arvidson, Wendy Berwick, Wayne Berwick, John Carpenter. 82 mins. (Loonic)

Kidd, star of the even rarer 1958 should-be cult item *Wink of an Eye* (n/a), is an adult-ed grad on a hot date with blond hussy Statten. After they plow into an oncoming car, Kidd wanders away from the wreck and, suffering from total amnesia, hooks up with an impoverished traveling preacher. Seven years later, Kidd's a veritable Jimmy Swaggart, equipped not only with elocutive but with genuine healing powers! When Statten, who did time for the accident, chances to see Kidd's picture in the paper, she cooks up a belated blackmail scheme, and it's here that the fun *really* begins. Look for obscure self-styled B-western hero and future Ed Wood actor John (*Night of the Ghouls*) Carpenter in a bit role.

SEXY PROIBITISSIMO (1963)
B&W **1/2

D: Marcello Martinelli. Karmela, Lilli de Saigon, Monique. 63 mins. (Something Weird)

This quaint Italo import purports to re-create the history of the striptease through the ages. While the filmmakers fall short of achieving that noble ambition, strip fans should enjoy their valiant efforts. Highlights here include Dracula and Frankenstein numbers, a girl-in-a-bottle tableau, an outer-space strip, and other doubtless historically impeccable segments. The American narration sounds like it's supplied by the same mental giant, one Carl Princi, who lent his vocal talents to George Weiss's priceless cheesecake short "Sin-erama Cuties." A few of his otherwise insightful comments border on sexist. To wit: "Maybe space driving is easier for dizzy dames. There's less traffic in outer space."

SHE-DEVILS ON WHEELS
(1968) ***

D: Herschell Gordon Lewis. Betty Connell, Pat Poston, Nancy Lee Noble, Christie Wagner, Rodney Bedell, Ruby Tuesday. 83 mins. (Something Weird)

"Sex, Guts, Blood and All Men Are Mothers!" That's the exotic rallying cry of the infamous Man-Eaters, biker bimbos whose exploits are captured in all their kick-butt glory in Lewis's infamous drive-in debauch. Lewis recruited several local South Florida bikerettes to play themselves. A wise move, since two of their number—Connell as gang leader Queenie and Poston as two-ton, cigar-smoking road hog Whitey—project a raw vitality that easily outdistances the emotive abilities of H.G.'s stiff "professional" thesps. The Man-Eaters, meanwhile, spend most of the movie staging cycle races to determine who gets first pick among the local "stud" population (a Hobson's multiple choice if ever there was one). A slim story line eventually evolves when relatively sensitive gang deb Karen (Wagner) grows disaffected with the Man-Eaters' rule forbidding members to have individual boyfriends. (As Karen warns prospective beau Bedell, "Ted, do you realize what could happen if Queenie found out you didn't come here to be a stud?") In addition to Connell's and Poston's perfs, highlights here include the theme song "Get Off the Road" and a scenic tour of lovely Medley, Florida. The usually violence-prone Lewis shows remarkable restraint in this outing—at least until the pic's requisite last-reel decapitation scene—but more than compensates with scuzzoid sociological insights galore.

SHE SHOULDA SAID "NO!" (1949)
B&W ***

D: Sam Newfield. Lila Leeds, Alan Baxter, Michael Whelan, Lyle Talbot, Jack Elam, David Gorcey. 70 mins. (Sinister Cinema)

Original ads for *She Shoulda Said "No!"* (a.k.a. *Wild Weed* and *The Devil's Weed*) promised patrons they'd witness how "the happy, normal laughter of physically adorable young girls gives way to the hysterical outbursts of dope-maddened women." (Hey, everybody's gotta grow up *some*time!) Star Leeds—who had recently been released after serving six months on an infamous marijuana bust that also netted better-known thesp Robert Mitchum—apparently accepted the role as part of her postpenal penance and frequently delivered in-person antidrug lectures following road-show screenings. Produced by Kroger (*Bob and Sally*) Babb, this already anachronistic "*Reefer Madness* Revisited" throwback is not without its high points, including the usual guided tour of marijuana's hopeless victims, plus a great hallucinatory piano-fantasy sequence (with "Chopsticks" performed by Rudolf Friml, Jr.) that puts *Reefer*'s keyboard scenes to shame. We likewise applaud Alicia Adams's choreographic contributions and the flick's special Theremin Effects. Besides Lila, Babb's "All-Star Hollywood Cast" includes Baxter as a big-time pusher, David (Brother of Leo) Gorcey as one of tea's tragic young victims, heavy Elam in his youthful-thug days, and perennial exploitation-pic authority figure Talbot as a cop.

STREET CORNER (1948)
B&W **1/2

D: Albert Kelley. Joseph Crehan, Marcia Mae Jones, John Truel, Billie Jean Eberhart, Greti Dupont, Jan Sutton. 62 mins. (Something Weird)

Something Weird serves up another camp-enriched dose of vintage celluloid saltpeter in *Street Corner*, a likely inspiration for scripter Ed Wood's far more spirited and thematically ambitious 1956 exploitation epic, *The Violent Years*. Her well-heeled parents' policy of benign neglect, facts-of-life-wise, leads 17-year-old Jones to surrender to a bout of lakeside prom-night passion with college-bound beau Truel. (Said passion is artfully symbolized by a close-up of Marcia Mae's hand rhythmically squeezing her own corsage.) Her subsequent pregnancy eventually lands her in the clutches of local abortionist DuPont (resembling something of a female Rondo Hatton). Concerned (and ever meddling) medico Crehan—an aged bachelor with a perhaps overly intense interest in the erotic habits of the local teenette population—interrupts the maudlin proceedings for a (color) "birth of a baby" reel (a real fast-forward special). More slickly produced than many of its cautionary carnal counterparts, *Street Corner* may be bald on sensual thrills but packs its fair share of cultural curio value.

STRIPORAMA   (1952) ***½

D: Jerald Intrator. Jack Diamond, Mandy Kay, Charles Harris, Betty Page, Lili St. Cyr, Georgia Southern, Rosita Royce, Mr. America, the Venus Beauties. 70 mins. (Something Weird)

When four geezers prepping an entertainment time capsule vote to exclude burlesque from the assembled treasures—as a mock *Variety* headline puts it, FUTURE DEPRIVED OF BUMPS AND GRINDS—a Burly-Q impresario and two baggy-pants comics (Diamond, Harris) force them at gunpoint (!) to watch a burlesque film, which, natch, turns out to be *Striporama.* The pic represents one of this vintage genre's best, from the terrific Times Square footage (circa 1951) to comics repping the last gasps of old-time immigrant humor to several cheesily lavish strip acts, including a harem bath routine by the peerless Page, Lili St. Cyr's fabled Cinderella number, a typically whirlwind turn by Georgia Southern ("the Fastest Girl in Burlesque"), and a one-of-a-kind ornithological act by the immortal "Rosita Royce and Her Clothes-Stealing Doves." A multitalented Mr. America also drops by to toot a harmonica and levitate a fat comedian using only his teeth. *Striporama* stacks up as a prime example of the type of good, clean, down-and-dirty fun they don't hardly make anymore. For more, including an evocative tour of Manhattan's erstwhile "Burlesque Boulevard"

(52nd Street), see *The Striptease Murder Case* (Something Weird).

TRAFFIC IN SOULS   (1913) B&W ***

D: George Lourie Tucker. Jane Gail, Matt Moore, Ethel Grandin, Arthur Hunter. 88 mins. (Kino)

While tame by later standards, *Traffic in Souls*—widely regarded as the American cinema's first true exploitation film, meticulously restored, with a new "musical setting" by Philip Carli—is anything but campy or primitive. Tucker's direction, on authentic NYC locations, boasts a precocious fluidity, particularly during several well-choreographed crowd scenes. The performances are naturalistic and the use of flash cards spare, beyond establishing the identities of a large cast of characters. Tucker employs almost a dramatized-documentary approach in dissecting the ins and outs of the "white slave" racket (or "traffic in souls"). He details how lowlifes in the employ of "the man higher up" (outwardly a respectable citizen whose own daughter is engaged to the society "catch" of the season) trick innocent immigrant girls fresh from Ellis Island and country gals adrift in the big city into accepting their "aid," then squirrel them away in well-guarded bordellos. Our central story line focuses on Gail and patrolman beau Moore's attempts to recover the former's younger sister from the organization's clutches, which they do with the help of her "invalid inventor" dad. (Per a flash card: "That night, they secure her father's invention for intensifying sound waves and recording dictagraph sounds on a phonographic record.") Indeed, *Traffic in Souls* relies as much on "modern" technology as such late-'40s *policiers* as *Call Northside 777* and *White Heat.* While *Traffic* unspools much like a contempo issue-of-the-week TV movie, it offers a fascinating view of a sensationalized social problem of the era, generates genuine suspense as a crime thriller, and presents a vivid picture of pre–World War I Manhattan life.

VIOLATED   (1953) B&W ***

D: Walter Strate. Wim Holland, Lili Dawn, Mitchell Kowal, Viki Carlson, William Martel, Jason Niles. 78 mins. (Something Weird)

In the '60s and '70s, Times Square bijou minimogul William Mishkin commissioned infamous Staten Island

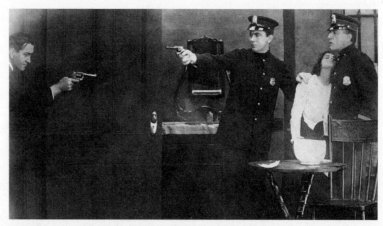

TRAFFIC *COP:* Policeman Matt Moore draws bead on bad guy in the American Cinema's first true exploitation feature *Traffic in Souls.*
© *Kino International Corporation 1999*

auteur Andy (*The Ghastly Ones*) Milligan to lens amateur-night fright flicks on budgets so low that the pics could turn a profit even if they only played Mishkin's limited venues. Apparently, Mishkin experimented with this practice as early as '53, when he coproduced and scripted this cheesily compelling exercise in verité noir about a Manhattan-based psycho who slays and scalps his female prey. The violence is discreetly handled as the focus swings between photographer-suspect Holland (who also produced) and a Dragnet-manqué police investigation conducted by fairly thick-witted NYPD dicks Kowal and Martel. A shrink (Niles) is also on hand to lend credibility and even a note of enlightened compassion to the fragmented proceedings. While the suspense angle is pretty much bungled, *Violated* succeeds in establishing its own eccentric, melancholy mood, one greatly abetted by Tony Mottola's mostly solo electric-guitar score, and provides a fascinating look at 1953 Greenwich Village (where Holland has his photography studio) and other Gotham locales.

A VIRGIN IN HOLLYWOOD (1948) B&W **½

D: Klayton W. Kirby. Dorothy Abbott, Thad Swift, Phil Rhodes. 55 mins. (Something Weird)

Based on the "shocking" book exposé of the same name, *A Virgin in Hollywood* (a.k.a. *Hollywood Confidential*) stars Abbott as a virginal reporter looking for the lowdown on the Tinseltown sin scene. She finds a cheesecake photo shoot, a bad John Barrymore impersonator, a lengthy lingerie show, and a surprise cameo by the African fertility mask that would later achieve lasting fame in Ed Wood's *Glen or Glenda*. As stimulating and educational as it sounds.

THE WEIRD WORLD OF LSD (1967) B&W ***

D: Robert Ground. Terry Tessem, Yolanda Morino, Ann Lindsay. 76 mins. (Something Weird)

"Under LSD, veins on your arm become an intense blue mountain range," drones the 'droidoid narrator of this bizarre exercise in B&W wackiness. "One's eye can be seen to grow until it fills a room and the walls close in on it until it is squashed, sending a symphony of colors into a sea of sounds." Bald on erotic elements, *Weird* nonetheless sheds vital light on the catfights, dismemberments, bouts of gluttony, girls-in-Halloween-ape-masks apparitions, and all the other LSD-inspired *hell*ucinations acid luminaries like Tim Leary, Ken Kesey, and Aldous Huxley so frequently reported. In a class by itself—and destined to be left back.

Wild Youth A Go-Go!
CELLULOID DELINQUENTS, HIPPIES, AND HOODS

"Go, cat, go—you're warming me!"
—wild youth, *BEAT GIRL*

AMERICAN HISTORY X   (1998) ***

D: Tony Kaye. Edward Norton, Edward Furlong, Beverly D'Angelo, Fairuza Balk, Stacy Keach, Avery Brooks, Elliott Gould. 119 mins. (New Line) DVD

Despite a somewhat messy structure—Brit director Kaye publicly petitioned to have his name removed from the film and replaced by the handle "Humpty Dumpty" (!)—*American History X* compensates with a gritty take on an ugly topic (native neo-Nazism) and intensely powerful performances. A bulked-up Norton fully earns his 1999 Best Actor Oscar nom via his wrenching portrayal of a frustrated, hate-poisoned California youth whose violent, dead-end values soften during a sobering prison stretch. Norton returns home to find younger bro' Furlong deeply entrenched in the local skinhead scene—supervised by a supremely creepy Keach—and seeks to extricate him from same. Kaye's overreliance on flashy visual techniques occasionally distracts from the drama (though relating flashbacks in black and white works well enough), but *American History X* represents the best examination of skinhead culture since Geoffrey Wright's 1992 Aussie import *Romper Stomper* (see index).

BAD BOYS   (1983) ***

D: Rick Rosenthal. Sean Penn, Ally Sheedy, Esai Morales, Clancy Brown. 123 mins. (HBO) DVD

Penn and Morales are strong as natural adversaries who find themselves behind the same bars in an effective update of the boys'-reformatory flicks of yore. We missed erstwhile Dead End Kid Billy Halop's presence, but *Bad Boys* is still tough, tense, top-of-the-genre stuff. No relation to the 1995 Martin Lawrence/Will Smith buddy-cop lovefest of the same name (Columbia/TriStar). For a lower-rung femme companion piece, try Tim Kinkaid's chicklets-in-chains opus *Bad Girls' Dormitory* (Active).

BEAT GIRL   (1960) B&W **1/2

D: Edmond T. Greville. Gillian Hills, David Farrar, Noelle Adam, Christopher Lee, Shirley Anne Field. 92 mins. (Kino)

Beat Girl (initially released stateside as *Wild for Kicks*) is an alternately daring and campy exposé of Brit Beats, who act more like Yank rockers (or "jiving, driveling scum!" as one character negatively appraises them) prone to uttering such pithy pronouncements as

"Go, cat, go—you're warming me!" Hills portrays a spoiled rich girl resentful of her divorced dad's (Farrar) new young wife (Adam), who herself harbors the "shocking" secret that she once worked as a Parisian stripteuse. That discovery entices our hep young heroine to try the same line of work in a Soho strip joint run by a sleazy Lee. Real-life rocker Adam Faith shows up as a James Dean wannabe, while Oliver Reed puts in an early appearance as a youth identified in the end credits only as "Plaid Shirt" (!). Brit rockabilly numbers and a railway chickie race supply other highlights. Kino has since released the recommended Brit '60s winners *The Leather Boys* and *The Girl-Getters*.

THE BEATNIKS   (1960) B&W **

D: Paul Frees. Tony Travis, Peter Breck, Karen Kadler, Joyce Terry, Charles Delaney. 78 mins. (Something Weird)

The only feature film directed and cowritten by multivoiced Paul Frees (of Boris Badenov fame), *The Beatniks* dramatizes how lowlife scum/singing talent Travis is held back from superstardom by his envious lowlife-scum friends, the most flipped-out of whom is future *Shock Corridor* crazy

Breck. Tony's impromptu, jukebox-backed rendition of the inspired ditty "Sideburns Don't Need No Sympathy" is of potential youth-anthem proportions. Many yawns frame this lone memorable moment.

THE BLACK REBELS
(1960/1965) ***

D: Richard L. Bare. Rita Moreno, Mark Damon, Gerald Mohr, Jay Novello, Richard Rust, Tom Gilson, Douglas Hume. 90 mins. (Something Weird)

About 95 percent of *The Black Rebels* is a 1960 juvenile-delinquent exposé titled *This Rebel Breed*, a bizarre-enough outing in its own right. To ferret out the facts about a burgeoning L.A. high school marijuana racket and prevent racial unrest at the same site from boiling over into serious violence, cop Mohr assigns two young undercover officers (Damon, Hume) to pose as students. The pic takes pains to explain the cop high-schoolers' comparatively advanced age, though the two thesps actually rank among the *younger-*looking pupils at this geriatric educational facility. Hume's mission is to work his way into the reigning Anglo gang, the Royals, led by grass retailer Rust. Damon, wearing some kind of weird berry stains, is supposed to pass as half Mexican, half black and join the local African-American contingent, headed by Freeman (who eyes Damon like he's from another planet—and *not* a brother from same). In fact, you can't keep track of the various ethnic strains without a scorecard. Damon tumbles for half Mexican, half Anglo coed Moreno (then 27), who's having a secret affair with a Royal gang member (Don Eitner). Moreno's Chicano gang-leader brother (Richard Laurier) warns off Damon because he's supposed to be half black, then becomes the prime suspect when Eitner is killed (by Rust) because the victim was white. ("He hates everyone but Mexicans," cop Mohr helpfully explains.) Meanwhile, a foxy Diane (soon to be *Dyan*) Cannon shows up as Rust's kicks-crazed squeeze, Wiggles, who's eventually exposed as being black (?!). Thematically, *This Rebel Breed* is all over the place, delivering surprisingly sensible sermons about American racism's ingrained class and economic roots one moment, spreading *Reefer Madness*–type panic about pot's pernicious influence the next. (One outrageous scene depicts Rust bullying three roughly eight-year-old black kids into smoking a joint!) The flick's crowded climax sees every major character *and* extra converge on the same suburban house for one of the most chaotic confrontations ever captured on celluloid. Still, it's the *other* 5 percent of the film that's truly out-there. A half decade after *This Rebel Breed* made its medium-profile bijou rounds in 1960, producer William Rowland lensed several new sleaze inserts, edited them into the existing film, retitled the resultant mess *The Black Rebels*, and sent it out, on the drive-in/grindhouse circuit, as a new flick. At regular intervals during this reasonably serious if muddled movie, rehired actor Hume walks around opening random doors and stumbling on the same group of characters, utterly unrelated to the original film, indulging in topless twist and heavy-petting parties (!). In short, they don't get much weirder than this.

THE BLOODY BROOD (1959) B&W **¹/₂

D: Julian Roffman. Peter Falk, Jack Betts, Barbara Lord. 80 mins. (Sinister Cinema)

According to the original ads, *The Bloody Brood* is "a Motion Picture That Peels Off the Dirty Sweaters Covering the Raw Emotions of Youth!" Falk makes his screen debut as a sort of beatnik Raskolnikov who kills a delivery kid for kicks by feeding him a burger mixed with ground glass during a wild Beat bacchanal; the victim's brother seeks revenge. Packed with all manner of Holy Profundities.

A BOY CALLED HATE (1995) **

D: Mitch Marcus. Scott Caan, Missy Crider, Adam Beach, James Caan, Elliott Gould. 96 mins. (Paramount)

Stop us if you've heard this before: Boy and girl "meet cute" when boy guns down girl's influential uncle for attempting to rape her in a saloon parking lot. Boy and girl take it on the lam, with the law in hot-to-lukewarm pursuit. The boy is the eponymous Hate, so called because he carved that word into his forearm with the aid of his trusty razor blade. Played by Scott (Son of James) Caan, Hate is your basic broken-home teen living in a remote white-trash Arizona outpost with his shiftless dad, portrayed by James (Father of Scott) Caan. It's their typical bickering that leads Hate out into the night on his bike, ultimately running into distressed damsel Cindy (Crider) and her abusive unk (Gould). In this road ode to aimless youngsters armed with bad attitudes, bald intellects, and big guns, the inarticulate Hate and the sullen, embittered Cindy share your typical de rigueur '90s-styled rites-of-passage adventures—jacking cars, trysting in gas-station rest rooms, partying down with wild and crazy Native American Billy Little Plume (Beach) and his desert homeys, and even, eventually, falling in old-fashioned love. Unfortunately, Hate reflexively kills a cop along the way, putting another serious damper on their trip. Debuting director/writer Marcus's parade of doom-generation clichés is occasionally uplifted by deft location lensing and an infectious performance by the charismatic Beach, who easily steals those scenes he shares with the bland Caan and irritating Crider. No relation to the French enraged-youth drama titled simply *Hate* (PolyGram).

THE BOYS NEXT DOOR (1985) ***

D: Penelope Spheeris. Maxwell Caulfield, Charlie Sheen, Hank Garrett, Patti D'Arbanville, Christopher McDonald. 88 mins. (New World, Starmaker)

The boys in question, surly Roy (Caulfield) and his passive partner, Bo (Sheen), are a pair of incorrigible recent high school grads who take off for a wild L.A. weekend before starting dead-end jobs at a local factory. Our working-class antiheroes let it all hang out, guzzling beer, stealing gum, and kidnapping a classmate's poodle before graduating to the requisite abrupt-and-senseless slaughter spree. *Boys* pretends at first to be a sober probe into *Psychopathia Americanus*. But have no fear: Spheeris, still a long way from her *Wayne's World* (Paramount) days, delivers an occasionally dim but never dull flick that's actually a thoroughly sleazy wild-youth rampage, long on random violence, high-speed car chases, and trashy rock songs but refreshingly low on redeeming social value.

CLASS OF 1984 (1982) ***

D: Mark L. Lester. Perry King, Roddy McDowall, Merrie Lynn Ross, Timothy Van Patten, Michael Fox. 93 mins. (Vestron, n.i.d.)

Lester's nearly peg-by-peg punk update of the seminal *Blackboard Jungle* (MGM/UA) stars King in the Mr. Daddy-O role (originally played by Glenn Ford), McDowall as a cynical fellow teacher (who packs a gun in class), Van Patten as a teen psycho with potential, and Michael Fox (so young in this one that he hadn't even grown his "J." yet) as a victimized student. While a fairly blatant rip-off, *Class* offers a decidedly different set of solutions for the teen troublemakers and rates overall as the sort of slick, sick trash entertainment sorely needed in our troubled world. The series went the sci-fi route with the 'droid-dominated sequels *Class of 1999* (see index) and *Class of 1999 II*.

CRACK HOUSE (1989) **¹/₂

D: Michael Fischa. Jim Brown, Anthony Geary, Richard Roundtree, Cheryl Kay, Gregg Gomez Thomsen, Angel Tompkins. 90 mins. (Cannon)

Crack House kicks off as a low-budget *Colors* clone, mutates midway into a typical backdate "blaxploitation" pic, enters a brief but intense *Reefer Madness* phase, and ends with a SWAT tank rolling over the title abode (!). In sum, *Crack House* covers all the B-movie bases, leaving no sleaze stone unturned or, with its emphasis on intoxicants of all kinds, no plot turn unstoned. At heart, though, *Crack House* is an updated good-girl-gone-bad tale. Anglo teen Melissa (Kay) and Chicano beau Rick (Thomsen) vow to escape their ethnically mixed West Coast ghetto. When Rick winds up in jail, Melissa hangs with crack dealer B.T. (Clyde R. Jones), who introduces her to hard drugs, which cause her to squabble with her alcoholic mom (veteran screen floozy Tompkins), run away, and degenerate into a crack-house hooker. (Then again, what's a girl to do in a world where her own self-righteous high school guidance counselor [Geary] turns out to be the area's chief drug supplier?) Luckily for Melissa, caring cop Richard (*Shaft*) Roundtree is determined, with a reformed Rick's help, to bust the local drug ring. *Crack House* is low in educational content, high on exploitation, and medium in low-rent entertainment value. Jim Brown buffs beware: Though toplined, the veteran black action hero doesn't show up until the flick's final reels, and then as an evil dealer/pimp.

DADDY-O (1959) B&W **1/2

D: Lou Place. Dick Contino, Sandra Giles, Bruno VeSota, Jack McClure, Gloria Victor. 74 mins. (Columbia/TriStar)

This quirky youth noir stars the ever-smooth Contino as a beer-swigging truck driver/singer stuck with the titular moniker. Dick belts a few rock tunes, develops an initially antagonistic, later amorous relationship with hard-driving femme Giles, and tangles with smack-trafficking club owner VeSota (doing his best Sebastian Cabot impersonation, which probably ran about even with his *worst* Sebastian Cabot impersonation) and his muscular, myopic minion (McClure). While Contino's career failed to soar, *Daddy-O* packs a lot of lowlife entertainment into 74 swift minutes.

DAMAGED GOODS (A.K.A. *V.D.*) (1961) B&W ***

D: Haile Chace. Dolores Faith, Mory Schoolhouse, Charlotte Stewart, Michael Bell. 91 mins. (T&A)

The T&A Video sleeve features a con-tempo shot of a suggestively posed model, making the tape—advertised as being "Rated RRR" (!)—look like a standard hard-core porn affair. The box credits list the already oddly monikered male lead, Mory Schoolhouse, as "Mary" (!), but the plot synopsis on the back is fairly accurate. In fact, the flick itself, with an excellent Ventures instrumental appropriately titled "Damaged Goods Theme," is an earnest, well-acted, and quite credible account of four soon-to-graduate high school seniors—lovebirds

Judy (Stewart) and Jim (the aforementioned Mr. Schoolhouse), their horny pal Monk (Bell), and newly arrived "bad girl" Kathy (Faith), who poses as Monk's squeeze to get closer to Jim. In the fullness of time, Jim, Monk, and a couple of buddies cruise to Seaview, where Jim gets drunk, laid, and infected, leading to a talk with the coach, a visit to the doc, and a five-minute U.S. Public Health documentary on the dangers of social diseases. While clearly the flick's hook, the VD angle actually constitutes only a small portion of this nonhysterical, low-key coming-of-age story, one well worth catching (so to speak) for its legit dramatic merits and time-capsule sociology.

DRAGSTRIP GIRL (1957) B&W **1/2

D: Edward L. Cahn. Fay Spain, John Ashley, Steve Terrell, Frank Gorshin, Russ Bender. 69 mins. (Columbia/TriStar)

AIP moguls Sam Arkoff and Jim Nicholson made a point of keeping adults at a distance in their teen-POV flicks, and *Dragstrip Girl* is no exception. Here hot-rodding rich kid Ashley (who would reprise virtually the same role in 1960's *High School Caesar*) resorts to underhanded tactics to keep poor but honest Terrell from winning the big race and buxom blond Spain's hand. One undeniable highlight finds Frank (the Riddler) Gorshin performing the rap-styled "Dragstrip Baby" in drag (!) while Ashley makes like an Elvis wannabe. *Dragstrip Girl* shapes up as a lively teen saga marred only by some cornball comic relief. Vintage-car buffs should get off on the pic's procession of primo wheels.

EXPRESSO BONGO (1960) B&W ***

D: Val Guest. Laurence Harvey, Sylvia Syms, Cliff Richard, Yolande Donlan. 108 mins. (Kino)

Adapted by Wolf Mankowitz from his hit play and directed by frequent

genre helmer Val (*The Quatermass Xperiment*) Guest, *Expresso Bongo* shapes up as a lively showbiz fable set in London's Soho strip- and music-club milieu and peppered with original tunes. A lean and hungry-looking Harvey stars as Johnny Jackson, a sleazily upbeat press agent bent on boosting a local teen singer (then-reigning Brit pop star Richard) to the top of the rock-'n'-roll heap. *Expresso Bongo* stirred some controversy in its day for its casual treatment of (semi-)nudity, sex, and shady media manipulation; while time has somewhat blunted its erstwhile edge, the pic, presented in a pristine wide-screen edition, succeeds in preserving a fascinating time-capsule portrait of the cradle of the coming Brit rock revolution.

THE FLAMING TEEN-AGE (1956) B&W **1/2

D: Irwin S. Yeaworth, Jr., Charles Edwards. Noel Reyburn, Ethel Barrett, Jerry Frank, Shirley Holmes. 67 mins. (Sinister Cinema)

Irwin (*The Blob*) Yeaworth, working from a Jean Yeaworth/Ethel Barrett screenplay "based on the true life story of Fred Garland," kicks off to a promising start as a no-budget account re the perils of teen drinking. (The opening segment, beyond being hosted by the same nagging '50s authority figure in an ill-fitting suit, has nothing to do with the rest of this celluloid disquisition, which was apparently filmed several years earlier.) When teenaged Tim turns up tipsy, Dad decides to exercise reverse psychology by taking him on a tour of several seamy bars, a field trip that, according to our on-screen authority figure, "saved him from, at worst, potential delinquency." That entertaining episode is followed by Fred Garland's advertised true-life tale of woe. Garland (Reyburn) is depicted as a vaguely ambitious, terminally aimless jerk (long past adolescence, by the way) who operates a small-town candy store, moves to New York (where we're treated to some all-too-brief vintage Times Square travelog footage), "drifts" into a dancing career (!), briefly becomes a booking agent, shoe salesman, swindler, hopeless alcoholic, junkie, jailbird, and, unsurprisingly, an evangelist. Yes, Fred is a man of many lives—all of them dull. On Sinister's tape, the feature is preceded by a priceless "girlie" short called "Nautical Nudes," as riveting an exercise in comatose minimalism as your Phantom's ever seen and well worth the price of admission for fanciers of this brand of brain-dead bare fare.

GIRL GANG   (1954) B&W ***½

D: Robert C. Derteno. Timothy Farrell, Joanne Arnold, Harry Keaton, Lou Monson. 60 mins. (Something Weird)

Created by the same Poverty Row personnel responsible for *Gun Girls* (see index)—directed/edited by Robert Derteno, photographed by camera ace William C. Thompson, and "Produced Under the Personal Supervision of George Weiss"—*Girl Gang* isn't quite as campy as *Gun Girls* but easily outsleazes it; indeed, the filmmakers seemed casually determined to violate every Code sanction on the books, especially when it came to drugs. Our story centers on dope pusher Joe (Farrell, whose slogan goes "Weed today, shots tomorrow!") as he cheerfully hooks the local teen population on heroin, masterminds gas-station heists, fences stolen cars, seduces his distaff customers, and (it's implied) brokers abortions with the help of boozy discredited sawbones "Doc." Joe also gives on-screen lessons in the art of smack preparation ("No, that's *too* much water") and injection (needling one girl in her exposed thigh), while gang recruits are forced to have "intimate relations" with five guys to join the club (after which they sit around a warehouse, smoking joints and grooving to a boogie-woogie piano). Derteno and crew even work in a contrived catfight right under the last-reel wire. (Production values are

so minimal that even the prop guns are tiny—barely credible as cap pistols!) Couchside '50s-sleaze historians won't want to miss this one.

GIRLS IN PRISON   (1956) B&W **

D: Edward L. Cahn. Richard Denning, Joan Taylor, Adele Jergens, Helen Gilbert, Lance Fuller, Raymond Hatton. 87 mins. (Columbia/TriStar)

While producer, film scholar, and onetime Ed Wood collaborator Alex Gordon occupies a highly respected niche in the B-movie pantheon, as a filmmaker he lacked fellow AIP auteur Roger Corman's knack for tapping into the youth market. One of the first true "fans" to make movies, Gordon frequently indulged his penchant for casting older thesps and beloved has-beens in what were supposed to be basically teen-oriented films. And rather than adopting Corman's streamlined rock-'n'-roll approach, Gordon favored a more leisurely '40s style; in short, he would have been more at-home at the by-then-defunct Monogram than at AIP. This early chicks-in-chains potboiler serves as a prime case in point. The flick exhibits some "modern" touches—like the primitive rock theme song "Tombeat"—and offers some memorable lines, as when one hard-boiled babe muses, "'S'funny how scum like us think alike" and "You helped bring this on, you little cesspool!" Gordon ultimately fared better in the sci-fi/horror genre via low-budget but effective efforts like *Atomic Submarine* (see index).

GIRLS IN PRISON   (1994) ***

D: John McNaughton. Missy Crider, Ione Skye, Anne Heche, Nicolette Scorsese, Bahni Turpin, Tom Towles, Jon Polito. 82 mins. (Dimension)

Girls in Prison is the second of several features from Showtime cable's 1994 *Rebel Highway* series to

INSIDE DOPE: Director Robert C. Derteno defies Code drug sanctions with his smack-happy wayward-teens celebration *Girl Gang.*
Courtesy of Something Weird Video

reach homevid (see also Robert Rodriguez's *Roadracers*). The idea was to give free rein to a wide range of directors to appropriate vintage American-International Pictures titles and do with them what they wouldst. *Girls in Prison* sports glittering credentials indeed—John (*Henry, Normal Life, Wild Things*) McNaughton directs a script credited to the late Sam (*Shock Corridor*) Fuller (!) and cowriter Christa Lang Fuller. While *GIP's* themes qualify as quintessentially Fuller-ian, the treatment seems way too winkingly postmodern for that offbeat but ever earnest maverick auteur. The '50s-set chicks-in-chains spoof tracks a trio of young gals convicted, in separate cases, of killing obnoxious older males and subsequently sent to a femme pen run by brusque, burly head guard Towles. Our story centers primarily on Crider, the only one of our justifiably homicidal heroines who's innocent of the charge brought against her—the brutal (if well-deserved) stabbing death of a sleazy music publisher

(Polito) who'd agreed to record her original song (actually Jody Reynolds's haunting 1958 suicide ditty, "Endless Sleep," heard repeatedly throughout the film in a new cover version). Produced by frequent John Carpenter partner Debra Hill and Lou (Son of Sam) Arkoff, *GIP* plays like a subversive underground comix–styled send-up and mostly succeeds on that level. The flick references everything from *Dragnet* to the McCarthy hearings, includes the requisite catfights and shower scenes (some pretty fair ones at that), and never allows its tongue to stray too far from cheek.

GIRLS TOWN   (1959) B&W ***

D: Charles Haas. Mamie Van Doren, Mel Torme, Paul Anka, Ray Anthony, Cathy Crosby, Gigi Perreau, Elinor Donahue. 92 mins. (Republic)

Dig that crazy cast! Too bad veteran sleazemeister/producer Albert Zugsmith didn't have a story to match. The one that's there does boast its share of camp value, though. When Mamie's dress-alike younger sister (Donahue, of *Father Knows Best* fame) accidentally pushes a fresh creep off a cliff, the law puts the blame on Mamie, who's framed and sent to a reform school run by nuns Maggie Hayes and Sheila Graham. Paul Anka sings to the rescue, crooning "Ave Maria" and "Girls' Town Blues" (an opening-credits duet with an off-key Mamie). Torme plays a 35ish wild youth, while Dick (*Daddy-O*) Contino, and celebrity sons Charles Chaplin, Jr., Jim Mitchum, and Harold Lloyd, Jr., likewise lend their talents. Gloria (*I Married a Monster from Outer Space*) Talbott plays the reformatory's token tough.

GUN GIRLS   (1956) ***1/2

D: Robert C. Dertano. Timothy Farrell, Jean Ann Lewis, Jeanne Ferguson, Jacqueline Park. 61 mins. (Something Weird)

"Here, for the first time, is a dramatic picture of the extent and nature of this new girl problem: The story of *Gun Girls*!" Thus spake the original trailer for *Gun Girls*. The pic—adapted by director Dertano from his own book *Girls on Parole*—is an ultra-minimalist antimasterpiece that unfolds in a world consisting of roughly four or five small rooms, a gas station, and the back of a warehouse. *Gun Girls* shares much with the Ed Wood–scripted classic *The Violent Years*—the same cinematographer (William C. Thompson), an appearance by actress Barbara Weeks (again cast as a wealthy but negligent mom), a rampaging girl-gang plot, and a long, droning lecture on the juvenile-delinquency plague orated by a rambling authority figure (e.g., "Continuous disrespect for law and order is a shortcut to a prison term"). The late, great Timothy Farrell—who actually worked in California law enforcement between acting jobs (i.e., most of the time)—adds another sterling perf to his celluloid-gangster résumé. Here Farrell plays Joe, a sleazy fence who never seems to leave his shabby digs (for the record, he does, *once*, to replenish his liquor supply), who deals guns to over-aged delinquents Ferguson and Park and seduces wayward "good girl" Lewis into the bargain. While the script lacks Ed's dizzying Wooden wordplay, Dertano proves no slouch in the redundant-dialogue department, providing such overexplanatory lines as "What 'clients' can a fence have? You're a seller of stolen goods!" and "C'mon, Doris, let's conceal these weapons." One priceless scene sees a hitherto silent radio apparently turn itself on, sans human intervention, long enough to announce a plot-advancing "bulletin," then immediately return to silence (!). The flick's chief raison d'être revolves around the girls' frequent sartorial changes, where they flash bras and slips but go no further. If you're in the mood for vintage deadpan camp, *you* need go no further than *Gun Girls*.

HEATHERS   (1989) ***

D: Michael Lehmann. Christian Slater, Winona Ryder, Shannen Doherty, Lisanne Falk, Kim Walker, Glen Shadix. 102 mins. (Anchor Bay) DVD

While we enjoyed Lehmann's high-school-hell satire, we probably would have liked it even better if we hadn't seen much the same story before, as 1976's *Massacre at Central High* (see index). *Heathers* replaces *Massacre*'s fascistic male clique with a femme one but otherwise clones the earlier flick pretty closely. Still, *Heathers* is witty enough in its own right to deserve its elevated status and has itself been ripped off by inferior fare like the 1999 Rose McGowan vehicle *Jawbreaker* (Columbia/TriStar).

HIGH SCHOOL CAESAR   (1960) B&W **1/2

D: O'Dale Ireland. John Ashley, Gary Vinson, Judy Nugent. 75 mins. (Rhino)

Neglected rich kid Ashley is a teen bully who cares more about his pompadour than about other people in this road-show *Rebel Without a Cause*. The pic packs enough punch-ups, drag races, and primitive rock 'n' roll into its brief running time to make it a worthwhile item for adolescents-amok buffs. Ashley went on to produce (and sometimes star in) countless bad Filipino genre flicks and later produced TV's *Werewolf* terror series.

HIGH SCHOOL CONFIDENTIAL. (1958) B&W ***1/2

D: Jack Arnold. Russ Tamblyn, Jan Sterling, John Drew Barrymore, Mamie Van Doren. 85 mins. (Republic)

Undercover narc Tamblyn poses as Van Doren's high school student nephew so he can "size up this townsville" and ferret out local dope pushers (who include bandleader Ray

Anthony and future Uncle Fester, Jackie Coogan). Hipster Barrymore offers a jive version of Columbus's discovery of America, while Jerry Lee Lewis bangs his 88s, in this warped time-capsule classic.

HOTHEAD (1963) B&W ***1/2

D: Edward Mann. John Delgar, Robert Glenn, Barbara Joyce, Steve Franklin, Linda Kane. 72 mins. (Sinister Cinema)

Less a delinquent exposé than an unpretentious, thoroughly unpredictable, surprisingly powerful slice-of-lowlife created and populated by total unknowns, Edward Mann's *Hothead* (scripted by Milton Mann) chronicles young Frank's (Delgar) encounter with a shifty (and shiftless) middle-aged drifter (Glenn) he believes to be his absentee dad. Credibly acted, with verité-sounding dialogue, *Hothead* takes us through a single day in Frank's troubled life, as he loses his menial job, scuffles with attendees at an upscale pool party, then heads for the beach with pal Franklin and his squeeze, Joyce, where his showdown with Glenn begins. Mann's meditation on the themes of guilt and responsibility kept us hooked from start to finish. If *Hothead* had been filmed in Italian or Spanish (*El Cabeza Caliente*, anyone?) with English subtitles, it would have been hailed as a minor neorealist art-house classic. Fortunately, Sinister Cinema has rescued this offbeat sleeper from oblivion.

HOT ROD RUMBLE (1957) B&W ***

D: Leslie H. Martinson. Richard Hartunian, Leigh Snowden, Brett Halsey, Wright King, Joey Forman, John Brinkley. 79 mins. (Foothill)

Unknown thesp Hartunian impresses via his Brando/Dean Method-styled perf as inarticulate racer Big Arnie, a leather-jacketed Neanderthal with a soul of solid gold. Arnie's status with the Road Devils (also the pic's original title) hot-rod club (headed by comic and longtime Mickey Rooney sidekick Forman) is seriously diminished when he's suspected of causing the vehicular death of a fellow member. It takes the dim but determined Arnie until the last reel to clear his name, nail the actual culprit, and reclaim former squeeze Snowden. Frequent B leading man Halsey costars as another Road Devil, but the show belongs to Hartunian, who brings surprising depth to his knuckle-walking role. Much superior to the tame 1956 track flick *Hot Rod Girl* (Goodtimes), with Lori Nelson and Chuck Connors.

IVY LEAGUE KILLERS (1962) B&W **1/2

D: William Davidson. Don Borisenko, Don Francks, Barbara Bricker, Jean Templeton, Barry Lavender. Introducing Ivors Gavon singing "Get Hep" and "Easy Rider." 69 mins. (Sinister Cinema)

A genuine biker movie from up Canada way—sort of a "Mild Angels"—*Ivy League Killers* finds fairly harmless Harley hounds (they even listen to folk music!) led by a mannered Borisenko (who was obviously taking his James Dean *and* Marlon Brando pills) mixing it up with an overaged preppie psycho (Francks). Francks and his pals later pull a heist that leads to murder and implicate Don B. and gang in the crime. Adding further complications is ingenue Bricker, a rich girl who falls for Don B., much to Don F.'s chagrin. A beach-set Hootenanny from Hell sequence supplies a time-capsule highlight—as long as you remember to turn the sound down.

JACKTOWN (1962) B&W **1/2

D: William Martin. Patty McCormack, Richard Meade, Douglas Rutherford, Mike Tancredi. 62 mins. (Something Weird)

Apparently lensed (by producer, writer, and director Martin) to further the glory of Michigan state authorities and the titular penal institution, *Jacktown* emerges as a short, if not especially sweet, cautionary fable featuring depressingly authentic locales on *both* sides of the prison walls. Lead Meade lends all the stiffness he can muster to his role as Frankie, a shiftless 21-year-old petty thief who draws a stretch in stir on a bogus statutory-rape charge—though *statuary* might be closer to it, since the actress portraying the underaged but consenting waitress he seduces is every bit Meade's equal in the petrified-perf department. In jail, Frankie's crime arouses the moral opprobrium of his fellow inmates. Fair-minded warden Rutherford plucks Frankie from this den of danger and assigns him to tend his garden. There Frankie encounters the warden's sweet young daughter (McCormack, apparently hard-up for work after her *Bad Seed* triumph), who develops an instant crush on the stoic lowlife. Noir, wild-youth, and Patty M. fans will want to see how it all sorts out. The pic incorporates newsreel footage of the then-infamous 1952 Jacktown riots.

KNIGHTS OF THE CITY (1986) **1/2

D: Dominic Orlando. Leon Isaac Kennedy, Nicholas Campbell, Michael Ansara, Janine Turner, Jeff Moldovan. 88 mins. (New World)

Our titular urban noblemen are your typical overaged, multiethnic rock-'n'-roll B-movie gang. Led by then-37-year-old (!) Kennedy (who also scripted), the Knights steal cars and play guitars, break-dance and bust heads with equal aplomb. As luck would have it, a seemingly ill-advised rumble with a rival outfit lands our heroes in jail, where they not only run into the Fat Boys (doing "Jailhouse Rap," natch) but meet a major-label mogul (all-purpose movie ethnic specialist Ansara). Soon the Knights are vying with other nabe rockers to win a talent contest that will send them first-rungward up the ladder of success. Given that the story line isn't exactly fresh, let alone def, *Knights of the City* could have been worse. The violence is surprisingly graphic; the rumbles and dances are well choreographed; Smokey Robinson and Denny Terrio turn in the best emotive moments of their motion-picture careers; and each scene finds the characters sporting a new set of colorful T-shirts (KILL 'EM ALL reads our fave). Even *Knights*'s end credits are livelier than most, listing three—count 'em— three dialogue coaches for Kennedy alone and a "production psychologist" (!). The jail sequence proved particularly prophetic, since the pic's exec producer, Michael Franzese, later landed in that very locale after pleading guilty to 65 counts of racketeering.

THE LIARS' CLUB (1993) ***

D: Jeffrey Porter. Wil Wheaton, Brian Krause, Soleil Moon Frye, Michael Cudlitz, Aron Eisenberg, Shevonne Durkin, Bruce Weitz. 91 mins. (New Horizons)

The most surprising thing about producer Roger Corman's slightly upscale knockoff of Tim Hunter's 1986 sleeper, *River's Edge* (see index), is that it's almost as well done as its model. Wheaton is believable in a variation on the Keanu Reeves role as a decent kid compelled to cover up the rape and subsequent slaying of a former classmate by two of his best friends (Krause, Cudlitz). *The Liars' Club* lacks the raging anomie of Hunter's loosely fact-based original, but this is a very tight, credibly acted, deftly scripted (by Jeff Yonis) and directed film in its own right, complete with a double-twist finale. *The Liar's Club*—like Adam Simon's *Brain Dead* and Katt Shea's *Dance of the Damned* before it—supports the contention that, as long as projects stay within budget, Corman doesn't mind if his hirelings get it right.

MASSACRE AT CENTRAL HIGH (1976) ***1/2

D: Rene Daalder. Andrew Stevens, Derrel Maury, Robert Carradine, Kimberly Beck. 85 mins. (MPI, n.i.d.)

Dutch émigré Daalder's horror-tinged high school *Death Wish* has acquired a strong cult rep over the years, and for good reason. What begins as a predictable nerds-versus-bullies plot takes several unexpected twists. Not at all the slasher flick its title suggests, *Massacre* is very definitely worth seeing. It's been ripped off several times, in *Dangerously Close, Summer Camp Nightmare* (New Line), *Heathers,* and *The Craft* (see index), to cite a few, but the original is still the greatest.

MENACE II SOCIETY (1993) ***

D: Albert and Allen Hughes. Tyrin Turner, Larenz Tate, Jada Pinkett, Bill Duke, Charles S. Dutton, Arnold Johnson, Samuel L. Jackson. 104 mins. (New Line) DVD

Despite their tender years, then-21-year-old twins Allen and Albert Hughes show they know what they're doing in their directorial debut. A *Boyz N the Hood* (Columbia/TriStar) variation that owes an equal debt to *Mean Streets, Menace* follows drifting South Central youth Turner (in the Harvey Keitel role) and his wired bud Tate (in the De Niro part) over the course of a crossroads summer. Aided by Tyger Williams's strong script and expert perfs from the entire cast (including Arnold [*Putney Swope*] Johnson as Turner's Bible-quoting grandfather), the Hughes brothers capture the randomness, boredom, and bursts of sudden violence that characterize L.A.-ghetto gang life. Despite a forced ending, *Menace II Society* shapes up as an effective blend of social drama and exploitation.

MOTORCYCLE GANG (1957) B&W **1/2

D: Edward L. Cahn. Anne Neyland, John Ashley, Steven Terrell, Carl ("Alfalfa") Switzer, Russ Bender, Raymond Hatton. 78 mins. (Columbia/TriStar)

Good guy Terrell and bad kid Ashley fight over Neyland in a flick that largely rehashes *Dragstrip Girl*, with cycles subbing for hot rods. In a *Wild One* twist, Ashley and his hog hench-teens terrorize a small town and its few inhabitants (extras cost money, and this *was* AIP, after all) until Terrell and pals arrive to bust it up: Former *Our Gang/Little Rascals* stalwart Carl Switzer (Alfalfa) surfaces here as Terrell's over-aged comic-relief sidekick. Like many former Tinseltown tykes, Switzer had little luck in landing decent adult roles. Of his handful of later films, the brooding 1954 Robert Mitchum western *Track of the Cat* (n/a) was easily the most bizarre—there, the then-27-year-old Switzer appeared as a silent, nonagenarian Native American (!). *Motorcycle Gang* proved to be one of the former Cowlick Kid's final films; in 1959, at age 33, he was fatally shot during an argument over—according to Mark Voger's *Asbury Park Press* interview with Switzer's fellow Rascal Spanky McFarland—a $50 reward posted for a lost dog.

THE NARCOTICS STORY (1958) ***

D: Robert W. Larsen. Sharon Strand, Darlene Hendricks, Herbert Crisp, Fred Marratto, Allen Pitt. 75 mins. (Something Weird)

A "Police Science" production, *The Narcotics Story* boasts the unique distinction of being the only theatrically released exploitation pic produced as an actual police training film. Using a *Dragnet*-styled framework and a matter-of-fact voice-over, the flick dramatizes controlled-substance dealing and use in the shabby pads, shady malt shops, and seamy back alleys of a small California city. According to Something Weird's press release, *Narcotics Story*'s initial L.A. bookings sparked controversy over whether the film should be screened for "nonprofessionals," since it doggedly violates every antidrug sanction of the Motion Picture Code with its detailed look at the preparation and injection of heroin. This fascinating, verité-styled one-of-a-kind convergence of law-enforcement documentary and pure sleaze rates as a must for couchside criminologists and camp followers alike.

NEW JERSEY DRIVE   (1995) ***

D: Nick Gomez. Sharron Corley, Gabriel Casseus, Saul Stein, Gwen McGee, Andre Moore, Donald Adeosun Faison. 98 mins. (Universal) DVD

East Coast indie auteur Gomez follows his funky Brooklyn-based *Laws of Gravity* (see index) with this Newark-set study of aimless black teens on an auto-theft binge. While slicker than *Laws,* with significantly augmented production values, *New Jersey Drive* reflects the same semi-improvisational, verité-style ensemble approach Gomez took with his earlier film. Here he concentrates on high-schooler Corley, who, after a couple of busts and a harassment campaign conducted by corrupt cop Stein, begins to lose his enthusiasm for the joy-riding exploits that often lead to injury, arrest, and, in the case of one friend, death. Gomez admirably avoids both cheap exploitation moves and conventional knee-jerk moralizing, preferring to let viewers draw their own conclusions.

OVER THE EDGE   (1979) ***

D: Jonathan Kaplan. Matt Dillon, Michael Kramer, Pamela Ludwig. 95 mins. (Warner)

Kaplan's look at teen anomie in a sterile suburban setting is not only a worthy flick in its own right, but it anticipated such similarly themed tract-house tragedies as *subUrbia* (Vestron), *Out of the Blue,* and *River's Edge* (see index).

POT, PARENTS, AND POLICE (1971) **½

D: Phillip Pine. Phillip Pine, Robert Mantell, Madelyn Keen, Arthur Batanides, Martin Margulies, Dawn Frame. 90 mins. (Something Wierd)

Produced, written, and directed by veteran character actor Pine, who also costars, *Pot, Parents, and Police* (originally *The Cat Ate the Parakeet*) was specifically geared to play the abortive Jerry Lewis Cinemas circuit, protoplexes designed to screen family-friendly fare. According to a lengthy postfilm interview host Johnny Legend conducts with Pine, hundreds of JLC theaters were built in malls across America, but most folded within months. (Ironically enough, many of these family-targeted screens were later leased as mini porn palaces!) *Pot, Parents, and Police* never made it past a few Indiana drive-ins near James Dean's birthplace, where Pine parlayed his onetime friendship with the famed Causeless Rebel to lure a few crowds. *Pot*'s paucity of takers arrives as scant surprise, since there was absolutely no conceivable audience for it—not on this planet, at least.

Our totally grotty tale charts the misadventures of a dysfunctional California-'burb family. Goofy 13-year-old Johnny (Mantell) suffers recurring nightmares of his dad, traveling sales rep Pine, burning him alive (!). Dad, in turn, bemoans the fact that he can't seem to communicate with his dense offspring. *Pot*'s scant plot finds Johnny hooking up with a reefer-toking couple (including a young Johnny Legend himself, acting under his real name, Martin Margulies). After ingesting too much grass and wine, Johnny's deposited at a bus stop, where he's found by under-standing cop Arthur (*The Unearthly*) Batanides. This leads to further communication breakdowns with Pop Pine and Johnny's return flight to the hippies' pad, where Legend/Margulies, high on mescaline, performs a scene-stealing "Look, I'm a bird!" routine and threatens to leap out a window (he compromises by falling down the stairs instead). Something Weird presents *PP&P* in a gala letter-boxed edition, the better to appreciate director Pine's efforts to enliven a flick in which little happens (and still less makes sense) via split-screen, freeze-frame, and other then-popular techniques. (There's even a clip that appears twice—at least one of those times out of sequence.) If lensed today, Johnny and family would doubtless be the center of an edgy black comedy rather than a mixed-up morality drama. (Hopefully, no remake's in the offing.) Still, between the off-the-wall film and the subsequent interview, SWV's video makes for fascinating viewing for weird-artifact aficionados.

THE PRIME TIME   (1960) B&W **

D: H. G. Lewis. JoAnn LeCompte, Frank Roche, James Brooks, Karen Black, Ray Gronwald. 76 mins. (Something Weird)

Black makes her screen debut in this 1960 youth exposé, as one of several reckless bimbos who hang at the Golden Goose Lounge waiting for a chance to squander the best years of their lives (i.e., the prime time) posing for a local Beat painter called "The Beard," who likes to answer his phone with the way-cool greeting, "Who disturbs?" He's also heard to remark, "I don't like fresh air, fresh milk, or fresh kids—and you stink of all of them." Perhaps the best line, though, belongs to the bitter teen who declares, "You're not dating *me,* you're dating my *car*!" A catfight and fleeting nudity supply other eye-blink highlights.

REBEL WITHOUT A CAUSE (1955) ***1/2

D: Nicholas Ray. James Dean, Natalie Wood, Sal Mineo. 111 mins. (Warner) DVD

Ray's classic tale of troubled 'burb teens, further elevated by Dean's peerless performance, helped define an entire generation and, along with its funky urban counterpart of the same year, Richard Brooks's *Blackboard Jungle* (MGM), jump-started the '50s wild-youth genre.

RIPE (1997) **

D: Mo Ogrodnik. Monica Keena, Daisy Eagan, Gordon Currie, Ron Brice, Karen Lynn Gorney. 93 mins. (Trimark)

Yet another twisted tale of teenettes who drift into violence (see also *Heavenly Creatures* and *Fun*), writer/director Ogrodnik's indie offers strong perfs by the young leads and an authentic atmosphere but comes up short in the story and credibility departments. After their worthless parents expire in a car crash, fraternal twin sisters Violet (Keena) and Rosie (Eagan) hit the road, ending up as sort of jailbait mascots at a remote, beat-out southern military base, where they move in with slovenly civilian handyman Currie. The rest of the pic charts their picaresque "progress," as the foxy Violet takes up with Currie while oft antisocial sis Ros'e receives gruff emotional support from avuncular drill sergeant Brice (who also teaches her how to shoot, a skill you know will be utilized before film's end). Ogrodnik steers her meandering story in an ultimately trite direction that undermines much of its earlier aura of tattered authenticity.

RIVER'S EDGE (1986) ***1/2

D: Tim Hunter. Keanu Reeves, Crispin Glover, Ione Skye Leitch, Daniel Roebuck, Dennis Hopper, Roxana Zal. 99 mins. (New Line) DVD

Based partly on a true incident wherein a Milpitas, California, high-schooler murdered his girlfriend and invited classmates to view the evidence over the course of several days, *River's Edge* is a funny, chilling chronicle of local teens' reactions (and nonreactions) to a similarly senseless killing perpetrated by alienated, overweight Samson (Roebuck). Glover excels (and accelerates) as Samson's speed-freak friend Layne, who desperately attempts to cover up the crime and protect his largely indifferent bud in a bid to give his own life—which is literally going nowhere fast—a hit of meaning. ("I feel like I'm in a Chuck Norris movie!" he excitedly confides to a cohort.) Reeves is likewise strong as the confused but basically decent Matt, who decides the slaying shouldn't go unpunished. *River's Edge* presents a compelling portrait of kids brought up on a nonnutritional diet of fast food and cheap prefab media-driven dreams. Hopper as a one-legged ex-biker and his faithful inflato doll, Ellie, meanwhile, easily copped The Phantom's 1986 Celluloid Couple of the Year honors. For a Mondo Milpitas double bill, scope out the 1975 amateur-night horror *The Milpitas Monster* (VCI).

ROADRACERS (1994) ***

D: Robert Rodriguez. David Arquette, Salma Hayek, William Sadler, John Hawkes, Jason Wiles, O'Neal Compton, Kevin McCarthy. 94 mins. (Dimension)

Roadracers represents director Robert (*Desperado, From Dusk Till Dawn*) Rodriguez's first pro feature following his impressive indie debut, *El Mariachi,* and the first of Showtime Cable-TV's 1994 *Rebel Highway* series to reach homevideo. Rodriguez wisely lifts little from the original (1958) *Roadracers* beyond the title; instead of remaking a routine teen race-car caper, he assembles a highly stylized, over-the-top, tongue-in-cheek tribute to the '50s "cool" ethos, where the constant creak of leather jackets and the audio-enhanced hiss of matches igniting dangling cigarettes vie for the audience's auditory attention with a rumbling Link Wray–dominated instrumental soundtrack. Future *Scream* costar Arquette goes all the way in his portrayal of guitar-playing, grease-caked nicotine fiend and diehard rebel "Dude," while Hayek offers somewhat more subdued work as his Mexican squeeze. Dude encounters opposition from town punk Wiles and the latter's bent-macho lawman dad (Sadler) while harboring a dream to join a local rockabilly band (led by real-life rocker Johnny Reno). Film homages play a major role here. In one scene, Dude's cinema-obsessed sidekick (Hawkes) convinces his friend to join him for an *Invasion of the Body Snatchers* showing, where original *Invasion* star Kevin McCarthy puts in an amusing cameo as a mysterious theater patron. A skating-rink sequence references Jack Hill's influential trashfest *Switchblade Sisters.* A contrived violent climax mars the mood a mite, but Rodriguez's gleeful sense of deconstructionist fun is fairly contagious for most of *Roadracers*'s wild run.

ROCK ALL NIGHT (1957) B&W ***

D: Roger Corman. Dick Miller, Abby Dalton, Russell Johnson, Bruno VeSota, Barboura Morris, Mel Welles. 62 mins. (Columbia/TriStar)

Authentically sawed-off AIP icon Miller plays Shorty, a pint-sized rebel with an attitude (he hates taller dudes, which includes nearly everyone) who hangs at the rock club Cloud Nine and eventually outwits two killers (including *Gilligan's Island*'s Johnson) who take refuge therein. Corman shot this hip quickie in five days on one set, but it's one of his best wild-youth efforts. The Platters and the Blockbusters provide musical accompaniment. *Little Shop of Horrors* author Charles B. Griffith penned the script.

ROMPER STOMPER (1992) ***

D: Geoffrey Wright. Russell Crowe, Daniel Pollock, Jacqueline McKenzie, Alex Scott. 88 mins. In R and unrated editions. (Academy n.i.d.)

Sort of an Australian *Clockwork Orange* Meets Penelope Spheeris's *Suburbia*, Wright's debut feature is a bleak but ultimately traditional urban actioner that tracks a gang of white-supremacist Melbourne skinheads on their self- and other-destructive lowlife rounds. The film focuses on leader/theoretician Hando (Crowe) and his best bud, the taciturn, somewhat more decent Davey (Pollock), as they bond, booze, brawl, and stage mindless racist raids against the city's Asian emigrants. The skins' downfall begins when an Asian family purchases the gang's fave pub. A brutal, all-out street battle ensues, reducing the skinheads' active ranks by half. Further trouble arrives in the form of neurotic, pill-popping, game-playing rich girl Gabe (McKenzie), who floats from the indifferent Hando to the appreciative Davey and leads the gang's remnants on an assault against her wealthy, incestuous filmmaker father's (Scott) manse. Writer/director Wright, working with a credible cast, manages to evoke interest in, if not sympathy for, his hopeless, dead-end characters, who are too dim and tunnel-visioned even to protect themselves from their Asian targets, the police, or Gabe's selfish, vengeful agenda. While Wright is meticulous in nailing down the details of the skinhead lifestyle—complete with its own twisted philosophy and rock-'n'-roll anthems—*Romper Stomper* is less a social document than a pointed, pol-

ished exploitation film in the Down Under tradition of *Mad Max, Shame, Vicious!*, and numerous other bashfests. The violence level, though high, doesn't approach mainstream Hollywood genre movies, and *Romper Stomper*'s original NC-17 theatrical rating seemed unwarranted in that context.

17 AND UNDER (1998) ***

D: Gregory William Morgan. Cesar Herrera, Sunny Lombardo, Rodrigo Obregón, Lena Gallegos, M. Lee White. 108 mins. (Spectrum)

Morgan's excellent indie is a complex urban fable dealing with such wide-ranging themes as bereavement, atonement, justice, and redemption. Young Herrera leads a cast of mostly unknown but effective thesps as Juan Sanchez, a 17-year-old convicted murderer given a last chance at normal life under a new California juvenile-offender law. The final phase of Juan's rehabilitation requires him to spend six months with a volunteer "bereavement family," a family that's lost a youthful member to gang violence. Director/cowriter Morgan charts Juan's experiences with the Romeros, a successful ex-barrio clan now comfortably ensconced in the suburbs, whose college-bound son was senselessly slain by a high school gangbanger. Hardworking patriarch Tom Romero (frequent Andy Sidaris action-movie villain Obregón, strong in a rare straight dramatic role) is openly hostile to Juan, while mother Maria (Gallegos) is friendly but consumed with grief, and somewhat unstable teen daughter Kate (Lombardo) develops a gradual, complicated crush on the newcomer. Morgan intercuts Juan's new home life with other aspects of his moral rehab, involving a hard-nosed but well-meaning teacher (White), flashbacks to his earlier turmoil, and scenes of the barrio he's temporarily left behind. What could easily have played out as a rote issue-of-the-

week TV movie instead evolves into a subtle, poignant drama that stresses that the consequences of violence are eternal for those responsible for, and suffering from, the permanent loss it inflicts.

SHOPPING (1994) **1/2

D: Paul Anderson. Sadie Frost, Jude Law, Sean Pertwee, Jonathan Pryce, Fraser James, Sean Bean, Marianne Faithfull, Danny Newman. 86 mins. (New Horizons)

Sort of a Brit variation on Nick Gomez's *New Jersey Drive, Shopping* chronicles the aimlessly destructive ways of youths who snatch cars and trash malls for status and kicks, while what appears to be the world's most pathetic police force either gives futile chase or runs for cover. After an impressive opening aerial view of spreading industrial squalor, a familiar story line emerges—rebel hero Law, semi-squeeze Frost, and mates James and Newman decide to pull one last stunt before abandoning their pointless pursuit. Pryce appears sporadically as a police inspector, while Pertwee turns in the best work as a professional thief who resents Law's amateur approach. Director Anderson betrays his *Mortal Kombat* roots when he intercuts the vehicular chase scenes with tableaux from a "Crazy Cars" video game.

SWITCHBLADE SISTERS (1975) ***

D: Jack Hill. Robbie Lee, Joanne Nail, Monica Gayle, Kitty Bruce, Asher Brauner, Monica Clark, Michael Miller. 91 mins. (Miramax) DVD

Thanks to the mighty Quentin Tarantino's Rolling Thunder branch of Miramax, Hill's camp classic *Switchblade Sisters* received a first-class theatrical resurrection in 1996, scoring the attention that had passed it by during its humble initial run two decades earlier. The flick rates as a high-energy exercise in Trash with your proverbial capital *T*. Hill lets us know what's on his mind in the film's very first shot: a still life of two back-alley trash cans (!). (We later learn, via an on-screen tabloid headline, that the entire flick unfolds during a "12-Week Garbage Strike.") Our story involves factional struggles that break out within the ranks of the dread Silver Daggers, led by Brauner—as sexy teen leader Lee (a Shirley Temple–voiced 'burbette who contributes one of *the* classic bad turns in genre history) sees her exalted position challenged by newcomer Nail. Hill takes a kitchen-sink approach to this exploitation gem, tossing in punch-ups, catfights, shoot-outs (including one at a crowded roller rink), switchblade duels, rampaging homemade tanks (!), sadistic lesbian prison matrons, and gratuitous nudity galore. He even incorporates a feminist message of sorts when the debs split from their male counterparts to form their own, all-girl guerrilla unit, the Jezebels, and forge an alliance with a distaff Black Power cell headed by Clark. Kitty (Daughter of Lenny) Bruce volunteers a memorable stint as Donut, a plump, passive deb who, in the course of our drama, is forced to give one of the best squealing-pig imitations captured on celluloid since Ned Beatty's legendary porcine performance in *Deliverance*.

TEENAGE BONNIE & KLEPTO CLYDE (1993) *1/2

D: John Shepphird. Maureen Flannigan, Scott Wolf, Bentley Mitchum, Tom Power, Don Novello, Jeffrey Olson. 90 mins. (Vidmark)

It would be hard to imagine a less convincing pair than Wolf and Flannigan as "alienated" teens who embark on a full-scale crime wave. Not for a nanosecond do we believe that these terminally edgeless kids could even cut school with a clear conscience, let alone blow away bank guards. Producer Menaham Golan, apparently determined to cover all perceived teen-culture bases, refuses to relinquish his movie's mindlessly cheerful tone (a bad "Woolly Bully" rip-off is endlessly repeated) even as our wild youths rob and kill to juice up their jaded sex lives (!). Former Father Guido Sarducci Novello is wasted in a straight cop role. And yes, B&C get theirs in slo mo just like in the "real" *Bonnie and Clyde*.

TEENAGE DOLL (1957) B&W ***1/2

D: Roger Corman. June Kenney, Fay Spain, John Brinkley, Collette Jackson, Barbara Wilson, Ziva Rodann, Sandy Smith, Barboura Morris, Richard Devon, Jay Sayer, Richard Cutting, Dorothy Neumann, Ed Nelson, Bruno VeSota. 71 mins. (Englewood)

Englewood unearths and beautifully packages a rough gem with Corman's ambitious juvenile-delinquent opus *Teenage Doll*. Unlike such relatively wholesome West Coast–flavored troubled-youth pics, like AIP's *Dragstrip Girl* and *Hot Rod Gang*, this Allied Artists production—penned by talented Corman collaborator Charles B. (*Little Shop of Horrors*) Griffith—represents a dark, downbeat descent into true Gritty City turf. Following a terrific, almost Edward Gorey–like illustrated title sequence, the flick opens with a classic noir image: An impervious Chicano kitchen worker empties a pan of dishwater into a back alley, unwittingly splashing the twisted corpse of a blond teenette. The dead girl is soon discovered by five fellow members of her gang, the Black Widows, sister aggregate of the male Tarantulas. The vengeance-bent gals—who include ever fetching Israeli actress Ziva Rodann (misspelled in the credits as "Rodan," as in Toho's famed winged monster) as Chicana teen "Squirrel," complete with a long black braid and an accent that's uncertain at best—know the culprit is Kenney, a middle-class "good girl" whose crush on rival Vandals gang leader (Brinkley) has unwisely led her across the metaphorical tracks. Black Widow leader Spain instructs each of her charges to go home and return with enough cash and valuables to bribe Brinkley into ratting out the elusive Kenney, a clever device that allows us intimate entry into the girls' individual (and mostly broken) homes. One of the gals lives in a newspaper-strewn dump with a neglected baby sister she addresses as "Slob," a dirty-faced, nearly feral five-year-old first seen seated on the floor gnawing on a piece of cardboard (!), an image that takes us into contempo Harmony (*Kids, Gummo*) Korine territory. Another Black Widow has a querulous heart-to-heart with her older sis (an excellent Morris), who's dating her wormy boss as part of her plan to flee "uptown." Kenney, meanwhile—whom we learn killed the late Black Widow purely in self-defense—enjoys an oddball domestic scene of her own, with a strict but cryptic white-collar dad and a wacked-out mater straight out of a John Waters flick, dressed in a juvenile ensemble topped by an outsized girlish bow. Mom, it seems, has yet to recover from her ill-fated affair with a bootlegger back in 1921 (!) and wistfully advises daughter Kenney, "Maybe someday *you'll* meet a man like that. You'll know he's cheap and worthless and treacherous, but you won't care. You'll do anything he wants, at any time, and be glad for the chance to do it." Withal, *Teenage Doll* rates as a riveting example of top-shelf trash art that also delivers the exploitation goods, including an all-out climactic rumble set in an auto graveyard.

TEENAGE PSYCHO KILLER (A.K.A. *TEENAGE PASSION*) (1970) ***1/2

D: Murray Markowitz. Andrew Skidd, Robb Judd, Karen Martin. 84 mins. (Something Weird)

Something Weird rescues this riveting Canadian courtroom drama, based on an actual 1959 case, from undeserved oblivion. When the body of a raped and strangled teenage girl is found dumped in the woods, circumstantial evidence points to her would-be beau, 14-year-old John (Skidd, in a convincing performance). Since the victim was the daughter of one of the town's most influential citizens, John barely stands a chance of proving his innocence, particularly when police confine their investigation to building a case against the kid instead of seriously exploring other possible leads. Frank but free of sensationalism, *Teenage Psycho Killer* is reminiscent of the earlier, equally excellent Canada-set Brit drama *Never Take Candy From a Stranger* (see index).

THE TRIP   (1967) ***

D: Roger Corman. Peter Fonda, Susan Strasberg, Bruce Dern, Dennis Hopper. 85 mins. (Vestron, n.i.d.)

Hippie Dern lays his trip on commercial director Fonda, who roams through forest sets left over from Corman's Poe movies and takes time out to dig an orange's aura. Heavy. The laundromat scene's the topper here.

THE WARRIORS   (1979) **1/2

D: Walter Hill. Michael Beck, James Remar, Thomas Waites. 94 mins. (Paramount)

Hill's stylized gang-war epic sparked riots and critical controversy during its initial release. You may find yourself slashing your couch with a switchblade as you watch the embattled title aggregate "bop" their way from the Bronx to Brooklyn. Remar impresses as an especially animalistic youth. Released the same year as Philip Kaufman's adaptation of Richard Price's early-'60s-set gang novel *The Wanderers* (Warner).

WILD IN THE STREETS   (1968) **1/2

D: Barry Shear. Christopher Jones, Shelley Winters, Diane Varsi, Richard Pryor. 97 mins. (HBO)

An overrated but still-essential youth fable from the deep thinkers at AIP, *Wild in the Streets* stars Jones as a rock idol who's elected president and subsequently consigns over-35ers to LSD camps (!). Boomers who found it funny 30-plus years ago may not be laughing now.

THE GREAT 1960 SUMMER BIJOU BINGE:

How The Phantom Got That Way

For some reason, 1960 shaped up as our marathon movie summer. Maybe it was a run of bad weather. Or a lust to cash in on under-12 prices while we still had the chance; we were, to a kid, notorious cheapskates, and on fixed incomes (not the best consumer combo). But the real reason, I suspect in retrospect, lay in the recent devastating loss of our true local bijou, the Belaire, just two blocks from our street in Hollis, Queens.

Nearly all the nabe kids went to the Belaire, but none as religiously as Steve and Fat Tommy and I. Movies were our mission, our passion, our bond. We knew we didn't quite fit in with the greater local kid network; we weren't big on sports or other active-type pursuits. I had asthma (luckily confined largely to the school year); Fat Tommy not only lived up to his name but wore a greasy, ersatz-Elvis pompadour; and Steve, though innately hip, was nearly two years our junior and small for his age. The movies kept us off the streets, where it was generally wholesome, and out of our homes, where it was frequently not.

We would try, in the freedom-and-heat-enhanced summer months, to catch every worthy show at the Belaire, as well as sample the area's four other, farther-flung theaters. We'd not only sit through the double feature, but if the first flick hooked us, we'd stay to watch it again; if either film rated as *great,* we'd go back the next day and, finances permitting, the one after that.

We'd often flash back to *our* last picture show, December '59. Though the previous summer hadn't, by our consensus, shaped up as a primo bijou season, we'd still snared our share of cool movies. We were *Famous Monsters of Filmland* kids, so horror films ranked as our top priority (though action, sci-fi, westerns, and Jerry Lewis comedies likewise demanded our attention and dough). *The Alligator People, The Mysterians,* and *The Mummy* had all drifted through, so it had been far from a total wash. But, as always, fall and school necessitated a radical change in our bijou-going habits. And the colder it got, the less willing we were to brave the frigid hikes to more distant theaters. So it was Saturday matinee at the Belaire, or it was nothing at all.

Sometimes we chose nothing at all over catching a dull double feature (e.g., mainstream musicals, serious dramas, the odd foreign film, anything with Doris Day). That infamous December Saturday, we debated all morning whether to bijou or not to bijou. The main feature was *The Horse Soldiers.* John Wayne movies posed a major dilemma; the vaunted Duke reminded us too much of who our dads wished they were (and, in worst-case scenarios, pretended to be). On the other hand, *The Horse Soldiers* was a violent, action-packed Civil War picture, close enough to a western that we really had no choice, Wayne's lame swaggering presence notwithstanding.

They didn't hit us with the bad news until after the show let out. We were shivering outside the lobby when we noticed a cheesy, handwritten banner spread across *The Horse Soldiers*'s glass-enclosed poster:

LAST SHOWS TOMORROW/
THEATER CLOSING

Steve's narrow shoulders slumped; Tommy clutched his ample gut; I reached for my inhaler. We launched a collective warhead of outrage and denial before cooler emotions prevailed. By the time we reached our street, we'd convinced ourselves that it was closing only temporarily, for repairs or some other bogus reason.

We returned the next day. Now a handwritten sign said:

LAST SHOWS TODAY/
THEATER CLOSING

This was harder to dismiss. We debated paying our way in for one last look, but that sounded way too depressing. Besides, we still weren't quite ready to buy into the paranoid theory that there really could be no more Belaire. Still, instead of going home, we parked our butts on the theater stoop, moping under a chilly, fast-fading December sun, until the last thin crowd drifted out. The stragglers were trailed by the janitor, an older black guy we'd never noticed before. He swept up, then unlocked the glass cases and began removing the posters.

"What's it mean by 'closed'?" I finally asked.

"Closed means closed," he said. "That's the last show here."

"But that doesn't mean it's for good," Steve insisted.

"Yeah," added Tommy, with impeccable logic. "That wouldn't be fair."

The janitor seemed like a guy who was used to disappointments, though not entirely immune to them. "It's not up to *me*." He shrugged. "Hell, I'm out a job." Rolling up the last of the posters, he easily read our minds. "I'd give you boys these, but you gotta know Mr. O'Leary."

We knew Mr. O'Leary, the Belaire's wormy manager; he must have slipped out the back like the little coward we took him to be. The janitor disappeared inside, locked the lobby doors behind him. A moment later the marquee went dark. So did we.

We missed the Belaire even more as the virtually movieless winter months wore on. Our nostalgia for our vanished bijou grew so extreme we even missed the mega-annoying Mr. O'Leary. Sort of a cross between Barry Fitzgerald and Percy Helton, Mr. O'Leary liked to roam the matinee aisles before the first feature came on. "I don't know what kind of parents would let their kids see trash like this," he used to muse aloud, although he obviously didn't object to taking our—*their*—money. (Besides, he knew full well what kind of parents we had; in his extracurricular activity as a church usher, he also collected their hard-earned when he passed the plate around.) Then, when the lights dimmed and the screen brightened, Mr. O'Leary, like a sawed-off warden, would turn us over to the grim, flashlight-wielding guards—the matrons—and the riot would begin on cue. We forced ourselves to participate peripherally, just to save face with the other kids, but mostly we sat and merged with the movie.

Over that winter, we'd sometimes walk over and watch the orphaned theater's noisy makeover into a 32-lane bowling alley. By the time spring showed up, we had slipped into an unhealthy nostalgia, reminiscing about the past delights the Belaire had brought us:

"We weren't emancipated enough to proceed either west, where it was said to be seedy, or underground to Manhattan, where it was rumored to be dangerous and decadent."
Photo © Kino International Corporation 1999

Christopher Lee's melting face in *Horror of Dracula,* the outsized ocular orbs emerging from radioactive alpine clouds in *The Crawling Eye,* and, going *way* back to our earliest days, the climatic id rampage in *Forbidden Planet.* Memories to die, or at least pine, for.

Fortunately for us, when summer finally arrived and school, like some Brigadoon from hell, retreated into the infernal mist, there were still those four other theaters within (long) walking distance. That summer we vowed to hit 'em all.

Our mission kicked off to a bright start. We trekked 15 blocks east up Jamaica Avenue to the cavernous, well-kept Queens to swoon over *Brides of Dracula,* with its bounteous bevy of bloodsucking beauties. We cut three blocks west to the less grandiose Community, where *Circus of Horrors* supplied us with a surfeit of thrills (from the neat knife-throwing scene to Donald Pleasence's doomed dance with an angry bear) *and* left us humming the melody to the hauntingly contrapuntal theme song, "Look for a Star." We headed a half mile north to the Hollis to enter the *House of Usher,* where a tormented Vincent Price did his hammy best to entertain us.

The only theater left in walking distance, about 20 blocks south across the tracks, was the funky old Island, the one that most resembled the extinct Belaire. Like our late, lamented bijou, the Island was a stripped-down affair with maybe 600 seats (most of them torn, a few repaired with plastic tape), antique ice cream and soft-drink machines, and a great dank aroma of musty rugs embedded with the ghosts of trampled popcorn past. Despite the evocative similarity, I wasn't crazy about going there—not so much because of the distance but because of the route. There was no way to get to the Island without passing the alfresco HQ—a small, crowded triangular park—of the eponymous Triangle Gang. The Triangles themselves, in their mid-to-late teens, were too busy listening to their tinny transistors, tossing back Boone's Farm, making out with their debs, and planning future turf wars to waste their time harassing punks like us. But surlier, less engaged members of the gang's junior division, the Little Triangles, some as young as 11, would sometimes intercept us. Usually they just wanted to talk privately with Steve, while Fat Tommy and I hung back, feeling sort of gratefully unwanted. Which is exactly what happened on this occasion, nearly making us late for the show.

We received our first shock even before we entered the Island when we encountered creepy Mr. O'Leary. He was working the weekday-matinee shift at the ticket booth, an indignity he'd never suffered during his Belaire tenure. He didn't seem especially glad to see us, though as always he was happy enough to take our money.

"Aren't you boys a little far from home?" he inquired in his best Percy Helton cackle. "Still watching the same kind of trash, I see."

"Still showing it," noted Steve, cocky from his Little Triangles flirtation.

The trash in question turned out to be *Black Sunday*. With its refreshingly unhealthy atmosphere, the provocative presence of sepulchral seductress Barbara Steele, and that supremely scary opening sequence, it quickly spider-crawled to the top of our nascent summer-1960 faves list. We suffered through a boring, badly dubbed sword-and-sandal second feature to watch *Black Sunday* again.

Outside, the sensual blast of summer heat and blinding sunshine sent shock waves through our air-conditioned bodies, a sensation that had become, over that summer, an addiction unto itself.

"The best part was when they nailed the mask into her face," I put forward.

"No," said Steve, "the best part was the way her face looked when they dug her up."

"It was the bat," Tommy insisted, "flapping around the tomb."

We continued to regress on the long walk home, reenacting bits from the flick. All of us wanted to be the executioner. After some heated discussion, Steve and I agreed to share the role. Tommy got to be his precious bat. Steve and I took turns pretending to nail the mask into his face.

It was also on the walk back that Steve and I first noticed a strange change in Tommy. Steve was still going on about Barbara Steele. "She's like really scary and sexy all at the same time. *Damn!*" he added for emphasis. Without warning, Tommy went nuts. The air seemed to go out of him, accompanied by a low exhaust sound. Then he collapsed into an almost zombielike trance, moving his chunky body in slow, agitated circles while chanting "Sin! Sin! Sin!" At first we laughed and chanted "Sin!" back at him. But when he kept it up, seemingly beyond his own control, Steve and I grew honestly scared. Were these the wages of two helpings of *Black Sunday*? The onset of early puberty? Summer Catholic-school withdrawal?

Eventually, Tommy calmed down, and we asked him in earnest if he was all right. "It's a sin to say bad words," he explained with a kind of measured urgency. "You'll burn in hell forever." Okay. We made a point of not provoking him again that day but filed the outburst away for possible future use against him should he ever tick us off.

While Tommy returned to normal, financing our bijou binge was becoming a major problem. Even cutting back on our other expenditures—baseball cards, comic books, rock-'n'-roll records, unhealthy snacks (Tommy had the hardest time here)—we were rapidly tapping out our meager allowances. So we hatched an entrepreneurial plan to collect empty bottles and trade them in for their 2-cent deposits (a quart container netted a whole nickel). We'd make our rounds in the A.M. before the theaters opened, usually finishing at the nearby Kent Dry Cleaners at lunch hour, where we routinely bagged our biggest haul of the day. Even though the mostly black and Hispanic workers were probably laboring for minimum wage, we hounded them relentlessly, even guilting those reluctant parties into surrendering their empties. (The whole *world* owed us its empties, is how we felt.) After cashing in our cache at King Kullen, we'd have over a dollar, sometimes two, enough to expand our celluloid horizons.

A 15-cent bus ride would take us into Jamaica, *the* downtown of Queens, where, under rattling El tracks, three additional theaters flourished. First was the Valencia, the borough's reigning picture palace, complete with ornate balcony and starry ceiling. Directly across the street stood the humbler Alden, known for its eclectic double bills, and four blocks west, the fairly nondescript Merrick. It was midway through that summer that we also discovered the Eighth Wonder of our Bijou World, the triple-feature Savoy.

The theater had no doubt been operating for years, virtually under our very noses, a few blocks south of Parsons Boulevard. But Parsons had marked the end of our known universe, at least the one we were allowed to travel as independent entities, unburdened by adults. The bus from Hollis made its final stop at the Parsons subway station; we weren't emancipated enough to proceed either west, where it was said to be seedy, or underground to Manhattan, where it was rumored to be dangerous and decadent. Thus, no sign of any Savoy.

As it turned out, *I* located the Savoy in the *Long Island Press* movie listings. Normally I monitored only those bijous already known to us, but the triple feature—three films not playing anywhere else, one of whose titles was new even to me (in addition to being a *Famous Monsters of Filmland* kid, I was a precocious *Screen World* addict)—caught my eye. When I checked the address, a leaping of the heart ensued. It was only *three blocks* west of the end of the known world!

It took some persuading to get Steve and Tommy to go that extra mile. Two of the films playing the day of my discovery were *Little Caesar* and *Public Enemy,* antiques from the dawn of the sound era that had already aired their musty selves on television. First I pretended not to know they were old movies; but Tommy, no cinematic slouch himself, recognized the titles. Next I reminded them that *King Kong,* which we'd watched every night it it had played on Channel 9's "Million Dollar Movie," was almost as old, and had still become one of our all-time faves. Then I stressed the third feature, *The Brain Eaters,* which was practically new and, they had to agree, sounded undeniably must-see.

Mission accomplished. We took the bus in, braved the three blocks, where the nabe *did* take a further turn toward the shabby, and there spied the grandest sight of our young moviegoing lives: a crowded, rundown marquee announcing the three films *plus* SHORTS, CARTOON, NEWSREEL.

The Savoy shaped up as pure Time Warp City, a perfect match for its elderly attractions. In the decrepit but spacious, linoleum-floored lobby, six large cases, arranged with obvious TLC, contained posters for the current show, along with the next five slated triple bills. The theater proper, a former vaudeville house that dated back to the '20s, proved a sprawling fleapit paradise. Two prominent signs assured patrons that the theater came equipped with a state-of-the-art, VOICE OF THE THEATER sound system (state of the art in 1931). The Savoy had once housed more than a thousand seats, but several entire rows had since been ripped out. Still, so much available seating remained in the nearly deserted theater that it took us a few minutes to decide where to settle down. Finally, we opted for our usual spot, roughly tenth-row center.

Steve and Tommy groaned when the first flick, *Little Caesar,* opened with the Warner Brothers Vitaphone logo: "If it isn't a Vitaphone, it isn't a talkie." The frayed print jumped, a "motorboat" buzz blurred the soundtrack, and the story and acting struck us as old-fashioned. The pace picked up with the edgier *Public Enemy,* which arrived in better physical shape; even my jaded buds had to agree the gunplay and final scene, where a nearly mummified Cagney is delivered DOA to his unwitting mom's home, rated as cool in any era. The ancient sound system added a harsh edge to the relatively contemporary (1958) cheapie *The Brain Eaters* that somehow worked to the threadbare pic's advantage, though we all laughed at the sight of the titular aliens, mobile little furballs with pipe-cleaner antennae. Add the promised cartoon (a recent vintage "Droopy"), newsreel, boring short (a Montreal travelog!), and three sets of coming-attraction trailers, and we couldn't complain about not getting our 35 cents' worth.

It was during the last trailer that Tommy, perhaps weakened by five-plus hours of staring at that flickering screen, again began to unravel. The trailer was for the caper flick *Seven Thieves.* When a scantily clad Joan Collins went into a racy dance routine, Tommy started anxiously tapping his feet. A moment later, we heard a whispered chant of "Sin! Sin! Sin!" When the tapping and chanting gained sufficient volume to attract the attention of those few fellow patrons not dozing, I nudged Steve, who nodded and sprang nimbly to his feet. I whispered to Tommy, "It's getting pretty late. We oughtta split." Tommy snapped out of his trance, wriggled from his seat, and croaked an urgent "Okay."

The Savoy's unknown owner/manager, obviously an underappreciated buff, also went to the incredible trouble and expense of printing illustrated eight-page foldout pamphlets advertising the theater's next eight bills. Steve and I each grabbed one.

No thrilling blast of summer heat and sun greeted us when we hit the street; the long show had taken us into deep twilight. On the bus ride home, Steve and I studied the pamphlet, gravitating toward an especially lurid poster for something called *Macumba Love.* A silent Tommy sat across the way, looking distracted and slightly sweaty.

"*Macumba Love* starts next Tuesday," I noted. "I'm going."

"Me too," said Steve.

"No matter *what*?" I extracted his sworn promise.

"No matter *what,*" he emphatically replied.

No vote from Tommy, who turned openly sullen. "You guys go. It's probably a MOIP anyway."

He meant Morally Objectionable in Part. One of our fave pastimes was to scan the Legion of Decency film ratings that ran in *The Tablet* each Sunday, telling us what films we could and couldn't see. Our main interest focused on two areas—the Morally Objectionable in Part (or MOIP) list and the dread, enticing "Condemned" roster. Since mainstream studios respected the Legion's then-considerable clout, few of their titles cracked that latter, commercially harmful category. There were a few high-profile exceptions, like *The Moon Is Blue* (partly for its use of the word *virgin,* a term and status the religion was normally quite enamored of), *Baby Doll* (for its provocative Carroll Baker jailbait poster), and just about every Brigitte Bardot movie, her very name being synonymous with exotic sex and sin. Since the vast majority of newly released titles fell into the other categories, the Condemned docket boasted a static, in some cases seemingly eternal, quality with the same timeworn titles appearing week after week for years on end. Said titles burned into our pulpy brains with a permanence reserved for little other data, save maybe rock-'n'-roll trivia and baseball stats: What exactly *were The Sins of Mona Kent*? What forbidden secrets had been recorded by *The Savage Eye*? What was the sinister connection between *Wasted Lives* and *The Birth of Twins*? We feared we'd never know: These tantalizing titles never played our nabe theaters.

I couldn't wait to check out *Macumba Love* in the Sunday listings. Steve and I vowed to see it even if it *was* a Condemned, the risk of eternal damnation be damned; as it turned out, we couldn't find it listed anywhere.

"Maybe it's too hot even for the Condemned list," Steve excitedly decided.

"Maybe," I agreed, though privately I had my doubts.

Condemned or not, *Macumba Love* didn't disappoint. To our minds, the movie had everything—lush tropical setting, exotic calypso soundtrack, arcane voodoo rituals, dancing native girls, crowd-pleasing corpse-in-the-water and needle-in-the-eye scenes, and an all-around ambience of sultry, sunny sleaze. I fell in instant love with sexy Israeli starlet Ziva Rodann, cast as a randy local heiress; Steve felt equally passionate about blond June Wilkinson and her 48-inch Amazing Colossal Bust. We'd caught a lot of cool flicks over the past few weeks, but *Macumba Love* had to be *the* movie of the summer-'60 season.

We stopped by Tommy's house, eager to apprise him of what he'd missed, though we suspected it was probably a lost cause. He'd been a lot less fun all around over the last couple of weeks. He'd even stopped performing his fabled Elvis impersonation, where he would shake his girth and greasy pompadour while rocking out to "Hard-Headed Woman" and "Teddy Bear."

When he answered the door, we saw his pomp had been replaced by a grotty new crew cut.

"Who mowed your head?" asked Steve.

Tommy struck a huffy pose. "Maybe you never heard of keeping your scalp cool in the summer." Tommy wasn't losing his religion, but his sense of humor was fast going the way of all flesh.

"You just missed the coolest movie of the whole summer." Steve filled him in.

"I don't wanna hear it," said Tommy. Which, of course, only egged us on.

"There's this great human-sacrifice scene," I related. "You couldn't really see her tits exactly, but you could see she had no bra on."

"Shut up." Tommy cupped his hands to his ears. We obligingly upped the volume.

"And there's this blonde with the biggest ones anybody ever saw," added Steve.

I guess we went too far. Tommy slammed the screen door in our faces. We heard a faint chanting of "Sin! Sin! Sin!" as he receded into the house.

"Let's go back tomorrow," Steve suggested.

Macumba Love was playing only one more day; I agreed we definitely had to see it again before it vanished forever from our exotica-starved lives. For some reason, maybe due to local *Macumba* word of mouth, a larger-than-normal crowd of night-shift workers, dozing derelicts, and value shoppers on a break assembled for that Wednesday matinee. Though we'd seen it only once, Steve and I had the pic pretty much memorized. As it had the day before, *Macumba Love* opened with the same extended voodoo sequence playing under the credits. The nocturnal beach, the mesmerized drummers, bubbling cauldron, frenzied dancers, slithering snakes…

"Here it comes," whispered Steve.

The camera panned to a shapely native girl tied to a tree, her arms clasped over her clearly naked breasts. When the lens crept around to confirm her topless status, we heard a sudden commotion some distance behind us. The sounds, indistinguishable at first, coalesced into a single word endlessly repeated: "Sin! Sin! Sin!"

We turned with the rest of the crowd to find our worst suspicions confirmed: A crew-cut Tommy was moving in his slow, agitated circles, his chant growing loud enough to compete with the voodoo incantations shrieking from the crackly old sound system.

"Holy shit!" whistled Steve.

I could barely acknowledge the living nightmare unfolding in the back row. "We definitely don't *know* that jerk," I said.

Steve and I hunkered down in our seats as the Savoy's elderly security guard led a trembling Tommy into the lobby and, presumably, out into the light.

Tommy was pretty much out of our picture after that, but Steve and I caught many more slick flicks at the Savoy over the remainder of that summer: *The Tingler, The Fiend Who Walked the West, I Was a Teenage Frankenstein, Diary of a High School Bride,* and even the untamed, unashamed *Liane, Jungle Goddess* (where we lost our Condemned-list cherry for sure). But *The End* was drawing nigh, and not only because we were drifting into late August, with school looming on the horizon.

It happened the week before the new term began, when Steve turned 11. Nothing hot was shaking at the Savoy, so we decided to trek to the Island to catch *Gorgo* and *The Amazing Transparent Man*. On our way past the Triangle, a trio of gang-jacketed Little Triangles motioned Steve aside. I hung back, feeling even jerkier without Tommy around to share my nonentity status, while Steve and the three Little T's disappeared into the crowded park. A few minutes later, a sheepish Steve returned by his lonesome.

"You best go on ahead," he said. "I'll catch up with you later."

"But the show starts in ten minutes."

"I just got somethin' I gotta do with these guys for a little bit." He shrugged.

I reluctantly went on alone. Mr. O'Leary was working the ticket booth. For once he seemed happy to see me.

"I'm expecting the Three Musketeers," he cackled, "and all I get is the Lone Ranger."

A half hour into *The Amazing Transparent Man,* it became clear to me that Steve wasn't showing. It was already growing dark when I passed the Triangle on the way home. I spotted Steve, in an official LT gang jacket, hanging with a knot of Little Triangles. They were yukking it up to a Redd Foxx "Laff of the Party" record. I knew Steve wouldn't get half the dirty jokes. I knew because I wouldn't either.

The next day I checked the Savoy listing in the *Press*. A total knockout: *Screaming Skull, Naked Youth, How to Make a Monster.* I passed Steve's house on the way to the bus stop and almost rang his bell. But hell, I hesitated, there was no law against going to the movies by yourself. Besides, something told me I'd better start getting used to it.

THE PHANTOM'S
"B" WARDS FOR THE '90S

Time to hand out those trophies—i.e., the Phantom's Video "B" wards—praising or burying, as the case may warrant, those titles, individuals, and institutions that made the '90s the home-vid decade it so undeniably was. The video sleeves, please…

Psycho of the Decade: Anthony Hopkins's Hannibal ("the Cannibal") Lecter, *The Silence of the Lambs*; Runner-up: Corbin Bernsen's Dr. Alan Feinstone, *The Dentist*

Best Alien: Vincent D'Onofrio's redneck alien insect, *Men in Black*

Worst Alien: Glowing-eyed Willie Nelson, *Starlight*

Monster for the '90s: Titular critter, *Killer Condom*

Genre Discovery of the Decade: José ("Coffin Joe") Mojica Marins

Edgiest Thesp of the Decade: Peter Greene, *Clean, Shaven, Pulp Fiction, Judgment Night*

Postmodern Power Woman of the Decade: Franka Potente, *Run Lola Run*; Runner-up: Eileen Daly, *Razor Blade Smile*

Most Unlikely New Action Star: Meryl Streep, *The River Wild*

The Arnold Schwarzenegger *Commando* Body Count Award: John Woo's *Hard-Boiled*

Worst Performance by a Close Personal Friend of Arnold Schwarzenegger: Franco Columbu, *Beretta's Island*

Dumbest B-Movie Villains: Casey Siemaszko's "The Breathtaker" and his army of evil asthmatics, *Black Scorpion*

Best Athlete-Turned-Actor: Dennis Rodman, *Double Team, Simon Sez*; Runner-up: Brian Bosworth, *Stone Cold*

Worst Athlete-Turned-Actor: Howie Long, *Firestorm*

Best Sports Sequence: Opening football scene, *The Last Boy Scout*

Best Animal Performer: Elvis the Cat, *Assassins, The Specialist, That Darn Cat*; Runner-up: Bart the Bear, *The Edge, Meet the Deedles*

Worst Animal Performer: Steven Seagal

Most Overworked Stunt Double: Charles Bronson's action stand-in, J. P. Romano

Comeback(s) of the Decade, Live Division: Robert Forster, Pam Grier, *Jackie Brown*; Peter Fonda, *Ulee's Gold, The Limey*

Comeback of the Decade, Dead Division: Ed Wood, *Ed Wood*, and the documentaries *Ed Wood: Look Back in Angora, The Ed Wood Story: The Plan 9 Companion (a.k.a. Flying Saucers Over Hollywood), The Haunted World of Edward D. Wood, Jr., On the Trail of Ed Wood*

Comeback(s) of the Decade, Killer-Doll Division: (tie) Chucky the Good Guy Doll, *Bride of Chucky;* Zuni fetish doll, *Trilogy of Terror II*

Comedown of the Decade: Actor Temuera Morrison, from charismatic star of *Once Were Warriors* to Pamela Anderson Lee's rejected ex *(Barb Wire)* and Marlon Brando's dog *(The Island of Dr. Moreau)*

Come-On of the Decade: "I was hoping to demo your unit." Cindy Crawford to stunned computer nerd, *Fair Game*

Best New Names to Remember: Miracle Unique Vincent, *Virtuosity;* Moriah Shining Dove Snyder, *The Prophecy*

Worst Jerry Lewis Imitation: Tim Roth, *Four Rooms*

Best Jerry Lewis Imitation: Jerry Lewis, *Funny Bones*

Ed Wood *Glen or Glenda* Memorial Award for Best Drag Performances, Male Division: Gary Busey, *Under Siege, Diary of a Serial Killer;* Runners-up: Jackie Chan, *Supercop 2;* Johnny Depp, *Ed Wood;* Iggy Pop, *Dead Man;* **Female Division:** Pam Grier, *Escape from L.A.;* Runner-up: Julia Roberts, *Sleeping with the Enemy*

Not a Pretty Sight, Gratuitous Male Nudity Department: Harvey Keitel, *Bad Lieutenant*

Worst Hair Days, Male Division: Gary Oldman, *Bram Stoker's Dracula, The Fifth Element;* Runners-up: Jim Carrey, *Dumb and Dumber;* Chris Tucker, *The Fifth Element;* John Travolta, Samuel L. Jackson, *Pulp Fiction;* **Female Division:** Demi Moore, *G.I. Jane;* Runner-up: Traci Lords, *Nowhere*

WINNING SMILE: Armed and dangerous Eileen Daly makes for a major power babe in *Razor Blade Smile. Courtesy of A-Pix Entertainment*

The Zsa Zsa Gabor Sartorial Splendor Award for Most Creative Costume: Marlon Brando's white robe, powder, and ice-bucket ensemble, *The Island of Dr. Moreau*

Best Video Trend: The ongoing Asian Invasion

Best Video Box: Talking box, *Frankenhooker;* Runners-up: Lenticular morph boxes, *The Phantom, The Lost World: Jurassic Park;* Bloodbag box, *Bleeders*

Best Movie Title: *Sex, Chocolate and Zombie Republicans*

Best Movie Mouthful: *The Bloody Video Horror That Made Me Puke on My Aunt Gertrude*

Most Unfairly Maligned Movie of the Decade: *Showgirls*

Most Fairly Maligned Movie of the Decade: *Hudson Hawk;* Runner-up: *Cutthroat Island*

Most Unnecessary "Special Edition": *Cutthroat Island*

Worst Remake: *Diabolique;* Runner-up: *Psycho*

Worst Remake by the Same Director: George Sluizer's Hollywood version of *The Vanishing*

Worst Rediscovered Video with a Topless Scene by a Since-Ascendant TV Personality: (tie): *The Turning,* Gillian Anderson; *Gypsy Angels,* Vanna White

We Have Met the Paranoids and They Are Us Award: *The X-Files*

Been There, Done That Citation: *Star Wars, Episode I: The Phantom Menace*

The William Castle's Kvelling in His Grave Award for Best Gimmick and Promo Campaign: *The Blair Witch Project*

Best Movie Gadget: Mallets-and-blades medieval obstacle course, *First Knight*

Best Prosthetic: Mark Wahlberg's public privates, *Boogie Nights*

Best Credit Lines: (tie): "Kathoga hair stylist," *The Relic;* "On-set Pinocchio wrangler," *Pinocchio's Revenge*

Lifetime Achievement Award, Spies & Thighs Division: Director Andy/producer Arlene Sidaris, *Guns, Fit to Kill, Do or Die,* et al.

Most Overused Buzzword of the Decade: Buzz

(Note to winners: Don't call us, we'll call you; your trophies are in the mail.)

VIDEO SOURCE GUIDE:

Mail-Order, Specialty, and
Full-Service Video and DVD Suppliers

The following VHS and DVD suppliers and innovative indie labels cover the entire home-viewing spectrum. If you can't find a title you're looking for among the below, then odds are it isn't findable. We've included addresses, phone numbers, and websites, where available.

All Day Entertainment, 3109 Batter Sea Lane, Alexandria, VA 22309 (703 360-5820). Specializes in quality vintage and genre DVDs—from an Edgar G. Ulmer collection to gems like *The Sadist* and *Ganja & Hess*—many with audio commentary and other extras. www.alldayentertainment.com

Alternative Cinema Video Shelf, P.O. Box 371, Glenwood, NJ 07418 (973 509-9352). Specializes in distributing sell-through horror, genre, and other low-budget indies, as well as rare vintage genre and horror imports. Catalog available. www.alternative cinema.com

Anchor Bay Entertainment, 1699 Stutz Dr., Troy, MI 48084 (800 745-1145). Has moved to the top of the collectors' line with exclusive remastered "collector's editions" of a wide range of horror, sci-fi, drama, and art-house fare, affordably priced in VHS and DVD.

AnimEigo (800 242-6463). Specializes in "Unedited, Widescreen, Properly Translated" samurai classics (e.g., *The Razor, Zatoichi*) on VHS and laser disc. The best in its field. www.videoz.com/samcin/

Belle & Blade, 124 Penn Ave., Dover, NJ 07801 (800 365-2104). Specializes in a wide array of historical, adventure, and combat classics, from *The Black Swan* to *Zulu*, along with documentaries. www.belleandblade.com

Bennu Multimedia (212 563-8020). Stocks a number of rare, exclusive titles ranging from genre to documentaries. bennumedia@aol.com

Blackest Heart Media, P.O. Box 3376, Antioch, CA 94531-3376 (925 753-0169). Specializes in "rare import soundtracks, videos, and T-shirts," as well as "gut-crunching books, magazines and more." Boasts an impressive collection of uncut horror imports. Giant catalog available. www.houseofhorrors.com/blackest.htm

Captain Bijou, P.O. Box 87, Toney, AL 35773-0087 (256 837-0049). Slogan: "The one-stop source for collectors worldwide!" Captain Bijou carries an astounding assortment not only of videos and DVDs covering everything from the latest mainstream sell-through releases to vintage B westerns, serials, and rare TV shows, but pop-culture collectibles (posters, radio shows, magazines, et al.) of every stripe. Catalog available. www.captainbijou.com

Cinema Classics, 332 E. 11th St., New York, NY 10003 (212 677-6309). Offers a complete array of titles, including genre rarities, many at discount prices. Catalog available. www.cinemaclassics.com

Cinemacabre Video, P.O. Box 10005, Baltimore, MD 21285-0005. Emphasizes genre titles, trailer collections, short feature compilations, and other offbeat fare. Catalog available.

Critics' Choice Video, P O. Box 749, Dept. 10363, Itasca, IL 60143-0749 (800 367-7765). This established supplier has more than 10,000 movies in stock, with an emphasis on classics (including exclusives), many available at deep discounts. Catalog available. www.ccvideo.com

Cutthroat Video, P.O. Box 27714, Las Vegas, NV 89126-1714. Slogan: "A cut above the rest…in quality and price!" Specializes in "hard-to-find horror, uncut, exploitation, and bizarre films from around the world." Catalog available.

Darker Image Videos, Box 479, Medway, ME 04460. Specializes in rare film noirs at low prices.

Eddie Brandt's Saturday Matinee, 5006 Vineland Ave., N. Hollywood, CA 91601 (818 506-4242). One of the nation's oldest video stores and one of the most complete, with thousands of titles in stock, including rare TV shows. Also sells posters and other film memorabilia. Catalog available.

Englewood Entertainment, 10917 Winner Rd., Independence, MO 64052 (888 573-5490). Slogan: "The legal source for science fiction, horror, film noir, cult and special interest motion picture entertainment." Specializes in handsomely packaged, frequently remastered vintage genre films (e.g., *Bride of the Monster, The Fabulous World of Jules Verne*), previously unreleased fare (e.g., TV's *Tom Corbett, Space Cadet*) and original, more recent genre indies. www.englewd.com

ETC Video, P.O. Box 12161, Spring, TX 77391-2161 (281 225-8031). ETC is the ultimate source for "the peak period of European exploitation and genre cinema, with special emphasis on amazing Italian films of the '60s and '70s." Catalog available. www.diabolik.demon.co.uk

Facets Video, 1517 W. Fullerton Ave., Chicago, IL 60614 (800 331-6197). *The* leading purveyor of foreign and art-house fare, Facets also stocks more general titles and distributes the animation-driven Whole Toon Catalog. Sales and mail-order rental. Exhaustive catalog available. www.facets.org

Festival Films, 6115 Chestnut Ter., Shorewood, MN 55331 (612 470-2172). Has an extensive roster of international and art-house titles. Sales and rental.

Foothill Video, P.O. Box 547, Tujunga, CA 91403 (fax: 818 353-7242). This veteran supplier specializes in older titles, ranging from horror and serials to mysteries and foreign fare, with a large list of B westerns and silent films. Catalog available.

Grapevine Video, P.O. Box 46161, Phoenix, AZ 85063 (602 973-3661). One of the leading specialists in rare silent films and early talkies of all kinds, including many exclusives. Catalog available. www.grapevinevideo.com

Hollywood Book & Poster Company, 6562 Hollywood Blvd., Hollywood, CA 90028 (323 465-8764) Movie maven Eric Caidin's justly famed Hollywood genre-fan haven offers current and classic videos, television and music collectibles, posters, photos, and "much more."

Hollywood's Attic, P.O. Box 7122, Burbank, CA 91510 (818 843-3366). Specializes in vintage titles, ranging from B westerns to serials to early black films. Catalog available. www.hollywoodsattic.com

Home Film Festival, P.O. Box 2032, Scranton, PA 18501 (800 258-3456). Stocks international, indie, documentary, and other titles. Catalog available. www.homefilm festival.com

The Incredibly Strange Filmworks, Dept. PM, P.O. Box 245, Jamestown, MO 65046-0245 (800 859-9238). ISF specializes in offbeat genre fare, with an emphasis on the films of T. V. (*Apartheid Slave Women's Justice*) Mikels, Steve (*Dracula in Vegas*) Millard, Fred Olen Ray and other B auteurs. www.incrediblystrangefilm.com

Ivy Video, P.O. Box 18376, Asheville, NC 28814 (800 669-4057). Stocks an eclectic roster of titles, from *The Great St. Louis Bank Robbery* to the 1960s documentary *You Are What You Eat*. Catalog available.www.ivyvideo.com

Kim's Video, 6 St. Marks Pl., New York, NY 10003 (800 617-KIMS). A treasure trove for genre fans, featuring extensive import, indie, and *animé* collections. Catalog available. www.kimsvideo.com

Kino Video, 333 W. 39th St., New York, NY 10018 (800 562-3330). Kino releases a wide range of art films, imports, silents, noirs, horror, and exploitation, often in digitally mastered form in VHS and DVD. One of the best. Catalog available. www.kino.com

Liberty/VCI Home Video, 11333 E. 60 Pl., Tulsa, OK 74146 (800 331-4077). Features an interesting assortment of both public-domain and exclusive licensed titles covering the vintage-genre spectrum (from *Gargoyles* to *Mr. Imperium*) on VHS and DVD. Catalog available. www.vcihomevideo.com

Loonic Video, P.O. Box 2052, El Cerrito, CA 94530 (510 526-5681). Offers an eccentric, eclectic collection of vintage genre films, westerns, noirs, and exploitation, along with obscure animation and comedy-short collections. Catalog available.

Luminous Film & Video Wurks, P.O. Box 1047, Medford, NY 11763. A leading purveyor of foreign imports, ranging from art-house to horror, with an especially impressive spaghetti-western collection. Catalog available. www.lfvw.com

Manga Entertainment. A leader in distributing cutting-edge *anime*, Asian, and cult films on video (e.g., *Perfect Blue, Six-String Samurai*). www.manga.com

Media Blasters (800 338-6827). Specializes in licensing and distributing sell-through *anime* and live-action Asian titles, including the cutting-edge "Asia Pulp Cinema" and "Tokyo Shock" lines. www.media-blasters.com

Midnight Video, 5010 Church Dr., Coplay, PA 18037. Slogan: "Your #1 professional source for uncut horror & gore." Specializes in vintage Euro horror titles (e.g. Franco, Fulci). Catalog available. www.midnight1.com

Milestone Film & Video, 275 W. 96th St., Suite 28C, New York, NY 10025 (800 603-1104). Like Kino and Water Bearer, Milestone excels at discovering and remastering worthy vintage titles, including *The Bat Whispers* and the 1927 documentary *Chang*. Catalog available.

A Million and One World-Wide Videos, P.O. Box 349, Orchard Hill, GA 30266 (800 849-7309). Specializes in rare and out-of-circulation videos. www.wwvideos.com

Moore Video, P.O. Box 5703, Richmond, VA 23220 (804 745-9785). Stocks an extensive sell-through video line, with emphasis on genre titles. Moore also licenses and releases classic genre films (e.g., *Lemora, Deranged*) and coproduces low-budget genre films (e.g., *Afterbirth*).

Movies Unlimited, 3015 Darnell Rd., Philadelpha, PA 19154 (800 4-MOVIES). Slogan: "The largest selection of out-of-print and hard-to-find video movies for the serious collector." This video pioneer produces an impressive (and enormous) annual catalog and stocks tens of thousands of titles in every conceivable category. www.most movies.com

Nashville Cinema, P.O. Box 293213, Nashville, TN 37229 (615 872-9190). Specializes in the films of Ron Ormond (e.g., *The Monster and the Stripper*), available at sell-through prices.

R.E.C. Video, 301 W. 46th St., New York, NY 10036 (212 397-8680). Slogan: "The movie collector's home." Specializes in "Combat, Sci-Fi Flicks, Foreign Films, Japanese Animation, Kung-Fu Flicks, Creature Features, Kooky Cartoons, Alien Encounters, Funky-Freakouts, Sexy Shockers."

The Right Stuf International, P.O. Box 71309, Des Moines, IA 50325 (800 338-6827). Devoted to *anime* and related products. Catalog available. www.rightstuf.com.

Scarecrow Video, 5030 Roosevelt Way NE, Seattle, WA 98105 (206 524-8554). Slogan: "We will search the world for any movie, any format!" Scarecrow stocks more than 40,000 titles in VHS, DVD, laser disc, and PAL (import). Catalog available. www.scare crow.video

Science Fiction Continuum, 1701 E. Second St., Scotch Plains, NJ 07067 (908 322-2010). Specializes in sci-fi, *anime*, and genre titles of all types, along with collectibles. Catalog available. www.sfcontinuum.com/sjvideo

Scorched Earth, P.O. Box 101083, Denver, CO 80210. Carries vintage horror, exploitation, and sci-fi titles, along with newer indies and offbeat fare. www.sepnet.com

Sinister Cinema, P.O. Box 4369, Medford, OR 97501-0168 (541 773-6860). Slogan: "The Leading Source of Horror, Mystery and Science Fiction on Video!" One of the true genre sell-through pioneers, Sinister Cinema carries thousands of titles covering the genre spectrum, including many rare mystery and horror films of the '30s and '40s. Catalog available. www.sinistercinema.com

Something Weird Video, P.O. Box 33664, Seattle, WA 98133 (206 361-3759). The last word on exclusive vintage-exploitation titles, including thousands of reel rarities, from silents to the Swingin' '70s. SWV also carries a wide range of genre films—horror, sci-fi, imports, sword-and-sandal, Euro noirs, martial arts—and rates as a reel treasure trove for the serious genre-and-sleaze fan. www.somethingweird.com

Spyguise, Box 205, 263 Central Ave., Jersey City, NJ 07307 (201 653-7395). Specializes in international-intrigue videos (James Bond, *The Man from U.N.C.L.E.*), along with related items, ranging from records and posters to toys and autographs. www.spyguise.com

Tai Seng Video Marketing, 170 S. Spruce Ave., Suite 200, South San Francisco, CA 94080 (888 668-8338). Tai Seng is the "largest official source" for Hong Kong films of all stripes, with more than 2,000 titles. Catalog available. www.taiseng.com

Tapes of Terror, P. Riggs, 11430 Mullins Dr., Houston, TX 77035. Specializes in rare horror, Asian, Euro, and exploitation films, with more than 1,800 titles in stock. Catalog available. www.morticiasmorgue.com/tot.html

TLA Video, 234 Market St., Philadelphia, PA 19106 (800 333-8521). A full-service supplier that stresses art-house, indie, and foreign fare. Book-length illustrated catalog available. www.tlavideo.com

Tropic Twilight Company, PMB 3203, 1142 Auahi St., #A7, Honolulu, HI 96814. Specializes in imported horror films, with a wide and varied selection. Catalog available. www.tropictwilight.com

Unearthly Video, P.O. Box 681914, Orlando, FL 32868-1914. Slogan: "For thrilling videos you can't get elsewhere at affordable prices!" Specializes in horror, exploitation, and other genre titles. Free catalog available.

Video International, West Hi 201, 65 Hideri-cho, Saiin, Ukyo-ku, Kyoto 615-0065, Japan. Specializes in extreme-TV shows from Japan, including the *Japanarama!* compilation cassettes. One-of-a-kind weirdness.

Video Junkie, P.O. Box 1794, Aurora, IL 60507. Slogan: "#1 worldwide in service and selection." Stocks a full range of "imports & oddities" running the genre gamut, in all formats, as well as collectibles, including scripts, posters, magazines, and T-shirts. Catalog available. www.vidjunkie.com

Video Library, 7157 Germantown Ave., Philadelphia, PA 19119 (800 669-7157). Slogan: "We rent-by-mail anywhere in the United States." Features an extensive array of titles of all kinds. Catalog available. www.vlibrary.com

Video Oyster, 149 W. 12th St., Box 663, New York, NY 10011 (212 989-3300). Specializes in video rarities of all kinds. Video Oyster operates two major on-line sites: Out-of-print video sales: www.videooyster.com; Movie auctions: www.bideo.com

Video Plus, 2 Brookline Pl., Brookline, MA (877 694-4400). Specializes in sell-through titles of all kinds, VHS and DVD. Catalog available.

Video Resources, 220 W. 71st St., New York, NY 10023 (212 724-7055). Offers one of the most eclectic collections extant, ranging from D. W. Griffith silents to TV-commercials collections and vintage animation tapes. Catalog available.

Video Screams, Box 443, Bellefontaine, OH 43311. Carries an impressive lineup of horror, sci-fi, and other genre obscurities, including many Indian (e.g., *Superman: The Hindi Version*), Turkish and other imports, at low prices. www.videoscreams.com

Video Search of Miami, P.O. Box 16-1917, Miami, FL 33116 (888 279-9773). A leading source for rare Euro and Asian genre imports, often in uncut editions, as well as a full range of other titles. Catalog available. www.vsom.com

Video Specialists International, 182-LM Jackson St., Dallas, PA 18612 (570 675-0227). Carries a wide range of vintage videos, with an emphasis on rarities. Catalog available.

Video Vault, 323 S. Washington St., Alexandria, VA 22314 (800 VAULT-66). Slogan: "Guaranteed worst movies in town!" Specializes in sales and mail order rental of genre, cult, and video rarities. www.videovault.com

Video Wasteland, P.O. Box 81551, Berea, OH 44017 (440 891-1920) Video Wasteland "offers a complete line of books, magazines, posters & paper, Mexican Wrestling Stuff, T-Shirts, Autographs and much, much more. Over 3,000 rare, out-of-print and hard-to-find horror, exploitation and schlock films" available for mail order rental. Catalog available. www.videowasteland.com

Video Yesteryear, Box C, Sandy Hook, CT 06482 (800 243-0987). Stocks more than 2,500 vintage titles, including many silents (with musical accompaniment), in the full range of formats. Catalog available. www.yesteryear.com

Water Bearer Films, 48 W. 21st St., Suite 301, New York, NY 10010 (800 551-8304). Slogan: "Presenting the finest in home videos." Water Bearer licenses and releases an eclectic array of exclusives, including gay and lesbian features, genre imports, contemporary indie features and even the ultra-rare 1915 French serial *Les Vampires*. www.waterbearer.com

HOT
CYBER-CINEMA SITES:

On-Line Video Sources and Entertainment Sites

Andy Sidaris: www.andysidaris.com

Astounding B-Monster:
www.bmonster.com

Blow-Out Video:
www.blowoutvideo.com

B-Movie Theater: www.b-movie.com

Chiller Theatre:
www.chillertheatre.com

Feo y Loco: www.feoyloco.com

Film Forum: www.filmforum.com

Gameroom Magazine:
www.gameroommagazine.com

Image Entertainment:
www.image-entertainment.com

Insound: www.insound.com

Movie Gallery: www.moviegallery.com

The Picture Palace: www.picpal.com

Posteritati: www.posteritati.com

Shocking Images:
www.shockingimages.com

Troma, Inc.: www.troma.com

Videoflicks: www.videoflicks.com

VIDEOBLIVION

The following video labels are no longer active; most of their titles are out of circulation. Well-stocked video stores, mail order rental outfits, and video Internet sites are the prime sources for copies.

Academy Home Entertainment

Active Home Video

AIP Home Video

All Seasons Entertainment

Axon Video Corp.

Cannon Video

Charter Entertainment	New World Video
City Lights Home Video	Nostalgia Merchant
Embassy Home Entertainment	Pacific Arts Video
Forum Home Video	Paragon
Fox Hills Video	Prism Entertainment Corp.
Fries Home Video	RKO Pictures Home Video
Genesis Home Video	Regal Video
Hal Roach Film Classics	SGE Home Video
Imperial Entertainment	Southgate Entertainment
Independent United Distributors	Star Classics
Interglobal Home Video	Studio Entertainment
International Video Entertainment	Today Home Entertainment
J2 Communications	Trans-World Entertainment
Kartes Video Communications	Trylon
Key Video	Unicorn Video
King Bee	Urban Classics Video
King of Video	VCII—Film Classics
Lettuce Entertain You	VCR Enterprises
Lightning Video	Vestron Video
Lorimar Home Video	VidAmerica
M.C.E.G./Virgin Home Entertainment	Vidcrest
Magnum Entertainment	Video Gems
Media Home Entertainment	Virgin Vision
Mogul Communications	Vista Home Video
Nelson Entertainment	WesternWorld Video
New Star Video	Wizard Video

FEATURE REVIEW, SIDEBAR, AND INTERVIEW INDEX

INTERVIEWS AND SOUND BITES AT A GLANCE

ABOUT THE AUTHOR

Born some time ago in a galaxy practically right around the corner, JOE KANE, The Phantom of the Movies, cut his genre-movie teeth as writer/managing editor of *The Monster Times* before joining the New York *Daily News* as a columnist in 1984. His work has appeared in *Maxim, The Washington Times, National Lampoon, Playboy, Penthouse, The Village Voice, Fangoria, High Times,* and numerous other publications. He currently publishes the quarterly magazine *The Phantom of the Movies' VideoScope: The Ultimate Genre-Video Guide*.